Regis College Library
15 ST. MARY STREET
TORONTO, ONTARIO, CANADA
M4Y 2R5

WITHDRAWN

LUKE

Baker Exegetical Commentary on the New Testament

MOISÉS SILVA, EDITOR

1	Matthew	*David L. Turner*
2	Mark	*Robert H. Stein*
3	Luke	*Darrell L. Bock*
4	John	*Gary M. Burge*
5	Acts	*Darrell L. Bock*
6	Romans	*Thomas R. Schreiner*
7	1 Corinthians	*David E. Garland*
8	2 Corinthians	*Scott Hafemann*
9	Galatians	*Moisés Silva*
10	Ephesians	*Harold Hoehner*
11	Philippians	*Moisés Silva*
12	Colossians, Philemon	*Greg Beale*
13	1–2 Thessalonians	*Jeffrey A. D. Weima*
14	1–2 Timothy, Titus	*Reggie M. Kidd*
15	Hebrews	*S. Lewis Johnson*
16	James	*Scot McKnight*
17	1–2 Peter, Jude	*Norman R. Ericson*
18	1–3 John	*Robert W. Yarbrough*
19	Revelation	*Grant Osborne*

LUKE

VOLUME 1:
1:1–9:50

DARRELL L. BOCK

Regis College Library
15 ST. MARY STREET
TORONTO, ONTARIO, CANADA
M4Y 2R5

BS
2595
.3
.B58
1994
v.1

Baker Exegetical Commentary on the New Testament

Baker Books

A Division of Baker Book House Co
Grand Rapids, Michigan 49516

©1994 by Darrell L. Bock

Published by Baker Books
a division of Baker Book House Company
P.O. Box 6287, Grand Rapids, Michigan 49516-6287

Printed in the United States of America

All rights reserved. No part of this publication may be reproduced, stored in a re-
trieval system, or transmitted in any form or by any means—for example, electronic, photocopy, recording—without the prior written permission of the publisher.
The only exception is brief quotations in printed reviews.

Library of Congress Cataloging-in-Publication Data

Bock, Darrell L.
    Luke 1:1–9:50 / Darrell L. Bock.
       p.   cm. — (Baker exegetical commentary on the New Testament ; 3A)
    Includes bibliographical references and indexes.
    ISBN 0-8010-1053-5
    1. Bible. N.T. Luke I,1–IX,50—Commentaries. I. Title. II. Series.
    BS2595.3.B58   1994
    226.4′077—dc20   94-33507

With Appreciation

Dave Krentel
William D. Taylor
Harold Hoehner
Don Glenn
Elliott Johnson
Eugene Merrill
Ken Barker
Ed Blum
Stan Toussaint
Howard Hendricks
Don Campbell
I. Howard Marshall
M. Daniel Carroll R.
Scott B. Rae
Craig A. Blaising

It has been a privilege to learn so much from you,
and a joy to know the Lord's fellowship and
share in the Lord's work with you.

Contents

Volume 1
Series Preface   ix
Author's Preface   xii
Abbreviations   xv
Transliteration   xix

Introduction to the Gospel of Luke   *1*
I. Luke's Preface and the Introduction of John and Jesus
   (1:1–2:52)   *49*
   A. Preface: Luke Carefully Builds on Precedent (1:1–4)   *51*
   B. Infancy Narrative: Forerunner and Fulfillment
      (1:5–2:40)   *68*
   C. Jesus' Revelation of His Self-Understanding (2:41–52)   *259*
II. Preparation for Ministry: Anointed by God (3:1–4:13)   *276*
   A. John the Baptist: One Who Goes Before (3:1–20)   *278*
   B. Jesus: One Who Comes After (3:21–4:13)   *331*
III. Galilean Ministry: Revelation of Jesus (4:14–9:50)   *386*
   A. Overview of Jesus' Ministry (4:14–44)   *389*
   B. Gathering of Disciples (5:1–6:16)   *446*
   C. Jesus' Teaching (6:17–49)   *548*
   D. First Movements to Faith and Christological Questions
      (7:1–8:3)   *629*
   E. Call to Faith, Christological Revelation, and Questions
      (8:4–9:17)   *715*
   F. Christological Confession and Instruction about
      Discipleship (9:18–50)   *837*

Excursuses
1. John the Baptist and Elijah (1:17)   *901*
2. The Census of Quirinius (2:1–2)   *903*
3. Date of John the Baptist's Ministry (3:1–2)   *910*
4. Sources and Synoptic Relationships   *914*
5. The Genealogies of Matthew and Luke (3:23–38)   *918*
6. The Son of Man in Aramaic and in Luke (5:24)   *924*

7. The Sermon on the Plain in Luke: Its Relationship
   to Matthew and Its Theological-Ethical Function
   (6:20–49)   *931*
8. The Parables of Jesus   *945*
9. Luke's "Great Omission" (9:18) from Mark 6:45–8:26   *950*
10. Authenticity of the Suffering-Son-of-Man Sayings
    and of the Passion Predictions (9:22)   *952*

Provisional Bibliography   *956*

Maps   *50, 277, 388*

Volume 2 *(forthcoming)*
IV. Jerusalem Journey: Jewish Rejection and the New Way
    (9:51–19:44)
 V. Jerusalem: The Innocent One Slain and Raised (19:45–24:53)

Excursuses
11. Last Supper: Nature and Timing of the Meal (22:7–13)
12. The Jesus Seminar and the Gospel of Luke

Bibliography
Index of Subjects
Index of Authors
Index of Greek Words
Index of Ancient Literature
Index of Scripture

Series Preface

The chief concern of the Baker Exegetical Commentary on the New Testament (to be known as BECNT) is to provide, within the framework of informed evangelical thought, commentaries that blend scholarly depth with readability, exegetical detail with sensitivity to the whole, attention to critical problems with theological awareness. We hope thereby to attract the interest of a fairly wide audience, from the scholar who is looking for a thoughtful and independent examination of the text to the motivated lay Christian who craves solid but accessible exposition.

Nevertheless, a major purpose is to address the needs of pastors and others who are involved in the preaching and exposition of the Scriptures as the uniquely inspired Word of God. This consideration affects directly the parameters of the series. For example, serious biblical expositors cannot afford to depend on a superficial treatment that avoids the difficult questions, but neither are they interested in encyclopedic commentaries that seek to cover every conceivable issue that may arise. Our aim, therefore, is to focus on those problems that have a direct bearing on the meaning of the text (although selected technical details are treated in the additional notes).

Similarly, a special effort is made to avoid treating exegetical questions for their own sake, that is, in relative isolation from the thrust of the argument as a whole. This effort may involve (at the discretion of the individual contributors) abandoning the verse-by-verse approach in favor of an exposition that focuses on the paragraph as the main unit of thought. In all cases, however, the commentaries will stress the development of the argument and explicitly relate each passage to what precedes and follows it so as to identify its function in context as clearly as possible.

We believe, moreover, that a responsible exegetical commentary must take fully into account the latest scholarly research, regardless of its source. The attempt to do this in the context of a conservative theological tradition presents certain challenges, and in the past the results have not always been commendable. In some cases, evangelicals appear to make use of critical scholarship not for the purpose of genuine interaction but only to dismiss it. In other cases, the interaction glides over into assimilation, theological distinctives are ignored or suppressed, and the end product cannot be differentiated from works that arise from a fundamentally different starting point.

The contributors to this series attempt to avoid these two pitfalls. They do not consider traditional opinions to be sacrosanct, and they are certainly committed to do justice to the biblical text whether or not it supports such opinions. On the other hand, they will not quickly abandon a long-standing view, if there is persuasive evidence in its favor, for the sake of fashionable theories. What is more important, the contributors share a belief in the trustworthiness and essential unity of Scripture. They also consider that the historic formulations of Christian doctrine, such as the ecumenical creeds and many of the documents originating in the sixteenth-century Reformation, arose from a legitimate reading of Scripture, thus providing a proper framework for its further interpretation. No doubt, the use of such a starting point sometimes results in the imposition of a foreign construct on the text, but we deny that it must necessarily do so or that the writers who claim to approach the text without prejudices are invulnerable to the same danger.

Accordingly, we do not consider theological assumptions—from which, in any case, no commentator is free—to be obstacles to biblical interpretation. On the contrary, an exegete who hopes to understand the apostle Paul in a theological vacuum might just as easily try to interpret Aristotle without regard for the philosophical framework of his whole work or without having recourse to those subsequent philosophical categories that make possible a meaningful contextualization of his thought. It must be emphasized, however, that the contributors to the present series come from a variety of theological traditions and that they do not all have identical views with regard to the proper implementation of these general principles. In the end, all that really matters is whether the series succeeds in representing the original text accurately, clearly, and meaningfully to the contemporary reader.

The present commentary on Luke treats matters of detail to a greater extent than will other volumes in the series. Because this is the first commentary to appear on the Gospels, it seemed prudent to give the author some flexibility in discussing source-critical and historical questions (this matter is set in smaller type to distinguish it from the actual exposition of the text; see excursus 4 for additional rationale for assigning this role to the commentary on Luke). Accordingly, the authors of the volumes on the other Gospels will be able to deal with such questions more selectively and briefly. As an additional help, shading has been used to assist the reader in locating salient sections of the treatment of each passage: the introductory comments, the discussion of structure, and the concluding summary.

Textual variants in the Greek text are signaled in the author's translation by means of half-brackets around the relevant word or phrase (e.g., ⌐Gerasenes¬), thereby alerting the reader to turn to the additional notes at the end of each exegetical unit for a discussion of the textual problem.

The documentation uses the author-date method, in which the basic reference consists of author's surname + year + page number(s): Fitzmyer 1981: 297. The only exceptions to this system are well-known reference works (e.g., BAGD, LSJ, *TDNT*). Full publication data are given in the provisional bibliography at the end of volume one. Volume two will contain a comprehensive bibliography, as well as indexes, for the entire commentary.

Moisés Silva

Author's Preface

Writing a commentary is a little like raising a family. Once assigned, it lives with you and is in your thoughts constantly. Since I was asked to do Luke, my three children—Elisa, Lara, and Stephen—have left diapers and have entered or are now approaching junior high. They do not know what life is without Daddy working on "the book." They have given up much playtime and have kept the house quieter on many an occasion so Daddy could think. Sometimes this required parental negotiation or coercion or both, but they have been great about being sensitive to "the project." They, along with my understanding partner and friend Sally, are to be thanked for allowing a fourth "child" to invade the house for a time. I love you all very much.

But what is this child like? A commentary is different things to different people. I have kept one metaphor in mind as I worked— that of "tour guide." When one scales great heights, sees a great city, or visits a beautiful church, a tour guide helps to orient the visitor to the sights by helping the tourist to appreciate the details of the locale's history and what others have said or experienced at the site. This is what I have tried to do. My major goal is to discuss the text and compare it to what Mark and Matthew wrote. Beyond this, I have tried to reflect the table talk about Luke. I have had many able companions and have tried faithfully to note whenever I have peered over the shoulders of others. I have benefited greatly from the commentaries of Marshall, Fitzmyer, Schürmann, Bovon, Plummer, Luce, Ernst, Klostermann, Grundmann, Nolland, Danker, Tiede, and C. A. Evans. These works were my constant companions on the journey, though along the way several others joined the tour and helped to make it enjoyable. My appreciation to them and others cannot be sufficiently expressed, except to say that in a day when the sometimes lonely and tedious endeavor of scholarship and study is not always appreciated, their labors have been highly esteemed. Recent commentaries by L. Johnson (1991), Stein (1992), and Nolland (vols. 2–3: 1993a, 1993b) were released after this manuscript was substantially completed. They are worthy of inclusion in a list of good treatments of Luke, though I have not interacted with them as fully as they deserve.

This work is longer than I originally anticipated. This is not only because Luke is the longest book in the NT, but also because studies of the Gospels are exceedingly complex, given the presence of parallel passages and the numerous discussions about the historicity of events. I have tried to highlight background and custom, so that anyone studying the Gospel of Luke can know what first-century customs and thinking were like, as well as which ancient texts describe such customs. Sometimes we cannot be sure of the exact nature of the ancient practice, but I have tried to be sensitive to our distance from the original setting and to give the reasons behind my description of the custom. The numerous references to ancient sources of all kinds should allow readers to follow the tour guide's trail, if they so wish.

I have tried to structure the treatment of each pericope consistently so that the reader may find information quickly. Each unit begins with a quick overview of how it fits in the movement of Luke. Then comes a discussion of sources and historicity, including summary observations about how Luke is like and unlike parallel passages. Questions of form briefly follow. Next a detailed outline traces the argument of the particular passage; these outlines substitute for detailed discussions of structure and develop the master outline. Then in one paragraph I summarize the unit's themes. A translation follows this. All this initial material concentrates on synthesis, thus orienting the reader to the verses under discussion and setting the stage for the exegesis. The exegesis proceeds one verse at a time. I have tried to note a full range of tools, so that excellent discussions of an issue can be quickly located. More-detailed comparisons to parallel texts, where they occur, are also treated here. The last paragraph or two of this section answers one question: How did Luke want the reader to respond to this event or teaching? The additional notes cover mostly text-critical questions. For the most part, I have made little use of formal literary studies of Luke. This discipline is new and holds great promise, but much of the commentary was already written before its recent emergence. In the future, it is likely that much of value for understanding Luke will emerge from this field of study. Finally, I have been selective in my use of periodical material, choosing to concentrate on monographs. Excellent bibliographies of periodical material may be found in Bovon, Schürmann, Fitzmyer, and Nolland (who makes good use of such resources). So this commentary is historical, exegetical, and (in the summary remarks of each exegetical section) pastoral.

My gratitude extends to many who encouraged me in this work. Gary Knussman, Robert Ramey, Joe O'Day, Allan Fisher, Jim

Weaver, Moisés Silva, and Ken Barker served faithfully in the editorial process, constantly exhorting me to say it more succinctly and helping me to avoid many pitfalls. Most faithful of all was David Aiken, my editor, whose keen eye, patience, and sense of style added immeasurably to this commentary. Special appreciation goes to Baker Book House for letting me lay out the commentary in the way I desired. Their total commitment to serious evangelical scholarship is much needed in this age. Herb Bateman read through a late draft with a careful eye and much encouragement. Max Turner and Howard Marshall saw brief portions and gave helpful critiques. Clay Porr, Jay Smith, and Tom Bailey helped me to convert my computer files into the proper format. Most appreciated was a sabbatical leave granted to me by Dallas Theological Seminary for the year 1989–90 so I could study at the University of Tübingen, during which time the most substantive work on the commentary was completed. This was also the year the Berlin Wall fell and to see that event firsthand with my family was special. My hosts in Germany—Martin Hengel, Otto Betz, and the colleagues at the Theologicum—made the stay very pleasant. Our friends in the villages of Neckartailfingen and Kirchentellinsfurt helped us to feel as much at home as possible. We cannot thank them enough. In sum, God was faithful to us in our journey.

I dedicate this work with gratitude to a collection of people who have had a significant impact on my Christian life. They come from a wide variety of backgrounds and show the diversity that makes the body of Christ so fascinating. I thank them for their ministry in my life. My prayer is that they might accept this expression of gratitude, though it is but a drop compared to what their labor has given to me.

One day all children leave the nest, and so it is with this commentary. I pray that its use will make the subject of Luke's Gospel, Jesus Christ, more real.

Darrell L. Bock

Abbreviations

Bibliographic and General

BAA   *Griechisch-Deutsches Wörterbuch zu den Schriften des Neuen Testaments und der frühchristlichen Literatur*, by W. Bauer, K. Aland, and B. Aland (6th ed.; Berlin: de Gruyter, 1988)

BAGD   *A Greek-English Lexicon of the New Testament and Other Early Christian Literature*, by W. Bauer, W. F. Arndt, F. W. Gingrich, and F. W. Danker (2d ed.; Chicago: University of Chicago Press, 1979)

BDB   *A Hebrew and English Lexicon of the Old Testament*, by F. Brown, S. R. Driver, and C. A. Briggs (Oxford: Clarendon, 1907)

BDF   *A Greek Grammar of the New Testament and Other Early Christian Literature*, by F. Blass, A. Debrunner, and R. W. Funk (Chicago: University of Chicago Press, 1961)

BDR   *Grammatik des neutestamentlichen Griechisch*, by F. Blass, A. Debrunner, and F. Rehkopf (Göttingen: Vandenhoeck & Ruprecht, 1984)

KJV   King James Version

LSJ   *A Greek-English Lexicon*, by H. G. Liddell, R. Scott, and H. S. Jones (Oxford: Clarendon, 1968)

LXX   Septuagint

MM   *The Vocabulary of the Greek Testament: Illustrated from the Papyri and Other Non-literary Sources*, by J. H. Moulton and G. Milligan (repr. Grand Rapids: Eerdmans, 1980)

MT   Masoretic Text

NA   *Novum Testamentum Graece*, edited by [E. Nestle], K. Aland, and B. Aland (26th ed.; Stuttgart: Deutsche Bibelstiftung, 1979)

NASB   New American Standard Bible

NIDNTT   *The New International Dictionary of New Testament Theology*, edited by L. Coenen, E. Beyreuther, and H. Bietenhard; English translation edited by C. Brown (4 vols.; Grand Rapids: Zondervan, 1975–86)

NIV   New International Version

NKJV   New King James Version

NRSV   New Revised Standard Version

NT   New Testament

OT   Old Testament

PG   *Patrologiae Cursus Completus, Series Graeca*, edited by J. P. Migne (161 vols.; Paris, 1857–66)

PL   *Patrologiae Cursus Completus, Series Latina*, edited by J. P. Migne (221 vols.; Paris, 1844–55)

RSV   Revised Standard Version

SB   *Kommentar zum Neuen Testament aus Talmud und Midrasch*, by H. L. Strack and P. Billerbeck (6 vols.; Munich: Beck, 1922–61)

TDNT   *Theological Dictionary of the New Testament*, edited by G. Kittel and G. Friedrich; translated and edited by G. W. Bromiley (10 vols.; Grand Rapids: Eerdmans, 1964–76)

UBS   *The Greek New Testament*, edited by B. Aland, K. Aland, J. Karavidopoulos, C. M. Martini, and B. M. Metzger (4th ed.; New York: United Bible Societies, 1993)

Hebrew Bible

Gen.	Genesis	2 Chron.	2 Chronicles	Dan.	Daniel
Exod.	Exodus	Ezra	Ezra	Hos.	Hosea
Lev.	Leviticus	Neh.	Nehemiah	Joel	Joel
Num.	Numbers	Esth.	Esther	Amos	Amos
Deut.	Deuteronomy	Job	Job	Obad.	Obadiah
Josh.	Joshua	Ps.	Psalms	Jon.	Jonah
Judg.	Judges	Prov.	Proverbs	Mic.	Micah
Ruth	Ruth	Eccles.	Ecclesiastes	Nah.	Nahum
1 Sam.	1 Samuel	Song	Song of Songs	Hab.	Habakkuk
2 Sam.	2 Samuel	Isa.	Isaiah	Zeph.	Zephaniah
1 Kings	1 Kings	Jer.	Jeremiah	Hag.	Haggai
2 Kings	2 Kings	Lam.	Lamentations	Zech.	Zechariah
1 Chron.	1 Chronicles	Ezek.	Ezekiel	Mal.	Malachi

Greek Testament

Matt.	Matthew	Eph.	Ephesians	Heb.	Hebrews
Mark	Mark	Phil.	Philippians	James	James
Luke	Luke	Col.	Colossians	1 Pet.	1 Peter
John	John	1 Thess.	1 Thessalonians	2 Pet.	2 Peter
Acts	Acts	2 Thess.	2 Thessalonians	1 John	1 John
Rom.	Romans	1 Tim.	1 Timothy	2 John	2 John
1 Cor.	1 Corinthians	2 Tim.	2 Timothy	3 John	3 John
2 Cor.	2 Corinthians	Titus	Titus	Jude	Jude
Gal.	Galatians	Philem.	Philemon	Rev.	Revelation

Jewish and Christian Apocrypha and Pseudepigrapha

Add. Esth.	Additions to Esther	Sus.	Susanna
Bar.	Baruch	T. Abr.	Testament of Abraham
2 Bar.	2 (Syriac) Baruch	T. Asher	Testament of Asher
Bel	Bel and the Dragon	T. Ben.	Testament of Benjamin
1 Enoch	1 (Ethiopic) Enoch	T. Dan	Testament of Dan
2 Enoch	2 (Slavonic) Enoch	T. Gad	Testament of Gad
1 Esdr.	1 Esdras	T. Iss.	Testament of Issachar
2 Esdr.	2 Esdras (4 Ezra)	T. Job	Testament of Job
Jub.	Jubilees	T. Jos.	Testament of Joseph
Jdt.	Judith	T. Judah	Testament of Judah
Let. Jer.	Letter of Jeremiah	T. Levi	Testament of Levi
1 Macc.	1 Maccabees	T. Moses	Testament of Moses
2 Macc.	2 Maccabees	T. Naph.	Testament of Naphtali
3 Macc.	3 Maccabees	T. Reub.	Testament of Reuben
4 Macc.	4 Maccabees	T. Sim.	Testament of Simeon
Odes Sol.	Odes of Solomon	T. Sol.	Testament of Solomon
Pr. Azar.	Prayer of Azariah	T. Zeb.	Testament of Zebulun
Pr. Man.	Prayer of Manasseh	Tob.	Tobit
Ps. Sol.	Psalms of Solomon	Wis.	Wisdom of Solomon
Sir.	Sirach (Ecclesiasticus)		

Rabbinic Tractates

The abbreviations below are used for the names of tractates in the Babylonian Talmud (indicated by a prefixed b.), Palestinian or Jerusalem Talmud (y.), Mishnah (m.), and Tosepta (t.). The last column gives the numbers of the order and tractate in the Mishnah.

ʿAbod. Zar.	ʿAboda Zara	4.8	Nazir	Nazir	3.4
ʾAbot	ʾAbot	4.9	Ned.	Nedarim	3.3
ʿArak.	ʿArakin	5.5	Neg.	Negaʿim	6.3
B. Bat.	Babaʾ Batraʾ	4.3	Nid.	Nidda	6.7
B. Qam.	Babaʾ Qammaʾ	4.1	ʾOhol.	ʾOholot	6.2
B. Meṣ.	Babaʾ Meṣiʿaʾ	4.2	ʿOr.	ʿOrla	1.10
Bek.	Bekorot	5.4	Para	Para	6.4
Ber.	Berakot	1.1	Peʾa	Peʾa	1.2
Beṣa	Beṣa	2.7	Pesaḥ.	Pesaḥim	2.3
Bik.	Bikkurim	1.11	Qid.	Qiddušin	3.7
Dem.	Demaʾi	1.3	Qin.	Qinnim	5.11
ʿEd.	ʿEduyyot	4.7	Roʾš Haš.	Roʾš Haššana	2.8
ʿErub.	ʿErubin	2.2	Šab.	Šabbat	2.1
Giṭ.	Giṭṭin	3.6	Sanh.	Sanhedrin	4.4
Ḥag.	Ḥagiga	2.12	Šeb.	Šebiʿit	1.5
Ḥal.	Ḥalla	1.9	Šebu.	Šebuʿot	4.6
Hor.	Horayot	4.10	Šeqal.	Šeqalim	2.4
Ḥul.	Ḥullin	5.3	Soṭa	Soṭa	3.5
Kel.	Kelim	6.1	Suk.	Sukka	2.6
Ker.	Keritot	5.7	Ṭ. Yom	Ṭebul Yom	6.10
Ketub.	Ketubot	3.2	Taʿan.	Taʿanit	2.9
Kil.	Kilʾayim	1.4	Tamid	Tamid	5.9
Maʿaś.	Maʿaśerot	1.7	Tem.	Temura	5.6
Maʿaś. Š.	Maʿaśer Šeni	1.8	Ter.	Terumot	1.6
Mak.	Makkot	4.5	Ṭohar.	Ṭohorot	6.5
Makš.	Makširin	6.8	ʿUq.	ʿUqṣin	6.12
Meg.	Megilla	2.10	Yad.	Yadayim	6.11
Meʿil.	Meʿila	5.8	Yeb.	Yebamot	3.1
Menaḥ.	Menaḥot	5.2	Yomaʾ	Yomaʾ	2.5
Mid.	Middot	5.10	Zab.	Zabim	6.9
Miqw.	Miqwaʾot	6.6	Zebaḥ.	Zebaḥim	5.1
Moʿed Qaṭ.	Moʿed Qaṭan	2.11			

Targumim

Targumim on the Writings and Prophets are indicated by the abbreviation Tg. placed in front of the usual abbreviation for the biblical book. Targumim on the Pentateuch use one of the following abbreviations:

Frg. Tg.	Fragmentary Targum
Tg. Neof. 1	Targum Neofiti 1
Tg. Onq.	Targum Onqelos
Tg. Ps.-J.	Targum Pseudo-Jonathan

Midrashim

Midrashim on the biblical books are indicated by the abbreviation Midr. placed in front of the usual abbreviation for the biblical book. Where a more common name exists, the title is spelled out (e.g., *Sipra, Mekilta de Rabbi Ishmael, Pesikta Rabbati*).

Qumran / Dead Sea Scrolls

1Q28a	Rule of the Congregation (1QSa or Rule Annex)
1QapGen	Genesis Apocryphon
1QH	Thanksgiving Hymns/Psalms (*Hôdāyôt*)
1QM	War Scroll (*Milḥāmâ*)
1QpHab	*Pesher* on Habakkuk
1QS	Manual of Discipline (Rule/Order of the Community)
4Q161	Commentary on Isaiah (A) (4QpIsaᵃ)
4Q174	Florilegium (4QFlor)
4Q175	Testimonia (4QTestim)
4Q246	4QpsDan arᵃ (formerly 4QpsDan Aᵃ or 4Q243)
4QEnGiantsᵃ	Book of the Giants
4QMMT	*Miqsāt Maʿăsê Tôrâ*
4QPBless	Patriarchal Blessings (formerly 4QpGen 49)
4QPrNab	Prayer of Nabonidus
11QMelch	Melchizedek text
11QTempleᵃ	Temple Scroll
CD	Damascus Document

Greek Manuscripts

Sigla for Greek manuscripts basically follow that laid out in UBS⁴, pages 4*–52*. The original hand of a manuscript is indicated by an asterisk (א*), successive correctors by superscript numbers (א¹, א², etc.). Nonbiblical papyri are abbreviated according to the following list (see BAGD xxxi–xxxii for bibliographic information):

P. Fay.	Papyrus Fayûm
P. Lond.	Papyrus London
P. Oxy.	Papyrus Oxyrhynchus
P. Tebt.	Papyrus Tebtunis

Greek Transliteration

α	a	ζ	z	λ	l	π	p	φ	ph
β	b	η	ē	μ	m	ρ	r	χ	ch
γ	g (n)	θ	th	ν	n	σ ς	s	ψ	ps
δ	d	ι	i	ξ	x	τ	t	ω	ō
ε	e	κ	k	ο	o	υ	y (u)	ʽ	h

Notes on the transliteration of Greek

1. Accents, lenis (smooth breathing), and *iota* subscript are not shown in transliteration.
2. The transliteration of asper (rough breathing) precedes a vowel or diphthong (e.g., ἁ = *ha*; αἱ = *hai*) and follows ρ (i.e., ῥ = *rh*).
3. *Gamma* is transliterated *n* only when it precedes γ, κ, ξ, or χ.
4. *Upsilon* is transliterated *u* only when it is part of a diphthong (i.e., αυ, ευ, ου, υι).

Hebrew Transliteration

א	ʾ	בָ	ā	qāmeṣ	
ב	b	בַ	a	pataḥ	
ג	g	חַ	a	furtive pataḥ	
ד	d	בֶ	e	sĕgôl	
ה	h	בֵ	ē	ṣērê	
ו	w	בִ	i	short ḥîreq	
ז	z	בִ	ī	long ḥîreq written defectively	
ח	ḥ	בָ	o	qāmeṣ ḥāṭûp	
ט	ṭ	בוֹ	ô	ḥôlem written fully	
י	y	בֹ	ō	ḥôlem written defectively	
כ ך	k	בוּ	û	šûreq	
ל	l	בֻ	u	short qibbûṣ	
מ ם	m	בֻ	ū	long qibbûṣ written defectively	
נ ן	n	בָה	â	final qāmeṣ hē (בָה = āh)	
ס	s	בֶי	ê	sĕgôl yôd (בֶי = êy)	
ע	ʿ	בֵי	ê	ṣērê yôd (בֵי = êy)	
פ ף	p	בִי	î	ḥîreq yôd (בִי = îy)	
צ ץ	ṣ	בֲ	ă	ḥāṭēp pataḥ	
ק	q	בֱ	ě	ḥāṭēp sĕgôl	
ר	r	בֳ	ŏ	ḥāṭēp qāmeṣ	
שׂ	ś	בְ	ĕ	vocal šĕwāʾ	
שׁ	š	בְ	–	silent šĕwāʾ	
ת	t				

Notes on the transliteration of Hebrew
1. Accents are not shown in transliteration.
2. Silent *šĕwâ* is not indicated in transliteration.
3. The unaspirated forms of ת פ כ ד ג ב are not specially indicated in transliteration.
4. *Dāgeš forte* is indicated by doubling the consonant. *Dāgeš* present for euphonious reasons is not indicated in transliteration.
5. *Maqqēp* is represented by a hyphen.

Introduction to
the Gospel of Luke

Overview

The Gospel of Luke is unique in at least two ways. First, it is the longest Gospel. In NA, Matthew occupies 87 pages, Mark (through 16:8) 60 pages, and John 73 pages, while Luke takes up 96 pages. A comparison of verses reveals a similar count: Matthew has 1,071 verses, Mark has 678 verses, John has 869 verses, while Luke contains 1,151 verses.[1] Second, it is the only Gospel with a sequel. As such Luke not only introduces Jesus and his ministry, but also shows how that ministry relates to the early church era. This linkage enables Luke to discuss how God brought his salvation in Jesus, how the earliest church preached Jesus, and how they carried out their mission to both Jew and Gentile. The two volumes and their message are virtually inseparable, despite the canonical division. Luke's Gospel often lays the foundation for many of the issues whose answers come in Acts.

Luke–Acts highlights God's plan. It explains how Jew and Gentile could end up as equals in a community planted by God, even though that community's roots were originally grounded in a promise to Israel. Four issues were particularly problematic in the church of Luke's time.

First was the question of salvation. How could Gentiles be included as God's people on an equal basis with Jews, extending even to matters like table fellowship and the exclusion of circumcision? How did the hope of God open up to include all races—to the exclusion of so much that was related to law and Jewish tradition? Luke answers these questions largely in Acts, as he explains how God directed this entire process.

Second, the seeming paradox exists that while God's plan was at work the most natural audience for the message, the Jewish nation, was responding largely negatively. Indeed Jews even persecuted Christians who preached God's hope to them. Why was God's plan

---

This introduction is an updated and expanded version of my 1992b article on the Gospel of Luke in the *Dictionary of Jesus and the Gospels*. I wish to thank the publisher, InterVarsity Press, for the use of this material.

1. The verse count is from Aland and Aland 1987: 29.

meeting so much hostility? Was this new community cursed for being too generous with God's promise or was it blessed? If blessed, where was evidence of such blessing? Had God ceased to reach out to Israel? Had the new community withdrawn itself from the old community of faith? The Lucan answer to this question is that the church did not separate itself from Israel; it continued to preach to the nation and did not withdraw. Rather, Israel turned the church out, forcing it to form a new community. Luke's Gospel lays the groundwork for this reply in detailing how the nation and especially its leadership reacted to Jesus.

The third issue was how the person and teaching of a crucified Jesus fit into God's plan. How could Jesus, despite his physical absence, continue to exercise a presence and represent the hope of God? How could the church exalt such an "absent" figure and regard him as the center of God's work? How could a slain figure bring the consummation of God's promises? How would and could consummation come through him? Acts supplies the major answers to these questions by emphasizing the exaltation of Jesus, but the Gospel lays the groundwork by presenting the Christology that underlies the exaltation.

Fourth, what does it mean to respond to Jesus? What is required, what can one expect in making such a commitment, and how should one live until the day Jesus returns and the hope is realized? In short, what are believers and the new community to be? This is a major burden of the Gospel of Luke: to define Jesus' mission and that of the disciples who follow him. The bulk of Luke explains how Jesus prepared the disciples for his departure and prepared them to minister in his absence. This is where the crucial Lucan section of chapters 9–19, the Jerusalem journey, fits into the Gospel and controls its purpose. Accordingly, one should not separate the teaching of this Gospel too greatly from the period of the church. In Luke 24:44–49 (see also Luke 5:31–32) Jesus equates his mission with that of the church. The ethic of the Jerusalem journey section and of the Sermon on the Plain comes into view because of the realities of impending rejection. Luke records them for Theophilus so that he can be reassured about what God's plan is, what a disciple is called to be, and how a disciple participates in the community's task to identify and proclaim Jesus, not only through the message that the new community delivers about Jesus, but also by the way that disciples live in a world hostile to that declaration.

Luke's Gospel and his sequel cover these questions. So Luke's task is to reassure Theophilus (Luke 1:4), especially concerning the disputed presence of Gentiles in a new community. Acts develops this question; the Gospel points out the hostility believers face, especially from Judaism. Jesus faced similar hostility, as did the faithful prophets of old. Most important to Luke's Gospel is the role of Jesus in God's plan and promise, while Acts describes the nature of the new community that emerged from his ministry. This new community has historical roots in Jewish promise but is under intense pressure from the ancient Jewish community. Additional pressure comes from Jewish Christians who want Gentiles to relate more favorably to some matters of the law. Much of Judaism rejected Christian claims of fulfillment in Jesus. Does a Gentile really belong in this new community? Can God really be behind a community that faces so much hostility and rejection? What was Jesus really about in his life and teaching? How do Jesus' life, teaching, death, and resurrection really reflect divine "events fulfilled among us" (Luke 1:1)? These questions about God's plan, his Chosen One, and the emerging new community are at the heart of Luke's Gospel.

So Luke's Gospel highlights the activity of a mighty and faithful God through Jesus, the Promised One who shows the way. God reveals himself, his elect one, his promise, and his plan through the one who is now the risen Messiah and Lord (Acts 2:36; 10:36). Luke's Gospel introduces the fulfillment figure and the note of hostility, while Acts chronicles the initial key chapter of the new community. Luke–Acts says Jesus is Lord of all, so salvation can go to all. Salvation comes on the terms the risen Lord sets. A new way, in contrast to official Judaism, had emerged. It was a way promised in the old sacred texts, though the promise's form was not originally understood. Even Jesus' disciples during his ministry had to learn how the plan worked (Luke 9:35, 44–45; 18:31–34; 24:44–47). The new community's separation from Judaism was not the Christians' fault. Jesus and the church always proclaimed the hope to the Jews. However, the offer met with intense opposition. Such hostility slew Jesus, and Christians can continue to expect such resistance until the end. The need is to be faithful. Nonetheless, God was and is behind this new movement. Jesus' work, teaching, death, and resurrection show this truth (Luke), while the new era shows the Word's expansion through the church from Peter in Jerusalem to Paul in Rome (Acts). Both Jew and Gentile are welcome in this new community. Indeed God has directed the entire affair, even down to how Jews and Gentiles should relate to one another in the new community (Acts 10–11, 15). Be assured: Jesus revealed God's will, way, and blessing. Blessings are available to all who realize they are lost and so turn to God through Jesus (Luke 5:30–32; 19:10). God has kept and will keep his promises to those who turn to him, promises whose roots extend into the hope of the ancient Scriptures (Luke

1:14–17, 31–35, 57–79; 4:16–30; 24:44–47) and whose realization has come and will come in Jesus (Acts 2:14–41; 3:11–26).

The next section in this introduction treats issues that normally belong in technical NT introductions, while the remaining units introduce the message of Luke.[2]

Origin and Purpose
Authorship

Neither the Gospel of Luke nor the Acts of the Apostles names its author. A combination of external and internal evidence suggests that Luke was the author of both works.

Internal Evidence. The internal features concentrate on two points. First, the author is not an eyewitness to most of the events in his two volumes, especially those tied to the ministry of Jesus (Luke 1:1–2). Rather, he has relied on his study of traditions, which came from "eyewitnesses and servants of the Word" (Luke 1:2–4). Second, Luke presents himself as a companion of Paul in those parts of Acts known as the "we" sections (Acts 16:10–17; 20:5–15; 21:1–18; 27:1–28:16). This feature, though debated with respect to its historical reliability, limits options about the author's identity.

A current debate surrounding the "we" sections is whether they reflect the testimony of an eyewitness (Ellis 1974: 43–44; Hemer 1989: 312–34) or are a literary device that gives the impression of the presence of an eyewitness (Haenchen 1971: 85–90; Vielhauer 1966: 33–34, 47–48). Wrapped up in this question also is the issue of how well the author of the Third Gospel knew Paul, since the "we" sections of Acts portray their author as a traveling companion of Paul. Those who reject such a connection attempt to compare Luke's picture of Paul with the self-portrait of the Pauline Letters. They argue that the two pictures do not match in historical detail or in theological emphasis. In addition, Luke fails to use the Pauline Letters to describe Paul's work and position. Vielhauer argues that the portraits are too far apart for the author of the Third Gospel to be a companion of Paul. But Fitzmyer (1989: 1–26) defends the connection, arguing that a creative literary device cannot explain how the "we" units appear and disappear in such an arbitrary manner. He also notes that several "sailing" references, which would be candidates for such literary insertions, lack them (Acts 13:4, 13; 14:26;

---

2. For many of the technical aspects of style and introduction it makes no sense to repeat the excellent introduction of Fitzmyer 1981: 1–283. In particular I defer to his treatment of the current state of Lucan studies (pp. 3–34), some aspects of his discussion of Luke's composition (pp. 63–106), and his treatment of Lucan style and language (pp. 107–27), as well as the details of the manuscript tradition behind Luke (pp. 128–33).

17:14; 18:18, 21; 20:1–2). He suggests that Luke may be only a "junior" companion, in contrast to Irenaeus's famous claim that Luke was "inseparable" from Paul (*Against Heresies* 3.14.1). In addition, Goulder (1989: 129–46) suggests that Luke may have known and alluded to Paul's First Letter to Corinth and, to a lesser extent, to his First Letter to Thessalonica. Others defend the compatibility of the two portraits of Paul (F. F. Bruce 1975–76). So internal evidence in Luke–Acts tells us that the writer knew Paul and was at least a second-generation Christian.

External Evidence. The Pauline letters name some of the potential candidates who traveled with Paul: Mark, Aristarchus, Demas, and Luke (Philem. 24; Col. 4:14). To this list, one could add figures such as Timothy, Titus, Silas, Epaphras, and Barnabas. Yet despite the wide selection of potential candidates available as companions of Paul, the tradition of the church gives attention to only one name as the author of these volumes—Luke. This tradition was firmly fixed in the early church by A.D. 200 and remained so without any hint of contrary opinion. The absence of any dispute about this detail is a strong reason to take the tradition seriously. Allusions to the Gospel appear as early as 1 Clem. 13.2; 48.4 (ca. 95–96); 2 Clem. 13.4 (ca. 100). In addition, a use of Jesus' teaching, as reflected in Luke 10:7, appears in 1 Tim. 5:18. Numerous texts comment on authorship. Justin Martyr (ca. 160) in *Dialogue with Trypho* 103.19 speaks of Luke writing a "memoir of Jesus" and notes that the author is a follower of Paul. The Muratorian Canon (ca. 170–180) attributes the Gospel to Luke, a doctor, who is Paul's companion. Irenaeus (ca. 175–195) in *Against Heresies* 3.1.1 and 3.14.1 attributes the Gospel to Luke, follower of Paul, and notes how the "we" sections suggest the connection. The so-called Anti-Marcionite Prologue to Luke (ca. 175) describes Luke as a native of Antioch in Syria (Acts 11:19–30; 13:1–3; 15:30–35). It says he lived to be 84, was a doctor, was unmarried, wrote in Achaia, and died in Boeotia. Tertullian (early third century) in *Against Marcion* 4.2.2 and 4.5.3 calls the Gospel a digest of Paul's gospel. The Monarchian Prologue (date disputed: either third or fourth century) gives Luke's age at death as 74. Finally, Eusebius (early fourth century) in *Ecclesiastical History* 3.4.2 mentions Luke as a companion to Paul, native of Antioch, and author of these volumes.

Fitzmyer (1981: 40) divides the external evidence handily into two categories: what can be deduced from the NT and what cannot be deduced from it. That Luke was a physician, was tied to Paul, was not an eyewitness, and wrote his Gospel with concern for Gentiles are facts the NT makes clear. That Luke was from Syria, proclaimed Paul's gospel, was unmarried, was childless, and died at an old age are ideas that are not in the NT. Though the differences about Luke's age at death tell us that not everything in these traditions is indisputably true, their unity about authorship makes almost certain the identification of Luke as the Gospel's author. The tradition's testimony also makes Luke's connection to Paul very likely.

Luke: A Gentile and a Doctor? Two other questions about Luke require discussion. Was he a Gentile? Was he a doctor? Most see Luke as a Gentile, though they debate whether he was a pure Gentile or a "non-Jewish" Semite. An exception is Ellis (1974: 52–53), who argues that Luke was a Hellenistic Jewish Christian because (1) Luke's knowledge of the OT was great; (2) Col. 4:10–11, with its reference to those "of the circumcision," does not suggest that Luke was not Jewish, but merely that he was a Hellenist; and (3) the use of Palestinian language shows Luke's Jewish roots. But Ellis's reading of Col. 4:10–11 is not a natural one, since all Jews received circumcision (McKnight 1991a: 78–82) and Luke (4:14) is not listed among the "circumcised." More recently, Salmon (1988) defends this view, noting that the author (1) distinguishes Jewish groups, (2) discusses Torah observances in detail, (3) is interested in Gentile mission as a Jewish problem, and (4) calls Christianity "a sect" of Judaism. To this can be added the author's thorough knowledge of the OT. One cannot rule out this ethnic possibility for Luke, but other factors, noted below, along with Col. 4:14, make it less likely.

Fitzmyer (1981: 42–47) suggests that Luke is a non-Jewish Semite because of (1) the Col. 4:10–11, 14 text, (2) the shortened form of Luke's name, a Greek form of a Latin name, and (3) the details of the church tradition, which place Luke in Antioch of Syria. This view is quite possible. In fact, when one puts Fitzmyer's points together with Salmon's, the possibility is that Luke was a former God-fearer or Jewish proselyte.[3]

Most commentators identify Luke as a Gentile without any further detail. They (1) point to Col. 4:10–11, 14, (2) note Acts 1:19, which mentions a field with a Semitic name and then speaks of "their" language, and (3) point out the attention to Hellenistic locales and the concern for Gentiles. This last argument is not strong, since a Jew like Paul could fit into such geographical locales and concerns. In sum, it seems very likely that Luke was a Gentile,

---

3. On "God-fearers," see the discussion below on Luke's audience. For more details of the recent discussion, see Sterling 1992: 328. However, I reject Sterling's proposal (p. 326) that the author of Luke–Acts was not Luke but only interviewed him and used him as a source for Acts 13–28. One must explain why tradition names only Luke as the author.

though it is unclear whether his cultural background was Semitic. In any case, he probably had religious contact with Judaism before coming to Christ.

Colossians 4:14 refers to Luke as a doctor. In 1882, Hobart tried to bolster this connection by indicating all the technical verbal evidence for Luke's vocation. Despite the wealth of references Hobart gathered, the case was rendered ambiguous by the work of Cadbury (1926), who showed that almost all of the alleged technical medical vocabulary appeared in everyday Greek documents such as the LXX, Josephus, Lucian, and Plutarch. This meant that the language could have come from a literate person within any vocation. Cadbury's work does not, however, deny that Luke could have been a doctor, but only that the vocabulary of these books does not guarantee that he was one. Ultimately the issue concerns how one views Colossians and the tradition about Luke that grew up in the early church. Since such a detail was not necessary to note and served no apologetic concern, it can be seen to reflect reality.

So Luke is Paul's "sometime" companion. He is likely to be a medical doctor, possibly from Antioch of Syria, who is not Jewish, though whether he is Syrian or a Greco-Roman is not clear. The tradition also indicates that he lived a long life.

Sources

Sources of the Gospel. The sources of Luke's work are a debated part of a complex area known as the Synoptic problem.[4] Numerous approaches to the issue have been suggested.

Some argue for the independence of the Synoptic documents, though the amount of agreement in wording and order between these Gospels is against this approach. In addition, Luke's mention of predecessors in his preface (Luke 1:1–4) suggests that this approach is too simple.

An old solution, known as the Augustinian hypothesis, argues that the order is Matthew–Mark–Luke. The major problem with this hypothesis is that it cannot explain the contents of Mark, as a summarizing Gospel, without appealing to its use of Luke.

The Griesbach or "two-Gospel" hypothesis argues that the correct order is Matthew–Luke–Mark (Farmer 1964). The appeal of this view is the absence of hypothesized sources and its agreement with early church tradition, which suggests that Matthew's Gospel was the earliest. Its major problems are demonstrating that Luke knew Matthew and explaining how Mark, as a summarizing Gospel, often has *more* vivid detail in pericopes that overlap with the

---

4. Excursus 4 discusses my use of sources in this commentary.

other Gospels (C. F. Evans 1990: 17 n. *w*). Mark's lack of an infancy narrative or extended teaching, like the Sermon on the Mount (or Plain), is also against Mark coming last, especially since Mark's use of the eschatological parables or discourses shows that he can report Jesus' discourses.

Most scholars hold to some form of the "four-source" theory, a view first formalized by Streeter (1924) and defended today by Tuckett (1983) and Fitzmyer (1981: 63–106; Fitzmyer's defense of this approach as it relates to Luke is the most detailed available). This view argues for the priority of Mark and the use of a "sayings" source known as Q. In addition, Matthew has special source material (M), while Luke has his special material (L). Thus the four sources are Mark, Q, L, and M, and Luke would have used Mark, Q, and L. It must be noted that the most challenged aspect of this approach is the nature and evidence for Q, a document containing only sayings, which has only the Gospel of Thomas as a possible ancient parallel in this genre.

A recent variation of the two-Gospel hypothesis, which maintains Marcan priority, comes from Goulder (1989: 3–71), who argues for the order Mark–Matthew–Luke. He maintains Marcan priority, while dispensing with Q, the major hypothesized source. Thus, his view requires that Luke used Matthew. This connection between Matthew and Luke can be challenged, a challenge that also impacts Farmer's approach. The argument that Luke used Matthew has several points against it. (1) It has trouble explaining the unique infancy material in Luke and the absence of any indication of knowledge about Matthew's infancy material. (2) It has trouble explaining the reorganization of Matthean-like material in the central section of Luke (9:51–19:44) and Luke's distinct use of the eschatological discourse and other Matthean discourses (Fitzmyer 1981: 75). (3) It also must posit significant recasting of several Matthean parables and sayings (pounds, lost sheep, great banquet, unfaithful steward, Beatitudes, Lord's Prayer). (4) Luke never has the Matthean portions of triple tradition material (Fitzmyer 1981: 75). (5) With two exceptions (3:7–9, 17; 4:2b–13), Luke never has material from Matthew in the same Marcan context as does Matthew. (6) The view is a denial of Luke 1:1–4 with its appeal to many predecessors: both the two-Gospel view and that of Goulder have only two sources, which is not the "many" of Luke 1:1. Goulder notes this problem (1989: 27–37), but argues that the other predecessors were not "authoritative documents which Luke accepted" as equal to Matthew and Mark. But how can this be assured, when Luke ties them to authoritative tradition in the same breath (1:2)?

So in all likelihood, Luke had access to Mark, special material (L), and traditions (which also are reflected in Matthew, though often with some, even significant, divergence). In fact, the Q material is so varied in character that some speak of two forms of Q: a Matthean version and a Lucan version (Marshall often makes this distinction in handling these texts in his 1978 commentary). This means that Q may not be a fixed, written tradition, but rather a pool of widely circulating traditions. Given the amount of teaching and parables that Matthew and Luke share, one cannot rule out that L and Q might have overlapped, with Matthew using Q and Luke using L. While noting that others speak of Q as a *bona fide* document or set of documents, I understand Q to be a fluid pool of traditions from which both Luke and Matthew drew.

To show how the material breaks down by paragraph units, I provide the following lists of passages and sources, modified from C. F. Evans 1990: 17–18 and Fitzmyer 1981: 67.[5] Those who have another view of Synoptic relationships can still benefit from the listings. The lists follow Lucan order, so rearrangements are easily spotted.

The first list shows Lucan parallels with Mark. Parentheses around a reference indicate that the dependence is subject to some doubt. This means that the Matthean version (and so Q) may have influenced certain texts, though the passion material (Luke 22–23) may reflect L.

Luke	Mark
(3:1–7)	(1:1–6)
(3:19–20)	(6:17–18)
(3:21–22)	(1:9–11)
(4:1–2a)	(1:12–13a)
4:14–15	1:14–15
4:31–44	1:21–39
5:12–6:19	1:40–3:19
8:4–9:17	3:31–4:25; 4:35–5:43; 6:6–16, 30–44
9:18–50, (51)	8:27–9:8; 9:14–41; (10:1)
18:15–43	10:13–34, 46–52
19:28–38	11:1–10
19:45–21:33; (21:37)	11:11, 15–18; 11:27–12:27;12:35–13:32; (11:18b–19)
22:1–13	14:1–2, 10–16
(22:14–23)	(14:17–25)

5. These lists are according to paragraph units, so some individual verses for each category may be excluded in the final totals.

(22:39–53)	(14:26–52)
(22:54–71)	(14:53–72)
(23:1–5, 18–25)	(15:1–15)
(23:26, 33–38)	(15:21–32)
23:44–49	15:33–41
23:50–56	15:42–47
24:1–12	16:1–8

Mark thus relates to 406 verses of Luke, or about 35 percent of Luke's whole. The most important observation is that the Marcan material tends to come in blocks, especially in the sections that describe Jesus' ministry. (This is one of the reasons that Mark is seen as a fundamental source.) A few texts related to Mark also have material from Q or L: Luke 3:7–14, 23–38; 4:2b–13; 5:1–11; 19:1–27; 22:28–33, 35–38; 23:6–16, 27–31, 39b–43, 47b–49.

The next list shows Luke's parallels with Q/Matthew, where the picture is more complex. Problematic texts involve sayings or parables where factors raise uncertainties about a direct connection. Three types of situations raise uncertainty: (1) one Gospel writer may place in one location what the other Gospel writer has in a different place; (2) one writer may bring together material that another writer has in separate locations; and (3) the accounts may be rendered in significantly different terms. Parentheses in the following list indicate where C. F. Evans (1990: 21–22) expresses uncertainty; an asterisk (*) indicates my own uncertainty. Such texts, in my view, reflect either a variant Q or a potential overlap with L or both. Those who hold to Matthean priority will see Matthew as the point of connection, not Q.[6]

Luke	Matthew/Q
3:7–9, 16–17	3:7–12
4:2–12	4:2–10
6:20–23, 27–30, 31, 32–36, 37–40, 41–46, 47–49	5:2–4, 6–7, 11–12, 39–40, 42; (7:12); 5:44–46; 5:48; 7:1–2; (15:14; 10:24–25); 7:3–5, 16–21; (12:33–35); 7:24–27
7:1–10	8:5–13
7:18–23	11:2–6
7:24–35	11:7–19
9:57–60	8:19–22
* 10:2–16	9:37–38; 10:16, 9–10a, 11–13, 10b, 7–8, 14–15; 11:21–23; 10:40

6. The references for Q/Matthew reflect Lucan order and therefore are sometimes out of sequence.

* 10:21–22	11:25–27
* 10:23–24	13:16–17
* (11:1–4)	(6:9–13)
* 11:9–13	7:7–11
11:14–23	12:22–30
11:24–26	12:43–45
11:29–32	12:38–42
* 11:33–35	5:15; 6:22–23
* 11:39–52	23:25–26, 23, 6–7; 23:27, 4, 29–31, 34–36, 13
* 12:2–12	10:26–33; 12:32; 10:19–20
* 12:22–34	6:25–33, 19–21
* 12:39–46	24:43–51
13:18–21	13:31–33
* 13:24–30	7:13–14; 25:10–12; 7:22–23; 8:11–12; 19:30
* 13:34–35	23:37–39
* (14:15–24)	(22:1–10)
* 14:26–27	10:37–38
* (15:1–7)	(18:12–14)
* (16:16)	(11:12–13)
* (16:17)	(5:18)
* (16:18)	(5:32)
* (17:1–4)	(18:6–7, 15, 21–22)
* 17:22–37	24:26–28, 37–41, 40, 28
* (19:11–27)	(25:14–30)

This material represents 241 verses in Luke that are not found in Mark, or about 21 percent of Luke. The questionable Q texts also tend to cluster in the central section of Luke's Gospel. This unit, Luke 9:51–19:44, is basically a combination of large amounts of L material with material that has seeming parallels with Matthew. Given the amount of unique L material and the thematic character of some parts of this section, it is hard to know if material is really from Q or from L. Goulder (1989: 73–128) suggests a large amount of Lucan rewriting of Matthean material, positing that little of L really comes from a source, but is actually reflective of Lucan emphases and elaboration. The problem with this approach is that it means that Luke handled Marcan material very differently from the way he handled Matthew (or Q), since Luke did little to change the substance of his Marcan material.

C. F. Evans (1990: 26–27) lists forty-seven L texts (parentheses indicate questions about influence either from Q [or Matthew] or Mark):

1:5–2:52	(10:25–28)	13:10–17	(17:28–32)
3:10–14	10:29–37	13:31–33	18:1–8
3:23–38	10:38–42	14:1–6	18:9–14
(4:16–30)	11:5–8	14:7–14	19:1–10
5:1–11	11:27–28	14:28–35 (33?)	19:41–44
(5:39)	(12:1)	15:1–10	21:34–36
7:11–17	12:13–21	15:11–32	22:15–18, 27,
(7:36–50)	(12:35–38)	16:1–15	(31–33), 35–38
(8:1–3)	12:47–48	16:19–31	23:6–16
9:51–55	12:49–50	17:7–10	23:27–31
9:61–62	12:54–56	17:11–19	23:39–43
10:1, 17–20	13:1–9	17:20–21	24:13–53

This unique material comprises 485 verses of Luke, or about 42 percent of Luke's whole. Much in Luke is not found elsewhere. This material contains not only a unique portrait of Jesus' infancy, but also many fresh sayings and parables of Jesus.

Four miracles are unique (7:11–17; 13:10–17; 14:1–6; 17:11–19). Three deal either with a Sabbath controversy or with the response of a non-Jew to Jesus. Several parables are indisputably unique to Luke (10:29–37; 11:5–8; 12:13–21; 15:1–7, 8–10, 11–32; 16:1–8, 19–31; 18:1–8, 9–14). Their content has great variety, stressing service (Samaritan: 10:29–37), humility (Pharisee and publican: 18:9–14), diligence in prayer and in eschatological hope (nagging friend: 11:5–8; nagging widow: 18:1–8), the preciousness of the lost and the joy at their recovery (lost coin and lost son: 15:8–10, 11–32), and care in the use of resources and/or kindness to the poor (rich fool: 12:13–21; crafty steward: 16:1–8; rich man and Lazarus: 16:19–31). The ethical thrust of Luke's Gospel emerges in this material. Four additional parables that emphasize God's plan have potential overlap with Matthew and yet are cast in fresh light by Luke: one should be faithful until Jesus returns (cruel steward: 12:39–46), one should rejoice to sit at the table (great banquet: 14:15–24), one should rejoice at the coming of the lost (lost sheep: 15:1–7), and one should be faithful with what the master supplies, resting on his goodness (pounds: 19:11–27). The breadth of topics in the Gospel and Luke's pastoral concern emerge in this unique or uniquely emphasized material.

The Gospel's Link with Acts. In thinking about the use of sources, one should also consider that Luke structured his Gospel to anticipate his sequel, Acts. This connection to Acts is seen in the repetition of the prologue (Luke 1:1–4; Acts 1:1). In fact, the Acts prologue looks back to Luke's Gospel in a style reminiscent of other ancient works (Josephus, *Against Apion* 1.1 §1). The connection is also noted in the parallel themes that dominate the two volumes (Maddox 1982: 9–12). Jesus heals and so do Peter and Paul. Jesus must travel to Jerusalem, while Paul must go to Rome. Jesus is slain by opposition and so is Stephen. The account of the ascension also links the two volumes tightly together (Luke 24:49–53; Acts 1:1–11). Efforts to note extensive parallels between Luke and Acts have often brought much discussion (Talbert 1974). Though each of these connections needs evaluation, there is no doubt that Luke intends to show parallels between the time of Jesus and the time of his followers. Both the story and the theology of the two volumes are linked together. To understand the emergence of the church, one must understand Jesus and the plan of God.

Luke as Historian. One other point emerges from a look at Luke's use of sources: he was careful with his material. Great debate rages about how good a historian Luke was. Many see him handling his materials with great freedom for theological (Goulder 1989; Haenchen 1971; Dibelius 1956) or sociological reasons (Esler 1987). Among the items under scrutiny are Luke's association of Jesus' birth with a census from Quirinius, his timing for the rebellion under Theudas, the authenticity of certain parables and sayings, the reality of the miracles, his portrait of the trials of Jesus, the details of his resurrection accounts, the faithful rendering of speeches, his portrayal of early church harmony, the uniqueness of the meeting with Cornelius, the reality of the Jerusalem council, and his portrait of Paul. The examination of such details must be done on a case-by-case basis. Differing judgments will be made in such matters, not just on the basis of the complexity of the evidence, which one must remember is not without its own historical gaps, but also because of philosophical worldview issues. Nonetheless an examination of Luke's use of his sources shows his general trustworthiness (Marshall 1970: 21–76). Investigations into his descriptions of settings, customs, and locales reveal the same sensitivity (Hengel 1980: vii, 3–49; Hemer 1989). Luke is a first-class ancient historian, and most good ancient historians understood their task well (see Fornara 1983: 142–68, on Thucydides and Polybius). Efforts to argue that Luke is exclusively either a theologian or a historian, with many opting to give history a lesser place, underplay the evidence in sources that show that Luke is careful with his material. He is not careless, nor is he a fabricator of events.

This point, however, does not mean that Luke cannot rearrange material for emphasis, summarize events in his own language, or bring out his own emphases as drawn from the tradition. A study of the above lists of Luke's sources and their arrangement reveals these traits. The Lucan speeches summarize and proclaim, as well as report. Luke is a sensitive observer of the events he describes. He is interested in both history and theology. He writes not just about the time sequence of events and teaching, but about their topical and theological relationship as well. He writes as a theologian and pastor, but as one whose direction is marked out by the history that preceded him. To underemphasize any element in the Lucan effort, whether pastoral, theological, or historical, is to underestimate the depth of his account.

Purpose, Readers, and Destination

It is debated whether Theophilus is already a Christian or is thinking of becoming one. Numerous intents for the Gospel and its sequel have been suggested (see Maddox 1982: 20–22):

1. an explanation of why Jesus has not returned (Conzelmann 1960: 95–234)
2. a defense brief for Christianity (Haenchen 1971: 100–102)
3. a defense of Paul before Rome (Mattill 1975)
4. a defense of Paul before the community (Jervell 1972: 17)
5. an anti-Gnostic concern (Talbert 1978: 13–15)
6. evangelism (O'Neill 1970: 172–85)
7. confirmation of the Word and the message of salvation (Van Unnik 1960; Marshall 1978: 35–36; O'Toole 1984: 17)
8. a theodicy of God's faithfulness to Israel (Tiede 1980: 27–28)
9. a sociological legitimation of full fellowship for Gentiles and a defense of the new community as not unfaithful to Rome (Esler 1987: 210–19; Sterling 1992 is close to this with his "apologetic historiography")
10. an effort at conciliation with Judaism by showing that the offer of salvation in Jesus Christ is the natural extension of Judaism (Brawley 1987: 155–59)
11. an anti-Semitic document and a total rejection of the Jews (J. T. Sanders 1987)

This plethora of credible suggestions shows the complexity of the Lucan enterprise. Of all of these suggestions, those centering on God's role in salvation and his new community are most likely to reflect the key aspects of Luke's comprehensive agenda (views 7–10). The examination of the Gospel's structure and theology will bear this out, as does a survey of Luke's unique material.

It is unlikely that Theophilus is just interested in becoming a Christian or is a Roman official who needs to have Christianity explained in order to accept it as a legitimate religion. Nor are Paul and his message of simple evangelism the object of defense. Too little of the Gospel deals with such legal, political concerns and too much exhortation deals with issues beyond simple evangelism. Paul is important to the last part of Acts only because of the mission and perspective he represents. Luke 1:3–4 suggests that Theophilus received some instruction. The detail in Luke–Acts about faithfulness, Jew-Gentile relations, and clinging to the hope of Jesus' return suggests a Gentile who is experiencing doubt about his association with the new community. The problems over table fellowship, Gentile inclusion, and examples of how rejection was faced in the early church also suggest this setting. Likewise the amount of ethical exhortation in the Gospel suggests this approach. Theophilus appears to be a man of rank (Luke 1:3) who has associated himself with the church, but doubts whether in fact he really belongs in this racially mixed and heavily persecuted community. In the Gospel, Luke takes Theophilus through Jesus' career in order to review how God worked to legitimize Jesus and how Jesus proclaimed hope. Luke also wishes to defend God's faithfulness to Israel and his promises, despite the rejection of the promise by many in the nation. (In this sense, Luke is not unlike Rom. 9–11.) The offer of the gospel openly includes Theophilus and calls him to remain faithful, committed, and expectant, even in the midst of intense *Jewish* rejection and with the hope that both Jews and Gentiles will turn to Jesus. What is very possible is that Theophilus had been a God-fearer before coming to Christ, since this can explain the interest in God-fearers in Acts (10:2, 22, 35; 13:16, 26, 43; 50; 17:4, 17; 18:7), as well as the extensive use of the OT in the two volumes.

Luke did not write, however, just for this one person, but for any who felt this tension. Any Gentile feeling out of place in an originally Jewish movement could benefit from the reassurance Luke offers. Any Jew (or Jewish Christian) troubled by the lack of Jewish response to the gospel or by the Gentile openness to the gospel could see that God directed the affair and that he gave the nation multiple invitations to join in God's renewed work. Christianity conflicted with Judaism not because the new movement consciously tried to isolate itself from the nation, but because it was forced out. This rejection is evident in Acts, but the seeds are sown in the rejection of Jesus so carefully detailed in Luke 9–13 and 22–23. For Luke, the new community is broad in its extension of blessing because Jesus preached that it be so (Luke 4:16–30; 5:30–32; 19:10; 24:44–47) and God directed that it be so (Acts 10:34–43; 15:1–21; 22:6–11; 26:15–20).

Date

The date of the Gospel's writing is disputed, but there are some limits. For example, the earliest possible date would be within years of the last recorded event in Acts, which takes place probably in 62. On the other hand, Irenaeus contains some indisputable citations, so that the latest possible date is around 170 (*Against Heresies* 3.13.3; 3.15.1).

On a comparison of Luke with material from Marcion, Josephus, Justin Martyr, and the Pseudo-Clementines, some scholars offer a date in the early to mid-second century (Knox 1942: 110, 120; O'Neill 1970: 19; Townsend 1984: 47–58). But the tone of Acts does not really fit the tone of other documents of this period, like 1 Clement (A.D. 95) and Ignatius (A.D. 117) (see Ellis 1974: 55). In addition, it is unlikely that such a late work would ignore Paul's letters as much as Acts does. Finally, possible allusions in 1 Clem. 5.6–7 (to Acts 26), 2.1 (Acts 20:35), and 18.1 (Acts 13:22) argue against this date. These allusions move the mid-second-century limit down to the mid-90s.

The most popular date is sometime after the fall of Jerusalem, usually 80–90.[7] The reasons set forth include the following: (1) Luke is said to be after Mark, which itself is a document of the 60s; (2) the picture of Paul as a hero figure needs time to emerge; (3) the portrait of churches like Ephesus requires a period before the Domitian persecution of the mid-90s; (4) the Lucan apocalyptic discourses with their description of siege and their focus on the city presuppose the fall and require a period after 70; and (5) some assert that the theology is late, even "early catholic."

Three of these arguments are less than central. The suggestion that Paul needs time to emerge as a hero is not clear. His letters and Acts agree that he was a central figure in the church, who generated some following and controversy. Paul's letters show that James gained respect rather quickly, so why not the same for Paul? The portrait of the churches, which are not yet under Roman persecution, can fit any time before Domitian (ruled 81–96) or any time outside of Nero's persecution (64; Tacitus, *Annals* 15.44). The debate about "early catholicism" in Luke–Acts continues, but it is by no means clear that Luke's theology reflects a "late" theology (Marshall 1970: 81–83, 212–15).

Two arguments have more substance. The suggestion that Luke follows Mark is likely (even if one thinks Matthew, not Mark, is the

---

7. Fitzmyer 1981: 53–57; F. F. Bruce 1988: 6–13 (of Acts); Bovon 1989: 23; Kümmel 1975: 151; Danker 1988: 17–18; Tiede 1980: 1–18, 70; Maddox 1982: 6–9; Esler 1987: 27–29; C. A. Evans 1990: 2; C. F. Evans 1990: 14; L. Johnson 1991: 2–3.

first Gospel in order, most still date Mark's work in the 60s or later). This date is close to the last event in Acts, which takes place in the early 60s. How quickly would Mark have been in circulation and thus accessible to Luke, especially if Luke had associations with major leaders of the church (Reicke 1986: 166–89)? The argument that time needed to pass for Mark to gain stature is similar to the argument that Paul as a hero figure needed time to develop. But Paul was a major figure almost instantly. Now if Mark had roots to Peter, then respect for the work would have been instant. Luke sought out whatever materials were in circulation (Luke 1:1). Since he mentions several such documents, "quasi-canonical" status was not a prerequisite.

The most central argument is that the eschatological discourses (Luke 19:41–44; 21:20–24) assume a post-70 date. These texts detail the siege and focus on the city, rather than on the temple alone, as the accounts in Matthew and Mark do. Esler recently (1987) has undertaken the most vigorous defense of this date. He argues that the details of these discourses cannot be attributed simply to "what inevitably happens in war," because some of the features, such as building a circumvallation, total destruction of the city, and the marching off of all the captives, were not inevitable results of war. In responding in this way, Esler challenges Dodd's assertion (1947: 49) that all war language in the discourse is possible for Jesus before 70, because the language fits ancient military operations against Israel, as well as parallels LXX descriptions of the sacking of Solomon's temple in 586 B.C. In making the critique, however, Esler misses a key point of the OT connection. The OT judgment was exercised because of *covenant unfaithfulness*. The parallel of Jerusalem's total destruction, with siege and total defeat, could be expected as a covenantal act of God. The result is that Esler's argument does not stand. There is no need to appeal to Jerusalem's fall as a *fait accompli* in the perspective of these texts.

In addition, proponents of an earlier date note that there is no direct reference to the fall of Jerusalem. That the fall is alluded to here is strictly an inference. Yet those who hold that an allusion to the fall is present also frequently hold that Luke often "updates" his material and perspective. If, as is claimed, he did this elsewhere, why not here with this major salvation-historical event in the divine calendar? Why the silence instead of a direct reference?

To sum up: the prediction of Jerusalem's fall is one that Jesus was capable of making solely on the basis of his knowledge of how God acts to judge covenant unfaithfulness. Luke makes no effort to "update" remarks here; he only clarifies that in the temple's collapse the city is not spared either. Thus, a major argument for a date in the 80s–90s does not work. Although a date in the 80s might seem possible and is popular, it is not the most likely.

This leaves another possibility, a date somewhere in the 60s (Hemer 1989: 365–410; Moessner 1989: 308–15; Ellis 1974: 57; Marshall 1978: 35). Reasons for this date include the following: (1) the picture in Acts that Rome, knowing little about the movement, is still deciding where Christianity fits; (2) failure to note the death of either James (62) or Paul (ca. late 60s); (3) the silence about Jerusalem's destruction, even in settings where it could have been mentioned editorially (e.g., Acts 6–7 [the Stephen account], 21–23 [Paul's arrest in Jerusalem]); and (4) the amount of uncertainty expressed about internal Gentile-Jewish relations, which fits a setting that parallels the Pauline Letters that deal with similar tensions (Romans, Galatians, 1 Cor. 8–10, Ephesians). This last reason is most significant and has not been developed enough in the discussion to date (Moessner 1989: 312–15). Acts presupposes a racially mixed community, which in turn suggests an earlier date, not a later one. Details about the law, table fellowship, and practices that may offend (Acts 6:1–6; 10–11; 15) also suggest an earlier time frame. That the Gentile mission still needs such vigorous and detailed defense further suggests this earlier period, since by the 80s the Gentile character of the Christian movement was a given. That believers need reassurance in the midst of intense Jewish pressure fits an early date as well.

More difficult to determine is when in the 60s Luke was written. Some argue that the ending of Acts indicates the date of completion in the early 60s. Others suggest that texts like Luke 11:49–51 presuppose the start of the struggle with Rome and offer a date in the later 60s. That Paul's death is not mentioned in Acts may be an indication that it is the early to mid-60s rather than the latter third of the 60s. On the other hand, the time required for Luke to receive and incorporate Mark might suggest a mid-60s time frame. Overall an early to mid-60s date is likely. Luke left the end of Paul's career open-ended, because that is where matters stood when he wrote.

Place of Writing

Where one fixes the place of Luke's writing depends on the date one fixes for the work. It is really unknown. Possibilities include Caesarea (60s), Rome (60s or 80s), Antioch (any date), or Greece (any date). The *"Anti-Marcionite" Prologues* and the *Monarchian Prologue* place its origins in Achaia (Greece), while Bovon (1989: 23) thinks Rome is likely. Fitzmyer (1981: 57) is right to say that the answer is "anyone's guess."

Ancient Manuscripts

In this section, I merely outline Luke's key witnesses according to the families in which major papyri, uncials, and minuscules are commonly classified.[8] Details on the contents of each manuscript can be found in Aland and Aland 1987, Fitzmyer 1981: 127–28, and NA. When I speak of geographic distribution in text-critical matters, I mean that a reading is found in more than one family. By the use of the abbreviation Byz, I refer to the Byzantine family as a group, the origin of which I date to the fourth century. The major manuscripts of the Gospel of Luke are the following (dates [by century] are given in parentheses):

Family	Manuscripts
Primary Alexandrian	$\mathfrak{P}^{75}$ (early 3d), ℵ (4th), B (4th)
Secondary Alexandrian	C (5th), L^e (8th), T (5th), W (5th), Ξ (6th), 33 (9th), 892 (9th)
Western	D^e (6th), Itala (4th), Syriac^s (4th), Syriac^c (4th)
Primary Byzantine	A (5th), E^e (8th), F^e (9th), G^e (9th), H^e (9th), N (6th), P^e (6th), W (5th), Γ (10th), Δ (9th), Θ (9th), 047 (8th), 055 (11th), 0211 (7th), Byz (4th)
Secondary Byzantine	K^e (9th), M (9th), R (6th), S (10th), U (9th), V (9th), X (10th), Y (9th), Λ (9th), Π (9th), Φ (6th), Ω (9th)

The majority of manuscripts are from the Byzantine family, but these are the later manuscripts. One problem in talking about the "majority text" is that what is being referred to depends on one's time frame. What is the majority text today may not necessarily have been the majority in the earliest period. The above chart reflects this reality in that the earlier manuscripts fall largely in the Alexandrian family and in versions reflecting the Western text. That Byzantine manuscripts now constitute the majority of available NT manuscripts is attributable to at least three factors: (1) severe Roman persecution caused vast destruction of the earliest manuscripts in the late first to early fourth centuries; (2) later Muslim persecutions in Middle Eastern and African regions after the seventh century did the same; and (3) only the Byzantine region of Christendom continued to use Greek as their religious language, while much of Christendom turned to Latin after the fourth century. For these historical reasons I prefer to weigh manuscripts, not

8. In the main, my classification follows Holmes 1989. Manuscript dates are given according to Aland and Aland 1987. Rather than giving priority to any one family of manuscripts, I prefer Holmes's "eclectic" approach to textual criticism.

count them.[9] One should also note that the Byzantine readings are frequently the most harmonistic in the Gospels. This basic internal feature is a stylistic reason for viewing the Byzantine family with some caution (details are in the additional notes). I use an eclectic approach, taking each variant on its own terms and weighing both external and internal considerations.

Structure and Argument

Luke's Gospel breaks down nicely into largely geographical divisions (the full outline is printed at the end of this introduction):

    I. Luke's preface and the introduction of John and Jesus (1:1–2:52)
    II. Preparation for ministry: anointed by God (3:1–4:13)
    III. Galilean ministry: revelation of Jesus (4:14–9:50)
    IV. Jerusalem journey: Jewish rejection and the new way (9:51–19:44)
    V. Jerusalem: the innocent one slain and raised (19:45–24:53)

The argument of Luke's Gospel emerges as one proceeds through it in literary order. With the basic structure and argument of the book in place, its major theological points can be examined. The most sensitive works that concentrate on the literary argument of Luke are those by Talbert (1982), Tiede (1988), and L. Johnson (1991: 3–24), while Tannehill (1986) treats the themes of Luke topically with a literary emphasis.

Luke's Preface and the Introduction of John and Jesus (1:1–2:52)

After a crucial preface in which Luke explains his task, the author launches into a unique comparison of John the Baptist and Jesus that shows how both represent the fulfillment of promises made by God. John is like Elijah (Luke 1:17), but Jesus has Davidic roles to fulfill and possesses a unique supernatural origin (Luke 1:31–35). John is forerunner, but Jesus is fulfillment. Everything in Luke 1–2 points to the superiority of Jesus.

Mary's hymn (Luke 1:46–56) praises the faithfulness of God to his promise and his blessing of those who are humble before him, setting up a major Lucan theme. Zechariah reiterates the hope in national, Davidic terms and sets forth the superior relationship of Jesus to John (Luke 1:67–79). In doing so, Zechariah links spiritual promises and national promises to Davidic hope.

Jesus' birth takes place in humble circumstances, but all the figures surrounding his birth are pious and responsive to the hope of

---

9. For more details on the relationships of the various textual families, see Holmes 1983 and Metzger 1992.

God. Jesus is praised by a priest, a humble virgin, shepherds, and a prophet and prophetess at the temple. These people, all of whom are portrayed as walking with God, have high expectations of Jesus. Only the word of Simeon to Mary gives an ominous ring. The old man notes that Jesus will be "a light for revelation to the nations and glory of your people Israel" (Luke 2:32). In fact, however, Jesus will also be a cause of grief for Mary and division in Israel (Luke 2:34–35). Jesus is the "salvation" of God (Luke 2:30), but in the midst of hope is the reality that fulfillment comes mixed with pain.

Jesus' own self-awareness concludes the introductory overture of the Gospel (Luke 2:41–52). Here the young boy declares that he must be about the work of his Father in the temple. Jesus notes his unique relationship to God and his association with God's presence and teaching.

This section, dominated by OT allusions, opens the Gospel with notes of fulfillment and God's direction—emphases that continue through the entire Gospel. John and Jesus are placed side by side in the pericopes of Luke 1; then Jesus has the stage in Luke 2. The structure imitates the theology of forerunner-fulfillment.

Preparation for Ministry: Anointed by God (3:1–4:13)

John and Jesus remain side by side in the next section on Jesus' ministry. John is the "one who goes before" (Isa. 40:3–5; Luke 3:1–6), while Jesus is the "one who comes" (Luke 3:15–17). Unlike Matthew and Mark, Luke lengthens his citation of Isa. 40 to make the point that salvation is seen by all people. Only Luke contains a section where the ethical dimensions of John's call to repentance in terms of response to others are made clear (Luke 3:10–14). John warns about judgment, calls for repentance, and promises the coming of one who brings God's Spirit. John baptizes Jesus, but the main feature of the baptism is the first of two heavenly testimonies to Jesus (Luke 3:21–22). John had promised that Jesus would bring the Spirit, but here Jesus is anointed with the Spirit. The first hints of fulfillment are here. The heavenly testimony calls Jesus the "beloved Son in whom I am well pleased." This fusion of Isa. 42 and Ps. 2 marks out Jesus as a regal, prophetic figure, who as a chosen servant of God brings God's revelation and salvation. The universal character of Jesus' relationship to humans is highlighted in the list of his ancestors (Luke 3:23–38). He is "son of Adam, son of God." His first actions are to overcome temptations from Satan (Luke 4:1–13), something Adam had failed to do. So the section shows Jesus as anointed by God, representative of humans, and faithful to God.

Galilean Ministry: Revelation of Jesus (4:14–9:50)

Jesus' teaching and miracles dominate the third section of Luke's Gospel. Major teaching blocks include his synagogue declaration of the fulfillment of God's promise (Luke 4:16–30) and the Sermon on the Plain (Luke 6:17–49). Elements unique to Luke are that the synagogue speech represents Jesus' self-description of his mission, while the sermon represents his fundamental ethic presented without the concerns related to Jewish tradition. The section's fundamental issue is, "Who is Jesus?" The unit pictures the growth of faith that comes to those whom Jesus gathers around himself. Their discovery is the vehicle that Luke uses to answer the question of Jesus' identity. Jesus follows their response with the first discussions of the hard road of discipleship. Following Jesus is full of blessing, but it is not easy.

In the synagogue speech (Luke 4:16–30), Jesus raises the note of fulfillment through the appeal to Isa. 61:1–2 and 58:6. He says that the anointing of God promised in Isa. 61 is fulfilled today. In the context of Luke, the anointing looks back to the anointing with the Spirit in Luke 3. Thus, the appeal to Isaiah is not just to the picture of a prophet, as allusions to Elijah and Elisha suggest, but it also asserts Jesus' regal role. He will bring salvation to all those in need: poor, blind, and captive. Rejection will be met with the taking of the message to others, an indirect allusion to the inclusion of Gentiles. The mission's scope is summarized here.

Luke 4–9 juxtaposes Jesus' gathering of disciples and the raising of opposition. Jesus' ability to bring salvation is pictured in a series of miracles (Luke 4:31–44), while disciples are called to be fishers of people (Luke 5:1–11). The first hints of official opposition come with the miracles of divinelike authority, when the Son of Man claims to be able to forgive sins and heals on the Sabbath (Luke 5:12–26). Levi, a hated tax gatherer, is called (Luke 5:27–28), and four controversies emerge, one of which involves the type of company Jesus keeps, while the others center on the Sabbath (Luke 5:29–6:11). Jesus gives a mission statement: his task is to call sinners to repentance (Luke 5:32). His authority is such that to do good is the real issue of the Sabbath (Luke 6:5, 9).

Jesus organizes the disciples and issues a call. The Twelve are chosen (Luke 6:12–16). Then Jesus offers blessing to the humble and poor, while warning the rich and oppressive (Luke 6:20–26). His Sermon on the Plain is a call to love others in the context of accountability to God. One is to respect the authority of Jesus' teaching and respond with obedience (Luke 6:27–49).

Luke 7:1–8:3 concentrates on "who is Jesus?" and the appropriate response to him. A Gentile centurion understands faith better than do those in the nation (Luke 7:1–10). The crowd believes Jesus is a prophet (Luke 7:11–17). John the Baptist wonders if Jesus is the Coming One, probably because of Jesus' style of ministry. Jesus replies that his eschatological works of healing and preaching give the affirmative answer (Luke 7:18–35; Isa. 29:18; 35:5–6; 61:1). An exemplary faith is displayed by the woman who anoints Jesus and by those women who contribute to his ministry (Luke 7:36–8:3).

Jesus can be trusted. With the parable of the seed and the image of the Word as light, a call is made to trust God and his Word, as revealed by Jesus (Luke 8:4–21). Jesus then shows his authority over nature (Luke 8:22–25), demons (Luke 8:26–39), disease and death (Luke 8:40–56). He sends out a mission of proclamation of the kingdom (Luke 9:1–6), as word about him reaches as far as Herod (Luke 9:7–9). The picture of Jesus' ability to provide comes in the multiplication of loaves (Luke 9:10–17).

This section moves from teaching and demonstration of authority to confession and call to discipleship. Peter confesses Jesus to be the Christ (Luke 9:18–20). Now Jesus explains what kind of Messiah he will be; he will suffer (Luke 9:21–22). Those who follow him must have total commitment in order to survive the path of rejection that comes with following Jesus (Luke 9:23–27). The second heavenly testimony to Jesus comes at the transfiguration (Luke 9:28–36). The divine voice repeats the endorsement made at the baptism with one key addition, the call to "listen to him" (Deut. 18:15). Jesus is a second Moses, who marks out a new way. This section closes with the disciples failing, showing their need for Jesus to instruct them. Jesus issues calls to trust and be humble, two basic characteristics of discipleship (Luke 9:37–50).

Jerusalem Journey: Jewish Rejection and the New Way (9:51–19:44)

As much as 49 percent of the fourth section contains material unique to Luke. There is a high concentration of teaching and parable. In fact, seventeen parables are in this unit, fifteen of which are unique to Luke. The "journey" is not a chronological, straight-line journey, since Jesus in Luke 10:38–42 is near Jerusalem, while later in the section, he is back in the north. Rather it is a journey in time, in the context of the necessity of God's plan. Journey notes dot the section (Luke 9:51; 13:22; 17:11; 18:31; 19:28, 41) as Jesus travels to meet his appointed fate in Jerusalem (Luke 13:31–35). The section's thrust is that Jesus gives a new way to follow God, which is not the way of the Jewish leadership. The theme is "listen to him." So this section discusses how Jesus' teaching relates to current Judaism. Jesus fulfills the promise and is the way, but his way is distinct from that of the leadership of the nation. The difference brings to the surface great opposition, a theme dominating Luke 9–13. All are invited, but some refuse. As the new way is revealed, the seeds of discontent leading to Jesus' death are also made manifest.

The journey starts with the disciples learning the basics of discipleship: mission, commitment, love for God, love for one's neighbor, devotion to Jesus and his teaching, and prayer (Luke 9:51–11:13). Also raised are notes of challenge to Judaism's leadership (Luke 11:14–36) and an indictment by Jesus (Luke 11:37–52). The leadership's way is not God's way. Fundamentally, discipleship is trusting God, not people or riches, for everything, while remaining faithful to him (Luke 12:1–48).

Jesus tells his followers to know the nature of the times (Luke 12:49–14:24). Israel is turning away, and the time for it to respond, without facing judgment, is short (Luke 13:1–9, 31–35). Nevertheless blessing will still come. Renewed condemnation of Jesus' Sabbath healings shows that the warnings and divine authentication are unheeded (Luke 13:10–17; 14:2–6). Jesus says that the door is closing, so be sure to enter the narrow way (Luke 13:23–30). He also warns that those at the table will not be those who were expected to be there (Luke 14:1–24).

From this point on, most of the journey section concerns discipleship. Disciples in the face of rejection need absolute commitment (Luke 14:25–35). Their mission, even though others grumble at it, is to seek the lost, just as God does (Luke 15:1–32). God rejoices in finding lost sinners, so Jesus' call is to pursue them. Discipleship expresses itself in service to others, so the disciple is generous with resources (Luke 16:1–31). Though false teaching is a threat, it is overcome with forgiveness of each other, deep faith, and service (Luke 17:1–10). The disciple is to look for the hope of the king's return, when the promise of the currently inaugurated kingdom is consummated (Luke 17:11–18:8). The return will bring severe judgment, but also vindication. The disciple is to be humble, give all, and trust all to the Father (Luke 18:9–30).

Now Jesus turns to Jerusalem. He again displays his authority when he predicts his suffering; he then heals as the "Son of David" (Luke 18:32–43). Zacchaeus pictures the transformed sinner and rich person (Luke 19:1–10). He is a picture of the mission of Jesus in seeking and saving the lost (Luke 19:10). The parable of the pounds shows the need for faithfulness and the reality that the disciple, as well as the nation of Israel, is accountable to the king (Luke 19:11–27). Jesus enters Jerusalem as a king, but the leadership rejects the claim (Luke 19:28–40). Jesus warns the nation that it has failed to respond to God's promise and faces judgment (Luke 19:41–

44). Its tragic fall draws near. Though opposition results in death for Jesus, opposition results in something much worse for the nation. Thus they are the loser, while God's plan advances in triumph.

Jerusalem: The Innocent One Slain and Raised (19:45–24:53)

In his concluding section, Luke explains how Jesus died, why apparent defeat became victory, and how God revealed who Jesus was. In addition, the task of disciples in light of God's acts becomes clear. Luke mixes fresh material with that found in the other Gospels.

The final battles in Jesus' earthly ministry occur here, recalling earlier confrontations in Luke 11–13. Jesus cleanses the temple, signaling his displeasure with official Judaism (19:45–48). The leaders fail to embarrass Jesus in various controversies concerning his authority, political-economic responsibilities, and resurrection (20:1–8, 20–26, 27–40).

A parable in the midst of these controversies (20:9–19) and a question at their end (20:41–44) overview God's plan. They reveal God's commitment to his Son, despite Jewish rejection. The nation's rejection will cost them. The kingdom will go to new tenants. The question about Ps. 110 gives the reason. The Messiah is not just David's Son; he is David's Lord, who is to be seated at God's right hand. Jesus' death is a transition, not an end to God's plan. Jesus reveals how things stand when he condemns the scribes' hypocrisy and praises a poor widow's simple, generous, and sacrificial faith (Luke 20:45–21:4). Blessing is not a matter of position, but of the heart.

In light of the nation's rejection, Jesus predicts the fall of the temple and of Jerusalem, events that are a foretaste of the end (Luke 21:5–38). The fall of Jerusalem will be a terrible time for the nation, but it is not yet the end, when the Son of Man returns on the clouds with authority to redeem his people (Dan. 7:13–14). Disciples are to watch and be faithful.

Luke 22–23 describes the moments before Jesus' death. Jesus, though betrayed, is innocent, but his death will bring the new covenant and is a sacrifice on behalf of others (Luke 22:1–20). In his last discourse, Jesus announces the betrayal, points out that greatness is in service, appoints eleven to authority, predicts Peter's denials, and warns of rejection (Luke 22:21–38). Jesus is in control, even as his death approaches.

As Jesus prays, exemplifying in the midst of rejection the trust that he calls for from disciples, he is betrayed and arrested (Luke 22:47–53). The trials center on who Jesus is. The answer comes in Luke 22:69. Jesus "from now on" will be manifest as the exalted

Lord, who is seated with authority at the side of God. Messiahship means lordship, authority over God's plan and salvation. No judgment the leadership makes can prevent that from happening. In fact, ironically and unwittingly, they help bring it to pass. Jesus is on trial, it seems; but in fact, he is the judge (Luke 22:54–71).

But it is not only the leadership that is guilty. As Pilate and Herod debate what to do about Jesus, the people are given the final choice (Luke 23:1–25). Despite Pilate's repeated protestations of Jesus' innocence and Herod's similar reaction, the people ask for Jesus to be slain and Barabbas to be freed. Justice is absent, both in the request and in the failure of the leaders to carry out what they know to be right. Passively and actively, the responsibility for Jesus' death widens. The innocent one dies, a criminal is freed—a cameo of the significance of Jesus' death. Jesus is crucified between two thieves: one derides, the other believes and receives the promise of life in paradise, providing yet another cameo of the significance of Jesus' death and the reactions to it. A centurion confesses the righteousness of Jesus, the final word at the scene of the cross (Luke 23:47). Luke describes Jesus' death with OT allusions that picture Jesus as an innocent sufferer who relies on God (Luke 23:26–56; Ps. 22:7–8, 18; 31:5; 69:21).

Luke closes with three scenes of resurrection and vindication. First, Luke 24:1–12 announces the empty tomb. The angels tell the women to recall the predictions of suffering proclaimed during the journey to Jerusalem. Luke 24 often notes that such events must be (δεῖ, dei; Luke 24:7, 26, 44). The news of the excited women is, however, greeted with skepticism.

Second, the experience of the Emmaus disciples pictures the reversal the resurrection brings to the disciples' despair (Luke 24:13–35). These two disciples mourn the departure of the prophet of Israel who might have redeemed the nation. But instruction in Scripture and the revelation of Jesus himself show that God had a plan, which included Jesus' death. God has indeed raised Jesus, vindicating both Jesus and the plan. Despair turns to joy upon understanding the nature of God's plan and Jesus' role in it, a major note in Luke.

Third, Luke reports Jesus' final commission, instruction, and ascension (Luke 24:36–53). Just as Luke 1–2 opened with the hope of OT promise fulfilled, so Luke 24:44–49 returns to the central theme of Jesus the Messiah as the fulfillment of God's plan and promise. Jesus' final appearance in Luke's Gospel yields a commission, a plan, and a promise. Reminding the disciples again that Scripture teaches the suffering and exaltation of Messiah, Jesus also tells them that they are called as witnesses to preach repentance. The plan is to go to all the nations, starting from Jerusalem. The promise is the Father's gift of the Spirit (Luke 24:49; 3:15–17). As the Baptist promised, so it has come to pass.

The ascension of Jesus (Luke 24:50–53) pictures the exaltation Jesus predicted at his trial (Luke 22:69). A dead Messiah does not represent the end of God's plan. In exaltation, Jesus is vindicated and the plan to reach all nations goes on. Jesus the Messiah is Lord of all, so the message can go to all (Acts 2:14–40; 10:34–43). The Gospel closes with the disciples rejoicing that, out of the ashes of apparent defeat, victory and promise have arisen. The new way is still alive and the risen Lord shows the way. Theophilus can be reassured (Luke 1:1–4).

Theology

Biblical theological treatments often compartmentalize an author's teaching. My brief survey outlines the major strands and connections that show Luke's theological and pastoral concerns: God's plan, Christology and salvation, and the new community.

God's Plan

The center of Luke's concern is a detailed discussion of God's plan. This theme is emphasized in Luke more than in the other Synoptics. Mark and Matthew speak of the role of John the Baptist as forerunner, the necessity of Jesus' suffering, and a plan concerning his return. They also have a series of parables that describe the kingdom, but Luke provides details concerning the connections and relationships.

A number of uniquely Lucan passages bring out this theme (Luke 1:14–17, 31–35, 46–55, 68–79; 2:9–14, 30–32, 34–35; 4:16–30; 13:31–35; 24:44–49). One key text does overlap with the other Gospels (Luke 7:18–35). In addition, Luke has the suffering Son of Man texts, a few of which are unique to him (Luke 9:22, 44; 17:25 [L]; 18:31–33 [L]; 22:22 [L]; 24:7 [L]). Acts also highlights the details of God's plan (Acts 2:23; 4:27–28; 10:34–43; 13:32–39; 24:14–15; 26:12–23). These passages make it clear that the major elements of the plan are the career of Jesus, the hope of the spiritually humble and needy, the offer of God's blessings, the coming of the new era, the defeat of Satan, the suffering that comes to Jesus, and the division that comes to Israel.

Luke 24:44–49 is a key passage because it divides the career of Jesus into three parts and appeals to the Scriptures: (1) Christ must suffer; (2) he must be raised from the dead on the third day; and (3) repentance for the forgiveness of sins must be preached in his name to all the nations, starting from Jerusalem. Also highlighted is the promise of the Spirit's coming. Thus, for all the beauty of Jesus' ethical teaching, the message of the gospel for Luke is more than ethics. It is a new way of relating to God by turning to him through Jesus. If one approaches God in repentance, the spiritual blessings of the Father are bestowed.

Promise and Fulfillment. The theme of God's plan is supported by the note of promise and fulfillment in the Gospel and Acts, especially as it relates to the Scriptures (Talbert 1982: 234–40; Bock 1987). Appeal to the OT concentrates on Christology, Israelite rejection/Gentile inclusion, and justice in the end. The latter two themes are more prominent in Acts, as "the Way" (Acts 24:14) is presented and defended from various charges, especially during Paul's efforts among Jews and Gentiles. Nonetheless, the theme of Gentiles and non-Jews responding to the gospel, while Israel stumbles, is present in numerous texts in Luke (2:34; 3:4–6; 4:25–27; 7:1–10; 10:25–37; 11:49–51; 13:7–9, 23–30, 31–35; 14:16–24; 17:12–19; 19:41–44). This racial concern, observed throughout Luke's Gospel, indicates how God's plan includes all races. The "today" passages enhance the plan motif and show the immediate availability of the promise (Luke 2:11; 4:21; 5:26; 13:32–33; 19:5, 9, 42; 23:42–43).

John the Baptist. John the Baptist is the "bridge," stretching between the old era of promise and the new era of inauguration (Luke 1–2 [esp. 1:76–79]; 3:4–6; 7:24–35; 16:16). Luke 7 is instructive here. John is the forerunner predicted by Malachi, but even more John represents the greatest prophet of the old period (Luke 7:27). Nonetheless, the new era is so great that the "lowest" member of the kingdom is higher than the greatest prophet of the old age (Luke 7:28). The passage presents the basic Lucan structure of God's plan: an era of promise or expectation followed by an era of inauguration. This two-stage structure is better than the three stages proposed by Conzelmann (1960: 12–17) and defended in modified form by Fitzmyer (1981: 185). Conzelmann's proposal makes the divisions between Jesus' era and the church's era too strong, especially in light of the parallels between the activities of Jesus and those of the church. The church's gospel message and Jesus' teaching about the end clarify the timing and structure of the newly inaugurated era. God's plan has future elements to be realized (Luke 17:21–37; 21:5–38), but the basic turning point has come. So the second portion of the plan has a subdivision, even though the entire era is one of fulfillment: inauguration (Acts 2:14–40) and consummation (Acts 3:14–26)—or what NT theology now calls "already–not yet." The "not yet" expectation is important to Jesus' ethical message and will be discussed later.

Mission Statements. Other elements of God's plan are seen in Jesus' mission statements, where he outlines his task. Jesus comes to preach good news to the needy (Luke 4:18–19); he comes to heal the sick (Luke 5:30–32); he comes to be heard, whether the message is through him or his representatives (Luke 10:16–20); he comes to seek and to save the lost (Luke 19:10). His career is reviewed again in Acts 10:36–43.

Geographic Progression. Geographic progression reveals the movement's growth under God's plan. The outline of the Gospel from Galilee to Jerusalem shows this growth, as does the necessity of Paul's going to Rome in Acts (Acts 19:21; 23:11).

"It Is Necessary." Many passages declare "it is necessary" that something occur. In fact, 40 of 101 NT uses of δεῖ (*dei*) occur in Luke–Acts. Jesus must be in his Father's house (Luke 2:49). He must preach the kingdom (Luke 4:43). He must heal the woman tormented by Satan (Luke 13:16). Luke shows that Jesus is not a mere moralist, but one struggling against cosmic forces opposed to God. Certain events must precede the end (Luke 17:25; 21:9). Jesus must be numbered among the transgressors (Luke 22:37). The Christ must suffer and be raised (Luke 24:7). The preaching of repentance for the forgiveness of sins must take place (Luke 24:43–47). The necessity of the Son of Man's suffering, already noted, is also a part of this emphasis. Acts also stresses this theme, sometimes using δεῖ, sometimes not (Acts 1:11; 3:21; 9:6, 16; 13:46; 14:22; 19:21; 23:11; 25:10; 27:24). Like a church bell's ring each hour, Luke chimes the note of God's design. God's plan expresses his compassion and effort to deliver. He directs what occurs. What has happened, God has designed. For Luke, it is reassuring to fall into the hands of an active, compassionate God.

Christology and Salvation

At the center of God's plan are Jesus and deliverance. Who is Jesus? What does he bring? How do we know he is God's chosen? These are central questions for Luke. There are also the message and the call to respond, along with the enablement of God. All these notes are wrapped in a package that makes it clear that the plan not only has a future, but is relevant for the present. Not only is one to know God, but one is responsible and accountable to him. Thus the plan not only delivers, but calls for a response of faith that has an ethical edge as well.

Messiah-Servant-Prophet and Lord. The portrait of Jesus is one that Luke carefully develops. Some say that Luke's Christology is a collection of a variety of traditions, "the most variegated in the NT" (C. F. Evans 1990: 65). It is argued that none of the titles dominates or is worked out in detail. In my judgment, this understates Luke's work.

Luke 1–2 introduces Jesus largely as a regal figure. Both the announcement to Mary and the remarks of Zechariah make the Davidic connection explicit (Luke 1:31–33, 69). Other functions, like prophet and servant, are also important to Luke. The anointing of Jesus at his baptism recalls a combination of Ps. 2 and Isa. 42, which brings together a regal-prophetic image (Luke 3:21–22). Servant and prophet imagery come together in Simeon's remarks (Luke 2:30–35; Luke 4:16–30 has the same mix), but the idea of a *leader*-prophet is dominant in Luke. Though the prophets Elijah and Elisha are raised as parallels (Luke 4:25–27), Luke also speaks of the anointing in the aorist tense (Luke 4:18), thus indicating that the anointing that Jesus says is fulfilled "today" (Luke 4:21) looks back to Jesus' baptism (Luke 3:21–22), which had a regal-prophetic mix. Still, the populace views Jesus as a prophet (Luke 7:16; 9:7–9, 19). But Peter's confession centers on Jesus as the Christ (Luke 9:20). Jesus qualifies this confession by introducing the inevitability of the Son of Man's suffering (Luke 9:22). Even Jesus' title as Son is uniquely related by Luke to Jesus' messianic role (Luke 4:41). This regal-prophetic mix reappears with the voice of the transfiguration (Luke 9:35; Ps. 2:7; Isa. 42:1; Deut 18:15). When Jesus is presented as a prophet, he is a leader-prophet, one like Moses. Even here the note of rule and direction is fundamental. In short, Jesus' messianic role is central for Luke's Christology. But Jesus' messiahship needs clarification and careful definition, so Luke places other expectations alongside that of Messiah. Nonetheless, messiahship is the foundational category around which the other concepts revolve.

The prophetic motif is strong in texts like Luke 11:47–51; 13:31–35; and 24:19, 21. But the appeal to Ps. 118 (in Luke 13) expands the Lucan presentation into a regal allusion (Luke 19:38), since "the one who comes" is fundamentally an eschatological and messianic figure (Luke 3:15–18; 7:22–23; 19:38). Luke 24 also presents the hope that Jesus would "redeem" the nation (Luke 24:21). Thus, the regal-deliverer picture is never very far from the prophetic one.

Toward the end of Jesus' ministry, Luke's portrayal is more focused. Luke now makes reference to the authority of the Son of Man and speaks of the Lord (Luke 20:41–44; 21:27; 22:69; Acts 2:30–36; 10:36). These concepts, mentioned earlier (Luke 5:24), now become the focus of the dispute about Jesus. Luke's citations of Ps. 110 show the centrality of this passage. In three steps, Luke raises the issue of lordship (Luke 20:41–44), gives Jesus' answer (Luke 22:69), and shows how Jesus' authority in lordship is proclaimed (Acts 2:30–36; see Franklin 1975: 40–41, 73–75, 119–24; Bock 1987: 128–32, 139–43, 181–87). The Synoptics share the first two texts, but unique to Luke is the detailed exposition found in

Acts 2. Luke 22:69 makes it clear that "from now on" Jesus, alongside God, will exercise authority as Lord. The Messiah-Servant-Prophet is Lord. In Acts, religious rites are done in his name. Jesus' authority is total and extends to believers calling on his name and acting in his name, just as OT saints acted on behalf of Yahweh. In other words, Luke develops his Christology from the earth up. Although hints of a heavenly connection exist at his birth, the Messiah-Servant-Prophet is gradually revealed as Lord in the context of his ministry and trial. The narrative brings the reader along: its portrait of Jesus deepens as events proceed. Luke enhances the portrait of Jesus' authority by uniquely speaking of "the Lord" in narratives introducing events in Jesus' ministry. Old Testament citations involving Christology and the use of κύριος (*kyrios*, Lord) within editorial narrative notes in the Gospel show that central to the Lucan portrait is the picture of Jesus as "leader-prophet" who is "more than Messiah" (Bock 1987: 262–70).

Obviously, other titles are present alongside this basic portrait. Jesus is "Savior" or deliverer (Luke 2:11; 1:70–75; 2:30–32; Acts 5:31; 13:23–25). He is Son of David (Luke 1:27, 32, 69; 2:4, 11; 18:38–39; Acts 2:25–31; 15:16) or King (Luke 19:38). He is the Son who relates to God as Father, even as divine testimony declares (Luke 1:35; 2:49; 3:22, 38; 4:3, 9, 41; 9:35; 10:21–22). Yet he is also the son of Adam who grows in grace (Luke 3:38; 2:40, 52; Acts 2:22). He is compared to Jonah (message of repentance) and Solomon (message of wisdom; Luke 11:29–32). As Son of Man he suffers, is exalted, and ministers (Luke 5:24; 6:5, 22; 7:34; 9:58; 11:29–32; 12:8; 19:10). He frequently is simply teacher (Luke 7:40; 8:49; 9:38; 10:25; 11:45; 12:13; 18:18; 19:39; 20:21, 28, 39; 21:7; 22:11). Luke's portrait of Jesus is variegated, but organized. Jesus bears authority and promise.

Kingdom in Jesus' Teaching and Work. The Messiah brings God's kingdom, God's rule manifested on earth (Luke 4:18, 43; 7:22; 8:1; 9:6; 10:11). The kingdom is present now, but comes in the future. It contains earthly hope and yet has spiritual dimensions. It has responsive, potential, and reluctant subjects.

The kingdom present is associated with Jesus' authority. Luke often mentions the kingdom's "already" presence when Jesus exercises authority over evil spiritual forces. This connection shows the spiritual character of the kingdom. The kingdom is near (Luke 10:9). The authority of the seventy-two disciples over demons is seen as Satan's fall (Luke 10:18–19). In fact, Jesus says that if he casts out demons by the finger of God, then the kingdom has come upon those who are present (Luke 11:20–23). The kingdom is "among you" (Luke 17:21). The king, in one parable, departs "to receive a kingdom," so he clearly possesses it before he returns (Luke

19:14–15). At his trial Jesus makes clear that he now will be at God's side (Luke 22:69). Luke's appeal to Ps. 110 depicts the presence of regal authority. Luke expounds on this theme in Acts 2:30–36, which involves the distribution of the benefits of salvation. Complementing the present aspect of the kingdom is its future nature. This "not yet" aspect includes a judgment that precedes the kingdom's coming (Luke 17:22–37), which is called the "time of redemption" (Luke 21:5–38). Day-of-the-Lord imagery abounds as evil is decisively judged. In Luke 21:25–27 are allusions to Isa. 13:10; Ezek. 32:7; Joel 2:30–31; Ps. 46:2–3; 65:7; Isa. 24:19 LXX; Hag. 2:6, 21; and Dan. 7:13. Old Testament hope and expectation is not dead (Acts 3:20–21). Jesus will return to bring the rest of the promise, a promise that will visibly show itself on earth to all humankind, as well as in the eternal benefits given to believers.

The kingdom is earthly. Jesus will rule as a Davidite on the earth and bring a total deliverance to it as he exercises his sovereignty over all. Such hope is most strongly expressed in Luke 1:32–33, 46–55, 69–75. The eschatological discourses and the remarks of Acts 1:11 and 3:18–21 show that the future hope has not been consumed in the present inauguration, but remains alive, connected to its OT roots. God is faithful and brings all of his promises to fruition, even those made to Israel. Spiritual deliverance, however, is also his. Jesus is the rising sun who shines on those in darkness and leads them into the path of peace (Luke 1:78–79). The promise of the Spirit (Luke 3:15–18; 24:49; Acts 1:8) and the hope of forgiveness of sins (Luke 24:47) are central here. Jesus' miracles over demons and other forces show that he is able to bring such promises to realization.

The most obvious subjects of the kingdom to benefit from its presence are the disciples (Luke 18:26–30). All of salvation's benefits are theirs. But potential beneficiaries exist; for example, anyone who enters (Luke 13:23–30; 14:16–24). There are, however, unwilling subjects who will face the reality of Jesus' rule one day and are accountable to him even now (Luke 19:27; 21:24–27; Acts 3:20–26; 10:42; 17:30–31). Thus, everyone has some relationship to the King and therefore to the kingdom. The issue is where they fit.

Holy Spirit. The Spirit as a central figure of redemption moves from the position of being promised (Luke 3:15–18) to being a testifier-enabler for Jesus (Luke 3:21; 4:16–18). The full promise finally comes later when the Spirit falls on all believers (Acts 2:1–13). Luke explains the event as the sign that the new era has come (Acts 2:14–21; Joel 2:28–32). The Spirit, therefore, is the gift of the Father through the exalted Son. He is power (or enablement) from on high (Luke 24:49; Acts 2:30–36; 10:44–47; 11:15–16; 15:8). His presence is evidence that Jesus is raised and that Jesus directs his new community from the side of God. Luke reassures Theophilus that, though the Messiah is dead and seemingly absent, he is present in the gift and presence of the Spirit he has sent.

Resurrection and Ascension. Central to the provision of the Spirit are the resurrection and ascension of Jesus. Luke alone mentions and develops the ascension. The ascension links Luke 24 and Acts 1 and is explained in Acts 2:23–24, 30–36; 3:14–15, 21; 4:10–12; 5:30 (17:31 mentions resurrection, not ascension). A raised Savior is one who can rule and can consummate his promise. He is one who can forgive and bestow blessing as a sign of that forgiveness (Acts 2:21; 4:12; 10:43). Jesus' authority is active and is demonstrated in those who work "in his name" (Acts 2:38; 3:6, 16; 4:7, 10; 8:11–12; 9:27–28; 10:48; 19:5). Thus, the ascension shows that he is Lord (Franklin 1975: 6, 35, 40–41, 48).

Salvation in Jesus' Teaching and Work. Jesus brings promise and salvation. Salvation involves sharing in hope, experiencing the kingdom, having forgiveness, and being enabled by the Spirit. Jesus reveals himself as the one who brings salvation, while his teaching and work explain what he hopes to bring through his ministry. Jesus is a teacher and wonder-worker (Luke 4:14–15, 31–32, 44; 6:17–19; 7:22). His teaching centers in the offer of the kingdom. The kingdom's coming is pictured as release and healing in the context of Jubilee (Luke 4:16–21; Lev. 25:10; Isa. 61:1–2), but it also includes a call to ethical honor as a result of experiencing blessing (Luke 6:20–49). The parables show the same combination. Some, where meal scenes dominate, deal with God's plan (Luke 13:6–9, 23–30; 14:16–24; 20:9–18). These texts not only show the joy of salvation but picture the table fellowship of the future, which the community can have now without racial distinction (Acts 10–11, 15). Thus, there is to be a unity among the people of God.

Beyond unity stands a call for ethical living, which involves relationship with God, mission, and ethical honor. Love, humility, service, and righteousness are to dominate relationships, as many parables show (Luke 10:25–37; 11:5–8; 14:1–12; 12:35–48; 15:1–32; 16:1–8, 19–31; 18:1–8; 19:11–27). Jesus did not come just to get people to heaven, to enable them to know the transforming activity of God in their lives. Thus, the community is accountable to God. This is why commitment is so prominent in Jesus' teaching (Luke 9:21–26, 57–62; 14:25–35; 18:18–30).

Cross. In surveying Jesus' work and teaching, I have said little about the cross, because in Luke's presentation exaltation is featured more than the cross. Some would deny a saving function for Jesus' work, preferring to argue that Jesus in his death is only an example (Pilgrim 1971; Büchele 1978; Glöckner 1976). Exemplary elements do exist for a church under pressure, but this ethical view of Jesus' death is too limiting (Sylva 1990). Tyson (1986) stresses how the portrayal of Jesus' death reveals the conflict between Judaism and the new way. The leaders debate Jesus' claims of authority, while Luke argues that Jesus' death is a necessary outcome of this conflict. Although the cross is less prominent for Luke than for Paul, the cross is important theologically in Luke's teaching; it does not have merely an ethical or historical function.

Jesus is the righteous sufferer (Luke 22–23). Two texts, however, especially define Jesus' death: Jesus' death inaugurates the new covenant with God (Luke 22:20) and Jesus' blood "purchases" the church (Acts 20:28). Covenant inauguration and a soteriological transaction occur with Jesus' death. Two other images reinforce this view. Jesus' substitution for Barabbas pictures Jesus' substitution for the sinner, especially since all share in the unrighteous choice (Luke 23:13–25). And the offer of paradise to the thief on the cross pictures Jesus' ability to offer life, despite his death (Luke 23:36–49).

Miracles. Jesus' authentication comes not only in resurrection, but also in miracles, which show the arrival of the new era (Luke 7:22; Acts 2:22–24). Miraculous healing demonstrates the scope of Jesus' authority. He heals the sick, exorcises evil spirits, and cures fever, leprosy, paralysis, a withered hand, epilepsy, dropsy, blindness, a flow of blood, and deafness. He resuscitates the dead and exercises power over nature. Jesus' work testifies to his person and task. His disciples also perform some of these works in Acts, demonstrating that such authentication continues (Acts 3:6, 16) and that Jesus' authority continues also.

Jesus and Salvation. Although Luke's portrayal of Jesus is fundamentally about his authority, Jesus also brings promise. Salvation inaugurates the kingdom, delivers the sinner, forgives sin, provides the Spirit, and calls for committed and faithful living in the context of the kingdom's future consummation. All of God's covenantal promises are inaugurated by Jesus. Realized are the Abrahamic promise (Acts 3:22–26), the Davidic hope (Luke 1:31–33, 69; 22:69; Acts 2:25–36; 13:23–39; 15:14–21), and the hope of the Spirit associated with the coming of the new era and new covenant (Luke 22:20; Acts 2:14–21). Theophilus should be reassured that Jesus can and does deliver on these promises. But who participates in such blessing, how do the members relate to one another, and what is the task of community members? Who makes up the new community and what is it to be? How does Luke view Christology's effect on the content and task of the new community? The answers to these questions are found in Luke's portrayal of the new community.

The New Community

Jesus' new community is not a totally organized entity in the Gospel. Beyond the twelve apostles and the seventy-two of Luke 10, there is no formal structure for some time. Rather, those who become the new community of Acts are called disciples. In the Gospel, this group is mostly Jewish, but there are a few hints that the benefits of Jesus' program can extend to Samaritans and non-Jews (Luke 3:4–6; 4:22–30; 7:1–10; 13:23–30; 14:16–24; 17:12–19; 20:15–16; 24:47). Although the racial theme is central in Acts, Luke's Gospel shows that the message is going out to those on the fringe of society.

Beneficiaries of Salvation. Luke focuses on the reception of the message by social outcasts and women. Luke features the poor, sinners, and tax collectors.

Luke has in view the materially *and* spiritually poor. This spiritual element is clear in Luke 1:50–53 and 6:20–23, where the poor and humble, like the mistreated prophets, are beneficiaries of God's covenant. The poor or rejected are mentioned in several texts (Luke 1:46–55; 4:18; 6:20–23; 7:22; 10:21–22; 14:13, 21–24; 16:19–31; 21:1–4). Sinners are also special objects of the gospel (Luke 5:27–32; 7:28, 30, 34, 36–50; 15:1–2; 19:7). Tax collectors are also offered hope. They are disliked because they are seen as traitors to Israel for collecting Roman taxes, but Jesus shows they can enter God's blessing (Luke 5:27–32; 7:34; 18:9–14; 19:1–10).

Finally, Luke features the responsiveness of women (Luke 7:36–50; 8:1–3, 48; 10:38–42; 13:10–17; 24:1–12)—not just women, but widows, who represent the most vulnerable in society (Luke 2:37; 4:25–26; 7:12; 18:3, 5; 20:47; 21:2–3). Whether in parable or by example, these women are sensitive to Jesus' message. Though they are on the fringe of first-century society, they are in the middle of Luke's story. Often they are paired with men (Luke 2:25–28; 4:25–27; 8:40–56; 11:31–32; 13:18–21; 15:4–10; 17:34–35; Acts 21:9–10), a clear indication that the gospel is for both genders.

In short, the makeup of this new community knows no boundaries. The message is available to all, but especially to those who are exposed in society and who, as a result, are often most suited to respond to the message of hope and reliance upon God.

Pictures of Response. Luke uses three terms to describe response to the message: *repent, turn,* and *faith.* "Repent" (μετανοέω, *metanoeō*) and "repentance" (μετάνοια, *metanoia*) have OT roots (Luke 11:32; 24:43–47), where the Hebrew equivalents (mainly שׁוּב, *šûb*) refer "to turning around." In Greek, the term has to do with a "change of mind." The point is that repentance involves a reorientation of perspective, a fresh point of view. When dealing with

God's plan, it means to see that plan in a new way and to orient one-self to it. Luke demonstrates that the fruit of repentance expresses itself concretely (Luke 3:10–14). Repentance expresses itself in life, especially in how one treats others.

Luke paints four pictures of repentance. (1) A sick patient in need of medical attention and totally reliant on the skill of the doctor comes to the physician for help. So the one who repents comes to God for spiritual healing and blessing (Luke 5:31–32). (2) The "repentance" of the prodigal's action in returning to his father indicates how repentance makes no claims, but is totally reliant on the mercy of the one to whom the request is made (Luke 15:17–21). Repentance is a change in attitude about sin, because one sees that only God and his mercy can provide relief. The centrality of repentance for Luke is indicated by its summation in Luke 24:47. "Repentance for the forgiveness of sins" means that one seeks God's mercy through Jesus as one approaches God on his terms, recognizing the need to be forgiven and that only God can provide forgiveness. (3) The tax collector shows this type of approach to God, though the term *repentance* is not used there (Luke 18:9–14). (4) Also instructive is the response of Zacchaeus (Luke 19:1–10). In Acts, the term is also key (Acts 5:31; 11:18; 13:24; 19:4; 20:21; 26:20). The verb is also frequent to indicate proper response (Luke 11:32; 13:3, 5; 15:7, 10; 16:30; Acts 2:38; 3:19; 17:30; 26:20).

The term "turn" (ἐπιστρέφω, *epistrephō*) appears primarily in Acts but is hardly visible in the Gospel (Luke 1:17; 17:4; 22:32; Acts 3:19; 9:35; 11:21; 14:15; 15:19; 26:18–20; 28:27). The term, however, is important because it pictures a change of fundamental direction, a reversal of estrangement, and portrays what happens with repentance. Acts 26 is particularly important because the three key concepts of repent, turn, and faith appear together and are related to each other.

"Faith" (πίστις, *pistis*) also describes actions that bring benefit to the bearer. Faith expresses itself concretely through the paralytic's friends (Luke 5:20), the centurion (Luke 7:9), and the sinful woman who anoints Jesus (Luke 7:47–50). The Samaritan leper and the blind man also have faith that Jesus can restore them to wholeness (Luke 17:19; 18:42). In sum, faith believes and so it acts. Faith also expresses itself concretely in Acts (3:16; 14:9; 6:5; 14:27; 15:9; 16:30–31; 20:21; 24:24; 26:18). Belief has various levels. It can be short-lived (Luke 8:12) or increased (Luke 8:50). In Acts, those who respond are sometimes called "believers" to show the centrality of faith and its dynamic ongoing quality (Acts 5:14; 15:5). In short, faith is the recognition and persuasion that God has something to offer through Jesus, namely, forgiveness and the blessings of promise. One must actively embrace faith and "call on the name of the Lord" (Acts 2:21; Rom. 10:13).

Blessings of the New Community. Luke uses various terms in the Gospel for blessings offered: forgiveness or release (Luke 1:77 and 3:3 [both tied to John the Baptist]; 4:18; 24:47; Acts 2:38; 5:31; 10:43; 13:38), life (Luke 10:25; 12:15 with 12:21 [not in possessions]; 18:29–30), peace (Luke 1:79; 2:14; 10:5–6; Acts 10:36), the kingdom, and the Spirit (both noted above).

These blessings and the way in which the promise is set forth show that Luke's agenda is not a political one. Consequently, liberation readings (e.g., Cassidy 1978)—especially those with a political ideological base or those that attempt to turn Jesus into a political activist—lack support. Jesus did not challenge the current political order of Rome. He worked "above" and "around" it. The church does not stand against the state or with it *per se*. The church should not be confused with the state (Luke 20:20–26). Nevertheless, the ethics of the community does have social implications. The transformation of people is to be exemplified in this new community, which stands alongside secular institutions. People of this new community—who love God—should manifest their love by caring for those in the community (Acts 4:32–38) and those "neighbors" outside of the community (Luke 10:25–37). If social concern and compassion are visible anywhere, it is in the hope that the new community and its message of blessing and transformation offer to all, as well as in the concrete expression of such care in the generosity, love, and activity of the community.

Opponents of Salvation. In contrast to those who are responsive stand those who oppose and pressure the new community. At the transcendent level, the spiritual forces of evil stand resistant, though powerless, before God's plan (Luke 4:1–13, 33–37; 8:26–39; 9:1; 10:1–12, 18; 11:14–26; 22:3). For Luke, God's struggle involves not only regaining human devotion, but also reversing the effects of evil forces.

On a human level, the opponents who are the biggest obstacle to the community are the scribes, Pharisees, and Sadducees—that is, the religious leadership of Judaism. Their opposition is virtually constant once Jesus claims to have authority to forgive sin and challenges Sabbath tradition (Luke 5:24; 6:1–11). The roots of this rejection go back to their refusal to respond to John the Baptist (Luke 7:29–30; 20:1–8). At various meals, they are warned (Luke 7:36–50; 11:37–52; 14:1–24). The leaders are at the center of Jesus' condemnation in the journey section, as well as in Jerusalem (Luke 11:37–52; 12:1; 14:1–4; 15:1–2; 16:14–15; 19:45–47; 20:45–47). Brawley (1987: 84–132) attempts to picture the Sadducees as the major opponents, with the Pharisees and scribes pictured more neutrally on the basis of Acts. For him, the Sadducees and high priests oppose Christ, while the Pharisees are less resistant and legitimate key aspects of the church's message by standing up for resurrection. Now there is no doubt that the Sadducees are portrayed more negatively, but the texts of Luke make it clear that the Pharisees and scribes are under severe criticism as well for rejecting the message. There are, however, exceptions—such as Jairus (Luke 8:41) and Joseph of Arimathea (Luke 23:50–53). But it is mostly the leadership who oppose Jesus and plot his demise (Luke 6:11; 11:53–54; 20:19; 22:3–6, 52–53; 23:3–5).

The crowd's reaction, however, is mixed. They have interest in Jesus, yet their response to him is superficial and sometimes fickle. The transition occurs in Luke 9–13. Jesus offers many warnings to them in Luke 12:49–14:24. He rebukes "this generation" (Luke 11:29–32), he condemns various cities of the nation (Luke 10:13–16), and he tells a few parables about the fault of the nation (Luke 13:6–9; 20:9–19). The crowd's eventual response typifies the general response of most in the nation. The rejection brings warnings of judgment, but such warnings do not represent anger. They picture prophetic regret, since Jesus weeps for those he warns (Luke 19:41–44). In fact, the crowd becomes responsible for Jesus' death when they ask for Barabbas (Luke 23:18–25). Jesus warns of the consequences in a final prophetic note of judgment (Luke 23:27–31). There is no doubt that the nation stands accountable for rejecting Jesus (Acts 2:22–24; 3:14–26; 5:30–31).

The response of Israel is a tragic one, at least for now (Tannehill 1986: 169–99). It was in line for blessing, but has missed the day of visitation (Luke 19:44). Now it is the "time of the Gentiles" (Luke 21:24). Israel is not, however, out of God's plan, for the faithfulness of God's promise to the nation cannot be denied, but Israel is "desolate" until it acknowledges the Messiah (Luke 13:34–35; Acts 3:14–21). In Acts, the nation is warned again to change its mind about Jesus and repent (Acts 2:22–24; 5:27–32).

Luke has been accused of anti-Semitism (J. T. Sanders 1987). But this is harsh. Luke does argue that the new community is persecuted by those who fail to respond to the message of hope. Jesus and the disciples consistently offer the gospel to the nation and suffer while making the offer. The disciples do not create the division and they do not bring violence to the Jewish community. Those who respond to Jesus are forced out, as the persecution of Acts shows and as Jesus predicted (Luke 12:1–12; 21:12–19). But the new community is not "anti-Jewish"; it is "pro-promise." Consistently in Acts, the new community continually returns to the synagogue at great risk to offer hope to Israel. These enemies are to be loved and prayed for, as Jesus made clear (Luke 6:27–36; 23:34; Acts 7:60).

Source of Tension: The Law. A primary cause of tension in Luke's Gospel and Acts is the new community's relationship to the law. This is a heavily debated area in Lucan studies. Some argue that Luke is very conservative in his attitude to the law (Jervell 1972: 133–51; Esler 1987: 110–30). Esler argues that Luke maintains this position, even though it is impossible to defend. Luke does so for sociological reasons, which serve to legitimate the new community. Others suggest that Luke is ambivalent on the law (Wilson 1983). Luke sees Jewish Christians keeping the law, while Gentiles are free on some matters (circumcision) and bound on others (idols, meat offered to idols, immorality). Others argue that the law is part of the old era and that the church slowly came to recognize this (Blomberg 1984a; M. Turner 1982). The last position is best. Most of these matters are made clear in Acts 10–11, 15, though the discussions of Luke 6:1–11 and 16:16 are also relevant. Law is not binding, though missionary considerations mean that it can be followed in matters where central issues of the new faith are not at stake. In Luke's complex view, the law needs to be seen in three different perspectives:

1. As a legal and sacrificial code and as a sociological distinctive, the law passes away (Luke 6:1–11; Acts 10–11, 15)—as evidenced by change in food regulations, circumcision, and perhaps Sabbath practice.
2. As a promise of the hope of the kingdom, the law is fulfilled (Luke 16:16–17; 24:43–47; 4:18–20 [on the law and Jubilee; perhaps the Sabbath is viewed as hope of rest now realized]).
3. With its ethical thrust in terms of loving God and loving one's neighbor and in relation to its moral commands (as distinct from the Sabbath command), the law is reaffirmed in ways that parallel the OT prophets (Luke 6:27–49; 10:25–37; 16:19–31; 18:18–30).

The law—or the traditions associated with it—are a central source of irritation in the Gospel, especially Sabbath regulation (Luke 6:1–11). In fact, Jesus makes the point that what David did on the Sabbath, which is his justifying example, is not allowed in the law (Luke 6:4). It is crucial that the Sabbath challenge comes after Jesus' proclamation that new wine must come in new wineskins and that those who like the old will not try the new (Luke 5:33–39). This remark is part of a dispute about Jesus' failure to follow traditions related to cleansing. Jesus challenged the law, at least in terms of how it was read in the first century, and his challenge helped produce the opposition to him.

Acts makes this challenge clear. The opening up of all foods, the full table fellowship with the Gentiles, and the refusal to circumcise Gentiles (Acts 10–11, 15) reflect a rejection of some elements of the law and the tradition that grew out of it. Luke's clear indication that members are charged with denial of Mosaic customs and his description of opposition within the new community show that issues related to Jewish roots are alive and a source of irritation, even within the community (Luke 13:10–17; 14:2–6; 23:2; Acts 6:11, 13; 15:1–5; 21:28; 25:8). Luke replies that the law pointed to promise (Luke 24:43–47; Acts 26:4–23; Acts 3:14–26 cites only Torah texts). He also openly describes differences with aspects of the law. The argument is that God gave evidence of his acceptance of this new community and its differences from the law by pouring out the Spirit on Gentiles, even though they were not circumcised (Acts 11:15–18). God shows his support of the new way with a vision that commands open table fellowship (Acts 10:1–33). Luke portrays the taking of vows and other elements of the law as optional, as long as one does not make these elements necessary (Acts 15:22–29; 21:17–26). The exercise of such options might promote unity on some occasions. Luke's resolution is that Jews are free to observe such customs, as long as they do not force Gentiles to do so. This distinction is key and is not unlike Paul's solution in Rom. 13–14. The law cannot be held as binding. The many texts in Acts dealing with this issue reveal some of the concerns that Luke wishes to treat; they presuppose a racially mixed community struggling with its relationship to ancient roots. One can suspect how much tension such racial differences raised in the new community. Luke is honest about these differences and about the complex solution and compromise that resulted for the sake of the church's unity, a compromise he endorses in his portrayal.

Pressure against God's Plan. Opposition calls for a strong commitment to Jesus. It is inevitable that with every decision for Jesus comes opposition. Notes about division come early (Luke 2:34–35) and are found throughout the Gospel (Luke 8:14–15; 9:21–23, 61–62; 12:4–9, 22–34; 22:35–38). Disciples shrink back from responding boldly in the Gospel, as Peter's denial exemplifies, but the presence of the Spirit in Acts makes them bold. Steadfastness and faithfulness are marks of a disciple. Luke's exhortations to steadfastness reveal an element of his purpose and setting. The pressure of this conflict within and about the community raised the need for Theophilus to be reassured. This troubled disciple belongs in this new movement, and he, along with any other Gentiles, has the right to be here. He needs to know that God's plan and blessing are at work in this new community. But if he belongs here, what is his call as a member of this new community? What is his relationship to Jewish promise, to Jewish Christians, and to Jews?

The new community did not choose to be separate. It presented itself as the hope of Israel, but it was forced to become distinct. In its distinctiveness it became steward of the Word of God (Acts 6:7). It now houses the true people of God, the repository of the promises given to the patriarchs and to David (Acts 13:21–39). Some features even mark it as distinct. The "newness" of the Spirit is responsible for this difference and is the source of enablement by which Jesus expresses his presence though he is physically absent (Acts 2:14–40; 11:15). Accordingly, the new community is to have a distinct character, unlike the present piety of the leadership or the current cultural standards (Luke 6:27–36; 12:1; 14:1–14; 22:24–27).

Faith and Dependence. The fundamental role of a reorientation to God is noted above (see under "Pictures of Response"). Such basic trust not only begins the walk with God, but sustains it (Luke 5:31–32; 15:17–21; 12:22–32).

Total Commitment. Disciples are to be totally focused on their walk with God. There are to be no higher priorities (Luke 9:23, 57–62; 14:25–35). This focus requires daily dedication and reflection about what is demanded. The reason for this commitment is that the path of the disciple is not easy. It involves "cross-bearing," which is a daily endeavor.

Commitment to the Lost. The community has a mission to the lost. Acts details the early accomplishments of this mission, but the Gospel spells out the call (Luke 24:47), the emphasis (Luke 5:31–32; 19:10), and the focus of the mission on "tax collectors" and sinners (Luke 15:1–32; 7:28–30). The church is not an inwardly directed body, but an outwardly reaching group. The theme of testimony and witness in Acts also underlies this point.

Love for God and for One's Neighbor. Devotion to God expresses itself in dependent prayer (Luke 11:1–13). Devotion to Jesus is shown in the "right" choice of Mary to sit at Jesus' feet, absorbing his teaching and presence (Luke 10:38–42). The care of one's neighbor is likewise an expression of such devotion (Luke 10:25–37). In fact, the call is to be a neighbor to everyone. Such care and compassion know no boundaries of race, gender, or class, as Jesus' own ministry showed.

Prayer. Prayer is noted by exhortation and example (Luke 11:1–13; 18:1–8, 9–14; 22:40). Prayer does not demand; it requests, humbly relying upon God's mercy and will. It looks to the return and consummation. It rests in God's care and provision of basic needs. It also recognizes that in seeking forgiveness one should be prepared to give it as well.

Persistence in Suffering. Many of the texts dealing with persistence have already been noted (Luke 8:13–15; 9:23; 18:8; 21:19). The church in Acts often exemplifies such persistence (Acts 4:23–31). This attitude of the disciple is related in turn to patience and expectation.

Watchfulness, Patience, Boldness. Disciples are to fear God, not people (Luke 12:1–12). They recognize that the Lord will return and that they are responsible to him (Luke 12:35–48; 19:11–27; 18:8). They cling to the Word and bear fruit (Luke 8:15).

It is here that eschatology makes its impact in Luke. Jesus represents both the present and the future. The promises that remain unrealized will come (Luke 17:22–37; 21:5–38). The judgment of Jerusalem, which came in A.D. 70, is seen as the guarantee and picture of the final judgment. The return will be a horrific period in which unbelieving humankind is severely judged and believers will suffer at the hands of those who do not believe. Luke emphasizes that the return's reality and the accountability that comes with it require that disciples be faithful and that all people respond to the good news. In Acts, Luke will note that Jesus is the "judge of the living and the dead" (Acts 10:42; 17:31). The Lucan eschatological discourse makes it clear that there is some time before the return (Luke 21:5–20). The time of the return is unknown, but will come quickly when it comes (Luke 12:35–40).

More problematic is how soon Luke anticipates the return. Some texts suggest a high level of immediacy (Luke 18:8; 21:32). But such texts can be read to suggest either that the return is "next" on the divine calendar (Luke 18:8; Acts 3:18–21) or that the return, when it comes, will come quickly and be resolved quickly (Luke 17:24–37; 21:25–36). Luke's position expresses uncertainty about the timing of the return and yet the possibility of its coming at any moment.

Luke uniquely notes the reality of "personal eschatology," that is, the awareness of being in Jesus' presence upon death. In two unique texts, Luke portrays death as a transition into paradise (Luke 23:42–43) or as the acceptance of a faithful witness by the Son of Man (Acts 7:55–56). Thus the issue of a current "interim" period without the consummation is somewhat softened by the presence of the intermediate reality for those who pass away before the return. In all of this, the future helps to give perspective to the present, especially perspective about the readiness to suffer.

Joy and Praise. Notes of joy resound throughout the Gospel; they are related to God's plan (Luke 1:14; 2:10), the Word (Luke 8:13), mission (Luke 10:17), heaven's reaction to sinners who repent (Luke 15:7, 10), and Jesus' resurrection and ascension (Luke 24:41, 52). The hope of the gospel fuels a basic joy and praise of God.

Hindrances to Discipleship. The role of money is a much discussed Lucan topic (Seecombe 1982; Pilgrim 1981; T. Schmidt 1987). Negative warnings and parables abound (Luke 8:14; 12:13–21; 16:1–15, 19–31; 18:18–25). But positive examples also exist (Luke 8:1–3; 19:1–10; 21:1–4; Acts 4:36–37). Especially debated is whether Luke decries wealth *per se*. The example of Zacchaeus, who generously repaid his misuse of funds, but hardly divested himself of every asset, suggests the issue is not what one has, but what is done with what one has. The disciples are said to have "left all" for Jesus (Luke 18:28–30), a remark that goes beyond resources to leaving family as well. Yet later in the Gospel, they exhibit failure, when the pressure of Jesus' arrest produces denial. The issue with resources (as with family and fearing people) is not the perfection of one's response or a literal following through to one's last coin, but a fundamental orientation, a recognition that all of one's life belongs to God and comes from his hand. The rich man would not even consider Jesus' request to sell all, while the disciples and Zacchaeus had entered into the process. In sum, Luke warns that the hindrances to discipleship include not only resources, but fearing people (Luke 12:1–12) and worrying about the cares of life (Luke 8:14).

Summary

Luke's Gospel is pastoral, theological, and historical. The reality of God's plan influences how individuals see themselves and the community to which they belong. Old barriers of race are removed. New hope abounds. There is to be no doubt that the message of Jesus is one of hope and transformation. Anyone, Jew or Gentile, can belong. At the center is Jesus, the promised Messiah-Lord, who sits at God's right hand exercising authority from above. He will return one day and all will be accountable to him. His life, ministry, resurrection, and ascension show that he has the ability to be trusted. He can bring God's promises to completion, just as he has inaugurated them. In the meantime, being a disciple is not easy, but it is full of rich blessing that transcends anything else this life can offer. This is the reassurance about salvation that Luke offers to Theophilus and others like him.

Outline

The following detailed outline of the Gospel of Luke reflects the basic exegetical units discussed in the commentary, except in a few cases where more precise divisions are beneficial to note.

I. Luke's preface and the introduction of John and Jesus (1:1–2:52)
  A. Preface: Luke carefully builds on precedent (1:1–4)
  B. Infancy narrative: forerunner and fulfillment (1:5–2:40)
    1. Announcement to Zechariah (1:5–25)
    2. Announcement to Mary (1:26–38)
    3. Meeting of Mary and Elizabeth (1:39–45)
    4. Mary's praise: the *Magnificat* (1:46–56)
    5. Birth of John (1:57–66)
    6. Zechariah's praise: the *Benedictus* (1:67–80)
    7. Birth of Jesus (2:1–7)
    8. Reaction to the birth (2:8–21)
    9. Witness of the man and woman at the temple (2:22–40)
  C. Jesus' revelation of his self-understanding (2:41–52)
II. Preparation for ministry: anointed by God (3:1–4:13)
  A. John the Baptist: one who goes before (3:1–20)
    1. Ministry of John the Baptist (3:1–6)
    2. Preaching of John the Baptist (3:7–14)
    3. Promise of John the Baptist (3:15–18)
    4. Imprisonment of John the Baptist (3:19–20)
  B. Jesus: one who comes after (3:21–4:13)
    1. Jesus' baptism (3:21–22)
    2. Jesus' genealogy: son of Adam, Son of God (3:23–38)
    3. Messianic preparation: resistance of Satan (4:1–13)
III. Galilean ministry: revelation of Jesus (4:14–9:50)
  A. Overview of Jesus' ministry (4:14–44)
    1. Summary of Jesus' Galilean ministry (4:14–15)
    2. Example of Jesus' preaching (4:16–30)
    3. Examples of Jesus' ministry (4:31–44)
      a. Setting summary (4:31–32)
      b. Unclean spirit cast out (4:33–37)
      c. Simon's mother-in-law healed (4:38–39)
      d. Jesus' healings; demonic confessions (4:40–41)
      e. Jesus' mission to preach the kingdom (4:42–44)
  B. Gathering of disciples (5:1–6:16)
    1. Miraculous catch and Peter (5:1–11)
    2. Two miracles of authority (5:12–26)
      a. Cleansing of the leper (5:12–16)
      b. Healing of the paralytic (5:17–26)
    3. Call of Levi and a complaint (5:27–32)
      a. Call of Levi (5:27–28)
      b. Controversy over association and mission (5:29–32)
    4. Rise of opposition: three controversies (5:33–6:11)
      a. Question about fasting (5:33–39)
      b. Question about plucking grain on the Sabbath (6:1–5)
      c. Question about healing on the Sabbath (6:6–11)
    5. Choosing of the Twelve (6:12–16)
  C. Jesus' teaching (6:17–49)
    1. Setting (6:17–19)

    2. Jesus' message: an offer and the call to love (6:20–49)
      a. Prophetic call: blessings and woes (6:20–26)
      b. Parenetic call to love and mercy (6:27–38)
      c. Parabolic call to righteousness, fruit, and wise building
        (6:39–49)
  D. First movements to faith and christological questions (7:1–8:3)
    1. Faith of a centurion (7:1–10)
    2. Resuscitation of a widow's son and questions about Jesus
      (7:11–17)
    3. Questions about Jesus and John the Baptist (7:18–35)
      a. John's question to Jesus about his ministry (7:18–23)
      b. Jesus' view of John (7:24–30)
      c. Jesus' view of this generation (7:31–35)
    4. Picture of faith: a sinful woman forgiven (7:36–50)
    5. Picture of faith: the ministering women (8:1–3)
  E. Call to faith, christological revelation, and questions (8:4–9:17)
    1. Call to faith (8:4–21)
      a. Issue of response: seed parable (8:4–15)
      b. Call to respond to light (8:16–18)
      c. True family of Jesus (8:19–21)
    2. Christological authority over all (8:22–9:17)
      a. Authority over nature: stilling of the storm (8:22–25)
      b. Authority over demons: Gerasene demoniac (8:26–39)
      c. Authority over disease and death: flow of blood and Jairus's
        daughter (8:40–56)
      d. Commissioned authority revealed (9:1–6)
      e. Herod's questions about Jesus (9:7–9)
      f. Authority to provide revealed (9:10–17)
  F. Christological confession and instruction about discipleship
    (9:18–50)
    1. Peter's confession (9:18–20)
    2. Prediction of Jesus' suffering (9:21–22)
    3. The "new way" of suffering (9:23–27)
    4. Transfiguration: divine confirmation and a call to hear
      (9:28–36)
    5. The disciples' failure and Jesus' instruction (9:37–50)
      a. The disciples' failure and Jesus' reversal (9:37–43a)
      b. Prediction of betrayal (9:43b–45)
      c. On greatness and cooperation (9:46–50)
IV. Jerusalem journey: Jewish rejection and the new way (9:51–19:44)
  A. Blessing of decision: privilege, mission, and commitment
    (9:51–10:24)
    1. Rejection at Samaria (9:51–56)
    2. Warnings about discipleship (9:57–62)
    3. Second mission of the seventy-two (10:1–24)
      a. Larger mission of the seventy-two (10:1–12)
      b. Jesus' woes on the unrepentant cities (10:13–15)
      c. Jesus' messengers (10:16)
      d. The messengers' report (10:17–20)
      e. Thanksgiving and blessing of Jesus (10:21–24)

B. Discipleship: looking to one's neighbor, Jesus, and God
   (10:25–11:13)
   1. Looking to one's neighbor: parable of the good Samaritan
      (10:25–37)
   2. Looking to Jesus: Martha and Mary (10:38–42)
   3. Looking to God: call to prayer (11:1–13)
C. Controversies, corrections, and calls to trust (11:14–54)
   1. Controversy: what do healings mean? (11:14–23)
   2. Warnings about response (11:24–36)
      a. Parable of returning spirits (11:24–26)
      b. Blessing for keeping God's word (11:27–28)
      c. No sign except Jonah (11:29–32)
      d. Two sayings about light (11:33–36)
   3. Rebuke of Pharisees and scribes (11:37–54)
D. Discipleship: trusting God (12:1–48)
   1. The need to avoid hypocrisy, fear God, and confess Jesus
      (12:1–12)
   2. Parable of the rich fool (12:13–21)
   3. Call to avoid anxiety (12:22–34)
   4. Call to be ready and faithful stewards: parable of the faithful
      and unfaithful servants (12:35–48)
E. Knowing the nature of the time: Israel turns away, but blessing
   still comes (12:49–14:24)
   1. Knowing the time (12:49–59)
      a. Jesus as a cause of division (12:49–53)
      b. Reading the times like the weather (12:54–56)
      c. Settling accounts with the accuser (12:57–59)
   2. Lessons for Israel (13:1–9)
      a. Tragedy and the need to repent (13:1–5)
      b. Parable of the spared fig tree (13:6–9)
   3. Sabbath healing of the bent-over woman (13:10–17)
   4. Kingdom parables: mustard seed and leaven (13:18–21)
   5. The narrow and soon-shut door (13:22–30)
   6. Lament for the nation as Jerusalem nears (13:31–35)
   7. Another Sabbath healing and silence (14:1–6)
   8. Lessons on humility and generosity (14:7–14)
   9. Parable of the great supper (14:15–24)
F. Pure discipleship in the face of rejection: basic elements (14:25–35)
G. Pursuit of sinners: heaven's examples (15:1–32)
   1. Parable of the lost sheep (15:1–7)
   2. Parable of the lost coin (15:8–10)
   3. Parable of the forgiving father (15:11–32)
H. Generosity: handling money and possessions (16:1–31)
   1. Parable of the crafty steward (16:1–13)
   2. Responses to the Pharisees' scoffing (16:14–18)
   3. Parable of Lazarus and the rich man (16:19–31)
I. False teaching, forgiveness, and service (17:1–10)
   1. Warning about false teaching (17:1–3a)

2. Sins and forgiveness (17:3b–4)
3. Faith (17:5–6)
4. Parable of the servant of duty (17:7–10)
J. Faithfulness in looking for the king, the kingdom, and its consummation (17:11–18:8)
    1. Healing of ten lepers and a Samaritan's faith (17:11–19)
    2. Question about the consummation (17:20–37)
        a. Basic reply (17:20–21)
        b. Its quick coming and accompanying judgment (17:22–37)
    3. Expectant prayer and promised vindication: parable of the nagging widow (18:1–8)
K. Humility and trusting all to the Father (18:9–30)
    1. Humility and arrogance: parable of the Pharisee and tax collector (18:9–14)
    2. Children received and faith (18:15–17)
    3. Jesus' discussion with a rich man and the disciples (18:18–30)
        a. Rich man and Jesus (18:18–23)
        b. Discussion with the disciples and a promise (18:24–30)
L. Turning to Jerusalem: messianic power, personal transformation, warning of responsibility, and entry with mourning (18:31–19:44)
    1. The passion prediction (18:31–34)
    2. Healing by the Son of David (18:35–43)
    3. Zacchaeus: faith's transforming power (19:1–10)
    4. Parable of stewardship (19:11–27)
    5. Jesus' controversial approach to Jerusalem (19:28–40)
    6. Weeping for Jerusalem (19:41–44)
V. **Jerusalem: the innocent one slain and raised (19:45–24:53)**
A. Controversy in Jerusalem (19:45–21:4)
    1. Temple cleansing (19:45–48)
    2. Question about authority (20:1–8)
    3. Parable of the wicked vinedressers (20:9–19)
    4. Question about temple tax (20:20–26)
    5. Question about resurrection (20:27–40)
    6. Jesus' question about Messiah (20:41–44)
    7. Jesus' condemnation of the scribes (20:45–47)
    8. Counterexample: the widow who gave all (21:1–4)
B. Jerusalem's destruction and the end (21:5–38)
    1. Setting (21:5–6)
    2. Signs before the end (21:7–11)
    3. Persecution (21:12–19)
    4. Picture of the end: Jerusalem's destruction (21:20–24)
    5. The end: coming of the Son of Man (21:25–28)
    6. Parable of the fig tree (21:29–33)
    7. Application: call to watch (21:34–36)
    8. Teaching at the temple (21:37–38)
C. Betrayal and farewell (22:1–38)
    1. Judas's plan to betray (22:1–6)
    2. Preparing for the meal (22:7–13)
    3. Last Supper (22:14–20)

    4. Last discourse (22:21–38)
      a. The betrayer (22:21–23)
      b. Greatness (22:24–27)
      c. Appointment to authority (22:28–30)
      d. Peter's denials predicted (22:31–34)
      e. Swords and rejection (22:35–38)
  D. Trials and death of Jesus (22:39–23:56)
    1. Preparation through prayer (22:39–46)
    2. Betrayal and arrest (22:47–53)
    3. Trials and denials (22:54–71)
      a. Jesus to the high priest (22:54)
      b. Peter's three denials (22:55–62)
      c. Jesus reviled (22:63–65)
      d. Jesus condemned before the Sanhedrin (22:66–71)
    4. Trial before Pilate (23:1–5)
    5. Trial before Herod (23:6–12)
    6. Sentencing by Pilate and release of Barabbas (23:13–25)
      a. Jesus' innocence declared (23:13–16)
      b. Demand: Jesus' death and Barabbas's release (23:18–23)
      c. Jesus condemned and Barabbas released (23:24–25)
    7. Crucifixion (23:26–49)
      a. To Golgotha (23:26–32)
      b. Crucifixion (23:33–38)
      c. Two thieves (23:39–43)
      d. Jesus' death (23:44–49)
    8. Burial (23:50–56)
  E. Resurrection and ascension of Jesus (24:1–53)
    1. Resurrection discovered (24:1–12)
    2. Emmaus road and the meal of discovery (24:13–35)
      a. Setting (24:13–16)
      b. Conversation (24:17–27)
      c. Meal and revelation (24:28–32)
      d. Report to disciples (24:33–35)
    3. Commission, promise, and ascension (24:36–53)
      a. Appearance at a meal (24:36–43)
      b. Commission, plan, and promise of the Spirit (24:44–49)
      c. Ascension (24:50–53)

➤ I. Luke's Preface and the Introduction of John and Jesus (1:1–2:52)
II. Preparation for Ministry: Anointed by God (3:1–4:13)
III. Galilean Ministry: Revelation of Jesus (4:14–9:50)
IV. Jerusalem Journey: Jewish Rejection and the New Way (9:51–19:44)
V. Jerusalem: The Innocent One Slain and Raised (19:45–24:53)

I. Luke's Preface and the Introduction of John and Jesus (1:1–2:52)

Luke introduces his account with three major units. The first, a preface, mirrors other ancient writing and describes the basis of his work (1:1–4). His account carefully builds on precedent and is grounded in a tradition from eyewitnesses. In addition, Luke has gone back through the events carefully and now sets about telling the story in a way that assures the reader about God's plan.

The second unit is a long and elaborately constructed section in which Luke introduces God's work of salvation (1:5–2:40). This section serves as a theological overture to many themes in Luke–Acts. The basic emphasis is God's fulfillment of promises made long ago. In addition, Luke introduces two key players in the plan: John the Baptist and Jesus. Everything about these two chapters shows Jesus' superiority to John. John is born of barren parents, but Jesus is born miraculously of a virgin. John is great before the Lord, a prophet of the Most High, but Jesus is greater, the promised Messiah from David. Numerous witnesses from heaven and earth testify to what is taking place as God's salvation arrives.

The third section is generally put with the "infancy material" of 1:5–2:40, but really is distinct. It represents Jesus' own testimony, showing his awareness that he must do his Father's work (2:41–52). Since Jesus is almost a teenager at the time, it hardly does the passage a service to place it with the infancy material. Rather, it is the last section in the overture, with Jesus sounding the final note. The account rightly moves Jesus to center stage. Until 2:41 others talk about Jesus. In this final passage, Jesus introduces himself and his authority.

Luke moves from describing his own task (1:1–4) to having Jesus reveal his call (2:49). Christology dominates these texts, as does the note of fulfillment. This fulfillment is painted in very national colors, as those around Jesus hope that he will deliver the nation. Jesus does that and more.

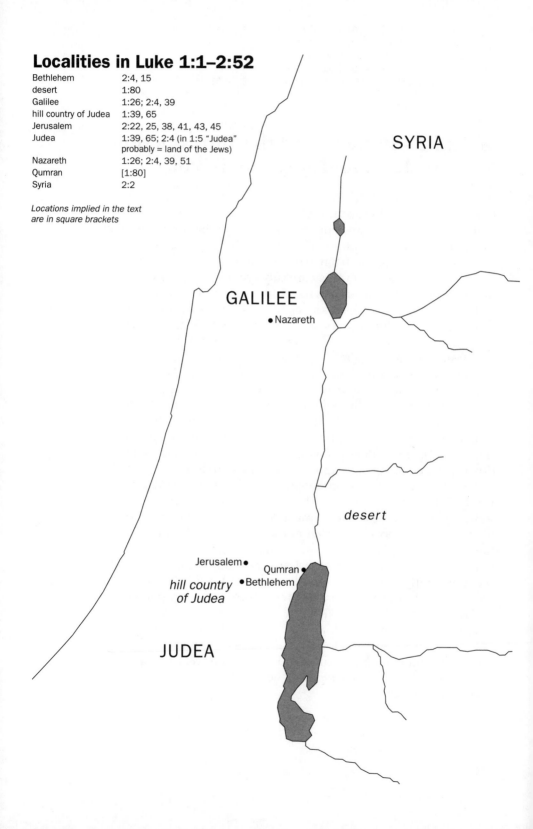

Localities in Luke 1:1–2:52

Bethlehem	2:4, 15
desert	1:80
Galilee	1:26; 2:4, 39
hill country of Judea	1:39, 65
Jerusalem	2:22, 25, 38, 41, 43, 45
Judea	1:39, 65; 2:4 (in 1:5 "Judea" probably = land of the Jews)
Nazareth	1:26; 2:4, 39, 51
Qumran	[1:80]
Syria	2:2

*Locations implied in the text
are in square brackets*

SYRIA

GALILEE

• Nazareth

desert

Jerusalem •   Qumran •
hill country   • Bethlehem
of Judea

JUDEA

I. Luke's Preface and the Introduction of John and Jesus (1:1–2:52)
➤ A. Preface: Luke Carefully Builds on Precedent (1:1–4)
   B. Infancy Narrative: Forerunner and Fulfillment (1:5–2:40)
   C. Jesus' Revelation of His Self-Understanding (2:41–52)

A. Preface: Luke Carefully Builds on Precedent (1:1–4)

Luke begins his work as other ancient writers do, with a preface. The entire paragraph is one long Greek sentence. Luke explains his connection to the past and his desire to give his readers assurance about the instruction they have received. Luke discusses in 1:1 the tradition he inherited. Then he traces in 1:2 the origin of that tradition in eyewitnesses and servants who preach the Word. As the main clause, 1:3 discusses how Luke wrote his account. The last verse reveals Luke's purpose. He desires to give his reader, Theophilus, assurance about the events surrounding Jesus. Theophilus had previous knowledge of these events and Luke wishes to reassure the recipient of his treatise that Jesus is the fulfillment of God's promises. Luke 1:1 speaks of fulfilled events to raise the note of God's activity at the very start. History makes it clear that Theophilus was not the only one who benefited from Luke's labor; the church was also a major beneficiary.

The structure of 1:1–4 reflects balanced Greek periodic style with a protasis in 1:1–2 ("inasmuch as" or "since") and an apodosis in 1:3–4 ("it seemed good also to me"; see BDF §464; BDR §464.4). BDF describes how the periodic parallelism works: "many" is parallel to "also to me," while "to compose a narrative" goes with "to write for you," and "even as eyewitnesses and servants handed down" is tied to "in order that you might have assurance." The parallelism in the third unit is not as clear as in the first two units (for a stylistic parallel, see Acts 15:24–25). Tiede (1988: 33) notes how the period is laid out in parallel lines, matching the suggestion of BDF. So Luke 1:1–4 goes as follows:

   a   inasmuch as many have undertaken (1:1a)
   b   to compile an account of the things . . . (1:1b)
   c   even as those . . . delivered to us (1:2)
   a' it seemed good also to me . . . (1:3a)
   b'   to write an orderly account for you . . . (1:3b)
   c'   that you might know certainty . . . (1:4)

The passage's balance provides an esthetic touch. The parallelism also reflects Luke's effort to create a culturally appropriate introduction.

There are ancient parallels to the prologue. Some are in Hellenis-tic-Jewish writings (Wiefel 1988: 38 n. 1). Here one can note 2 Macc. 2:19–31. The writer of 2 Maccabees cites a predecessor and then explains what his own goal is in writing a new summary work (2:23). He compares his work to painting an already constructed house (2:29). He wishes to entertain and provide facts for the profit of the reader (2:25). Josephus's *Antiquities* 1 *proem* §§1–4 and the *Letter of Aristeas* 1–8 should also be mentioned. There is also the prologue to Sirach, where the writer likewise explains the rationale for his work.

Josephus says that he writes to set out events in which he took part and to remove the prevailing ignorance that exists about im-portant events. Josephus's introduction in *Against Apion* 1.1 §§1–5 even has a dedicatory line to "most esteemed Epaphroditus" and describes the quality of the witnesses on whom Josephus relies. He writes this work to convict detractors of the truth who spread false-hood, to correct ignorance, and to instruct all who desire to know the truth. The prologue to the *Letter of Aristeas* speaks of a "trust-worthy" narrative of memorable matters (1, 6). Sirach simply tries to present to the outside world the legacy of Israel's traditions of wisdom and discipline.

Greek parallels also exist for this form. The later work by Lucian of Samosata (ca. A.D. 125–180), *How to Write History* 53–55, states that unlike the orators he will not appeal for a favorable hearing. He desires to interest his audience and instruct them. Earlier, he had said that the only task of a historian is to tell the truth (39–40; Tiede 1988: 34). Fitzmyer (1981: 16) notes that the ancients knew how to distinguish between fact and fiction. The goals of many Greek writ-ers were like those of 2 Maccabees and other Jewish historian-theo-logians. Lucian argues that, if what is said is important and essen-tial, it will receive attention. The goal is to be clear, set forth causes, and outline the main events. Luke writes with similar goals.

Alexander (1986: 60–63) argues that Luke is a writer in the clas-sic "ancient scientific" mold.[1] This places Luke in the "middle brow" of classical writing. In Alexander's view, such a work re-spects tradition and uses sources, but also has some reworking of tradition. Sterling (1992: 311–89) argues that Luke–Acts is apolo-getic historiography, like Josephus and other Hellenistic Jewish works. Luke is trying to define the church's place within Hellenistic culture and to explain how its roots relate to divine promise. Hengel (1980: 49) argues that Christian history is not designed to present a

---

1. Bovon 1989: 30 n. 1 notes that these comparisons with ancient prologues date back to the eighteenth century with G. Raphelius and J. J. Wettstein. C. F. Evans 1990: 116–19 cites several of these "scientific prefaces."

"rational means of proof for the church" (i.e., pure apology), but is an "invitation to understanding in faith." This is the best way to understand Luke's historiography, provided one does not divide too greatly between history and theology or between rationality and persuasion.

Among the ancients, various terms are tied to writing history. The term ψυχαγωγία (*psychagōgia*, persuasion) is related to a verb that can be pejorative: ψυχαγωγέω (*psychagōgeō*, to lead astray, delude; LSJ 2026 §II). It refers to the goal of some writers, while others refuse to adopt it. Another term is ὑπόμνημα (*hypomnēma*, records, memorial, commentary, or minutes; LSJ 1889 §II.4).[2] Still a third idea is ἱστορία (*historia*, inquiry, information, narrative, or history; LSJ 842 §II). But Luke chose none of these terms to describe his work. His term is διήγησις (*diēgēsis*, narrative account; see BAGD 195 and BAA 392; LSJ 427 defines the verb form broadly as "to describe"; Büchsel, *TDNT* 2:908, defines a related verb as "to recount").

Büchsel (*TDNT* 2:909) notes that the term διήγησις simply means "narrative." It does not refer to some form of an incomplete literary work that one could compare to the individual, detached traditions of modern form criticism. Luke has longer materials in mind than individual pericopes. Büchsel gives some extrabiblical texts using the term (*TDNT* 2:909 n. 3). Some texts describe oral reports; others refer to written reports or historical accounts: Sir. 6:35 (oral); 9:15 (oral); 22:6 (oral); 27:11, 13 (oral); 38:25 (oral); and 39:2 (discourses of famous men); *Letter of Aristeas* 8, 322 (written); 2 Macc. 2:32 (written); 6:17 (historical narrative). LSJ adds Plato, *Republic* 392d and *Phaedrus* 246a, and one should also note Hab. 2:6 LXX (oral). The verb διηγέομαι (*diēgeomai*) in the NT speaks of both oral and written accounts: oral in Mark 5:16; 9:9; Luke 8:39; 9:10; Acts 8:33; 9:27; 12:17; written in Heb. 11:32. So whatever type of narrative Luke alludes to in 1:1, it is not clear whether the sources are oral or written or both. What is clear is that these prior works are long and that Luke's work is similar to them, as 1:3 makes clear (Tannehill 1986: 10). This association might suggest, but does not guarantee, that they are written sources.

So Luke explains why he has written and establishes that his work has precedents. Luke makes other points as well: he highlights the eyewitness origin of tradition; he points out that his account results from a careful consideration of the events; and he notes that the study was carefully done. In fact, the account begins at the start and is thorough. Luke's contribution is signifi-

---

2. These are often unpolished materials; see Lucian, *How to Write History* 47–48.

cant not only because of his careful work, but also because only he writes a sequel, Acts, tying fulfillment in Jesus to the church.

The basic outline of Luke 1:1–4 is as follows:

1. The precedents (1:1–2)
   a. Existence of other accounts (1:1)
   b. Source of the accounts: apostolic eyewitnesses (1:2)
2. Luke's contribution (1:3–4)
   a. Luke's method of composition (1:3)
   b. Purpose of Luke's composition (1:4)

Luke stresses his accuracy and reveals his goal of providing assurance to the reader. His care reflects his aim. Though others have gone before him, Luke attempts to give additional detail to Jesus' ministry, so that Theophilus and those like him can know that God was at work in Jesus. Luke's Gospel is about Jesus and salvation, but it is more than that. Behind the events stands the God of design and concern, who will not abandon his people, his promises, or his plan.

Exegesis and Exposition

[1]⌐Inasmuch as⌐ many have undertaken to compile an account of the things that have been fulfilled among us, [2]even as those who were from the beginning eyewitnesses and servants of the Word delivered to us, [3]it seemed good ⌐also to me⌐, having followed all things carefully from the beginning, to write an orderly account for you, most excellent Theophilus, [4]that you might know certainty concerning the things about which you were instructed.

1. The Precedents (1:1–2)
a. Existence of Other Accounts (1:1)

1:1 Luke's work is not novel. His Gospel notes the precedent of others recounting what Jesus did. The conditional term ἐπειδήπερ (*epeidēper*, inasmuch as) is usually causally related to the action of the main clause: "*since* many have undertaken" (BDF §456.3). Those accounts laid the groundwork for why Luke writes. Ancient writers loved to show that what they were doing had precedents.

Luke's introduction has stylistic parallels with other ancient writings. Fitzmyer cites similar beginnings from Josephus, *Jewish War* 1.6 §17, and Philo, *Embassy to Gaius* 25 §164.[3] No LXX usage

3. See the introduction to §I.A above for more examples; also cf. Fitzmyer 1981: 290–91.

exists for the introductory term ἐπειδήπερ, but this style of intro-duction is common. The causal nuance is defended by Marshall (1978: 41) and Schneider (1977a: 38).

So Luke is not the first to write about Jesus. "Many" (πολλοί, *polloi*) refers to his literary or oral predecessors or both. For most scholars today, this would allude, at least, to Mark and Q (from German *Quelle*, source). Q is a posited source or set of sources contain-ing Jesus' teaching that both Luke and Matthew used. Those who hold to the existence of Q usually think that Mark was the first Gos-pel written. Others believe that Matthew is a source that precedes Luke; some of these scholars do not think an appeal to Q is neces-sary. Scholars who hold to the Griesbach or Augustinian hypothe-sis consider Matthew as the first written Gospel (Griesbach: Mat-thew, Luke, Mark; Augustinian: Matthew, Mark, Luke). Fitzmyer (1981: 91) and Schneider (1977a: 38), with most, hold to the "four-source theory," which advocates Marcan priority and the use of Q, along with a special set of Lucan sources called L. The fourth source (called M) in the four-source view is a special Matthean source, which is material that only the First Gospel writer used. Caird (1963: 23–27) argues for a proto-Luke hypothesis, that is, Mark became a Lucan source at a late stage. In this view Mark had a minor role as a source.[4]

Ἐπεχείρησαν (*epecheirēsan*, have undertaken, set their hand to, attempted) describes the work of Luke's predecessors. "Setting the hand" to tell a story might well suggest written accounts here, ex-cept that other terms in the context suggest organized oral reports. So Luke's remark suggests the presence of written materials, but need not be limited to such sources. Is ἐπιχειρέω neutral or pejora-tive? Did Luke think Jesus' story was well served by previous ac-counts? First, the term is the natural one to use for composing an account (BAGD 304; BAA 617; Cadbury 1922a: 493). Κἀμοί (*ka'moi*, and I also) in 1:3 has Luke join himself to his predecessors (Leaney 1958: 77; Marshall 1978: 42; Creed 1930: 3; Plummer 1896: 4).[5] But Fitzmyer (1981: 291–92) argues that the stress on accuracy and re-search shows Luke still thought work needed to be done. Kloster-mann (1929: 2) also views a critique as implied.

However, another fact complicates the discussion. Luke's sequel makes his task unique, by joining Jesus tradition to church history.

---

4. For evaluation of this issue, see the introduction to the Gospel of Luke under "Sources" and excursus 4. See also McKnight 1991b and Stein 1987.

5. Delling, *TDNT* 8:32–33, esp. n. 3, makes it clear that a censure of the predeces-sors is not in view. He cites the first-century B.C. historian Diodorus Siculus 1.1.1–3 as a parallel. To this Conzelmann, *TDNT* 9:596, adds from the same work 1.2.7 and 1.4.4–5.

Luke adds more accounts to Jesus' ministry and includes discussion of the church's rise (L material comprises over one-third of the Gospel). He does so without necessarily downgrading his predecessors, who blazed a difficult trail ahead of him.[6] One can note the neutrality in ἐπεχείρησαν by citing common usage from MM 250–51.[7] Acts 9:29 and 19:13 represent other NT uses, which are more negative, but κἀμοί in Luke 1:3 is the key to the problem. The phrase is not as pejorative as Danker (1988: 24) suggests when he includes the possibility of heretics in this group.[8] Along with 1:3, the connection of these accounts with the apostolic eyewitnesses shows that they are seen mostly in a good light (1:2).

Luke calls the previous accounts orderly (ἀνατάξασθαι διήγησιν, *anataxasthai diēgēsin*). Fitzmyer (1981: 292) has a detailed lexical survey of διήγησις (*diēgēsis*), which refers to historical narrative.[9] Ἀνατάξασθαι refers to an orderly account (BAGD 61; BAA 122). Delling (*TDNT* 8:32–33) suggests that the term refers to the movement from oral to written tradition. Taken with this sense, the Lucan reference is exclusively to written sources, but it is not guaranteed that this is the point. Ἀνατάσσομαι itself can refer to oral or written accounts, so the idea that only written accounts are in view cannot be defended merely from the use of this term.[10] This term is a technical expression of ancient historians for different kinds of recounting.[11]

It was not just any set of events that were recorded. They had a special character. Περὶ τῶν πεπληροφορημένων ἐν ἡμῖν πραγμάτων (*peri tōn peplērophorēmenōn en hēmin pragmatōn*) means "concerning the events fulfilled among us." The meaning of "fulfilled" is disputed (Fitzmyer 1981: 293). Does it mean *completed*,[12] *assured*

---

6. For a defense of the unity of Luke–Acts and the prologue as serving both volumes, see Maddox 1982: 4–6. Sterling 1992: 341–45 is balanced, arguing that whatever criticism is present is "subdued."

7. Cadbury 1922a: 494 has a list of texts using ἐπιχειρέω; some are neutral, others pejorative. As always, context determines the proper force.

8. For Bovon 1989: 34, the usage in Acts is decisive for a negative sense, but he calls the criticism "discreet."

9. Note also the discussion in the introduction to §I.A above.

10. For more on διήγησις as meaning oral and written accounts, see the introduction to §I.A above and *TDNT* 2:909, where Büchsel provides a nice summary of usage. One parallel to note is Polybius 5.31.4.

11. Van Unnik 1979: 40–42, esp. n. 23, cites Lucian's use of ἀνατάσσομαι in *How to Write History* 47–48. See also Van Unnik 1973. It should be said, however, that when used in a prologue and tied to a word like ἐπιχειρέω, ἀνατάσσομαι suggests written or at least well-organized reports. Also in favor of written predecessors is Du Plessis 1974: 262–63. Written sources are still the most likely referent here. My point is that we cannot be sure that Luke did not mean more than that, especially since multiple sources are mentioned.

12. So Cadbury 1922a: 495–96. rsv and nasb: "the things (which have been) accomplished." Similar is *Neu Luther* and *Zürcher Bibel*.

(Rengstorf 1968: 14), or *fulfilled*[13] events? The third meaning, "fulfilled," is the best since Luke's emphasis in his volumes is the fulfillment of God's plan (1:20, 57; 2:6, 21–22; 4:21; 9:31; 21:22, 24; 24:44–47). The passive participle πεπληροφορημένων (that have been fulfilled) suggests God's acts with its use of the "theological" passive (Marshall 1978: 41). These fulfilled events from the past continue to color how one should see the present. The effect of Jesus' life, death, and resurrection lives on. Luke will chronicle one of the immediate effects, the rise of the church, in his second volume. In Acts, Luke makes the point that Jesus continues to work in the world as the exalted Lord (Acts 1:1–5).

These divinely wrought events did not occur in a corner. Ἐν ἡμῖν describes "events fulfilled *among us*." At the minimum, the first-person plural pronoun refers to those believers who saw the initiation of salvation history, the "first generation." Both Fitzmyer (1981: 293–94) and Leaney (1958: 77) stress that the reference here is to those who observed these events. Leaney is more narrow, taking ἡμῖν to refer only to this original group. But Fitzmyer correctly extends the reference to all affected by salvation history, as does Marshall (1978: 41). Dillon (1978: 271 n. 115) argues that this phrase moves one's attention away from a reference only to the original events to the effect of those events in a later time for all who came to believe. It refers to the second and third generations (the perfect participle suggests a broader time frame for the remark). He notes correctly that the perfect tense of the participle "fulfilled" can include a reference to a group that was not present at the original events. Past and present believers, united by these events, share in their significance. The historical ground that produced this impact is the topic of Luke's two volumes.

b. Source of the Accounts: Apostolic Eyewitnesses (1:2)

Luke now details the ultimate source for these accounts. The conjunction καθώς (*kathōs*, even as) describes how the accounts originated by comparing the previous accounts to their point of origin (Fitzmyer 1981: 294; BDF §453). The term stresses the reliable basis on which these accounts rested: traditions passed down to the reporters by the eyewitnesses and ministers of the Word. There is a two-step process described here; but the nature of the sources guarantees the quality. Luke is still discussing the earlier accounts here, not his own study, which he will describe in 1:3–4.

1:2

---

13. Fitzmyer 1981: 293; Marshall 1978: 41; Schweizer 1984: 11; Du Plessis 1974: 263–64; Sterling 1992: 334; L. Johnson 1991: 27. NIV and NKJV: "things that/which have been fulfilled." *Einheitsübersetzung* speaks of events that occurred among us and were fulfilled, combining the first and third meanings.

The ultimate sources of the Jesus tradition are described by two terms, αὐτόπται (*autoptai*, eyewitnesses) and ὑπηρέται *(hypēretai,* servants). Here is a clear allusion to the original oral level of the tradition. This is the only NT use of αὐτόπτης. These servants served Jesus' cause as eyewitnesses who preached the Jesus they saw.[14] Fitzmyer (1981: 294) notes that the word order favors a reference to one group that holds a twofold role: early witnesses who became ministers of the Word (also Nolland 1989: 7). The single article οἱ *(hoi,* the) and the trailing participle γενόμενοι (*genomenoi,* were, became) argue for this view, though the plural makes it less than certain, since the Granville-Sharp rule does not apply in plural constructions. Fitzmyer (1981: 294) suggests that the reference is to those disciples who became apostles. These eyewitnesses go back to "the beginning" (ἀπ᾽ ἀρχῆς, *ap' archēs*) of Jesus' ministry, a ministry that started after Jesus' baptism by John the Baptist (Acts 1:21–22; 10:37–41). One group is referred to as they functioned in two stages of church history: they saw, and then they reported.[15]

Fitzmyer (1981: 294) argues that Luke is a third-generation Christian because before him there were (1) those present at the beginning and (2) those who ministered the Word (also Goulder 1989: 201). But, if the same group is in view in these two descriptions, then Luke could be a direct descendant of the original group. Even though Luke may be second generation, he is describing three stages of history in the tradition: (1) the experienced events, (2) the witnesses' formulation of tradition concerning the events, and (3) the recording of that tradition and the reflection upon those events. Ellis's description (1974: 65) of Luke as second generation is more accurate than seeing Luke in the third generation.

The Word refers to the message about Jesus and divine events (Luce 1933: 82). The Word preached as God's authoritative message is powerful.[16] The ministers served not their own ends, but the cause of God's message.

The message was preached and was passed on, as παρέδοσαν ἡμῖν (*paredosan hēmin,* delivered to us) indicates. The verb παρα-δίδωμι (*paradidōmi*) is a technical term for passing on official tra-

14. Rengstorf, *TDNT* 8:543; also Michaelis, *TDNT* 5:348, 373. Luke will call these men "witnesses" later in Luke–Acts (Luke 24:44–48; Acts 1:8). Such eyewitnesses were important to ancient historians: Thucydides 1.22.2; Josephus, *Against Apion* 1.10 §55; and Lucian's parody in *How to Write History* 4. See Du Plessis 1974: 265.

15. Ellis 1974: 65. For details, see Dillon 1978: 270–71, esp. n. 114. The title of Dillon's volume, *From Eye-Witnesses to Ministers of the Word,* alludes to the unified view of this phrase.

16. Leaney 1958: 77 mentions the responses to Jesus and the apostles throughout this book as examples of this theme; Luke 4:22; 6:17; Acts 2:36–37; 4:13–14.

dition.[17] Since an account (1:1) was made of what these ministers passed on (1:2), it is likely that the reference in 1:2 is to apostolic oral tradition (Creed 1930: 4). The reference to "us" in 1:2 alludes to the tradition's transmission to a later generation of the church, to those of Luke's time. The appeal to eyewitnesses is more than mere literary convention. Creed (1930: 4) notes against Cadbury (1922a: 497) that one mentions eyewitnesses in the hope that one's account will be believed. The recording of this tradition preserves this important material for all time.

2. Luke's Contribution (1:3–4)
a. Luke's Method of Composition (1:3)

Introducing the main clause, 1:3 gives Luke's view of his own work. **1:3** Ἔδοξε κἀμοί (edoxe kamoi) means "it seemed good also to me."[18] Luke joins himself to those others who have catalogued Jesus' life. They drew from the apostolic tradition for these accounts. Most agree that Luke wishes to add to this tradition of writing because he feels he has something to contribute (Schneider 1977a: 39; Fitzmyer 1981: 296; Dillon 1981: 207–8). Any interpretation that Luke is contrasting himself to his predecessors does not honor the presence of καί (kai, and) in the verse.[19]

Luke notes four characteristics of his work in 1:3, but the meaning of several terms in the verse is disputed. The first key term is παρηκολουθηκότι (parēkolouthēkoti), whose literal rendering is "having followed along closely." The verb basically means "to follow," but its precise force here is disputed (Fitzmyer 1981: 296). Though six possible meanings exist for the term, the dispute boils down to three options. (1) The term may refer to "following closely the progress of certain events," so it means "to keep up with a movement."[20] In this view, it refers to following something with interest or by association, as opposed to doing research. (2) It may refer to the investigation of past events.[21] (3) Some church fathers took the

17. 1 Cor. 11:2, 23; 15:3; Mark 7:13; Jude 3; Fitzmyer 1981: 296. On the verb's aorist form, cf. BDF §95.1.

18. The grammatical parallels to the ἔδοξε κἀμοί construction are Acts 15:22, 25, 28.

19. Κἀμοί is crasis for καί plus μοι. It means "and to me" or "also to me."

20. So Cadbury 1956–57: 131, who argues that the meaning "to investigate" is unattested in Greek; so also Ropes 1923–24: 70–71; Luce 1933: 82; Maddox 1982: 4–5; and RSV. Cadbury's argument has roots in an earlier article (1922b), where he notes the six possibilities for the verb.

21. So most take it, including Fitzmyer 1981: 297; Creed 1930: 4–5; Ellis 1974: 66; Schweizer 1984: 12; Marshall 1978: 43; and Kittel, *TDNT* 1:215–16, who cites Polybius 3.32.2; Josephus, *Against Apion* 1.10 §53 and *Life* 65 §357. Cadbury 1922a: 501–2 challenges the first two examples directly. This view is present in NIV, NASB, *Neu*

term differently, referring it to Luke's role as an apostolic follower. They argued that it means "to accompany," a meaning that is close to the first sense found here, but that stresses Luke's direct involvement more than the first view would (Irenaeus, *Against Heresies* 3.10; Justin Martyr, *Dialogue with Trypho* 103). If this third sense were the meaning, one wonders why Luke would appeal so strongly to the testimony of others as eyewitnesses, since he would have been one himself. Why would Luke be so obtuse about his own direct involvement?

Haenchen argues strongly for the second view, asserting that the meaning "to investigate" is present in Josephus and that Cadbury's interpretation does not fit the Lucan context.[22] Josephus uses the verb to mean "to follow," but with a catch. The idea is to follow an account or events so as to understand them. If Luke's meaning parallels that of Josephus, then the Gospel writer is asserting here that he gave careful attention to the events, something that implies investigation, since he did not experience all the events.

Haenchen continues his case by noting that one cannot be intimately associated "carefully," which is the resultant meaning when one links Cadbury's sense of παρηκολουθηκότι to ἀκριβῶς (*akribōs*). Also, ἄνωθεν (*anōthen*) is unlikely to mean "a long time," which is what it must mean for Cadbury's definition of the term to stand.[23] Now Luke is not an eyewitness, so his ability "to follow" the events carefully can result only from investigation.[24]

Robertson (1923–24) also enters the discussion, noting that the choice for "investigation" is contextually generated because of the perfect participial form of the verb, since the meaning is that Luke "followed along" (i.e., studied) before he wrote.[25] So Luke declares first of all that his work is the fruit of investigation.

The second description applies to the extent of the investigation. It is tied to ἄνωθεν in the phrase ἄνωθεν πᾶσιν ἀκριβῶς (*anōthen pasin akribōs*, from the beginning all things [or events] carefully).

Luther, and *Einheitsübersetzung.* NKJV and KJV speak of having a "perfect understanding," the most emphatic of all translations, which is really a separate view.

22. Josephus, *Against Apion* 1.10 §53 and 1.23 §218; Haenchen 1961.

23. Cadbury 1922a: 504 takes ἀκριβῶς with γράψαι in order to solve the contextual problem of his view. So in his view, Luke writes carefully. But word order makes such a connection grammatically unlikely, as Creed 1930: 5 makes clear.

24. See Plummer 1896: 4 for a defense of παρακολουθέω with this meaning; BAGD 619 §3 cites other ancient texts; also BAA 64. Among them are the already noted texts by Josephus: *Against Apion* 1.10 §53 and 1.23 §218. See Du Plessis 1974: 267.

25. Robertson believes that Luke may have been an eyewitness to some events, but the language of the earlier verses makes this unlikely for the events in Luke's Gospel. The "we" sections of Acts are another matter.

However, ἄνωθεν can mean either "from the beginning"[26] or "for a long time."[27] If the latter translation is chosen, Luke refers to the length of study. The solution comes from Lucan usage. The parallelism of this expression with ἀπ' ἀρχῆς in Luke 1:2 and Acts 26:4–5 suggests the first meaning here.[28] An emphasis on the length of the study would make the later reference to the care of the study somewhat redundant. So Luke makes a temporal reference back to the earliest events.

Fitzmyer (1981: 298) raises the question if ἀρχή here refers to the births of John the Baptist and Jesus or to the start of the apostolic tradition. He opts for the latter but gives no clear reasons. The first option is better (Schneider 1977a: 39; Plummer 1896: 4; Creed 1930: 5). If one notes the emphasis on fulfillment in the infancy material and thus Luke's unique contribution in regard to this period of Jesus' life, then it would seem natural that Luke intends to refer back to this beginning. Though Jesus' ministry does not begin until after John the Baptist, the fulfillment starts with John's coming to earth. Luke viewed his new material on the infancy as contributing to the church's information about Jesus.

The reference to "everything" (πᾶσιν, *pasin*) gives a third characteristic of Luke's work. It tells what he studied. He not only investigated the accounts and went back to the beginning, but he also looked at everything. A question exists whether πᾶσιν is masculine, referring to the study of all the sources, or neuter, referring to the study of events (Fitzmyer 1981: 297 opts for the latter). If ἀπ' ἀρχῆς refers to the events starting from the infancy narrative, then it is most natural to see a reference to events here as well. Fitzmyer (1981: 297) seems inconsistent in taking the previous phrase to refer to apostolic tradition, while referring this phrase to events. Luke examined all the events going back to Jesus' birth (Klostermann 1929: 3). Given Luke's associations in the church, he could make such inquiries. We should not think of Luke as a student locked up in a library, especially since written material was so rare in the ancient world. Here was an inquiring student, who took in whatever he could, oral or written.

Ἀκριβῶς (*akribōs*) describes a fourth characteristic of Luke's study. It tells how Luke did his work.[29] He investigated the material "carefully." Some commentators see this as a description of

26. So most hold, including Büchsel, *TDNT* 1:378. So read NKJV ("from the very first"), NIV, NASB, *Neu Luther, Zürcher Bibel, Einheitsübersetzung*.

27. So Cadbury 1922a: 502–3; Marshall 1978: 42; and RSV. For options, see BAGD 77 §2; BAA 153 §2a.

28. Luce 1933: 82–83. Even though ἄνωθεν in Acts 26:5 means "a long time," it looks back to ἀπ' ἀρχῆς in 26:4, which refers to the earliest point of Paul's ministry.

29. Josephus liked this term to describe his work; see *Against Apion* 1.10 §53; *Jewish War* 1.6 §17; Du Plessis 1974: 268 n. 50.

how Luke wrote his material (i.e., modifying γράψαι) rather than as a description of his investigation. But the word order of the sentence makes this connection less likely. So, Luke's study is the fruit of a careful and thorough investigation that went back to Jesus' birth.

Luke describes his undertaking with καθεξῆς σοι γράψαι (*kathexēs soi grapsai*, to write an orderly account for you). The connection of καθεξῆς could be disputed. Does it describe the manner of study? If so, it goes with παρηκολουθηκότι and means "having investigated in an orderly manner." Or does it describe the nature of the account? If so, it goes with γράψαι and means "it seemed good to write an orderly account for you." The parallel structure of the prologue argues for the second view: καθεξῆς describes what Luke wrote for Theophilus.[30] Luke wrote an orderly account of these events.

But to what does καθεξῆς (an orderly account) refer? Is the order (1) "broadly chronological" (Marshall 1978: 43; Plummer 1896: 5), (2) "a literary systematic presentation" (Fitzmyer 1981: 298–99, citing Acts 11:4), (3) "a salvation-historical linkage" (Schneider 1977b), (4) "a complete presentation" (Klein 1974: 194–96), (5) "a continuous series" (Völkel 1973–74), (6) the presentation that follows the prologue (Kürzinger 1974), or (7) a presentation without gaps (Mussner 1975)?[31]

One can answer this question only by examining what Luke has done. The first three views all have some merit; but each, by itself, is inadequate. Luke is broadly chronological in its flow, but there is some rearrangement of material (e.g., Luke 4:16–30 from Mark 6:1–6; Luke 4:1–13, where the order of the temptations differs from Matthew; and the placement of John the Baptist's imprisonment by Herod in Luke 3:19–20). These rearrangements and others rule out a strictly chronological arrangement, though a general chronology is present, as I argue in the introduction to the Gospel of Luke.

There is a geographical arrangement to the material as well. This movement is from Galilee, to Samaria, Jerusalem, Judea-Samaria, and then Rome. This arrangement is not artificial, since it represents the broad geographical sweep of Jesus' ministry and the church's growth. However, the organization of this material with this clear emphasis is Luke's work.

30. Fitzmyer 1981: 298 correctly notes that on the other view the parallel line starting with σοι would be very short. Almost all translations go this way.

31. Evaluation and rejection of views 4–7 can be found in Schneider 1977b. To determine the difference between views 4 and 7 is hard, except view 4 says the account is full, while view 7 might suggest it is exhaustive. Dillon 1981: 218–23 agrees with Schneider (view 3 above) and argues that view 5 is incorporated into it.

Luke's order is also salvation-historical in that it shows the progress of salvation under God's direction. This growth starts from its founder and continues with one of the most representative messengers of the faith, Paul. It runs from Israel to the Gentiles. It moves from promise in the infancy material to fulfillment in Jesus and the church. This two-part promise-fulfillment structure for God's plan has more merit than does the threefold division advocated by Conzelmann (promise, Jesus, church), since it is not entirely clear that Luke separates the Jesus period from the church period as sharply as Conzelmann implies (see the discussion in Marshall 1970: 77–83; Bock 1994c). Thus, the order of Luke's account works on many levels.[32] It is broadly chronological and geographic, and deals with sacred history.

Schneider (1977b) correctly argues that the focus is salvation-historical. Luke does not just link the events, but shows that what has been fulfilled gives assurance about what is still to be fulfilled: worldwide proclamation of the gospel and Jesus' return. Schneider appeals especially to Acts 3:17–24 and 11:4 for this concept of sacred history told "in order." He puts his finger on a significant part of Luke's concern but his restriction of assurance to future events is too limiting when one looks at 1:4 in light of the whole of Luke–Acts. Luke is also interested in Christology, and he details Gentile mission and inclusion.

The recipient of the book comes next with κράτιστε Θεόφιλε (*kratiste Theophile*, most excellent Theophilus). The identity and spiritual status of Theophilus are unknown. Some have suggested that the name is symbolic of "pious Christians," since the name means "beloved of God" (Plummer 1896: 5, with uncertainty). However, the address to him with the vocative κράτιστε seems to indicate a specific person of high social standing (Acts 23:26; 24:3; 26:25).[33] This greeting could suggest that Theophilus is the patron or monetary backer of Luke's work (so Ellis 1974: 66), but there is no clear way to determine this point. Marshall (1978: 43), Caird (1963: 44), and Fitzmyer (1981: 299–300) mention traditions and speculation about his exact identity (see the introduction to the Gospel of Luke under "Purpose, Readers, and Destination"; Pseudo-Clementine, *Recognitions* 10.71).

---

32. Tiede 1988: 37 alludes to Lucian's comparison of a historian's work to a work of fine sculpture.

33. This is the polite form of address; see BDF §60.2. However, that Theophilus is of high rank is not guaranteed; see Bovon 1989: 39 n. 64. See Theophrastus, *Characters* 5, who says that the address is "simple flattering speech." Nonetheless, Luke's usage does strongly lean toward a greeting of respect.

Is Theophilus a believer or an interested unbeliever? This question turns on 1:4 and the meaning of κατηχήθης (katēchēthēs, you were instructed or you were informed). Caird (1963: 44) argues that an unbeliever is in view, because the dedication is too formal for a reference to a believer and because Luke's work is apologetic in character (also Beyer, *TDNT* 3:639). But these arguments are not convincing. Luke's prologue is formal, because it purposely has taken on a literary character. Accordingly, the formality need not indicate the audience, beyond suggesting someone of high culture. Luke's goal, as stated in the preface, is to give knowledge or assurance (see the exegesis of ἀσφάλειαν in 1:4). The characterization of the Gospel as apologetic is not the best description of the work. The contents of the Gospel and Acts do not represent a defense but a proclamation of Jesus, a review of his teaching and that of the church about which Theophilus has already heard (1:4). So, edification and encouragement are Luke's goal. If this description is correct, then Luke is probably addressing a new believer or one whose faith needs bolstering. Since Theophilus is a name used by both Greeks and Jews, the name does not indicate his nationality (Fitzmyer 1981: 299). However, his social station suggests that he is probably a Gentile, as does the amount of energy Luke spends in Acts defending the Gentile mission. The amount of Jewish material and interaction with devout pagans in Acts may also suggest a former God-fearer (see the introduction to the Gospel of Luke under "Purpose, Readers, and Destination"). Nevertheless, that the work is dedicated to Theophilus does not mean that Luke intended his work just for him. Other ancient writers dedicated their works to individuals, knowing full well that they were writing for a larger audience (Josephus, *Against Apion* 1.1 §§1–5).

b. Purpose of Luke's Composition (1:4)

1:4   Luke's purpose is that he wants Theophilus to realize something about the material.[34] What is realized is ἀσφάλειαν (asphaleian). However, the meaning of ἀσφάλειαν (truth, trustworthiness, assurance) is disputed. Does it vouch for the message's (1) correctness or (2) reliability, or (3) is it giving certainty (or assurance) to the reader? Is Luke interested in accurate facts (view 1) or more (views 2–3)? The Greek word's position at the end of the sentence is emphatic, so it is a key term. Lucan usage of ἀσφάλεια and related

---

34. So one should understand ἐπιγνῷς. Bultmann, *TDNT* 1:704, argues that it means "to confirm," but this comes more from the context than from the term itself; see Acts 22:24; 23:28.

terms answers the question. In Acts 2:36, 21:34, 22:30, and 25:26, he consistently uses these terms in reference to assurance or determining the facts with certainty.[35] Thus, Luke wishes Theophilus, and those who have questions like his, to be certain of the teaching's truth (i.e., either view 2 or 3).

The resulting assurance is probably not of a political nature. Luke is not writing an apology to a Roman official who wonders if Christianity should be granted a legal status. Schweizer (1984: 13) notes that these volumes are too long and deal too little with political issues to have been written for that purpose. What official, he asks, would wade through all this information for just that point? Rather, it seems that the assurance is of a religious, theological nature (Schneider 1977a: 40). Theophilus's question would seem to be, "Is Christianity what I believed it to be, a religion sent from God?" Perhaps such doubt resulted from the judgment the church suffered, especially as a result of including Gentiles. Why should a Gentile suffer frustration for joining what was originally a Jewish movement? Is the church suffering God's judgment because it has been too generous with God's salvation? Will the rest of God's promises come to pass? Has most of Israel rejected the promise? Questions like these are Luke's concern in Acts, where Gentile mission and Paul's ministry as a fulfillment of OT hope receive detailed review. Can one really be sure Jesus is the fulfillment of God's promise and that he brings God's salvation both now and in the future? By the emphasis on fulfillment in Jesus and the truthful character of the tradition (1:1), Luke intends to answer these questions with a resounding "yes." The gospel of Jesus is from God and is available for all, Jew and Gentile alike (Marshall 1978: 43–44).

The phrase περὶ ὧν κατηχήθης λόγων (*peri hōn katēchēthēs logōn*, concerning the things about which you were instructed) tells us Theophilus knows something about Jesus. The meaning of this phrase is disputed, but that meaning is clarified once ἀσφάλειαν is shown to mean "certainty" or "assurance." Λόγων can mean "matters" and refer to the events of salvation (Luke 7:17; Acts 8:21; 15:6), or it can refer to "instruction" (Luke 4:32; 10:39), or it can refer to a message received (Luke 1:20; 6:47). Κατηχήθης can refer to "a report of information" (Acts 21:24; so Cadbury 1922a: 508; RSV) or to "receiving instruction" (Acts 18:25; NKJV, NIV, NASB, *Neu Luther, Ein-*

---

35. Fitzmyer 1981: 300; Creed 1930: 5; Marshall 1978: 44. K. Schmidt, *TDNT* 1:506, cites the Lucan usage noted above. In the LXX, ἀσφάλεια normally refers to something that is safe or secure (2 Macc. 3:22), as it does in Acts 5:23. Its use in Luke with a verb of knowing points to a psychological goal. It refers to knowing the truth, but doing so securely.

heitsübersetzung, Zürcher Bibel).[36] The difference in sense surrounding κατηχήθης is that the first meaning could refer to a report of information given to anyone, including an unbeliever, while the second sense looks more to received teaching and would imply that a believer is addressed. Since the reference to assurance suggests that a new believer is addressed, a reference to instruction is more likely. More importantly, Luke's Gospel-wide pressing for commitment and for remaining faithful until Christ returns also suggests this force. Luke is not pressing for decision, but for faithfulness.

Whether λόγων means events or teaching is less certain, since either meaning can fit. Fortunately, the difference between the two senses is slight. Whether Theophilus was taught about the events or simply given teaching, the result is virtually the same. If teaching is in view, then the significance of the events may have been included in it, but since the events are seen as fulfillments anyway (1:1), the difference becomes almost meaningless. Luke's point is that Theophilus be reassured about the teaching he had previously received. Ellis (1974: 66) suggests that heretical teaching, perhaps of a protognostic flavor, was circulating in the church, but it is more likely that the assurance deals with the pressures felt by a church suffering rejection and persecution. Concern about the nature and extent of God's salvation is a major subject of Acts. Luke's goal is to reassure Theophilus about salvation's fulfillment in Jesus, a salvation that involves even the Gentiles.

Summary

In sum, the goal of Luke's prologue is to place his work alongside other church materials that have recounted the eyewitness, apostolic testimony about Jesus. Luke's unique contribution is found in a fresh presentation of this salvation history, starting from John the Baptist's birth and running through the extension of the church into Rome. Luke's work involved investigation that was thorough and careful. In the orderliness of the account and in its careful, systematic presentation, Luke hoped to reassure Theophilus and those like him about the certainty of what the apostles taught about Jesus. Jesus is the fulfillment of God's promise and the fulfillment of salvation, which is now available directly to all nations.[37]

Many suggest that the use of a literary convention in the prologue to make claims about accuracy proves nothing about the

36. For options, see also Fitzmyer 1981: 301. This is not a reference to a formal catechism, though κατηχέω can refer to a catechism, but rather it means simple instruction (Gal. 6:6; Rom. 2:18; 1 Cor. 14:19).

37. Bovon 1989: 31 compares this emphasis on the account's trustworthiness to John 20:30–31; 21:24–25; Rev. 1:1–3; 22:18–19. Note also 2 Pet. 1:16–18.

real historical character of Luke's work. The argument goes, Luke makes great claims for accuracy, as did other ancients, who in fact were not very accurate (Cadbury 1922b: 419; Talbert 1982: 10–11). It must be noted, however, that the goal of what Luke wishes to accomplish, assurance, is greatly affected by his accuracy. Also, unlike many of the historians to whom Luke is compared, his writing is virtually contemporary to the events he describes. As a result, his ability to be careless with the facts is limited. Assurance grounded in "propaganda" that can be exposed by eyewitnesses is not any great comfort to the doubting. For Luke to produce false propaganda in a period when people experienced what had happened would be counterproductive.

One could also question the morals of a writer who believes in a religion that stresses the telling of the truth, and who yet misrepresents the history he describes. Such religious constraints did not exist for many ancient secular writers. Thus, comparison of Luke to their prefaces, though superficially compelling, does not deal with the unique personal and religious factors that control Luke's account. Whether Luke achieved his goal of accuracy may be tested by an analysis of his work. However, a cavalier dismissal of his claims is not advisable. Neither does a quick appeal to extrabiblical parallels do justice to the statement of the author's goals. Luke's desire is to assure Theophilus, or anyone who reads his Gospel, of the truth of the apostolic teaching about Jesus. His claim is that he was careful about his task in order to achieve this goal. In examining the account to see if Luke met his own standard, we must presume that he tried to do so.

Additional Notes

1:1. Though ἐπειδήπερ appears nowhere else in the NT, the style of the Lucan period is not unique. Acts 15:24–25 has a parallel "since . . . it seemed well to us" construction (Creed 1930: 3).

1:3. Three Latin manuscripts (b, g¹, q) add *et spiritui sancto* (and to the Holy Spirit) after κἀμοί. Mention of the Holy Spirit (probably influenced by Acts 15:28) is designed to add a reference to inspiration in the prologue, but such an idea is not original to the Lucan text nor is this issue explicitly addressed in this text (Klostermann 1929: 3). The reading is too poorly attested to be original.

1:4. The relative pronoun ὧν has been attracted to the genitive case of λόγων. It would normally be accusative since it functions as an object to κατηχήθης. Grammatical attraction has produced the use of the genitive case (Klostermann 1929: 3; Fitzmyer 1981: 301; BDF §294.5).

I. Luke's Preface and the Introduction of John and Jesus (1:1–2:52)
    A. Preface: Luke Carefully Builds on Precedent (1:1–4)
➤ B. Infancy Narrative: Forerunner and Fulfillment (1:5–2:40)
    C. Jesus' Revelation of His Self-Understanding (2:41–52)

B. Infancy Narrative: Forerunner and Fulfillment (1:5–2:40)

Luke's infancy narrative is a major section of his Gospel, since it introduces many key themes. Biblical narrative uses a variety of means to present its point of view: (1) reviewing or previewing events, (2) using Scripture to reveal God's purpose, (3) revealing God's purposes through commissioned agents, and (4) giving testimony through reliable characters within the account (listed in Tannehill 1986: 21–22). Luke's infancy material utilizes all of these: (1) the account is obviously a preview of Luke's Gospel; (2) OT allusions dominate the two chapters; (3) two key agents are revealed and commissioned: John the Baptist and Jesus (the role of each emerges in announcements from Gabriel the archangel and through the hymns of Mary and Zechariah); and (4) additional testimony comes from Simeon and Anna, prophets of Jewish piety.

The narrative's major goal is to give an overview of God's plan by showing the relationship of Jesus to John. John is the forerunner who announces fulfillment's approach, but Jesus is the fulfillment. In every way, Jesus is superior to John. John is born out of barrenness; Jesus is born of a virgin. John is great as a prophet before the Lord; Jesus is great as the promised Davidic ruler. John paves the way; Jesus is the Way. The key stylistic feature used to develop this contrast is parallelism with interchange. John is the major figure in 1:5–25, 46–80; Jesus is the subject in 1:26–38 and 2:1–40. The announcements of the births are laid side by side for contrast. Also, the naming of John is placed alongside the birth of Jesus to set these events together (the chapter break here is a little unfortunate in that it hides the parallelism). After the infancy unit, there is a concluding episode about Jesus in the temple (2:41–52), which underscores how well the Chosen One understands his own mission. No such parallel exists for John. The absence of this parallelism reveals the uniqueness of Jesus.

A key link in the unit is Mary's meeting with Elizabeth (1:39–45). This event ties the two strands of the section together as John and Jesus meet through the interaction of the two mothers.[1] Following

---

1. Bovon 1989: 46–47 demonstrates the linking nature of 1:39–45 as follows:
   a   declaration of the birth of John the Baptist (1:5–25)
   a'   declaration of the birth of Jesus the Messiah (1:26–38)
   b   meeting between Mary and Elizabeth (1:39–56)
   c   birth of John the Baptist (1:57–80)
   c'   birth of Jesus the Messiah (2:1–40)

this, Mary's hymn details what God is doing in Israel (1:46–55). Another link is the hymn of Zechariah (1:67–79), which places the two figures side by side and shows how John leads to Jesus. Once Luke 2 arrives, John is left behind and everything is about Jesus. The forerunner hands the baton to the Promised One.

Luke 1:5–2:40 serves as a theological overview of the work of God. It is in every sense an "overture" and "introduction" orienting the reader to God's work of salvation. A careful study of these two chapters must be a part of any treatment of Luke's two volumes, for they set the table for Luke's account. The outline of the entire unit is as follows:

1. Announcement to Zechariah (1:5–25)
2. Announcement to Mary (1:26–38)
3. Meeting of Mary and Elizabeth (1:39–45)
4. Mary's praise: the *Magnificat* (1:46–56)
5. Birth of John (1:57–66)
6. Zechariah's praise: the *Benedictus* (1:67–80)
7. Birth of Jesus (2:1–7)
8. Reaction to the birth (2:8–21)
9. Witness of the man and woman at the temple (2:22–40)

Events 3 and 4 occur at the same time, as do events 5 and 6, but their significance and stylistic differences require that each be treated as a separate unit. The events move from John to Jesus and back again, with some events mixing the two:

1:5–25	John
1:26–38	Jesus
1:39–45	both
1:46–56	both
1:57–66	John
1:67–80	both
2:1–7	Jesus
2:8–21	Jesus
2:22–40	Jesus

1. Announcement to Zechariah
(1:5–25)

The first unit is, strictly speaking, an angelophany: an angel appears to Zechariah to announce John's birth and his commission as forerunner. The account records the reversal of the couple's barrenness. Zechariah's doubting reaction will bring God's short-term discipline, during which he will learn to trust God and believe his word. Zechariah's expression of faith comes in the *Benedictus* (1:67–79). Luke 1:5–25 shows God moving to save, his individual concern for the couple, and John the Baptist's call.

Sources and Historicity

Whereas the sources and historicity sections will normally treat only the unit under consideration, this section treats sources and historicity issues for the entire infancy narrative (1:5–2:40) as well as for 1:5–25.

Discussion of the genre of the infancy narrative has become very complex, and various names have been given to the genre of Luke 1:5–2:40. Some use the label "legend," because of the highly supernatural features in the account (Klostermann 1929: 4). Some speak of "imitative historiography," because Luke's style parallels OT accounts.[1] Others speak of Midrash or Haggadah, because the major reference point for the unit's concepts is the OT (Schürmann 1969: 22–23; Nolland 1989: 18).[2] Still others, appealing to Greek categories, call the account a "pre-public heroic account," because the

---

1. So Fitzmyer 1981: 309, who notes that the title goes back to E. Burrows. Bovon 1989: 45–47 belongs here, though he sees the presence of legend (1:57–80; 2:1–40), a declaration scene (1:26–38), a meeting account (1:39–56), and two hymns (1:46–56, 67–79). Bovon also sees parallelism in form to Acts 10, though there is no hymnic material there. In addition, he accepts the description of the material as Midrash, provided Midrash is defined as actualizing existing revelation.

2. Fitzmyer 1981: 308–9 correctly dislikes the use of the term *Midrash* for the material, since that genre technically does not actualize an event, but a sacred teaching that is recorded. When Luke wrote, the infancy tradition was not yet old enough or circulated widely enough to be seen in this light. Whether the description *midrashic* applies to Luke's infancy account is more difficult to decide, since the tendencies of a literary form can be reflected without having the genre present. The strong links with OT passages may justify such a description, though not at the expense of the account's historical base.

account exalts the major figure before he has done anything.[3] Perhaps it is best to describe the material as "confessional history," because it clearly has a point of view of faith and yet sets forth the roots of God's work of fulfillment (Schneider 1977a: 77–78). The unit is very complex, using various types of subgenres: angelophany, hymn, narrative, and prophetic pronouncement. Luke uses a variety of genres to depict the start of God's work.

The discussion of sources is equally complicated and numerous propositions and combinations exist (R. Brown 1977: 244–50; Marshall 1978: 47–48; Fitzmyer 1981: 309–11; Nolland 1989: 21–24). Some argue for material created from oral tradition. Others seek origins in a pre-Lucan document, in either Hebrew or Aramaic. Various other sources are posited, especially an appeal to sources from circles associated with John the Baptist for the material in 1:5–25, 57–66. The discussion reaches back as far as 1911 and includes as major contributors D. Völter, R. Bultmann, M. Dibelius, P. Winter, and H. Schürmann (see Schürmann 1969: 18–19 n. a). Schürmann's detailed analysis (1969: 140–45) of the issue concludes that the resolution is still wrapped in darkness, a point that is still true today. The division of sources is very speculative at points, though it does seem likely that Luke would have found some of his material in the Jewish-Christian church, perhaps from believers with roots in the movement started by the Baptist. The contacts within the Jewish-Christian church may well have included family members of Jesus, like Mary or James.[4]

The issue of historicity in these accounts is a judgment that reflects the worldview of the interpreter. Numerous similarities and differences exist between Matthew's account and Luke's version. The differences and the heavy supernatural flavor of both accounts cause many to doubt their historicity, or at least many individual aspects of the accounts. Still, there are numerous similarities in the accounts (Schneider 1977a: 78; Fitzmyer 1981: 307):

1. John is a forerunner of Jesus.
2. Events surrounding Jesus involve eschatological fulfillment.
3. There is no Mary typology.
4. Jesus' origin is grounded in God.
5. There is no adoptionism in the Christology of the passages.

---

3. Talbert 1982: 15–16, who compares Luke's account to Suetonius's *Lives of the Twelve Caesars*, noting how portents, dreams, prophecies, and childhood prodigies dominate the latter source. However, the real literary points of contact with Luke are very few: only the prophecies overlap; Talbert's other points of contact are forced. Another problem with this analysis is that Talbert extends the unit to 4:15, which clearly mixes two Lucan sections together.

4. Most recently Bovon 1989: 22 tentatively suggests this possibility for some of Luke's special material, but he disdains (p. 66) a Marian connection for the Luke 1 material because of the Synoptic portrait of family doubt in Mark 3:21, 31–35. However, Mary's response in Mark may be a reaction to the type of Messiah that Jesus was turning out to be versus what she had assumed he would be.

6. In fact, there is Davidic Christology: Jesus is the promised Davidic redeemer.
7. Jesus' human origins are rooted in righteous parents.
8. The pious recognize Jesus.
9. Grace comes into Israel.
10. Mary is a picture of faith.
11. Jesus is born in the time of Herod.
12. Mary is a virgin and is engaged to Joseph.
13. An angel makes the announcement.
14. Jesus is named by the angel.
15. The Holy Spirit is involved in the birth process.
16. The birth is in Bethlehem.
17. Both accounts call Jesus "Savior."
18. Jesus is born after Mary and Joseph are together.
19. The family settles in Nazareth of Galilee.

The differences in the accounts have raised much discussion. Matthew's account is from Joseph's perspective, while Luke focuses on Mary. How could two announcements have come in isolation? Would not Jesus' parents have told each other? The differences in content are so great that one cannot really place the accounts side by side. This is where the real complaint about historicity lies. Matthew's infancy account has a genealogy; Luke's does not. When Luke does give a genealogy, it differs from Matthew's. Matthew has the magi and a trip to Egypt; Luke has no such details. On the other hand, only Luke has details about John the Baptist's family, events in the temple, the shepherd account, the hymns, and the prophetic remarks of Simeon and Anna. These differences make determining sequence difficult, but one must recognize the possibility of independent, complementary presentations. Clearly one of Luke's goals was to supplement what was already known about Jesus (1:1–4), so such differences are not entirely unexpected. We may not get the neat unity of presentation that we might wish to have, but each account is helpful in revealing elements of the situation.

With regard to possible discussion between Joseph and Mary, two points can be made. First, marriage in the ancient world was more formal and arranged than in current Western culture. Their contact may have been limited. In addition, it seems clear in Matt. 1:18–19 that Joseph did know about Mary's condition. But would he really have believed her explanation had she given it to him? The Matthean account serves as a confirmation to Joseph to go ahead despite Mary's pregnancy.

Many interpreters do speak of a core of historicity in these accounts, but they tend to demur at different points. Nonetheless, one's judgment about historicity, especially in view of the presence of angels and a miraculous birth, depends more on how one sees God's activity in the world than on the data of the text. In other words, philosophy, how one views other ancient historical-literary materials, and theological viewpoint determine how one sees the text, though there can be no doubt that the text's perspective sees the events as historical realities and calls the reader to see them in the same way.

The outline of Luke 1:5–25 is as follows:

a. Tragic situation: a childless couple (1:5–7)
b. Answer: announcement of John's coming birth (1:8–23)
   i. Setting: evening temple offering (1:8–10)
   ii. Event: angelic announcement, doubt, and judgment (1:11–20)
   iii. Aftermath: a wondering crowd and the silent priest (1:21–23)
c. Resolution: Elizabeth's pregnancy (1:24–25)

The structure of 1:13–17 calls for additional comment. NA lays these verses out in strophic lines, a layout that reflects the generally held belief that the material is poetic.[5] Since there is no agreed upon poetic division, it seems best to present the movement of thought in the passage.[6] In fact, it is not entirely clear a hymn is in view. Rather, what is present is a formulaic announcement, which takes on a fixed structure.

R. Brown (1977: 156) lists the five parts of a biblical birth annunciation:

1. appearance of an angel or of the Lord
2. fear of the one to whom the appearance comes
3. the message
4. objection by the recipient of the vision
5. a sign given for reassurance

Luke contains all of these elements. Brown notes that the divine message in biblical birth annunciations also has a typical style:

1. the person is addressed by name
2. a qualifying phrase describes the person
3. the person is urged not to be afraid
4. an announcement is made that a woman is or soon will be with child
5. a promise is made that she will give birth to the child

---

5. The repeated use of καί and future verbs suggests this idea. See R. Brown 1977: 261 for options.

6. Marshall 1978: 56 points out that the material cannot reflect a church hymn, since it is clearly directed to the situation. Bovon 1989: 51 agrees with Marshall that a nonpoetic approach is best.

6. the name of the child is given
7. an etymology of the name is given
8. the future accomplishments of the child are predicted

Of these elements, only the second, third, and seventh are missing in Luke 1:13–17. Here is the four-part movement of thought in the verses:

promise of a child in answer to prayer; his name (1:13)
personal and corporate response to the child (1:14)
position and character of the child (1:15)
mission of the child (1:16–17)

The announcement of John's birth begins a series of great events that ring through the corridors of time and eternity as God's salvation comes to fruition. The themes of this unit are the return of God's promised work of salvation, the promise of a righteous prophet for the nation, God's power exercised for righteous people, and the piety of John's parents in the midst of disappointment. There is a reversal of that disappointment, for God does respond to personal prayer offered in pain. Although answers to such prayer may take time, God may respond positively. In addition, there is the portrayal of God's disciplining grace to a doubting Zechariah. In short, God's promise begins to be realized and its presence brings joy.

Exegesis and Exposition

[5]In the days of King Herod of Judea, there was a certain priest named Zechariah, of the division of Abijah; and he had a wife out of the daughters of Aaron and her name was Elizabeth. [6]And they were both righteous before God, following in all the commandments and ordinances of the Lord with blamelessness. [7]And they had no children, because Elizabeth was barren, and both were advanced in years.

[8]When Zechariah served his course as priest before God while his division was on duty, [9]the lot fell to him to sacrifice in the Holy Place of the Lord, according to the custom of the priesthood. [10]And the full multitude of the people were praying outside at the hour of incense. [11]And there appeared to him an angel of the Lord standing on the right side of the altar of incense. [12]And when he saw the angel, he was afraid and fear fell upon him.

[13]The angel said to him, "Do not fear, Zechariah, because your prayer is heard, and your wife Elizabeth will bear you a son, and you shall call his name John. [14]And it shall be joy and gladness for you, and many will rejoice at his coming, [15]for he shall be great before the Lord, and he shall drink no wine nor strong drink, and he shall be filled with the Holy Spirit, even from

the mother's womb. [16]He shall turn many sons of Israel to the Lord their God. [17]And ⌜he shall go⌝ before him in the spirit and power of Elijah, to turn the hearts of fathers to the children, and the disobedient to the wisdom of the just, to make ready for the Lord a people prepared."

[18]And Zechariah said to the angel, "How shall I know this? I am old and my wife is advanced in years."

[19]And the angel replied to him, "I am Gabriel, who stands in the presence of God, and I have been sent to speak to you and bring you this good news. [20]And behold, you shall be silent and not be able to speak until the days all these things happen, because you did not believe my words, which will be fulfilled in their time."

[21]And the people were waiting for Zechariah and wondered at his delay in the Holy Place. [22]And when he came out, he was not able to speak to them, and they knew that he had a supernatural encounter in the Holy Place, and he made signs to them and remained deaf and mute. [23]When his days of service ended, he went to his home.

[24]After these days his wife Elizabeth conceived, and for five months she hid herself, saying, [25]"Thus the Lord has done to me in the days when he looked on me, to take away my reproach among men."

a. Tragic Situation: A Childless Couple (1:5–7)

Luke places the events in the context of Palestinian history (references to Roman history are saved until 2:1–2; 3:1). Ἐγένετο . . . ἡμέραις (egeneto . . . hēmerais, it came about in those days) is reminiscent of LXX style and ethos (Judg. 13:2; Jdt. 1:1; Tob. 1:2; Marshall 1978: 51; C. F. Evans 1990: 145). The reference to "days" refers to the period of Herod the Great, who reigned as a Jewish ruler for Rome in 37–4 B.C. He is correctly described as a "king" (Marshall 1978: 51; Plummer 1896: 8; Tacitus, *Histories* 5.9). Herod received his commission to rule from Mark Anthony and the Roman senate in 40 B.C., but did not actually return to rule until 37 B.C. (Josephus, *Antiquities* 14.14.4–5 §§383–86; 14.15.1 §469; Fitzmyer 1981: 321). He is described as the king of Judea in its broad political sense, with "Judea" referring to Judea proper, Galilee, much of Perea, and much of Syria (so Luke 4:44; 6:17; 7:17; 23:5; Acts 2:9; 10:37; 11:1, 29; Klostermann 1929: 6; Plummer 1896: 8).

1:5

When all the NT data are put together, these events are dated near the end of Herod's rule, around 4 B.C. Matthew 2:15, 19–20 notes that Jesus was born near the time of Herod's death (see Josephus, *Antiquities* 17.8.1–3 §§191–99). Schweizer argues that Herod wanted to see himself as the Davidic king, yet the one who would get that designation was born in his reign in a little Israelite village.[7]

---

7. Schweizer 1984: 20. Herod's reaction in Matt. 2 seems to confirm that this is Herod's view, although the Josephus reference (*Antiquities* 14.9 §§156–84) cited by

The meaning of Zechariah's name, "Yahweh has remembered again," fits the account, but Luke makes no effort to exploit the point, since he offers no translation for his audience, which included Gentiles (Marshall 1978: 51–52). The name is common, especially in the OT.[8]

Zechariah was a righteous and faithful Jewish servant of God (1:6). As a priest, he served in the temple for two one-week periods each year, excluding festival periods (SB 2:55–68; Marshall 1978: 52; Plummer 1896: 8–9). Josephus describes the twenty-four divisions of first-century priesthood.[9] Each division was further subdivided into orders, and each order served a daily rotation during its week of service at the temple. Each rotation consisted of four to nine priestly houses or families.[10] Zechariah was not a high priest as the Protevangelium of James 8 portrays him.[11] In 1 Chron. 24:10, the order of Abijah (or Abia) comes eighth in the list; the evil reputation that they came to have centuries later was not true of Zechariah (SB 2:68 cites an eighth-century rabbinic elegy).

Elizabeth was also of priestly blood, since she was a daughter of Aaron.[12] It was very common for a Jewish priest to have a wife of the same background, and such a union was regarded as a sign of special privilege.[13] The mention of Elizabeth's lineage underlines her pious origins and strengthens the pedigree behind John the Baptist. That Elizabeth was also the name of Aaron's wife (Exod. 6:23) may explain why the Protevangelium of James referred to Zechariah as a high priest.

The meaning of Elizabeth's name is disputed. It means either "my God is the one by whom I swear" or "my God is fortune" (Fitzmyer

---

Schweizer appears not to make a Davidic point; rather, it highlights his regal self-awareness.

8. 1 Chron. 15:24; 2 Chron. 35:8; Neh. 11:12; Fitzmyer 1981: 322; Leaney 1958: 79; Creed 1930: 8. The *Anchor Bible Dictionary* 6:1057–61 records thirty-one individuals with the name *Zechariah* in the OT and Judaism, four of whom are also mentioned by Josephus (who knows of two more); Schalit 1968: 49.

9. *Life* 1 §2 and *Antiquities* 7.14.7 §§363–67 attribute the twenty-four groups to David and allude to 1 Chron. 24:31; see also *Against Apion* 2.8 §108.

10. For details, see Schürer 1973–87: 2.246–50, 287; Wiefel 1988: 47; Schrenk, *TDNT* 3:262; and esp. Jeremias 1969: 199.

11. Bovon 1989: 52 n. 30 notes that a high priest would not be one of those who were chosen by lot to give this offering.

12. The wording "daughter of Aaron" is not found in the OT, Josephus, Philo, or the rabbis; see K. Kuhn, *TDNT* 1:4.

13. Lev. 21:7, 14 discusses the laws regarding priestly marriages and restricts the priests to virgins (Marshall 1978: 52). SB 2:68–71 notes that this type of priestly union was encouraged; Plummer 1896: 9. For ancient Jewish rules of marriage, including reference to some Jewish texts after the first century, see G. Moore 1927–30: 2.119–22 and Safrai 1976a: 752–60.

1981: 322). The choice is not certain, but both possibilities indicate trust in God. Elizabeth's response later shows her faith (1:24–25). The parents of John the Baptist are of the best spiritual ancestry.

This couple not only had the right heritage, they also had a commendable spirituality. Both were "righteous before God," an expression describing a moral righteousness that conforms to God's standards, as the following reference to a blameless conduct shows.[14] This use of δίκαιοι (*dikaioi*, righteous) is different from Paul's use of the term to refer to those who are positionally righteous before God (Rom. 3:21–31). The righteousness described here fits its precross setting; it is righteousness from the perspective of God's law. In contrast to Pauline justification, righteousness here is concrete and visible and is seen in consistent acts. The phrase ἐναντίον τοῦ θεοῦ (*enantion tou theou*, before God) depicts God's positive evaluation of their lives. They are faithful saints who have an approved walk before him. The wording also has OT parallels (Gen. 6:8; 7:1; Ezek. 14:14; Klostermann 1929: 6; Luce 1933: 84; Creed 1930: 9; Plummer 1896: 9). **1:6**

Luke further defines this couple's righteousness: Zechariah and Elizabeth were blameless with respect to God's commands and requirements. The participle πορευόμενοι (*poreuomenoi*, following), which depends on ἦσαν (*ēsan*, were), describes how John's parents were obedient: they faithfully and consistently obeyed God.[15] The OT also refers to following after God's commandments (Deut. 28:9; 1 Sam. 8:3, 5; 1 Kings 3:14; Plummer 1896: 9). Ἐντολαῖς καὶ δικαιώμασιν (*entolais kai dikaiōmasin*, the commandments and ordinances) is another OT phrase.[16] Luke loves to note obedience to the law and faithfulness to the temple.[17] The adjective πάσαις (*pasais*,

14. Marshall 1978: 52; Schrenk, *TDNT* 2:189 §C2c (who notes Lucan parallels to the expression in Luke 2:25 and Acts 10:22). In addition, Schrenk notes NT parallels: Abel in Matt. 23:35; Lot in 2 Pet. 2:7–8; prophets in Matt. 13:17; 23:29; and martyrs in Matt. 23:35. The phrase has parallels in the OT (Deut. 6:25; 24:13; Ps. 106:31) and Judaism (Sus. 3; Sir. 44:17); Nolland 1989: 26.

15. Isa. 33:15; Prov. 28:18; Jub. 7.26; Hauck and Schulz, *TDNT* 6:571. Marshall 1978: 52 notes that this description for spiritual integrity carried over into Judaism; T. Reub. 1.6; 4.1.

16. Gen. 26:5; Exod. 15:26; Num. 36:13; Deut. 4:40; 10:13; 27:10; 2 Kings 17:13. In Judaism: 1 Macc. 2:21; T. Levi 14.4; T. Judah 13.1; Schrenk, *TDNT* 2:220; Klostermann 1929: 6; Plummer 1896: 9 (who notes that the terms are synonymous in this usage).

17. Luke 2:23–24, 27, 37, 39, 46; 16:17; 19:45, 47; 20:1; 21:37–38; 23:56; 24:53; Tiede 1988: 41. These emphases are less pronounced in Acts; consider, e.g., Stephen's critique of the temple in Acts 7 and Peter's warning about the law in Acts 15:10–11. For Luke's complex view of the law, see the introduction to the Gospel of Luke under "Theology—The New Community—Source of Tension: The Law."

all) shows that this couple's righteousness covered the full range of God's commandments. They earned the right to be called ἄμεμπτοι (*amemptoi*, blameless; BAGD 45; BAA 87). They were a spiritually exemplary couple. Zechariah and Elizabeth were of honorable priestly origin and were faithfully righteous before God, but there was one thing that was a disappointment: despite their blamelessness, they were barren (1:7).

1:7   The pious couple lacked children and were troubled as a result (1:18, 25). The absence of children was generally seen as a reproach in Judaism and in the OT.[18] But the couple's righteousness (1:6) shows that their barrenness was not the result of judgment or sin. Rather, God had something special in mind, as he had with many of the great OT saints who were born under similar conditions. Among the OT parallels are Isaac born to Sarah (Gen. 18:11), Samson born to the wife of Manoah (Judg. 13:2, 5), and Samuel born to Hannah (1 Sam. 1–2). If a curse was not present, then perhaps God was preparing to do something great. To those readers who knew the rest of this account, the reversal was a cause of joy and wonder. For those who did not know the outcome, Luke proceeded to set forth the gracious outcome of the couple's dilemma.

The phrase beginning with καθότι (*kathoti*, because) is explanatory, just as was the participle πορευόμενοι in 1:6: they were childless because Elizabeth was barren. To make matters worse, both (ἀμφότεροι, *amphoteroi*) were now old (προβεβηκότες ἐν ταῖς ἡμέραις, *probebēkotes en tais hēmerais*, advanced in their days).[19] The age factor makes this account parallel to the Abraham-Sarah-Isaac birth account. There, as here, the birth is seen as God's act, since the child is born despite the excessive age of the parents (Schneider 1977a: 45). The rabbis make the point that whenever Scripture says "she had not," God gave her a child.[20] The indications of the situation leading up to the announcement of John's birth prompt the reader to expect great things from God's hand as he begins the execution of the "events of fulfillment" (1:1). God's action now parallels the way God often introduced the greats of the OT. A new great period begins with God's grace toward this faithful couple.

18. Lev. 20:20–21; Jer. 22:30; 1 Sam. 1:5–6; 2 Sam. 6:23; Plummer 1896: 10; Fitzmyer 1981: 323; J. Schneider, *TDNT* 5:239. Contrast Gen. 1:28; Ps. 127, 128.

19. Stylistically this is like some OT phrases, e.g., "advanced in days" (Gen. 18:11; 24:1; Josh. 13:1; 23:1; 1 Kings 1:1); BDF §197; N. Turner 1963: 220 (dative of respect using ἐν); Luke 1:18; 2:36; Delling, *TDNT* 2:947–50, and esp. n. 42.

20. Leaney 1958: 80; SB 2:71. Midr. Gen. 38.14 (23c) attributes the remark to Rabbi Levi, an ascription that dates the remark to ca. A.D. 300.

b. Answer: Announcement of John's Coming Birth (1:8–23)
i. Setting: Evening Temple Offering (1:8–10)

Zechariah is in the midst of his biannual temple ministry as one of **1:8**
approximately 18,000 priests (see additional note) who served at
the temple (SB 2:71–75). The setting is the temple ministry of Zechariah, but his week of ministry is not a normal one, as 1:9 makes
clear.[21] In offering the incense, Zechariah is performing the greatest ministry of his priestly career. At this special moment, God
makes an announcement for the pious priest and for the nation of
God's people.[22]

By the casting of lots Zechariah received the honor of giving the **1:9**
sacrifice. The custom of casting lots—required because of the large
number of priests (*m. Tamid* 5.2–6.3)—occurred twice a day to determine which priest would offer the incense with the whole burnt
offering. Only once in his life would a priest receive the special
honor of offering incense in the Holy Place as part of the preparation for the sacrificial offering.[23]

The times of the twice-daily offering were at sunrise and dusk.[24]
In first-century Judaism the time of the evening offering, which was
known as "the perpetual offering,"[25] was altered so that prepara-
tions for it started around 2:30 in the afternoon. Taken to the altar
about an hour later,[26] this offering coincided with the time of
evening prayer at the temple, so that it was often well attended
(Dan. 9:21; Acts 3:1). Details of the offering, both the offering of the
incense and the sacrificial offering, are found in the Mishnah (see
Tamid 6–7 and the exegesis of 1:22). The chosen priest went into the
Holy Place, where the altar of incense, the lampstand, and the
showbread were found. The priest offered the incense with its
"sweet savor" on behalf of the people. The incense was a symbol of
intercession proceeding up to God (1:10). It is at this high moment
in Zechariah's career that God speaks to him. It is not clear whether
a morning or evening offering is in view here, though the presence

21. This is the one NT use of the verb ἱερατεύω (to serve in the temple); Schrenk,
TDNT 3:249.
22. On the structure of this verse and Luke's use of ἐγένετο, see Creed 1930: 9;
Klostermann 1929: 6–7; Marshall 1978: 54; BDF §472.3.
23. Exod. 30:1–9; Marshall 1978: 54; Michaelis, *TDNT* 4:264. For this narrow use
of ναός as "Holy Place," see 1 Macc. 1:21–22; Fitzmyer 1981: 323; Schrenk, *TDNT*
3:232.
24. Schürer 1973–87: 2.287 n. 74; *m. Yoma* 2.2–4; *m. Tamid* 1.2; 3.1; 5.2; Safrai
1976d: 887–90; Hanse, *TDNT* 4:1.
25. Exod. 29:38–42; Num. 28:3–8; Schürer 1973–87: 2.301–3.
26. Schürer 1973–87: 2.300–301, esp. n. 30; Josephus, *Antiquities* 14.4.3 §65;
m. Pesaḥ. 5.1.

of the large crowd tends to favor the evening offering (Klostermann 1929: 7; Schneider 1977a: 45). At a moment of prayer, God acts for his people.[27]

1:10　The people gathered at the temple were praying, while Zechariah was busy offering sacrifices to God.[28] The offering of sacrifices inside the temple reflected the action of the people outside. A solemn mood of corporate piety is present in the narrative. A later tradition from Tg. Song 4:16 says that the people prayed during the offering: "May the merciful God enter the Holy Place and accept with favor the offering of his people" (SB 2:79; Marshall 1978: 54; Klostermann 1929: 7). Though this tradition is later than the first century, it may accurately reflect the people's sentiments during this offering, especially since eschatological hope was high in Judaism during this period. What happened to Zechariah would be witnessed by a pious throng (1:21–22). Luke paints the background of the announcement in pious, worshipful colors. In the midst of this worship, the angel Gabriel (1:19) comes.

ii. Event: Angelic Announcement, Doubt, and Judgment (1:11–20)

1:11　The account returns to Zechariah, and the drama begins in earnest. As Zechariah goes to place the incense on the altar and offer up a prayer (*m. Tamid* 6.3), an angel appears to him. He stands at the right of the altar, the side of favor.[29] This position places the angel between the altar and candlestick in the Holy Place (Plummer 1896: 12). The verb ὤφθη (ōphthē, there appeared; from ὁράω, horaō, to see) is frequently used in Luke of supernatural appearances.[30] Arguing that the discussion about angels is "characteristic of the naive supernaturalism of primitive and popular thought," Luce (1933: 85) explains the event in terms of Zechariah's spiritual, psychological perception. But Plummer (1896: 11–12) rightly raises the question whether such an explanation works here. If only an internal psychological event were intended, it would be easy to depict God speaking to Zechariah in a vision or in a voice without an angel present. Luce's explanation reveals more about the interpreter than the event. As to the reality of the event, one's view of God's ability

27. The theme of prayer is key for Luke: 5:16; 6:12; 9:18, 28; 18:1–8; 22:41.

28. On the connection between incense and prayer, see Ps. 141:2; Rev. 5:8; 8:3–4.

29. Ps. 110:1; Mark 16:5; Marshall 1978: 55; Klostermann 1929: 7. Danker 1988: 29 is wrong to call it the side of divine authority; this is the meaning only when one is at the right side of God, though the altar does represent approaching God.

30. Luke 24:34; Acts 2:3; 7:2, 30, 35; 9:17; 13:31; 16:9; 26:16; Fitzmyer 1981: 324; Michaelis, *TDNT* 5:358. Acts 7:26 is an exception to this consistent usage.

to reveal his will and one's view of the spiritual world will determine how one sees the reality of what is described here. But the biblical perspective about the reality of angels is clear. In the view of the entire NT, such beings do exist (Luke 2:9; Matt. 1:20; Acts 5:19; 1 Cor. 4:9; Heb. 1:4; 1 Pet. 3:22; Jude 6; Rev. 5:2).

Parallels for this event are often noted. The most popular parallel is found in Josephus, *Antiquities* 13.10.3 §282, where the high priest Hyrcanus (135–104 B.C.) hears God's voice reporting the victory of his sons in battle during the offering of a sacrifice. But this parallel is not as strong and intense as the Lucan account in that hearing a voice is different from seeing an angel. So the appeal to parallel "heavenly voice" accounts is not a precise comparison to make with Luke 1:11.[31]

The angelic report to announce a birth recalls OT figures like Ishmael, Isaac, Jacob, Esau, and Samson.[32] But against those who argue that Luke created the parallelism, it is to be noted that usually those appearances were to the mothers of the children, not to the fathers. Thus, if Luke had wished to construct a parallel, Elizabeth, not Zechariah, would have been the likely subject of the announcement. The similarity with this OT motif does, however, show that God is active for his people again.

1:12 Zechariah reacts. When he saw (ἰδών, *idōn*) the angel, he was terrified with fear (ἐταράχθη, *etarachthē*; φόβος, *phobos*).[33] In the Scriptures, an encounter with the Divine or his agents usually produces fear (Exod. 15:16; Judg. 6:22–23; 13:6, 22; 2 Sam. 6:9; Isa. 6:5; Dan. 8:16–17; 10:10–11). Luke consistently records this response to God's presence, his activity, or the presence of his messengers (Luke 1:29–30, 65; 2:9; 5:8–10; 9:34; Acts 5:5, 11; Tiede 1988: 42). Other things producing this or a similar response are the gospel message alongside apostolic wonders (Acts 2:37 ["cut to the heart"], 43; 19:17), Jesus' teaching and work (Luke 5:26; 7:16; 8:37), and the resurrection event (in the other Synoptics, but not in Luke; Balz, *TDNT* 9:209–12).

The priest's response is real terror, as is indicated by the verb ἐταράχθη (*etarachthē*, he was afraid; Tob. 12:16; Mark 6:50; Luke 1:29

31. See Klostermann 1929: 7 for more examples; Marshall 1978: 55 mentions 2 Macc. 3:22–40 as a parallel, where Heliodorus, chief minister to the governor of Syria, suffers a vision that prevents him from entering and defiling the temple. Nolland 1989: 29 suggests that the closest parallel is Dan. 8:17; 9:20–21; 10:7, 15.

32. Gen. 16:10–11 (Ishmael announced to Hagar); 17:15–19 (Isaac announced to Abraham); 18:10–15 (Isaac announced to both parents, though Sarah's response is the focus); 25:23 (Jacob and Esau announced to Rebekah); and Judg. 13:3–21 (Samson announced to the wife of Manoah).

33. Fear is slightly emphatic in the sentence; BDF §472.2.

[uses the intensified form διαταράσσω]; 24:38). The description is not a mere literary touch, for when humans contact the "unseen world" they often respond with fear at the unknown.[34] This response reveals that Zechariah is taken aback by the angel's appearance. He does not expect it, nor does he view it as a common occurrence. Rather it places him in deep anxiety. The angel's presence heightens the drama. God is at work.

1:13 The angel announces the child's arrival with a word of comfort. The call not to fear is typical of an annunciation scene and seeks to relieve the anxiety that the encounter with God or his messenger has produced.[35] As Zechariah is about to find out, there is no need to fear what the angel will say or do. He brings good news (1:19).

The reason that Zechariah need not fear is that his prayer has been heard.[36] There is much discussion about the content of this prayer, and it is hard to be sure. Views include that (1) he had prayed for a son as part of his prayer in the Holy Place (Creed 1930: 10; Danker 1988: 29; Klostermann 1929: 8); (2) he had prayed for the redemption of Israel (Plummer 1896: 13; Marshall 1978: 56); and (3) the angel referred to a previous prayer for a child (Schürmann 1969: 32–33; Schneider 1977a: 45). Although the immediate context starts out as if the answer were to a prayer for a child, the nature of Zechariah's reply in 1:18 makes it unlikely that he had prayed for a child in the Holy Place or even that he still hoped to have a child. So view 1 is not likely.

The choice between the other two options is more difficult. In the context, both personal and national concerns are addressed. Prayer for the nation is the point of the evening offering, so that event itself suggests view 2. The term δέησις (*deēsis*, prayer) suggests specific petition, a definition that fits either view (2:37; 5:33; Greeven, *TDNT* 2:41). It is perhaps more likely, in light of the personal focus of the angel's reply and in light of Zechariah's question about the promised son, to see a reference to his old prayer for a child, as 1:13 suggests (view 3). Plummer (1896: 13) argues against any reference to past prayers, insisting that a reference to a past set of requests in the singular δέησις is unusual. However a collective reference for δέησις can occur (see Rom. 10:1—surely Paul prayed for Israel more than one time!). In fact, God was tackling two problems at

---

34. Plummer 1896: 12; Marshall 1978: 55. The reaction to Orson Welles's broadcast of the "War of the Worlds" is a good illustration of this phenomenon.

35. In Luke's writings: Luke 1:30; 2:10; Acts 18:9; 27:24; elsewhere in the NT: Matt. 1:20; 28:5, 10; Mark 6:50; Rev. 1:17; in the OT: Gen. 15:1; 26:24; Josh. 8:1; Isa. 43:1, 5; 44:2; Jer. 46:27–28; Dan. 10:12. See Balz, *TDNT* 9:212 §D2c; Marshall 1978: 56; Plummer 1896: 12; Creed 1930: 10.

36. Διότι is causal, so it translates as "because."

once. He was dealing with something absent from Zechariah's personal life, while dealing with Israel's prayer and plea. God's answers sometimes come at a surprising time, in a surprising place, and in a surprising way.

The birth announcement reflects OT announcements.[37] The father usually names a child (1:62); God's naming a child shows that the child is important to his work (Gen. 16:11; 1 Kings 13:2; Isa. 7:14). Luke is not concerned with the meaning of John's name; but the name is appropriate enough, seeing that it means "Yahweh has been gracious." The child is special and significant, as the angel's further explanation will reveal.

The angel announces the personal joy that will be Zechariah's because of the child's coming. Terms are chosen that suggest the great joy usually associated with God's great acts. Both χαρά (*chara*, joy) and ἀγαλλίασις (*agalliasis*, gladness) often refer to the response associated with God's work. Bultmann makes the point that ἀγαλλίασις in this context describes the reaction to the position and mission of the child.[38] Conzelmann shows that χαρά and its variants frequently appear in Luke (*TDNT* 9:367–68). Joy comes with finding the lost (15:5–7) and at knowing one's name is written in the book of life (10:20). Joy is a reaction to the acts of Jesus (13:17; 19:6), to the events associated with the ascension (24:52), and even to suffering for proclaiming and believing God's message (Acts 5:41). Zechariah will rejoice not only because he is a father, but also at what the mission of this child means for his people. John's coming means that salvation nears. The fundamental Lucan theme of God's work of salvation emerges.

1:14

John will bring joy not only to his formerly barren parents, but also to the "many" (πολλοί, *polloi*). There is a minor debate over whether πολλοί means "all" (Danker 1988: 30; Jeremias, *TDNT* 6:541) or "a lot" (Marshall 1978: 57). Luke 1:16 seems to settle the matter, for it speaks of "many" (πολλούς, *pollous*) who will turn to the Lord. Since not every Israelite responded to John's ministry (e.g., the Pharisees in Luke 3), πολλοί means "a lot." The rejoicing is on the basis of (ἐπί, *epi*, because of) his γενέσει (*genesei*, birth or coming). Since the rejoicing is corporate, the verb χαρήσονται (*charēsontai*, will rejoice) is a term suggesting eschatological joy for John's entire ministry (summarized in 1:13–17). The term γενέσει here refers to the response to John's coming and not just to his

37. Gen. 16:11; 17:19; 1 Kings 13:2; Isa. 7:14; 49:1; also Luke 1:31; Matt. 1:21; Marshall 1978: 56. On the grammar, see BDF §157.2; Matt. 1:21, 23, 25; Luke 1:31; 2:21.

38. *TDNT* 1:20. Used elsewhere in Luke 1:44 and Acts 2:46, ἀγαλλίασις is typically associated with the celebration of God's goodness (Heb. 1:9; Ps. 44:8; 51:12).

birth.[39] This eschatological and comprehensive reference receives confirmation in 1:15, which begins with γάρ (*gar*, for) and gives the explanation for this statement by the angel. The explanation is focused on the position, work, and ministry of John the Baptist (1:15–17). Thus, a paraphrastic way to render 1:14 in light of the description of the following context is this: "And many of the Lord God's people will rejoice because of his ministry of preparing them for the Lord." Joy comes because John's ministry signals the Lord's decisive work for salvation.

1:15   Next, the angel describes John's character and ministry. His position before God is that he will be great. Μέγας (*megas*, great) anticipates what will be said of John in 7:28, that there is no one greater born of a woman. The reason for his greatness rests in his character and mission (1:15b–17). God will use John for his own purposes (Danker 1988: 30). The term μέγας by itself need not suggest that John is a prophet, just that he is significant in God's plan.[40] John's prophetic role is made clear by the rest of the announcement. Fitzmyer (1981: 325) notes that when the term appears by itself in an absolute sense it describes an attribute of God (Ps. 48:1 [47:2 LXX]; 86:10 [85:10 LXX]; 135:5 [134:5 LXX]; 145:3 [144:3 LXX]). So the unqualified description of Jesus with just this term in Luke 1:32 suggests Jesus' superiority to John and implies that Jesus is closer to Yahweh than is John.

The phrase *before the Lord* places John's greatness in perspective. He is great in God's judgment because John lives to serve him. R. Brown (1977: 273) sees an allusion here to Mal. 3:1, which is explicitly picked up in Luke 7:27. Fitzmyer (1981: 325) rejects this allusion, but gives no reason for his view. John is perceived through this allusion as an eschatological messenger of salvation.

John lives a life of discipline. The restriction from wine represents special consecration. In the OT, such a restriction existed for priests when they were performing their duties (Lev. 10:9). A more permanent restriction existed for the Nazirite, who could make a

39. There are three allusions to eschatological joy in this verse: χαρήσονται, χαρά, and ἀγαλλίασις; Leaney 1958: 80; Marshall 1978: 57. Or as Bovon 1989: 55 says, the joy is for the birth of a prophet. His office is the source of joy. The joy may well start with Elizabeth (1:39–45).

40. Μέγας is used derisively of Simon Magus in Acts 8:10, but positively of Isaiah in Sir. 48:22; R. Brown 1977: 273 n. 33. It is used of Mordecai (Esth. 10:3), who was not a prophet. Bovon 1989: 56 compares the remarks to the "great" priestly figures in T. Levi 17–18. "Greatness" comes for the first priest of Jubilee in being able to talk to God (17:2), while for the last priest, the eschatological priest, it involves anointing by the Spirit (18:7). It is clear that greatness has to do with being specially endowed to serve God.

vow not to drink during his or her whole life (Judg. 13:4–5) or could vow to refrain for special periods (Num. 6:1–21). The strongest OT parallel to the wording here is 1 Sam. 1:11, an allusion to Samuel, who was presented as Israel's first prophet.[41] By this parallel, John's office is implicitly affirmed.

The term σίκερα (*sikera*, strong drink) is a Semitic loanword, going back ultimately to Akkadian *šikaru* (Klostermann 1929: 8). It refers to intoxicating drink not made from grapes and includes drinks like barley beer (Fitzmyer 1981: 326). The restriction does not say anything inherently evil about drink, but points to a special consecration that is above the call of the normal person.[42] The vow receives emphasis through the use of οὐ μή (*ou mē*, shall not).[43] Such a vow usually was voluntary; but in the rare cases where it was not, the imposition of the vow revealed a special person called of God.[44] R. Brown (1977: 269, 273–74) suggests that Luke framed the account after the OT parallels, but if that had been the case would not Zechariah have committed John to the vow? It cannot be denied that a pattern of God's actions with great individuals is present here. However, the variations argue against Lucan creation of a parallel, since more agreement might be expected if the details were fabricated.

From this verse some conclude that John is a Nazirite (Leaney 1958: 41; Plummer 1896: 14; Fitzmyer 1981: 326). For others the absence of an instruction not to cut his hair shows that John is not a Nazirite, but an ascetic (R. Brown 1977: 274; Marshall 1978: 57; Klostermann 1929: 9; Gray 1899–1900). It is hard to be sure, since nothing more is made of his abstinence. Rather the stress is on John's prophetic office. If Luke 7:25, 33 is any guide, the asceticism of a prophet is the point of the description here. John is specially set apart to God, as his lifestyle will indicate.

The presence of God's Spirit with John underscores his prophetic role. Such an association is used elsewhere to refer to great people of God.[45] God's Spirit is very active in the infancy events (1:35, 41, 67; 2:25–27; Marshall 1978: 58; Tiede 1988: 43). The

41. 1 Sam. 3:20; Acts 3:24. On the OT background, see R. Brown 1977: 273; Fitzmyer 1981: 326; Marshall 1978: 57.

42. The Bible condemns excess drink, not drink per se: Eph. 5:17–18; John 2:1–11; esp. Deut. 14:26; 29:6 [29:5 MT]; Prov. 20:1; 23:20–21, 29–35; 31:6.

43. On the grammar of this emphatic command, see N. Turner 1963: 96; BDF §365.3; the LXX of Num. 6:3 and 1 Sam. 1:11 lacks μή.

44. So it was for Samuel, who had it imposed upon him by the vow of his mother, and Samson, whose mother vowed it of herself during her pregnancy.

45. Samson in Judg. 13:5, 7; 16:17; the Servant in Isa. 49:1; Jeremiah in Jer. 1:5 and Sir. 49:7; Klostermann 1929: 9.

Spirit's presence before the birth expresses God's sovereign choice of one to serve him.

An intensification of the usual OT practice is seen in the Spirit's permanent residence in John the Baptist, since in the OT the Spirit came and went freely in a person (1 Sam. 10:10; 2 Kings 2:9–16). R. Brown (1977: 274) notes that the association of John with a permanent filling of the Spirit is not a Christianized account about John, since the association of God's Spirit with his prophets is strong (Isa. 61:1; Ezek. 11:5; Joel 2:28 [3:1 MT]). The point is, yet again, that a prophet is present. Luke commonly uses πίμπλημι (*pimplēmi*, to fill) to indicate filling, whether in reference to being filled with the Spirit (Luke 1:41, 67; Acts 2:4; 4:8, 31; 9:17; 13:9), being filled with fear or anger (Luke 4:28; 5:26; 6:11), or to the fulfillment of a law, a time period, or a scriptural passage (Luke 1:23, 57; 2:6, 21–22; 21:22; Acts 13:33 [uses ἐκπληρόω]).

Reference to the Spirit's filling is largely absent from Luke's Gospel, but makes an appearance again in Acts. Such a contrast tends to indicate that John is a transitional figure, since he is regarded as part of the OT prophets (7:26–28). The Spirit's provision for him in this period is unique. This intensification may explain why Jesus calls him "more than a prophet" in 7:26. Luke's presentation of John as a transitional figure tends to dilute the attempt to make clean breaks in the "periods" of Luke's portrayal of salvation history. John represents a bridge between promise and fulfillment.

Some discussion exists whether filling "from the mother's womb" means "from birth" (Isa. 48:8; Ps. 22:10 [22:11 MT]; Plummer 1896: 14) or "while still in the womb" (Judg. 13:3–5, 7; 16:17; Isa. 44:2; Marshall 1978: 58; R. Brown 1977: 261; Fitzmyer 1981: 326).[46] Luke 1:41, with the testimony of the kicking fetus in the womb, argues for the rendering "while still in the womb." Elizabeth's testimony in that scene makes clear that John performs as a "witness" before his birth.[47] The witness idea is something that will appear explicitly in Acts (1:8). John's lifestyle and early provision of the Spirit reveal a special man of God, the transition figure from promise to fulfillment. In his intimate relationship with the Spirit, John the Baptist is a precursor of God's coming ministry of the Spirit in the church when the Spirit will be given not just to a few but to all who believe.

46. On the grammar, see N. Turner 1963: 180; Matt. 19:12; Acts 3:2; 14:8.
47. See the exegesis of 1:44. Could this reflect the ancient Jewish view of the fetus as an existing child? Exodus 21:22 fines a person for causing a miscarriage, though with a lesser penalty than if the mother is also slain. The life of the mother took precedence over a fetus until the moment of birth; *m. ʾOhol.* 7.6.

John the Baptist's mission is prophetic. Danker (1988: 30) com- **1:16**
pares the ministry of John to the high priest effecting reconciliation, but John offers no sacrifices and has no mediatorial role.
Rather, his ministry involves proclaiming God's message by calling
for repentance that expresses itself in a changed life (3:1–14), a ministry like the OT prophets. In fact, in 7:26, John is called a prophet.
Nothing in this section indicates that John was ever treated as a
messianic figure in Luke's source material (Fitzmyer 1981: 318–
19). The picture is of a prophet in the OT mold.

John, the prophet, calls the nation to reform—to turn to God and
live differently. Ἐπιστρέψει (*epistrepsei*, he shall turn) alludes to a
change of orientation or of direction in life (1 Thess. 1:9–10). But
John's message is not the universal ministry that is a part of the
church's call. Rather, it involves πολλοὺς τῶν υἱῶν Ἰσραήλ (*pollous
tōn huiōn Israēl*, many sons of Israel). It is a ministry calling Israel
to prepare for the work of God. Κύριον (*kyrion*, Lord) is not a Christianized reference here to Jesus, since the Lord is clearly identified
as τὸν θεὸν αὐτῶν (*ton theon autōn*, their God) (Friedrich, *TDNT*
2:719; Stein 1992: 76 takes the opposite view) and Jesus has not
been mentioned yet. This verse recalls language like that in Mal.
2:6, while Luke 1:17 parallels the description of Elijah found in Mal.
3:1; 4:5 [3:24 MT]; and Sir. 48:10. In fact, the "turning" role of the
prophet recalls the prophetic mission expressed in 2 Chron. 15:1, 4
and a prophetic message not responded to in Sir. 48:15. The idea of
"turning to God" is a standard OT phrase for repentance of the covenant people, a return to the God of salvation (Deut. 30:2; Hos. 3:5;
7:10; Bertram, *TDNT* 7:727). Variations of this theme are also tied
to the prophets' messages (Jer. 3:7, 10, 14; 18:8; Ezek. 3:19; Dan.
9:13; Plummer 1896: 15). The idea of turning is picked up in the NT
to describe conversion (Acts 9:35; 2 Cor. 3:16; 1 Pet. 2:25; Marshall
1978: 58; R. Brown 1977: 275). In fact, repentance is part of the
content of the great commission in Luke (24:47). This is the second
note of continuity between John and the period of fulfillment, with
the role of the Spirit being the first.

Thus, the opportunity for salvation comes in the call to turn—or
return—to God. Whereas in the church's language turning indicates an initial reorientation of one's life to God's way, here John's
call is for the covenant nation to return to the way of living that God
expects of his people. This distinction between John and the Christian message is as important as the similarities between John and
the period of the church. Luke 3:7–14 discusses the details of this
turning and suggests a reliance on God for a new way of living. It is
a life conducted in righteousness and in kindness to one's fellow humans. The prophets called Israelites to live a faithful, righteous life

before their covenant God and reminded them of this call when they turned away. John has this same role.

1:17   The angel details John's prophetic mission with three descriptions: "going before," "turning," and "preparing." The first means leading or going before the Lord (the reference to "him" goes back to 1:16 and means God). Plummer (1896: 15), R. Brown (1977: 261), and Fitzmyer (1981: 326) make the point that only God can be meant here since the Messiah has not yet been introduced. Of course, the reader knows that the coming of the Lord is tied to Messiah, but John's role is to represent the Lord God before his people. The phrase's wording is similar to Mal. 3:1, indicating a parallelism between the end-time ministry of Elijah and the reforming ministry of John. Because of this prophetic parallelism, there is no need to posit an original messianic view of John in the source that Luke used. As the succeeding lines show, John's message prepares the people for God's work through Jesus. But for Luke, it is God's plan. God is the main player; Jesus is his right-hand man.

The manner in which John shall go before the Lord God is explicitly compared to Elijah's prophetic ministry. Ἐν πνεύματι καὶ δυνάμει (en pneumati kai dynamei, in the spirit and power) is a common association (Luke 1:35; 4:14; Acts 1:8; 10:38; Marshall 1978: 59). The phrase denotes that the character and the power of John's ministry are parallel to Elijah's ministry. The comparison, instead of being a total equation between the two ministries, focuses on John's powerful message. Elijah's ministry involved the miraculous, as well as a powerful declaration of the need of God's people to return to a faithful walk with God (1 Kings 17–18). However, John the Baptist is not portrayed as performing miracles. He parallels only Elijah's call to repentance (Klostermann 1929: 9). It is interesting that the association of message and power is also emphasized by Paul when he describes his gospel preaching in Corinth (1 Cor. 1:18–2:5). The Word of God, especially the salvific Word, contains power to change one's view of God, self, and the world. It also changes how one lives.

The phrase in Luke's next line, "to turn the hearts of fathers to the children," is virtually a quotation of Mal. 3:24 LXX and Sir. 48:10. It appears to refer to the reconciliation between families that occurs through the ministry of reform. Both Luke and the MT of Malachi use the plural in speaking of the fathers and the children, in contrast to the singular nouns in Sirach (Bock 1987: 59–60; N. Turner 1963: 23). The next phrase, "[to turn] the disobedient to the wisdom of the just," recalls wisdom motifs and describes a turning back to the way of the Lord (Fitzmyer 1981: 327). The preposition ἐν (en) can be translated "into." It indicates the change of perspective from disobedience to righteousness that John's powerful preaching will effect.[48]

But what is the force of both lines together? Views vary on the nature of the parallelism. (1) Marshall (1978: 59) cites the options and, seeing Mal. 3:24–25 as the key allusion, supports a loose conceptual parallelism where families and neighbors are reconciled to one another. (2) Others associate the fathers with the patriarchs, while the children are interpreted as disobedient people. This view sees a chiasmus in the lines.[49] (3) Conversely, some hold that the reference to fathers alludes to the disobedient, while children are the obedient. This approach sees a natural parallelism here (R. Brown 1977: 278; Schweizer 1984: 22). Brown, arguing that Luke sees children positively and in contrast to the old in 3:7–8 (also 7:31–35), says that children are an anticipated reference to Gentiles, a view that Schweizer rejects. One could add conceptual examples of the recent as "good" (e.g., 5:36–39, where the new is not mixable with the old; 7:31–35 goes both ways). (4) Leaney (1958: 80) holds that children's hearts are a figure for what will happen to the parents.

Which view expresses Luke's intention? Leaney's view (view 4 above) that children's hearts are figurative is too complicated in that it takes parents literally but the children as a figure. The appeal to the fathers as the patriarchs is not supported by the context. Thus, the chiastic view is unlikely (view 2). R. Brown's view that Gentiles are intended, a form of view 3, cannot work, since John's ministry is portrayed solely as a ministry to the nation (1:16). Thus, whatever reconciliation John brings, it involves the people of Israel. As well, the links between 3:7–8 and 1:17 are not exact; since in Luke 3 the father is a patriarch, while in Luke 1 the fathers are the tradition-laden groups that are straying.

Schweizer's approach (view 3) seems possible. The fathers represent the old generation set in the ways of tradition and needing a call to reform, while the children, as the new generation, are naturally open to the new things of God. In the parallelism, fathers line up with the idea of disobedience and children are paired with the righteous. The parable of the impossibility of putting new wine in old wineskins is a similar idea (5:37–39). For reconciliation to take

48. On ἐν substituting for εἰς and meaning "into," see BDF §218; N. Turner 1963: 257.

49. Chiasmus is a pattern that pairs the first and last ideas in a unit and the second and third ideas (e.g., a-b-b′-a′). When a chiasmus has more than four lines, the pairings continue until the ideas merge at the middle. The thought reverses at the middle back up the chain in the opposite direction. Creed 1930: 11 cites A. Loisy as holding this view.

place, a change in the old traditional way of thinking and living must occur. John's role is to call the nation to reform this traditional thinking and have a change of heart. The only problem with this approach is that the symbolic connection is not readily apparent. If this father-children motif were well attested then it might be possible to accept the idea.

What is the meaning then? Marshall's "loose" connection is still the best option. But is it as loose as he suggests? Maybe a synthetic parallelism is present that states John's reform in terms of basic horizontal and vertical relationships. John's ministry will bring families together (horizontal) and bring righteousness before God back to the disobedient (vertical). This Godward-human duality is a basic characteristic of righteousness that is pleasing to God and reflects OT law (10:27; elsewhere in the NT: Col. 1:4; Philem. 5; Eph. 1:15). If Malachi controls the background of the passage, then such a reform is the point. Since a first-century Jew had many religious sectarian options, the reference to family division may allude to family members choosing different individual sects. Thus, families would split as sons chose to belong to sects to which their fathers did not belong. John's mission was to call people back from the other options to *the* way of God.

John's final task speaks of him "making ready for the Lord a prepared people" (1:16; "Lord" here is God, not Jesus). This phrase is not found in either the OT or the NT, but it is a combination of ideas from several OT passages. Malachi 3:1 speaks of the messenger of the Lord, later identified as Elijah, coming to prepare the way before the Lord. The LXX uses the term ἐπιβλέψεται (*epiblepsetai,* shall show) to describe this preparatory work, whereas Luke uses ἑτοιμάσαι (*hetoimasai,* shall prepare). Thus, if Mal. 3:1 is in view, the LXX has not influenced Luke's wording. The reforming Elijah motif is the prevalent one used to describe John's ministry.

The verbal term used in Isa. 40:3 LXX for preparation is ἑτοιμάσατε (*hetoimasate*), the same term Luke uses. Mark 1:2–3 combines Isa. 40 and Mal. 3 to introduce John the Baptist. Thus, this pairing represents a traditional association that the church made between John and the OT. Its distinct attestation in a variety of Gospels shows it to be a strongly held tradition. But Luke has a twist on the OT motif. The OT called on the people to prepare for the Lord, while Luke reverses the image to speak about a prepared people for God. The idea is similar but the emphasis is on the product that emerges from the response to the prophet's call.

The idea of a prepared people comes from Isa. 43:7. With its reference to the preparation of Israel for the coming of the Lord, Isa. 43 serves to complement Isa. 40 and refers to the elect status of the nation Israel, a people whom God prepared. But perhaps more relevant is 2 Sam. 7:24, where the context is Davidic covenant and hope. Here the Lord speaks of a prepared people, a nation that God has called to himself. The Samuel and Isaiah passages stress that "a prepared people" are a special people that God has drawn to himself for his own purposes. In light of the Davidic emphasis in 1:31–35, it is quite probable that this wording is alluded to here (Fitzmyer 1981: 327).

So John's ministry in Luke 1:17 is heavily influenced by OT ideas. John calls out of Israel a prepared and responding group of people who are ready to follow the Lord's way of salvation. This description of a "prepared people" has a "remnant" tone to it. God prepares a responding remnant, which is called out from the nation. The call to reform and the creation of a prepared remnant people summarize the basic ministry of John the Baptist. In this Elijah-like ministry, he establishes his "great" position before the Lord and brings joy to many in Israel (see excursus 1). From it emerges a people who are ready for God's salvation.

1:18 A human touch enters with Zechariah's response. He questions what the angel says about a child, because of his age (πρεσβύτης, presbytēs, old) and his wife's advanced years (προβεβηκυῖα, probebēkuia, advanced [in years]). Unlike some legendary accounts, where the miraculous occurs as a matter of course, in this narrative the angel's announcement catches Zechariah off guard. His response is typically human: he asks for a confirming sign. The request for a sign has OT precedent in that Abraham (Gen. 15:3–8; 18:11–12, also pleading age), Gideon (Judg. 6:37), Hezekiah (2 Kings 20:8), and Ahaz (Isa. 7:11) requested signs from God. King Saul was told of signs to look for to guarantee what was said (1 Sam. 10:2–7; Wiefel 1988: 48). In Luke 1:20 the Lord grants the sign, but also issues a rebuke about unbelief. The sign delays any revelation of the miracle until it comes to pass (1:63; Marshall 1978: 60).

Danker (1988: 22) argues that Luke is particularly hard on those who seek signs (11:16, 29–30). Yet Danker's references indicate that the motif belongs to the NT (Matt. 16:1; Mark 8:11; John 4:48; 20:24–29, esp. v. 29; 1 Cor. 1:22). The difference between Zechariah and later Synoptic examples, where sign-seekers are more strongly rebuked, is that Jesus' ministry was full of signs that should have authenticated his claims; but Zechariah had no personal precedent for response. So God granted the sign and yet called on Zechariah to believe his word (1:20).

1:19 The objection about the parents' ages yields a remark about the messenger's position and authority. Zechariah may be old, but

God's message comes from the angel Gabriel, who stands in God's presence and has direct access to God.[50] The meaning of Gabriel's name is disputed. It means "man of God," "God has shown himself strong," or "God is my hero" (Fitzmyer likes the latter; 1981: 328). But the name is not an issue for Luke, nor does the action of the narrative seem to suggest any significance for it.

Gabriel's career is tied biblically to eschatological events (in Dan. 8:15–16; 9:21 he is the giver of the prophecy of the seventy weeks). Jewish tradition regards him as one of the more significant angels who served next to God. The number of angels who stand in God's presence varies from four to seven.[51] Because Gabriel has a major function in God's work and direct access to him, the angel's message carries credibility.

Gabriel describes his task as being one of God's commissioned messengers (ἀπεστάλην, apestalēn, I have been sent). Gabriel speaks to Zechariah and proclaims good news to him. The use of the plural ταῦτα (tauta, these things) helps determine whether εὐαγγελίσασθαι (euangelisasthai) means simply "to report good news" or has an additional nuance of reporting "eschatological good news." The plural shows that the entire angelic message of 1:13–17 is in view, and therefore the good news includes a reference to God's salvific good news (Danker 1988: 22). Zechariah is challenged to believe and respond to this good news. As Danker expresses it, "To ignore the knell of judgment is disastrous, but to question the divine procedure, as Zechariah does, is to invite the tolling of the bell." Luke 1:20 points out Zechariah's lack of faith. It is better to say that Zechariah leans toward unbelief here, rather than that he is entirely unbelieving. His asking for a sign suggests that he is attempting to respond positively to the angel's message, though he has grave doubt and needs prodding. Thus the angel's reply calls Zechariah to faith instead of doubt.[52]

1:20   Gabriel gives Zechariah a sign to remind him of his lack of faith—both the inability to speak and deafness, the latter evident from the hand signs used to ask him a question in 1:62 (against this view is Klostermann 1929: 10; see Fitzmyer 1981: 328–29;

---

50. See Dan. 7:16 and Job 1:6 for the idea of direct access to God or his angels; R. Brown 1977: 262; Danker 1988: 32.

51. 1 Enoch 40.9 names four angels: Michael, Raphael, Gabriel (the angel of strength), and Phanuel (alternately called Uriel); 1 Enoch 20 names these four as well as Saraqael, Raguel, and Suruel (Gabriel is described as caring for the Garden of Eden and the cherubim). See Tob. 12:15; Fitzmyer 1981: 327–28; Bousset 1926: 325–31; SB 2:89–97.

52. Doubt is not unbelief, but it is not faith either. When it comes to what God has promised, doubt hangs in a dangerous canyon between faith and unbelief.

R. Brown 1977: 263). The expressions ἔσῃ σιωπῶν (*esē siōpōn*, you shall be silent) and μὴ δυνάμενος λαλῆσαι (*mē dynamenos lalēsai*, not able to speak) emphasize by repetition the inability positively and negatively. The angel declares the sign's duration. Zechariah is handicapped "until" (ἄχρι, *achri*) the days when these things begin to happen. Γένηται (*genētai*, it shall be) is clearly inceptive in the context, for Zechariah is silent until the birth of John and not until the time of his ministry. R. Brown (1977: 280) suggests that the presence of muteness in Dan. 10:15 and the literary need for a sign led Luke or his source to include the detail of the sign of judgment, but such a deduction is unlikely. There is a difference between going speechless from the awe that one has at seeing a revelation, a silence that is quickly removed by the angel (Daniel), and being affected because of one's unbelief by a temporary sign of judgment that lasts for months (Zechariah). If this detail were created, why did not the angel simply say, "The silence (from your awe at this revelation) shall remain until you leave the temple"? The motivation for this detail is not reflection on the OT text.[53]

The reason, ἀνθ᾽ ὧν (*anth' hōn*, because), for the sign was Zechariah's lack of faith. He did not believe the angel's message. However, the sign also performs another function. It serves to conceal the revelation from the crowd and all others until the proper time (Marshall 1978: 61). In fact, the angel notes that God's word will be fulfilled at the proper time, a comment showing God's sovereign control over these events. The term πληρόω (*plēroō*, to fulfill) denotes the completion or realization of God's word or plan. This verb appears at key points in Luke's account (Luke 4:21; 9:31; 24:44; Acts 1:16; 3:18). The use of καιρός (*kairos*, time) in the sense of appointed time is also frequent (Luke 12:56; 18:30; 19:44; 21:8, 24; Acts 1:7; 3:20; 17:26; though it is to be noted that Luke 12:56 and 18:30 have Synoptic parallels: Matt. 16:3 and Mark 10:30).

In discussing this sign and its challenge, which also reflects disciplining judgment, Schweizer (1984: 23) notes, "A salvation that does not reveal and thereby change what stands in its way would not be real salvation. . . . That God opened someone's eyes to that which is distorted in such a way that the person is re-formed, not simply shattered, is a demonstration of the living God." In other words, through the temporary judgment, Zechariah (and the reader with him) is to learn something about trusting God's message.

---

53. For other OT or Jewish uses of the motif of silence or being struck silent, see Ezek. 3:26; 24:27; 2 Macc. 3:29; Marshall 1978: 61.

iii. Aftermath: A Wondering Crowd and the Silent Priest (1:21–23)

1:21 Luke shifts the scene to outside the Holy Place and the people's anticipation of Zechariah's return and blessing. The durative periphrastic imperfect ἦν . . . προσδοκῶν (ēn . . . prosdokōn, were waiting) depicts the wait as an ongoing, lingering affair.[54] The waiting turns to amazement when Zechariah does not emerge from the Holy Place quickly. Ἐθαύμαζον (ethaumazon, were wondering) continues the sequence: "They were waiting and they were wondering as he delayed in the Holy Place."[55] If the Jewish tradition of the Day of Atonement is any guide, then such a delay in the Holy Place is a cause for worry for those outside. M. Yomaʾ 5.1 mentions that a short prayer is expected of the high priest, lest the nation worry.[56] In fact, if the Mishnah reflects first-century practice, Zechariah was accompanied by four other priests, who waited for him to complete the offering.[57] On his departure, Zechariah and the priests would give the people a blessing, but little did those outside realize what was occurring.

1:22 In a resolution of the drama, when Zechariah emerged from the Holy Place, not only was it clear that something unusual had happened, but the first fulfillment of the angel's prediction came to pass. When Zechariah came out (ἐξελθών, exelthōn) of the temple, he was unable to speak. Most likely he was silent as the other priests gave the Aaronic blessing (Num. 6:24–26) required by Jewish practice.[58] Luke focuses on Zechariah, because he is the only one relevant to the movement of divine events. If the mishnaic requirements existed in the first century, then Zechariah could have been in the Holy Place by himself at any one of four points in the offering process: to clear away the ashes from the previous offering

---

54. Plummer 1896: 18; the plural English verb is a result of the collective noun λαός, which though singular in form is plural in sense. Luke loves to use a vivid, progressive imperfect.

55. Ἐν τῷ χρονίζειν is probably a temporal infinitive and translates as "as he delayed" or "while he delayed," though a causal idea is possible, which would mean they wondered "because of" his delay. Plummer 1896: 18 argues for a temporal infinitive.

56. The premise was that it is dangerous to be too near and too long in God's presence; Bovon 1989: 60.

57. M. Tamid 7.2; also 5.4–6.3; Creed 1930: 12; Fitzmyer 1981: 328. See the exegesis of 1:22 for details.

58. M. Tamid 7.2, though a later text, probably reflects a first-century practice of several priests sharing in the offering itself, as well as individually helping to prepare for it. Although the Mishnah was written ca. A.D. 170, this tradition is likely to reflect long-standing practice since it deals with temple liturgy—practice that was suspended with the fall of Jerusalem and its temple in A.D. 70.

(*m. Tamid* 6.1), to fix the candlesticks and relight them if necessary (*m. Tamid* 6.1), to take in the cinder pan and place new burning material on the altar (*m. Tamid* 6.2), or to spread the incense over the altar (*m. Tamid* 6.3). A delay at any of these points would have slowed up the entire offering-blessing process.

Luke 1:9 tells us that Zechariah drew the lot to make the incense offering.[59] Thus, it is possible that he spread the incense over the altar (i.e., the instruction of *m. Tamid* 6.3). Luke portrays Zechariah's experience as private. Such a private moment in the offering sequence is possible in the prescribed order of events, so the suggestion that Luke erred in not citing the custom of multiple priests being present is not correct. On the other hand, if the meeting occurred during the offering itself, then Luke may be suggesting a private encounter like Paul's on the Damascus road.

The crowd drew the correct conclusion. The priest had a vision or a supernatural encounter. Ἐπέγνωσαν ὅτι (*epegnōsan hoti*, they knew that) suggests an appropriate conclusion and is a Lucan expression.[60] The term used for the meeting, ὀπτασίαν (*optasian*, vision or appearance), differs from the passive form of ὁράω (*horaō*, to see; i.e., ὤφθην, *ōphthēn*, appeared) and often refers to supernatural appearances.[61] The crowd's conclusion is a natural one in light of the delay and the traditions about what causes a person to be struck mute (Ezek. 3:26; Dan. 10:7–8, 15; 2 Macc. 3:29; Josephus, *Antiquities* 13.10.3 §§282–83; SB 2:77–79; Creed 1930: 12).

When faced with the dilemma of his priestly responsibility and his inability to utter the blessing, Zechariah signs the blessing. Again a periphrastic imperfect is used (ἦν διανεύων, *ēn dianeuōn*, was making signs). But Zechariah's disability is not temporary like the OT parallel (Dan. 10:7, 15–16); rather his condition lingers as the angel predicted (διέμενεν κωφός, *diemenen kōphos*, was remaining mute).[62] The immediate fulfillment of the punitive sign suggests that the rest of God's word will come to pass as well.

R. Brown mentions the possibility of an intentional Lucan literary contrastive parallel between the inability to give blessing here and Jesus' bestowal of blessing in Luke 24:50–52, but such a sugges-

59. On θυμιᾶσαι, see BAGD 365, BAA 741, MM 294 (where the verb is used of fumigating with herbs), LSJ 809.

60. For this meaning, see Luke 5:22; 7:37; 23:7; 24:16, 31, as well as six times in Acts (with a different force); Plummer 1896: 18; Marshall 1978: 61.

61. Luke 24:23; Acts 26:19; 2 Cor. 12:1; Dan. 9:23; 10:1, 7, 8, 16 [all Theodotion]; Plummer 1896: 18. The experience is called a vision because Zechariah saw an angel, a being that normally goes unseen; Michaelis, *TDNT* 5:372. Luke is not psychologizing here; it is an angelophany. See Luke 1:11.

62. On κωφός signifying deafness and muteness, see 1:62 and Philo, *Special Laws* 4.38 §§197–98; Marshall 1978: 61; Fitzmyer 1981: 329.

tion is unlikely in light of the lack of any Lucan portrayal of Jesus as a priest.[63] Appeals to Sir. 50:19–23 also falter, since clear allusions are lacking and the event is a common one.

The judgment functions as a sign (1:18–20), as Elizabeth's pregnancy serves as a sign to Mary (1:34–38). A Lucan warning about signs will emerge later in the Gospel, but is not dealt with here. For Luke, signs confirm the word of God and are in God's sovereign control, rather than being subject to popular demand (11:29–32), a view shared with the early church tradition (Matt. 12:39–42).

Zechariah stayed and completed his week of temple duty. The καὶ ἐγένετο (kai egeneto) or ἐγένετο δέ (egeneto de, and it came to pass) construction with a verb is common in Luke.[64] When he fulfilled his priestly responsibility, he went home. The term ἐπλήσθησαν (eplēsthēsan) has the nontechnical sense of the "completion" of a set number of days, while λειτουργίας (leitourgias, time of service) denotes priestly service related to the worship of God, a sense paralleled in the LXX.[65]

1:23 Zechariah, on finishing his task, went home, which was located in the hill country, south of Jerusalem (1:39). No more details are given. In the infancy material, Luke often ends a unit with a journey or a return home. These endings set up a transition to the next event.[66] Before Luke moves to the next event, he notes the reaction of Zechariah's previously barren wife, as she prepares to give birth. This returns the reader's attention to God's personal concern (1:6–7, 13, 18), a complementary theme to what God is doing for his plan of salvation.

c. Resolution: Elizabeth's Pregnancy (1:24–25)

1:24 The initial fulfillment of the angel's promise (1:13) comes in Elizabeth's conceiving (συνέλαβεν, synelaben, she conceived).[67] How quickly this fulfillment came is not stated, since the phrase μετὰ . . . ταύτας τὰς ἡμέρας (meta . . . tautas tas hēmeras) means simply "after these days" and refers to the general time period after Zechariah's return. The brief reference to conception parallels the reference to Samuel's conception (1 Sam. 1:19–20; Fitzmyer 1981: 329).

---

63. R. Brown 1977: 280–81. The blessing at the end of Luke also does not occur at the temple, another key omission against any claim for literary symmetry with Luke 24.

64. Examples include Luke 5:1, 12, 17; 8:1, 22; 9:28, 51; see Fitzmyer 1981: 119. It is classical style; BDF §472.3.

65. Num. 8:22; 16:9; 18:4; 2 Chron. 31:2; also Heb. 8:6; 9:21; Plummer 1896: 18; Fitzmyer 1981: 329; Strathmann, *TDNT* 4:219–22, 227.

66. So also within the infancy material: 1:56; 2:20, 39, 51; R. Brown 1977: 263.

67. The term is used with a similar sense in 1:31, 36; 2:21; Plummer 1896: 19.

As a result of the conception, Elizabeth consciously decides to hide herself, as seen in the reflexive pronoun in περιέκρυβεν ἑαυτήν (*periekryben heautēn*, she hid herself). For five months, she hid herself from the public by remaining at home (1:39–40). Why did she withdraw?

1. Some say that the pain of reproach from her neighbors caused her to hide (Plummer 1896: 19; Ellis 1974: 70; Marshall 1978: 62). But would she still grieve when she had become pregnant? Only if she were worried that she might not deliver a healthy child and be proven wrong. But the text gives no hint of anxiety or a lack of faith. Rather, it suggests joy and relief, so that this explanation seems less likely.
2. Others argue that adding together all the chronological notes in the infancy sequence results in an allusion to Daniel's seventy weeks (five months noted here, a sixth month in 1:26, three months in 1:56, and eight days in 2:21).[68] R. Brown rejects this view, because the addition is based on seeing a nine-month rather than a lunar ten-month pregnancy. The view also fails because Luke gives approximate time references. Luke 1:56 says that Mary's visit with Elizabeth lasted about (ὡς, *hōs*) three months. An effort to extract exact days from an approximate reference cannot work.
3. Creed (1930: 12) cites J. Weiss's suggestion that Elizabeth went into seclusion to give herself to praise to the Lord, as 1:25 suggests. It may be added that perhaps Elizabeth set herself to prepare for the birth of this important child, much as the wife of Manoah vowed to do (Judg. 13). This suggestion has some contextual merit (SB 2:98; Alford 1874: 446).
4. Most recent commentators suggest that Luke uses this detail for one of two reasons. (a) Luke may wish to set up the confirmation of John's work, which comes when John kicks in his mother's womb when she sees Mary, the one bearing Messiah Jesus (R. Brown 1977: 282; Klostermann 1929: 10–11; Danker 1988: 34; Leaney 1958: 42; 1 Sam. 1:19–20). This detail allows John to react to Jesus' presence and serve as forerunner. (b) The withdrawal keeps the birth a secret until the proper time, and thus serves the same purpose as Zechariah's muteness (Fitzmyer 1981: 329; Schneider 1977a: 46).

The purpose of Elizabeth's action is obscure, as the many views show. It seems that Luke sees the withdrawal as a time of praise

---

68. The view is mentioned and refuted by R. Brown 1977: 282; it is held by Laurentin 1967: 56–64.

(view 3), though the action also seems to explain why the mother of the Lord went to the home of the forerunner's mother (view 4a; Luke 1:36, 39–40). View 4b cannot work on a literary level, since Mary knew about Elizabeth before they met. To put the matter simply, Elizabeth withdrew and Luke does not tell why. During this time of seclusion Mary heard of her own impending pregnancy and of the state of her relative Elizabeth (1:26–38).

R. Brown (1977: 282) argues that the verses linking 1:24–25 to 1:36 are Lucan compositions. This contention, however, is hard to prove since Brown's argument is structural and there is no peculiar Lucan terminology in these verses. But the position cannot be rejected either, since Luke may be responsible for the parallel arrangement of events in the narrative, an arrangement that, if it reflects Luke's research, would indicate the timing and sequence of the actual events.[69] That such an arrangement is the product of Luke's own research does not seem improbable at all. In the withdrawal of Elizabeth, Luke notes her pious response to her pregnancy, clearing the stage for the birth annunciation to Mary.

1:25   Luke briefly reports Elizabeth's reaction to her pregnancy. The introductory ὅτι (*hoti*, that) has been taken to express content; thus the reader sees the report as an expression of Elizabeth's heart. Another possibility is to view ὅτι as causal, giving the reason for her withdrawal.[70] Most commentators argue that the participle λέγουσα (*legousa*, saying) in 1:24 expects ὅτι to express content. Alford (1874: 446) notes that, although the nuance is slightly different, the basic sense is not affected by the choice. Whether a report is present or the cause for her withdrawal is expressed, the verse still depicts Elizabeth's attitude to the end of her barrenness.

Elizabeth expresses both relief and joy that God removed this source of public shame (barrenness was commonly viewed this way; SB 2:98). Expressing thanks to the Lord for the provision of a child is a common OT theme (Sarah in Gen. 21:6; Rachel in Gen. 30:23). Creed (1930: 13), however, distinguishes between this narrative and these two OT examples in that both OT praises come at the birth of the child, not before it, as here. Therefore, such a distinct detail argues against Luke creating this response from an OT parallel.

69. As was noted in the historicity discussion to the infancy material, positions on Luke's approach to this infancy material ultimately will be influenced by one's general view of God's ability to act directly in history and the interpreter's specific view of Luke's accuracy. Luke can tell the story in his own words without creating the events.

70. So Winter 1955; also mentioned by older commentators such as Luce 1933: 86 and Alford 1874: 446.

The language of her praise is interesting. Elizabeth notes what the Lord "has done" in these days. Πεποίηκεν (*pepoiēken*, he has done) is a perfect tense form, which indicates a finality to God's lifting of her burden. She stresses God's active and personal involvement in her life by choosing the term ἐπεῖδεν (*epeiden*, he looked on me). This term comes from ἐφοράω (*ephoraō*, to gaze upon something) and is often used in Classical Greek of the actions of the Greek gods in relationship to humans (BAGD 331; BAA 576; LSJ 746; Plummer 1896: 19–20; Luce 1933: 86). This is an unusual term for Luke (his only other use is in Acts 4:29); ἐπισκέπτομαι (*episkeptomai*, to visit) is the normal Lucan expression (Luke 1:68, 78; 7:16; Acts 6:3; 7:23; 15:14, 36; Leaney 1958: 81). This argues against a Lucan creation of this material (against this view is R. Brown 1977: 283–85). The Lord has watched over Elizabeth so that her reproach among people is gone.[71]

The remark's brevity leads some to doubt if Zechariah informed Elizabeth about the significance of the child. Hence Elizabeth discovered the child's importance with the events of 1:39–45.[72] Such a conclusion is unlikely, since at Mary's visit she possessed knowledge about the other child (1:41–44). Also, it seems unlikely that Zechariah would withhold information from his wife about the cause of his deaf-muteness. Luke is purposely brief here. In fact, it may be that Elizabeth's knowledge about the child's significance is the cause for her withdrawal.[73]

Two themes dominate this final unit. First, there is a sense of joy and relief since God has removed a source of Elizabeth's pain. God has acted in her life. The second theme is God's personal attention to Elizabeth, a point expressed in the idea of God's visitation (1:25). As God deals with his salvation plan, he is also meeting human needs. John may have a special role for Israel, but the child also met a personal need for Elizabeth.

Summary

The major concern of 1:5–25 is the renewed salvific work of God for his people. John will be a prophet who in the spirit of Elijah calls Israel to reform. The numerous allusions to Malachi and to Elijah suggest an end-time event. In fact, John will prepare a

---

71. Ἀφελεῖν is the object of ἐπεῖδεν and functions as a purpose infinitive, while ἐν ἀνθρώποις is tied to ὄνειδος, as the positive note in 1:36 shows; Fitzmyer 1981: 329–30; Plummer 1896: 20. Acts 15:14 is a grammatically parallel verb-object-infinitive construction.

72. Marshall 1978: 62, citing H. Sahlin; Klostermann 1929: 11 cites B. Weiss, while he seemingly rejects the view.

73. See the "withdrawal" discussion in the exegesis of 1:24, where a clear explanation for the withdrawal is said not to be Luke's concern, though it does seem that reflection is a goal.

remnant people for the coming of the Lord. Many in Israel will be reconciled to one another as they turn to righteous thinking (1:14–17).

But alongside these cosmic, national, and salvific themes is the simple personal story of Zechariah and Elizabeth. They were a righteous, childless couple who prayed for a child. God visited them and heard their prayer of pain. The answer took time, but God honored their request. Luke depicts God's sovereign involvement in the lives of believers. Scripture reveals requests answered immediately, requests answered eventually, and requests denied for a better way. In this case, the answer to a personal prayer comes after years of waiting and calls forth a response of praise.

An additional theme is that God's message comes to pass. The patterns of God's salvific ways are being reestablished, as God reaches to his people now in a way that parallels how he reached out to OT saints. In addition, the rebuke of Zechariah and the judgment upon him call the reader to believe that God's Word and plan will come to pass. The fulfillment of the angel's message in two phases also underscores this theme. In the birth announcement of John, God renews his work of salvation for his people, as the patterns of salvation are reenacted. God's promises are revealed and then partially fulfilled. Surely, the fulfillment of the rest of the plan is secure.

Additional Notes

1:8. The number of priests in first-century Jerusalem is variously estimated, but the best number comes from the *Letter of Aristeas* 95 (noted by Jeremias 1969: 200). There are about 700 priests per order outside the 50 or so who handle the sacrifice for the week. Thus, 750 times 24 equals 18,000.

1:9. The grammar is somewhat difficult in that the aorist participle εἰσελθών (coming) is tied to the infinitive θυμιᾶσαι (to sacrifice), not to the verb ἔλαχε (it fell) (Plummer 1896: 11). The verse reads, "According to the custom of the priests, the lot fell [to him] to offer incense after going into the Holy Place."

1:17. Προελεύσεται is the verb to be read here on the basis of superior manuscript support, rather than two other less well attested verbs. Supporting it are ℵ, D, and Byz, showing the presence of the reading in all major textual families (this text-critical problem is not discussed in UBS[4]).

1:25. One source question needs to be handled. R. Brown (1977: 283–85) argues that 1:5–25 was composed by Luke. His argument has three points:

(1) the stylistic parallelism between the John the Baptist and Jesus units in the infancy material, especially in the epilogues to each unit, (2) numerous OT parallels, and (3) the problem of reconciling John's being a relative to Jesus with John the Baptist's statement in John 1:31, 33 that he did not know Jesus. Brown argues that Luke, having a Jesus annunciation tradition, composed a parallel Baptist tradition. Now it may well be that Luke brings together various traditions to show the parallelism of these accounts, but does that mean that he created a new event from a Jesus tradition and the OT?

It is unlikely that this is a proper explanation for this pericope's origin. (1) Though there are many details that parallel the OT, there usually is a significant variation in the Zechariah event that shows that Luke did not work merely from the OT (see the exegesis of 1:11, 20, 25). (2) Some details in this event seem unnecessary to the parallelism of the story, so that composition cannot explain their presence. Among the questions that composition cannot explain are (a) why a temple setting? (b) why a priestly background? (c) why appear to the father and not the mother? (d) why the praise of the Lord at the withdrawal and not at birth? and (e) why the withdrawal at all? Such details do not help the parallelism and are not explained by a theory of Lucan creation. If one wishes to argue that only some details are historical, then how is one to choose which details are historical and which are not? (3) Some vocabulary in alleged Lucan units is not Lucan (see the exegesis of 1:25). (4) The most powerful point raised for this view is the problem of John 1:31, 33. However, it seems possible that in these verses John the Baptist is referring to the decisive knowledge of God's personal confirmation about who Jesus is, rather than making a comprehensive statement about never knowing Jesus personally. Luke 1:41–44 would not contradict this Johannine distinction, since that passage has a prenatal act by John that Elizabeth interprets for him. Though the baby is prompted by the Spirit (1:15), the fetal John is hardly conscious of performing a confirming sign from God. John 1 is only making the point that John could not definitely know the Messiah was Jesus, until God showed him directly. Thus, Brown's theory about Lucan composition is to be rejected.

2. Announcement to Mary
(1:26–38)

The announcement to Mary has two key parallels. First, there is the parallel to OT birth announcements (Ishmael: Gen. 16:7–14; Isaac: Gen. 17:15–22; 18:9–15; Samson: Judg. 13:2–23; Samuel: 1 Sam. 1:9–20; Schürmann 1969: 59; Wiefel 1988: 50). The account recalls God's past great acts. Second is the parallel with the announcement to Zechariah (Luke 1:5–25). The entire passage stands in parallelism to the earlier birth announcement, but the unusual nature of the birth and the future call of the child show that Jesus is superior to John. The mood of the passage is very different from the earlier announcement. In contrast to the public setting of the temple in the middle of Jerusalem, Mary receives her announcement privately in a village setting.

The parallels to the Zechariah announcement are striking, as seen in the following list:[1]

1. The scene is set and the angel comes (1:5–11, 26–27).
2. The person fears (1:12, 29).
3. The angel gives assurance (1:13a, 30).
4. The birth is promised and the child is named (1:13b, 31).
5. The significance of the child is described (1:14–17, 32–33).
6. A question expresses some doubt (1:18, 34).
7. The Spirit's role is noted (1:15b–c, 35).
8. A sign or an instruction is given (1:19–20, 36–37).
9. A remark about the significance of the angel's words is present (1:20, 38).

There also are major differences (Schweizer 1984: 25–26; R. Brown 1977: 293; Nolland 1989: 40–41). In the announcement to Mary, no need for the birth is mentioned, nor is there any note about the parent's pious background, other than a brief remark that Mary is a virgin and that there are Davidic connections. In this announcement, the angel controls the literary movement in that most of the account records his words. There is less activity than in 1:5–25; the scene in 1:26–38 has a calmer tone. The an-

---

1. There are various ways to list the parallels. With only minor variations, I follow Schürmann's list (1969: 59 n. 132). For other arrangements and discussions, see Tiede 1988: 45–47; R. Brown 1977: 293–98; Schneider 1977a: 48; and Creed 1930: 13.

nouncement in 1:26–38 goes to the mother, not to the father. No fulfillments occur within the announcement, unlike the judgment on Zechariah. There is no rebuke for lack of faith, despite a question. Most importantly, where the previous birth is the reversal of barrenness, here there is a virgin birth. The announcement setting here is simple, but the miracle is great. Everything rests on God's fresh creative power. This child is his in a way no child since Adam has been, a point Luke makes more directly in 3:38 (Wiefel 1988: 51).

Sources and Historicity

The question about sources and historicity for this account runs headlong into its supernatural character. Many express doubt or agnosticism about aspects of historicity in this unit and deny the possibility of sources in Jesus' family.[2] For many its origins are obscure. They argue that the account arose in Hellenistic Christian circles or was influenced by Isa. 7:14 LXX, and that a divine birth for the Messiah was not known in Judaism (Schneider 1977a: 52–53). The differences between this account and the one in Matthew are another factor causing doubt about any tradition with roots back to Mary.[3] Still more troublesome to most is the absence of the expression of a virgin birth in the NT outside of Matthew and Luke. Why did it not make its mark more strongly? This omission causes some to argue that the origin of the most miraculous part of the account must be found in circles outside of Judaism and that the virgin birth was the product of reflection about Jesus, rather than a part of the original tradition about his birth.[4] Some even argue that Luke put together separate traditions here by adding the virgin birth account to a simple birth narrative.[5] Most regard the

2. Danker 1988: 34, more agnostic, says an attempt to trace the account back to Mary is "pure speculation," but the attempt to argue Lucan invention is "sheer conjecture." Tiede 1988: 47 notes that the argument that the tradition had contact with Mary cannot be proved or disproved.

3. This issue is discussed and evaluated in the introduction to the infancy narrative in 1:5–25. See also the additional note on 1:26.

4. This comparative-religions approach was very popular in the early part of the century. Numerous parallels have been noted, though none of them are exact. For a list of such parallels see Ernst 1977: 76 and Marshall 1978: 72–75, both of whom note the parallels and argue that such outside accounts are not the basis of this account (so also esp. Nolland 1989: 47). This is the current consensus, whatever else is said about the material. Machen 1930, though now dated, is the strongest critique against the comparative-religions approach.

5. The arguments here are complex, based on a variety of suppositions, and thus come in a variety of forms. Schürmann 1969: 56–57; Bovon 1989: 64–70; and Schneider 1977a: 48–49 have brief discussions of the details, as does Marshall 1978: 63. Most discussions center on 1:34, so more detail awaits treatment of that verse. Other details related to the discussion are treated as they arise in the verses.

virgin birth as a natural product of later Christianity, influenced either by reflection on Isa. 7:14 LXX, application of Ps. 2:7, or reflection on Jesus' baptism (Schürmann 1969: 56 for Isa.; Schneider 1977a: 52 for Ps. and baptism).[6]

However, one should not forget that oral traditions about Jesus' origins were in circulation. Most accept that Luke inherited his material, so something about Jesus' birth was in circulation. The absence of details about Jesus' birth and origins in the NT corresponds with the general absence in the NT of material about the life of Jesus outside the Gospels. The only omission that is surprising is Mark's, but he ignores Jesus' childhood entirely, so his omission may be explained simply as literary choice. John's omission is the result of his presenting an even higher Christology at the start of his Gospel: the incarnation of the preexistent Word. Those NT passages that tie Jesus to Joseph are natural in light of Joseph's responsibility for the house in which Jesus grew up.[7]

In sum, the discussion boils down to worldview. The text clearly presents the virgin birth as the origin of Jesus. Marshall aptly says that belief in the virgin birth is not unreasonable, if one can accept the reality of the incarnation.[8] This keen observation does not solve entirely the issue of sources. Mary is not the only one who could have related this material to the church, but ultimately the tradition that arose must go back to her or her family. It may also be that the church came to understand the significance of the event to God's plan through later reflection on OT texts, but deepening one's understanding through scriptural reflection is a different question from accepting the reality of the event. There is no need for the church to have created the event. To exalt Jesus' birth falsely would have been of no benefit to the message about Jesus. In fact, the absence of this emphasis in the kerygma shows that the concept was not emphasized in the church's preaching. Such a claim would only bring derision, unless something genuine generated it (see the exegesis of 1:31). Why place another stumbling

6. Bovon 1989: 66–67 (also n. 13) speaks of Isaiah and the development of Jewish speculation like Pseudo-Philo's portrait of Isaac and Moses (*Biblical Antiquities* 8–9) and Philo's view of Isaac (*Cherubim* 12–15 §§40–52), though Bovon notes that for Philo this detail was allegorical. One could add Pseudo-Philo's portrait of Samson's birth (*Biblical Antiquities* 42). None of these accounts are virgin births: they only supply details of the event not in the original accounts. Bovon also argues for Hellenistic influence. C. F. Evans 1990: 156–57 surveys divine paternity in the ancient world, but denies its value for this passage. He prefers to speak of a retrojection, which means he thinks later reflection has produced the tradition.

7. Some argue that Luke 2 betrays this tension in that Joseph is seen as the father of Jesus in 2:1–7. It is suggested that Luke 2 betrays no knowledge of the virgin birth. But Joseph's precise relationship to Jesus need not be mentioned every time Joseph and Mary are discussed.

8. Marshall 1978: 76. Marshall's discussion (pp. 72–77) of the question is the best brief treatment currently available, though it is not clear that a "birth secret" is present. Nolland 1989: 46–48 also defends a "traditional" view of historicity.

block in the message? Ancients were not as gullible as many suggest. A concrete event must have generated this belief about Jesus, even if its significance emerged slowly.

The outline of Luke 1:26–38 is as follows:

a. Setting of the appearance (1:26–27)
b. Announcement: birth of the Davidic Son of God (1:28–37)
    i. Fear before the angel and a calm greeting (1:28–30)
    ii. The announcement proper, part 1 (1:31–33)
    iii. Mary's question (1:34)
    iv. The announcement proper, part 2 (1:35)
    v. A confirming sign and assurance of God's ability (1:36–37)
c. Acceptance by a willing servant (1:38)

A closer look at the structure of the announcement proper reveals the following:

an angelic word of calm (1:30)
announcement of the birth of the Davidic ruler (1:31–35)
    the promise: a son will be conceived (1:31)
    his call: Jesus the Davidic son who rules forever (1:32–33)
    Mary's inquiry (1:34)
    answer: he will be a Spirit-conceived Son of God (1:35)
announcement of a sign: Elizabeth's pregnancy (1:36)
lesson: nothing is impossible with God (1:37)

Numerous themes dominate the passage: the simple form of God's coming, the coming of the Davidic king's reign, the fulfillment of Israel's hope, the creative power of God and his Spirit, the uniqueness and superiority of God's son, the uniqueness of the Son's birth, and the certainty of God's word and power. As the angel says, "Nothing is impossible with God" (1:37). Most of these themes focus on God and the figure of fulfillment, Jesus. There also are themes tied to Mary. Her example represents the humble acceptance of God's word (1:38). In addition, she pictures one touched by God's grace.

Exegesis and Exposition

[26]In the sixth month, the angel Gabriel was sent by God to a city of Galilee named ⌜Nazareth⌝, [27]to a virgin betrothed to a man whose name was Joseph, of the house of David; and the name of the virgin was Mary.

²⁸And coming to her, he said, "Greeting, ⌐O favored one⌐, the Lord is with ⌐you⌐!"

²⁹⌐But she was greatly perplexed⌐ at this saying and pondered what sort of greeting this might be.

³⁰And the angel said to her, "Do not fear, Mary, for you have found favor before God. ³¹You shall conceive and shall give birth to a son and shall call his name Jesus. ³²This one shall be great, and shall be called Son of the Most High; and the Lord God shall give to him the throne of his father David, ³³and he shall rule over the house of Jacob forever; and of his kingdom there will be no end."

³⁴And Mary said to the angel, "How can this be since I do not know a man?"

³⁵The angel replied, "The Holy Spirit will come upon you, and the power of the Most High shall overshadow you; therefore ⌐the one who is born⌐ shall be called holy, the Son of God. ³⁶Behold Elizabeth, your relative, in her old age has also conceived a son; and this is the sixth month with her who is called barren. ³⁷For nothing is impossible ⌐with God⌐."

³⁸And Mary said, "I am the servant of the Lord. Let it be to me according to your word." And the angel departed from her.

a. Setting of the Appearance (1:26–27)

1:26 God commissions the angel Gabriel, who made the birth announcement to Zechariah, to deliver a similar message to Mary (on Gabriel, see the exegesis of 1:19). There is some question as to whether the phrase ἀπὸ τοῦ θεοῦ (apo tou theou) means sent "from God," emphasizing the place from which Gabriel came, or sent "by God," emphasizing who commissioned the angel. The phrase usually emphasizes location, but it is possible that ἀπό substitutes for ὑπό (hypo) (BAGD 87; BDF §210.2). Fitzmyer (1981: 343) notes that the preposition may be influenced by the Semitic preposition מִן (min, from, by), which can be used for both separation and agency. The preposition's natural meaning makes good sense and ought to be preferred.[9] Thus, Gabriel is sent from God's heavenly realm to Mary.

The meeting takes place in the sixth month of Elizabeth's pregnancy, a note that connects this angelic visit with 1:5–25. The visit occurs in the Galilean region, about 45 to 85 miles north of Jerusalem. About 30 miles in width, it contained within its borders the Sea of Galilee and was situated just north of Samaria. The region may be mentioned because Nazareth was a very small village (πόλις, polis) and Luke's readers may not have known even its general location (Marshall 1978: 64).

9. Some copyists of the NT (A, C, Byz), perhaps sensing that ἀπό was not strong enough or personal enough, substituted ὑπό.

Contrast with the preceding account sets the announcement's tone. The previous announcement about John came to a priest in the midst of a public worship service at the high holy place of Israel's capital. The announcement about Jesus comes privately to a humble woman in a little rural village. Luke contrasts the greatness of the setting of the announcement about John with the simplicity of the announcement about Jesus. The tone of the setting of Jesus' birth matches the tone of his ministry. The great God of heaven sends the gift of salvation to humans in a serene unadorned package of simplicity.

The angel appears to a young woman, Mary. Luke uses two simple **1:27** descriptions of her. First, she is a virgin. Παρθένον (*parthenon*, virgin) expresses her chaste state. Her condition receives confirmation in 1:34, where she confesses her lack of sexual experience. Matthew 1:23 agrees with this description of Mary.

Second, Mary is engaged to Joseph (Matt. 1:18 also expresses Mary's relationship to Joseph in these terms). The phrase about betrothal is worded like Deut. 22:23 and refers to the first stage of a two-stage Jewish marriage process. The initial stage of engagement (or betrothal) involves a formal witnessed agreement to marry and a financial exchange of a bride price (Mal. 2:14; Fitzmyer 1981: 343). At this point, the woman legally belongs to the groom and is referred to as his wife. About a year later, the marriage ceremony takes place when the husband takes the wife home.[10] A woman could become betrothed as early as age twelve (Marshall 1978: 64; Schürmann 1969: 42; SB 2:374–75). Luke does not give Mary's age.

Her name, Μαριάμ (*Mariam*, Mary), probably means "excellence" (Fitzmyer 1981: 344). Mary's descent is disputed. Since she is a relative of Elizabeth, a daughter of Aaron (1:5), many argue that she has Levitical roots (Creed 1930: 17). Some suggest that Eli is the point of Levitical connection to Mary in the Lucan genealogy (see 3:23).[11] Others connect her roots to David (Protevangelium of James 10.1; Ignatius, *Ephesians* 18.2; Justin Martyr, *Dialogue with Trypho* 45.4). It is hard, in light of the limited data, to make a choice, though her Levitical roots are clearer in Luke 1 than her

---

10. SB 1:45–47; *m. Ketub.* 4.4–5; Jeremias 1969: 364–67; Safrai 1976a: 752–60. The mishnaic text is suggestive for Matt. 1, since the initial realization of her pregnancy might suggest that Mary should be punished (Deut. 22:23–26) or, more leniently, be betrothed, given that premarital intercourse could result in betrothal (Deut. 22:28–29). Cases of rape were handled differently (Deut. 22:25–27).

11. The view is mentioned by R. Brown 1977: 287–88, who cites Hippolytus for it; see also the discussion of the genealogy in 3:23–38.

Davidic roots are, because of her tie to Elizabeth. Of course, a mixed lineage is also a possibility with one line supplied by Mary's mother and another by her father (Creed 1930: 17).

It is debated whether the virgin reference in Luke comes from or reflects Isa. 7:14.[12] Such an allusion is clearly present in Matt. 1:23, but there is nothing particularly Isaianic in Luke 1:27. Παρθένος is the natural term for a virgin, and Mary's virginity need not necessitate a reference to Isaiah (e.g., a passage like Gen. 16:11 shows that Luke frames the description of the birth in typical OT language). It may be in Luke's mind, but he makes no clear effort to point to this text. Nevertheless, Luke intends Jesus' birth to be seen as a virgin birth (1:34). R. Brown (1977: 300–301) argues persuasively that the superiority of Jesus to an elder John the Baptist assumes a supernatural conception of Jesus that is greater than the "out of barrenness" miracle that brings forth the Baptist. God will do an unprecedented work in a chaste young woman. God sets up salvation as he did in the OT, as he will do with John, except that even more will be done with Jesus.

Mary is engaged to Joseph of the house of David. Although some attempt to attribute the reference to the Davidic house to Mary's ancestry, the word order in the Greek is against such a view because the second use of παρθένος makes the reader aware that Luke has returned to discussing Mary after giving Joseph's lineage.[13] Luke 2:4 attributes Davidic background to Joseph also (Lohse, *TDNT* 8:485). Creed (1930: 16–17) regards the Joseph–virgin birth combination as problematic since Jesus derives his Davidic heritage from Joseph, even though Jesus is not truly Joseph's son (so also Luce 1933: 87). But this is not as great a problem as Creed and Luce make of it. Legally, since Mary at the time of her engagement is Joseph's wife, any child born to Mary would be regarded as Joseph's, if he accepted care for the child.[14] Precedent for moving ancestry exists in levirate marriage, though it goes the other direction (Deut. 25:5–10), that is, a levirate child is credited to the dead brother's and earlier husband's line, even though that brother did not produce the child.

---

12. So Schneider 1977a: 49. Against a reference to Isaiah in Luke are R. Brown 1977: 300 and Fitzmyer 1981: 336. The NT sees the virgin state as honorable (Acts 21:9; 1 Cor. 7:25; Rev. 4:14); Bovon 1989: 72.

13. Klostermann 1929: 13. A reference to "her name" or "whose name" following the mention of the Davidic house would have made a Davidic reference to Mary clear; Strathmann, *TDNT* 4:238.

14. Schweizer 1984: 27–28; see the earlier discussion of Jewish engagement in this verse. On a possible Davidic tie through Mary, see 1:69.

b. Announcement: Birth of the Davidic Son of God (1:28–37)
i. Fear before the Angel and a Calm Greeting (1:28–30)

Gabriel greets Mary and declares her a recipient of God's favor. He **1:28** appears to her in an unspecified indoor setting.[15] He greets her with two alliterative terms that emphasize grace (χαῖρε, *chaire*; κεχαριτωμένη, *kecharitōmenē*).

The vocative χαῖρε is variously understood: (1) a Greek greeting out of place in a Semitic setting (Creed 1930: 17); (2) a Semitic greeting of peace reflecting either Aramaic שְׁלָם (*šĕlām*) or more probably חֲדָי (*hadāy*);[16] (3) a Semitic call to rejoice;[17] or (4) a Greek greeting that had found its way to first-century Palestine and so was used in a Semitic setting naturally (Fitzmyer 1981: 345).

Fitzmyer (1981: 344) argues that Mary ponders over the reference to grace (1:30). Yet he also concedes that Semites are recorded in the NT as using the grace greeting (Matt. 26:49; 28:9). Paul, a Semite, gives greetings of both peace and grace (Rom. 1:7; 1 Cor. 1:3). It is hard to know whether Luke or his source has translated an originally Semitic expression into an equivalent Greek expression (view 2) or whether one is dealing with a Greek phrase that was part of the original tradition (view 4). The term is not foreign to the setting either way (contra view 1). The expression is a greeting (1:29), not a call to rejoice (contra view 3). Although the expression has precedent in the LXX as a rendering of various Semitic verbs for rejoicing, in this Lucan context that meaning is unlikely (Zech. 9:9; Zeph. 3:14; Joel 2:21; Lam. 4:21; Marshall 1978: 65). Regardless of its origin, the greeting means "hail to you" or "hello" (BAGD 874 §2a).

After the greeting, Mary is addressed as the "favored one" (κεχαριτωμένη). In this context, Mary is the recipient of God's grace, not a bestower of it (Fitzmyer 1981: 345; Alford 1874: 446). She is simply the special object of God's favor, much as John the Baptist was a special prophet of God.

With his greeting, Gabriel assures Mary by promising the presence of the Lord God. The phrase lacks a verb, but by supplying ἐστίν (*estin*) for the ellipse the declaration "the Lord *is* with you" emerges. Support for supplying this indicative verb, rather than a

15. Εἰσελθών suggests an entry into a room or a house. Most of the fifty uses in Luke's Gospel speak of entering a house or a city or of demons entering a person. The term simply means "to enter."

16. Marshall 1978: 65, who cites H. Gressmann through Klostermann 1929: 13, who in turn prefers חֲדָי. Greetings of peace are found in Luke 10:5; 24:36; John 20:19, 21, 26.

17. Laurentin 1967: 75–82, who also cites S. Lyonnet as holding this view. Note also the remark of Zimmerli, *TDNT* 9:367 n. 66.

subjunctive ("may the Lord be with you"), comes from the context, which asserts the certainty of God's involvement with Mary in bringing forth a great child. There is no uncertainty here, so the indicative is intended. The OT parallels divide between supplying a declarative verb (Judg. 6:12) and a subjunctive verb (Ruth 2:4), but context (Luke 1:30) is the key to this decision. The phrase expresses God's aid, as he is at her side (Fitzmyer 1981: 346). It has been interpreted as a reference to the moment of conception, which is said to occur while Gabriel addresses Mary.[18] However, the future tenses in 1:31–35 are against such an understanding of this verse in that both 1:31 and 1:35 put God's visitation in the future. Gabriel wishes only to encourage Mary that God will be with her through all the events the angel reveals.

1:29   Mary is perplexed by the angel's initial remarks. The compound verb διεταράχθη (*dietarachthē*, was greatly perplexed) reflects a more intense curiosity and concern than the use of ἐταράχθη (*etarachthē*, was perplexed) expressed for Zechariah in 1:12.[19] The cause of her confusion is the angel's greeting (ἐπὶ τῷ λόγῳ, *epi tō logō*, at this saying).[20] Some suggest that a man speaking to a woman is what troubles her, since later rabbinic tradition looks down on such conversation, but the evidence for this Jewish view is late, though John 4:27 suggests that it is possible (*b. Qid.* 70a; Fitzmyer 1981: 346). However, only the greeting is cited as the cause of the problem, not the nature or gender of the speaker (Marshall 1978: 66).

Mary begins to consider what is happening to her and ponders the greeting.[21] The imperfect διελογίζετο (*dielogizeto*) translates as "she was pondering" and portrays her as giving some ongoing reflection to the greeting (Schrenk, *TDNT* 2:96 §B1). She was mulling over the question ποταπὸς εἴη ὁ ἀσπασμός (*potapos eiē ho aspasmos*, what sort of greeting might this be?). She heard that God was with her and that she was an object of his grace. What was God going to do to her?

1:30   The angel deals with Mary's concerned curiosity by telling her "not to fear," just as he had told Zechariah in 1:13. More precisely, the use of the present imperative μὴ φοβοῦ (*mē phobou*) probably indi-

---

18. Sibylline Oracles 8.459–72. Klostermann 1929: 13 and Creed 1930: 17 note this ancient interpretation.
19. See BAGD 189 and BAA 380 for the term here. The prepositional prefix intensifies the force of the verb.
20. For a textual issue that affects this conclusion, see the additional note.
21. The use of the article as a pronoun is rare, but usually involves the singular "he" or "she"; Plummer 1896: 22; BDR §3.6.

cates that she is to stop fearing (Fitzmyer 1981: 346; BDF §336.3). This word of comfort shows that her curiosity about the greeting also caused her anxiety. But the following announcement makes clear that she has no need to be concerned.

Before turning to the discussion of the coming child, Gabriel adds one note of explanation (γάρ, *gar*, for) to his call to be calm. Mary has "found favor" (εὗρες . . . χάριν, *heures . . . charin*) with God. This expression is a Semitism (Gen. 6:8; 18:3; 39:21; 43:14; Judg. 6:17; 1 Sam. 1:18; 2 Sam. 15:25; Marshall 1978: 66). It is also common as a secular OT expression (Gen. 33:9–10). Whether the person showing favor is pleased because of an earlier action by the favored one or just chooses freely to display kindness depends on the context. As an expression of divine working, favor signifies God's gracious choice of someone through whom God does something special (Noah is spared from the flood; Gideon is chosen to judge Israel; Hannah is given a child in barrenness; David receives back the ark of the covenant). In the OT, the phrase often involves a request granted on the condition that someone had favor with God (so Gideon, Hannah, and David). However, here this favor is announced without any hint of a request. It is freely bestowed. The noun χάρις (*charis*, grace or favor) is used only by Luke in the Synoptics. It becomes a key term in Acts to describe what God does for his people out of his good pleasure (Luke 2:40; Acts 7:10, 46; 11:23; 13:43; 14:3; Conzelmann, *TDNT* 9:392–93). Mary is about to receive freely the special favor of God. She is a picture of those who receive God's grace on the basis of his kind initiative.

ii. The Announcement Proper, Part 1 (1:31–33)

Mary receives a specific word about the grace that God will extend to her. The first part of this announcement is in 1:31–33: 1:31 predicts the birth of a child and 1:32–33 describes his ministry. The form of the angelic announcement that the virgin Mary shall bear a son follows the OT pattern: Gen. 16:11; Isa. 7:14; and Judg. 13:5 (Creed 1930: 18; Fitzmyer 1981: 346–47; Marshall 1978: 66). The declaration of her approaching conception and bearing of a son is followed by instruction about what to name the child. This pattern also exists with Ishmael (Gen. 16) and Immanuel (Isa. 7:14), but with Samson (Judg. 13) the name of the child is lacking. Also, Hagar is already pregnant, while the mother of Samson and the woman referred to in Isaiah are not. Thus, the first part of an angelic birth announcement can appear in either present or future tense. Luke's use of the term συλλήμψη (*syllēmpsē*, shall conceive) points to a possible Semitic and Palestinian origin behind this part of the tradition, since the LXX verb, ἔχω (*echō*), is not used (Bock 1987: 296 n. 36).

1:31

The angel tells Mary that she will conceive. Is Luke consciously alluding to Isa. 7:14?[22] The reasons asserted for an Isaianic connection are the reference to the Davidic house in 1:27, the reference to παρθένος in 1:27 and 1:34, and the wording of the birth announcement here. But none of these reasons is decisive. The reference to the house of David may emerge from Christian tradition without requiring an allusion to Isa. 7:14. Mary is called a παρθένος because that is her condition on receiving the announcement. The mere presence of the term does not require an allusion to Isa. 7:14. The wording of the announcement is not distinctively parallel to Isa. 7:14, since Gen. 16:11 also looks parallel. It may be that Luke has Isa. 7:14 in mind, but he certainly is not making an effort to draw the reader's attention to this text. Unlike Matt. 1:18–25, he makes no mention of the Immanuel concept, which is a key idea of the Isaiah passage. If Isaiah is in mind, Luke does not note its fulfillment.[23]

Luke's possible lack of an allusion to Isa. 7:14 does not mean that he did not hold to a virgin birth. The language of Luke 1:27 and 1:34–35 makes it clear that he saw Jesus' conception as a work of God's Spirit. Ellis (1974: 73) notes that the virgin birth plays only a minor role in Luke and is largely absent from the writings of the early church and the church fathers. He suggests that the apostolic church did not make much use of it, given that it could cause offense to Jews about Jesus' origins or could be misunderstood by Greeks. The virgin birth was not, then, the creation of the later church. Only when Jesus' integrity was attacked directly by Jews or his humanity and divinity were attacked by Docetists and Adoptionists respectively did the virgin birth become a major issue of discussion in the postapostolic church.

Καλέσεις (*kaleseis*, shall name) has virtually an imperatival force (Fitzmyer 1981: 347; Zerwick 1963: 94 §280). The phrase in which it occurs is a Semitism (R. Brown 1977: 289). Luke merely cites the name *Jesus*. Unlike Matt. 1:21–23, throughout this material Luke never comments on the name. In this characteristic, Luke is distinct from many OT narratives. The description of the child's position, role, and origin follow in the rest of the birth announcement.

1:32 The significance of Jesus' birth is laid out in two stages. The early part of the announcement describes Jesus' future ministry and po-

---

22. For this allusion, see Marshall 1978: 66; Leaney 1958: 83; Schneider 1977a: 50; Schürmann 1969: 46, esp. n. 40; uncertain of it is R. Brown 1977: 299–300; Laurentin 1967: 115.

23. Bock 1987: 61–62. On conceptual ties reaching back at least to the Palestinian church, see Delling, *TDNT* 5:836 n. 66. On the issue of possible Jewish parallels, see Delling, *TDNT* 7:760 n. 6.

sition. The two stages (1:32–33 and 1:35) of the description are divided by the question of Mary in 1:34. The OT background to this announcement is strongly regal and Davidic, with much of the language having a parallel in 2 Sam. 7:9, 13–14, 16 (Fitzmyer 1981: 338; R. Brown 1977: 310–11). The individual focus of the regal declaration parallels 1 Chron. 17:11–14. Both 2 Sam. 7 and 1 Chron. 17 announce the Davidic covenant. Fulfillment comes in Jesus.

Jesus surpasses John the Baptist. The Baptist is "great before the Lord" (1:15), while Jesus is simply "great." Laurentin points out that μέγας (*megas*, great), when used by itself to describe someone, refers only to God in the OT. But although a reference to God is the prevalent use, it is not the exclusive use of absolute μέγας.[24] Moses (Exod. 11:3) and Mordecai (Esth. 10:3) are described as great men of God with absolute μέγας. In fact, the allusion here may be to Mic. 5:4 [5:3 MT], where the Davidic figure is portrayed as "great from the ends of the earth." Laurentin uses his evidence to suggest that Luke implies Jesus' divinity in this description. In light of the other parallels, however, such a conclusion cannot be regarded as certain, but only as possible (Bock 1987: 62–66). Jesus' greatness is really defined by further descriptions in this context. At the minimum, Jesus is an extremely significant figure before God; his unqualified position before God makes him greater than John.

The name υἱὸς ὑψίστου (*huios hypsistou*) occupies an emphatic position because it precedes the verb. "Son of the Most High" is simply another way of saying "Son of God," since ὑψίστου is another way to refer to God's supreme authority as "the Most High." The title appears in the OT, in Judaism, and at Qumran (Gen. 14:18–20, 22; Num. 24:16; Ps. 7:17 [7:18 LXX]; 2 Sam. 22:14; Dan. 4:24 [4:21 MT]; Jub. 16.18; 1 Enoch 9.3; 10.1; 46.7; 60.1, 22; T. Levi 16.3; 1QapGen 12.17; 20.12, 16; Fitzmyer 1981: 347–48). All but two of the NT uses of the genitive ὑψίστου are in Luke–Acts (Luke 1:35, 76; 6:35; 8:28; Acts 7:48; 16:17; Mark 5:7; Heb. 7:1; Marshall 1978: 67; Bertram, *TDNT* 8:619–20). Some attribute the phrase to a Greek setting, but Qumran makes this description of the title's origin unlikely. The title *Son of the Most High* is clearly attested at Qumran in an Aramaic document that has several phrases parallel to Luke 1:31–35. A Qumran fragment (formerly 4Q243, now 4Q246

24. Laurentin 1967: 36; Ps. 48:1 [47:2 LXX]; 76:1 [75:2 LXX]; 86:10 [85:10 LXX]; 96:4 [95:4 LXX]; 135:5 [134:5 LXX]; 145:3 [144:3 LXX]; 147:5 [146:5 LXX]; Fitzmyer 1981: 325, 347. Laurentin may mean by "absolute" that μέγας has no prepositional modifiers, in which case his statement is correct. Μέγας has no modifying role as a dependent adjective.

[= 4QpsDan ar^a = 4QpsDan A^a] 2.1) contains an interesting parallel. However, the passage is enigmatic because it is a fragmentary text containing only a few intriguing lines. The Qumran data clearly show the title in Luke to be a natural one for a Jewish setting (Schweizer, *TDNT* 8:381 n. 346). What is minimally present in Qumran's use of this title is the description of a regal figure (Fitzmyer 1973–74: 391–94; Marshall 1978: 67). The contemporary use of this phrase for a king is significant in revealing the regal context in which the term operates.[25] A king is about to be born.

The phrase *Son of the Most High* also has parallels in the plural *sons of the Most High*. Psalm 82:6 [81:6 LXX], Luke 6:35, and Matt. 5:9 show the phrase applying to special men of God. The psalm describes the OT judges, while the NT texts describe believers (R. Brown 1977: 289). Again, the term need not require a reference to deity. Rather, it describes someone with a special, intimate relationship to God.

A regal reference to Jesus is also indicated by the description υἱός (son). The term *son* is used in various connections in the OT, including that of the Davidic king (2 Sam. 7:14; 1 Chron. 22:9–10; Ps. 2:7; 89:26 [88:27 LXX]). It also is used regally and messianically at Qumran (4Q174 [= 4QFlor] 1.10–11; Brooke 1986: 111–14, 197–205, esp. 202–3). As Jesus' birth is announced, regal imagery abounds to describe the coming Messiah.[26]

Jesus' Davidic origin and his reign's permanence receive attention in the next part of the announcement. He is to receive the throne of his father David, a picture of majestic rule.[27] The connection to the house of David seems to be made through Jesus' relationship to Joseph (1:27), though an additional connection through Mary cannot be dismissed categorically (Alford 1874: 447). The Davidic throne is clearly a regal image drawn from the Davidic covenant's promise of a son, a house, and an everlasting rule (2 Sam. 7:8–16, esp. vv. 13, 16; on Solomon's accession, 1 Kings 1:48; 2:24). The promise in 2 Sam. 7 also begins with a declaration of the greatness of the one addressed, just as the announcement here begins with the greatness of the coming child. The promise to David found its initial fulfillment in Solomon, the king who built the temple. However, the ultimate fulfillment of the everlasting character of this line of rulers is clearly realized in Jesus (1:33). The initial prom-

25. For a brief discussion of the Qumran texts and an evaluation of Fitzmyer's 1973–74 article, see Bock 1987: 65, 298 n. 51 and Collins 1993 (who challenges Fitzmyer's claim that *Son of God* lacks a messianic nuance).

26. Discussion of the Lucan relationship of the phrase *Son of the Most High* to *Son of God* will be deferred until the discussion of the latter phrase in 1:35.

27. Majestic rule is suggested by the term *throne*; Schmitz, *TDNT* 3:164 §B2.

ise to David is elaborated and reiterated throughout the OT (1 Kings 2:24, where Solomon is seen as fulfilling the promise; Ps. 89:14, 19–29, 35–37; 132:11–12; Isa. 9:6–7 [9:5–6 MT]; 11:1–5, 10; Jer. 23:5–6; Marshall 1978: 67; Tiede 1988: 49). The announcement clearly recalls a deeply held hope that emerges from the OT. Fitzmyer (1981: 206–7, 338–39) contends that the first linkage in Jewish literature between the Son of God and Messiah is made in the NT, but the association is not surprising, since both terms describe Davidic figures in Palestinian Judaism (Lohse, *TDNT* 8:480–82; see n. 25 above). If a regal figure was a son of God, surely the Messiah is Son of God *par excellence* (Bock 1987: 297 n. 41).

Luke will make much of Davidic descent in this section. The house of David is mentioned in 1:69, the city of David and his house in 2:4, and the city of David in 2:11. Luke's genealogy goes through David in 3:31. Jesus' regal Davidic connection is the basic christological starting point for Luke's presentation of the person of Jesus (Bock 1987: 262; Lohse, *TDNT* 8:485 §B.II.3b). The concept of David's throne is mentioned again by Luke in the crucial enthronement declaration of Acts 2:30, where Peter describes the resurrection-ascension as pointing to the rule of Jesus, the Lord-Messiah. In this resurrection event, Jesus' rule goes public for all to see, as the evidence of the pouring out of God's Spirit makes clear. In Acts 2 Jesus' kingship is obvious, but it is also recognized during the time of his ministry (Luke 18:39; 19:38). However in the unique resurrection-ascension, the initial fulfillment of what the angel announces here becomes visible to all and is proclaimed to all by those who testify to the significance of Jesus Christ (so also Paul in Rom. 1:3–4).

A fundamental concept of Lucan theology is the kingdom rule of the promised Davidic son. The regal presentation of Jesus is foundational to what is said about the risen Lord and the message of the kingdom in Acts, a kingdom that has both present and future elements for Luke.[28] With the coming of the king, the kingdom draws near. How this concept is presented and developed in Luke is key to understanding Luke's portrayal of God's plan. Luke's kingdom portrait is a complex one that cannot be transformed merely by declaring that while Jesus spoke of a spiritual kingdom in the present, we are to await the outward manifestation of the new heaven and the new earth (against Hendriksen 1978: 87).

---

28. Present elements are found in Luke 11:20; 17:21; future in Luke 13:28; Acts 14:22; future and delayed in Luke 19:11; Acts 1:6, 11. In Acts 1, esp. v. 11, the answer to the apostles' question about total restoration is found in the angelic promise of a return; see also Acts 3:18–21; Marshall 1970: 134; Bock 1992c; and Bock 1994c.

The statements of this verse lead to all types of speculation about the nature of Jesus. Does Luke intend the references to the Son of God to be seen in a full divine light at this point? Marshall (1978: 67–68) suggests that the answer here is yes, because divine sonship is the foundation behind Davidic sonship, since it is mentioned first. On the other hand, R. Brown (1977: 310–16) argues that the language of 1:32–33 reflects merely the description of a Jewish hope of the Davidic Son of God, unlike 1:35, which contains fresh Christian ideas that were read back into this event. The question of the Lucan description of Jesus' nature in 1:31–35 cannot be answered until the entire announcement is studied and the Lucan usage of the Davidic motif is surveyed, but a few preliminary observations can be made. Luke clearly understands Jesus as the fulfillment of fundamental Jewish hopes for a ruler and redeemer. The ruling position and activity of Jesus in God's plan is the fundamental point of the angelic description of Jesus. The christological debate about the nature of Jesus is whether what is explicitly stated about Jesus is a high Christology, or whether Luke only implicitly lays the groundwork for a later declaration of a high Christology. Luke's language seems to focus on Jesus' Davidic connection, but it may also suggest even more (Bock 1987: 65–66).

1:33 Jesus not only has a regal position (1:32), but he also has a realm and an everlasting reign (1:33). His position is ruler over the nation of Israel. Βασιλεύσει ἐπί (basileusei epi) means "to reign over" a people.[29] The phrase *house of Jacob* is another way to refer to the nation of Israel (Exod. 19:3; Isa. 2:5–6; 8:17; 48:1; Fitzmyer 1981: 348). Some see allusion to Jesus gathering a "fresh Israel" or a "new Israel" here (Danker 1988: 38; O'Toole 1984: 18, who says it means Christians). There is, however, nothing in this context to suggest this broader reference. In fact, Mary's hymn expresses purely national sentiments (1:46–55), as does Simeon (2:29, 32, 34–35).[30] Jesus comes as King of the Jews, whether or not they recognize him. Godet (1875: 1.91) clearly argues that theocratic royal expectation is present here and notes that such a hope makes it impossi-

---

29. BDF §177, §233.2; BDR §177.1–2; Marshall 1978: 68; Klostermann 1929: 14. Luke 1:33 is the only use of the verb in the Gospels with reference to Jesus; K. Schmidt, *TDNT* 1:590. References to his "kingdom" are found in 22:30 and 23:42. Despite the absence of this term, regal reign imagery is found in several other terms and concepts, especially in Luke's use of Ps. 110:1 in Luke–Acts, as well as in the picture of Jesus' victory over Satan. In the OT, 2 Sam. 2:4 comes closest to this wording; Nolland 1989: 52.

30. The one reference to the nations in 2:32 is still expressed in very OT terms and is no real exception to this point, since the distinction between Israel and the nations is clear.

ble to see in this text a "prophecy" written in the late first century.[31] The Davidic king comes to his own. How this theocratic relationship works itself out, how the nation responds to it, and how God deals with the response is another major burden of Luke's work.

The duration of Jesus' rule is forever. Again, the details are not presented here, only the facts. The idea of an eternal rule in the NT develops the promise of an eternal line of kings from the OT (2 Sam. 7:12–16; 1 Kings 8:25; Isa. 9:6 [9:5 MT]; Ps. 110:4; 132:12; Marshall 1978: 68; Grundmann, *TDNT* 9:569 n. 483). Later in the OT the potential for a long dominion and an eternal ruler emerges (Isa. 9:6–7 [9:5–6 MT]; Mic. 4:7 with 5:1–4 [4:14–5:3 MT] portrays God's regal rule; esp. Dan. 7:14). This idea was also present in Judaism (Ps. Sol. 17.4; 1 Enoch 49.1; 62.14; 4Q174 [= 4QFlor] 1.11; 2 Bar. 73 [early second century]). The phrase εἰς τοὺς αἰῶνας (*eis tous aiōnas*, into the ages; i.e., forever) parallels οὐκ ἔσται τέλος (*ouk estai telos*, shall not be an end) and clarifies the everlasting duration of Jesus' rule.[32] Nothing will overcome Jesus or bring a halt to his reign. Luke–Acts makes clear that neither official Jewish rejection nor crucifixion will stop the plan of God for his Davidic king.

The eternality of this reign suggests something unique about Jesus. The hope of resurrection to eternal life was something that the OT had mentioned (Dan. 12:2). The hope of an unending rule for David's house also fits in with the OT, as already noted. Here the combination comes together in one person. Again the point is stated and no implications are drawn, at least not yet.

The fact is he will reign. When the reign commenced or commences is not noted or explored here by Luke. Jesus in the announcement is simply presented as the Davidic son (Marshall 1978: 68). The issue is when he will manifest his reign to Israel. That this question is still an issue later in Luke is indicated by the disciples' question in Acts 1:6 and Peter's speech in Acts 3:18–21. There is a sense in which the reign becomes visible in Acts 2:30–36 with the ascension and its corollary, the Father's bestowal of the Spirit, which initially fulfills the new covenant promise. But a full manifestation of authority to all people is still anticipated beyond this initial manifestation (Luke 17:20–37; 21:5–38; Acts 10:42–43; 17:31). Another major burden of Luke's writings is to show how the Davidic ruler comes to have such comprehensive authority over all humans. Luke will develop this theme throughout his Gospel.

31. Plummer 1896: 23. Godet's argument is correct, since a Christianized version would not focus so exclusively on Israel. The remarks belong in the context in which Luke has them.

32. On εἰς τοὺς αἰῶνας as a plural expression that stresses eternality, see Sasse, *TDNT* 1:199. For the grammar of the phrase, see BDR §141.1.3.

iii. Mary's Question (1:34)

1:34 Mary questions how this birth can occur, given her lack of sexual experience. She does not doubt the announcement, for she does not ask for a sign as Zechariah did.[33] Rather she is puzzled as to how (πῶς, *pōs*) this birth can occur, a question that causes the angel to elaborate (1:35). The reason Mary raises her question is that she does not know a man. Ἐπεί (*epei*, since) is used only here in Luke and appears rarely in the Gospels.[34] Mary uses the term γινώσκω (*ginōskō*, know) as a figure for sexual relations (Matt. 1:25; Gen. 4:1; 19:8; Judg. 11:39; 21:11; Num. 31:17–18). Contextually the present tense focuses on her current status of inexperience as opposed to a perpetual state of virginity, a view that shall be discussed in detail below. Mary does not currently know a man and thus cannot expect to be pregnant. She understands normal biology!

Mary's question has brought much discussion and is seen as historically problematic. Three factors are involved here:

a. In light of the prospect of her marriage to Joseph, it seems odd that Mary ponders over how the birth would occur. Surely, it is argued, she would have deduced that the angel meant her future husband would provide the means for a child.

b. The Davidic connection through Joseph, who is not actually Jesus' father, suggests a tension in the passage that does not correspond with the declaration of a virgin birth. Thus, some see an interpolation here that is not Luke's or that he carelessly inserted (Luce 1933: 88–89; Schneider 1971). The issue of Joseph as Jesus' "father" is discussed above (at 1:27), where it is concluded that there is no tension. The presence of a problem with this linkage is rejected, because legal precedents in Jewish culture allow for associating lineage to a nonbiological father.

c. In manuscript b of the Old Latin version, 1:34 is omitted and 1:38 appears, leading some to suggest that 1:34 is not original to Luke's Gospel, but is a later insertion. Others tie this variant with the previously noted objection about the Davidic connection through Joseph in order to support the interpolation view.[35] It is argued that a virgin birth does not fit a declaration of Joseph's fatherhood. With the omission of 1:34, it can be ar-

---

33. Zechariah asks "how shall I know this?" versus Mary's "how can this be?" Zechariah asks for a sign; Godet 1875: 1.92; Plummer 1896: 24; Schürmann 1969: 49.

34. Three times in Matthew, once in Mark, twice in John; R. Brown 1977: 289.

35. The early critical history of the view is mentioned by Klostermann 1929: 14.

gued that Luke saw the fulfillment of the angel's promise coming to pass in married relations between Joseph and Mary.

The possibility of an interpolation is to be rejected. First, the textual evidence for the view is weak, limited to versions in the Western family. Second, the question's removal destroys the parallelism with the account of Zechariah, where he too responds to the announcement with a question. Third, the question's presence follows the standard form of birth announcements where the announcement often sparks a question or a request (Gen. 17:17; Judg. 13:8; R. Brown 1977: 307–8).

So what causes Mary to ask her question? Various solutions have been proposed:

1. Mary questions Gabriel because of a vow of perpetual virginity that she does not wish to violate (see additional note on 1:34). Parallels for such a platonic approach to marriage are sometimes suggested from Qumran and the Essenes, especially the Therapeutae mentioned by Philo.[36] However, the present tense of γινώσκω argues against this sense. If the idea of a perpetual virgin were intended, a future verb would appear.
2. Mary knows that Isa. 7:14 teaches that the mother of Messiah is a virgin, so she questions Gabriel, since she would be marrying (Audet 1956). However, the absence of a clear allusion to Isa. 7:14 in Luke makes it unlikely that Luke intended this idea. Luke 1:34b with its emphasis on Mary's current status, not her future one, is also against this understanding. If this view were correct, would not Mary have asked about marrying Joseph?
3. Luke inserts the verse with 1:35–37 in order to set forth the virgin birth (Klostermann 1929: 14 cites many who hold this view). But this view expresses an overconfidence in what the tradition said and what Luke added. The defense for Luke's addition is that 1:35 has a higher Christology than 1:32. The literary "seam" is obvious, because of this christological difference. But the christological point, which is the basis for arguing for Luke's insertion, cannot be sustained. There is no distinction in the Christology of the two verses (see the exegesis of 1:35).

36. R. Brown 1977: 305 rejects this Jewish evidence, noting that the Qumran community did not have a permanent celibacy but a temporary one for priests offering sacrifices. The texts in Philo are *Contemplative Life* 8 §68 and *Hypothetica* 11.14–17 §§380–81.

4. The question is merely a literary device. It is not to be examined to give the psychological state of Mary, but provides Luke the opportunity to elaborate on his announcement.[37] This view seems to be overly skeptical in dealing with the assertions of the text, as the fifth and sixth views show.

5. Marshall (1978: 70) argues that the question cannot simply be a literary device to introduce 1:35 because Luke could have just continued the announcement after 1:33 with the data of 1:35. In other words, 1:34 need not be supplied to get to the assertions of 1:35. Marshall argues that a verbatim account of the announcement is not being given, so Luke is free to retell the event in this form. This view is possible, but it seems to leave the tension of the awkwardness of the question unresolved.

6. A traditional view, still held by a few recently, is that Mary understood the angel to be announcing an imminent pregnancy (Godet 1875: 1.93; Plummer 1896: 24; Arndt 1956: 53; Gaechter 1955: 92–98). The future tenses of 1:31, 35 could argue against such a near-term view (Fitzmyer 1981: 349–50); nevertheless a case can be made for it, because several terms in 1:28–30 suggest a near fulfillment. Mary is addressed with the perfect tense in 1:28 as κεχαριτωμένη (kecharitōmenē), that is, as one who is in a "favored state." In the same verse, she is told ὁ κύριος μετὰ σοῦ (ho kyrios meta sou), that is, "the Lord is with you." Finally, in 1:30 she is told εὗρες γὰρ χάριν (heures gar charin), that is, she "has found grace" with God. The exchange of tenses suggests a potential immediacy. So she takes the announcement not to be of a future birth in her marriage, but of an immediate birth. In addition, she may have concluded that Joseph came from too humble a background to be the source of such a child. So Mary asks her question.

Luke supports the concept of the virgin birth. God is marvelously at work and has taken the initiative (Tiede 1988: 50). This miraculous explanation for Jesus' birth has also been the object of much critical discussion (R. Brown 1977: 517–33 and Fitzmyer 1981: 341–42 see it as "unresolved"). The birth is often rejected because of presuppositions about limits of God's activity in the world.

37. Creed 1930: 19; Schneider 1977a: 50; Schürmann 1969: 49–50; Fitzmyer 1981: 348–50; Wiefel 1988: 51–52; Ernst 1977: 72; R. Brown 1977: 309. Gewiess, in an appendix to Laurentin's German 1967 edition, interestingly takes a view opposite of Laurentin in the French original and omits Laurentin's own discussion of the question.

Though it is true that outside of Matthew and Luke the NT does not address this issue, no adequate explanation for the origin of the concept, outside the event itself, has been posited.[38] If one accepts the possibility of a virgin birth, then the problem of the human father and Jesus' Davidic lineage is also solved, since the only human father associated with Jesus is Joseph. He would naturally be regarded as Jesus' father and, as a practical matter, the source of Jesus' ancestry.

iv. The Announcement Proper, Part 2 (1:35)

Gabriel replies and proclaims direct divine involvement in the coming Davidic ruler's conception. The verse has a three-part structure: the divine work of conception comes in two parallel lines, while descriptions of the result and significance of that conception follow. Some see the anarthrous reference to Holy Spirit (πνεῦμα ἅγιον, *pneuma hagion*) as equivalent to the "divine spirit," like the OT references in Gen. 1:2 and Ps. 91:4,[39] while others see a specific appeal to the Holy Spirit (Ellis 1974: 74; Marshall 1978: 70; R. Brown 1977: 124–25, 289–90). The parallelism with "power of the Most High" (δύναμις ὑψίστου, *dynamis hypsistou*) and Luke's general portrait of the Spirit suggest a reference to the creative power of God, God's active Holy Spirit (24:49).[40] To make a distinction is too subtle in light of the major role that Luke gives to the Holy Spirit.

1:35

This work parallels the reference in 1:15 to the Spirit's filling of Elizabeth's womb. God's Spirit is the active, life-giving agent. Such a reference corresponds with the OT and Jewish picture of God's Spirit (Ezek. 37:14; Jdt. 16:14; 2 Bar. 21.4; Ellis 1974: 74). The verb ἐπελεύσεται (*epeleusetai*, will come) should not be overpressed as a sexual allusion, since God can create life without a sexual act (Gen. 1 or the process of resurrection; Nolland 1989: 45, 54). God's work in Mary will result in a child. Technically speaking, this verse proclaims a virgin "conception" for Mary.

Jesus' birth will be the work of God's creative power. The power of the Most High (δύναμις ὑψίστου) will overshadow Mary. Putting the parallel lines together indicates that God's Spirit acts with cre-

---

38. Machen 1930, though somewhat dated, is still helpful both in rejecting explanations that are grounded in a history-of-religions approach and in evaluating the arguments surrounding the rejection of this teaching; see esp. pp. 126–34, 380–81.

39. Fitzmyer 1981: 350. Bovon 1989: 76 speaks of a reference to the creative power of God. Isa. 32:15 LXX (A, ℵ) mentions the Spirit's "coming upon" someone. See also 1 Sam. 10:6; 16:13 ("leap upon"); and Ezek. 37:14; C. F. Evans 1990: 163.

40. Bovon 1989: 76 notes that the combination of Spirit and power is frequent in Luke–Acts: Luke 1:17; 4:14; Acts 1:8; 10:38.

ative power.[41] The Creator God who brought life out of nothing and created humans from the dust is also able to create human life in a womb. God's act involves his overshadowing Mary. Ἐπισκιάσει (*episkiasei*, shall overshadow) in the OT refers either to the Shekinah cloud that rested on the tabernacle (Exod. 40:34–35; Num. 9:18; 10:34) or to God's presence in protecting his people (Ps. 91:4 [90:4 LXX]; 140:7 [139:8 LXX]).[42] In Luke 9:34, the term refers to the cloud of the transfiguration overshadowing the disciples. Thus, overshadowing refers to God's glorious presence before his people.

Attempts have been made to give ἐπισκιάζω a more specific reference:

1. Creed (1930: 20) argues against attempts to equate the term with Philo's usage in describing Gen. 6:4–6, since Philo spoke of overshadowing as a negative moral influence of evil spirits (*On the Unchangeableness of God* 1.3).

2. Daube (1956: 27, 32–36) thinks the term has sexual connotations. Connecting it with Semitic טלל II [*ṭll*, to cover over; BDB 378], he notes that the rabbis understood the phrase "to spread a טַלִּית (*ṭāllît*, mantle) over a woman" as a euphemism for sexual intercourse (*b. Qid.* 18b). Though the Semitic term may be so used, ἐπισκιάζω never carries this connotation (R. Brown 1977: 290).

3. Leisegang (1922: 25–33) sees a parallel between the Spirit's overshadowing of Mary and the Greek mystery religions, in which spirits were said to overcome female worshipers. But appeal to the ecstasies of a mantic or sibyl is unnecessary when biblical parallels provide a more satisfying explanation (R. Brown 1977: 290; Menzies 1991: 37, 122 n. 2).

4. Laurentin (1967: 85–91) compares Mary to the ark of the covenant, viewing her as a holy receptacle (cf. Exod. 40:35). But Ps. 91:4 offers a closer OT parallel to Mary's experience. As R. Brown (1977: 327) notes, it is the cherubim that are said to overshadow the ark. In addition, the ark and the tabernacle are not the only objects overshadowed by God's presence: Mount Zion (Isa. 4:5), the Israelites (Num. 10:34 [10:36 LXX]),

---

41. Bertram, *TDNT* 8:619 n. 48, cites 1QH 7.6–7 (where God's power as Most High and the Spirit are linked; see 1QH 6.33) and T. Levi 16.3 (where a man who brings renewal to the Law is said to work by "the power of the Most High"). Some think that T. Levi 16 has been reworked by a Christian editor to allude to Jesus; H. Kee in J. Charlesworth 1983–85: 1.794 n. 16a. Grundmann, *TDNT* 2:300, 311 n. 91, notes the tie between power and the Spirit. Procksch, *TDNT* 1:101, speaks of a "supranatural origin."

42. Marshall 1978: 70–71; Schweizer 1984: 29; Wiefel 1988: 53; Schulz, *TDNT* 7:400; Schweizer, *TDNT* 6:405; Justin Martyr, *Apology* 1.33.6.

and the chosen ones (Deut. 33:12). It seems unlikely that this parallel is intended. Rather, overshadowing merely says that the conception of Jesus results from God's creative work.

The child produced by divine conception will be holy, the Son of God. This verse is one of the most christologically significant verses in the book. The divine conception results, διό (*dio*, therefore), in two descriptive terms being applied to Jesus: *holy* and *Son of God*.

The first, ἅγιον (*hagion*), is taken by many to refer to Jesus as "set apart for special service."[43] This sense does convey the basic meaning, but is there more significance to the term? Godet (1875: 1.94) suggests that the term alludes to Jesus' unfallen state at creation, in that he was the only person created by God's hand besides Adam. This view seems unlikely and extremely subtle until one examines 3:38 and finds that Luke's genealogy ends with a reference to Adam as τοῦ θεοῦ (*tou theou*, of God), a phrase that in the context of a genealogy would be equivalent to "son of God." So, Godet's suggestion may be an implication of the verse, but it is hardly explicit. If he is correct, then Jesus is portrayed through his birth as the True Man, the Second Adam.

Marshall raises another option, arguing that ἅγιον leads into the description *Son of God* and should be taken as a reference to Jesus' divinity or at least his "divine relatedness."[44] This meaning depends on whether Son of God is taken as a term of divinity by Luke. As the meaning of Son of God is the crux problem in the passage, the exact force of ἅγιον must await its consideration.

Until this verse, Jesus is clearly portrayed as the Davidic son, the regal messianic figure in whom all Israel hoped. But does the addition of the title *Son of God* to the context make the passage explicitly contain more than a simple declaration of Jewish hope? The evidence for a deeper significance to the sonship reference is twofold. (1) The Holy Spirit's action on behalf of Jesus shows that his human origins are grounded in God's creative activity: Jesus' superiority to John is grounded in a superiority of position and manner of birth, which is of a supernatural origin. (2) Verbally and linguistically there is a linkage between *Son of God* and *Son of the Most High* that makes them synonymous and points to a deeper role for Jesus than that of fulfilling the Jewish Davidic hope (Marshall 1978: 67–71;

43. Fitzmyer 1981: 352 mentions Luke 2:23 and Isa. 4:3; Schweizer 1984: 30 adds Isa. 35:8; 62:12; Exod. 13:12; and Lev. 23:2 to show the variety of objects called "holy"; Schürmann 1969: 54 notes that 1 John 2:20 and Rev. 3:7 apply the description to Jesus.

44. Marshall 1978: 71 uses the German term *Gottgehörig* to describe his view. In the NT, the title appears in John 1:34; 20:31; Acts 9:20; 2 Cor. 1:19; Gal. 4:4; Heb. 4:14; 1 John 4:15; Rev. 2:18 (C. F. Evans 1990: 165).

Michel, *NIDNTT* 3:636–37, 642; and Marshall 1970: 168). Initially, these arguments look quite compelling.

But historical linguistic factors and, more importantly, Luke's own usage raise questions about an explicit reference to a divine Son of God. The "birth from God" terminology appears at Qumran in 1Q28a [= 1QSa = Rule Annex] 2.11.[45] The exact meaning of this passage is disputed, but it describes a nondivine child who is born with a special kinship to God through an anointing by God's Spirit. Thus, in contemporary Judaism, the phrase could describe a person, without necessarily requiring ontological overtones.

The most crucial factor is Luke's usage of the phrase. In 1:32, Jesus is described as υἱὸς ὑψίστου (*huios hypsistou*, Son of the Most High), a phrase that anticipates 1:76. Jesus is "a Son of the Most High" in contrast to John the Baptist, who is προφήτης ὑψίστου (*prophētēs hypsistou*, a prophet of the Most High). Jesus functions as a son, while John functions as a prophet. The context makes clear that the distinction is grounded in Jesus' Davidic office (1:69, 76). The contrast is one of role, not one necessarily of nature. The same Davidic emphasis continues in 2:26, 29–31. Jesus as Son is confessed at the baptism and the transfiguration. The baptismal confession contains regal imagery (Ps. 2:7), while the transfiguration follows a messianic confession (Luke 9:20). *Son* also appears in texts where exorcism is present or an attack by Satan is made (4:3, 9, 41; 8:28). In 4:41, which is particularly significant because the verse is unique to Luke, Luke explains the title *Son of God* by the following ὅτι (*hoti*, because) clause. Luke says that the meaning of "Son of God" is that Jesus is χριστόν (*christon*, the Christ). Thus, Luke's usage consistently has a messianic thrust.

Thus, Luke presents the title *Son of God* consistently as the Davidic deliverer, the regal and messianic Christ. For Luke, the Son of God is Messiah, at least at this point of his presentation. The presence of a divine element in Jesus' birth does not require or focus upon an *explicit* statement of Jesus' metaphysical divinity, but asserts that Jesus' origins are divinely grounded in the Spirit's creative power. Jesus is uniquely from God. Luke has heightened the Jewish conceptual use of being born of God by tying it to a virgin conception. Jesus is from God in a unique way.

Luke's Davidic focus in the title *Son of God* may also imply an ontological conclusion, but the point is simply that Luke does not emphasize ontology by his use of this title, as his later usage of *Son of God* also shows. One must distinguish between what Luke's lan-

---

45. Dupont-Sommer 1973: 108; Michel and Betz 1960: 11–13, 15–17; Michel and Betz 1962–63. This usage also shows that a Hellenistic origin for the phrase is not required.

guage focuses on and what his language may imply. One cannot say that Luke did not believe Jesus to be divine. Luke's use of other titles reveals his Christology. His use of the title *Lord* in Acts makes clear and Jesus' own portrayal of God as his Father in Luke 2:41–52 suggests that Luke did see Jesus in this deeper light. However, it seems that Luke did not seek to make this deeper christological point from his early usage of the title *Son of God*.[46] The nature of Luke's usage also explains why the hymns of Mary and Zechariah in Luke 1 concentrate on Davidic themes, and it serves to explain why at points Mary was troubled with the form of Jesus' ministry. She certainly is not portrayed as perceiving an announcement of a divine child here.

So, Jesus as a result of God's creative power comes as the Son of God. This portrayal views Christ's birth from the perspective of the start of his human existence. Luke builds his Christology from the ground up. R. Brown (1977: 291, 314 n. 48) makes the point that there is no mention of Jesus' preexistence in Luke, a point that is correct enough, but neither is there a denial of such a role. Luke portrays merely the earthly ministry and history of Jesus. The absence of a fully theologically developed presentation of Jesus in the infancy material is a defense of its authenticity in that no effort has been made to Christianize or to theologically deepen Jesus' portrait to conform to what was later more clearly perceived about him. The account fits the Jewish setting from which it emerged. The divine conception of Jesus is a supernatural work. His description as Son has a messianic and nativistic meaning. The messianic thrust comes from the Davidic messianic context, while the nativistic or birth thrust comes from 1:34 and 3:38. As Son, Jesus is a Holy Messiah and possibly also is seen as True Man, Second Adam. Later texts will make it clear that his messiahship and sonship have even greater connections, which transcend Jesus' earthly sonship ties. But Luke does not make such points explicit here.

v. A Confirming Sign and Assurance of God's Ability (1:36–37)

Gabriel notes a confirmation of what he has proclaimed: Elizabeth's pregnancy. The use of "behold" (ἰδού, *idou*) forms a parallel with 1:20 and turns attention to work that God performed in tandem with his work in Mary. Luke 1:36 also shares the term for conception with 1:24 (συλλαμβάνω, *syllambanō*, to conceive) and ties the events to the previous section, since "barrenness" here recalls 1:24 (Schneider 1977a: 51). Mary does not request a sign, but one

1:36

---

46. Bock 1987: 65–67. The theme of Jesus' sonship in Luke, outside of the use of the title *Son of God*, does push Luke's imagery toward a higher Christology, but that is not his point yet. See the exegesis of 2:49.

is given to her anyway for encouragement (Klostermann 1929: 15; Fitzmyer 1981: 335). Elizabeth, Mary's long-barren relative, has conceived and is in the sixth month of her pregnancy.[47] The reference to Elizabeth's pregnancy shows that nothing is impossible with God (1:37) and prepares the reader for the next event, Mary and Elizabeth's meeting. In God's plan, Mary and Elizabeth are woven together through miraculous births.

1:37 Gabriel explains that Elizabeth's pregnancy (and thus also Mary's pregnancy) is possible because (ὅτι, *hoti*) nothing is beyond God's power. The angel affirms God's power to accomplish what is said. Most see evidence of two Semitisms in the verse: (1) The term ῥῆμα (*rhēma*, thing) is used with the broad sense of דָּבָר (*dābār*, thing; i.e., event; Acts 10:37) and (2) the use of οὐκ (*ouk*, not) with πᾶν (*pan*, all) and a verb makes an emphatic statement.[48] Schneider (1977a: 51) notes that ῥῆμα in this context refers to all God does, both by word and by action. The concept of God's total power reflects an OT motif (Gen. 18:14; Job 10:13 LXX; 42:2; Zech. 8:6; Jer. 32:17 [39:17 LXX]).[49] In a major theological statement of the pericope, the angel affirms God's total power to accomplish these miraculous births. Godet (1875: 1.95) cites J. Oosterzee as saying, "The laws of nature are not chains which the Divine Legislator has laid upon Himself; they are threads which He holds in His hand, and which He shortens or lengthens at will."

c. Acceptance by a Willing Servant (1:38)

1:38 Mary responds to Gabriel's message with submission and obedience. She identifies herself as δούλη (*doulē*, bondservant).[50] In everyday speech, this word describes one of humble station who addresses a superior in recognition of their position. As God's handmaid, Mary accepts openly what God asks of her.

Mary is exemplary in the way she responds to God's message of grace. God can do with her what he wishes. This acceptance is sig-

47. The relationship between Mary and Elizabeth is not specified. Wycliffe seems to be responsible for associating the two as cousins; Plummer 1896: 25; R. Brown 1977: 292. On the problem of a supposed contradiction between John and Jesus as relatives and the statements of John 1:31, 33, see the additional note on 1:25.

48. Creed 1930: 21; R. Brown 1977: 292; Klostermann 1929: 15; BDF §302.1; BDR §302.1.2. The force is that "nothing at all is impossible" for God.

49. Jer. 32:17 MT is close in force to the genitive expression here. So the genitive may reflect a Semitic original behind Luke and suggest that he is not responsible for the material in the section; Marshall 1978: 72; Danker 1988: 40; see additional note.

50. BAGD 205; BAA 413; Acts 2:18 from the Joel 2 citation; 1 Sam. 1:11 (Hannah). Mary's remarks recall Hannah. The figure also is used of Israel in Isa. 65:13–15 (Danker 1988: 40).

nificant, taken at possible personal loss. Such a step might involve her in potential problems with Joseph and with her reputation (Matt. 1:18–19; Plummer 1896: 26; Hendriksen 1978: 90). There is risk in agreeing to go God's way, but as the Lord's servant, she willingly goes.

His job completed, the angel departs. Now Luke turns to the meeting of Mary and Elizabeth. There is no counterpart in Mary's story to 1:24, since the moment of Mary's conception is not revealed, though there are verbal overlaps in the promise "to conceive" (1:24, 36; Klostermann 1929: 15; Creed 1930: 21). However, by the time of the meeting Mary is pregnant (1:42–43).

Summary

Luke 1:26–38 describes Gabriel's announcement to Mary of Jesus' birth. The heavenly messenger sets forth the promise of a miraculous birth, which will produce a child who fulfills the Davidic promise for the nation (1:31–35). The emphasis of the passage is not the manner of Jesus' birth, though it is clearly a virginal conception. Rather, the focus is God's gracious work in fulfilling his promise to deliver his people (Schweizer 1984: 31). For Luke, the birth's miraculous character serves only to demonstrate God's power in carrying out this plan. The birth also serves to point, through his unique conception, to Jesus' uniqueness. The nature of Jesus' birth and his regal, messianic position explain Jesus' superiority to John the Baptist. Jesus reigns over Israel as a result of the Spirit's work. His birth may also indicate a connection to Adam. Jesus represents the fulfillment of God's promise and the renewal of God's activity on behalf of humanity. As such, Jesus is the hope of humanity.

In the middle of all this drama stands Mary, God's listening, humble, willing servant, who comes to see that God has the power to bring his plan to pass. So Mary has the attitude of a model saint. God can do great things for his cause and can use anyone or anything to accomplish it (1:37). Mary is ready to be such a vessel.

Additional Notes

1:26. A few Western manuscripts (D, Itala) omit Ναζαρέθ. This leads some to wonder if Luke cited the specific locale (Leaney 1961–62: 161–62), but Alexandrian and Byzantine texts attest that he did (R. Brown 1977: 287).

1:26. R. Brown (1977: 287) sees a discrepancy between Matthew and Luke about the parents' original home. Matthew, he argues, knows only of a Bethlehem birth and vision, while Luke portrays Joseph and Mary's home as Nazareth, a locale Jesus is brought to in Matt. 2:22–23 only after his birth. But this reconstruction places Joseph's vision in a locale that is not expressly stated by Matthew. Only Jesus' birth is tied to Bethlehem in Matt. 2:1. Brown's is thus an argument from silence. Joseph's vision has no named locale. Luke may have supplied additional details as a result of his going over the tradition, as he does when he discusses how the couple got to Bethlehem (Luke 2:4–5). The problem in Matthew of Joseph's initial inclination to return to Judea and not to Nazareth (Matt. 2:22) may have been influenced by three factors: (1) Jesus was born in Bethlehem, (2) it was an ancestral home, and (3) it was the city of David. After all, the family did remain in Bethlehem for the full time of Mary's purification (Luke 2:39). Unlike Matthew, Luke does not mention the journey to Egypt, an omission that can be explained either by Luke's lack of knowledge about the journey or by his choosing not to mention it, given that Matthew had already recorded it. By giving Mary's perspective, Luke seems to supplement Matthew and does not duplicate any of Matthew's infancy events beyond agreement on the most basic elements.

1:27. Joseph's name means "may Yahweh add (sons)," but Luke makes nothing of this point (Marshall 1978: 64). The name became very popular, starting with postexilic Judaism (Fitzmyer 1981: 344; Gen. 37–50). Luke mentions Joseph to establish a Davidic connection to Jesus.

1:28. Language in 1:28 may recall Zeph. 3:14–15. The potential allusions are the greeting and the note that God is with Mary (μετὰ σοῦ). Some argue that the Zephaniah allusion is part of a string of allusions that identify Mary as "daughter Zion," a type of redemption (Laurentin 1967: 75–82). But Fitzmyer (1981: 345) replies that the allusions cited for this view come from an array of variant versions of the MT and LXX. This view also requires a suspect rendering of קֶרֶב (qereb) in Luke 1:31 from Zeph. 3:17 as meaning both "in your midst" and "in your body." Thus, this association is unlikely.

1:28. Is Mary the "bestower" of God's grace? An important translation variant is found in the Vulgate, which suggests that Mary possesses grace, so that in some sense she is "full of grace." Against the Vulgate rendering, 1:30 clearly portrays Mary as "finding grace" with God, as the object of grace, not the possessor or bestower of it (Klostermann 1929: 13; the key phrase is εὗρες γὰρ χάριν). What God will do in giving her this special child is his act of grace. Mary is a simple humble object of God's work, without any idea of personal merit on her part (Danker 1988: 35–36). However, this Lucan phrase, along with that in 1:42, serves as the basis for the Catholic *Ave Maria*, a liturgical prayer to Mary: "Hail Mary, full of grace; the Lord is with thee. Blessed art thou among women, and blessed is the fruit of thy womb. Holy Mary, Mother of God, pray for us sinners now and at the hour of death." The first two sentences have roots in Luke and appear to go back to Gregory the Great, but they were not authorized as a creedal formula until 1198. The third portion of the saying, with its plea for Marian intercession, was authorized by Pope Pius V in 1568 (Plummer 1896: 21–22 n. 1). The theological speculation derived from these verses is unrelated to 1:28, which treats Mary as an object of blessing, not a source of it (Caird 1963: 53; Delling, *TDNT* 5:834–35).

1:28. A textual problem involves the additional phrase, which also definitely appears in 1:42, that Mary is "blessed among women."[51] Most text critics regard the phrase as a scribal addition influenced by 1:42, arguing that it is easier to see how it was added to 1:28 than to explain its removal (Metzger 1975: 129). The shorter reading, supported by ℵ, B, L, W, Ψ, and a few versions, is probably original.

1:29. The text-critical problem involves the addition of a participle, ἰδοῦσα (seeing), which suggests that, in addition to the message, the mere appearance of the angel caused confusion. A, C, Θ, and Byz contain this term (so also Godet 1875: 1.89–90). It is possible that this term was originally in the text in light of the frequency of participial ἰδών (seeing) in Luke's Gospel (twenty times in this form; esp. 1:12). However, most regard the word as superfluous here, since the greeting is named as the reason for Mary's confusion (1:29–30). Omitting the participle are ℵ, B, D, L, W, and Ψ. The agreement of the major Western uncial with ℵ and B is impressive (Fitzmyer 1981: 346). Thus, it is more likely that only the angel's greeting caused Mary concern.

1:29. Luke often uses the optative mood (εἴη) with an indirect question to express a participant's thought (3:15; 8:9; 18:36; 22:23; Marshall 1978: 66; BDF §65.2, §386).

1:31. The meaning of Jesus' name is disputed. In fact, the name *Jesus* goes back to the OT name *Joshua* and was popular in postexilic Judaism. In the second century, it fell out of use both in Judaism and among Christians (Marshall 1978: 67; Foerster, *TDNT* 3:285–86). The etymology of the name is a complex issue, as etymologies of Hebrew names often are (Fitzmyer 1981: 347; Foerster, *TDNT* 3:289; Noth 1928: 154–55 n. 2). Many tie the name to the Hebrew verb שָׁוַע (*šāwaʿ*, to cry for help) or the root ישׁע (*yšʿ*, to deliver). Thus the original name is said to mean "Yahweh, help," while the popular etymology reads the name as "Yahweh delivers." Since wordplays on related verbal roots or terms are common in the Jewish handling of etymologies, this explanation of the etymology is possible. However this two-level explanation for the etymology can be questioned, since *Joshua* literally means "Yahweh, cry out for help," which is awkward in

---

51. A, C, D, Byz, and many versions. R. Brown 1977: 288 notes that the phrase's presence in these manuscripts influenced the *Ave Maria* and its juxtaposition of the terms *Mary, full of grace,* and *blessed.*

sense. In addition, an imperatival verbal element in a name is unusual.[52] It may be that the etymology is "Yahweh is salvation" (BDB 221).

1:34. The meaning is straightforward, yet it has occasioned a long discussion in Catholic theology. Traditional Catholicism argues that Mary's reply is based on a vow of virginity that she had taken and expected to maintain even in her marriage to Joseph.[53] This argument was popularized by key fathers of the West—Ambrose and Augustine. Alongside this view there also developed the view that Mary stayed an intact virgin, even in birth,[54] a teaching that appears in the NT apocryphal work the Protevangelium of James 19–20 (Schneemelcher 1991–92: 1.433–34). When combined, these views led to the three-part mariological confession that Mary was *virginitas ante partum, in partu, et post partum*, that is, "a virgin before birth, in birth, and after birth." The creed goes back to the fourth century (R. Brown 1977: 518 n. 2). The Lucan text supports only the prebirth virginity (Marshall 1978: 69; Fitzmyer 1981: 348–49). Brown notes that many current Catholics take "a more nuanced position."

1:35. A minor textual problem involves the inclusion of ἐκ σοῦ after γεννώμενον, which would translate as "the one who is born *from you*." The reading is early, as its presence in Tatian's Diatessaron shows. The reading is also found in C and Θ. But the external evidence is largely for the omission of the phrase, since manuscripts of each text family support the simple reading that translates "the one who is born" (ℵ, B, D, L, Byz, Lect, and most Itala).

1:35. The syntax is disputed, with three options being put forward. Some take the participial phrase τὸ γεννώμενον (which is born) as the subject of the sentence with ἅγιον (holy) serving as an adjective to the participle. This view reads the verse as "the one born holy [or, the holy one born] will be called the Son of God" (Alford 1874: 448; Godet 1875: 1.93; NIV). The view is attractive because it creates a parallelism with 1:32. But normally an adjective like ἅγιον in 1:35 is found with the definite article when it follows the word it modifies. Since there is no article here, it seems that ἅγιον serves as a predicate.[55] Thus, it reads, "The one who is born is holy."

---

52. Thanks to my former colleague Allen Ross for this evaluation.

53. Laurentin 1957a: 176–88 (this discussion is only in the French edition). The view is first attested in Gregory of Nyssa in A.D. 386; *PG* 46:1140D–41A; R. Brown 1977: 304; and Delling, *TDNT* 5:834–35, esp. n. 55, who prefers to speak of a "virgin conception" as the most accurate way to describe Luke's portrayal. Wiefel 1988: 53 refers to Ambrose, *Expositio Evangelii Secundam Lucam* 2 (Corpus Scriptorum Ecclesiasticorum Latinorum 32:99), and Augustine, *De Sancta Virginitate* 4 (Corpus Scriptorum Ecclesiasticorum Latinorum 41:327). For the full history of exegesis, see Graystone 1968: 3–36.

54. This view is why Delling makes the distinction described in the previous note.

55. Moule 1953: 107. Bovon 1989: 77 argues that the predicate position is supported by the OT allusion to Isa. 4:3.

Others argue that a parallel copula verb should be supplied for ἅγιον (Fitzmyer 1981: 351). The copula would be future with the other verbs of the context, so that the verse reads, "The one who is born shall be holy and shall be called the Son of God." This possible rendering makes good sense, but if there is no need to supply a verb one should not do so.

The third option holds that both ἅγιον and υἱὸς θεοῦ are predicates to the verb, a view that translates the verse, "The one who is born shall be called holy, the Son of God" (Plummer 1896: 24–25; Schürmann 1969: 54–55; Leaney 1958: 83; Marshall 1978: 71; R. Brown 1977: 291). This rendering also parallels 1:32a in having two predicates. The phrase *to be called holy* will reappear in 2:23 and has an OT precedent in Isa. 4:3. Thus, this construction of the verse seems the most natural option.

1:37. Does the text read τοῦ θεοῦ (so ℵ, B, D [with a different word order], L, W) or τῷ θεῷ (so A, C, Δ, Θ, Ψ, Byz, Lect, some Itala)? The first reading translates, "No promise from God is impossible"; the second, "Nothing is impossible with God." However, what confuses the discussion is that ῥῆμα can be seen as a reflection of Hebrew דָּבָר, because the verse recalls Gen. 18:14. If this is the case, then either reading can be translated as "nothing is impossible with God." The more difficult reading is taken to be the genitive because it does not conform to Gen. 18:14 LXX (Metzger 1975: 130). However, it is possible that the dative should be read here because of the distribution of witnesses for that reading. Regardless, the sense of the passage is the same (this text-critical problem is not discussed in UBS[4]).

1:38. Γένοιτο as an aorist optative expresses not so much a wish as it expresses an acceptance that God may do with Mary what he wills.[56] The remark reflects an openness as to when God may do this. Thus, the sentence means, "Let this be whenever he pleases" (Godet 1875: 1.95).

1:38. Did Luke compose 1:38? The verse need not be seen as a Lucan redaction to stress the theme of Mary as obedient (but so R. Brown 1977: 316–19). In order to defend his "obedience" view, Brown must soften Jesus' remark in 8:19–21. In addition, some response in 1:38 by Mary is natural, given that the announcement comes in two stages. An indication of Mary's reaction is called for and expected. Brown overpresses the argument from form by insisting that it must always cohere in an exactly parallel manner, which is something that these announcements do not do. A variation does not require a conclusion of Lucan redaction.

---

56. Not, "I wish it would be to me according to your word," but, "let it be according to your word"; BDF §384; BDR §384.3; Fitzmyer 1981: 352.

3. Meeting of Mary and Elizabeth (1:39–45)

Mary and Elizabeth's meeting brings together John and Jesus as represented through their mothers. The account emphasizes Jesus' superiority, since the mother of the elder John blesses Jesus' mother. The fetal John testifies to Jesus' presence by leaping in Elizabeth's womb. Such fetal testimony recalls Gen. 25:22–26, though there are differences in the two passages (Wiefel 1988: 54; SB 2:100–101). Luke 1:39–45 is the union of fulfillment and sign, with Elizabeth functioning as the revealer of God's plan.[1]

The passage is also intimately linked with the hymn of 1:46–56. In fact, one could treat that passage as a part of this one, since the two events are associated with the same occasion. Nonetheless, a separation has been made, for this passage has the testimony of the Baptist's mother, while the next contains the testimony of Jesus' mother.

Sources and Historicity

The account's source is disputed. Many argue that Luke creates the scene to bring the two mothers together and to bring together his parallelism (Luce 1933: 91; R. Brown 1977: 251–52, 339–40; Fitzmyer 1981: 357–59). Luce reasons that this passage conflicts with Mark 1:9–10; Luke 3:21–22; 7:19; and especially John 1:29–34, where John the Baptist denies knowing the Messiah's identity. Discussed above in the additional note on 1:25, this problem is not an obstacle to the event's historicity.

Others argue that when the material came to Luke, this linkage was already present (Schürmann 1969: 69, esp. nn. 194–95; Ernst 1977: 81; Marshall 1978: 77; Wiefel 1988: 54; Machen 1930: 75–101). Schürmann argues that the passage's Semitisms, non-Lucan expressions, and Jewish parallels are against a Lucan composition (he mentions parataxis, the method of citing place-names, and the use of ἵνα as examples). Bultmann (1963: 296) also argues that the tradition came to Luke in this form, noting as evidence the lack of a specific allusion back to 1:36. It is possible that

---

1. Schürmann 1969: 64 notes that the sign of the leaping baby is explicit in the passage, while the fulfillment is implicitly presented in the sign. C. F. Evans 1990: 168 rightly calls this a "linchpin" passage.

Luke brought together this material with other infancy traditions, but there is no reason to regard it as a Lucan creation.

The outline of Luke 1:39–45 is as follows:

a. Mary's greeting (1:39–40)
   i. Setting (1:39)
   ii. Greeting (1:40)
b. Elizabeth's response (1:41–45)
   i. The baby's reaction: leaping (1:41a)
   ii. Elizabeth's explanation (1:41b–44)
   iii. Elizabeth's blessing (1:45)

Elizabeth functions as a prophetess, and Mary receives honor as the bearer of Messiah. Mary is an example, an object of God's grace. Her blessing is not because she has merit; rather, the reason for her blessing is the child. John the Baptist begins his prophetic function from the womb. The lesson is in the final remark: blessing comes to the one who has believed God. Mary's example of faith is to be emulated.

Exegesis and Exposition

[39]In those days, Mary rose up and went in haste into the hill country to a city of Judea. [40]She came to Zechariah's house and greeted Elizabeth.

[41]When Elizabeth heard Mary's greeting, the baby leapt in her womb, and Elizabeth was filled with the Holy Spirit, [42]and she exclaimed with a ⌜loud cry⌝, "Blessed are you among women, and blessed be the fruit of your womb. [43]How is it that the mother of my Lord comes to me? [44]For behold, when the greeting came into my ears, the baby in my womb leapt in joy. [45]Blessed is the one who believes that there shall be a fulfillment of what was spoken to her from the Lord."

a. Mary's Greeting (1:39–40)

Mary's visit to Elizabeth serves two literary purposes. First, it ties together the birth announcements, since John and Jesus are brought together. Second, it sets up the births of John and Jesus, since this account ends with Elizabeth in her ninth month (1:36, 56; Marshall 1978: 77; Klostermann 1929: 15). The note of praise celebrates fulfillment.

i. Setting (1:39)

Mary goes immediately to her relative's side. She had been told of Elizabeth's condition (1:36) and now travels to see God's sign. Her

1:39

journey is made with haste (μετὰ σπουδῆς, *meta spoudēs*) into the Judean hill country, to a city south of Jerusalem. The journey, covering 80–100 miles, would take three or four days (Schürmann 1969: 65 n. 164). Several reasons for this hasty journey have been posited (R. Brown 1977: 331). (1) Some suggest that Mary left to prevent the Nazareans from discovering her pregnancy. If this were the case, she would hardly return at the three-month period when she would just be revealing her condition, so this view is unlikely. (2) Hospodar (1956) suggests that hasty action is out of character for such a pious figure, so he translates the phrase μετὰ σπουδῆς "with serious intent." As R. Brown notes (1977: 331), the context suggests that Mary's haste reflects her obedience, so an unusual rendering of σπουδῆς is not required. (3) Mary's departure reflects an instant response to God's leading. This view is the most satisfying.

The city's location within Judah is unknown. The reference is very indefinite. Some argue for a reference to the "province of Judea," but that sense is not historically possible, for the term present here is not the term for "province" (ἐπαρχεία, *eparcheia*).[2] Rather Luke uses ὀρεινήν (*oreinēn*, hill country).[3] The exact location of the city is still a mystery (Schürmann 1969: 66). Luke's point is simply that Mary goes to greet Elizabeth.

ii. Greeting (1:40)

1:40 The meeting is initially described in simple terms. Mary comes to Zechariah's home and greets Elizabeth (ἀσπάζομαι, *aspazomai*, to greet; BAGD 116; BAA 233). Mary's arrival and the word of greeting bring a response of blessing and praise.

b. Elizabeth's Response (1:41–45)
i. The Baby's Reaction: Leaping (1:41a)

1:41a Elizabeth's response to Mary's greeting has three subjects: Mary and her child Jesus (1:42), Elizabeth and the response of her son (1:43–44), and Elizabeth's blessing of Mary (1:45; Godet 1875: 1.98). Mary's greeting brings a "leaping" response from the baby in the womb.[4] The term for leaping occurs in Gen. 25:22 of fetal move-

2. Fitzmyer 1981: 363; BAGD 283; BAA 574. But so argues Jeremias, *TDNT* 7:92 n. 29. Ἐπαρχεία is used in Acts 23:34 and 25:1.
3. BAGD 580; BAA 1175. Luke 1:39, 65 are the only two NT uses. Josephus, *Jewish War* 4.8.2 §451 has this use.
4. Καὶ ἐγένετο (or ἐγένετο δέ) with a verb is a common Lucan expression: 1:5, 8, 23, 41, 59; 2:1, 6; 6:1; 8:22; Fitzmyer 1981: 363; Klostermann 1929: 16–17. On the grammar with ἀκούω, where the genitive indicates the speaker and the accusative the thing heard, see BDF §173 and BDR §173.1–2. Luke 11:31 and 15:25 are grammatically parallel to 1:41.

ment and in Ps. 114:4 [113:4 LXX] of mountains leaping like rams. The fetal response recorded in Gen. 25 describes the struggle of Esau and Jacob for position within Rebekah (Talbert 1982: 22; R. Brown 1977: 332). Concerning this text, Marshall (1978: 80) correctly points out that the older serves the younger, but the parallel is not identical, since the Genesis image is of an internal struggle between twins (Schweizer 1984: 34). No such tension exists in Luke. A rabbinic parallel similar to this Genesis idea speaks of the fetuses of Jewish mothers at the exodus singing hymns at the parting of the sea.[5] The baby's response is taken as a sign by Elizabeth (1:44). Many speculate that Elizabeth's excitement caused fetal movement. But such attempts at physiological explanation miss the point of the narrative. John is seen as beginning his forerunner ministry by his response (1:15).

ii. Elizabeth's Explanation (1:41b–44)

As was noted above, some see the supernatural work of the unborn John's identification of Jesus as contradicting the teaching of the other Gospels about John not knowing Jesus (John 1:31; R. Brown 1977: 341, esp. n. 7). But does such an objection overpress the narrative? Elizabeth interprets the significance of the movement. She functions as a prophetess, declaring the divine significance of an action.[6] In addition, John's reference is about not knowing Jesus before the sign was given to him at the baptism (John 1:31). This remark may relate only to knowing Jesus' position in God's plan through the confirmation of a divine sign. John's later question whether Jesus was "the one who comes" (Luke 7:18–22) was raised because Jesus was not the kind of Messiah that John expected, causing him to wonder if he had it right (see the additional note on 1:25 and the exegesis of 7:18–20).

1:41b

Elizabeth is filled with the Holy Spirit as she speaks to Mary. Such filling is common in the infancy account as various people address the key figures of the account and explain God's plan (Zechariah in 1:67; Simeon in 2:27 is led by the Spirit). Thus, her response is not only an enthusiastic welcome of Mary, but it is a revelation of

5. *Y. Soṭa* 5.4 (20c) (= Neusner et al. 1982–93: 27.153); Creed 1930: 21; SB 2:101. The idea of singing babies does represent a major expansion of this motif, not paralleled in the OT or NT. On βρέφος as fetus, see Oepke, *TDNT* 5:637; BAA 293–94; Luke 1:44; Sir. 19:11. In later Judaism, Tg. Ps. 68:27 calls on the fetus in the womb to praise God, while Odes Sol. 28.2 speaks of a child leaping in the womb; Bovon 1989: 85 n. 35.

6. Friedrich, *TDNT* 6:835 §D.III.2, notes that Elizabeth is filled with the Spirit and cries out like a prophet, actions parallel to Anna in Luke 2 and to Zechariah in his hymn; see also Delling, *TDNT* 6:130.

God's mind. The Spirit for Luke is a Spirit who reveals, speaks, and guides (Luke 4:1; 12:12; Acts 15:28).

1:42   Elizabeth addresses Mary and explains the significance of the moment. A few features of the narrative deserve comment. First, is Elizabeth's reply to be viewed as a hymn? Plummer (1896: 27) lays the text out in two stanzas of four lines. Hendriksen (1978: 95) argues that the parallelism of 1:42 is appropriate for a hymn. R. Brown agrees and adds that the verb ἀναφωνεῖν (*anaphōnein*, to cry out) is used of liturgical singing in the LXX.[7] Fitzmyer (1981: 358) argues against the presence of a hymn since 1:43–44 is not poetic. It may also be added that the verb ἀναφωνεῖν and related constructions are used in Koine Greek of a solemn or significant announcement (MM 39; P. Fay. 14.2; LSJ 126; Gen. 27:34 LXX [using ἀνεβόησεν φωνήν]; Bovon 1989: 85 n. 38). Thus, a hymn is not likely here. Rather, the remark is a significant statement, opened with a solid refrain.

Second, how does Elizabeth know about the child that Mary bears? It is possible that Mary's greeting included more than a mere hello. Perhaps Mary said something that suggested she bore a special servant, a special dignitary of the Lord (Ellis 1974: 76; Windisch, *TDNT* 1:496, 500). If so, Luke chooses not to narrate it. Rather, he literarily leaves the impression that it is by the Holy Spirit that Elizabeth perceived who was visiting her (Fitzmyer 1981: 363; Hendriksen 1978: 94; Marshall 1978: 80; Schneider 1977a: 56).

Elizabeth initially addresses Mary as the "blessed among women." To be blessed is to receive special favor from God.[8] Usually the blessing is given as a wish, as in a benediction, but in this context God has already acted and Mary is already blessed. The phrase ἐν γυναιξίν (*en gynaixin*) can be taken as comparative (more blessed among women) or superlative (most blessed among women) (for options, see BDF §245.3). Mary is specially blessed because of the child that she will bear. She is a special vessel, chosen by God's grace (Fitzmyer 1981: 364; Godet 1875: 1.98–99; Schürmann 1969: 67–68). In either sense, and the choice is not clear, the use of the phrase itself does not denote Mary as more blessed than any other woman ever. The phrase functions almost proverbially and was also used of others: Jael (Judg. 5:24) and Judith (Jdt. 13:18;

---

7. 1 Chron. 15:28; 16:4, 5, 42; 2 Chron. 5:13; R. Brown 1977: 333. On the verb, also see O. Betz, *TDNT* 9:303 n. 7, who makes the same association.

8. Bertram, *TDNT* 4:366 n. 36 and 367; Luke 1:28; Matt. 21:9; 25:34; Ps. 1:1; Deut. 33:29; Isa. 56:2. Bovon 1989: 86 notes that the Gospel starts with blessing on Mary and Jesus, while it ends with blessing on the disciples (24:50).

R. Brown 1977: 333). In each context the mother is bearing or being a deliverer for the nation (cf. Song 1:8; 1QapGen 20.6–7). Elizabeth knows that Mary has been graciously chosen to bear the Deliverer. Luke 11:27–28, depicting an event that only Luke records, argues against making too much of Mary's status, since what counts is obeying God.[9]

Elizabeth also blesses the child. The idiom *fruit of the womb* is a Hebraism (R. Brown 1977: 333). In the OT, a fruitful womb was considered a blessing from God and was related to faithful obedience to God (Deut. 7:13; 28:1, 4; contrast Lam. 2:20) or to God's sovereign provision (Gen. 30:2). The child Mary bore was special.

Elizabeth counts it an honor to be a part of these events. Her question, "How has this come upon me?" expresses her humility. How is she worthy to share in this visit and in these events? This expression shares OT parallels in 2 Sam. 6:9 (the ark of the covenant returns to David) and 24:21 (Araunah at King David's visit). However, to suggest that Mary is a type of the ark (Laurentin 1967: 91–94) is too subtle, in that the ark for David was a cause for fear, not joy, since that ark was an instrument of God's judgment (so correctly R. Brown 1977: 344). Araunah's response is more illustrative of Elizabeth's tone of amazement. **1:43**

The description of Mary as ἡ μήτηρ τοῦ κυρίου μου (*hē mētēr tou kyriou mou*, the mother of my Lord) has also caused some discussion. Alford (1874: 449) argues that Jesus' divine nature is alluded to here. But such a comprehensive understanding of Jesus this early in his ministry is unlikely. Rather, the term κύριος is a term of respect for distinguished people of various types (Danker 1988: 41). Elizabeth sees the child as her superior and so speaks of "my Lord." Most opt for a messianic perception in the term (Klostermann 1929: 17; R. Brown 1977: 344; Plummer 1896: 29; Hendriksen 1978: 96). Elizabeth's focus is not on Mary, but on the child, as the following explanation makes clear (γάρ, *gar*, for; 1:44). There is no need to posit a presentation of Mary as "queen mother" (Stanley 1959–60). Such regal motifs do not exist anywhere in Luke's presentation of Mary. Also, the liturgical phrase *mother of God*, which alludes to this verse, overstates what the verse says.[10] Though the title *Lord* will take on significant proportions in the latter part of the Gospel, here the term is one of messianic respect. Elizabeth marvels that Messiah visits her and that her relative bears this significant child. She does not take the visit of her Lord as an everyday, insignificant matter.

9. Talbert 1982: 24 traces Luke's portrayal of Mary and notes that she is set forth as a model disciple who obeys God's Word; Luke 1:38; 8:19–21; 11:27–28; Acts 1:14.
10. R. Brown 1977: 344 n. 17 notes the allusion to this verse in the *Ave Maria*.

1:44   Luke explains (γάρ) Elizabeth's blessing and her sense of amazement that the mother of her Lord is present. The combination ἰδοὺ γάρ (*idou gar*) is common in Luke (Luke 1:44, 48; 2:10; 6:23; 17:21; Acts 9:11; otherwise only 2 Cor. 7:11) and brings emphasis to Elizabeth's declaration. It is a "for behold" declaration (Marshall 1978: 81–82; Fitzmyer 1981: 365; R. Brown 1977: 333–34). She tells Mary that upon hearing her greeting the baby leapt with joy in her womb.[11] The term ἀγαλλιάσει (*agalliasei*, joy) is significant because of its earlier association with John the Baptist. Its mention here recalls 1:14 and anticipates 1:47, where Mary rejoices in God her Savior. It expresses joy related to salvation (Fitzmyer 1981: 365; Bultmann, *TDNT* 1:19–21). Joy is engendered by these salvific events. Elizabeth feels honored to be used of God.

John's leap suggests that he has initiated his work as the forerunner (1:15). Hendriksen (1978: 97) expresses doubts whether John's action is conscious, arguing that such speculation and discussion are not the narrative's point. Rather, Elizabeth is seen as the interpreter of the baby's movements. Luke clearly intends the reader to see the movement as special and significant by his remark in 1:15, but beyond this connection, Hendriksen says, it is wise not to go. However, Luke's thrust is on the divine sign present in the baby's action and the motive attributed to his action; that is, that the baby responds with joy (ἐν ἀγαλλιάσει). Elizabeth introduces the idea of motive for the baby, so Luke clearly wishes the reader to perceive that the action belongs to the child as forerunner. Though John's consciousness is certainly not an explicit point, the action belongs to the child. Jesus' superiority to John is clearly set forth in the action and recalls the allusion to being filled from the womb in 1:15.

iii. Elizabeth's Blessing (1:45)

1:45   Elizabeth gives a final blessing to Mary for her faith. She expresses her own confidence that God will bring to pass everything he revealed. Μακαρία (*makaria*) addresses Mary as fortunate, happy, or blessed.[12] It is the first beatitude in the Gospel.[13] There is something laudable and beneficial in faith. Elizabeth expresses the beatitude in a generalized form when she uses the participle ἡ πιστεύσασα (*hē pisteusasa*, the one who believes), rather than using a

---

11. On κοιλία as womb, see Behm, *TDNT* 3:787. The only NT uses of the term σκιρτάω are in 1:41, 44; 6:23. The context of joy for each of the uses is consistent with Lucan usage; Fitzer, *TDNT* 7:402.

12. R. Brown 1977: 333; Danker 1988: 41; BAGD 486; BAA 988 §1b; Luke 6:20–22.

13. Plummer 1896: 30. Other beatitudes are 6:20–22; 7:23; 10:23; 11:27–28; 12:37–38, 43; 14:14–15; 23:29.

second-person direct address, "Blessed are you" (Klostermann 1929: 17). This expression makes Mary an example of faith. She stands in contrast to Zechariah, who was rebuked for lacking trust (1:20). The theme of obeying God's word or responding to it in faith occurs in other Lucan texts that involve Mary (8:21; 11:27–28).

The thought of the certain completion of God's promise is related to Elizabeth's blessing of Mary. The nature of the thought's connection to the blessing of Mary is disputed. Some treat the ὅτι (*hoti*) clause as giving the content of Mary's faith: "Blessed is the one who believes *that* fulfillment will come" (Marshall 1978: 82, notes that Acts 27:25 is parallel to this verse and supports this rendering). Others treat the ὅτι clause as causal, giving the reason why Mary is blessed: "Blessed is the one who believes, *because* the fulfillment will come" (Plummer 1896: 30; Creed 1930: 22; Hendriksen 1978: 97–98). This approach argues that a causal connection is clearer in that Mary is blessed because God will perform an act. Also, in 1:49 the relationship between blessing and the ὅτι clause is one of blessing followed by God's action (Alford 1874: 450). But reading a content ὅτι here is natural, since Mary is blessed for her response. Her hymn in 1:46–55 evidences her faith. Although the choice is difficult, a content nuance is more likely. Mary's blessing as a faithful one is a result of her trust that God will act.

God's word coming to completion is part of Luke's fulfillment motif. The key term is τελείωσις (*teleiōsis*, completion, fulfillment). It refers to the final execution or completion of God's promises. Once again, trusting in fulfillment is emphasized. God's promise, conveyed by the angel Gabriel in 1:31–35, is what Mary believes will occur and is the ground for her being blessed. She believes God's promise that she will bear the messianic child. The fulfillment of promise to her is the reader's assurance that the rest of God's promise will come to pass.

Summary

Two themes dominate this section. The first stresses faith in God's promise and word. Mary is a forerunner of the true believer who trusts and responds to God's word (Schneider 1977a: 56). The second is the realization that blessing is grounded in God's bringing his promises to completion. Some aspects of the promise awaited fulfillment at the time of Luke's writing (just as they await fulfillment today). Luke writes to assure Theophilus about such promises (1:3–4). Part of the assurance comes from knowing what God has done already, so one can trust in what God will do. Blessing comes to those who rely on those promises. To share in the events that Jesus brings is an honor worthy of joy and praise. Mary is the example of one with faith. Elizabeth pictures the joy a participant in salvation should have. Together they show that trust and joy are a vital part of a walk with God. Their shared joy pictures how the believing community should respond together, since they also partake in the blessings that come from Jesus.

Additional Notes

1:39. Where is the city of Judea? Two locations have been the center of speculation, although neither commends itself. (1) The traditional location as far back as the sixth century is ʿAin Karim, some five miles west of Jerusalem. This site has a long history as the home of Zechariah, but there is no way to confirm the tradition. (2) Taking Ἰούδα as an indeclinable noun, another view suggests Juttah, five miles south of Hebron. This view goes back to A. Reeland in 1714 (Plummer 1896: 28). Again, there is no way to confirm such an identification. (3) R. Brown (1977: 332) suggests that Luke drew the reference from 2 Sam. 2:1. But why create such a detail? The place is not exploited at all; thus there was no rationale for creating the detail. Despite uncertainty about the exact locale, R. Brown (1977: 332) and Marshall (1970: 71) note that the reference to Judea does not reflect a geographical error, as Conzelmann argues (1960: 69). Judea can have a regional sense, as Roman materials show (Tacitus, *Annals* 12.54; so Ἰουδαία in Luke 4:44 and Γαλιλαία in Mark 1:39).

1:42. A small textual problem concerns *loud cry*. Some manuscripts (A, D, Ψ, family 1, Byz) read φωνῇ (voice), while others (B, L, W, Origen) read κραυγῇ (loud cry). A third reading (supported by א, C, Θ, family 13) has a different verb, ἀνεβόησεν (he cried out) with φωνῇ, but the evidence for this reading is weak (O. Betz, *TDNT* 9:303 n. 7, appears to accept this reading). Though the external evidence is not overwhelming, most regard κραυγῇ as the more difficult reading and see the use of φωνῇ as a return to Luke's more common term, especially since κραυγῇ could be regarded as harsh in this context (Plummer 1896: 29). It is possible, however, that φωνῇ should be read, since it has Western and Byzantine support. Κραυγῇ is perhaps a stronger term since it suggests a significant announcement made "with a loud cry."[14] The reading is hard to determine, but the meaning is little altered by the choice.

1:43. The syntax of the question is a little unusual. One needs to supply γέγονεν to fill out the idea of the sentence.[15] Also, ἵνα explains τοῦτο in

---

14. Rom. 8:15; John 1:15; Mark 9:24; Marshall 1978: 81. The dative here is a dative of means; BDR §198.4–5.

15. Plummer 1896: 29; Marshall 1978: 81. BDF §189.3 speaks of an ellipsis in the verse.

the question and indicates that Elizabeth sees Mary's visit in particular as significant in that she is the mother of the Lord.[16] Thus: "From where has come about this thing, that is, that the mother of my Lord comes to me?"

1:45. Τελείωσις has four possible meanings in the LXX: (1) execution of a plan (2 Chron. 29:35); (2) completion in the sense that nothing need be added (Sir. 34:8); (3) completion of a task (e.g., a building; 2 Macc. 2:9); and (4) one who is sexually mature.[17] In Luke 1:45, the first sense is present.

---

16. Plummer 1896: 29. Luke 10:11 and 12:39 are syntactically parallel but use ὅτι, not ἵνα; BDF §394; BDR §394.3.3. Ἵνα is epexegetical.

17. This last meaning must be clearly indicated by the context, as in Jer. 2:2 (A, B); Delling, *TDNT* 8:85.

4. Mary's Praise:
The *Magnificat* (1:46–56)

Elizabeth's blessing produces a reaction from Mary. She bursts into praise, offering a hymn of thanksgiving. The hymn gives thanks for God's gracious dealings with her, actions that reflect how he has treated humanity through all generations. The hymn has a very nationalistic focus, which fits its setting. The point is that God's mercy and power are exercised for the humble who fear him. The hymn adds to the note of joy and thankfulness present in 1:39–45. It reveals the mood of those who share in God's blessing, as well as makes clear that Mary partakes richly from God's consistent character. Mary speaks for herself and echoes the feelings of the community at the same time. God is worthy of praise for what he will do in taking care of his own.

Sources and Historicity

The source of the hymn is a much discussed and controversial matter (Farris 1985 is the most detailed recent study of the hymns in 1:46–55, 68–79; 2:29–32). Five options exist:

1. The hymn is a free composition by Luke (Harnack 1900; evaluated by Machen 1930: 75–86). This position has seen a recent resurgence.[1] The argument says that the hymn imitates the LXX, while its many allusions and themes fit the larger emphases of Luke. Farris (1985: 14–30) examines the stylistic argument behind this view and shows that it is not likely (such hymns are lacking elsewhere in Luke–Acts). Repetition of themes is not sufficient grounds for establishing authorship.

2. The hymn is an adaptation of a Jewish hymn of praise (Gunkel 1921). This view is based on the presence of Semitisms in the passage, noting the hymn's nationalistic perspective.[2] Winter (1954) contends that the source was a hymn of the Maccabean period. But this view fails to win acceptance because the praise of the hymn is

---

1. Drury 1976: 49–51 and Tannehill 1974; earlier Cadbury 1958: 192–93. For a fuller list, see Farris 1985: 15.

2. Schürmann 1969: 78 at nn. 259–60, though holding a different view, raises the Semitism issue.

so Davidic in character and the Hasmonean leaders were Levites (Farris 1985: 86–89).

3. The hymn is an adaptation from a source that concentrated on the Baptist (Bultmann 1963: 296–97; Klostermann 1929: 15–16; Grundmann 1963: 63). With this view often comes the additional opinion that Elizabeth was the original speaker of the hymn, an issue examined below. The major argument is that the hymn is more natural on the lips of an older woman who was barren than in the mouth of a younger expectant mother. It is also argued that the Baptist is the focus of this pericope. But the textual evidence for Elizabeth as speaker is weak (see n. 9), and the hymn's emphasis is on Davidic roots and a second figure superior to John. No amount of editing can remove these obstacles without so altering the hymn as to make the position unacceptable (Farris 1985: 91–94).

4. The hymn comes from a Jewish-Christian source, perhaps from the "poor" (the *Anawim*); this may be the most popular current view.[3] The emphases on God's raising the humble and on God's covenants are key to this view. R. Brown sees Luke taking an originally Jewish-Christian hymn and reapplying it to an earlier setting. Thus, Mary embodies the situation of the *Anawim* (the Christian poor like those in Jerusalem), as the group's condition parallels and is projected back into her setting. Brown sees 1:48 as redacted into the hymn. Although it is true that the hymn's perspective certainly is similar to the *Anawim* (see 6:20–23), there is nothing in the hymn that requires such a setting. The hymn fits naturally enough in the setting it describes. The major arguments for the view are (a) that most of the hymn's praise is general, (b) that the choice of Mary as the hymn's source is motivated by a certain view of biblical historicity, and (c) that the hymn appears to be inserted into the narrative.[4] None of these objections is decisive. (a) The general praise

3. R. Brown 1977: 346–55; Wiefel 1988: 57; Farris 1985: 86–98; Fitzmyer 1981: 359–62; Jones 1968; Bemile 1986: 36. Fitzmyer, agreeing with Winter and Schneider, notes that the hymn is parallel to the psalms in 1 Maccabees, the Qumran Thanksgiving hymns, and the Qumran War Scroll. The hymn also resembles the OT hymns of praise (Ps. 33, 47, 48, 113, 135, 136; one could add to the list 1 Sam. 2:1–10; Jon. 2:2–9 [2:3–10 MT]; Isa. 38:9–20; Tob. 8:15–17; and Sir. 51:1–12). Fitzmyer (p. 359) regards 1:48 as a Lucan insert. In fact, he seems favorable to R. Brown's position that the hymn emerged out of the Jewish-Christian community. Schneider 1977a: 56 sees a Hellenistic Jewish-Christian rewrite of Jewish material or a reworking by Luke himself; so also C. F. Evans 1990: 171–73.

4. Farris 1985: 14 makes the latter two charges. Grigsby 1984 argues that the aorist tenses of the hymn are against its proposed Marian setting and give evidence that the hymn was inserted by Luke. The *Magnificat*, he believes, originally was a Semitic hymn that came to Luke in Greek through the Jewish-Christian church, but Grigsby's approach ignores the hymn's Semitic roots and setting, as well as making too much of the aorist tenses. See the exegesis of 1:51 and n. 22 below.

may reflect the corporate solidarity that one feels with others who share God's mercy. Such generalization is natural to praise. One praises God not only for one's own blessings, but also for his similar treatment of all the faithful. (b) The charge about a certain view of the Bible may be true in some cases, but it is not in itself a reason to reject biblical claims. So this charge is *ad hominem*. Farris knows this and raises textual and historical reasons against a Marian connection that need evaluation. (c) The argument about insertion also proves nothing. Almost all agree that Luke combines sources; such weaving might have been necessary. Farris argues that one could remove the hymn and the story would fit nicely, but this proves only that Luke drew from a variety of materials, not that the sources must be postcross. An earlier source connection is possible.

5. The hymn goes back to Mary, either uttered in this situation or composed later to reflect a poetic description of what she thought or said in this situation. Many suggest the latter.[5] Marshall argues that the combination of eschatological hope and personal thanksgiving is Jewish in character. The hopes are Jewish rather than characteristically Christian, national rather than universal. The lack of Christian universal coloring suggests a pre-Christian hymn and makes Mary a possible candidate for composition, though not necessarily in this setting.

Machen notes the possibility that Mary composed the hymn later as a reflective response to Elizabeth's blessing (perhaps during her three-month stay). To insist on an extemporaneous hymn immediately in this setting is not necessary; an "instant" hymn would be the result of Mary's reflecting on the annunciation and conception before her coming to Elizabeth. Either option reflects a historical description of the event. What is clear is that the *Magnificat* is a pre-Christian hymn of nationalistic proportions and fits nicely into a setting before Jesus' ministry. There is no evidence of tampering by the Christian community, since postcross hymns and creeds are less nationalistic in tone (Eph. 1:3–14; 1 Tim. 3:16; 6:15–16; 2 Tim. 1:9–10). Accordingly, the event's historicity need not be rejected.[6] The hymn would naturally be retained and cherished in the Jewish-Christian church, so efforts to place the hymn in this setting have merit, provided they do not ignore the ultimate origin in Mary or someone in her family.

5. Machen 1930: 95–97; Marshall 1978: 79; Schürmann 1969: 79 (who argues that Mary is related to 1:46–49 and that the additional elements came from the community).

6. For a brief presentation of the argument that rejects historicity, see Luce 1933: 90.

Some find it difficult to attribute the hymn to Mary because of its poetic quality. Could a country girl compose such a work? However, given the existence of OT parallels from the Psalter and the influence of the singing of the Psalms in the popular culture, such a talent for composition need not be beyond Mary.[7] In sum, Mary cannot be ruled out as the source for this material.

It is clear that Elizabeth was not the original speaker of the hymn.[8] Nonetheless, the position that she was the speaker is popular enough to need treatment and critique. The position has historical roots, since a few manuscripts and church fathers attribute the hymn to Elizabeth.[9] The argument is that Elizabeth's barren position parallels the OT hymn of Hannah, as does the reference to the woman's humble state. It is natural for Elizabeth to give praise here and then for Zechariah to do so in 1:68–79. Some argue that the mention of Mary in 1:56 implies a change of subject.

All these arguments can be refuted (Marshall 1978: 78). Elizabeth's offering the hymn is not natural after the tone of her blessing on Mary; it would be self-serving. Luke 1:48 need not refer to barrenness. Luke 1:48b, with its promise of generations of praise, is exaggerated if it describes Elizabeth. A reply from Elizabeth is more natural at 1:25, not here. The repetition of the speaker's name in 1:56 has OT precedent (Num. 24:25; Deut. 32:44; 2 Sam. 2:1). Seeing the hymn as evidence of Mary's response to Elizabeth and as a reflection of Mary's faith is quite natural. The hymn is so loaded with OT parallels that to focus on Hannah is not appropriate. The textual evidence for the variant is weak. The effort to gain parallelism through Elizabeth destroys a chiasmus in the structure (Wiefel 1988: 58):

a proclamation to Zechariah (1:5–25)
b proclamation to Mary (1:26–38)
b′ Mary's hymn (1:46–56)
a′ Zechariah's hymn (1:67–80)

---

7. Godet 1875: 1.100–101 may overstate the case, but his point about the exposure of the populace to the Psalter is well taken; Hendriksen 1978: 101.

8. But so argues Creed 1930: 22–23, who draws on the position of Harnack. Also in favor of this view are Danker 1988: 41; Klostermann 1929: 17–18; Bultmann 1963: 296–97; and Luce 1933: 91–92.

9. Three Old Latin manuscripts (a, b, and l*) attest to Elizabeth, as does the Latin version of Irenaeus, *Against Heresies* 4.7.1. Jerome refers to this view as contained in Origen's seventh homily on Luke. About A.D. 400 Niceta of Remesiana (in the area of the former Yugoslavia) knows of this reading (*De Psalmodiae Bono* 76 or 9.11). Wiefel 1988: 56 and Fitzmyer 1981: 365–66 note the texts. Farris 1985: 108–13 has a detailed look at the issue, as does Bemile 1986: 5–19. Bemile correctly notes that the testimony of the fathers is for Mary (pp. 12 and 266–68 nn. 54–61), including Irenaeus, *Against Heresies* 3.10.2; Tertullian, *On the Soul* 26; and Athanasius, *In Lucam* (*PG* 3:26:1393).

The desire to have both the father and mother speak probably produced the textual variant by a copyist, who thought that that was the likely structure. All these factors show Mary to be the original speaker.

Though it is called an "eschatological hymn" by Gunkel (1921), a better description of the form is "hymn of praise" or "psalm of thanksgiving." The personal nature of the praise, the general appeal to God's actions, and the absence of a call to praise, as is present in eschatological hymns, suggest this classification.[10] One of a very few NT psalms (perhaps the longest in the NT is Eph. 1:3–14), the hymn is full of joy for God's actions. The outline of Luke 1:46–56 is as follows:

a. Mary's hymnic response of praise (1:46–55)
   i. Praise for God's work for Mary (1:46–49)
   ii. Praise for God's acts to all (1:50–53)
   iii. Praise for God's acts for his people Israel (1:54–55)
b. Departure: three months and then home (1:56)

The hymn proper has three parts: 1:46–49 focuses on God's actions for Mary the humble woman; 1:50–53 generalizes God's acts to include God-fearers, proud, humble, hungry, and rich;[11] 1:54–55 repeats the covenant context and highlights God's faithfulness to his promises to Israel.

10. Farris 1985: 67–85 surveys the parallel examples in the OT and Judaism; Berger 1984: 242–43; Fitzmyer 1981: 359; Schneider 1977a: 56–58. Bovon 1989: 82–83 notes that the *Magnificat* focuses on the victory of the righteous; it does not praise God as Creator, as do the Qumranic hymns, and has less harsh criticism of enemies than do the Psalms of Solomon. Bovon notes many verbal parallels to the Psalms of Solomon:

Motif	Magnificat	Psalms of Solomon
fearing God	1:50	2.33; 3.12; 4.23; 15.13
Israel or the nation as servant	1:54	12.6; 17.21
Abraham and his descendants	1:55	18.3
the proud	1:51	2.1–31; 17.13, 23
contrast of rich and poor	1:53	5.11
reversal	1:52	11.4
refrain	1:50	13.12
power of God	1:51	17.3
arm of God	1:51	13.2
God's seeing	1:48	18.2
God's help	1:54	16.3, 5
God's remembering	1:54	10.1, 4
God's speaking	1:55	11.7

11. The focus on the covenant and the God-fearer is key, for it shows that Luke is not generalizing about all people here, but about those in covenant with God through faith. Thus, the hymn is not a political manifesto.

There are many themes in the passage. God is merciful to those who fear him. God's power overcomes the proud. God exalts the humble. God responds to the hungry with his hands open. God resists the proud rich. The contrasting fates of the rich and the poor picture "eschatological reversal," where God's ultimate justice is hoped for and declared as coming in his actions. God mercifully keeps his promise to his people Israel.

Personal themes also exist. Mary exemplifies a life of praise and faith in God's word. The faithful are blessed, because God will bring his promises to completion. The passage stresses the readiness to praise God for the constant character of his goodness manifested in a variety of ways to the faithful. Confident faith knows that God will resolve issues of justice in his coming and in his judgment. The *Magnificat* is rich in describing God's attributes, not as abstractions, but in terms of his everyday actions. Assurance comes from knowing that God acts in this way: faithful to his word and stretching out his mighty hand for those who stand humbly before him.

Exegesis and Exposition

46 And Mary said,
> "My soul magnifies the Lord.
47 My spirit has begun to delight in God my Savior,
48   for he has looked upon his lowly servant.

> "For behold, from now on all generations shall call me blessed;
49   for the Mighty One did great things for me,
> and holy is his name.
50   His mercy is from generation to generation to those who fear him.

51 "He exercised power with his arm,
>   and scattered the proud in the thoughts of their hearts.
52 Powers were cast down;
>   he exalted the humble.
53 He has filled the hungry with good things;
>   the rich he sent away empty.

54 "He helped Israel, his servant,
>   because he remembered mercy
55 to Abraham and his seed forever,
>   even as he spoke to our fathers."

⁵⁶Mary remained with her three months and returned home.¹²

a. Mary's Hymnic Response of Praise (1:46–55)
i. Praise for God's Work for Mary (1:46–49)

1:46 Mary offers praise to the Lord in a hymn called the *Magnificat*, a name reflecting the Latin translation of the term μεγαλύνει (*megalynei*, magnifies). The hymn has numerous phrases that recall wording in OT and apocryphal hymns. The strongest literary parallel to the hymn is Hannah's word of praise in 1 Sam. 2:1–10. The praise of God by women occurs often in the OT (e.g., Deborah in Judg. 5).¹³ Mary's hymn contains personal and eschatological praise.

Mary begins her praise with parallelism common to hymnic genre. The parallelism extends into 1:47, linking 1:46–47 together. The phrase ἡ ψυχή μου (*hē psychē mou*, my soul), which is another way to refer to the personal praise that comes from deep inside a person, is in synonymous parallelism to τὸ πνεῦμά μου (*to pneuma mou*, my spirit) in 1:47. Ἡ ψυχή μου is another way to say, "I extol the Lord" (Marshall 1978: 82). Old Testament parallels include Ps. 35:9 [34:9 LXX] (which has a ψυχή reference to the self); Hab. 3:18; and 1 Sam. 2:1–2. The latter two texts match more the spirit than the wording of this Lucan text.

The verb μεγαλύνω means "to make great, to praise, to extol" and so parallels the idea of rejoicing in 1:47. Mary lifts up the Lord God as she praises his work on her behalf (1:38). Old Testament parallels include Ps. 34:3 [33:4 LXX] and 69:30 [68:31 LXX]. Luke also uses μεγαλύνω in Acts 5:13 (of the apostles); 10:46 and 19:17 (both of God) (Plummer 1896: 31; Grundmann, *TDNT* 4:543). The reference to the Lord addresses God as the sovereign Master and Ruler of the world. The address shows that Mary's approach to God reflects her awareness of her humble position (1:48).

---

12. I lay out the hymn in thought units so the parallelisms are visible. Note the chiasmus in 1:52–53: powers–humble–hungry–rich. This declaration of eschatological reversal in very rhetorical style also opens the hymn (1:46–48). With the refrain about the generations, the hymn broadens its worldview to include all who trust God. God's commitment to Israel and to his promise closes the passage. The parallelism in the passage is both synonymous (as in the opening line) and antithetical (as in the opposition of the hungry and the rich). The best discussion of structure is Bemile 1986: 37–62, esp. 47.

13. Charts detailing the various OT parallels in the hymn can be found in Plummer 1896: 30–31; Klostermann 1929: 18–19; and R. Brown 1977: 358–60. The fullest chart including Qumran parallels is Bemile 1986: 116–33. For the connection to 1 Sam. 2, see Goulder 1989: 225–29, who also notes parallels to Ps. 88 and 102.

Mary repeats her praise, as her spirit rejoices in the Lord. Πνεῦμα **1:47**
(*pneuma*, spirit) functions in this verse as ψυχή did in the last verse,
as a personal reference (Gen. 6:3; Ps. 143:4 [142:4 LXX]). These
terms are often linked in parallelism (Job 12:10; Ps. 77:3–4 [76:3–4
LXX]; Isa. 26:9; Wis. 15:11; R. Brown 1977: 336; Marshall 1978: 82;
Fitzmyer 1981: 366).

Mary offers praise to God her Savior. The picture of God the deliverer is common in the OT (Ps. 25:5; Isa. 12:2; Mic. 7:7; Fitzmyer
1981: 367). Hendriksen (1978: 103–4) tries to define "deliverer" primarily in spiritual terms, but the hymn itself spells out the deliverance in terms of eschatological reversal and the promises to Israel.[14] Mary's language is best taken in the national categories in
which it is introduced, though of course such language has spiritual
implications.[15]

Mary rejoices in God her Savior. The verb of praise, ἠγαλλίασεν
(*ēgalliasen*, rejoiced), is a term of eschatological rejoicing, as 1:14
and especially 1:44 suggest. God's special work produces this rejoicing. An unusual feature, however, is that ἠγαλλίασεν is aorist (or
past) tense, while the parallel verb μεγαλύνει in 1:46 is present tense.
Fitzmyer (1981: 366) argues that the parallelism intends a "timeless" or gnomic aorist and nothing more in the verb.[16] He rejects any
attempt to posit a Semitic original behind the hymn, an unfortunate
position in light of the hymn's setting. Surely the possibility of such
a setting should be considered, not quickly dismissed.

Other explanations for the aorist include the following: (1) it is
an ingressive aorist translated "my spirit has begun to delight" (Nolland 1989: 69; see BDF §331); (2) it reflects a Hebrew *waw* consecutive translated as an English present tense;[17] and (3) it is intended
to refer to initial reaction at the conception of the child or at the
message of the angel (Godet 1875: 1.102). In favor of this last approach it could be argued that chiasmus is present:

present tense	Mary lifts up the Lord (1:46b)
past tense	she praised her Savior (1:47)
past tense	he saw her humble position (1:48a)
future tense	all the generations shall praise her (1:48b)

14. Applying the remarks only to the church is exactly what Luke did not do!

15. Plummer 1896: 32. The remarks made here are always true of God's character (1:50) and apply to anyone who shares in the promise of the covenant.

16. BDF §333.2; BDR §333.1b.6, §331.1. The frequency of such tense shifts in
Hebrew poetry is demonstrated by Buth 1984, who argues, on the basis of this feature, that the hymn was originally in Hebrew.

17. Zerwick 1963: 85 §260; Wiefel 1988: 58. Nolland 1989: 69 also sees this as
possible.

The present, backward, and forward reference in these verses seems possible, but the major feature against it is the parallelism.

The best explanation is to take the aorist in an ingressive sense (view 1), since if a present had been intended it could have been written to make an exact parallelism explicit. If taken in this sense, verses 46–47 together mean that Mary praises the Lord now, even as she has begun to find eschatological joy in her Savior God. Such a rendering suggests that Jesus' story is just beginning. The ingressive influences the precise force because it emphasizes more clearly not just that Mary stands praising her God (which a present tense would emphasize), but that she has entered into praise, because of what he has done. From the call to praise, Mary turns in 1:48 to review what God has done for her.

1:48 Mary sets forth the basis, ὅτι (*hoti*, for), of her praise. God has been gracious to look upon his lowly servant. The verb ἐπέβλεψεν (*epeblepsen*, he looked upon) refers to God's loving care in selecting Mary to bear the child. The OT also uses the idea of God's looking on his own in acts of love (1 Sam. 1:11; 9:16); Luke 9:38 also uses the verb to express a call to Jesus for compassion for a sick son (Marshall 1978: 82). The aorist tense refers back to the event of messianic conception.

Mary describes herself as God's handmaiden (the repetition of δούλης connects this verse to 1:38), which acknowledges her subordinate position before God. She did not expect or assume that she should be the object of such special attention from God, so she is grateful for the attention. She also describes herself as of "low status," which term (ταπείνωσιν, *tapeinōsin*) many see as a more natural reference to barrenness. Seeking support from OT parallels in 1 Sam. 1:11, Gen. 16:11, and especially Gen. 29:31–32, they argue that the term is more suitable for Elizabeth.[18] But the term can also quite naturally refer to one's low social position, as Luke 1:52 makes clear. In fact, the social terminology throughout the hymn argues for a broader reference here and supports an original reference to Mary (Alford 1874: 450; Godet 1875: 1.102; Grundmann, *TDNT* 8:21). Ταπείνωσις as social-status terminology also has OT parallels to describe both Israel and individuals (Gen. 29:32; Deut. 26:7; 1 Sam. 9:16; 2 Sam. 16:12; 2 Kings 14:26; Ps. 9:13 [9:14 LXX]; 25:18 [24:18 LXX]; 31:7 [30:8 LXX]). This use also has parallels in Judaism (Jdt. 6:19; 2 Esdr. [= 4 Ezra] 9:45; Nolland 1989: 69). Mary is able to praise God her Savior, because he looked

18. See the discussion of sources in this unit. Klostermann 1929: 19; Luce 1933: 92; Danker 1988: 43; and Creed 1930: 23. The term can be translated "humiliation" (James 1:10; Acts 8:33), as well as "humble state."

upon her low social state and yet in love let her bear the Messiah. What God did for her is like what he does for others in the same state (1:52).

Mary recognizes that God has given her a special place by having her bear the Messiah. She explains, γάρ (*gar*, for), that generations of all time, πᾶσαι αἱ γενεαί (*pasai hai geneai*, all generations), shall bless her. They, too, shall perceive her fortune in receiving this special role. She is an example of one graced by God, an example of faith (Fitzmyer 1981: 367; Gen. 30:13 is a conceptual parallel). Elizabeth's blessing in Luke 1:45 is the first of many blessings that Mary receives as an exemplary servant touched by grace.

The expression *from now on* (ἀπὸ τοῦ νῦν, *apo tou nyn*) is an important Lucan phrase. It indicates that a significant change has taken place in God's plan, so that "from now on" things will be different (Luke 5:10; 12:52; 22:18, 69; Acts 18:6). Once Mary is touched by the gracious act of God, things are different (Stählin, *TDNT* 4:1111, 1113). They are never the same.

The promise of future blessing as indicated by the future tense has one other implication. It shows that the aorists in 1:47–48 are not prophetic and thus do not refer to future events, but to past ones. If future events were intended by the aorists, then this verb would be in the past tense as well (Farris 1985: 117).

Mary gives a second reason, ὅτι (*hoti*, for), for her praise (the first is in 1:48): the Mighty One acts both on her behalf and on behalf of God-fearers. Marshall (1978: 83) relates ὅτι to 1:48b and argues that the verse gives the reason she will be called blessed by all generations (with Schürmann 1969: 74). However, the reasons in 1:49 focus on God's attributes of power, exalted holiness, and mercy—descriptions designed to focus attention on God, not on Mary. Thus, Mary explains why she praises God, a connection that looks back to 1:47 (Fitzmyer 1981: 367–68; Farris 1985: 118). **1:49**

The reference to God as the Mighty One (ὁ δυνατός, *ho dynatos*) recalls 1:35 and alludes to his power in creating the child and giving Mary this role (Godet 1875: 1.103). What God promised and what seemed impossible (1:37) was possible for God, as he delivered on his commitment (Deut. 10:21; 34:11 [of the exodus]; Ps. 71:19 [70:19 LXX] [of the "great things" his power does]; Grundmann, *TDNT* 4:531). For such power exercised on her behalf, Mary gives praise and others will bless her. The title *Mighty One* often alludes in the OT and in Judaism to the warrior God who fights on behalf of his people and delivers them (Ps. 44:4–8; 89:9–10; 112:2, 9; Zeph. 3:17; 2 Macc. 3:24; 3 Macc. 5:51; R. Brown 1977: 337; Wiefel 1988: 59; Schürmann 1969: 74). In Luke, God creatively exercises his power to deliver his people.

The exercise of God's power demonstrates his authority as an exalted, holy ruler. Holiness means to be set apart. As the rest of the hymn stresses, God is holy, not in the sense that his holy moral attributes receive praise, but in the sense that he displays his unique sovereign authority as ruler over people. Such emphasis on sovereignty is also present in the OT (Ps. 99:3; 111:9; Lev. 11:44–45 [giving the covenant ground of such holiness and stressing God's unique holiness as deliverer]; Isa. 57:15). As Mary sets forth the high sovereign authority of God, his acts on her behalf take on a more gracious light.

ii. Praise for God's Acts to All (1:50–53)

1:50 Mary turns from describing the ground of her praise in terms of God's holiness to a consideration of his mercy. One attribute leads into the other. God's unique character is not separable from his mercy, for holiness expresses itself in mercy. Ἔλεος (*eleos*, mercy) is used in the LXX to translate the Hebrew term חֶסֶד (*ḥesed*), which refers to the loyal, gracious, faithful love that God has in covenant for his people (Ps. 103:2–6, 8–11, 13, esp. 17; R. Brown 1977: 337; Marshall 1978: 83; Schürmann 1969: 75; Bultmann, *TDNT* 2:483 n. 95; see also Ps. Sol. 15.13). Such gracious faithfulness characterizes God's dealings with those who acknowledge him. God's timeless and changeless faithfulness is behind the reference to "generation to generation," a phrase that appears in various ways in the OT (Ps. 49:11; 61:6; 90:1; 100:5; Isa. 51:8; the wording here is found in T. Levi 18.8).[19] Thus, what Mary experienced parallels what believers throughout time experience. Mary is counting on such faithfulness for future generations (1:54–55).

God's favor is specifically directed to those who fear God (τοῖς φοβουμένοις αὐτόν, *tois phoboumenois auton*). "Fearing God" and conceptual parallels are common OT descriptions of anyone who acknowledges God's position and authority (Deut. 7:9 [those who love God and keep his commandments follow his ways]; Ps. 25:12; 103:17; Isa. 55:3, 6; 57:15 [those of contrite (broken) heart seek God]). The description and others like it also existed in Judaism (Ps. Sol. 10.4 [of servants that God remembers with mercy]; 13.12; Plummer 1896: 32). Mary is a God-fearer who acknowledges the holy and exalted position of her God. The hymn shows the spirit of a God-fearer in recognizing the sovereignty of God (Danker 1988: 43; R. Brown 1977: 337; Josh. 24:14, 19–24). The picture of the God-

---

19. R. Brown 1977: 337; BDF §493.2; BDR §493.2–3; Büchsel, *TDNT* 1:663. This is called "distributive doubling." Schürmann 1969: 75 n. 231 prefers the translation "for many generations" with BDF.

fearer is common in Luke.[20] Those who see the most of God, says Mary, are those who acknowledge him. She has seen, as other God-fearers have seen, God's work and so she offers praise.

Luke 1:50 forms a transition in that Mary turns from a consideration of God's specific action for her (1:47–49) to a consideration of God's actions for his people (1:51–53). Such transitions from the individual (first-person singular) to the community (third-person plural) are common in the Psalms (Ps. 9, 30, 66, 68, 72, 117, 137; Nolland 1989: 71). In fact, one can see in these subsequent verses an expansion of the divine acts that apply to Mary, as the return to the theme of God's power in 1:51 makes clear (Schneider 1977a: 57). The acts of mercy described in 1:51–53 show that Mary is but one of many such blessed God-fearers. Luke wants his readers to appreciate this point, so they too might fear God and see him work. Such an identification with the promise of God's faithfulness should be assuring to the reader.

Mary turns from a consideration of God's mercy (1:50) to his acts **1:51** of power toward different groups of people. God's dealings with the proud and the mighty demonstrate his power toward those on the independent end of the social scale: he punishes the mighty, but lifts up the humble. God's exercise of power is described with anthropomorphism, comparing God's acts with the actions of people. Thus, the reference to the arm of God and the working of power points to the visible demonstration of God's authority.

The figure of God's arm is common in the OT (Deut. 4:34; Ps. 44:3; 89:13; 118:15; Hendriksen 1978: 107). The expressions ἐποίησεν κράτος (*epoiēsen kratos*, he performed mighty deeds) and ἐν βραχίονι αὐτοῦ (*en brachioni autou*, with his arm) are Semitisms (Isa. 53:1). Their presence here gives evidence that the hymn is not of Lucan or Greek origin (Luce 1933: 92). Reference to the power of God's arm appears in key texts describing God's work, especially in the exodus period (Exod. 6:1, 6; Deut. 3:24; 7:19; 2 Kings 17:36; Isa. 30:30).[21] God will extend his salvific power to those who fear him; no one can oppose him (Michaelis, *TDNT* 3:907).

Unlike the following verses, this line ("he exercised power with his arm") does not mention a specific group. So it refers back to "the generations who fear him" in 1:50b. It also introduces the discussion of various groups in 1:51–53 (R. Brown 1977: 337; Plummer 1896: 33). The referring back to 1:50b helps to define who the

---

20. Luke 12:5; 18:2, 4; 23:40. In Acts, the God-fearer is a person who respects God but does not know Jesus, often a non-proselyte Gentile favorable to God (10:2, 22, 35; 13:16, 26, 50 [probably]), or a Jew (16:14); Balz, *TDNT* 9:212–13.

21. Schlier, *TDNT* 1:639–40. God's arm is also an image for the second exodus (Ezek. 20:33–34; Isa. 51:5, 9; 53:1); Nolland 1989: 71.

poor, mighty, proud, humble, hungry, and rich are. These lines contrast those who are open and responsive to God with those who are not. Often the social circumstances of the powerful make them independent of and insensitive to God or to their fellow humans, while the poor often are more dependent on God (so also Paul in 1 Cor. 1:26–29).

The reference to God's powerful working by his arm is presented in the aorist tense, ἐποίησεν, along with the five verbs that follow in 1:51–53. This feature has generated much discussion, since the grammatical issue determines the meaning of the passage (Plummer 1896: 33 and Marshall 1978: 83–84 have summaries). To what is Mary referring? Views include the following:

1. Past events are under consideration here. This approach can take two forms. (a) Mary is referring to God's past acts for OT saints. Although this view is possible, it is not commonly held, because, despite the generalized form of the language here, the hymn seems to have specific groups and eschatological acts in mind. (b) The aorists reflect the context of an original Jewish-Christian hymn and refer to the work of Messiah Jesus in exalting the poor of the Christian church. This popular view has severe problems. Why is there an absence of specific messianic references? Why does the language describe a total political and social victory for Israel, which the resurrection set the stage for but did not as yet provide (Acts 3:19–22)? The victory mentioned in this hymn and the eschatological reversal of the proud and the humble had not totally occurred. According to this view, such a perspective was projected back into Mary's mouth as her utterance (R. Brown 1977: 352–53; Fitzmyer 1981: 361; Farris 1985: 120–21). However, the hymn's national focus is not entirely appropriate to the setting described by this view, especially since this victory is expressed in the past tense.

2. The aorists are gnomic aorists describing what God habitually does, and they should be translated as present tenses.[22] It is argued that 1:49 is a past event and that Luke could have expressed a future tense if he had wanted to do so. In favor of the position is the contrast to the future tense in 1:48b and the

---

22. BDF §333; Hendriksen 1978: 108, 112 defends this sense and cites Robertson 1923: 836–37, though Robertson says "maybe" to this view. For Grigsby 1984: 167 n. 29, this force is impossible, and he notes that the BDF discussion of the gnomic aorist does not mention the *Magnificat*. He apparently failed to read the fine-print portion of §333.2, where the hymn is mentioned. His omission undercuts the key reason he offers for rejecting a pre-Christian setting for the hymn.

supplied present tense in 1:50, which sets up the section. Hendriksen (1978: 108) lists a series of examples from the OT of God's lifting up the lowly in the past. Nevertheless, three problems exist for this approach. (a) This meaning of the aorist is rare in Hellenistic Greek. The present tense is much more natural for this sense (e.g., Hannah's song, 1 Sam. 2). (b) It tends to ignore the introduction of a future perspective by Mary's initial praise. The temporal note in 1:48b, "from now on" (ἀπὸ τοῦ νῦν, *apo tou nyn*), turns Mary's attention to the future and controls the discussion that follows, thus providing a key transition of thought. (c) Most importantly, this view ignores the theme of covenant fulfillment expressed in 1:54–55, a reference that looks at what Jesus will achieve in the future. This concluding reference supports 1:48b as a transition of perspective and nullifies the value of appealing to 1:50 as the key temporal reference.

3. The aorists are reflective of an iterative perfect in Hebrew; this position would also regard the verses as descriptive of God's standard of behavior toward humanity through time (Schmid 1960: 55). This view is possible, except that it seems not to deal adequately with the context of 1:54–55, which places the declarations of the hymn in terms of covenant promise to Abraham and its ultimate fulfillment.

4. The most satisfying approach is to take the aorists as prophetic aorists, that is, portraying the ultimate eschatological events tied to Jesus' final victory. These consequences result from his past conception (1:49). These events are seen as so certain that, even though they are future events, they can be portrayed as past realities. Paul has this force with the verb *glorified* in Rom. 8:30. Such an approach unifies the context and ties together nicely with the idea of the realization of the covenant promise to Abraham (Gen. 12:1–3). In this sense, the hymn parallels the expression of Zechariah in Luke 1:72–74. The total salvation of those who fear God is so certain that it can be viewed as having taken place.[23] What God will do (view 4) is like what God always does (view 2), but Mary is interested in what Jesus' coming will mean. In a real way, God is setting up a new world order. Those who are on his side can look for a reversal of current fortune.

---

23. Danker 1988: 43–44; Ellis 1974: 76; Klostermann 1929: 20; Godet 1875: 1.104–5; Plummer 1896: 33; Marshall 1978: 84. It must be remembered that Luke presented the passage as Mary's words, so he must expect them to be read prophetically. Here is another failure of the view (1b) that argues for a reference to Jesus' work in the past.

Thus, Mary looks forward to God's vindication of the God-fearers and regards it as a matter of faith that it will come to pass (1:45). What this vindication will involve is the scattering of the proud, those who see no need for God nor for treating fellow humans with compassion. The idea of God's dispersing the arrogant or having sovereignty over social status is a popular OT theme (Num. 10:35; 1 Sam. 2:7; Ps. 68:1; 89:10; Bertram, *TDNT* 8:528). The judgment is against the proud. Ὑπερηφάνους (*hyperēphanous*, the proud) is consistently negative in the NT (James 4:6; 1 Pet. 5:5; Rom. 1:30; 2 Tim. 3:2; Schoonheim 1966).

The arrogance of the proud is described in the following phrase, διανοίᾳ καρδίας αὐτῶν (*dianoia kardias autōn*), where διανοίᾳ is a dative of reference or respect: "proud with respect to the thoughts of their heart."[24] The heart is seen as the center of feeling (1 Sam. 16:7; Prov. 4:23) and as the base of reasoning power (1 Chron. 29:18; Job 12:3; R. Brown 1977: 337; Behm, *TDNT* 3:612 §D2b). This pride is deep-seated and reflects their innermost being. God will judge such pride. Luke 18:9–14 is to be seen as a commentary on the contrast between the proud and the humble, which serves as testimony concerning whom God accepts and whom he does not. God will scatter those who feel no need for him, but are proud of their spiritual or material attainments and capabilities.

1:52 The reversal of social position will occur in the final exercise of God's power. Who is described? Ταπεινούς (*tapeinous*, humble) stands in contrast to δυνάστας (*dynastas*), a term that refers to rulers (Gen. 50:4). That rulers are removed from their thrones (ἀπὸ θρόνων, *apo thronōn*) makes the nuance of ταπεινούς clear. The powerful are governing rulers. The humble are those oppressed by these rulers. Mary has in mind God's covenant people, which is evident from 1:54–55 and the mention of God-fearers in 1:50. R. Brown (1977: 363) sees a reference to the spiritually oppressed, a reference that is correct in light of the emphasis on God-fearers in the hymn. All the injustice of the ruling classes against God's people will be reversed as the humble are lifted up by God. The rulers' oppression and lack of compassion will be dealt with by God, who desires that people treat their neighbor with compassion. The rulers deny God and oppress his people. Mary has in mind the Romans and those like them, who use their secular power to keep God's people at bay. Those who think they have authority do not have ultimate authority. A major theme of the OT is the oppressed people of

---

24. Διανοίᾳ is singular according to Greek idiom, an idiom that English renders in the plural, "thoughts"; Ps. 75:6 LXX is a grammatical parallel; Klostermann 1929: 20; N. Turner 1963: 23.

God described as poor and humble (Ps. 9:11–12, 17–20 [9:12–13, 18–21 MT]; 10:1–4, 17–18; 12:1–5 [12:2–6 MT]; 18:25–29 [18:26–30 MT]). These few references are part of a consistent theme of the OT, especially in the Psalter.

The idea of the removal of rulers is expressed in the OT and in Jewish hope (Job 5:11; 12:19; 1 Sam. 2:7; Sir. 10:14; Jdt. 9:3; 1QM 14.10–11; R. Brown 1977: 337; Plummer 1896: 33; Danker 1988: 44; C. Schneider, *TDNT* 3:412 §3). The exaltation of the humble is also a key OT and Jewish theme (Ps. 147:6; Sir. 10:14; 1 Sam. 2:7). Mary uses the language of the faithful. She trusts God's just vindication in the approaching messianic reign. Hendriksen (1978: 108) makes reference to how the humble were lifted up in the past, but this shows only that what God will do is like what he has done. However, Mary is looking to the future, not the past. She is anticipating, in the child she bears, total vindication. The way God will accomplish this vindication has some other intermediate requirements of which she is not aware, namely Messiah's suffering. First Peter 1:11 summarizes the emerging career of Jesus in two stages: "The sufferings of Christ and the glories that . . . follow." Mary longs to share in the days of glory.

The social consequences of God's work are now set forth. God will **1:53** fill the hungry with good things, a promise paralleled in the OT (1 Sam. 2:5; Ps. 107:9; 146:7) and Judaism (Ps. Sol. 5.10–11; Plummer 1896: 33). In the beatitude of 6:21, Luke returns to the theme of the poor being filled, and in 11:13 he mentions that God will give the Spirit to those who ask for good things (Hauck, *TDNT* 4:389; Ps. 34:10 [34:11 MT]).

In contrast, God will send the rich away empty, another theme with OT precedent (1 Sam. 2:5; Job 15:29; Jer. 17:11). Luke is strong in his denunciation of the independent rich (6:24–26; 12:19–20; 16:25; 21:1–4). Luke 12:21 is clear that independence from God tends to characterize the wealthy, making them an object of condemnation. Danker (1988: 45) argues that Luke (6:20–26; 16:19–31) expresses traditional Jewish hope for political vindication, a hope that is redefined by Jesus when those inside the nation are warned. But one must be careful not to interpret the eschatological reversal solely in a spiritualized form, so that the context of the national hope is lost (1:54–55). Luke 16:19–31, with its contrast between poor Lazarus and the unbelieving rich man serves as a commentary on this passage's ultimate teaching of the reversal at the time of judgment. The rich man's self-focus reflects his lack of faith and his spiritual insensitivity toward the God to whom he is responsible. Such self-focus produces a lack of concern for one's neighbor, which God condemns. Nonetheless, the reversal also applies to national hope. It is the nation that is helped (1:54).

Luke's point is that one should keep material things in perspective and use them generously to serve one's neighbor. Two errors of interpretation must be avoided. One is to spiritualize the material references to the point where the warning about excessive attachment to riches and the dangers it can hold is ignored (Marshall 1978: 85 and Nolland 1989: 72). On the other side, one can ignore the hymn's covenant background and context to such an extent that the spiritual element in the context is lost. The hymn exalts God-fearers. When one ignores this background, the temptation is to make the hymn a manifesto for political action, devoid of any spiritual content.[25] This empties the teaching of its central thrust, the need to turn to God. The context requires that both extremes be avoided. Luke 1:53 looks to the ultimate eschatological reversal that God will bring in the end-time. But care with regard to material things and power is what his followers ought to pursue with good spiritual balance. Such an attitude reflects what God desires in light of what he will judge.

iii. Praise for God's Acts for His People Israel (1:54–55)

1:54 Mary gives the basis of God's vindication for God-fearers: God's covenant mercy and loyal love for his people Israel. God will support the nation. Ἀντελάβετο (antelabeto) means "to take hold of, to hold up, to support" (Isa. 41:8–10; 42:1; Sir. 2:6; Acts 20:35; Plummer 1896: 33). God extended his support to his people Israel. The verb is an aorist tense, as are the other verbs in 1:51–53. As argued in the exegesis of 1:51, the tense is a prophetic aorist—a reference to all that God will do through Christ for his people. Mary's reference looks for the fulfillment of the nation's hope in Jesus. Mary's nationalistic perspective is not to be interpreted as referring directly to the church, but rather to her national covenant hope. Godet (1875: 1.106–7) notes that the lack of direct Christian references in the verse argues against a setting for the hymn after Jesus' ministry. Nonetheless, it can be said that God's treatment of people as described here will be applicable to the church as well, since they will also experience God's protection, vindication, and participation in covenant.

Israel is referred to as the servant (παιδός, paidos). Παῖς (pais, servant) refers to the chosen position of the nation as God's repre-

---

25. So err many liberation movements that appeal to Jesus' teaching about the poor. For a balanced discussion that applies the text to South America and Africa without succumbing to political ideology, see Bemile 1986: 237–53.

sentative people, a description from the OT (Isa. 41:8–9; 42:1; 44:1–2, 21; 45:4; 48:20; 49:3; Marshall 1978: 85; see Jeremias, *TDNT* 5:680 n. 174, 684 n. 213, for possible Jewish references outside the OT). This concept also was held in Judaism (Ps. Sol. 12.6; 17.21; Plummer 1896: 33–34). The phrase clearly reveals Mary's national focus and suggests that she is awaiting a political deliverance, as well as a spiritual one from Jesus.[26] In fact, the blessed nation here is really a remnant, for only the God-fearers can count on this deliverance (Godet 1875: 1.106; Ellis 1974: 76; against this view is Fitzmyer 1981: 361, who extends this blessing to a reconstituted Israel; so also R. Brown 1977: 364). God will take special care of his remnant nation in Jesus, though the sequential outworking of that ministry will yield some surprises as well. Christ will suffer and others will be included in the blessings that come to the faithful in Israel. (On distinguishing between Israel and the church, so that the church is not reconstituted Israel, see Blaising and Bock 1993.)

The ground of God's response is his covenant mercy and loyal love. The infinitive μνησθῆναι (*mnēsthēnai*, to remember) is best taken as a causal infinitive connected with ἀντελάβετο, not as a purpose infinitive. It provides the *basis* for God's acting for his people, not his *purpose* in acting for them.[27] The point is that God's action is motivated by his loyal love. "He remembered mercy" declares that God's actions grew out of his faithful regard for his covenant promises (1:55). Ἐλέους (*eleous*, mercy) recalls the reference in 1:50 and speaks of God's *hesed* love (Schneider 1977a: 58). God is faithful to his promise and loyal to his people.

1:55

The content of God's remembrance of mercy is grounded in his covenant promise as given to the fathers (Plummer 1896: 34). How one handles the following syntactical problem will determine how the verse is taken. The problem involves the presence of two phrases that begin with "to": πρὸς τοὺς πατέρας (*pros tous pateras*, to the fathers) and τῷ Ἀβραάμ (*tō Abraam*, to Abraham).

1. Some take the Abraham reference as appositional to the fathers. The resulting translation is, "He remembered mercy, even as he spoke to our fathers, that is, to Abraham and to his seed forever" (Creed 1930: 24; Schürmann 1969: 77 n. 252; NASB; NKJV).

26. Such a tone is paralleled in the *Benedictus* of Zechariah in 1:68–79 and in Simeon's comments in 2:29–32.

27. Fitzmyer 1981: 368 sees a purpose infinitive here; BDF §391.4 argues for result; Marshall 1978: 85 and Michel, *TDNT* 4:676, opt for a causal reference.

2. Some hold that 1:55a is a parenthetical remark about where the promise of mercy is recorded, while the phrase τῷ Ἀβραάμ goes back to the idea of remembering mercy. In addition, τῷ Ἀβραάμ is usually taken as a dative of interest or advantage (Zerwick 1963: 20 §55). This view translates, "Because he remembered mercy for Abraham and his seed forever, even as he spoke to our fathers" (NIV; discussed but rejected by R. Brown 1977: 338; for this view: Plummer 1896: 34; Marshall 1978: 85; Godet 1875: 1.107). This view is supported by the following points: (a) the idea in view 1 of God speaking to Abraham and his seed *forever* is awkward and (b) a dative following an accusative does not normally indicate apposition. Thus, Mary declares that the covenant to Abraham is the basis for God's acts of loyal love, acts that were promised to the fathers of the nation.

Abraham is a major Lucan OT figure, mentioned twenty-two times in Luke–Acts.[28] The covenant promises of Mary's hymn are those of the Abrahamic covenant (Gen. 12:3; 17:7–8; 18:18; 22:18; 26:3; Exod. 2:24; Mic. 7:20). The reference made to the nation has remnant overtones because of Luke 1:50 (see also 3:8–9); there is no universalism (Marshall 1978: 85). Such covenant acts extend into the culmination of the messianic era. Εἰς τὸν αἰῶνα (*eis ton aiōna*, into the age) refers to the messianic age of deliverance, the eschaton. Since what is found in that age will continue forever (Plummer 1896: 34), one can speak idiomatically of God remembering his mercy forever, of his constancy extending to the end.

This age is introduced here without any reference to its duration or its stages of development. Mary sees one age, but, as Luke will show, the kingdom program of God has two distinct stages. Luke makes no effort to update the hymn's perspective, a point for its authenticity. Mary ends her hymn by recalling that God's action for his people resides in covenant promise, as he never forgets his merciful, loyal love (Godet 1875: 1.107; Hendriksen 1978: 109).

b. Departure: Three Months and Then Home (1:56)

1:56 The visit ends with Mary's return to her home. Mary's visit with Elizabeth lasted three months, so Elizabeth's pregnancy is now at nine months (1:26, 36). R. Brown (1977: 338) argues that a ten-month lunar calendar is being used by Luke. However, Fitzmyer (1981: 369) correctly objects that a lunar month is 29.5 days long,

---

28. Dahl 1966 studies Luke's presentation of this figure and argues that Luke faithfully presents Abraham as the OT did.

making a 295-day pregnancy, a total that is too large. In stating that Mary remained with Elizabeth, Luke uses a favorite preposition, σύν (*syn*, together or with), which he often prefers to μετά (*meta*, with), as a comparison of pericopes with Synoptic parallels shows (8:38, 51; 20:1; 22:14, 56; Plummer 1896: 34). Just before John's birth, Mary returns to Nazareth (1:56).[29]

Much discussion surrounds Mary's departure. Arguing that Mary would not have left so close to John's birth, many suppose that Luke has moved the account of Mary's return forward to take Mary off center stage before John's birth. Such a shift would parallel how John the Baptist's arrest is presented in 3:19–20.[30] Although it is possible, the impression of the narrative does not fit this interpretation (Fitzmyer 1981: 369). Mary might have withdrawn early to avoid drawing attention to herself, but the text does not state the motive. Mary simply returns home before John's birth.

In sum, Mary's visit to her relative Elizabeth and her subsequent **Summary** hymn serve as a foretaste of many Lucan themes. John testifies to the baby Jesus by leaping in the womb. Mary's faith in God's promise is praised. The blessing of Mary leads into a hymn of praise that is a declaration of faith. God will vindicate the God-fearers in the nation in remembrance of his covenant promises to Abraham. The national focus of the remarks reflects a setting before the church's ministry, fitting the scene. Mary knows not only that God has shown mercy to her, but that this mighty, merciful, and holy God will manifest himself to his faithful people. The hymn's major burden shows that Mary trusts in the fulfillment of God's promises, especially those to Abraham. They will come to pass. The reader is to identify with Mary's confidence, her faith, and her sense of joy. Whether a God-fearer from Israel or from the nations, the reader should know that God will vindicate his promise to his nation and to those who fear him. His promise will come to pass.

Additional Notes

1:46. There is no hint of a play on words involving the description of Mary and Hab. 3:16–18. Laurentin argues that Mary's rejoicing in the Lord and her name in the Hebrew substratum point to making her a personification of Israel. (R. Brown 1977: 336 argues correctly against Laurentin 1957b

---

29. The term ὑποστρέφω is used thirty-two times in Luke–Acts and three times in the rest of the NT (Gal. 1:17; Heb. 7:1; 2 Pet. 2:21). Considered alongside the use of σύν, this verb may show 1:56 to be a Lucan linkage.

30. R. Brown 1977: 345–46 notes this but makes no effort to answer the historical issues.

and 1967: 96.) This suggestion requires a Semitic original source for the hymn, which is possible. However, the association is problematic because it requires a specific Semitic verb for the wordplay to work. Though there are three possible Semitic verbs that could be used here (*mĕrîmâ* or *merîm*; *rômēmâ*; or *mĕrabbyâ*), the suggestion is not to be taken seriously, especially since it involves Luke, a Gentile author (if wordplay was intended in Luke's source, a firmer link with OT terms would be expected).

1:48. Some suggest because of the direct references to 1:26–38 that Luke redacted or inserted this entire verse into an existing hymn (R. Brown 1977: 356–57, 360; Fitzmyer 1981: 360, apparently). Brown's argument includes the observation that Lucan phrases are present in the verse (ἰδοὺ γάρ and ἀπὸ τοῦ νῦν) and that a double ὅτι in 1:48–49 is awkward. However, one can argue for Lucan editing in the emphasis on ἀπὸ τοῦ νῦν without arguing that he inserted the entire line. Luke only highlights what the future tense μακαριοῦσιν implies. There is precedent for double ὅτι in the OT Psalter (Ps. 116:7–8 [114:7–8 LXX]; 135:4–5 [134:4–5 LXX]; 138:5–6 [137:5–6 LXX]; 143:2–3 [142:2–3 LXX]). Given the way in which the social perspective of this verse fits nicely into the hymn, there is no need to posit a totally creative redaction in the verse (Marshall 1978: 83; Jones 1968: 21–23).

5. Birth of John (1:57–66)

Luke 1:57–66 turns the spotlight back on John the Baptist and his parents. The unit has two parts: John's birth (1:57–58) and John's naming (1:59–66). The event fulfills 1:5–25, especially 1:13–14. The promised child comes and so does the promised joy (Schürmann 1969: 82). The child's naming makes two key points: (1) Zechariah learned during his period of silence to trust God and (2) the child receives a name God gave him, and not a traditional name, indicating that this child is special.

Just like the pairing of 1:39–45 with 1:46–55, this passage pairs with the following passage. Just as the meeting between Elizabeth and Mary followed with a hymn, so here the birth and naming of John follow with a hymn. The hymn gives the significance of the event. The parents are pious, obedient Israelites, having the child circumcised on the eighth day (Fitzmyer 1981: 376). God's plan works itself out from within Israel. God's mercy reveals itself in the coming of the child to the barren family. The response to that mercy is joy. The wonder of the crowd is three-fold: the joy at the child's birth to such an old couple, the unusual circumstances of his naming, and especially the freeing of Zechariah's tongue. God's discipline of the priest is over. The sign has passed away because fulfillment has come.

The account also forms a pair with the birth of Jesus in 2:1–40 (Ernst 1977: 89). Both accounts follow the pattern of birth, circumcision, and naming. Each has special events at or after the circumcision. For John, there is the freeing of Zechariah's tongue and the hymn. For Jesus, it is the testimony of the prophets. But there are also differences. John receives praise from his own father, because he will function as a prophet. Zechariah also praises Jesus (1:78–79). Jesus receives testimony from prophets and praise from heaven. Jesus' testimony comes from outside his family and encompasses angels, men, and women. The complexity of the structure in 2:1–40 shows Jesus' superiority, as do the multiple testimonies for him. Thus, Luke expresses Jesus' superiority literarily and esthetically, giving more attention to Jesus than to John.

Sources and Historicity

Not much discussion exists about sources of this unit. The options parallel the previous pericopes: many opt for a source from John the Baptist's community (Fitzmyer 1981: 372; Grundmann 1963: 67); others argue that the unit comes from Jewish-Christian sources.[1] The account could have come to Luke from either community. Luke 1:66 mentions many people laying these events on their hearts, and any of these witnesses could have been the source. The remark also recalls what Luke will say of Mary in 2:19, 51. A source could be alluded to here. So either option is possible.

The event's historicity is straightforward, since such a naming and celebration were common. Judgments about 1:57–66 parallel judgments about 1:5–25. The only obstacle for some in 1:57–66 is the miraculous sign. Judgments about it reflect worldview issues rather than textual evidence.

The outline of Luke 1:57–66 is as follows:

a. John's birth is accompanied with joy (1:57–58)
b. Circumcision: the chosen name brings speech and wonder (1:59–66)
  i. Setting: circumcision on the eighth day (1:59)
  ii. The crowd's protest to Elizabeth's naming of John (1:60–61)
  iii. Surprising confirmation of name by Zechariah (1:62–63)
  iv. The immediate restoration of Zechariah's speech (1:64)
  v. The crowd's wonder at the hand of God (1:65–66)

This passage has many themes. The child's arrival brings much joy to parents and neighbors as they experience God's mercy. With Zechariah's obedience, which is against normal custom, comes restoration by God. Zechariah represents one who has learned to have faith and trust God's word. The question about the kind of child John might be calls for the reader's reflection. The note about wonder describes the reaction to God's activity and expresses the mood that surrounds these unusual events.

Exegesis and Exposition

[57]When the time of Elizabeth's pregnancy was complete, she bore a son. [58]The neighbors and relatives heard that the Lord had magnified his mercy to her, and they rejoiced with her.

[59]And on the eighth day, they came to circumcise the child and they wished to name him Zechariah after his father. [60]But the mother said, "No, rather he shall be called John." [61]And they said to her, "Not one of your rel-

---

1. Schürmann 1969: 96 notes the possibility of a Baptist origin, but thinks the source is more likely to be Jewish Christian. R. Brown 1977: 376 opts for a Jewish-Christian source as well. Marshall 1978: 86 is uncertain where the origin lies.

atives is called by this name." [62]They made signs to the father about what he might wish to call him. [63]After asking for a wax tablet, he wrote, "John is his name." And they all marveled. [64]Immediately his mouth and tongue were loosed, and he was speaking, giving praise to God. [65]And fear came upon all his neighbors and they were discussing all of these events throughout the hill country of Judea. [66]And all who heard laid it on their heart, saying, "What then will this child be?" For indeed the hand of the Lord was with him.

a. John's Birth Is Accompanied with Joy (1:57–58)

The time of fulfillment has come. Elizabeth gives birth to the predicted son.[2] The reference to "the time of the birth being full" (ἐπλήσθη ὁ χρόνος τοῦ τεκεῖν, *eplēsthē ho chronos tou tekein*) is a Hebraism (Gen. 25:24) and will be repeated in Luke 2:6 (Klostermann 1929: 22; R. Brown 1977: 368; BDR §400.1.3). After nine months, it is time to give birth (1:24, 26, 56). The verse gives the first note of fulfillment of Gabriel's words about the prophet-son's arrival (1:13), even repeating the term *bore* (ἐγέννησεν, *egennēsen*; Schweizer 1984: 38). God is performing his word.

1:57

Word about the baby's arrival draws a joyous crowd. They rejoice that God has removed Elizabeth's barrenness. The idea of the Lord magnifying his mercy (ἐμεγάλυνεν κύριος τὸ ἔλεος, *emegalynen kyrios to eleos*) has OT precedent (Gen. 19:19; also "to do mercy": Gen. 24:12; 40:14; 47:29; Ruth 1:8; 2:20; Klostermann 1929: 22; Plummer 1896: 36; Schürmann 1969: 82 n. 2). Both elements, the magnifying and the mercy of God, are key concepts in the infancy section. Earlier in this chapter, Mary magnified the Lord and his salvation in her hymn (1:46). But here the emphasis is on God's action in magnifying or displaying his mercy to Elizabeth by allowing her to bear a child (Gen. 21:1–6; Marshall 1978: 88; R. Brown 1977: 369). The theme of God's mercy is repeated several times in the section (1:50, 54, 72). As the *Magnificat* showed, God's mercy refers to his loving action.

1:58

The name *John* suggests a play on words, since it means "God is gracious" (Fitzmyer 1981: 325, 373). However, there is no term for grace in the passage, an absence that makes such a connection unlikely, at least for Luke and his audience.[3] What does occur is the rejoicing of neighbors and family. Συνέχαιρον (*synechairon*, they

2. The reference to Elizabeth is in the emphatic position; BDF §472.2; BDR §472.2.6.

3. One cannot say if there was a wordplay in an original source, since if it had Semitic roots, wordplay is possible. However, Luke, unlike Matthew, does not discuss the meaning of names (cf. Matt. 1:23).

rejoiced) refers to this shared joy and points to the second fulfillment of the angel's words (1:14). God's word is coming to pass, and
some are rejoicing in it. Joy and praise run from the beginning of
the infancy section to the end (1:14, 64; 2:14, 28).

b. Circumcision: The Chosen Name Brings Speech and Wonder (1:59–66)
i. Setting: Circumcision on the Eighth Day (1:59)

1:59 The time to name the child comes, and it yields a surprise for the
gathered witnesses. The naming takes place in conjunction with the
circumcision on the eighth day (ἐν τῇ ἡμέρᾳ τῇ ὀγδόῃ, *en tē hēmera
tē ogdoē*; Gen. 17:10–12; 21:4; Lev. 12:3). In the OT and in Judaism,
the normal time to name a child appears to have been birth (Gen.
4:1; 25:25–26; 29:32–35; perhaps Tob. 1:9). Later Jewish tradition
attributed the naming of Moses to the time of his circumcision.[4]
Greek children were normally named in the seven-to-ten-day period following birth (Fraenkel 1935: 1615–16; Ellis 1974: 78; Marshall 1978: 88). In the OT, Abram received the name *Abraham* upon
the occasion of his circumcision, but he was not a baby (Gen. 17:5).
Thus, it seems, although a naming on the eighth day is unusual, it
is not to be regarded as a historical problem, since cultural and biblical precedents do exist for the practice (Luce 1933: 93). The circumcision takes place before a crowd of witnesses. In later times,
at least ten witnesses were normally present.[5]

Ellis (1974: 78) suggests that the circumcision takes place over
the "throne of Elijah" in the hopes that this child might be the
hoped-for end-time prophet (Mal. 3:1; 4:5 [3:23 MT]). But nothing
in this text suggests such a reference or such a context, and Luke
makes nothing of this point (Marshall 1978: 88).

The crowd's expectation that the child might be named Zechariah is not surprising. In fact, as Luke pictures the event, the
crowd agrees that this will be the name. Ἐκάλουν (*ekaloun*) is a
conative imperfect and suggests that the crowd *"was wishing to
name* the child Zechariah" (so NIV, NKJV, NASB; RSV: "would have
named him"; Marshall 1978: 88). A child was customarily named
after a relative, usually the father or the grandfather.[6] The Lord

4. *Pirqe de Rabbi Eliezer* 48 (= Friedlander 1916: 378), an eighth-century text that
is too late to be of real help; R. Brown 1977: 369. Gen. 21:3 may belong here in light
of Gen. 21:4–5, but it is hard to be sure; R. Meyer, *TDNT* 6:82.

5. R. Brown 1977: 369; SB 4:23–40. M. *Šab.* 19.5 indicates that circumcision
could take place between the eighth and twelfth days. So important was this act that
rabbinic texts speculated why it had not been included among the Ten Commandments; *Pesikta Rabbati* 23.4 (117a) (= Braude 1968: 479).

6. Fitzmyer 1981: 380; Klostermann 1929: 23; SB 2:107. Efforts to prove that the
grandfather was the most frequent choice, as argue Creed 1930: 24 and Nolland

chose a different name, so that the custom of parents' choosing did not apply.

ii. The Crowd's Protest to Elizabeth's Naming of John (1:60–61)

Elizabeth knows what the child is to be called and surprises the crowd. The Hebraic redundancy ἀποκριθεῖσα . . . εἶπεν (apokritheisa . . . eipen, replying . . . she said) introduces her response (N. Turner 1963: 155–56; BDR §420.1–2). Luke records her rejection of the crowd's suggestion, using the negative particle οὐχί (ouchi, no). Rather, the child's name is John. She shows her obedience to Gabriel's giving of the name (1:13).

1:60

That Elizabeth knew the name has caused some discussion. How did she know? Some suggest that Luke intends a miraculous revelation to her about the name (Creed 1930: 24; Klostermann 1929: 23; R. Brown 1977: 369; Goulder 1989: 238). It is argued that such a revelation heightens the miraculous tone and that any other approach makes the movement of events comical. But is such an emphasis necessary? Surely would not Zechariah have somehow communicated with his wife about his experience in the temple? Such communication is natural to expect as background to this event. It might also explain how Elizabeth knew about Mary in 1:39–45 (Schweizer 1984: 38; Plummer 1896: 36; Fitzmyer 1981: 381; Hendriksen 1978: 115; Marshall 1978: 88). The passage highlights the family's obedience in the face of societal custom (custom explains the crowd's reaction). As with significant figures in the OT, this is a special child, so he receives a special name. Confirmation of what the family is doing follows in the succeeding verses.

The crowd protests the choice, complaining that no one in Zechariah's family bears this name. Such a name is not customary! Since Elizabeth offers the name and Zechariah is mute, the crowd may be thinking that Elizabeth is picking a name without Zechariah's consent, and so they wish to appeal the choice to the father (Marshall 1978: 88). Of course, the name that Elizabeth selected is the one that God had given the child (1:13). The name *John* or variations of it were not unusual in priestly families (Neh. 12:13, 42; 1 Macc. 2:1–2; R. Brown 1977: 369; Fitzmyer 1981: 381). The appeal to Zechariah will confirm Elizabeth's choice.

1:61

1989: 79, are not substantiated. Examples of naming after a relative are numerous: after the father: Tob. 1:1, 9; Josephus, *Life* 1 §5; *Jewish War* 5.13.2 §534; *Antiquities* 14.1.3 §10; after a grandfather: 1 Macc. 2:1–2; Jub. 11.15. C. F. Evans 1990: 179, positing Hellenistic assimilation, is entirely too skeptical about the details here.

iii. Surprising Confirmation of Name by Zechariah (1:62–63)

1:62 The appeal is made to Zechariah through the signing of a message to him. Ἐνένευον (*eneneuon*, they motioned) refers to communication with a deaf person, though it normally means "to motion to someone" (Acts 24:10; John 13:24). The verb is a source of dispute. Is Zechariah portrayed as both deaf and mute? Hendriksen (1978: 115) and Godet (1875: 1.108) reject this understanding, arguing (1) that only Zechariah's speech is dealt with in 1:20, 64, (2) that nowhere else in the NT does the term κωφός (*kōphos*) (1:22) mean deaf and mute, and (3) that it is only natural to sign to someone who is mute. But it seems unnecessary to limit Zechariah's condition to muteness. Κωφός can mean deaf and mute and refers to idols that cannot hear or speak (Hab. 2:18–19; 3 Macc. 4:16).[7] Certainly if Zechariah could be addressed, why go to the trouble of signing the question to him? The term here suggests that Zechariah is deaf and mute.

Luke presents the crowd's question in his common style of using the article τό for a repeated question (9:46; 19:48; 22:2, 4, 23, 24; Marshall 1978: 89; BDF §267.2). The less definite mood of the optative indicates that Zechariah has many names from which to choose. With this expectation they ask him, "What would you wish to call him?"[8] Zechariah demonstrates his faith by his choice.

1:63 The crowd consults Zechariah, who writes his message on a tablet because he is unable to speak. Πινακίδιον (*pinakidion*) describes a wood tablet covered with wax (Danker 1988: 46; Plummer 1896: 37; SB 2:108–10; Ezek. 9:2 [Symmachus]). The verbal combination ἔγραψεν λέγων (*egrapsen legōn*, he wrote saying) is a Hebraism (2 Kings 10:6; 1 Macc. 10:17; 11:57; Josephus, *Antiquities* 11.4.7 §104). Zechariah does not speak until after he gives the name in 1:64 (Klostermann 1929: 23; Creed 1930: 25).

Zechariah's reply is emphatic. His name *is* (ἐστίν, *estin*) John. Zechariah does not say it *shall be* John. The change in tense between 1:60 and 1:63 is significant. For Zechariah, the child had a name from the time of the angel's announcement. There was no choice for him. His reply indicates obedience and submission to God's message.

---

7. BAGD 462 mentions this meaning, though it does not place Luke 1:22 here; BAA 938. For idols, the emphasis is on their inability to answer, but this is a function of more than being unable to speak. See also Philo, *Special Laws* 4.38 §197. Sibylline Oracles 4.27–28 also refers to idols.

8. Luke reports the question in the third person, making it grammatically an indirect question.

Two reactions follow. The first reaction is that of the crowd marveling or being amazed. The basis of the amazement is debated. (1) They marveled at Zechariah's agreement with Elizabeth in giving the unusual name. This view regards the verse as confirmation that Zechariah was deaf, for why would there be amazement if he had heard his wife name the child (R. Brown 1977: 370; Alford 1874: 452)? (2) They marveled as a reaction to the firmness of Zechariah's reply (Plummer 1896: 37; Godet 1875: 1.109). What the amazement really reflects is the insistence on the unusual name. It is hard to be sure that this is an either/or proposition. It may well be that the combination is what produced the wonder, though the wonder is more understandable if Zechariah is deaf as well as mute (Fitzmyer 1981: 381; Marshall 1978: 89). The key point is that Zechariah learned from his period of silence. The sign of silence worked; he, even as an already righteous man (1:6), learned to trust God's word even more.

iv. The Immediate Restoration of Zechariah's Speech (1:64)

There is another reaction to Zechariah's confirmation of John's name. His speech returns immediately (παραχρῆμα, *parachrēma*) following his reply. This term is frequent in Luke and often accompanies miraculous works.[9] The sign accomplished its divinely given task, so the handicap disappears as the angel promised (1:20; R. Brown 1977: 370). God's word comes to pass.

1:64

In the account, three unusual events occur: (1) the old give birth, (2) the child receives a strange name, and (3) the silence of Zechariah is removed. Zechariah responds with praise to God. Whether this praise is distinct from the *Benedictus* or serves as an initial introduction to it is not clear. The account's mood reflects Zechariah's joy. The restoration of his speech leads to praise.

v. The Crowd's Wonder at the Hand of God (1:65–66)

The birth, the unusual name given to John, and the return of Zechariah's speech brought a twofold response: fear and discussion. The realization that God was near produced the fear (1:66). Such a response to God's presence is common (1:12, 30; 5:26; 7:16; 8:37; 21:26; Acts 2:43; 5:5; Marshall 1978: 89). All the neighbors who witnessed the event reacted in the same way.[10] The universality of the

1:65

9. It occurs ten times in Luke (1:64; 4:39; 5:25; 8:44, 47, 55; 13:13; 18:43; 19:11; 22:60) and six times in Acts; in the NT outside of Luke–Acts, it is found only in Matt. 21:19–20; Fitzmyer 1981: 381.

10. The term τοὺς περιοικοῦντας recalls the related term οἱ περίοικοι in 1:58.

neighborhood's response is highlighted by the unusual word order
ἐγένετο ἐπὶ πάντας φόβος (*egeneto epi pantas phobos*).[11] Fear fell
upon all as they realized that God was in their midst.

Word of the event spread through Judea. The imperfect verb δι-
ελαλεῖτο (*dielaleito*, they were discussing) describes the spread of
the news. The subject of discussion is the ῥήματα (*rhēmata*, the
events) that surrounded the birth.[12] Something different is happening.

1:66 Another reaction follows. In addition to the neighborhood fear and
the regional report, a question lingered for those who heard about
these events. They set them in their heart (ἔθεντο ... ἐν τῇ καρδίᾳ
αὐτῶν, *ethento ... en tē kardia autōn*), an expression that all who
heard about the events had a strong and deep emotional reaction to
the news ("to take to heart" or "to put in the memory"; 1 Sam. 21:12
[21:13 LXX]; 2 Sam. 13:20; Mal. 2:2; Luke 2:19, 51; Hendriksen
1978: 118; Plummer 1896: 38). But along with the events' lasting
impression, they also raised a question about what this child would
come to be. The use of τί (*ti*, what) shows that the focus of concern
is the role that John will have in God's plan.[13]

To the popular response, Luke adds an explanatory note (καὶ
γάρ, *kai gar*, for indeed [the hand of God was with him]). The figure
of God's hand is common in the OT, especially when depicting deliverance.[14] God's power and guidance are with John, who is a special instrument for his service. The figure is a metonymy. The hand
pictures and represents strength (BDR §495.4.4). God is at work,
doing something very special, and the crowd senses it.

Summary The unit stresses that God's word comes to pass. Zechariah pictures one who learns his lesson and submits in trust to God's
promise. His period of pain and reflection led him to realize that
God does what he says. The reader sees that what God has promised he will do. But what is God going to do? For those who are
reading the account for the first time and who do not know the
story, the question raises a note of mystery. To those who know

11. BDF §472.2 and BDR §472.2.6 note that this word order is emphatic, since
the reference to fear is delayed and the reference to *all* is moved forward. Literally
the word order translates "there came upon all, fear."

12. For ῥήματα as events see Gen. 24:66; Luke 2:19, 51; Klostermann 1929: 24.
It can also refer to words (1 Sam. 3:1, 7).

13. On the grammar of the predicate use of τί see BDF §299.2 and BDR §299.2.2.

14. Exod. 13:3; 15:6; Isa. 5:12; 26:11; 31:3; Ps. 28:5; 1 Chron. 28:19; Creed 1930:
25; Marshall 1978: 90. In the NT, Acts 7:50; Lohse, *TDNT* 9:431 §C3. Schürmann
1969: 83 n. 20 notes that only Luke uses the phrase "the hand of the Lord" in the NT
(Acts 11:21; 13:11; in the LXX, Isa. 41:20; 66:14).

the story, the question calls for joyous reflection about what amazing things God did through this key child.

Additional Note

1:64. Στόμα and γλῶσσα are the double subject of the singular verb ἀνεῴ-χθη, an abbreviated construction known as zeugma. The redundancy emphasizes the total return of speech to Zechariah.

6. Zechariah's Praise:
The *Benedictus* (1:67–80)

The naming of the child John brings praise. Zechariah's hymn, the *Benedictus*, forms one of the theological keys to the infancy material. With Mary's hymn and the other angelic and prophetic statements in Luke 1–2, it sets the theological tone of Luke–Acts.[1] Zechariah's scope is more comprehensive than Mary's hymn in that her praise was personally stated and then took a broader look at God's work. This hymn goes the opposite direction. It starts with God's activity in raising up the Davidic horn for the nation. Then it narrows to discuss the child and the one who follows him.

The hymn is Spirit-filled (1:67) praise and prophecy. The praise (1:68–75) describes the coming of the Davidic ruler and elaborates on 1:31–35, while the prophecy (1:76–79) concentrates on John's relationship to Jesus and develops both 1:13–17 and 1:31–35 (Schürmann 1969: 90; Fitzmyer 1981: 385). The hymn answers the question of 1:66b: John is the preparer and forerunner to Jesus, in that his message sets up Jesus' work (1:76–77). It is John's preaching that interests Luke. John the Baptist makes ready a people by speaking to them of forgiveness of sins. Jesus' coming also gets attention in that he is the incarnation of Davidic hope. Jesus brings salvation for the nation and fulfillment of covenant promise (1:69–75). Jesus' work is to free God's people to serve God in holiness. John is the prophet of the Most High and Jesus is the bright Morning Star who lights the path of peace to God. The father, Zechariah, points to Jesus, as will his son.

Sources and Historicity

Sources for the *Benedictus* are as debated as for the *Magnificat*, and the options are similar. Three features make this discussion more complex. First, the hymn's grammar raises questions: the praise section (1:68–75) is one long Greek sentence, so the syntax is difficult to analyze. Second,

1. Tannehill 1986: 31 refers to the *Magnificat* as an operatic aria, where the action stops and the situation is assessed with a flourish. That description may be applied to the *Benedictus* as well.

the hymn's transitions are abrupt; the move to John in 1:76 and the shift to Jesus in 1:78 complicate the picture. Third, there is a shift of form between 1:75 and 1:76. The first portion of the hymn is a psalm of praise;[2] the second part is a prophecy in honor of the birth of a child, a *genethliakon*.[3] This break in form has led to five hypotheses about how the two parts were combined either in the tradition or by Luke:[4]

1. Some argue that Luke wrote the hymn (Harnack 1907: 206–17). Although many of the phrases have LXX parallels, there is an absence of Lucan wording.[5] The only verses with traces of Lucan style and emphasis are 1:70, 76–77. This view simply cannot work.

2. Others argue for an altered Baptist tradition (Vielhauer 1952; Bultmann 1963: 296 sees either a Jewish or Baptist background). To posit such a source is natural, given the topic. Against it are the references to the Davidic horn (which cannot be about John), the absence of reference to baptism, and the presence of 1:77. If the material came from Baptist sources, it has been heavily altered to its current form. This suggestion is not a comprehensive solution.

3. Others suggest an adaptation of an original Jewish hymn praising recent Jewish success (Gunkel 1921; Winter 1956: 239–40 n. 41; Klostermann 1929: 24). The major arguments against this view are the same as in the case of the *Magnificat*. The Davidic thrust argues against a Jewish setting of the recent past, since recent hope was grounded in Maccabean or Hasmonean models, which tended to be priestly and regal (T. Levi 18.5; negatively, T. Moses 6.2). In addition, recent Jewish rule contradicted Davidic emphases, because of its Levitical priestly thrust in distinction from Melchizedekian expectation. This view does not work since Luke lacks priestly themes, and Davidic themes are so prominent.

4. The most popular recent suggestion is that the hymn emerged from a Jewish-Christian setting, though there is discussion whether some

---

2. Marshall 1978: 86 speaks of the Jewish *berāka*. Berger 1984: 243 calls the *Benedictus* a psalm of thanksgiving, as does Bovon 1989: 96–97.

3. Marshall 1978: 86; Berger 1984: 243. Bovon 1989: 99 notes that the expressions here have similarities to the Testaments of the Twelve Patriarchs: *compassion* (Luke 1:78; T. Zeb. 7.2–3; 8.2) and *to visit* (Luke 1:68, 78; T. Levi 4.4; T. Judah 23.5; T. Asher 7.3).

4. The most detailed recent survey of the issues is Farris 1985: 26–30. Other treatments include R. Brown 1977: 377–78; Fitzmyer 1981: 376–78; Marshall 1978: 86–87; Ernst 1977: 92–94; Wiefel 1988: 62–64; Nolland 1989: 82–85; and Schürmann 1969: 84–85, 88–89, 93–94.

5. R. Brown 1977: 377. Schürmann 1969: 84 n. 26 notes traces of non-Lucan style and argues for a Palestinian setting. Bovon 1989: 98 and n. 8 argues that the terms *to make redemption*, *horn of salvation*, and *to remember covenant* are not Lucan expressions, though the terms *to go before*, *knowledge*, and *salvation* are like Lucan usage.

of the material might be even older.[6] A variety of positions exist on what was inserted into old material by Luke or perhaps in earlier stages of the tradition. The candidates mentioned most often are 1:70, 76–77.[7] The major reasons for this view are that the form shifts in the middle of the hymn and that traces of Lucan emphasis are found in some verses (e.g., 1:70, 76–77). But hymns can have mixed forms as Ps. 90 and 128 show.[8] The Lucan emphases are really not so Lucan, but are traditional Christian motifs. For example, the clear ordering of John under Jesus is traditional in Christian thought (Mark 1:2–8; Matt. 3:1–12). Tying John to forgiveness of sins (Luke 1:77) is not a Lucan emphasis, since Jesus and forgiveness of sin are linked in other Lucan texts (Luke 24:47; Acts 5:31; 10:43; 13:38; 26:18). Behind this position stands a belief that John's subordination to Jesus was not such an early idea, a position that depends on evaluation of issues treated in the introduction to this unit and the additional notes at 1:25.

5. Still others argue that the hymn is a unit and emerged through the Jewish-Christian church (Marshall 1978: 86–87 [if not through Baptist sources]; R. Brown 1977: 378 [though opting for a Jewish-Christian origin, Brown notes the absence of the developed Christology of the later NT]). This position is like the one mentioned in regard to Mary's hymn in 1:46–56. It need not deny the influence of Jewish expression on the hymn's wording. Zechariah is a pious Jew offering hymnic praise. Most who hold this position do not comment on historicity beyond this connection. However, the text presents a Spirit-filled burst of praise. Such material could have been preserved or summarized at a later time to express accurately Zechariah's words and feelings.[9] My point is that there is nothing against the hymn's

---

6. R. Brown 1977: 377–78; Fitzmyer 1981: 377–78; Farris 1985: 27–28. The formative articulation of the view is Benoit 1956–57: 182–83. His work not only formulated the basic position, but is regarded as having challenged the unity of the hymn as well.

7. Among the hypotheses are the following:

	Added to	Adherents
1:76–79	Jewish or Jewish-Christian hymn	Winter 1956: 239 n. 41
1:76 or 1:76–77	early Christian hymn	Benoit 1956–57: 182–91
1:68–75	Christian hymn	Schürmann 1969: 88–90
1:76–77, 79b	Baptist hymn	Hahn 1969: 242–43, 365–66
1:76–77	Jewish-Christian hymn of the *Anawim*	R. Brown 1977: 377–78; Farris 1985: 27–28
1:70, 76–77	Jewish-Christian hymn probably from the *Anawim*	Fitzmyer 1981: 378

8. The shifts occur at Ps. 90:14; 128:5. Marshall 1978: 87 notes that Daube 1956: 201 speaks of mixed forms.

9. In other words, one need not think that there was a stenographer present to take down the words on this occasion. But a faithful recollection of remarks at some

origin reaching ultimately into the original setting. Godet (1875: 1.110) argues that Zechariah himself had time to reflect on these events during his period of silence and then uttered the hymn. But Fitzmyer (1981: 377) objects that such a family tradition would not be preserved in Greek. However, there is nothing to prevent such a tradition being translated into Greek. Such traditions, if they existed, would be of interest to all the church. So this objection does not stand. There is no serious challenge to the traditional view, though mediation of the tradition through the Jewish-Christian church is quite likely.

The structure of Luke 1:67–80 is a hymn of mixed form: thanksgiving and praise for a newborn child:

a. Setting (1:67)
b. Praise for messianic deliverance (1:68–75)
    i. Redemption for Israel through David's house (1:68–69)
    ii. In accordance with the prophets (1:70)
    iii. Salvation from enemies (1:71)
    iv. Mercy and covenant remembrance (1:72)
    v. In accordance with Abrahamic promise (1:73)
    vi. Goal: to serve God in holiness after rescue (1:74–75)
c. Prophecy about Jesus and John (1:76–79)
    i. John: prophet of the Most High to prepare the way (1:76)
    ii. John: to give knowledge of forgiveness of sins (1:77)
    iii. Jesus: Dayspring Visitor by the mercy of God (1:78)
    iv. Jesus: to bring light and to guide into the way of peace (1:79)
d. Growth of John (1:80)

One could divide the praise (§b) and prophecy (§c) parts of the hymn into four subunits: the first (1:68–70) contains the basic praise; the second (1:71–75) tells what God will do; the third (1:76–77) describes John the Baptist; and the fourth (1:78–79) presents Jesus.

The major theme of God's redemption through the Davidic ruler dominates the passage. One feature is particularly significant. The Davidic redemption described in the hymn has both political and spiritual aspects. This union is crucial to Luke's

---

later point is possible. Machen's remarks about Mary's hymn may well apply to Zechariah's praise; see the discussion of sources in 1:46–56.

view. God has not abandoned covenant commitments and promises made to Israel. Salvation unites the real world with the world of the heart and the world of heaven. To remove any element is to miss the Lucan picture of salvation. To remove the heart and heaven demotes salvation to politics. To remove the earthly hope leaves a chasm between justice in the world and individual response to God. God's salvation is not intended to be a private affair, but is designed to show God's greatness to all the creation. Heaven and earth cannot be divorced in redemption. Zechariah's praise shows that when God delivers he brings salvation to the earth as well as to the heart. Salvation is tied to God's mercy, to forgiveness of sin, and to rescue from enemies. The hope expressed here fits the reversal pictured in 1:50–53. One other point is crucial. The goal of redemption is not a rest in heaven or material prosperity, but service to God in holiness and reverence (1:73–75). Here is Luke's call to his reader. God does many things: he saves, redeems a people, and keeps his word. But he also grants the saved a privilege: to serve him (Bovon 1989: 97). Salvation leads to service; it is a means to an end.

Exegesis and Exposition

[67]And Zechariah, his father, was filled with the Holy Spirit and prophesied:

[68] "Blessed be the God of Israel,
     because he visited and made redemption for his people,
[69] and raised up a horn of salvation for us
     in the house of David, his servant,
[70] even as he spoke
     through the mouth of his holy prophets from the beginning,
[71] deliverance from the hands of our enemies
     and from the hands of those who hate us,
[72] to do mercy to our fathers
     and to remember his holy covenant,
[73]   the oath that he swore to Abraham, our father,
     to grant us,
[74]   having rescued us from the hands of ⌐our⌐ enemies,
     fearlessly to serve him
[75]   in holiness and righteousness before him all our days.

[76] "You shall be called prophet of the Most High,
     for you shall go before the Lord to prepare his ways,

^{77} to give knowledge of salvation to his people
   in the forgiveness of their sins,
^{78} through the deep tender mercy of our God,
   in which mercy the rising sun from on high ⸢will visit⸣ us,
^{79} to shine on those seated in darkness and in the shadow of death,
   to guide our feet in the way of peace."

^{80}And the child was growing and was being strengthened in spirit and was in the desert until his appearing to Israel.[10]

a. Setting (1:67)

Whereas Mary gave praise for God's meeting personal needs (1:46–55), Zechariah gives praise for God's raising up a Messiah for the nation. The hymn is traditionally called the *Benedictus*, a name that comes from the first word of the hymn in the Latin version. Zechariah's note of praise answers the crowd's question concerning the role of John the Baptist in the context of God's plan (1:66; Nolland 1989: 82–83 opposes this view). John is the prophet who precedes the long-awaited son of David. The hymn's language reflects OT expressions throughout, as well as expressions in Judaism (for charts showing the OT parallels, see Klostermann 1929: 25; Hendriksen 1978: 122–23; Creed 1930: 25–27; R. Brown 1977: 386–89).

1:67

Zechariah gives his praise while full of the Spirit.[11] Most see the hymn as detailing the praise mentioned in 1:64. The reference to Zechariah as the father leads some to see this verse as a Lucan insertion because the description is viewed as superfluous in light of 1:5–24a and 1:59 (Fitzmyer 1981: 382; R. Brown 1977: 370). But the repetition suggests an extant source, which Luke did not alter, since otherwise the reason for the repetition is less than clear.

The hymn is not only given under the Spirit's inspiration, it is also called prophecy, serving as inspired commentary on the events.[12] In John's birth, Zechariah is certain that God's plan of salvation is beginning to move to completion.

---

10. The first part of the hymn is one long sentence, making it more difficult than the *Magnificat* to lay out in strophic lines. Four infinitives in 1:72–74 are key: ποιῆσαι ἔλεος (to do mercy), μνησθῆναι (to remember), δοῦναι (to grant), and λατρεύειν (to serve).

11. In this chapter, both Elizabeth (1:41–44) and Zechariah give Spirit-directed remarks. The name *Zechariah* is in the emphatic position in the verse; BDF §472.2 and BDR §472.2.

12. Friedrich, *TDNT* 6:835. Again, the Spirit serves as "testimony bearer" and "revelator"; Acts 2:17–18; 11:27; 13:1; 19:6; 21:9; Nolland 1989: 85. On the Lucan theme of the Spirit as the Spirit of prophecy, see Menzies 1991: 119–22.

b. Praise for Messianic Deliverance (1:68–75)
i. Redemption for Israel through David's House (1:68–69)

1:68 Zechariah's praise begins by focusing on God's visitation in messianic redemption. The call to praise God for a specific act is the common introduction for a praise hymn.[13] God is to be blessed, to be honored with praise (Beyer, *TDNT* 2:764). The language of the verse is that of OT national salvation, as the God of Israel is blessed in terms that are commonly used in the OT (Gen. 9:26; 1 Sam. 25:32; 1 Kings 1:48; Ps. 41:13 [41:14 MT]; 72:18; 89:52 [89:53 MT]; 106:48) and Judaism (Tob. 3:11; Ps. Sol. 2.37). It is interesting that the parallel in 1 Kings is in David's blessing of Solomon, a decidedly regal and national context. The nationalistic blessing is also seen in the Qumranic eschatological hymns (1QM 14.4; 1QH 5.20; 10.14; R. Brown 1977: 384, 386). Such nationalistic features argue against reading these verses as containing only "transferred Christian significance" for Luke.[14] The people (λαῷ, *laō*) in view here are the nation Israel, as 1:71–73 shows (Strathmann, *TDNT* 4:53).

The aorists in this hymn are clearly prophetic aorists, since there is reference to the raising up of a delivering Messiah (1:69) and the hymn is described as prophetic (1:67; Schürmann 1969: 87 [against this view]; Klostermann 1929: 26; Marshall 1978: 90). Luke 1:68b gives the basis of the praise (ὅτι, *hoti*, for). The reason is God's visitation, specifically God's making redemption for (setting free) his people. As the entire hymn will show, God's visitation will occur through the visitation of Messiah. Though Zechariah speaks in the past tense in part because Messiah is already conceived, his focus is on what is yet to happen through that Messiah (see the future tense verb *shall visit* in 1:78).

A reference to God's visitation (ἐπεσκέψατο, *epeskepsato*) can refer either to a gracious act (Ps. 8:4 [8:5 MT]) or to judgment (Jer. 44:13; Marshall 1978: 90; Beyer, *TDNT* 2:605). Here the reference is to God's gracious visit. The expression is common in contemporary Judaism (Bovon 1989: 104; Schweizer 1984: 42; R. Brown 1977: 371; Nolland 1989: 86; Wis. 3:7; Ps. Sol. 3.11; 10.4; 11.6; 15.12; T. Levi 4.4; T. Asher 7.3; CD 1.7) and is also found in the OT (Gen. 50:24–25; Exod. 3:16; 4:31; 13:19; 30:12; Isa. 23:17; Ps. 80:14 [80:15 MT]; 106:4; Ruth 1:6). The phrase is important to Luke as a description of God's coming salvation in the Messiah Jesus (Luke 1:78; 7:16; 19:44; Acts 15:14). Within the hymn, the repetition of

---

13. Εἴη (not ἐστίν) should be supplied, yielding "blessed *be* the God of Israel"; BDR §128.5.8.

14. The remarks do have application for the church, but this language also includes notes of hope for Israel. On this text's two levels of meaning, see Bock 1993.

ἐπεσκέψατο in 1:68 and ἐπισκέψεται (*episkepsetai*) in 1:78 makes it clear that God's visitation comes in Messiah's visitation.

What Messiah's visitation means for God's people is redemption. As the following verses make clear, the redemption in view here is a deliverance from enemies, so that God's people are free to serve their God in righteousness and holiness. Redemption is release to a Redeemer who frees (Büchsel, *TDNT* 4:351). Luke 1:71 and 1:74–75 make it clear that a political tone exists in this reference, especially since the God of Israel is addressed in terms that parallel the political notes of the Psalms (Plummer 1896: 40; Marshall 1978: 90–91). But is a political deliverance really in view?

Hendriksen (1978: 123–24, 127–28) argues that 1:77–78 reveals a purely spiritual reference, citing 2:38 in support of this point. However, the context of Luke 2 includes references to Israel's consolation (2:25), to Jesus as a light to Gentiles and a glory for Israel (2:32), and to Jerusalem's redemption (2:38). The latter phrase goes beyond spiritual overtones, as Luke 21:28; 24:21; Acts 1:6; 3:19–26 suggest.[15] The Lucan texts, especially Luke 21:28 and Acts 3:19–26, show that Jerusalem's redemption includes the Son of Man's coming to rule and judge the earth. The political emphasis is not absent in Luke. What has happened is that the political redemption is delayed, because of the failure of much of the nation to respond (13:31–35; 19:44).[16] But this delay is not clear at this point in Luke and is not alluded to directly by the hymn. Luke saves these details for later.

Thus, redemption has both political and spiritual elements, since the hymn includes not only nationalistic themes (1:71, 74), but also a statement (1:77–78) about the forgiveness of sins (Klostermann 1929: 27). What Zechariah praises God for is the expectation of a total deliverance for God's people. Such a linkage between spiritual and political blessing is not surprising, since it parallels the blessing-and-curse sections of Deuteronomy. What will be new is the division of the deliverance into two distinct phases tied to two comings of Jesus. Of course, Zechariah has no such twofold conception here: he simply presents the total package. Only subsequent events explain how the plan has two parts.

15. For OT and Jewish parallels, see Ps. 111:9; for the verb *redeem*, see Sir. 48:20; 50:24; 51:2 (twice).

16. The delay is one of appearance only and applies to the generally held Jewish expectation that when God came in Messiah he would accomplish all things at once. Luke 24:44–47 and Acts 2:22–24 make it clear that Israelite rejection was always part of God's plan, while the NT clarifies how two comings were also always in view. Contrary to the Jewish perspective of OT hope and presentation, the political consummation was delayed; but it was not canceled. Alongside the delay of political consummation, spiritual redemption was inaugurated.

1:69   Along with God's visitation of redemption, Zechariah also praises the raising up of a powerful Messiah who will deliver the nation. The idea of God's raising up (ἤγειρεν, ēgeiren) someone is the way the OT expresses God's sending a significant figure to his people: a prophet (Deut. 18:15, 18), judge (Judg. 3:9, 15), priest (1 Sam. 2:35), or king (2 Sam. 23:1). The expression is also common for Luke (Acts 3:22, 26; 13:22). The figure in view is clearly regal, as the reference in the next line makes clear: (ἐν οἴκῳ Δαυίδ, en oikō Dauid, the house of David). David is described as God's servant (παιδὸς αὐτοῦ, paidos autou), a description that Luke earlier applied to the nation of Israel (1:54; also Acts 4:25). Such a description of David occurred in contemporary Judaism (1 Macc. 4:30; 2 Esdr. [= 4 Ezra] 3:23; R. Brown 1977: 371). David is the prototype of Israel's regal dynasty, whose foundational place in God's plan was revealed in the Davidic covenant (2 Sam. 7:13–14; Fitzmyer 1981: 383). The decisive Davidite for Judaism is Messiah. Covenantal promises of Scripture are being inaugurated with Jesus' coming. Marshall (1978: 91) notes that this messianic reference makes it impossible for the original hymn to have referred to John, who has no Davidic connection.

Messiah is a picture of power and strength. The reference to the "horn of salvation" (κέρας σωτηρίας, keras sōtērias) is drawn from the OT, where it pictures an ox with horns that is able to defeat enemies with the powerful thrust of its protected head (Deut. 33:17). The image was transferred to the warrior who had a horned helmet to symbolize the presence of power (Ps. 75:4–5, 10 [75:5–6, 11 MT]; 148:14 [in reference to the nation of Israel]; 1QH 9.28–29).[17] The figure is also used to describe God himself (2 Sam. 22:3; Ps. 18:2 [18:3 MT]). In particular, the term was often used for a powerful regal figure. In some of these references the horn is specifically tied to the Davidic house, which is portrayed as delivering the nation (1 Sam. 2:10; Ps. 132:17; Ezek. 29:21; the fifteenth benediction of the Jewish prayer Shemoneh Esreh [Eighteen Benedictions] [= Schürer 1973–87: 2.458]).[18] The nature of the powerful messianic deliverance is spelled out in the following verses, especially Luke 1:71, 74. Zechariah portrays a Messiah of great power and strength who will deliver God's people from their enemies.

Some suggest that these verses clearly portray the Messiah's Davidic connections as coming at least in part through Mary (Godet 1875: 1.111; Hendriksen 1978: 124). Although such a conclusion cannot be regarded as absolutely certain, the suggestion is proba-

17. Foerster, *TDNT* 3:670, notes that the combination *to raise up a horn* does not appear in the LXX.

18. Michel, *TDNT* 5:129; Jeremias, *TDNT* 5:681 n. 184, 700; SB 4:213. Lohse, *TDNT* 8:481, cites the Jewish benediction; cf. also pp. 482, 485.

ble. Zechariah, as portrayed by Luke, would be aware of Mary's pregnancy, because of her visit to Elizabeth (1:39–56), and this despite her not yet being married to Joseph (exactly when Joseph and Mary married is not clear in the timing of these events). If such is the case and if Zechariah is not making merely legal associations in his reference to David's house, then Jesus' Davidic connection also comes through Mary, not just through Joseph, as was noted earlier in 1:27. In spite of the lack of explicit Lucan references to such a Davidic connection through Mary, the implicit reference here may suggest that Luke does see such a double connection.

ii. In Accordance with the Prophets (1:70)

Zechariah now brings in the theme of promise. The coming of a **1:70** powerful Messiah corresponds (καθώς, *kathōs*, even as) to the promise of the prophets. This idea is close to that of 1:55: what is taking place is according to what God predicted.

The predictive element is emphasized by the multilayered description of the prophets. First, the promises that were spoken came διὰ στόματος (*dia stomatos*, through [their] mouth). The singular reference to the *mouth* of the prophets (repeated in Acts 3:18, 21; Plummer 1896: 41) portrays them as secondary agents in the presentation of God's promise. It also presents their message as unified: they speak from God "with one mouth" about Messiah. Second, the prophets are holy prophets. The term ἁγίων (*hagiōn*) is adjectival, meaning "holy," not a noun meaning "saints," a rendering that is too complicated in this context (Plummer 1896: 41; Godet 1875: 1.111). This description is present in Judaism: the prophets are set-apart instruments of God (Wis. 11:1; 2 Bar. 85.1; R. Brown 1977: 371). Third, the prophets who uttered this promise date back to "of old" or come "from early times": ἀπ᾽ αἰῶνος (*ap' aiōnos*; lit., from the age) characterizes the prophecies as laid out in a long succession of prophets, dating back to the early days of the nation.[19] If the citations in Acts detail this point, then the prophecies date back to Moses' promise in Deut. 18 and include many of the prophets dating from Samuel (Acts 3:18–26; 10:43; Luke 24:27, 32, 44–47).[20] This specific reference to the prophets of old is found again in Acts 3:21 and 15:18 (conceptually related by mentioning the covenant promise are Acts 7:8 and Luke 22:20). The basic prophetic promises are the two alluded to in this hymn: the Abrahamic

19. Bovon 1989: 54 prefers the translation "the entire time" or "always," but the point is the same. The promise through time has been consistent.

20. Hendriksen 1978: 125 includes a chart of various texts about Messiah. For covenant references in the OT, see Exod. 2:24; Lev. 26:42; Ps. 106:45; Ezek. 16:60; Bovon 1989: 106 n. 62.

oath of Gen. 12 (Luke 1:73) and the Davidic covenant of 2 Sam. 7 (Luke 1:69).

iii. Salvation from Enemies (1:71)

1:71 Zechariah specifies the nature of the messianic salvation set forth by the prophets. Σωτηρίαν (*sōtērian*, salvation) stands in apposition to 1:69, especially the reference to the horn of salvation, and explains the type of salvation Zechariah hoped for in Messiah (Godet 1875: 1.112; Creed 1930: 26). The term itself means deliverance or preservation, whether it be physical preservation of health, deliverance of a nation, or the spiritual deliverance of salvation before God (Exod. 14:13; Job 5:4; 2 Macc. 3:32; Ps. 106:10; Ps. Sol. 10.8; 12.6; Plummer 1896: 41). Here the reference is to the deliverance that comes through Messiah, a deliverance promised by the prophets so that it contains an earthly element as well as spiritual overtones. Here is another "exodus" for the nation. In fact, one can view 1:68–70 as announcing the theme that the rest of the hymn explains. The political emphasis is present also in contemporary Judaism (1QM 14.4–10; 11.5–6 ["the Star of Jacob"]; 18.6–11; Ps. Sol. 17.23–27; *Shemoneh Esreh* [Eighteen Benedictions] nos. 7, 10, 12 [= Schürer 1973–87: 2.457]; Marshall 1978: 91; Bovon 1989: 98). Hendriksen (1978: 125), because he sees a spiritual emphasis in the passage, takes the reference to enemies to refer primarily to Satan. Schweizer (1984: 42) argues that Luke has made something spiritual out of an originally political reference. However, it seems better in light of OT and contemporary usage to include a political reference in the verse alongside the reference to satanic forces, as the OT background of the following phrases in the hymn make clear (Ps. 18:17 [18:18 MT]; 106:10; 2 Sam. 22:18; Danker 1988: 48; Marshall 1978: 91).[21] It is difficult to limit the phrase *those who hate us* to evil spiritual beings, as this description also fits human agents who bear animosity (Luke 6:22, 27). When the hymn is considered as a whole, both spiritual and political rescue are present in the salvation that Messiah brings (see the exegesis of 1:68).

The salvation is from enemies and from the hand of those who hate. The twofold mention of "us" refers to those who are godly like Zechariah and generalizes the hymn beyond the psalmist. Godet (1875: 1.112) argues that the terms ἐχθρῶν (*echthrōn*, enemies) and μισούντων (*misountōn*, those who hate) refer to two distinct

---

21. For a reference to satanic enemies, see 10:18; 11:14–23; 13:16. They are part of the opposition, since in first-century Judaism they both move the human opposition and are responsible for "darkness." They should be included because of the literary role of the hymn in Luke–Acts in introducing themes developed later in the book.

groups. The first refers to foreign enemies, while the second refers to local Jewish tyrants who hated the faithful. But the appearance of these terms in parallel in the Psalms (18:17 [17:18 LXX]; 106:10 [105:10 LXX]) argues against making such a distinction. The reference in both cases is to religious and political enemies of all types who oppose God's people (Fitzmyer 1981: 384). The reference to the hand of those who hate us is a figurative allusion to the power of the opponents, from whom the faithful are rescued by Messiah (Lohse, *TDNT* 9:430; Josh. 2:24; Judg. 4:2; Luke 24:7; Acts 12:11 [a figure for the exercise of authority or control]). The Messiah will deliver the faithful from the clutches of the enemy. Luke 1:74 elaborates this with the idea of rescue.[22] Zechariah's hope is that the Messiah will deliver the people and will exercise authority over them.

iv. Mercy and Covenant Remembrance (1:72)

God's mercy and his covenants are brought together; his actions re- **1:72** flect both: in saving his people through Messiah, God is faithful to his covenant promises. The OT also connects mercy and covenant (Deut. 7:9; 1 Kings 8:23). He keeps his promises with the ancestors of faith (Danker 1988: 48). The expression ποιῆσαι ἔλεος (*poiēsai eleos*, to do mercy) gives the result of the coming of salvation. Some argue that the phrase either explains the salvation of 1:71 (Fitzmyer 1981: 384) or gives the purpose of the coming of salvation (Marshall 1978: 92; Plummer 1896: 41). But 1:72 does not really describe messianic salvation, as that is done in 1:71, 74. Nor is the point that the goal of God's salvation is to display his mercy, though it does do that. Rather, the result of messianic salvation is that mercy is displayed and covenant is remembered (BDF §391.4). Thus, the verse is not so much interested in God's motivation for salvation (the purpose view), as it is in articulating what salvation shows or produces, the display of God's mercy and faithfulness.

The expression *to do mercy* is similar to 1:54–55. As mentioned there, mercy describes God's loyal, faithful, gracious love, his חֶסֶד (*ḥesed*), as he acts for his people. The idiom *to do mercy* has OT precedent (Gen. 24:12; Judg. 1:24; 8:35; Ruth 1:8), while the idea of showing mercy to the fathers also appears in the OT and in Judaism (Mic. 7:20; 1 Macc. 4:10; Schürmann 1969: 88; Fitzmyer 1981: 384; a Hebraism, BDF §310.1). Luke repeats the idea in Acts 3:25.[23]

---

22. The terms ῥύομαι (to rescue) and σῴζω (to save) occasionally appear together to express the idea of deliverance; Foerster, *TDNT* 7:990–91; Kasch, *TDNT* 6:1002; Ps. 7:1–2 [7:2–3 LXX]; 71:2 [70:2 LXX].

23. The fathers/patriarchs are mentioned in John 7:22; Acts 3:13; 7:32; Rom. 9:5; 11:28; the promise is noted in Acts 13:32; 26:6; Rom. 15:8; Schrenk, *TDNT* 5:976 nn. 178 and 182. In Judaism, see 4 Macc. 16:20; 2 Esdr. [= 4 Ezra] 2:5–7; 3:10–17.

God's performing mercy means that he takes decisive action for his own. The same idea occurs when Luke speaks of God's making redemption (1:68). What is interesting is the idea of doing mercy "to the fathers."[24] The reference to a current action done to the fathers implies strongly that the fathers are alive or, at least, are aware of covenant fulfillment (16:23, 27).[25] What God has promised they are seeing come to pass. God keeps his word.

Messianic salvation also results in God's remembering his holy covenant. Again, the description ἁγίας (*hagias*, holy) marks out the covenant as special or set apart (Marshall 1978: 92). To "remember covenant" or "confirm an oath" is an OT expression (Ps. 105:8; 106:45; Gen. 22:16–18; 26:3; Exod. 2:24; Schürmann 1969: 88 n. 47). The covenant in view is the Abrahamic covenant (1:73). The idea of remembering (μνησθῆναι, *mnēsthēnai*) is not merely cognitive, but refers to God's bringing his promise into operation. The phrase could well be rendered "to act" or "to effect" his holy covenant (Michel, *TDNT* 4:676). God's acting for his covenant should encourage Luke's readers that he will act on the rest of his promises.

v. In Accordance with Abrahamic Promise (1:73)

1:73 The particular covenant that God remembers is his promise to Abraham (Gen. 12:1–3; 17:7; 22:16–18; 26:3, 24; Deut. 7:8). The recollection of the oath made to the fathers is an OT and Jewish theme (Ps. 105:8–9, 11; Jer. 11:5; Exod. 2:24; Lev. 26:42; 1 Macc. 4:10; 2 Macc. 1:2; CD 8.18; Behm, *TDNT* 2:132; R. Brown 1977: 372). The mention of Abraham recalls that God is faithful to his original commitments. Through Jesus' coming, God keeps promises made to both of the key OT figures highlighted by the hymn: Abraham (1:73) and David (1:69).

The rest of the verse, along with 1:74, teaches that God committed to the Abrahamic covenant so that the faithful could serve God. Δοῦναι (*dounai*, to grant) introduces 1:74, serving as a purpose infinitive explaining why the covenant commitment was given (Plummer 1896: 41–42). As the next verse shows, God made covenant commitments and rescued his people in order to gather a people that would serve him. That God "grants" such service adds a note of "gift" to the image. Some see here the abandonment of OT hope and draw attention to the spiritual emphasis in the passage (Creed 1930: 26; Fitzmyer 1981: 385), but the reference to the rescue from

24. For μετά meaning "to," see BDF §206.3 and BDR §206.3.5; "with" cannot be meant here because the fathers do not cooperate with God in this action.

25. SB 1:892; Schweizer 1984: 42; Plummer 1896: 41. One could argue that the figure means "for the sake of the fathers," but this rendering seems too soft in light of the belief that the righteous experience resurrection (16:19–31).

enemies so his people can serve God is not out of touch with OT expression. Many psalms request rescue and then promise to worship God in response (e.g., Ps. 70, 71, 72). The expectation of the devout for a political and spiritual rescue is not merely because of a pragmatic desire to be politically free, but also because of a wish to serve God. God's covenant people were constituted as a theocracy in the OT. Some wished to return and serve God as a united, sovereign people without the burden of domination by those who did not know the God of Abraham. The nature of OT promise always had physical and spiritual elements. How God will fulfill this OT expectation in Christ is part of the burden of Luke–Acts. Here, fulfillment's certainty is expressed, so that one raises a note of praise because that reality is drawing near.

vi. Goal: To Serve God in Holiness after Rescue (1:74–75)

In a restatement of the idea of 1:71, Zechariah describes the messianic salvation that delivers him so he can serve God. The desire to be rescued from the enemy has OT roots, as well as being a theme of Judaism (Ps. 97:10; 18 superscription [18:1 MT]; Jer. 30:8; 2 Sam. 22:18; Ps. Sol. 17.30, 45; 3 Macc. 6:10).[26] The enemies in view here are opponents of God's nation and people (Leaney 1958: 89–90; Godet 1875: 1.112). The community prayer of Acts 4:25–31 indicates the type of enemies that opposed Messiah, although in Zechariah's time the enemy would have been seen primarily in the foreign domination of Palestine. What God will do through Messiah is rescue God's people from the hands of these enemies.[27] Zechariah anticipates physical deliverance as a part of messianic salvation. Such expectation belongs to the salvific perspective of those who trust Messiah. Luke will explain in his two volumes how the expectation works itself out.

1:74

The idea of being rescued is subordinate to the idea of serving God. The covenant (1:72–73) is made and granted to the faithful in order that once the faithful are rescued they may fearlessly serve God. The term ἀφόβως (*aphobōs*, without fear), even though it begins the verse, modifies λατρεύειν (*latreuein*, to serve), so that the hymn speaks of "serving God fearlessly" (Hendriksen 1978: 131). The position of the term at the start of the sentence means that the reference to fear's absence is emphatic. It reflects a life without the

---

26. Foerster, *TDNT* 2:813. Kasch, *TDNT* 6:1002, notes that rescue in the NT always refers to God as the rescuer. Rescue texts have strong OT roots; seven of seventeen NT uses of ῥύομαι have OT influence: Luke 1:74; Matt. 27:43; Rom. 11:26; 2 Cor. 1:10a; 2 Thess. 3:2; 2 Tim. 3:11; 4:17.

27. For χειρός as a figure for power, see the exegesis of 1:71. On the grammar, see BDR §217.5.

distraction of oppression. In turn, λατρεύειν is tied to the infinitive δοῦναι (*dounai*, to grant) in 1:73 as an epexegetical infinitive.[28] It explains precisely what God has granted his people to do. Thus, God fulfills covenant so they can serve him fearlessly.

God saves for service. The term λατρεύω is significant because it refers to the total service one gives to God, not just to the worship or sacrificial service that a faithful Jew would render in the temple or synagogue. In the NT, the term is used exclusively of service given to a deity, whether it be to God or, in pagan settings, to the gods (Luke 2:37; 4:8; Rom. 1:25; Exod. 3:12; Deut. 11:13; Strathmann, *TDNT* 4:62–63). God's deliverance enables one to serve God with one's life. At least, that is Zechariah's desire.

In regard to the hymn's original setting, the political emphasis, alongside the spiritual emphasis, is interesting. Godet (1875: 1.113) asks the following penetrating question: "How, after the unbelief of Israel [as portrayed in the rest of the Gospel account] had created a gulf between the expectation and the facts, could a later writer, attributing to Zacharias just what words he pleased, put into his mouth these fond hopes of earlier days?" What Godet suggests is that the only appropriate setting for such unqualified hope is one involving an expectant Jew, a Jew looking at messianic events before Jesus' life made the picture more complex. The hymn is appropriately attached to Zechariah.

1:75 The purpose of deliverance is to allow continuous service before God; but such service is not merely activity on behalf of God. There is a moral quality to this worship. God's people are to serve "in holiness and righteousness" before him. The combination ὁσιότητι καὶ δικαιοσύνῃ (*hosiotēti kai dikaiosynē*) reflects an attitude that respects God's moral demands in obedience and conforms to his call to righteousness.[29] The essence of worship is responsiveness to God's demands. Zechariah desires undefiled, undistracted worship of God, a worship that is both personal and moral. It is conducted with the realization that all service is done before (ἐνώπιον, *enōpion*) God. Such worship is not tied to a locale, but is related to all of life. In addition, it is a continuous worship that spans the lifetime of the delivered faithful, thus, the reference to service given "all our days" (πάσαις ταῖς ἡμέραις ἡμῶν, *pasais tais hēmerais hēmōn*). Zechariah wishes to be a useful servant of God. Deliverance, in his

---

28. Marshall 1978: 92 cites Luke 8:10; Acts 2:4; 4:29 as grammatical parallels.

29. Danker 1988: 48–49; Plummer 1896: 42; Hauck, *TDNT* 5:491 n. 24, 493. The combination is found elsewhere in Wis. 9:3 and Eph. 4:24. God seeks righteousness and worship even among the heathen: Acts 13:10, 16; 24:25; 10:35, 43; Schrenk, *TDNT* 2:199. In the OT, Josh. 24:14 is similar in thrust; Nolland 1989: 88.

mind, will make this desire more possible; that is why he rejoices at its prospect.

c. Prophecy about Jesus and John (1:76–79)
i. John: Prophet of the Most High to Prepare the Way (1:76)

Zechariah now turns his attention to his child (καὶ σὺ δέ, παιδίον, **1:76** *kai sy de, paidion,* but you, child). John is God's prophet. John prepares the way for God, who himself comes to his people through Jesus' messianic visitation. This verse begins the second major unit of the hymn, as the topic shifts from what God is doing for the righteous, to what he will do through John and the Messiah. The sectional shift is indicated by the change of topic and by the shift from aorist tenses to future tenses (Fitzmyer 1981: 385).

This child shall be known as the prophet of the Most High. The Most High (ὑψίστου, *hypsistou*) refers to God as the exalted transcendent deity and repeats the reference to him found in 1:32.[30] John's description contrasts with the earlier reference to Jesus (1:32–35). Whereas Jesus is the Son, John is a prophet. Thus John's subordination to Jesus is clear.

The topic of John as a prophet reappears in 7:26–35, where the point is made that John is more than a prophet, because he has a special role. The latter text stresses that John is the last of the line of prophets who looked forward to Messiah's coming. John, as a prophet, heralds the arrival of salvation and introduces the figure of this new era.

The title *prophet of the Most High* occurs in T. Levi 8.15, where it has a messianic connotation, a point that has led some to suggest that John is seen messianically here.[31] But Luke clearly does not see John in this way, since the Davidic connection is limited to Jesus, as is the regal emphasis. In addition, this hymn goes on to describe Messiah as a figure separate from John (Marshall 1978: 93; Fitzmyer 1981: 385). This title had a fluid meaning within Judaism, with the exact nuance determined by the community and context in which it was used.

The explanation (γάρ, *gar,* for) of this prophet's role comes next. John will go before (προπορεύσῃ, *proporeusē*) the Lord for the pur-

---

30. "Most High" is another way to speak of heaven. To speak of "glory in the highest" (2:14; 19:38) is to call heaven to praise; Matt. 21:9; Luke 1:32, 35; Acts 7:48; Schrenk, *TDNT* 5:985 n. 253.

31. Danker 1988: 49; Leaney 1958: 24 (who suggests that this hymn originally was tied to Anna [2:38], but then the question is why move it and bring in John the Baptist). Levi is referred to as a priest-king, fulfilling the Maccabean model. Evil king-priests of the Most High appear in T. Moses 6.1.

pose of preparing the way for him.[32] How John prepares the way is explained in 1:77. John prepares for all that God will do through the Messiah. The preparation involves a message, the proclamation of the knowledge of salvation, and the forgiveness of sins.

The idea of going before the Lord repeats the idea of 1:17, where John functions like the Elijah end-time prophet. The verbs of 1:76, προπορεύσῃ (Mal. 3:1 [conceptually, not lexically]) and ἑτοιμάσαι (Isa. 40:3), reflect OT wording. The Malachi passage, in particular, discusses the Elijah figure (Godet 1875: 1.114). The picture of John as a forerunner and preacher of forgiveness is consistent with the picture of the other Gospels (Mark 1:2, 4; Matt. 3:3) and also reflects later Lucan references (Luke 3:4–6; 7:27). What is unique to Luke is the highlighting of salvation (1:77). Luke notes this point of continuity between what John does and what Messiah will do (Acts 10:38; 13:24). The Qumran community saw Isa. 40 as a text fulfilled in the end-time (1QS 8.13–14; 9.19–20), though they thought they were that end-time community. Thus, an allusion to Isa. 40 as an end-time text would not be a surprising association for first-century Judaism.

One debated item in the passage is the identity of *Lord* (κυρίου, *kyriou*): is the way prepared for God or Jesus? Those who argue for Jesus point out that Jesus is alluded to as the Lord in 1:43 and that Jesus is the natural association for Christian readers (Fitzmyer 1981: 385–86; Marshall 1978: 93; Michaelis, *TDNT* 5:70 n. 94). But a reference to God is more likely contextually (Klostermann 1929: 28; Schneider 1977a: 62; Danker 1988: 49; Schürmann 1969: 90–91, who distinguishes between the original meaning [God] and Luke's [Jesus], which distinction I reject). This is anticipated in 1:16–17 with its allusions to Mal. 3:1 and Isa. 40:3, where God is clearly meant (see esp. 1:16). Now in this hymn, if "his people" (1:77) is a reference to God's people—and that is virtually certain—then the natural reference of "his ways" (1:76) is also to God. In both cases the antecedent would be κυρίου in 1:76. That his people (τῷ λαῷ αὐτοῦ, *tō laō autou*) refers to God is seen in 1:68, where the redemption of his people is mentioned and the term clearly refers to God. The importance of this interpretation is that there is no basis of appeal to a post-Christian understanding of the OT hope by Zechariah at this point. The hope is one of an OT saint looking for messianic redemption. In this hymn, there is no retrogression of a later faith into an earlier period.

But in what sense can John be said to go before the Lord, if God is meant? The clue is found by the double use of the idea of visita-

32. Ἑτοιμάσαι, a purpose infinitive, goes back to προπορεύσῃ.

tion in the hymn (1:68, 78). God's redemption visits his people in the person of Messiah. John goes before the God of Israel, because he goes before the salvation that is tied to the Messiah.[33] In the Messiah, God's plan and design are found, so that when Messiah comes, God comes. John as a prophet will prepare for God's coming by clearing the way for him as he delivers his own in the Messiah.

ii. John: To Give Knowledge of Forgiveness of Sins (1:77)

John prepares the way for God through the message of salvation   **1:77** that he brings, a message that declares the forgiveness of sins. As Zechariah describes it, John's basic task is to give knowledge of salvation to God's people. Δοῦναι (*dounai*, to give) functions as an epexegetic infinitive to the final phrase of 1:76, explaining how John prepares the way.[34] Since ἑτοιμάσαι in 1:76 is itself a purpose infinitive, 1:77 also elaborates the purpose of John's "preparatory" mission. John communicates the knowledge of God's offer of salvation to God's people, that is, to Israel. The national focus of the reference to his people (λαῷ, *laō*) is clearly indicated in the hymn's introduction, where the God of Israel is praised (1:68). Though the wording about salvation here has no exact OT parallel (R. Brown 1977: 373), most see in the spiritual emphasis an allusion to the new covenant (Jer. 31:34; 33:8; Acts 5:31; Leaney 1958: 90; Schürmann 1969: 91 n. 71).

John's message centers on the forgiveness of sins. There are three suggestions for how the reference to forgiveness, ἐν ἀφέσει (*en aphesei*), relates grammatically to the verse.[35] (1) Some tie the reference to δοῦναι, the idea of giving knowledge, so that the sense of the verse is "to give in forgiveness of sins a knowledge of salvation" (Creed 1930: 26–27). Plummer objects to this approach, arguing that John does not forgive sins, which is what the wording of this view suggests. (2) Others tie the term to γνῶσιν (*gnōsin*, knowledge), yielding "to give a knowledge in the forgiveness of sins of salvation." This view is grammatically awkward in that it is not clear how knowledge, forgiveness, and salvation relate to one another.[36]

33. Luke 1:69 and 2:30 express this idea explicitly; Bock 1987: 73–74.

34. Schürmann 1969: 91 n. 67; Hendriksen 1978: 131; Wiefel 1988: 65; BDF §400.6. Bovon 1989: 108 correctly states that John has a foot in each era, since as the last of the prophets of promise he sets the table for the new era (Luke 7:26; 16:16).

35. Plummer 1896: 42. The NT refers to this concept in alternative ways: Mark 1:4; Matt. 26:28; Luke 1:77; 24:47; Acts 2:38; 5:31; 10:43; 13:38; 26:18; Col. 1:14; Heb. 10:11 ("take away sin"); Eph. 2:17 ("peace"); Bultmann, *TDNT* 1:511.

36. Plummer does not cite anyone who argues for this option. "Knowledge of salvation" in Hebrew idiom refers to the experience of salvation; Ps. 98:2; Nolland 1989: 89.

(3) The best connection ties the term to σωτηρίας (*sōtērias*, salvation), so that the verse reads "to give a knowledge of salvation in the forgiveness of sins" (Plummer 1896: 42–43; Godet 1875: 1.115; Schürmann 1969: 91 n. 69; Marshall 1978: 93). Thus, the stress of the verse is on the intimate connection between salvation and forgiveness of sins. John brings an experience of forgiveness with his message, an experience his baptism portrayed, not because of the rite, but because of what the person brought to the rite—a repentant heart (Bovon 1989: 108). The key spiritual operation of salvation is in the sphere of forgiveness of sins.[37] Forgiveness of sins is a precondition to peace with God (C. Brown, *NIDNTT* 3:212). This wording has no explicit OT background and is Luke's first mention of this key concept (Foerster, *TDNT* 7:990–91; R. Brown 1977: 373).

John's mission as a preparer of the way fits the portrait of the other Synoptic writers, but Luke is the clearest in associating the forerunner role with the content of John's message: salvation, the forgiveness of sins, and baptism of repentance (Luke 3:3; 24:47; Acts 10:37). In Luke's eyes, the emphasis on forgiveness is also a major part of Jesus' ministry (Luke 4:18, a double use of ἄφεσις, *aphesis*, forgiveness). In addition, Jesus' ministry and the apostolic preaching emphasize repentance (Luke 24:47 [the message of Luke's Great Commission]; Acts 5:31; 13:38; 17:30; 20:21). Luke presents the messages of John, Jesus, and the apostles as being in essential continuity with regard to a call to repentance. However, Jesus and the apostles have additional details because of the revelation associated with Jesus' ministry. Such revelation the church will incorporate into its message. Luke will spend some time developing this theme. Luke 1:77 highlights John's proclamation of a salvation of forgiveness. This forgiveness is the product of repentance, a responsive turning to God alone to deal with sin (5:31–32).

This strong spiritual emphasis within salvation differentiates the Christian hope from that of contemporary Judaism, which tended to emphasize the earthly and physical elements of salvation (Hendriksen 1978: 127; Fitzmyer 1981: 386; Foerster, *TDNT* 7:991). But the redemption present in the hymn does not lack physical elements, as the use of λύτρωσιν (*lytrōsin*, redemption) in 1:68 shows. To some, the unique spiritual emphasis is so strong that it is considered impossible that this hymn could have emerged from a pre-Christian or John the Baptist source (R. Brown 1977: 373). But el-

---

37. Godet 1875: 1.115. Bovon 1989: 108 n. 74 notes that the expression *forgiveness of sins* is like neither the OT nor the Christian expression. Jewish usage does occur: Philo, *Life of Moses* 2.29 §147; *Special Laws* 1.35 §190; Josephus, *Antiquities* 6.5.6 §92 (which discusses God's reaction to Israel's desire to elect a king in 1 Sam. 12 and the nation's confession of sin after God revealed his displeasure).

ements of this spiritual conception are present at Qumran (Ring-gren 1963: 120–25; 1QH 9.32–36) and the association between spiritual condition and blessing is a part of OT theology (Deut. 28–32), so that these remarks are not impossible for a Jewish speaker.

iii. Jesus: Dayspring Visitor by the Mercy of God (1:78)

One word, *mercy*, characterizes the entire plan. Both the forerunner's and Messiah's tasks are the concrete expression of God's mercy. The phrase *through God's mercy* (διὰ σπλάγχνα ἐλέους θεοῦ, *dia splanchna eleous theou*) relates to the description of John's call. The grammatical connection is debated and affects the sense of the passage: does it go back to προπορεύσῃ (*proporeusē*—John "goes before" by God's mercy), σωτηρίας (*sōtērias*—John gives knowledge "of salvation" by God's mercy), or ἀφέσει (*aphesei*—"the forgiveness of sins" is by God's mercy)? Since all of these actions are interrelated, it seems best not to specify the point of connection, but rather to regard mercy as a general qualification of all of these actions (Marshall 1978: 94; R. Brown 1977: 373). As 1:78b also makes clear, the entirety of Messiah's coming also occurs in the context of God's mercy (ἐν οἷς, *en hois*, in which—referring back to mercy).

Σπλάγχνα (*splanchna*) refers literally to the bowels, but the LXX and Judaism used the term to refer to deep-seated personal feeling, especially compassion.[38] Combining this term with ἐλέους (*eleous*) is unique and refers to a compassionate mercy.[39] Mercy as the ground of God's actions repeats a key theme (1:50, 54, 72; Eph. 2:4). Salvation is ultimately an act of God's mercy. Not only is John's ministry conducted on the ground of God's mercy, but the sphere (ἐν οἷς) of Messiah's ministry is also the mercy of God.

The visit of the "rising sun from on high" introduces a new figure. The phrase *rising sun* has produced much discussion. It is significant that the previous mention of visitation in the hymn is associated with Messiah, the horn of David (1:68–69; R. Brown 1977: 373–74). This observation makes it likely that Messiah is intended by "rising sun," which is confirmed when one examines the messianic background of the term ἀνατολή (*anatolē*). God will visit his people in Messiah, the coming light.

The reference to ἀνατολή is important. The Greek term, which literally means "that which springs up," has a rich and varied OT background. On the one hand, it referred to the Branch or Sprout

1:78

---

38. Prov. 12:10; Sir. 30:7; T. Naph. 4.5; T. Levi 4.4; 1QS 1.22; 2.1; Plummer 1896: 43; Marshall 1978: 94; Fitzmyer 1981: 386; Köster, *TDNT* 7:556. The English equivalent term is *heart*.

39. Col. 3:12 is a grammatically parallel verse where οἰκτιρμοῦ (mercy) is a genitive of quality, as ἐλέους is here.

in dependence on the Hebrew term צֶמַח (*semaḥ*; Jer. 23:5; 33:15 [not present in the LXX]; Zech. 3:8; 6:12; Isa. 11:1–10).[40] It also referred to the rising sun or star when the verbal form ἀνατέλλω (*anatellō*, to rise up) was used (Num. 24:17; Mal. 4:2 [3:20 MT/LXX]).[41] At Qumran and in contemporary Judaism, the former sense of Branch was predominant and was understood messianically.[42] Interestingly, both Philo (*On the Confusion of Tongues* 14 §§60–63) and Justin Martyr (*Dialogue with Trypho* 100.4; 106.4; 121.2; 126.1) saw the term as messianic and tied it to the picture of a heavenly light (Schlier, *TDNT* 1:353). T. Judah 24.1, 6 appears to mix both images. Thus, the title was clearly messianic in the first century, though the picture in the term varied.

But which image is key in this text, branch or sun? The context clearly marks the image of light as key. Ἀνατολή is qualified by the phrase ἐξ ὕψους (*ex hypsous*, from on high), a reference to the heavens. In addition, 1:79 goes on to speak of the light guiding in the midst of darkness, so that the picture is of a beacon from heaven. Nolland (1989: 90) may be right in appealing to Isa. 60:2–3 and 58:8–10 as important conceptual background.

But many think that the first-century association of the term with the messianic Branch was so strong that double entendre is present, that is, Luke intends to evoke both associations, though the rising sun association is the dominant idea (Bock 1987: 73; so also Bovon 1989: 109). By God's mercy, God's regal Messiah visits and serves people as a guiding heavenly light, leading them into God's way of peace. Marshall (1978: 95) summarizes: "The imagery is thus that of the Davidic Messiah, the Shoot from Jesse (Is. 11:1ff.) and the star from Jacob (Nu. 24:17) who is to visit men from on high, i.e. from the dwelling place of God (2 Sa. 22:17)." God sends his Messiah as the bright dawn of salvation shining upon the face of people.

iv. Jesus: To Bring Light and to Guide into the Way of Peace (1:79)

1:79   Zechariah concludes the hymn and describes Messiah's mission of guiding the lost, those dwelling in darkness, into God's way. The

---

40. Schlier, *TDNT* 1:352–53; Schürmann 1969: 92; BDB 855. When a plant is the image in the OT, a Davidite is in view; Nolland 1989: 90.

41. Marshall 1978: 94–95. On God or his word as light, see 2 Sam. 22:17, 29; Ps. 119:105; Goulder 1989: 242.

42. CD 7.18–19; 1QM 11.6; 4Q175 [= 4QTestim] 12; 4Q161 [= 4QpIsa^a]; T. Levi 18.3. T. Levi 4.3–4 is an interesting parallel, but it is debated whether a Christian interpolation is present; H. Kee in J. Charlesworth 1983–85: 1.789 n. 4b. Fitzmyer 1981: 387 cites the texts. On the tribe of Judah as the locale of the messianic, regal hope, see T. Naph. 8.2; T. Sim. 7.1–2; Wiefel 1988: 65.

task is presented in the two infinitival terms ἐπιφᾶναι (*epiphanai*, to shine) and κατευθῦναι (*kateuthynai*, to guide). Both infinitives explain the role of the rising sun's visitation (1:78), but in addition they seem to describe in particular the purpose for his coming. The imagery of the shining heavenly light continues in the reference to ἐπιφᾶναι. The OT commonly pictures God as a light who shines on his people and enlightens them (Deut. 33:2; Ps. 118:27; Bultmann and Lührmann, *TDNT* 9:10; Marshall 1978: 95; C. F. Evans 1990: 187; note Acts 26:17–18). The image of light appearing in the darkness to aid people is also common, whether the light is God himself or an agent of God (Isa. 9:1–2 [8:23–9:1 MT]; 42:6–7; 49:6; Plummer 1896: 43; Conzelmann, *TDNT* 7:440–41). The idea of Messiah's shining describes his coming to humans, his teaching on their behalf, and his ministering to them (Fitzmyer 1981: 388).

The need for such ministry is described in bleak terms. People sit in darkness and in the shadow of death. These OT images appear to refer to those who are oppressed spiritually and physically, like Israel before the exodus (Ps. 107:10; Isa. 9:2 [9:1 MT]; 42:7; 49:9–10; 59:8–9; Mic. 7:8). They refer to people locked up in ignorance, on the edge of death. Threatened with rejection, they lack righteousness, do not demonstrate justice, and stand in need of release and forgiveness.[43]

It is interesting that the "righteous" Zechariah (1:6) includes himself among the needy when he speaks of "our feet" being guided by the messianic light into the way of peace.[44] People in the nation of Israel (1:68) stand in need of repentance, a picture that Luke continues to describe throughout his two volumes (Luke 24:47; Acts 5:31). Those who are uncertain of God's way have in Messiah a light by which they can see the road.

Messiah's task also involves guidance (κατευθῦναι). The purpose of his appearing is to lead others to God, into the way of peace. The consequence of deliverance is a full life, which is able to serve God (1:74–75; Schneider 1977a: 62). The description of salvation in terms of peace is another common theme in Luke.[45] The OT also had this theme with שָׁלוֹם (*šālôm*; Jer. 14:13; Isa. 48:18; 54:10; Ezek. 34:25–29). The OT idea refers to a person's total well-being as a re-

43. This is the point of the connection to Luke 1:77; Godet 1875: 1.117. On the verse as a whole, see Danker 1988: 50–51. C. Schneider, *TDNT* 3:443, argues that the image is a figure for mourning. Those who sit in darkness are those who mourn the presence of death. Whether this particular picture is present is less likely given the OT background.

44. Fitzmyer 1981: 388. A similar exhortation for the "straight walk" is found in T. Sim. 5.2, but in Luke, God supplies the way; Bovon 1989: 110 n. 89.

45. Luke 2:14, where peace is limited to people of good will, that is, to those who respond to Messiah's coming as did the shepherds; Luke 10:5; 24:36; Acts 10:36.

sult of being in harmony with God. Luke's picture differs little from the OT. For Israel, the way to peace was through the guidance provided by the Messiah. The question was, "Would the nation come to its Messiah?"[46]

In 1:76–79, John and Jesus come by God's mercy to God's people. John will prepare the way for God's visitation in Messiah. He will instruct them about salvation and the forgiveness of sins. But Messiah will go beyond John. For he will serve like a bright guiding light that takes the people out of the darkness and brings them into God's way. John will proclaim salvation, but Jesus can take them into it (Schürmann 1969: 92; Fitzmyer 1981: 387).

d. Growth of John (1:80)

1:80 Luke summarizes the Baptist's growth, who is not mentioned again until his ministry begins in 3:2. Such summaries are common in the infancy section (2:40, 52) and have parallels in the OT. The accounts of Isaac (Gen. 21:8), Samuel (1 Sam. 2:26), and Samson (Judg. 13:24) also have growth summaries (R. Brown 1977: 376–77; Tiede 1988: 64). John was growing physically and spiritually. Luke uses his preferred imperfect for both verbs (ηὔξανεν, *ēuxanen*, was growing; ἐκραταιοῦτο, *ekrataiouto*, was becoming strong). Some regard the reference to πνεῦμα (*pneuma*) as a reference to the Holy Spirit (1:15, 41, 67; R. Brown 1977: 374; Schweizer 1984: 44). But the reference more naturally refers to John's personal spirit, since it is placed next to the idea of physical strength (Hendriksen 1978: 132; Godet 1875: 1.117; Schweizer, *TDNT* 6:415).[47] Such growth is related to God's Spirit, but the primary point is John's growth (Luke 2:40; Eph. 3:16; Danker 1988: 51).

John spent his preministry days in the wilderness. The plural reference to "wildernesses" (ἐρήμοις, *erēmois*) is not a reference to several places, but is an abstract plural that looks at one general locale (Godet 1875: 1.117; BDF §263). Luke is fond of the plural expression (5:16; 8:29). The area is probably the Jordan Valley, the barren Judean wilderness west of the Dead Sea. John spent his days there

---

46. Tannehill 1986: 34–35 speaks of the reader's sense of tragedy in Luke, since the reader knows that Israel's release did not happen, because it rejected Messiah. A successful outcome of the promise is not yet realized, though Luke still has hope for Israel; cf. Tannehill 1985. The account as a whole is almost a theodicy, explaining what God is doing, despite Messiah's apparent failure. Tiede 1980 develops this idea, including issues tied to the fall of Jerusalem. His view of Luke's understanding of Jerusalem's fall requires that the Gospel of Luke be dated after A.D. 70, which is debatable. However, the term *theodicy* does apply to the assurance Luke–Acts seeks to give. Tiede's insights on how Luke saw Jerusalem and Israel are valuable.

47. Apparently, Schweizer's view changed.

until he came to minister to Israel. Luke again notes the national and exclusive focus of John's ministry ("to Israel"), a reference that is clearly intended to describe a historical reality. The phrase *the days of his appearing* looks forward to the beginning of his ministry.[48] At this point, Luke leaves the story of John until 3:2. It is time to turn to Jesus.

Summary

The infancy sections on John's birth contain two distinct events: John's naming (1:57–66) and Zechariah's hymn of praise (1:67–80). The first major point is that Zechariah has learned from his period in silence that God is at work in amazing ways. The selection of an unusual name for John, which is immediately confirmed by Zechariah, shows that he has learned to trust God and his word. Rather than give the child a traditional name, the name that God chose (1:13) is selected. Instantly, Zechariah regains his speech, a confirmation of his obedient response. The first account closes by reflecting on the events surrounding the entire naming incident and raising the question of who this child is.

The answer follows in the hymn.[49] John raises the curtain on God's salvation, a prelude to the main act. This salvation involves a prophet who will prepare the people for God's visit in Messiah. This prophet will inform the people about salvation and the forgiveness of sins. He will have a message of repentance that is in continuity with what Jesus will preach. Yet John's message will lack the detail that Messiah's life and ministry will provide. Thus John prepares the way, rather than being the way.

The hymn glorifies God for completing the salvation that was promised to Abraham and to the nation. That salvation centers in the Davidic Messiah, who will function like a shining heavenly light in the midst of people who sit in death and darkness. The Messiah will guide many into the way of peace, a whole and harmonious relationship with God. Instruction on "the way" will be a major burden of the book, especially §IV (9:51–19:44).

Included in this salvation hope is not only a spiritual emphasis, but also the expectation of a physical deliverance from enemies. The outworking of this element of salvation will also concern Luke, though his answer to this issue is not fully developed until Acts. At this point in Zechariah's thinking, the salvation at both the spiritual and the physical levels is unified in time and

---

48. The phraseology is Semitic in style, both in using the term ἡμέρα as meaning "time" (BDF §165; Delling, *TDNT* 2:950) and in using the genitive ἀναδείξεως (R. Brown 1977: 374). The use of ἀναδείξεως to describe his manifesting himself to Israel is the only NT use of the term (Sir. 43:6).

49. Bovon 1989: 111 notes that salvation history is narrated and sung. The mood of praise is important.

emphasis. Such a view is only natural for a hymn that does not have the perspective of the cross to draw upon. In maintaining this unified emphasis, Luke has been faithful to the perspective of his source. What John's birth shows, above all, is that God's promised messianic salvation draws near. The events continually emphasize that God's promise and God's word come to pass. Luke's readers can be assured that God can and will do what he promises in his Messiah Jesus (1:4). In addition, they can learn from Zechariah's praise that salvation's goal is to serve God in holiness and righteousness (1:74–75).

There is one other major lesson in this unit. The maturing of pious Zechariah's faith pictures one who struggles to accept what God has promised. Zechariah shows that even the faith of pious people can pause, and then develop added depth. It is important that the example is a man whose piety was praised at the start (1:6). Now Zechariah has assurance about God's promises. He is to trust that God can deliver on his promises—which is an important lesson for the doubting Theophilus. Zechariah also responds in obedience, obedience that Mary gave without hesitation. Faith for some comes slowly and for others more naturally, but in the end, the call is to emulate these saints with their notes of joy, expectation, and belief. The curtain comes down on Luke's first act, John's birth. The second act follows, as Jesus finally arrives to take center stage in God's program.

Additional Notes

1:67. Is Zechariah's subordinated viewpoint of John different from Jesus' and evidence of a later Christian perspective? There are two considerations against the theory that Zechariah's prophetic perspective is a Christian reference in hindsight, written without knowledge of Jesus' praise of John as "greater than a prophet" (but so R. Brown 1977: 378; see 7:26). First, Jesus accepts that John is a prophet. The remark in 7:26 is rhetorical and really says John is the "greatest" of the prophets, because he is the bridge into the new era. Second, Zechariah need not articulate his view in the same way Jesus does, since Jesus' perspective is addressed from the total perspective of God's plan as eras change.

1:70. A minor textual issue (not discussed in UBS[4]) concerns an article τῶν before ἀπ'; attestation for its inclusion is as strong as for its omission. Its presence makes no difference in the translation.

1:70. The number of conceptual parallels in 1:70 to other portions of Luke–Acts, some of which are unique to Luke, have led a few interpreters to see this verse as a Lucan insertion into the hymn (Schneider 1977a: 61; Fitzmyer 1981: 384). In fact, Fitzmyer regards this verse as the major evidence against a Jewish origin for this hymn. But when one looks at the hymn as a literary unit, the argument is much less compelling. The idea expressed here is that what occurs is according to God's promise, a concept paralleled in 1:73 and reflective of the hymn's conceptual balance. The structure in both cases involves an assertion followed by the note that the teaching is just as God promised. When one takes this verse as a Lucan gloss, this conceptual balance in the first part of the first stanza of the hymn is lost. It is significant that the Acts parallels are limited to Jewish-Christian speakers and Jewish-oriented audiences (Acts 1:20 and 3:24 [Peter]; 4:25 [the Jerusalem community]; 15:15 [James]), which indicates that the Jewish-Christian community expressed fulfillment in these terms. In other words, the expressions belong to Jews who came to see Jesus as God's promise. Thus, Luke presents a Jew looking for the hope of Messiah, though it is possible he has accurately paraphrased Zechariah in some of his own language. If Wilcox (1965: 74–76) is right that the language is somewhat liturgical, then a need to appeal to a Lucan paraphrase is minimized. The key idea is that fulfillment of divine promise comes in Messiah Jesus (Luke 1:1). This theme is central to this infancy section, as well as to Luke–Acts.

1:73. The style reflects a Semitic word order with the relative clause connected as a descriptive phrase (Klostermann 1929: 27). In addition, ὅρκον in the accusative case is inversely attracted to the accusative case of the next relative pronoun, ὅν (BDF §295; BDR §295.2). Grammatically, ὅρκον is in apposition to διαθήκης in 1:72 and so specifies that the covenant to which Zechariah refers is the oath that God made with Abraham.

1:74. The text is somewhat uncertain, although the variants do not alter the meaning. The major question is whether the reference is to "our" (ἡμῶν) enemies (so A, C, Θ, Ψ, Byz, D [with additional variant]) or simply "enemies" (so ℵ, B, L, W). Many see the longer text as an expansion made explainable by 1:71, especially in light of the variations on the addition, but the external evidence for including the reference to "our" enemies includes two major textual families. It is possible the text here parallels 1:71 and personalizes the opposition that God's people face. However, it is more likely that the shorter text is original, given the variations on the addition.

1:76. That ὁδούς is plural yet is usually translated as a singular is not a problem, since its use wavers in grammatical number without greatly altering the sense (plural OT uses: Deut. 30:16; Ps. 16:11 [15:11 LXX]; Prov. 8:20). The plural is perhaps slightly more descriptive of all that God is doing to save.

1:78. A textual problem centers on the tense of ἐπισκέψεται, a future tense read by most modern texts. Although its manuscript evidence is not broad (ℵ, B, L [with a misspelling], Θ), it is perceived as the harder reading.

Most see the variant, the aorist ἐπεσκέψατο, as an assimilation to the same verb in 1:68 and regard the presence of a future tense as more natural in a context where the verbs are future (Luce 1933: 95; Metzger 1975: 132). R. Brown (1977: 373) argues that the aorist is the harder reading, because the aorist does not fit the context of future verbs and because Jesus in the time frame of the account is not born yet. Although a future seems more stylistically natural and is probably original, there is not a great difference in sense, since an aorist would be a prophetic aorist or would look at Jesus' conception in light of what he will become.

1:80. Was John a member of the Dead Sea Qumran community? This verse raises an interesting historical question. Does the description of John spending time in the wilderness indicate that he was a member of the Essene sect of Judaism, the probable religious party of the Qumran community and the source of the famous Dead Sea Scrolls? A case for John's association with the Qumran community is made by J. Robinson (1957), while Fitzmyer (1981: 389) regards the view as plausible. There are serious objections to this view:

1. Since the Qumran community strongly opposed the Jerusalem priesthood, John would have rejected his parents if he were a part of that community.
2. John is portrayed as being more like a prophet than like the holy ones of Qumran.
3. John held to one baptism, not several washings as Qumran did.
4. John's message was not a message of separatism (3:10–14), whereas Qumran was a strongly separationist community.
5. John's preaching does not display the legalistic or ritualistic concern present at Qumran.

Thus, John probably was not a former Qumranian, though his presence in the deserts allows for the possibility that he knew the community.[50]

---

50. See discussions in Schürmann 1969: 94–95; Schweizer 1984: 44; R. Brown 1977: 376 n. 2; Bovon 1989: 110. Godet 1875: 1.118 refutes the older view that John was an Essene. The similarity between the two groups suggests that if John did not belong to one group, he probably was not a member of the other either.

7. Birth of Jesus (2:1–7)

The unit about Jesus' birth is the first of two that deal with Jesus' arrival: 2:1–7 recounts the circumstances of the birth and 2:8–20 notes the angels' announcement of the birth and the shepherds' visit. One could place these units together, but the shift in perspective suggests viewing them as separate units. Luke 2:1–7 places Jesus in the perspective of world history and concentrates solely on the family's activity. Luke loves to make such connections to the world (Luke 3:1–2; Acts 26:26).[1] In divine history, the important element is Jesus' Davidic heritage, hence Luke's note that Bethlehem is the city of David. Jesus' parents are obedient to Rome and proceed to register for the census. This results in a humble birth for the great child. Luke 2:8–20 focuses on heaven's reaction to the birth and human testimony to it. A short note in 2:21 ends the narration of Jesus' birth, making a transition to the trip to the temple in 2:22–40.

Sources and Historicity

The sources for 2:1–7 and 2:8–21 are typically treated together.[2] Many comparisons are made to birth stories of other significant children, but none of these comparisons prove compelling.[3] Accordingly, scholars have come up with four basic alternatives:

1. Some argue that the OT allusions and the use of certain terms suggest a Hellenistic origin for some material. This view is usually combined with the suggestion that Luke is responsible for at least

---

1. Wiefel 1988: 68–70 gives some background on Caesar Augustus. For an evaluation of the Lucan notes that place Luke within the sphere of ancient history writing, see Büchsel, *TDNT* 3:395–96, and Strathmann, *TDNT* 4:492 n. 53.

2. Major discussions can be found in Fitzmyer 1981: 392–93; R. Brown 1977: 411; Klostermann 1929: 31–32; Creed 1930: 30–32; Schürmann 1969: 103–4, 108–9, 118–19; Marshall 1978: 96–97; Plummer 1896: 46; Nolland 1989: 98–103; and Ernst 1977: 99.

3. Among the candidates for comparison are Cyrus, Romulus and Remus, Mithras, Osiris, Aion, Virgil, Semiramis, and Moses. For discussions see Creed 1930: 30–32; Klostermann 1929: 31–32; Bultmann 1963: 298; Gressmann 1914; and Machen 1930: 348–58 (who has a detailed critique). Virtually no one argues for any direct connection, though most speak of the account's legendary features, because of its supernatural elements.

2:1–5.[4] The major evidence for this view is the OT allusions and the use of εὐαγγελίζω and σωτήρ in 2:10–11. The allusions must be evaluated individually, and the use of the terminology is not decisive for the whole of 2:1–21. In fact, another issue also comes into consideration: the argument that Luke has erred in giving the data about the census (but see excursus 2). This view generally is the most skeptical of historicity, though a few details might be historical (e.g., the parents' names, the birth in Bethlehem).

2. Others argue for Lucan composition based on traditional material.[5] The major factor here is the census. The text shows the movement of Jesus' parents from Nazareth to Bethlehem. Both views 1 and 2 argue that Luke 2:1–40 and Matt. 2:1–23 are so different as to be irreconcilable; both passages cannot belong to tradition. In addition, both views argue that Luke 2 shows no knowledge of Luke 1, since the parents are introduced a second time. The problem with these suggestions about style is that the unit's style is not particularly Lucan and its Palestinian-Jewish coloring is like previous accounts (Marshall 1978: 97). Allusions are cited indirectly, as in Luke 1. Nothing in the account requires a Hellenistic origin; in fact, the naming of Bethlehem as the city of David is against such a connection, since that description is not from the LXX (see 2:4). Also, the concept of a Savior is not an exclusively Hellenistic idea.

3. Marshall (1978: 97) argues for roots in Palestinian or Jewish Christianity.[6] Palestinian coloring is the only argument that he brings forward for this view. This position is a natural consequence of rejecting a Hellenistic background. This view tends to see more historicity than do the previous views. Doubts tend to center on the timing of the census. This view also tends to discuss historicity less directly than does the following approach.

4. Finally, others appeal more specifically to a connection with Mary.[7] Mention is made of 2:19 for support; in addition, the account—if historical—can have such detail only through a family member or through the shepherds involved. This view emphasizes that Luke 2

4. Bultmann 1963: 299; Grundmann 1963: 76. Luke is given credit for 2:1–5 because of the note that alludes to history. Such notes are unique to his Gospel and recall the historical notes common in the OT historical books, esp. Kings and Chronicles.

5. R. Brown 1977: 411. Fitzmyer 1981: 393 argues for traditional elements in the material, specifically the names of the key characters, the birth in Bethlehem, the parents' tie to Nazareth, and a tie between Galilee and the census. Generally, more of these details would be seen as historical than in view 1.

6. Schürmann 1969: 108–9, 118 also argues that the shepherd motif is Palestinian and that OT allusions reflect the MT.

7. Plummer 1896: 46. Mary is not the only possible option, since sources could include the family or the shepherds, making this view more like view 3.

is historical, though some who hold it might question details about the census. If one does not insist on a Marian connection, which may be too specific, this view is attractive. The major obstacles to this view are the census issue and the problem of unifying Matt. 1:18–2:12 with Luke 1–2. The arguments here are so complex that they must be treated in a detailed excursus and in the exegesis of the individual verses.[8]

View 4 (at least in its expanded form) or view 3 appears to be the most satisfactory. The only qualification is that Luke may be responsible for much of the wording in 2:1–5; but Luke's facts reflect historical realities.

This unit is a simple birth account that places Jesus in world history.[9] The outline of Luke 2:1–7 is as follows:

a. Historical setting: the census (2:1–3)
b. Journey to the Davidic city (2:4–5)
c. Humble birth (2:6–7)

The unit's themes reveal the fulfillment of the promise of a child for Mary (1:31–35) and the entry of the Davidic son into the world. John's birth is superseded by that of Jesus. The detail about Jesus' birth and the heavenly revelation that accompanies it show this superiority. Heaven and earth give praise to this child. God is in control of these events. Bethlehem may be a little town and the baby may have a humble birth, but God's presence behind the birth makes this event one of the greatest in all history.

Exegesis and Exposition

[1]It came to pass in those days that a decree went out from Caesar Augustus to register all the empire for taxes. [2]This was the first census while Quirinius was governor of Syria. [3]And all were going to register themselves, each to their own cities.

[4]And Joseph went up from Galilee from the city of Nazareth into Judea to the city of David, which is called Bethlehem, because he was out of the

8. Fitzmyer 1981: 398 argues specifically against this view. He rejects the idea that 2:19 discloses a source. Arguing that there is no evidence for such a Marian memoir, he suggests that 2:19 means Mary kept these things to herself. He may be right that Mary is not the source, but other options exist for this account's historical roots.

9. Berger 1984: 349 calls this passage biography—a child history that places the baby in the framework of larger world history.

house and family of David, [5]in order to register himself. He went up together with Mary, his ⌐betrothed⌐, who was pregnant.

[6]And it happened when they arrived there that the days of her pregnancy were completed. [7]And she gave birth to her firstborn son and wrapped him up and laid him in a feed trough, because there was no place for them in the guest room.

a. Historical Setting: The Census (2:1–3)

2:1 Luke notes a policy requirement issued by the Roman leader. A decree of registration goes out from Octavian, Caesar Augustus. The Lucan reference to "those days" (ταῖς ἡμέραις ἐκείναις, *tais hēmerais ekeinais*) ties the census to the period of John's birth as it looks back to 1:80.[10] Δόγμα (*dogma*, decree) and its Latin equivalents *placitum* and *decretum* refer to a formal action of the Roman Senate (Klostermann 1929: 31; Kittel, *TDNT* 2:230–32; Marshall 1978: 98; Josephus, *Jewish War* 1.20.3 §393). Luke uses the term to refer to formal actions of various types (Acts 17:7; 16:4).

The decree calls for the registration of provincial citizens for the purpose of assessing taxes (i.e., Jews would not be registering for military service).[11] The decree follows Jewish custom in requiring a journey to the ancestral homeland. (The nature of the decree is discussed in detail in excursus 2.)

In calling the census one of the "whole world" (πᾶσαν τὴν οἰκου-μένην, *pasan tēn oikoumenēn*), Luke uses the standard description of any event that covered much of the Roman Empire.[12] Nonbiblical history knows of Augustan censuses in Gaul, Cyrene, and Egypt (Fitzmyer 1981: 400; Tacitus, *Annals* 1.11, 31, 33; Dio Cassius 53.30.2).

Octavian became known for his administrative organizing of the empire after an interesting rise to power (Fitzmyer 1981: 394, 399; Schürmann 1969: 99; R. Brown 1977: 394). He was born in September 63 B.C. and was the great nephew of Julius Caesar. After the murder of Julius Caesar, he was named chief heir and ruled in a triumvirate with Mark Antony and Lepidus. Lepidus fell from power in 36 B.C. and Antony's involvement with Cleopatra of Egypt brought him into conflict with Octavian. In 31 B.C. Octavian won a

---

10. The phrase ἐν ταῖς ἡμέραις is common in Luke: Luke 1:5, 39; 6:12; Acts 1:15; 6:1; 11:27.

11. Hoehner 1977: 14–15; K. Weiss, *TDNT* 9:81 n. 12. For the force of ἀπο-γράφεσθαι as a middle verb, "to register oneself," see BDF §317; in favor of the middle voice are 2:3, 5.

12. Acts 11:28; Michel, *TDNT* 5:157; P. Oxy. vol. 7 #1021 line 5; Fitzmyer 1981: 400. The remark may be rhetorical and partially hyperbolic (cf. Col. 1:6: "to the whole world").

decisive victory over Antony at Actium and was finally acknowl-edged as Augustus Caesar by the Senate in 27 B.C. when they gave him the honored Greek name *Sebastos* (= Latin *Augustus*). His reign was known for its peaceful character, as his accession ended a long period of civil strife. He died in A.D. 14 and was succeeded by Tiberius, the ruler of Rome during Jesus' ministry.

Luke portrays Augustus as the unknowing agent of God, whose decree leads to the fulfillment of the promised rise of a special ruler from Bethlehem (Mic. 5:1–2 [4:14–5:1 MT]). In the period of the emperor known for his reign of peace, God raises up the child of peace. For many interpreters, Luke is not only placing Jesus' birth in the context of world history, but he also is making a play on the theme of the peaceful emperor (Schürmann 1969: 102; Fitzmyer 1981: 393–94; R. Brown 1977: 415–16). The real emperor of peace is Jesus, not Octavian. But in the absence of Lucan comment about Augustus, the point, if present, is subtle.

In addition to the historical connection, the mention of the cen-sus explains how a couple from Nazareth gave birth to a child in Bethlehem. The accidental events of history have become acts of destiny. Little actions have great significance, for the ruler was to come out of Bethlehem and only a governmental decree puts the parents in the right place.

2:2 The problems surrounding Luke's mention of the census are cov-ered in excursus 2. Only a few additional items need attention. The reference to the "first" (πρώτη, *prōtē*) census here can be taken most naturally to mean either that this census was the first ever done in the province or that it was the first of at least two censuses done un-der Quirinius. The second meaning is more natural.

Quirinius had a noteworthy career. An able administrator and soldier, he was appointed counsel in 12 B.C., was victorious over the Homonadensians in south Galatia, and was legate over Syria in A.D. 6–9 after Herod's son Archelaus was deposed. He died in A.D. 21.[13] The reference to his governing need not refer to official office as governor, but could refer to administrative authority as a represen-tative of the emperor (MM 276–77; Josephus, *Antiquities* 18.4.2 §88; Fitzmyer 1981: 402). The mention of the census is another way to refer to the tax registration of 2:1.

2:3 In Luke's description of the response to the census, no mention is made of trouble that could suggest that this census is the A.D. 6 census, which Luke knows produced problems (Acts 5:37). All

13. References to Quirinius are found in Tacitus, *Annals* 2.30; 3.22–23, 48; and Strabo, *Geography* 12.6.5; Luce 1933: 95–96; Fitzmyer 1981: 402; R. Brown 1977: 395.

who were subject to the census went to be registered in their own cities.

The allusion to Joseph's journeying to his ancestral home is unusual for a Roman census, but there are examples of journeying to locales where one has property. In A.D. 104 in Egypt, Vibius Maximus issued an edict for such a journey in connection with a provincial census (Kenyon and Bell 1907: 124; P. Lond. 904; for other examples, see Creed 1930: 33; Klostermann 1929: 32; and Schürmann 1969: 100 n. 8). Journeying to one's ancestral home is unprecedented, but fits nicely with Jewish custom. The census, which could be controversial, uses customs that would be the least offensive. For Jews, an ancestral registration would be a most natural way to sign up for taxes (2 Sam. 24). So each one travels to his own city to register, and Joseph heads for the Davidic city of Bethlehem.

b. Journey to the Davidic City (2:4–5)

2:4 The attention narrows specifically to the family of the child, Joseph and Mary. The reference to their "going up" from Nazareth to Bethlehem is natural, since ἀναβαίνω (*anabainō*, to go up) is often used for journeys (2:42) and since Bethlehem is at a higher elevation than Nazareth. If they bypassed Samaria, Bethlehem was some ninety miles from Nazareth and almost seven miles south-southwest of Jerusalem. In going to Bethlehem, Joseph is obedient to the Roman government.[14] The choice of different prepositions in the verse to describe leaving (ἐκ, *ek*) Nazareth, the town, and leaving (ἀπό, *apo*) Galilee, the district, makes clear the distinction between departure from two distinct types of geographical units (Plummer 1896: 52; cf. Luke 10:30; 23:55; Acts 7:4; 8:26; John 1:44; 7:42; 11:1).

The focus of 2:4 is the Davidic connection, since Joseph's Davidic ancestry is mentioned alongside Bethlehem as the city of David. The mention of Bethlehem as the city of David is a little surprising, since in the OT this description is normally limited to Zion, that is, to Jerusalem (e.g., 2 Sam. 5:7, 9; 6:10, 12, 16; Marshall 1978: 105; Fitzmyer 1981: 406). In fact, the description argues strongly against Lucan creation of this material and for his use of tradition from a Semitic source, since the LXX does not refer to Bethlehem as the city of David.[15] Thus, Bethlehem as the city of David argues

14. Bovon 1989: 118 argues that the parents' obedience shows that they are not nationalists, like the later Zealots.

15. Only one LXX context refers to Bethlehem as David's city: 1 Sam. 20:6 ("his city"). David's connection with Bethlehem is noted in the MT of 1 Sam. 17:12, 58, but these verses are absent from the LXX; 1 Sam. 16:18 LXX connects the city with Jesse, not David. Even Judaism did not have a Bethlehem-Davidic-Messianic connection; SB 1:82–83; Plummer 1896: 52; Bock 1987: 75.

strongly for a Palestinian source for Luke 2:1–20, with 1 Sam. 17:12, 58 supplying the background.

Bethlehem's association as the birthplace of the ruler is suggested by Mic. 5:1–2 [4:14–5:1 MT]. Luke does not explicitly mention this prophetic connection, so whether he is consciously alluding to this text, as Matt. 2:6 does, is not certain. Luke may be only presenting the event and allowing those who know the Scripture to make the association (Bock 1987: 75). What is clear is that the Davidic and regal connections of Jesus are again being stressed by Luke, as they were in 1:31–35.

The journey comes because Joseph is of the Davidic family. But does Luke agree with Matthew about Joseph's home? Some try to solve the difference in geographical focus between Matthew and Luke either by arguing error or by positing that Joseph owned property in Bethlehem. The former view argues that Matthew (2:11) apparently regards Bethlehem as the home of Jesus' parents at the birth, while Luke (2:39) is clear that the home is Nazareth (Fitzmyer 1981: 406; R. Brown 1977: 396). This difference raises a question, since it does not follow that Bethlehem is their residence just because they have found a place to reside by the time the Magi arrive. Thus, to argue error deduces too much from the accounts. On the other hand, it is clear that Joseph did not own a home in Bethlehem, since if he did they would hardly have stayed at an inn, much less a stable, upon their arrival (2:6–7).[16] Thus, this view also founders. Ancestral registration is the only possible explanation for the trip. Significantly, the ancestry goes back to David.

Joseph did not make the census trip alone. Mary was with him despite her condition. The phrase σὺν Μαριάμ (syn Mariam, together with Mary) belongs naturally to the main verb, ἀνέβη (anebē, he went up), of 2:4 and not to the idea of registration in 2:5 (so Fitzmyer 1981: 406–7; Marshall 1978: 105; against this connection is Klostermann 1929: 35). Luke's point is not that they registered together, but that they traveled together. If the verse is read in this way, it does not insist that Mary *had* to come up for the census, though that may have been the case (so correctly Schürmann 1969: 103 n. 39).

2:5

The reference to Mary as betrothed (ἐμνηστευμένη, emnēsteumenē) may have a motive. It does not suggest that Mary is not yet married to Joseph, since this trip in a betrothal situation would be unlikely (Plummer 1896: 53; Ellis 1974: 81; Marshall 1978: 105; Hendriksen 1978: 142). Rather, it means that the marriage is not yet

16. Ellis's suggestion (1974: 81) that this region was Mary's former home also faces similar problems at this point. Where are the friends or relatives?

consummated and thus implies a virgin birth (Marshall 1978: 105; Matt. 1:20, 24).

The description of Mary's pregnancy at the end of the verse sets up the reference to the birth in 2:6. Although the extent of her pregnancy is not given, her condition may suggest why she accompanied Joseph. Plummer (1896: 53) argues that she would not want to give birth in Joseph's absence. Both Fitzmyer (1981: 407) and R. Brown (1977: 397–98) argue that such an understanding is overpsychologizing the text. It is not possible to state that this is Luke's intention, but it cannot be ruled out either. The reference is so brief that it is hard to be certain of the point, though it does seem more likely that a couple in the midst of such an important period early in their marriage would not desire to be separated. In any case, when Joseph comes to Bethlehem to register, a pregnant Mary is with him.

c. Humble Birth (2:6–7)

2:6 The birth of Jesus is told with simplicity (Schweizer 1984: 48–49). The days of her pregnancy were fulfilled (ἐπλήσθησαν, eplēsthēsan) on her arrival.[17] Jesus' birth clearly occurs in Bethlehem and not along the way, as the apocryphal Psalm of Matthew 13 and the Protevangelium of James 17.3–18.1 suggest.[18] In the Protevangelium of James, Mary is in birth pangs in the middle of the journey, and the child is delivered in a cave in the Bethlehem region (Fitzmyer 1981: 407).

The birth itself is told briefly without any details as to why the couple stays in the stable (Schürmann 1969: 103; R. Brown 1977: 418–19). There is no account of a search for a place, an idea that erroneously leaves an impression that the couple find the last place in town. There is no speculation about a harsh innkeeper who cannot provide a room. Neither is there a suggestion that the parents are too poor. Rather, Mary's time comes; so she bears the child in a stable, wraps him up, and places him in what probably is an empty feed trough (2:7).

2:7 Luke describes Jesus' birth in very simple, unadorned terms. Many issues are raised by the verse, mainly because of traditional associations tied to the birth event. But the setting presents a very humble beginning for the future messianic king.

17. For such language to express the end of pregnancy, see Gen. 25:24; Luke 1:57; R. Brown 1977: 398. This is yet another Hebraism; Delling, *TDNT* 2:950 n. 42.
    18. Plummer 1896: 53. Bovon 1989: 120 n. 36 notes that expansions on the birth miracle occur in the second-century Protevangelium of James 4–10, 19–20.

Mary gives birth to a firstborn (πρωτότοκος, *prōtotokos*) son, a description that is handled in various ways:

1. He is called firstborn to indicate that Mary had other children later (Hendriksen 1978: 143; Matt. 12:46–47; Luke 8:19–20).
2. The reference to the firstborn prepares for 2:23–24 (Marshall 1978: 106; Godet 1875: 1.130).
3. The term is equivalent to calling Jesus the "only begotten."[19]
4. It refers to Jesus' right to inherit David's throne as the first son in a Davidic family (Danker 1988: 55; Schürmann 1969: 104).
5. It refers to Jesus' right as the firstborn son to the benefits of inheritance.[20]

Almost all see a literary function for the term that prepares the reader for 2:23–24 (view 2), but which of the other senses is likely here? It is unlikely that Luke explicitly intends to refer only to the ultimate size of Mary's family, so that an explicit reference to Jesus' siblings is not the point (view 1), though the implication exists (8:19). Πρωτότοκος can mean "first" without any reference to others who follow.[21] Used in this way, the term refers to a special relationship to God. But the term cannot be so specific as to suggest a unique or messianic relationship to God (view 3), since Luke has no interest in the term as a title anywhere else. In fact, Luke's lack of interest in the term as a title suggests that a special relationship at any level is probably not intended. Thus, a reference to the general rights of Jesus as a firstborn is likely (view 5). This is the most natural way to take the term in the context (2:23–24). Thus, Jesus has all the rights of a firstborn son, including any regal rights.

The newly born child is wrapped in swaddling clothes. The custom was to take strips of clothes and bind them around the child to keep the limbs straight (Marshall 1978: 106; Safrai 1976a: 766; Ezek. 16:4). Swaddling prepares us for the shepherds' recognition of the child (2:12), as does the mention of φάτνη (*phatnē*, manger). There is no idea of a painless birth in the account's silence, as some

19. This used to be the Catholic understanding of the term and is still held by some today; Blinzler 1967 discusses the options and the subject of Jesus' family. R. Brown 1977: 398 hints at this view, citing Ps. Sol. 13.9 [mistakenly cited as 13.8 by Brown]; 18.4; 2 Esdr. [= 4 Ezra] 6:58 as examples of πρωτότοκος meaning "only begotten." Bovon 1989: 121 speaks of a privileged relationship to God.

20. Exod. 13:2; Num. 3:12–13; Deut. 21:15–17; Schürmann 1969: 104 n. 43. Both Fitzmyer 1981: 406 and R. Brown 1977: 398 note that the term shows only that no one preceded Jesus.

21. Exod. 13:2; Num. 3:12; Schürmann 1969: 104 n. 43; Fitzmyer 1981: 407–8; Frey 1930; Michaelis, *TDNT* 6:876–77 and n. 36; Bovon 1989: 121 n. 38.

of the church fathers suggested, nor is the idea of abject poverty for Jesus' family suggested by the setting (Plummer 1896: 53; Klostermann 1929: 35).

The child is laid in a φάτνῃ, probably a feed trough normally used for animals, since that is the normal meaning of the term (Creed 1930: 34; MM 665; Hengel, *TDNT* 9:53–54). Some suggest that the reference is to being laid down in a stable, but the reference to being wrapped up and then laid down suggests a specific locale within the stable (so correctly Schürmann 1969: 104). The mention of the feed trough does suggest that Jesus was born in an animal room of some sort.

But what kind of animal room was it and why were the child's parents there? The passage tells us that they were there because (δι- ότι, *dioti*) there was no room at the καταλύματι (*katalymati*, public shelter). Κατάλυμα suggests that a formal inn is not in view here. The LXX refers to the public shelters where many people might gather for the night under one roof.[22] Luke 22:11 uses the term of a guest room in a house, while 10:34 uses πανδοχεῖον (*pandocheion*) to describe a formal inn. The ancient formal inn usually took two forms: either a two-story house where the first floor housed animals and the second floor took travelers, or a one-story building with the stable next to it. The Christmas associations of an inn and an innkeeper, however, do not reflect the language of Luke's text.[23] Rather, κατάλυμα seems to refer to either some type of reception room in a private home or some type of public shelter. Since this place was full, refuge was sought elsewhere.

The animal room that Joseph and Mary found may have been either a stable next to the place of lodging or a cave, since the use of caves for stables was common (Godet 1875: 1.130; Marshall 1978: 107). Ancient tradition associates Jesus' birth with a cave (Protevangelium of James 18; Justin Martyr, *Dialogue with Trypho* 78.4; Origen, *Against Celsus* 1.51). A basilica was erected over a cave site in Bethlehem in the time of Constantine (fourth century), at the site of the present Church of the Nativity. The Lucan text does not specify that the animal room used for the birth was a cave, but it is possible that the traditional cave site is correct and that the traditional association between Jesus' birth and a cave is accurate. The Lucan text and first-century customs do not prevent the association, but it cannot be regarded as established.

22. Exod. 4:24. The meaning "dining room" is found in 1 Sam. 1:18 and Sir. 14:25; BAGD 414; BAA 841; Schürmann 1969: 105; Stählin, *TDNT* 5:19–20 nn. 136, 143.

23. Hendriksen 1978: 144–45. On the ancient house, though inns are not explicitly discussed, see Safrai 1976a: 728–35.

The simple birth of Jesus Christ is somewhat paradoxical, since **Summary** the Messiah is born in a room normally reserved for animals. From such humble beginnings will emerge the "rising morning sun from on high" (1:79). Jesus Christ has the right heritage: he is born of pious Davidic parents in the city that the OT promised would be the birthplace of a ruler. The "chance" of a census had made it happen. Rome was an unconscious agent in God's work. The profane decree of a census had yielded a divine event. A stable was the Messiah's first throne room.

Additional Notes

2:2. Is the census a midrashic creation? R. Brown (1977: 417–18) considers the census to be the product of midrashic messianic speculation (he calls this approach "possible"). In Judaism, there is evidence of Messiah's association with a census in the Midrash's citation and discussion of Ps. 87:6 [86:6 LXX]. Evidence is also found in the Quinta column (the fifth Greek column) of Origen's Hexapla and in a late targum on Ps. 87:6, an association that seems to be reflected in the Midrash on the Psalms as well. Thus, the addition of a census is seen as an attempt to add a messianic flavor to the narrative.

This theory has problems. First, the Quinta reading is one textual reading of the Psalms among many. As such, the reading points only to the existence, not prevalence, of a tradition in the second century. It is a rather distant witness. Second, the locale in the Psalms targum is Zion, that is, Jerusalem. Thus, the argument would have to be that Luke or his source took a possibly obscure Jewish tradition and changed the locale of the fulfillment, a procedure that would obscure, not clarify, the messianic association. Third, none of the terms in the Lucan text match the LXX reading. These problems make a midrashic origin for the census quite unlikely (Bock 1987: 76). The census in Luke is best explained as a reference to an actual census. Though a Quirinian census before the turn of the era lacks extrabiblical testimony, excursus 2 shows that it can be fit into the historical movement and customs of the period.

2:4. The meaning of Bethlehem's name is disputed. Plummer (1896: 52) suggests that the name means "house of bread," while Fitzmyer argues that an Amarna letter (#290) refers to the town as "Bit-Laḥmi," which means "house of [the god] Laḥmu."[24] The identification by Fitzmyer has been challenged, so the Amarna connection is not certain (Marshall 1978: 105; D. Payne 1962: 144). The debate is not important, since Luke does not make anything of the name.

24. Fitzmyer 1981: 406; ANET 489. Schürmann 1969: 102 n. 30 notes that Plummer's option is a popular etymology.

2:4. The difference in meaning between οἶκος and πατριά is debated. Hendriksen argues that οἶκος is a broad term (house) that is qualified and narrowed by πατριά (family), since a difference in meaning is the only reason one can give to explain the presence of both terms.[25] Marshall (1978: 105) argues that the terms are synonymous references to ancestry (Acts 3:25; Eph. 3:15).[26] A synonymous reference, which would be emphatic, seems more natural, since there is so little difference between the distinctions noted. Either way, the point is to connect Joseph to David.

2:5. The description of Mary as "betrothed" (ἐμνηστευμένη) reflects a textual problem. Ἐμνηστευμένη is attested by ℵ, B, C, D, L, and W. Some versions (Syr[s] and Itala manuscripts aur, b, c) read γυναικὶ αὐτοῦ (his wife), which is accepted by Creed (1930: 33) and Klostermann (1929: 35) as original. Many manuscripts (Θ, Ψ, and Byz) have a combination reading: τῇ μεμνηστευμένῃ αὐτῷ γυναικί (the betrothed-to-him wife), which is accepted by Godet (1875: 1.129). It is generally regarded that γυναικί is inserted, because it avoids a possibly offensive reference to Mary's pregnancy while betrothed. But it is hard to explain, despite the parallel in 1:27, how this betrothal description was inserted into this context, if another description were already there (Luce 1933: 99; Marshall 1978: 105; R. Brown 1977: 397). If γυναικί had been present, ἐμνηστευμένη is not needed. It is easy to explain, however, why the term γυναικί would have been added. Thus, ἐμνηστευμένη is likely the original reading.

25. Hendriksen 1978: 141; Godet 1875: 1.129; Plummer 1896: 52. Schrenk, *TDNT* 5:1016–17, esp. n. 7, argues similarly. The term οἶκος refers to the whole house of a ruler, while πατριά is added, so that the reference to the whole house is clearly seen as a specific reference to ancestry.
26. Luke 1:33 and Acts 7:46 are against οἶκος in a narrow sense.

8. Reaction to the Birth (2:8–21)

Luke 2:8–21 is closely bound to 2:1–7, since it tells the reaction to Jesus' birth. Heaven responds with praise and announces the birth to shepherds (2:8–14), who then visit the child (2:15–20). The visit includes wonder and praise. The naming of Jesus at his circumcision closes the account (2:21), showing that Mary and Joseph are faithful, pious parents.

The note of joy and the proclamation of the arrival of promised salvation dominate the account. The scene is full of common people. The child in a feed trough, the shepherds in their fields, and the family with a new child are all themes of simple life. In stark contrast to the setting's humble, everyday character stands the activity of heaven in praise and adoration. Heaven confesses the identity of the child (2:10–11, 14). This is the Davidic child who brings good news and peace to God's people. He is Savior and Lord. As with the earlier announcements to Zechariah and Mary, there also is a sign to see: the child in a feed trough. The shepherds pursue the sign and tell their story. They respond to the call to see the child. A mood of wonder, praise, and expectation fills the account.

Sources and Historicity

The discussion of sources for Luke 2:8–21 parallels the discussion of sources for 2:1–7 and need not be repeated here. Judgments about historicity are influenced once again by worldview (e.g., do angels appear to humans?). Luke tells the story with a mixture of awe and simplicity that indicates he takes the account seriously.

The account's form combines angelophany (2:8–14) and birth story (2:15–21). Doxology (2:14), proclamation (2:10), and visions of heaven (2:9, 13) are found within the account (Berger 1984: 230, 236–37, 282–83).

The outline of Luke 2:8–21 is as follows:

a. Heavenly annunciation (2:8–14)
   i. Setting (2:8–9)
   ii. Angelic announcement (2:10–12)

iii. Heavenly praise (2:13–14)
b. Earthly confirmation (2:15–20)
i. The shepherds' confirmation of the angelic word
(2:15–17)
ii. Astonishment, remembrance, praise (2:18–20)
c. The obedient naming of Jesus at circumcision (2:21)

The passage shows creation praising the birth of the king. God's word, promised in 1:31–35, comes to pass. The sign promised to the shepherds also comes to pass. Events occur according to the word (2:15, 20, 21). God is at work, while heaven speaks and watches. Shepherds are amazed, while parents reflect. Before a vast audience of varied responses, salvation comes into the world. Luke 2:8–21 is a simple picture of a profound truth, painted with a flurry of activity. The mood of 2:18–20 should influence the mood of the reader. With a song in its heart, heaven sent Jesus to earth.

Exegesis and Exposition

[8]And there were shepherds in that region, who lived outdoors and kept guard over their flocks by night. [9]⌜And⌝ an angel of the Lord stood near them; and the glory of the Lord shone around them; and they were afraid.

[10]But the angel said to them, "Do not fear, for behold, I proclaim good news to you of great joy, which is for all the people, [11]for a Savior, who is Christ, ⌜the Lord⌝, was born for you today in the city of David. [12]And this shall be the sign for you, you shall see a baby wrapped up and lying in a feed trough."

[13]And suddenly there appeared together with the angel a multitude from the heavenly host, praising God and saying,

[14]   "Glory to God in the heavenly places,
          and on earth peace among men of his good pleasure."

[15]And it came to pass, when the angels departed from them to heaven, ⌜the shepherds⌝ were saying, "Let us go indeed to Bethlehem and see this thing that has come to pass, which the Lord has made known to us." [16]And they went out hurriedly and found Mary and Joseph and the child, who was lying in the feed trough. [17]And when they saw this, they made known the matter spoken to them concerning the child.

[18]And all who heard it wondered at what the shepherds told them. [19]And ⌜Mary⌝ was pondering all these matters, trying to put them together in her heart. [20]And the shepherds returned, glorifying and praising God for all they had heard and seen, even as it was spoken to them.

²¹When the eight days were completed for him to be circumcised, they called his name Jesus, the name that was given by the angel before he was conceived in the womb.[1]

a. Heavenly Annunciation (2:8–14)
i. Setting (2:8–9)

Luke turns from the birth to its proclamation. The account shifts attention to shepherds who hear a heavenly announcement of Messiah's coming (2:11). This is the third announcement pericope in Luke 1–2 (the others are 1:5–25 and 1:26–38). The announcement is not just to a family member, but to people who represent all people.[2] The verse reveals the setting of the proclamation.

2:8

Shepherds are in the field at night watching over their flock. If the field is located near "Shepherds' Field," it is two miles from the town (R. Brown 1977: 401). The shepherds kept night watches in turn and were said to "live outdoors," as they protected the sheep from robbers and wild animals.[3] It is possible, but not certain, that these sheep were destined for the temple (*m. Šeqal.* 7.4 and *m. B. Qam.* 7.7 might suggest this point).

The shepherds are often characterized as representing the "downtrodden and despised" of society, so that the first proclamation of the gospel is said to have come to sinners (Hendriksen 1978: 149; Godet 1875: 1.130; R. Brown 1977: 420 n. 38). The evidence for this view draws on material from rabbinic Judaism (SB 2:113–14; *b. Sanh.* 25b; Midr. Ps. 23.2 [99b]). But there are two problems with reading the shepherds as symbols of the hated. First, the rabbinic evidence is late, coming from the fifth century. More importantly, shepherd motifs in the Bible are mostly positive. The NT (Luke 15:4; Mark 6:34; Matt. 18:12; John 10; 1 Pet. 2:25; Heb. 13:20; Eph. 4:11) portrays shepherds in a favorable light, even describing church leaders with this figure. In the OT, Abraham, Moses, and David were all shepherds at some point in their lives.[4] Thus, the presence of the shepherds is not a negative point. Rather, they pic-

---

1. In my translation, I have sacrificed literary flow in an effort to bring out the precision of some of the terms. Also, the brief note of praise in 2:14 is laid out in poetic lines to show the parallelism.

2. Tannehill 1986: 38 makes this observation and speaks of the birth as more than a family affair.

3. Ἀγραυλοῦντες means "to make one's field [into] one's courtyard or house"; BAGD 13; BAA 23; Schürmann 1969: 108. Shepherds would often work together to provide this protection; Jeremias, *TDNT* 6:499. Jeremias (pp. 490–91) also points out that the account is not influenced by any literary traditions.

4. Schürmann 1969: 108–9. Ezek. 34 is a negative OT text, but even here it is the perversion of the shepherd's care that is in view. Israel's leaders are portrayed as doing something unnatural in their care for the nation.

ture the lowly and humble who respond to God's message (1:38, 52; 4:16–18; Fitzmyer 1981: 408).

Jesus' birth is followed immediately by a proclamation to an everyday group: shepherds in a field. Of course some (as mentioned in the additional note) do not see any historical basis for mentioning the shepherds. But one is hard pressed to suggest a clear motive for the creation of such a detail through an appeal to Greek and Jewish culture and literature.[5] If Luke is creating this motif, it is not at all clear why shepherds are picked as representatives of humble people over other, better-attested possibilities, like the poor or the widows. The shepherds' presence in the text reflects their presence in fact.

2:9 The heavenly announcement begins with the angel's arrival. The structure of the announcement is in a standard sequence: appearance (2:9a), fear (2:9b), a "do not fear" announcement (2:10–11), and a sign (2:12). A word of testimony comes from heaven with the arrival of an angel of the Lord. The angel is not named and is not to be confused with the OT "angel of the Lord."[6] The term used to describe his arrival, ἐπέστη (epestē, appeared; from ἐφίστημι), is a common Lucan term for "standing near or beside someone" and is often used to describe angelic or supernatural appearances.[7] Classical Greek also used the term for meeting the supernatural (Plummer 1896: 55; Homer, *Iliad* 10.496; Herodotus 1.34; 7.14). The term itself need not suggest a sudden appearance, but the nature of an angel's arrival certainly implies this (so Schürmann 1969: 109 n. 98).

With the messenger came the bright presence of the Lord's glory surrounding the shepherds.[8] Δόξα (doxa) refers to the כָּבוֹד (kābôd) of God, the bright Shekinah glory, God's majestic presence (Exod. 16:10; Ps. 63:2 [63:3 MT]; Isa. 40:5; Ezek. 1; Kittel, *TDNT* 2:247; also Luke 2:14). Such glory will appear again at key points in Luke–Acts in association with Jesus (Luke 9:30–31; Acts 7:55). Such a bright light in the midst of the evening would have been an impressive sight; Luke intends the reader to visualize the contrast.

5. R. Brown 1977: 420–24. Marshall 1978: 107–8 rejects this approach. Fitzmyer 1981: 395–96 sees OT influence but rejects a midrashic view. So correctly Jeremias, *TDNT* 6:490–99, also rejects such connections.

6. Klostermann 1929: 37. Ἄγγελος is introduced without the definite article. Bovon 1989: 124 thinks that the angel may be Gabriel, but the text does not say.

7. All but three NT uses are Lucan: Luke 21:34; 24:4; Acts 12:7; 23:11; 1 Thess. 5:3; 2 Tim. 4:2, 6; Marshall 1978: 109; Danker 1988: 56–57.

8. Oepke, *TDNT* 4:22–24. Kittel, *TDNT* 1:84 n. 67, argues that the white-robed angels in Luke 24:4 and Acts 1:10 serve to indicate angelic glory. Their radiance finds its source in heaven.

The response to this stirring divine sign was a natural one: great fear. Such fear is emphasized by Luke's cognate construction ἐφο-βήθησαν φόβον (*ephobēthēsan phobon*, they were filled with fear; BDF §153.1; Fitzmyer 1981: 409). It is like the fear that overcame both Zechariah and Mary when the angel came to them (1:12, 29), and such fear gripped the disciples at the transfiguration (9:34). The encounter with the divine is initially startling and unsettling. With the angel's coming and God's bright presence, the announcement follows.

ii. Angelic Announcement (2:10–12)

The angel begins his announcement by calming the shepherds' fear, **2:10** as is common in such appearances (1:13 [Zechariah]; 1:30 [Mary]; 5:10 [Peter]). The initial encounter with God or his messenger frightens most who experience it, but the grace of God is such that this fear is quickly removed as an obstacle. God wishes to interact with his creation.

The announcement itself contains two descriptions. The announcement is good news, and the birth causes great joy. Εὐαγγελί-ζομαι (*euangelizomai*) means "to proclaim good news" and its verbal and noun forms are especially frequent in Luke and Paul (Hendriksen 1978: 152; Plummer 1896: 56; Friedrich, *TDNT* 2:710, 717, 727). All uses of the verb in the Gospels are found in Luke except one (Matt. 11:5; Luke 1:19; 2:10; 3:18; 4:18, 43; 7:22; 8:1; 9:6; 16:16; 20:1). The response to this news will be great joy. Luke's commonly placing joy next to salvation is a key idea in his Gospel (10:17; 15:7, 10; 24:52). This combination of good news and joy is also found in the earlier announcement of John the Baptist's birth in 1:14.[9] Clearly the good that God is about to do should meet with great expectation. The ideas of announcing good news and of a savior's presence are also used to describe the emperor Augustus in an inscription about the celebration of his birthday (Creed 1930: 35; Klostermann 1929: 37; Marshall 1978: 109; Dittenberger 1903–5: #458). It is probably too much to see a conscious polemic against the emperor of Rome here since Luke–Acts does not engage in challenging the Roman leadership. But a declaration of the greatness and significance of Jesus is intended.

The joy is for all the people (παντὶ τῷ λαῷ, *panti tō laō*)—which is not a statement about both Jews and Gentiles. The entire context up to this point in Luke has been about the people of Israel (1:68, 72–74; 2:32). In addition, in Luke–Acts the term for people (λαός, *laos*)

---

9. Friedrich, *TDNT* 2:721. The tie between humans and good news appears in a variety of texts: Matt. 26:13; 28:19; Acts 1:8; Mark 14:9; 16:15; Sasse, *TDNT* 3:890.

is used of Israel except twice in Acts (15:14; 18:10; Schweizer 1984: 50). Thus, the reference here speaks of blessing Israel (R. Brown 1977: 402; Marshall 1978: 109; Wilson 1973: 34–35; Strathmann, *TDNT* 4:53). The relationship of Jesus' coming for Gentiles is something that Luke presents later in his two volumes, especially in Acts. The only exception to this Israelite focus is Luke 2:31, but even here it is but a hint of things to come. The national focus still dominates Luke 2, though implications exist that the circle of inclusion is becoming wider. For now, Luke is interested in how Jesus fulfills national expectations, a focus clearly controlled by historical concerns. Of course, the nature of this blessing for the nation is tied very much to the nature of the person who comes, the angel's next topic.

2:11   The announcement is significant for three reasons. First, it explains (ὅτι, *hoti*, for) that the reason the message is good news and a cause for great joy is that a messianic Savior is born. This event is not a distant reality; it comes even now. Second, Luke repeats the note of fulfillment (2:4) that the birth occurs in the city of David. Third, the description of Jesus contains three key christological terms—Savior, Christ, and Lord.

The shepherds as common people benefit from the Savior's birth. Ὑμῖν (*hymin*) is a dative of advantage, so the birth is "for you (i.e., the shepherds)." The reader should identify with the shepherds' perspective as they hear this good news. What is for all the people (2:10) is also for the shepherds. The personal nature of the address to them is significant, since it individualizes the message.

What is currently taking place in Bethlehem is of timeless significance. Thus, Luke uses one of his favorite terms: σήμερον (*sēmeron*, today). In addition, the presence of the past tense ἐτέχθη (*etechthē*, was born) shows that what was anticipated as future in 1:31–35 is now realized. Σήμερον is significant to Luke, stressing the currentness of the saving event as it occurs "today" (2:11; 4:21; 5:26; 13:32–33; 19:5, 9; 23:43; Schweizer 1984: 50–51).

The combination of titles present here is unique. *Savior, Christ,* and *Lord* do not appear together in any other NT text. The reader is prepared for the use of *Savior* and *Christ* here by previous Lucan discussion (pointedly in 1:31–35; conceptually in 1:67–79). But the title *Lord* applied to Jesus appears for the first time as a comprehensive title.[10] All three titles appear frequently in the OT, which sup-

---

10. Luke 1:43 is not a formal comprehensive use of the title *Lord*, but is a reference of respect for the baby, who will be Messiah; the uses of *Lord* in 1:17, 76 are best understood contextually as referring to God. See the exegesis of these verses and the discussion below.

plies important background to their meaning here. In addition, some of the terms have undergone development in Judaism—a development that NT usage also reflects.

The σωτήρ (*sōtēr*, Savior) word group, when referring to people in the OT, describes a deliverer from enemies, such as a judge (Judg. 3:9, 15; 12:3; Neh. 9:27).[11] The only OT king called σωτήρ is Jehoahaz (2 Kings 13:5). Its primary OT reference, however, is to God, who delivers from various types of peril: enemies that seek to destroy and disease that seeks to kill (Deut. 20:4; Josh. 22:22; Ps. 24:5 [23:5 LXX]; 25:5 [24:5 LXX]; Isa. 25:9). In the OT, Messiah is never called σωτήρ. In fact, Messiah as a technical term for the Davidic Anointed One is clearly developed in intertestamental literature (Ps. Sol. 17), though its roots go back to Ps. 2:2. In Greek culture, σωτήρ referred either to gods who delivered or to humans who saved other humans from dangers; for example, doctors, rulers, and philosophers could be labeled σωτήρ. The term was popularly used of Roman rulers (Foerster and Fohrer, *TDNT* 7:1003–21).

Luke intends the reader to see the meaning in terms of rescue or delivery from peril, in both its physical and spiritual senses. In 1:47, σωτήρ is used to describe the God who delivers by sending Messiah. He is the God who remembers Israel and exalts the humble who fear him, while casting down rulers (1:47–55). In Zechariah's hymn, God is praised for sending the horn of salvation to the nation (1:69). Again, the picture includes a portrait of deliverance from national enemies (1:68–74). Since Jesus is the one who brings God's salvation, he can be called "Savior" in his own right. He is God's deliverer for God's people (Bock 1987: 78–79). It is perhaps significant that Jesus is described by a title that is often applied to God, but the major point here is Jesus' function as deliverer.

The combination χριστὸς κύριος (*christos kyrios*, Christ, the Lord) serves to further describe the Savior. The rendering of the phrase is variously presented: (1) "Messiah, Lord" (where κύριος is in apposition to χριστός); (2) "Anointed Lord" (χριστός is an adjective modifying κύριος); (3) "the Messiah, the Lord" (the titles are highlighted as being uniquely applied); and (4) "an anointed one, a lord" (no technical terms are present). The most natural rendering, given 1:31–35, sees the terms as appositionally related (#1). The third option is possible, but in fact is only a more emphatic form of the first rendering.

---

11. Foerster and Fohrer, *TDNT* 7:1015–24. Foerster (7:1015 n. 63) regards the phrase *who is Christ the Lord* as a possible Lucan explanatory gloss. See Acts 5:31 and 13:23 and the related ruler ideas in Acts 3:15 and 7:35. The variety of traditions drawing on the concept is against a gloss here.

In the OT, the combination χριστὸς κύριος occurs only in Lam. 4:20, while in Judaism it is also present in Ps. Sol. 18.7. Other eschatological Jewish uses of the title *Lord* for the redeemer include T. Levi 2.11 and T. Sim. 6.5. However, there is no explicit OT allusion present in the wording here. Rather, titles are presented that draw on general OT ideas.

The use of χριστός is not surprising, since much of the infancy material sets forth Jesus as heir to the Davidic office of regal deliverer (1:27, 31–35, 68–72; 2:4, 11; Bock 1987: 79–80). It is important to note that the term *Messiah* in ancient Jewish thought was not automatically a technical term for this Davidic figure. M. De Jonge (1966) shows the variety of persons to whom the term could refer in the OT and in Judaism (see also Rengstorf, *NIDNTT* 2:334–43). But for Luke the term *Christ* (or *Messiah*, the Semitic equivalent) clearly has regal, Davidic, and messianic connotations (1:31–35, 69).

What does the third term, κύριος, mean? The use of κύριος for Jesus has occurred so far only in 1:43, where it indicates that Elizabeth realizes that Jesus is a more significant figure than John the Baptist. Otherwise, the term in the infancy material (e.g., 1:16, 46, 68, 76) is used of God as sovereign deity, which fits its predominant OT usage.[12] For Luke this title will become the key christological term to describe Jesus (Luke 20:41–44; Acts 2:33–36), and these later texts will define what κύριος means. For now, Luke is content merely to present the term from the angelic announcement and not explain it. Thus, it here serves a literary foretaste of what is to come (Bock 1987: 81–82). The term will clearly come to refer to the absolute sovereignty and divine relationship that Jesus possesses as the one who brings salvation (Bock 1986). The title does not detract from the main declaration of Jesus as the Davidic Messiah; but its presence here suggests that there is more present in Jesus than his merely being Messiah. The presence of this title serves to tip Luke's hand about how he sees Jesus, but Luke does not define the title here. He merely introduces it as a descriptive title of the messianic Savior. Luke defines his Christology mainly from the earth up, since that is how most people of his time came to see who Jesus was. He allows the readers, through exposure to Jesus, to grow in their understanding of who Christ is. In this way, the readers experience christological understanding, much as those around Jesus had.

The verse ends by localizing the birth in the city of David, a reference to Bethlehem (2:4). This repeats the Davidic and regal focus that Luke attaches to Jesus' birth.

12. Κύριος is used more than nine thousand times in the LXX, of which around 6,150 render the divine name יהוה (Yahweh).

Luke now presents a sign of the birth. As with the other angelic an- **2:12**
nouncements in this infancy section (1:19–20, 36), a sign comes
with the announcement (Fitzmyer 1981: 410). The sign's unusual
character, the baby in a feed trough, confirms the announcement's
truth. The expression *this will be a sign* has OT roots (Exod. 3:12;
1 Sam. 2:34; 14:10; Isa. 37:30; 38:7; Rengstorf, *TDNT* 7:231 n. 213).
The shepherds are to look for a newly born child lying in a feed
trough (2:7).[13] Βρέφος (*brephos*) refers to a newly born child (1 Pet.
2:2), though it can refer to the unborn (Luke 1:41, 44) or to a young
child (Luke 18:15; Acts 7:19; 2 Tim. 3:15) (Plummer 1896: 57 also
cites LXX usage). What is amazing is not that the child is wrapped
up, but who the child is and where he is. One hardly expects to find
Messiah in an animal room. One would expect a palace. But the
Messiah's humble and common origins fit nicely with the task that
he shall bear for all his people, including especially the humble,
hungry, and poor (1:50–53). Messiah's life will contain an unusual
bookend for a king, since he was born in an animal room and will
die with robbers (Danker 1988: 58).

iii. Heavenly Praise (2:13–14)

Luke gives a rare glance at heavenly praise. Shepherds see a por- **2:13**
tion of the angelic host praising God. Ἐξαίφνης (*exaiphnēs*), which
may be translated either "suddenly" or "unexpectedly," often refers
in the NT to actions associated with the supernatural world.[14] It is
difficult to translate because the emphasis is as much on the un-
usualness of the action as it is on how quickly it occurs. What is
unusual in this case is the appearing of a portion of the heavenly
host—the angelic entourage that serves God (Dan. 7:10; 1 Kings
22:19; 2 Chron. 18:18; 4 Macc. 4:11).[15] Στρατιᾶς (*stratias*, host) is a
partitive genitive, which means that the multitude is a select group
that comes from the entire heavenly array of angels.[16] Such experiences usually come in the midst of visions. Angelic praise serves
the same function literarily for Luke as do choruses in Greek dra-
mas (Schneider 1977a: 67)—they supply commentary. Thus, angels reveal to the shepherds through praise what the result of

13. On εὑρίσκω in the NT, see Preisker, *TDNT* 2:769.
14. BAGD 272; BAA 549; Mark 13:36 (of the return of the Lord); Acts 9:3 and 22:6
(both of the Lord's appearing to Paul); Luke 9:39 (of a spirit crying out to Jesus).
15. Marshall 1978: 111; Leaney 1958: 96. The appearance of the angel is an angelophany, while the experience of heaven is more like a vision; Michaelis, *TDNT*
5:351.
16. Plummer 1896: 57. Traub, *TDNT* 5:537–38, discusses the "heavenly host." A
singular noun joined to a plural participle is an *ad sensum* construction; BDR
§134.1b.

Jesus' coming should mean. Heaven addresses earth about Jesus' significance.

2:14 The angels offer a brief heavenly note of commendation. The structure is debated, but a twofold structure is most likely (see the additional note). The word pairs *glory-peace*, *heaven-earth*, and *God-men* relate literarily to one another.

Δόξα (*doxa*, glory) can have one of two meanings. It may refer to an attribute of God, describing his majesty (Marshall 1978: 112), or it may be used to ascribe praise to God.[17] The latter sense of praise is more likely here, since this concept appears in 2:13.

The praise is offered in heaven, ὑψίστοις (*hypsistois*), which can be translated "the highest way" or "the highest place" (i.e., heaven). The parallelism dictates the meaning in the context: since ὑψίστοις is opposite to γῆς (*gēs*, earth), "heaven" is meant. These terms are often contrasted in the NT and have OT roots (Matt. 6:10, 19; 16:19; 18:18; 23:9; Heb. 8:1–5; Sasse, *TDNT* 1:679; Traub, *TDNT* 5:513 nn. 118–19).

While heaven offers praise, humans are to have peace. Εἰρήνη (*eirēnē*) connotes the harmonious relationship that can exist between God and humans, the biblical "shalom" of the OT (Ps. 29:11; Isa. 26:3; Jer. 16:5; Ezek. 34:25–31; Nolland 1989: 108). The peace that God provides in Jesus is a key concept for Luke (Luke 1:79; 10:5–6; 19:38, 42; Acts 9:31; 10:36).[18]

God's peace extends to ἀνθρώποις εὐδοκίας (*anthrōpois eudokias*, men of his good pleasure), which is almost a technical phrase in first-century Judaism for God's elect, those on whom God has poured out his favor.[19] In this context, God's elect would be the God-fearers mentioned in the *Magnificat* (1:50–53), those who will respond to Jesus' coming (Danker 1988: 60). Thus, to argue that the term should be seen as broad, almost universal, in light of 2:10 fails to note its technical force. It also fails to note the difference between those whom Jesus comes for (all people; 2:10) and those who benefit from his coming (men of his good pleasure; 2:14).[20] In summary, the angelic praise contains two basic ideas: (1) the heavens

17. Fitzmyer 1981: 410 cites the formulas of praise or confession in Bar. 2:17–18; 1 Esdr. 9:8; 4 Macc. 1:12; Rom. 11:36; and Heb. 13:21. See also Schürmann 1969: 113. Nolland 1989: 108 mentions Ps. Sol. 18.10. The formula corresponds to the Semitic "Hosanna"; Lohse, *TDNT* 9:683, esp. n. 14.

18. Swartley 1983 is too broad in his perception that the scope of peace automatically encompasses all people; see the introduction to 4:16–30.

19. 1QH 4.32–33; 11.9; *Shemoneh Esreh* [Eighteen Benedictions] no. 17 (= Schürer 1973–87: 2.458); Marshall 1978: 112; Fitzmyer 1981: 411–12; Jeremias 1929a; Jeremias, *TDNT* 1:364; Schrenk, *TDNT* 2:745–50; Fitzmyer 1958; Nolland 1989: 109.

20. The term ἐν could be rendered as a simple dative: "*to* men of his good pleasure"; BDR §220.1.1.

rejoice and praise God for salvation's outworking and (2) the people to whom God draws near through Jesus will experience the harmony and benefits that God bestows on his own.

b. Earthly Confirmation (2:15–20)
i. The Shepherds' Confirmation of the Angelic Word (2:15–17)

The angels' departure leads the shepherds to discuss what they have heard, and their discussion resolves into the decision to go to Bethlehem. Their use of the particle δή (dē) adds a note of emphasis: "Indeed or surely, let us go. . . ." Their simple desire is to see this very thing that God has "made known."[21] Ῥῆμα (rhēma) here means "this matter," like the use of λόγων (logōn) in Luke 1:4 and ῥῆμα in Acts 10:37 (Creed 1930: 36), while ὁ κύριος (ho kyrios) here clearly refers to God, not Jesus (Klostermann 1929: 39). God is present since he revealed his plan through his spokesmen, the angels.

2:15

The announcement sets off a chain reaction. First, the shepherds respond in faith and go to find the child (2:16). They tell others what caused them to seek the child (2:17). The shepherds' response in faith and testimony is similar to Mary's instant response to the word in 1:39 (Marshall 1978: 113; Schürmann 1969: 116 n. 150; Danker 1988: 60). The shepherds' reaction causes the audience to react to their testimony (2:18), which in turn leads to a response by Mary (2:19).

2:16

The shepherds move hastily to find the child. Σπεύσαντες (speusantes) has an intransitive sense and functions almost like an adverb: "Hurriedly they went out . . ." (R. Brown 1977: 406; Plummer 1896: 59–60; BDR §435.2.2). The haste fits nicely with the urgency of their decision to go, which δή reflects in 2:15. They search for the child and find him with the family. Ἀνευρίσκω (aneuriskō) means "to search with the result of finding what is sought" (Acts 21:4). Mary is named first, probably because the narrative is focused on her throughout (Luke 1:26–2:19).[22] The use of the connective particle τε (te), an untranslated enclitic particle, expresses the family connection more tightly, so all the members are seen together (Marshall 1978: 113). What the shepherds see is exactly what the angel promised (2:12), a baby lying in a feed trough. The shepherds reflect a vibrant faith, where the sequence is God's word, faith, and then testimony (Schweizer 1984: 51). When God's word comes to pass, testimony should follow (2:17).

---

21. So γνωρίζω often in the NT (Rom. 9:22–23; Acts 2:28), and often tied to the idea of making known a mystery (Col. 1:27; Eph. 1:9; 3:5, 10; 6:19); Bultmann, *TDNT* 1:718.

22. On the unusual spelling of Mary's name, see BDR §53.4.12.

2:17   The shepherds' testimony follows. When they had seen the sign of the baby in a feed trough, they related or "made known" (ἐγνώρισαν, *egnōrisan*) all that the angel had said about the child. Many commentators call them "the first evangelists" (Danker 1988: 61). In looking at the totality of their response, Danker (p. 60) points to the lesson of the narrative: "Depth of spiritual commitment is determined by the quality of one's fidelity after the majestic voice is no longer heard." The audience for the testimony is unspecified, though 2:18 makes clear that it was more than the child's family (Marshall 1978: 113). Mary, Joseph, and others hear that this child shall be a Savior for them, Christ, the Lord (2:11). What the shepherds see and testify to is something that prophetic words and angelic testimony have addressed (1:31–35; 2:4, 11, 14; Schürmann 1969: 117). The full understanding by people will come later. But for now to the voices of the angels is added the testimony of humans. What they see and hear, they report (Tiede 1988: 73). These testimonies are notes of assurance to a man like Theophilus (1:4).

ii. Astonishment, Remembrance, Praise (2:18–20)

2:18   The response of all who heard the testimony was wonder. This response of marvel or wonder occurs frequently in the infancy section (1:21, 63; 2:33; ἐθαύμασαν, *ethaumasan*, they marveled). However, its presence need not suggest the presence of full faith (Acts 3:12; Luke 4:22; 24:41; Danker 1988: 61). Rather, marveling reflects the surprise of those who encounter God's act or revelation (Bertram, *TDNT* 3:39).

     Luke's choice of terms in 2:18–19 contrasts this corporate response and Mary's private response. The particle δέ (*de*) in 2:19 presents Mary in contrast to the hearers in 2:18 ("the hearers marveled, *but* Mary . . ."), and the use of ἐθαύμασαν to summarize the hearers' response stands in contrast to συνετήρει (*synetērei*, she was keeping) in 2:19 to describe Mary's ongoing meditation. This contrast indicates that she reflected on the events in a way that the hearers did not (Godet 1875: 1.134; Plummer 1896: 60). Luke is saying that the report was circulated and caused a stir, but it is not certain that he is saying the city responded concretely to the birth. The report tickles the crowd's ears, but it may have missed their hearts. However, the shepherds did believe (2:20). Jesus' birth brings a variety of responses.

2:19   Mary's response follows. In contrast (δέ) to those of 2:18, she engaged in deep reflection on what was taking place. Συνετήρει indicates an ongoing contemplation of these events (Danker 1988: 61; Klostermann 1929: 39; R. Brown 1977: 406). The wording reflects other texts where a figure ponders over significant events (Gen. 37:11

[Jacob recalling Joseph's dream about the coat]; Dan. 4:28 LXX and 7:28 [Theodotion] [where the prophet reflects on his vision]; T. Levi 6.2; Sir. 39:2; Prov. 3:1; Ps. 119:11).[23] This reflection is described more fully by the participle συμβάλλουσα (*symballousa*, pondering), which in this context refers to a type of contemplation that attempts to put thoughts together into an understandable whole (Josephus, *Antiquities* 2.5.3 §72; Fitzmyer 1981: 413; Van Unnik 1964). It is debated whether this term suggests that Mary did put the events completely together. In light of passages like Mark 3:20–35, it seems unlikely she figured them all out in these early days. Luce (1933: 101) is so impressed by this Marcan text that he argues the Lucan text cannot be historical if Mark is. But the wording here need not preclude that Mary wrestled later with the exact character of Jesus' messianic ministry. In fact, the revelation from Simeon causes Mary some pause as well (Luke 2:33). Luke's point is not on the success of Mary's reflections, as much as on their presence. The reference is simply to her pondering these "matters" (so ῥήματα, *rhēmata*, should be translated, as it was in 2:15). The idiom *pondering in her heart* does not translate well into English, since in English one would normally speak of pondering in one's mind. However, the idea of the Greek is essentially the same as the English idiom *mulling things over.*[24]

Some view the presence of this remark as a possible indication of Luke's source (Ellis 1974: 38; Marshall 1978: 114). Others regard the remark as purely literary, in that Mary is portrayed as a symbol of a disciple who ponders the revelation of God in Jesus (Schneider 1977a: 68; R. Brown 1977: 428). It cannot be doubted that Mary is an example of a proper response to the message of Jesus. Her contemplative response is contrasted to that of the hearers in 2:18. However, the personal focus may also reflect the potential contribution either of Mary herself or of one close to her (perhaps James?). An ultimate source from within the family is not out of the question, though some terminology is Lucan in character, so it may be a Lucan summary note.[25] Regardless, the reader is to identify with Mary's response.

23. Schürmann 1969: 117 n. 160; Riesenfeld, *TDNT* 8:151; B. Meyer 1964: 43. The remark argues that the events, like revelation of an apocalyptic secret, transcend human understanding and require reflection.

24. The term καρδία describes the place of reflection; Luke 1:51; 9:47; 24:38; Acts 8:22; Mark 11:23; Behm, *TDNT* 3:612.

25. Schürmann 1969: 117–18 notes the unique Lucan usage in 2:19 involving the specific form of Mary's name; fourteen of the twenty-seven uses of Μαριάμ are in Luke–Acts (but eleven of these are in the infancy material, so the usage may reflect sources). In addition, all six NT uses of συμβάλλω are in Luke–Acts. Also tied up in this point is a textual issue (see the additional notes on 2:19). I read Μαρία here, a reading that makes the possibility of Lucan composition less likely.

2:20   The shepherds, having seen the sign, returned home. But they returned with their faith confirmed and deepened. All they had heard, they had also seen come to pass. This produced a sense of joy in them, as they honored God with glory and praise. The realization of the message led to praise, just as the angels offered praise in 2:13–14 (Fitzmyer 1981: 413). The remark sets the passage's mood. The reference to glory and praise is a combination that is also present in the OT (Josh. 7:19; 1 Chron. 16:35; Ps. 66:2; 106:47; Isa. 42:8, 12; Jer. 13:11; Hab. 3:3; Dan. 4:34, 37 [4:31, 34 MT]). Glory can be offered in a variety of relationships, but here it refers to verbally giving honor to God for his acts.[26] What the shepherds saw in Bethlehem was in agreement with what they had heard from the angels.[27] God's message through the angels had come to pass, leading to praise for God's work. The shepherds had witnessed the start of God's work in Jesus and felt honored to share in the event.

c. The Obedient Naming of Jesus at Circumcision (2:21)

2:21   Functioning as a transition, 2:21 could be regarded as the beginning of a new section or as the conclusion to this unit. Schneider (1977a: 70) argues that it belongs with the next section, because it parallels 1:59, which ties John's circumcision and naming to a prophetic description of his mission. But the claim of parallelism will not stand, since the prophecy tied to Jesus' mission occurs at purification, not circumcision. In addition, the accounts differ in that John's parents have a major role in the circumcision event, while Jesus' parents are not mentioned (R. Brown 1977: 431). Most likely the verse concludes the birth narrative and forms a transition between the birth and the purification visit.

Jesus' parents fulfill the law when they bring the child in for circumcision. They do what any Jewish parent would do with any Jewish son. Ἐπλήσθησαν (eplēsthēsan, were fulfilled) points to the completion of a number of days set by nature or the law (1:23, 57; 2:6, 22). In the OT, it was instructed that any son of Abraham should be circumcised on the eighth day (Gen. 17:11–12; Lev. 12:3; Luke 1:59). That Jesus underwent circumcision has led many commentators to speculate on the event's significance. They speak of Jesus' identifying with his people as their representative leader or as a representative human (Rom. 8:3; Gal. 4:4; Heb. 2:17; Alford 1874: 460; Hendriksen 1978: 158–59; Plummer 1896: 61–62). Such a theologi-

---

26. Plummer 1896: 60 gives all the combinations: human to human (1 Sam. 15:30); human to God (Exod. 15:2); God to human (Ps. 91:15 [90:15 LXX]).

27. Καθώς compares what they heard with what they saw and thus connects only to εἶδον; Godet 1875: 1.134.

cal significance for this event is not Luke's concern, though it is a valid theological point implied by these other passages. However, when Jesus undergoes circumcision, he identifies with Israel, not all humans, since circumcision is a national rite.

The parents name the child with the name the angel gave (1:31). The giving of the name is more important than the significance of Jesus' circumcision, since it reflects a faithful response to the angel's message of 1:31–35, just as Zechariah had responded faithfully with the naming of John in 1:57–66. The word of God was obeyed (Schweizer 1984: 55).

The verse has many terms or features that are frequent in Luke or are particularly Lucan (Plummer 1896: 61): (1) the combination καὶ ὅτε (kai hote, and when) (1:22, 42; 6:13; 22:14; 23:33); (2) πίμπλημι (pimplēmi, to fulfill);[28] (3) the infinitive of purpose (1:74, 77, 79; 2:24; 4:10; 5:7; 8:5; etc.); (4) καί expressing a consequence (5:1, 12, 17; 7:12; 9:51; etc.); and (5) συλλαμβάνω (syllambanō, to conceive) (eleven of sixteen NT uses are in Luke–Acts, including Luke 1:24, 36). It is possible that Luke has summarized a larger set of material to isolate the main point of obedience.

Summary

Luke 2:1–21 portrays Jesus' birth with a simplicity that belies the event's universal significance. The birth of the Davidic Savior and Messiah occurs in a room normally reserved for animals. His crib is a feed trough. And yet the birth in Bethlehem is the beginning of the fulfillment of God's most significant act for humans. From this simple setting emerges the Lord Jesus, the focus of all of God's promises and of all human hopes.

Fundamental to this section is the Christology of 2:11. Jesus' life is introduced in terms of three titles: *Savior* points to his role as deliverer; *Messiah* points to his office in terms of the promised Anointed One of God; and *Lord* indicates his sovereign authority. Both *Messiah* and *Lord* will be key titles in the presentation of Luke's two volumes. Jesus' birth is set in the middle of Roman history, in the reign of Caesar Augustus. However, for Luke the key historical figure is not the powerful Roman ruler; it is the frail child, Jesus, the Christ, who is Lord.

In the angelic exchange with the shepherds, the major point is heaven's testimony to simple folk. The shepherds seem to represent humankind. After hearing angelic testimony of heaven's joy over the birth, they respond admirably and go to see the child. They share the joy of heaven upon fulfillment of the word. They

28. Twenty-two times in Luke–Acts and two times in rest of NT; in Luke at 1:15, 23, 41, 57, 67; 2:6, 21, 22; 4:28; 5:7, 26; 6:11; 21:22; the non-Lucan examples are Matt. 22:10; 27:48.

see, hear, and testify. Other bystanders at the event marvel at what is happening as the birth produces a variety of responses. In Jesus, heaven and earth come together.

Mary represents the response of a faithful one. She sees the events and contemplates their significance. She wrestles to understand all that is happening. We know she is faithful because the name revealed by the angel in 1:31 is now given to the child. She is intimately acquainted with these events, and yet she too struggles to understand what it all means.

Events often happen "just as was spoken" by the angels. This concept dominates the account and leads to the emergence of two ideas: God is in control of these events, and God's word comes to pass just as he promised. Here is the note of assurance for Luke's reader. God can be believed.

Joy surrounds all the events, whether it be in the angelic call to glorify God or in the shepherds' praise. All are to share in the joy of Jesus' coming. These are special events; God's hand is actively and uniquely at work. Just as the heavens rejoice, so should the earth.

Additional Notes

2:8. Some suggest that rather than a historical account, the pastoral scene with shepherds is a product of midrashic reflection that linked messianic associations in Tg. Ps.-J. Gen. 35:21 with the "tower of the flocks" (Mic. 4:8) and its association with Jerusalem.[29] The view has severe problems. First, it is not entirely clear that the targum refers to Bethlehem instead of Jerusalem, especially if the basis of the association is Tg. Mic. 4:8. Second, it is not clear that Gen. 35:21 refers to Bethlehem instead of a locale between Bethlehem and Jerusalem (A. Cohen 1948: 171). T. Reub. 3.13 sees *Eder*, the Hebrew name for the tower of the flocks, as distinct from Bethlehem. Creed's statement (1930: 31–32) that the tower was at Bethlehem oversteps the evidence. This probable lack of association between Bethlehem and the ancient exegetical sources makes a midrash developed on the basis of such material highly unlikely.

2:8. The presence of flocks in the field raises questions about the traditional December date for Christmas. Some argue that grazing sheep presupposes a milder climate than December offers. Also, some Jewish traditions argue for grazing in the period from April to November (SB 2:114–16; *b. Beṣa* 40a; *b. B. Qam.* 79b–80a; *y. Beṣa* 63b [= Neusner et al. 1982–

---

29. Some add an association between swaddling clothes and Messiah in Midr. Lam. (*Ekah Rabbah*) 1.51, an approach discussed and rejected by Marshall 1978: 107.

93: 18.128]; Edersheim 1889: 1.186–87, esp. n. 2). However, Edersheim notes that these restrictions are limited to sheep "in the wilderness." *M. Šeqal.* 7.4 implies year-round grazing, because the Passover lambs graze in February, which has the harshest weather of the year. Thus, this reason for rejecting the tradition is not definitive (Schweizer 1984: 49; Hoehner 1977: 26; Plummer 1896: 55).

The Lucan text does not indicate a season or a date for the birth. The tradition of December 25 as the date of Jesus' birth and of the Christmas holiday arose in the time of Constantine (A.D. 306–337). It coincided with a pagan feast of Saturnalia, or the rising of the sun from darkness (Hendriksen 1978: 150). But the tradition for the date may go back even further, since it may be mentioned by Hippolytus (A.D. 165–235) in his *Commentary on Daniel* 4.23.3 (Hoehner 1977: 25). However, Hippolytus's meaning is disputed, as it is unclear whether he is referring to the date of the birth or the date of the conception. If it is the latter, then a December date is presented, but the reference is unclear.[30] Alongside the possible third-century testimony for a December date stands Clement of Alexandria's testimony (ca. A.D. 200) for an April/May date (*Stromata* 1.21 §§145–46; R. Brown 1977: 401). The Eastern church celebrates January 6 as the day of both the birth and the coming of the Magi. In the West, by the time of Augustine (*On the Trinity* 4.5) a December date for the birth was fixed. Thus, the testimony of the early church is mixed as to Jesus' exact date of birth. A December date, though possible, is not certain.

It is impossible to know for sure Jesus' exact date of birth. The ancient indecision between spring and winter leads many scholars to cite Jesus' birth year as 5/4 B.C. Given the lack of detail in Matthew or Luke, such caution is appropriate.

2:9. Ἰδού is probably not original, since its absence is hard to explain if it had been originally present. It is the normal introduction to such events.[31]

2:11. The text reads χριστὸς κύριος, not χριστὸς κυρίου; the external evidence that supports the latter reading (as does Winter 1958 and possibly Klostermann 1929: 37) is weak. Only a few witnesses read χριστὸς κυρίου: two Old Latin manuscripts, two Syriac versions, Diatessaron, and Ephraem (rejecting χριστὸς κυρίου are Metzger 1975: 132; Schürmann 1969: 111; and Grundmann, *TDNT* 9:533 n. 276).

2:11. Is the use of the term *Lord* an explanatory gloss by Luke? The presence of κύριος has caused much discussion, with some suggesting that

---

30. Lake 1910: 606. Hippolytus was a disciple of Irenaeus, who studied under Polycarp, who in turn studied under the apostle John. As such, Hippolytus might be a significant witness, if one could be sure exactly what he meant.

31. Marshall 1978: 108. Supporting the addition are A, D, Θ, Ψ, family 13, Byz, and some Latin and Syriac versions. The harder-reading rule is against it, though it has wide attestation.

Luke added the term to describe for his Greek audiences what χριστός means (Schürmann 1969: 111–12 and n. 117). This explanation is possible, but is not very likely. Κύριος occurs thirty-seven times in Luke with reference to Jesus. Often it is used in the address of others to Jesus and simply means "master" (twenty-one times). Even the earlier use in 1:43 is a title of respect, not a statement of Jesus' divine nature. It took Jesus' family a while to realize exactly who Jesus was, as Mary's pondering in 2:19 suggests. The title often appears in the introduction to events where Luke is describing the context of an action. These texts describe Jesus as the Lord (eleven times). This narrative, editorial use of the term *Lord* points to a title for Jesus; but in the Gospel it is not found on the lips of others in a titular sense except here and at 24:34. It is combined with other terms in a titular sense at 6:5 ("Lord of the Sabbath," where Jesus is the speaker) and 24:3 ("Lord Jesus," where it appears in the narrative). The only other use of κύριος for Jesus is in the crucial passage of 20:42–44, which is traditional material.

The point is simply that Luke is very restrained in his use of the title *Lord* and its scope *when it involves the address of others* (only 19:31, 34 are debatable). Speakers in the ministry narratives of Luke's Gospel do not call Jesus "Lord" in the full sense. When one considers how many opportunities there were for this type of insertion as some conceive of it, the number of uses noted above is not great. Thus, the conclusion that Luke inserted this term is open to doubt, since Luke shows a restrained use. Further, Luke uses κύριος in a completely different way in the infancy material by retaining its primary usage as a reference to God (fifteen times). When one includes the κύριος parables, only two of the seven passages where these parables occur are unique to Luke (Bock 1987: 80–81, 305 n. 108). In sum, the evidence for Luke's independent use of κύριος in reference to Jesus' ministry is meager. Luke did not insert κύριος here.

2:14. It is debated whether 2:14 divides poetically into three or two parts.[32] The three-part line reads, "(1) Glory to God in the highest (2) and on earth peace, (3) good will toward men." The two-part line reads, "(1) Glory to God in the highest (2) and on earth peace among men of his good pleasure."[33] Part of the debate is text-critical. Key manuscripts of the Alexandrian and the Western families read a two-part line (ℵ, A, B, D, and many Itala manuscripts). Internally, the clearer parallelism involves three pairs of concepts in a two-part line: glory matches up with peace (condition), heaven matches up with earth (locale), and God matches up with the men of his good plea-

---

32. The KJV reflects a three-part division by reading nominative εὐδοκία; so Godet 1875: 1.132–33. Many recent translations reflect a two-part division by reading genitive εὐδοκίας; so Plummer 1896: 57–58; Fitzmyer 1981: 410–12; and R. Brown 1977: 403–5.

33. On the options, see Schrenk, *TDNT* 2:747–50, who also opts for the two-part line.

sure (persons). Thus, a two-part division seems more likely (Metzger 1975: 133). Attempts are made to trace this part of the tradition back to an Aramaic original (Klostermann 1929: 39 [who cites H. Gressmann]; Black 1967: 168).

2:15. The exact text is uncertain, since a variety of witnesses (A, D, P, Byz) insert the words καὶ οἱ ἄνθρωποι before the reference to shepherds (this text-critical problem is not discussed in UBS[4]). The shorter reading of UBS–NA also has good support (א, B, L, W, and versions) and is slightly more likely (Metzger 1975: 134). The choice makes no great difference to the meaning, which simply states the shepherds' resolve to go and see the child.

2:17. Fitzmyer (1981: 311) argues that the absence of a reference to virgin birth suggests the original independence of the Luke 2 narrative from the events of Luke 1. But this seems speculative. Why does the virgin birth need mention here? It is not necessary to this pericope and its absence says nothing about the question of sources. In fact, it may suggest that the stories about Jesus were an original unit, since this concept is not reintroduced.

2:19. Μαρία is the slightly better reading, since it is the harder reading and has good attestation (א*, B, D, Θ). The longer Μαριάμ (adopted in UBS–NA) is supported by א[2], A, L, W, Ξ, Ψ, family 1, family 13, and Byz. This normal spelling of the name (see 1:27, 34, 38, 39, 46, 56; 2:5, 34) makes Μαρία the harder reading. Either reading is quite possible and the choice makes no difference.

2:19. Plummer (1896: 60) raises the possibility that perhaps the shepherds were a source for this account, while Fitzmyer (1981: 398) rejects this conclusion in his discussion and rejection of Mary as a possible source for this material. Fitzmyer uses the same reasoning as does Luce (1933: 101), citing Mark 3:20–35 as a contradiction to a Marian source, as well as arguing that identifying a source is not the point of the verse (see the exegesis of 2:19). But can one really demonstrate a denial of the material's possible ultimate origin in sources such as Mary, the family, or the shepherds? Certainty of the source cannot be argued from these verses, but that such sources would have been unavailable to Luke cannot be categorically asserted either.

9. Witness of the Man and Woman at the Temple (2:22–40)

Further reaction to Jesus' birth comes at the temple. Jesus' parents are pious and law-abiding. At the temple, Mary receives purification after the birth, and Jesus is presented to the Lord as a firstborn son. The scene has four elements: the setting (tied to Mary's faithful following of the law; 2:22–24), the description and prophecy of Simeon (2:25–35), Anna's reaction (2:36–38), and a note about Jesus' growth (2:39–40). This final note provides a transition into the next passage (2:41–52), where Jesus speaks for the first time.

The account shows the superiority of Jesus to John the Baptist. John's career was described at his naming and circumcision, but Jesus' praise continues long after his circumcision. It requires additional scenes to describe his work. In fact, this scene and the next one break the parallelism between the two accounts and show that the major attention in Luke 1–2 belongs to Jesus. In this account, prophets of Jewish piety speak. In the next, Jesus speaks for himself.

In this pericope two prophets, a man and a woman, offer their evaluations of Jesus. Simeon declares that Jesus is God's salvation, who is set before his people. He is light for the nations and glory for Israel. For the first time Jesus' mission is explicitly related to the Gentiles. In Simeon's further remarks to Mary, more new details occur: Jesus' presence will result in the fall and rise of many in Israel, and his coming will bring a sword that will pierce Mary's soul. Here is Luke's first hint of coming rejection and suffering. Anna's testimony is brief: She preaches to all of Israel's coming redemption, and she is thankful to God for the child. In these two scenes, humankind—male and female—offers praise to God for Jesus.

Sources and Historicity

The treatment of sources and historicity in this account is complex. The absence of Lucanisms makes it unlikely that this material is from Luke.[1] The only possible exceptions to this are 2:22–24, with its explanation of Jewish

---

1. Farris 1985: 30 notes that A. von Harnack admitted this stylistic feature in the *Nunc Dimittis*. There are some, however, who hold out for Lucan redaction, merely because of the Gentile emphasis.

practice, and the hymn-prophecy of 2:29–35, which has a Gentile emphasis. Luke 2:22–24 is often considered to have come to Luke through Hellenistic Judaism, that is, if he did not write it himself.[2] This controversy can
be settled only through examination of the passage. As will be shown,
2:22–24 contains no error and so a Hellenistic origin is not required,
though that portion of the tradition containing an explanation of the custom
may reflect Lucan sensitivity for a Hellenistic audience.

This tradition's ultimate roots are old, though how old and from where are
disputed.[3] In the early part of the twentieth century, associations were raised
between this birth account and that of Buddha, but these have been rejected.[4] Many see the hymn of 2:29–32 and the prophecy of 2:34–35 coming
from similar sources, so the discussion here parallels that of the earlier
hymns.[5] Because of the allusions to Gentile salvation, many argue that these
are "after the fact" prophecies with roots in Hellenistic Christian circles (so
Klostermann 1929: 40). There is also debate about whether they were originally tied to the narrative about Simeon. But others argue that the details are
too Palestinian to have originated in the Gentile church (Schürmann 1969:
122, 126, 131; Marshall 1978: 144).[6]

This brief overview shows how difficult it is to unravel the issue of sources
because of the different types of material in the passage. However, certain

2. Bultmann 1963: 299, 304 regards this setting as artificial and erroneous, since
the firstborn child is presented at the temple, which was not required by the law.
Schürmann 1969: 119–20, 131 speaks of editorial work from Hellenistic Christianity, though he still insists that the bulk of the tradition is Jewish-Christian because
of its heavy emphasis on Israel and its traces of a Palestinian setting (the only other
verse he questions is 2:27). He places the origin in a setting similar to 1:5–25 and
1:57–79. Nolland 1989: 115 argues for Luke's hand in 2:22–24, 39; but the non-LXX
form of the OT citation is against 2:22–24 being from Luke's hand. In Nolland's view
(p. 116), the rest is substantially from a source, with 2:25, 38 serving as Lucan editorial links. He also sees possible Lucan elements in 2:33–35.

3. There are many suggestions about Lucan redaction at various spots. Klostermann 1929: 40 sees Luke's hand in 2:22b–23, 29–32, 34–35. R. Brown 1977: 445–47,
452–55 argues for an original tradition that contained what is now 2:27–34; Luke,
however, added the hymn. For Brown, the hymn is from the Jewish-Christian
Anawim, as were the earlier hymns of Luke 1–2.

4. Creed 1930: 37–38 mentions these associations and rejects them, as do Bultmann 1963: 299–300 and Schürmann 1969: 131 n. 244. The comparison was described by Aufhauser 1926 and defended by Garbe 1959: 47–49, but there are just
too many differences between these accounts.

5. Fitzmyer 1981: 420 speaks of several stages in the construction of the account.
He thinks it likely that Luke added the hymn, but he is unsure whether the hymn's
origin is the same as the origin of the hymns of Luke 1. See the earlier discussion of
hymns in the sources and historicity sections of 1:46–56 and 1:67–80.

6. The major reason for separating 2:22–40 from the earlier material in Luke 1–
2 is the additional note of parental surprise, which is regarded by many as a doublet
to the surprise in 2:18–19. This explanation can be challenged, as the information
Simeon supplies is new and could create the reaction, since there was no universalism in the earlier passages and Mary's hymn was so national in focus.

points should be made. The appeal to "after the fact" prophecy is a worldview issue that inevitably affects historical judgment.[7] If one rejects the concept of prophecy, then all such texts must have their origin in the church, where Gentile mission is already a fact. However, other factors suggest that this approach is inappropriate. The remarks about Gentile inclusion are framed in OT terms, so there is nothing "postcross" about these remarks. Only the predictions of suffering lack OT antecedents, but they are expressed circumspectly, emphasizing division in the nation more than suffering. In fact, even the suffering is tied mainly to Mary. Surely the idea that Messiah's coming would be controversial is possible in this era of many messianic claims, especially when many such claims proved false. The ultimate source of such tradition, taken historically, would have to be a setting of Jewish piety, for Anna's remarks are still very national, speaking only of the redemption of Jerusalem. This does not fit the alleged category of later created prophecy, which would focus on all nations. One suspects that it is the predictions for a baby, rather than merely the prophecies' content, that causes questions about historicity. One other point supports an older tradition. Unlike many Lucan citations, the citation of the law in 2:23 does not follow the LXX.

As with the other parts of the material, this tradition gives evidence of reaching back into the earliest parts of Jesus' life. It should be noted, however, that it is possible Luke has narrated these historical details in a highly condensed fashion, at times giving explanations or summaries of actions taken. So it is entirely possible that 2:22–24, 27, which explain how the parents fulfilled the law, are narrative notations by Luke to make precisely this point. Such an explanation might also apply to the summary of 2:39–40 with its parallelism to 1:80.

> The form of the account is actually a mixture. The prominent forms are hymn (2:29–32) and prophecy (2:34–35). The hymn is a hymn of praise before an approaching death.[8] One could also speak of a "fate" text in that the career of the child is summarized (Berger 1984: 327). The account could also be called a "prodigy" account, since a baby's greatness is extolled (Berger 1984: 349).
>
> The outline of Luke 2:22–40 is as follows:
>
> a. Setting of the prophecies: the law of purification (2:22–24)
> b. Witness of the man: Simeon (2:25–35)

7. Marshall 1978: 114, very clear on this point, argues for a Palestinian setting. That is as far as he goes.

8. Berger 1984: 243, 350. Bovon 1989: 137 speaks of a God-directed meeting (other examples are Luke 1:39–45; Acts 9:10–18; 10:17–29). He observes that meetings before a death have parallels in the OT (Gen. 46:30 [Jacob with Joseph]; Deut. 32:49–50; 34:1–5 [Moses and the land]) and in Judaism (Tob. 11:10–15). Bovon also notes Greek parallels.

     i. Simeon's righteousness (2:25)
     ii. The Spirit's promise (2:26)
     iii. Simeon's reception of the child (2:27)
     iv. The *Nunc Dimittis* (2:28–32)
       (1) Praise (2:28–29)
       (2) Reason for praise (2:30)
       (3) "A light for the nations, glory for Israel" (2:31–32)
     v. The parents' marvel (2:33)
     vi. Blessing for parents and a prophecy of division (2:34–35)
  c. Witness of the woman: Anna (2:36–38)
     i. Anna's piety (2:36–37)
     ii. Her prophecy to all (2:38)
  d. Transition: return to Galilee; Jesus' growth (2:39–40)

Many themes dominate this crucial text. Jesus is the promised child who represents God's coming salvation to Israel and the nations. However, the first ominous note also comes: Jesus will divide Israel. There are promise and fulfillment, but not all is good. Jesus forces choices and, as a result, some people will fall rather than rise.

Jesus' parents are seen as faithful to the law. The locale for this blessing is significant: the temple. Just as the infancy events started in the temple, they also end there. The nerve center of Jewish worship is the site of this praise to Jesus. He is not an outsider, but is received by the pious who worship God. Men and women offer commendation. In fact, the old—like Simeon and Anna— find comfort in his coming. Simeon can die in peace, knowing that Jesus has come. Thus, the mood of the passage is both joy and peace. God's promise has come. Prophets declare it and people can rest in the hands of the sovereign God who brings it to pass. The actions of these prophets are directed by God through his Spirit (this unit has numerous references to the Spirit's presence: 2:25, 26, 27). God is in control of what has taken place. Such are the notes of assurance Theophilus is to have about Jesus.

Exegesis and Exposition

²²And when the days of ⌜their⌝ purification were fulfilled according to the law of Moses, they took him up to Jerusalem to present him to the Lord, ²³even as it is written in the law of the Lord that "all males who open the womb shall be called holy to the Lord," ²⁴and to give sacrifice according to what is said in the law of the Lord, "a pair of turtledoves or two pigeons."

²⁵And behold there was a man in Jerusalem whose name was Simeon, and this man was righteous and devout, awaiting the consolation of Israel, and the Holy Spirit was upon him. ²⁶And it had been revealed to him by the

Holy Spirit that he would not see death before he saw the Messiah of the Lord. [27]And he came in the Spirit to the temple courts, and when the parents brought the child Jesus to do to him according to the custom of the law, [28]then Simeon took him into his arms and blessed God and said,

> [29] "Now release your servant, Master, according to your word in peace,
> [30] because my eyes have seen your salvation,
> [31] which you prepared in the presence of all the people,
> [32] a light, for revelation to the nations
> and for the glory of your people Israel."

[33]And his ⌜father⌝ and mother were amazed about the things spoken about him.

[34]And Simeon blessed them and said to Mary his mother, "Behold, this one is set for the falling and the rising of many in Israel and for a sign of contradiction [35](and a large sword will pierce through your own soul also) so that the hostile thoughts shall be revealed out of the hearts of many."

[36]And there was Anna a prophetess, daughter of Phanuel, from the tribe of Asher. She was very old, having lived with a man seven years from her youth. [37]And she was widowed eighty-four years and she did not leave the temple, giving service, fasting, and praying night and day. [38]And in that hour she drew near and offered praise to God and was speaking concerning him to all who were awaiting the redemption of ⌜Jerusalem⌝.

[39]And when they completed all the things according to the law of the Lord, they returned to Galilee into the city of Nazareth. [40]And the child grew and ⌜became strong⌝, filled with wisdom, and the favor of God was upon him.

a. Setting of the Prophecies: The Law of Purification (2:22–24)

2:22   The setting of Simeon's and Anna's prophecies about Jesus involves three separate ceremonies that have been summarized together in 2:22–24: the purification ceremony involving the wife, forty days after birth (Lev. 12:2–4, 6; Luke 2:22a, 24); the presentation of the firstborn to the Lord (Exod. 13:2, 12, 15; 34:19; Num. 18:15–16 [which notes the ransom payment of five shekels]; Luke 2:23); and the dedication of the firstborn to the Lord's service (1 Sam. 1–2). This third ceremony is suggested by the absence of any allusion to the ransom payment and the mention in Luke 2:22b of Jesus' being dedicated to the Lord (Marshall 1978: 117; Schürmann 1969: 121–22; Reicke, *TDNT* 5:841, esp. n. 14). The Lucan context argues for a dedication to Jesus' messianic ministry, but this association is more explicitly expressed in the later messages of Simeon and Anna than it is connected with the parents' action. Jesus is a firstborn, but with a difference.

Jesus' parents are presented as pious, law-abiding Jews as they journey from Bethlehem to Jerusalem to fulfill the law of purification. The law stated that the mother of a male child was unclean for seven days and then was to be confined for thirty-three days before journeying to the temple to offer a sacrifice of a lamb and a turtledove (Lev. 12:2–4, 6)—the lamb as a burnt offering and the turtledove as a sin offering. If she could not afford a lamb, then her sacrifice was to be two turtledoves or two pigeons, one bird for the burnt offering and the other for the sin offering (Lev. 12:8). From Luke 2:24 it is clear that Joseph and Mary offered the offering of the poor, an offering that identifies them with the very people whom Christ portrays himself as saving (1:52; 4:18–19; 6:20; Greeven, *TDNT* 6:69; Danker 1988: 62). However, it should not be concluded from this that Joseph lived in abject poverty, since he had a trade as a carpenter (Hendriksen 1978: 165; Plummer 1896: 65; Mark 6:3). The lamb seems to have been offered only by the fairly wealthy. It is quite possible that Jesus' parents bought their offering in the temple courts (R. Brown 1977: 437; Luke 19:45–48).

In addition to coming for cleansing, the parents came to Jerusalem to dedicate Jesus to the Lord. The child need not be brought along, if they wished only to pay the prescribed ransom for the firstborn. What Jesus' parents did was above what the law instructed for a firstborn.

This "more than the law" element may explain a peculiarity in the text that is also reflected in a text-critical problem (not discussed in UBS[4]). As the solution to the textual issue is important to the historical issue, both are treated here. The better-attested text reads the plural αὐτῶν (*autōn*, their), which relates the purification to both Mary and Joseph or to both Jesus and Mary.[9] Some copyists, who knew that the purification law applied to the woman only, altered the text to αὐτῆς (*autēs*, her), the feminine pronoun.[10] Others tried to attach the purification to Jesus or to Joseph only (e.g., D has αὐτοῦ, *autou*, his). The external evidence and the most-difficult-reading canon indicate that αὐτῶν is original. But two questions need attention: (1) Who is addressed by αὐτῶν? and (2) How could the purification be associated with both, when only the woman needs purification?

On the first question of whom the plural refers to, Creed (1930: 39) argues that the reference includes Jesus and Mary, because in 2:22–24 the major figures are Jesus and Mary (also Schneider 1977a: 71). But the verse's syntax suggests that Luke means Mary

---

9. So א, A, B, L, Byz; so read most translations. Schürmann 1969: 121 n. 180 and Marshall 1978: 116 discuss this textual problem.

10. So 76, the Complutensian Polyglot of 1514, and possibly some Itala manuscripts and Vulgate, a reading also adopted in the KJV.

and Joseph (*"they* brought him up for *their* purification"). The most natural way to understand the verse is to see the subject and the third-person pronoun in agreement (Plummer 1896: 63; Fitzmyer 1981: 424).[11]

How can one reconcile a plural reference to the law that applied only to women? Numerous suggestions have been made. The first is to suggest that Luke as a Hellenist either erred or was confused about the law (Bultmann 1963: 299; perhaps Schneider 1977a: 71, who says Luke is "not precise"; Fitzmyer 1981: 424). But better solutions exist:

1. It could be argued that Joseph, because he aided in the delivery, was himself made unclean, since according to the Mishnah contact with blood in the delivery made one an "offspring of uncleanness" (Bock 1987: 83–84; Blackman 1977: 6.10–11; *m. Nid.* 5.1; 2.5; 1.3–5). If this was the case then he would have needed to make such an offering in order to be ready to present the child.
2. An equally plausible explanation is that if the child was dedicated, then both parents would have participated in the dedication, just as Elkanah, the husband, paid Hannah's vow for Samuel, even though it was the mother's vow (1 Sam. 1:21). The only problem with this approach is that a vow is not present in Luke. One could, however, argue that only the dedication aspect is parallel.
3. Machen takes a grammatical solution, arguing that αὐτῶν should be taken as a subjective genitive, which refers succinctly to "their participation" in purification. Thus, the word only makes the point that Joseph was included in the process (Machen 1930: 73, as noted also by Schürmann 1969: 121 n. 180). The problem is that this view is vague in explaining how Joseph is involved. Views 1 and 2 are more complete.
4. Others simply say the problem arises from summarization. Luke is combining several events in a short space, and the combination has produced a lack of clarity (Ernst 1977: 114; Schürmann 1969: 122).

There is obviously a compressed account here, but it also seems natural that if the parents were dedicating the child to the Lord, they would want to be ceremonially clean at the time of dedication. Thus, either view 1 (the birth-cleanliness view) or view 2 (the parental-

11. Most commentators note that Mary's association with purification argues against a view that sees her as an "intact virgin" after Jesus' birth; see 1:34; Creed 1930: 39; Plummer 1896: 63; R. Brown 1977: 436; Fitzmyer 1981: 421.

dedication view) could explain the plural reference. The point of the passage should not be missed in the debate: Jesus' parents are piously following the law by bringing the child before the Lord.

Jesus' dedication to the Lord is tied to the law's instruction about presenting the firstborn as recorded in Exod. 13:2 (Reicke, *TDNT* 5:840–41). The citation's wording does not depend on the LXX version, since the syntax of the Lucan citation is very different from that of the LXX (Bock 1987: 82–83; Holtz 1968: 82–83). This feature of the text suggests a non-Hellenistic origin for this material. The wording is such that no one specific text is clearly in view. What is referred to is the sanctified position that the firstborn son has in the Jewish family. In Num. 18:1–16, only Levi's family was required to give their sons for priestly service, but a redemption price of five shekels for the firstborn were required of other families. The absence of a ransom allusion has led many to see Jesus' dedication as a reflection of Exodus rather than Numbers (see Luke 2:22). Luke's point lies in the description of Jesus as holy (an initial fulfillment of 1:35). However, within the pericope itself, Jesus' fulfillment comes as a firstborn Jewish son rather than with his messianic function. In the dedication, the child is said to belong truly to the Lord. How much Jesus belongs to the Lord is something the parents will only slowly come to understand, as their confusion in 2:41–52 shows.

2:23

Luke now introduces the second way in which the parents fulfilled the law: participation in the sacrifice of purification (see 2:22). The wording, though alluding to the instruction of Lev. 12:8, is closer to the wording of Lev. 5:11 LXX regarding the sin offering (Bock 1987: 83). The peculiar wording means either that a Semitic source is present (so Holtz 1968: 82–83) or that Joseph's offering is alluded to as well through the Lev. 5 reference. The piety of Jesus' parents is the point. They obeyed the law. In making their offering with the birds instead of the lamb, they chose the sacrifice that was to be offered by the poor (C. Brown, *NIDNTT* 1:172). As they drew near to the temple to make the offering, startling words of testimony came from two elderly prophets.

2:24

b. Witness of the Man: Simeon (2:25–35)
i. Simeon's Righteousness (2:25)

Jesus' parents meet Simeon, the first of two pious saints who give Spirit-led testimony to Jesus at the temple. Such testimony reveals strong divine sanction of Jesus (Schürmann 1969: 122). Simeon is presented as a simple man, a layman, not a priest, who dwells in Jerusalem. Simeon was a common name, since it was the name of one of Jacob's sons (Gen. 29:33). Speculation that this is Simeon,

2:25

son of the great rabbi Hillel and father of Gamaliel, the teacher of Paul, is unlikely.[12] The name Simeon means "God has heard," but the meaning plays no role for Luke (Fitzmyer 1981: 426).

The postbiblical tradition that developed around Simeon is interesting. In the Protevangelium of James 24.3–4, he is treated as a priest, a point that may have led to speculation that he had rabbinic ancestry,[13] but the Lucan text doesn't call him a priest. In the Gospel of Pseudo-Matthew 15.2, his age is given as 112 years, but Luke mentions neither his age nor that he is old. At best, old age is inferred from the text where Simeon says he is ready to die after seeing the baby Messiah (2:26, 29).

What is revealed about Simeon is neither his vocation nor his age, but his spiritual condition. He was a devout believer in God. The description of Simeon as δίκαιος (dikaios, righteous) and εὐλαβής (eulabēs, devout or pious) shows him to be an exemplary saint (Matt. 10:41; 13:17; 23:29, 35; 2 Pet. 2:7–8).[14] Others called δίκαιος were Job (Job 1:1), Zechariah the father of John the Baptist (Luke 1:6), and Cornelius (Acts 10:22). Εὐλαβής in secular literature describes the "ideal statesman" who was "conscientious and cautious."[15] The term refers to the spiritually sensitive God-fearer, the faithful law-abider (Marshall 1978: 118; Schürmann 1969: 123 n. 191; Acts 2:5; 8:2; 22:12). Clearly Simeon is seen in a favorable light.

Simeon not only is righteous, he also lives in the hope that God's promise will come to pass: he is awaiting the consolation of Israel (cf. Luke 2:38; Mark 15:43).[16] Israel's consolation (παράκλησιν τοῦ Ἰσραήλ, paraklēsin tou Israēl) was a key element in many strands of OT and Jewish eschatology, referring to the hope of deliverance for the nation (Isa. 40:1; 49:13; 51:3; 57:18; 61:2; 2 Bar. 44.7). Later, the rabbis would refer to Messiah as Menahem (comforter) because they saw him as the one who would bring this consolation (Schmitz and Stählin, TDNT 5:793; SB 1:66, 83, 195; y. Ber. 2.3 [= Neusner et al. 1982–93: 1.87–89]). In the OT, various agents brought God's con-

---

12. Godet 1875: 1.137; Plummer 1896: 65; Fitzmyer 1981: 426. In favor of this view is Cutler 1966. New Testament uses of the name include Luke 3:30; Acts 13:1; 15:14; 2 Pet. 1:1; Rev. 7:7. Simon is a variation of the name.

13. Bovon 1989: 141 n. 22 notes that Simeon is a teacher or rabbi in the Acts of Pilate 16:2, 6.

14. Schrenk, TDNT 2:189 §C2c. Δίκαιος is often used in the NT of the prophets or martyrs.

15. Bultmann, TDNT 2:753; Plato, Statesman 311B; Luce 1933: 101; Plummer 1896: 66, who notes that Philo used the term to describe Abraham in Who Is the Heir? 6 §22.

16. Grundmann, TDNT 2:58. Schmitz, TDNT 5:798, argues that the phrase is Palestinian.

solation, but a primary agent in eschatological contexts was the Servant of God (Schmitz and Stählin, *TDNT* 5:789–90, 792–93; SB 2:124–25). This desire for consolation characterizes the believer or God-fearer in Luke (6:23–24; 17:22–37; 21:25–36). Interestingly, while Luke associated consolation with Messiah, John will associate it with the Spirit (John 14–16).[17] One also can associate this hope with the idea of messianic comfort given to those in darkness (1:79; Plummer 1896: 66). God was expected to complete his promise, and Simeon looked forward to the arrival of that day.

Simeon was not only pious and expectant, he was blessed, having received a special work of the Holy Spirit. This last note prepares the reader for the revelation that Simeon receives in 2:26 as well as for his prophetic statements in 2:29–32, 34–35. The separation of πνεῦμα (*pneuma*, Spirit) and ἅγιον (*hagion*, holy) by ἦν (*ēn*, was) probably serves to make the statement of the Spirit's special work slightly more emphatic (Godet 1875: 1.137). The one through whom God speaks is a righteous man of rare spiritual quality and gift.

ii. The Spirit's Promise (2:26)

Simeon's prophecy is described further as God's promise to Simeon **2:26** "by the Holy Spirit" (ὑπὸ τοῦ πνεύματος τοῦ ἁγίου, *hypo tou pneumatos tou hagiou*). Simeon received a revelation from the Spirit. Κεχρηματισμένον (*kechrēmatismenon*, had been revealed) refers to God's direct revelation to his people (Jer. 25:30 [32:30 LXX]; 33:2; Job 40:8; Matt. 2:12). The association between God's Spirit and prophecy is strong, as Judaism looked to an active Spirit in the new age accompanying God's act of deliverance.[18] In this case, Simeon received a promise that God would not let him die without seeing Messiah. The remark ties together the messianic idea (Luke 2:26) with the idea of Israel's consolation (2:25). Only when this is fulfilled is the prophet ready to die (2:29–30). As in all the other cases in this infancy section, God's word comes to pass for the prophet.[19] Jesus' coming reflects regal messianic hope, the basic initial category for Luke's presentation of Jesus.

17. Note the similar description of Joseph of Arimathea in Luke 23:51, while Acts 4:36, 9:31, and 15:31 describe consolation or encouragement as a characteristic of the believer in day-to-day life, a different force than here. Danker 1988: 64 notes the contact with Luke 6.

18. Jer. 31:31–33 [as writing the law on the heart]; Joel 2:28–32 [3:1–5 MT]; 1QS 4.21–22; Danker 1988: 64; SB 2:126–27; R. Meyer, *TDNT* 6:816–20, 826–27. On the view of some in ancient Judaism that the Spirit's revelatory work ceased sometime before the Maccabean period, see 1 Macc. 9:27; 14:41.

19. For the grammar of the temporal phrase πρὶν ἢ ἂν ἴδῃ, see BDF §383.3, §395.

iii. Simeon's Reception of the Child (2:27)

2:27 The prophecy's specific setting involves Simeon's going to the temple by the divine leading of the Spirit (cf. 4:1, 14). Though the phrase ἐν τῷ πνεύματι (en tō pneumati, by the Spirit) in other contexts speaks of prophetic vision (Rev. 1:10), here the reference is to the Spirit's prompting that guides Simeon to the temple (Plummer 1896: 67; J. Schneider, *TDNT* 2:671 §B1f). God is responsible for this meeting.

Luke distinguishes between two terms in referring to the temple. Ναός (*naos*) refers to "the Holy Place," where only the priests are allowed to go (1:9, 21, 22), while ἱερόν (*hieron*), the term used here, refers to the entire temple area (Fitzmyer 1981: 427; R. Brown 1977: 439; Plummer 1896: 67; C. F. Evans 1990: 215). In the context of this event, Simeon is located either in the court of the Gentiles or in the court of women, since Mary could be present only at these two locales. Despite the picture of many contemporary portrayals of this event, it seems unlikely that Simeon is a priest (see the exegesis of 2:25).

The parents were proceeding into the temple to dedicate the firstborn according to the law, when Simeon stopped them. The allusion here to parental action that corresponds to the law looks back to 2:22–24 (see the discussion there on Jesus' dedication), showing that the account is unified in its perspective and suggesting that distinct sources for 2:22–24 and 2:25–35 should not be posited. This unity argues against seeing different sources in the stylistic variation of the terms used for Jerusalem in 2:22 and 2:25.

In fact, the idea here continues into 2:28, since the combination of ἐν τῷ εἰσαγαγεῖν (en tō eisagagein) and an aorist infinitive (τοῦ ποιῆσαι, tou poiēsai) introduces a dependent temporal clause that is completed in 2:28: "When the parents brought him in to do . . . , Simeon took him in his arms . . ." (Marshall 1978: 119). This fulfilling of the law serves once again to point out the pious obedience of Jesus' parents. But the basic idea of the verse centers not on the parents but on a revelation about Messiah that is given in the temple (Schürmann 1969: 124). While Jesus is brought to God for dedication, God testifies to Jesus the Messiah through the prophet (Schweizer 1984: 56). For pietistic Jews, there could hardly be a more solemn locale for the testimony.

iv. The *Nunc Dimittis* (2:28–32)
(1) Praise (2:28–29)

2:28 Simeon takes the child and expresses his gratitude to God for sharing in this special moment. Καί (*kai*) is translated "then" to express the completion of the sequence of the parents entering the temple area, meeting Simeon, and handing him the child. The sequence is described in a very abbreviated way (Plummer 1896: 67). In church tradition, Simeon received the name *Theodochos* (God-receiver) for his role in this event (R. Brown 1977: 439; Plummer 1896: 67). What follows is a hymn of prophetic praise to God for the joy of seeing the Messiah in fulfillment of God's word. Simeon's reception of Jesus is intended to picture the arrival of messianic hope for Israel. The prophet represents the nation and, beyond that, all humanity (Bovon 1989: 142 also notes the nation's rejection of the opportunity, starting in 4:24).

2:29
The third hymn of the infancy section is known as the *Nunc Dimittis*, a name that comes from the hymn's opening phrase in the Latin version. The hymn is composed of three pairs of lines (vv. 29a–b, 30–31, 32a–b). In the narrative the hymn completes a promise-fulfillment-praise chain, where the promise of seeing Messiah is made in 2:26, while the fulfillment comes in holding the child in 2:28 (Kittel, *TDNT* 4:113 §D5a). The hymn is a joyful response of praise for the fulfillment of God's promise, a pattern that is related to the function of each of the hymns in Luke 1–2 (Farris 1985: 144–46). Thus, the hymn says that God acts "according to his word." Here God's word is the promise that death would not come until Messiah was seen (2:26).

Simeon declares that he can now rest, because in seeing Jesus he has seen God's salvation. Simeon is like the watcher who can leave an assigned post because the anticipated event has come. Some mention the literary parallel of the watcher in the opening lines of *Agamemnon* by Aeschylus (R. Brown 1977: 457; Godet 1875: 1.138). As Godet says, Simeon is a sentinel whose job is to announce the appearance of a great star in the world. With his task performed, God can do with Simeon what he wishes.

When tied to νῦν (*nyn*, now), the reference to ἀπολύεις (*apolyeis*, release) in the present tense serves to express the readiness of the watcher to die ("now release your servant"; Marshall 1978: 119–20). Ἀπολύω is used to express death in various texts (Gen. 15:2 [Abraham]; Num. 20:29 [Aaron]; Tob. 3:6 [Tobit]; 2 Macc. 7:9 [a martyr]).[20] The picture describes a servant's release from a task, though the reference to the master is not a declaration of a desire for manumission (against this view are Creed 1930: 41 and Plummer 1896: 68). Simeon would never dream of wanting to be freed from God's gracious sovereignty. The requested release is simply from the

---

20. Procksch, *TDNT* 4:328 n. 3; Creed 1930: 41. Bovon 1989: 143 n. 35 adds Sophocles, *Antigone* 1268, 1314.

earthly post of service (Hendriksen 1978: 167 n. 144). When Simeon describes himself as δοῦλος (*doulos*, servant-slave), he uses common OT imagery for a faithful and righteous servant (Ps. 27:9 [26:9 LXX]; Luke 1:38 [Mary]; Acts 4:29; Rengstorf, *TDNT* 2:273). The reference to God as "Master" (δέσποτα, *despota*) points to a recognition of God's sovereignty, since this word occasionally translated אָדוֹן (*ʾādôn*, Lord) in the OT (Isa. 3:1; 10:33; Schweizer 1984: 56; Schürmann 1969: 125 n. 199).[21] R. Brown (1977: 439) notes that the term is rare in the NT and may reflect Semitic influence (Acts 4:24; Rev. 6:10).

The reference to God's word looks back to the promise of 2:26, but more interesting is the idea of being released "in peace" (ἐν εἰρήνῃ, *en eirēnē*). Is this an allusion to death as peaceful sleep (A. B. Bruce 1897: 475; Creed 1930: 41; Gen. 15:15)? It seems better to see peace as referring to the comfort of knowing that God's work comes to fulfillment. Simeon's life can come to an end with him at peace in this knowledge. Elsewhere in this section Luke has much to say about the Messiah's association with peace, an association that has OT roots, as well as roots in intertestamental Judaism (Luke 1:79; 2:14; Zech. 8:12 LXX; Ps. 71:7 LXX; Ps. Sol. 17.26–42 [through the picture of restoration]; Schürmann 1969: 125; Marshall 1978: 120). God again has brought his word to pass, a source of encouragement and assurance not only to Simeon but also to Luke's readers.

(2) Reason for Praise (2:30)

2:30 Simeon's having seen God's salvation is the reason (ὅτι, *hoti*, because) he can ask for release from his post. The interesting feature of this verse is that seeing God's salvation is linked directly to seeing Jesus, so that a strong tie exists between salvation and the one who personifies it. This connection in turn relates to the idea of Israel's consolation in 2:25. Fulfillment has come in Jesus, and so Simeon can die in peace. The idea that the person of Jesus is at the center of soteriology is a keystone of Lucan Christology. With Jesus' birth, salvation comes (Schneider 1977a: 71–72). Fitzmyer (1981: 422) objects to associating an incarnational soteriology with Luke, limiting its expression to John.[22] But though the motif is not explicit incarnation like John's, it is clear that in Lucan theology salvation comes and God comes because Jesus the Messiah has come.

21. Δεσπότης is used ten times in the NT, twice in Luke–Acts (here and Acts 4:24).
22. Technically Fitzmyer is correct. Luke gives no hint of Jesus' preexistence, so the idea of "God come in the flesh" is not explicitly present in Luke–Acts. But Luke's idea is close to this concept, especially later in Luke–Acts, when Jesus addresses God as his Father, is called Lord, and is treated much like God the Father.

The idea of one's seeing God's salvation has OT echoes (Isa. 40:5; 52:10; Ps. 98:2; Luke 3:6; conceptually 1QH 5.12).[23] The association of joy with seeing God's salvation appears again in Luke 10:23–24. For Luke, Messiah's coming is at the center of salvation (1:69; 2:11; Schürmann 1969: 125 n. 203). The mood of joy in this text dominates the rest of the passage.

(3) "A Light for the Nations, Glory for Israel" (2:31–32)

Simeon turns to describe the divinely promised salvation. The relative pronoun ὅ (*ho*, which) refers back to the salvation mentioned in 2:30. It is a salvation that God prepares. The reference ὅ ἡτοί-μασας (*ho hētoimasas*, which you prepared) points to God's design of salvation in history, a design that included a deliverer coming through Israel.[24] Jones (1968: 42) notes that one of Luke's major themes is suggested by the term: "The idea of the preparation of *salvation* is unique, and in the light of what follows, this must mean the providential preparation of salvation through Israel's history, according to prophecy and promise, until the time of fulfilment which is now recognized." This salvation should not catch people by surprise, since it was expected.

2:31

The salvation was not only designed, it was prepared before a vast throng. The phrase κατὰ πρόσωπον πάντων τῶν λαῶν (*kata prosōpon pantōn tōn laōn*, in the presence of all the people) identifies a large audience and has produced some discussion.[25] Does λαῶν refer only to Israel, as the plural reference to λαοῖς (*laois*, peoples) in Acts 4:27 suggests (so Kilpatrick 1965b)? Or does the term refer to both Israel and the Gentiles, suggesting a note of universalism in Luke for the first time (Farris 1985: 148)? Both the OT background and the parallelism of Luke 2:32, which refers to both racial groups, indicate a universal reference (Isa. 55:5; 60:5; 61:9; Schweizer 1984: 56; Fitzmyer 1981: 428; R. Brown 1977: 439–40). Thus, God intends to extend to all the salvation that comes in Jesus. Though the language looks at salvation's preparation in the sight of all, the following verse makes clear that participation in that salvation also extends to every racial group. All will see what Jesus has done, and each group will share in its benefits.

---

23. Marshall 1978: 120. Bovon 1989: 144 notes conceptual parallels in Ps. 31:19 [31:20 MT; 30:19 LXX] and Isa. 64:4–5 [64:3–4 MT]. Nolland 1989: 120 cites Bar. 4:24 and sees Isa. 52:10 as the key point of connection. Goulder 1989: 257 sees Isa. 40:1–5 as the key text.

24. Farris 1985: 148. God's direction runs through this entire scene, whether it be in Messiah's coming or in the timing of Simeon's meeting with Joseph and Mary.

25. On the grammar of κατὰ πρόσωπον, see BAGD 406 §II.1b; BAA 825 §II.1b; BDF §140; Plummer 1896: 69.

2:32   Luke describes this salvation in further detail. Solving a grammatical problem will determine the text's meaning. Most commentators see φῶς (*phōs*, light) and δόξαν (*doxan*, glory) in parallel and both in apposition to salvation in 2:30 (Plummer 1896: 69; Schürmann 1969: 126 n. 209; Bovon 1989: 145; NASB; NKJV). If this view of the syntax is adopted, then the idea is that salvation is a light to Gentiles, while it is glory to Israel. In support of this view, one can argue that glory and light are paired in parallelism in the OT (Isa. 60:1–3) and either term is associated with God's salvation in the OT (Isa. 49:6; 51:4–5; 42:6; Farris 1985: 149). The tenor of Luke is regarded as supporting this view (Acts 13:47; Plummer 1896: 69). In addition, the alternative syntax (see below) requires the addition of certain terms to clearly express its sense.

A second approach argues that ἀποκάλυψιν (*apokalypsin*, revelation) and δόξαν are parallel and both are in apposition to φῶς, which in turn refers back to salvation in 2:30 (Fitzmyer 1981: 428; R. Brown 1977: 440; TEV; RSV; NIV; *Neu Luther*). If this view is accepted, then salvation is described as light for all people, but in particular it is revelation to the Gentiles and glory for Israel. In support, it can be argued that in Isa. 60:1–3 the relationship between light and glory is one of cause and effect. Israel receives the light of salvation and thus can be called God's glory, so that the two concepts are distinct, with glory tied to Israel. In addition, Luke 1:78–79 describes Messiah as a light that comes to the nation. Light comes; revelation and glory result. Further, in Acts 26:22–23 the light is portrayed as coming to both Jews and Gentiles. Thus, it is a fundamental characteristic of salvation that it is light for all people, not light just for a particular group. These arguments seem to favor slightly this second view, which would be translated "light, for revelation to the Gentiles and for the glory of your people Israel."

Light suggests the coming of illumination into a place of darkness (1:79; Luce 1933: 102). It is a frequent NT image of Jesus and his task (Acts 13:47; Matt. 4:16; 5:14; John 1:7; 12:35, 46; 2 Cor. 4:6). In rabbinic Judaism, especially in the midrashim, the image of Messiah as light was also frequent (SB 1:161–62).

Light as illumination means this light is revelation for the Gentiles. Though usually in this type of noun-genitive construction with ἀποκάλυψιν the genitive gives the source of the revelation, in this context it is clear that the Gentiles are portrayed as recipients of the revelation.[26] God's revelation dwells in a person, an idea that implies some of what John says explicitly when he calls Jesus the

---

26. See Plummer 1896: 69 for four grammatical options for the genitive; Farris 1985: 149. R. Brown 1977: 440 notes that the peculiarity of the syntax here is a reflection of Semitic style; BDF §259.3.

Word. Old Testament ideas abound. Some passages suggest that the Gentiles are passive observers of this process, while others see them participating (passive: Isa. 49:6; 52:10; Ps. 98:2; participating: Isa. 42:6–7; esp. Zech. 2:10–11 [2:14–15 MT]). Intertestamental literature also expressed this idea in both forms (passive: Bar. 4:24; participating: Ps. Sol. 17.34–35). The rest of Luke's Gospel and Acts reveal that Gentiles participate as equals (esp. Acts 10–11; 15; also Eph. 2:11–22; 3:3–6). Jesus as light brings salvation to all humankind, illuminating them into God's way (Marshall 1978: 121).

If Jesus is revelation for the Gentiles, he is more than that for Israel. He is its glory. As Isa. 60:1–3 shows, the nation's hope was that, with the coming of salvific light to Israel, the attention of all people would be drawn to Israel. Isaiah 46:13 makes clear that Israel's task makes it special and that God's righteousness approaches it (Rom. 10:5–8). At the heart of what makes the nation special is that salvation comes through it. Paul shares this special view of Israel (Rom. 9:1–5). In fact, the roots of salvation extend into the nation of Israel and give it a special place. Simeon's note contains a hint of joy that the nation's vindication comes in Jesus.

Schürmann (1969: 126) notes that these verses argue against seeing the hymn as a Lucan creation: 2:29 answers the expectation mentioned in 2:26 and the hints of Semitic and Jewish-Christian perspective also argue against it. In sum, Simeon is a picture of redemption's joy in that he senses the significance of who Jesus is and rests in that knowledge.[27]

The hymn as a whole repeats basic themes of all the hymns in the infancy narrative. God is acting for his people Israel. He is saving them according to his plan and promise. That salvation is found in Jesus. But the *Nunc Dimittis* also adds to these themes. Jesus is now directly associated for the first time with the "Servant" hope of Isa. 40–66. However, it is not the suffering elements of this figure that are brought to the fore, as in other NT uses of this theme; rather it is the note of victory, vindication, and hope (Bock 1987: 85–87; Schneider 1977a: 72). In addition, the hymn adds the universal scope of Jesus' work. The regal, Davidic, messianic Savior-Servant has come to redeem more than the nation of Israel; he has come for the world.

v. The Parents' Marvel (2:33)

Luke records the parents' response to Simeon's words. The description of Jesus' universal task produces amazement. Some suggest

2:33

---

27. Farris 1985: 147 and Grundmann 1963: 90 argue that Simeon is the "first redeemed man," but Zechariah's hymn also reveals Jesus' role in salvation (1:69–78). What Simeon portrays is the one who can rest in Jesus.

that the note of wonder indicates that Luke 2 was originally separate from the Luke 1 narrative, since it does not know of the virgin birth (Creed 1930: 42; Schneider 1977a: 72; Luce 1933: 102). However, the wonder may be explained by two factors. First, the note of universality was a new point to make about Jesus' ministry (Godet 1875: 1.140–41; Hendriksen 1978: 169; Plummer 1896: 70). Second, the motif of amazement after revelation was typical (R. Brown 1977: 440; Marshall 1978: 121; Luke 2:18). The parents' response was natural since revelation about Jesus just kept coming.

vi. Blessing for Parents and a Prophecy of Division (2:34–35)

2:34 Simeon gives a blessing to the parents and then gives a special word to Mary. It is not entirely encouraging. His topic is Jesus, division, and Israel.

Jesus' ministry is summarized in two images. He is the one who is set for the falling and rising of many in Israel, and he is a sign. The first image is drawn from passages in Isaiah, where God is portrayed as setting up a stone of stumbling over which some fall (Isa. 8:14–15), a precious cornerstone that will not disappoint those who trust in it (Isa. 28:13–16, esp. v. 16). The use of these texts was common in the NT (Rom. 9:33; 1 Pet. 2:6–8; Luke 20:17–18). The image of a figure of division or of a figure who causes rising and falling was used at Qumran (1QH 2.8–10; 1QM 14.10–11). The linking of Isa. 8 with Isa. 28 is possible either through recourse to the MT's use of the verbal element שָׁבַר (šābar, to break) or through the LXX text's use of πίπτω (piptō, to fall) and συντρίβω (syntribō, to break).[28] Since Messiah was the personification of God's deliverance and the agent of his justice, these texts were easily related to the Messiah.

The nature of the "falling and rising" picture is disputed. Is there one group that falls only to rise again, a reference relating only to the believers' suffering and vindication?[29] Or are there two groups, unbelievers who fall and believers who rise on the basis of their response of faith to Jesus?[30] Those who argue for one group make the point that in the OT the image of rising and falling refers to the same group (Amos 5:2; 8:14; Isa. 24:20; Mic. 7:8; Prov. 24:16). In addition, the picture of falling only to rise sets up a perfect contrast to the image of the sign of contention later in the verse. Thus, it is ar-

28. BDB 990; Bock 1987: 87, 310 n. 145. This is a clear example of the Jewish hermeneutic *gezerah shewah* (i.e., comparison of similar things).

29. Schweizer 1984: 57; Marshall 1978: 122. Jeremias in his earlier *TDNT* article, 4:271–72, 276–77, stresses that the dividing point is the presence or absence of faith.

30. R. Brown 1977: 461; Hendriksen 1978: 170; Danker 1988: 68. Jeremias in his later *TDNT* article, 6:541–42, revised his view.

gued that the image is of the humble (Luke 1:52), who start out low but are exalted by God.

Against this view is the context, which seems to suggest a note of deep pain in Mary in 2:35. If the note of this saying is evenly positive and negative for one group, then the focus on her pain seems inappropriate. In addition, the normal force of the stone image in the NT is one of division (Luke 20:17–18; Rom. 9:33; 1 Pet. 2:6–8). Finally, a consistent NT note about Jesus' ministry is that it divides people into two groups (Luke 4:29; 6:20–26; 13:28–29, 33–35; 16:25; 18:9–14; 19:44, 47–48; 20:14–18; esp. 12:51; Fitzmyer 1981: 422–23; Hendriksen 1978: 170). Thus, it seems better to see an allusion to two groups in falling and rising, with those who reject Jesus headed for a fall, while those who accept him in faith are headed for vindication. The qualification ἐν τῷ Ἰσραήλ (en tō Israēl, in Israel) shows the nationalistic and Jewish perspective of the account. Jesus will divide the nation.

The emphasis on opposition continues in the reference that Jesus will be a sign of contesting. Ἀντιλεγόμενον (antilegomenon, that is opposed) has a future sense, since Simeon is discussing how people will respond to Jesus (R. Brown 1977: 441; BAGD 73 §2; BAA 148 §2; BDF §339.2b). Humans will resist Jesus. For them, Jesus will not be a hope of promise fulfilled, but a figure who is to be opposed.[31] The sign is characterized best as one of contention, not only rejection, because the point of the context is division (Rengstorf, TDNT 7:238–39). The incident in 4:28–29 illustrates this situation. Simeon knows that although Jesus is God's hope, not everyone will respond positively to him. The raising of this aspect of Jesus' fate is Luke's first indication that all will not go smoothly for God's Anointed.

2:35   Simeon turns from the effect of Jesus on the nation to the effect that Jesus will have on Mary. There is some debate whether 2:35a is parenthetical. If the remark is taken as parenthetical, then the purpose clause of 2:35b, introduced by ὅπως (hopōs, so that), refers back to 2:34. Given this syntax, the revealing of the hearts describes the goal of Jesus' ministry to the nation (Plummer 1896: 70; Marshall 1978: 123; most translations). Others see the remark to Mary as not being parenthetical and take it as representative of what the nation will face. In this view, the thoughts that are revealed include those of Mary, as Simeon notes the purpose for the sword passing through the nation.[32]

---

31. Acts 13:45; 28:19, 22; Danker 1988: 69. In the OT, examples of the image of opposition are found in Isa. 65:2 and Hos. 4:4.

32. Godet 1875: 1.141–42 argues that the other construction is too violent; that is, too far removed to be likely.

It is best to see the remark as parenthetical. As Fitzmyer (1981: 439–40), R. Brown (1977: 441), and Bovon (1989: 148) note, the construction goes from a broad audience in 2:34, to a personal reference in 2:35a, and then back to a broad audience in 2:35b. Thus, the personal remark (2:35a) is to Mary, while 2:35b describes the effect of Jesus' ministry on all.

The personal focus of Simeon's remark in 2:35a is made clear by the reference to σοῦ δὲ αὐτῆς τὴν ψυχήν (*sou de autēs tēn psychēn*, your own [i.e., Mary's] soul), where ψυχή refers to the seat of emotion (Plummer 1896: 71; BAGD 893 §1bγ; BAA 1781 §1bγ). He tells Mary that the child shall cause a sword to pass through her own soul, a figure that is made more graphic because the term chosen for sword, ῥομφαία (*rhomphaia*), designates a very large, broad, two-edged sword (Luce 1933: 103; Plummer 1896: 71; BAGD 737; BAA 1475; Michaelis, *TDNT* 4:525 n. 14, 6:995 §B1 and n. 17). The figure points to Jesus' bringing extreme emotional pain to his mother.

The figure's exact force has attracted much attention. To what specifically does the image refer? Views abound (Fitzmyer 1981: 439–40; R. Brown 1977: 462–65).

1. An ancient interpretation, going back to Origen (*Homilies on Luke* 17) and still held by some recently, sees the sword as a metaphor for doubt. The view argues that Mary doubted during Jesus' ministry and passion (Alford 1874: 462–63; Schweizer 1984: 57; Creed 1930: 42). But Luke's positive view of Mary (Luke 8:21; Acts 1:14) and the absence of biblical parallels for a sword as a metaphor of doubt argue against this view.
2. Epiphanius (*Heresies* 78.11) argued that the sword is a figure for Mary's own martyrdom. But there is no evidence that Mary was martyred.
3. Mary was rejected and contradicted by people as Jesus was, though she was not killed (Schürmann 1969: 129 mentions this view; some cite the woman of Rev. 12:4–6, 17 as support for it). The problem with the figure is that if Mary is seen as pierced, she is pierced by Jesus in 2:35a, not by his opponents, as this view would seem to require. Also, Jesus is not depicted as pierced by the sword in this passage.
4. Mary is pierced by being slandered for bearing an illegitimate child. This idea requires the contribution of Matt. 1:18–19 or John 8:41 to work (E. Burrows 1940: 43). Nothing in the entirety of Luke's Gospel expresses this idea.
5. Mary lives to see Jerusalem's fall and the defeat of her own people (Winandy 1965). Such an interpretation cannot explain how Jesus sends the piercing unless Jerusalem's fall is

seen as the act of Jesus, an idea that is not present in the Gospels. Jerusalem's fall is God's judgment on the nation (13:34–35; 19:41–44).

6. Ambrose (*Expositio Evangelii Secundam Lucam* 2.61 [Corpus Christianorum, Series Latina 14:4:57]) understands the sword to be a reference to the piercing work of God's word; but this too is unlikely, because it is not clear when this happens in Luke–Acts.

7. Some see a fulfillment of Gen. 3:15 (A. De Groot, cited by Schürmann 1969: 129 n. 229). The problem with this view is with the figure, since Mary does not fight others, but Jesus pierces her soul.

8. Mary is a figure for "daughter Zion" and represents the nation so that the reference again is to the nation of Israel (Leaney 1958: 100; Laurentin 1967: 103–4; Black 1967: 154, citing Ezek. 14:17 and Sibylline Oracles 3.316 as parallel for the sword and nation image). But the personal pronoun in 2:35a makes the verse look like a personal reference. In addition any Lucan reference to Mary as daughter Zion is unlikely (see 1:34–35).

9. The sword refers to the pain or sorrow that Jesus brings to his mother in undertaking his ministry with such dedication that it results in his tragic death.[33] The major problem is that Luke in his passion account does not explicitly mention Mary as present at the cross (23:49). If this is the prophetic idea, Luke fails to note its fulfillment. However, it could be argued that Luke included her among those present, so that there is no need to mention her or the fulfillment.

10. The reference is to the pain that Jesus' ministry causes Mary, as Jesus creates his own family of disciples and his own priorities (R. Brown 1977: 464; Fitzmyer 1981: 430). This view would be stronger if either the note of dissension and family questioning (Mark 3:31–35) or the reference to Jesus' bringing the sword (Matt. 10:34–36) were present in Luke. The sword in this view is seen as a sword of discrimination that Jesus wields in his ministry, like the picture in Ezek. 14:17 (where the discrimination occurs in the nation) or in Sibylline Oracles 3.316. Supporting this view is Luke 2:41–52, a point that R. Brown (1977: 479) underplays because of his theory that this passage fulfills nothing found earlier in Luke. There we see Jesus causing his parents grief because he lingers in

---

33. John 19:25–27; Godet 1875: 1.141; Hendriksen 1978: 170–71; Marshall 1978: 123. Nolland 1989: 122 cites Ps. 22:20 [22:21 MT]; 37:15; Zech. 12:10; 13:7; and Ps. 37:15 as conceptual background.

the temple. He must be in his Father's house (2:49). This pericope, it would seem, is the fulfillment, or at least an initial fulfillment, of Simeon's prophecy. As such, it represents another promise that is fulfilled in Luke 1–2, showing the unity between the prophecy and the following narrative. Jesus' ministry will bring choices that will be hard for Mary to bear. An ultimate allusion to the cross is possible within this view, because the rejection by some in Israel is mentioned in this context; but it is not the exclusive point of reference. The passage emphasizes the division Jesus brings, not the nature of his suffering. This view seems to be the most satisfactory. (According to C. F. Evans 1990: 219–20, either option 9 or 10 is possible.)

After this brief personal remark, Simeon returns to the broad picture. The purpose (ὅπως) of Jesus' having a ministry that divides is so that the thoughts of the hearts might be made manifest. In Luke, διαλογισμοί (dialogismoi) is an indication of hostile thoughts (5:22; 6:8; 9:46–47; 20:14; Marshall 1978: 123; Schrenk, TDNT 2:97; Bovon 1989: 148 speaks of the presence of tragedy). Jesus' ministry shows where hearts really are before God. Jesus will expose those who do not believe. He is a litmus test for the individual Jewish responses to the fulfillment of their promise. Do they believe it or not? The reference to the heart (καρδία, kardia) points to the deepest seat of thought (see also 2:19 for the figure; Plummer 1896: 71; BAGD 403–4; BAA 819 §1bβ; Behm, TDNT 3:612 §D2b). The "manifestation" (ἀποκαλυφθῶσιν, apokalyphthōsin) of these thoughts alludes to judicial exposure by Jesus. How humans respond to God's promise is made evident by how they respond to Jesus, whose presence reveals their true colors (Marshall 1978: 123; Oepke, TDNT 3:590). Simeon focuses on the exposure of those who will not respond to God, as the mention of hostile thoughts makes clear. Jesus comes; humans choose. Some oppose him and fall. Luke is honest about the tension and God's response.

When Simeon's prophecy is viewed as a whole, one sees a prophet at peace because he knows that God's salvation has come. Salvation's light has come in Messiah; Simeon rejoices. But the picture is not entirely rosy. For the Promised One is variously perceived, and many in Israel will reject him. In the path the child takes, his mother will feel pain; but his ministry will expose who is hostile to God. The messianic Son will be a light to the world, but his shining will bring division as he shines forth. Many will be raised to the Light, but tragically others will fall in judgment, having missed the promise.

c. Witness of the Woman: Anna (2:36–38)
i. Anna's Piety (2:36–37)

Luke turns to the testimony of a pious woman. The biographical **2:36** data detail her credentials as a woman of devotion to God (for a similar *vita* listing, see Phil. 3:5–6). The name Hannah (or Anna as most translations render it) is the Greek spelling (Ἅννα) for a Semitic name that means "grace," but Luke makes nothing of her name (for other uses of the name, see 1 Sam. 1–2; Tob. 1:20; 2:1; Bovon 1989: 149). What he does tell us is that she is a prophetess. In Acts 21:9, Luke will mention the daughters of Philip as prophetesses and Paul knows of prophetesses as well (1 Cor. 11:3–6; Acts 2:17–18). In Jewish tradition, seven women were mentioned as prophetesses: Sarah, Miriam, Deborah, Hannah, Abigail, Huldah, and Esther (*b. Meg.* 14a; Ellis 1974: 84). Of these, Miriam (Exod. 15:20), Deborah (Judg. 4:4), and Huldah (2 Kings 22:14), together with Noadiah (Neh. 6:14) and Isaiah's wife (Isa. 8:3), are portrayed this way in the OT.[34] Anna is a vessel for revelation from God.

Additional personal references indicate that Anna was Phanuel's daughter from the tribe of Asher. These details add little to the story, though they do indicate that tradition anchored the event in its historical framework. Her father's name is a variant of the Hebrew name Penuel or Peniel, which means "face to face with God" or "the face of God." This is the name of the place where Jacob wrestled with God's angel (Gen. 32:22–32 [32:23–33 MT]). Once again, Luke makes nothing of this name. Asher was one of the ten northern tribes of Israel, yet this woman was a faithful Israelite.

Anna was very old. The redundant Greek construction αὕτη προβεβηκυῖα ἐν ἡμέραις πολλαῖς (*hautē probebēkuia en hēmerais pollais*) translates literally as "she was very old in her many days" and is a Hebraism (Gen. 18:11; 24:1; Josh. 13:1; 23:1; Delling, *TDNT* 2:950 n. 42; BDF §197; BDR §197.5). She was married for seven years. If we assume marriage at the age of thirteen or fourteen, which was normal in the ancient Near East, she would have been widowed by her early twenties. As the next verse makes clear, she remained a widow the rest of her life.

In the midst of describing her piety, Luke notes that Anna had been **2:37** a widow for a long time. Exactly how long is debated. The Greek

---

34. Wiefel 1988: 80. These texts show that God used women as revelatory agents. Several texts, including Luke 2:36–38, have audiences that include both men and women. There is no indication in the Bible that prophetesses had a gender-restricted audience. In fact, the recording of their prophecies for all to read suggests the opposite. On Luke and women, see Flanagan 1978: 292–93, who notes thirteen Lucan texts where man and woman are paralleled as Simeon and Anna are here; Nolland 1989: 122.

phrase ἕως ἐτῶν ὀγδοήκοντα τεσσάρων (heōs etōn ogdoēkonta tessarōn, until eighty-four years) is ambiguous. Does it mean her widowhood lasted eighty-four years, which would make her around 105 years old (Marshall 1978: 123–24; Schürmann 1969: 130; Leaney 1958: 101; Danker 1988: 71; Wiefel 1988: 80–81)? Some argue for this view on the basis of parallelism with the age of Judith in the Jewish work of that name. However, Marshall notes that the numbers in Judith, though similar, are not laid out in a parallel way (Jdt. 16:22–24; 8:4–8), and Judith is 105 at her death, while Anna is quite active. Another view takes the phrase to mean that Anna was a widow until the age of eighty-four.[35] If the latter view is taken, Anna was a widow for almost sixty-five years. It is hard to make a choice. The most direct impression is that her widowhood was eighty-four years long, since widowhood is the subject of the sentence (R. Brown 1977: 442; Stählin, TDNT 9:450–51; John 1975). For someone to live into her second century is not unprecedented. Regardless of the view taken here, Anna was a woman who chose a lifetime of service to God over remarriage, an action that was highly regarded in the first-century religious community (1 Tim. 5:5; Jdt. 8:4–8; Bovon 1989: 149).

Anna's daily activity reflects piety. She is at the temple daily, fasting and offering prayers all day. Λατρεύουσα (latreuousa) describes this labor as religious service and is often used in the OT of priestly cultic activity (Strathmann, TDNT 4:62–64; 1 Esdr. 8:49). In the NT, all of life is service offered to God, sometimes in contrast to OT cultic service, which cannot cleanse a conscience from sin (Rom. 1:9; 12:1; Heb. 9:9; 10:2). Anna's activity pictures a person totally focused on serving God. The reference is not to be overpressed as if Anna lived on the temple grounds, since there would be no place for her to stay there.

Just as the prophet Simeon testified to Jesus, so this woman, the highest example of female piety, will point to him. In Luke 2, all types of people testify to Jesus: the simple folk of the field, the devout men of the city, and pious women of the city.

ii. Her Prophecy to All (2:38)

2:38 Unlike Simeon who addresses the child's parents, Anna approaches the parents and then turns to offer thanksgiving to God (ἐπιστᾶσα, epistasa, from the verb ἐφίστημι, ephistēmi; BAGD 330 §1a; BAA 668 §1a; Luke 2:9). Ἀνθωμολογεῖτο (anthōmologeito, she was offering

---

35. Hendriksen 1978: 172–73; Schneider 1977a: 72. The omission of the term ἕως in D and the Itala shows some ancient manuscripts had this view too. But the omission is not attested widely enough to be taken seriously as original.

back praise) is a *hapax legomenon* that refers to the giving of praise (Ps. 79:13 [78:13 LXX]; Dan. 4:37; Sir. 17:27; 3 Macc. 6:33). The prefixed verb sees Anna's praise as a response given in exchange for God's act (Alford 1874: 463; Godet 1875: 1.143; Hendriksen 1978: 177; Michel, *TDNT* 5:213; Marshall 1978: 124).

Along with her praise, Anna addressed the crowd concerning Israel's redemption. The phrase λύτρωσιν Ἰερουσαλήμ (*lytrōsin Ierousalēm*, redemption of Jerusalem) refers to the redemption of Israel, since the capital stands for the nation. Equivalent to the phrase *consolation of Israel* (2:25), it has OT background in that it refers to God's decisive salvific act for his people (Isa. 40:9; 52:9; 63:4).[36] The focus is on the Redeemer and the time he brings (Büchsel, *TDNT* 4:351). In Luke, Anna's expectation is like Joseph of Arimathea who is said "to await the kingdom of God" (23:51). It also parallels the description of the Emmaus travelers, who were disappointed at Jesus' death because they were awaiting Israel's redemption (24:21; Luce 1933: 103; Danker 1988: 72; Schürmann 1969: 131). In addition, the content and mood of Anna's remarks parallel ideas already expressed in the *Magnificat* and the *Benedictus* (1:46–55, 68–79; also Acts 1:6; 26:6–7; Tiede 1988: 78). For Luke, the ultimate expectations for Jesus' ministry change little between the start and finish of the Gospel.

Simeon and Anna show that before Messiah came, God's people lived a good but unfulfilled life (Schweizer 1984: 60). In addition, they reflect the twofold testimony to the truth of an event (Deut. 19:15; Schneider 1977a: 73). Jesus fulfills the expectations of pious saints and prophets. Anna's message hints at a remnant concept, since she addresses her remarks only to those who await the consummation of God's plan. For those ready to hear, fulfillment has come.

d. Transition: Return to Galilee; Jesus' Growth (2:39–40)

Luke 2:39–40 provides a transition out of the infancy material proper, since in the next event Jesus is twelve years old. In discussing the return to Nazareth, Luke appears to be telescoping events in Jesus' life (see the third additional note on 2:22). The actual order of events between Luke and Matthew is difficult to establish, since chronological facts are limited. Alford (1874: 464) notes that one cannot state for certain that a contradiction with Matthew is present. Hendriksen (1978: 178–79) suggests that Luke's limiting of

2:39

36. Conceptually, Isa. 43:3–4; 45:14; 49:26; 54:1–8. National redemption is the point. The picture is of a "new exodus," also paralleling the Jubilee image of release; Lev. 25:47–54.

a Gentile emphasis to Acts explains why he omitted the Matthean material, but it is possible that Luke did not know Matthew or his tradition at this point.

In returning to Galilee and to Nazareth, Mary goes back to her original home (1:26). This verse also notes that the parents treated the baby in a way that fulfilled the law, a continual emphasis of Luke 2.

2:40 Luke notes Jesus' physical (ηὔξανεν, *ēuxanen*, he grew) and spiritual (ἐκραταιοῦτο, *ekrataiouto*, he became strong) growth. The spiritual focus of the remarks is shown by the qualifying participial phrase, πληρούμενον σοφίᾳ (*plēroumenon sophia*, being filled with wisdom), which shows that Jesus grew in his perception of God's will. Luke's description emphasizes Jesus' humanity. The verse parallels what was said of John the Baptist (1:80), but what is said about Jesus is more extensive. John is said simply to grow in his human spirit, but Jesus grows in the wisdom of God.

Since Jesus is filled with wisdom (Wis. 7:7), he is portrayed as deepening in his perception of God's will and his fear of God. Jesus as the wisdom of God will be a minor point of emphasis in Luke (11:49; on the Spirit supplying wisdom, see 21:15). Jesus is specially favored as well. The reference to God's favor is like the reference to God's favor being on Mary in 1:28, 30. Jesus is the object of God's special attention. The extent of this growth, especially in respect to wisdom, will be demonstrated by Jesus' wise perception in 2:41–52 (Fitzmyer 1981: 432). The language has both OT (Judg. 13:24; 1 Sam. 2:21, 26) and NT parallels (Acts 6:8; 7:10; Bovon 1989: 150 n. 79). Jesus grows into his ministry. The brief remarks about Jesus' childhood stand in stark contrast to what is said in the apocryphal gospels, which relate many childhood stories about Jesus, including many that portray him as causing miraculous events from his earliest days.

Summary Luke 2:22–40 is the first of two passages that break the parallelism between John the Baptist and Jesus. Here Luke presents the testimony of a prophet and a pious old woman. By narrating additional events about Jesus, Luke indicates his superiority. The double testimony comes as obedient parents dedicate their first-born to the Lord. When the testimony of the man and the woman is placed alongside the testimony of the shepherds, one can see a triad of witnesses. They come from the country and from the city; they represent both male and female; they picture the common person of the field along with the pious saints of great devotion. Many appreciate Jesus.

Simeon can leave this life in peace, because in Jesus he has seen the coming of God's salvation. As God had promised, Simeon did not die before seeing Messiah. God's word comes to pass, a note that gives assurance to the readers. In the fulfillment, there is present a revelation from God. The Light of God has come in Messiah. He is a revelation to Gentiles, revealing that God's plan includes them. This is the first clear hint in the Gospel that salvation includes every nationality. Jesus also is Israel's glory in that all the nation's hopes come to fruition in him. Simeon's imagery describes Isaiah's Servant, but it is not the Suffering Servant of so many NT texts. Rather, Jesus is proclaimed as the Victorious Servant in whom the exaltation of God is realized. Of course, these are not two distinct descriptions of two different figures, but Simeon concentrates on victory.

However, an initial ominous note also exists in Simeon's remarks to Mary. Jesus will cause division, as well as bring victory. Mary will suffer great pain, as she sees what the choices associated with Jesus' ministry will bring. The road to Messiah's victory will require a journey down a road of pain.

Anna's presence fits two key Lucan emphases. First, it represents a continued focus on women who respond to Jesus. Second, with Mary and Elizabeth (1:39–56), she rejoices in Jesus. So, the note of thanksgiving that comes from Anna adds to the notes of joy and gratitude that have characterized the infancy material. She testifies to the fulfillment of the nation's hope for consolation. The concern for Israel expressed throughout these two chapters manifests itself once again.

The section closes with a few transitional notes as Luke leaves his presentation of Jesus' birth and infancy. The family returns to Nazareth, having performed duties prescribed by the law. Jesus grows physically and spiritually, setting the stage for the final event of this introductory section. An event in the temple twelve years later (2:41–52) shows just how far Jesus' self-understanding goes. Jesus is a Messiah-Servant, who knows himself to be the Son of God.

Additional Notes

2:22. On the text-critical problem of αὐτῶν vs. αὐτῆς, see the exegesis.

2:22. Luke uses two spellings for Jerusalem in his two volumes: Ἱεροσόλυμα (*Hierosolyma*), the Greek spelling, as here, is used twenty-six times, while the more Semitic spelling, Ἱερουσαλήμ (*Ierousalēm*), is used sixty-four times (Fitzmyer 1981: 425 counts sixty-five uses of the Semitic form, the difference involving textual decisions). Josephus uses both spellings as well, so no point can be made about the source of this material from this term (*Antiquities* 7.3.2 §67; *Against Apion* 1.22 §179). The Greek spelling is found four times in Luke and the rest are in Acts; the Semitic spelling is found twenty-seven times in Luke and thirty-seven times in Acts.

2:22. A few commentators tackle the issue of reconciling the timing of the Lucan purification visit to Jerusalem with the Matthean Magi episode (many commentators ignore the question or reject the historicity of one of the accounts). Plummer (1896: 64, 73–74) argues that the Magi incident must come after this visit, on a later journey of the family to Bethlehem, reasoning that the family would never have risked a journey to Jerusalem after the Magi's visit to Herod and also positing that the family, after the temple visit, originally planned to live in Bethlehem, thinking it was right to raise Jesus there. Only after the Magi visit, which was after the temple visit, did they flee. Such a view is possible, but the impression of the Lucan text is that Bethlehem was not Jesus' home after the temple visit. This Lucan implication probably argues against the solution of Thomas and Gundry as well (1978: 30–31, who differ from Plummer only in arguing for a residence in Bethlehem for the family). They argue that the family lived briefly in Bethlehem after the temple visit, then saw the Magi there, and planned to return there to live after the flight to Egypt (Matt. 2:21–22) only to be warned away. However, another possibility is suggested by Matthew's implication of some delay between the Magi's visit and Herod's action against Jesus in that it took the ruler time to realize that he had been tricked. There is no indication when Joseph received his dream, other than that it was after the visit. It is quite possible that the Magi's visit came before the trip to Jerusalem and then afterward, perhaps immediately afterward, the family escaped to Egypt, having been warned by the dream.

Luke seems to have used material that Matthew did not know, while Matthew has material that is unique to his Gospel. Either Luke does not know Matthew's Gospel, and thus the events of that Gospel, or Luke chose not to narrate the Matthean events for reasons we cannot ascertain. Of course, those who reject the essential historicity of these accounts make no effort to bring the Gospels together, rejecting either Matthew's picture or Luke's or both. In addition, some on literary grounds avoid drawing any implications from these accounts for Synoptic studies.[37]

Though the reconciliation of these two accounts cannot be established with certainty, two plausible scenarios exist. However, the point of the section is not found in these related historical issues.

---

37. Fitzmyer 1981: 421 regards such historical questions as beside the point of the narrative. Technically this is correct, since the Gospels do not try explicitly to solve such questions. Each writer tells his own story with his own emphases. But such historical questions do have value in helping us wrestle with the early days of Jesus' life. R. Brown 1977: 448–51 sees Luke creating much of this event.

There is one other implication here. The differences in the description of the early days of Jesus' ministry suggest that Luke did not know of Matthew's infancy material. If he did, it is hard to understand why he made no mention of many of the issues Matthew raised. This omission and others like it (e.g., the Sermon on the Mount) are reasons why many think that Luke did not use Matthew. If this is correct, it is hard to argue that Matthew is the earliest Gospel. This leads many to posit that Mark is the first Gospel, while Luke and Matthew shared a common source(s) of sayings, known as Q.[38]

2:27. Some make a conclusion about sources from the plural reference to parents in Luke 2 by arguing that this chapter does not know of Jesus' virgin birth as presented in Luke 1 (Leaney 1958: 100; Bovon 1989: 115). They argue that Luke has clumsily put together two distinct accounts. This is hyper-criticism at its worst, since the language used here is the language of daily life and reality. Joseph functioned as Jesus' father! As Marshall (1978: 119) points out, only a long and distracting note could make a point about virgin birth here, a point that is not necessary to this story, especially in light of the presence of Luke 1 (also Godet 1875: 1.138; Plummer 1896: 67; Hendriksen 1978: 167; R. Brown 1977: 453 n. 25).

2:32. Some argue that Luke mistranslated a Hebrew original into Greek, because there is no Hebrew noun for "revelation" (so Sahlin 1945: 254). However, Farris (1985: 150) shows that the Hebrew that Sahlin suggests may be behind the Greek can be translated in a way that yields the meaning of the Greek. Of course, such argumentation assumes that Hebrew and not Aramaic is being spoken and that only single-term equivalents must be posited for terms present in the translation. The Hebrew term גָּלָה (gālâ, to uncover or reveal) shows that the concept of revelation is not beyond Semitic expression (Num. 22:31; 1 Sam. 9:15; Ps. 119:18; Jer. 11:20; 20:12; Dan. 2:22; 1QH 1.21). There is no mistranslation here.

2:33. A grammatical peculiarity is present in the verbal element ἦν, which is singular, though it is linked to a plural participle in a periphrastic construction. This is unusual, since normally the number of the verb and participle would match. But the effect of the mixed number may be to tie together the subject more intimately and to suggest a unified response by the parents (A. B. Bruce 1897: 476). Constructions with mixed number occur occasionally in the NT (Matt. 22:40; Luke 8:19; Acts 11:14; BDF §135.1d, which cites Matt. 17:3 as the closest parallel).

2:33. A textual problem centers on the subject: is ὁ πατὴρ αὐτοῦ or Ἰωσήφ original? The external evidence is rather evenly divided. Most argue that

---

38. McKnight 1991b outlines the current discussion of the Synoptic problem. See also the introduction to the Gospel of Luke under "Sources" and excursus 4. There is debate whether Q is a single teaching source similar to the collection of sayings in the Gospel of Thomas, or whether this teaching tradition existed in various forms. Those who see Matthew as the first Gospel generally deny the existence of Q.

scribes would be aware that Joseph is not Jesus' real father and so a change to Ἰωσήφ is easy to explain. On the other hand, if Ἰωσήφ was original, why would one alter the reading to ὁ πατὴρ αὐτοῦ? Since a change to Ἰωσήφ is easier to explain, the reference to ὁ πατὴρ αὐτοῦ is seen as more likely to be original (Fitzmyer 1981: 429; Metzger 1975: 134).

2:38. A small text-critical problem concerns the last word: λύτρωσιν ἐν Ἰερουσαλήμ is supported by A, D, L, Θ, Ψ, Byz, Lect, and λύτρωσιν Ἰσραήλ by 1216, some Itala. Λύτρωσιν Ἰσραήλ is clearly a later reading, in that it reflects harmonization with 2:25 and has little external attestation. The first reading has better attestation, but is not likely on internal grounds. A third option, the text printed in UBS–NA, λύτρωσιν Ἰερουσαλήμ (supported by א, B, W, Ξ, most Itala), is Semitic in flavor and is more likely to be original, since the inclusion of the preposition ἐν makes the variant reading more acceptable in terms of Greek style (Fitzmyer 1981: 432 supplies the linguistic data; see especially Lev. 25:29, 48 and Mur 25 i 1 [Discoveries in the Judaean Desert 2:135 #25], a Wadi Murabbaʿat text from the Dead Sea collection).

2:38. Marshall (1978: 124) rejects as speculation arguments that the *Benedictus* was positioned here in the original tradition. If this were so, it is not clear why Luke would then have taken the prophecy of a woman associated with Jesus' dedication and put it in the lips of the Baptist's father before Jesus was born. Such an unlikely movement would be required for this critical approach to stand. If the setting were Jesus' birth, there are also the problems of direct address to John in 1:76 and the hymn's distinguishing this prophet from the rising star to come.

2:38. Luce (1933: 104) suggests that Anna is not historical. But Godet (1875: 1.144) notes that the creation of this account is unlikely, since if it had been created one could have expected a hymn in parallelism to Simeon. Plummer 1896: 73 notes that F. Schleiermacher also made this point.

2:40. A textual variant reflected in some English translations (e.g., κjv) is supported by some manuscripts (A, Θ, Ψ, 053, family 1, family 13, Byz, some Itala, Syriac) that read πνεύματι, thus saying that Jesus grew strong "in spirit." This looks like a harmonizing addition to make 1:80 and 2:40 parallel. Godet 1875: 1.145, who often accepts Byzantine readings, rejects this one as a gloss. The UBS–NA text is supported by א, B, D, L, N, W, 1241, and some Syriac—a strong collection of external evidence.

I. Luke's Preface and the Introduction of John and Jesus (1:1–2:52)
    A. Preface: Luke Carefully Builds on Precedent (1:1–4)
    B. Infancy Narrative: Forerunner and Fulfillment (1:5–2:40)
➤ C. Jesus' Revelation of His Self-Understanding (2:41–52)

C. Jesus' Revelation of His Self-Understanding (2:41–52)

Luke 2:41–52 is the concluding note of Luke's prelude. It is not an infancy account, since Jesus is on the edge of adulthood as far as the ancients are concerned. Rather, the story is both a high point and transition into the body of Luke's Gospel. If the Gospel were a play, there would be a "fade to black" before this account and a pause to reflect the passing of twelve years. Now Jesus will speak for himself. The account is a high point in Luke 1–2, because Jesus speaks for the first time, revealing how he sees his own task.

The point of the passage is Jesus' unique attachment to the Father (Schürmann 1969: 133; Fitzmyer 1981: 437). In addition, this relationship has priority over all other relationships so it will require certain painful obligations (Tannehill 1986: 53). This account continues the serious note of Simeon's remarks in 2:34–35. In fact, it could be seen as the first fulfillment of it, since Jesus causes his mother pain. Jesus knows what he is about and that he must do the task his Father has given him. The necessity of his carrying out the task shows his resolve and his recognition that God is sovereign (2:49). In this sense, Jesus is an example to those who follow him. They too must be faithful to the call of their Father.

In addition, there is the initial picture of Jesus as very wise and knowing (Schneider 1977a: 74, 76). This is the first of many scenes where Jesus is with the teachers of the faith. Nothing is shared about the contents of the discussion. Rather, there is only the amazement at the quality of Jesus' participation.

Sources and Historicity

Luke 2:41–52 is generally regarded as having a tradition history separate from the previous units in Luke 1–2.[1] Some reasons for this conclusion are

---

1. The view is old. Those who hold it include Bultmann 1963: 300; Creed 1930: 44; Klostermann 1929: 45; Schürmann 1969: 139; Schneider 1977a: 76; Wiefel 1988: 82; and Fitzmyer 1981: 435–36. About the only one who raises doubts is Marshall 1978: 126. Despite the remarks about sources, Coleridge 1993: 187–213 is certainly correct that from a narrative viewpoint this pericope could not be dropped without substantial loss to the infancy narrative. Jesus' remarks about himself are a fitting climax to the prologue. In Coleridge's words (p. 189), this unit is "the most important" of the infancy narrative.

more valid than others. Most raise two details: (1) There is no mention of the virgin birth and (2) the shock of the parents at Jesus' self-revelation is indicative that the account was not written in connection with other parts of Luke 1–2. The second reason is slightly more valid than the first, but both are suspect. The insistence that the virgin birth be mentioned every time Jesus' parents appear is tedious. Joseph was the everyday, practical father to the child. So this reason is not compelling. And the shock of Jesus' parents is not entirely surprising from the narrative's viewpoint. Jesus has said nothing to this point. There have been twelve long years of silence since the events of 2:1–40. Jesus' first set of remarks is shocking, because of his strong sense of identity with God in 2:49. There may also be shock that the remarks come after he has caused his parents such pain. Thus, it is unlikely that these objections to unity are decisive.

More revealing, however, are stylistic features. The style of this pericope is more like the body of the Gospel than the infancy narratives. There is almost no recollection of the OT here. Moreover, there seems to be less trace of Semitisms in the account.[2] These differences suggest that a distinct tradition is present, though they do not argue for Lucan creation, since the perspective is still very Jewish and there are still some traces of earlier roots.[3] Luke may have brought the various materials together, but this account does seem to come out of Palestinian circles (Marshall 1978: 126). Jesus' family or friends could be the ultimate source.

There is some debate about whether Luke is responsible for some individual verses. Most see 2:52 as a Lucan summary built in parallel to 2:40 and 1:80. This is very likely, especially if these separate traditions were originally detached.

It is suggested that 2:47 is a Lucan creation, as the note of astonishment appears to be added, but such notes are common in various traditions (1:65–66; 2:18, 33). The shift of subject from "they" (2:46) to "all" (2:47) and then back to "they" (2:48) is also raised as evidence of either an editor's or Luke's hand (see Schürmann 1969: 135, who argues it is not Luke's). Remarks like 2:47 do normally come at the very end of pericopes, but one cannot rule out a variation in form here (as also in 2:33). And the subject shift is not that abrupt when the issue is how others are perceiving Jesus. (This is little different from the reaction of the synagogue figure to Jesus' healing in 13:14 in the midst of 13:10–17.) In fact, to continue to speak of "they" would exclude amazement on the part of anyone but the family. However, the point is that even the teachers sitting with Jesus were amazed. How else could this be said?

2. Schürmann 1969: 139 notes numerous Semitisms in earlier accounts and says this account has more unmistakable traces of Greek and Lucan expression. The most influential study here is Van Iersel 1960.

3. Schürmann 1969: 139, esp. n. 300, notes the positive attitude to the law, the temple focus, and the possible traces of Semitic elements.

Luke 2:44 is also usually posited as a Lucan creation because such a "lost child" situation is considered unlikely. But it is credible that a trustworthy child was assumed to be with other family.

The account's form has received various descriptions, some of which reflect judgments about historicity. Bultmann (1963: 244, 300) places it in his section on legend, by which he means a form that is not a miracle, but that is told for religious and edifying purposes rather than historical ones. Such accounts also have supernatural touches to them.[4] Bultmann's term and description are unfortunate. Other names are better, since there is no reason to reject historicity.[5]

What is the form of the account? Berger (1984: 253, 349) speaks of a childhood-prodigy story and of a revelatory dialogue. Such accounts of significant figures were common in the ancient world.[6] Another good description of the account's form is "pronouncement story," since Jesus' saying is key to the pericope.[7]

The outline of Luke 2:41–52 is as follows:

4. Such a classification is also used for other sections of Luke 1–2. On such motifs in the Greco-Roman biographical tradition, see H. De Jonge 1977–78; Nolland 1989: 127; C. F. Evans 1990: 222–27. See n. 6 for the ancient texts.

5. Marshall 1978: 125–26. One can only note the restraint in this account compared to the apocryphal gospels. In contrast, the Jesus Seminar puts Jesus' saying in 2:49 in black type (meaning that it does not go back to Jesus); Funk and Hoover 1993: 275–76. They see the unit as Luke's production, drawing on the child-prodigy genre, the Lucan emphasis on design, and its lack of attestation elsewhere. But these criteria ignore the potential of a unique source surfacing in Luke's research and the evidence for the unit's origins in Palestinian settings (see the discussion above and n. 3). Its enigmatic expression also reflects Jesus' style (see also Nolland 1989: 127–28, who speaks less directly on the issue of historicity in 2:49). That this is the only use of δεῖ relating Jesus to the Father speaks against a Lucan origin. On the historicity of the entire scene, see the exegesis of 2:50.

6. Creed 1930: 44 and Nolland 1989: 129 have typical lists of examples: Cyrus (at ten) in Herodotus 1.114–15; Alexander the Great in Plutarch, *Life of Alexander* 5; Apollonius in Philostratus, *Life of Apollonius* 1.7; Moses in Josephus, *Antiquities* 2.9.6 §230, and in Philo, *Life of Moses* 1.5 §21; Samuel (at twelve) in Josephus, *Antiquities* 5.10.4 §348; Solomon (at twelve) in 1 Kings 2:12 LXX; and Josephus (of himself!) in *Life* 2 §§8–9. To this can be added the account of Augustus in Suetonius, *Augustus* 94, as Klostermann 1929: 45 notes. Luke's account of Jesus is restrained in comparison to most of these accounts.

7. Fitzmyer 1981: 436. Bovon 1989: 154 prefers to speak only of a biographical interest, calling the account an anecdote. He compares it to the Infancy Gospel of Thomas 2, an account of a five-year-old Jesus fashioning twelve sparrows from clay. Though this account is much more fanciful than the Lucan pericope, its ending (19), stressing Jesus' wisdom, is similar to but less restrained than Luke's emphasis on wisdom (Schmahl 1974; see the exegesis of 2:46). In this case, the Infancy Gospel of Thomas is influenced by Luke (R. Brown 1977: 481).

1. Introduction (2:41–42)
   a. The faithful parents' custom (2:41)
   b. The journey in Jesus' twelfth year (2:42)
2. Problem: search for the missing Jesus (2:43–45)
3. Encounter: instruction but no understanding (2:46–50)
   a. Amazement of those who hear Jesus (2:46–47)
   b. Parental complaint (2:48)
   c. The point: Jesus must be in his Father's house (2:49)
   d. The lesson not understood (2:50)
4. Resolution: return home for a time (2:51)
5. Transition: Jesus' growth (2:52)

Many themes have already been noted. Jesus' relationship to his Father and his wisdom are the keys to the passage. Jesus knows the reason why he has come, part of which revolves around teaching. The account continues the note of wonder that has been a part of Luke 1–2. There is also a note of perplexity and pain in this text. People will struggle to understand Jesus' task and person. What is clear is that Jesus does not struggle to know either God or his own mission.

Exegesis and Exposition

[41]And his parents would go down each year to Jerusalem at the time of the feast of the Passover. [42]And when he was twelve years old, they went up according to the custom of the feast. [43]When the days of the feast had ended, upon the parents' return, Jesus, the child, remained in Jerusalem and the parents did not know it. [44]But thinking he was in the caravan, they went a day's journey and sought him among relatives and friends, and [45]when they did not find him, they returned to Jerusalem and were searching for him.

[46]And it came to pass after three days of separation, they found him in the temple seated in the midst of the teachers, listening to them and questioning them, but [47]all those who heard him were amazed at his understanding and his answers.

[48]And when they [his parents] saw him they were amazed and his mother said to him, "Child, why did you do this to us? Behold, your father and I sought you with great pain."

[49]And he said to them, "Why do you seek me? Do you not know that it is necessary for me to be in the things of my Father?"

[50]And they did not understand the words he spoke to them.

[51]And he returned with them and came into Nazareth and was submissive to them. And his mother kept all things in her heart.

[52]And Jesus grew in wisdom and stature and grace before God and men.

1. Introduction (2:41–42)
a. The Faithful Parents' Custom (2:41)

Luke 2:41–52 completes the Lucan introduction to Jesus. The section ends, as it begins (1:5), in the temple. The account really makes a transition into Jesus' ministry and gives testimony to the early insight that Jesus had about his relationship to God. However, despite the move into a later period of Jesus' life, structurally the repetition of the growth theme in 2:52 shows that Luke intends the story to conclude the initial section. The growth note about Jesus in 2:40 and a parallel note about John in 1:80 together indicate that the passages are part of the same section. Thus, this account is a preministry account of Jesus' life that serves as a prologue and foretaste of what will come in the rest of the Gospel. Just as the infancy section begins and ends in the temple, so also the events of the entire Gospel begin and end in the temple (1:5; 24:53). Luke often relates Jesus and his ministry to Judaism's center of religious worship. Jesus never sought to turn his back on Judaism.

2:41

The piety of Jesus' parents comes to the fore again in this account, just as it did in the temple presentation of Jesus (2:21–40). The OT commanded Jewish men to come to Jerusalem for three festivals: Passover, Pentecost, and Tabernacles (Exod. 23:14–17; 34:22–23; Deut. 16:16). But in light of the nation's scattering, the custom of first-century Judaism was that the pious who lived some distance away from the city journeyed to the temple only once a year.[8] The annual character of the family's journey to celebrate the Passover is indicated by κατ' ἔτος (*kat' etos*, each year). Jesus' parents were faithful adherents to the traditional faith.[9]

The Passover, the major feast celebrated at the beginning of the Jewish year, begins on the fifteenth of Nisan, which in our calendar falls in March or April (Fitzmyer 1981: 439–40). It recounts the miraculous deliverance of the nation from Egypt, which led to the exodus (Exod. 12:1–36). It was sometimes called the Feast of Unleavened Bread, since that celebration followed it immediately and the two feasts were celebrated together (Luke 22:1, 7; Matt. 26:2; Mark 14:1).[10] Men were required to go, but the journey was not a require-

---

8. Jeremias 1969: 76–77; Josephus, *Life* 65 §354 (which notes how few Tiberians [two thousand] were in Jerusalem on one key festival occasion); *Antiquities* 17.9.3 §§213–14; *Jewish War* 2.14.3 §280; 2.1.3 §§10–12.

9. Danker 1988: 74; Plummer 1896: 74. BDF §305 discusses the distributive use of κατά that is present here.

10. Josephus, *Antiquities* 17.9.3 §213; Jeremias, *TDNT* 5:898 §1. The reference in the verse to the Passover, τῇ ἑορτῇ τοῦ πάσχα, is grammatically to be taken as a dative of time: "at the time of the feast of the Passover" (Plummer 1896: 74; Luke uses a dative of time at 8:29 and 12:20).

ment for women (*m. Ḥag.* 1.1). Thus, for a woman to go was a sign of great piety (Klostermann 1929: 46; Hendriksen 1978: 183; SB 2:141–42; Preisker, *TDNT* 2:373). This note of piety is reinforced in 2:42.

If the travelers went around Samaria, the journey was about an eighty-mile trip from Nazareth. The journey often included roads that were exploited by highway robbers, so the pilgrims often traveled in large caravans for protection. Some commentators mention that women and children often traveled in front, with the men in the back.[11] There is, however, no cited evidence for this practice from the period itself. The journey would be a three- or four-day affair, as the caravan would make around twenty miles a day.[12] This verse sets the background to the account. Such an annual visit was a custom for the family. Some speculation exists whether this was Jesus' first trip with the family, but the text provides no answer. All that concerns Luke is that Jesus went this time.

b. The Journey in Jesus' Twelfth Year (2:42)

2:42 The journey occurred in Jesus' twelfth year, which was before the normal age (i.e., thirteen) for Jewish boys to be responsible before God (*m. Nid.* 5.6; *m. Meg.* 4.6; Schürmann 1969: 134 n. 257; Hendriksen 1978: 183; R. Brown 1977: 472–73). Instruction toward this goal would be intensive for twelve-year-olds (*m. ʾAbot* 5.21; *b. Ketub.* 50a; SB 2:144–47). *M. Nid.* 5.6 is particularly enlightening, for it says that twelve-years-olds can be taught concerning vows, but they are not responsible for them until age thirteen. The custom of Bar Mitzvah, common today for Jewish boys, began at a period after the time of Jesus (Fitzmyer 1981: 440).

This verse introduces the next passage by giving the setting of the events. The participle ἀναβαινόντων (*anabainontōn*, going up) is grammatically subordinate to the verb ὑπέμεινεν (*hypemeinen*, he remained) in 2:43 and serves as a genitive absolute with temporal force: "When they were going up" (Marshall 1978: 126–27). The parents' taking the twelve-year-old Jesus on the Passover journey is, once again, a picture of faithful Jewish parents instructing their child in the faith on a very important holy day.

2. Problem: Search for the Missing Jesus (2:43–45)

2:43 Luke introduces a family problem. Although some pilgrims only celebrated Passover and then returned after two days, the phrase τελει-

---

11. Ellis 1974: 85–86. Plummer 1896: 75 cites a source describing contemporary, not ancient, Bedouin.

12. Marshall 1978: 127; R. Brown 1977: 474; Jeremias 1969: 58–60; Josephus, *Life* 52 §269; *m. Maʿaś. Š.* 5.2.

ωσάντων τὰς ἡμέρας (*teleiōsantōn tas hēmeras*, when the days were completed) seems to suggest that Jesus' parents stayed for the whole seven-day period of the celebration (A. B. Bruce 1897: 478; Hendriksen 1978: 183; Alford 1874: 465). The length of the stay also reveals the family's devotion to Jewish custom and the worship of God.

The nature of the returning caravan might well have been parallel to the journey into Jerusalem. If so, Joseph and Mary may have traveled separately, or, more likely, they may have assumed that Jesus was with relatives (2:44). Whatever the exact situation, the account is clear that the parents did not worry about Jesus (Plummer 1896: 75). Only at the end of the first day of travel, when all would have come together for the night, did the parents realize that there was a problem (2:43–44).

Luke merely mentions that Jesus "remained behind" (ὑπέμεινεν, *hypemeinen*) in Jerusalem. The verse's structure shows that this idea is the key one, alongside the parents' being unaware (οὐκ ἔγνωσαν, *ouk egnōsan*) of his absence. Speculation that Jesus' parents were careless or that the incident is unbelievable is not profitable,[13] and there is no reason to engage in either side of this debate. Jesus remained behind and the text makes no effort to blame the parents for the incident. Neither does the text contain any elements that would suggest Luke sees anything but a historical account here (Marshall 1978: 126). The parents returned and Jesus remained behind without their knowledge.

One detail is interesting. The term used to describe Jesus is παῖς (*pais*, child). Danker (1988: 74) argues that an allusion, a double entendre, is present because of Luke's use of this term in Luke–Acts to refer to the "Servant of God" (παῖς θεοῦ, *pais theou*). However, three literary reasons argue against a reference to the Servant here: (1) the title παῖς has not yet been used with reference to Jesus; (2) in this passage παῖς stands in contrast to οἱ γονεῖς (*hoi goneis*, the parents), thereby reminding the reader that the event comes relatively early in Jesus' life; and (3) the contrast between παῖς and παιδίον (*paidion*, little child, baby) in 2:17, 27, 40, a diminutive form of παῖς, stresses the growth that Jesus has undergone since the previous event in Luke 2. Thus, Luke's use of παῖς simply indicates that when Jesus' parents returned to Nazareth the child Jesus did not accompany them.

The parents had a problem: they had mistakenly assumed that **2:44** Jesus was somewhere in the caravan. Συνοδίᾳ (*synodia*, in the com-

---

13. For the latter, see R. Brown 1977: 473, 486, who speaks of the literary character of the account, by which he means one should not spend too much time looking for historical or psychological detail.

pany [i.e., in the caravan]) is present only here in the NT (BAGD 791; BAA 1577). As was mentioned in the exegesis of 2:41, some suggest that men and women traveled separately during the daytime. The problem with this approach is that the evidence cited for this custom is modern.[14] Only if nomadic customs like those practiced today were followed then would this explanation fit. Since villages traveled together, a more likely explanation is that the parents assumed that Jesus was safe with family and friends. That such a possibility fits the setting is noted by SB 2:148–49 in citing how such vast caravans worked (see also Safrai 1974: 191–204; Safrai 1976d: 898–904). A day's journey passed before the problem emerged, as the parents sought Jesus among relatives and friends but could not locate him.

2:45 Luke notes how the parents reacted to Jesus' absence: they headed back to the temple city to look for Jesus. The participles and the verb present an interesting picture. Both the participle εὑρόντες (*heurontes*, [not] finding) and the verb ὑπέστρεψαν (*hypestrepsan*, they returned) are aorist. They did not find him in the caravan and made a decision to go back to Jerusalem, their failure to locate him being expressed in summary tenses. In contrast, ἀναζητοῦντες (*anazētountes*, searching) is a present participle. When they got to Jerusalem, they began *the process* of searching for him—language reflecting the passing of time as they anxiously hunted for the missing child.

3. Encounter: Instruction but No Understanding (2:46–50)
a. Amazement of Those Who Hear Jesus (2:46–47)

2:46 After three days the parents find Jesus in the temple. There is disagreement about this chronological reference. Alford (1874: 465) holds that the "three days" began with the search in Jerusalem rather than with the discovery that Jesus was missing. But most regard the phrase as referring to the first day out by caravan, the second day back from the caravan, and the third day in Jerusalem (Hendriksen 1978: 184; Creed 1930: 45; Marshall 1978: 127; R. Brown 1977: 474). Danker suggests that the reference to the third day is an allusion to resurrection, but Fitzmyer rightly rejects the connection, noting that the phrase used in reference to the resurrection is different.[15] R. Brown (1977: 487) concludes that the wording

---

14. Plummer 1896: 75 cites H. B. Tristram. Wight 1953: 121 also mentions a split travel custom of children spending time with kin and neighbors, but without citing ancient evidence.

15. Danker 1988: 75 notes the difference in wording, but still thinks a hint exists about the future; Fitzmyer 1981: 441. Luke 9:22 is an example of the different phrasing. Bovon 1989: 156 also sees no allusion to the resurrection.

Luke uses here is strictly chronological in meaning, for the other uses of this phrase have only a temporal sense (Acts 25:1; 28:17). Thus, Jesus was found three days after the caravan started home.

Mary and Joseph find Jesus in the temple, sitting at the feet of the teachers. Teachers in the ancient world normally sat with their students (C. Schneider, *TDNT* 3:443 §2d, §3b). The custom in Judaism was that pupils entered into question-and-answer dialogue with their mentors (SB 2:150–51; *b. Sanh.* 88b). It is not clear where Jesus is within the temple. Is he in the "house of instruction" or in the "outer court"? The text does not say.[16]

This is the only account in Luke where Jesus takes instruction from Jewish teachers. He is the listener; he does not instruct, as some popular renditions of the event suggest, except to enter into discussion with the teachers. As 2:47 shows, everyone is impressed with his understanding. In fact, apocryphal accounts of this incident make Jesus' teaching the point of the event. The Infancy Story of Thomas 19.2 has Jesus' comments silencing the teachers (Creed 1930: 45; Schneemelcher 1991–92: 1.449). The Arabic Gospel of the Infancy 50–52 has Jesus instructing the teachers on subjects like medicine and astronomy (Plummer 1896: 76). Such accounts differ from the simplicity of Luke's material.

The term διδασκάλων (*didaskalōn*, teachers) is unusual for Luke in that this is the only place he uses it of Jewish teachers; his preferred terms for Jewish teachers are νομικός (*nomikos*, lawyer) and γραμματεύς (*grammateus*, scribe) (R. Brown 1977: 474). The unusual usage probably suggests a source. For the most part Luke reserves διδάσκαλος for Jesus, though John the Baptist is its referent in 3:12 (Rengstorf, *TDNT* 2:152–53). Its use here is strictly neutral, not negative. Jesus is portrayed as a boy with a thirst to understand and discuss spiritual questions. The tranquillity of this dialogue will be shattered later by the disputes that Jesus will have with the religious authorities. As Danker (1988: 75) says, "One day his questions will pierce to the very core of the religious establishment, and he will give answers to his own questions" (e.g., 11:19–20; 13:2–5; 20:41–44 with 22:69). For now, Jesus is a boy at the instructors' feet. However, as the rest of this section will show, Jesus is already aware that he is more than a mere student of an ancient and venerable faith.

Jesus' wisdom astonishes the crowd. Luke frequently uses ἐξ-   **2:47**
ίσταντο (*existanto*, were amazed) to describe the wonder that emerges from an action associated with God's presence (Luke 8:56;

16. Rengstorf, *TDNT* 4:435 n. 152. Bovon 1989: 157 believes that the probable locale is the portico of Solomon (Acts 3:11; 5:12, 21, 25).

Acts 2:7, 12; 8:13; 9:21; Ellis 1974: 86; Fitzmyer 1981: 442). But this meaning does not suggest an awareness of Jesus' divinity, since the pericope itself shows that even Jesus' parents do not understand him yet in these terms. Rather, he is a person gifted by God. What produces the astonishment is the dialogue that Jesus has with the teachers.[17] The insight of his answers is what draws their attention. Συνέσει (*synesei*) speaks of understanding that is able to penetrate to the heart of an issue, and the term can be rendered "insight" (Isa. 11:2; 1 Chron. 22:12; R. Brown 1977: 475). Other figures of the era were portrayed in this way, but often the portrayal was autobiographical and, as a result, self-serving (so Josephus, *Life* 2 §§8–9; Plutarch, *Life of Alexander* 5; Danker 1988: 75–76). Jesus is not portrayed as God's wisdom, as he will be later (11:49–51), but he is seen as endowed with wisdom. Thus, the verse illustrates Jesus' growth in wisdom (2:40; Schürmann 1969: 135; R. Brown 1977: 475). As Sir. 11:1 says, those who have wisdom are regarded with respect, taking their seat among the great, even if they are poor. The audience's amazement shows respect for the quality of Jesus' insight.

b. Parental Complaint (2:48)

2:48 Their discovery of Jesus leads the parents to a mild complaint, though they are amazed to see Jesus talking with the temple teachers. The term chosen here is different from that used in the previous verse. Ἐξεπλάγησαν (*exeplagēsan*) refers to a reaction of being overwhelmed by events (BAGD 244; BAA 492; Luke 4:32; 9:43; Acts 13:12) and probably indicates both amazement and relief, since the verse goes on to mention that Mary and Joseph were anxious about finding Jesus.

As in the other accounts in the infancy section, Mary is the key parental figure. The exchange is rather direct, and her words leave no doubt that Jesus had really troubled his parents. She mentions that they searched for him with anxiety. Ὀδυνώμενοι (*odynōmenoi*, anxiously) describes deep mental pain or trauma. Only Luke uses this term in the NT (Hauck, *TDNT* 5:115; Luke 16:24–25; Acts 20:38). Mary, speaking for both parents, wants to know why he has done such a seemingly insensitive thing. Jesus' reply in the next verse addresses both of them as well. The form of Mary's question may have OT roots (Gen. 20:9; 12:18; 26:10; Exod. 14:11; Num. 23:11; Judg. 15:11).[18] This is the language of complaint. The ques-

---

17. For an example of the form of rabbinic teaching, see *Pirqe ʾAbot* 6.5–6 (= Hertz 1945: 111); Klostermann 1929: 47.

18. Wiefel 1988: 84 n. 20. Bovon 1989: 159 notes that the idiom suggests the questioner's belief that an error has been made.

tion prepares for a key teaching about Jesus' identity. Even his parents must come to understand his mission.

c. The Point: Jesus Must Be in His Father's House (2:49)

Jesus' reply represents his first statement in the Gospel. It reveals Jesus' sense of priority and includes a reference to the necessity of his task. The key Lucan term δεῖ (*dei*, it is necessary)—used strategically in the Gospel where elements of Jesus' mission are set forth[19]—is included in the statement. This is the only use of δεῖ that suggests Jesus' relationship to the Father. His parents need to understand his mission.

2:49

The thrust of the reply has been debated. The issue turns on filling in a missing element in the passage. The key phrase ἐν τοῖς τοῦ πατρός μου (*en tois tou patros mou*) is literally translated "in the . . . of my Father." What is to be supplied in the ellipse is at issue (Fitzmyer 1981: 443–44; R. Brown 1977: 475–77):

1. The least held view is that Jesus says that he must be among those of his Father's house, that is, among the Jewish teachers of the law. This view is attributed to some church fathers, though R. Brown questions this association.[20] Jesus makes reference to an "eschatological family" in Luke (8:19–21; 11:27–28). But the fatal blow against this view is that it is highly unlikely that Jesus would refer so positively to teachers of the law (or that the church would retain such a tradition). There is too much conflict with these figures later in Luke's account for them to be so exalted here (11:37–54; 20–23).

2. Another view, reflected in some translations, is a reading that translates, "I must be about my Father's business" (KJV; NKJV; Erasmus; see discussion in R. Brown 1977: 476). This view can amass many parallel texts: Mark 8:33; 1 Cor. 7:32–34; 1 Tim. 4:15. The idea then becomes that God's ministry is paramount to Jesus and that his parents must understand this. But this reading is contextually less than satisfying. The issue up to this point was the pain in searching for Jesus. Why should Jesus raise the broad issue of the Father's business when Mary simply wanted to know why he stayed behind at

---

19. Luke 4:43 [to preach the kingdom of God]; 9:22 [to suffer, die, and be raised]; 13:33 [he must go to Jerusalem]; 17:25 [to suffer]; 19:5 [to remain with Zacchaeus]; 22:37 [to be reckoned with criminals]; 24:7 [to suffer, die, and be raised]; 24:26 [to suffer and come into glory]; 24:44 [that Scripture about him be fulfilled]; Danker 1988: 77.

20. Theodoret, *On the Incarnation of the Lord* 24; see *PG* 75:1461CD. R. Brown 1977: 477 cites J. Döderlein as a modern exponent.

the temple? To put it another way, Jesus could do the Father's business in lots of places other than the temple, as his ministry will prove (Creed 1930: 46). Thus, this reading is not clearly supported from the context. Also, Luke 2:49 uses a construction (ἐν and the neuter plural definite article) that is not used in the parallel texts cited for the view: Mark 8:33 and 1 Cor. 7:32–34 do not use ἐν and 1 Tim. 4:15 uses ἐν and the neuter plural demonstrative pronoun. This view is unlikely to be correct.

3. The most widely held view today is that the phrase translates, "I must be in my Father's house." Jesus must be involved with instruction in divine things, since the temple as presented by Luke is above all a place where instruction occurs (Luke 20–21). An additional point here is that Jesus' parents should have known where to look. The construction of ἐν, the neuter plural definite article, and a genitive fits this view best. This is an idiom for being in one's house (Gen. 41:51; Esth. 7:9; Job 18:19; Josephus, *Against Apion* 1.18 §118; *Antiquities* 16.10.1 §302; P. Oxy. vol. 3 #523 line 3).[21] Thus, Jesus declares the necessity of being in God's house, where God's presence is held to reside and where instruction about God is given.

The way in which Jesus asks his question is really designed to make a statement. The "do you not know" introduction is designed to produce an affirmative reply. The parents need to see that Jesus must be about the work of discussing what God desires. To limit the reply's force to "you should have known where I was," as Creed (1930: 46) does, is to remove the rationale for keeping the story in the tradition. Surely the point of δεῖ and the mention of God's house is to emphasize that Jesus must discuss what humankind's task before God is.

But the reply has another additional element of teaching. When Jesus refers to the temple as *his Father's* house, a note of intimacy is raised that is significant. This idea of sonship has been variously explained:

1. Some suggest that the idea of God as Father is the language of the pious and faithful (Winter 1954: 146–47 cites Frg. Tg. on Exod. 15:2). Jesus is alluding to his relationship to God as a faithful follower. Schürmann (1969: 137 n. 280) notes the key texts outside the Fragmentary Targum that may suggest

---

21. See BAGD 552 §II.7; BAA 1120 §II.7; BDF §162.8; Fitzmyer 1981: 443. Literally, the phrase translates as "in the things of my Father," with the things referred to being determined by the given context.

such an idea (Sir. 23:1, 4; 4:10; Wis. 2:16, 18; Ps. 71:15–17). The problem with this association is that the targum's date, even though disputed, comes too late to be of value for a first-century meaning, while most of the other references imply only a Father concept. The Sirach parallels, however, are strong and may suggest an aspect of connection; but given Jesus' emphasis on his task, his being a faithful follower cannot be the major point.

2. Others limit the reference to a messianic sense since the "Son of God" in the OT is a regal idea (Ps. 2:7). This connection is possible, but nowhere else does the king address God as his Father as Jesus does here.[22]

3. It seems best to see an intimate allusion to the filial relationship that Jesus has to God (10:21–22; Godet 1875: 1.149; Hendriksen 1978: 185; Marshall 1978: 129). "My Father" suggests the mystery that is a part of Jesus' person (Schneider 1977a: 75). Jesus has a strong sense of identity with the Father and is committed to the mission God sent him to do. The reference here is personal versus messianic, for it is not clear why Messiah would be needed in the temple. Like the Gospel of John's portrayal, Jesus recognizes himself as sent by the Father to reveal his will. How this view of Jesus fits into the trinitarian language and discussion of the postapostolic church, however, is not Luke's explicit concern. The relationship is merely presented; it is not developed or explained. Thus, what Schürmann (1969: 137) calls the "high point" of the infancy section is that Jesus introduces himself to the reader for the first time. Jesus declares that he is called to instruct humans because he has a close, personal relationship to the Father and has a mission to carry out from him. The implication for the reader is clear, "Let anyone who has ears listen to what is taught by the Son!" As for Jesus' parents, they too must come to understand this mission (note Nolland's remarks [1989: 132] that Jesus' reply was not so much a reproach about having the right priorities as it was a declaration of mission). Of course, Jesus' parents were not alone in trying to come to grips with who Jesus was. The disciples also came along very slowly in perceiving that following God's will took priority for Jesus (Luke 9:59–62; 14:26; Mark 10:29–30).

---

22. This view is really a variation of view 1. It simply focuses on the king. Numerous commentators criticize it, though none mention who holds it. Bovon 1989: 160–61 comes close in mentioning the activity of Messiah in the context and in speaking only of God's love relationship to Jesus.

d. The Lesson Not Understood (2:50)

2:50 The parents do not understand Jesus' remarks. Their ignorance relates to the exact nature of Jesus' mission as well as to his identity. If they had understood his mission better, then his presence in the temple would not have been so surprising (Ellis 1974: 86). Again the parents' ignorance will be matched by that of the disciples, showing that understanding God's calling is not a natural thing into which one falls (9:45; 10:21–24; 18:34; Danker 1988: 78).

This ignorance, especially Mary's, has caused problems for some commentators, who find it hard to believe that Mary, in light of all she experienced, could have failed to understand Jesus' mission. Some try to explain the passage by referring the ignorance to someone other than Mary (see R. Brown 1977: 477 for the options). Three such efforts exist. (1) Some relate the ignorance only to Joseph, but the reference to "they" (αὐτοί, *autoi*) is against this limited connection. This view is centuries old (Brown cites a sixteenth-century work by Cardinal Cajetan). (2) Others relate the ignorance to bystanders, but the dialogue before the verse involves the parents, as does the reference to Mary following the remark (M. Power 1912). (3) Still others allude to an unmentioned saying of Jesus being the source of the ignorance, but such an appeal is special pleading and cannot honor the literary flow of the passage.[23] None of these views is satisfactory. Rather the parents' ignorance demonstrates that it was hard to fathom the new ground Jesus was breaking.

The parents' ignorance has also produced a more skeptical response. Luce (1933: 106) and R. Brown (1977: 482–84) both regard it as unlikely that the full account of this event is historical. Luce believes the ignorance to stand in contradiction to the annunciation narrative, while Brown argues that it reflects a postresurrection understanding about Jesus projected back into the infancy setting. For Brown the ignorance motif is designed to explain why no one recognized Jesus as the Son of God earlier in his earthly ministry and life, a view that goes back at least to W. Wrede's 1901 work on the messianic secret in Mark. One is hard pressed, however, to see the need to explain away a person struggling to accept the identity of a man who had a unique relationship to God and to understand as well all the aspects of his mission. Is it any wonder that those around Jesus were slow to realize fully who he was? If such a man were to come today, would not the uniqueness of the claim give us pause, especially if the view existed that such a man would be a great regal figure? The prob-

---

23. M. Power 1912 mentions this approach, while Cortés and Gatti 1970 and Bover 1951 suppose that the missing saying was that Jesus told his parents he would remain in Jerusalem, but they had not understood him on that point.

lem of people wrestling to comprehend who Jesus actually was and what he might be doing in a place like the temple was a real one in the face of Jewish national hope. What association would that person have with necessary activity in the temple? The struggle to understand and accept Jesus for who he was in the comprehensive scope of his mission was a problem not only for Jesus' parents. It was a problem that continued into Luke's own day. For Luke, the uncertainty was resolved by a study of Jesus' life and ministry (1:1–4). The parents may well picture the struggle of Luke's readers.

4. Resolution: Return Home for a Time (2:51)

The incident at the temple was an isolated affair, after which Jesus   **2:51** returned home with his parents to Nazareth. There he lived, one may assume, a normal life. That the account speaks of Jesus' submitting himself to his parents shows the narrative's respect toward Jesus. Children were to be submissive and yet Jesus' submission is worthy of note, because of who he is. Jesus' piety in this self-submission is the point. In fact, the submission appears to have lasted at least seventeen years, and in the intervening time Joseph died.

After the mention of the return, Luke adds a note about Mary's response to this event and others like it: she keeps all these things in her heart. The plural phrase πάντα τὰ ῥήματα (*panta ta rhēmata*, all things) shows that more than the temple scene is referred to here. The idea recalls 2:19 and, although worded differently, makes the same point. The reference to keeping (διετήρει, *dietērei*) has to do with careful recall, keeping a close eye to something (Gen. 37:11 [Jacob of Joseph's dream]; Acts 15:29; BAGD 189; BAA 381). This mention of Mary's recollection indicates that she took note of the events about Jesus and did not take unkindly to his retort, but rather reflected on it. Thus, Mary's reputation, which may have been hurt by the exposure of her ignorance, receives some restoration. In fact, the pondering that Mary does may well be a call to the reader to do the same, in that she pictures what the faithful should do when they encounter truths about Jesus (Schneider 1977a: 76; Schürmann 1969: 138).

The remark creates speculation about the source for the infancy material. Plummer (1896: 78) and Godet (1875: 1.163) take the remark to be a Lucan clue that Mary is the source for much of this material. Klostermann (1929: 48) feels that such a conclusion is pressing the language of the verse. It is difficult to resolve the dispute. Although it is possible that the material goes back to Mary, such a conclusion cannot be established definitively, since Luke does not name a source. However, it is likely that at some point she did contribute to this material, since she would be a major source for such information about Jesus. Even if this material emerged from Jewish Christianity, as some scholars argue and as has been argued at points in this commentary, there would, given such a setting, likely have been contact with Jesus' mother or a member of the family. The comment in this verse suggests this connection.

5. Transition: Jesus' Growth (2:52)

2:52 A second note about Jesus' growth concludes the introductory section (cf. 2:40). It may well be a Lucan summary. That Jesus receives two such notices while John the Baptist receives only one suggests Jesus' superiority. The wording is like 1 Sam. 2:21, 26. The mention of both God and humans is a way of saying all perceived this growth. Whereas John grew in spirit (Luke 1:80), Jesus grew in wisdom, stature, and favor (Hendriksen 1978: 186). This difference is yet another indication of superiority. The reference to wisdom has to do with a growth in Jesus' insight (see the exegesis of 2:47 on συνέσει). Ἡλικίᾳ (*hēlikia*, stature) probably addresses growth in physical stature (19:3; Marshall 1978: 130; J. Schneider, *TDNT* 2:941–43). Such a note of physical growth for a major figure is not unusual (see Josephus, *Antiquities* 2.9.6 §230, of Moses). The reference to grace (χάριτι, *chariti*) has to do with moral growth and favorable perception (Prov. 3:3). Luke pictures Jesus' growth very naturally. His terms for Jesus change from one pericope to the next: βρέφος (*brephos*, baby; 2:16), παιδίον (*paidion*, little child; 2:40), παῖς (*pais*, child; 2:43), and finally just his name (2:52; Plummer 1896: 78).

Summary Luke 2:41–52 reveals Jesus' self-testimony and calls the reader to consider who Jesus is. At a young age, he remained behind in the temple and entered into exchange with the teachers of the faith. Both his questions and his answers brought attention to him for their insight. Of course, what was troublesome was that Jesus had entered into this encounter without his parents being aware that he had remained behind in Jerusalem. His absence caused them anguish, and when they found him, Mary did not hesitate to make the point. This in turn led to Jesus' crucial remark about the necessity of his involvement with religious discussion like that at the temple. His sonship demanded it. Such self-understanding the parents could not comprehend, nor did they perceive as yet Jesus' total sense of priorities toward the things of the Father. Yet the event is but a foretaste of Jesus' later ministry. The remarks are significant as Jesus' first words in the Gospel. The struggle that the parents had is similar to the disciples' struggle. Others also will wrestle to understand who he is. All will have to wrestle with Jesus' identity and decide exactly who Jesus is. Jesus returns to normal life for a time and submits to his parents until later. But Mary ponders the remarks of her child as he grows up.

The reader of Luke's Gospel is left to ponder the same things. One reads on with interest to see what Jesus' ministry itself will reveal about him. With such a preview of Jesus as Messiah-Servant-Son, one can only look forward with expectation to the teaching and wisdom that Jesus will display. The time of fulfillment comes.

When considered as a whole, these two chapters show that whatever God promised came to pass. The passage provides not only expectation, but assurance concerning the things to which Luke testifies. In Jesus, God is at work.

I. Luke's Preface and the Introduction of John and Jesus (1:1–2:52)
➤ II. Preparation for Ministry: Anointed by God (3:1–4:13)
III. Galilean Ministry: Revelation of Jesus (4:14–9:50)
IV. Jerusalem Journey: Jewish Rejection and the New Way (9:51–19:44)
V. Jerusalem: The Innocent One Slain and Raised (19:45–24:53)

II. Preparation for Ministry: Anointed by God (3:1–4:13)

Luke's second major section introduces Jesus' ministry through the ministry of John the Baptist. This section has two major units: John's ministry as the "one who goes before" (3:1–20), followed by the introduction of the "Mightier One who is to come" (3:21–4:13).

John's ministry (3:1–20) has three major themes. John comes, as the OT promised, to announce the way of the Lord and to baptize for the forgiveness of sins (3:1–6). John preaches a message that warns about judgment if one does not respond in concrete repentance (3:7–14). John promises that one is coming who will bring the promised Holy Spirit (3:15–18). This unit closes with a short note about how John was imprisoned (3:19–20).

Jesus arrives to be baptized by John (3:21–22), an event that contains the first "voice from heaven" remark about Jesus (9:35 is the other). The voice describes Jesus in terms that recall OT promise: he is the beloved, regal Son-Servant. Luke then introduces a genealogy that goes back to Adam, the son of God (3:23–38). Jesus comes for all people as the second (but successful) Adam. Then Jesus goes into the wilderness to suffer through Satan's temptations (4:1–13). This first cosmic confrontation is not really about temptation but victory. Unlike Adam, Jesus does not succumb to the devil, but resists him. Satan's challenge of Jesus' faithfulness as Son fails. Jesus is qualified to minister God's salvation. He obeys God and resists self and Satan.

This section introduces John's and Jesus' ministries. As with the infancy material, Jesus' superiority is the point. After this unit John the Baptist disappears from the stage, except for a brief appearance in 7:18–35. The main figure comes center stage and dominates the account.[1]

---

1. Marshall 1978: 131 defends a break in Luke's Gospel before 4:14 by noting that Jesus' ministry really begins at this verse. Schürmann 1969: 146–48 sees the break at 4:44.

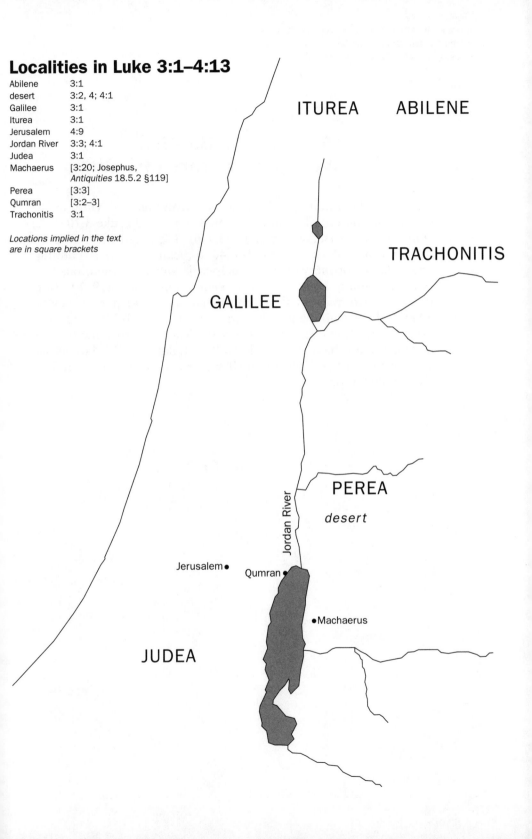

Localities in Luke 3:1–4:13

Abilene	3:1
desert	3:2, 4; 4:1
Galilee	3:1
Iturea	3:1
Jerusalem	4:9
Jordan River	3:3; 4:1
Judea	3:1
Machaerus	[3:20; Josephus, *Antiquities* 18.5.2 §119]
Perea	[3:3]
Qumran	[3:2–3]
Trachonitis	3:1

Locations implied in the text are in square brackets

ITUREA   ABILENE

TRACHONITIS

GALILEE

PEREA

desert

Jordan River

Jerusalem●   Qumran●

●Machaerus

JUDEA

II. Preparation for Ministry: Anointed by God (3:1–4:13)
➤ A. John the Baptist: One Who Goes Before (3:1–20)
   B. Jesus: One Who Comes After (3:21–4:13)

A. John the Baptist: One Who Goes Before (3:1–20)

Luke 3:1–20 contains much uniquely Lucan material. Only Luke details the content of John the Baptist's teaching (Luke 3:10–14). Only Luke cites Isa. 40:4–5 (Luke 3:4–6). The lengthened citation (Matthew and Mark cite only Isa. 40:3) means that Jesus' coming offers the opportunity of salvation for all. Only Luke mentions the imprisonment of John so early in the account (Luke 3:19–20). But there are also traditional materials that have clear parallels elsewhere. The warning about judgment to the Jewish leaders has a clear parallel (Luke 3:7–9; Matt. 3:7–10). The promise of the Mightier One to come has conceptual parallels (Luke 3:15–17; Matt. 3:11–12; Mark 1:7–8). Both old and fresh material describe John's ministry of preparation.

1. Ministry of John the Baptist (3:1–6)

This pericope has a twofold purpose: to place Jesus' ministry in the midst of world history (3:1–2a) and to set the ministry of John the Baptist in the midst of OT hope (3:4–6). The word of God comes to John in the wilderness as his ministry renews God's direct activity for people (3:2b–3). By beginning in the wilderness, the account picks up where the infancy section left off with John (1:80).

The teaching about John the Baptist extending to 3:20 represents what Schürmann (1969: 148) calls the "pre-kerygma" of John. John's message prepares the people for the coming of salvation with a call to repent.

The position of John the Baptist in Luke's Gospel is a much discussed issue. Some consider John the last of the prophets, the last of the age of promise. So Conzelmann (1960: 18–27) argues by noting that the Baptist account is self-contained in Luke. He notes that Luke moves the account of John's imprisonment up, so that Jesus is the exclusive focus of the period of fulfillment (so also Ernst 1977: 146; Schürmann 1969: 149, 183–84; and Fitzmyer 1981: 450–51, but with some qualification). Luke 16:16, with its "clear" break between John the Baptist and Jesus, is Conzelmann's major support text. Others consider John a bridge figure in whom the transition from promise to fulfillment is made.[1] The key to the debate is the infancy section. If one includes its teaching as a part of Luke's perspective—and there is no reason to exclude it—then John is closely linked to the time of fulfillment, so that the best description of him is as a bridge. In addition, 7:18–35, where John reappears, also serves to give a close linkage between John and Jesus. Whether the exegesis of 16:16 sustains a "clear" break between John and Jesus is debatable (Marshall 1970: 146; see the exegesis of 16:16).

A problem in this discussion is a failure to distinguish between figures of fulfillment and the time of fulfillment. With John's ministry, the time of fulfillment comes. The "precursor" is indivisibly linked to Jesus, even as the use of Isaiah in this peric-

---

1. So Marshall 1978: 132; Marshall 1970: 145–46; Bovon 1989: 165 (who sees John as a "bridge" figure); Wink 1968: 42–86. Other Lucan texts on the Baptist are Luke 7:18–35; Acts 1:5, 22; 10:37; 11:16; 13:24–25; 19:3–4.

ope shows. But for Luke, Jesus is the only figure who brought the eschaton. John's ministry fulfills the promise only in pointing to Jesus and his ministry.

Sources and Historicity

The sources of this pericope can be determined by a quick comparison with Mark 1.[2] Whatever the source of Mark's material, Luke clearly had additional material or has given John's ministry his own additional reflections. (1) He lengthens the OT citation to include Isa. 40:4–5, so that the universal manifestation of salvation is clear (see the exegesis of 3:5–6). (2) He also uniquely places the ministry in its historical setting, working from the greatest rulers down. He starts with Tiberius Caesar, goes to the Roman governor Pilate, then to the Jewish tetrarchs, ending with religious high priests. (3) Unlike the Marcan tradition, Luke does not engage in a description of John's ascetic lifestyle, though the later description of John in 7:33 shows that Luke knows about it. He also notes with Mark that John performed his baptism in the Jordan River. Mark and Matthew also share the points about lifestyle and place of ministry. Thus, though much of what Luke writes agrees with Mark and Matthew, he adds additional features to the portrait (Aland 1985: §13). In later pericopes, Luke is closer to Matthew than to Mark. Luke 3:7–9 and 3:15–17 have Matthean parallels. Thus, Luke's material has traditional roots.

With regard to historicity, John's ascetic lifestyle and baptism are generally accepted. When challenges come, they revolve around the Gospels' portrait of him as forerunner, especially since as late as the period covered in Acts 19:1–7 there were some people who had only John's baptism. The issues surrounding John 1 and Luke 1 also raise questions. But all that the Acts 19 passage shows is that some who had heard John did not yet know of Jesus. They are not "John's disciples" carrying his flame despite the presence of Jesus, which is how some describe them. The issues surrounding John 1 and Luke 1 were treated in the additional note on 1:25. One can accept the account's trustworthiness (see the additional note on 3:3).

As the next few pericopes show, Luke is interested not only in John as the precursor and baptizer, but also in giving John's message (see esp. 3:10–14). In doing so, Luke presents John as a prophet more fully than do the other Synoptic writers. All the writers agree that John was a man whose ministry anticipated

---

2. For characteristic approaches to this issue, often appealing to Q, see Klostermann 1929: 50; Creed 1930: 46–48; Schneider 1977a: 82. Bovon 1989: 165–66 speaks of Q, Mark, and other material. Distinctive is Goulder 1989: 271–72, who argues for Luke's use of Matthew.

Jesus, but Luke explains how John prepared for Jesus. In addition, Luke's placement of these events on the stage of world history communicates that they were of international significance; they did not occur in a corner (Acts 26:26; Schürmann 1969: 150; Danker 1988: 81).

The text combines various forms. It has a historical note in 3:1–2a. There is a brief historical description in 3:2b–3. Then in 3:4–6 there is a comparison with the OT, which announced what God's coming salvation is like. This OT text explains what the events mean (Berger 1984: 114, 347, 352). In literary terms, these notes make up the narrative's framing of John the Baptist's ministry.

The outline of Luke 3:1–6 is as follows:

a. Historical setting of John's ministry (3:1–2a)
b. John's preaching a baptism of repentance (3:2b–3)
c. Isaiah's promise of a preparer for salvation (3:4–6)

Four points dominate the pericope. First, God's promise comes in the context of history. Second, the word of God is once again active. Third, the preparation for salvation requires personal repentance of one's sins. Fourth, John's coming was anticipated in the Scriptures; it is a clearing of the way for God. The story of the good news really begins in earnest when John prepares a people for God's salvation (1:17, 76–77).

Exegesis and Exposition

[1]And in the fifteenth year of the reign of Tiberius Caesar, when Pontius Pilate was governor of Judea, and Herod was tetrarch of Galilee, and Philip his brother was tetrarch of the region of Iturea and Trachonitis, and Lysanius was tetrarch of Abilene, [2]during the high priesthood of Annas and Caiaphas, the word of God came to John, the son of Zechariah, in the wilderness. [3]And he came into all the region of the Jordan preaching a baptism of repentance for the forgiveness of sins, [4]even as it is written in the book of the recorded words of Isaiah the prophet, "A voice is crying in the wilderness, 'Prepare the way for the Lord, make straight his paths. [5]All valleys shall be filled and all mountains and hills shall be lowered, and the crooked places shall be straight and the rocky places shall be smooth, [6]and all men shall see God's salvation.'"

a. Historical Setting of John's Ministry (3:1–2a)

Luke gives the setting of John's ministry. In fact, seven rulers are mentioned, working from the most comprehensive ruler down to

3:1

the regional spiritual leaders. This type of synchronic approach to dating fits ancient style (Thucydides 2.2; Polybius 1.3), as well as being a part of OT dating, where the prophet's call is placed alongside the rulers who governed during his ministry (Jer. 1:1–3; Isa. 1:1; Amos 1:1; Schürmann 1969: 151 n. 31; Nolland 1989: 138; C. F. Evans 1990: 231).

Tiberius ruled this region from a distance, so that the effect of his reign was present only through the governors and others under him. Tiberius inherited his governmental system from Augustus, his stepfather, in A.D. 14. Tiberius had been an effective general, but withdrew and pursued academic studies in Rhodes when it appeared that Augustus was grooming the son of his daughter Julia as the next emperor. When that son died in battle, Tiberius quite logically became the heir. The empire was divided into imperial provinces directly under the emperor's care (e.g., Syria and Galatia) and senatorial provinces under the care of the Senate (e.g., Asia, Macedonia, and Achaea).[3] Rulers in these regions were either legates (military men in charge of the army) or prefects (also called procurators, administrative financial officers in charge of collecting taxes and keeping the peace). Prefects were usually of lesser stature than legates.[4] Pontius Pilate was a prefect.

Sometimes rule was shared with regional figures who had developed a good relationship with the emperor. Such had been the case for Antipater (the grandfather of Herod Antipas), who ruled Idumea from 63 B.C. to 43 B.C. and was accorded a function like that of a prefect in 55. Antipater had received authority to rule from Julius Caesar for helping the emperor suppress rebellion in Syria. Thus, in Judea of Jesus' time, Herod Antipas ruled Galilee and Perea as tetrarch from 4 B.C. to A.D. 39. He was a third-generation ruler of a family with deep ties to Rome. His father, Herod the Great ("king" from 37 B.C. to 4 B.C.), ruled a vast region that encompassed much of what had been ancient Israel. Herod the Great rebuilt much of the city of Jerusalem and started the restoration of the great temple. Education and economic vitality came to the region, intermixed with bouts of internal unrest. But with his death in 4 B.C., his kingdom was split among his three sons: Archelaus, the eldest, received Judea and Samaria until his banishment in A.D. 6 (he died in A.D. 18). Herod Antipas inherited Galilee and Perea, and their benevolent half-brother Philip received

---

3. Reicke 1968: 228–34. On these distinctions, see Sherwin-White 1963: 1–23 (who cites a variety of relevant ancient texts); C. F. Evans 1990: 233; Tacitus, *Annals* 15.25.

4. Reicke 1968: 138, 228–29. F. F. Bruce 1972: 16–17 notes that the term *procurator* is later than this period, coming into use with the emperor Claudius (41–54).

the northern Transjordan area. Technically, they were all te-trarchs or, in effect, regional rulers. With Archelaus's banishment, the governing of the region became the domain of a succession of Roman prefects, but wise policy required that the prefect cooperate with his Herodian neighbors and be sensitive to his predominantly Jewish subjects. John's ministry stepped into this complex political situation (Schürer 1973–87: 1.336–98; Reicke 1968: 84–137).

The major ancient source for this period is Josephus, who discusses each of the key figures: Pontius Pilate, Herod Antipas, and Philip.[5] Philo also discusses Pilate (*Embassy to Gaius* 38 §299). In addition, an inscription referring directly to Pilate as prefect is evidence that he was popularly regarded as holding this position.[6]

Luke's mention of Lysanius of Abilene has often been regarded as historical error. Wellhausen (1904: 4) believes that Luke blundered by citing the Lysanius mentioned by Josephus in *Antiquities* 14.13.3 §330 and 15.4.1 §92. This ruler is too early to be mentioned here since he died in 36 B.C. But the accusation of error ignores evidence of other inscriptions (Böckh 1828–77: #4521, #4523) that attest to a later Lysanius who lived in the time of Tiberius. In fact, the inscriptions may suggest that several dynasts of this period bore this name (Creed 1930: 307–9; Godet 1875: 1.168–69; Plummer 1896: 84; Schürer 1973–87: 1.567–69). Fitzmyer (1981: 457–58) notes that one cannot categorically identify the figure in the inscriptions with the figure mentioned by Luke, but what the evidence does show is that there is clearly more than one Lysanius in this region in this period. Thus, even external evidence suggests that Luke's mention is accurate (Marshall 1978: 134). The inscriptions seem to be confirmed by vague Josephean references to a Lysanius in a time period before Herod Agrippa I, Herod Antipas's nephew and successor who ruled from A.D. 40 to 44 (*Antiquities* 19.5.1 §275; 20.7.1 §138). As to the dates of Lysanius, the references are so few and obscure that they cannot be determined.

The final figures mentioned in Luke's synchronic dating are Annas **3:2a** and Caiaphas, who are not political figures but the key Jewish religious authorities. The reference has an interesting peculiarity, as Luke refers to the period of the ἀρχιερέως (*archiereōs*, high priest) Annas and Caiaphas. That is, Luke uses a singular term to refer to

5. For Pilate, see Josephus, *Jewish War* 2.9.2–4 §§169–77; and *Antiquities* 18.3.1 §§55–59. For Herod Antipas, see *Jewish War* 1.33.8 §§668–69; 2.9.1 §§167–68; *Antiquities* 17.8.1 §188; 17.11.4 §318; 18.5.2 §§116–19. For Philip, see *Antiquities* 17.2.2 §§27–28; 17.4.2–3 §§78–80; 17.8.1 §189; 17.11.4 §319.

6. Sherwin-White 1963: 12 n. 4. Tacitus, *Annals* 12.60, is the ancient source that discusses the key terminology.

two men. But there were not two high priests in this period. Annas had been high priest from 6 to 15.[7] After a few short tenures by other high priests, Caiaphas, Annas's son-in-law, came to power and remained there until 36. Thus, Caiaphas was the formal high priest during this time.

What is Luke suggesting by his use of the singular ἀρχιερέως? He is communicating that actual power was really shared and that the religious authority of the region was really a two-man affair, with Annas exercising great power behind the scenes (Ellis 1974: 88; Marshall 1978: 134). The picture of John 18:13–27 confirms this description and shows the accuracy of Luke's reference (on Caiaphas, see Acts 4:6; John 11:49; Bovon 1989: 168–69). It may well be also that Annas, though not officially in office, retained the title for life, much as American presidents or governors do. Thus, one could speak of the time of the high priests Annas and Caiaphas without speaking of their official time of holding office. Josephus also exhibits plural references with regard to the high priests (on Annas, see *Antiquities* 20.9.1 §§197–200; on the "college" of high priests, see *Antiquities* 20.10.4–5 §§244–51). Thus, Luke accurately gives insight into the real power structure of religious Judaism in Jerusalem.

The data show the complexity of the political and religious setting into which John's ministry came. There were many parties and concerns with which one had to deal. One lived in the contexts of Roman rule, the allies of Rome, and religious Judaism. Israel was under subjection, but there was cooperation. The detail shows Luke's universal perspective. In this setting the word of God came through a prophet. The data place us in the time of A.D. 29, as God began to move in history and manifest his salvation (Luke 3:6). These events occurred in the public square (Acts 26:26).

b. John's Preaching a Baptism of Repentance (3:2b–3)

3:2b The extended effort to date John's arrival shows this event's importance. The Baptist's call to prophetic ministry is more than the call of any OT prophet (7:26; Schürmann 1969: 152–53). Rather, what is present for Luke is the beginning of the epoch of fulfillment, for if the speeches of Acts are considered, one can see how closely Luke links John to Jesus (Acts 1:22; 10:37; 13:24–25; Plummer 1896: 84–

---

7. Josephus mentions Annas's appointment (*Antiquities* 18.2.1 §26) and discusses the interim priests after Annas was deposed by Valerius Gratus (*Antiquities* 18.2.2 §§33–35). Five sons of Annas as well as his son-in-law Caiaphas succeeded to this office, so it is easy to see why Luke sees Annas as key. He is a patriarch to the high priesthood. The interim priests were Eleazar, son of Annas, and Simon, son of Camith, who each served one year.

85). John and Jesus should not be totally separated in the description of Luke's salvation-historical presentation.[8]

External ancient sources testify to the existence of John the Baptist. Josephus makes explicit mention of him (*Antiquities* 18.5.2 §§116–19). As Fitzmyer (1981: 451) notes, there is no contradiction between the portrait of Josephus and the portrait of the Gospels. Josephus stresses the political fears that John aroused in Herod, while the Gospels focus on his moral preaching, even against the political leadership.[9]

Around A.D. 29, the word of God came to John. The significant reference to ῥῆμα θεοῦ (*rhēma theou*) describes the coming of clear revelation and direction from God (Godet 1875: 1.171; Oepke, *TDNT* 3:585). God promised that John would be a prophet of the Most High (1:76). He had grown up in the desert (1:80). Now in language reminiscent of the call of the OT prophets, John is directed to begin his ministry (Jer. 1:1–2; 11:18–20; 13:3; Isa. 38:4; Hos. 1:1; Fitzmyer 1981: 458; Wiefel 1988: 88).[10] God intervenes again in history and calls John to give his message to humans.

The choice of ῥῆμα rather than λόγος (*logos*) for "word" of God has been taken in two ways. Some argue that ῥῆμα suggests a particular message of God rather than the entire scope of his message, as λόγος would do (Plummer 1896: 85; Liefeld 1984: 858). In addition, the term is particularly Lucan in that nineteen of its twenty-six Synoptic uses are in Luke (and Luke–Acts together have thirty-three of sixty-eight NT uses). On the other hand, Schürmann (1969: 152 nn. 36–37) relates ῥῆμα to the specific call to begin ministry, as the verbal parallelism to Jer. 1:1–4 suggests. This latter sense gives a specificity to ῥῆμα that is quite plausible here. God calls John to begin the ministry that was predicted for him. God's word again comes to pass.

The description of John as Zechariah's son recalls the story of Luke 1, where the ministry was predicted. Some suggest that the repetition of the father's name here shows that originally this pericope began Luke's Gospel, since there would be no need to mention the name if the infancy account had been written already (Schürmann 1969: 153). But this suggestion ignores one stylistically crucial feature of introducing a prophet's ministry. It was the custom in the OT to mention a prophet's father's name when introducing his ministry (Hos. 1:1; Joel 1:1; Zech. 1:1; Ernst 1977: 138–

---

8. Against this view is Conzelmann 1960: 18–27. See the introduction in §II.A above.

9. For discussion of Josephus's text, see Creed 1921–22; F. F. Bruce 1974: 34–35.

10. Note especially how John's father is named again in Luke 3:2, a style reminiscent of the OT.

39).[11] Thus, the name's inclusion reinforces the prophetic theme and, accordingly, inclusion need not suggest that Luke's Gospel originally started here. Marshall (1978: 135) notes that the form in which the reference to Zechariah is made may have Semitic origins since the use of υἱόν (*huion*, son) is superfluous in Greek style. If this is correct, then the tradition that Luke is dealing with could be an old one.

God's call comes in the desert, which is where John has been for some time (1:80). The use of ἐρήμῳ (*erēmō*, desert) raises the question of John's locale. Some pit the Gospel writers against one another or suggest that the remark is strictly a theological creation to achieve a parallel to Isa. 40 (Bultmann 1963: 246). Others argue that Luke limits John to the Jordan wilderness region, so that John does not minister where Jesus does. Regarded by Luke as the last of the OT prophets, John belongs exclusively to the era of Israel and promise (Conzelmann 1960: 18–27). But such exclusively theological approaches to the term are not profitable (Creed 1930: 50).

The Gospels are united on where John baptized and therefore where he must have ministered. Mark 1:5, Matt. 3:6, and Luke 3:3 suggest a ministry by the Jordan River. Matt. 3:1 also notes a ministry in the "wilderness of Judea," a region characterized as wilderness by Josephus (so *Jewish War* 3.10.7 §515 describes the area south of Lake Gennesaret [Sea of Galilee]). Luke's language that the word "came" (ἐγένετο, *egeneto*) to John may suggest that the call was initially received in the wilderness and followed by the mission to a broad locale, the Jordan. Thus, John's ministry involves the area just west of the northern Dead Sea (near Qumran) and extending north into the Jordan Valley proper.

But is there a theological sense to wilderness as well? The separation and ascetic motifs argued for by Conzelmann (1960: 20) are not to be accepted, since Jesus, a nonascetic (7:31–35), also clearly ministers in the wilderness, including this area (Luke 4:42; 5:16; 9:12; Wink 1968: 49; Fitzmyer 1981: 459). Any effort to see the wilderness as a figure for demonic attack (4:1–13; 8:29) is also to be rejected, since positive ministry occurs there too (3:2; 4:42; 9:12). It is possible to see the wilderness as a place of special reflection and reception of revelation: Israel received the law there, John receives his call there, and Jesus often retreats there (3:2; 4:42; 5:16; Schürmann 1969: 153 n. 40). But a unique theological emphasis on ἔρημος is not present, since many similar types of events occur in other locales. The wilderness is but one place where God works his salvation.

---

11. 2 Kings 18:1 names the father of a king discussed previously in 15:30!

Luke's summary of John's ministry contains two key features: its **3:3** itinerant character and its message of repentance as tied to baptism. The locale of John's ministry was discussed in the exegesis of 3:2b, but here Luke details the scope of John's ministry, which encompassed "the entire region of the Jordan" (πᾶσαν τὴν περίχωρον τοῦ Ἰορδάνου, *pasan tēn perichōron tou Iordanou*). Some argue that Luke separates the wilderness from the Jordan region, but this conclusion is not necessary. The "coming" (ἦλθεν, *ēlthen*) into all the region does not so much suggest entry into a new area as the scope of a wide-ranging ministry.[12] Given the Gospel of John's comments, the ministry involved both sides of the Jordan River, since Perea was also included in the ministry (John 1:28; 3:23; 10:40; Marshall 1978: 135).

The Lucan portrayal of John stresses John's message more than it does his baptism. Luke 3:7–18 details the message. Here is a prophet who brings God's message to his people. But even in 3:3, the baptism that John brings is also associated with a message—"repentance" (μετανοίας, *metanoias*) This is not only a characteristic of John's ministry, but also a key term for Luke. The product of repentance, as far as John is concerned, is elaborated in the comments found in 3:10–14. It is reflected in a concern for one's fellow humans, which makes an effort to meet needs. It is motivated by a preparation for God's coming and the possibility of God's wrath (3:7–9). Repentance produces a life lived with a sense of responsibility before a sovereign God. It is an internal attitude that aims at a product. The term itself, given the Semitic setting of John's ministry, is related to the Hebrew term שׁוּב (*šûb*, to turn). This idea in a religious context speaks of a reorientation of one's perspective from sin to God (1 Kings 8:47; 13:33; 2 Kings 23:25; Ps. 78:34; Isa. 6:10; Ezek. 3:19; Amos 4:6, 8).[13] Though μετάνοια does not occur in these OT passages in the LXX, the term *repentance* probably summarizes best the Semitic prophets' calls to the nation about what is necessary to deal with sin. John's call is parallel. The term will be a part of Jesus' Great Commission in Luke 24:47, showing that the reorientation to which John calls his audience is part of the apostolic ministry. The emphasis existed throughout Jesus' ministry (the noun in 5:32; 15:7; the verb in 10:13; 11:32; 13:3, 5; 15:7, 10; 16:30;

---

12. Against this view is Schürmann 1969: 155; in favor of a wide-ranging minstry is Marshall 1978: 135. The reference to the entire region suggests that Marshall is correct.

13. The OT term is often translated "turn" or "return." One could easily paraphrase the idea as a change in one's point of view. Such a change manifests itself concretely in action according to Luke 3:10–14 and Acts 26:20. On the ethical thrust of such rites in Judaism, see Dahl 1955. Jesus made it clear that the church's concept and message of repentance are rooted in the OT (Luke 24:44–47).

17:3, 4).[14] The Lucan passages tied to Jesus' ministry have a prophetic ring to them, since events of Jesus' ministry often compare to the prophets' work in Israel. John challenged his Jewish audience to change their thinking. Such reorienting of their relationship to God meant they were to live differently.

Comparisons with other washings of the first century are among the proposals regarding the nature of John's baptism:

1. As suggested in the additional note on 3:2, John's baptism is sometimes compared with the Essene practice at Qumran (Fitzmyer 1981: 459–60; Gnilka 1961–62; Nolland 1989: 141–42). Fitzmyer argues that it is not clear that John's baptism was a once-and-for-all exercise, and so the comparison to multiple baptisms at Qumran is possible. However, the nature of John's baptism, which we shall consider shortly, suggests that it was a one-time rite.

2. Another suggested comparison is proselyte baptism, which was an initiatory ceremony for Gentiles who decided to become Jews (Jeremias 1949; Jeremias 1929b). This comparison also has major problems. First, it is not clear that such a baptism was practiced in the first century (Fitzmyer 1981: 460), although the Ethiopian eunuch's response to Philip in Acts 8 might suggest an awareness of such a practice. More importantly, John's appeal is made to children of the covenant, to Israelites, not to outsiders. What seems to be in view here is not so much an initiatory rite as a reaffirmation of one's commitment to God, a reaffirmation that also reflects one's true relationship to God (or else the warning of Luke 3:7–9 does not make sense). However, another point is important. Failure to heed John is serious and results in judgment. To reject God's prophet is to show one's real position, a position outside covenant blessing regardless of one's heritage. In this sense, the baptism does have an "entry" flavor to it. John's call is aimed at the true remnant, while those who refuse him expose where they really are.

3. Schürmann's proposal (1969: 156–57) seems the most satisfactory. John's baptism is unique to him and is grounded in his prophetic office. It is a call to commitment and includes a recognition that God is coming. It is neither the washing of a separated covenant community (Qumran) nor an initiatory rite (proselytes). Unlike traditional Judaism, it is not a reli-

14. Creed 1930: 50; Nolland 1989: 141. Tiede 1988: 86 notes the emphasis this idea has in Acts (2:38; 3:19; 5:31; 8:22; 11:18; 17:30; 20:21; 26:20).

gious act related to bringing sacrifices. Rather, it is an affirmation, a washing that looks with hope for God's coming and lives in light of one's relationship to him. This attitude is much like the NT emphasis on a life of faith.

The final characteristic mentioned about this baptism is its goal. It is directed toward, εἰς (*eis*, for), the forgiveness of sins. This statement could be read to suggest that some type of total forgiveness and efficacy is found in John's baptism that makes the experience one of "becoming saved." However, this understanding reads back more into the event than the time of the event and the presentation of Luke will allow. John is a preparatory figure (1:17, 76–77; Schürmann 1969: 154–57). He prepares a people for God. Most importantly, John says that his baptism is nothing compared to the baptism that the Mightier One brings (3:16). So John's baptism is a prophetic eschatological washing; that is, it is a baptism of promise that looks to the greater baptism of the Spirit (Schürmann 1969: 158–60). It points forward to the cleansing that comes to those who respond to Messiah's offer with faith. This association of Spirit and cleansing was mentioned in the OT (Ezek. 36:25–27; Zech. 13:1). The washing in the Jordan adds symbolism, picturing either repentance (Isa. 1:16–17; Jer. 4:14) or divine cleansing (Ps. 51:7–9 [51:9–11 MT]; Isa. 4:2–6; Ezek. 37:23; Jer. 33:8; Jub. 1.23) or, perhaps, both (Nolland 1989: 141).

If there be any doubt that Luke understands John in this prophetic and eschatological fashion, a glance at Acts 19:1–10 ends any such uncertainty. Disciples who know only of John are to accept immediately the baptism tied to Jesus. Acts 19:4 makes it clear that John's baptism is not complete in itself, but points to faith in Jesus (also Acts 13:24). Thus, John's baptism represented for its precross Israelite audience a commitment to a new approach to God resulting in a life of fruitfulness for God and expectation of the eschaton. Such life expressed compassion to all and looked for the definitive Spirit baptism. This baptism to come is "the promise of the Father," the baptism that comes to all who turn to Jesus (Luke 24:44–49 with Acts 2:1–39). This fundamental promise and indicator of the arrival of God's eschatological kingdom was a constant hope offered in the preaching of John, Jesus, and the church. In short, John's baptism was a step on the way to the Promised One's forgiveness. The repentance in view here will not only make one alter the way one lives, but also will cause one to see "the Mightier One to come" as the promise of God. To submit to this baptism is to confess one's commitment to this perspective. This is the essence of John's baptism of repentance for the forgiveness of sins.

c. Isaiah's Promise of a Preparer for Salvation (3:4–6)

3:4 Luke 3:4–6 describes the divine significance of John's ministry. Luke sees here the fulfillment of Isa. 40:3–5. The formula ὡς γέγραπται (*hōs gegraptai*, as it is written) introduces the fulfillment that Luke sees present here (Acts 13:33; Schürmann 1969: 154 n. 49). The formula is a standard way for Jewish writers to cite venerated texts (2 Chron. 35:12; 1QS 5.17; 8.14; 4Q174 [= 4QFlor] 1.15; Fitzmyer 1981: 460). Luke sees in John the fulfillment of the "teaching" (λόγων, *logōn*) of Isaiah. In mentioning the OT text at this point, he parallels the presentation of Matt. 3:1–4 in describing John the Baptist first and then mentioning the OT. Mark, on the other hand, mentions the Isaianic fulfillment first and also notes Mal. 3:1 before describing John. Luke saves the Malachi text for Luke 7:27, which describes an Elijah-like figure who will precede the coming of God's deliverance. Danker (1988: 87) argues that Luke is purposefully removing any apocalyptic expectations for his audience. But this is overstated in light of Luke's use of Malachi in 7:27 and the use of returning Elijah imagery in 1:17. The Synoptics see John as a fulfillment figure pointing to salvation's arrival. Luke is most explicit since only he includes Isa. 40:3–5.

Luke's usage of the text is debated. Some claim that Luke and the early church before him used the LXX version to indicate that the Baptist's desert ministry was a fulfillment of this passage (Stendahl 1954: 48). At issue here are four points: (1) the syntax of the phrase ἐν τῇ ἐρήμῳ (*en tē erēmō*, in the wilderness), (2) the figure of "clearing the way of the Lord," (3) the mention of salvation, and (4) the event of the Isaiah context (see the additional note and Bock 1987: 95–97).

Several points are worth noting about the syntax of the phrase ἐν τῇ ἐρήμῳ. First, the phrase is important to Luke, since it recalls the wording of 3:2b (by *gezerah shewah*). Next, the dispute whether Isaiah said, "A voice crying in the wilderness" (so LXX), or, "A voice is crying, 'Prepare a way in the wilderness'" (so MT), is an old one, but Jewish materials can be found supporting each rendering. Qumran texts (1QS 9.19–20; 8.14) support the MT, while rabbinic texts can be cited that support the LXX, showing that the Greek translation reflects an ancient Semitic dispute.[15] Thus the LXX may preserve the original sense; but to insist on this is not appropriate, since the MT parallelism is against it. Finally and most importantly, that John's desert ministry fulfilled Isaiah is possible with either render-

---

15. SB 1:96–97; 2:154; Midr. Lam. 1.2 (49a); *Leqaḥ Tob* on Num. 24:17 (2.129b, 130a) (see Strack and Stemberger 1991: 389–90); *Pesikta Rabbati* 29/30B.4 (139b) (= Braude 1968: 587–90). On the OT roots of the concept of renewal in the wilderness, see Ezek. 20:33–38; Hos. 2:14–23 [2:16–25 MT]; Nolland 1989: 143; Mauser 1963.

ing, since if a call were made to prepare in the desert, the response would include a desert locale. A ministry in the desert is not ruled out by the MT's wording. Thus, the LXX is not necessary to establish the text's fulfillment. Stendahl (1954: 48) is wrong to insist on the LXX's necessity for the development of this teaching, though it is fair to say the point is clearer in the LXX. Nonetheless, the tradition of John's association with Isa. 40 can predate the church's expansion into Greek-speaking regions.

In regard to point 2, the figures concerning the clearing of the way are standard ancient Near Eastern metaphors about clearing the way for the entry of a king or a god (Westermann 1969: 38; Godet 1875: 1.173). The clearing prepares for the glorious entry of the sovereign figure. It is usually taken in Isaiah to refer to God's going before his exiles and allowing them to return to the land following the Babylonian captivity (Luce 1933: 109; Ernst 1977: 140; Westermann 1969: 38; Isa. 35:8; 62:10; 57:14). To take the figure exclusively in this physical, pictorial sense has problems. If the people are led by God (Isa. 40:11), how can they clear a path in front of him? And how is the physical leveling described in the passage humanly possible for people? Von Rad's proposal (1962–65: 2.243) that the passage addresses angels seems to ignore that the message given here is to the nation (Isa. 40:2–9). The text seems to be a call for creation to prepare for God's coming. But if so, how do people get prepared? It would seem better to take the figure as more than a metaphor for preparing a road for a sovereign's entry. In other words, the actual picture has a more significant spiritual referent.

Seeing the passage as the introduction to the whole of Isa. 40–66 may help. The figures in the verse are better taken as a call for a morally prepared people, as Isa. 49:8–11, 52:11–12, 62:6–10, and especially 57:14–17 show. Preparation is a call to prepare morally for God's coming (North 1964: 74–75, who looks back as well to Isa. 35:8–10). In other words, the highway that clears the way for God's coming is a purified heart.

In regard to the third point, Luke's reference to salvation is the rendering of a term (Isaiah's "glory") by a contextual equivalent. This technique was common in Judaism and need not be seen as a violation of the passage's sense. In fact, if one reads on in the MT, one can see that Isaiah's topic in this section is salvation (Isa. 40:10–11). Thus, to refer earlier in the text to God's salvation is not a violation of the passage's sense, especially since Isa. 40:1–11 argues that God's glory is demonstrated to all because he brings salvation. Thus, a reference here to salvation is entirely appropriate.

The fourth and last question is the key one. What event is in view for Isaiah? First, it ought to be noted that in first-century Judaism this text was seen by various groups of Jews as referring to ultimate salvation.[16] A salvific understanding of this text is found at Qumran, where the text is seen to be a call to study the law before the Lord comes (1QS 9.19–20; 8.14–15). A reference to the end is also seen in Bar. 5:7 and T. Moses 10.3–4. Rabbinic materials continue this trend (*Pesikta Rabbati* 29/30A, 29/30 B, 30, 33 [= Braude 1968: 570–97, 625–61]; and Midr. Lev. 1.14). The question is whether this understanding emerged from Isaiah.

Clearly much of Isa. 40–66 deals with the setting of the Babylonian exile, as the specific reference to Cyrus as God's anointed makes clear (Isa. 45:1–2). However, the description of events in this section pictures a new exodus (Isa. 42:13; 48:21; 52:12; esp. 43:16–19). This section of Isaiah declares that God is repeating the fundamental pattern of his salvation, an exodus like that which formed the nation. Such action suggests the faithfulness of God (Isa. 40:6–8). The salvation depicted here is comprehensive, so complete that anyone reading in Isaiah and thinking of God's faithfulness would be led to see a reference to God's ultimate work of salvation. What Isaiah describes is not just a reference to release from the Babylonian captivity, but to what it pictures—a salvation so complete that one is driven to think of God's decisive act of salvation as well (Hendriksen 1978: 202; Geldenhuys 1951: 137).[17] When one reads Isa. 40:3–5 in the light of the entire section, a broad-ranging prophecy emerges from the wording.

The problem of explaining the Isaiah passage may emerge from asking too narrow a question: What *event* (singular) is in view here? The text seems to speak of various periods (and thus *events*) at the same time. Isaiah discusses how God repeatedly saves his people in a pattern like the exodus. God did it in the Babylonian period, but the language of these texts looks for a more complete vindication that Luke now proclaims is about to be fulfilled. Therefore, when Luke sees in John's ministry the fulfillment of Isaiah, he sees fulfillment of a section that ultimately hoped for God's final salvation. Clearly, Luke is faithful to the long-term hope of the OT.

Now the Lucan usage of this text becomes clear. The fulfillment figure who cries out in the wilderness is John the Baptist. The prep-

---

16. Snodgrass 1980 analyzes the use of this text in the OT, LXX, Targums, Dead Sea Scrolls, Apocrypha, Pseudepigrapha, and rabbinic literature. In the Jewish view, it often looked to end-time salvation.

17. Such a "pattern" rendering of OT events fits the OT prophetic hope, where the message of a prophet is read in light of a larger context of the book or in light of the whole of the OT. It is biblical typology in the proper sense of the term; Foulkes 1958 and Goppelt 1982. For more on the hermeneutics of the OT use in the NT, see Bock 1985.

aration of the Lord's way and the making of straight paths for him mean clearing the way for God's coming. The heart that turns in repentance is to express itself in concrete acts and await God's deliverance. The reuse of Isaiah's verb ποιέω (*poieō*, to make) in Luke 3:8, 9, 10, 11, 12, 14 makes it clear that this ethical sense of repentance is primarily in view. This kind of stitching together of OT text to NT exposition is common (2 Cor. 3; Eph. 4:7–11; 1 Pet. 2:4–10; by *gezerah shewah*). It helps to explain why Luke lengthened the quotation. To "make" a highway for the Lord is to be morally ready for his coming (Luke 1:17). John's ministry centers in a call to repentance. In other words, Luke is not just interested in the universal emphasis in 3:6; the whole quotation is important.

Luke's text differs from the LXX in one respect, which he shares with Mark 1:2 and Matt. 3:3. Rather than speaking of going before "our God," as the MT and the LXX do, the evangelists speak of going before "him." Virtually every recent commentator takes this change to be christologically motivated, so that the idea is that John goes before Jesus (Danker 1988: 84 is the only exception). However, such a conclusion, though possible, does not seem likely, at least for Luke. As was pointed out earlier, αὐτοῦ (*autou*, him) in Luke 1:17 is God. In the Luke 3 context, the nearness of God's judgment follows this citation (3:7–8). In the Baptist's view, this is something that God does. Even more to the point is that all flesh see God's salvation in 3:6. When one puts 3:6 with 3:15–16, Luke is saying that God's salvation is seen in the Spirit baptism that Christ brings. This idea parallels the infancy section; namely, that in Christ the salvation of *God* comes (2:26, 30). Luke's presentation of salvation is consistent. John, the herald of God, calls for moral preparation in the wilderness before God brings his salvation in Messiah. God again is at work, bringing his promise to pass. What people see—and are to see—in Jesus are the hand and coming of God himself.

3:5 Isaiah's picture of preparing for God's salvation is a supernatural preparing of a highway. The leveling of the geographic obstacles is a way of portraying God's coming as powerful and without obstruction. Just as God parted the sea in the exodus, so he will remove all of creation's obstacles for his people as he delivers them. There are several key passages in Isaiah that use one or another of these images. The highway as a means of access to God and his city is found in Isa. 57:14 and 62:10. Isaiah 57:14–17 is especially important, since the image of clearing the way for God's people is present alongside a picture of his people as humble and lowly. Thus, the way is cleared for a humble and righteous people; the imagery has ethical dimensions.

Other passages give background. Isaiah 2 presents the fundamental picture of the Lord's mountain raised up for all to see. All nations are to come to the mountain to learn the ways of God. There will be a period of peace and harmony, which pictures the total salvation that God brings. But in the latter portion of the chapter, the haughty and proud are brought low, as the Lord shakes the earth (Isa. 2:6–22). Thus, the geographic leveling not only clears a path for God's entry, it pictures the severity of God's coming as well. It shows the prospect of judgment for the proud. The expression *brought low* in Isa. 2:9, 11, 12, 17 is the same term used in Isa. 40:4 for the laying low of the mountains.

The clearest passage on geographical reorganization is Isa. 42:14–17. God clears a path to lead the blind, as he will not forsake his people. But those who pursue idols will be put to shame. Isaiah 42:16 repeats an image of Isa. 40:4 in making the rough places smooth (see also Isa. 63:11–14, for God's clearing a path in the exodus).

These texts in Isaiah explain the image. God is preparing to clear a highway for his people, as he comes in power to redeem them. Total victory is in view. Those who will share in the victory are the humble and the blind, those who recognize the need for and who depend upon God. But such leveling of obstacles also will crush the proud and destroy those committed to idolatry. Physical and ethical images merge. The images call the hearer of John's message to realize that God is coming in judgment and that only the humble who rely on him will be spared.

Other images of Luke 3 support this call "to be ready or else." The message in 3:7–9 points to the nearness of God's judgment and issues a call to prepare for it. But alongside the warning are promises about the forgiveness of sins (3:3) and about the Spirit's coming for anyone who realizes that John points to another (3:10–17).

Interestingly some terms in this citation or their synonyms turn up in other Lucan passages with a distinctly ethical force. Εὐθύς (*euthys*, straight; Luke 3:4, 5) is used in Acts to evaluate key figures who are rebuked for not making their paths straight or "right" (Acts 8:21 [Simon Magus]; 13:10 [Sergius Paulus]). Ταπεινόω (*tapeinoō*, to bring low; Luke 3:5) also has an ethical flavor later in Luke 14:11 and 18:14, a usage that looks like some of the passages from Isaiah (2:9, 11, 17; 13:11; 26:4–6). Finally, σκολιός (*skolios*, crooked; Luke 3:5) in Acts 2:40 describes the character of the current generation that faces the prospect of God's judgment. Other NT writers also use the term this way: Phil. 2:15; 1 Pet. 2:18. The point is not that all these images are present in Luke 3, but that this leveling imagery has ethical overtones. The physical imagery conveys ethical realities.

One more observation is key. In 3:4b there is a call to others to prepare the road, while in 3:5 the stress is on what will happen as a result of God's activity. Luke 3:5 pictures God's powerful coming to his people, a coming for which humans are to prepare themselves ethically. This arrival, as understood by first-century Jews, would have brought expectations of the great day of the Lord (Isa. 2:6–22). The Isa. 40 picture of geographic leveling suggests the day's coming, but the sequence of related events was to work itself out in a surprising way, as Luke will develop in his two volumes. Luke will show that some aspects that anticipate the day come now, while others come later.

Luke concludes the citation with a focus on all people. This conclu-   **3:6**
sion is crucial for him and is a major reason for citing a longer portion of Isa. 40. The reference to σωτήριον (sōtērion, salvation) reflects the LXX and replaces the MT's reference to the glory of God (see additional note on 3:4). Speculation exists about the change. Marshall (1978: 137) suggests that Luke possibly did not see God's glory revealed in Jesus' earthly ministry, but this explanation seems very unlikely in light of 19:37, where praise is offered for God's powerful work in that ministry. It is better to see salvation as the consciously chosen, less abstract equivalent for manifesting the glory of God. The LXX's rendering, which Luke follows, may have been motivated by a desire to show how God's glory is manifested; that is, God's glory is seen in his salvation. It also may have resulted from the LXX's tendency to make God more distant and transcendent. The choice of the alternative rendering, however, accurately reflects Isaiah. God's display of salvation before all is something Luke has already suggested (2:30–31). It is a fundamental concern of his book.

Putting the entire Isaiah quotation together, one sees that John calls the humble to prepare for God's powerful coming. After John's ministry comes a manifestation of power, the salvation of God. As 2:30 shows, God's salvation resides in Jesus. This salvation is available to all (2:31–32). While the people are called to prepare (ἑτοιμά-σατε, hetoimasate) in 3:4 for God's salvation, in 2:31 God prepares (ἡτοίμασας, hētoimasas) salvation for them in a special person (Acts 28:28; Foerster, TDNT 7:1023).

Is Luke directly responsible for the lengthening of the Isaiah citation? Most see Luke's interest in the universality of salvation as sufficient reason for arguing that he is the source of the expansion (Ernst 1977: 140; Fitzmyer 1981: 461; Marshall 1978: 137). Schürmann (1969: 161) is the only recent voice of dissent, suggesting an omission by the other evangelists. He notes that nowhere else do we see Luke expanding Synoptic material using the OT. He also argues that Matthew does not see John as a salvation messenger, but merely as a preacher of repentance. The question is complex since the citation that Luke uses does not seem to be from his own hand, as the additional note on 3:4 shows. However, Schürmann's attempt to explain why Matthew would omit the longer text is not convincing, since John in Matthew does preach the nearness of God's kingdom (Matt. 3:2). Schürmann does not explain why Mark also has a short quotation.

The question is this: Did the full Isa. 40 citation come as part of a tradition associated with John the Baptist? There is no way to answer the question. It is possible that Luke came in contact with traditional materials that Matthew or Mark lacked. It is possible he made the association himself. What is clear is that only Luke develops the Isa. 40 citation so fully. John's ministry is a call to repent, as God's powerful and promised salvation draws near.

Summary   Luke 3:1–6 shows that in about A.D. 29, God sent a prophet to the northern Dead Sea and the Jordan River. John the Baptist preached a unique baptism, a washing of preparation for the coming of God's salvation. Such preparation involved a change of thinking that in turn changed the way one lived before God. The baptism's goal looked forward to the forgiveness of sins that God would offer in his salvation. This forgiveness is tied to the greater, yet-to-come baptism brought by one stronger than John (3:15–17). The language by John here is vague, but the event, set as it is after Luke 1–2, makes it clear that the one to come will be Jesus. John's ministry reflects the repetition of a basic salvation pattern of God, a second exodus, which Isaiah describes. It fulfills the promise of a voice calling the people to prepare for God's powerful coming in salvation. Those who wish to see God's hand must be prepared to listen for him. Part of that readiness means knowing one's real spiritual status before God and having a sense of humility that drives one to seek God's forgiveness. Those who submitted to John's baptism were not proud but realistically humble. They sensed that God's coming demands preparation from the heart. Luke wishes the reader to note this exemplary attitude. For God comes to the humble who will acknowledge who they really are before him. In fact, God exalts the humble who rest in his promise (1:52–54).

Additional Notes

3:2. In the additional note on 1:80, I concluded that John was not an Essene. Another related issue is the historical significance of this Jordan location. If John ministered and lived in this region, did he have contact with what was probably an Essene separatist sect at Qumran? The possible connection is suggested by this movement's also seeing its ministry in terms of Isa. 40 and by its washings of purification tied to repentance.[18] Such contact is possible, but it is less than likely that the sect influenced John. For one thing the character of the washings at Qumran seems to be different from John's baptism, in that Qumran had more than one washing. In addition, such washings were required to maintain a good standing before God, as well as for establishing membership in the community.[19] In contrast, John seems to be pointing to a singular baptism for a specific event, the coming of God (LaSor 1972: 149–51). The use of Isaiah at Qumran focused on commitment to the study of the law and separation from the world, while John's message is directly ethical and assumes loving involvement with people (1QS 9.19–21 vs. Luke 3:10–14). In addition, it is to be noted that John's ascetic lifestyle, which Luke does not mention here but is noted in Mark 1:6, differs from that of Qumran (LaSor 1972: 146). It is possible that John had contact with the Qumran community, but it is unlikely that he was a disciple of the sect or that he lived with them at any time, if his beliefs here indicate his background. What Qumran does show is that when John preached, he approached the Jewish people in terms they could understand. Not only did he call them as a prophet would, but he also made use of rites and concepts that were similar to those used in the contemporary culture. It is to be noted that John's use of these concepts took on unique emphases that were distinct from contemporary alternatives, emphases that involved humility before God and sensitivity to others (3:10–14). Yet his message was well contextualized.

3:3. John's role as baptizer and prophet has recently received detailed attention. Webb's 1991 study, a careful consideration of the historical John the Baptist, places John in the context of second-temple practice.[20] Webb (pp. 214–16) argues that John's baptism had six functions. (1) It expressed a "person's conversionary repentance," a turning to God from a sinful lifestyle. This new relationship with God was to produce a new, righteous lifestyle. (2) God's response to this choice to be baptized was to give forgiveness of sins. (3) The past life was understood as a "moral contagion" that made the person "unclean," so the washing of baptism was required for

---

18. On Isa. 40: 1QS 8.12–15; 9.19–21; on repentance: 1QS 5.13–14; 3.1–9; on the baptisms of cleansing: CD 10.10–13.

19. 1QS 5.13; Josephus, *Jewish War* 2.8.2–13 §§119–61. Bringing Josephus's description into consideration assumes that the Qumran community is Essene, a stance defended by Dupont-Sommer 1961: 39–67. Despite recent objections raised because of the find of *Miqsāt Maʿăśê Tôrâ* (4QMMT) at Qumran, this is still the best option.

20. This book appeared too late to integrate well into the exegetical discussion, so I note it here. His general view parallels the "eschatological prophetic" role I described.

cleansing. (4) The baptism foreshadowed the expected figure's greater baptism. (5) It separated the repentant from the unrepentant. (6) It represented a protest against temple abuse and so questioned the validity of some temple activity. In Webb's view (pp. 261–306), John saw the expected figure as the agent of Yahweh who represented Yahweh's coming. This figure would bring judgment and restoration. That this expectation explicitly included for John a "messianic" element is less certain for Webb, given the six possible categories a Jew might have thought of for such eschatological activity.[21] However, Webb avers that this is the interpretation of the NT and that "it may well be that this interpretation has historical validity after all" (p. 383). With regard to John's prophetic function, Webb (pp. 307–48) sees John functioning like a "leadership popular prophet." Prophets in this category led large peasant movements, faced opposition that led eventually to martyrdom, preached deliverance, surrounded themselves in symbolism to depict this deliverance, drew pictures from the history of the nation, and delivered some form of oracle that was perceived as coming from God.

3:4. The Isa. 40 citation is closest to the LXX reflected in manuscript Alexandrinus (Holtz 1968: 37–39). There are four points where this version is followed against the MT. Two are key: (1) the connection of ἐν τῇ ἐρήμῳ to the voice and not to the call of preparation and (2) the insertion of a reference to salvation. However, the MT is followed at one point over the LXX.[22] Also, Luke alters the LXX rendering at two key points: (1) the reference to "the paths of our God" is rendered "his paths" and (2) the phrase about the glory of God is omitted. The significance of the LXX/MT differences and of the Lucan alterations was treated in the exegesis of 3:4. The differences indicate that Luke uses a somewhat independent text. The trace of a Semitic connection makes it unlikely that the text is a Lucan formulation. Rather, the text is probably drawn from a traditional source.

---

21. His six categories (pp. 254–60) are Yahweh returning through a future agent, Davidic Messiah, Aaronic Messiah, Michael/Melchizedek, Son of Man, and Elijah *redivivus*. Of the focused categories that Webb examines, the closest correspondences occur in the Son of Man and Davidic Messiah categories, though the category that has the most contact with John's expectation is Yahweh returning through an agent.

22. Bock 1987: 94–95 discusses the details and shows that the plural term τραχεῖαι of 3:5 is closer to the Hebrew plural than to the LXX's singular.

2. Preaching of John the Baptist (3:7–14)

After introducing John the Baptist in 3:1–6, Luke now gives the reader a glimpse of his ministry. In the next two sections, Luke highlights two elements of that ministry: in 3:7–14 John preaches about the approach of God's judgment and about the need for repentance, and in 3:15–18 Luke presents John's preaching about the Coming One and the greater baptism that comes with him. These two sections show how John's ministry fulfilled what Isaiah promised about a preparatory prophet (Isa. 40:3–5 in Luke 3:4–6).

Luke 3:7–14 may be divided into two sections. Luke 3:7–9 gives John's prophetic preaching on God's coming wrath. Here John uses day-of-the-Lord imagery. The nearness of judgment causes John to call for true repentance, while warning that racial heritage alone is not good enough to escape God's wrath. Luke 3:10–14 gives the crowd's response, along with John's elaboration on what repentance means. In addition, this section ties into the previous one through the repeated use of ποιέω (poieō, to do or make) in 3:8, 9, 10, 11, 12, 14. It probably also ties back to 3:4b, where making the paths for the Lord has an ethical thrust. John's goal is "a prepared people" (1:17). Preparation means humble submission before God.

Sources and Historicity

The two sections of this pericope reflect two distinct sources. Luke 3:7–9 agrees almost verbatim with Matt. 3:7–10.[1] So Luke either uses Matthew or a source shared with Matthew. It is unlikely that independent or oral testimony is present, since independent testimony would not have been so exact. In many scholarly treatments, the source that Luke and Matthew are said to have in common is called Q.[2] Whatever one may think of Q as a uni-

---

1. Aland 1985: §14. After the introduction to the pericope, there are only three differences: Luke 3:8 has the plural *fruits*, while Matt. 3:8 has the singular *fruit*; Luke 3:8 has *do not begin to say*, while Matt. 3:8 has *do not think to say*; and Luke 3:9 has an extra conjunction *and*.

2. See, e.g., the treatments of Creed 1930: lvi–lxx; Klostermann 1929: 49; Fitzmyer 1981: 75–81. Detailed studies are Schulz 1972; Polag 1982; Kloppenberg 1988; and Kloppenberg 1987. A commentary on Q is Manson 1949. On the rationale for Q, see Stein 1987. These analyses differ in detail and approach, but all agree that an independent source or set of sources is involved.

fied written document or even as a historical entity, it is clear that in 3:7–9, Matthew and Luke are working with a similar tradition. A consideration of how this commentary handles Matthew and Q as sources for Luke may be found in excursus 4.

The material in 3:10–14 is unique to Luke. The tradition's origin is uncertain, though to regard it as late, as Bultmann does, because of the mention of soldiers in 3:14 is incorrect.[3] Neither is Schulz's reason of the anti-Jewish polemic persuasive, since John's conflict with Israel's leadership is clearly historical.[4] John's presence in Josephus shows that he made an impact on Israel (*Antiquities* 18.5.2 §§116–19). Luke clearly had access to old material in both 3:7–9 and 3:10–14.[5] Luke 3:10–14 shows how John explained his baptismal rite. John does not discuss the mode of baptism but only the spiritual, ethical response that one is to have as a result of being baptized. The point shows where John's interest lies. Unlike Matthew and Mark, Luke does not have John cry out about the nearness of the kingdom. Rather, he leaves kingdom preaching to Jesus (Liefeld 1984: 855). However, the account coheres with the Synoptics and is authentic.

One final feature to note about this section, especially 3:7–10, is the presence of wilderness imagery: stones, barren trees, snakes (Plummer 1896: 89). John uses the setting of his surroundings as he speaks about spiritual realities.

In thinking of the form of the material, various descriptions are helpful. Luke 3:7–9 is a prophetic warning, like those in the OT (Berger 1984: 195). Luke 3:10–14 is an exhortation about the product of repentance. Both sayings together could be called pronouncement accounts, since authoritative sayings dominate

---

3. Bultmann 1963: 145 argues that the account is a product of the late Hellenistic church. See the first additional note on 3:10.

4. Schulz 1972: 371 n. 321, who also regards the material as late because of its pronouncement form and its orientation of John as subordinate to Jesus. However, the OT prophets are loaded with such pronouncements, and the view that the subordination of John to Jesus reflects late material turns on an approach that rejects the historical character of the tradition of Luke 1–3, a position discussed in the sources and historicity sections of 1:5–25 and 3:1–6, the additional notes on 1:25 and 3:3, and excursus 1.

5. It is possible that Luke described the dialogue in 3:12–14 with his own words, but the call for concrete repentance fits the work of a prophet. Ernst 1977: 143 argues that the question-and-answer style and the theme of care for fellow humans are like Luke. However, more likely is that the material has a traditional base, since the style is not as Lucan as Ernst suggests. So correctly argues Schürmann 1969: 169 n. 53, who with Marshall 1978: 142 notes numerous peculiarities that Luke does not have elsewhere. The Semitisms in 3:7–9 suggest the age of the material; see the exegesis of 3:8–9 for details.

(Berger 1984: 81).[6] Bovon (1989: 171) prefers the description "chain of sayings" for 3:7–9 since there is no dialogue or challenge to set up the saying.[7] Wiefel (1988: 89) speaks of a call to turn and an ethical exhortation.

The outline of Luke 3:7–14 is as follows:

a. Warning of God's judgment and a call to repentance (3:7–9)
    i. The rebuke that is a warning about judgment (3:7)
    ii. The call to make fruit worthy of repentance (3:8a)
    iii. The warning not to rely on ancestry (3:8b)
    iv. The second reminder of judgment (3:9)
b. The appropriate fruit of repentance (3:10–14)
    i. Fruit of repentance described for the crowd (3:10–11)
    ii. Fruit of repentance described for tax collectors (3:12–13)
    iii. Fruit of repentance described for soldiers (3:14)

Luke 3:7–14 argues that the times tied to John (and Jesus) are inseparably linked to God's eventual judgment and that Jewish heritage does not exempt one from responding properly to God. Salvation and preparation for God's coming involve a ready heart responding to God on his terms. Religious heritage and ancestry are irrelevant before God in comparison to proper response. As a result the children of Abraham (i.e., those who know God) are not limited to a certain race, because God is able to create his children, even "out of stone." God's children are not born at physical birth, but are transformed from the heart. Finally, the fruit of appropriate repentance shows itself in how one treats others. The concrete character of the exhortation leads to many practical themes about walking with God.

John's call for repentance is preparatory for the greater baptism and message of God to come in Jesus (3:15–18). Though their ministries function in continuity to one another, John's ministry is not in itself normative today, since it was a precross ministry that could not address salvation in terms of resurrection realities or expectations. Nevertheless, the attitude demanded by John is illustrative of key concepts that Luke will develop, and thus his ministry foreshadows work that Jesus and his followers will do (3:10–18; 24:44–49).

6. The technical name used for such pronouncement accounts is apophthegm. Luke 3:7–9 is more a controversy or polemic saying, since it challenges. The other sayings in 3:10–14 are exhortations. For an examination of form criticism and its terminology, see Bock 1991b.
7. He sees these remarks as inserted into the account.

Exegesis and Exposition

[7]Now he was saying to the crowd, which had come out to be baptized by him, "Sons of snakes, who told you to flee from the coming wrath? [8]Therefore make fruit worthy of repentance; and do not begin to say within yourselves, 'We have a father, Abraham,' for I say to you that God is able to raise up children for Abraham from these stones. [9]And already the ax is laid and aimed at the root of the tree; therefore every tree not making good fruit is cut down and cast into the fire."

[10]And the crowd was asking him, "What shall we do?" [11]And he said to them, "The one who has two undergarments, let him give to the one who does not have any; and the one who has food, do likewise."

[12]And the tax collectors also came to be baptized by him and said to him, "Teacher, what shall we do?" [13]And he said to them, "Exact nothing more than has been appointed to you."

[14]And the soldiers also were asking him, "What also shall we do?" And he said to them, "Do not rob anyone by violence or by fraudulent extortion, and be content with your wages."

a. Warning of God's Judgment and a Call to Repentance (3:7–9)
i. The Rebuke That Is a Warning about Judgment (3:7)

3:7   John turns and addresses the crowd, which sought his baptism. The imperfect ἔλεγεν (*elegen*, he was saying) has been taken in a couple of ways. Plummer (1896: 88) argues that the durative tense suggests a summary of what John said on several occasions (also Godet 1875: 1.175). This sense is possible, but not likely. Luke uses the imperfect ἔλεγεν so often that a vivid usage is more likely (6:20; 9:23; 10:2; 12:54; Marshall 1978: 138). The imperfect tense, if vivid, presents the action to the reader as in progress. The point Plummer wishes to make, however, is legitimate, even if it is not specifically made by the tense. Luke clearly intends to represent what is typical of John's preaching. Luke 3:18, which probably is a Lucan summary note, says as much. It shows that John's teaching involves more teaching than the examples of 3:7–14.

John's audience is simply called "the crowd" (ὄχλοις, *ochlois*). This may represent a summary of what the other Gospels note at other points in their presentation of John's ministry. Matthew 3:5 and Mark 1:5 note that people from throughout Judea and Jerusalem came out to him. In addition, Matt. 3:7 mentions that John specifically addressed the Sadducees and Pharisees. Some regard Luke as expanding the audience, a point that is possible, since ὄχλος is a popular word for Luke and the change fits the broad audience mentioned at other points in the other Gospels (see esp. 3:10–14).[8] Fitzmyer (1981: 467) argues that a broad audience fits the Lucan emphasis that the message is for all. Marshall (1978: 139), however, observes that Matthew tends to single out the Pharisees and Sadducees for criticism (Matt. 16:1, 6, 11–12; also Schürmann 1969: 163). So it is hard to be certain who beyond them may be in view.

The situation itself is clear enough when one looks at Matthew's wording. Matthew 3:7 says that John looked to the Pharisees and Sadducees as he spoke. One has the impression that John spoke to the crowd but focused on the Pharisees and Sadducees as he made his remarks. Or perhaps the remarks came correctly to be regarded as appropriate for the leadership, given their lack of response. What John said was said to all, as Luke notes, while Matthew points out that the religious leaders needed to heed the warning.

John's words are harsh, shocking the listeners like a prophetic woe. They are called the "sons of snakes" (of Pharisees: Matt. 12:34; of scribes and Pharisees: Matt. 23:33). The snake's poisonous and destructive nature is the point of comparison.[9] This exact figure is absent in the OT, Josephus, and the rabbis.[10] Nevertheless, the OT does have figures that refer to God's enemies as vipers (Isa. 59:5 [of Israel]; Jer. 46:22 [Egypt]; Isa. 14:29 [Philistines]). The figure appears at Qumran in 1QH 3.12–17, where it refers to the sons of Belial (Ellis 1974: 89; Schürmann 1969: 164 n. 15). If this later conceptual association is the point for John, then rather than calling his Jewish audience the chosen people, he is calling them children of the devil. They need to change or face the wrath of God (John 8:44). John addresses his audience as opposed to God if they do not prepare for his coming. Given such a condition, a remedy is needed.

Before John turns to the remedy, he makes a final comment. Retaining the figure of snakes, he mentions fleeing the coming wrath. When brush fires surface in the desert, snakes often come out of the ground to flee. John asks a provocative question as he inquires about who told them to flee the coming wrath: Are they ready to run from their holes in recognition that destructive fire draws near? The reference to wrath (ὀργῆς, *orgēs*) is an allusion to the day of the Lord when judgment comes (Isa. 13:9; 30:27; Amos 5:18–20; Zeph.

---

8. Luke uses the singular form of ὄχλος twenty-five times and the plural sixteen times in his Gospel; in Acts, the singular occurs fifteen times and the plural seven times; Marshall 1978: 138; Fitzmyer 1981: 467. Schulz 1972: 366 n. 285 is confident the change is Luke's because of his usage of this term.

9. Ps. 58:4 [58:5 MT]; 140:3; Matt. 3:7 [the parallel to this pericope]; Luce 1933: 110; Danker 1988: 86; SB 1:114–15; Foerster, *TDNT* 2:815–16. Acts 28:3 refers to a poisonous snake.

10. Fitzmyer 1981: 467; Büchsel, *TDNT* 1:672; Nolland 1989: 147. The image parallels the expression *offspring of asps* in the LXX: Isa. 11:8; 14:29; 30:6; 59:5.

2:2; Mal. 3:2; 4:1, 5 [3:19, 24 MT]; Creed 1930: 51; Nolland 1989: 148). In the NT one's position in relation to Jesus is the key to avoiding the wrath of judgment (Acts 17:29–31; 1 Thess. 1:9–10; Rom. 5:9). John sees the judgment coming, because with salvation's hope the day of judgment also comes. This is normal OT thinking.

Discussion exists over John's question, "Who told you to flee the coming wrath?" Is this a legitimate inquiry as to how they have come to sense that the day draws near?[11] Or is it a rhetorical and ironic question that doubts the sincerity of those who are coming (Marshall 1978: 139; Stählin, *TDNT* 5:444–45)? The following positive response suggests the former, while the greeting that calls them snakes favors the latter. There seems to be another way to read the question. One can see in it a real rebuke that is not designed ironically, but seeks to grab their attention and raise the question, "Do you really understand what my baptism is about?" The question is a call to see that John's message about wrath requires repentance, regardless of one's station in life. Such a response is necessary in order to escape God's judgment. The stakes in John's ministry are high. In fact, they are the highest stakes of all. Those who understand who really calls them through John will escape. Those who do not understand face God's wrath. The question presents a choice and warns the audience that God's judgment is linked to their decision.

ii. The Call to Make Fruit Worthy of Repentance (3:8a)

3:8a Luke elaborates on the need for reflection. In assessing the significance of John's ministry, the one coming to be baptized needs to consider the significance of the baptism. The issue is not a washing by water, but the response that baptism depicts. The aorist imperative ποιήσατε (*poiēsate*, make) denotes a specific call to produce fruit that is the appropriate product of repentance (Plummer 1896: 89). Real repentance manifests itself in concrete action.[12] John is after more than participation in a religious rite. The use of the plural καρπούς (*karpous*, fruits) suggests a repetitiveness to the action, while the singular καρπόν (*karpon*, fruit) in Matt. 3:8 looks at the product as a collective unit (Plummer 1896: 89). The Baptist says there is an appropriate product of repentance. Submitting to baptism from John is a commitment before God to change one's life, while awaiting the approach of God's salvation.

---

11. Schürmann 1969: 164 n. 21. On "coming wrath" in Judaism, see Jub. 15.34; Ps. Sol. 15.6; 1 Enoch 84.4–6; C. F. Evans 1990: 239.

12. Ernst 1977: 142. On "doing," see Luke 6:43–45; 13:6–9; James 1:19–25; 3:12–18; 1 Cor. 9:23; Col. 3:17.

iii. The Warning Not to Rely on Ancestry (3:8b)

In pressing for a concrete response, John offers a warning against a   **3:8b** great potential error—to rest in one's heritage rather than respond to God. The temptation to rest in Abrahamic heritage is something that ought not enter their minds. This warning is expressed with the imperative μὴ ἄρξησθε λέγειν (*mē arxēsthe legein*, do not begin to say). Such a thought should not cross their mind or their lips. The expression *speak to oneself* may reflect an original Semitism, as well as represent a common Lucan expression.[13] Abrahamic heritage was a source of pride in Judaism (2 Esdr. [= 4 Ezra] 6:56–58 [conceptually]; Josephus, *Antiquities* 3.5.3 §§87–88; Ps. Sol. 9.9; 18.3; Jub. 22.10–24; SB 1:116–21). Such heritage was thought to bring protection from God since judgment comes on the nations, not on the people of Abraham.[14] John's warning is that—at an individual level—Abrahamic heritage guarantees nothing before God. The best religious pedigree by itself is not an adequate source of protection before him. Each individual must assess himself or herself aright. By itself the richest of biological connections is worthless spiritually if the spiritual environment and exhortation are ignored.

The issue of becoming God's child is not a matter of inheritance, but of God's power and work. The explanation of the Abraham remark is introduced with the solemn phrase "for I say to you" (λέγω γὰρ ὑμῖν, *legō gar hymin*). The picture of God producing life out of an inanimate object attributes adoption into God's family to the work of God and not to the natural rights of having a certain genealogy. The stones picture dead, inanimate creation, which God brings miraculously to life. A similar vivifying of inanimate objects will reoccur in Jesus' picturesque remarks upon entering Jerusalem in 19:40. The allusion here has conceptual similarities to Isa. 51:1–2, where Abraham is referred to as the rock from which those who seek God are cut.[15] Of course, the centrality of Abraham emerges

---

13. Marshall 1978: 140; Luke 7:39, 49; 16:3; 18:4; Black 1967: 302. Manson 1949: 40 notes that the Semitism is reflected in Luke's wording, while Matthew has a more stylized Greek. The verb ἄρχω occurs in the middle voice, ἄρχομαι, meaning "to begin," thirty-one times in Luke and thirteen times in Matthew.

14. Schürmann 1969: 164; Tannehill 1986: 50, 145. The failure of such an appeal is evident in 16:24, 27, 30.

15. Fitzmyer 1981: 468. Jeremias, *TDNT* 4:269–71, notes that in later Judaism the imagery describes the creation of the nation, as Tg. Isa. 51:1 shows. Bovon 1989: 172 does not consider the allusion likely, since he sees Luke alluding to the Gentiles here. Bovon also distinguishes between a stone (here) and a rock (the OT image). Bovon is right that Luke has an implication here about Gentiles, but that still need not deny the background of the OT, especially since the Greek wording is translated out of the original setting. The OT allusion is possible, though not certain. This remark is also against a view of "covenantal nomism"; see Allison 1987. Placement into blessing is not a matter of election through mere biology.

from the promise of Gen. 12:1–3. The NT frequently charges that people rely, perhaps too much, on such a connection at a natural level, and yet there is a connection to Abraham in terms of faith that has eternal significance (Luke 16:24; John 8:33–39; Acts 7:2; Rom. 4:1; Gal. 3:29). In John's view, all must repent and come to God. Becoming a child of God is a matter of responding to God on his terms, terms that involve repentance. Comments about God's ability to produce children from rocks may suggest the possibility that God can raise up anyone of any race to respond and be his child. Luke may well be including Gentiles here.

Two notes should be made about the stone figure. First, in the picture John uses, the stones do not become children of God. Rather, God creatively produces children from them, a description that places adoption into God's family in the hands of the creator God. Second, the contrast between children and stones may conceal what would have been a wordplay in Aramaic between בְּנַיָּא (*bnyʾ*, children) and אַבְנַיָּא (*ʾbnyʾ*, stones), a second Semitism in this material that suggests its authenticity.[16] The only possible obstacle to this suggestion of wordplay is that there are two Aramaic terms for *stone*.[17] If a wordplay is behind the text, the wording betrays even more the wilderness setting and argues for an old tradition.

iv. The Second Reminder of Judgment (3:9)

3:9 John follows with an eschatological warning of great significance, since he focuses on the nearness of the approaching judgment (Fitzmyer 1981: 469). Ἤδη (*ēdē*, already) serves along with the present tense κεῖται (*keitai*, is lying) to stress the nearness of God's decisive judgment. Hendriksen (1978: 206 n. 172) notes correctly that ἤδη is in the emphatic position, since it comes first in the sentence, an emphasis heightened by its isolation from the verb it modifies. (Of its sixty-one NT uses, ἤδη begins a sentence ten times [counting the second occurrence in 1 Cor. 4:8]; of its twenty-five uses in the Synoptics, it has this position only in the parallel [Matt. 3:10] and Luke 7:6.) The implication is that John's audience may not think God's decisive judgment is near. However, it is nearer than they think, since the ax is ready to fall (Plummer 1896: 90).

The ax primed to fall is a very explicit figure for the clearing away of those who are not fruitful. The passive verb κεῖται may well suggest that God is the agent who will wield the ax (Marshall 1978:

16. Marshall 1978: 141; Black 1967: 144–45 (who notes other traces of Semitisms in Matthew).

17. Jeremias, *TDNT* 4:268, 270, tends to think NT usage is against the wordplay and cites Mark 15:46 as well as Syriac evidence as support.

141). The picture is of the ax aimed at the root.[18] If the ax falls, it will chop away at the roots, and the tree will be destroyed (Danker 1988: 87; Bovon 1989: 173; Deut. 19:5).

The removal of the fruitless vine pictures destruction, and it parallels OT use. Hosea 10:1–2 and Jer. 2:21–22 use the image to depict the nation's destruction in judgment, while Isa. 10:33–34 uses the figure to depict the removal of the Assyrians, and Amos 2:9 uses it of the Amorites (Fitzmyer 1981: 469; Creed 1930: 52; Ellis 1974: 89). The image of the fruitless or uprooted tree also occurs in the intertestamental period (Sir. 6:3; 23:25; Wis. 4:3–5 [of illegitimate children]; Marshall 1978: 141). The image of the ax that destroys also has OT roots (Ps. 74:5–6; Jer. 46:22 [by the enemy]; Bovon 1989: 173). As Luke 7:29–35 will explain, John the Baptist's ministry, like Jesus' ministry, forces choices and creates a division among people.

Black (1967: 144–45) notes that φυγεῖν (*phygein*, flee) in 3:7 and ῥίζαν (*rhizan*, root) in 3:9 make a nice wordplay in Aramaic: אֲרַק (*ᶜrq*, flee) and אִקָּר (*ᶜqr*, root).[19] The possibility of a Semitic wordplay adds to the evidence already noted for the ancient character of this tradition (see the exegesis of 3:8b).

The ax will make distinctions similar to those mentioned in 7:29–30, since it is aimed only at fruitless trees. The conclusion concerning the image of a tree and its produce is introduced by οὖν (*oun*, therefore). More than one tree is in view, since John speaks of every (πᾶν, *pan*) tree. John stresses that only the unfruitful, the unrepentant, need to be concerned about the ax's falling (3:8). They are the ones who will be cut down.[20] Jesus uses this same imagery (Luke 6:43–49; 13:7, 9; John 15:1–6). The later Lucan parallels link the produce to a proper response to Jesus, showing a continuity between John and Jesus on the theme of repentance.

The fruitless trees are not only cut down, they are cast into fire. The image of the fire of judgment also has OT roots. Both Jer. 11:16 and Ezek. 15:6–7 used the image to speak of the consuming destruction that crushed the nation and produced the exile (as a general image of judgment upon all: Isa. 66:15–16, 24; upon various nations: Amos 1–2 [seven times]; see also Nah. 1:6; Zeph. 1:18; 3:8). In

---

18. Note πρός, whose basic directional meaning is "toward"; so here "toward [at] the root."

19. Black goes on to argue that 3:9 originally followed 3:7, but such an argument is unnecessary since the imagery of 3:8–9 is the same; Schürmann 1969: 166 n. 33.

20. Grundmann, *TDNT* 3:545, though he overemphasizes baptism here. The fruit is submission to God through repentance, which in turn is productive; also Behm, *TDNT* 4:1001. The presence of more than one tree argues against seeing trees as a corporate image equal to Israel, as Maurer, *TDNT* 6:988 §4a, holds. What John says about the day of judgment applies to any unproductive person, though it is clear that John's audience is a Jewish one.

the NT as well, fire is a picture of consuming destruction (Luke 3:17; 9:54; 17:29; Matt. 5:22, 29; John 15:6). Once the ax falls in a judgment that is near, there is no hope (Lang, *TDNT* 6:941–42). Thus, the summary of John's message on repentance finishes where it started—with a graphic warning about God's coming wrath in judgment for those who fail to discern the times correctly. As Schürmann (1969: 166 n. 32) notes against H. Conzelmann, it is wrong to speak of Luke's John as preaching just about Messiah and not about judgment. For Luke, John's ministry refers to both Messiah and judgment. In fact, it is judgment that makes preparation for Messiah so imperative.

Hendriksen (1978: 206–7) raises a practical question about this unit. How is one to evaluate John's message in light of the delay of the final judgment? He posits several elements to an appropriate answer: prophetic foreshortening; a foreshadowing of the fall of Jerusalem, which did in fact come soon; and the importance of repenting.[21] But when John's teaching is put together with Jesus' use of this imagery in Luke 6, 7, 13, a slightly different answer seems to emerge. The point is that John called for personal decisions that would determine one's fate. How one decided about the source of John's preaching and about John's view of being rightly related to God through repentance was a personal eschatological decision of the greatest importance. With the ministries of John and Jesus came the critical time of decision.

The ultimate die is cast with regard to God by how one relates to the message about forgiveness of sins in the context of repentance. Jesus' coming will force people to look at themselves and make decisions that determine their eternal fate. One can be aided in understanding Jesus by understanding how John prepared the way for him. The judgment of God draws near in that however one decides on the message of John and Jesus will represent how one responds to God's message and thus how God will deal with that individual. Just as in John's Gospel the cross can be viewed as the source of the decisive defeat of Satan, even though the ultimate defeat is yet to come, so the Baptist's coming (and that of Jesus) can be regarded as judgment drawing near, even though the actual judgment they discuss is yet to come. For the decision that one makes about John's ministry and about his greater successor Jesus will determine precisely whether God's judgment will fall.

This is not to say that John is the decisive eschatological figure for Luke; indeed, Jesus' superiority to the Baptist is portrayed in Luke 1–2 and 3:15–18. But John prepares for Messiah in noting the

---

21. Bovon 1989: 173 also sees a "past" reference to Jerusalem's destruction, since he believes that Luke was written after the city's fall in A.D. 70.

decisive nature of the times. John warns the crowd to see their need for repentance and to live fruitfully. John opens the door for Messiah, who will bring the forgiveness that the responsive know they need.

b. The Appropriate Fruit of Repentance (3:10–14)
i. Fruit of Repentance Described for the Crowd (3:10–11)

John's message does not fall on deaf ears. The response of three **3:10** distinct groups in 3:10–14 constitutes a section unique to Luke's Gospel.[22]

The crowd is the first to press John for elaboration. If the crowd is to make fruit worthy of repentance, what are they to do? In asking the question, the crowd understands that John is not calling them to participate in an efficacious rite, but he is calling on them to respond with action. The washing pictures what happens in the heart. They are asking him in effect, "What is the product that reflects true repentance?" Ποιήσωμεν (*poiēsōmen*, shall we do?) here plays off ποιήσατε (*poiēsate*, make) in 3:8. The crowd wishes to know what repentance entails.

John's reply about the product of repentance is exceedingly practi- **3:11** cal. He does not call the crowd to his ascetic lifestyle, nor does he call for a commitment to a series of ritual religious acts, nor does he point to the sacrifices associated with the Jewish faith. Rather, he points to meeting the needs of others.

Giving an undergarment to the one in need fits the OT prophets' concern about the proper treatment of one's fellow humans, especially the poor (Job 31:16–22; Isa. 58:7–8; Ezek. 18:7–9; Mic. 6:8; Danker 1988: 87; Schürmann 1969: 168 n. 47; Creed 1930: 52). The literature of contemporary Judaism also retains this theme (Sir. 4:1, 4, 8; 7:32; 10:23; 11:12; 34:21; 35:2 [conceptually, by reference to alms]; Tob. 1:17; 4:16). Repentant individuals are not to worry about social separation or sacrifice; they are to care for the needs of their neighbors. Such exhortations to caring are also present in Jesus' ministry (Luke 16:19–31) and in the teaching of the early church (James 1:26–27; Eph. 4:28). The fundamental ethic involves an unselfish approach to life, which sees a person in basic need and gives a spare possession to meet it (Danker 1988: 88).

The exact picture is of taking an extra item from one's garments to clothe the unclothed. Χιτών (*chitōn*, undergarment) was basically a short undershirt worn underneath the longer outer garment or ac-

---

22. On Luke's love of triads, see Delling, *TDNT* 8:223–24, esp. n. 58; also Sparks 1936. Of sixty-four such groupings in the NT, seventeen are peculiar to Luke. The note in *TDNT* argues that the technique goes back to Jesus.

tual tunic (ἱμάτιον, *himation*).[23] Numerous passages reflect the distinction (Luke 6:29; Matt. 5:40; Josephus, *Antiquities* 17.5.7 §136; SB 1:343). Both were usually worn, but that was not necessary (Mark 6:9; Luke 9:3). John is saying that members of the crowd should seek to clothe anyone whom they notice lacks an undergarment (i.e., lacks clothes). This call to share is voluntary, but it also is a reflection of a morally appropriate concern for one's neighbor (Ellis 1974: 90). Refusing the call reveals what is in the heart. There is a prophetic ethical demand in John's reply. The one who understands the proper product of repentance will attempt to meet such needs. Is it any wonder that both John and Jesus were popular with the masses, who could appreciate the importance of meeting such needs?

What applies to clothing also applies to food. John does not elaborate here, but simply exhorts "do likewise" (ὁμοίως ποιείτω, *homoiōs poieitō*) with the need for food. Paul notes that with food and clothing one can have material contentment (1 Tim. 6:8). John says that sharing basic needs with one's neighbor is the proper fruit that grows out of repentance.

ii. Fruit of Repentance Described for Tax Collectors (3:12–13)

3:12 Luke next reports the specific request of two groups that were among the least popular in Jewish society: toll collectors (3:12–13) and soldiers (3:14). Only the toll collectors are said by Luke to have come forward to be baptized. Either this is stylistic variation, or Luke is highlighting that this group was responsive, as other Lucan references to them seem to suggest (5:27–30; 7:29, 34; 15:1; 18:9–14; 19:1–10).

To understand a little about the reply that John gives to the toll collectors, one must examine the background of the office.[24] Taxes in the Roman Empire were a complex affair. There were different ranks of collectors, and there were different taxes to collect. The system of collection was known as tax (or toll) farming. City rulers leased the right to collect taxes to an individual or group, who had bid for this right and had paid for it in advance. Thus, the collector would not only have to collect the tax that Rome had stipulated, but

23. On χιτών, see BAGD 882; BAA 1759; Matt. 5:40; 10:10; Mark 6:9; Luke 6:29; 9:3; Acts 9:39; Jude 23. On ἱμάτιον, see BAGD 376; BAA 763–64; Luke 8:44; 22:36.

24. Michel, *TDNT* 8:94–105; Stern 1974: 330–34; Donahue 1971; Fitzmyer 1981: 469–70; Badian 1972. E. Sanders 1992: 146–69 notes that the tax system in Palestine was not more oppressive than in other regions. He estimates that taxes consumed somewhere between 20 percent and 30 percent of one's income. For a more skeptical view that sees toll collectors as a symbolic representation of Jesus' outreach to archetypal sinners, see Neale 1991: 110–15. I regard Neale's dichotomy between symbolic representation and history as false for reasons made clear below. In this approach Neale follows Horsley 1987, and both underestimate the connections between John and Jesus in terms of audience. See also 5:29–32.

he also would have to add a surcharge to meet his expenses, an additional charge over which he had total control.[25] In most of the empire this job of collection went to wealthy Romans who were designated "publicans." They in turn would hire others to do the actual collection, the "tax collectors" proper (τελώνης, *telōnēs*; BAGD 812 and BAA 1619 are clear on the distinction between these groups). And at times these tax collectors would hire subordinates, becoming "head tax collectors."

Because of the political situation, in 44 B.C. Julius Caesar reduced taxes in Palestine, so that publicans ceased to operate there (Donahue 1971: 44; Josephus *Antiquities* 14.10.5–6 §§200–209). Collecting direct taxes for Rome became the responsibility of the prefect, who hired a δημοσιώνης (*dēmosiōnēs*, state or public tax official; lit., farmer of the revenue)—a term that does not appear in the NT—to collect taxes.[26] Direct taxes included the poll tax (a general citizen's tax) and the land tax (a tax on one's harvest) (Michel, *TDNT* 8:97–98). In addition to these direct taxes, there also was a set of indirect taxes on all items purchased or leased in a region, including a type of sales tax, which involved the hiring of τελῶναι, the term Luke uses here.[27] Dues were collected at major cities such as Jerusalem, Jericho, and Caesarea.[28] As one can see, this system of multiple collectors, each of whom could add his own surcharge, could create great abuse. In fact, a Palmyrene inscription from a slightly later period records an attempt to control abuses (Dittenberger 1903–5: #629).

Judaism reacted with extreme distaste to those who took up this vocation. One of the reasons was that people whose business required them to travel might be taxed at each locale throughout a region, and they regarded these surcharges as robbery (Michel, *TDNT* 8:101–2). Of all the taxes, the indirect taxes were the least liked.[29]

---

25. In *Antiquities* 12.4.2–9 §§160–220, Josephus has a vivid story of such a crafty collector, Joseph, who extorted much money during the rule of Ptolemy V.

26. Fitzmyer 1981: 470; LSJ 387; BAA 358. Some of these figures in Palestine would be Jews. A related term, δημόσιος, occurs four times in Acts (5:18; 16:37; 18:28; 20:20).

27. In *Antiquities* 17.8.4 §205, Josephus says that these taxes were "ruthlessly exacted"; in 18.4.3 §90 he notes the temporary lifting of the taxes under Caesar.

28. Michel, *TDNT* 8:98–99. The rate ranged from 2 percent to 10 percent in the empire itself. Josephus describes some tax decrees (*Antiquities* 14.10.5–6 §§200–209), explains the bidding for tax collection (*Antiquities* 12.4.3 §169), and mentions some exemptions (*Antiquities* 12.3.3 §143). See also 1 Macc. 10:26–31; 11:28, 34–36; 13:34 for exemptions and relief in an earlier period.

29. Michel, *TDNT* 8:102. In *b. Sanh.* 25a–b tax collectors appear with dice players and Sabbath breakers; *m. Ned.* 3.4 and *m. B. Qam.* 10.2 pair them with murderers and robbers; and *m. Ṭohar.* 7.6 says a tax collector who enters a house makes it unclean. One can see, in light of the historical setting, why the NT derogatory phrase *toll collectors and sinners* was so common.

Lucian, a second-century non-Christian writer, in describing people who "only stir up great confusion," referred to "adulterers, pimps, tax collectors, yes-men, and informers."[30] Even non-Jews disliked them. Jews excommunicated toll collectors because they were regarded as robbers (Donahue 1971: 49–53). Only a few of these men were commended for how they carried out their tasks.[31] A group of such tax collectors were sensitive to John's message and asked him what they should do.

In addressing John, the toll collectors used the word διδάσκαλε (*didaskale*, teacher), a term that was often used of a rabbi to denote deep respect (Ellis 1974: 90). In fact, in Luke nondisciples often address Jesus with this title (9:38; 10:25; 11:45; 12:13; 18:18). John apparently touched a nerve. The description is apt, since in 3:1–18 we see John offering prophecy, preaching apocalyptic, and giving exhortation and wisdom (Bovon 1989: 174). The tax collectors were basically asking, "What needs to change?"

3:13   John's reply is straightforward: the toll collectors are not to give up their profession. Rather, they are to conduct themselves honorably and fairly. John is not a political revolutionary, for he does not attack the right to collect taxes. What John argues is that taxes should be collected without extortion, surcharges, kickbacks, payoffs, or bribes. The tax collectors are to do their job and not take advantage of their authority. They must exact only what has been appointed (διατεταγμένον, *diatetagmenon*) to them to collect. In short, they are to be honest stewards. Πράσσετε (*prassete*) is a commercial term that means "to transact business" (BAGD 698 §1b; BAA 1399–1400; Luke 19:23). The fruit of repentance in a toll collector would be fair business practices, in contrast to corrupt toll collectors. The call is one of fairness to one's neighbor. It parallels the call made to the crowd. The penitent one lives differently, manifesting an appropriate response in his or her vocation.

iii. Fruit of Repentance Described for Soldiers (3:14)

3:14   The third group, the soldiers, ask how they should respond. It is generally agreed that these soldiers were Jewish rather than Roman (Fitzmyer 1981: 471; Bovon 1989: 174 n. 39; Marshall 1978: 143; Schneider 1977a: 86–87; Plummer 1896: 92). They could have come

30. *Descent into Hades* 11. Other notations from ancient writers include Tacitus, *Annals* 2.42; and Pliny, *Natural History* 12.32 §§63–65. Emperors sometimes warned against abuses: Tiberius said, "The sheep are to be shorn, not fleeced"; Dio Cassius, *Roman History* 57.10.5; Suetonius, *Tiberius* 52; Danker 1988: 88.

31. Josephus, *Jewish War* 2.14.4 §287 commends a tax collector for trying to solve a dispute, but notes that he had little alternative.

from one of three groups: Antipas's army in Perea, which included foreign troops as well (on the international nature of this army, see Josephus, *Antiquities* 17.8.3 §§198–99); the Judean "police"; or soldiers who assisted and protected the toll collectors. The last possibility may be indicated by καὶ ἡμεῖς (*kai hēmeis*) at the end of the question: What shall "we also" do? (i.e., we *alongside* the toll collectors). It may also be supported by John's reply focusing exclusively on money. These two factors indicate a possible connection between the groups of 3:12–14, though one cannot be certain (so Leaney 1958: 107; Geldenhuys 1951: 139; Hendriksen 1978: 208). The possibility for abuse of authority by law enforcement personnel was very real (Heidland, *TDNT* 5:592). The soldiers, sensing a need to change as a result of John's warning in 3:7–9, ask what they should do.

The reply comes in three parts: two prohibitions and an exhortation. First, they are not to intimidate anyone so as to extort money violently. Διασείσητε (*diaseisēte*) means "to shake violently" and is equivalent to our slang expression *to shake someone down* (BAGD 188; BAA 377–78; MM 153; 3 Macc. 7:21; Marshall 1978: 143–44). John commands the soldiers not to use strong-arm tactics to gain financial advantage. The term is used only here in the NT but was commonly used this way in Koine Greek (P. Tebt. vol. 1 #43 lines 26, 36 [118 B.C.]; P. Oxy. vol. 2 #284 line 5 and #285 line 13 [both A.D. 50]). In P. Tebt. 43 διασείω appears with Luke's next verb, συκο-φαντέω. Extortion is the basic idea and is strictly prohibited by John. John's answer about the product of repentance reflects itself in practical ethics and an absence of abuse of power.

The meaning of the second prohibition, συκοφαντήσητε (*sykophantēsēte*), is debated. It seems originally to have meant "to shake figs," that is, to expose figs by shaking the tree (Fitzmyer 1981: 470–71; BAGD 776; BAA 1549; MM 596). Two approaches have been applied to this meaning: it means simply to be an informer against someone else (Alford 1874: 471; A. B. Bruce 1897: 483) or, more strongly, it means to falsely accuse or to gain monetary advantage, that is, to extort by fraud (Luce 1933: 111; Plummer 1896: 93; Creed 1930: 53). The term is used in the NT only here and in 19:8. Since the context surrounding the verb is monetary, the second idea of extortion by fraud or false representation seems to be the likely meaning (Marshall 1978: 144; Fitzmyer 1981: 471; Nestle 1903; Hunzinger, *TDNT* 7:759). Again, this sense conforms to everyday uses found in the ancient papyri.[32] Thus, the soldier is not to abuse his

32. P. Tebt. vol. 1 #43 lines 26, 36; P. Oxy. vol. 3 #472 line 33 (A.D. 130). BAGD 776 cites Lysias 26.24 as well as Luke 19:8, though it interprets the term in Luke 3:14 as "harass, accuse falsely."

position so as to take monetary advantage of those under his authority. He is not to seize additional money by force to supplement his basic wage. Being a soldier itself is not considered to be unlawful, but the soldier should not take advantage of the citizenry.

The exhortation is to be content with one's wage. Ὀψώνιον (*opsōnion*) is almost exclusively a military term for the provisions given to a soldier.[33] The military wage of the day was a basic provision of food and minimal subsistence—a level of support that might tempt one to take advantage of position and to supplement income through excessive use of civil authority. If one was content, then one would be less tempted by this possibility. John's counsel is similar to that of Josephus in discussing soldiers (*Life* 47 §244; Fitzmyer 1981: 471).

John's response to the three groups says to be compassionate, loving, and fair to fellow human beings and not to take advantage of another or leave another in destitution for one's own gain. Rather, one is to be content with what one has. Look to meet needs, rather than to aggravate them.

Summary   Luke 3:7–14 represents a sample of John's call to repentance. It emphasizes the nearness of God's coming wrath. In one sense, it is the negative side of saying the kingdom draws near (Matt. 3:2). With the opportunity of promise comes also the risk of judgment for rejecting the promise. Matthew notes the positive experience, while Luke notes the danger. The declaration makes it clear that crucial times are approaching; key decisions need to be made. The best way to prepare is to answer John's call to repentance. One should live in light of an awareness of God's coming and his judgment.

John's message involves a unique setting not to be confused with the postcross perspective of the NT Letters. John preached to the Jewish people and prepared them for the promise, by helping them to understand sin and their relation to it (1:17, 76–77). Religious heritage, even Abrahamic heritage, is no guarantee against that day when the ax will fall against those who are not fruitful. The recognition of one's need for repentance is crucial. In 3:15–17, the Baptist speaks of a greater baptism that Jesus brings, a baptism that is later called (24:49) the promise of the Father from above. This is the bestowal of the Spirit, which embodies God's response to those who come to him through Jesus (Acts 2:17–39). The Spirit is God's gift of enablement for those who turn to him. In addition, the recognition of one's need for re-

---

33. BAGD 602; BAA 1217–18; 1 Cor. 9:7; 1 Macc. 3:28; Heidland, *TDNT* 5:591; Caragounis 1974.

pentance paves the way for response to the Lord Jesus later (Acts 19:4). John's ministry and baptism ultimately point to Jesus and find their culmination in him.

But in practical terms, what is true repentance? Three groups ask John this question, and in each case the response is not given in terms of ascetic lifestyle nor in terms of a particular feeling of remorse nor in partaking of religious rites nor in some form of mere mental acknowledgment. Rather, true repentance responds to God and treats fellow humans justly. If a repentant person sees someone who is hungry or in need of clothing, the call is to feed and clothe that person. A repentant person who collects taxes must do so without excessive surcharges. A repentant person who is a soldier must not intimidate or extort money, but be content with one's own wage. It is interesting that two specific replies in 3:12–14 deal with money, an area where it is easy to be most protective of one's own resources and interests. John's repentance expresses itself neither in separation from the world nor in selfish pursuit of it. Rather, repentance exhorts people to be fair with others and meet basic needs with fundamental aid. This is what God desires of those who know he is present and coming: a concern for him is expressed through concern for others.

Additional Notes

3:8. Some suggest this material may have been used for baptismal instruction in the early church (Schürmann 1969: 179). However, it seems that Luke's concern is historical, not catechetical, since Jewish heritage would hardly be an issue for Luke's audience. There is instructional value, however, in the material, since it shows that what repentance involves is something more concrete than mere intellectual assent. Repentance is pictured as producing a personal appropriation and commitment, which expresses itself in concrete acts (5:32). Another crucial element that speaks against a baptismal association is the absence of an effort to relate repentance to Jesus or to Messiah, something that is quite evident in Acts as one moves toward Christian baptism (Acts 2:38–40; 19:1–4). John's baptism may have analogies to Christian baptism, but it is only a pointer to a greater period of God's dealing with people. It is a precursor of a greater baptism, as Luke himself will make clear in agreement with Christian tradition (Luke 3:15–18; Matt. 3:11–12; Mark 1:7–8). The setting of these remarks is not baptism in the early church or Christian preaching; it is John the Baptist.

3:10. The source of 3:10–14 is much discussed. In the early part of this century, some argued that the section must be a late creation of Luke, since the passage contained what was judged to be "low moral content" in comparison to Jesus' teaching (6:29; so Wellhausen 1904: 5). Some question the possibility of soldiers listening to John in a Semitic context (Bultmann 1963: 145), a view that has not gone unchallenged. Ernst (1977: 143) argues that the material was found in Luke's special source and that the question-answer format along with the social concern fits Luke's perspective. In addition, the question, "What shall we do?" follows typical Lucan style. Luke often presents a crowd asking for guidance in response to a speaker (Acts 2:37; 16:30; 22:10). However, Ernst gives no indication why he refers this material to a special Lucan source rather than to Luke himself.

A better solution is that of Schürmann (1969: 169; for lexical details, see n. 54) and Marshall (1978: 141–42). They argue that Luke included material from a traditional source that Matthew chose to omit. The evidence that the material comes from a source about John the Baptist is that in no other place does the uniquely Lucan material show a concern for John the Baptist alone. Marshall goes on to note that the reply's morality is not low as Wellhausen claims, but is revolutionary (also Danker 1988: 89–90). Marshall notes that Bultmann's statement about the impossibility of soldiers being present before John is sheer speculation. Schürmann (1969: 169 n. 53) adds that the reply of 3:11 has clear OT roots as well as some non-Lucan expressions.[34] Thus, Luke is using traditional material about John the Baptist. The question of whether Matthew had this material seems less certain. The point is that Luke presents unique material, and there is no reason to question the connection of the material to John.

3:10. The grammatical dispute concerning the use of the imperfect tense ἐπηρώτων influences the meaning of the verb. Plummer (1896: 90) and Godet (1875: 1.178) suggest that it indicates repeated questions on repeated occasions. Creed (1930: 52) suggests that it simply and vividly presents the past action as still in progress. The latter is to be preferred, since a later verse uses the aorist tense (3:12). What Luke describes is a single representative scene from John's ministry (3:18). Schweizer (1984: 73) makes the correct observation that 3:10–11 gives the general exhortation while 3:12–14 mentions specifics that apply to two groups.

---

34. See the exegesis of 3:11 and the introduction to this unit. Among the peculiarities are "the one who has," "likewise," and use of the verb "he said" with the dative.

3. Promise of John the Baptist (3:15–18)

Luke completes the presentation of John's ministry with two brief sections. Where 3:1–6 introduced John in the context of history and OT fulfillment and 3:7–14 gave an illustration of his preaching about repentance, 3:15–18 gives his preaching about the Christ and 3:19–20 contains a brief note about his imprisonment. The first section (3:15–18) shows that John is subordinate to Jesus and points out that the real promise and hope come with the one who is mightier than John. Luke presents this emphasis more elaborately than do the other Synoptics. Where Matt. 3:11–12 and Mark 1:7–8 give John's teaching about "one to come" without any introduction, Luke 3:15 presents the teaching in a context of popular speculation about whether John was the Christ. So a stronger note enters into John's eschatological teaching.

Sources and Historicity

The connection between the traditions in the various Gospels is a complex issue. Luke combines various sources here. Luke 3:15 is unique to Luke, but it has terminology that is not Lucan, which leads Schürmann to consider the introduction as traditional in origin.[1] Luke 3:16 parallels material in Mark 1:7 and Matt. 3:11. The reference to the Stronger One stands verbally closer to Mark, while the material on baptizing with water is sequentially parallel to Matthew, though it is in all three Gospels. All mention the future baptism of the Spirit. Luke's presentation is more condensed. Luke 3:17 is very close in wording to Matt. 3:12, agreeing almost exactly except that Luke has an infinitive (συναγαγεῖν) where Matthew has a verb (συνάξει). In addition Matthew has an extra καί, and there is one reversal of word order. Luke 3:18 is unique to Luke and serves as a clear summary to the discussion about John's active ministry. Luke is responsible for this summary. Judgments about historicity parallel the discussion of 3:1–6 (see the exegesis of 3:16).

The form of this account is prophetic pronouncement (Berger 1984: 260). It is laid out in an "I but he" comparison, which

---

1. Schürmann 1969: 171 n. 64 notes that most of the terms from 3:15–18 (which is §16 in Aland 1985) show up elsewhere in Luke predominately where he has parallels. Ernst 1977: 145 calls the introduction Lucan, but with less rationale.

shows how John compares to Jesus. The form contrasts Jesus and John, while the nature of the different baptisms shows that Jesus is superior to John.

The outline of Luke 3:15–18 is as follows:

a. John's promise of a greater one to come (3:15–17)
   i. Popular messianic speculation about John (3:15)
   ii. Promise of a greater baptism (3:16–17)
b. Summary: John preached good news (3:18)

Numerous themes dominate this short passage, John's relationship to Jesus through John's own prophetic testimony being the most important one. John's baptism is a prelude to Spirit baptism, which is the greater baptism of the Mightier One to come. In addition, no one, not even a prophet, compares to Jesus. In fact, all are unworthy in comparison. There is a somber note as well as promise. With the coming of the Stronger One who brings promise, there is also judgment. So the goal of the warning is to lead each one to decide where he or she stands in relation to the hope.

Exegesis and Exposition

[15]And the people were expectant and all were questioning in their hearts whether John might be the Christ. [16]John replied to all, "I shall baptize you with water; but there comes one who is stronger than I, the thong of whose sandals I am not worthy to untie; he shall baptize you with the Holy Spirit and fire. [17]He has the winnowing fork in his hand to clear the threshing floor, to gather the wheat into the storehouse but the chaff to burn with unquenchable fire."

[18]Now also with many other exhortations he preached good news to the people.

a. John's Promise of a Greater One to Come (3:15–17)
i. Popular Messianic Speculation about John (3:15)

3:15 Among the Synoptics, only Luke at this point mentions that John's preaching created a stir of popular speculation. John's mention of God's coming wrath as a time of vindicating judgment would naturally suggest that Messiah and deliverance might be near (3:7–9). Such eschatological speculation was natural for a Jewish audience sensitive to OT hope. Thus Luke mentions that the people were expectant. Προσδοκάω (*prosdokaō*, expecting) is used frequently by Luke (Luke 1:21; 7:19, 20; 8:40; 12:46; Acts 3:5; 27:33; 28:6; Plummer 1896: 93; Marshall 1978: 145; BAGD 712 §3; BAA 1427). It usually denotes a high level of expectation about an event that draws near. The parallel in Luke 7:19–20 shows that it can speak of end-time expectation, in which a sense of nearness is key (Matt. 11:3; 2 Pet. 3:12–14). Such was the hope that John created in the people.

Speculation went beyond the nature of the times to John himself; this speculation is expressed by the phrase διαλογιζομένων πάντων ἐν ταῖς καρδίαις αὐτῶν (*dialogizomenōn pantōn en tais kardiais autōn*, all were questioning in their hearts; Mark 2:6–8; Luke 5:22; 12:17; Matt. 16:7–8; 21:25; Schrenk, *TDNT* 2:96 §B1). The reference to the heart probably should not be interpreted as an indication that only internal private speculation was involved. The other passages about the popular view of John make it clear that thoughts about John's role were a matter of public discussion (7:19–35 [where Jesus is dealing with such speculation]; 9:7–9). Surely if the people discussed the issue of the nature of the times, the possibility of a messianic connection was also considered. Thus, καρδίαις refers to the deep personal level at which the question was raised. All were reflecting fully on the matter.

Some wish to make a theological point of the use of λαοῦ (*laou*, people). In a few contexts in Luke–Acts the term clearly means the special people of God (Luke 1:77; Acts 15:14), though in many contexts it is a way to refer to Israel (Luke 1:68; 2:32; Acts 4:10, 25, 27). But the usage in Luke 3:18, 21 seems to envision John's general audience, and so a specialized meaning of the term is unlikely here. It is only a stylistic variation for ὄχλοι (*ochloi*, crowd) in 3:10, as in 23:13.

The question the people raised concerned John as Messiah. The combination μήποτε αὐτὸς εἴη ὁ χριστός (*mēpote autos eiē ho christos*, perhaps he might be the Christ) has been seen as a statement of denial by Luke, since the interrogative particle μήποτε contains the particle μή, a particle that expects a negative answer (Danker 1988: 91). Thus, Luke raises the question about John, but states it in Greek in such a way that the answer is not left in doubt. John is not the Christ. However, most interpret μήποτε as referring purely to uncertainty, because of the optative εἴη (Creed 1930: 53; BAGD 519 §3bα; BDF §370.3, §386.2; BDR §370.3.5, §386.2.3; Robertson 1923: 938–39). The uncertainty is laid out in a way that suggests unlikelihood, but that the possibility is even raised shows how seriously some took John. John will reject this association (3:16–17). However, the raising of the messianic issue points out to the reader that these are special times and that Jesus is the Messiah (Acts 13:24–25; John 3:25–30).

ii. Promise of a Greater Baptism (3:16–17)

3:16   The question about whether John is the Christ leads into the Baptist's response. The response of 3:16–17 will declare a threefold superiority for Jesus: he is stronger than John; he brings a better baptism than John; and he is the Judge (Schneider 1977a: 88). The order of Luke's remarks is like Matt. 3:11, where the sequence is baptism in water, the Stronger One, and baptism in the Spirit. Mark 1:7–8 mentions the Stronger One first and then contrasts baptism of water with baptism of the Spirit. Luke, however, is aware of the direct contrast, as Acts 1:5 and 11:16 show (Creed 1930: 53). Thus, the statement of Jesus' superiority and the contrast of the two baptisms of John and Jesus is something all the Synoptics share. Jesus' ministry is in a different class than John's. John's teaching prepares for rather than parallels Jesus' teaching.

John baptizes *with* water (ὕδατι, *hydati*, is an instrumental dative; Plummer 1896: 94). Ὕδατι is thrown forward in the construction, making it slightly emphatic.[2] The mention of water baptism serves to set up the initial contrast, which expresses Jesus' superiority. Luke gives no details about mode, since it is not his concern.[3]

A Stronger One is coming. Ἰσχυρότερος (*ischyroteros*) has been seen as a title by some, but a technical meaning is not intended here; only a description is present. The association of strength with a redeemer is an OT idea: Deut. 10:17; 2 Sam. 22:33 (= Ps. 18:32 [18:33 MT]); Isa. 11:2; Jer. 50:34 (Danker 1988: 92; Ernst 1977: 145). In a couple of these passages, the Redeemer is clearly God (so also Philo, *Special Laws* 1.56 §307), but Isa. 11:2 is a reference to the root of Jesse, while 2 Sam. refers to God's giving David strength. Acts 10:38 makes the point that Jesus' strength emerges from his anointing by the Spirit. Thus, the figure of the Strong One for Luke is tied to an anointing with power, a picture that looks not so much at divinity as it does at Jesus' regal office.[4]

Next, John's humility and identity in comparison to Jesus come out clearly. John is not worthy to untie a sandal from Jesus' feet. Most people in the first century went barefoot or wore sandals (Oepke, *TDNT* 5:310–11). One duty of a slave was to untie the sandals from the master's feet (SB 1:121; Ellis 1974: 90). In Judaism this

---

2. Marshall 1978: 146 compares its position to that of ἐν πνεύματι ἁγίῳ καὶ πυρί later in the verse. There is a balance here. The reference to water comes early, while the reference to the Spirit trails in its clause. Both are emphatic and the distinction marks a clear contrast not only in content but in presentation.

3. Matt. 3:11, 16 seems to be clearer in picturing the mode as immersion; Acts 8:39 also suggests this.

4. Schürmann 1969: 172 n. 75. See the exegesis of 3:21–22 and note the OT background there.

was such a degrading act that a Hebrew slave was not to undertake it (Schneider 1977a: 88; *Mekilta de Rabbi Ishmael*, tractate *Nezikin* 1 on Exod. 21:2 [= Lauterbach 1933–35: 3.5 = Neusner 1988a: 112]). Thus, John is saying that he is so inferior to the Coming One that he is not worthy to perform even the most menial task for his master.[5]

A key factor in the difference between John and Jesus is the baptism that each brings. Standing in contrast to John's baptism with water is Jesus' baptism of the Spirit and fire. Scholarly discussion about the two-part description of Jesus' baptism is dominated by two issues: what John said in the original tradition and the meaning of "fire."

On the issue of what John said, there are two approaches. Some regard the reference to fire (πῦρ, *pyr*) as a Lucan explanation of the significance of Spirit baptism, since Mark 1:8 does not mention fire (Ellis 1974: 90, citing a connection to Acts 2). Others regard the reference to the Spirit as an addition that must have been a part of the tradition since it occurs in all three Gospels.[6] Those arguing that John predicted only a judgment and did not foresee the Spirit's coming use three pieces of evidence to support this view: it is argued that Acts 19:1–10 shows that the disciples who knew John did not know of a coming Spirit baptism; it is claimed that Luke 3:17 looks only to a judgment; and it is asserted that the association of Messiah with the Spirit is not likely for Judaism in John's time.

Both approaches can be challenged. Against the view that Luke added a reference to fire are two points. (a) The appearance of πῦρ in Matt. 3:11 shows that Luke did not add the phrase for the sake of Acts. (b) More importantly, the use of the image of fire in Acts 2:3 is exactly that, the use of a picture. Acts 2:3 does not say that the baptism associated with the Spirit's distribution is *of* fire, but that it spread through the crowd *like* a fire. Thus, the Acts image of fire discusses only the Spirit's spreading through the crowd and does not discuss the nature of the baptism itself. The attempt to appeal to the image of fire in Acts 2:19 also fails, for there heavenly signs are in view. Thus, the baptism with fire in Luke 3:16 does not have literary contact with Acts.

Against the view that Luke added a reference to the Spirit are the following points. (a) Acts 19:1–10 does not argue that the disciples who knew John's baptism did not know about a Spirit baptism at all. Rather it shows that they did not know that Spirit baptism had

---

5. Plummer 1896: 94 n. 1 notes that the use of the redundant αὐτοῦ is a Semitism. In translation the repetition is omitted, because it sounds awkward.

6. Bultmann 1963: 246; Creed 1930: 53–54; Lang, *TDNT* 6:943; Manson 1949: 41. This view usually denies that the historical John saw himself as a precursor to Jesus the Messiah. John was only a prophet warning that the end was near.

come.[7] (b) Luke 3:17 is not only about judgment, since there is mention that wheat is gathered by the "one who comes." (c) One can assume that John the Baptist's ministry had positive notes as well as warnings. In declaring the kingdom's nearness or in announcing God's coming, John would be using terminology that noted the approach of God's promise (Dunn 1970a: 9–10; Witherington 1990: 41–42). The association of Spirit and the end-time was strong in the OT (Isa. 32:15; 44:3; Ezek. 36:25–27; Joel 2:28–32 [3:1–5 MT]; Marshall 1978: 147) and also present at Qumran (1QS 4.20–21). Thus, an association of the Spirit with the end-time is not at all unlikely for John. The theme was available to him from first-century Judaism. John could look forward to a baptism of the Spirit and fire. Since in Judaism both Messiah and Spirit baptism are associated with the end-time, only some reflection on the OT hope is needed to put the two elements together.

What does the image of fire mean? All commentators agree that this image is the key to understanding the baptism. Four views exist:

1. The reference is to Pentecost, and the distribution of the Spirit belongs to those who trust Jesus (Ellis 1974: 90; Bovon 1989: 177; Wiefel 1988: 92). This view is old, going back to Chrysostom, *Homilies on Matthew* 11.6–7 (citing Luke 12:49–50; 24:32; and Acts 2:3). The major problem with this approach is that it is too specific in linking up the promise to Acts 2. As was mentioned above, the fire terminology of Acts 2 does not support this view.

2. Others see a mention only of judgment. The picture of the Spirit is seen as an allusion to a mighty wind that brings destructive judgment (Isa. 40:24; 41:16; Jer. 4:11–12; 23:19; 30:23; Ezek. 13:11–13). The reference to the chaff in Luke 3:17 is seen as supporting this view (so Eisler 1931: 274–79; Barrett 1947: 125–26). The major problem with this approach is that it tends to limit the scope of John's ministry to a note of warning and thus conflicts with 3:18 (Fitzmyer 1981: 474).

3. The reference is to two distinct baptisms, one of salvation (Spirit) and one of judgment (fire). This position goes back at least to Origen, *Homilies on Luke* 24 (it is also held by Lang, *TDNT* 6:943; Schürmann 1969: 174–75; Scobie 1964: 71). By far the strongest argument for this view is that fire is a consistent image for judgment in the OT, especially the final judgment associated with the eschaton (Isa. 29:6; 66:15; Ezek.

---

7. Marshall 1978: 147; Scobie 1964: 73 n. 1. As Nolland 1989: 152 says, the argument "proves too much." Acts 19 shows people whose tie to Spirit hope is remote, not intimate.

38:22; Amos 1:4; 7:4; Zeph. 1:18; 3:8; Mal. 3:2; 4:1 [3:19 MT]), an imagery that continues in Jewish literature.[8] The extent and consistency of this imagery make this view attractive. Of course, the mention of the Spirit refers to the provision of New Covenant hope that associates the Spirit with the end-times (Joel 2; Ezek. 36; Isa. 32; esp. Jer. 31:31–33). The fulfillment of this element is not seen so much in Pentecost as in the provision of the Spirit to all who come to Messiah. However, two points seem to be against the two-baptism view. First, there is only one grammatical object (ὑμᾶς, *hymas*, you), which speaks against a division into two groups according to two distinct baptisms (Fitzmyer 1981: 473). Second, two explicit baptisms would seem to require ἤ (*ē*, or) and not καί (*kai*, and) in Luke 3:16. Thus, this view, though initially compelling, does have problems.

4. View 3 musters strong rationale, but the best option seems to be a reference to a single baptism. The Spirit purges and thus divides humankind (Marshall 1978: 146–47; Fitzmyer 1981: 474; Dunn 1970a: 12–13). The key OT text here is Isa. 4:4–5, which sees a purging of peoples so that some may dwell in God's presence. The key connection is that the Isaiah passage is the only OT text to use Spirit and fire together. Some who hold this view tend to discuss the purging of the righteous at the expense of the judgment concept, but it seems best to keep both in view in light of Luke 3:17 and the nature of OT fire imagery.[9] The Christ comes with the πνεύματι ἁγίω (*pneumati hagiō*, Holy Spirit). The Mightier One will test all people and divide them. This approach to the passage is also supported by other texts in Luke: 12:49–53 speaks of the division by fire that Jesus came to bring; 17:29–30 speaks of the day of the Son of Man as a day of fire that divides people; and 12:10, which mentions the blasphemy against the Spirit, may well belong here in that the failure to respond to the offer of the Spirit creates an irreversible division among people, with some ending up rejected. So the offer of the Spirit divides people into two camps. One baptism is offered to the world, but it has two consequences. Which consequence a person experiences depends on the individual's decision in regard to the baptism.

8. Jub. 9.15; 36.10; 1 Enoch 10.6; 54.6; 90.24–27; 2 Esdr. [= 4 Ezra] 7:36–38; 13:4; Ps. Sol. 15.4–7; 2 Bar. 48.39; T. Abr. (A) 14.11; 1QH 3.28–31; 6.18–19; 1QS 2.8, 15; 4.13; Dunn 1970a: 12 n. 11; Schulz 1972: 376 n. 347 (who rightly notes this is an apocalyptic image applied to Jesus, not something that describes his first coming).

9. For fire as purging, Dunn 1970a: 12 n. 12 mentions Isa. 1:25; Zech. 13:9; Mal. 3:2–3; 1QH 5.16.

Thus, in the baptism of Spirit and fire there are two sides to Jesus' offer of God's promise. It divides people into two groups. Those who accept it, by accepting the one who brings it, are purged and taken in. Those who do not are thrown to the wind, as 3:17 suggests. The offer of this decisive baptism, revealed at Pentecost but offered continuously thereafter, shows Jesus' superiority to John. The offer of the Spirit began with the message of salvation, which was preached at Pentecost. With acceptance come the gift and the presence of the Spirit, who protects one from judgment (Acts 2:38–40). John is only a precursor to him who brings this baptism.

Comparison of Luke 3:16 with the Synoptic parallels reveals one other theological point. John's remark indicates how one will know that the coming kingdom has arrived (Matt. 3:2). If John is not the Christ, but the kingdom approaches with the Christ who baptizes with the Spirit (Matt. 3:11; Mark 1:8; Luke 3:16), then the kingdom's arrival must be associated with this baptism. Though Luke does not make this point here, he suggests it later in Acts 2:16–39, where the bestowal of the Spirit indicates proof of the activity of the Christ, who is also Lord. Peter also indicates as much when he speaks of "the beginning" in Acts 11:15–18, looking back to Acts 2 as a point of comparison with what God had just done for Cornelius and his Gentile friends.

3:17   John explains the baptism of Spirit and fire through the picture of sifting grain at harvest time (Godet 1875: 1.180). Πτύον (*ptyon*, winnowing fork) was a wooden forklike shovel used to lift the grain in the air, so that the wind or a winnowing fan could separate the wheat from the chaff (BAGD 727; BAA 1456). The heavier, usable grain would fall directly down onto the threshing floor, while the lighter, useless chaff would be blown away (for ἅλωνα, *halōna*, threshing floor, see BAGD 41; BAA 81; MM 24). Of course, the sifting illustration is the point. Jesus is ready to divide among people. Just as wheat is saved for the storehouse, so those who draw near to Jesus will be spared. But also just as the chaff is tossed to the wind, gathered, and burned, so will be the fate of those who refuse him. Jesus separates between people, and the winnowing fork is in his hand already. The picture indicates not only a separation within humanity, but a cleaning up of the threshing floor. His purging brings decisive judgment.

These images have an OT background. The picture of harvest occurs in Prov. 20:26, Jer. 15:7, and Isa. 41:15–16 (Marshall 1978: 148). In addition, the picture of the fire as unquenchable (ἀσβέστῳ, *asbestō*) uses OT imagery (Job 20:26; Isa. 34:8–10; 66:24), which is also found in Judaism (Jdt. 16:17). The image of fire tied to eternal judgment occurs also in Mark 9:43–44 (Lang, *TDNT* 6:945). The picture of the unquenchable fire alludes to the fierce and unending quality of an inescapable judgment that will be decisive and irreversible. There is one difference between this image and that of the OT. The purge here applies to everyone, not just to Gentiles. People in Israel are at risk too (Schulz 1972: 378; Midr. Song 7.3).

What is interesting to note about John's remarks is that Jesus institutes the judgment for God, an image that will reappear in Acts (10:42–43; 17:31; Marshall 1978: 148). Thus, Jesus' position is grounded in his superior authority.

The idea expressed here agrees with Matt. 3:12 exactly, though Matthew uses verbs where Luke has infinitives—a difference that is only stylistic (Creed 1930: 54). Another note about the verse is that the combination of relative and personal pronouns is a reflection of Semitic style (Black 1967: 101, 144; Schürmann 1969: 177 n. 105).

b. Summary: John Preached Good News (3:18)

3:18 Luke wraps up the overview of John's ministry by a summary verse that functions like 1:66, 80; 2:40, 52 (Godet 1875: 1.181; Plummer 1896: 96). The transition to a summary is indicated by the μὲν οὖν καί (men oun kai) construction: "now also."[10] Some suggest that ἕτερα (hetera) means messages of a character "different" from the message presented here (Plummer 1896: 96). However, it seems more likely that Luke is using the term to indicate that John preached about much more than what is present here, since Luke prefers ἕτερος (heteros, other; used thirty-two times) to ἄλλος (allos, other; eleven times) (N. Turner 1963: 197). John's ministry is characterized by exhortation to his audience. Λαόν (laon, people) is not a technical term here for those who respond to John. Rather, it refers to John's audience (3:15, 21).

John's message involves preaching good news (εὐηγγελίζετο, euēngelizeto, to give a good-news message). Fitzmyer (1981: 475) argues that a technical reference to the salvation message is not present in that the use here is parallel to 1:19. But this approach ignores the allusions to salvation in 1:77 and 3:6, and the announcement of the Mightier One in 3:15–17. There is an allusion to the precursor of the salvation message, a point that does not suggest that John's message equals that of Jesus, but that John introduces what Jesus will actually bring (Godet 1875: 1.181; Creed 1930: 54; Schürmann 1969: 178; Marshall 1978: 149; Wink 1968: 52–53).

Summary There is continuity between John and Jesus. They share in breaking ground for God's message. Luke often emphasizes continuity

---

10. Though this is its only use in Luke, the construction occurs twenty-seven times in Acts; BDF §451.1; BDR §451.1.3; Marshall 1978: 149.

alongside the distinctions that he maintains, and the transition figure of John is no exception to this rule.[11] John is a part of the movement toward salvation and sets the table for it.

Additional Notes

3:16. Many commentators note that Luke, unlike Matt. 3:11 and Mark 1:7, omits the phrase ὀπίσω μου (Schürmann 1969: 173 n. 77; Fitzmyer 1981: 472; Wink 1968: 55). They explain the omission as an attempt by Luke to avoid any potential admission that Jesus may have been a disciple of John and thus might be inferior to him (the phrase is used for discipleship in Luke 9:23; 14:27). But is this theological motive behind the difference? Luke has made it abundantly clear by this point where John fits. More importantly, Luke is capable of expressing the idea that Jesus came after John (as in Acts 10:37; 13:25; 19:4, where in each case the preposition μετά is used). It may be that Luke removed ὀπίσω μου for stylistic reasons to avoid a repetition, since the idea of "there comes one" already suggests that he comes after John. Although the omission involves a preposition different from the one used in Acts, a stylistic change seems more likely. Thus, Luke's shorter line really does not differ from the Synoptics' point.

3:18. Schürmann (1969: 179–81) argues in detail that the message Luke gives here has more than a salvation-historical function. Luke is giving a catechetical teaching about baptism. But Luke does not emphasize baptism. His points of focus are the message, the proper response to that message, and a gift that comes with it. John's baptism is a temporary rite sandwiched between the OT expectation of God's coming salvation and the announcement of the coming Mighty One. Jesus' baptism is not a rite, but is the gift of the Spirit. Thus, the salvation-historical context is never lost for Luke, and his perspective is future-oriented. Luke does not focus on the past, as a catechetical perspective would seem to require. Thus, Schürmann's suggestion for the passage's setting is not helpful.

---

11. Luke 16:16 emphasizes a note of distinction in presenting John, as does 7:24–30, while 7:31–35 is able to compare John to Jesus in the midst of distinction. For Luke, John is a bridge between the old and the new eras. Sometimes he emphasizes one side of the relationship, while other times he notes the other side.

4. Imprisonment of John the Baptist
(3:19–20)

Luke concludes the overview of John's ministry by recounting his arrest in a short summary note. Luke has placed this short unit about John's imprisonment earlier in his Gospel than the later position it has in Mark 6:17–18 and Matt. 14:3–4. The Lucan wording of this event is unique and looks like a summary, though it adds substance to the accounts of Mark and Matthew. Whereas Mark and Matthew quote John's charge that Herod's marriage to Herodias was not lawful, Luke notes that this was only one of the things for which John was arrested. Luke omits the quotation of John entirely and never includes the details about John's death. Luke says only that Herod beheaded the Baptist (9:7–9). Thus, Luke summarizes John's ministry in one spot. This arrangement serves to focus on the Coming One more explicitly by staying on Jesus' ministry once it is introduced. Luke sees John functioning in a context of popular messianic speculation. John deflects this speculation, but does not remove it, because John points to the one who follows him. By broadening the nature of John the Baptist's condemnation of Herod, Luke emphasizes that John was a prophet who preached a moral message for all.

Sources and Historicity

This account is clearly moved forward chronologically, as is evident from comparison with Matthew and Mark and from the subsequent account of a baptism over which John presides (Hendriksen 1978: 213). The placement may be influenced by a tradition like that in Mark 1:14, which mentions John's imprisonment before Jesus' Galilean ministry (Fitzmyer 1981: 476). Thus, the accounts of Matt. 14:3–5 and Mark 6:17–20 give a more temporally focused perspective on this event. Much speculation exists about Luke's motive for this chronological transposition, including the argument that he wished to separate totally the period of John from the period of Jesus' ministry. But Fitzmyer rightly warns against reading too much theological or theological-geographical significance into this placement. Luke 7:24–35 shows that John can be discussed in the context of Jesus' ministry, while 9:7–9 notes the effect that John's death had on Herod. The order probably represents a literary preference to present John and then focus on Jesus.

The ancient historian Josephus also recounts the arrest of John (*Antiquities* 18.5.2 §§116–19). His account parallels the Gospels, mentioning that John's baptism was tied to a call to righteousness and that Herod saw John as a political threat. Josephus lacks two points: John's ultimate eschatological focus and the forerunner motif. However, given that Josephus is attempting to placate the Romans and yet not make Jewish movements look too bad at the same time, these omissions are natural in a politically focused treatment (Geldenhuys 1951: 141). Josephus gives us one other piece of information: the locale of John's prison was Machaerus on the east end of the Dead Sea.

The account's form is a summary (Berger 1984: 334).[1] There is no need to outline the verses, since the unit is self-contained. One theme, the faithfulness of John's preaching, dominates the passage. Such faithfulness led to arrest, but God's moral standards were not to be left behind for the sake of personal safety. Here is an exemplary prophet who carries out his call.

Exegesis and Exposition

[19]But Herod the tetrarch was rebuked by him concerning Herodias, his brother's wife, and concerning all the evil that Herod did, [20]and he added this above all: he locked up John in prison.

3:19 Incarceration was the result of John's preaching and challenge to the moral character of the Jewish political leadership. Luke, in discussing the reason behind John's imprisonment, is clear that the Baptist rebuked Herod Antipas for his marriage to Herodias. A change in tone is evident in that John is said to have exhorted the people (3:18), but Herod he rebuked (3:19): παρακαλῶν (*parakalōn*, exhorting) in 3:18 contrasts with δὲ . . . ἐλεγχόμενος (*de . . . elenchomenos*, but . . . rebuking) here. The rebuke involved public (1 Tim. 5:20; 2 Tim. 4:2) condemnation of Herod's act.

The marriage was objectionable on at least two grounds. Both Herod Antipas and Herodias left previous marriages to enter into this marriage. But in addition, Herodias had been married to a half-brother of Herod, also known as Herod. (Herod Antipas had been married to the daughter of Aretas IV of Nabatea.) Thus, not only were two marriages destroyed in the remarriage, but Herod Antipas ends up marrying the wife of a near blood relative in violation of Lev. 18:16 and 20:21 (Fitzmyer 1981: 477–78). Of course, Herod

---

1. Technically, Luke does not mention the death of John and so martyrdom is not in view. This text shows the price that John paid for his preaching and the persecution he suffered.

lacked an exemplary background, since his father, Herod the Great, had ten wives. Luke's explanation of the imprisonment agrees with the other Gospels (Matt. 14:3–5; Mark 6:17–20).

Luke does not mention the marital history of Herodias, as the other Gospel writers do in referring to Herod Philip. Many think that Luke is correcting what he realizes is an error in the tradition (so Creed 1930: 54), but such a conclusion is not required since the reference to Philip is not necessarily incorrect, as Hoehner argues (1972: 131–36).

Luke does not limit the cause of imprisonment to this one issue. He alone notes that the rebuke included all the evil that Herod had done. The term used for this broad category is πονηρῶν (*ponērōn*), which refers to vice in general.[2]

In light of such criticism of Herod's lifestyle, it is easy to see why Josephus said that Herod regarded John as a political threat, since such a moral attack would undermine Herod's credibility. What this additional criticism involved cannot be determined. It is interesting to note that, in making such a condemnation, John's ministry takes on a quality that parallels other divine prophets who challenged the blatantly immoral activity of their rulers. An outstanding example of this type of prophetic challenge is the ministry of Elijah (1 Kings 21:17–26; Schürmann 1969: 184).

3:20 Luke describes the worst crime of all. Herod silenced the criticism of his morals by locking John up. The expression προσέθηκεν ... ἐπὶ πᾶσιν (*prosethēken ... epi pasin*, he added ... above all) is a Septuagintalism that shows what in Luke's judgment was the greatest atrocity (on the Septuagintalism, see BDF §419.4; N. Turner 1963: 227; Marshall 1978: 149–50). The decision to suppress John the Baptist was an utter rejection by Herod of the prophet's critique. Often sin seeks to remove the source of exposure rather than heed a warning of love. John was placed in prison at the edge of the Dead Sea, and there he met a death that was the product of Herodias's anger at John's condemnation (Matt. 14:1–12; Mark 6:14–29).

Summary Luke 3:15–20 shows that John's ministry points to Christ as the superior one. Jesus is superior because he will bring a greater baptism associated with the Spirit. This ministry will separate people from one another. So great is the one to come that John does not feel worthy to be his slave. Such is the exemplary humility of John. In pointing to Jesus, John clearly "witnesses" to the coming Mighty One in a manner reminiscent of the later

2. See BAGD 691 §2c; BAA 1386 §2c; Gen. 6:5; Matt. 9:4; Mark 7:23. Grammatically the plural ὧν is attracted to πονηρῶν, while it refers back to πάντων; BDF §294.5; Marshall 1978: 149.

Gospel of John's portrayal of the Baptist as the μάρτυς (*martys*, witness; Schürmann 1969: 187; John 1:7–8, 15, 19, 32, 34; 3:26; 5:33–36).

John did not have a "successful" ministry by external standards. His straightforward rebuke of Herod's morality landed him in prison. But the arrest is not a sign of failure for this faithful prophet. Rather, it represents a condemnation of a ruler who when confronted with personal sin did not respond in repentance as the people before him had done (3:10–14). In concluding the overview of John's ministry, Luke portrays John as the first of many servants of God who will suffer at the hands of those who reject the message. Some cannot stomach God's message confronting their approach to life. Sin is ugly and some cannot stand to have it exposed, even when forgiveness is offered at the same time. That is the tragedy of Herod's response.

II. Preparation for Ministry: Anointed by God (3:1–4:13)
   A. John the Baptist: One Who Goes Before (3:1–20)
➤ B. Jesus: One Who Comes After (3:21–4:13)

B. Jesus: One Who Comes After (3:21–4:13)

Luke completes the introduction of Jesus' ministry with a three-part unit. He briefly describes Jesus' baptism, where the divine voice confirms Jesus' status (3:21–22). Then he lists the genealogy of Jesus, tracing Jesus back to the starting point: Adam's creation by God (3:23–38). This means that Jesus is son of Adam, Son of God. Finally, there is Jesus' temptation by the devil (4:1–13), where Jesus proves his faithfulness and shows that he is ready to assume the task.

My analysis of the unit could be debated. For example, it could be argued that 3:21–22 really belongs with the previous section on John the Baptist. However, Luke does not name the Baptist in this section, so it is clearly Luke's intention to focus on Jesus (Schürmann 1969: 191). It should also be noted that 3:21–22 is really a transition paragraph and that in it Luke makes a fifth point about John's ministry:

ministry (3:1–6)
preaching (3:7–14)
promise (3:15–18)
imprisonment (3:19–20)
baptism of Jesus (3:21–22)

With regard to the end of the unit, the break at 4:13 recognizes that after this verse Jesus enters into active ministry. Everything up to this point is preparatory. Luke 4:14–15 is an introductory summary of Jesus' activity, and 4:16–30 is an initial representative description of his teaching. So a break at 4:13 is appropriate.[1]

---

1. For more detail on the discussion about structure, see the first additional note on 3:21.

1. Jesus' Baptism (3:21–22)

This short paragraph completes the transition from John the Baptist to Jesus. The event is one of the most christologically significant in the entire Gospel, because it presents one of two divine testimonies given during Jesus' ministry (the transfiguration account, 9:28–36, is the second such event). The force of the Lucan and Matthean testimony is not as striking as is the material in Mark, because Mark, unlike the other Gospels, lacks an infancy account. Thus, this event for Mark is the first direct divine testimony to Jesus. As such it stands in contrast to Matthew and Luke, who give angelic testimonies in their infancy material (Matt. 1:20–21; Luke 1:31–35; 2:10, 14).

Nevertheless, the baptism is significant for all the writers, since it marks the preparation point for Jesus' ministry, a ministry that begins with divine endorsement. Acts 10:37–38 acknowledges that this event was significant. The endorsement is marked by two elements: the divine word from heaven and the anointing by the Spirit (Schürmann 1969: 189). Together, these signs mark Jesus as the agent through whom God will work. So Jesus receives confirmation by revelation from God.

Sources and Historicity

The Lucan account's sources are the subject of some discussion. It is clear that for each of the Synoptic writers Jesus' baptism is a key event. It is also one of the few events that the Gospel of John refers to with the Synoptics (Aland 1985: §18; Matt. 3:13–17; Mark 1:9–11; John 1:29–34). Matthew has the fullest account, while each writer has some peculiarities. A particular element in this discussion is whether Matthew and Luke share a similar additional tradition at points. Some suggest that Q-like material is shared between the two writers (Marshall 1978: 150; Schürmann 1969: 197, 218–19; Ernst 1977: 151 ["perhaps"]).[1] Schürmann argues that this source combined the baptism with Jesus' wilderness temptation experience. The problem is that Q normally contains only Jesus' teaching, which is not present here. Others argue that no shared independent source was available to them, so Luke is using only Mark

---

1. There are two places where Luke's wording matches Matthew's: both have ἐπ' αὐτόν and both use the aorist passive βαπτισθῆναι. Those who hold to a two-Gospel hypothesis argue that this is evidence that Matthew preceded Luke and Mark.

(Fitzmyer 1981: 479; Schneider 1977a: 91; Wiefel 1988: 95; Bovon 1989: 179).[2]

Perhaps the most significant piece of agreement between Matthew and Luke is that they both use the same term, ἀνοίγω, to describe the opening of the heavens, though Matt. 3:16 has a verb (ἠνεῴχθησαν) and Luke 3:21 an infinitive (ἀνεῳχθῆναι), a grammatical difference also paralleled in Luke 3:17 and Matt. 3:12. But the difference in vocabulary with Mark is probably stylistic, since Mark uses ἀνοίγω only once in his Gospel (Mark 7:35), while Matthew uses it eleven times and Luke six times. In fact, ἀνοίγω has some theological value for Matthew, for he uses it to speak of the opening of ears, eyes, or mouth so that one can give or receive revelation from God (Matt. 5:2; 9:30; 13:35; 17:27; 20:33). Luke, on the other hand, does not share this Matthean force. This may well suggest that Matthew and Luke are independently agreeing with one another here. There is no need to appeal to an additional source for Matthew and Luke. Most of the differences are choices of style and narrative detail. The only additional detail, Jesus' prayer, fits an emphasis that Luke likes to make (see the exegesis of 3:21). But the association of invocation or prayer with religious ritual is normal in a Jewish setting (note the association of blessing and oath with covenant and washing at Qumran [1QS 2.1–26; 5.8–23]).

Even the often highly skeptical Crossan (1991: 232-33) accepts the historicity of John's baptism of Jesus. In his judgment, the tradition evidences much "theological damage control," which shows it took place. The tradition goes out of its way to make clear that, although John baptized Jesus, Jesus possessed no sin nor was he inferior to John.

When it comes to the historicity of the text's christological affirmations, Nolland (1989: 159) notes three reasons why scholarship is now taking early christological affirmations more seriously and why more scholars are viewing such declarations as grounded in preresurrection phenomena. (1) It is clear that Jesus elicited strong responses from others, so something must have caused such reaction. (2) Jesus' challenge in texts like Mark 8:38 contained implicit Christology. (3) Jesus' speaking of God as "Abba" and the use of the introductory double "Amen" show that he was conscious of a unique authority and relationship to God. It is clear that Christian tradition reflected on this event, as the distinct wording of the voice in the different Gospels shows. It is also clear that the tradition takes the event seriously and views it as significant. Nolland's approach stands in contrast to

---

2. But Goulder 1989: 281–82 sees Luke drawing both on Matthew and to a lesser degree on Mark. Fitzmyer 1981: 479–80 lists five major differences between Mark and Luke: (1) Luke omits references to Jesus' coming from Galilee (Mark 1:9) or being baptized in the Jordan; (2) Luke does not name John (Mark 1:9); (3) Luke uniquely notes Jesus' prayer; (4) Luke has the heaven "open" versus being "rent" (Mark 1:10); and (5) only Luke notes that the Spirit descended "in bodily form" like a dove (with Matt. 3:16). Wiefel 1988: 94–95 notes that Luke uses the singular "heaven" instead of the Semitic plural "heavens."

the view of C. F. Evans (1990: 246) that Jesus was baptized by John, but the heavenly declaration was exclusively the product of "theological reflection . . . judged according to the Spirit." He is skeptical that Jesus was the ultimate source of the account. I prefer Nolland's approach to that of C. F. Evans. Something concrete happened to Jesus to make this event such a vivid memory. As Nolland (1989: 159) says, "Something set Jesus apart from all the other baptismal penitents!"

In considering the form of this key passage, numerous inappropriate suggestions have been made. Bultmann (1963: 247–48) uses the combination of the miraculous voice and the pericope's "edifying purpose" to call it legend.[3] The problem is that the edifying purpose of the account is not so clear, since no general exhortation appears. If the edification comes merely through the christological declaration, then that is not reason enough to classify the material as legend, since christological declarations occur in a variety of forms. Also inadequate is the idea that 3:21–22 is a prophetic call like Jer. 1 or Isa. 6, since there is no task to which Jesus is called (Schürmann 1969: 197 #3; Fitzmyer 1981: 480). The account is not a theophany or epiphany, since God does not appear to anyone (so correctly Wiefel 1988: 94).

What is present then? Berger (1984: 235), noting the direct address using "you," speaks of an "identification acclamation," which is a correct way to describe the message of the voice (so also Ernst 1977: 152). Schürmann (1969: 190 n. 8, 197) calls it a "Christ-*Geschichte* revelatory event," a form that lacks parallels.[4] Bovon says it is an explanatory vision that has contact with apocalyptic, since the heavens are said to open up.[5] The term *vision* is perhaps not the best, since Luke does not emphasize what was seen in heaven, as much as he describes the Spirit's descent as being like a dove.[6] When everything is said, Schürmann's description, a revelatory event, is the best.

3. It is important to recall that the term *legend* is not always used in form criticism with the negative connotation it often has in English (i.e., supernatural, made-up, false). Nonetheless, Bultmann's use of the term here is not appropriate.

4. I have left untranslated the term *Geschichte*, which normally means "the significance of history" as opposed to mere "event." Schürmann's point, it appears, is that the event is not so much described as explained. It is a "Christ-history revelatory event."

5. Bovon 1989: 179 n. 65. He notes Isa. 64:1 [63:19 MT]; T. Levi 18.6–7. One could add 3 Macc. 6:18; 2 Bar. 22.1; Traub, *TDNT* 5:530 n. 263. Also seeing the presence of apocalyptic elements is Witherington 1990: 149, who compares the text to Rev. 1 and defends the event's authenticity as a vision.

6. This is a supernatural revelation, but it is not a glance into heaven or into the future. Neither does the opening up of the heaven serve to bring comfort in the

God sends the Spirit to come upon Jesus. For Luke, John drops entirely out of this pericope. His name is not explicitly mentioned, so that attention is placed exclusively on Jesus' prayer and the divine voice. So notable is this absence that Leaney (1958: 109) suggests that Luke's John does not baptize Jesus, but this ignores Acts 10:37–38 and 13:24–25. The omission stresses that this event is entirely God's work. The endorsement of Jesus is uniquely his.

The unit divides nicely into four parts:

setting of the endorsement: Jesus' prayer after baptism (3:21a)
opening of the heavens (3:21b)
descent of the Spirit (3:22a)
divine word (3:22b)

Each break is introduced by either a verb or an infinitive. The outline of Luke 3:21–22 is as follows:

a. Setting (3:21)
b. Testimony (3:22)

The major focus of the unit is christological. God gives a sign of endorsement to Jesus. Jesus' ministry has God's enablement behind it. The exact Christology of the heavenly pronouncement is a matter of much debate, as the exegesis of 3:22 will show. At the least, the OT allusions in the divine remark suggest a regal and messianic endorsement for Jesus, as opposed to a merely prophetic description.

The nature of the Spirit's anointing is also a subject of discussion. It seems to serve as a visible sign of the endorsement, a stamp of trustworthiness and enablement. Much of this significance is developed in Acts 10:36–38, where the Spirit's anointing of Jesus is associated with power.[7] The portrait in the Gospel itself supports this point, since power is tied specifically to the person of Jesus (Luke 4:36; 5:17; 6:19; 8:46; 9:1; 10:19; 21:27; Acts 2:22). In Jesus, one encounters a unique agent who bears God's authority and promise.

---

midst of persecution. Rather the Spirit is revealing himself to some on earth. For this reason the use of "vision" for Luke is less precise. For some texts from the second-century church fathers that briefly mention the event, see Ignatius, *Ephesians* 18.2 and *Smyrneans* 1.1; Justin Martyr, *Dialogue with Trypho* 88.2–8; 51.2; 103.6; and Irenaeus, *Against Heresies* 3.9.3; 3.17.1. See also Bertrand 1973 and Bovon 1989: 183–84.

7. See also 24:49, where the promised Spirit is associated with power.

Exegesis and Exposition

[21]When all the people were baptized, after Jesus was baptized and while he was praying, the heaven opened [22]and the Holy Spirit descended in bodily form like a dove upon him, and a voice came from heaven, "┌You are my Son, my beloved, in whom I am well pleased┐."

a. Setting (3:21)

3:21 Luke gives the divine testimony's setting. The verse's structure sets up 3:22. The grammar indicates that all the clauses of this verse are subordinate to the confession in 3:22 (Liefeld 1984: 859; Marshall 1978: 152). As a point of transition Luke mentions that all the people were baptized, a reference that underscores the Baptist's popularity by picturing a vast throng responding to his call. The use of "all people" (ἅπαντα τὸν λαόν, *hapanta ton laon*) is hyperbolic in that 7:30 shows that not every person responded to John. The hyperbole pictures the large size of the response and not the total number that responded.

Jesus gets baptized. Luke, unlike Matthew and Mark, does not mention here that Jesus came from Galilee. Luke may have excluded this note, since Jesus' home was already presented in 2:39. The baptism itself is underplayed, since Luke makes clear that the important event followed the actual baptism. The temporal order is indicated by a contrast between an aorist participle, βαπτισθέντος (*baptisthentos*, after he was baptized), and a present participle, προσευχομένου (*proseuchomenou*, while he was praying). The sequence shows that the only ongoing event at the time of the heavenly voice was the prayer (BDF §404.2; Plummer 1896: 99).[8] Thus, in contrast to Matt. 3:14–15, Luke makes no point about why Jesus should get baptized.

The theological significance of Jesus' partaking in the baptism has been much discussed throughout church history (for the options, see the second additional note on 3:21). The noncanonical traditions of this event show Jesus agreeing to the baptism only at the insistence of his family (Jerome, *Against the Pelagians* 3.2, citing the Gospel of the Hebrews; Plummer 1896: 99; Schneemelcher 1991–92: 1.160). The later church's concern over this event was motivated by the desire to avoid any suggestion that Jesus needed to repent and confess sin. Some argue that Jesus began to take on sin for humans here (Hendriksen 1978: 216–17; Geldenhuys 1951: 146;

---

8. My translation of 3:21–22 is deliberately nonidiomatic in the bracketed portion above to show this point. The mention of prayer fits a decidedly Lucan emphasis: 1:10, 13; 2:36–38; 5:16; 6:12; 9:18, 28; 10:21–23; 11:2–4; 22:32, 41, 44; 23:46. Note also the parables in 18:1–8 and 11:5–13. On this theme, see Plymale 1991. Jesus' attitude of prayer shows the solemnity with which he takes the baptism.

John 1:29). This view removes the dilemma and might seem logical, but it has a biblical obstacle. The NT never suggests that John's baptism had this soteriological function (Liefeld 1984: 859 [who argues that Jesus was baptized in order to identify with sinners]; Godet 1875: 1.190–91). Even the remarks in John 1 are general personal testimony about Jesus and not about the baptism's significance.

Jesus' choice to partake in John's baptism probably has a threefold role. First, it represents an endorsement of John's ministry and message (20:1–8). Jesus by accepting baptism links his cause to that of John. Second, it shows how Jesus identified himself with people as he began his ministry. He identifies with John's message of repentance (1:76–77; 3:3) and so endorses the need of people to repent. Third, in the Spirit's descending, Jesus emerges as the Coming One to whom John pointed and who brings this greater baptism (Luke 3:15–18; Acts 10:37–38). Luke reflcts only the first and third purpose.

Luke places the heavenly voice after the actual baptism, as do Matt. 3:16 and Mark 1:10. But Luke uniquely notes that Jesus was praying when the voice came. This focus on prayer is an emphasis of Luke. Many key events in Jesus' life are noted as having been accompanied by prayer.[9] The prayer adds solemnity to the setting, as if Jesus knows he is about to embark on his mission. The Coming One stands in supplication before the Father as he receives the Father's endorsement and enablement.

God begins to act. The picture of the heavens opening is a common figure for God's dramatic action, usually a vision from heaven, or merely for the breaking in of revelation.[10] Stephen's vision in Acts 7:56 starts with the opening of the heavens. The picture is of God stepping out of heaven to address people, of God entering into their everyday world. This adds to the event's mood. Clearly God takes the initiative to show humanity the way to him.

b. Testimony (3:22)

The revelation following Jesus' prayer comes in two parts: the physical sign of the Spirit descending upon Jesus and the heavenly, verbal testimony to him. Luke's account is short and simple in contrast to accounts in the later apocryphal tradition.[11] In each

3:22

---

9. Luke 6:12 (choosing of the Twelve); 9:18 (Peter's confession); 9:29 (transfiguration); 11:1 (Lord's Prayer); and 22:41 (Gethsemane).

10. Ezek. 1:1; Isa. 24:18; 64:1 [63:19 MT]; Gen. 7:11; Mal. 3:10; 3 Macc. 6:18; T. Levi 2.6–8; esp. 18.6–7 (a Christian interpolation?); Apocryphon of John 47.30; Maurer, *TDNT* 7:962; Schweizer 1984: 78; Bovon 1989: 180 n. 66; Godet 1875: 1.186–87 (who also treats the Synoptics' relationship to the account in John's Gospel).

11. Gospel of the Ebionites in Epiphanius, *Haereses* 30.13.7–8; Gospel of the Hebrews in Jerome, *Commentary on Isaiah* §4 (on Isa. 11:2); Gospel of the Nazareans

of these other accounts the voice from heaven speaks more fully. The Gospel of the Ebionites repeats the saying twice, while the voice in the Gospel of the Hebrews calls Jesus God's rest and first-begotten Son. In the Gospel of the Nazareans, Jesus goes to be baptized at the encouragement of his parents and will admit only to the possibility of sins of ignorance. In contrast to these accounts, Luke produces a simple heavenly endorsement, which shows the arrival of the Coming One of 3:16. God is with his agent and has bestowed his Spirit upon him. Thus, this event is on a higher scale than a prophetic call, though it bears a few similarities to such accounts (Schürmann 1969: 197 #3). There is no vision of heaven as with Ezek. 1 nor a tracing of the prophet's life as in Jer. 1. There is only the declaration of who Jesus is. The event is without parallel, but the anointing with the Spirit reveals the presence of divine wisdom.

The Spirit's descent comes with the opening of the heavens. Luke alone emphasizes the concrete nature of the experience by speaking of a descent in bodily form. The unique reference to σωματικῷ εἴδει (sōmatikō eidei, in bodily form) shows that the coming of the Spirit was a visible experience.[12]

Depictions of this event tend to overplay the metaphor. Ancient sources retelling the story make this error (Odes Sol. 24:1–2; Greeven, *TDNT* 6:68 n. 56). What was visible was not a dove, but rather what was seen is compared to a dove, since ὡς (hōs, as) is an adverb of manner (Schürmann 1969: 190). The manner of the Spirit's descent was like the way a dove floats gracefully through the air. Luke alone lacks a verbal reference to the sighting of a dove-like entity, in that he does not use εἶδεν (eiden, he saw) as Matt. 3:16 and Mark 1:10 do. In this way, Luke minimizes the visionlike aspects of the account (Michaelis, *TDNT* 5:353).

The association of a dove with the Spirit is a topic of some discussion (Marshall 1978: 153–54; Creed 1930: 57; Glickman 1983: 44–71; Keck 1970–71; Lentzen-Deis 1970: 170–83). Numerous points of connection have been suggested:

1. In Greek culture, birds and the gods were often associated (Greeven, *TDNT* 6:64–66).[13] But the account's setting and imagery are Semitic, not Greek, in character.

---

in Jerome, *Against the Pelagians* 3.2; Funk 1985: 1.316; Schneemelcher 1991–92: 1.169, 177, 160.

12. For εἶδος, see BAGD 221. Σωματικός is found in the NT only here and in 1 Tim. 4:8; BAGD 800.

13. Greeven, *TDNT* 6:64–65, details this background and shows that the dove was the bird of the gods. Aphrodite was "the dove goddess" on many coins.

2. Some associate the Spirit with the *Bath Qol* (בַּת קוֹל, daughter of a voice), a teaching in Judaism of a heavenly voice that was not directly God's and that came after the prophetic period of the OT.[14] The problem with this association is that the Spirit is not portrayed as speaking, and the voice is not to be seen as a substitute for God.[15] The voice is God's (*"my* Son"; 3:22).
3. Some tie this image to God's Spirit brooding over the creation waters in Gen. 1:2, a figure that in some later texts is tied to a dove.[16] Other Jewish materials tie the Genesis reference to a more general reference to a bird (Midr. Gen. 2.4 [3c]). But Luke identifies the descending creature too narrowly as a dove. An additional problem is the appeal to a rather late Jewish tradition, unless an allusion does exist at Qumran.
4. Another possible approach is the comparison to Noah's dove in Gen. 8:8–12, where the dove symbolizes the end of judgment and the beginning of grace (Dunn 1970a: 27 n. 13). The association has problems. First, the baptism that Jesus brings, according to Luke 3:16–17, includes judgment so that the symbolism argued for in the dove is opposite to the ministry that John the Baptist promises for Jesus. Second, the passage in Genesis does not mention God's Spirit.
5. Others attempt an association with the nation of Israel (Hos. 11:11), but this association is not a part of the context at all.
6. Others attempt a connection to Deut. 32:11 and a call to a new exodus, but in this OT passage the bird is an eagle.

These attempts to make a theological symbol out of the dove seem flawed. The closest plausible associations are the two Genesis passages where something new is begun, but even these connections may be too distant. It seems best to leave the figure of the dove as a simple metaphor without theological significance. The Spirit descended on Jesus with the grace of a dove.

14. O. Betz, *TDNT* 9:288–90, 298. Some cite Tg. Song 2:12; SB 1:123–24, but Sjöberg, *TDNT* 6:382, notes that the Spirit never appears in the form of a dove in rabbinic writings.

15. O. Betz, *TDNT* 9:288, makes clear that the *Bath Qol* is a voice inferior to God and the prophets. In Luke, angels have this intermediary role.

16. Keck 1970–71. B. Ḥag. 15a, a talmudic reference of later origin, makes this connection. More recently, Allison 1992 argues vigorously for a connection to Gen. 1:2. The Messianic Vision fragment from Qumran (see photograph and R. H. Eisenman's translation in *Biblical Archaeology Review* 17.6 [Nov.–Dec. 1991]: 65) might contain an allusion to Messiah and Gen. 1:2. If so, the objection to the lateness of the other Jewish parallels is removed. The image would suggest a "new" beginning in God's work, though I disagree with Allison that the remark is only symbolic, as if one must choose between history and symbol.

The Spirit is said to come down upon (ἐπ᾽, *ep'*) Jesus. Here Luke agrees in terminology with Matt. 3:16, while Mark 1:10 has εἰς (*eis*, into). The difference is one of perspective not substance. Mark emphasizes in his language the "anointing of the Spirit," an act that Luke recognizes is present in this event (Luke 4:18; Acts 10:36–38; Schürmann 1969: 195). For Mark, the Spirit comes into Jesus. Luke and Matthew word the account in light of the figure of the dove, since a dove cannot go into, but can alight upon someone. The nature of the anointing must await the discussion of the declaration by the voice.

The voice came from heaven. Clearly God's voice is meant, for it is a voice distinct from the angelic messengers who appeared directly to people in the infancy section. As such, the voice cannot be the *Bath Qol*, since that voice is distinct from God. The voice's presence raises the question of what type of experience is present here.

The question about the kind of experience is compounded when one compares the Synoptic accounts. Luke 3:22 and Mark 1:11 have σύ (*sy*, you) as the subject of God's address, while Matt. 3:17 has οὗτος (*houtos*, this one). Thus, Luke and Mark have a direct address to Jesus, while Matthew's wording broadens the audience being addressed. John's Gospel, which reports the event through John the Baptist, does not mention the wording of the voice, but does make clear that John the Baptist saw the Spirit descend as a dove (John 1:32–33).

A simple solution taken by the apocryphal Gospel of the Ebionites is that the voice makes two statements, first using σύ and the next time using οὗτος (Schneemelcher 1991–92: 1.169). Such a composite might seem possible, but is unlikely, since all the Gospel accounts have only one statement.

Another approach argues that Matthew's broad perspective gives the utterance and that Mark and Luke have personalized the reference to Jesus alone for emphasis and christological focus. This approach is also possible, more so in my judgment than the previous one, but it means that two writers independently made the same type of alteration, a result that, though possible, is not very likely.[17]

Though certainty is impossible on this issue, it seems more likely that Mark and Luke recorded the tradition's original thrust of the voice addressing Jesus alone. Matthew "applied" accurately the significance of the event by pointing out that "this one," Jesus, is the beloved Son. Matthew, by making the change, shows the event's

---

17. Even if Luke is perceived as merely copying Mark, the agreement is significant, especially if Mark is the earliest Gospel. On the other hand, if Matthew is the first Gospel, what caused Luke and Mark to go the same way together?

significance in terms of his readers. They are to realize who this Jesus is (Carson 1984: 109). By broadening the reference, Matthew also suggests that the experience was not limited to Jesus. His rendering also rules out that it was merely an internal psychological experience. It is easier to see Matthew being responsible for a single change than to see two authors independently making the same change. The nature of the event emerges. Jesus had a private experience of the Spirit, but it was not an entirely private or internal vision, for John the Baptist also could testify to the event (Godet 1875: 1.186–87).

The voice's saying consists of three parts: a reference to the Son (υἱός, huios), a reference to the beloved (ἀγαπητός, agapētos), and a reference to God's being pleased with the Son (ἐν σοὶ εὐδόκησα, en soi eudokēsa). The OT background to the saying is much discussed and is important, since the nature of the allusions determines the christological point made about Jesus. Six positions are possible (Bock 1987: 100–105):

1. The only OT text involved is Ps. 2:7. This position is tied to the textual problem discussed in the additional note and is rejected on text-critical grounds.
2. The only OT text involved is Isa. 42:1 (Jeremias 1971a: 53–55; Cullmann 1963: 66; Hahn 1969: 337–41). This position argues that, where υἱός is now present, there was originally present in the tradition the title παῖς (pais, servant), an allusion to Isa. 42 (see Matt. 12:18). Marshall (1968–69) examines the six arguments used for this view and finds them less than compelling. Most significant is the lack of any text variant citing παῖς.
3. Bretscher (1968) argues that the phrase υἱὸς πρωτότοκός μου Ἰσραήλ (huios prōtotokos mou Israēl, my firstborn son, Israel) in Exod. 4:22–23 is behind the passage, with Jesus presented as idealized Israel. He argues that πρωτότοκος was switched to ἀγαπητός, a common word pair in Jewish parallelism (2 Esdr. [= 4 Ezra] 6:58; Ps. Sol. 13.9; 18.4). This view cannot work, since there is no evidence in the NT that Exod. 4:22–23 was ever used as a christological proof-text, while both Ps. 2:7 and Isa. 42:1 have such traces in the NT tradition (Acts 13:33; Matt. 12:18). In addition, Bretscher's explanation of the origin for ἀγαπητός, though possible, is complicated and should be dropped if an easier solution exists.

The next three approaches agree on two points: that the reference to υἱός comes from Ps. 2:7 and the reference to God's being pleased from Isa. 42:1. Only the source for ἀγαπητός is disputed.

4. A phrase in Gen. 22:12, 16, τοῦ υἱοῦ σου τοῦ ἀγαπητοῦ (*tou huiou sou tou agapētou*, your beloved son), may be behind the reference.[18] Thus, the idiom here, ὁ υἱός μου ὁ ἀγαπητός, should be rendered "only Son." The emphasis is on the uniqueness of Jesus' sonship. However, υἱός has a double meaning in this view, since it would be drawn from both Ps. 2:7 and Gen. 22:12 and would refer both to Messiah and to the Isaac typology. Such a multilayered allusion is possible, but is complicated since two distinct types of sonship are in view. Second, Luke has no Isaac typology clearly present in his material. In fact, in the NT, only Paul comes close to this allusion by his wording of Rom. 8:32, though Heb. 11:17–19 might also apply. Third, Luke can use μονογενής (*monogenēs*, only begotten or unique) when he wishes to express the idea (Luke 7:12; 8:42; 9:38). Fourth, the shift from ἀγαπητός to ἐκλελεγμένος (*eklelegmenos*, chosen) in 9:35 is against the connection. That saying parallels this account and serves to give a clue as to the meaning of ἀγαπητός in 3:22. It does not suggest the Gen. 22 reference.

5. Isa. 41:8 and 44:2 may be behind ἀγαπητός with their association of being chosen and being loved. Gundry (1967: 30–31) argues for this approach from Tg. Ps. 2:7. The targum includes a reference to ἀγαπητός, a point that Gundry makes, drawing support from material noted by Schweizer (*TDNT* 8:368). However, the targum is of a late date and its reference to sonship is too indirect to have been of influence (Marshall 1968–69: 333–34). In addition, Isa. 44:2 cannot be a part of the connection, because the reference to the concept of love is absent in that passage.

6. It seems best to tie the reference to ἀγαπητός, if it has OT origin, to Isa. 41:8. In this passage the ideas of Servant, chosen, and beloved are tied together. The Isa. 41 passage links up with Isa. 42 in that the ideas of Servant and chosen are repeated. In Matthew, the concept of chosen in Isa. 42 is translated as "beloved," which is a reflection of this earlier linkage. It may be that the saying links only a targum-like rendering of Isa. 42 with Ps. 2, but if so, the hidden point of contact is still the concept of Isa. 41. Thus, the reference to ἀγαπητός speaks

---

18. C. Turner 1925–26: 113–25; Glickman 1983: 86–87. Stegner 1989: 15–31 stresses this Genesis connection over the regal motifs, tying ἀγαπητός to the Jewish motifs of the binding of Isaac. Currently, this may well be the most popular explanation. Gen. 22:2 is also mentioned as having the same basic phrase, though the expression there is in the accusative case. Other LXX uses of this phrase occur in Jer. 6:26; Amos 8:10; and Zech. 12:10.

of Jesus' intimate and chosen position. It also may imply that Jesus represents the nation, since Isa. 41:8 refers to the nation.

Thus, Ps. 2:7, Isa. 42:1, and possibly Isa. 41:8 are the OT elements behind the voice's endorsement. But what does the saying, with these allusions, tell us about Jesus? Psalm 2 is a regal psalm that looks ideally at the king's total rule. The allusion to "my Son" in terms of Ps. 2 says that Jesus is this regal figure. This allusion is essentially messianic, when it is placed alongside John the Baptist's declaration in Luke 3:16. This position is confirmed within Luke by the regal and rule images that appear in the other usages of the messianic concept. "My Son" appears in 9:35, after a section where Jesus is confessed as "the Christ"; the messianic concept occurs in Acts 4:25–30, where similar "anointed" sentiments are expressed, and anointing is used with similar force in Acts 10:36–38. Thus, a key part of the endorsement is a messianic one.

This messianic interpretation may be challenged as inadequate in two ways. First, Fitzmyer (1981: 485–86) argues that the term *my son* is only a nonmessianic regal allusion. But, at least in Luke, this seems unlikely in light of the evangelist's emphases noted above, and especially in light of the messianic thrust of the infancy section leading up to this material. If Jesus is a regal figure who follows an eschatological prophet like John the Baptist, who can he be but Messiah? Fitzmyer (1981: 482) concedes as much for Acts 10:37–38 and its view of this event, but distinguishes this interpretation from the self-contained event itself. But on the assumption of a traditional background for this material in Luke, a messianic thrust also emerges for the second evangelist (Mark 1:1, 7). A similar conclusion is possible for Matthew, since John the Baptist announces the approach of the kingdom with the one who baptizes with the Spirit (Matt. 3:1, 11). Jewish tradition may also speak against this distinction in its use of Ps. 2 (Ps. Sol. 17.23–24; 4Q174 [= 4QFlor]; Nolland 1989: 163). So a regal nonmessianic understanding is unlikely, both from Luke's standpoint and from the tradition he inherited. To connect Jesus to regal texts in an eschatological setting makes an implicit messianic claim. Fitzmyer is right that the title alone cannot make the point, but it is the title coupled with the setting that leads to this conclusion.

Second, others argue that the point heads in the direction of the full ontological sonship of Jesus.[19] Marshall's approach is possible, but is not clearly indicated by the allusions themselves. It is my con-

---

19. Hendriksen 1978: 218 (who alludes to eternal generation); Geldenhuys 1951: 147; Marshall 1978: 155–56 (who more cautiously speaks only of a more than Messiah perspective, while refusing to emphasize ontology as such).

tention that Luke purposefully and gradually reveals who Jesus is. Thus, his Christology in this section is still essentially messianic, though the nature of this messiahship is such that Luke can later show who Messiah really is. One can hold to this view of Luke's presentation of Jesus without denying Jesus' own self-understanding to be more than this.[20] Luke's allusions to the Christ are consistently messianic up to this point and for some period after the account (see the exegesis of 4:41). So, then, a messianic focus is in view here.

The possible connection to Isa. 41:8 alludes to the chosen and intimate relationship that Jesus has to the Father, while also suggesting a point of connection with the nation. The allusion to Isa. 42:1 also emphasizes the Father's pleasure in the Son, while identifying the Son with the Servant figure, who does God's will and has God's anointing. The Isaianic Servant is a complex figure, mixing prophetic qualities with deliverance images. So Jesus' connection to the Servant suggests that Jesus' task is complex. Luke 9:35 will also have this mix of regal and prophetic elements, but will use Deut. 18 to make the prophetic element more explicit. Thus, the OT background present here serves to fuse together the distinct portraits that existed in the infancy material. Jesus is the Messiah-Servant.

In describing what took place in the baptism, some have spoken of adoption; that is, Jesus is made Messiah at this point in his life. In fact, some argue that the time of Jesus' entry into his messianic office has been pushed back in the tradition from its original locale at the resurrection to this time of baptism.[21] But it is better to speak of legitimation for Luke. Jesus is not becoming Messiah at his baptism (Schürmann 1969: 191–92). This point is especially clear in Luke's presentation, where Jesus' position as a promised Davidic ruler is clear from the start in 1:31–35. Rather, what is present is the first testimony to Jesus from heaven, as God's agent prepares to embark on his mission. The baptism is like an inauguration, a call to begin the mission for which Jesus was always headed.

When one sees the voice in this light, one also can speak of the Spirit's anointing not just in terms of wisdom, power, and enablement, but also in terms of endorsement and confirmation (Schürmann 1969: 194–95). The power that Jesus exhibits in Luke–Acts is attributed to his own authority, person, or name, and not solely to the Spirit (Luke 4:36; 5:12, 17; 6:19; 8:46; 9:1; 10:19; Acts 3:12, 16;

20. Marshall 1978: 155–56 links the two positions together unnecessarily. One can distinguish between how Jesus saw himself and how a Gospel writer chose to reveal that understanding. For example, 2:41–52 shows hints of the deeper view of Jesus, but it is not explained until late in the Gospel and in Acts.

21. Acts 2:32–36 is said to reflect such a resurrection tradition, as does Rom. 1:3–4.

4:7). Even the power that the disciples receive is sent by Jesus to them so that he has authority over it (Luke 9:1 and 24:49 with Acts 2:32–34). The Spirit is associated with power in Acts 2:38, not so much because the Spirit is the source of the power, but because the Spirit shows that God is with Jesus (Acts 10:38). The same "chosen by God" emphasis is seen in Luke 4:18–19, a passage that speaks of Jesus' anointing and looks back to this baptism. After the baptismal confirmation come the presence and direction of God's Spirit into the task (4:1, 14). The Spirit leads and confirms more than he empowers Jesus in Luke.[22] Both ideas—power and confirmation—are present, but the emphasis is on direction, identification, and support for Jesus rather than on provision. This distinction is important, because the disciples have a fundamentally different relationship to the Spirit than does Jesus. The disciples are totally subject to the Spirit, who comes to them through the agency of Jesus (Acts 2:32–34). Thus, Jesus' baptism is an endorsement and confirmation of him in terms of his Messiah-Servant mission. Jesus is the Coming One to whom John looked. Now, with God's confirmation having come to Jesus, the introductory figure, John, passes off Luke's stage almost entirely. It is time for the main character to step forward.

Summary

Luke 3:21–22 shows that with Jesus' baptism comes the divine confirmation that Jesus is the Messiah-Servant. What his task will be, how he will rule, and how he will deliver are questions that the rest of the Gospel will answer. But the emphasis here is that heaven has spoken. God has revealed his choice. Much as a political party puts its stamp on a presidential candidate, so here God has shown who will accomplish his plan. Having received God's confirmation in the Spirit's testimony, Jesus can prepare for ministry.

Before tackling the ministry proper, Luke has two final items of introduction to cover. First is the genealogy of Jesus, a genealogy that will identify Jesus not only with the nation as the chosen Son, but with all people, since he is the son of Adam, the Son of God. Here Jesus' roots show him to be the representative of humanity (3:23–38). Second is the matter of Jesus' righteousness and faithfulness to God as he stands up against the great opponent, Satan (4:1–13). Jesus is qualified to serve. In the baptism of Jesus, God has shown his hand and registered his vote. The testimony of heaven is that Jesus is the beloved Son. When God speaks, the reader is to listen.

22. However, the Spirit is associated with empowerment in Luke. Luke 24:49 does see the Spirit as a source of power for disciples; also 4:14.

Additional Notes

3:21. Commentators differ on where to break this and the adjoining sections, since Luke does not give us his own outline. For example, Wiefel (1988: 86) has a unit extending from 3:1 to 4:30, since he calls part of the section the beginning of Jesus' work, a title that justifies his larger boundaries. Bovon (1989: 162) has a subsection entitled "The Work of John and the Baptism of Jesus," which extends from 3:1 to 3:22. Bovon does not attempt to construct a larger-level outline other than to group a few pericopes together, so it is hard to sense how he sees this unit fitting into the whole. Nonetheless, the title matches the unit. On the other end, Schürmann (1969: 187) has a unit entitled "The Beginning of the Kingdom Preaching of Jesus," which extends from 3:21 to 4:44. Again the title matches the unit, but why stop the "beginning" at 4:44? The beginning should probably include the first gathering of disciples in 5:1. Thus, in my judgment, it is better to distinguish between where Jesus prepares for ministry and where he actually does it. Marshall's division (1978: 131) agrees with mine and is called "John the Baptist and Jesus." This division allows one to focus more clearly on the geographical orientation of the book, with 4:14–9:50 being the ministry in Galilee, while 9:51–19:44 is the journey to Jerusalem.

3:21. Fitzmyer (1981: 482) notes four basic approaches to the issue of Jesus' submitting to baptism. Stein (1992: 139) has six possibilities, while noting that the very difficulty of explaining the event's rationale is a reason to take its historicity seriously. Two of Stein's options are (1) that Jesus did this to fulfill all righteousness (Matt. 3:15), but what that means still needs explanation, and (2) that we do not know the purpose of the baptism. This leaves Fitzmyer's four approaches. (3) Jesus is shown to be conscious of personal sin, a view that Fitzmyer notes is counter to the entire Christian tradition (John 8:46; 2 Cor. 5:21; Heb. 4:15; 7:26; 9:14). (4) The baptism shows Jesus' approval of John's ministry. This has "an element of truth," according to Fitzmyer, but is more suited to Matthew's version. (5) Jesus is a sort of disciple of John's, a view Fitzmyer argues is possible from John 1:29–50 and 3:26. Against this is that none of the Gospels anywhere suggests that Jesus ever "followed" John. (6) The baptism is a symbolic anticipation of Jesus' passion and expiation (Luke 12:50; Isa. 53:12; Mark 10:38–39). Fitzmyer argues that this sees too much in the text. Most likely Jesus' act has two functions: (a) to identify with and endorse John's ministry and thus (b) to show people's need to have sin forgiven (so Justin Martyr, *Dialogue with Trypho* 88.2), that is, views 1 and 4 above.

3:22. In considering the divine voice's testimony, the wording must be determined. Many interpreters argue that the voice, as cited by Luke, uttered Ps. 2:7 alone (Luce 1933: 113; Klostermann 1929: 55; Leaney 1958: 110–11; Rese 1969: 193–95). Those who see only Ps. 2:7 here argue that it is the harder reading, since it diverges from Matthew and Mark. Only D and some Itala have this reading, along with some fathers such as Hilary and Augustine. Those who favor this position argue that it is an ancient reading, since it is cited as the message of the voice by Justin Martyr in *Dialogue with Trypho* 88, 103. It is also the more difficult reading, because it might imply adoptionism and thus a copyist would have been likely to change it.

The argument for Ps. 2:7 alone is not as strong as it might look at first.[23] The issue of the divergence from Matthew and Mark is balanced by the possibility that a copyist was influenced by Acts 13:33 to conform this citation to Luke's other usage of this passage. The evidence of Justin is clouded by his mention only of details from Matthew—and Matthew has no textual variant about what the voice said nor does he cite Ps. 2:7. Justin mentions only Ps. 2:7 because he brings out the OT background more clearly. In favor of an alteration in light of Acts 13:33 is the point that manuscript D and its Western family relatives have universalistic tendencies in their textual tradition that caused them to cite Ps. 2:7–8 in Acts 13:33 (Epp 1966: 79–81). So Ps. 2:7 was important to D. As well, D often assimilates a text to conform to the LXX (Mark 15:34 and Ps. 22:1 [22:2 MT]; Acts 13:33 and Ps. 2:8; Jeremias, *TDNT* 5:701 n. 349; Schürmann 1969: 193–94). Thus the text that appears in UBS–NA is original.

---

23. Bock 1987: 99–101. Note also the discussions rejecting this reading in Schürmann 1969: 193–94 and Marshall 1978: 154–55.

2. Jesus' Genealogy: Son of Adam, Son of God (3:23–38)

Jesus' genealogy performs an important role in Luke's Gospel. The account concludes with the name *Adam* and then mentions that Jesus is the Son of God. This connection indicates Jesus' relationship to all humankind as their representative. The universal perspective fits very nicely with the Lucan emphasis on salvation for all (Acts 10:34–43; 17:22–31). In tracing the genealogy all the way back to Adam, Luke distinguishes his genealogy from that of Matthew, who goes back only as far as Abraham (Matt. 1:1–17), a choice that focuses on the national promise of a king to Israel. Danker (1988: 96) notes that tracing the genealogy back to God would impress Hellenistic readers with the importance of Jesus.[1]

Some argue that the Adamic connection is not really significant (M. Johnson 1988: 234–52). Johnson rejects the Adamic association for three reasons. First, the Pauline motif of the second Adam (Rom. 5:12–21; 1 Cor. 15:20–28, 45–49) appears nowhere else in Luke–Acts. Second, any attempt to connect Adam to the temptations in Luke 4 must be regarded as a failure. Third, the genealogy does not end with Adam, but with Jesus the Son of God, so that Adam is not the point. In place of Adam, Johnson argues that the genealogy highlights two key features: that Jesus is the Son of God and that Jesus is a prophet, since his line passes through Nathan.[2]

But this rejection of the Adamic connection misses the big picture. The key feature of the genealogy is that it goes past Abraham to Adam. The addition of that perspective alone is significant and is not to be ignored. As Marshall (1978: 161) argues, "To regard all the names from Joseph to Adam as one gigantic paren-

---

1. On the Jewish use of genealogies, see C. F. Evans 1990: 251–53. Such lists were available to some in the first century. Josephus, *Life* 1 §§3–6 and *Against Apion* 1.7 §§30–36 limits such lists to priestly families.

2. Fitzmyer 1981: 497 rejects M. Johnson's verdict, noting that this alternative requires that Nathan son of David equal Nathan the prophet. Fitzmyer argues that there is no evidence of such an identification in pre-Christian Judaism or in the pre-Lucan Christian community. Zech. 12:12 is key here. Nolland 1989: 170, 172 agrees and argues that the line of Nathan is opened up by the curse on Jeconiah (Jer. 22:30), alternately called Jehoiachin (NIV) or Coniah (NRSV), which prompted Luke to ignore Jewish kings. Nolland does not emphasize a prophetic connection to Nathan. If this view is to be held, this is the way to argue for it.

thesis . . . misses the point of the genealogy, and to regard divine sonship as mediated to Jesus through his ancestors conflicts with the birth story. Hence the point of the genealogy is rather to show that Jesus has his place in the human race created by God." Outside of Jesus, Adam is the only one related to the title *son of God* in Luke.

Glickman (1983: 407–9) notes that Adam's placement next to "the son of God" is one of five unusual elements about the genealogy, a point that shows the connection was planned. (1) Placement of the genealogy not at the start of the Gospel but between the baptism and temptation is unusual. With this placement, the genealogy comes between two events where Jesus' sonship is the issue. (2) Rather than starting with the original ancestor, the order goes from the present back to Adam—a choice that allows Adam's name to fall nearer the temptation account. This argument goes against M. Johnson's separation of the genealogy from the temptation. (3) The use of the υἱὸς τοῦ (*huios tou,* son of) formula sets up this descending order. (4) The extension of the genealogy all the way back to Adam reflects a universal point of view. (5) The unique inclusion of sonship to God brings the reader back to creation, giving a comprehensive temporal perspective. Glickman (1983: 410–24) examines Johnson's arguments in detail and finds them lacking (Marshall 1978: 161 also notes there is no Nathan-as-prophet motif in the NT). If the Adamic connection is rejected, it is hard to see how the prophetic connection through Nathan can be substituted for it, since that name is less prominently located than Adam's. It is better to see an Adamic focus (Ellis 1974: 93; Marshall 1978: 161; Schürmann 1969: 210–2; Danker 1988: 98). In the genealogy, Jesus is identified with the entire human race. In mentioning this idea, Luke highlights God's design in the outworking of salvation (so the use of δεῖ [*dei,* it is necessary] or other sovereignty-related terms for Jesus' activity in other texts: Acts 2:22–24; 17:31).

Sources and Historicity

This account is unique to Luke, though it draws on OT genealogies, esp. Gen. 10–11 and 1 Chron. 1–3. The issue of its historicity is largely related to the list's function, the value of the OT sources it draws upon, and its relationship to Matthew's ancestral list. This latter connection is the subject of excursus 5.

An outline of this section is not really necessary, since it proceeds through a list of names. As is mentioned in excursus 5, if one excludes the reference to the son of God, there are eleven groups of seven names, though nothing structurally notes this breakdown. The basic structural marker is the repeated use of the trailing genitive τοῦ (*tou*) to indicate paternity. The key names are David, Abraham, Adam, and son of God. The passage's form is obvious: we are dealing with a genealogy.

The major theme is that Jesus possesses the proper roots to be the promised agent of God. He is in David's line, pointing to a regal figure. He is Abraham's seed, pointing to the Abrahamic promise. He is Adam's seed, relating him to all humanity. And he is the Son of God. God has created this line to culminate in Jesus. Salvation, then, is the product of God's design and the object of his careful planning. In Jesus, there are no historical surprises.

Excluding Joseph in 3:23 (because of the "supposed" note) and the reference to the son of God in 3:38 (because it is a descriptive title, not a person), there are eleven groups of seven names. The translation is laid out in columns for easy reference.

Exegesis and Exposition

[23] Jesus, when he began his ministry, was about thirty years of age, being (as it was supposed) the son of Joseph,

    the son of Heli,
[24] the son of Matthat,
    the son of Levi,
    the son of Melchi,
    the son of Jannai,
    the son of Joseph,

[25] the son of Mattathias,
    the son of Amos,
    the son of Nahum,
    the son of Esli,
    the son of Naggai,
[26] the son of Maath,
    the son of Mattathias,

    the son of Semein,
    the son of Josech,
    the son of Joda,
[27] the son of Joanan,
    the son of Rhesa,
    the son of Zerubbabel,
    the son of Shealtiel,

    the son of Neri,
[28] the son of Melchi,
    the son of Addi,
    the son of Cosam,
    the son of Elmadam,
    the son of Er,
[29] the son of Joshua,

    the son of Eliezer,
    the son of Jorim,
    the son of Matthat,
    the son of Levi,
[30] the son of Simeon,
    the son of Judah,
    the son of Joseph,

    the son of Jonam,
    the son of Eliakim,
[31] the son of Melea,
    the son of Menna,
    the son of Mattatha,
    the son of Nathan,
    the son of David,

³² the son of Jesse,	the son of Abraham,
the son of Obed,	the son of Terah,
the son of Boaz,	the son of Nahor,
the son of ⌜Salmon⌝,	³⁵ the son of Serug,
the son of Nahshon,	the son of Reu,
³³ ⌜the son of Amminadab,	the son of Peleg,
the son of Aram,	the son of Eber,
the son of Admin,	the son of Shelah,
the son of Arni,⌝	³⁶ ⌜the son of Cainan⌝,
the son of Hezron,	the son of Arphaxad,
the son of Perez,	the son of Shem,
the son of Judah,	the son of Noah,
³⁴ the son of Jacob,	the son of Lamech,
the son of Isaac,	³⁷ the son of Methuselah,

the son of Enoch,
the son of Jared,
the son of Mahalaleel,
the son of Cainan,
³⁸ the son of Enos,
the son of Seth,
the son of Adam,

the son of God.

3:23 At the start of the genealogy Jesus is named in a rather emphatic, solemn way: αὐτὸς ἦν Ἰησοῦς (*autos ēn Iēsous*, he, namely Jesus, was) (BDF §277.3). Jesus' age at the start of his ministry was about thirty.[3] Beginnings are important to Luke, and he notes them regularly.[4] The beginning of Jesus' ministry follows his baptism, as the Spirit's coming marks out Jesus' call (Nolland 1989: 171).

The age of thirty has been taken as symbolic of the appropriate age for the beginning of service, since many OT offices could be filled at that age. Among the OT references to thirty are the age for priesthood (Num. 4:3), the age of Joseph on entry into Pharaoh's service (Gen. 41:46), the age of Ezekiel when called to ministry (perhaps Ezek. 1:1), and, most importantly, the age of David when he started reigning (2 Sam. 5:4). However, the number should not be taken as merely symbolic or theological, since Luke gives only an approximate number.[5] If Luke created the number, why did he not

3. Ἦν connects grammatically with ὡσεί, since that is the only possible predicate for the verb.

4. For ἀρχή, see Luke 1:2; Acts 11:15; 26:4; for the verbal equivalent, see Acts 1:21–22; 10:37. For the participle ἀρχόμενος, present here, see Luke 24:27; Acts 8:35; 11:4; Bovon 1989: 189.

5. Ernst 1977: 155 speaks of a theological, not a biographical, reason for the number. Schürmann 1969: 199 nn. 76, 79 sees only the Davidic reference as key and

make it exactly thirty? In rabbinic tradition (*b. Sanh.* 106b [where Jesus is probably referred to by the code name Balaam]; SB 2:155), Jesus' age during his ministry is 33–34, which is entirely possible, even though Schürmann (1969: 199 n. 81) calls the figure speculative and probably dependent on Luke 3:23. The age of thirty connects Jesus with OT notables.

Jesus' sonship to Joseph comes with a remark showing that this sonship is strictly a legal one, since Joseph was "supposed" (ἐνομίζετο, *enomizeto*) to be Jesus' father—a remark suggestive of the virgin birth. In the first century, legal status depended on the father, so the most natural way to take the reference to Joseph is as a genealogical reference. The genealogy is not Mary's, given the consistent structure of focusing on the fathers and the exclusion of women throughout the list.[6] The reference to the supposition of Joseph's paternity may be a Lucan note, since Luke uses νομίζω (*nomizō*, to suppose) nine times (here; Luke 2:44; and seven times in Acts), while NT usage outside Luke–Acts has only six occurrences (Matt. 5:17; 10:34; 20:10; 1 Cor. 7:26, 36; 1 Tim. 6:5; Schürmann 1969: 199 n. 82). The genealogical line is Joseph's, despite the virgin birth. It is merely a legal line.

Before discussing the genealogy proper, a few general points need to be made. First, most of the people mentioned in 3:24–31 are unknown, until one reaches the name *Nathan* in 3:31. For example, Fitzmyer (1981: 500, 501) notes that seventeen people from Matthat to Rhesa (3:24–27) are unknown, as are eighteen people from Melchi to Mattatha (3:28–31). Only Zerubbabel (1 Chron. 3:19; Ezra 2:2; Hag. 2:23) and Shealtiel (Hag. 1:1, 12, 14; 1 Chron. 3:19 LXX) in Luke 3:27 are known. Second, Ernst (1977: 156) notes that similarities in the names make for three groups of seven names each from Joseph to Shealtiel: Joseph to Joseph, Mattathias to Mattathias, Semein to Shealtiel. There follow another three groups of seven names each: Neri to Joshua, Eliezer to Joseph, Jonam to David (all names in these three groups diverge from Matthew's listing until David). Marshall (1978: 160) has an alternative grouping of the names, which differs slightly from mine because of text-critical decisions. Schürmann (1969: 200) notes that, though the structure is not accidental, Luke makes no real point of it.[7] Third, only

---

does not deny a historical value to the number. In the Greco-Roman world, men were called to public service at thirty; Dionysius Halicarnassus, *Roman Antiquities* 4.6; C. F. Evans 1990: 254.

6. For defense of a Marian genealogy, see Hendriksen 1978: 222–25. Marshall 1978: 162 gives the grammatical refutation of the notion that the reference to Joseph is parenthetical, which would make the genealogy Mary's.

7. The structure may belong to Luke's source, whose presence is suggested by the lack of any comment by Luke in the face of such a conscious structure.

Luke includes names between Adam and Abraham. Luke shares with Matthew the list from Abraham to David, though textual variation exists with Arni and Admin in 3:33. Luke diverges from Matthew in the David-to-Joseph listing, except for Zerubbabel and Shealtiel (Plummer 1896: 103). How the lists converge at this one point will be discussed in the exegesis of 3:27. Throughout the exposition, individual consideration will be given to each name to note that name's presence or absence elsewhere in Scripture. Many of the people mentioned here are largely unknown.[8] Where the name is discussed but not the individual, the person referred to is otherwise unattested.

Ἠλί (Heli)—This individual is the father of Joseph, although the nature of this connection is disputable, as excursus 5 shows. Heli may be the physical father or, possibly, the legal father by marriage or through a female relative. There is no way to be certain. Some have associated Heli with a rabbinic reference to Miriam, the daughter of Heli, to defend the view that the tradition of Mary's connection to this genealogy is old. But as noted in the excursus, this association is unlikely.

3:24 Μαθθάτ (Matthat or Mattatha)—The spelling of this name is close to several names (cf. Ματταθά in 3:31 and Ματταθίου in 3:25, 26), though it reappears in the NT only in 3:29. Similar names occur in the OT at Ezra 10:33 and 2 Chron. 23:17. This name was omitted from Africanus's list of Lucan names, a factor that complicates his solution to the genealogical issue (see excursus 5).

Λευί (Levi)—This name has a disputed morphology. It is either an indeclinable Hebrew term (BDF §53.1) or a genitive form (BDF §55.1e). This name was omitted from Africanus's list of Lucan names, a factor that complicates his solution to the genealogical issue (see excursus 5).

Μελχί (Melchi)—This name appears again in 3:28.

Ἰανναί (Jannai)—This name is a *hapax legomenon*.

Ἰωσήφ (Joseph)—This name appears again in 3:30, as well as in 3:23. The popularity of the patriarch who is the focus of Gen. 37–50 made this name common.

3:25 Ματταθίου (Mattathias)—This is a common Jewish name (1 Esdr. 9:43; Ezra 10:43; Neh. 8:4; 1 Chron. 9:31; 1 Macc. 2:1, 14).

Ἀμώς (Amos)—This name has both regal (2 Kings 21:18) and prophetic ties (2 Kings 19:2; Amos 1:1).

---

8. Marshall 1978: 162–65 also has a detailed presentation of this material. In the following discussion, I do not transliterate the Greek names because in almost every case the English name is the same as the transliteration. The only differences involve case endings or transliterations that are drawn from the Hebrew.

Ναούμ (Nahum)—This name has a prophetic background (Nah. 1:1).

Ἐσλί (Esli)—This name is a *hapax legomenon*.

Ναγγαί (Naggai)—This name appears in 1 Chron. 3:7.

3:26　Μάαθ (Maath)—This name appears in 1 Chron. 6:35 [6:20 MT] and 2 Chron. 29:12.

Ματταθίου (Mattathias)—This name occurred in 3:25.

Σεμεΐν (Semein)—This name is a *hapax legomenon*.

Ἰωσήχ (Josech)—This name is a *hapax legomenon*.

Ἰωδά (Joda or Joiada)—This name has an uncertain background, but may go back to names mentioned in 1 Esdr. 5:58; 9:19; Neh. 12:10–11 (Marshall 1978: 163).

3:27　Ἰωανάν (Joanan or Jehohanan)—This name appears in Ezra 10:6 and 2 Chron. 23:1. Marshall (1978: 163) suggests that Ἰωανάν could be equivalent to Anania (or Hananiah) in 1 Chron. 3:19, since the divine name is attached to both: a prefix on Ἰωανάν and a suffix on Anania. If so, this child is the son of Zerubbabel. A problem to this approach is the presence of the next name, Rhesa, which intervenes between Joanan and Zerubbabel.

Ῥησά (Rhesa)—It has been argued that this is not a personal name, but an Aramaic form of the word for prince used to describe Zerubbabel (Plummer 1896: 104). However, two problems exist for this suggestion. First, if this is a comment, then one must posit a very early textual corruption for which there is no extant manuscript evidence. Second, this would be the only name in Luke's list to receive elaboration. And if the suggestion were correct, it would indicate that Luke's source was Aramaic and was laid out in standard genealogical order. However, the lack of other comments in the genealogy and the history of the text are against this suggestion. It is to be noted, nonetheless, that the retention of the name is regarded as a problem as well, since other genealogies of Zerubbabel do not list Ῥησά as a descendant. Either there is a textual problem in Luke or Luke gives an additional descendant at this point.

Ζοροβαβέλ (Zerubbabel)—This individual is well known as the head of the tribe of Judah at the time of the return from Babylonian captivity under Cyrus the Great (Ezra 2:2), around 539–519 B.C. Luke shares this name with Matt. 1:12, and its presence in both lists raises some questions. In 1 Chron. 3:19 MT, Zerubbabel's father is called Pedaiah, who is a brother of Shealtiel and the third son of Jeconiah. However, Matthew, Luke, and 1 Chron. 3:19 LXX call Zerubbabel the son of Shealtiel (see also Hag. 1:1, 12, 14; 2:2, 23; Ezra 3:2, 8; 5:2; Neh. 12:1). Either the LXX text is the original and correct text (Fitzmyer 1981: 500) or a levirate marriage of a childless Shealtiel explains the difference (Plummer 1896: 104; Machen 1930: 206; adoption is possible as well). A clear choice between these options is not possible. The solution of Jeremias (1969: 295–96), which posits the Chronicler's erroneous placement of a grandson of the king as a restorer of the temple, is less satisfactory.

Σαλαθιήλ (Shealtiel)—As noted, this name is also shared with Matthew, where he is also presented as Zerubbabel's father.

Νηρί (Neri)—To call Neri the father of Shealtiel introduces a small problem, since the father of Shealtiel is called Jeconiah (= NIV's Jehoiachin) in the OT (1 Chron. 3:17). This latter connection is also made in Matt. 1:12. A couple of approaches exist here as well (again, lack of data makes it impossible to obtain certainty here). Luke may have taken Jer. 22:30 either as disqualifying Jeconiah from having a role in the official line or as indicating that the king was childless or, at least officially, heirless. Jeconiah did, in fact, have children according to 1 Chron. 3:17, and at least one of them is listed as having heirs. Thus, of these options, a conscious "legal omission" is more likely. Under this scenario, the line got to Shealtiel through Neri's line, who in turn goes back to Nathan. The first view, disqualification of Jeconiah, has some support in ancient tradition. M. Johnson (1988: 243–45) notes that Eusebius in *Gospel Questions and Solutions Addressed to Stephanus* 3.2 is aware of the curse on Jeconiah and argues for an official line through Nathan as a result of it. The genealogy now enters the period before the exile.

Μελχί (Melchi)—This name appeared earlier in 3:24.   **3:28**
'Αδδί (Addi)—This name represents the LXX form of the name (1 Chron. 6:21 [6:6 MT]).

Κωσάμ (Cosam)—This name is a *hapax legomenon*.

'Ελμαδάμ (Elmadam)—This name is found in Gen. 10:26.

"Ηρ (Er)—This name is somewhat common in the OT (Gen. 38:3; 1 Chron. 2:3, 4:21).

With this verse the genealogy starts to have some overlap with the   **3:29**
initial part of the list. Of the next sixteen names, four parallel earlier names and occupy a similar position, while two other names are close (Marshall 1978: 159). This led G. Kuhn (1923) to suggest that Luke repeated himself here, but it is obvious that four or six out of sixteen does not exactly qualify as repetition.

'Ιησοῦ (Joshua)—This name is the same form as the name *Jesus* (1:31). However, this Joshua is unknown.

'Ελιέζερ (Eliezer)—This name appears in Gen. 15:2, where it refers to Abraham's servant, and in Exod. 18:4. This Eliezer is unknown.

'Ιωρίμ (Jorim)—It is suggested that this name is another spelling for Ἰωρείμ (Joreim), which appears in some manuscripts of Ezra 10:18.

Μαθθάτ (Matthat)—This name occurred in 3:24.

Λευί (Levi)—This name occurred in 3:24.

3:30   Συμεών (Simeon)—This name appeared in 2:25. In the OT, Simeon was one of the twelve tribes of Israel (Gen. 35:23). The specific figure mentioned here is unknown.

Ἰούδα (Judah)—This name appears in 1:39. Judah was one of the twelve tribes of Israel (Gen. 35:23) and was one of the two tribes that made up the southern kingdom of Israel (1 Kings 12:20–21).

Ἰωσήφ (Joseph)—This was the name of Jesus' legal father (Luke 3:23), as well as the name of one of the patriarchs (Gen. 37–50).

Ἰωνάμ (Jonam)—This name is usually associated in form with Ἰωνάν (Jonan; variant readings in 1 Chron. 26:3 and Neh. 6:18).

Ἐλιακίμ (Eliakim)—This name also appears in Matthew's genealogy (Matt. 1:13). It is used in 2 Kings 18:18.

3:31   Μελεά (Melea)—This name is a *hapax legomenon*.

Μεννά (Menna)—This name is a *hapax legomenon*.

Ματταθά (Mattatha)—This name occurred in 3:24.

At this point the genealogy picks up again with known figures. The figures of Nathan and David are of some significance.

Ναθάμ (Nathan)—This individual was David's third son, born to him in Jerusalem (2 Sam. 5:14; 1 Chron. 3:5; 14:4; Zech. 12:12). The same spot in Matthew's genealogy is occupied by Solomon. As was noted in the introduction to this pericope, some argue that Nathan's inclusion is an attempt to make a prophetic connection in the genealogy. This connection is unlikely, since Luke and the NT have no evidence of such a tradition tied to Nathan. More likely, the difference is the effect of the curse preventing Jeconiah from producing a legal line, as mentioned in the exegesis of 3:27. It is to be noted that reading the text this way complicates the distinction often made between the "royal" line of Matthew and the "physical" line in Luke. It is better to see the line in Matthew as depicting the "royal and physical line," while the line in Luke is "legal but still royal," in light of the curse.

Δαυίδ (David)—The mention of David is also significant, since this connection puts Jesus in the regal line from which the Messiah was to emerge. Luke makes much of this connection throughout his work, just as he made a point of regal and Davidic connections in the infancy material (Luke 1:27, 31–35, 69; 2:4, 11; 18:38–39; Acts 2:25–31; 13:34–37; Schürmann 1969: 201 n. 97). All but one of these texts are unique to Luke. Luke does not elaborate here on the name. He simply mentions it and moves on. Of course, the name itself would draw great attention from anyone who knew Israel's history. David needed no introduction.

With David, there begins a long string of agreements with Matthew, **3:32** as both proceed down to Abraham. The OT base for this portion of the genealogy is 1 Chron. 2:1–15 and Ruth 4:18–22.

Ἰεσσαί (Jesse)—This individual is David's father, who came from the tribe of Judah and lived in Bethlehem (1 Sam. 16:1; 17:12; 20:27; Ruth 4:22; Acts 13:22; Rom. 15:12; Fitzmyer 1981: 501).

Ἰωβήδ (Obed)—This name is a variant spelling for Ὠβήδ in 1 Chron. 2:12. Matthew 1:5 also has this longer spelling. In the Book of Ruth, Naomi is said to have nursed this child (Ruth 4:16–17, 21–22; Fitzmyer 1981: 501).

Βόος (Boaz)—This individual, the main male figure in the Book of Ruth, ends up marrying the Moabitess. He also appears in the genealogy of 1 Chron. 2:12.

Σαλμών (Salmon)—The spelling of this name is disputed, though the variants refer to the same person (see the additional note).

Ναασσών (Nahshon)—This individual is mentioned in Ruth 4:20 and 1 Chron. 2:10–11, and he appears also in Matt. 1:4. The name is used as well in Exod. 6:23 and Num. 1:7. This earlier figure probably was one of the chiefs of the twelve tribes who helped Moses take the census in the wilderness (Num. 1:7). If so, his sister married Aaron (Exod. 6:23).

Ἀμιναδάβ (Amminadab)—This individual is the father of Nah- **3:33** shon (Exod. 6:23; 1 Chron. 2:10; Ruth 4:19–20). Matthew 1:4 also has this listing.

The next few names are disputed and are part of a difficult textual problem treated in the additional note. I have adopted the order Ἀράμ (Aram), Ἀδμίν (Admin), and Ἀρνί (Arni).

Ἐσρώμ (Hezron)—This individual is present in Ruth 4:18–19; 1 Chron. 2:5, 9; and Matt. 1:3. Genesis 46:12 also notes the name. The intervention of two names (Admin and Arni, between Aram and Hezron) in Luke's list in comparison to Ruth's list need not be a problem, if one recognizes that skips in the genealogy exist, a situation that is likely, for example, in Ruth's listing of names. Ruth's mention of one person's "fathering" (הוֹלִיד, *hôlîd*) another can involve skips in the line.

Φάρες (Perez)—This individual is found in Gen. 38:29; 46:12; Ruth 4:18; 1 Chron. 2:4–5; and Matt. 1:3. He was Judah's son through Tamar. Ruth's list starts with Perez.

Ἰούδα (Judah)—This individual is the ancestor of the tribe of Judah, a son of Jacob through Leah (Gen. 29:35; 35:23). This name was mentioned in Luke 3:30 and is present as well in Matt. 1:2–3.

3:34   Ἰακώβ (Jacob)—This individual was the son of Isaac and Rebekah, as well as the twin brother of Esau (Gen. 25:19–26). He is called Israel in Gen. 35:10, and the twelve tribes of Israel take their names from his twelve sons. Luke mentions him in 1:33; 13:28; and 20:37. The listing of Jacob, Isaac, and Abraham agrees with Matt. 1:2.

Ἰσαάκ (Isaac)—This individual was the long-awaited promised son of Abraham and Sarah (Gen. 21:1–7). His name also appears in 1 Chron. 1:34.

Ἀβραάμ (Abraham)—This individual was the patriarch of promise, who is the focus of Gen. 12–25. He is merely mentioned here, but the presence of his name alone is significant. Matthew's list ends here.

Luke now moves beyond Matthew's listing with the mention of Terah and Nahor. The names running from Terah to Adam come from a combination of sources: Gen. 11:10–26; 5:1–32; 1 Chron. 1:1–26 (esp. 1:24–26). The names on the list are well known, as they come from the Book of Genesis with its account of the beginning of Israel's history.

Θάρα (Terah)—This individual is the father of Abraham in Gen. 11:26–27. His name also appears in Josh. 24:2 and 1 Chron. 1:26. He was a Semite whose name may reflect the region from which he came (Fitzmyer 1981: 502).

Ναχώρ (Nahor)—This individual probably bears the name of the region from which he came, the area of Naḫuru in Mesopotamia (Fitzmyer 1981: 502). He is mentioned in Gen. 11:22 and 1 Chron. 1:26.

3:35   The sources for the names in this verse are largely confined to the two genealogical lists of Gen. 11 and 1 Chron. 1.

Σερούχ (Serug)—This individual is mentioned in Gen. 11:20 and 1 Chron. 1:26.

Ῥαγαύ (Reu)—This individual appears in Gen. 11:18 and 1 Chron. 1:25.

Φάλεκ (Peleg)—This individual appears in Gen. 11:16 and 1 Chron. 1:25.

Ἕβερ (Eber)—This individual is mentioned in Gen. 11:14; 10:24; and 1 Chron. 1:25.

Σαλά (Shelah)—This individual is noted in Gen. 11:12; 10:24; and 1 Chron. 1:24. A variant reading of the name appeared in Luke 3:32.

3:36   Καϊνάμ (Cainan)—This name lacks a Hebrew equivalent in the MT. It is, however, present as Καϊνάν in the LXX of Gen. 11:12 and 10:24 and in manuscript A of 1 Chron. 1:18. Most take this as evidence that Luke is using the LXX (Marshall 1978: 165; Schürmann

1969: 201 n. 101). More difficult is the order of names in the LXX, for there Cainan appears as the father of Sala, not his son, as here (Plummer 1896: 104). Plummer regards the name in the LXX text as possibly a late insertion, since it is not attested independently until Augustine. However, he is clear that the LXX addition cannot find its source in Luke, since the order differs. The possibility that Luke had access to a different source containing this name in a different order cannot be excluded. There is good possibility that the name should be omitted in Luke, since $\mathfrak{P}^{75}$ and D omit the name here and it reappears in 3:37. If it is omitted, then the eleven groups of seven noted in the translation include Joseph. Again, there is too little evidence to make a clear decision.

Ἀρφαξάδ (Arphaxad)—This individual appears in Gen. 11:10 and 1 Chron. 1:24.

Σήμ (Shem)—This name is derived from the individual in Gen. 5:32, though the name also appears in Gen. 9:26–27 and Sir. 49:16.

Νῶε (Noah)—This is the famous figure of the flood whose name appears frequently in OT and Jewish materials (Gen. 5:29; 6:9; 7:1–8:22; 1 Chron. 1:4; Wis. 10:4; Sir. 44:17; Tob. 4:12; 1QapGen 6).

Λάμεχ (Lamech)—This individual appears in Gen. 5:25; 4:18–22; and 1 Chron. 1:3. In the Genesis Apocryphon from Qumran, the tradition concerning him is expanded (1QapGen 2.3, 19; 5.4, 10, 25–26; Fitzmyer 1981: 503).

3:37 Μαθουσαλά (Methuselah)—This individual is mentioned in Gen. 5:21 and 1 Chron. 1:3.

Ἐνώχ (Enoch)—This individual is mentioned in Gen. 5:18, 24; Sir. 49:16; and 1 Chron. 1:3. Because of his unusual life, Enoch was the object of much discussion in the intertestamental period and in the NT (Jude 14; 1QapGen 2.20; 4QEnGiantsª 8.4; 1 Enoch; Fitzmyer 1981: 503–4).

Ἰάρετ (Jared)—This individual is found in Gen. 5:15 and 1 Chron. 1:2.

Μαλελεήλ (Mahalaleel)—This individual is found in Gen. 5:12 and 1 Chron. 1:1.

Καϊνάμ (Cainan)—This individual is found in Gen. 5:9 and 1 Chron. 1:1. The name is present in Luke 3:36.

3:38 Ἐνώς (Enos)—This individual is referred to in Gen. 5:6 and 1 Chron. 1:1.

Σήθ (Seth)—This individual is mentioned in Gen. 4:25–26; 5:3; 1 Chron. 1:1; and Sir. 49:16.

Ἀδάμ (Adam)—The genealogical table ends with the mention of Adam, the first man created by God's hand in Gen. 1. He is made in God's image. According to Genesis, from him all the human race

descends. It is probably this connection that allows Luke to conclude the list with the unparalleled τοῦ θεοῦ (*tou theou*, son of God).
No example of such an ending exists in genealogies in the OT,
Pseudepigrapha, Qumran writings, or rabbinic literature.[9] Nearly
all commentators see an identification of Jesus with all humanity
in this reference.[10] This universal perspective fits the Lucan concern for Gentiles.

The sonship in view here is related to but distinct from the sonship of 3:21–22. There the sonship was largely regal and messianic.
Here the sonship is more universal, grounded in God's having
formed humanity. In the baptism, Jesus is king and is related especially to Israel, since John the Baptist's ministry was designed to
prepare the nation for Messiah (1:14–17). In the genealogy, Jesus is
related to all people in a way that expands the scope of his ministry
to include the hopes of all. So Jesus' sonship in its narrow and
broad senses links 3:21–22 to 3:23–38. Another key point emerges
from the reference to sonship with God. In God's plan, Jesus is the
main figure who puts humanity's creation from God's hand into
perspective.

Summary   Jesus' genealogy in 3:23–38 ties all humankind into one unit.
Their fate is wrapped up in Jesus. His ministry, as seen from
heaven, represents the focal point of history. The introduction of
the genealogy right before the commencement of his ministry
serves to highlight the scope of Jesus' concern for humans. It
points to his universal perspective. Jesus is not some isolated
minister to Israel; he does not merely minister to a tiny nation of
subjected people seeking political deliverance from a dominating Rome. Rather, he is the culmination of a line of descendants
stretching back through the great men of promise like Adam,
Abraham, Isaac, Jacob, and David. The lineage confirms his position and suggests his ministry's comprehensive character. In
him, the entire hope of the OT is inseparably and eternally
bound. In him, as well, the fate of all divinely created humans is
bound together.

Additional Notes

3:32. A text-critical problem concerns the fourth name in this verse. Many
texts (𝔓[4], B, ℵ*, some Syriac and Coptic versions) have Σαλά (Sala or

9. Philo, *On the Virtues* 37 §§204–5, is close in tying Adam's descent to the eternal
Father, but Philo sees Adam as unique in this role.
10. Acts 17:28–29 is clearly conceptually parallel; Schürmann 1969: 202. The
idea of God as Creator of all humanity is the basis of Paul's approach to Gentiles
with the gospel; less specific but similar in force is Acts 14:15.

Shelah), a name that appears as well in Gen. 10:24; 11:13–15; and 1 Chron. 1:18, 24. UBS–NA accepts this as the harder reading, since Matt. 1:4 has Σαλμών (Salmon), as does 1 Chron. 2:11 (Ruth 4:20–21 has Σαλμάν, another variant of this name). Σαλμών, however, has good distribution among the textual families: א², A, D, L, Θ, Byz, Itala, Vulgate, some Syriac, and some Coptic versions. Thus, it would seem the NIV, which adopts this reading, has some reason for doing so. The alternative reading is present in my translation, and I believe it is slightly more likely to be original. Σαλά could have come into the text through confusion with the names in Genesis. Since Luke and Matthew are so close in this section, one should hesitate to adopt a divergent reading here. If Σαλά is original, it may reflect the Syriac tradition, which reads this name in Ruth 4:20–21 (Metzger 1975: 136). It would be referring to the same figure as Σαλμών does.

3:33. The most difficult text-critical problem of the genealogy concerns three names: Ἀράμ (Aram), Ἀδμίν (Admin), and Ἀρνί (Arni). This problem is important because the structure of the genealogy is influenced by the reading chosen. UBS–NA goes with the reading given in my translation, except that they exclude Ἀράμ on the apparent reading of $\mathfrak{P}^4$ and the clear readings of L, family 13, and one Coptic version—an unimpressive extent of witnesses. The problem is that eleven other variants exist, a situation that suggests that the transmission of this text was disturbed early in its copying. Metzger (1975: 136), in accepting the UBS–NA text, calls it the "least unsatisfactory form of text"—hardly a ringing endorsement.

A breakdown of the variants shows that eight include reference to Ἀμιναδάβ (Amminadab), five have Ἀδμίν, six have Ἀρνί, and eight have Ἀράμ (whose name also appears in Matt. 1:4 and 1 Chron. 2:10). What complicates the picture is that no Alexandrian manuscript has Ἀράμ. The NIV accepts the Ἀράμ reading, but drops both Ἀδμίν and Ἀρνί—names that are otherwise unattested, though Marshall (1978: 165) takes Ἀρνί as corresponding to Ἀρράν (Arran) in Ruth 4:19. Marshall argues that the exact textual transmission is uncertain at this point, which is quite possible, given the number of distinct variants. It is interesting to note that Ἀράμ is read by family 1, Θ, Δ, C, Byz, A, D, P, Itala, Vulgate, and Syriac versions. Though attested in various combinations, Ἀράμ appears to have a wide variety of support. On the other hand, the presence of Ἀδμίν and Ἀρνί is hard to explain in the textual history if they were not originally present. Why would they be added?

The best text seems to include all three names, a reading adopted by Θ and the Armenian and Georgian versions. א is close to this reading, if one sees an orthographic confusion in its use of the name Adam here. If P (*rho*) is read as the second letter instead of Δ (*delta*), then the reading would match my suggestion and an Alexandrian witness would be joined to the other families attesting Aram. It would be natural to confuse Aram for Adam, given the prominence of Adam's name.

If any name among the three names is to be omitted, it is most likely Admin, because of the more limited testimony for it. Once the confusion of the name Adam comes into the transmission, it is easier to explain how Admin could come into the transmission. However, the inclusion of all three names seems better, since it preserves the pattern of eleven groups of seven names, if one excludes Joseph in the view of the "supposed" note in 3:23. Thus, the reading adopted has internal structural support as well.

There is another possible option, but to be original it requires at least three copying errors early in the tradition (Heater 1986). Heater argues that only Ἀράμ should be read and derives it from the Hebrew רַם (Ram) of 1 Chron. 2:10. Such a reading would bring Luke in agreement with Matthew, Ruth, and 1 Chronicles at this point, which is one reason some hesitate to accept it, since it looks like harmonization. Heater explains the presence of some names in the textual tradition, but only with difficulty. (1) He calls Ἀδμίν a variant of Adam. (2) It is necessary that the article be assimilated into Ἀράμ and then misread as α in the LXX, or else the name was confused with אֲרָם (Aram) in Gen. 10:22–23. (3) He argues that Ἀρνί came from Ἀράν or Ἀρράν, but this also requires assimilation or a misreading of the article. All these are possibilities, but it is the combination that makes the option difficult. However, the text history in this passage is so confused, as the list of variants in 1 Chronicles and Luke shows, that one should be slow to express certainty about any option. Only probabilities exist. Heater's use of internal criteria in looking for the eleven groups of seven spanning from Christ to God is also a point in favor of his option, as is Luke's general parallelism to the other genealogies in most of his list.

3:36. For the text-critical problem concerning Καϊνάμ, see the exegesis.

3. Messianic Preparation: Resistance of Satan (4:1–13)

Jesus' temptations serve as a major prelude to his ministry. The account also brings together the baptism, genealogy, and the start of his ministry. The focus is on Jesus as the beloved Son (3:22, 38), who is obedient to God in a way that other people—including Adam—are not. Schürmann (1969: 205) points out three levels at which the account works: (1) Jesus is the pious Son who has unswerving allegiance to God; (2) the battle between Satan and Jesus will run through the entire Gospel; and (3) the success of Jesus in the wilderness recalls Israel's failure there. Jesus is qualified to lead the nation, and his success gives promise of ultimate success against all spiritual enemies. The focus on Deuteronomy, the book of the nation, serves to underscore this reversal motif concerning Israel. Jesus begins his ministry having overcome the initial onslaught of the evil one, while showing his commitment to living in a way that may not be the easiest road to travel, but is the way that most pleases God.

Another focal point is how Jesus overcomes the evil force by his reflective application of the written Scripture and its truth. In so doing, he serves as an example of the spiritual person (Schürmann 1969: 207). The christological note in the account is clear, since the narrative presents Jesus as one who is faithful to God—an important point in light of the possibility of perceiving his ministry as a failure because of his tragic death.

Tannehill (1986: 59) adds another important observation about the account: The temptations reveal Jesus' approach to his mission. Here is a man who pursues God's call. Jesus is dedicated to God's mission, not his own purposes, desires, or self-advancement. The account is, then, an introduction to how Jesus will not pursue his mission. His goal is not to draw attention to himself, but to focus on God's work and God's truth, which he is called to carry out. The next large pericope, 4:16–30, will reveal what Jesus' mission is. Jesus will not use his power to serve himself, but he will lift up others and minister to both their physical and spiritual needs.

Sources and Historicity

The historicity of this event has been variously approached. Marshall (1978: 168) speaks of an inward experience expressed in dramatic form. Fitzmyer (1981: 509) sees a qualified connection back to Jesus, but regards historicity as a less significant question than the account's theological and symbolic value. He suggests that Jesus spoke of this experience parabolically or dramatically. One should not read the experience with "naïve literalism" or seek to "salvage" its historicity (p. 510). The hesitancy to see a direct experience is hard to justify, and the separation of symbol and history is something, as seen in other accounts, that reflects a worldview judgment. Tiede (1988: 97–98) offers a warning that interpreters should not be drawn into excessive historical or psychological speculation that reduces the account to hallucinations due to lack of food. I prefer an approach that does not divorce symbolism from history quite so much. To religiously sensitive eyes, history is full of symbolic import. To say this is to acknowledge that some of these experiences may have been inward or supernatural in character (see Luke 4:8).

The account's source ultimately must go back to Jesus himself.[1] It is hard to see how or even why the early church would create such an account. There are numerous ways to show how Jesus overcame demonic opposition other than to produce a story like this one, which lacks any real parallels. The absence of such encounters by other NT luminaries, not to mention the lack of any OT parallels, speaks against its creation by the community. In fact, the closest NT parallel is Paul's failure to get relief from his "harassment" by a messenger from Satan, where dependence on God's grace is the issue (2 Cor. 12:7–10). The closest OT parallel is Job. But neither of these accounts is a face-to-face battle with dialogue between the combatants. The temptation account is unprecedented, which speaks for its connection to Jesus. The critical criterion of "dissimilarity" may apply here.

Given that the basic account has roots in Jesus, the issue of verbal agreement and divergence in the various Synoptic accounts still remains.

---

1. Plummer 1896: 106; Manson 1949: 46 (who strongly defends this view); Dupont 1968: 97–115 (who argues for a middle course between literalism and parable); Carson 1984: 111; Nolland 1989: 177 (who defends the plausibility of Jesus' reporting this event to his disciples). On the other end of the spectrum apparently is Crossan (1991), who does not even discuss this event in his portrayal of Jesus. The Jesus Seminar (Funk and Hoover 1993: 133–34 [Matt.], 278–80 [Luke]) places all the sayings of this unit in black type, thereby indicating rejection of a tie to Jesus. The consensus of the seminar is that the text is legendary, like Greco-Roman biography, and that the sayings were authored by Q following the LXX. The seminar calls it an "ordeal story," but this generic form category does not explain the explicit uniqueness of this confrontation account, a point that negates this argument. Manson 1949: 45–46 rightly challenges the description of the account as legendary (see the discussion of form below). LXX citations reflect only Luke's sensitivity to his Greek audience and are not evidence of the text's origin, since MT renderings would work (Nolland 1989: 177).

Mark 1:12–13 contains only a brief remark about this event and lacks dialogue and detail. On the other hand, Matt. 4:1–11 is so close to Luke's account that most commentators see a written source shared by Matthew and Luke (most speak of Q here: Creed 1930: 61; Luce 1933: 115; Manson 1949: 42–43; Wiefel 1988: 99; Bovon 1989: 193; Fitzmyer 1981: 507; Tiede 1988: 98; C. F. Evans 1990: 256). However, a key point of agreement with Mark 1:12–13—the association of testing with the wilderness and with the period of forty days—suggests that Luke is also aware of material like that in Mark.[2] Yet Mark's failure to give details about this event leads some to suggest that Mark did not know the body of tradition that Matthew and Luke share.[3] In fact, there are enough small, but theologically irrelevant differences between Matthew and Luke that to posit the same exact written source for both of them seems difficult. For example, why do Matt. 4:3 and Luke 4:3 differ on the name of Satan (the tempter versus the devil)? Or why does Matt. 4:3 work with the plural stones and loaves, while Luke 4:3 has the singular? Why is Luke's version of the offer of the kingdoms (4:6) much fuller than Matthew's? Why is Matthew's citation of Deut. 8:3 so much longer than Luke's (see the additional note on 4:4 for details)? What about the differences in Matt. 4:7 and Luke 4:12 (see the additional note on 4:12)? Why does Luke 4:9 alone say "from here" (see the exegesis of 4:9)? Why does Luke omit a reference to angels in 4:13? In this pericope Matthew and Luke are dealing with distinct yet very similar traditions (distinct versions of Q?). Luke is probably responsible for the account's introduction and conclusion (4:1–2, 13).

The major distinction between the accounts is the order of the temptations. In Matthew, the trip to the mountain to see the kingdoms of the world is the final temptation, while for Luke the trip to the top of the temple is the last temptation. Since it is clear that six temptations are not to be posited, it is also clear that one of the Gospel writers has rearranged the order for literary reasons. The event shows that the Gospel writers are not averse to arranging materials for the sake of topical or theological concerns, a point that must be kept in mind when examining other pericopes as well.

Which writer rearranged the sequence? Schürmann argues that Matthew rearranged the account because he develops the site of the mountain as a significant theological locale of revelation, a point that is supported by the ending of Matthew's Gospel (28:16–20) on a mountain.[4] But Fitzmyer (1981: 507–8) and Schulz (1972: 177 esp. n. 2, who also traces the de-

---

2. Schürmann 1969: 218–19 sees both Mark and Q as contributing to Luke, as does Bultmann 1963: 254.

3. Luce 1933: 115. On the other hand, Matt. 4:11 and Mark 1:13 both note the ministry of angels to Jesus at the end of the temptation, a note that Luke lacks.

4. Schürmann 1969: 218; so also Schneider 1977a: 99; C. F. Evans 1990: 256 (who incorrectly calls this the majority view); and Manson 1949: 42–43 (but with no details other than the claim that Matthew's order makes "a fine dramatic climax" so it is hard to imagine Luke's altering it if it were the original).

bate's history) argue more persuasively for a Lucan rearrangement. Fitzmyer notes that Matthew's order is a natural progression—desert, building pinnacle, mountaintop—and that the Matthean citations of Deuteronomy appear in reverse canonical order (Deut. 8:3; 6:16; 6:13). In addition, the clearest temporal adverbs occur only in Matthew (e.g., πάλιν in 4:8, τότε in 4:10, and the summary dismissal of Satan—details that Luke lacks). Finally, as Schulz makes clear, Luke has a theological motive for his rearrangement. For Luke, Jerusalem is the climactic locale of conflict in Jesus' life (19:45–24:53). Luke's rearrangement places the emphasis on the Jerusalem temple temptation as the decisive one. Goulder (1989: 294) agrees, but prefers to see the phrase *you shall not tempt the Lord your God* as climactic, forming an *inclusio* on temptation, rather than seeing Jerusalem as the motive. Most commentators accept Matthew's order as original (Ellis 1974: 94; Schweizer 1984: 82; Hendriksen 1978: 232; Tiede 1988: 98). Plummer 1896: 110 refuses to choose either way.

This account has caused much speculation, especially in the early church. Hebrews 2:17–18 and 4:15 speak of Jesus' being tempted as a high priest and perfected. In a period of high christological controversy, the question was raised about how Jesus could be sinless and yet be truly tempted. Some modern expositions still focus on this question, as if it were the major issue for Luke.[5] It must be noted, however, that Luke is not concerned with ontological questions here. He simply presents the temptations as an event in Jesus' life, as an important encounter in which Satan was successfully rebuffed. Plummer (1896: 105–6) rightly notes that some questions raised by this passage are not answered for us; he also notes that to resist temptation is harder than to succumb to it. Jesus' achievement, as far as Luke is concerned, is that Jesus resisted giving in to Satan. Jesus represents in his rejection of evil what a son of God in the Adamic sense is capable of when he follows God's desire. The second Son of God succeeds, where the first son of God failed.[6]

> There is general agreement about the account's basic form, but not about its roots. Bultmann (1963: 254–57) calls it a "story about Jesus" and classifies it as scribal Haggadah, since God's Word is used to refute the devil, but he also says (p. 253) that it possesses "the rudiments of an originally detailed legend" like those about Buddha or Zoroaster, a point that Manson (1949: 45)

---

5. Hendriksen 1978: 230 has a full discussion. He tends to emphasize a perceived priestly theme in Luke, but this is the point of the writer to the Hebrews and not a part of Lucan Christology at all (see Schweizer 1984: 81–82).

6. Jeremias, *TDNT* 1:141, alludes to the second Adam motif here, a point supported by the extension of Luke's genealogy back to Adam. That the close of the temptation account involves the temple shows a Palestinian, as opposed to a Hellenistic, viewpoint (see the exegesis of 4:9).

explicitly rejects. Bultmann goes on to argue that the text is against the selfish use of miracles, arguing that Jesus' work can be distinguished from magic on that basis. Because of the controversy, he sees the text emerging from Palestinian roots, but it has Hellenistic touches in that it rejects the portrayal of Jesus as a Greek miracle-working "divine man" (also Schulz 1972: 182, 187).

Rejecting Bultmann's description as too limited, Fitzmyer (1981: 508–9) sees the unit as the work of Christian scribes to produce an account that is primarily symbolic; it cannot have been produced by the community. The original setting is a set of parables or a dramatic depiction of experience that shows a Jesus who refuses to do signs. Bovon similarly sees a response to Jewish critics that Jesus is a magician or a false Messiah.[7]

Marshall (1978: 166) correctly notes, against Bultmann, that the issue is neither dialectical skill nor scribal debate. There is no scriptural controversy here, only confrontation (see also Schürmann 1969: 209). Rather, the issue is obedience to God's will as recorded in Scripture. Thus, it is right to call the account simply a "temptation of the righteous," whose closest parallel is Job.[8] Whether one needs to appeal to wider polemics with Jewish or Hellenistic opponents is debatable; but it is clear that the account renounces the raw use of miraculous power for any whim. Thus, it may explain what kind of divine agent Jesus would be: one who served others. The account should also be read as an example of how faithfulness overcomes the temptation to sin and avoids becoming allied with Satan. But it is not just personal temptation that is in view. Jesus as the Son of God represents a whole line of humanity (Tiede 1988: 98–99). Jesus was righteous and ready for his task.

The outline of Luke 4:1–13 is as follows:

a. Setting (4:1–2)
b. Temptation of bread and God's care (4:3–4)

---

7. On Fitzmyer's view, see the opening paragraph of the sources and historicity section. Bovon 1989: 202 also argues that the account depicts the victory of faith in the face of opposition. In his view only two texts parallel this account's point about refusing miracles as signs: Dan. 3 and *Sipra* 22.32 (99d) on Lev. 22:29–33 (= Neusner 1988b: 3.231). But only the latter is really parallel in showing that one does not reveal signs to someone who is unworthy. On Jesus' resisting temptation or persevering in trial, see Luke 22:28; John 6:15, 26–34; 7:1–4; on his refusal to do signs, see Luke 22:39–46; Heb. 2:17–18; 4:15; 5:2. For the history of this text's exegesis, see Köppen 1961.

8. Berger 1984: 337 §7, who also notes a parallel to T. Job 27.3–5. There is one distinction here: Job never talks with his adversary, so the parallel is not exact.

    c. Temptation of rule through false worship (4:5–8)
    d. Temptation to test God's protection (4:9–12)
    e. Departure of the devil (4:13)

Numerous themes dominate the passage. Jesus is the pious, obedient Son. Jesus is successful in temptation where others, like Israel and Adam, failed. Jesus is qualified to represent both the nation and humanity. Jesus refuses to rule on the wrong premises. His success shows the value of a reflective knowledge of God's Word. In fact, when God is obeyed in compliance to the Spirit, Satan can be resisted. Nonetheless, one should note that the road of resisting temptation is not always the easiest or most obvious road to take; in fact, it often means self-denial. Power is not to be accepted without careful consideration of the terms. Finally, God is not to be tested concerning his faithfulness.

Exegesis and Exposition

[1]But Jesus, full of the Holy Spirit, withdrew from the Jordan and was being led by the Spirit in the desert, [2]while being tempted for forty days by the devil. And he ate nothing in those days, and when they were completed, he was hungry.

[3]And the devil said to him, "If you are the Son of God, speak to this stone that it might be a loaf of bread." [4]And Jesus replied to him, ⌜"It is written that 'not by bread alone shall a man live.'"⌝

[5]And the devil took him up and showed him all the inhabited kingdoms in an instant. [6]And he said to him, "To you I will give all this authority and their glory; for to me it has been delivered and I give it to whom I will. [7]Therefore, if you bow down and worship me, all shall be yours." [8]And Jesus said to him, "It is written, 'You shall worship the Lord your God and serve him alone.'"

[9]And he led him into Jerusalem and set him on the pinnacle of the temple and said to him, "If you are the Son of God, cast yourself down from here, [10]for it is written, 'He shall give his angels charge over you to protect you'; [11]and 'on their hands they shall lift you up, lest you strike your foot against a stone.'" [12]And Jesus replied to him, "It is said, 'You shall not test the Lord your God.'"

[13]And when he finished every temptation, the devil departed from him for a time.

a. Setting (4:1–2)

4:1   The double reference to the Spirit is the prominent feature of Luke's introduction to the temptations. Jesus was full of the Holy Spirit and was led into the wilderness by the Spirit. Such an emphasis makes clear that Jesus' being exposed to temptation was not his fault in any way. Rather, this withdrawal was a direct result of God's leading. The characterization of Jesus as full of the Spirit is typical Lucan terminology to describe a spiritual person (Luke 1:15, 41, 67; Acts 6:3, 5; 7:55; 11:24). Just as Simeon was led to the temple in Luke 2:27, so Jesus is taken into the wilderness. Wisdom residing in or filling a wise person also occurs in Judaism (Wis. 1:4–5; 7:7; Sir. 39:6). The account itself will serve to verify why Jesus can be described in these terms.

Though each of the Synoptics speaks of Jesus' being led by the Spirit into this situation, each uses different terminology to express the same idea. Matthew 4:1 speaks of Jesus' being "led by the Spirit" (ἀνήχθη . . . ὑπὸ τοῦ πνεύματος, anēchthē . . . hypo tou pneumatos). In Mark 1:12 "the Spirit cast him out" (τὸ πνεῦμα αὐτὸν ἐκβάλλει, to pneuma auton ekballei) into the wilderness. And in Luke 4:1, Jesus is "led by the Spirit" (ἤγετο ἐν τῷ πνεύματι, ēgeto en tō pneumati).[9] In addition, Luke's double reference to the Spirit makes the point with more emphasis. It makes clear that the spiritual impulse that guided Jesus was an internal, spiritual one from God.

Ὑπέστρεψεν (hypestrepsen) can be taken in one of two ways: either Jesus "returned" to Galilee or he "withdrew" from the Jordan area. Since Luke does not mention from where Jesus came to the Jordan River, it is more natural to see here a reference to a withdrawal from the Jordan (Fitzmyer 1981: 513). Only Luke names the Jordan as the general locale, but even he does not specify the exact location of the temptations beyond its being called the wilderness. Often the wilderness is a region of demonic activity, and yet it is here that Jesus goes to commune with God. Luke 8:29 and 11:24 show that demonic forces looked on the wilderness as a haven (Schürmann 1969: 208 n. 145). While in other settings the wilderness is a place to retreat and find God (1:80; 3:2; 5:16; 7:24), on this occasion Jesus fasts and faces the devil in spiritual battle.

Luke notes that the duration of wilderness testing took forty days, but does the forty days go with being led or with tempting? Was Jesus led for forty days in the wilderness or was he tempted for forty days? Hendriksen (1978: 232) believes the former arrangement prevents a problem with Matthew and Mark in that Mark speaks of forty days in the desert, while Matthew speaks of the temptations coming at the end of the forty days. However, the construction in Mark 1:13 is similarly ambiguous. Plummer (1896: 107) notes cor-

4:2

---

9. Bovon 1989: 194 notes that the anaphoric use of the article with πνεῦμα in each Gospel argues for the age of the tradition; Bovon cites Jeremias 1980: 115; Deut. 8:2. On ἤγετο, see Wiefel 1988: 100. Paul has this expression: Rom. 8:14; Gal. 5:18.

rectly that, since πειραζόμενος (*peirazomenos*, being tested) is a present participle, the idea is that tempting occurred over forty days, regardless of where the phrase is placed in the sentence. This indicates that the tempting is contemporaneous with the leading, which negates Hendriksen's view. Jesus was tempted over a forty-day period. The three tests recounted here may be but the concluding act of the drama, since Luke says that these three tests came at a point of hunger after forty days of fasting, which is in agreement with Matt. 4:2. Mark 1:12–13 either does not know of or ignores the reference to specific temptations.

The reference to forty days is interesting, given the uses of the number forty in the OT. Forty years was the period of Israel's wilderness wanderings (Num. 14:33; 32:13; Deut. 8:2). Forty lashes was the most a person could receive (Deut. 25:3). Forty days was the period of uncleanness after birth (Lev. 12:1–4). Forty days was the duration of the flood (Gen. 7:4, 12). Ezekiel had to bear the iniquity of Judah for forty days (Ezek. 4:6). Most importantly, forty days was the length of the fasts of Moses (Exod. 34:28; Deut. 9:9) and Elijah (1 Kings 19:8) at key points in Israel's history (Plummer 1896: 108–9 n. 1). In fact, Moses spent forty days on the mountain to receive the covenant (Exod. 24:18; 34:28). The parallels of Moses and the nation (Deut. 8:2) are significant, since Jesus' reply to the temptations will come from Deuteronomy. Marshall (1978: 169) notes, however, that none of these OT passages attribute the periods directly to God's or the devil's testing, which means a purely symbolic parallel is unlikely. A note of design is present in the event; it is a time of significant action.[10]

Luce (1933: 116) would like to make the temptation a strictly internal psychological experience for Jesus, arguing that Jesus reflected in private on his baptismal call. However, it is clear that Scripture portrays this event as a battle between real beings. In the OT, the devil is portrayed as inquisitor in the heavenly courts (Job 1:6–12; 2:1–7), as an accuser (Zech. 3:1–2), and as a tempter (1 Chron. 21:1). In the NT, he is consistently portrayed as a personal foe: John 8:37–44; 2 Cor. 11:3; 12:7; Rev. 12:3–9; 20:1–4.[11] First-century Palestinian angelology depicted as real the realms of

10. Bovon 1989: 195 speaks of a time of divine revelation, but this is too specific for Luke 4. Jesus is simply "led" by the Spirit. For a study emphasizing the parallels with Israel, see Brawley 1992.

11. Carson 1984: 112. In Bovon's short excursus (1989: 196–97) on the term *devil*, he notes that Luke uses διάβολος and σατανᾶς seven times each in Luke–Acts. The reference to διάβολος in Luke 4:2 is possibly Luke's choice, though Matt. 4:1, 8 renders this judgment as less than certain. Matt. 4:3 uses ὁ πειράζων and Matt. 4:10 σατανᾶ, which Luke lacks. In 4:1–13, Luke speaks only of the διάβολος, avoiding Matthew's variation of terms and Mark's reference to Satan.

faithful and fallen angels: 1 Cor. 4:9; 6:3; 10:20; 11:10 (faithful angels who observe the worship of the church); 1 Pet. 1:12; Eph. 3:10; 6:10–20. Luke 1 records Gabriel's visit to Mary, and Luke 24 the angelic figures' announcement of Jesus' resurrection. In addition, Fitzmyer (1981: 514) notes the focus on a personal "arch-demon" in this period (see also H. Kelly 1964). The encounter is much more serious than a mere issue of internal, psychological reflection. Whatever form the confrontation took, it was clear that two personalities were in the ring of battle.

Jesus' condition at the time of the final encounter was one of weakness. He had had nothing significant to eat for forty days. The phrase οὐκ ἔφαγεν οὐδέν (ouk ephagen ouden, he had not eaten anything) has been pressed literally by some, so that Luke is more emphatic in portraying Jesus' rejection of food than is Matthew, since it is argued that Matthew has him only fasting (Luce 1933: 116–17). Others (Schürmann 1969: 209–10) suggest that Luke's emphasis is Jesus' immunity from hunger pangs, showing the wonderful fullness of this time, for nothing is impossible with God (1:37; 18:27).[12] Schürmann is correct: Luke's point on the nature of the fasting is not clear. Did Jesus take only drink or did he eat only what the desert supplied, so that nothing substantive was consumed? But Klostermann (1929: 59) is correct to see the phrase as a popular way to express fasting. In other words, Matthew and Luke are probably saying the same thing. As a clear example of Luke's idiom, Klostermann cites Matt. 11:18, which speaks of John's eating and drinking nothing, an expression that cannot be meant in absolute terms. In addition, Matthew prefers the term he uses for fasting, νηστεύω (nēsteuō).[13]

So Jesus fasted for this period and at the end of it he was hungry. Jesus' situation at his test contrasts with Adam's. Adam had not fasted at all, while Jesus had suffered lack for forty days. Adam could eat from any tree in the garden but one, while Jesus was denying himself food. Adam was in paradise, while Jesus was in the wilderness (Hendriksen 1978: 233–34). Certainly if environment was the determining factor in overcoming temptation, Jesus was playing at a disadvantage. The devil made his move with Jesus in this exposed condition.

12. Schürmann also rejects any repetition of the manna miracle as being in view here. For details on the Jewish practice of fasting, see the exegesis of 5:33.

13. Matthew has eight uses to Luke's four, and Luke never uses this term for Jesus fasting: Matt. 4:2; 6:16 (twice), 17, 18; 9:14 (twice), 15; Luke 5:33, 34, 35; 18:12. See also Exod. 34:28, as Schulz 1972: 179 notes, where wilderness fasting means only no water or bread as opposed to no food at all.

b. Temptation of Bread and God's Care (4:3–4)

4:3 The first temptation fits the setting. Jesus is hungry, and he ought to feel free to provide himself with food. Surely this is a simple and straightforward request to meet one's basic needs. Satan's request is to transform a stone (λίθῳ, *lithō*) into a loaf (ἄρτος, *artos*), both singular nouns in contrast to the plurals in Matt. 4:3. It would seem that Luke chose to use the singular to focus the request and to bring it into direct conformity with the singular (ἄρτῳ, *artō*) of the OT quotation in Luke 4:4. Perhaps the singular was regarded as an appropriate reference to a meal for one (Fitzmyer 1981: 515; Nolland 1989: 179), whereas a plural might seek to add a corporate element to the provision that would highlight Jesus' role as the nation's son, a point that fits Matthew (Glickman 1983: 334–35). Schürmann (1969: 209 n. 161) argues that three loaves were made available to guests in Palestine (cf. 11:5). If he is right, then it is hard to explain the singular (but his suggestion in n. 160 that Matthew gets his plural from Matt. 3:9 is unlikely). Regardless of how the change in number occurred, the request is the same: Jesus is to provide food for himself by the miraculous transformation of a natural object. The number difference influences only the possible implications one might draw from the event.

What is the temptation? The question turns on the "if" clause. Since it is introduced with the indicative mood, εἰ (*ei*) is a first-class condition. In other words the statement presents the "if" clause as potentially true or with a heightened vividness ("if you are Son now"). Given this, attempts to suggest that the temptation is designed to challenge Jesus' sonship are probably overstated (Luce 1933: 117; Geldenhuys 1951: 159). The devil is not directly doubting Jesus' sonship. The temptation is more subtle than this.

If one realizes that the assertion of sonship is acknowledged by the devil, then the temptation can be taken in a variety of ways (Glickman 1983: 218–27; Marshall 1978: 170–71):

1. Jesus is tempted to satisfy his hunger in an inappropriate manner (Gerhardsson 1966: 52). But surely the mere miraculous provision of food in itself is not sin or else the feeding of the five thousand by Jesus would have to be viewed similarly. This view is too vague.

2. The satisfaction of hunger represents a distrust of God's provision and protection of his Son (Fitzgerald 1972: 156). In favor of this approach is the context of the Deut. 8:3 citation in Luke 4:4.

3. Jesus is tempted to satisfy his hunger by miraculous power. This view takes various forms. (a) Such power is an expression

of self-gratification, which is an inappropriate use of Jesus' miraculous powers (Marshall 1978: 170–71; Schürmann 1969: 209; Fitzmyer 1981: 510). (b) The exercise of power would prove Jesus' sonship, which the tempter doubts (Luce 1933: 117; Geldenhuys 1951: 159). This view incorrectly reads the conditional clause and is therefore suspect. (c) The satisfaction of hunger through miraculous means brings into question God's provision for and protection of Jesus, and it questions the way God is leading him with regard to self-denial and service.[14] This latter approach is really a combination of views 2 and 3a.

Which of these approaches to the temptation is best? Much is to be said for the combination approach (i.e., view 3c). First, the citation of Deut. 8:3 has to do with God's provision for the nation. God promised he would protect his people Israel and had demonstrated his protection by providing manna for them (Exod. 16). God had demonstrated his faithfulness for forty years. In Deuteronomy, Moses was reminding the nation not to doubt God's goodness upon entering the land. Jesus too had a promise that he was God's Son (Luke 3:22), and surely God would protect his Son. Thus, if food were to come to the Son who had been led into the desert to fast, surely God could give it to him. Thus, the Deuteronomy parallel centers on God's promise and its truth, a promise that is related to his provision.

Second, by providing himself with food, Jesus would be operating independently of God, something that the Son was not to do, as Jesus' acknowledgment of God's will at Gethsemane shows (22:39–44). Jesus' miraculous provision of food for himself would represent a challenge of God's protection for his Son and a rejection of the Son's dependence on him, especially since God had led him into the desert.

The devil was really suggesting that perhaps God was abandoning Jesus, and so he had better look out for himself. Is not God treating you poorly? If so, take care of yourself. You can look out for yourself better than God can look out for you! Given the self-sacrificial mission the Son was to have and the suffering he would face, such a test of self-denial was appropriate. As Jesus' reply shows, he

14. Glickman 1983: 226–27. Nolland 1989: 179 says that the test is exploitation of Jesus' privilege of sonship, since the Son has access to the powers of the Father. "Son of God" here has a special force for Jesus' unique filial relationship to God, since Jesus can access such power. But C. F. Evans 1990: 258 ties υἱός to 3:22, so that it means "servant of God" or "king." Nolland's view is more likely. Satan is not testing regal authority, but something more significant.

knew the devil's attack on God's goodness and protection was wrong.

4:4   Jesus' reply is short and to the point: human livelihood consists of more than the mere meeting of daily needs. The citation is from Deut. 8:3, the original point of which was to call Israel to remain fixed on God's faithfulness in delivering his promises and protection (cf. Luke 12:31). The "word of God" by which people are ultimately to live is even more fundamental than the provision of food. Jesus will rest on God's sustenance and provision, given in God's own way. He will not short-circuit God's path. Here is how the Son of God (3:38) lives. In fact, for Jesus, life is doing God's will, not providing for self. Luke cites a shorter portion of Deut. 8:3 than does Matthew (see the additional notes for textual and critical issues tied to this difference).

c. Temptation of Rule through False Worship (4:5–8)

4:5   The second temptation begins with a glimpse of the world. Matthew places this temptation last, which is probably the original order. Creed (1930: 63) notes in support of Matthew's order that what is present are two tests grounded in sonship followed by a final effort to offer Jesus all things, a natural progression (see the introduction to this unit).

The nature of this experience is disputed, mainly because Matt. 4:8 mentions Jesus' being taken to a very high mountain, while Luke speaks only of his going up and seeing the kingdoms in an instant. Luke focuses on the quickness of the special appearing of the kingdoms, while Matthew simply presents the place. But most commentators, going back as far as Calvin, note that no mountain gives a view of the entire world. So most posit some type of vision here. Arguing that the language in Matthew and Luke is too spatial to refer merely to a vision, Schürmann (1969: 210) challenges this approach and speaks of a "diabolical rapture" in Luke. The mountain image has apocalyptic connections in Ezek. 40:2, Rev. 21:10, and 2 Bar. 76.3, while 1 Enoch 25.3, 77.4–5, and 87.3 refer to the mountain(s) of God, a mountain of great elevation that sits above all as paradise.[15] So Jesus is given a perspective from above—whether by vision or by rapture—which allows him to see a great expanse of territory.

---

15. Liefeld 1984: 864; Schulz 1972: 187 n. 98; Foerster, *TDNT* 5:486; Manson 1949: 44. The picture of the "high mountain" is almost regal imagery and recalls how rulers often lived high on a mountain over their subjects. Such "heavenly journeys" are not unusual: 2 Cor. 12:2–3. C. F. Evans 1990: 258 cites as parallel Deut. 34:1–4, where Moses sees the promised land from a mountain.

The reason for Luke's omitting the reference to the mountain, that is, if he in fact knew of it, has been variously explained. (1) Plummer (1896: 111) says that Luke knew a vision was present, so he removed the mountain reference. (2) Conzelmann (1960: 29) argues that the mountain was a place of revelation for Luke, so he removed it since a reference to a mountain here would not fit this motif. But one could argue that a revelation was present, though it was a diabolical one. (3) Many note that Luke focuses on time over place, because he realizes no mountain is high enough to see all the kingdoms (Creed 1930: 63; Fitzmyer 1981: 515–16; Schürmann 1969: 210; Dupont 1968: 55). The first part of this approach is likely, though the rationale for it interprets the text in a overly literal manner and ignores the possible apocalyptic origin of the figure. Luke may have merely opted for a stylistic equivalent. Glickman (1983: 464–65) notes that Luke's change allows for a steadier progression toward Jerusalem (Nolland 1989: 179).

This observation about Jerusalem, if stated carefully, is correct. In the three Lucan temptations the only locale mentioned is Jerusalem. Probably stylistic reasons cause omission of the mountain reference. Perhaps Luke is simply working with a different source.

What is clear is that Jesus had a view of all the inhabited earth and that all earthly power was presented to Jesus (Schneider 1977a: 101). Luke's use of οἰκουμένης (*oikoumenēs*, inhabited world) may well be a reference to the Roman Empire, in that Rome was basically regarded as the world of that day (cf. 2:1–2). Οἰκουμένης occupies the place of κόσμου (*kosmou*, of the world) in Matt. 4:8 and is a Lucan term with a comprehensive scope (Luke 21:26; Acts 11:28; 17:6, 31; 19:27; 24:5).[16] As Marshall (1978: 171) notes, like a prospective seller, the devil points out the goods. In a place where Jesus has nothing, he is about to be offered everything.

4:6 The offer highlights its scope. Σοί (*soi*, to you) is in the emphatic position: "Look, Jesus, at what can be yours!" The use of τὴν ἐξουσίαν ταύτην ἅπασαν (*tēn exousian tautēn hapasan*, all this authority) underscores the extent of the offer. All the earthly kingdoms under Satan's authority are available to Jesus, for Satan can give them to him.[17] The offer precedes the actual condition of the contract, which will reveal the intent of the offer. The bait is placed in the trap.

It is interesting to note the perspective that this verse brings concerning the kingdoms of the world. Political and institutional

16. Sasse, *TDNT* 3:888 §C3a; Michel, *TDNT* 5:158; Bovon 1989: 199 n. 35. Κόσμος is found in Luke 9:25; 11:50; 12:30; and Acts 17:24.

17. Note that ἐμοί is also in the emphatic position; Plummer 1896: 111. Matt. 4:8 speaks of the kingdoms and their glory, while Luke stresses what they have: "authority."

power is related to Satan's power and authority in a way that is unusual for Luke, in that Luke normally is quite benevolent toward Rome. This suggests that Luke is using a source whose perspective he accepts.[18] The assumption behind this perspective is that until the earth is redeemed by God's power, it lies in the hands of the evil one. Satan's influence is still significantly present in the world (Rom. 8:18–30; John 12:31; 14:30; 16:11; 1 John 5:19; Eph. 2:2; 2 Cor. 4:4; Rev. 13:2; Ernst 1977: 159). Here arises the question of whether Satan had the authority to make this offer. Was Satan offering something he could deliver?

It is probably best to say that the devil's offer is a mixture of truth and error. He is pictured as wielding great authority on the earth, so much so that some interpreters regard the offer as totally genuine (Godet 1875: 1.215). He certainly claims such authority in saying he can give these things to whomever he wishes.[19] It is possible that Satan believes the claim, so that the offer should be seen as involving diabolical self-delusion.

But there is evidence in the Gospel that suggests the offer is exaggerated. Jesus' expulsion of demons is against such a view of Satan's absolute authority. Later in Luke, Jesus' authority triumphs over the demons, and the demons respond to his rebuke (4:31–37; 8:26–39; Hendriksen 1978: 236; Godet 1875: 1.244–46). Their fear shows that the demons are aware of a limitation on their power. That Satan can be dismissed, as he is in Matt. 4:10, may also suggest this limitation. From the text's perspective, Satan's offer is at best characterized as an oversell (John 12:31; 14:30; 16:11), and at worst it is a lie (John 8:44). Nonetheless, the temptation was real. Would Jesus be drawn into seizing power and turning his back on God, or would he receive it from God's hand graciously, as the ruling Son had been promised in Ps. 2:8 and Dan. 7:14? These OT passages use terms that are used in Luke 4:6: δώσω (dōsō, I will give) and ἐξουσία (exousia, authority). The temptation was ultimately about seizing power on one's own, apart from God's promise and provision. Of course, as later passages show, Jesus realized that there was only one source that could make this offer and that source was not the one addressing him now (10:22; 22:29; Schürmann 1969: 211).

18. Schürmann 1969: 211 n. 176 notes that this difference suggests a source and also notes some ten passages in Luke–Acts where Rome is treated mostly positively: Luke 3:12–14; 20:20–26; 21:12–13; 22:25; 23:4, 13–16, 22; Acts 10:1–11:18; 13:6–12; 16:11–40; 18:12–16; 25:1–26:32. However, Luke is capable of attacking the leaders of Rome, though that is not his usual approach; see Acts 4:24–29.

19. Fitzmyer 1981: 516 notes that ᾧ ἐὰν θέλω is a technical phrase in Aramaic legal documents. Satan claims that he has this right.

In offering Jesus all the kingdoms' authority and glory, Satan was attempting to suggest that all the power, wealth, glory, and fame that the world could offer were there for Jesus' taking.[20] The offer made here was a much easier route to go than the one by which Jesus would obtain all these things from God. But it was also a dead end. Danker (1988: 102–3) gives a beautiful contrast between Jesus' refusal to seize this authority and Alexander the Great's claim to deity (Lucian, *Dialogues of the Dead* 14).

It also should be noted that Luke's description of Satan's words is much fuller than that in Matt. 4:9, even if one allows that the description of Matt. 4:8 has been brought into the statement of Luke 4:6. If Luke and Matthew had a common source, there is no adequate way to sort out or explain the differences here. Marshall (1978: 171–72) admits that it is a moot point whether Luke expanded the text (Dupont 1968: 53–55) or Matthew abbreviated the text (Schürmann 1969: 211). There is no way to tell. The difficulty suggests that perhaps the Gospel writers were not dealing with exactly the same source material. The differences are not significant for the meaning, but they may be revealing at a source-critical level.

Satan's condition is that the Son renounce his allegiance to the Father. He is to bow down and worship Satan, an act that would not require just a momentary action, but that would change his life. Often the temptation is described as if all Jesus had to do was hit his knees once and all would be his. But the challenge represents a defection from God, and such a defection would have lifetime consequences. Jesus was to give the devil the respect and honor due to God alone (Marshall 1978: 172). For by bowing down (προσκυνήσῃς, *proskynēsēs*) before (ἐνώπιον, *enōpion*) the devil, Jesus would be accepting his authority and sovereignty.[21] In Luke, προσκυνέω appears only here (including v. 8) and in 24:52, where the risen Lord is the object, a rare usage of christological significance, since in that context there is no doubt who Jesus really is.[22] The meaning of the offer was clear: if Jesus would give Satan his heart and bow down before him, Satan would let Jesus rule. It was a high

4:7

20. On δόξα, see BAGD 204 §2; BAA 410 §2; Schweizer 1984: 83; and Hendriksen 1978: 235–36 (who cites 2 Chron. 9:9–28; Eccles. 2:1–11; Rev. 18:12–13). Kittel, *TDNT* 2:237, suggests translating the term "radiance." The term alludes to the splendor and value of these kingdoms.

21. Greeven, *TDNT* 6:763–64 and n. 59, observes that the objects of such actions in the NT are God, his agents, or false gods. The agents always tell the supplicant to rise, and the bowing to false gods is always condemned (Acts 14:13–16; Isa. 41:5–7, 21–22).

22. Bovon 1989: 200 n. 36. Προσκυνέω is also found in Acts 7:43; 8:27; 10:25; 24:11. It always has a religious force for Luke. Ἐνώπιον with a genitive is common in Luke (twenty-two times, including 1:15, 17, 19, 75, 76; 5:18, 25; Plummer 1896: 112).

price to ask for an empty claim, but the response would reveal where Jesus' priorities were.

4:8   Jesus again replies with Scripture that gets right to the issue: God alone is worthy of allegiance. The citation is a summary of Deut. 6:13. Only the word μόνῳ (*monō*, alone) is not in that passage. But the presence of the term summarizes well the force of the command to give honor only to God and not to idols (Hendriksen 1978: 237 n. 193; Nolland 1989: 180). The attitude expressed is like that in John 5:19, 5:30, and 6:38, where Jesus pledges that he does nothing except in subjection to the Father. His "religious service" (λατρεύω, *latreuō*, to serve) is only for God. Λατρεύω is also usually limited to God or to idolatrous religious service (BAGD 467; BAA 949–50; Strathmann, *TDNT* 4:62; Luke 1:74; Acts 7:42).

Some believe that Jesus rejected the principle of an earthly political rule (Plummer 1896: 112). This represents an overinterpretation. What is rejected is ruling at Satan's side now, not an earthly rule per se. Satan's temptation is an attempt to break the Son's relationship to the Father. The problem is the nature of the proposed alliance, not the issue of the rule's locale or character. Luke 17:20–37, 21:5–38, and Acts 3:19–21, which look forward to Jesus' return, suggest a time when Jesus will rule the earth, beyond his current rule in ascension. Jesus will display his sovereign authority. He will rule on the earth, but that authority will come from God, not the devil. The Son's loyalty will be rewarded with sovereignty, because of the Father's loyalty (Acts 10:42; 17:31). No offer is great enough to persuade Jesus to abandon his Father. Such total allegiance to God is exemplary.

d. Temptation to Test God's Protection (4:9–12)

4:9   The third temptation also involves an element of travel. As noted earlier, this is Matthew's second temptation. This is probably a visionlike experience, since a real trip would involve witnesses unless it took a special form.[23] The devil takes Jesus to Jerusalem, or what Matt. 4:5 calls the holy city (τὴν ἁγίαν πόλιν, *tēn hagian polin*). Since both writers use the name Ἰερουσαλήμ (Jerusalem) frequently and the phrase ἡ ἁγία πόλις is rare in the Gospels (only Matt. 4:5; 27:53), it is possible that Matthew made the change, since he alone uses the phrase (Marshall 1978: 172). However, the motive for such an alteration is not clear. But if τὴν ἁγίαν πόλιν was the original wording, a change to Jerusalem for a Gentile audience is a little more likely, though hardly

---

23. Even if one is uncertain about or uninterested in what can be known exactly about the event, one still has to describe the narrative's perspective on what is taking place.

necessary, since the temple is named explicitly (Fitzmyer 1981: 516; Nolland 1989: 181). This absence of motive for the change again raises the possibility that the traditions used are distinct. Luke presents this temptation last, because it places the climax in the city where ultimately the drama surrounding Jesus' life will be resolved. Luke makes much of Jerusalem (Luke 9:53; 17:11; 18:31; 19:11).

Jesus ends up on the temple's pinnacle, but the exact locale is uncertain.[24] Some think it is a high temple gate (Jeremias 1936), but many think it is the Royal Porch on the temple's southeast corner, which loomed over a cliff and the Kidron Valley, creating a drop of some 450 feet (Hendriksen 1978: 237–38; Godet 1875: 1.218; Plummer 1896: 113). Josephus mentions that the height of this locale made people who peered over its edge dizzy (*Antiquities* 15.11.5 §§411–12). Despite uncertainty about the exact location, the point is clear: Jesus is at a height where, if he were to cast himself down, it would take special protection to emerge unscathed.

The devil's request is simple enough. He again calls Jesus the Son of God in a first-class Greek conditional clause, a statement that does not in itself assume doubt, but presents the current potential of sonship quite vividly (see the exegesis of 4:3): "If you, Jesus, are currently the Son, cast yourself down." The rationale of the request comes in 4:10–11, but clearly Jesus is intended to place the protection of his life and limb in God's hands. According to church tradition, James the Just died from a similar fall from the temple's pinnacle (Eusebius, *Ecclesiastical History* 2.23.11).

The request's significance is disputed. Why is the temple brought in? Surely if only protection from a fall is in view, then a wilderness cliff would do. Some suggest that the temple scene describes a public act.[25] This view holds that Jesus is to make a public, miraculous confirmation of his sonship and test the faithful protection of God (Fitzmyer 1981: 517). Some go on to argue that Jesus' messianic status is what will be proved, since there is a Jewish tradition that ties Messiah to signs at the temple.[26] A flashy display of power, not the cross, is the devil's offer to Jesus. However, the idea of a public demonstration is unlikely, unless the event is also a representation. There is no mention of an audience or any hint that this action is public (Schürmann 1969: 213 n. 195; Nolland 1989: 181). As with the other temp-

---

24. Schrenk, *TDNT* 3:236; Hyldahl 1961. The expression for the locale is almost unique for Jewish sources.

25. Plummer 1896: 113 raises the suggestion, but is not sure of it, while Glickman 1983: 234 is for it.

26. *Pesikta Rabbati* 36.2 (162a) (= Braude 1968: 680–83); Kirk 1972: 95–98; Wiefel 1988: 102. However, the Jewish text is late and it speaks only of his standing on the roof of the temple.

tations, this is a private affair between the devil and Jesus. In addition, the Jewish tradition about messianic works is late.

Another parallel often mentioned, *Acts of Peter* 32 (ca. 180–190), serves as a contrast to the temptation account. It does not suggest an explicit messianic connection to the act described there and in fact makes a polemical point (Marshall 1978: 173; Schneemelcher 1991–92: 1.312–13). In that text, Simon Magus flies over the temples and hills in Rome, until Peter's word of judgment causes him to crash to the ground. Though Simon claims to fly by the power of God, Peter shows that the reality is different. The *Acts of Peter* text actually rebukes the kind of miraculous display that Jesus refuses to engage in here.

What is the nature of the challenge then and why the temple? It would seem that the challenge is a private test of God's faithful protection. If Jesus is the Son and is righteous, then God will protect him as the citation from Ps. 91 in Luke 4:10–11 suggests. This temptation is really a test of God's care and of Jesus' trust of God (Danker 1988: 104; Hendriksen 1978: 238; Marshall 1978: 173). The temple is a locale that pictures God's closeness. It is where he is to be found as a refuge of protection (Gerhardsson 1966: 56–58). Surely if God will rescue anyone, he will do so at the temple where he is said to dwell.[27]

In light of God's proximity, Jesus can feel free to cast himself down. Luke alone among the Synoptics uses the term ἐντεῦθεν (*enteuthen*, from here [only here and 13:31]). The rest of the NT uses the term eight times, seven of which are in John and Revelation. Again, the addition is hard to defend as Lucan, and it may suggest another source.[28] As Jesus looks over the high pinnacle's edge, he is exhorted to cast himself down and rest in God's hands. He is to let go and let God!

4:10–11 Satan takes a new approach. Having been bested twice by Scripture, he now invokes the text on his own behalf (Schneider 1977a: 102). The Son is to cast himself into the open air because of God's promise of protection for the righteous in Ps. 91:11–12 [90:11–12 LXX].[29] As Liefeld (1984: 864) notes, the mere use of biblical words and promise may not convey God's will.[30]

---

27. Perhaps this is one of the touches of the account that guarantees its ancient origin. In general, Hellenistic Jews cared less about the temple than did Semitic Jews (Acts 7:47–48). The Semitic point of view fits the setting.

28. Schulz 1972: 180 regards the addition as Lucan, but the evidence is not there to make this conclusion.

29. C. F. Evans 1990: 260 says Luke sees the psalm as about the Son of God, but this is not necessary. It need refer only to the righteous for the point to apply.

30. Satan's argument appears to be that "there should be no martyrs"; so Nolland 1989: 181.

The citation is given fairly faithfully, though Luke has the phrase τοῦ διαφυλάξαι σε (*tou diaphylaxai se*, to protect you), which Matthew does not possess. Both writers omit the phrase ἐν πάσαις ταῖς ὁδοῖς σου (*en pasais tais hodois sou*, in all your ways) after the mention of protection. Luke's additional line (τοῦ διαφυλάξαι σε) highlights the protection on which the demonic challenge turns. Again, the reason for its inclusion is hard to explain if Matthew and Luke share the same source. An addition, if present, can only be for emphasis. Some argue that the omission of ἐν πάσαις ταῖς ὁδοῖς σου is designed to suggest that the devil twisted the Scripture, since the protection applies only to "all the righteous ways" in which one goes (Hendriksen 1978: 238); but this reads into the line the word *righteous*, an idea that is clearly in the context, but is not present verbally in the line itself. Thus, the omission is like many OT citations where a nonessential line is omitted without influencing the argument (Danker 1988: 104; Schürmann 1969: 213 n. 192).

The citation's point is clear. Satan argues: "God will protect those who are his, so go ahead and jump. If you are God's Son, Jesus, you need not worry a bit." In first-century culture, this type of miraculous protection was expected of wonder workers and would be a testimony of Jesus' special position.[31] Jesus should trust God, and his position would be confirmed. In addition, God's goodness would be substantiated. Again a lie is present, since those who were possessed by demons or followed the suggestion of evil spirits often ended up with bodily damage (9:39; 8:33).

4:12

Jesus refuses the devil's attempt to test God's miraculous protection. Such a test would be presumptuous of Jesus, because it would be artificially created and really would be unbelief masquerading as faith. The premise behind the test is that maybe God will not protect the Son (Liefeld 1984: 864; Stählin, *TDNT* 6:752). Jesus recognizes the offer for what it really is and, citing Deut. 6:16, refuses to jump.

In its OT context, Deut. 6:16 is a reminder to the nation, as it enters the land, not to test the Lord as it had done at Massah (Exod. 17:1–7). In Exodus, the nation had presumed on the Lord's guidance and deliverance by complaining that they never should have come out of Egypt. Freedom and manna were not enough. Jesus is comparing the devil's offer to such a test. It says in effect, "I do not think you will take care of me as Son, so to be sure I am going to place you in a situation where you must take care of me now and on my terms." The demanding of miraculous protection, where it is

31. Creed 1930: 63 cites *Acts of Peter* 32 and Lucian, *Lover of Lies* 13, while Fitzmyer 1981: 511 notes Josephus's description of Theudas in *Antiquities* 20.5.1 §§97–98.

not needed, is not faith or loyalty. It is sin. So Jesus refuses. God had proclaimed Jesus to be the Son at his baptism, so Jesus will rest on his promise. Jesus will need such loyalty and faith in light of what he will face.

e. Departure of the Devil (4:13)

4:13   The reference to completing the temptation adds evidence to the suggestion that Luke saw these three temptations as the end of a string of temptations (Plummer 1896: 114). The construction πάντα πειρασμόν (*panta peirasmon*, every temptation) denotes a comprehensiveness to the trials and thus the comprehensiveness of Jesus' refusal to fall into the trap (a similar use of πᾶς is found in Matt. 3:10 and 12:31; Plummer 1896: 114).

The reference to the devil's departure (ἀπέστη, *apestē*) for a time (ἄχρι καιροῦ, *achri kairou*) is provocative.[32] Conzelmann (1960: 28) suggests that Luke portrays the period from 4:13 to 22:3 as "Satan free" (this interpretation predates Conzelmann, being held by Plummer 1896: 114 and Klostermann 1929: 61). Stated this way the view cannot work, since Jesus' ministry is loaded with demonic challenges (4:33–37; 8:12; 9:38–42; 10:17–18; 11:14–22; 13:11–17; S. Brown 1969: 5–19; Marshall 1970: 87–88). What one can say is that satanic pressure intensifies in Luke 22, as numerous references in that chapter show (22:3, 28, 31, 53). The battle between the adversary and Jesus is a constant one in the Gospel, as 22:28 makes clear. Nevertheless, the conflict rages more heatedly in the final moments of the drama. Fitzmyer (1981: 518) notes that 4:13 is the only place in the entire Gospel where direct temptation is successfully withstood—and Jesus is the one who succeeds.

A final peculiar omission of material occurs here. At the end of this account, Luke omits the reference to angelic ministry, even though he readily refers to angelic activity (Luke 1:11, 26; 2:9; Acts 5:19; 8:26; 12:7; 27:23).[33] It could be argued that Luke omits the reference because the angels are primarily a vehicle for revelation or guidance. But the Acts passages show the angels active in deliverance. So the omission in light of the reference to angels in both Mark and Matthew is peculiar and might again suggest an independent source.[34]

---

32. The verb ἀφίστημι is used only by Luke in the Gospel tradition. Luke also loves to make temporal notes using ἄχρι: Luke 1:20; 17:27; 21:24; Acts 13:11; Nolland 1989: 182.

33. Luke 22:43 involves a text-critical problem and thus is disputed, though I regard it as Lucan.

34. For a defense that most changes are Luke's altering of Matthew, see Goulder 1989: 291–97.

On the other hand, the Lucan omission of Jesus' instruction to Satan to depart, which appears in Matt. 4:10, can be explained more easily, since that command belonged to the final temptation of Matthew, which Luke has earlier. Thus, it dropped out in Luke's rearrangement of the temptation's order.

Summary

In Luke 4:1–13 Jesus shows his qualities as a loyal and beloved Son. He refuses on three occasions to enter into activities that would show a lack of trust toward God's care. These temptations have been compared to texts like 1 John 2:16, so that Jesus is tempted with regard to the lust of the eyes, the lust of the flesh, and the pride of life. Others see the tests of Jesus at the level of Priest (temple), Prophet (stone to bread), and King (kingdoms of the world). However, both of these arrangements are unlikely for Luke. The Prophet, Priest, and King model fails because two of the tests are explicitly tied to the same title (Son), and because there is no priestly motif for Jesus in Luke. The comparison to 1 John 2:16 fails because it is not clear how to align the temptations to the three categories.

All three tests challenge God's promise about Jesus' sonship as revealed at the baptism (Luke 3:22). Did Jesus believe that God would care for his very needs or should the Son go his own way and provide for himself (stone to bread)? Did Jesus hold God in the first place of priority? If an offer for all the world came Jesus' way at the cost of worshiping another, would he refuse it (kingdoms of the world)? Did Jesus believe God's word and realize that God would protect him, rather than put God to a staged test (temple)? The issues of Jesus' faith, focus, and loyalty were at the center of the tests. Jesus emerged as a faithful Son, despite the less-than-ideal environment.

Some argue that these tests are unique to Jesus and should not be read as exemplary (Fitzmyer 1981: 518; S. Brown 1969: 17). It is true that the forms of the temptations are unique to Jesus and are related to his unique position. What Satan asked of Jesus would not be repeatable. But the issues of the tests are fundamental ones that can be repeated for anyone. Previous to entering this unit, Luke had tied Jesus to Adam as Son of God. If one is literally sensitive to Luke's order, then there must be a significance to the Adamic reference between the two events of baptism and temptation, both of which discuss Jesus' sonship. What Jesus does is exemplary and representative. The ultimate way to avoid falling into temptation is not to go one's own way. Faithfulness to God involves trusting him, worshiping him alone, and refusing to create a test of his goodness. Jesus knew the lesson and served as the teacher. As such he showed that he was ready for the ministry that the Father had given to him. He also shows the reader the path to a faithful walk with God. Life is defined as doing God's will and walking in God's way, even if it entails suffering and self-denial.

Luke 4:1–13 concludes the second major portion of Luke's Gospel. The ministry of John the Baptist pointed the way to Jesus and told all to look for the coming of a Mightier One who would bring God's Spirit. The baptism showed that God had cast his lot with Jesus, the beloved Son. The genealogy tied Jesus to all humanity through Adam. The resistance of temptation showed that Jesus was righteous and faithful. Jesus was introduced and was ready for ministry. The next major pericope will let Jesus speak for himself about his mission (4:16–30). As he enters that ministry, one thing is not in doubt. Jesus faithfully serves God and is qualified to represent his hope. He is ready to undertake his mission.

Additional Notes

4:4. Some manuscripts cite the whole of Deut. 8:3 (Byz, A, D, Θ), but the different forms that the longer version of Luke 4:4 has in the manuscript tradition argue against the presence of this longer reading (see UBS on this text).

4:4. Different theories exist for how the original temptation tradition was worded, given Matthew's long citation and Luke's short version. Schürmann (1969: 210 n. 164) argues that Luke shortened the original: (1) Luke 4:22 shows that Luke knew the concept of "words proceeding out of the mouth of God," which is present in Matthew's OT citation; and (2) Luke's understanding of God's word did not allow him to use the term to refer to preservation of life; instead he referred it more specifically to God's utterances (also Wiefel 1988: 101).

On the other hand, Holtz (1968: 61) argues that Matthew filled out the citation to bring out clearly the point intended in the reference to Deut. 8:3. Fitzmyer argues that Matthew expanded the text to bring in wisdom motifs about the teacher who feeds his disciples.[35] These explanations are possible, but less than convincing. Did Luke really avoid the idiom of God's word, as Schürmann suggests? Is the passage's point really clearer by the text's expansion, as Holtz suggests? Interestingly, no pattern emerges as to

---

35. Fitzmyer 1981: 515 cites Prov. 9:1–5; Sir. 24:19–27; and Wis. 16:26. These texts reveal the general theme, but they have no teacher-disciple context, so this explanation is problematic. Bovon 1989: 198 also argues for a Matthean lengthening but gives no reason.

whether Luke 4 or Matt. 4 possesses the longer OT citations. Luke 4:10–11 has the longer OT text versus Matt. 4:5–7. Neither Gospel writer is inclined to abbreviate or expand quotations in this account. It may be that the tradition has produced these variations. This difference may illustrate only that slightly distinct, but similar, sources have been used, since there is no clear evidence that one or the other is original. This is the first of many such details in this pericope, as noted in the exegesis above.

4:12. A few stylistic characteristics in this verse may be attributable to variant sources. Luke uses ἀποκριθείς to refer to Jesus' reply, while Matt. 4:7 uses ἔφη. It can be argued that there was a parallel in the source and that Matthew departs from it with ἔφη.[36] But it could also be argued that Luke created the parallel uses of ἀποκριθείς, since the term is present in Luke 4:4, 8. This is another stylistic alteration that is difficult to pin down to a common source.

A second curious difference in Luke is the absence of γέγραπται (Matt. 4:7), along with the Lucan use of εἴρηται. Dupont argues that this is a stylistic variation.[37] However, the rationale for the difference is not clear, since Luke uses γέγραπται frequently (e.g., Luke 4:4, 8, 10). Here is more evidence that suggests perhaps the material that Matthew and Luke used was not common material or that one of them had additional material (Ernst 1977: 162).

36. Marshall 1978: 173 notes the options. Schulz 1972: 180 argues that Matthew is secondary.

37. Dupont 1968: 58–59. So also Schulz 1972: 180, citing for the use of this verb Acts 2:16 and 13:40, which themselves may reflect traditional expressions. Nolland 1989: 181 gives the most plausible explanation: Jesus refuses to match γέγραπται, which the devil used in 4:10. The form εἴρηται does not appear elsewhere in the NT, which suggests a traditional use more than a Lucan change.

I. Luke's Preface and the Introduction of John and Jesus (1:1–2:52)
II. Preparation for Ministry: Anointed by God (3:1–4:13)
➤ III. Galilean Ministry: Revelation of Jesus (4:14–9:50)
IV. Jerusalem Journey: Jewish Rejection and the New Way (9:51–19:44)
V. Jerusalem: The Innocent One Slain and Raised (19:45–24:53)

III. Galilean Ministry: Revelation of Jesus (4:14–9:50)

Luke 4:14–15 is the first summary note in the body of the Gospel. These verses introduce Jesus' ministry and note his initial popularity, and they also introduce a new section of Luke's Gospel, Jesus' Galilean ministry, which runs to 9:50. Schürmann (1969: 147) disagrees, running the section that started in 3:1 to 4:44, but the summary serves as an introduction to a geographical shift that is significant in Luke's structuring of the Gospel (also correctly Nolland 1989: 186). Wiefel (1988: 86–87, 108) also has a different division, breaking the section after 4:30. He regards 4:31 as beginning the Galilean ministry, but it is not clear why 4:16–30, which is set in Nazareth, does not belong here.

This section of 4:14–9:50 describes Jesus' Galilean ministry. If one accepts the outline of John's Gospel, then this ministry comes about a year after the temptations and follows the Judean ministry, which only John records (Plummer 1896: 115–16; Carson 1984: 116).[1] Carson suggests that the incident with Martha and Mary in Luke 10:38 points to such a Judean ministry and presupposes Jesus' previous contact with the southern part of Israel, but it is hard to know exactly why the Synoptics speak so little about this period.

A few features of Luke 4–9 are Jesus' gathering of disciples who will serve as his witnesses in Acts (Acts 10:37–39) and two major presentations of Jesus' teaching in Luke 4:16–30 and 6:17–49. Luke 4 presents Jesus proclaiming in the synagogue the reality of fulfillment, while in Luke 6 one finds Jesus' moral teaching about love in the context of grace.

The section's basic theological question is, "Who is Jesus?" Who can do such works and teach with such power? The unit describes the awakening of the disciples' faith and the subsequent teaching to them about discipleship, especially about rejection and suffering. Miracles are also prominent, as Jesus reveals his power and authority.

There are some interesting peculiarities concerning parallels with the other Gospels. Luke 6:20–8:40 contains no Marcan paral-

---

1. Those who do not accept Johannine chronology do not discuss the timing of these events, since they believe that one cannot determine the timing.

lels, while Mark 6:45–8:26 is omitted from the Lucan material.[2] The omission is unusual in that much of Mark's material is paralleled in Luke. It may suggest a more complex source situation than the standard four-source theory allows. The omission has been explained as allowing Luke to keep a Galilean focus, but this explanation works for only a few of the pericopes. It cannot explain the entire omission, for Luke does have Jesus journey outside of Galilee in 8:26–39. The removal of Marcan doublets is another explanation that is often offered; but parallelism is something that is not beyond Luke, as the infancy section showed and as Luke 15 will show (not to mention events like Paul's conversion and the Peter-Cornelius visit in Acts).

Attempts to outline this unit are difficult, since as Marshall (1978: 175) notes, Luke tends to flow his sections into one another by using bridge passages. Nonetheless, emphases clearly include the movement to the disciples' confession and then Jesus' response to it. One of the major ideas at the end of the section is how much the disciples have to learn, even after their confession of Jesus. Such an emphasis suggests a rationale for Luke's effort to reassure Theophilus and also explains Luke's emphasis on teaching in Luke 4, 6, and 9–19. After coming to faith, there is still much to learn.

A study of the whole section and its outline reveals the movement from the teaching and revelation of Jesus to confession of him. Jesus' reaction to the confession produces the declaration that he will suffer and so will his disciples. Disciples must stand together and have commitment in order to withstand the forces gathered against them. Luke's word to those who need assurance is this: see the power of Jesus and note that suffering is in God's plan. He will deliver on his promises. In the meantime, have faith, love one another, and work together, knowing that the opposition is strong, but your God is stronger.

---

2. Details on such questions and form issues will be taken up in each pericope, but a general observation is made here. For the significance of the Marcan parallels, see the introductions to 9:7–9 and 9:18–20 and excursus 9. Of course, these remarks are most relevant to those who hold to Marcan priority. Those who see Matthew as first and Mark as last will not discuss what Luke has done to the Second Gospel, but rather what Mark has added.

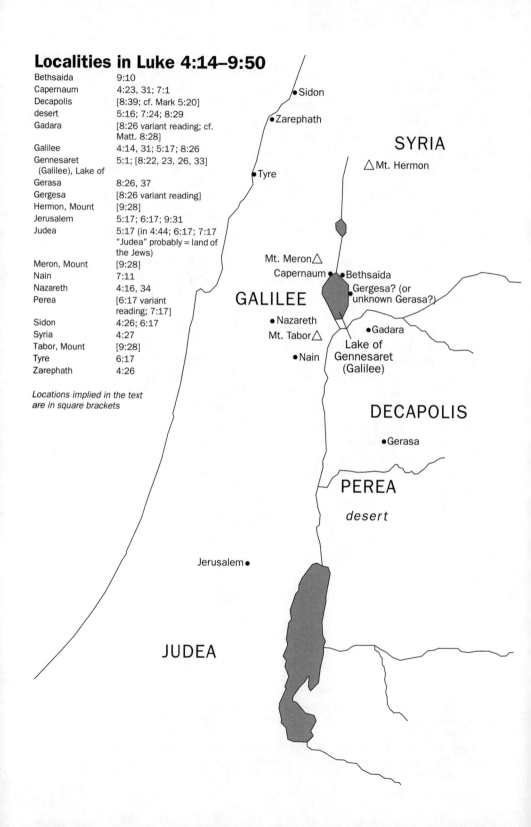

Localities in Luke 4:14–9:50

Bethsaida	9:10
Capernaum	4:23, 31; 7:1
Decapolis	[8:39; cf. Mark 5:20]
desert	5:16; 7:24; 8:29
Gadara	[8:26 variant reading; cf. Matt. 8:28]
Galilee	4:14, 31; 5:17; 8:26
Gennesaret (Galilee), Lake of	5:1; [8:22, 23, 26, 33]
Gerasa	8:26, 37
Gergesa	[8:26 variant reading]
Hermon, Mount	[9:28]
Jerusalem	5:17; 6:17; 9:31
Judea	5:17 (in 4:44; 6:17; 7:17 "Judea" probably = land of the Jews)
Meron, Mount	[9:28]
Nain	7:11
Nazareth	4:16, 34
Perea	[6:17 variant reading; 7:17]
Sidon	4:26; 6:17
Syria	4:27
Tabor, Mount	[9:28]
Tyre	6:17
Zarephath	4:26

Locations implied in the text are in square brackets

• Sidon

• Zarephath

SYRIA

△ Mt. Hermon

• Tyre

Mt. Meron △

Capernaum • • Bethsaida

Gergesa? (or unknown Gerasa?)

GALILEE

• Nazareth

Mt. Tabor △

• Gadara

Lake of Gennesaret (Galilee)

• Nain

DECAPOLIS

• Gerasa

PEREA

desert

Jerusalem •

JUDEA

III. Galilean Ministry: Revelation of Jesus (4:14–9:50)
➤ A. Overview of Jesus' Ministry (4:14–44)
  B. Gathering of Disciples (5:1–6:16)
  C. Jesus' Teaching (6:17–49)

A. Overview of Jesus' Ministry (4:14–44)

The initial section introduces Jesus' ministry in three steps. First, there is an introductory summary in 4:14–15. Then comes the example sermon in 4:16–30, with its universal thrust and hostile reaction. Finally, there are a series of miracles and further summaries in 4:31–44. Most of the events take place in one day. They show Jesus busy with healing and reveal the initial interest in his ministry. Two parts of this final unit are particularly striking: the encounter with demonic forces in 4:40–41 shows the conflict that Jesus' coming introduces and the "mission statement" of Jesus in 4:42–44 declares that he must preach the kingdom of God. Thus, Jesus' message not only is about promise and fulfillment, it also deals with the promised realization of the rule of God. Luke 4:16–30 is a sample of such preaching, while his healings evidence his power and the coming of his rule (10:9, 18; 11:14–20).

1. Summary of Jesus' Galilean Ministry (4:14–15)

A short note introduces and summarizes Jesus' ministry. The emphasis here is on Jesus as teacher. In addition, Jesus is still led by the Spirit. There also is the first note of reaction to Jesus. He is being praised by all.

Sources and Historicity

Some discussion exists concerning the source of 4:14–15. Many explain the passage as a variation of Mark 1:14–15 (Fitzmyer 1981: 521; Schneider 1977a: 104; Wiefel 1988: 103 [who says that it is difficult to say]; Bovon 1989: 207; Nolland 1989: 184–85; Delobel 1973). Mark's four elements are the arrest of John, the entry into Galilee, the preaching of the gospel, and the call to repent because the kingdom is near. Matthew 4:13–17 is similar, except that Matthew adds a note about OT fulfillment, as is typical of his Gospel. On the other hand, Schürmann (1969: 223–24) argues for an independent source (see Schürmann 1964 for a detailed argument). Luke's summary is somewhat different from Mark's, with the only common element being an entry into Galilee.

At least five terms in 4:14 show Lucan influence (Plummer 1896: 116–17): (1) ὑπέστρεψεν (4:1), (2) δύναμις as the Spirit's power (1:35 and esp. 4:36), (3) καθ' ὅλης in this sense (Luke 7:17; 8:39; 23:5, 44; Acts 5:11; 7:10, 11; 9:31, 42; 11:28), (4) περιχώρου (Luke 3:3; 4:37; 7:17; 8:37), and (5) πάντες (1:63; 2:18, 20, 47; 4:22, 28, 37). These terms suggest that Luke has written the summary, which is not too surprising in light of the numerous summaries found in Acts (Acts 6:7; 12:24–25; 16:4–5).

The differences from Mark do not necessarily resolve the question whether it is the source for this Lucan summary. The omission of a mention of John's arrest can be plausibly explained by Luke's earlier coverage in 3:19–20 (Nolland 1989: 185). If Mark was used, the omission of a call to repent because of the kingdom's nearness is more difficult to explain, unless one sees the detailed preaching of 4:16–30 as taking its place.[1] The difficulty with arguing that 4:16–30 explains why repentance is missing in

---

1. Goulder 1989: 299, accepting both omissions as likely explanations, believes that Luke used Mark. For a different view on the kingdom omission based on an alleged Lucan reduction of a connection between the kingdom's coming and repentance, see Conzelmann 1960: 114.

4:14–15 is that the sermon does not mention repentance. Goulder (1989: 300) appeals instead to a link with Matt. 13:54, which is possible.[2]

The question of sources is difficult to resolve, but it would seem that either an independent source has been used or Luke has supplied a summary that adequately captures the initial response to Jesus' early ministry. Mark may not have been used (so also Marshall 1978: 176).

There is no need to produce an outline for this unit, since it is only two verses long. Its form is a summary text. Its themes include a focus on Jesus as a popular teacher and the note that he is led by the Spirit.

Exegesis and Exposition

[14]And Jesus withdrew by the power of the Spirit into Galilee. And a report concerning him went throughout the entire region. [15]And he was teaching in their synagogues, being glorified by all.

4:14 Jesus enters Galilee, the home of his parents (1:26), to begin ministry. This region will be a key one for Luke (Luke 23:5; Acts 10:37; 13:31; Fitzmyer 1981: 522–23; Schneider 1977a: 104–5). Jesus will gather disciples in this region and from them select his apostles. Early contact with Jesus will be a criterion for apostleship later when Judas is replaced (Acts 1:21–22). The key, official witnesses must know Jesus' ministry from its beginning (Acts 1:8; 10:36–43).

Jesus comes into the region under the Spirit's guidance. In this section of Luke, the Spirit's main role is to guide Jesus or equip him for teaching (4:1, 14, 18); this is related to how the Spirit worked in the infancy material (1:15, 41, 67; 2:25).[3] The Spirit is present at the start of Jesus' ministry, just as the Spirit will aid the earliest church's ministry in Acts 2 (Fitzmyer 1981: 522). This point of continuity between Jesus' ministry and the church's is the first of many that Luke will note.

The report about Jesus went out into the whole region. Φήμη (*phēmē*), the source of the English term *fame*, refers to the report that spread about Jesus (Matt. 9:26 is the only other NT use of the term). The region's grapevine poured with news about Jesus. His ministry drew quick attention, and Luke 4:15 will explain why. This is the first of several notes about how people initially responded to

2. Goulder also notes how this fits the use of the phrase *their synagogues* in Matthew (4:23; 9:35; 10:17; 12:9; 13:54). On Jesus' authority and teaching, see Matt. 7:29; 11:1. Still, such summaries may not be sourced in Matthew only, but in oral tradition about Jesus' teaching.

3. Bovon 1989: 208 says that the Spirit in Luke is primarily the Spirit of prophecy and filling. Another way to say this is that the Spirit is the enabler.

Jesus (4:22, 28, 32, 36–37). The response was varied. But initially, it was a type of honeymoon period that often greets a new, significant figure. Luke also notes such reports about Jesus elsewhere (5:15; 7:17). Jesus' work received a lot of attention (cf. Acts 26:26).

4:15   The source of the public's interest was his synagogue teaching. The origin of synagogues is still shrouded in mystery. In all probability, synagogues arose during the Babylonian captivity, when the temple could no longer be a focus for worship.[4] Taking the temple's central place, they served as locales for teaching and prayer among the dispersed Jewish people. Each week the OT was read and men of the community would address the body about the text's relevance. Luke 4:16–30 shows how this process worked, as do key passages in Acts (Acts 13:5–45; 14:1; 17:1, 10).

Jesus' teaching in such synagogues brought him notice. Ἐδί-δασκεν (*edidasken*, was teaching) indicates that his regular teaching in the synagogues caused the crowds to give him "glory" or praise. Marshall (1978: 177) and Schürmann (1969: 222) suggest that works of power may have contributed to his fame; their evidence is the reference in 4:14 to the power of the Spirit (also Nolland 1989: 187; Grundmann, *TDNT* 2:301).[5] However, Luke can make such references to the miraculous clear (5:17; 6:19; 8:46). Since the phrase describes the return to Galilee, the mention of the Spirit in 4:14 refers more to the Spirit's guidance about where Jesus ministers than to the activity of his ministry (Delling, *TDNT* 6:285; Schweizer, *TDNT* 6:408 n. 492).

It is better to see Jesus' teaching as the exclusive cause of the initial fame. This fits in nicely with the teaching emphasis in the chapter (4:18–19, 21, 24–25, 31–32, 43–44). Miracles are clearly associated with Jesus in the chapter and are known to the populace, as 4:23 shows. They also draw attention, but it is the teaching that Luke wishes to emphasize. Luke's Gospel stresses Jesus' teaching ministry (4:31; 5:3, 17; 6:6; 11:1; 13:10, 22, 26; 19:47; 20:1, 21; 21:37; 23:5; Fitzmyer 1981: 523). The synagogue is a natural place for Jesus to present his teaching, though 6:17 shows that Jesus was not averse to teaching in other public settings. The synagogue will be a center for the apostolic teaching as well, especially that of Paul. Luke will illustrate the nature of Jesus' teaching frequently in his Gospel, with the parables having a prominent role in Luke 9–19.

---

4. Fitzmyer 1981: 524 has a bibliography on the synagogue. See also Safrai 1976c; C. F. Evans 1990: 264–65.

5. Nolland 1989: 186 notes the variety of phrases used to describe the Spirit's activity: 4:1, 14, 18; 5:17; 10:21.

The positive response to Jesus follows the reference to δοξαζό-μενος (*doxazomenos*, being glorified). This verb is usually reserved for God and only here does Luke use it of Jesus (Schürmann 1969: 223).[6] At this early moment a wave of popularity is sweeping Jesus, but the initial reaction to a public figure is often not the ultimate reaction. It is with this positive note that Luke introduces Jesus' ministry.

Summary

In Luke 4:14–15 Jesus comes to Galilee and immediately receives much popular attention. His teaching ministry leads to a regional report about him. The Galileans are interested to know what this Jewish teacher is all about. Some news about his miracles may have circulated, but it is his teaching that is drawing most of Luke's attention. A figure of significance is emerging. The reader is supposed to feel this sense of interest and excitement about Jesus. This one who resisted the devil is now moving among the people and bringing his message. What could that message be? The next passage will give a glimpse.

6. But praise of God for Jesus or his work also appears in 2:13, 20, 28; 7:16; Wiefel 1988: 103.

2. Example of Jesus' Preaching (4:16–30)

The Nazarean synagogue account exemplifies Jesus' teaching and claims. It is the second step in a three-part introduction to Jesus' ministry. The summary was in 4:14–15, while the example of Jesus' ministry of healing and service appears in 4:31–44. The account's major features are Jesus' declaration that he fulfills the promise of Scripture, the local rejection of Jesus, Jesus' warning that God's wonders can be limited (as in the period of Elijah and Elisha), the Jewish hostile reaction to that warning, and Jesus' departure from that hostility. In fact, this account is one of Luke's most detailed events and contains many themes that he will continue to develop. Luke 4:16–30 is a representative sample of Jesus' ministry, a paradigm for his ministry.

The passage portrays God's plan and Jesus' role in it. It also shows how Jesus' teaching exposes the reaction of human hearts to that plan (2:34–35; Tiede 1980: 23–33). In this case, the response is wonder along with rejection. The note of the people's failure to respond to God's plan recalls the message at the end of Deuteronomy, as well as the OT theme of how the nation treated God's prophets. Luke will return again and again to this parallel with the prophets, the outstanding examples being Luke 11:47–51 and Stephen's speech in Acts 7.[1] The nation misses a significant opportunity if it rejects Jesus' message.

Sources and Historicity

Luke 4:16–30 has received much attention because of its location in the Gospel in comparison to its Synoptic parallels: Mark 6:1–6a and Matt. 13:53–58 (Aland 1985: §33). Various explanations have been given for this location. Most see Luke positioning this event earlier in order to show its typical character. Like Mark and Matthew, Luke contains a synagogue message, a question about heritage, a reference to a prophet without

---

1. Tiede 1980: 30–47 develops this theme along with other OT prophetic portraits that influence Luke's perspective. He argues that the Gentile issue and its defense is a major Lucan concern that is a motivation for this critique, a point with which I totally agree; so Bock 1987: 259, 277–78. The people not only reject Jesus, but they also refuse to be sensitive to his expanded, inclusive mission.

honor, and the comment about rejection in unbelief. But the picture is more complex than this. In the Marcan and Matthean accounts, the sequence has eight parts:

1. entry into the synagogue
2. astonishment at Jesus' teaching
3. source of Jesus' wisdom questioned[2]
4. Jesus' kinship questioned
5. the offense that some took at Jesus
6. a prophet's lack of honor
7. Jesus' stoppage of works there[3]
8. Jesus' marveling at their unbelief

In contrast, the Lucan account has thirteen elements, including three overlaps with the Synoptic parallels (nos. 1, 7, and 9):

1. entry into the synagogue on the Sabbath (Luke 4:16; Matt. 13:54; Mark 6:2)[4]
2. Jesus' standing to read Isaiah
3. citation of the passage
4. closing of the book
5. Jesus' declaration that fulfillment has come today
6. the crowd's speaking well of Jesus' gracious words
7. Jesus' relationship to Joseph questioned (Luke 4:22; Matt. 13:55–56; Mark 6:3)[5]
8. the proverb that a physician should heal himself and do great works
9. a prophet's lack of honor (Luke 4:24; Matt. 13:57; Mark 6:4)[6]
10. the Elijah-Elisha parallel
11. the crowd's filling with anger[7]
12. the crowd's desire to throw Jesus over a cliff
13. Jesus' passing through the crowd

One can see in this listing the amount of detail that Luke has brought into his account. What approaches are available concerning this material?

2. Matthew repeats the question about the source of Jesus' wisdom after the questions about his kinship.

3. Mark notes a few exceptions.

4. In fact, Luke differs from the potential parallels here. Matthew and Mark both mention that Jesus taught in the synagogue, while Luke speaks only of entry. But the difference may be because of Luke's additional detail about reading Isaiah.

5. Again, there are small differences: Mark does not mention Joseph, the father, while Luke and Matthew do.

6. Luke notes this citation in a shorter form than do Matthew and Mark.

7. One could argue that this equals the crowd's offense in Matt. 13:57 and Mark 6:3, but the Lucan reaction comes later in his account.

1. Some argue that two distinct events are present (Godet 1875: 1.240–41 [with some uncertainty]; Lane 1974: 201 n. 2; Carson 1984: 335 and Liefeld 1984: 866 are uncertain). In addition, they argue that the summary of Jesus' ministry in 4:15 is background for the reference to the Capernaum miracles in 4:23. Without the summary, this allusion to Capernaum is a problem, since no event has yet occurred there. The view's appeal centers on the degree of difference between the other Synoptic accounts and Luke's portrayal. Alford (1874: 477) forcefully lists the objections to this approach. (a) If Luke gives the first visit, where rejection was so strong, how could one marvel at the unbelief the second time in Mark 6 and Matt. 13? It will not do to say that the amazement is at the constancy of unbelief, for the rejection present in the accounts looks like a response to present events and the tenor of the remark in Luke does not suggest a constancy of unbelief. (b) Why is there the parallel of the family connection in both accounts? This looks like surprise raised at an initial encounter. (c) The reference to Capernaum in Luke 4:23 is raised without any qualifying description. This stands in contrast to 4:31, where Capernaum is described as a city in Galilee, a type of note that usually accompanies the introduction of a city for the first time (also Leaney 1958: 50). This probably indicates that the reference in 4:23 has been relocated ahead of where the first reference to Capernaum existed in the tradition. (d) The reference to previous miracles in Capernaum assumes previous miraculous ministry, but the summary in 4:15 mentions only teaching. Any appeal to previous miraculous activity in Capernaum must read into the summary allusions to the city and to the presence of miracles in the Spirit's ministry, both of which are possible but not likely. Thus, this view has too many hurdles to overcome.

2. Many attribute the additions simply to Luke's hand for his own theological purposes.[8] Often this position suggests that Luke's additions are only theological, not historical, since the Gentile theme alluded to in the Elijah-Elisha reference is not a major theme in the other Gospels. But such a capricious treatment of material is not in character for Luke, as Marshall shows (this is one of the major theses of his 1970 work). In addition, the Gentile theme is present in Gospel tradition and is a part of Jesus' teaching (Luke 20:9–19;

8. Bultmann 1963: 31–32 (where he calls the account an apophthegm or pronouncement story, which he believes grew into this full-blown account); Creed 1930: 65; Schneider 1977a: 106–7; Klostermann 1929: 62; Fitzmyer 1981: 527; Tannehill 1972; C. F. Evans 1990: 266–67 (who notes a series of Lucan expressions in the account); Goulder 1989: 299. For a summary of the recent discussion and a full bibliography on this passage, see Shreck 1989, while Corrington 1993 evaluates a redactional reading of this text with other types of readings.

Matt. 15:21–28; 21:33–46; Mark 7:24–30; 12:1–12). The presence of this theme in various sources reflects the possibility of multiple attestation and suggests its authenticity.

3. Luce (1933: 121) suggests that Luke combined two distinct events into a single event. This suggestion is difficult, since one has no indication of how to sort out the events.

4. Luke has used an additional non-Marcan source with material from Mark 6.[9] This approach is possible, though Mark may have a minor role. Schramm shows that Mark cannot be the source for Luke 4:24, which on the surface looks like the strongest point of contact with Mark.[10] Mark's direct influence on the account is less than clear in light of such considerations. This may suggest that Luke, instead of using Mark, has independent information.

5. Luke knows Mark 6, but chooses to use another source for this event.[11] Marshall notes that the event is historically plausible and should not be challenged because of the presence of these additional features in Luke. This approach to the problem is the most satisfying, since it recognizes Luke's research and summarizing hand in the material, while explaining how the parallels between the accounts can exist. It explains how the accounts can run so similarly without having much verbal overlap. If this is the correct view, Luke chose to follow his other source because of its greater detail.

The historical analysis by the Jesus Seminar rates all of the sayings in this passage as Lucan and not from Jesus, except for 4:24, which Jesus probably said (Funk and Hoover 1993: 279–80). The claim is that the scriptural-citation-and-fulfillment scene in 4:18–21 was invented by Luke and would not have circulated independently. But those who argue for the input of another source would differ with this view (see views 4 and 5 above). The passage's concepts are similar to those in 7:22, which is not as disputed (Dunn 1975: 54–62), though Dunn is more skeptical about 4:18–21 than

9. Leaney 1958: 50–54. Schürmann 1969: 227–28, 241–42 says the source is Q; so also Busse 1978: 113–14 (though he sees Q's influence as more conceptual than verbal, which makes Luke very responsible for the account); Nolland 1989: 192.

10. Schramm 1971: 37 n. 2 shows that the word order and word choice in Mark 6:4a are not close to Luke 4:24. Note especially Mark's use of ἄτιμος in contrast to Luke's δεκτός, which is the key term in the verse. However, Luke's term may be influenced by Luke 4:19.

11. Schramm 1971: 37; Marshall 1978: 179. Ernst 1977: 168–69 sees Luke's hand in many but not all changes. Bovon 1989: 207–8 sees an additional source beyond Mark, either Q or special Lucan material, and despairs of being able to sort out what came from where, beyond the basic elements in 4:18–22 and 4:25–27 originating in the additional source. Crossan 1991 fails to discuss this text, a significant omission in a life-of-Jesus study. This omission may well suggest that Crossan regards none of it as going back to Jesus.

I am. If Jesus can speak in terms like 7:22, can he not preach in terms of Isa. 61:1–2? Note also the possible traditional points of contact in the citation (as discussed in the exegesis of 4:18). The rejection in 4:22 has a possible traditional note (see n. 36 and the exegesis of 4:22). The Jesus Seminar rejects the "Doctor, cure yourself" saying because it is a popular proverb. But if so, why can Luke but not Jesus use it? The displacement of the Capernaum remark in 4:23b suggests a relocated saying of tradition, not a Lucan creation. Luke 4:24 fits Jesus' teaching and reflects the kind of inevitable response he must have given to the presence of opposition. As noted above in view 2, the Gentile theme that relates to Elijah and Elisha in 4:25–27 was widely attested in the tradition. Even a scholar as skeptical as Bultmann (1963: 32) sees a pre-Lucan unit in 4:25–27 (Nolland 1989: 194). The Synoptic reference to Elisha is a *hapax legomenon*, so how can a Lucan creation be determined by a unique use? The thrust of the passage reflects the voice of Jesus.

If the account does represent a single event, then Luke moved the account forward to highlight its importance, allowing it to introduce the entire Galilean ministry. Jesus' ministry will not meet with universal approval. In fact, he will be rejected by the very people who are closest to him. On the other hand, his message will go to those who are not racially close to him, but all of this is still a central part of God's plan.

The form of the account is variously described. Bultmann (1963: 31–32) and Bovon (1989: 208) call it an apophthegm or pronouncement story. Fitzmyer (1981: 527–28) sees a conflated form and seems undecided whether a pronouncement story or a story about Jesus is the best category.[12] He speaks of a combination of fulfillment story and rejection story, a good description as long as it is not suggested that two distinct accounts were merged together, which is what Fitzmyer's presentation implies. Berger (1984: 30, 113, 115, 262–63, 347) speaks of subforms. He mentions "I words" of commission (4:18–21), a proclamation account, an account that explains one's identity, a scriptural call account (Isa. 61:1–2), and an example account, drawing on Elijah-Elisha (Luke 4:25–27).

The outline of Luke 4:16–30 is as follows:

12. This latter category is also called legend, where the point is to tell about and exalt the main figure, rather than to give teaching. The term *legend* in form classification is not necessarily pejorative, though the other name for the form, "story about Jesus," is less susceptible to confusion and misunderstanding. Both terms are often applied where there are strong supernatural elements. Many times the classification does express doubt about historicity, but this is not necessarily the case. There is no doubt that this account exalts Jesus, but there is nothing overtly supernatural about it, outside of the revelatory claims that Jesus is making. Given the prominence of teaching, a pronouncement account is likely.

a. Setting of the Scripture reading (4:16–17)
b. Cycle 1: Scripture reading and its exposition (4:18–21)
c. Cycle 1 response: the initial questioning of the crowd (4:22)
d. Cycle 2: a proverb and a historical picture of their rejection (4:23–27)
e. Cycle 2 response: the crowd's anger and hostile desire (4:28–29)
f. Jesus' departure (4:30)

Some argue for a chiastic structure within this account.[13] In this view the center of the account is found within the citation:

a   the synagogue (4:16b)
b   standing (4:16c)
c   receiving the Scripture (4:17a)
d   opening the Scripture (4:17b)
e   preaching the good news (4:18c)
f   proclaiming release to the captive (4:18d)
g   giving sight to the blind (4:18e)
f'   setting free the oppressed (4:18f)
e'   proclaiming acceptable year of the Lord (4:19a)
d'   closing the Scripture (4:20a)
c'   returning the Scripture (4:20b)
b'   sitting (4:20c)
a' the synagogue (4:20d)

The broad outline of the chiasmus is possible, though there are breaks at points. It is better to speak of two cycles of presentation and rejection: cycle 1 is the speech and the crowd's doubt (4:18–22), and cycle 2 is the proverb with its following warning and the crowd's anger (4:23–29; Tiede 1988: 103). The crowd's hostility grows in the account. The two cycles are bracketed by an introduction (4:16–17) and a conclusion (4:30), both of which may be Lucan narrative summaries.

Many ideas dominate the account: the synagogue presentation of the message to Jews and the first hint of Jewish rejection (the mention of Elijah and Elisha alludes to Gentile inclusion and national judgment). The dominant themes are Jesus as fulfillment of OT promise and the present as the time of salvation and Jubilee. Three concerns dominate the passage: Jesus' teaching, the christological revelation about Jesus' mission, and the

---

13. Combrink 1973; Talbert 1982: 54–55; Tiede 1988: 103. I present Tiede's suggestion. See also the further discussion in 4:18.

reaction to Jesus. Jesus is the Anointed One with a message of good news. He is light and liberator to the poor, captive, and blind.

Jesus' portrayal as light and liberator to the poor, captive, and blind is a crucial point in the passage and has been the subject of much discussion, even spawning a theology—liberation theology—focused around passages like Luke 4 (for a healthy evaluation of liberation theology, see Núñez C. 1985). The images of Luke 4 cannot be treated as individual promises and broken up from each other, so that one isolates social elements from spiritual elements. The imagery operates as a unit, picturing the totality of Jesus' deliverance. All the images have to do with the comprehensiveness of Jesus' message and the hope that he offers people.

Reflective of a liberation approach, which underplays the spiritual connection in deference to more sociological emphases and breaks up these categories, is Swartley's 1983 study. For example, Swartley argues that in 2:14 peace on earth is envisioned for people everywhere, but he fails to note that the peace is for those "of God's good pleasure," a reference to God's electing hand that is making distinctions among people. Speaking of the work of R. J. Cassidy and J. H. Yoder, Swartley says, "Their portrait of Jesus' mission as revolutionary—socially, economically, and politically—fits well with the Lukan teaching on the rich and the poor, with Luke's universal outlook which puts the despised Samaritans and the enemy Gentiles in positive light, with Luke's positive emphasis on women, with Luke's accent on God's and Jesus' love for sinners, with Luke's emphasis on salvation (*sōtēria*) and with Luke's highlighting of the Holy Spirit as God's agent to create a new order. Luke's well-known missionary vision and imperative also fit well with this emphasis" (p. 33).

There is much truth in this quotation, but how Jesus' mission is nuanced is crucial. Is Jesus a social, economic, and political revolutionary? Is the mission of the church primarily to confront society's structures so they can be transformed? Or is its primary goal to confront individuals within these structures and pursue changes in individuals that impact the structures they serve? Placing this Luke 4 text in its proper literary context is a key to determining Luke's thrust. Arguing that peace is not merely individualistic, by which he means salvation is not just for the individual, Swartley concludes: "To be sure these points are not wrong, but they are abortive when viewed against Luke's major attention to social themes which show the *eirēnē*-gospel to be of revolutionary consequence, socially, economically, and politically—here and now" (p. 35).

Jesus' social teaching in Luke 4 is certainly challenging, but the spiritual dimension and its individual character cannot be overlooked or understated, since it is Jesus' starting point. He preached to people and did not speak out directly against political structures or leaders. Jesus did seek to create a new community of people before God who would be called out from the ways of the world and would reflect a different, even revolutionary, way of life to the world. The revolutionary call of that community was to show God's love for all and to offer comfort to those of God's people who suffered oppression. So, the oppression in view in Luke 4 is largely aimed against spiritual aspirations, as the light and blindness imagery makes especially clear. However, at the same time the scope of Jesus' deliverance has implications for one's relationship to fellow humans, as well as one's relationship to God. The church must face these implications and reflect aspects of its mission. The gospel does have societal implications, not so much directly for society, as it does for how the redeemed community approaches humans and social structures. Compassion, concern, love, truth, and service are to be concretely expressed by the church, just as they were evidenced in Jesus. Many in stressing the individual have missed these elements of ministry, which reach out to a full range of people's needs. Such elements are important to the church's task, despite their being overstated and often misapplied by perspectives that underplay the spiritual dimensions of Jesus' call.

More balanced and thought-provoking is the 1984 study by Ford entitled *My Enemy Is My Guest*, which contrasts Jesus' message in Luke 4 with the note of vengeance struck in 11QMelch at Qumran (pp. 53–64). Jesus is the bringer of God's grace. The point of Jesus' imagery is that those who sense need and who have deep basic human needs are more likely to hear the message. Jesus cannot heal those who feel they are not in need, for they are happy with their position and condition in life. Jesus' mission sought to deal with needy people at all levels of their life. The church can learn from Jesus' description of who needs the good news. These texts cannot be spiritualized. The poor and the blind in these texts do not exclude the poor and the blind![14]

14. The examples set by "medical missions" or by Christian "food drives" are instructive about how to apply Luke 4, and they are but the tip of the iceberg. Much more could and should be done by the church in these areas if it is to reflect those concerns. Jesus' teaching does possess a "poor-ology"—a concern for the theology of the poor and to the poor.

Exegesis and Exposition

[16]And he came into ⌜Nazareth⌝, where he had been brought up, and he went into the synagogue on the Sabbath according to his custom, and he stood up to read. [17]And the book of the prophet Isaiah was given to him, and he ⌜unrolled⌝ the book and found the place where it was written,

[18] "⌜The Spirit of the Lord is upon me
    because he has anointed me
       to preach good news to the poor,
    he has sent me
       to proclaim
          to the captives forgiveness and
          to the blind sight,
       to set free those who are oppressed,
[19]   to proclaim the acceptable year of the Lord⌝."

[20]And rolling up the scroll, he gave it to the attendant, and sat down; and the eyes of all were fixed upon him. [21]And he began to speak to them, "Today in your hearing this Scripture is fulfilled."

[22]And all were testifying about him and were amazed at the gracious words that proceeded from his mouth. And they were saying, "Is this not the son of Joseph?"

[23]And he said to them, "Surely you will say this proverb to me, 'Physician, heal yourself; what we have heard you did in Capernaum, do here also in your own country.'" [24]And he said, "Truly I say to you, no prophet is acceptable in his homeland. [25]But truly I say to you, many widows were in Israel in the days of Elijah, when the heavens were closed for three-and-one-half years, when there came a great famine in the land, [26]and to none of them was Elijah sent except to a widow in Zarephath of Sidon. [27]And there were many lepers in Israel in the time of Elisha the prophet, and none of them were cleansed except Naaman the Syrian."

[28]And all in the synagogue were filled with anger when they heard these things. [29]And rising up they cast him outside the city and led him to the brow of a mountain on which their city was built, so that they might cast him over the side.

[30]But he went out through their midst and went on his way.

a. Setting of the Scripture Reading (4:16–17)

4:16   Jesus goes to his home town, Nazareth. Luke 4:14–15 made a point about Jesus ministering in Galilee. Now Luke zooms in to look at his message.

Jesus is a pious Jew, who attends synagogue regularly. On this occasion Jesus goes to the synagogue as was his habit (εἰωθός, eiōthos; BAGD 234; BAA 471; Acts 17:2; Matt. 27:15; Mark 10:1; Num. 24:1) on the Sabbath (Ernst 1977: 169). This point is especially important, because Jesus' controversy with the Jewish religious leadership may have left him with a reputation of being a religiously insensitive rebel. In fact, many of the six Sabbath passages in Luke end up in some controversy.[15] Jesus may be pious, but the character of his piety is different from that of the Jewish leadership. On the Sabbath, Jesus will heal, meet people's needs, and instruct them. The synagogue as a center of Jesus' activity parallels the church's activity around the synagogue or temple (Acts 3–4; 13). Christianity did not attempt immediately to isolate itself from Judaism. Rather, it saw itself as the natural fulfillment of Judaism's hope. So a part of its mission was to call Jews to enter into the time of fulfillment.

A synagogue service had various elements (*m. Meg.* 3–4; *m. Ber.* 2): recitation of the *Shema* (Deut. 6:4–9), prayers (including some set prayers like the Tephillah and the *Shemoneh Esreh* [Eighteen Benedictions]), a reading from the Law, a reading from the Prophets, instruction on the passages, and a benediction.[16]

The exact nature of the synagogue service—including how fixed it was in this period—has been the subject of discussion.[17] Though some speak of a fixed cycle of readings every three years, such a schedule in this period seems unlikely (Crockett 1966). The Hebrew Scripture would be read in a standing position in one- to three-verse units. Then the text was translated into Aramaic, the local language, an oral procedure that often involved targumic renderings of the text (i.e., Aramaic paraphrases of the Hebrew OT), though the translator did not read from a text in the assembly (Neh. 8:8–9; Acts 13:15, 27; 15:21; *m. Meg.* 4.1–5, 10). The Torah was always read, and often a reading from the Prophets followed (*m. Meg.* 4.1–2; *b. Meg.* 31a–b).[18] After the reading came an invitation for someone to instruct the audience. Based on texts already read or on new texts, this instruction could be done by any qualified male in the audience, provided ten males were present.[19] Jesus stood up apparently to indicate that he could speak about a passage. Jesus gave

15. Schweizer 1984: 88 incorrectly says that all six Sabbath passages (4:16–30; 4:31–37; 6:1–5; 6:6–11; 13:10–17; 14:1–6) lead to dissension, but there is no mention of controversy in 4:31–37.

16. Schürmann 1969: 228; Ellis 1974: 96; Marshall 1978: 181. For the wording of the *Shemoneh Esreh*, see Schürer 1973–87: 2.456–61.

17. Schrage, *TDNT* 7:810–26, 828–33; Schürer 1973–87: 2.423–63, esp. 447–54; Safrai 1976c: 927–33; Billerbeck 1964.

18. For a variety of regulations on the reading of the Law, see Josephus, *Against Apion* 2.17 §175; Acts 15:21; *m. Meg.* 2.4; 3.4; 4.1–2, 4, 6, 10. I draw heavily on the Mishnah here, despite its later date (ca. A.D. 170), because synagogue tradition as liturgy was likely to have been conservative in its development and because the synagogue was an old institution by this point.

19. *M. Meg.* 4.3 indicates what happens if ten men are not present.

such a lesson from the Prophets, what was called the Haftarah (a reading from the Prophets).

4:17 Jesus takes the scroll and unrolls it to the place from which he will give instruction. It seems that Jesus chose the reading from the Prophets and "found" (εὗρεν, *heuren*) the place in Isaiah from which he wanted to teach (Luce 1933: 120; Fitzmyer 1981: 531; Schürmann 1969: 228–29). If the text was part of a fixed reading schedule, then the scroll would have been opened at the appropriate place. This detail suggests that a reading schedule was not used, but that Jesus chose his text.

b. Cycle 1: Scripture Reading and Its Exposition (4:18–21)

4:18 Before discussing this important text, which outlines in scriptural terms Jesus' mission and proclaims its fulfillment (4:21), some background issues need treatment to help explain the passage's meaning.

Jesus' citation comes from Isa. 61:1–2 and, probably, from Isa. 58:6 (the reason for this mix will be discussed below). In its textual form, the citation is very close to the LXX in omitting repeated references to the divine name and in rendering a difficult MT phrase as "sight to the blind" (Holtz 1968: 39–41; Bock 1987: 106–7). The more significant differences with the LXX are as follows:

1. In Luke 4:19, Luke uses the synonymous κηρύξαι (*kēryxai*, to preach) in place of the LXX's καλέσαι (*kalesai*, to call). Luke's term, which suits his picture of Jesus' preaching ministry, was used traditionally to describe his work (Bock 1987: 316–17 n. 55).
2. Luke omits the phrase *heal the brokenhearted* (Isa. 61:1). This change involves a text-critical problem, but the evidence is strong for the line's omission (see the additional note). One possibility for the omission is that the line *to set free those who are oppressed*, which may be from Isa. 58, is in fact a targum-like rendering of this omitted line from Isa. 61. Such a view is possible, but it is hard to prove. If so, then Jesus reads from and alludes to only Isa. 61. The problems with the suggestion are that there is no evidence of such a targumic reading of Isa. 61 in Jewish materials and the use of such a paraphrastic reading is a little out of character for Luke's citations. If such a reading is present, Luke adopted it from a source.
3. If there is no targumic reading of Isa. 61 here, then there is a probable insertion of Isa. 58. The linkage (via *gezerah shewah*) that creates the association of these texts could emerge from various terms: ἄφεσιν (*aphesin*) and ἀφέσει (*aphesei*) are parallel in the Greek texts (both terms mean forgiveness and differ

only in case); שָׁלַח (*šālaḥ*, to send) appears in both passages; and רָצוֹן (*rāṣôn*, acceptable) appears in Isa. 61:2 and Isa. 58:5. These Hebrew links make it possible that a traditional source is present (J. A. Sanders 1993: 21–25; Bock 1987: 317 n. 59; Violet 1938: 258–69; Chilton 1981: 162–63). There is also the parallel Sabbath–Jubilee-year imagery in both Isaiah texts, a conceptual link to the Jubilee theme of Luke 4.[20] In addition, Judaism linked Isa. 58 and Isa. 61 (Tanenbaum 1974: 65; Westermann 1969: 337).

4. Many note an additional change: Luke's omission of the line in Isa. 61:2 where God's vengeance appears. This is not so much a textual issue, as a literary-theological one. It reflects a choice about how much of the passage to cite and why. The omission is theologically significant in that Jesus characterizes the current time as one primarily of release, and not of judgment, though he does have a warning later (Luke 4:24–27).

None of these changes alter Isaiah's basic sense; but they might indicate that Luke is summarizing textual material used by Jesus in his synagogue address, since a normal synagogue reading would not mix passages quite like this, and the description of Jesus' remarks here is decidedly brief and dramatic (see the exegesis of 4:21). Jesus likely used both passages in the actual setting.

Some see a chiasmus in 4:16–20 (see the layout in the introduction to this unit).[21] A chiastic structure works if the reading is treated as a unit. But within the Isaiah passage, however, it fails because the dual references to the Spirit's anointing would have to be put together in a single line. In addition, the center of the chiasmus is the reference to the blind, which does not receive emphasis as the center in the larger passage. Nonetheless, the broader chiastic structure of this unit shows the citation's centrality for the paragraph.

Liefeld (1984: 867) summarizes the three key ideas of the citation: (1) Jesus is a bearer of the Spirit (3:22; 4:14); (2) Jesus is an eschatological prophet who declares good news; and (3) Jesus is the one who brings release, a messianic function. Each one of these ideas describes the nature of Jesus' task. Of these three, only the third is debated.

The OT background of the passage is significant, as is the history of the interpretation of Isa. 61. This Servant Song–like passage describes the prophet's role in terms used of the Servant of Isaiah, es-

---

20. Sloan 1977: 39–41; Rese 1969: 219. Isa. 58 has Sabbath imagery, while Isa. 61 has Jubilee imagery.

21. Talbert 1982: 54–55; Tiede 1980: 35. For a definition of chiasmus, see the exegesis of 1:17.

pecially in 42:1–4 and 49:1–11.[22] The figure of Isa. 61 brings a message of God's deliverance to exiles. The deliverance imagery parallels the description of the Jubilee year (Lev. 25: 8–17), when debts were canceled and slaves were freed every fiftieth year. It is a picture of forgiveness and spiritual liberation, which is at the center of Jesus' message (Plummer 1896: 121; Sloan 1977: 4–27; Shin Kyo-Seon 1989).

Isaiah 58 contains a prophetic rebuke of the nation for not exhibiting justice toward those in their nation who are in need. God declares in Isa. 58 that the fast he prefers is one that treats one's neighbor properly. Isaiah 61 proclaims a time like that envisioned but not carried out by the nation in Isa. 58. The two passages belong together because the release pictured in Isa. 58 has Jubilee overtones and also describes release in Sabbath terms, an event much like the year of Jubilee.[23] When Jesus applies the passage to himself, he is saying that the present time is like the message of comfort that Isaiah brought to the nation. In fact, the totality of the deliverance that Isaiah described is now put into motion with Jesus' coming. He is the Servant *par excellence*.

Fitzmyer (1981: 529) denies a Servant or messianic understanding of this passage, preferring a reference to the eschatological prophet.[24] If one reads the passage without consideration of the larger Lucan literary context, then such a position could be defended. Jesus is using prophetic texts to make declarations as an eschatological prophet. He compares his ministry to Elijah and Elisha. There is nothing inherently messianic in the subsequent explanation of the OT text. So it is true that the prophetic element exists in the passage and is a significant part of the picture of Jesus' ministry. In fact, it is likely that the audience in the synagogue saw nothing more here than a prophetic eschatological claim.

22. For details, see Bock 1987: 319 n. 68; J. A. Sanders 1975: 80–81. The idea of anointing, the establishment of justice, and the picture of restoration are shared in Isa. 42:1, 3–4; 49:4, 7; 61:1–2. Tg. Isa. 61:1 clearly reads the text this way: "The spirit of prophecy from before Lord Elohim is upon me." But it is wrong to read the OT passage as only about Isaiah, as C. F. Evans 1990: 269 does. Salvation in Isaiah is depicted in terms of God's exodus pattern and is too comprehensive to refer only to Isaiah. Judaism was right to read the text ultimately in terms of the eschaton. This is another typologically fulfilled text like Luke 3:4–6; see the discussion of typology there.

23. Sloan 1977: 38–41. One could also suggest that the Isa. 58 connection was made to underline the very type of ministry that Jesus did exhibit on the Sabbath. His activity fulfilled expectation in line with the general ethical call of Isa. 58:1–13, esp. v. 13, where the Sabbath theme appears; see Carroll R. 1992.

24. Nolland 1989: 196 sees both ideas present, with the prophetic note dominant. This is a better way to see the passage, though whether the prophetic note is primary for Luke (as opposed to its use in the original setting) is questionable.

However, it is clear that Luke has not understood the anointing picture in just this way. He has correctly linked it to other events in his Gospel. The infancy narrative, the baptism, and the following section (4:38–41) all strongly emphasize Jesus as the anointed Son and proclaimer of the kingdom (4:43–44) (Bock 1987: 319 n. 70, 320 n. 74). In fact, the term ἔχρισεν (echrisen, he anointed) in the citation looks back in the flow of Luke's Gospel to the baptism, which was not just prophetic, but was regal as well, since it was grounded in allusions to Isa. 42 and Ps. 2.[25]

One other background issue remains. What is the nature of the audience for whom Jesus came? The picture here should not be pressed in exclusively material or sociological terms, since the history of Jewish interpretation of Isa. 61 shows that by the first century this text was seen to picture the dawning of the new eschatological age.[26] That this interpretation of the passage also continued in rabbinic Judaism suggests that this interpretation is old and deeply rooted in the tradition.[27]

Thus, when one cited Isa. 61, the audience would think immediately of the coming of God's new age of salvation. Jesus proclaims himself to be the bearer of this new age, though whether it is as a prophet or Messiah or both is yet to be fully discussed. The time of deliverance for humankind is present. It is a time when much of what the prophets called for can be realized among those who respond. The audience is not described in purely sociopolitical terms. What is in view is a spiritual and social transformation in a new community.[28]

The citation begins with a reference to the speaker's anointing with God's Spirit, which Jesus sees as an allusion to his baptismal experience (Acts 10:36–38; Schürmann 1969: 229–30). The Spirit has been repeatedly mentioned since Luke 3:22 (4:1, 14), and his placement on Jesus points to a special anointing and a special task: an election to do God's business on behalf of people (Tiede 1980: 43–44). The nature of the task is marked out by the four infinitival phrases. Their merger pictures a prophet and regal deliverer.

25. Note also the commentary on these events in Acts 10:35–43 with its image of Jesus the anointed Lord promised in Scripture. More support for this point comes later in the discussion of the infinitives of the citation.

26. 11QMelch applies Isa. 61 to Melchizedek; J. A. Sanders 1975: 89–91 (who adds 1QH 18.14–15); M. Miller 1969; Nolland 1989: 196 (who notes CD 2.12 and 1QM 11.7). In 1QM 11.7, the figure has priestly and messianic qualities.

27. J. A. Sanders 1975: 83–88, where he mentions six passages, three of which have an eschatological focus: Midr. Lam. 3.50 (73a), Yalqut ha-Makhiri on Isa. 61:1, and Tg. Ps.-J. Num. 25:12, where Isa. 61 is linked with Mal. 3:1.

28. For a balanced treatment of this passage as it relates to current sociopolitical issues, see Pilgrim 1981: 64–84.

Fundamental to Jesus' task is the call to preach good news to the poor (the first infinitive: εὐαγγελίσασθαι πτωχοῖς, *euangelisasthai ptōchois*). This prophetic role fits nicely with Luke's emphasis on Jesus as prophet or teacher (Liefeld 1984: 867; Deut. 18:18 in Acts 3:22; Acts 7:37, 52; Luke 4:24; 7:16, 39; 9:8, 19; 13:33; 24:19). Εὐαγγελίσασθαι recalls 3:18 and puts a note of continuity between Jesus and his forerunner. The good news, or gospel preaching, is detailed in what follows.

The reference to the poor is also key. The use of πτωχός is best described as a "soteriological generalization"—that is, it refers to those who most often responded to Jesus (1 Cor. 1:26–29), and in an invitation context it refers to those who are open to God. The use of ταπεινός (*tapeinos*, humble) in Luke 1:52 is parallel and significant, since it shows that a covenant relationship is part of the background to the description. The key to πτωχός for Luke is found in the Beatitudes. In 6:23, the poor are compared to the prophets (i.e., those who bear and believe the message of God) and in 6:26 the rich are compared to false prophets (i.e., those who reject the message of God). In 6:23, it is clear that Jesus' message and benefits are not given *carte blanche* to the poor, but are related to their developing a proper response to him. In other words, the good news is an announcement and an invitation. In fact, 6:23 is worded in such a way that *anyone*—rich or poor—who comes to Jesus receives the benefits he offers. Given that general invitation, the description of the poor in 4:18 emerges as a generalization, not as an exclusive reference. Nonetheless, the description applies because it is the poor in general who sense their need in the greatest way and, as a result, respond most directly and honestly to Jesus. They characterize concretely the person in need. Their material deprivation often translates into spiritual sensitivity, humility, and responsiveness to God's message of hope. The message is offered to them and they tend to be the most responsive to it.

A strictly material and political interpretation of these verses often ignores this crucial spiritual element and also tends to forget that Jesus spoke in 6:23 of the reward existing in heaven for those who suffer. This is not the language of violent revolution, but of individual transformation within a new social perspective. On the other hand, it is significant that the poor get singled out as a particularly appropriate audience for the gospel. The outsider often related to Jesus' message the best (see also 1 Pet. 2:11–25). The church is certainly called to minister to such people and to do so with a sensitivity to their plight and poverty, since a major ethical call for the church is that Christians are to meet one another's needs and to love their neighbors, as the church expresses its love concretely to all (Luke 10:26–28, 36–37). The example of Paul's collection for the Jerusalem saints shows that this responsibility knew no regional or racial bounds (Rom. 15:14–29). The church is to be the place where such total concern is expressed most visibly. Other human institutions are subsidiary to this institution of God as the vehicle of such concern.

Jesus was sent, a perfect tense verb (ἀπέσταλκεν, *apestalken*) that looks to God's commission, which still directs him. The idea of commission is commonly found in this verb in Luke (1:19, 26 [Gabriel]; 4:43 [Jesus]; 7:27 [John]; 9:2 [the Twelve]).

Jesus' message involved proclaiming release to the captives (the second infinitive: κηρύξαι αἰχμαλώτοις ἄφεσιν, *kēryxai aichmalōtois aphesin*). Again, a more prophetic focus is in view. In the OT, reference to captives meant the exiled, but often it had spiritual overtones, especially since the OT viewed the exile as the result of sin (Deut. 28–32; Ps. 79:11; 126:1; Isa. 42:7; Kittel, *TDNT* 1:196). The image is of release from captivity; but in Luke, the picture includes release from sin and spiritual captivity (Luke 1:77; 7:47; 24:47; Acts 2:38; 5:31; 10:43; 13:38; 26:18; Pilgrim 1981: 68). Of course, since the judgment of captivity is tied to sin, such an association is natural. Jesus' call is to come to God on his terms and accept his forgiveness as provided in Jesus, who sets free the oppressed.

Jesus proclaimed sight to the blind (τυφλοῖς ἀνάβλεψιν, *typhlois anablepsin*). Again, on the surface, one might be led to think only of physical miracles here (e.g., 7:22 and events like 4:31–37, 40–41, which, although not involving the healing of the blind, show Jesus' power to heal; 18:35–43). But the light and darkness imagery also has spiritual overtones, as does the idea of seeing (1:77–80; 6:39 [where the image is negative]; 8:10 [seeing but not seeing]; 10:23–24; 18:41–43). The work envisioned here is not merely physical.

The reference to setting at liberty the oppressed (the third infinitive: ἀποστεῖλαι τεθραυσμένους ἐν ἀφέσει, *aposteilai tethrausmenous en aphesei*) is probably from Isa. 58:6. While a prophet could proclaim the message of liberty for the oppressed, he could not bring it to pass. It is a deliverer who brings deliverance to reality. Again Lucan theology makes the point clear. Luke 3:15–18 spoke of the Stronger One to come who is greater than the prophet John. This Coming One brings with him the Spirit's baptism, which represents salvation's presence and the covenant's arrival (Jer. 31:31). Thus, this passage describes a messianic function. The messianic function also serves to make clear why Isa. 58 was added to the list. It guarantees that Jesus' mission is seen in messianic terms.[29] The healings by Jesus picture this deliverance and are related to his authority, an authority that is greater than prophetic authority (Luke 11:14–23 [where the kingdom arrives]; 11:31–32 [where one greater than Solomon and Jonah arrives]; 18:38–39 [where the Son of David heals]; 19:37–38 [where God is praised for his mighty works through Jesus who enters like a king]).

Jesus will do what Israel was rebuked in Isaiah 58 for not doing: Jesus will meet in love the needs of those who need God. The picture again is of Jesus reaching out to the needy and giving them aid. It is a declaration of injustice reversed (Pilgrim 1981: 70).

In the next line, which returns to Isa. 61, the Jubilee year image of release (ἀφέσει) is again present. Jesus' ultimate role is not only to proclaim deliverance: he brings that release. In this description of his mission, he is seen as both eschatological prophet and Messiah.

4:19 Concluding the OT appeal, the reference to κηρύξαι ἐνιαυτὸν κυρίου δεκτόν (the final infinitive: *kēryxai eniauton kyriou dekton*, to proclaim the acceptable year of the Lord) clearly ties the passage to the Jubilee theme (the concept of acceptable year appears also in 2 Cor. 6:2 and Isa. 49:8).[30] Because of the comprehensive character of the deliverance that Isaiah described, Jubilee was interpreted in Judaism as a reference to the dawn of God's new age. The citation in Luke, then, is not a call to fulfill literally the legal requirement of Jubilee. Rather, the passage takes that picture of freedom to show what God is doing spiritually and physically through his commissioned agent, Jesus. Jubilee, by analogy, becomes a picture of total forgiveness and salvation, just as it was in its prophetic usage in Isa. 61.

The allusion to Isa. 61 has led to speculation about the exact time and setting of this event. Starting with Strobel (1972), attempts have been made to tie the event to a specific year (Strobel posits A.D. 26/27 as a Jubilee year and suggests that Jesus' sermon came about this time). Efforts also exist to discover a specific Torah reading for this event (Finkel 1963: 108 n. 1; Perrot 1973; Bovon 1989: 211; such efforts go back to Mann and Sonne 1940: 283–85). Strobel's dating, though surfacing much background material, must be regarded as a failure since the chronology of Luke 3:1 suggests that Jesus' ministry began about A.D. 30, which is too late for the pro-

---

29. Bock 1987: 109. In Isaiah, the announcement of the prophet coincides with the salvation, but the deliverance is God's, not the prophet's (Isa. 40:9; 41:27; 52:7; esp. 51:16).

30. Sloan 1977: 33–36. Grundmann, *TDNT* 2:59, sees a clear messianic allusion (Isa. 49:8–11; 58:6–8), though what the Isaiah texts show is the presence of decisive deliverance more than a direct allusion to Messiah. Ἐνιαυτός recalls not only Isa. 61:2, but also Lev. 25:10, which teaches Jubilee.

posed setting (see the exegesis of 3:1). Finkel and Perrot both mention Gen. 35:9–15 as the Torah reading for this event, an interesting suggestion but with minimal support.

Hill (1971: 173–75) questions whether a Haftarah reading is present at all, noting that Isa. 61 does not appear in Jewish lectionary lists and pointing to Jesus' mixed citation. But three possibilities exist for seeing a Haftarah reading in the background. (1) If the reading cycle was not fixed in the first century beyond a Torah reading and a Prophets reading and Jesus chose his text, as Luke 4:17 implies, then a Haftarah reading of Isa. 61 is possible, with Jesus adding commentary from Isa. 58. (2) If Jesus simply gives the commentary after the Torah and Prophets readings and reads a text to set the context of his remarks, then the mixed oral citation becomes even more explainable without having to posit here a summary citation from Luke or his source. (3) Finally, if Jesus is using only Isa. 61, then the line about freeing the oppressed might reflect a targumic form. Although the event's details are not certain because we lack information on first-century worship practices, it is clear that Jesus presented himself as the fulfillment of Isa. 61.

The remaining issue in Luke 4:19 is the omission of a reference to judgment. One of two explanations is possible. First, the omission may have been made to delay the allusion to judgment until Jesus' warnings in 4:24–27. As mentioned earlier with John the Baptist, the time of salvation is also a time of division (3:7–9, 16–17; 2:34–35). But another reason is more likely: the ultimate time of God's vengeance is not yet arrived in this coming of Jesus (9:51–56; 17:22–37; 21:5–37). The division of deliverance and judgment in God's plan, alluded to by the omission, is sorted out later in Luke. This omission represents part of the "already–not yet" tension of NT eschatology, and a Gospel writer can discuss an issue from either side of the temporal perspective. Jesus' mission is placed initially in terms of hope, but it also brings an implication of judgment about which he will warn in 4:24–27.

4:20 The drama intensifies now that the eschatological passage has been read, but its exposition remains. The scroll is rolled up and returned to the attendant, who is responsible for getting and returning the scroll to the ark where it is kept (πτύξας, ptyxas, to roll up a scroll; BAGD 727; BAA 1456). In all probability he is the ḥazzan of the synagogue (Acts 13:5; Fitzmyer 1981: 533). Jesus then sits down to teach. Teaching in a sitting position was customary (Luke 5:3; Matt. 5:1; 23:2; 26:55; Mark 4:1; Danker 1988: 107; C. Schneider, *TDNT* 3:443).[31] As he prepared to speak, he had the crowd's attention. The

---

31. One could also stand; Philo, *Special Laws* 2.15 §62; Acts 13:16.

common Lucan term ἀτενίζοντες (*atenizontes*) depicts intense, focused emotion by describing the crowd's gaze of attention. Luke uses it twelve times in Luke–Acts, while the rest of the NT uses it twice (Schürmann 1969: 231 n. 64). It appears at key moments such as Jesus' ascension (Acts 1:10), Stephen's vision (Acts 7:55), Paul's rebuke of Elymas (Acts 13:9), and Paul's look as he addresses the Sanhedrin (Acts 23:1). What will Jesus say? Everyone senses the moment and is attentive.

4:21   Jesus declares that the time of fulfillment for Isa. 61 is now. The sequence of verses indicates that Luke is summarizing the events. Luke only notes Jesus' brief declaration here, but the following verse indicates that the crowd was impressed with his message of gracious words, a remark that suggests that Jesus said more than what Luke recorded (Alford 1874: 479; Marshall 1978: 185; Plummer 1896: 123). The text also says that Jesus began (ἤρξατο, *ērxato*) to speak, suggesting that he gave more than one sentence of exposition.

Jesus says the fulfillment is present today (σήμερον, *sēmeron*). The emphasis falls on fulfillment's current availability, as the position of σήμερον at the head of the sentence shows. Σήμερον is a key term in Luke's theology and stresses that the opportunity for salvation is this very moment. Luke uses σήμερον repeatedly in his Gospel to make this very point (2:11; 5:26; 12:28; 13:32–33; 19:5, 9; 22:34, 61; 23:43; and nine times in Acts; Liefeld 1984: 868). Conzelmann (1960: 36–37) argues that the term limits the time of fulfillment and salvation to Jesus' earthly ministry. However, the idea of current fulfillment in Acts 1:6 and 3:18 shows that the period associated with the church is a part of this "today" (Fitzmyer 1981: 533–34). Its recurrence in many passages also makes the point that the "today" is not so much a "now and only now" affair, as much as it is a timeless "now," a reference to the immediate present, when fulfillment is available and a life-changing decision can be made (Schweizer 1984: 89; Marshall 1978: 185; Fuchs, *TDNT* 7:274). Hope can become a reality "today."

The fixedness of fulfillment is further stressed by the use of the perfect tense πεπλήρωται (*peplērōtai*), which refers to an existing state of fulfillment. Alongside the reference to σήμερον, this verb tends to function much like a present tense (Marshall 1978: 185): "This Scripture is being fulfilled today." The fulfillment is tied explicitly to the promise of Scripture, just as it will be in 24:44–46. In Luke 4 it is Isa. 61 that stands fulfilled.[32]

The message's availability is also made clear by the reference to being fulfilled "in your ears" (ἐν τοῖς ὠσὶν ὑμῶν, *en tois ōsin hymōn*).

---

32. Note the definite construction: ἡ γραφὴ αὕτη: "this scripture."

Jesus is completing his commission to preach good news as outlined in Isa. 61. What is preached is also heard (Schürmann 1969: 232). Here is the dawn of a new era, but with the hearing comes the responsibility for a decision (Horst, *TDNT* 5:554).

Of course, the era of fulfillment is very much tied to Jesus' person. He brings a special time. Whereas Mark 1:14–15 puts Jesus' message in terms of the nearness of the kingdom, Luke stresses the nature of the time in the nearness of the person. However, the two ideas are related and are very similar, since with the king comes the kingdom (Luke 11:20; 17:21; Gärtner 1970–71). Jesus is saying to his hometown audience, "The time that all people faithful to God have been waiting for is now here and it is found in me."

c. Cycle 1 Response: The Initial Questioning of the Crowd (4:22)

The crowd gives a twofold response: they recognize Jesus' rhetorical skill and gracious words, but they also remember his ancestry. Some interpreters have been bothered by the contrast. The audience is so positive in 4:22a, but it seems so skeptical in 4:22b. Three suggestions exist for handling this tension:

4:22

1. Luke has rather unskillfully combined sources or perhaps even events (Luce 1933: 121). This suggestion is excessively skeptical, since the context itself gives help with regard to the attitude of the audience and shows the unity of the passage (view 3 below).

2. The phrase ἐμαρτύρουν αὐτῷ (*emartyroun autō*, they were testifying about him) should be taken negatively, not positively, so that αὐτῷ is seen as a dative of disadvantage. In this case the verse would read, "They were testifying *against* him," as in constructions like Matt. 23:31 and John 7:7.[33] In addition the amazement mentioned in the next line is really anger at Jesus' omitting Isaiah's reference to vengeance. Thus, the hostility would exist from the initial point of their response and no abrupt change of mood exists. Against this view is the phrase *gracious words out of his mouth*, which looks to be a positive statement (Fitzmyer 1981: 534). Thus, the view shifts from negative ("all testified against him") to positive ("and they marveled at the words of grace") and then back to negative ("and they asked, 'Is this not the son of Joseph?' "). This view is possible, but less than likely.

33. Jeremias 1958: 44–46; Marshall 1978: 185–86, who notes (though leaning to this view) that the next is also possible.

3. The initial statements represent the crowd's positive reaction to the message's rhetorical power and hopeful character. However, the question about sonship is the product of the crowd's reflective thought since Jesus' heritage does not match, in their view, the nature of the claim (Hendriksen 1978: 256; Geldenhuys 1951: 168). That such a shift is possible, even with the presence of a term like θαυμάζω (*thaumazō*, to marvel), can be seen in 11:14–15, where amazement and skepticism are also side by side. Marveling at his words is a positive response to rhetorical skill, not to his claims. It must also be remembered that this is a summary. The remark is very much like the reaction a strong political or ideological opponent might get: "He is an effective speaker, but I do not accept his point of view." Another parallel might be how one can appreciate a slick defense attorney without necessarily accepting the claim of innocence made for a client. The attorney makes a nice argument, but is it the truth? The skepticism argues that Jesus' claims are excessive for a Galilean Jew. The retorts to Jesus in other settings (e.g., "what good thing can come out of Nazareth?" or "we were not born out of fornication") speak clearly to the attitude that Jesus had to overcome (John 1:46; 7:41; 8:41).

Still, the power and positive thrust of Jesus' message were appreciated: the people were amazed at his gracious words. Ἐθαύμαζον (*ethaumazon*) should be translated "amazed" and not "wondered" or "marveled" (Mark 6:6; Luke 11:38; John 7:21; A. B. Bruce 1897: 490; Godet 1875: 1.236).[34] His rhetorical skill was recognized by all. This positive response with opposition is like the one Stephen receives in Acts 6:15 and the one the apostles get in Acts 4:13 (Schweizer 1984: 90; Leaney 1958: 119; Bovon 1989: 213 mentions Acts 2:7, but attributes the note to Luke's redaction). That the attitude is positive is seen by the use of scriptural language from Deut. 8:3: ἐκπορευομένοις ἐκ τοῦ στόματος αὐτοῦ (*ekporeuomenois ek tou stomatos autou*, proceeded out of his mouth) reflecting this OT text.

The phrase λόγοις τῆς χάριτος (*logois tēs charitos*) should be seen as a description of his message: Jesus speaks gracious words. It is not grammatically an objective genitive linked to grace ("words about grace"; Creed 1930: 67; Plummer 1896: 124–25; Bovon 1989: 214).[35] This positive note in the passage with its allusion to Deut.

---

34. The word *marvel* suggests too much approval to English ears.
35. Ps. 45:2 [44:3 LXX]; Col. 4:6; Acts 14:3; 20:32; Schürmann 1969: 234 n. 92. Nolland 1989: 198–99 argues that it refers to the cause of marvel: the words were endued with the power of God's grace. But this also is too positive, given their rejection.

8:3 is so strong that it causes some to suggest that Luke sees Jesus' word as a "divine message" (Schürmann 1969: 234–35). This description may be too strong for the crowd, but the expression does suggest a very positive mood about the message's hopeful content.

Others suggest that the amazement results from shock or offense that Jesus omits the reference to vengeance in his reading of Isa. 61. However, there is no indication that the reading bothers the crowd (Marshall 1978: 186 mentions this possibility, as does Jeremias 1958: 45). The issue is not what Jesus said, but who Jesus claims to be.[36] How could "this neighbor" be the fulfillment?

Doubt emerges with the question about parentage. That doubt centers in Jesus' person. The use of οὐχί (*ouchi*, is not?) in the question shows that a positive answer is expected: Jesus is the son of Joseph. Mark 6:3 and Matt. 13:55–56 express the question with reference to Mary, brothers, and sisters. This may evidence different sources among the Synoptics, but the point remains the same. Luke has condensed the presentation to a single question. If the crowd raised this issue, it surely was stated in various forms. The point is simply this: How could a common man's son make such claims? Familiarity breeds contempt (Luce 1933: 121; Hendriksen 1978: 256).

Luce (1933: 121) argues that the form of the question shows the absence of a belief in the virgin birth. But this is clearly overinterpretation. Jesus grew up in Joseph's home. He is Joseph's son in the practical sense of the term.

d. Cycle 2: A Proverb and a Historical Picture of Their Rejection (4:23–27)

The message produces the crowd's desire for visible signs of the new era, though it is Jesus who expresses the thoughts of his audience. Jesus operates as a prophet here. Fitzmyer (1981: 528) describes the escalation of hostility in 4:23–29: personal challenge through a proverb (4:23), personal rejection from the region as recorded proverbially (4:24), Jesus' response with its hint of rejection (4:25–27), and the desire to toss Jesus over the cliff (4:28–29).

4:23

Some regard the mention of asking Jesus to perform signs as out of place here (Fitzmyer 1981: 528). But signs were suggested by the use of Isa. 61. The topic is appropriate when one recalls that by using Isa. 61 Jesus is suggesting that the new era has come (Luke

---

36. Schürmann 1969: 236 §d notes that the expression υἱὸς Ἰωσήφ might conceal an Aramaism. He also sees a connection to John 6:42 and suggests that Luke's version is old.

7:21–22). In fact, as the passage makes clear, what Jesus did at Capernaum is precedent for the request.[37]

Jesus responds by noting what the audience will ask of him. The future tense ἐρεῖτε (*ereite*, you will say) is not so much the use of a prophetic future (looking to what they will think) as it is vivid (telling what they are thinking). Jesus, the prophet, is reading their collective mind. He cites a proverb. Παραβολή (*parabolē*) normally means parable, but here it is clear that a proverb is presented, so the term takes on the force of מָשָׁל (*māšāl*) (Wiefel 1988: 106; Plummer 1896: 125–26; Bovon 1989: 214; BAGD 612 §2; BAA 1238–39 §2; 1 Sam. 10:12; Ps. 49:4 [48:5 LXX]; Luke 6:39). The proverb is a popular one.[38]

The proverb's meaning is variously interpreted. Many suggest that the request is, "Do at home what you have done elsewhere" (Hendriksen 1978: 257; Schürmann 1969: 236–37; Schneider 1977a: 109; Mark 6:1). The only problem with this view is that it requires the word σεαυτόν (*seauton*, yourself) be read as a reference to the town or else as a figure meaning "heal your own people" (a corporate force to the proverb that is unlikely). This point comes in the next line, not in the proverb itself.

Others suggest that Jesus is asked to prove his claims. He is to show his stuff, so he may be believed. It is a "you profess, so now produce" mentality (Godet 1875: 1.237; Ellis 1974: 97; Plummer 1896: 126). This is probably the way the remark is intended, since it fits the proverb more directly. Jesus has asked the townspeople to believe that he is a significant figure, and they are hesitant until he shows them. Schweizer (1984: 90) notes that the test of a prophet is in his message, not in his signs (Deut. 13:1–3 [13:2–4 MT]). The request to do signs will linger throughout Jesus' ministry (Luke 4:3; 11:16; 22:64; 23:8, 35–37; Ellis 1974: 97).

However, that an element of regional jealousy is present is not to be excluded. The line immediately after the proverb requests that Nazareth receive the same treatment as Capernaum. It is clear that Jesus' work at Capernaum, a Galilean town located on the west shore of the Lake of Gennesaret, did not go unnoticed in Nazareth. The town of Capernaum will become the center of Jesus' ministry (4:31; 7:1; 10:15).

4:24   Jesus presents a rebuke to the crowd's desire for signs. It is introduced by ἀμήν (*amēn*, truly), a term that Luke uses in solemn state-

---

37. It is important to recall that the passage has probably been relocated here to reflect a typical scene; see the introduction to this unit.

38. Euripides, *Fragments* 1086, 1071; Oepke, *TDNT* 3:205; Creed 1930: 68; Marshall 1978: 187; Cicero, *Letters to His Friends* 4.5.5; Midr. Gen. 23.4 (15c); SB 2:156; P. Oxy. vol. 1 #1 logion 6; Gospel of Thomas 31; Nolland 1979. On ἰατρός, see BAGD 369 §1; BAA 750.

ments.[39] Jesus clearly presents himself as a prophet by this remark. He notes that he is not accepted in his country. In the OT, God's prophet was often rejected by the people. Jesus is no different.

The use of δεκτός (*dektos*) presents an interesting contextual wordplay. In 4:19, Jesus declared the acceptable (δεκτόν) year of the Lord (Tiede 1980: 36–39). But he, as a prophet (4:24), is not acceptable (δεκτός) to the crowd. God offers to accept all who come to him through Jesus' message (Acts 10:35–36); but people will not accept Jesus (Liefeld 1984: 869). This saying is present in Matt. 13:57, Mark 6:4, and John 4:44, but only Luke uses δεκτός. The local rejection is but a picture of the larger rejection to come.

4:25 The stakes in the discussion escalate with the introduction of a warning and a historical analogy. Jesus does not elaborate on the theme of a prophet's being without honor in his land. Rather, he goes on to note what the prophet may do as a result of rejection. He cites a low point in Israel's history: the time of Elijah and Elisha. In this historical comparison, the threat is that those closest to Jesus may miss God's blessing, while others, who are far away, will receive it. Luke 4:25–27, which alludes to the period of the evil king Ahab, is unique to Luke's portrayal of the synagogue account.[40] The OT text alluded to here is 1 Kings 17–18, which refers to a specific famine and judgment for covenant unfaithfulness. Such unfaithfulness brought Israel under judgment at this time, so God's provision and prophetic signs were absent from the land.

4:26 The analogy continues. The absence of God's work is stressed by two indicators. First, the passive voice reappears. Three theological passives allude to God's direct work in restricting blessing: ἐκλείσθη (*ekleisthē*, were closed [4:25]), ἐπέμφθη (*epemphthē*, was sent [4:26]), and ἐκαθαρίσθη (*ekatharisthē*, were cleansed [4:27]). A lack of faith may alienate God, as it did in the past.

The second indicator is the use of οὐδεμίαν (*oudemian*, no one) in 4:26 and οὐδείς (*oudeis*, no one) in 4:27. This double usage stresses that no Israelite received positive benefit from the prophets' presence in this period. Rejecting a prophet is risky. The choice was Israel's, and it paid a heavy price in the past. It risks paying

---

39. O'Neill 1959; Luke 4:24; 12:37; 18:17, 29; 21:32; 23:43. On the authenticity of these statements, see Marshall 1978: 187–88. Ἀμήν, transliterated from אָמֵן (*ʾāmēn*), means "let it be so."

40. Plummer 1896: 128 notes two grammatical-stylistic points: ἐπί plus the accusative refers to duration of time: "the heavens were closed *for* three-and-a-half years" (Acts 13:31 and 19:10 are stylistically parallel); and λιμός is masculine, which reflects common usage over the use of the feminine. These points do not influence the passage's meaning.

again (13:32–35; 19:41–44). The analogy to Jesus is strong and clear: now people must decide again about God's messenger.

Jesus notes that not a single widow received blessing except for a Gentile woman in Zarephath, a town located north of Israel between Tyre and Sidon (1 Kings 17:9).[41] In the OT account, the woman is described in terms of her faith (1 Kings 17:12, 16, 18, 24). This Gentile is an exception to the rule, and she is the last person one would expect would be blessed by an Israelite prophet.[42]

The parallelism with Elijah is popular in the NT and in Luke.[43] In a dire period of Israel's history, Elijah ministered outside the nation. The exact point of the comparison can be stated in various ways (Marshall 1978: 188). (1) The comparison shows that Nazareth does not have exclusive claim to Jesus. This point, though true, is too narrow to develop the major idea. (2) Elijah and Elisha show that, because of Nazareth's refusal, Jesus will go elsewhere. This point also is true yet lacks specificity. (3) The prophetic example teaches that, although the homeland rejects him, others will respond and see God work.[44] This approach is probably accurate, since not everyone in the homeland or in the nation will reject Jesus. Again as in 4:18, the language is in generalized form, but the warning is serious. Salvation will open up to all kinds of people. Liefeld (1984: 869) argues that rejection is not explicitly the point here. This is correct, but the comparison to this bleak time of famine and to Elijah's period certainly warns, through clear implication, that the consequences of rejecting Jesus may involve God's rejection.

4:27   The message is reinforced by a second illustration, this one about Elijah's successor, Elisha (2 Kings 5:1–14), the only time he is named in the NT. No Israelite leper was healed. Rather, a Syrian Gentile named Naaman received God's cleansing in the Jordan River. The point about the danger of potential rejection is driven home through an illustration about a second category of needy people, lepers. God was working with those outside Israel and with the sick who were unclean (Lev. 14:2–31). Those ostensibly distant

41. On Zarephath, see Josephus, *Antiquities* 8.13.2 §320; Fitzmyer 1981: 538.
42. For εἰ μή (in this context: adversative "but"), see Klostermann 1929: 65; Marshall 1978: 189; BDF §448.8.
43. Luke 7:11–17; 17:12–19; Wink 1968: 44; Jeremias, *TDNT* 2:928–41; France 1971: 48.
44. Brawley 1987: 6–27 challenges the argument that the passage is a paradigm for the rejection of the nation or for the inclusion of Gentiles. The view that Brawley rejects is probably overstated, but his critique may also go too far. Brawley is right that Israel is not permanently rejected in Luke's view, but an allusion to potential inclusion of outsiders, including Gentiles, cannot be excluded. Such an allusion can exist without insisting that it must also include the idea that Israel is cut off.

from God could become the blessed, while those hearing his message now risked an experience like Israel of old. Those ostensibly near to God had better hear the warning. Jesus' audience did react, but with something other than a positive response.

e. Cycle 2 Response: The Crowd's Anger and Hostile Desire (4:28–29)

Jesus' comparison to the ministries of Elijah and Elisha did not bring a positive reaction. The crowd knew their biblical history and got the point. The idea that Jesus might reach out to outsiders produced anger. In effect, Jesus was saying that the Nazareans were worse than Syrian lepers and Phoenician widows (Hendriksen 1978: 258; Ernst 1977: 174). Θυμοῦ (*thymou*) is used by Luke for angry reactions to speeches of major figures (Acts 19:28; Büchsel, *TDNT* 3:167–68). Like Paul's message about going to the Gentiles, this warning also left its audience displeased (Acts 13:46, 50; 22:21–22; Plummer 1896: 129). Outsiders might end up being blessed, while insiders are left out.

4:28

The crowd rises up to take hold of Jesus and remove him from the synagogue. Ἀνίστημι (*anistēmi*, to rise up), from which the term ἀναστάντες (*anastantes*, rising up) comes, is sometimes used of a hostile reaction or the surfacing of a contentious figure (Acts 6:9; 5:36–37; Marshall 1978: 190; BAGD 70 §2d; BAA 139 §2d). The crowd takes him outside the city to the brow of the mountain. The exact locale of this incident is not known. A site commonly mentioned is an overhang of some thirty to fifty feet in height (Godet 1875: 1.239–40; Plummer 1896: 129). Some accuse Luke of a vague (Fitzmyer 1981: 538) or erroneous (Schneider 1977a: 110) reference here, but there are many such locales in the region. Luke is not concerned about the specific site.

4:29

The crowd desires to cast Jesus over the edge. The conjunction ὥστε (*hōste*, so that) indicates their purpose and reflects their unfulfilled desire (Marshall 1978: 190).[45] The desire to execute Jesus might seem excessive, but there is some precedent for the attempt. In all likelihood, Jesus is the object of the "lynch law," where a person who is seen as flagrantly violating the law is executed on sight and without a trial (John 8:59; 10:31; Acts 7:54–58; 21:31–32; Plummer 1896: 129). If Jesus is viewed by the crowd as a false prophet, he could be subject to such a slaying according to Deut. 13:5 [13:6 MT] (also Jer. 11:21; Danker 1988: 110; Schürmann 1969: 239). Such a situation might presuppose a stoning (Blinzler 1970). Re-

---

45. Luke 9:52 and 20:20 are grammatically parallel; BDF §390.3, §391.3.

gardless, Jesus' life is seriously threatened in this incident, and the division first predicted in 2:34–35 is coming to fruition. The hostility shown him will also be displayed in Acts against his followers, as the incidents involving Stephen and Paul show.

f. Jesus' Departure (4:30)

4:30 Jesus walks away from his second encounter with the edge of a high locale (cf. 4:9–12). It is debated whether a miracle is implied here, and it is hard to tell. But Jesus escapes this threat, since it is not yet his time to suffer at the hands of rejecters. The idea of divine direction found in ἐπορεύετο (*eporeueto*, he went on his way), which is used often by Luke, suggests that Jesus is on a divinely led journey that will end in his death and resurrection.[46] This event is but the first act of conflict and the first of several conflicts on the Sabbath. Nonetheless, Jesus departs and the story picks up with him in Capernaum.

Summary The synagogue incident of Luke 4:16–30 summarizes the nature of Jesus' ministry. Jesus is the Spirit-anointed prophet who announces the new era and brings to pass this salvation as the anointed Messiah (Isa. 61:1–2; 58:6). He is to proclaim the acceptable year of the Lord. He brings release to those held captive and to the needy. His own people demand that he display signs, yet they reject his claims. This is the first of many such rejections. His response will be to minister to outsiders, and eventually his message will be taken to Gentiles. The conflict will be one of life and death. But Jesus will emerge from the conflict.

In one pericope Jesus' ministry is outlined. Every reader faces a choice upon reading this account: to identify with Jesus and his message of hope or to side with those who reject Jesus. Jesus' safe departure suggests where the decision ought to reside. As Luke will show, people cannot bring Jesus to his death. Rather, Jesus will choose to offer himself up in their behalf. Will the reader accept the offer Jesus makes? Will the reader enter into the Lord's Jubilee and the acceptable year of the Lord? Or will the reader reject him, as the Nazareans did, with all the risk that that entails? Is Jesus the fulfillment of promise or an imposter full of empty words?

Additional Notes

4:16. The spelling Ναζαρά occurs twice in the NT: here and Matt. 4:13 (cf. the more common Ναζαρέθ; Luke 1:26; 2:4, 39, 51). It may represent a

46. See the use of πορεύω in 4:42; 7:6, 11; 9:51, 52, 56, 57; 13:33; 17:11; 22:22, 39; 24:28; Fitzmyer 1981: 539; Ernst 1977: 174–75. "Jesus' hour had not yet come"; Nolland 1989: 201.

more Semitic spelling of the term (Schaeder, *TDNT* 4:874–79; Zenner 1894). As such it may reflect a trace of the original source material for this account.[47]

4:17. A minor textual problem involves ἀναπτύξας (to unroll) (BAGD 60; BAA 118), a reading that occurs in ℵ, D* (in a variant spelling: ἀπτύξας), Δ, Θ, Ψ, family 1, family 13, Byz, Lect, and Itala. The variant ἀνοίξας (to open) is read by A, B, L, W, 33, Syriac, and Coptic. The verbal idea of unrolling the text is natural since an ancient scroll like those found at Qumran is present. A later copyist, being more used to books, changed the term to a more appropriate term for them (Metzger 1975: 137).

4:18. Manuscripts that include an additional line of Isa. 61:1, ἰάσασθαι τοὺς συντετριμμένους τὴν καρδίαν, are A, Θ, Ψ, family 1, Byz, some Vulgate, and some Syriac. Those omitting the line are ℵ, B, D, L, W, family 13, 33, and some Syriac. Reicke (1973: 49) argues for its inclusion; but it looks like a doublet in the passage to "releasing the oppressed" where one is not needed. It also reflects assimilation to the LXX. This variant is not discussed in UBS[3].

4:25. The reference to three-and-a-half years for the Elijah famine agrees with James 5:17 and contrasts to the mention of only three years in 1 Kings 18:1. There are three possible explanations for the difference. (1) Some see three simply as a round number (SB 3:760–61). (2) Others see three and one-half as a symbolic reference to national calamity or the presence of an end-time-like misfortune (Danker 1988: 109–10; Schürmann 1969: 238 n. 122; Klostermann 1929: 65; Plummer 1896: 128; Dan. 7:25; 12:7; Rev. 11:2–3 [= 42 months = 1,260 days]; 12:6, 14; 13:5). (3) Others, taking Luke's number more seriously, argue that the half-year emerges from a difference between the April and October rains, as well as noting that a famine is not removed immediately with the return of rain. The production of food would follow after some time (Plummer 1896: 128; Godet 1875: 1.239; Hendriksen 1978: 258; Bishop 1949–50). The latter explanation seems best, though the significance of the number (view 2) may also be important.

---

47. On the elements of Lucan and non-Lucan style in the verse, see Schürmann 1969: 227 n. 45. He argues that the name *Nazareth* and the reference to Jesus' being reared in Nazareth are not Lucan, since ἀνατρέφω is used in Acts 7:20–21 and 22:3. Τρέφω (to rear) occurs only here in the NT with this meaning, though Luke 23:29; Rev. 12:6, 14 are close in sense: "to nourish, nurture" (BAGD 825; BAA 1645–46).

3. Examples of Jesus' Ministry (4:31–44)

Luke 4:31–44 contains the third part of Luke's introduction to Jesus' ministry. Luke has summarized the ministry (4:14–15) and has given an example of Jesus' preaching (4:16–30). Now he shows how Jesus ministered. The passage concentrates on miraculous works. Jesus has power over disease and demons, two enemies that grip humankind. There are brief allusions to his teaching as well. The mission statement in 4:43–44 serves as a bracket to the teaching emphasis in 4:14–15, a "bookend" rounding out this introductory section of 4:14–44 (Tannehill 1986: 83).

Luke details Jesus' ministry in a series of miracles that take place on a single Sabbath in Capernaum. The section begins with the healing of a demon-possessed man (4:31–37), which is Jesus' first miracle in Luke's Gospel. This is followed by the healing of Peter's mother-in-law (4:38–39) and a series of healings in the evening involving a variety of maladies (4:40–41). Unlike Nazareth, the people ask Jesus to stay, but he must depart to other points in Galilee because of the nature of his mission (4:42–44). Luke 4:43–44 provides a second short mission statement from Jesus in the Gospel; 2:49 was the first, while his synagogue speech of 4:16–30 represents a more comprehensive mission statement. In fact, this ministry shows in concrete terms what the synagogue statement meant.

The healing of the demon-possessed man is the first of five Sabbath healings in Luke (4:31–37, 38–39; 6:6–11; 13:10–17; 14:1–6). It is no accident that this event occurs after a declaration of fulfillment on the Sabbath through an appeal to Sabbath themes (see 4:17–19). Much of Jesus' activity sparks reaction from those sensitive to observing rest on the Sabbath day. Many lessons emerge from these Sabbath confrontations about God's new way and about the failure to heed the new hope.

Not only does Luke concentrate on Capernaum with the next few sections, but he also begins to differentiate between groups. Some respond; others do not. The three sets of miracles in 4:31–44 are received positively. Then follows the passage on Peter's call (5:1–11) with its miraculous catch and its call to discipleship. Next is the healing of the leper (5:12–16), a miracle that shows Jesus' intent to be faithful to the law, as well as his efforts to curb excessive focus on his miraculous work. The healing of the paralytic follows (5:17–26), a miracle that introduces notes of conflict and represents the start of formal opposition to Jesus. Not everyone will welcome Jesus. These six miracles of Luke 4–5 reflect the scope of Jesus' power to deal with a variety of conditions and trace how he revealed himself. Jesus is teaching, healing, and gathering disciples. The reactions to the miracles, along with Jesus' comments about them, explain why some rejected him.

Sources and Historicity

Luke 4:30–6:19 follows Mark's order of events fairly consistently, with only Luke 5:1–11 having a different location. Two options exist for explaining the relationship of Luke 5:1–11 to Mark 1:16–20. (1) If these passages describe the same event, then Luke moves this account back in order to start his survey of Jesus' ministry with the illustrative teaching in Nazareth and then follow it with a demonstration of that ministry in Capernaum. By holding back on the call, Luke can also contrast directly how one group of people responded to Jesus as opposed to those in his hometown. (2) However, it can also be argued that Luke 5:1–11 is an event distinct from Mark 1:16–20, so that Luke has not moved the event as much as he has chosen to narrate a fresh account of Jesus' contact with some of his disciples.[1]

The exorcism of Luke 4:33–36 is introduced with a description of the setting in 4:31–32, which is very close in wording to Mark 1:21–22.[2] The introduction is not to be compared with Matt. 7:28–29, which though similar in wording is a summary belonging to a different setting.[3] The healing itself also parallels Mark 1:23–28, though with seven minor differences that will be noted in the exegesis of the verses (Matthew lacks this miracle).[4]

---

1. See the discussion of sources in 5:1–11, where this latter option is slightly preferred. Those who hold to Matthean priority have a similar view of Luke's placement, since Matthew's order is temptations (Matt. 4:1–11), summary of Galilean ministry using a citation from Isa. 9 unique to Matthew (Matt. 4:12–17), and then the disciples' call (Matt. 4:18–22), which parallels Mark 1:16–20. Aland 1985: §§20, 30, 32, 34.

2. Aland 1985: §35. Note especially Mark 1:22a and Luke 4:32a. The latter part of Luke 4:32 is a condensed version of Mark 1:22b. Those who see Mark coming from Luke speak of expansion. One difference is that Luke repeats the point that Capernaum is in Galilee, while Mark lacks such a note.

3. Fitzmyer 1981: 542. Those who opt for Matthean priority see Mark following Luke here, because only Luke narrates the miracle that follows and so Mark simply took Luke's introduction to that miracle. Actually Matt. 4:13 is closer to this introduction than is Matt. 7, but in sequence Matt. 4:13 belongs with Luke 4:14–15 and Mark 1:14a.

4. Aland 1985: §36. For the list of differences, see Fitzmyer 1981: 542; Schramm 1971: 85–88.

The Capernaum healings underscore Jesus' authority as the Anointed One of God (Acts 10:38; Luke 4:18–19). The mighty works point to his person, as he confronts both personal and spiritual foes in the form of spirits and disease.

After the exorcism, Luke continues his presentation of Jesus' Sabbath activity in Capernaum. This part of the unit contains the healing of Peter's mother-in-law (4:38–39), a summary of Jesus' healing of the sick and possessed (4:40–41), his withdrawal and refusal to stay in Capernaum (4:42–43), and his preaching in Judean synagogues (4:44). The material parallels Mark 1:29–39, though at numerous points the wording of the events' description differs slightly (Aland 1985: §§37–40; details await the exegesis of these verses and the additional note on 4:35b–37). Nolland (1989: 210) notes that the healing of Peter's mother-in-law is often regarded as a Petrine reminiscence.

Matthew places this material at what appears to be a later point in his Gospel, since the healing of Peter's mother-in-law is found in Matt. 8:14–15. However, his placement is really very similar to the other Gospels, except that the leper's healing in Capernaum (Matt. 8:1–4) precedes this event, which Luke has later in Luke 5:12–16, as does Mark in Mark 1:40–45 (see the discussion of sources in 5:12–26). In addition, Matt. 8:5–13 has the healing of the centurion's slave, an event that Luke does not have until Luke 7:1–10. So both Luke and Matthew have the miracle after the Sermon on the Mount/Plain (Mark lacks this miracle). It appears that Matthew has singled out the slave's healing as representative of Jesus' work and as an example of faith. In addition, the cluster of events in Matt. 8 occur in Capernaum, suggesting a type of topical arrangement for Matthew. Matthew's order in chapters 4–8 begins with an introduction to Galilean ministry, then the disciples' call, a summary of Galilean ministry, an exemplary teaching of the Sermon on the Mount, the leper cleansed, and finally the day at Capernaum. Thus, in Matthew these events represent Jesus' early ministry and have a placement similar to the other Gospels, but without strict chronological sequence. Whatever the relationships, it is clear that Luke is closer to Mark than to Matthew here. Either he is following Mark, as Marcan prioritists believe, or Mark has followed Luke.[5]

I reserve comment on the historicity of these actions until we consider the theme of Christology later in this introduction. Since this ministry scene is introductory and summarizing of all of Jesus' ministry, I cover historicity in conjunction with the theology that these events teach. History and theology are tightly wed in this text and should be discussed together.

5. It should be noted that the rationale for Mark's following Luke over Matthew here is not clear. The Marcan omission of the Sermon on the Mount or the Sermon on the Plain is hard to explain, if Mark is a summary Gospel, even given that Mark records less teaching of Jesus than do the other Gospels. He does possess the Olivet discourse, which shows he is not averse to presenting teaching as such.

The form is really straightforward. Three miracle stories appear in 4:33–37, 4:38–39, 4:40–41.[6] Summaries appear in 4:31–32 and 4:42–44, so that three miracles are bracketed by the summaries. One could also call 4:42–44 a pronouncement since the punch line is in Jesus' saying, but it is not a pronouncement story because there is no real controversy or issue in the account.[7] Perhaps 4:42–44 is best called a pronouncement summary, though seeing it as a commission statement is also accurate.

Goulder (1989: 312) suggests a plausible chiastic structure for this passage:

a   teaching (4:31–32)
b   exorcism (4:33–37)
c   healing (4:38–39)
c'   healing (4:40)
b'   exorcism (4:41)
a' preaching (4:42–44)

The outline of Luke 4:31–44 is as follows:

a. Setting summary (4:31–32)
b. Unclean spirit cast out (4:33–37)
    i. Demonic cry of recognition and confession (4:33–34)
    ii. Rebuke by Jesus (4:35a)
    iii. Departure of the demon (4:35b)
    iv. The crowd's amazement at Jesus' authority (4:36)
    v. Spread of the report (4:37)
c. Simon's mother-in-law healed (4:38–39)
d. Jesus' healings; demonic confessions (4:40–41)
e. Jesus' mission to preach the kingdom (4:42–44)

Numerous themes appear in the unit. Most dominant are Jesus' authority in teaching and his authority over disease and the spirit world. The instantaneousness of the healings shows in another way the totality and consistency of this authority. An important confession from the supernatural world states that Jesus is God's Holy One, a messianic confession that Jesus mysteriously silences. The populace is amazed at the uniqueness of Jesus' authority with respect to his teaching and healing. Jesus' individ-

---

6. One can specify their form: 4:33–37 is an exorcism, 4:38–39 is a healing, and 4:40–41 is a summary miracle account; Fitzmyer 1981: 542, 548, 552. On the classification of miracles, see the first additional note on 4:33.

7. Fitzmyer 1981: 555 calls this account a pronouncement story, while Bultmann 1963: 155 is more specific, calling it an "I-saying," which is his category for a commission statement.

ual concern shows as he heals people one by one. Luke continues his focus on Jesus' mission to spread the word of the kingdom.

Turning to the figures around Jesus, one sees a willingness to receive Jesus' aid and to serve (e.g., Simon's mother-in-law). Jesus is approachable. People have confidence to ask Jesus for help. In turn, he is meeting essential needs.

In Luke 4:31–44 Jesus meets the needs of a variety of people. He deals with individuals, crowds, women, and men. The breadth of Jesus' audience matches the breadth of his message (Schür-mann 1969: 244). The events read like personal recollections, because of their detail; for example, some regard the Marcan account of Peter's mother-in-law's healing to have come from Peter (Marshall 1978: 194; Roloff 1970: 115–16). The miracles show that Jesus' authority over both spirits and disease is not incomplete or the result of chance. They point to the nature of the times and the identity of his person (Luke 7:22–23; 24:19; Acts 2:22; 10:38; Theissen 1983: 203, 223–24). Theissen notes three characteristics of Lucan miracles: (1) the power is an active not static force;[8] (2) Jesus' healings are charitable in character; and (3) these healings fulfill Scripture and promise (Luke 5:26; 7:16, 22). In Jesus, the time of fulfillment for God's plan has come.

The emphasis in this section is christological. Luke wishes the reader to focus on Jesus' power, which liberates humanity. That some of these healings involve supernatural forces implies a most fundamental liberation—one from the power of evil. Two factors inhibit readers today from appreciating this type of exorcist authority.

First, the spirit world is minimized in Western culture by the use of abstract terms: "fate" or "the stars." Demonic forces are explained away, rationalized as being simply vestiges of an ancient worldview, or placed in modern categories of mental illness. The latter category may have something to offer at times, but it does not tell the whole story, since some mental illness may be the product of deeper realities. The perspective of these accounts is harder for us to understand than for many in the so-called Third World.[9] They are more open to the reality of such forces, while the miracle accounts often strike the modern Westerner as odd.

---

8. However, Theissen's conclusion that this description reflects Luke's subordinationism is imprecise; see Bock 1987: 66–69. In Luke, Jesus emerges with authority and a role equal to that of God, but Luke builds his Christology from the "earth up" for the benefit of the reader. See Bock 1994c: 102–17.

9. The term "Two-Thirds World," although etymologically at odds with the derivation of "Third World," has achieved considerable currency in and better describes those countries.

But Jesus' genuine authority over such beings is what gives the account its point, power, and relevance. If the spirit world does not exist, then Jesus is merely a motivator or encourager and these stories lack substance. In fact, the accounts would be lies, since Luke presents Jesus as having authority over such forces.[10] In other words, without a basis in history, these accounts have no basis to teach theology or their fundamental Christology. Luke's goal is surely not just to place Jesus in the mundane category of encourager or psychologist. Luke 4:18–19 tells us that Jesus is more than a "positive thinker." To lower Jesus to such levels destroys the biblical portrait of him and rids the gospel of one of its connections to God's power, which can reverse evil (see note on demon possession in Arndt 1956: 146–47).

Second, and perhaps more tragic, the stories about Jesus tend not to strike us as fresh events because they are so well known. Most know that the Bible teaches that Jesus did wonders; so these events no longer amaze. But to read the story as Luke wishes it to be experienced, one must read it as a fresh account. Luke's perspective places the reader into the event as a spectator. The reader is in the synagogue or in the crowd, watching the event take place. He or she is to see it as happening anew. The reader is to identify with the characters in the account and sense their reaction and amazement. Jesus is not just another run-of-the-mill ancient wonder worker. The variety of his wonder working points to something more, as does his different style. It is this freshness and the variety of miraculous activity that give the story its emotional power. Luke says, "Imagine what it would be like if you, dear reader, were the one who witnessed these events or were among the ones healed by Jesus."

10. Nolland 1989: 204 notes that in the ancient world exorcism falls between magic (Paris Magic Papyrus, lines 3007–85) and medicine (Philostratus, *Life of Apollonius* 4.20; Josephus, *Jewish War* 7.6.3 §185). Jews and non-Jews believed in magic (Josephus, *Antiquities* 8.2.5 §§45–49; Lucian, *Lover of Lies* 16, 30–31). But these healings often included potions or other aids that Jesus does not use. The healer in Lucian's account, a Syrian from Palestine, charged a large fee for the service. Lucian also notes the exorcist's use of "Egyptian works" and "imprecations in the Egyptian language." Surveying recent work on the question, Crossan 1991: 304–10 compares magic, miracle, and medicine and equates miracle to magic. But this grossly underestimates Jesus. The range of Jesus' miracles suggests the presence of power far beyond anything magical. Jesus does not rely on potions or aids, but uses only his word. The Jesus Seminar (Funk and Hoover 1993: 42) argues that because Jesus did not use magical formulas or incantations, the disciples did not preserve his actual words for the exorcism. But the logic of this argument for a lack of remembrance is not clear or compelling. The very dissimilarity of Jesus' style compared to other such events in the ancient world might make what he did say memorable.

Exegesis and Exposition

³¹And he went down to ⸀Capernaum⸤, a city of Galilee, and was teaching them on the Sabbath. ³²And they were astonished at his teaching, because his word was with authority.

³³And in the synagogue there was a man having an unclean demonic spirit and he cried out in a great voice, ³⁴"Ah, what have you to do with us, Jesus of ⸀Nazareth⸤? Have you come to destroy us? I know who you are, the Holy One of God." ³⁵And Jesus rebuked him, saying, "Be silent and come out of him." And the demon threw him down in their midst and went out of him without doing him any harm.

³⁶And amazement came upon all, and they were saying to one another, "What is this word, that he commands the unclean spirits with authority and power, and they come out?" ³⁷And the report about him went into all the areas of the region.

³⁸And rising up from the synagogue, he came into Simon's house. But Simon's mother-in-law was afflicted with a high fever, and they were asking him about her. ³⁹And standing above her, he rebuked the fever and it left her; and immediately rising up she ministered to them.

⁴⁰Now while the sun was setting, all those who had any who were sick with various diseases brought them to him; and he laid his hands on each one of them and was healing them. ⁴¹And also the demons came out of many crying, "You are the Son of God." And he rebuked them and would not allow them to speak because they knew him to be the Christ.

⁴²And when it became day, he went out and proceeded to a deserted place. And the crowd was seeking him and came to him and would have kept him from leaving them. ⁴³But he said to them, "To other cities also it is necessary for me to preach the kingdom of God, for it was for this reason I was sent." ⁴⁴And he was preaching in the synagogues of ⸀Judea⸤.

a. Setting Summary (4:31–32)

4:31 Jesus comes to Capernaum, located on the northwest shore of the Sea of Galilee, some 680 feet below sea level (Marshall 1978: 191). A journey there from virtually anywhere in Galilee is a journey down into the city. The town was a major Jewish center in the northern Galilean region, which boasted a trade economy centered in agriculture and fishing (Josephus, *Life* 72 §403; *Jewish War* 3.10.8 §519; Godet 1875: 1.242; Plummer 1896: 131). Luke alone notes that Capernaum is a Galilean city, since this is his first detailed discussion of ministry there. The exact location of the ancient village in today's world is somewhat uncertain, though the two sites suggested are within three kilometers of each other. Most feel it is at Tell Ḥum (Fitzmyer 1981: 535; Schürmann 1969: 246 n. 174).

Jesus again goes to the synagogue. One may question whether 4:31–32 is an introduction to this incident or is another Lucan summary. The point of a summary, if present, is that Jesus regularly went to this Capernaum synagogue. This dispute exists because σάββασιν (*sabbasin*, Sabbaths) is plural, which raises the question whether Luke is speaking of Jesus' teaching on a number of Sabbaths (Schweizer 1984: 98; Schürmann 1969: 246 n. 175). What complicates matters is that the plural term clearly has a singular sense in many passages (Matt. 28:1; Luke 4:16; the singular is used in 6:1, 7, 9). Plummer (1896: 132) notes that, when the term has a plural meaning, it is qualified by a numeral, as in Acts 17:2. But that rule does not always work, as Matt. 28:1 and Mark 1:21 show (Klostermann 1929: 66 notes that Luke 4:16 is paralleled in Mark 1:21). In addition, Plummer claims that the term is plural because it is a transliteration from Aramaic. This cannot work either, since a plural definite article often accompanies the word (Fitzmyer 1981: 544; BDF §141.3; BAGD 739; BAA 1480 §1bβ). Finally, the reference in the parallel Mark 1:21 is clearly intended as singular, since it is qualified by εὐθύς (*euthys*, immediately). Thus, it is most likely that Luke refers to one Sabbath, so that 4:31–32 introduces the event. It is not a separate summary, but sets up the associated events in 4:33–37. As in Nazareth, Jesus has come into the Capernaum synagogue to teach.

The reaction to Jesus' teaching was similar to the reaction in Nazareth. In fact, ἐξεπλήσσοντο (*explēssonto*, were astonished) is the same term used in Matt. 13:54 and Mark 6:2 of Jesus' teaching in Nazareth, as well as in Mark's description of the Capernaum episode (Mark 1:22). The verb also recalls the astonishment felt at the answers of the younger Jesus (Luke 2:48; other Lucan uses are Luke 9:43; Acts 13:12). **4:32**

The reason for the reaction was the authority (ἐξουσίᾳ, *exousia*) of Jesus' word. Two ideas are key here. First, Jesus' authority is what impressed the people. Hendriksen's long list (1978: 263–64) of items that make up the difference between the scribes and Jesus is too generalized to be helpful (e.g., truth versus evasive reasoning, preaching versus system, raised curiosity through illustration versus speeches dry as dust, teaching spoken as a lover of people versus teaching with a lack of love). The issue, as Luke puts it, is simply a matter of authority. What probably caused the reaction is that the scribes would teach from tradition, while Jesus would handle the text directly and independently. His word alone was sufficient.

The second key idea involves the use of λόγος αὐτοῦ (*logos autou*, his word), which is another way to draw attention to Jesus as a teacher with God's message. The theme of the word's progress is key for Luke, especially in Acts where the word of God grows (Luke 5:1; 7:7; 22:61; 24:19; Acts 6:7; 8:4; 12:24; 19:20; Danker 1988: 111;

Leaney 1958: 120). The focus on the word and on Jesus' authority keeps the attention right on Jesus and his teaching (Kittel, *TDNT* 4:106). The idea of Jesus' authority reappears in Luke 4:36 to describe his miraculous work, but here the attention is only on his teaching. In short, Jesus speaks from God (Friedrich, *TDNT* 6:843). Liefeld (1984: 871) notes that the omission of any comparison between Jesus and the scribes, as in Mark 1:22, may be explained in one of two ways: Luke's audience is basically Gentile and so would not be interested in the scribes (Wiefel 1988: 110), or Luke's desire is to focus on Jesus alone. Jesus' teaching makes an impression on the crowd, but later, Luke will reveal that this impression does not last (10:15).

b. Unclean Spirit Cast Out (4:33–37)
i. Demonic Cry of Recognition and Confession (4:33–34)

4:33 Luke 4:33–37 marks the first miracle in Luke's Gospel. That it is a battle with demonic forces is appropriate, for it is evil and Satan that Jesus seeks to overcome through his ministry. A man has a πνεῦμα δαιμονίου ἀκαθάρτου (*pneuma daimoniou akathartou*, an unclean demonic spirit). Δαιμόνιον (*daimonion*, demon) is used twenty-three times in Luke's Gospel.[11] The combination πνεῦμα δαιμονίου ἀκαθάρτου is unique, since usually one refers just to an unclean spirit (πνεῦμα ἀκάθαρτον, *pneuma akatharton*).[12] This phrase has been variously translated, depending on how the genitives are taken (Plummer 1896: 132). Some see a genitive of quality: "a spirit consisting in an unclean demon" (Alford 1874: 482; Leaney 1958: 120). Others see a reference to a genitive of apposition or epexegesis: "a spirit that is an unclean demon" (Bovon 1989: 222 n. 24). Still others suggest a genitive of possession: "a spirit possessed by an unclean demon." Regardless of the classification chosen, the idea is that an outside evil force exercises its authority on this man.

The demon's description as unclean (ἀκαθάρτου) is also taken in a variety of ways. Some suggest that the reference is material and alludes to the man's filthy personal habits (Alford 1874: 482; Leaney 1958: 120). Others suggest that the term is moral in force

---

11. Luke 4:33, 35, 41; 7:33; 8:2, 27, 29, 30, 33, 35, 38; 9:1, 42, 49; 10:17; 11:14 (twice), 15 (twice), 18, 19, 20; 13:32. These references tend to cluster in the Galilean ministry section, as Luke shows less interest in demons when he moves into Jesus' teaching in Luke 9–19. On demon possession, see the second additional note on 4:33.

12. Luke 4:36; 6:18; 8:29; 9:42; 11:24; Foerster, *TDNT* 2:16; Hauck, *TDNT* 3:428. On demons in Judaism, see Josephus, *Jewish War* 7.6.3 §185 ("spirits of wicked men who enter the living and kill them unless aid is forthcoming"); 1 Enoch 19.1; Jub. 10.5; T. Ben. 5.2; C. F. Evans 1990: 279. In the OT, δαιμονίου occurs in Ps. 90:6 [91:6 Engl.] and τὸ πνεῦμα τὸ ἀκάθαρτον in Zech. 13:2.

and refers to the demon's evil character, since in Greek thought spirits could be good or evil.[13] Some see both ideas present (Liefeld 1984: 872).

It seems that ἀκάθαρτος should be seen primarily in a moral light. It refers to the spirit's evil character, since no personal habits are described. Luke's description is not any different from Mark's (against equating Luke's meaning to Mark's is Schneider 1977a: 114; but see Luke 8:2, 27, 29). Mark 1:23 simply presents the more common description in its more concise form: ἐν πνεύματι ἀκαθάρτῳ (en pneumati akathartō, with an unclean spirit).

The presence of demon possession makes the issue of the passage clear. A confrontation exists between Jesus and the forces of evil, like his earlier encounter with the devil in 4:1–13. God's power manifested in the anointed Jesus and the power of evil face off. The spiritual nature of this conflict is highlighted in 1 John 3:8, but in Luke the conflict is put in terms of personal confrontation. Judaism knew that demonic power would be crushed in the messianic age (T. Zeb. 9.8; T. Moses 10.1; Luke 7:22; SB 4:527). The die of cosmic confrontation is cast. The nature of the times and the victor are revealed by the battle.

The demon's reaction to Jesus' presence occurs in the midst of Jesus' **4:34** teaching: he cries out and challenges Jesus.[14] Such cries by demons who meet Jesus are common (Mark 3:11; 5:7; Matt. 8:29; Luke 4:41; 8:28; Grundmann, *TDNT* 3:900; O. Betz, *TDNT* 9:294). Except for ἔα, Luke 4:34 corresponds exactly in wording to Mark 1:24. The man begins with an emotional interjection. The origin and meaning of ἔα (ea) are uncertain (A. B. Bruce 1897: 492): is it an interjection meaning "ah!" or an imperative form of ἐάω (eaō, to leave alone) meaning "let me be!"?[15] It is clear from its use in 1 Clem. 39.5 that it is an emotive expression with imperatival force, for there it means "away then" (BAGD 211; BAA 425 ["a cry of unwillingness": *oho*!]; Creed 1930: 70). BAGD regards a connection to the imperative here as possible. Either way, the remark is emotive, expressing surprise and/or displeasure. The line of emotion introduced here continues through the entire response. Jesus' presence leaves the spirit feeling opposed and threatened (Van Der Loos 1965: 379).

The spirit prefers that Jesus leave him alone, since he is afraid of what the teacher might do. The phrase τί ἡμῖν καὶ σοί (ti hēmin kai

---

13. Foerster, *TDNT* 2:8–9. Marshall 1978: 193 notes this contrasts to Jesus, the Holy One, in 4:34.

14. Ἀνέκραξεν in 4:33 gives the remark's urgent mood in contrast to 1:42, where a synonymous verb (ἀναφωνέω) is used positively of praise.

15. Schürmann 1969: 247–48 n. 194 prefers the imperative and cites Luke 22:51 and 4:41 as conceptual support. He says the use of the interjection in prose is rare.

soi, what have you to do with us?) is a somewhat idiomatic expression for saying, "We have nothing to do with one another" or "Why interfere?" or "Why bother me?" or "Why bug me?" (Danker 1988: 111). The phrase appears in OT settings where one is surprised (Judg. 11:12; 1 Kings 17:18; 2 Kings 3:13).[16] The plural reference to "us" is idiomatic and will be discussed below.

A vocative is used to address Jesus of Nazareth. A. B. Bruce (1897: 492) argues that Luke's using the term Ναζαρηνέ (*Nazarēne*, of Nazareth) shows that he is using Mark, because Luke prefers to use Ναζωραῖος (*Nazōraios*, Nazarean) (BAGD 532; BAA 1077). The personal reference to Jesus leads into the expression of the spirit's real fear.

The note of conflict comes in the question about whether Jesus has come to destroy. Such conflict between forces of good and evil is common (Isa. 11:4 [of the root of Jesse against the wicked]; 1 Cor. 15:25 [of Jesus' ultimate victory]; Luke 8:28; 10:8–9, 17–19; 11:14–23; Mark 3:22–27; Matt. 12:22–30). The spirit fears Jesus' power.

The antecedent of the twofold us (ἡμῖν, *hēmin*, and ἡμᾶς, *hēmas*) is debated. (1) Van Der Loos (1965: 379–80) suggests that it refers not just to the spirit, but to all in the synagogue audience, as the spirit attempts to alienate the audience from Jesus by raising the threat of destruction. But the recognition of Jesus as the Holy One is against this approach to the verse, for that remark is too positive to inspire fear in the audience. That the confession is given in the first person also speaks against this view. (2) Most opt for a reference to Jesus' power over all evil spirits and see here an allusion to all evil forces that Jesus will tame (Plummer 1896: 134; Hendriksen 1978: 264; Fitzmyer 1981: 545–46; Schürmann 1969: 247; Luke 8:27, 30, 35, 38). As Schürmann notes, this is a reason why Jesus is called the Stronger One (3:16; 11:21–22). This view is certainly possible and reflects the note of conflict that dominates the passage. (3) Intriguing, and perhaps more unifying to the passage, is the view of Danker (1988: 111), who argues that ἡμᾶς is a reference to both the demon and the man. Thus the man, possessed by evil, is potentially subject to destruction. The demon, in effect, is challenging Jesus by saying, "In order to get me, you also have to destroy the man." This interpretation explains the Lucan note about the man's emerging unhurt (4:35). The miracle, then, would be not only the exorcism, but also the safe delivery of the man in the process. Luke knows that the possessed can be harmed by their tormentors (8:29; 9:39, 42;

---

16. Schürmann 1969: 248 n. 195. Seesemann, *TDNT* 5:117–18, rightly calls it a "defensive formula," not a confession.

11:14; 13:10–17; Schürmann 1969: 249 n. 214). But in this case, Jesus will extract the evil force without harming the man. The power exerted involves Jesus' total control of evil. Both Jesus and the man emerge victorious, a point the reader is to appreciate. It is hard to know whether view 2 or 3 is better here. It is possible that both may be correct: the demon senses that he is in trouble, but believes that for Jesus to get the demon and what he represents Jesus must also destroy the man.

The spirit reveals the basis of his fear: Jesus is not just a Nazar-ean, he is the Holy One of God. He has a special anointing from God and is his servant. In the OT, similar titles refer to Aaron (Ps. 106:16 [105:16 LXX]) and Elisha (2 Kings 4:9) (cf. the description of Samson in Judg. 13:7). Thus, some suggest that Jesus is seen only as a prophet or a commissioned figure here (Fitzmyer 1981: 546; Bovon 1989: 223). If one takes the passage by itself, such an allusion might be possible, but this association ignores Lucan literary factors. Luke makes a connection between the Holy One and the Davidic Messiah in 1:31–35. This connection appears again here in the conjunction of Son and Christ in 4:41 (Schneider 1977a: 114, 117; Ernst 1977: 179; Schweizer 1984: 99; Schürmann 1969: 249; Creed 1930: 70). Luke clearly sees a messianic conflict. The Lucan connections also make likely the view of Procksch (*TDNT* 1:101–2) that the Holy One of God refers to Jesus as the bearer of the Spirit.[17] Thus, we have a battle between the unclean spirit and the one who has the Holy Spirit. As James 2:19 notes, demons have knowledge about God (Hendriksen 1978: 265). They also appear to know who Jesus is and to have some awareness of his power. This unclean spirit is very nervous about what Jesus will do. Evil has severe angst in the presence of righteousness ready to be exercised.

ii. Rebuke by Jesus (4:35a)

Jesus' response is quick. He exercises his authority and rebukes (ἐπε-τίμησεν, *epetimēsen*) the spirit. Fitzmyer (1981: 546) notes that in Semitic this key word is a technical term for calling evil into submission and that this emphasis is absent in Greek sources.[18] This Semitic lexical point argues against a Hellenistic θεῖος ἀνήρ (*theios anēr*, divine man–wonder worker) approach to Jesus' miracles. Ἐπιτιμάω is common in Luke (4:39; 8:24; 9:42). Jesus, unlike other

4:35a

---

17. Procksch underplays, however, the messianic sense of the title. Note especially 1:35.

18. Ellis 1974: 100. The Hebrew term is גָּעַר (*gāʿar*, to shout at, exorcise), the Aramaic גְּעַר (*gĕʿar*, to exorcise); Zech. 3:2; Ps. 68:30 [68:31 MT]; 106:9; Jub. 10.5–9; 1QapGen 20.28–29; 1QM 14.10; Kee 1967–68; Stauffer, *TDNT* 2:625–26; Jastrow 1903: 261; BDB 172.

exorcists, uses only his word and forgoes the usual rituals or incantations.[19] Jesus' word is powerful and shows that he is indeed the "bearer of the Spirit."[20]

Jesus calls on the unclean spirit to be silent and come out, a rebuke that many regard as preventing the spirit from making any more christological remarks about Jesus. Scholars speculate as to why Jesus would silence the spirit in these accounts (Mark 1:25 = Luke 4:35a; also Mark 4:39). Liefeld (1984: 872) gives three possible reasons for Jesus' not wanting his position publicly declared: (1) He is not going to be a revolutionary against Rome; (2) he prefers his works to testify for him (Luke 7:18–23); and (3) Judaism had a belief that only certain types of self-proclamation were appropriate for Messiah (Longenecker 1970: 71–74). To this list could be added a hesitation to have positive testimony from such an inglorious figure. Such a confession might lead to the wrong conclusion about the source of Jesus' power. However, it is not entirely certain that the silencing is only because of demonic confession (Theissen 1983: 144). Jesus may well be responding to the entire set of demonic remarks, including the demon's hesitation to have Jesus deal with him. This comprehensive approach to Jesus' call for silence is in harmony with the passage's note of conflict.

iii. Departure of the Demon (4:35b)

4:35b The demon throws the man down. The description includes a term unique to exorcisms, ῥίπτω (*rhiptō*, to throw down).[21] Luke's account here is condensed in comparison to Mark 1:26, which speaks of convulsions and the voice's crying out. The exorcism occurs amid the synagogue crowd. Luke's note stresses the public character of the act. The demon departs, and the man is unharmed. The devil is defeated, and the man is protected. God's power overcomes evil. God expresses his power dynamically through Jesus. Round one goes to Jesus. Such synagogue healings are frequent in the Synoptics (Mark 1:23–27 = Luke 4:33–36; Mark 1:39 = Matt. 4:23; Mark 3:1–5 = Matt. 12:9–13 = Luke 6:6–10; Matt. 9:35; Luke 13:10–17; Schrage, *TDNT* 7:830 n. 210).

---

19. Ellis 1974: 100; Plummer 1896: 134. Compare Tob. 8:1–3; Josephus, *Antiquities* 8.2.5 §§45–49 (where the reference is to the powers that Solomon—a regal figure—possessed over evil forces); Justin Martyr, *Dialogue with Trypho* 85. Nolland 1989: 210 notes eight different methods that Jesus used in his various healings in Luke, all of which involve his word or personal touch.

20. Grundmann, *TDNT* 2:301–2; Tannehill 1986: 83. On power: Luke 4:14; 5:17; 6:19; 8:46; Acts 10:38; on miracles: Luke 19:37; Acts 2:22; on authority: Luke 10:19.

21. Bieder, *TDNT* 6:992. The other NT uses are Matt. 9:36; 15:30; 27:5; Luke 17:2; Acts 22:23; 27:19, 29.

iv. The Crowd's Amazement at Jesus' Authority (4:36)

The crowd's reaction to the exorcism is straightforward: they are **4:36** amazed and begin to discuss the significance of what they have seen. The amazement reflects the occurrence of a work of divine power.[22] These are not everyday events. The crowd wonders, "What is this matter?" Λόγος (*logos*, matter; lit., word) describes the entire action surrounding the exorcism. The event is characterized as teaching, because it is a lesson in action. Mark 1:27 makes clear that the idea of teaching is a focus in the discussion. The question by the crowd reflects a curiosity about Capernaum's situation, especially in light of their dealing with a person with such power. The reason for their reaction follows. They are curious because (ὅτι, *hoti*) his teaching has authority and power. The phrase ἐν ἐξουσίᾳ καὶ δυνάμει (*en exousia kai dynamei*, with authority and power) is in an emphatic position in its clause, showing that Jesus' power is the point. Δύναμις is used often by Luke for this miraculous type of exercise (Luke 5:17; 6:19; 8:46; 9:1; Acts 3:12; 4:7; 6:8). Jesus is the Stronger One about whom John the Baptist talked (Luke 3:16; Schürmann 1969: 247, 250). He possesses command over the world of evil. The evil forces obey him, even while they dominate people. Jesus' first miracle, appropriately enough, is against the forces of evil, for he offers that which is good and holy to humanity.

v. Spread of the Report (4:37)

The action made an impression, and news circulated about Jesus **4:37** throughout Galilee (identified in 4:31 as the region referred to in this verse). The expression εἰς πάντα τόπον τῆς περιχώρου (*eis panta topon tēs perichōrou*) emphasizes that the report went into each part of the region (Reicke, *TDNT* 5:888 n. 9). The report would highlight how the demon testified to Jesus' power and authority. The event would raise questions about Jesus, and as a Sabbath healing it may have raised legal questions as well. But the word was out about Jesus, and yet Jesus' work in Capernaum for this Sabbath was only starting.

c. Simon's Mother-in-Law Healed (4:38–39)

From the synagogue, Jesus proceeded to the home of Simon (i.e., **4:38** Peter). This is Luke's first mention of him. That he is introduced

---

22. Bertram, *TDNT* 3:6, notes that the crowd's reaction is a typical ending to a miracle story; Mark 1:27; Luke 5:9. C. F. Evans 1990: 281 notes that the reaction is like the comment of a chorus in similar accounts.

without comment probably suggests that he is so well known that no comment is needed. Unlike Mark, Luke does not mention anyone besides Peter, perhaps because Luke has yet to narrate the disciples' call.

Peter's home is in Capernaum. In John 1:44, his hometown is said to be Bethsaida, which is close to Capernaum. What we may have here is the difference between a boyhood town and a current residence, with Capernaum being Peter's current home (Godet 1875: 1.248).

Peter's mother-in-law lay ill at his house. Πενθερά (*penthera*) indicates that Peter was married, since it refers to a mother by marriage (Matt. 8:14; Ruth 1:14; 2:11; Plummer 1896: 136). First Corinthians 9:5 also indicates that Peter was married. In fact, tradition says that Peter's wife was actively involved in women's ministry and that Peter had children (Eusebius, *Ecclesiastical History* 3.30.1).

The mother-in-law lay ill with a high fever. Συνεχομένη (*synechomenē*) refers to affliction with disease (Marshall 1978: 194; Köster, *TDNT* 7:877–85), and most see in this word an ancient medical term for a high-grade fever (πυρετῷ μεγάλῳ, *pyretō megalō*) that might have included dysentery.[23] Some reject a medical classification here, because Galen is said to reject the distinction between high- and low-grade fever, but his rejection of the distinction does not mean it did not exist.[24] Regardless, her serious condition led some unspecified people to ask Jesus about her, and they knew he could do something about it.[25]

Schramm (1971: 88) notes that two terms are Lucan: συνέχω (*synechō*, to afflict), which occurs nine times in Luke–Acts and once in Matthew, and ἐρωτάω (*erōtaō*, to ask), which occurs twenty-two times in Luke–Acts, four times in Matthew, and three times in Mark. Luke has put the incident in his own words.

4:39 Jesus shows his control and power when he stands over Peter's mother-in-law and rebukes the fever. Ἐπετίμησεν (*epetimēsen*, he rebuked) repeats the verb of 4:35 and leads many to suggest that Luke has an exorcism here (Ernst 1977: 181). Theissen (1983: 185) notes

23. On πυρετός, see BAGD 730–31; BAA 1462; Van Der Loos 1965: 553; K. Weiss, *TDNT* 6:956–59; Galen, *De Differentiis Febrium* 1.1; SB 1:479; Hobart 1882: 3–5.

24. Rejecting a medical term are Fitzmyer 1981: 550 and Cadbury 1926: 194–95, 203; but see also Hengel and Hengel 1959: 340–41. Cadbury shows that the terminology itself is not limited to physicians, but is quoted by laypeople, e.g., Aulus Cornelius Celsus and Alexander of Aphrodisias, the second of whom cites Galen almost verbatim (the source of both citations appears to be Archigenes). Thus, this language had come into popular use.

25. On how the ancients attempted to treat fever, see Van Der Loos 1965: 553–54 and n. 3.

that the language is close to exorcism, but lacks a major motif for that classification (i.e., the description of the demon's departure). Luke 8:24 uses the verb for a nature miracle, so that a demonic connection is not necessary. Rather the fever is personified, suggesting a connection between sin and disease (Deut. 28:22; T. Sol. 18.20, 23).[26] In short, if this is an exorcism, Luke has not pointed it out by the form.

The healing here is instantaneous, as the woman rises up and immediately ministers to those in the house. Her service to others indicates the totality of the instant recovery, while also showing a grateful response to the healing (Plummer 1896: 137; Schneider 1977a: 116; Fitzmyer 1981: 550). The use of παραχρῆμα (parachrēma, immediately) is Lucan, as is the use of the verb ἐφίστημι (ephistēmi, to stand at).[27] In one day, Jesus has shown his authority over the demon-possessed and over illness. These are special days.

d. Jesus' Healings; Demonic Confessions (4:40–41)

Jesus continued his healing activity after the sun had gone down and the Sabbath had passed.[28] Luke moves from describing a public healing of a demon-possessed man (4:34–37), to a semiprivate healing of a woman with a severe illness (4:38–39), to a public healing of people with a variety of diseases (4:40–41). The scope of what Jesus does gets broader and broader. Luke will also distinguish between the sick in 4:40 and the possessed in 4:41.[29]

4:40

The account is similar to Mark 1:32–34, though Luke's description of the event's timing is simpler than Mark's by taking only one of Mark's two temporal phrases (the sunset). Interestingly enough, Matthew 8:16 has Mark's other phrase, a reference to its becoming night, a point that adherents of Marcan priority say shows that Mark is the first Gospel.[30] Five elements distinguish Luke's presentation:

26. Danker 1988: 112 (who calls it a demonic effect); Marshall 1978: 195; Creed 1930: 71; Nolland 1989: 211–12 (who speaks of the presence of "demonic force" as opposed to possession). On the idea of rebuke, see Luke 9:21, 42, 55 (other Lucan uses of ἐπιτιμάω are 4:41; 17:3; 18:15, 39; 19:39; 23:40).

27. Παραχρῆμα occurs sixteen times in Luke–Acts and elsewhere in the NT only twice at Matt. 21:19–20; Plummer 1896: 157; Creed 1930: 71. Ἐφίστημι appears eighteen times in Luke–Acts and not at all in Mark or Matthew; Schramm 1971: 88.

28. Luke never uses ὄψιος, which is found in Mark's account five times and in Matthew's seven times, including the parallels in Mark 1:32 and Matt. 8:16; Schramm 1971: 88.

29. On νόσος, see Oepke, TDNT 4:1091; Matt. 4:23–24; 8:17; 9:35; 10:1; Mark 1:34; Luke 6:18; 7:21; 9:1.

30. Plummer 1896: 138; Schneider 1977a: 116; Fitzmyer 1981: 553. Against this argument is Farmer 1964: 128–30, who sees Mark combining both Matthew and Luke; but see Fitzmyer 1972.

(1) shortening the temporal reference, (2) separating the sick from the possessed, (3) omitting the setting at the city gate, (4) mentioning of the laying on of hands, and (5) specifying the confession of the possessed (Fitzmyer 1981: 552).

Jesus attends to each of the sick individually, an act that shows his concern and compassion. He also lays hands on them (so also Luke 13:13; Mark 5:23; 6:5; 7:32; 8:23, 25; 16:18).[31] The significance of this act is variously understood. Some see a magical quality in the laying on of hands, but this ignores Jesus' healing by various means; for example, he did not always touch the person (Plummer 1896: 138; Luke 7:1–10). More likely it represents the touch of personal care (Godet 1875: 1.250), or is a sign of blessing (Ernst 1977: 182; Plummer 1896: 138; Gen. 48:14; Lev. 9:22–23; Luke 13:13), or pictures the connection between Jesus and the one healed so that the sick one is "recreated" (Van Der Loos 1983: 321). The use of hands for healing is rare in Judaism, but does exist (Marshall 1978: 196; Fitzmyer 1981: 553; 1QapGen 20.28–29; Lohse, *TDNT* 9:428; Flusser 1957).

Jesus' care here has a personal touch to it. Luke often mentions this "to each one" character of Jesus' ministry.[32] The summary's presence indicates that the healings specifically referred to in the Gospel are but a sample of Jesus' work. The response to Jesus shows his initial popularity.

4:41   Jesus deals not only with the possessed, but also with the sick. He exorcises these hostile spirits and can do so on a regular basis. Such battles are common for Jesus (Luke 8:2; Mark 1:34; 3:10–11; Matt. 12:22; 17:18; Beyer, *TDNT* 3:130). As they depart, the demons confess Jesus to be the Son of God. The world of spirits knows who Jesus is. This perception stands in contrast with the man's struggle to determine who he is (Liefeld 1984: 874). The spirits' confession shows that they recognize the presence of the program Jesus outlined in Luke 4:18–19. Once again, Jesus rebukes the spirits as he exorcises them (4:35, 39). That the rebuke is heeded shows his authority.

With the rebuke comes a call to be silent. The most likely reasons why the silence might have been commanded are that the demons represented an "undesirable" endorsement (Danker 1988: 113) and that the popular reaction to a Messiah might have included political

31. Maurer, *TDNT* 8:161; Schrage, *TDNT* 8:288 n. 129; Lohse, *TDNT* 9:431–32 §C4. In the Marcan examples, this is often requested of Jesus; Nolland 1989: 213.

32. On ἕκαστος, see BAGD 236; BAA 476. Εἷς (μία/ἕν) ἕκαστος is used in Luke–Acts eight times (of which six are in Acts); Matthew once; and Mark not at all; Schramm 1971: 88.

expectations that Jesus wished to avoid.[33] The description here is paralleled in another summary, Mark 3:10–11.

The key to this passage is the christological confession of 4:41. What does Luke intend by his use of the terms ὁ υἱὸς τοῦ θεοῦ (*ho huios tou theou*, Son of God) and τὸν χριστόν (*ton christon*, Christ)? Many see a confession of Jesus' divinity in the first title, citing 1:31–35, while the second title refers to his regal office (Godet 1875: 1.251; Marshall 1978: 197; Schürmann 1969: 253–54). Others see the terms as synonymous here (Schneider 1977a: 117 [who calls the two almost identical in force]; Klostermann 1929: 67; Fitzmyer 1981: 554). The key is given at the end of the verse, where the reason for the silence is indicated by the second use of ὅτι (*hoti*, because). The silencing is because the demons knew him to be τὸν χριστόν. This additional explanation appears only in Luke, and it argues against seeing the terms ὁ υἱὸς τοῦ θεοῦ and τὸν χριστόν differently here. It is Jesus' anointed position as the Christ that Luke stresses, though the christological presentation later in Luke–Acts indicates that Luke sees even more in Jesus. If the titles had been reversed then a more comprehensive christological confession could be defended. Luke's christological presentation is well thought out and is designed to let the reader see who Jesus is one step at a time (Bock 1987: 63, 66, 262–70). Again, the issue in the exorcisms is the authority of Jesus, which points to the presence of a special time.

e. Jesus' Mission to Preach the Kingdom (4:42–44)

The citizens of Capernaum attempt to keep Jesus in their city, but fail. Luke 4:42–43 is paralleled in Mark 1:35–38. Luke has five differences in the paragraph, but the changes do not alter the passage's basic meaning (Fitzmyer 1981: 556). Jesus begins the new day by venturing out to a secluded locale,[34] which he often did (Matt. 14:13; Mark 1:35, 45; 6:31; Luke 5:16; John 11:54; Kittel, *TDNT* 2:658). Mark tells us that he goes specifically to pray. That Luke lacks this point is interesting in light of his emphasis on prayer (3:21; 5:16; 6:12; 9:18, 28). The normal explanation for this omission is that Luke wanted to focus only on the issue of mission here and so will refer to prayer in 5:16 (Creed 1930: 72; Luce 1933: 125). This explanation seems lame. Luke uses references to prayer close

4:42

---

33. Marshall 1978: 197; Ernst 1977: 182; Hendriksen 1978: 269–70. See the exegesis of 4:35a for fuller discussion. Other demonic confessions are Mark 1:24; 3:11; 5:7; Luke 4:34; 8:28; Acts 16:17; 19:15; Matt. 8:29; Friedrich, *TDNT* 3:708; Grundmann, *TDNT* 3:900 §B1.

34. Luke has only one of Mark's two temporal descriptions here and has different wording by referring to the coming of day. Mark speaks of "in the morning, before the day," that is, daylight.

together (9:18, 28), while the mention of it here would fit his tendency to speak of it at key transition points. It seems better to see an additional source here distinct from Mark. Marshall (1978: 197) and Lohmeyer (1959: 42) allude to such a traditional source.[35] It might even be possible that Luke did not use Mark here at all for this summary.

The crowd seeks out Jesus. Mark refers specifically to Simon and company, but goes on to mention in Mark 1:37 that they represent others. Luke's version is compressed (Hendriksen 1978: 272). But only Luke points out that they wish for him to stay. This desire stands in contrast to the Nazareans' reaction to Jesus in Luke 4:28–29. Jesus will reply that his mission requires that he move on.

4:43   Jesus refuses to stay in Capernaum, because staying in one place would be counter to his mission. It is interesting that two of the terms appearing here also were found in the description of Jesus' mission in 4:18: εὐαγγελίσασθαι (euangelisasthai, to preach the good news) and ἀπεστάλην (apestalēn, I was sent). Jesus has a commission, which he must heed. It involves the message of the kingdom's nearness (Danker 1988: 114; Schürmann 1969: 255). There is a necessity to his work, as the use of δεῖ (dei, it is necessary) indicates.[36] The message is the powerful means that Jesus uses to announce salvation's approach.

Jesus' message concerns God's kingdom (ἡ βασιλεία τοῦ θεοῦ, hē basileia tou theou), a phrase that appears thirty-one times in Luke and six times in Acts. In addition, the single term βασιλεία appears with reference to the kingdom of God six more times in the Gospel (Fitzmyer 1981: 557; on the Jewish concept, see C. F. Evans 1990: 284–85). The kingdom's meaning in Luke is complex. It has both a present and a future element in it and at any point either emphasis or both ideas together can appear, depending on the context (Marshall 1970: 128–36; Ellis 1972). The kingdom is the topic not only of Jesus' preaching but also of his disciples. The messages of the apostles, including Paul, include the message of the kingdom (Luke 8:1, 10; 9:2; 10:9; Acts 8:12; 28:23, 31; K. Schmidt, *TDNT* 1:583; Friedrich, *TDNT* 2:718). The carryover of this term into Acts shows a key point of continuity between Jesus' message and the apostolic preaching. Some passages emphasize the kingdom's nearness or its having come (Luke 10:9, 11; 11:20; 12:32; 16:16; 17:20–21; 23:42–43), while other texts clearly look to the total manifestation of that

35. Matthew has no parallel to this summary; Aland 1985: §39. Matthean priorists who see Mark as the last Gospel argue that Mark followed Luke.
36. See the exegesis of 2:49 for a discussion of δεῖ, which is also found in 9:22; 13:33; 17:25; 19:5; 22:37; 24:7, 26, 44.

rule in the millennium and thereafter (21:31; 13:29).[37] This "already–not yet" quality to the kingdom is like many other areas in NT theology,[38] and one should not seek to remove either side of the tension. In the "already" period come the demonstration of Jesus' authority over evil, his ability to deal with sin, and his reign at the right hand of God (Luke 10:9; 11:20; Acts 2:30–36). In the "not yet" period will come the total demonstration of that authority on earth and the fulfillment of all the promises made to Israel, as Acts 1:10–11 and 3:19–25 suggest. In terms of contemporary theological systems, amillennialism tends to minimize the "not yet" period, while older dispensationalism has tended to understate the "already."[39] It is the message of this total program that Jesus brings.

So Jesus takes his message into the synagogues of other cities and **4:44** preaches there. Conzelmann (1960: 38–41) argues for Lucan imprecision here, since Luke clearly sees Jesus in Galilee. But it is better here to see a broad meaning for Ἰουδαία (Judea), which refers to the entire land of the Jews, as occurs in Luke 1:5; 6:17; 7:17; 23:5; Acts 10:37 (Creed 1930: 73; Klostermann 1929: 68; Ernst 1977: 183–84; Fitzmyer 1981: 558). So Jesus preaches his message in Galilee and Judea. But Luke will also use Ἰουδαία more narrowly (Luke 1:39, 65; 2:4; 3:1; 5:17; 21:21). Jesus ministers to all the Jews. Luke's summary is broader geographically than Mark's or Matthew's. Luke highlights the scope of Jesus' ministry.

---

37. Though *millennium* is not a Lucan term, it is used to describe the earthly character of this future rule; Bock 1992a. The kingdom of God in Luke refers to a total program—promised in the OT and detailed in the NT—that is inaugurated and then realized in stages. There are not two different kingdoms offered during Jesus' ministry: one before rejection like the OT earthly kingdom and another more spiritually focused kingdom offered after Israel's rejection. Jesus always offered the *same* kingdom. It was always coming in two stages, since Jesus' suffering and rejection by his own were in the OT design (Isa. 52:13–53:12). This view is contra Saucy 1994 and his explanation of Matthew. To make his distinction work, Saucy underplays the kingdom of heaven/God language and its implication in Matt. 18:1, 3–4, 23; 19:12, 14, 23–24; 21:31, 43; 23:13; esp. the parable introduced in 20:1—texts that come after Israel's rejection. The kingdom to come is the full kingdom, with Israel possessing a central role. But the present kingdom is grounded in the messianic hope presented in Ps. 110:1 and 132:11, 17 (Acts 2:14–41; Eph. 1:19–23; 4:7–10). The arrival of the Spirit is the sign of the arrival of the Christ and his kingdom with blessing (Luke 3:15–18; 24:49; Acts 2:30–36). One should be careful about stating Matthew's theology without reflecting on how the Book of Acts contributes canonically to the biblical teaching about the church and the kingdom. The change in emphasis within Matthew's kingdom portrait does show the changing role for Israel in that program during the church era.

38. One simple example is the picture of glorification as "already" in Rom. 8:30 and "not yet" in almost all other NT uses.

39. On this theme of Luke, see Bock 1992a and Feinberg 1988. See the exegesis of 10:9, 18; 11:17–20; 17:20–21.

Summary   Luke 4:31–44 shows that Jesus' ministry is a mixture of authoritative teaching and healing. Jesus' first miracle is an exorcism. The conflict that it depicts is fundamental to the Lucan picture of Jesus. The Anointed One has great authority and power. His power extends into the hidden world and rules cosmic forces. Such power can free a person from the evil forces that affect life. It is teaching in action, an illustration of his power. Jesus is no mere moralist. Neither is he merely a great motivator and psychologist. He is one with authority to defeat the evil forces that can dominate humanity. The reader is put in the place of those in the synagogue who ask about Jesus' power and authority. The story makes clear where ultimate power resides. It is not in the spirits of evil that oppress humans. Jesus can deal with the evil one and restore people.

   In addition, Jesus' authority is presented in an ever-widening scope. He heals the relative of a friend, Peter; he ministers to multitudes, heals the sick, and exorcises the demon-possessed. So impressed are those around him that they ask him to stay. But Jesus' mission calls him to all of his people, so he must journey through Israel with the message of God's approaching rule. Jesus' call requires that he press on. As he goes he will continue to demonstrate the authority that allows him to lay claim to people's devotion and commitment. Any reader who does not know Jesus is challenged to see that Jesus came to minister and present God's kingdom. One need only respond to him. Those who know him stand reassured that he delivers what he offers.

Additional Notes

4:31. Variant spellings of the ancient city's name lead to a minor text-critical problem. The spelling Καπερναούμ is found in A, C, L, Θ, Ψ, family 1, family 13, and Byz. Greater distribution between families exists for the spelling Καφαρναούμ, which is found in ℵ, B, D, and W. In either case, the village is clearly Capernaum.

4:33. Fitzmyer (1981: 542–43) classifies miracles in various forms: exorcism, healing, resuscitation, and nature. Theissen (1983: 81–118) divides miracles into six categories: exorcism, healing, epiphany, rescue, gift, and rule. The differences are easy to explain. Theissen further classifies some of the nature miracles in terms of their express purpose, that is, to rescue or to give provision. Rule miracles involve healings whose goal is not just to heal, but to show authority (e.g., the healing of the paralytic; see the exegesis of 5:24). The epiphanies, on the other hand, are postresurrection phenomena and do not involve the presence of an outside figure who needs healing. The difference between exorcisms and healings is determined by the express mention of evil forces in the case of possession, a biblical distinction that is interesting in light of modern attempts to reduce all the miracles to physical or psychological explanation.[40] Healings have no mention of hostile forces. What is present in this account is an exorcism, since a being possesses this man. The next account, in contrast, is a healing (4:38–39).

4:33. What is demon possession of a person? It is clear that something other than just sickness is in view, since a distinction between illness and possession exists (Matt. 4:24; Luke 4:40–41; 7:21; 9:1; 13:32). On the other hand, some overlapping also exists, for a possessed person can exhibit physical consequences (11:14; 13:11, 16; 9:39; 8:29). Hendriksen (1978: 264) resists any attempts to tie these possessions to illness or insanity, probably out of fear that the supernatural character of the description is then removed. The dispute is a worldview issue. Those who reject the spirit world seek natural or literary explanations for these exorcisms and regard naturalistic classification as exhausting the issue. Others recognize that possession may manifest itself in various ways, which may look on the surface like simple illness or psychosis. Yet though noting the presence of physical symptoms, they realize that more is here than mental or physical illness. This latter approach is taken by Van Der Loos, who (1983: 371–78) sees the manifestation of possession as akin to multiple personality. Hendriksen (1973: 437) rejects such a description, arguing that in exorcisms the spirit is portrayed as physically departing (as into the swine) and that the healing is instantaneous and not prolonged, as in psychotherapy. Hendriksen speaks instead of distinct "personality possession." But neither of Hendriksen's objections is decisive in proving that it is wrong to describe a possessed person's appearance and behavior in physical or psychological terms. As long as the description is not reduced to purely natural terms, illness may describe how the possessed one manifests his or her condition.

The work of Van Der Loos has the merit of comparing accounts of how people in the Third World describe such phenomena. What demon possession looks like to the outside observer may be little different from other purely medical or psychological conditions, but it is clear in Luke's view that sometimes there is a spiritual presence behind the scenes that is the real cause of the problem.

4:34. Luke uses Ναζαρηνός in Luke 4:34; 24:19; and Ναζωραῖος in Luke 18:37; Acts 2:22; 3:6; 4:10; 6:14; 22:8; 24:5; 26:9. Interestingly, the uses in Acts tend to come in speech material, which may suggest that Luke's us-

---

40. Van Der Loos 1965: 78–79, 110–13 notes that not all disease is possession nor is all possession disease. On the distinction between miracles and magic, see Witherington 1990: 156–60; on Luke's antimagic polemic, see Garrett 1989, who defers from answering any historical questions, staying at the literary level.

age is also traditional. Mark prefers Ναζαρηνός (Mark 1:24; 10:47; 14:67; 16:6), while not using Ναζωραῖος at all—which suggests that Luke follows Mark here.

4:35b–37. The wording of Luke 4:35b–37, though very close to Mark 1:25–28, is distinct from it. In fact, the two accounts almost paraphrase each other while dealing with similar matters in similar sequence. Bothered by the claim that Mark was used by Luke, Godet (1875: 1.247) asks why Matthew would omit this account, which would seem to suggest that Luke used an independent source, a question that on the surface looks quite valid. Most reply that Matt. 8:28–34 with its healing of a demoniac is sufficient in Matthew's mind to show how Jesus dealt with the possessed.[41] But the omission is a little out of character for Matthew. Those who prefer Matthean priority and place Mark last must attribute the account of this miracle to a Lucan special source, which Mark has taken over and altered in wording. If Mark is the second Gospel in order, then Mark still had access to a source which Luke drew from through Mark.

The issue of whether Luke used an independent source can be discussed with more confidence. Schramm (1971: 87) and Plummer (1896: 135–36) together list six elements in these verses that are characteristic of Luke:

1. The combination ἐγένετο and ἐπί occurs five times in Luke's Gospel (1:65; 3:2; 4:25, 36; 23:44), once in Mark (15:33), and once in Matthew (27:45). Since the two non-Lucan examples are parallel to Luke 23:44, the expression's use in those Gospels is probably a reflection of tradition.
2. Θάμβος is unique to Luke (Luke 4:36; 5:9; Acts 3:10).
3. Πρὸς ἀλλήλους occurs twelve times in Luke–Acts, four times in Mark, and not at all in Matthew.
4. Συλλαλέω occurs in Matt. 17:3; Mark 9:4; Luke 4:36; 9:30; 22:4; and Acts 25:21. However, the sample for this point is small.
5. Of the thirteen uses of ὥστε in Mark, none are repeated in Luke, though Luke does use the term four times himself (Luke 4:29; 5:7; 12:1; 20:20).
6. Ἦχος is used by Luke alone among the Gospel writers (Luke 4:37; 21:25; Acts 2:2; Heb. 12:19).

These arguments are of varying weight, but suggest that Luke has done some stylistic work on his sources and that he is probably responsible for the wording of Luke 4:36–37. Both Mark and Luke make the same point about Jesus' authority, despite these differences of style and wording.

---

41. Gundry 1982: 138 notes that Matthew will mention exorcisms later. Carson 1984: 204 argues that Matthew omits the account to condense the presentation of Jesus' authority. The omission is still odd, because the passage fits Matthew's theme.

4:44. Most manuscripts (Byz, D, Ψ, A, Δ, Θ, family 13) read Γαλιλαίας (Galilee) instead of Ἰουδαίας (Judea) (D, Ψ, and family 13 also read the accusative τὰς συναγωγάς, not the dative ταῖς συναγωγαῖς). Godet (1875: 1.252–53) favors this reading. Nevertheless, most scholars see Ἰουδαίας as the original text here, because it is hard to explain how it came into the text tradition as a variant. Thus, it is the harder reading and more likely to be original, as UBS–NA indicates. Manuscripts supporting this reading are $\mathfrak{P}^{75}$, ℵ, B, and Lect. Γαλιλαίας as a variant can be explained as assimilation to Mark 1:39 and Matt. 4:23.

B. Gathering of Disciples (5:1–6:16)

Luke introduces a new key element in Jesus' ministry: the gathering of disciples. In fact, much of 4:31–6:16 reflects this focus. Luke 4:31–44 relates one day's ministry in Capernaum and explains why people became interested in Jesus. But where should Jesus' mission and an interest in him lead? What type of people come to him? Luke 5:1–11 gives Jesus' answer in the picture of the miraculous catch of fish. Here is the first discipleship passage, which also is a call to mission. Those who respond to Jesus are to follow him in calling people to God. They are to be "fishers of people," even though they, as fishers, are sinners. Luke 5:12–26 contains two more miracles of authority, further confirming the scope of the leader's power. Luke 5:27–32 describes the call of Levi, the hated tax collector, who joins the cause. Luke 5:33–6:11 presents three controversies surrounding Jesus. They show that his way is a new way, which cannot be mixed with the current form of Judaism. The new way rests on the Son of Man's authority and ministers to the needs of all with compassion. Luke 6:12–16 narrates the call of the Twelve, as Jesus singles out a group of disciples for a special role. Theobald (1984) argues for a sevenfold structure in this unit: Luke 5:1–11, 5:27–39, and 6:12–16 are call scenes; 5:12–16 and 5:17–26 are healings; 6:1–5 and 6:6–11 are Sabbath episodes. The contrast is between gathering disciples and the rise of opposition.

With the disciples in place and apostles chosen, 6:17–49 presents Jesus' teaching to those disciples in the Sermon on the Plain. The disciple is to trust God and love people. Jesus' earthly ministry has three elements: teaching, miraculous work, and gathering of disciples. In addition, there is hostile reaction to Jesus, because he does not follow all of the Jewish customs. Jesus brings a new way and is forming a new community, but he also brings God's promise and rule. Those whom Jesus calls come from various backgrounds: fishers, tax collectors, lepers, paralytics, and other people in need (like the man with a withered hand). His ministry is open to all, and the disciples who follow him are to gather even more people, like themselves, to him. The means that God uses to "catch" others include the disciples' faithful walk with God, their message, and their ministry of love and compassion to all.

Though these disciples come from various backgrounds, they all have one thing in common: They do not come because they deserve God's gift; they come because they know that they need his grace.

Peter, at first, thinks that his sin means that he can have nothing to do with Jesus. But Jesus, by his actions and teaching, shows that the realization that one is a sinner is fundamental to spiritual growth. In fact, this sinful condition is the very reason one should experience God's grace and encourage others to enter into it. Disciples are sinners who consciously enter into the Physician's transforming care (5:30–32). They are fish rescued by the saving net of God's grace. Peter is a sinner, but the Son of Man has authority on earth to forgive sin (5:24) and, as the Great Physician, to bring healing to the wounds caused by it (5:31–32). Jesus gathers disciples not because he needs them, but because they need him.

1. Miraculous Catch and Peter (5:1–11)

In Luke 5:1–11, the focus is on Jesus' knowledge, the human condition, and the opportunity to share in God's task. Jesus can be trusted. In fact, he knows people better than they know themselves. This is pictured in Jesus' knowing how to fish better than the fishermen do. What they could not do the night before, even though fishing was their profession, Jesus enables them to do with amazing results. More importantly, despite the presence of sinfulness in the fishermen, Jesus still asks sinful people like Peter to join him in fishing for people. To be a "fisher of people" is to be a "fish" who is able to relate what it means to be pulled out of dangerous waters by God's grace.

In the event itself, several points are worth noting (Liefeld 1984: 876). (1) The focus in this account is largely on Peter. He is isolated as the first disciple chosen by Jesus. In fact, this account may well explain the prominence that Peter will come to have. Jesus called Peter early in his ministry. (2) The miracle highlights Jesus' knowledge and holiness. Peter knows that he stands as a sinner before Jesus. Peter knows that such a catch is possible only because Jesus has access to divine power. (3) When the account ends, a change of vocation is suggested. The called follow Jesus and leave their nets. The response to Jesus' ministry is not all negative, despite the setback of the Nazareth incident (4:16–30). Many are responding to Jesus and some are responding completely. Jesus ministers to sinners and calls them to let him transform them. They have new lives and vocations as a result of knowing him.

Sources and Historicity

The nature of the event and its relationship to other events in the Gospels (in particular, Mark 1:16–20 and John 21:1–14) are much discussed. Some see this account as a postresurrection event projected back into the life of Jesus;[1] conversely, others see it as an event from Jesus' life that John projected forward into the postresurrection period (Schweizer 1984: 103).

---

1. Fitzmyer 1981: 561–62, who regards Peter's cry to the Lord and acknowledgment of sin in Luke 5:8 as problematic in a preresurrection setting. He regards it as a postresurrection event that was already a simple miracle story when Luke received it (in L).

R. Brown (1970: 1090) notes ten points of connection between John 21 and Luke 5:[2]

1. The disciples have fished all night and have caught nothing.
2. Jesus tells them to cast their nets (in John: from the beach; in Luke: from the boat).
3. Directions are followed, and a large catch results.
4. The catch affects the nets (but differently in each Gospel).
5. Peter reacts to the catch (though the beloved disciple also speaks in John).
6. Jesus is called Lord (but the sense of this title in the two Gospels differs).
7. The other fishermen say nothing (only if one excludes the beloved disciple's comments in John).
8. The theme of following Jesus ends each account (Brown appeals to John 21:19, 22, which, however, belongs to a subsequent event).
9. The catch symbolizes a successful missionary endeavor.
10. Some vocabulary overlaps, especially the name Simon Peter, which appears only here in Luke.
11. To Brown's list, Fitzmyer (1981: 561) adds the absence of any mention of Andrew in either account (cf. Mark 1:16).

Though the miracles in Luke 5 and John 21 are similar, they are distinct and should not be identified (Van Der Loos 1965: 670). The main reason for the separation is not only the clearly distinguished settings, but also the differences in the description of the nets, Peter's reaction, and Jesus' location during the event. In Luke 5:6 the nets are breaking; in John 21:11 they are not. In Luke 5:8 Peter bows before Jesus; in John 21:7 he flees. In Luke 5:3 Jesus is in the boat; in John 21:4 he is on the beach. Surely if the same event were in view, these differences would not be present.

The relationship to Mark 1 is much more difficult, and its resolution is less than certain. Many see Luke developing Mark 1:16–20 by filling in details that Mark chose not to discuss.[3] This approach is possible because the call to become fishers of people is shared in both texts and the same group of people are present in the accounts, with the exception of Andrew. In addition, the setting at the Sea of Gennesaret (Galilee) is the same.

2. Plummer 1896: 147 lists seven points of dissimilarity between these accounts. My parenthetical comments in Brown's list above show some of the questions raised about this connection. Note also the similarities listed by Bovon 1989: 228–29: Jesus face to face with Peter, Peter's prominence, Jesus' instruction, the new attempt to catch fish, the obedience of the fishermen, the miraculous catch, the reaction of Peter, and the promise. He sees an original promise to Peter, which the church expanded in two directions: Luke in terms of discipleship and John in terms of call.

3. Godet 1875: 1.255 (who is not shy about seeing distinct events elsewhere); Liefeld 1984: 876. As already noted, Fitzmyer and Schweizer tie the account to John 21.

Nevertheless, seeing two events is also possible (Carson 1984: 119; Alford 1874: 484–85; Geldenhuys 1951: 180–81; Marshall 1978: 201 [apparently]). (1) In Mark 1:19 the fishermen are mending nets, not washing them as in Luke. This difference is not great, as both might occur at the same time, but the difference in detail is noteworthy. (2) In addition, a distinct set of nets may be in view in each account (Marshall 1978: 202; see the exegesis of 5:5). (3) The absence of Andrew is peculiar, if Mark's account is being developed by Luke, since the structure of two pairs of fishermen from Mark is ignored here. Good arguments can be assembled either way. It is quite possible to explain the differences simply as Mark's telescoping his account, especially since the mended nets belong not to Peter, but to James and John (Luke 5:2 with 5:7; Matt. 4:21; Mark 1:19).[4] Nevertheless, it can also be argued that Luke is narrating a distinct account here, one that gives rationale for why these disciples were so quick to leave all for Jesus. The difficulty is that Luke could simply be filling in details for an event that Mark told in summary form. If one event is present, then Luke has probably delayed his account, so he could first give a summary of Jesus' preaching and active ministry. The delay allows him to develop the theme of gathering disciples in one section. On the other hand, seeing two events here may explain Jesus' previous contact with Peter in Luke 4:38–39 in that they also had contact in the Mark 1 account, which Luke has omitted. Two events may suggest that Jesus' teaching and activity, as noted in Luke 5:1–11, helped to solidify the association between Jesus and these men. It is a difficult choice. Matthew 4:18–22 parallels Mark in terms of its placement and description of a nonmiraculous call. It may be that two events are in view here, with Luke narrating the final event of the pair.

In fact, Fitzmyer (1981: 560) notes three differences between Mark and Luke that seem to suggest distinct events. (1) Jesus teaches in Luke 5:1–3 and is not merely passing by as in Mark 1:16 and Matt. 4:18. (2) In Luke, the call is made after the miracle (Luke 5:4–9); in Mark 1:16–17, 19–20 and Matt. 4:18–19, 21–22, the nets are merely being cast and washed. In other words, in Luke's Gospel Jesus causes the men to fish, while the other Synoptics have them fishing already. To Fitzmyer's observation on this point, I add one more detail. In the one-event view, it is strange that the "developed" Lucan account has only one call, while the "simpler" Matthew and Mark have two. (3) The call in Luke 5:10 is made exclusively to Simon but all follow, whereas in Mark and Matthew, all are called. In Mark 1:17 and Matt. 4:19, the call to be fishers of people is made to both Simon and Andrew. Though Fitzmyer explains the differences in his own way (see below), they seem significant enough to suggest distinct events.

4. Such would be the view of anyone who thinks that Mark is later than Luke. They would also mention Matt. 4:18–22 in this discussion. See Aland 1985: §41.

Obviously, the source issue relates to the discussion of parallel texts (Luce 1933: 127; Marshall 1978: 199–200; Fitzmyer 1981: 559–62). Four approaches exist: (1) Luke represents a mixing of John and Mark (Creed 1930: 74); (2) the account is strictly Lucan and allegorical;[5] (3) Luke uses an independent source; or (4) Luke uses mostly an independent source but with touches of Mark.[6] The position one takes here is determined by how one sees the relationship between the events, though positions 3 and 4 are each possible. If one sees an independent event, then an independent source becomes likely (view 3). The differences in the accounts lean in this direction.[7] Of course, Matthean prioritists will see Luke as either independent or as drawing on Matt. 4:18–22.

One's view of the event's historicity is tied to one's view about miracles. The Jesus Seminar (Funk and Hoover 1993: 281–82) rejects the sayings in the scene by arguing that the account is a rewrite of Mark (5:4, 10 is printed in black type). Though they acknowledge that Jesus may have used the metaphor of fishing to catch people, they argue that such a saying would not have circulated in the oral tradition. But this is a mere assertion. Did not the oral tradition tell miracle stories? Could not such a saying be included in this type of account? Most scholars see a developed tradition-history here. Even Crossan (1991: 410) argues that the miracle was deleted from the tradition at a later stage, with Mark at the end of a John–Luke–Mark sequence! Against Crossan, my earlier analysis questions linking this event to John or seeing a strong link to Mark. Something other than fabrication must explain this account's miraculous thrust, unless one's worldview shuts out the option of miracle. Nolland (1989: 220) rightly argues that the saying and miracle are tightly linked and cannot be separated. I prefer to see the account this way and to acknowledge that the event has historical roots. (On the historicity of 5:8, see the additional note on that verse.)

The form of the account is discussed by Bultmann (1963: 217–18) in his section on miracle stories, where he calls it a nature miracle.[8] Theissen (1983: 321) calls it a gift miracle, because of

---

5. Creed 1930: 73 mentions J. Wellhausen as holding this view. Luce 1933: 127 also discusses this option.

6. So hold most scholars. For discussion, see Schneider 1977a: 122–23; Marshall 1978: 199; Fitzmyer 1981: 561 (who speaks of L, where the postresurrection tradition was already moved back; Luke simply used L and joined it to Marcan material); Ernst 1977: 184–85 (who goes on to say that Luke is not merely embellishing Mark); Van Der Loos 1965: 670; Schramm 1971: 37–40 (who sees mostly Marcan material); Dietrich 1972: 25–38 (who explains why Mark alone cannot be the source).

7. Tiede 1988: 116–17 cites OT parallels from Exod. 3, Judg. 6, and Isa. 6 as similar in tone, since they are also "call" texts.

8. Bultmann goes on to note that the account is really a legend because of its supernatural flavor. He regards John 21:1–14 as a later variant of this tradition. Bultmann's legend classification reflects his worldview, which shuts out the possibility of miracle.

what is provided. Fitzmyer (1981: 562) prefers the classification "pronouncement story" because of the key saying at the end. What this debate really evidences is the presence of a mixed form: miracle and pronouncement. Talbert (1982: 60–61) describes the account as a "commission narrative," which also emphasizes the importance and function of the pronouncement.[9] There is no need to insist that a form must be simple and have only one point of focus. The miracle lays the basis for the realization about who Jesus is in comparison to other people. In doing so, it lays the groundwork for the commission.[10]

The outline of Luke 5:1–11 is as follows:

a. Setting: teaching from Simon's boat (5:1–3)
b. The marvelous fisherman and his promise (5:4–11)
   i. Miracle of the catch (5:4–7)
      (1) Jesus' command (5:4)
      (2) Peter's trust (5:5)
      (3) Full catch (5:6–7)
   ii. Response to the miracle: confession and commission (5:8–11)
      (1) Peter's confession and fear (5:8–10a)
      (2) Promise of new fish (5:10b)
      (3) Departure to follow Jesus (5:11)

Numerous themes dominate the account. The knowledge of Jesus stands out as he points the way to the catch. Jesus' greatness is clearly confessed by Peter. The gathering of a special group of disciples begins. Peter is the first among many who will follow him. So, Jesus' call to mission is compared to fishing. Luke does not hide the key role of Peter in this gathering of disciples. But more significant still is Peter's transformation from sinner to "fisherman."

Though the call of these disciples is the call to a special group, many of their responses are exemplary. Peter's humble perception of himself as a sinner before the Lord is a key realization about Jesus' greatness and humanity's condition. It leads to a sense of

---

9. This classification describes its function most precisely. See also Hubbard 1977 and Tiede 1988: 117 (who prefers to call the account an "epiphany-call" story to emphasize the disclosure of divine presence).

10. Berger 1984: 272, 281, 316 speaks of Peter's realization of sin here as a religious self-witness. He sees the account as related to commission. It is one of many miracles on the sea (John 21:1–14; Mark 4:35–41 = Luke 8:22–25; Mark 6:45–52 = Matt. 14:22–23); Berger 1984: 309–10. Interestingly, all the sea miracles involve only disciples.

dependence on which discipleship is based. Peter's faith is also exemplary. The importance of mission is a key theme. The picture of Peter's transformation from sinner to "fisher" is significant. The transformation results in action when Peter leaves his nets, with others following. Jesus is the one capable of leading people; accordingly, they should respond totally to what he asks of them.

Exegesis and Exposition

[1]While the people pressed upon him to hear the word of God, he was standing by the Lake of Gennesaret. [2]And he saw two boats by the lake; but the fishermen, having gone out from them, were washing their nets. [3]And getting into one of the boats, which was Simon's, he asked him to put out a little from the land and, sitting down, he taught the crowd from the boat.

[4]And when he finished speaking, he said to Simon, "Put out to sea and let down your nets for a catch." [5]And Simon replied, "Master, we have labored through the entire night and caught nothing; but upon your word I shall let down the nets." [6]And when they did this, the nets enclosed a great many fish, and the nets began to break. [7]And they signaled to their partners in the other boat to come and help them. They came and filled both boats so that they began to sink. [8]And when Simon Peter saw it he fell at Jesus' knees, saying, "Go away, for I am a sinful man, Lord." [9]For he was astonished, and all that were with him, at the catch of fish that they had taken; [10]and so also were James and John, sons of Zebedee, who were partners with Simon. And Jesus said to Simon, "Do not be afraid; for you will be fishers of men." [11]And when they had brought their boats to land, they left everything and followed him.

a. Setting: Teaching from Simon's Boat (5:1–3)

5:1

Before telling about the miraculous catch, 5:1–3 contains a summary to indicate that Jesus was teaching the crowd. Τὸν ὄχλον (*ton ochlon*) here refers simply to the curious masses, not to the responsive (R. Meyer, *TDNT* 5:586; Luke 6:19; 7:9; 8:40; 9:18; 19:3; 23:48). Jesus obviously was becoming a popular figure, for the crowd pressed near him, straining to hear him (ἐπίκειμαι, *epikeimai*; BAGD 294 §2b; BAA 597 §2b; Luke 23:23; Acts 27:20). Eventually Jesus will withdraw to Peter's boat to avoid the crush (5:3).

What the crowd has come to hear is the word of God (τὸν λόγον τοῦ θεοῦ, *ton logon tou theou*). This is probably a genitive of source—"the word from God"—that is, a message based on revelation from the heavenly Father. The phrase is a key one for Luke in that he later applies it to apostolic and early church teaching (Luke 8:11, 21; 11:28; and fourteen times in Acts; Fitzmyer 1981: 565; note that three of the fourteen uses in Acts [13:44, 48; 16:32] are disputed on text-critical grounds). The phrase in the other Synoptics occurs clearly only once in Mark 7:13 and probably also in Matt. 15:6, so it reflects a Lucan emphasis.[11] The expression stresses not only the source but also the authority of Jesus' message. It also serves, by its usage in Acts, to suggest continuity between what the apostles offer and what Jesus has taught. Their message is nothing less than revelation.[12]

The locale of the teaching is the Lake of Gennesaret, also known as the Sea of Galilee (Matt. 4:18; Mark 1:16). It was named after a region south of Capernaum that was situated on a fertile and thickly populated plain (BAGD 156; BAA 312; Josephus, *Antiquities* 18.2.1 §28; *Jewish War* 3.10.7–8 §§506–21; 1 Macc. 11:67); the current name is el-Ghuweir. In the OT, the site was called the Kinnereth or Chinnereth (Num. 34:11; Josh. 11:2; 19:35; Leaney 1958: 123; Marshall 1978: 201). Fitzmyer (1981: 565) notes that the description of Gennesaret as a lake (λίμνην, *limnēn*) is precise.[13] The lake is about eight miles by fourteen miles in size and was a popular locale for fishing. This is the only time in Luke that Jesus teaches by a lake, but Jesus is often portrayed as teaching in natural settings (Matt. 5:1; Luke 6:17; Mark 8:1, 4; Hendriksen 1978: 281). Conzelmann (1960: 42) says that the lake represents a locale of the manifestation of power, but Jesus' miracle here is not a particularly powerful display. Rather, the miracle shows his knowledge and ability to guide.

5:2 Jesus is looking for a place to get away from the crowd and spots two boats (Schürmann 1969: 267 notes that this detail differs from John 21). However, the fishermen are away from their vessels, washing their nets. Evidently Luke is describing the nets used for evening fishing in deep water (see the exegesis of 5:5; Marshall 1978: 202). It is not clear that this verse is a Lucan modification of Mark 1:19, with its description of the fishermen repairing their nets (so argues Fitzmyer 1981: 566). As 5:4 shows, when Jesus calls them to cast their nets, the fishermen are ready to go.

5:3 The attention turns to Peter. Jesus goes out of his way to involve Peter by consciously choosing to enter his boat. Peter becomes representative of the others with Jesus in the boat. Yet Peter is clearly portrayed as the first of the inner circle of the disciples, a portrayal that

11. The Matthean text has a textual problem, but the phrase is probably present, since it has excellent distribution.

12. Danker 1988: 115 argues that the phrase equals the expression *good news of the kingdom* in 4:43. This is possible, given the Lucan form of the parable of the seed in 8:4–15. For Bovon 1989: 230–31, it is God's saving message and covenant promise that are in view.

13. Other Gospel writers call it simply a sea (θάλασσα; Matt. 4:18; 15:29; Mark 1:16; 7:31; so also the LXX: Num. 34:11; Josh 12:3; BAGD 350; BAA 711 §2). Luke's language is precise, while the other evangelists' language reflects popular usage. Luke uses θάλασσα only three times: Luke 17:2, 6; 21:25.

legitimizes his key role in the church despite his denials at Jesus' trial and his struggle to respond to Gentile table fellowship (Luke 22:54–62; Gal. 2:11–14; Danker 1988: 115; Schweizer 1984: 101; Marshall 1978: 199; Cullmann, *TDNT* 6:101–2).[14] That Peter allows Jesus to use the boat indicates his positive response, and it will be the first of many such responses from him. The boat is probably about twenty or thirty feet long, since later it will hold several men at once (Ellis 1974: 102).

Jesus sits and teaches the crowd, a posture that he often takes when he teaches (Matt. 5:1; 13:1–2; 15:29; 24:3; 26:55; Mark 4:1; 9:35; 13:3; John 6:3; 8:2; C. Schneider, *TDNT* 3:443). The specifics of his message are not related, but everywhere that Jesus goes, Luke consistently shows him teaching to any who will hear (Luke 4:31–32; 5:17; 6:6). As Plummer (1896: 143), puts it, "Christ uses Peter's boat as a pulpit, whence to throw the net of the Gospel over His hearers."

b. The Marvelous Fisherman and His Promise (5:4–11)
i. Miracle of the Catch (5:4–7)
(1) Jesus' Command (5:4)

At this point, Jesus begins to draw in his initial group of disciples. **5:4** After speaking to the multitudes, Jesus begins to form a more intimate group of associates. With the completion of his teaching, he calls on Peter to take them out to fish. The first command, ἐπανάγαγε (*epanagage*, put out), is a second-person singular directed at Peter, who is steering the vessel. But the second command, χαλάσατε (*chalasate*, let down), is plural, so that all are called to help in casting the nets (Creed 1930: 74; Danker 1988: 116).[15] The son of a carpenter is telling the fishermen where to toss their nets!

This instruction begins a miracle that Theissen (1983: 104–5) calls a gift miracle. Jesus initiates the whole affair, guides it, and in the end gives provision to those around him. In such an account, the details of how the provision occurs are not specified. The provision just comes. Theissen also calls the account allegorical, because it depicts material need transcended by Jesus and points to spiritual realities. But the term *allegory* is best avoided here (Van Der Loos 1965: 674 n. 2). It might be better to speak of the action's parabolic or illustrative quality, since not every feature in the miracle has a

---

14. Peter is always listed first: Mark 3:16; Matt. 10:2; Luke 6:14; Acts 1:13. Peter has the key role in Matt. 14:28; 17:24; 18:21; 26:40; Mark 5:37; 8:29–33; 9:2–5; 14:37; Luke 22:8.

15. Δίκτυα is also plural, indicating that there is a crew on this boat. On the use of δίκτυον, see T. Dan 2.4; T. Abr. (A) 8.10 (= J. Charlesworth 1983–85: 1.886) (BAGD 198; BAA 399). Perhaps these negative figurative uses in Judaism help set up Jesus' positive metaphors later? On fishing in Palestine, see Bishop 1951.

spiritual point to make. Nonetheless, the miracle points to Jesus' guiding power in giving people the gospel. It also pictures a call to mission (5:10b). Such a missionary thrust is the call of disciples in the Gospel and of believers in Acts (as well as being the call of the church today). Blomberg's characterization of miracles as parables is correct; they point to Jesus' spiritual work and call the reader to respond to Jesus and his mission.[16]

(2) Peter's Trust (5:5)

5:5   Peter responds with respect and openness to Jesus' request. The term of address, ἐπιστάτα (*epistata*, Master), is Lucan. It is often used in place of ῥαββί (*rhabbi*, rabbi) and is always found on the lips of disciples, except in 17:13 (8:24, 45; 9:33, 49; Danker 1988: 116; Oepke, *TDNT* 2:622–23; Lohse, *TDNT* 6:965 n. 40; Glombitza 1958). That Peter uses a title that recognizes Jesus' authority is important since Peter is clearly in charge of the boat (see Peter's reference to his issuing a command at the end of this verse).

Peter speaks from two perspectives. First, Peter the fisherman speaks as he notes the lack of success his crew had on the previous evening. The participle chosen to express their labor, κοπιάσαντες (*kopiasantes*), refers to wearisome work.[17] The plural reference almost certainly includes Andrew, and possibly James and John (5:7, 10). They had worked to the bone, but had caught nothing. Though night was the best time to fish, last night had been fruitless. So Jesus' daytime request that they cast their nets has two strikes against it. The description of the premiracle conditions is common to these accounts and serves to set up the action's greatness when the miracle brings the reversal.

Second, Peter the man of faith responds. Despite the fisherman's professional view of the situation, at Jesus' word Peter gives the command to his companions to cast the nets.[18] This part of the verse shows that Peter is in charge, since χαλάσω (*chalasō*, I will let down) is first-person singular. Peter's responsiveness to the word reflects a proper reaction to God's messenger (1:38; 6:46; 8:21; 11:28). Δίκτυα

16. Blomberg 1984b, where he also raises the additional question of a purely metaphorical, not historically intended, miracle in Matt. 17:27. Even if Blomberg is right about Matt. 17 as a saying, which is uncertain, his category of "metaphorical miracle" to describe it seems unhelpful by introducing confusion in the classification of genuinely miraculous material that also has metaphorical elements. What this miracle and the saying tied to it show is that the miracles served as "audiovisuals" of deeper realities (see also Luke 5:19–26; 8:26–39; 11:14–23).

17. BAGD 443 §2; BAA 901 §2; Luke 12:27; Acts 20:35; John 4:6; Matt. 6:28; Josh. 24:13; Plummer 1896: 143.

18. On Jesus' word as powerful, see Matt. 8:8, 16; Luke 7:7, 14; Mark 1:24–25; 2:10–12; 4:39; Kittel, *TDNT* 4:107.

(*diktya*) describes nets used for evening fishing in deep water, in contrast to the terms for nets in Mark 1:16 (ἀμφιβάλλοντας, *amphiballontas*) and Matthew 4:18 (ἀμφίβληστρον, *amphiblēstron*), which refer to nets used for shallow-water, day fishing (Van Der Loos 1965: 671 n. 1). And so, willingly, they cast their nets to see what they might find.

(3) Full Catch (5:6–7)

The good response met with such immediate success that disaster almost resulted. The nets found the fish, but they were so full that they were breaking. This situation, if allowed to continue, would have meant the loss of the catch. Διερρήσσετο (*dierrēsseto*) is best taken as ingressive in force, so Luke says the nets "began to break" (Luce 1933: 128; Plummer 1896: 144). The rope is straining and fraying to bring in the load. **5:6**

The miracle's nature is somewhat disputed. Is it a miracle of knowledge (Jesus knew the fish would be there), of will power (Jesus brought the fish there), or both? No detailed discussion occurs in the account, but usually in a nature miracle, when forces are taken over by Jesus, there is some verbal indicator in the account. That is, Jesus rebukes the wind or gives some other indication that he is acting on nature. Thus, it seems better to see it as a miracle of Jesus' knowledge (with Godet 1875: 1.257; but against Hendriksen 1978: 282, who sees both). Whatever the exact nature of the act, it makes a strong impression.

Now the action gets somewhat frantic. The fishermen signal for help.[19] The partners in view are probably James and John (5:10; Creed 1930: 75). Such team fishing in the lake is common when making big catches (Hauck, *TDNT* 3:804 n. 49). It is not clear whether the partners are in the water or on shore. Help is needed to pull in the catch, and, as is mentioned next, space is also required. The catch's size is emphasized: not only are both boats filled, but the catch's weight begins to pull both boats down. Βυθίζεσθαι (*bythizesthai*) is also ingressive, meaning that the boats "began to sink" (BDF §338.1; BDR §338.1.1; on the term, see 2 Macc. 12:4; Polybius 2.10.5). What a day at the lake! God is working through Jesus. The teacher has guided the fishermen to the catch, so he will guide them in other matters of a more spiritual nature. God in all his power is present and expressing himself through Jesus. Jesus knows their vocation better than do the fishermen. He knows their needs better, **5:7**

19. Does κατένευσαν refer to signaling with their heads or voices because their hands are busy, as Nolland 1989: 222 suggests? Cf. the use of signals in 1:62. Μέτοχος appears only here in the Gospels; Hanse, *TDNT* 2:831.

too. Even in the chaos and strain that following God often means, there will be opportunity if one depends on him.

ii. Response to the Miracle: Confession and Commission (5:8–11)
(1) Peter's Confession and Fear (5:8–10a)

5:8 All the repercussions of the miracle follow. Simon Peter's reaction to the catch is immediate. The use of the full name Σίμων Πέτρος (Simon Peter) is unique in Luke.[20] Until now, he has been Simon, so the expanded name may point to the developing importance of this figure, since traditionally Peter is the name he came to receive as a result of his encounter with Jesus (John 1:42; Matt. 16:17–18). Falling to his knees pictures the humility that one displays before a superior of any kind (Mark 5:22 = Luke 8:41; Luke 17:16; Matt. 17:6; 1 Cor. 14:25). Peter recognizes Jesus' authority in this action. In the presence of God's agent, the chaos becomes secondary to sorting out where he stands with the one who has made himself known.

Peter's confession falls into three parts. First, he asks Jesus to depart. The amazement (Luke 5:9) of God's working through Jesus produces the request. The awareness of God's presence, directly or via a surrogate, produces such a response in people; it yields a sense of unworthiness at receiving God's bounty (Luke 1:13, 30; Isa. 6:1–6; Ezek. 1:1–2:3; Nolland 1989: 222; Danker 1983: 401).

Second, the reason (ὅτι, hoti, for) Peter bows before Jesus is his realization that he is a sinful man. This is not a confession of individual transgressions; rather it is a recognition of his character before the divine and his representative. So Peter responds with respect and honesty (Luke 3:15–18). One's mortal frailties stand exposed in the face of such total knowledge. God's presence means the presence of power, knowledge, and purity (Tiede 1988: 118). Peter's reaction is a confession of unworthiness before God's chosen Holy One (4:34; Liefeld 1984: 877). Such confessions are the means to acceptance by God (7:37–50; 15:18, 21; 18:9–13; 19:1–10; Grundmann, *TDNT* 1:304; Rengstorf, *TDNT* 1:330–31). It is disputed whether part of this confession includes the first-century cultural perspective that fishermen had a less than honorable profession.[21]

---

20. For Luke's normal way of naming Peter ("Simon . . . called/named Peter"), see Luke 6:14; Acts 10:5, 18, 32; 11:13. On the text-critical problem that this unique wording produces, see Marshall 1978: 204. A few manuscripts (e.g., D, W, family 13) omit Πέτρος. The uniqueness of the phrase speaks to its originality.

21. Rengstorf, *TDNT* 1:330, says that Peter is regarded as a sinner "by the community." Van Der Loos 1965: 671 agrees with the above assessment of the fishing occupation, while Schürmann 1969: 270 n. 54 disagrees, noting that no evidence exists for this view of fishermen in the first century; so also SB 1:187. Schürmann is surely right here.

Peter correctly has a definite sense that there is a vast difference between Jesus and him.

Third, Peter addresses Jesus as Lord (κύριε, *kyrie*). The title's use reveals a confession that recognizes Jesus' authority along with God's working through him. Κύριος is a key term and stands as a stronger term in contrast to the use of ἐπιστάτα (*epistata*, master) in 5:5. In its nonvocative forms, κύριος does not appear on people's lips with reference to Jesus before the resurrection, but the vocative form is common, because it was a form of polite address equivalent to "Sir" (5:8, 12; 6:46 [twice]; 7:6; 9:54, 59, 61; 10:17, 40; 11:1; 12:41; 13:23, 25; 17:37; 18:41; 19:8; 22:33, 38, 49; Fitzmyer 1981: 568). It was used to recognize one of a higher station or authority. Here, in combination with the act of bowing, it is more than mere polite address. It is a recognition of sovereignty, but how much is intended in that recognition is not clear.

What does Peter mean by the title? Some see a full confession of deity here, but this is unlikely at this point in Peter's understanding (against this less-than-deity view is Nolland 1989: 222, who sees Peter's use of κύριε as a reference to the "supreme Lord" of 1:43; 2:11). The disciples are still discussing who Jesus is in 8:25, where they wonder what type of person Jesus is because he calmed the wind. If they had his deity already in mind, this would not be a question. The great confession of Jesus as the Christ and the pondering of the significance of his miraculous works have yet to occur. But this catch begins a series of events that start the disciples to thinking. Jesus is recognized as God's agent here, and the beginning of the disciples' growth in understanding starts with this confession. God is manifesting himself through this Galilean. In fact, one can say that as a result of actions like this tensions are introduced about who Jesus is. These tensions will be resolved as Luke proceeds. What is more interesting is how Jesus does not turn his back on the sinner, but includes the sinner in his task. What a reversal and what a token of God's grace this is.

5:9 It is the size of the catch that amazes the disciples (γάρ indicates the explanation of 5:8). Here is a carpenter-teacher delivering the goods as a professional fisherman. They all know something is going on. God's goodness is bringing them to an awareness of who they are (Acts 17:25–28; Rom. 2:4). Repentance is not mentioned in the account and should not be inserted into it to make Peter's act a full paradigm of believing confession. But there is a significant spiritual point here. Jesus will take the faith and humble attitude exhibited in Peter and turn them into a call to serve. Peter's attitude reflects an openness that allows Jesus to transform the sinner. Peter's responsiveness and humble approach to Jesus' word reflect exemplary attitudes about how people should respond to God's message. Peter reflects the essence of faith. Luke does not so much emphasize responsiveness to personal sin as stress that one should change one's mind about Jesus and thus become humbly obedient to him. Jesus can transform the sinner's life and vocation, as the disciple comes to serve God.

Grace is at work. An unworthy Peter and his companions receive and observe the benefits of a gracious God through his agent. They are overwhelmed. Thus, the awe in view here is focused first of all on the visit of the holy God—much like Elizabeth's awe in 1:43. Holiness and awesome knowledge are displayed in God's working through Jesus. Second, the awe is fueled by the recognition that this God would be so kind to them in providing the bountiful catch. Third, the catch also points to Jesus' greatness and power (Van Der Loos 1965: 671; Schürmann 1969: 270). Jesus is the agent of God's beneficence (Acts 10:38).

5:10a Attention now turns away from Peter. Peter and those with him (probably Andrew) were not the only ones amazed at these events. James and John, the sons of Zebedee, also were amazed. Κοινωνοί (*koinōnoi*) probably identifies James and John as business companions of Peter (Schürmann 1969: 270). The term differs from μετόχοις (*metochois*, companions) in 5:7, and the change may well suggest this additional idea, provided that the terms are not synonymous, which also is possible.

Jesus does not chastise the humble sinner. He calms him with the call not to fear (1:13, 30; 8:50; 12:32; Balz, *TDNT* 9:212 §D2c; Ellis 1974: 102; Fitzmyer 1981: 568). Seeing God's power is not a cause to fall back and withdraw from God, but is an opportunity to draw near to him. Thus, Jesus comforts the fishermen (Creed 1930: 75). They will share in his work and vocation. The call to share in the mission is the call to participate in the building of the current form of the kingdom.

(2) Promise of New Fish (5:10b)

5:10b Jesus again addresses Peter only, though the response of 5:11 suggests that the promise applies to more than him. Again, Peter represents the disciples. Jesus does not call Peter, as in Mark 1 and Matt. 4, and ask Peter to follow him in discipleship. Rather, Jesus promises him what his vocation will be. This difference may well confirm that this event is different from the formal call in Mark and Matthew and that the Lucan event serves, historically speaking, to confirm that call. In other words, Luke presents this event to explain the call to discipleship found in Mark 1 and Matt. 4, an event that is well known if either of the other Gospels is known to his audience (Luke

1:1). Again, the knowledge and directing work of Jesus are stressed here. The disciples are in capable hands. The Lucan ἀπὸ τοῦ νῦν (*apo tou nyn*, from now on) stresses, as Luke often does, that things change from this moment on as a result of encountering Jesus (Luke 1:48; 12:52; 22:18, 69; Acts 18:6; Marshall 1978: 205). A genuine meeting with Jesus alters one's perspective. We can see why Luke presents this account as a key description of the disciples' gathering in the Galilean ministry.

The promise specifically is that Peter will catch people (ἀνθρώ-πους ἔση ζωγρῶν, *anthrōpous esē zōgrōn*).[22] The figure is one of rescue from danger, as the OT and Jewish usage of the concepts "to let live" and "to save alive" show (Num. 31:15, 18; Deut. 20:16; Josh. 2:13; 2 Macc. 12:35; for the concept of the "fisher," see Jer. 16:16; Ezek. 29:4–5; Amos 4:2; Hab. 1:14–17; Fitzmyer 1981: 569; Schürmann 1969: 271 n. 64; Marshall 1978: 205–6; Wuellner 1967: 114). The figure focuses on the catch. Some have been bothered by the figure in that fish are caught to die, while people are rescued for God. Others are bothered that much of the OT imagery is negative (cf. the verses listed just above). However, the point is the idea of gathering and rescue. The reversal of the normal imagery is revealing as well as surprising. God is in the business of saving humanity, and some will help him in the catch. The idea of being caught alive pictures an entry into a new and vibrant life and does not describe just the moment of saving (Schneider 1977a: 126). In addition, ἔση ζωγρῶν (will be catching alive) portrays the mission as an ongoing task. The promise is one of being engaged continually in evangelism. This account concludes a series of contacts between Jesus and this small group of disciples (John 1:35–42; Mark 1:16–20; Luke 4:38–39 [Peter's family]).

(3) Departure to Follow Jesus (5:11)

So, the life of discipleship begins for all the witnesses of this event. **5:11** Upon returning to shore, they leave their ships behind. The subject here is plural, so other men leave in addition to Peter. The priority of their lives is no longer fishing, but following Jesus (14:27) and fishing for people. At the height of surely one of their greatest catches, certainly the most memorable one, they leave their profession behind. Danker (1988: 117) notes that Peter is now the amateur fisherman! The idea of following (ἀκολουθέω, *akoloutheō*) will be a standard image for discipleship, one that is grounded in tradition (Luke 5:27–28; 9:23, 49, 57, 59, 61; 18:22, 28, 43; Mark 1:18; 2:14;

---

22. On ζωγρέω, see BAGD 340; BAA 688. The term is used only twice in the NT: here and 2 Tim. 2:26.

Matt. 8:1; 9:9). In Jewish idiom, students or protégés often followed their teachers (Kittel, *TDNT* 1:213). The nature of the commitment is stressed in the idea of "leaving all" (ἀφέντες πάντα, *aphentes panta*). Now the center of their lives is Jesus.

Summary For Luke, the gathering of disciples begins with the fishing bonanza of Luke 5:1–11. These disciples will become the great witnesses of the Book of Acts. They will declare with great boldness the way to Christ. Fishing for people will become a dangerous calling. The miracle of the catch depicts Jesus' knowledge and authority as the agent of God, who guides the disciples into the great haul. The account focuses on Peter as the leader and representative of the group. Peter has simple faith. He responds to Jesus' call to go into the deep and cast the nets, despite a failure to catch fish the previous night. After the catch, the initial realization that God is working through Jesus brings a confession of unworthiness from the professional fisherman. Yet Jesus does not put him off. Rather, Jesus promises Peter a ministry that will share in the task of gathering people. In turn, Peter and those with him drop their nets and begin the lifelong task of following Jesus in the pursuit of catching people. Jesus has company, as he undertakes his mission. Those who know they are unworthy at the time of Jesus' gracious invitation undertake to follow him in ministry. A higher call causes them to abandon their nets. God transforms sinners into servants.

Additional Notes

5:8. Many regard 5:8 as an insertion, perhaps from a postresurrection account (Fitzmyer 1981: 561).[23] As such, its historicity is challenged. Objections to its originality have three elements: (1) the confession is postresurrection in character with the use of the term κύριος and the mention of sin; (2) Peter would not fall to his knees in a boat full of fish; and (3) Jesus could not depart from the boat, thus the request is unrealistic (Klostermann 1929: 70). Others suggest that Luke combined two accounts here, with the original miracle ending at 5:7 and the confession occurring on land in another account (Schneider 1977a: 125).

None of these objections is substantial and some reflect overrationalization. The encounter between humans and the divine often produces fear and the awareness of human finitude (1:13, 30). Falling before Jesus is natural in such an encounter (Isa. 6:1–6; Ezek. 1:1–2:3), and there is no reason to press the language so much as to suggest that there was absolutely no room to move on the boat because of the fish. In addition, a fisherman is

23. For the relationship of Luke 5 to John 21, see the introduction to this pericope.

used to fish, so falling on them would not be a problem! The detail is important, because the action shows just how overwhelmed Peter had become. The problem of the sinking boat and the abundance of fish had become clearly secondary to dealing with who Jesus was and the risk that that entailed for a sinful Peter. Next, the request to depart need not be taken as a command to be heeded literally in an instant, but to be acted on after arrival on shore. It would be a request equivalent to "please pack your bags" (Luke 8:37). So the need to posit an additional source with a "land-based" action is unnecessary. The account fits together very nicely as is. Danker (1983: 401) notes that in a first-century setting God's beneficence is sufficient to produce this kind of humble prostration. What the reaction depicts is Peter's extreme sensitivity and emotional character.

5:10. Allegories of various kinds have been constructed from this account throughout church history. The water is seen to represent evil from which people are rescued (Mánek 1957–58a). More elaborately, fishing in deep water is seen as a reference to Gentile mission, so that the fish represent the many Gentiles who come to faith (noted and rejected by Plummer 1896: 147–48). The latter idea is refuted because James and John, in helping Peter in the Gentile mission, must picture Paul and Barnabas, a connection that is hardly obvious. Also, there is no corresponding fishing in shallow water to depict Jewish mission (Nolland 1989: 222). The former allegory tends to portray people as neutral entities who need only to be removed from their evil environment. As long as this suggestion is avoided, seeing the sea as picturing evil is possible, since the catch is a rescue. A third variation speaks of the boats as picturing the church, and the mention of two boats indicates the two missions of the church to Jews and Gentiles (Bovon 1989: 235). This goes in the right direction, but also goes too far. The most one has here is the picture of Jesus as leader of the mission to rescue people. The boat can picture rescue, but the real metaphor is the "catch," which rescues people from death and brings them into life. The gospel brings people safely to shore. Jesus says laborers will be brought together for this task.

2. Two Miracles of Authority (5:12–26)

Luke turns from the call of the new disciples to a fresh display of Jesus' authority. He does so by recounting two miracles: the cleansing of the leper (5:12–16) and the healing of the paralytic (5:17–26). Both healings raise questions. Jesus touches the leper, an act that would make him unclean by tradition, but he also commands the healed man to go to the priest, which is in accordance with the law. Jesus claims to forgive sins as he heals the paralytic, a claim of unique authority. This claim brings the first opposition from organized Judaism. The Pharisees and scribes, making their first appearance in the Gospel of Luke, complain that no one has the authority to forgive sin except God. The confrontation of the second miracle sets the stage for Luke's fundamental question about Jesus: Who exactly is this one who claims to minister for God? Much of the rest of the section until 9:50 wrestles with this question, as units alternate among miracles, teaching, and controversy over Jesus' claims.

Talbert (1982: 63) makes an interesting point about structure here: just as Jesus' activity in 4:31–44 helps to set up Peter's response in 5:1–11, so also the activity of 5:12–26 sets up Levi's response in 5:27–32. Thus, the interplay between Jesus' activity and the gathering of disciples is still present. In fact, just as 5:10 had a mission statement for disciples, so also 5:31–32 has a mission statement for Jesus.

The two miracles of 5:12–26 are so related to each other that it is good to bracket them together, even though they are clearly distinct pericopes. I will introduce each pericope's background separately, but treat the outline and themes at the same time. This bracketing allows one to see the escalation between the miracles.

Luke 5:12–16 describes Jesus' second encounter with a socially ostracized outcast,[1] the first being the demoniac in 4:33–37 (Danker 1988: 118). The healing of the leper is the last miracle before a series of events where Jesus finds himself in direct controversy with the Pharisees (5:17–6:11). This larger grouping parallels Mark 2:1–3:5. Even the order is the same, except that Luke has a summary right before the Sermon on the Plain rather than before the selection of the Twelve, as in Mark 3:7–12 (see the in-

---

1. The only other leper healing in Luke occurs in 17:11–19. In addition, Luke 7:22 and Matt. 10:8 mention such healings in summary remarks.

troduction to Luke 6:17–19). This is merely a stylistic rearrangement to note Luke's transition into a teaching section.

Luke focuses more narrowly on Jesus' positive desire to heal the leper in contrast to Mark's more complex account, which stresses some negative elements of the healing (e.g., Jesus' strong tone in warning the leper and his subsequent disobedience). Luke's positive emphasis argues that Jesus aids those who sense they have need. Those who appeal to him for help find grace. This positive focus fits this entire chapter's picture of Jesus' ministry (5:8–9, 12–13, 20, 27–32).

The healing of the leper is told briefly in a relatively straightforward style. Jesus' ministry is to those on the outside, those who have nothing. The action illustrates the ministry announced in 4:16–30. The sequence of healings shows the breaking in of messianic times (7:22; Marshall 1978: 207; Schneider 1977a: 130). Belief in a relationship between healing the ill and the messianic times was prevalent in Judaism (SB 1:593–96; 2:747–50; Schürmann 1969: 276; Jub. 23.26–30; 1 Enoch 5.8–9; 96.3; 2 Esdr. [= 4 Ezra] 7:123; 2 Bar. 29.7). The only biblical precedent for healing a leper was Elisha's ministry (2 Kings 5:1–14, esp. vv. 13–14; 7:3–9). Of course, the parallelism of Jesus' ministry to this period of Israel's history was already alluded to in Luke 4:25–27. The connection shows Jesus functioning as a prophet of old. He touches the leper, an act that makes him unclean, but that visualizes his desire to show compassion, even at a cost. In addition, Luke shows Jesus instructing the healed man to follow the law, since Jesus tells him to go to the priests and give testimony to God's work. The healing also produces a large popular reaction to Jesus, which apparently he tries to avoid. Jesus' power successfully exercised on behalf of those in desperate straits is Luke's major concern.

On the other hand, Luke 5:17–26 reveals the fuller significance of Jesus' ministry. The healing of the paralytic raises the stakes as it takes Jesus' theological claims to higher levels, escalating the tension in the narrative. The issue is not just his power, but the extent of his authority. The theological ramifications of Jesus' ministry become clearer and the reaction to him becomes more diverse and defined. According to this account, the authority of Jesus includes the right to forgive sins (5:20, 23–24).

This claim produces the first reaction from organized Judaism. They immediately oppose Jesus and consider such claims to be an affront against God. They think Jesus is guilty of blasphemy. Meanwhile, Jesus is claiming prerogatives that point to the full identity of his person (Marshall 1978: 210–11). Clear christological lines are being drawn that dominate the rest of the Gospel. Is Jesus ultimately a teacher, a prophet, a Messiah, or someone much greater?

What is interesting about this account is that it is Jesus who initiates the confrontation and, to a great extent, has control over events. The account is loaded with contrasting characters: the authoritative Jesus, the believing paralytic and his friends, and the questioning religious leadership. The healing, of course, means that Jesus has reached out to another man in need, a need different from the previous ones he has met. Jesus is able to overpower a variety of maladies.

Sources and Historicity (5:12–16)

The healing of the leper has parallels in Mark 1:40–45 and Matt. 8:2–4 (Aland 1985: §42). Its placement in relation to the chronological progress of Jesus' ministry is disputed and difficult to set precisely.[2] Godet (1875: 1.259) and Plummer (1896: 148) argue that, since Matthew gives the only chronological context, the event must come after the Sermon on the Mount. But this approach ignores certain factors in the construction of Matt. 8–9 (Carson 1984: 196–97). This section of Matthew depicts the early phase of Jesus' ministry without concern for exact chronological order, so that Matt. 8:1 should be read merely as a general transition marker out of the sermon section. Matthew 8–9 clearly shows a sequence different from Mark and Luke. The healing of Simon's mother-in-law's fever comes in Matt. 8:14–15 and it in turn is followed by the summary of Jesus' work in Matt. 8:16–17, which places these events after the healing of the leper. Mark and Luke both place the healing of the fever earlier in their account, before the leper account (Mark 1:29–31; Luke 4:38–39). A double healing of the same person for the same ailment is unlikely, since it might raise questions about the quality of Jesus' first effort. So it becomes clear that at least one of the Gospel writers has reorganized the order of these events and has proceeded in a more topical fashion. Who has done so?

Matthew has only three short pericopes about Jesus' Galilean ministry before giving the rather lengthy Sermon on the Mount. But these early pericopes are summaries or introductions.[3] Thus, the healings in Matt. 8–9 are the first detailed Matthean descriptions of Jesus' activity. Creed (1930: 76) suggests a plausible motive for the Matthean arrangement by

2. Many regard the tradition as circulating so loosely with regard to chronological placement and/or historical reality that they do not pursue such questions.
3. Matt. 4:12–17 is a summary of the Galilean ministry and OT promise; Matt. 4:18–22 is the call of the first four disciples; and Matt. 4:23–25 describes in broad terms Jesus' ministry of preaching and healing.

arguing that a story where Jesus is careful about following the law's requirements would naturally be placed after his potentially controversial Sermon on the Mount. Matthew 8–9 gives detail about the early phase of Jesus' ministry, without concern for exact order, moving along topical and broadly chronological lines. The leper incident is a particularly illustrative healing for Matthew, which also shows that Jesus is not callous toward the law. Thus, at this point Mark and Luke probably reflect the chronological sequence.[4]

The wording of the three accounts is very close, especially in the dialogue. Where differences do occur, it is hard to tell who influenced whom. Sometimes Matthew and Luke agree against Mark;[5] sometimes Matthew and Mark agree against Luke;[6] and sometimes Luke and Mark agree against Matthew.[7] Perhaps this event was a well-known tradition that circulated orally as well as in written form (Schneider 1977a: 130; Marshall 1978: 206).[8]

Fitzmyer (1981: 572) notes five differences between Mark and Luke,[9] two of them being key: (2) Luke does not describe Jesus' emotion, as Mark 1:41 does (but Mark is often alone in noting Jesus' emotion) and (5) only Luke 5:16 mentions a withdrawal to the wilderness, while Mark 1:45 mentions that Jesus was out in the country and could not go into the towns because of the crowds. Otherwise, Luke and Mark are very similar. Matthew's version is more condensed and is introduced in a distinct setting. He lacks any mention of the report that circulated as a result of this healing, possibly because it is the first event in his sequence.

As far as historicity goes, Marshall (1978: 207) correctly notes that one's evaluation of the account will be determined largely by preconceptions about what Jesus could do. He rightly rejects attempts by Pesch (1970b: 78–80) to argue that the account's literary form as a miracle story is alone sufficient to rule out its claims to being historical. The Jesus Seminar (Funk and Hoover 1993: 43, 282) handles the sayings of these texts as they did

---

4. So also Hendriksen 1978: 289; for a set of parallel units where Matthew seems more chronological, see the introduction to 5:27–32.

5. Matthean and Lucan agreements include their use of κύριε (Luke 5:12; Matt. 8:2); their spelling the Greek term for "immediately" as εὐθέως (Luke 5:13; Matt. 8:3) versus εὐθύς in Mark 1:42; and their lack of the double negative (μηδενί in Luke 5:14 and Matt. 8:4 versus μηδενὶ μηδέν in Mark 1:44, which is more emphatic).

6. Luke omits a second mention of cleansing, and Matt. 8:4 and Mark 1:44 share the verb ὕπαγε versus ἀπελθών in Luke 5:14.

7. So the wording of Mark 1:44 and Luke 5:14, which includes a specific reference to cleansing that Matthew lacks.

8. Only Schramm 1971: 91–99 suggests that Luke used a written source.

9. Fitzmyer's other three points are stylistic alterations: (1) Mark 1:40 has the leper fall at Jesus' feet, while Luke 5:12 has him falling on his face; (3) Luke omits any mention of sending the leper off, unlike Mark 1:43; and (4) Luke 5:15 notes the crowd's reaction and gathering, while Mark 1:45 stays focused on the leper's talking to others.

4:31–37 (see the discussion of sources and historicity of that unit). In their view, these miracle-story sayings did not circulate as aphorisms and so could not be historical. Apparently they believe that early traditions about Jesus circulated where he said much and did nothing—unlike the Synoptic Gospels we possess! Also, did the miracle stories circulate without dialogue? The seminar's rejection of these sayings is strictly presuppositional. Interestingly, Crossan (1991: 322) accepts the traditional origin of the request to be healed, but rejects Jesus' sending the leper to the priests as Lev. 13–14 and Deut. 24:8–9 require. But it is not clear why following the law in giving testimony to God's work is beyond a pious Jesus.

There is no reason to reject the account, since all levels of the tradition contain remarks about Jesus' miraculous work with the sick. The critical criterion of multiple attestation supports the miraculous background of a healing like this one.

Sources and Historicity (5:17–26)

The event recorded in Luke 5:17–26 is recounted in all the Synoptics (Mark 2:1–12; Matt. 9:1–8; Aland 1985: §43). Luke's presentation is very full, as is Mark's, though there are numerous differences of wording that are mostly stylistic in character. This similarity leads most to reject the idea of multiple sources for this pericope (Marshall 1978: 211 and Fitzmyer 1981: 578 against Schramm 1971: 99–103; Bovon 1989: 245 discusses a possible source in oral tradition). Fitzmyer (1981: 578) notes nine differences between Mark and Luke, most involving small details.[10] These details complement one another.

The exact placement of this event in Jesus' ministry is hard to determine. All the Synoptics have the event early in the Galilean ministry, but Matthew has included the account relatively late in his topical overview of Jesus' ministry in Matt. 8–9.[11] Mark and Luke have many of these Matthean events later in their Gospels, so someone has rearranged the material.

It would seem that Mark's and Luke's general placement reflects the event's timing (Carson 1984: 221). However, there are no firm chronologi-

10. For example, Luke does not mention Capernaum as the site; he does not note specifically the presence of four men; and Luke is the only one to note that the Lord's power was with Jesus (5:17), to describe the roof as having tiles (5:19), to specify the scope of the audience (5:17), and to note how quickly the healing occurred (5:25). The omission of a specific site and the mention of Jesus' power reflect consistent Lucan style.

11. It comes in Matt. 9:1–8 after these events: the leper's cleansing (Matt. 8:1–4 = Luke 5:12–16 = Mark 1:40–45), the centurion's slave's healing (Matt. 8:5–13 = Luke 7:1–10), a summary (Matt. 8:14–17, like Luke 4:38–41 and Mark 1:29–34), Jesus' rejection of some who wish to postpone discipleship (Matt. 8:18–22 = Luke 9:57–62), the stilling of the storm (Matt. 8:23–27 = Luke 8:22–25 = Mark 4:35–41), and the Gadarene demoniac's healing (Matt. 8:28–34 = Luke 8:26–39 = Mark 5:1–20).

cal indicators in any of the Gospels for this event, so any conclusion is only a probability (Plummer 1896: 148 prefers Matthew's timing "just after . . . the Sermon on the Mount"; Van Der Loos 1965: 441). I regard the Marcan-Lucan placement as more chronological. In all the Synoptic Gospels, the call of Levi follows this miracle (Matt. 9:9–13 = Mark 2:13–17 = Luke 5:27–32). Though all the Gospels add the dinner at Levi's home at the same time as they narrate his call, this dinner event appears to have been later, after the Gadara healing. This placement is preferred because it appears likely that the even later dispute about disciples' fasting stems from this dinner, where they ate and drank with sinners (Luke 5:33 = Mark 2:18 = Matt. 9:14). All the Synoptics mention that the dinner got the Pharisees' attention (Matt. 9:11 = Mark 2:16 = Luke 5:30; see the introduction to Luke 5:27–32). Mark and Luke placed the dinner before Gadara to describe topically the significance of Levi's call. Matthew waited to narrate all the Levi events until after the Gadara account, since the final events followed that incident (Carson 1984: 221). In other words, each writer worked topically to some extent but in different directions, with Mark and Luke moving the dinner up and Matthew delaying the call. But the events preceding Levi's call appear in all the Gospels to be connected to the call. If Mark and Luke moved up the dinner, then the call seems to be in its proper relative location and the events related to the call—the two miracles of Luke 5:12–26—appropriately precede it.

The historicity of this event and the passage as a whole is tied to the Son of Man saying in 5:24, a question that is treated in detail in excursus 6. One view to be noted is that of the Jesus Seminar (Funk and Hoover 1993: 283). They reject the saying because it would not have circulated independently as a "true aphorism." Apparently they regard as suspect a miracle account that has sayings circulating with it. The logic of this exclusion is not clear. Crossan's attempt (1991: 324–25) to see the event without its theology is not much more satisfying. The Son of Man saying is the key to this passage. It seems that if one can explain its presence here, one can defend the whole account.

The account of the healing of the leper in Papyrus Egerton 2 is generally regarded to be based on Luke 5:12–16 (Fitzmyer 1981: 572–73; Schneider 1977a: 130). Attempts to locate an early church application in a specific baptismal setting (Schürmann 1969: 275) are overdrawn. The picture of cleansing suggests Jesus' power to heal the effects of sin, since leprosy was often regarded as picturing the presence of sin (Lev. 13–14; Num. 5:2–3; 12:10–12; Deut. 24:8), but baptism narrows the focus too much. The cleansing pictured here has analogies to what baptism represents, but it does not picture only baptism.

Luke 5:12–16 is a miracle story, specifically, a healing.[12] It has the standard structure of need (5:12a), request (5:12b), healing (5:13a), sign of the healing's presence (5:13b), and popular reaction (5:15).

Luke 5:17–26 combines a healing miracle and a theological pronouncement.[13] By emphasizing the account's form, some insist that the tradition merged two distinct accounts, on the premise that different types of stories are not combined in the original setting. A second reason is that one verse (Mark 2:10 = Matt. 9:6 = Luke 5:24) is seen as problematic to the original setting (Fitzmyer 1981: 579). However, the claim about sin is key to the account and cannot be attributed to just one form of the story. Both Jesus' remarks during the healing and his challenge to the Pharisees mention sin and forgiveness (Marshall 1978: 211; Carson 1984: 220). Because of this factor, Theissen (1983: 322) calls it a rule miracle.[14] Bovon (1989: 245) speaks of a miracle account and a controversy account. It is best to see a rule miracle and a controversy account. Jesus is doing two things at one time: showing his authority and exposing the Pharisees' opposition. Regardless of the name given to the account's form, there is no reason to divide it into two separate sources in an original tradition or to insist that a story originally can have only one form. Surely healing and pronouncement can go together, both in terms of event and especially in a tradition summarizing the event.

The outline of Luke 5:12–26 is as follows:

a. Cleansing of the leper (5:12–16)
   i. Healing (5:12–14)
      (1) Setting: a Galilean city (5:12a)
      (2) Condition and request of the leper (5:12b)
      (3) Jesus' willing healing (5:13)
      (4) Call to go to the priest (5:14)
   ii. Reaction to the healing (5:15–16)
      (1) Result: report and crowds (5:15)
      (2) Jesus' withdrawal for prayer (5:16)

12. Bultmann 1963: 212, 240; Fitzmyer 1981: 572; Berger 1984: 314; Theissen 1983: 321. Fitzmyer notes that M. Dibelius's classification of this account as a tale is certainly wrong. Dibelius classifies many miracle stories as tale, reflecting perhaps other presuppositions.

13. Bultmann 1963: 66, in describing Mark 2:1–10. The pronouncement is in Luke 5:20, 23–24.

14. Theissen notes that such accounts combine healing and exposition but that exposition dominates. Similarly, Berger 1984: 85 speaks of the binding together of Chrie (his term for "sayings") and miracle.

b. Healing of the paralytic (5:17–26)
   i. The healing explained (5:17–24)
      (1) Setting: teaching before the Pharisees (5:17)
      (2) Faith: the paralytic through the roof (5:18–19)
      (3) Jesus' response: sins are forgiven (5:20)
      (4) Official reaction: only God can do this (5:21)
      (5) Explanation: the Son of Man's authority (5:22–24)
   ii. Healing and the response (5:25–26)
      (1) Healing: the paralytic departs with joy (5:25)
      (2) Crowd's reaction: praise and awe (5:26)

Numerous themes are present in these two pericopes. The healings show that the messianic times are arriving. They indicate Jesus' care for those who sense their need. In his work, Jesus faithfully points to God's power working through him. The leper's healing pictures cleansing from sin. The leper exemplifies one who humbly approaches Jesus. Jesus does not wish to draw undue attention to his healing ministry, but this desire is having little success. On occasion, to avoid the crush, Jesus withdraws to be alone with God.

In the account of the paralytic, additional themes arise. The most important point is Jesus' authority over sin. Also present are the first official objections to Jesus' claims. The events also exhibit Jesus' control, since he initiates the challenge. The paralytic's friends demonstrate the powerful and active character of faith, while the miracle itself pictures Jesus' spiritual power. The reaction leads to praise for God's saving work. God responds to aid and intercession from others. There also is the recognition of Jesus' uniqueness.

Exegesis and Exposition

[12]While he was in one of the cities, behold, there came a man full of leprosy; and, behold, when he saw Jesus he fell on his face and implored him, "Lord, if you are willing, you can make me clean." [13]And stretching out his hand, he touched him, saying, "I will; be clean." And immediately the leprosy went out from him. [14]And he commanded him not to speak to anyone; but, "Go and show yourself to the priest, and make an offering for your cleansing, as Moses commanded, for a testimony to them."

[15]But even more the report went abroad concerning him; and great crowds gathered to hear and be healed of their infirmities. [16]But he was withdrawing to the wilderness and was praying.

[17]On one of those days, he also was teaching, and there were seated Pharisees and teachers of the law, ⌜who had come⌝ from every village of Galilee, Judea, and Jerusalem; and the power of the Lord was with ⌜him⌝ to heal.

[18]And, behold, men were bringing a man who was paralyzed on a bed, and they were seeking to bring him and place him before Jesus, [19]and finding no way to bring him in because of the crowds, they went up on the roof and let him down with his bed through the tiles, into the midst before Jesus. [20]And when he saw their faith he said, "Man, your sins are forgiven." [21]And the scribes and the Pharisees began questioning by thinking, "Who is this who utters blasphemies? Who is able to forgive sins but God alone?" [22]But Jesus, knowing their reasonings, said to them, "Why do you question in your hearts? [23]What is easier to say, 'Your sins are forgiven you,' or to say, 'Rise up and walk'? [24]But in order that you might know that the Son of Man has authority on earth to forgive sins"—he said to the paralytic—"I say to you, rise up, and taking up your bed, go home."

[25]And immediately rising up before them, taking up that on which he lay, he went out to his house, glorifying God. [26]And amazement seized them all and they glorified God and were filled with awe, saying, "We have seen wonderful things today."

a. Cleansing of the Leper (5:12–16)
i. Healing (5:12–14)
(1) Setting: A Galilean City (5:12a)

5:12a The healing has a general setting but lacks a specific locale. In mentioning "one of the cities," Luke alludes to the continuation of Jesus' commission presented in 4:43–44, where πόλις (*polis*, city) also appears. Galilee is still in view here, because the context of the previous account describes an event on the Lake of Gennesaret in Galilee.[15]

(2) Condition and Request of the Leper (5:12b)

5:12b The approaching man is full of leprosy. Λέπρα (*lepra*) appears to be a broad term for a whole series of skin diseases, rather than referring just to Hansen's Disease (*Bacillus leprae*), as it came to be known in the nineteenth century.[16] The disease comes in various forms and creates lesions or swollen areas on the skin. It can attack the nerves as well. Besides what is technically known as leprosy, the term could also refer to psoriasis, lupus, ringworm, and favus. Sup-

---

15. So Fitzmyer 1981: 573 and Wiefel 1988: 116 rightly, against Conzelmann 1960: 43 and Schneider 1977a: 130, who see a reference to Judea, no doubt because of 4:44. Of course, if Judea is broadly understood in that verse, then Galilee is included in that earlier reference as well. See the exegesis of 4:44.

16. BAGD 471 (with bibliography); BAA 957; Van Der Loos 1965: 465–68; Michaelis, *TDNT* 4:233–34; Harrison, *NIDNTT* 2:463–66; SB 4:745–63; Pousma 1975: 138–39. Λέπρα occurs in the NT only in Matt. 8:3 = Mark 1:42 = Luke 5:12–13. A related term, λεπρός, appears in Luke 4:27; 7:22; 17:12; Matt. 8:2; 10:8; 11:5; 26:6; Mark 1:40; 14:3.

port for a broad sense here is indicated by the description for identifying a leper in Lev. 13–14, where the disease described has more variation than the disease called leprosy today.

To have leprosy was to face ostracism, which was commanded in Lev. 13:45–46 (also 2 Kings 7:3; Luke 17:12). To have leprosy and be excluded from normal society was difficult both socially and psychologically. The ostracism was not cruel; it was necessary because the condition was contagious. The disease's association with ritual uncleanness also produced associations of the disease with sin. Godet (1875: 1.259) describes the overall effect of the disease as a form of "living death." Leviticus 14 details what happens if and when the uncleanness passed, but in the OT the priests were not expected to provide healing for a leper (Bovon 1989: 239). Thus, for this man to approach Jesus was not only brave, it put the leper's entire self-esteem at risk. Whatever hope that he might have about a return to normal life was wrapped up in Jesus' power. The leper must have heard that Jesus was healing those in need. Great emotion underlies the passage. An ancient reader or observer would sense the tension and pathos. One might compare this situation to the situation with AIDS today (Tiede 1988: 119–20).

The humility of the man is evident: he bows before Jesus as someone would to any superior in this culture. Ἐδεήθη (edeēthē, he implored) describes the tone of his request. Δέομαι (deomai) is often used of prayer and suggests an urgent request (Luke 8:28; Acts 4:31; 10:2; BAGD 175 §§3–4; BAA 350). The address κύριε (kyrie, Lord) is more than polite address. It reflects a recognition that Jesus has the capability to deal with the problem, though a reference to full deity is unlikely, given that even Jesus' disciples did not see him this way yet (Hendriksen 1978: 289; Marshall 1978: 209). Jesus is addressed with respect because God is working through him. The leper probably sees Jesus as a prophet.

The request centers on Jesus' willingness to heal, not on his capability to do so (Hendriksen 1978: 289; Schürmann 1969: 276). The question in Greek is put in a third-class condition form (indicated by ἐάν, ean), that is, the leper is not sure what Jesus might do. Custom and law suggest that the leper should be isolated, maybe even that he is guilty of severe sin, but the isolated man knows that Jesus can reverse his condition and cleanse him. The reference to cleansing places a spiritual focus over the entire event. It is an abnormal and polluted condition with which Jesus is asked to deal. The request for healing is clear, and any suggestion that the man is simply asking for recognition of an already accomplished natural healing is clearly wrong. If that were the case, all the leper would need to do is see a priest. This "recognition" view—rightly rejected by Godet

(1875: 1.261)—attempts to remove the miraculous character of the healing. Such a view is naturalism gone awry when it encounters Jesus' works in the Gospels. Luke 5:13–14 leaves no doubt that the leper had the disease before coming to Jesus and that he left without the disease.

(3) Jesus' Willing Healing (5:13)

5:13 Jesus answers the question with a gentle touch. The stretch of his hand depicts physically his willingness to respond to the request. The leprous man is not sent away nor is he warned about coming near to Jesus. Rather, he hears and feels Jesus' tender willingness. Luke often mentions touch (7:14; 13:13; 18:15; 22:51). Jesus' word would have been sufficient, but his touch confirms his care. So Jesus touches the man, despite the tradition that said such an act would render him unclean (Lev. 14:46; *m. Neg.* 3.1; 11.1; 12.1; 13.6–12; SB 4:745–63).[17] Charity has taken precedence over a strict application of tradition, since Jesus can reverse the condition and his ministry involves meeting needs. Jesus' expression of willingness serves to calm the leper, much as Jesus' word calmed Peter in Luke 5:10. God's agent is approachable. The healing itself comes simply with an expression of willingness (θέλω, *thelō*) and the command to be clean (καθαρίσθητι, *katharistheti*) (Matt. 8:2; 10:8; 11:5; Mark 1:40, 42; Luke 4:27; 7:22; 17:14, 17; 2 Kings 5:13; BAGD 387 §1bα; BAA 785 §1bα).

Luke notes the instantaneous nature of the leper's healing with εὐθέως (*eutheōs*; also Matt. 8:3). Such was also the case when Jesus healed Peter's mother-in-law of fever (Fitzmyer 1981: 574–75; Luke 4:39 notes her immediate service). Mark 1:42, with its variant spelling, εὐθύς (*euthys*), also emphasizes this point. Luke does not discuss Jesus' emotion, as Mark does, but Jesus' actions reveal his compassion clearly enough. Unlike Mark 1:42, there is no mention of cleansing at this point in describing the healing. All the Gospels mention that the leprosy left the man, but only Mark adds that he was cleansed. Luke's focus is solely on the healing, as Luke often is more concise in his style (Creed 1930: 77; Klostermann 1929: 71; as in Luke 4:40, where Luke also has only half of what Mark says). Schürmann (1969: 276 n. 17) notes that there is no high priestly language in the account. In Jesus, God's power is at work, but there is no hint within the account as to his office. In the larger scope of Luke's Gospel, he is Messiah and prophet (4:18–20, 25–27; 7:22).

---

17. On the role of purity in Judaism as a stage on the way to holiness, see Neusner and Chilton 1991; *m. Soṭa* 9.15. On the Pharisees' concern for purity, see Witherington 1990: 56–59, who speaks in particular of the *ḥăbērîm*, the overly strict Pharisees.

The power of disease is not only nullified but is reversed at his word. Only disease is in view here, not exorcism.[18]

(4) Call to Go to the Priest (5:14)

Jesus gives explicit instructions about what the leper should do. **5:14** Luke lays out the instruction first in indirect language and then in the middle of the verse goes to a more direct form of discourse, as my translation makes clear (Godet 1875: 1.262; Marshall 1978: 209; BDF §470; BDR §470.2.3). Luke's description continues the note of authority. Παρήγγειλεν (*parēngeilen*, he commanded) is rarely used in Matthew (Matt. 10:5; 15:35) and Mark (Mark 6:8, 8:6), but is a Lucan favorite (Luke 8:29, 56; 9:21; Acts 1:4; 4:18; 5:28, 40; 10:42; 15:5; 16:18, 23; 17:30; 23:22, 30; Plummer 1896: 149).[19] The instruction has three parts.

First, the leper is to be silent. Various reasons are suggested for Jesus' command of silence (Plummer 1896: 149–50):

1. Jesus wants him to be silent until he is officially declared to be clean (Schürmann 1969: 277; Marshall 1978: 209; Wiefel 1988: 117).
2. Jesus wishes to prevent the leper from becoming proud. However, there is no hint of such a concern in the account.
3. Jesus wishes to prevent the priests from hearing about the healing early and thus stopping the leper's return to society. However, up to this point in Luke's Gospel, there is no hint of official opposition.
4. Jesus wishes to prevent excessive popular excitement as a result of his healing ministry (so Marshall 1978: 209, with view 1). This point is quite possible, as the following verse suggests.
5. It shows Jesus' humility. This idea is not developed in relationship to miracles anywhere else.
6. Jesus wants to avoid having to offer himself to be ritually cleansed for touching a leper. This motive, too, seems unlikely. When Jesus did not follow tradition, he did not hide his actions. It is also probable that since Jesus is a prophet he has the freedom to touch these people, as the Elisha example suggests.

The most likely explanations are that the silence was appropriate until the leper went to the priest (view 1) and that such silence also

18. Busse 1979: 110–14 argues that the idea of the leprosy "going out" of the man in 5:13 suggests an exorcism (he also notes Luke 4:32, 36; Acts 10:38). Bovon 1989: 240 is uncertain. However, the departure of the fever of Luke 4:39 is described in different but similar terms: ἀφῆκεν.

19. Matt. 8:4 and Mark 1:44 use the simple λέγω here.

would prevent undue popular excitement over Jesus' miraculous work (view 4). The account vividly shows how Jesus downplays his miraculous work. Often he tries to restrict the spreading of a message about miracles (Luke 4:35, 41; 8:56; Matt. 9:30; 12:16; Mark 1:34; 3:12; 5:43; 7:36; 8:26; Plummer 1896: 150).

Second, the leper is to show himself to the priest, a command paralleled in Matt. 8:4 and Mark 1:44 (Schrenk, *TDNT* 3:264). The healing of a leper in Luke 17:14 also carries this instruction with it (Creed 1930: 77; Fitzmyer 1981: 575; Luce 1933: 130). The instruction reflects Lev. 14:1–32. Getting the priest to declare one clean was a weeklong process.[20] The process began with two birds, one of which was sacrificed, while the other was released after being dipped in the blood of the sacrificed bird. The person was sprinkled seven times with the blood of the sacrificed bird. The entire ritual portrayed the cleansing and removal of sin. On the eighth day, a sacrifice was required, either two lambs or, if one was poor, a lamb and two doves. Jewish practice of the second century A.D. is recorded in tractates *Toharot* and *Nega'im* of the Mishnah. The mishnaic material describes how priests diagnosed leprosy, and *m. Neg.* 14 deals with the process of declaring a leper clean. After the eight-day period, the leper was free to return to society.

Third, the leper is to offer sacrifice before the priest. The sacrifice is specifically described as being for cleansing, the third time this idea is mentioned. To be offered in fulfillment of what Moses commanded, the sacrifice is designated "a testimony to them" (εἰς μαρτύριον αὐτοῖς, *eis martyrion autois*). The meaning of this phrase and the antecedent of the plural αὐτοῖς have created some discussion:

1. The testimony about Jesus' power is for the priests (Danker 1988: 119).
2. The testimony to the priests is that Jesus does not disregard the law (Geldenhuys 1951: 186; Hendriksen 1978: 291; Godet 1875: 1.262–63; Danker 1988: 119). This explanation is difficult in the contexts of Luke and Mark, where legal conflict has yet to emerge. But it is possible that Jesus is anticipating a problem.
3. The testimony is for the leper's return into society. This explanation is difficult, because the testimony is specified as directed to the priests, not to the leper.
4. The testimony is to the people, not just to the priests, that Jesus does not disregard the law (Plummer 1896: 150; Nolland 1989:

---

20. Hendriksen 1978: 291. Fitzmyer 1981: 575 notes a Qumran text on this topic: 11QTemple[a] 48.17–49.4. At Qumran, lepers were also isolated to prevent additional defiling.

228). However, the absence of legal conflict to this point applies here just as it did against view 2.

5. The testimony, which is for all, is to the presence of messianic times (Schürmann 1969: 276–78).

The problem is that αὐτοῖς can refer to priests or to all people. Those who see a reference to all argue that only one priest is referred to in the verse, so "priests" cannot be in view. But this explanation assumes that no one will talk about the testimony given to the priest. On the other hand, if the leper obeys Jesus, then the only one who hears the testimony is the priest who handles his cleansing (so Lev. 14). But surely such a dramatic testimony will be shared, as were reports of other miracles. Thus, it seems best to restrict the testimony to the priestly circle, though it must be remembered that the priest is a representative of the nation. What Luke is suggesting is that the religious leadership, as representatives of the people, should come to know that God is at work in Jesus. It may be no accident that some of the leadership are present in the next pericope (Luke 5:17). But does such testimony refer to Jesus' obedience to the law? This conclusion is unlikely, because Jesus has had no legal conflicts up to this point in Luke. The testimony most naturally would be to God's power expressed through Jesus in cleansing the man. The command does evidence Jesus' obedience to the law, but it is hardly the major concern. This type of cleansing might well testify to the presence of messianic times (7:22). So the combination of views 1 and 5 seems most likely. The leper is one of the "signs of the times" that declare God's power in Jesus.

ii. Reaction to the Healing (5:15–16)
(1) Result: Report and Crowds (5:15)

The reaction to the healing was the gathering of greater crowds. Mark **5:15** 1:45 tells us that the leper was not silent. Luke does not contain that remark, but notes instead the consequences of the word getting around. Διήρχετο (diērcheto) indicates that the news about Jesus spread through the public grapevine (Klostermann 1929: 71; Thucydides 6.46.5; Xenophon, Anabasis 1.4.7). Schürmann (1969: 278) notes that the news about Jesus extends ever wider in Luke's portrayal (first to Galilee and Capernaum in 4:14–15, 37, and then to Judea and Jerusalem in 5:15, 17). The mission of 4:44 is being fulfilled. The crowd comes to hear the message and to be healed. In such simple terms, Luke summarizes the expanding influence and response to Jesus' work (other summaries are 4:14–15, 40; 6:18; 7:21). Mark notes that the crush of people trying to see Jesus is so great that Jesus can no longer enter the city. He must minister in the country (Mark 1:45).

(2) Jesus' Withdrawal for Prayer (5:16)

5:16 The large gatherings did not prevent Jesus from withdrawing habitually and finding time to commune with God or his disciples (Luke 4:42; also Matt. 14:13; Mark 1:35, 45; John 11:54). Luke regularly notes Jesus' praying (Luke 3:21; 6:12; 9:18, 28–29; 11:1; 23:46; Leaney 1958: 124). Despite all the activity, Jesus is portrayed as seeking time with God, rather than fanning his fame. Perhaps the activity's very scope and importance required that time be spent with God. Jesus' prayers tend to come at key times, and this summary is no exception. Jesus was headed for a series of conflicts in the events that followed. Luke makes clear that before Jesus got into trouble, he was spending time with God (Danker 1988: 120).

b. Healing of the Paralytic (5:17–26)
i. The Healing Explained (5:17–24)
(1) Setting: Teaching before the Pharisees (5:17)

5:17 The description of the healing's setting is given in general terms. Καὶ ἐγένετο (*kai egeneto*, and it happened) is a frequent Lucan transition phrase into a new event,[21] and it simply refers to one of the days that Jesus was teaching. Mark 2:1 mentions that the event was in Capernaum. Schürmann (1969: 281) argues that Luke purposely omitted Capernaum to keep the reference to geographical expansion clear, but this is speculative, especially in light of Luke's already clear indication that Jesus' audience has come from various locales.[22] In fact, Luke 5:17 shows that people came from Galilee, Judea, and Jerusalem. Luke does not need to omit the locale to make the point Schürmann raises. The difference has no clear motive, other than Luke's tendency not to mention a locale. As was his custom, Jesus teaches with others seated about him.

The audience now has some new members. The Pharisees and teachers of the law come from the entire region, even from as far as Jerusalem. The officials of organized Judaism are starting to take an interest in Jesus. The Pharisees were one of four major religious groups in first-century Judaism—Sadducees, Essenes, and Zealots being the others.[23] The Pharisees were a nonpriestly or lay separatist

---

21. This phrase is not always translated. It appears in Luke in various combinations fifty-one times. Ἐγένετο with an additional καί and a finite verb occurs twelve times, including 5:1, 12; 8:1, 22; 9:28, 51.

22. Luke mentions Capernaum in 4:23, 31; 7:1; and 10:15. The reference in 7:1 negates Bovon's inference (1989: 243) from 4:42–44 that in the rest of Luke Jesus does not return to Capernaum. Jesus' itinerant ministry does bring him back to his home base. Luke just chooses not to note that detail.

23. Josephus, *Antiquities* 13.5.9 §171; 13.10.6 §§293–98; 17.2.4–3.1 §§41–51; 18.1.2 §11; *Jewish War* 2.8.14 §§162–63; C. F. Evans 1990: 298–99.

movement whose goal was to keep the nation faithful to Mosaic faith. In order to do this, they had a very developed tradition that gave rulings on how the law applied to a variety of possible situations not addressed directly by Scripture (Marshall 1978: 212; Fitzmyer 1981: 581).[24]

The teachers of the law (νομοδιδάσκαλοι, nomodidaskaloi) were religious lawyers who supported the development of this extrabiblical tradition. Their motive was to preserve and contextualize the biblical teaching into new settings. Usually called scribes (γραμματεύς, grammateus), they are often linked with the Pharisees (5:21, 30; 6:7; 11:53; 15:2) or the chief priests (9:22; 19:47; 20:1, 19; 22:2, 66; 23:10). They could rule on the religious legality of an issue from a pharisaic point of view, although, as the Mishnah attests, the opinions on any given issue were hardly unanimous. This is the only occurrence of νομοδιδάσκαλος in the Synoptics, but it does appear elsewhere in the NT (Acts 5:34; 1 Tim. 1:7; Jeremias, TDNT 1:740–42; Rengstorf, TDNT 2:159). These legal assistants helped in recording the tradition for future generations. They functioned like religious parliamentarians for the sect and were Pharisees themselves. The Pharisees were a strict movement that had little popular appeal, but they held much influence in key places.[25]

As already noted, this is Luke's first mention of the Pharisees' observing Jesus' ministry. Mark will introduce them in his Gospel in the next event, the call of Levi (Mark 2:16), though Mark 2:6 does mention the presence of scribes at this healing.[26] Matthew 9:9–13, Levi's call, is Matthew's first mention of these figures in reference to observing Jesus' ministry. Their presence at these events shows that the reports about Jesus were not going unnoticed. News had reached the highest levels of Judaism.

After mentioning the future opponents, Luke adds another unique note: the Lord's power to heal is with Jesus. What Jesus is about to do is in conjunction with God's power working through him (Luke 4:14, 36; 6:19; 8:46; Acts 10:38; Grundmann, TDNT 2:301; Danker 1988: 120; Plummer 1896: 152). It may be one teacher versus

24. The Mishnah is an anthology of the tradition, and the Talmud is commentary on the Mishnah. I have consistently noted these sources as background to the ancient Jewish perspective on various events. Since it is an older work, the Mishnah is of more value here than the Talmud. Yet, one must also be careful with mishnaic references since it is a late-second-century document. Still, the Mishnah's roots in a conservative theological tradition suggest that much of what is present in it may be older.

25. Schürer 1973–87: 2.381–403; R. Meyer and H. Weiss, TDNT 9:11–48. For Luke and the Pharisees, see Carroll 1988.

26. Mark will not specifically mention Pharisees from Jerusalem until Mark 3:22, the Beelzebub incident.

several religious authorities, but God is working through the teacher, who is also a healer. Jesus is teaching. The Pharisees are present. Jesus is ready to heal and make great claims in the process.

(2) Faith: The Paralytic through the Roof (5:18–19)

5:18 As the crowd congregated, some men (four according to Mark 2:3) brought a paralyzed man on his bed toward Jesus. Matthew and Luke use the same term to describe the bed, κλίνη (klinē; nine times in the NT), while Mark 2:4 uses a different term, κράβαττος (krabattos, pallet; eleven times in the NT). Both terms refer to the stretcher on which the lame man rested (BAGD 436, 447; BAA 887, 909). Luke describes the man as crippled, using one of four NT terms to describe this condition.[27] The men were coming to bring him before Jesus. But, as the next verse makes clear, getting access to the teacher proved difficult.

5:19 The normal entry into the house was blocked by the crowd. However, that would not stop this group of men. The typical house in Palestine had two stories, with the roof area serving as the second story. Steps up to the roof often lay in the open (Safrai 1976a: 730–32). The roof was usually somewhat flat and about six feet above the ground. Wooden beams were laid across the top of the stone or mud walls, with a layer of reeds, thorns, and several inches of clay on top of them. Such a roof was the answer for the blocked path to Jesus.

Luke gives the most detail at this point. The men go up on the roof, make a hole, and begin carefully to lower the man through the "tiles" (κεράμων, keramōn). This account is challenged on two levels: (1) how could the crowd watch such a thing? and (2) many claim that Luke erred in saying that the roof had tiles (Schürmann 1969: 282 n. 17; Creed 1930: 79). The scene, however, is not impossible. To cut through the mud layer above the beams would not be a major problem and debris would not be a factor (Plummer 1896: 153). As long as Jesus remained calm, the action would proceed. The reference to the tiles has been explained as Luke's accommodating the description to his Greek audience; but this is not necessary. The term κέραμος can also mean clay, and Luke may be describing the removed lumps of clay with a word that also indicated their func-

27. The four terms are χωλός (lame), used fourteen times in the NT, six times in Luke–Acts (e.g., Luke 7:22; 14:13, 21); κυλλός (maimed), used four times in the NT (e.g., Matt. 15:30–31), not used by Luke; παραλυτικός (stricken with palsy, paralytic), used ten times in the NT (e.g., Matt. 4:24), not used by Luke; and παραλελυμένος (paralytic), a perfect passive participle of παραλύω, used five times in the NT, four of which are in Luke–Acts (Luke 5:18, 24; Acts 8:7; 9:33). See Van Der Loos 1965: 436 n. 3.

tion.[28] It is also suggested that tile roofs were used in ancient Palestine.[29] What is clear is that this man's friends went to great lengths to get him before Jesus. Not only did they clear the roof, they also had to rig a way to lower him. Obviously, Luke gives these details to underline their faith's persistent character. With this effort, the man gets to Jesus.

The reference to "before Jesus" (ἔμπροσθεν τοῦ Ἰησοῦ, *emprosthen tou Iēsou*) is very dramatic, trailing at the end of the verse. Now the man sits right before Jesus. The detail of the account leads the reader to identify with various figures in the story. What would Jesus do? How would the paralytic and his friends feel? What is the crowd thinking?

(3) Jesus' Response: Sins Are Forgiven (5:20)

Jesus responds with more than healing. All the Synoptics explain that Jesus sees the faith of the friends and addresses the paralytic. The help of others has aided this man (Liefeld 1984: 880). Faith (πίστις, *pistis*) is often mentioned by Luke, and this is its first mention in the Gospel (7:9, 50; 8:48, 50; 17:19; 18:42; Plummer 1896: 154; Fitzmyer 1981: 582–83). Faith in this context emerges clearly as the belief that Jesus can provide graciously to meet the paralytic's need. God's help can be found through him (Nolland 1989: 235). Turning to God for help means that he will reply. These men understand what Luke notes in 4:18. Jesus has God's power to heal. Just how much healing authority Jesus possesses they are about to discover. He has more than they bargained for.

5:20

Despite the aid and the notation about the faith of many, Jesus addressed only the ailing man. The vocative, ἄνθρωπε (*anthrōpe*, man), is not derogatory as it is in American English (Marshall 1978: 213). It is like saying "friend" (BAGD 68 §1aγ; BAA 135 §1aγ). Mark 2:5 and Matt. 9:2 have τέκνον (*teknon*, child or son). Luke is paraphrasing, perhaps for his audience, which either may not appreciate τέκνον as a term of affection or may mistakenly conclude that the man was a boy. Bovon (1989: 244) rightly prefers the latter explanation.

The man's sins are forgiven (ἀφέωνται, *apheōntai*), a key term in Luke. The passive voice indicates that God does the healing and forgiving (7:48), while the perfect tense emphasizes the state of forgiveness into which the paralytic enters through Jesus' declaration

---

28. Both BAGD 429 and BAA 872 define κέραμος in Luke 5:19 as "roof tile" (see their bibliographies for details); LSJ 940. Nonetheless, the meaning "clay" is possible, as in 2 Sam. 17:28 and *Shepherd of Hermas* 4.1.6 §22.

29. If so, the less natural lexical meaning is not necessary; Marshall 1978: 213; Kelso 1962: 544; Van Der Loos 1965: 441 n. 3.

(Danker 1988: 122; Fitzmyer 1981: 583). The significance of this statement is not lost on the professional theologians in the audience (5:21). The hope of 1:77–79 is beginning to be realized. Jesus is showing that his miraculous work carries a message about spiritual realities (Marshall 1978: 213).

It is not clear whether specific sin is in view in the healing or whether Jesus indicates that disease is a reflection of a fallen created order. Numerous texts in Judaism saw paralysis as the product of sin (1 Macc. 9:55; 2 Macc. 3:22–28; 3 Macc. 2:22; C. F. Evans 1990: 301). But John 9:2–3 shows that one should not be quick to make a one-to-one correspondence between specific, personal sin and disease. The general disorder of creation is more likely the point (Danker 1988: 122; Liefeld 1984: 880–81; Hendriksen 1978: 296).[30] What is clear is that Jesus claims to have the power and authority to reverse the unfortunate situation. The theme of forgiveness of sin or of accepting the spiritually needy is frequent in Luke and the emphasis is on who provides it, namely Jesus or God (5:29–32; 7:34, 36–50; 15:3–7, 11–32; 18:10–14; 19:8–10; 23:40–43).[31] The claim to forgive means that Jesus' ministry has taken on a greater significance. Jesus begins gradually to reveal what his ministry is all about.

(4) Official Reaction: Only God Can Do This (5:21)

5:21 Jesus' comment gains a reaction, especially since the man, for now, remains paralyzed before him. Luke here refers to γραμματεῖς (grammateis, scribes), a different term from that used in 5:17 for this same group of people. In the OT, scribes served as legal counselors (Ezra 7:6, 11; Neh. 8:1; Jer. 8:8; Fitzmyer 1981: 583). Their legal, scriptural training causes them to react to Jesus' statement theologically, correctly understanding Jesus' claim to be significant. But they reject the claim, the first of many such rejections. Matthew 9:3 briefly recounts their thinking with one statement: "This man is blaspheming." Mark 2:7 is very close to Luke, but he states their thinking with a question-statement-question format: "Why does this man speak thus? It is blasphemy. Who can forgive sins but God alone?"

---

30. Tiede 1988: 122 notes that to always associate disease with a specific sin can be cruel. In this text, the condition is present as evidence of the fallen state of the human race and the disorder in creation, which Jesus has come to put right again. Luke 13:1–5 is also against assuming a specific reference here. That sin is a general reality in the creation explains why creation groans until full redemption comes (Rom. 8:19–25). When James (5:16) calls for confession of sin in the face of sickness, he simply recognizes that sin may be involved (note the third-class condition in James 5:15; so also conceptually 1 Cor. 11:30). Illness may or may not be related to specific sin.

31. On the noun ἄφεσις, see Luke 1:77; 3:3; 4:18 (twice); 24:47; Acts 2:38; 5:31; 10:43; 13:38; 26:18.

Luke has two questions: "Who is this that speaks blasphemies? Who can forgive sin but God only?" The idea in all these passages is the same, with each writer summarizing events in his own way.[32] The leaders' questioning involves their private reflection. It is not an open, verbal objection, as the comment of the next verse about the attitude of their hearts makes clear (Plummer 1896: 155; Fitzmyer 1981: 584; Marshall 1978: 214; Schürmann 1969: 283 n. 28).

Blasphemy is a serious charge, one that will eventually become the basis of Jesus' conviction. It involves an overt defilement of the divine name, that is, abusive speech or action directed against God (Isa. 66:3; 1 Macc. 2:6; 2 Macc. 8:4; 10:34–36; Van Der Loos 1965: 445 n. 3; Beyer, *TDNT* 1:622; SB 1:1008–9; Bock 1994b: 184–86; see the exegesis of Luke 22:69). Conviction was punishable by death, which involved stoning in the OT (Lev. 24:10–16, 23). What exactly constituted blasphemy in the first century is uncertain. Some rabbinic materials that define blasphemy are slightly later than the NT period and have a narrow definition of the term, one not followed by other later rabbinic sources. The Mishnah's narrow definition requires that the divine name be used (*m. Sanh.* 7.5), while other materials suggest three possible ways to blaspheme: (1) speaking ill of the Torah (*Sipre* 112 on Num. 15:30 [= Neusner 1986: 2.168–70]), (2) engaging in idolatry (*Sipre* 112 on Num. 15:31 [= Neusner 1986: 2.170]), or (3) bringing shame on Yahweh's name (*b. Pesaḥ.* 93b). The point in all of these possible ways to blaspheme is that God's majesty is somehow violated.

Such a violation is what the leadership claims is present, as the next question shows. They see Jesus claiming a divine prerogative and therefore violating God's majesty by taking to himself something reserved for God. Forgiving sin is God's work only (μόνος, *monos*, is somewhat emphatic). Their reading of what Jesus is doing and claiming is largely correct, though there is some precedent for God's having an agent who communicates this forgiveness (Nathan in 2 Sam. 12:13 or the priests' sacrificial work; Godet 1875: 1.267; Marshall 1978: 214; Plummer 1896: 155; Ernst 1977: 193). However, forgiveness itself is the work of God (Exod. 34:6; Ps. 103:12; Isa. 1:18; 43:25; Jer. 31:34; Hendriksen 1978: 297).[33]

What probably causes the reaction is the directness of Jesus' claim, coupled with his lack of any official tradition or training. Jesus

32. This is a good example of three-way variation that clearly deals with the same event. The tradition about Jesus was preserved, but there was not an insistence that it always be verbally fixed. The thrust of what was said and thought was key in the preservation.

33. On Jewish views of forgiveness of sin, see Nolland 1989: 236, who notes key studies: Sjöberg 1938; Thyen 1970; Gradwohl 1974; and Klauck 1981.

introduces a theological tension into his ministry. Those who observe him must wrestle with who he is. He also fulfills the commission laid out in 4:18. Jesus' claim to perform God's role and have authority over God's prerogatives forces Jesus' (and Luke's) audience to a decision. A healing would be seen as an act of forgiveness by God, but it is another thing to claim to give that forgiveness directly (James 5:15; *b. Ned.* 41a; Ellis 1974: 104).[34] Jesus will repeat this "crime" in Luke 7:48–49. Even the use of the passive voice, which lays forgiveness at God's feet, does not prevent the sense that Jesus is too direct here.

(5) Explanation: The Son of Man's Authority (5:22–24)

5:22 Jesus is not unaware of the religious leaders' thinking. He knows their reasonings.[35] Jesus' ability to see the heart is an initial fulfillment of 2:35. Division comes to Israel, and Jesus knows his listeners' hearts. Mark 2:8 closely parallels Luke, except that Mark includes an additional reference to Jesus' knowing these things in his spirit (τῷ πνεύματι αὐτοῦ, *tō pneumati autou*).

What Jesus' insight reveals about him is a matter of debate. (1) Some argue for natural insight because Jesus has just observed the religious leaders' response. He is simply portrayed as perceptive (Fitzmyer 1981: 584; Luke 4:23; 6:8; 7:40; 9:47). (2) Others argue for prophetic understanding (Schneider 1977a: 134). (3) Still others hold that divine insight is alluded to here. Jesus reflects "divine knowledge" (Schürmann 1969: 283) or is revealing his divinity (Hendriksen 1978: 298). It is hard to be certain of the specific nature of the intention here. The theme's consistency in Luke suggests more than natural perception, as does the use of ἐπιγνούς (*epignous*), which means he "knew fully" their thoughts. At the least, Jesus operates like a prophet.[36] Jesus' description of his authority in 5:24 as tied to the Son of Man suggests someone who is more than a prophet. Jesus decides to challenge the Pharisees directly, having realized what they are thinking. He simply begins by asking why they should question him.

5:23 Jesus issues the challenge in language that is virtually the same in all three Gospels. Mark 2:9 has an additional phrase when he speaks

34. Forgiveness expressed as a passive (as in James 5:15: "he will be forgiven") shows that God does the forgiving. *B. Ned.* 41a reads, "No one gets up from his sickbed until all his sins are forgiven."

35. On διαλογισμός, see BAGD 186 §1; BAA 372 §1; Schrenk, *TDNT* 2:97 §B1. The term is often negative in the NT (Rom. 1:21; 1 Cor. 3:20; Mark 7:21; Matt. 15:19; Luke 2:35; 6:8; 9:47), with Rom. 14:1, where it means "reasoning," being the only neutral use of the term. Matt. 9:4 has a synonymous term: ἐνθύμησις.

36. Friedrich, *TDNT* 6:844 n. 400, notes that such ability was seen as prophetic by later Judaism.

of the man's taking up the mat (καὶ ἆρον τὸν κράβαττόν σου, *kai aron ton krabatton sou*), a detail that highlights the presence of a cure. Luke is often more concise than Mark. Each Gospel repeats Jesus' earlier statement in the exact words used originally, with Matt. 9:5 (9:2) matching Mark 2:9 (2:5), while Luke differs slightly. The renderings mean the same thing and are merely stylistic differences.

The question that Jesus raises is asked from the observer's perspective (Marshall 1978: 214; Schürmann 1969: 283): "What is easier to say?" Εὐκοπώτερον (*eukopōteron*) means "easier labor" (16:17; 18:25). The logic of the question is easy to follow: it is easier to say something that cannot be visually verified than to say something that can be visually substantiated. The easier claim from the observer's point of view is the claim to forgive sins, since one cannot prove it wrong![37] The issue is this: Is Jesus' claim an empty word or the real thing? Does Jesus' declaration of forgiveness have God's word and power behind it? In this way, Jesus links the healing tightly with the spiritual message he bears in his person. One will reveal the truth of the other, as he is about to show. Such a challenge shows that the miraculous character of Jesus' ministry was not a peripheral matter that could be easily discarded from the early church's portrait of Jesus. These works had a crucial function against the objector in substantiating Jesus' claims. The miracles also served as pictures of deeper spiritual realities. Material and spiritual realities could be compared to one another. Miracles put rejection into the "without excuse" category, since miracles provided divine attestation (Acts 2:22; 3:6, 17; 4:9; 10:38).[38]

5:24 Jesus places the miracle in the context of his own authority. The wording of the verse, with the unusual parenthetical break in the middle, is virtually identical in all three Gospels, which suggests a similar source (Hendriksen 1978: 301; Plummer 1896: 156). This is Luke's first use of the title *Son of Man* (ὁ υἱὸς τοῦ ἀνθρώπου, *ho huios tou anthrōpou*). Mark's first use of the title occurs in the parallel Mark 2:10; Matthew's first use is Matt. 8:20 (which is not parallel to this account), and his second use is 9:6 (= Luke 5:24).[39] Luke uses the title twenty-five times. The text is also unique, since it is the only

---

37. Tiede 1988: 122 compares the statement rhetorically with other such "easier" statements in 16:17 and 18:24–25. Common in Judaism, this kind of remark involves difficult comparisons and is to be pondered over. Jesus connects the two issues by his remarks and actions. The remarks make his miracle an audiovisual of a more basic spiritual reality.

38. Even when Peter graciously says that the nation acted in ignorance against Jesus (Acts 3:17), the miracles stand as testimony against those who rejected Jesus. In fact, Peter's speech in Acts 3 is a presentation of Jesus in light of a healing.

39. As noted in the introduction to this unit, Matt. 8–9 has some rearranging in it.

Son of Man saying tied directly to a miracle (as opposed to a summary passage that mentions miracles). The Aramaic background of this title, its character, and its importance in Jesus' ministry are discussed in detail in excursus 6.

Ὁ υἱὸς τοῦ ἀνθρώπου is Jesus' favorite way to refer to himself. Jesus eventually will reveal that the designation comes from Dan. 7:13–14, where the Son of Man is simply a human figure in contrast to the four beasts. Yet his authority, derived from the Ancient of Days, is extensive, since this figure rides on the clouds and brings vindication to the saints. All of this background emerges explicitly through Jesus' later use and development of the phrase, as argued in excursus 6. In Luke 5, Jesus simply introduces the cryptic designation, a term that in Aramaic can also be an idiomatic way to say either "me" or "someone." By his actions, Jesus reveals himself as the Son of Man and indicates the extent of the authority he possesses. If the paralytic walks, the miracle talks about the Son of Man's authority to forgive sin. If the Son of Man possesses such unique authority, then who is the Son of Man other than God's unique agent of salvation? That is the question that the miracle raises.

Jesus turns to the paralytic and gives him three commands: get up, take the mat, and go home. The man's being able to walk home attests to his healing, and it should cause the observer and the reader to reflect on what this healing says about Jesus and what Jesus' claim to have authority over sin really means. If God is the source of healing, what does this healing mean? Moreover, since God does not work through impostors or liars, what does this healing mean? The miracle's success narrows the options. It leaves the audience both of the event and of Luke's Gospel to ponder the appropriate conclusion.

ii. Healing and the Response (5:25–26)
(1) Healing: The Paralytic Departs with Joy (5:25)

5:25   The healing is narrated in a rather simple form. Though the wording of each Gospel differs, the message is the same: the paralytic got up and walked away. Both Luke and Mark note the immediacy of the healing. Luke 5:25 says he got up immediately (παραχρῆμα, *parachrēma* [Matthew twice, Mark never, Luke ten times]), while Mark 2:12 notes that he picked up his mat immediately (εὐθύς, *euthys* [Matthew five times, Mark forty-one times, Luke once]). Matthew 9:7 simply notes he went out to his house. The differences are a matter of style in summarizing. Each of the three commands given in Luke 5:24 is paralleled with a fulfillment in 5:25: the paralytic got up, took up his mat, and went to his home. Luke adds an additional note. As the formerly paralyzed man walks home, he is praising God. Luke often notes that with the saving action of God, there comes gratitude and joy (Luke 2:20; 4:15; 5:26; 7:16; 13:13; 17:15; 18:43; 23:47 [at the cross!]; Acts 4:21; 11:15–18; 21:20). God's saving work brings a song to one's heart.

(2) Crowd's Reaction: Praise and Awe (5:26)

5:26 Luke concludes the account with the crowd's response: amazement gripped them. Mark 2:12 has distinct but parallel language, which makes the same point.[40] The crowd gave God praise, a common Lucan note that is shared by all the Gospels at this point.[41] The audience was filled with awe, a reaction that Luke's readers should have as well (Schürmann 1969: 285; Marshall 1978: 217). Luke notes the crowd's comment about seeing παράδοξα (paradoxa, wonderful things), a common LXX word that appears only here in the NT.[42] The term also appears in Josephus's description of Jesus as performing surprising works (*Antiquities* 18.3.3 §§63–64; F. F. Bruce 1974: 36–41). In Matt. 9:8, the amazement centers on such authority being given to humans, a comment that suggests that the crowd did not get the event's uniqueness. They failed to see (or focus upon) Jesus' uniqueness. Luke's comment makes it clear that the unusual character of Jesus' ministry was noted. The events of today (σήμερον, *sēmeron*) were unusual. The crowd knew it was dealing with God's surprising presence. The positive implication in this remark means that people other than the leadership saw the event and took note. They may not have understood everything, but they could see that something was happening. Σήμερον recalls Luke 4:21 and is a note that Luke frequently makes (2:11; 13:32–33; 19:5, 9; 23:43). Jesus' present ministry means that God is doing something unique, and even today this crowd has had the privilege of seeing it.

Summary Luke 5:12–16 showed Jesus ministering to the rejected of society. Perhaps no one pictures this separation more than lepers. These people were isolated socially and physically so that others would not contract their contagious disease. Jesus' power overcomes the disease and reverses the man's condition. The healing is placed in a context of Jesus' willingness to cleanse. The man is to give testimony to God for his goodness through Jesus. The result is more crowds. As his ministry grows and enters into a new pub-

---

40. Mark reads ὥστε ἐξίστασθαι πάντας (so that they were all amazed). Matt. 9:8 speaks of the crowd's fear, as well as of their glorifying God.

41. Matt. 9:8 uses an aorist verb for glorify, while Luke 5:26 has an imperfect and Mark 2:12 a present infinitive.

42. Jdt. 13:13; Wis. 5:2; Sir. 43:25; 2 Macc. 9:24; 4 Macc. 2:14. Παράδοξος means something beyond belief or explanation; Kittel, *TDNT* 2:255.

lic phase, Jesus is found alone with God in prayer. The healing of the leper is but another evidence of Jesus' power and compassion. It points to a special time and to God's special agent. Just how special the time is will be seen in the controversy that his continuing ministry generates as the issue of his person emerges even more in the miracle that follows.

The healing of the paralytic in 5:17–26 is a turning point in Jesus' ministry, as Jesus measures his ministry in terms of forgiveness of sins. Accordingly, the healing takes on an additional importance beyond the mere reversal of physical ills. The paralytic's restoration shows that God is committed to Jesus' ministry. The healing substantiates Jesus' claims about the extent of his authority. The faith of the paralytic and his friends moves Jesus to act and exercise his authority on behalf of people who recognize their need.

But the event also represents a more ominous development as Luke describes the first official rejection of Jesus. The charge of blasphemy is raised, and the lines of opposition are forming. Decisions about Jesus are being made. The inexorable movement toward the cross is beginning as the Lucan "it is necessary" plays itself out in Jesus' ministry. Readers are confronted with the choice of how they will respond to God's agent, who has authority to forgive sins. Is he a blasphemer or is he sent from God with authority to forgive transgression? Would God support a fraud with such works? Or is someone else behind him? Is Jesus the one that God promised? This event forces such questions and does not permit anyone to sit on the fence about the answer.

Additional Notes

5:17. The reading οἳ ἦσαν ἐληλυθότες has the best manuscript distribution: B, C, L, W, Δ, Θ, Byz, Lect. ℵ and D omit the relative pronoun οἳ but differ between themselves.

5:17. The more difficult reading is αὐτόν as the subject of the infinitive ("in order that *he* might heal"); it is supported by ℵ, B, L, W, Ξ. However, the reading αὐτούς ("in order that he might heal *them*") has better manuscript support: A, C, D, Δ, Θ, Ψ, Byz, Lect, family 1, family 13, most Itala. It is hard to be sure which reading is original, but the sense is not greatly influenced by the decision. Either God's power enables Jesus to heal or God's power enables him to heal *others*.

3. Call of Levi and a Complaint (5:27–32)

Jesus' outreach to outcasts continues. But now he deals with the social outcast rather than the physically handicapped (Danker 1988: 125; Liefeld 1984: 883). The section focuses on Jesus' association with sinners, an association that he initiates. The action produces a negative response from the Pharisees and scribes, since they reject such fellowship with the unrighteous. The contrast between the separatism of these Jewish officials and the outreach of this single teacher is clear. Jesus' example teaches the church community that they need to seek and associate with the outcast as a part of their mission, even though there might be some who would frown on such personal relationships (Fitzmyer 1981: 589; Michel, *TDNT* 8:105; Luke 15:1–32; 19:1–10; 18:9–14 [for the contrast]; Matt. 20:13–16). Jesus has gone from forgiving sinners to openly associating with them. Mission requires more than casual contact. Jesus engages with those in the culture. They sense that he cares for them and does not just preach at them. Thus, this passage exposes the personal character of his mission.

An additional significant note is the change in the sinner. This idea, though only alluded to here, is still of great significance for Luke. Levi will leave all. Jesus asks for repentance (pictured in 5:31–32). The sick need healing and are made well by Jesus' ministry. Levi pictures such a transformation and represents the model disciple. Luke's description of Levi shows that discipleship is part of Jesus' goal in reaching out to the sinner.[1] Fitzmyer (1981: 588) notes eight differences between Luke and Mark.[2] But none of these differences, as shall be seen, are substantive, though Luke is able to emphasize discipleship and repentance through his unique material.

Sources and Historicity

The texts parallel to Luke 5:27–32 are Mark 2:13–17 and Matt. 9:9–13 (Aland 1985: §44). There are no additional written sources to appeal to be-

---

1. Levi's leaving all (5:28) and the note on repentance (5:32) are uniquely expressed by Luke.
2. For the two important unique Lucan features see n. 1. Others include the lack of a setting (cf. Jesus' moving along the sea in Mark 2:13), the absence of a reference to the son of Alphaeus (Mark 2:14), and Luke's being clear that Levi's banquet is for Jesus (Mark and Matthew simply speak of a banquet). Other differences are stylistic touches. Matthew's version is closer to Mark's than to Luke's.

sides the sources that stand behind the Synoptic accounts. Two events are in view here: Levi's call in Luke 5:27–28 is followed by a banquet where Jesus dines and fellowships with tax collectors and sinners in Luke 5:29–32. As noted in the chronological discussion at Luke 5:12–26, the later placement of the call and the meal in Matthew makes it likely that the call preceded the dinner by some break in time (Marshall 1978: 217–18 discusses the source issue as it relates to Mark; Matthew differs from both Mark and Luke here). However, the events' clear relationship to one another has caused all the Synoptics to place them side by side, though in two distinct time frames.

Levi's call and association with Jesus create a controversy between Jesus and the Pharisees about personal relationships. Jesus does not shy away from the opportunity to challenge social outcasts with the gospel of the kingdom and the call to discipleship. Jesus sees what looks bad to the Pharisees as an opportunity for significant healing and restoration. His ministry reconciles people to God and preaches peace to them (Acts 10:36–39).

The two parts of the passage display different forms. Luke 5:27–28 is a brief story about Jesus that is also a call narrative.[3] Bultmann (1963: 28) calls the Marcan parallel a biographical apophthegm, which means a pronouncement story. However, that no climactic teaching is present speaks against this classification (Fitzmyer 1981: 588).

Luke 5:29–32 is a pronouncement story that is also a controversy account.[4] Luke 5:31–32 also has a mission statement or an "I-saying." Fitzmyer (1981: 588–89) argues that the tradition's setting is a product of the early church, though the sayings themselves apparently are from Jesus. He notes that the shift of persons to the disciples in 5:30 shows that they are the real objects of complaint in the original tradition. In addition, the Pharisees' appearance at the meal is impossible and shows that the setting is a later product. The tradition, in his view, served as a polemic for the Palestinian church to defend their association with undesirables.

Interestingly, the Jesus Seminar is less skeptical about these sayings than they are about most of the other sayings up to this point in Luke (Funk and Hoover 1993: 284–85). On the basis of Jesus' challenge to disciples in 9:57–62, they question Jesus' call to be followed. But they misread that text as Jesus' refusing to have disciples. Surely Jesus called disciples (6:12–16; 9:23, 59; 18:22). The presence of disciples, especially figures like Peter, is too well attested at various source levels to be rejected. The Jesus Seminar accepts as likely (using pink type) the saying, comparing

---

3. Mark 1:16–20 and Luke 5:1–11 are two form parallels; Bovon 1989: 252; Berger 1984: 316 (discusses the parallel in Mark 2:14); V. Taylor 1935: 75. Schürmann 1969: 287 speaks of an apophthegm for the whole account, which combines a call with a controversy account.

4. Bultmann 1963: 18. Berger 1984: 80–81 speaks of a "Chrie," which is his category for apophthegm.

Jesus' work to that of a physician; they do so on the grounds of the saying's proverbial character. But they question (using gray type) the mission statement about Jesus' calling others to repentance. They regard it as too similar to 19:10 and the parables in chapter 15. But would Jesus engage in a controversial ministry of outreach without a rationale for doing so? These grounds are not sufficient to deny authenticity. The authenticity of such mission statements is well defended by Jeremias (1967: 166–67) and Van Iersel (1967: 223); see also the additional note on 5:31–32.

Fitzmyer's point that Luke 5:29–32 is a teaching message about the church's association with undesirables is correct, at least in part. The issue of association is a major theme. However, there is no need to question the setting's authenticity. The Pharisees are not attending the dinner; rather, they are grumbling about what they know about Jesus. Their apparent presence at the meal in 5:30 is a result of literary compression, as their reaction probably followed their learning about the meal.

In addition, the Pharisees' address of the disciples is natural enough. They may have feared taking on Jesus directly at this point, especially given his recent successes and their limited exposure to the teacher. The approach to the disciples is one of timidity and does not indicate an original early church setting. The tradition about Jesus is full of his association with what the Pharisees saw as reprobates. The sayings relate directly to that tension. One suspects that an unwarranted assumption is creeping into the analysis, that is, that an unmixed form was the original form. However, traditional reflection may have put together these two distinct events into a sequence, an association that was natural, given the relationship of the events.[5] These events are historical. The sayings fit the occasion, revealing a key emphasis in Jesus' ministry.

The outline of Luke 5:27–32 is as follows:

a. Call of Levi (5:27–28)
    i. Jesus calls Levi to follow him (5:27)
    ii. Levi leaves all to follow Jesus (5:28)
b. Controversy over association and mission (5:29–32)
    i. Dinner with tax collectors and sinners (5:29)
    ii. Controversy: Jesus' company (5:30)
    iii. Reply: Jesus is called to the sick and the sinner (5:31–32)

Several themes are key. Jesus associates compassionately with the outcast in need, despite the impression this gives to outsiders. Such association is necessary because Jesus' mission is to call the

---

5. That Matthew differs in placement from Luke and Mark speaks for this conclusion. The events were tightly linked, but where to speak of them, at the time of the call or the time of the meal, was left open to choice.

outcast to be healed. He offers an accepting hand, while calling on them to turn to God. Levi pictures a called outcast, who in turn leads others to hear Jesus. The Pharisees and scribes picture those who are too concerned about separation to reach out to those in need. It is clear that their approach to mission comes in for rebuke by Jesus' remark.

Association with outcasts is a part of outreach. Jesus sees in the outcast an opportunity for God to show his grace. He extends to Levi the chance for fellowship with God. He communicates that, like any sinner, Levi can have a walk with God. In contrast, the Pharisees want nothing to do with these sinners. How do those who associate with Jesus view those who do not know his message? Isolation from sinners is not the call of the disciple. Jesus rejects the approach of the Jewish leadership to this question. Engagement, willingness to associate with sinners, and offering them hope are the role of the one who follows Jesus. There is also an awareness that spiritual and emotional healing can be offered to such people. They are accepted first as people, as the challenge and invitation to walk with God come. In fact, God's invitation to experience his grace can be offered only to those who realize that they are sinners in need of God's help. Everyone experiences God's healing grace the same way—because they realize they need it, not because they earn it through their own merit. Before God, all stand equally in need (Rom. 3:9–31).

Exegesis and Exposition

²⁷And after these things he went out and observed a tax collector named ⌜Levi⌝, who was seated at the tax office, and said to him, "Follow me." ²⁸And leaving all, Levi arose and was following him.

²⁹And Levi prepared a great feast for him in his home; and there was a large company of tax collectors and others reclining at the table with them. ³⁰And the Pharisees and their scribes were grumbling to the disciples, saying, "Why do you eat and drink with tax collectors and sinners?" ³¹And Jesus replied to them, "Those who are well do not have a need for a physician, but those who are sick. ³²I have not come to invite the righteous but sinners to repentance."

a. Call of Levi (5:27–28)
i. Jesus Calls Levi to Follow Him (5:27)

5:27   Luke describes Levi's call. With more detail at this point, Mark 2:13 notes that this event followed a teaching setting and occurred as Jesus passed beside the sea. Luke often lacks such details about the setting. As Jesus goes along, he spots Levi. Ἐθεάσατο (*etheasato,* looked at, observed) indicates that Jesus consciously singles this man out.[6] It is no accident that Jesus selects Levi. Jesus shows the type of person to whom he wishes to minister and to whom he wishes to show God's way. Jesus takes the initiative with the rejected. The action takes into account that tax collectors were held in the lowest esteem (see the exegesis of 3:12). Levi is called a τελώνης (telōnēs), which is not a chief tax collector (ἀρχιτελώνης, architelōnēs) like Zacchaeus (19:2), but a lower-level tax collector who would have reported to someone like Zacchaeus. He was one of the men at the tax booth who collected the levy as people traveled from city to city. The controversy this call will produce is no accident, since the conscious selection of this man challenges all cultural views of who is the potential object of God's mercy.

Matthew 9:9 calls this tax collector Matthew. Since at least the days of Origen in the third century, there has been debate whether Levi and Matthew are the same person (Plummer 1896: 158; Fitzmyer 1981: 590; the gnostic Heracleon [in Clement of Alexandria, *Stromata* 4.9] and Origen, *Against Celsus* 1.62, distinguish Levi and Matthew). Two factors lead many to equate these two names: (1) the detailed agreement between Luke's and Matthew's accounts and (2) the inclusion on the list of the Twelve of only one tax collector (Matt. 10:3). Others argue that two figures are present. Pesch (1968a) suggests that the Levi story is used in Matthew's Gospel but that the name Matthew is substituted for Levi, so that the story can be about one of the Twelve.[7] This approach is not likely since many figures in the first century had double names.[8] Godet (1875: 1.271) suggests that Levi was given the name Matthew by Jesus, while Hendriksen (1978: 302) argues that he had the double name all along. There is

6. Mark 2:14 and Matt. 9:9 have εἶδεν. Luke's term, also found in Luke 7:24 and 23:55, is more intense than the other Synoptics. Matthew uses θεάομαι four times, Mark twice, and Luke three times. Its presence seems to reflect Luke's conscious choice of wording.

7. Matthew never mentions Levi, while Mark 2:14, agreeing with Luke, calls this man Levi. Mark 2:14 gives the fullest name, calling him Levi son of Alphaeus. James son of Alphaeus is listed with the Twelve in Matt. 10:4; Mark 3:18; Luke 6:15; Acts 1:13 (see the exegesis of 6:15). In addition, Mark's list of the Twelve has Matthew, not Levi. These factors have produced the discussion. Strathmann, *TDNT* 4:234, calls Mark's description of the name more accurate, but it is unclear why this contrast to the other Synoptics is necessary. What is present are alternative names for the same person. Mark simply has more detail.

8. Carson 1984: 223–24, in critique of Pesch's view. Fitzmyer 1981: 590 is uncommitted, though he appears to lean toward equating the two names, calling two names "theoretically possible," while noting the debate of the early church. For examples of double names, see Acts 1:23; 12:25; 13:9; double Semitic names include Joseph Barnabas (Acts 4:36) and Joseph Caiaphas (Josephus, *Antiquities* 18.2.2 §35).

no way to answer this subquestion about the name's origin. However, there is no need to challenge the names used in the accounts.

Jesus issues Levi a call to follow him. Other such calls occur in Luke 9:23, 59; 18:22. The account runs similar to 5:10–11, except for the mention of an additional promise. There, Peter receives a promise that he will share in Jesus' mission of seeking people. In contrast, Jesus asks Levi simply to join his cause. But these are really the same request.

ii. Levi Leaves All to Follow Jesus (5:28)

5:28 Levi accepts Jesus' invitation. Great commitment is expressed with amazing brevity: Levi leaves all and follows Jesus. Luke alone notes that he leaves everything behind.[9] For Luke, discipleship means a priority commitment to Jesus, which is what Levi's leaving the tax booth describes.[10] The call of Jesus has taken priority over the old vocation.

Some see a problem in the "leaving all" language. How could Levi leave his job and still throw the elaborate dinner of the following verses? Fitzmyer (1981: 589) notes that asking this question undermines the story, since it does not address such issues (his literary point is correct). However, the event need not be out of character with the later action. One does not know if Levi was an efficient man with his share of the tax revenue. That such a question is raised reveals excessive skepticism. There is no rule that says a tax collector must be a financial fool with his earnings. What is clear is that after meeting Jesus and receiving a call from him, Levi puts his relationship and responsiveness to Jesus first.

b. Controversy over Association and Mission (5:29–32)
i. Dinner with Tax Collectors and Sinners (5:29)

5:29 Levi holds a feast with Jesus as the honored guest. The phrase ἐποίησεν δοχὴν μεγάλην (epoiēsen dochēn megalēn, he made a great feast) occurs in the LXX.[11] Only Luke explicitly refers to a feast. Levi takes his call seriously and opens up his home to his friends to introduce them to Jesus. As in Mark 2:15 and Matt. 9:10, the reference is clearly to Levi's home. Mark's language is a little more ambiguous

9. Luke 14:33 has a similar phrase. The parallels of Matt. 9:9b and Mark 2:14b are otherwise virtually identical. Luke uses a vivid imperfect tense, which he prefers, instead of the aorist of Matt. and Mark to say that Levi "followed" Jesus. Note also Mark 1:18, 20; 14:50; and Luke 5:11; Schürmann 1969: 288 n. 9.

10. Bammel, *TDNT* 6:907 n. 203, notes that those who fail to leave all behind fail to be in the inner circle.

11. Gen. 21:8; 26:30; Esth. 1:3; 1 Esdr. 3:1; see also Luke 14:13. Δοχή refers to a meal given with hospitality: "a banquet"; Grundmann, *TDNT* 2:54.

than Luke's as to who is the host; but the need to insert a specific reference to Jesus in Mark 2:15 shows that Jesus' own home is not in view (correctly Godet 1875: 1.272; Plummer 1896: 160; Creed 1930: 81; incorrectly Leaney 1958: 126). Luke often likes to mention events at meals (7:36–50; 9:10–17; 10:38–42; 11:37–54; 14:1–24; 19:1–10; 22:7–38; 24:29–32, 41–43; Danker 1988: 125). The table is a place where spiritual points are made and fellowship occurs. Levi seeks to use his home and resources to bring the message of Jesus to his friends.

The issue is not the party, but who is invited to it. Luke speaks of a large company of tax collectors and others, identified as sinners by the Pharisees in 5:30.[12] Luke lets the Pharisees make the full charge against Jesus and his disciples. Levi has gone to great trouble to bring Jesus to many who might not normally be expected to have contact with a religious dignitary. The turnout is clearly not the moral upper crust of society. Nevertheless, Jesus reclines with them in meal fellowship. In doing so, he is carrying out his ministry to the spiritually needy. At the same time, Jesus offends the separatism of the Pharisees, who would have never shared a meal with such rabble.[13]

ii. Controversy: Jesus' Company (5:30)

The official response to the meal occurs some time after the event **5:30** when the Pharisees and their scribes approach the disciples with a question. That this encounter comes after the party is clear, because the Pharisees would not have come to such a party, as their question shows, even in the unlikely event that they had been invited (Marshall 1978: 220; Tiede 1988: 128). The appearance that the leaders are near or at the party is a result of literary compression.

---

12. Matt. 9:10 and Mark 2:15 are explicit from the start about tax collectors and sinners.

13. Liefeld 1984: 883–84. E. Sanders 1985: 174–211 connects the idea of sinners to those who charge interest against the command of Lev. 25:36–38 and argues that, whoever they are, not all of them are "common people." He sees Jesus' offense as offering sinners hope of God without requiring the legal restitution that Judaism asked for from sinners. If later Jewish materials are a help in understanding the Jewish attitude, the view was that such sinners would have used their money or their bodies for immoral purposes: Tg. Onq. Gen. 13:13; t. Dem. 3.4–9 (= Neusner 1977–86: 1.88–89); SB 1:498–99. On a difference of opinion within Judaism about association with "common people," see m. Dem. 2.2–3. This last text shows that clean food was also a key concern. Not every religious Jew would have been disturbed by Jesus' effort, but some clearly would have been. Table fellowship, along with clean and unclean food, would be a key concern to some of Jewish background. Appeal may have come from a broad reading of Lev. 10:10. As the rest of the passage makes clear, Jesus does not ignore the need to turn to God (Luke 5:32), but he emphasizes God's grace and its availability to help as the first step, rather than as a later result.

The leaders wish to register a complaint. The verb chosen, ἐγόγ-γυζον (*egongyzon*, were grumbling), is a graphic, emotive verb whose pronunciation sounds like the action. One can almost hear the grumbling described by ἐγόγγυζον. Luke reserves this word group (γογγύζω and διαγογγύζω) for complaints about Jesus' relationship to outsiders (15:2; 19:7; Schweizer 1984: 111; Rengstorf, *TDNT* 1:733 §C1). It was also used in the OT to describe Israel's complaining against God in the desert, so that often the term describes inappropriate grumbling (Exod. 15:24; 16:7–8; Num. 14:2, 26–35; 16:11; 17:6, 20). In Judaism, some grumbling was wise (Sir. 31:24, grumbling about injustice in the distribution of food), while other grumbling was unwise (Sir. 10:25, grumbling about a wise ruler).

In Luke, the complaint attacks Jesus indirectly by aiming at the disciples, while Mark 2:16 and Matt. 9:11 complain only about Jesus. In addition, only Luke mentions both eating and drinking with undesirables, slightly intensifying the charge. When Luke speaks of Jesus' and his disciples' association with tax collectors and sinners, the charge is expanded in its natural direction, since Jesus *and* the disciples engaged in this behavior. The Pharisees' complaint was with Jesus, but they also questioned anyone who had such associations.

The problem in their view is not mere contact with sinners, but table fellowship that seeks out and welcomes these people. As Jesus' reply in 5:32 makes clear, ἁμαρτωλῶν (*hamartōlōn*, sinners) refers to a wide group of people, including the potentially impious, like tax collectors. In other words, it refers to any who need to be healed and not only to the worst sinners in the harshest possible sense. The judgment by the Pharisees is not necessarily harsh. It may accurately describe these people, but for Jesus, recovery is the issue, not quarantine.[14] The Pharisees regard the disciples' and Jesus' association with such people as inappropriate for any religious leader. Luke 7:34, 36–50 and 15:1–32 also treat the theme of associating with sinners, explaining why Jesus does so (Ernst 1977: 198).

As noted, Luke alone mentions drinking alongside eating, which strengthens the complaint. The issue of eating and drinking is a frequent charge against Jesus in Luke (5:33; 7:33–34; Marshall 1978: 220). Thus, both additional details about the disciples and about drinking are unique to Luke, expand the charge in scope, and heighten it in tone.[15] Jesus extends an acceptance that the Pharisees reject, especially since Jesus is taking the initiative. In the Pharisees'

---

14. Strathmann, *TDNT* 4:235; Luce 1933: 134; Fitzmyer 1981: 591; Schürmann 1969: 289–90; Völkel 1978; Jeremias 1931; E. Sanders 1985: 174–211.

15. This point is true regardless of what one believes the original order of the Gospels was, since Matthew and Mark both lack these details.

judgment, he reclines with those to whom he should respectfully decline fellowship.

Some argue that the table fellowship of the early church is the issue here, even the Lord's Supper, which, it is argued, is the event suggested by the meal with Jesus. The question would be, "Who is worthy of this meal?" But the association with the Lord's table, though an implication of the passage, is not what is directly in view, since an attendee at the Lord's table would be a believer who is already forgiven, an insider (1 Cor. 11:17–22, 27–34). What Luke makes clear is that outsiders should be invited to become "insiders." A direct connection to the Lord's table is too narrow an approach. This suggestion reflects an effort to press for a setting in the early church for these traditions. The accounts may have implications for the early church, but this approach does not explain the origin of these traditions.

Also to be rejected is the view of Walker (1978) that Jesus was not as close to these groups as the texts suggest.[16] As Carson (1984: 160) keenly observes, Walker makes an either/or choice out of a both/and situation. Jesus associated with sinners *and* condemned all sin— their sin as well as the sins of others. Jesus aggressively formed relationships that would help lay the basis of an acceptance from which the challenge about lifestyle could be made.

Thus, the issue is the scope of Jesus' mission and the focus of the disciples' concern, not table fellowship in the church. Disciples should seek the lost and relate to them in a way that allows the offer of God's grace to be extended to them. If Jesus sought to save the lost (19:10), how much more should his followers?

iii. Reply: Jesus Is Called to the Sick and the Sinner (5:31–32)

Jesus responds in wording that is virtually identical in all three Gospels. The only difference is that Mark 2:17 and Matt. 9:12 have οἱ ἰσχύοντες (*hoi ischyontes*, the strong), instead of Luke's οἱ ὑγιαίνοντες (*hoi hygiainontes*, the healthy), but the meaning is virtually synonymous.[17] Luke's reference to the healthy fits with the picture of Jesus as a physician, helping those in need.

5:31

---

16. Walker suggests that openness and challenge of sin cannot be put side by side. He opts for the challenge to sin.

17. Schürmann 1969: 291 n. 28 notes that Mark and Matthew reflect an Aramaism with οἱ ἰσχύοντες. If so, the alteration of wording is Luke's rendering of the figure. The other difference is that Matt. 9:12 and Mark 2:17 agree against Luke in their introductions to Jesus' saying: "and hearing, Jesus/he said," versus Luke's "and replying, Jesus said to them." All the Synoptic writers use ἰσχύω (Matthew four times, Mark four times, Luke eight times in his Gospel and six times in Acts), but Luke is the only Gospel writer to use ὑγιαίνω (Luke 5:31; 7:10; 15:27). Two of Luke's three uses have Synoptic parallels.

The reply adopts the Pharisees' perspective, and there is a note of sarcasm in it, as the later account of 18:11–14 shows. Jesus' reply shows that he is not seeking direct confrontation, because he keeps his answer solely in terms of the sinners' need and does not yet criticize the Pharisees explicitly (Danker 1988: 126). Danker notes the later comment of Greek philosopher Antisthenes: "Doctors associate with the sick but do not contract fevers" (Diogenes Laertius 6.6 [A.D. third century]). Jesus probably uses well-known proverbial imagery.[18] Jesus seeks out those in need who sense their position before God. The Pharisees, as the "healthy," are not prepared to be treated for something they do not recognize as diseased. As the following verse makes clear, Jesus' remarks have a metaphorical, ethical thrust (Mark 2:17; Matt. 5:45; Luke 15:7; Schrenk, *TDNT* 2:189; Preisker, *TDNT* 4:717). The tax collectors and sinners have no physical ills, but they need another kind of cure.[19]

5:32 Jesus elaborates on his physician remark with a description of his mission. Such mission declarations are common (Luke 7:34; 12:49, 51; 18:8; 19:10; Mark 1:38; 10:45; Matt. 5:17; 20:28; J. Schneider, *TDNT* 2:668; Fitzmyer 1981: 592). Ἐλήλυθα (elēlytha, I have come) shows his attitude about the mission and can have the force of a present tense ("I am come"; Fitzmyer 1981: 592; this is the only mission text to use the first person with the perfect tense of ἔρχομαι). Jesus' mission is not to the "righteous," but to sinners. Such concern for sinners is the burden of the Luke 15 parables as well.

The object of the mission—repentance—makes clear why this is so. The righteous cannot repent, but sinners can. There is a tight link between this and the previous verse. The healthy are the righteous and allude to the Pharisees' picture of themselves, while the sick and the sinners are those to whom Jesus seeks to minister. The remark is rhetorical and reflects the Pharisees' perspective. It is not an endorsement of their righteousness. Jesus goes to those who perceive their needs and he seeks to meet them. The point is not that the Pharisees are "justified" already, so that Jesus will leave them alone, but that they are not open to their own need of a physician, so he

18. Jewish imagery includes Isa. 3:7; Jer. 8:22; 2 Chron. 16:12; Sir. 10:10; and esp. Sir. 38:1–15 (a fascinating text that thanks God for doctors and medicine, while also calling for prayer and sacrifice); Bovon 1989: 259 n. 24. Note Luke 4:23 for another use of physician imagery. In the list above, positive physician imagery occurs in the Isaiah, Jeremiah, and Sir. 38 texts. Isaiah and Jeremiah allude to the image of the physician as a figure for the leader who heals.

19. Matt. 9:13 at this point uniquely adds an allusion to Hos. 6:6. Mark and Luke lack it perhaps because the allusion would not be clearly perceived by their Greek audience.

cannot appeal to them nor can he heal them. That they are not justified before God becomes very clear later in Luke's account, in Luke 11–13 (esp. 11:37–52).

The end of the passage includes a note that only Luke has: the call to sinners is for repentance.[20] Matthew 9:13 and Mark 2:17 speak only of calling sinners, but the point is the same. Luke is simply more explicit. Jesus accepts the sinner as a person who needs God and who can approach him, given the right frame of mind. However, Jesus' goal is to transform the sinner's way of thinking about life, as well as the way the sinner relates to God. Repentance, as noted, is a key Lucan theme and refers basically to a change of mind, a shift of view (3:3, 8; 13:1–5; 15:7, 10; 16:30; 17:3–4; 24:47). Luke 24:46–47 shows that the roots of repentance reach back to the OT. The change of mind involves not just Jesus but an embracing of God that changes one's orientation in life, like the OT concept of turning (שׁוּב, šûb; see the exegesis of 3:3). Repentance is part of Jesus' and the apostles' gospel message. Indeed, Acts includes many summary calls to repent: Paul describes his gospel message in these terms (Acts 26:20), and one responds to his call with faith (26:18). Such turning to God brings one into light (26:18, 23).

Luke also makes explicit what the call to sinners requires. The sinner is challenged to look at things in a way that is pleasing to God. What is involved in this change of mind, in reorienting oneself to God on his terms? Jesus challenges people to respond to God with humble openness before him about what their previous behavior means. They must know that it renders them guilty before God and places them in need. But Jesus also proclaims the possibility of finding forgiveness and God's grace by coming honestly, openly, and humbly to him. Those who recognize they are "sick" come to the Great Physician, Jesus, so he can exercise his power to heal and change them.

The perspective here is very similar to the contrastive parable of Luke 18:9–14, where the attitudes of a Pharisee and a tax collector are compared. The "sinner," the tax collector, comes out better; the tax collector called on God to have mercy on him a sinner, and Jesus says that the tax collector walked away from his prayer justified. Just as 5:32 is unique to Luke, so is the parable in 18:9–14. The two texts show how one in need can humbly come to God. For Luke, the spiritually sick coming for spiritual healing is a fundamental portrait of genuine repentance.

Thus, the physician imagery of 5:31–32 shows that we must recognize our need to be "treated." This type of humble openness to

---

20. Only Luke explicitly mentions repentance. Mark 2:17 and Matt. 9:13 are very similar otherwise. On repentance, see Behm, *TDNT* 4:1001–2 §E.II.2.

God for healing is what Jesus will commend in the tax collector of Luke 18. A repentant heart is open, not closed, to God. The physician seeks to call people to see themselves honestly, as they really are. They are ready to let God work on them. This willingness to rest in God and have him enter one's life is the essence of repentance. The Pharisees' attitude prevents this type of work from being done on them. So, Jesus goes where an opportunity for response exists. Spiritual restoration and healing can be accomplished only where the acceptance of "illness" is present. These tax collectors and sinners come to the table in the clinic, and the Physician is not about to reject their response.

Summary

In Luke 5:27–32, Jesus shows the universal scope of his ministry: he reaches out to all types of people. When one looks back at 4:31–5:32, one sees a variety of people who have received the benefits of Jesus' labor: the demon-possessed are exorcised; the sick are restored; the fishermen find a great catch, only to be invited to cast a new kind of net; the leper is cleansed; the paralyzed rise; the tax collector is called; the sinners are invited; and, last of all, paradoxically, the Pharisees stand in shock. In all of this activity, Jesus Christ's authority stands out, as it sits in judgment over the spirit world, disease, and most importantly sin and humanity. But how will this message go out? Can those in need really come to Jesus? Or will they need to be cleansed first, as the Jewish leadership suggests?

In this event, Jesus showed that his mission is not accomplished by separatism. Jesus will not wait for sinners. He will seek them out. He will accept them as persons; but he will challenge sinners to meet the God who can bind up wounds and bring them back to health.

Some may be startled at the ministry's openness. They may react that such associations taint the teacher's credentials and raise questions about his spiritual integrity. But what Jesus' actions show is the extent of his compassion and the depth of God's grace. The Physician seeks out the sick and calls them into the hospital room of God's care. In the context of personal acceptance, they may begin to listen, open up to God, and find the way to spiritual health. What Luke wishes his readers to see is that a gracious door of care is offered to all. Sinners are asked to sense their need. Thus, the mission extends to all and takes the initiative in seeking them out. It takes an open door to create open hearts. It is that openness that Jesus exemplifies in his willingness to risk ridicule and associate with sinners. Should not his disciples do likewise?

Additional Notes

5:27. In agreement with Mark 2:14, Levi's identification as son of Alphaeus is found in manuscript D and the Gospel of Peter 14.60. Manuscript D also provides a setting for the account: Jesus is walking by the sea (cf. Mark 2:13). The longer reading of D is not sufficiently attested; rather, it brought Luke into verbal agreement with Mark, perhaps because Mark is the most detailed.

5:31–32. Pesch (1970c) argues that 5:31 and 5:32 were originally separate in the earliest tradition, because 5:31 does not answer the Pharisees' question. He also argues (pp. 74–75) that other pronouncement stories do not end with two pronouncements, so that Luke's unique ending becomes suspect. But such a separation is not necessary. As noted, 5:31 sets up 5:32, which is relevant to the complaint, so that what is present is really one intertwined pronouncement. Even if two sayings were present, Pesch overapplies form methodology, since many individual NT passages do not fit entirely the ideal description of the form to which they belong. Thus, Pesch's approach is to be rejected. The original saying was a unit.

4. Rise of Opposition:
Three Controversies (5:33–6:11)

The opposition against Jesus becomes more resolute in Luke 5:33–6:11, which contains three pericopes that raise the tension between Jesus and the Pharisees.

The first controversy emerges from a question about fasting (5:33–39). This discussion leads Jesus to declare that a new era is present and that many in the old order will not respond to it. This is followed by two Sabbath controversies. The first has to do with plucking grain on the Sabbath; the Pharisees again register a broad complaint against Jesus and the disciples (6:1–5). Jesus' reply underlines his authority, even over something as sacred as the Sabbath. The new order is asserting itself. In the second controversy, Jesus takes the initiative by healing a man with a withered hand on the Sabbath (6:6–11). He knows that the Pharisees are watching him as he comes into the synagogue; yet, he acts with instant compassion just the same.

The three parts of 5:33–6:11 show their unity not only by sharing the issue of controversy but by concluding with the note that the scribes and Pharisees discussed what they might do to Jesus. Thus, in the space of three short events the opposition moves from mere protest to a resolve to stop Jesus. Luke has now recounted five consecutive controversies: Jesus' claim to forgive sins (5:17–26) and his openness in eating with sinners (5:27–32) were not his only provocative activities; now we learn that he does not fast (5:33–39), that his disciples pluck grain on the Sabbath (6:1–5), and that he heals on the Sabbath (6:6–11). Jesus' authority creates a reaction and meets with rejection.[1]

Sources and Historicity (5:33–39)

All the Gospels place the controversy over fasting immediately after the meal at the tax collector's home (Luke 5:33–39 = Mark 2:18–22 = Matt. 9:14–17; Aland 1985: §45). The issue of its placement is made complex by Matt. 9:18, where this teaching is tied temporally to the healing of Jairus's daughter, an event that is somewhat later in Mark and Luke (Mark 5:21–43 = Luke 8:40–56). Hendriksen (1978: 307) fully discusses this po-

---

1. Although each pericope could be discussed separately, I introduce them here consecutively so that the overall unit remains clear.

sitioning and suggests that the Matthean placement seems more precise, with Mark and Luke moving this event up because topically and logically it is associated with issues of Jesus' practice. These issues were first made public at the meal at Levi's house, so Mark and Luke associated the later events with that catalyst event. If this placement is correct, as seems likely, then each Gospel engaged in some topical arranging in its sections on Jesus' early ministry. Matthew 8–9, Luke 5:1–6:17, and Mark 2:1–3:6 basically proceed in chronological sequence, but each has rearranged some events because of their conceptual associations, rather than for purely sequential reasons.[2] Each writer exercised his own judgment as to when to arrange his account along more topical lines, but traces of the chronological arrangement are often left clear by notes in a given Gospel.

The Gospel accounts of the question about fasting are very similar, but still some differences remain. The following list of the key differences is based on Fitzmyer 1981: 594–95 and Marshall 1978: 222–23:

1. Luke includes or at least suggests that the Pharisees participated in the questioning.
2. Luke alone ties prayer to the fasting issue.
3. Like Matt. 9:15, Luke 5:34 relates a shortened form of the wedding image reply.
4. Luke alone calls the final verses parabolic.
5. Like Matthew, Luke has no allusion to the fasting practice of others before the event, in contrast to Mark 2:18.
6. Luke 5:35 speaks of *days* when fasting will occur, while Mark 2:20 speaks of a *day* of fasting, a remark that is clearly intended nonetheless to refer to a period of time, as the plural at the beginning of Mark 2:20 makes clear.
7. Luke 5:33 alone speaks of eating and drinking as the issue, a remark that alludes back to 5:30.
8. Luke 5:36b refers to "a patch cut out of a new garment," a variation of Mark 2:21 ("a piece of unshrunk cloth").
9. Luke 5:39 is a proverb unique to Luke's version.

None of these differences significantly alter the basic portrayal of the event, but they do allow Luke to make additional points, as well as to make some clearer associations with earlier events. The differences lead some to suggest that Luke had access to additional material, either oral or written (Marshall 1978: 222; Schramm 1971: 105–11; against this except for 5:39 is Fitzmyer 1981: 595). In addition, the few cases of Matthew's and Luke's standing together in agreement against Mark are interesting for those who

2. Other rearrangements may be found in 4:16–30; 5:12–26; and 6:12–16. For details, see the introductions to these units.

favor Marcan priority.[3] Later allusions to the event are found in the Gospel of Thomas 104, 47b–c.[4]

The authenticity of some of the sayings is questioned, especially Luke 5:34–35, because it assumes Jesus' death so early in his ministry.

The Jesus Seminar (Funk and Hoover 1993: 285–87) rates the verses differently: 5:34 (pink); 5:35 (black); 5:36 (gray); 5:37–39a (pink); and 5:39b (black), thus indicating that some of the teaching goes back to Jesus (5:34, 37–39a), while much does not (5:35–36, 39b). They reject Jesus' allusion to his death (5:35) for the reason noted above. They reject 5:39b because Jesus is in effect contradicting the common proverb that older is better (Sir. 9:10 is noted as an example). But Jesus' twist on the normal use of an ancient expectation is typical of his teaching (e.g., his positive use of Samaritans in 10:29–37 or the characteristic twists in his parables). Thus the reversal of the normal ancient-young imagery in 5:39 coheres with Jesus' teaching. His combative engagement of traditionalism is precisely the kind of issue that would have sparked opposition. Something must have caused the officials' rejection of Jesus, and dialogues like this one are a good candidate for explaining their rejection.

In addition, two factors argue against any skepticism about Jesus' foreseeing his departure. First, the real, historical position of the event probably comes slightly later, so we may be further along in the historical sequence of events. Second, the rising tide of the opposition surely left Jesus aware of the possibility that his ministry might be accomplished in his absence, through a forced departure (Marshall 1978: 223; Schürmann 1973). Marshall notes that the absence of fasting was not an issue that the early church would seek to defend, since in fact it fasted (e.g., Acts 13:2–3). Jesus' remark is dissimilar to Jewish and church practice. The Jesus Seminar (Funk and Hoover 1993: 48) speaks of the early church's reverting back to the old practice. But if the early church was as creative in altering the tradition as the Jesus Seminar claims, why did it retain the saying unless it was authentic? If changes were so readily made, why keep a record of Jesus' difference? This setting would not have been created to explain church practice. The sayings are authentic.

Sources and Historicity (6:1–5)

The exact chronological placement of the disciples plucking grain (Luke 6:1–5 = Mark 2:23–28 = Matt. 12:1–8; Aland 1985: §46) is difficult to determine, more because of Matthew than Mark. Luke's sequence parallels Mark's in that this event and the healing of the man with the withered hand follow the fasting issue. The succeeding event in Mark 3:7–12 is a summary

---

3. Fitzmyer 1981: 595 attempts to explain these agreements; but their presence suggests the complexity of the source problem.

4. In the Gospel of Thomas 47b–c, the Synoptic order is reversed.

of Jesus' ministry, followed by the choosing of the Twelve in Mark 3:13–19a. Luke reverses the order of those two pericopes, placing the choosing (Luke 6:12–16) before the summary (Luke 6:17–19). A general topical order is being followed in each Gospel, and each writer chooses when to summarize Jesus' ministry.

But the problem of placement of the grain-plucking incident is made difficult by Matthew's positioning. Matthew has the disciples plucking grain (Matt. 12:1–8) after the gathering of the Twelve (Matt. 10:1–4), whereas Mark and Luke both have it before that event (Mark 3:13–19a = Luke 6:12–16). It is quite possible that this Matthean gathering of the Twelve is a topical arrangement whereby he associates the choosing of the Twelve with their sending. Nonetheless, the problem of the relative position of this grain-plucking incident remains.

It is clear that all the Gospels have engaged in some topical rearranging; but where is this grain incident to be placed in terms of Jesus' general ministry? By introducing the next event with the comment that it occurred on a different Sabbath (6:6), Luke is the only Gospel to put a chronological note on either event. Plummer (1896: 165) makes no choice, being content simply to note Matthew's later placement and Luke's agreement with Mark. Hendriksen (1978: 317–18) prefers Matthew's placement, though he gives no explicit reasoning.

At the end of the next event, there is a resolve to destroy or deal with Jesus (Matt. 12:14 = Mark 3:6). Luke 6:11 is less explicit, for he says nothing about destroying Jesus, only that the Pharisees wish to deal with him. This softening of the account may be a clue to a later actual chronological placement. The decisive resolve looks like something that would occur later in Jesus' ministry, rather than earlier, especially if the Herodians were also involved (Mark 3:6). Thus, although either option is possible, it would seem that Matthew's order is slightly more likely to reflect the real relative placement of the event. If so, Mark and Luke have a more topical arrangement in order to keep the Sabbath controversies together. The wording of Luke 6:11 may omit mention of a plot to prevent a reader from making too strong a chronological association at this point. This resolve, though it was associated with the withered-hand controversy, as Mark notes, is not to be placed very early in Jesus' ministry, since Mark's and Luke's arrangement may be more topical. As such, Luke's work complements Mark's here. Matthew's placement of the grain incident is, thus, more likely to be relatively chronological, because of Jewish resolve and Herodian presence, although his placement of the choosing of the Twelve is likely to have been delayed because of topical concerns in Matthew related to mission (see also the discussion of 6:6–11 below and the introduction to 6:12–16).

The accounts in Mark and Luke are very close. Most see Luke working primarily with Mark's account (Marshall 1978: 229; Fitzmyer 1981: 605), but Schramm (1971: 80–81, 111–12) suggests that another source might be present. Fitzmyer notes four differences between Mark and Luke: Luke has no references to (1) being on the way, (2) Abiathar, or (3) the Sabbath's being for humans (Mark 2:27); in addition, (4) Luke 6:5 has a word order different from Mark 2:28. Matthew agrees with Luke in each of these points. Fitzmyer notes these differences and tries to explain them on the basis of Marcan priority, but he realizes that the common omission of the Sabbath saying about humans is particularly difficult to explain. It is difficulties like these that make the view of Marcan priority with four relatively fixed sources so difficult to accept. Some of these differences are not really explained by the data. Luke 5:33–39 exhibited similar problems (see above).

Two verses come in for debate with regard to authenticity. One of them is the verse peculiar to Mark, Mark 2:27, while the other is the line that follows it in Mark 2:28 (= Matt. 12:8 = Luke 6:5). One suspects that Mark 2:27 is regarded as not going back to Jesus because Matthew and Luke do not include it. Marshall (1978: 209) suggests that it may have come into the tradition at a later time, which is possible but not necessary, as the points below show. He defends the authenticity of the general setting by rejecting the two arguments often advanced against the event: the setting is not tied to Jesus and the argument looks too scribal for Jesus. Interestingly, the Jesus Seminar goes the opposite direction, arguing that the remark about humans probably has connection to Jesus (Mark 2:27–28 is in pink type), while the application of the Son of Man title to Jesus does not (Luke 6:5 is in gray type) (Funk and Hoover 1993: 49, 288; so also Nolland 1989: 254). The Jesus Seminar also rejects Jesus' appeal to Scripture and David as inauthentic, placing Luke 6:3–4 in black type (Funk and Hoover 1993: 287–88).

But Marshall notes that the bread typology of the event fits Jesus, because of its Davidic overtones and because Jesus' appeal to Scripture in other texts is similar (Mark 12:10, 26). He also notes that the issue of plucking grain on the Sabbath is hardly an issue that would have troubled the early church enough for them to create this controversy. One might also note that the type of ruling that Jesus makes here is not substantially different from the one he made in the withered-hand incident, where compassion has priority (Matt. 12:12 = Mark 3:4 = Luke 6:9).[5] Accordingly, there is no reason to reject the tie of this saying to Jesus or to this Sabbath setting. It would take a great authority to cause the church to forget such a deeply rooted tradition. The change of "holy day," because of the resurrection,

---

5. So V. Taylor 1966: 214–15 defends the authenticity of Mark 2:23–26 and suggests that the time of the event is somewhere between late April and June, because the grain is ready for harvest. Concerning the move from a saying about a human to a saying about the Son of Man (like that in Mark), all that is required is for Jesus to see himself as God's representative to humanity, a concept bound up in the Son of Man discussion and a connection that is quite possible for Jesus here. Matthew and Luke drop the humanity remark because it is an intermediate step in the argument (see excursus 6).

does not alter the point about practice on such a holy day. The early church did not carry over the effort to define labor for the new holy day and never treated Sunday as the Sabbath in the way Judaism had. They never tried to treat the subject of Sunday and labor in a way similar to the way the Jews did the Sabbath. The only adequate source for the change is Jesus.[6] There is no reason to doubt the account's authenticity.

Sources and Historicity (6:6–11)

In all three Gospels the controversy over healing the man with the withered hand is placed immediately after the grain incident (Luke 6:6–11 = Mark 3:1–6 = Matt. 12:9–14; Aland 1985: §47). As mentioned above with reference to Luke 6:1–5, it is likely that Matthew, who has this sequence slightly later than do Mark and Luke, has given the relative placement of the event in terms of the chronology of Jesus' ministry, while Mark and Luke are more topical.

When one compares the accounts, Mark and Luke are close, while Matt. 12:11–12 has some details unique to him (i.e., the remark about saving the sheep who falls in the pit). Luke also has unique details (Fitzmyer 1981: 605):

1. Luke 6:6a notes that the event is on another Sabbath.
2. Luke 6:6b notes that Jesus was teaching in the synagogue.
3. Luke 6:6c alone mentions the right hand of the man.
4. Luke 6:7 specifies that the Pharisees and scribes were present.
5. Luke 6:8 mentions uniquely that Jesus knew their thoughts.
6. The man's obedient response to Jesus is noted only in Luke 6:8.

However, only Mark mentions the officials' silence (3:4b) to Jesus' question and the Herodians' presence (3:6). None of these details alter the essential points of the account.

There is almost no dispute over the historicity of the account's setting (Marshall 1978: 233–34). But debate about its details are a different matter.

The Jesus Seminar (Funk and Hoover 1993: 289–90) questions the dialogue within the miracle, placing 6:8b, 9, 10b in black type and arguing that the words were created with the miracle narrative. But the logic of such an approach to miracles and the dialogue connected with them was criticized above in the discussion of sources for 5:17–26. What is curious about the Jesus Seminar's position is that they acknowledge the existence of Sabbath controversies, but they appear to argue that the tradition did not try to record

6. On this passage and various views on the authenticity issue, see also Roloff 1970: 55–62; Lohse, *TDNT* 7:21–24; Lohse 1960: 84–85; Daube 1972–73: 7–8; and France 1971: 46–47.

the events and dialogues that were a part of them (Funk and Hoover 1993: 50). This position seems self-contradictory.

Sabbath healing was not a topic of such concern for the early church that it would have formulated an account to deal with the issue. However, some do see this account and Luke 14:1–6 as doublets drawn from Mark 3:1–6 (Bultmann 1963: 12, 48; Lohse, *TDNT* 7:26). Part of the reason for this conclusion is that Luke 14 shares the illustration of falling into the pit with the Matt. 12 parallel to Luke 6. But it is suspect to assume that a teacher never does something twice or never uses the same material twice, especially since Matthew refers to a sheep and Luke refers to an ox or a son. The details in the rest of the event are sufficiently different to exclude an identification (Marshall 1978: 578, on the Luke 14 parallel and the attempt to connect it to Mark 3:1–6). Jesus' "new way" seems to have made a practice of Sabbath healing, as 4:31–37 suggests and as 13:10–17 and 14:1–6 show. Nolland (1989: 259) cites Roloff (1970: 63–64) as arguing for historical reminiscence here because of unique elements in the form of the account.

Luke 5:33–39 moves from Jesus' associations to his lack of religious asceticism. The issue now becomes the lack of fasting and prayer. Interestingly, Luke ties this account closely to the previous one by the reference to Jesus' eating and drinking (5:33), recalling the uniquely Lucan remark of 5:30. It is more than Jesus' associations that are bothersome. Jesus' meal with sinners is the tip of the iceberg. For Luke, the first direct challenge of Jesus comes here. Questions were raised as early as 4:22 and musings appear in 5:21; but in 5:30 public grumbling emerges against Jesus' associates. Such grumbling continues in reaction to Jesus' seeming lack of piety. Jesus is emerging as a controversial figure.

To understand the controversy over fasting, one needs to appreciate the significance of fasting in first-century Judaism. Fasting had a rich heritage in Judaism and was a highly regarded act of worship. Fasts were tied to the Day of Atonement in the OT (Lev. 16:29). In addition, four daylong fasts were held to recall the destruction of Jerusalem (Zech. 7:3, 5; 8:19). Fasts were also used for penitence (1 Kings 21:27; Joel 1:14; 2:15–27; Isa. 58:1–9) and mourning (Esth. 4:3). The Pharisees had developed fasting into a regular practice. Twice a week, on Mondays and Thursdays, they would fast and intercede for the nation (Luke 18:12; *Didache* 8.1; SB 4:77–114; Behm, *TDNT* 4:924–35). John's disciples fasted in imitation of the lifestyle of their mentor (Luke 7:33). In fact, Jesus fasted (Luke 4:2; 22:16, 18; Matt. 6:16–18), as did the early church (Acts 13:2–3; 9:9; 14:23). Clearly, for many in this period, fasting was a practice of the pious (for more details on fasting, see the exegesis of Luke 5:33). Jesus could not be a man of God and ignore such practices, but he only rarely engaged in them.

Into this setting comes Jesus' practice of open association with sinners, mixed with no apparent fasting (or at least a lack of frequent fasting). Jesus in dealing with the issue does not let the question remain simply at fasting. He basically says that there is a time appropriate for fasting and that the present is not such a time for his disciples. However, there will be time for fasting (5:34–35). Jesus then presses on to the deeper issue through his short parables. He notes that what is associated with him is different from both old and current Judaism (5:36–39). In fact, his new movement cannot really mix with the old without the new movement being lost. New wine must have new wineskins to last. Finally, he notes that those attached to old wine will not like the taste of the new wine and will prefer the old. Thus, in response to the indirect attack on his practice, Jesus begins to assert his distance from current religious views of piety, rich as its heritage might be. An increasing distance between Jesus and his opponents is present, and this distancing will eventually produce a separation. It is often said, and rightly so, that Luke emphasizes Jesus' continuity with the past; but in doing so Luke does not ignore the fundamental differences that also emerged from Jesus' ministry.

The structure of 5:33–39 is clear: an encounter over the issue of fasting followed by an additional explanation, which comes through two extended metaphors and a concluding proverb (the proverb is unique to Luke). The form of the passage is a pronouncement story, which is also a controversy.[7] Some argue that several sayings and forms were added later, since there is such a mix of sayings. In this view, 5:35 is regarded as a secondary announcement, 5:36–38 as extended metaphors, and 5:39 as a proverb.[8] This argument assumes that the tradition carried no mixed or multiple-layered forms within it and that the pronouncement story ends with a single key saying. But is this sustainable? The very linkage of the thought in a topical way is something that

---

7. Bultmann 1963: 18–19; Fitzmyer 1981: 595; Berger 1984: 80. Bultmann believes that even the first saying was added to this setting, which was created by the church, arguing that the situation in the saying is "indefinite." But all metaphors (which Mark 2:19a is) are allusions and indirect statements. The objection does not have force.

8. Bultmann 1963: 18–19, 103, where he argues that Luke's addition is clearly secondary because of its absence in the parallels. But can one rule out Luke's finding such material in his additional research? See Fitzmyer 1981: 595.

could have circulated in this form from the beginning and that could have emerged as a full response in a single setting. This is the way that oral tradition treated topical ideas, as a look at mishnaic texts shows. Surely Jesus talked in more than one-liners, and he certainly loved parables.[9] Others argue that the cloth and wine material in Mark 2:21–22, and thus its parallels, is independent in its own right, because it is more radical than the previous statement in Mark about fasting after the groom departs (V. Taylor 1966: 212). Taylor argues that it was added as a remnant from another pronouncement story. Nonetheless, he sees the remarks reaching back to Jesus. This view is possible, though it is just as likely that Jesus on this occasion elaborated his reasoning why fasting was done differently by his disciples. If remnant pronouncement stories were in circulation, then it is also possible that multiple versions of the same event or of similar disputes were in circulation.

Luke 6:1–11 moves to consider two Sabbath controversies after the introduction of the theme of the new way in 5:33–39. The first controversy involves the disciples' gathering grain on the day of rest (6:1–5). It leads Jesus to cite a scriptural example involving David where human needs supersede an issue of law. The Son of Man saying that concludes the pericope is at the heart of the argument and is a difficult saying whose exact meaning will be treated in the exegesis. Jesus functions in this passage as an authority in interpreting the law's scope. As such, he indicates aspects of the new way he is bringing, so the event is an elaboration on 5:33–39. Here the new way and its view of the law become clearer. The form of 6:1–5 is a pronouncement story. It is also a controversy.[10]

The last of the three controversies (6:6–11) marks the second consecutive Sabbath controversy. Some call it a conflict account

---

9. For a defense of the authenticity of Mark 2:18–20, and thus of its parallels, see V. Taylor 1966: 208–12 (who argues that the Marcan tradition has roots in an eyewitness and was told to reveal Jesus' mind about fasting); Cranfield 1959: 107–11; Marshall 1978: 223 (though he regards it as possible that Luke 5:36–39 may be a separate tradition). Bovon 1989: 256 also sees a distinct tradition, since Luke's saying has a parallel in the Gospel of Thomas 47, though in a different order (Luke: garment [5:36], then wine [5:37–39]; Thomas: the reverse). Teaching through word linkage was popular in Judaism. When done with the Scriptures, it was called *gezerah shewah*.

10. Bultmann 1963: 16–17, who argues that the passage is the work of the church to justify its "Sabbath customs" (or, rather, its lack of them). This view was rejected in the discussion of authenticity. Bovon 1989: 269 sees the church drawing on an authentic saying in the tradition. Berger 1984: 80, 309 calls the passage apophthegm, Chrie, and Sabbath conflict.

like 5:17–26.[11] Theissen (1983: 113, 322) calls the event a rule miracle, since Jesus is giving teaching and revealing his authority as he heals the man with the withered hand. Both descriptions are correct. Jesus is clearly in controversy with the scribes and Pharisees. In the midst of it, his healing also makes points about God's intention for the Sabbath and Jesus' authority in relationship to that day. When one considers the passage's placement in Luke, the confrontation surrounding the Sabbath is not the only issue. Following Jesus' claim to be Lord over the Sabbath (6:5), this healing demonstrates and confirms that authority and claim. The other Gospels agree on this emphasis (Matt. 12:9–14 = Mark 3:1–6). Jesus also confirms an additional claim that he made at the end of Luke 5: he brings a new way. Jesus is the issue in Luke 6, since the disciples' practices are no longer in view. The event is a turning point, because after this embarrassment the officials decide they must deal with Jesus. Luke 6:11 is less specific than Mark 3:6 or Matt. 12:14, speaking only of plans in a general sense (see the discussion of sources for Luke 6:1–5). But all the Gospels agree: Jesus' handling of the Sabbath made him a threat to traditional Judaism as the leaders sought to preserve it.

The outline of Luke 5:33–6:11 is as follows:

a. Question about fasting (5:33–39)
   i. Question: why do others fast and pray but not you? (5:33)
   ii. Reply: a wedding is not for fasting, but . . . (5:34–35)
   iii. Jesus' explanatory parables (5:36–39)
      (1) One cannot sew new cloth on old (5:36)
      (2) One cannot put new wine in old wineskins (5:37–38)
      (3) Those attached to old wine do not want new (5:39)
b. Question about plucking grain on the Sabbath (6:1–5)
   i. Setting: the disciples pluck grain on the Sabbath (6:1)
   ii. Pharisees' complaint: this is not lawful (6:2)
   iii. Jesus' reply: David and the place of the Son of Man (6:3–5)
      (1) Example: The needs of David and his men come above the law (6:3–4)

---

11. Schürmann 1969: 300–301, 306 speaks of a Sabbath conflict for both 6:1–5 and 6:6–11. In addition, a controversy saying is the focus of 6:6–11. It is hard to know whether a conflict pronouncement story or a miracle account is present, since both elements exist. The issue is whether the miracle or the saying is more central, which is a tough call. Bultmann 1963: 12 calls it a controversy account occasioned by a healing of Jesus. Bovon 1989: 273 rightly calls it a mixed form, combining a controversy with a miracle account.

(2) Authority of the Son of Man (6:5)
c. Question about healing on the Sabbath (6:6–11)
    i. Setting: officials waiting to make a Sabbath charge
       (6:6–7)
    ii. Jesus' response: a question (6:8–9)
    iii. Act: Jesus heals (6:10)
    iv. Reaction: decision to deal with Jesus (6:11)

A variety of themes are present in each pericope. Luke 5:33–39 notes the distinctness of what Jesus is offering and pictures it as new. As a result, pietistic practice is redefined and refocused. Fasting is argued to be inappropriate during Jesus' earthly ministry, though it may be appropriate after it. In this unit comes the first Pharisee-initiated challenge of Jesus, though it is made indirectly by questioning the disciples' practice as well. Jesus' reply gives the first hint of his future departure. It also is becoming clear that some will not respond.

The major point is the recognition of Jesus' distinctive person and teaching. The distinctiveness is so strong that even the appropriateness of fasting is tied to his personal presence. Of course, the issue of religious asceticism is also tackled here. The issue is neither its presence nor its necessity, but its rationale. Fasting is less than central. More important is why it is done. The impossibility of a syncretistic approach to traditional Judaism and the new way is also highlighted by the account. What Jesus offers is not mixable, even with a venerable faith like Judaism.

Luke 6:1–5 has its own set of emphases. Law must submit to need. Put another way: law is not designed to prevent one from meeting needs. In addition, the passage supplies pictures of Jesus' position. Jesus' role is compared to David, and the disciples are placed in parallel to men under the king. Jesus is also the evaluator of tradition and the one who comprehends the law's scope. In fact, Jesus is the one with authority over the Sabbath.

A major issue is how to apply law and tradition. Is law given as an absolute or is it designed to aid and serve people? The action of David, though technically illegal, was designed to meet a fundamental need. The law is to serve people, not to be master over them when fundamental needs are at stake. There is no reason to make the meeting of these needs difficult or to delay their being met because of tradition or restraints of law. A limited type of hierarchical ethic is implied here, where people are placed over rules. A more difficult issue is determining if Jesus is saying that this is the way the law should have always been read or whether he is exercising his claim to have interpretative authority over the law.

In Luke 6:6–11, Jesus demonstrates the Sabbath authority he claimed in 6:1–5. The approach of the new way reflects an ethical norm at the base of the movement. It was the "law of love," which in turn demands that one do good on the Sabbath. This passage contains the first direct challenge to Jesus without reference to his disciples. The account closes with the initial plot to deal with Jesus.

The passage's major interest is Jesus' person. However, out of the text comes an approach for understanding what the law about the Sabbath was designed to do. It was not to restrict one's ability to love people and meet their basic needs. The healing could have been put off; but it was not. The man had the right to be healed—and as soon as possible. Such considerations are not a violation of the concept of Sabbath rest. Thus, Jesus highlights the importance of acts of love. However, unlike the previous text, here it is not clear that Jesus makes an explicit challenge to the law. The text is concerned with Jewish issues. It does not attempt to answer the question of a Sabbath rest for Christians, other than to show how a basic ethic of compassion should cause the Christian to serve those in need.

Exegesis and Exposition

⁵:³³And they said to him, "⌐The disciples of John fast often and offer prayers, likewise also those of the Pharisees, but yours eat and drink.⌐" ³⁴But Jesus said to them, "Are the attendants of the groom able to fast while the groom is with them? ³⁵But there will come days, when also the groom is taken from them, then they will fast in those days."

³⁶And he told them a parable also, "No one having a piece of torn cloth from a new garment puts it on an old garment; but if he does, he will tear it because the new does not match the old. ³⁷And no one puts new wine in old wineskins; if he does, the new wine tears the skins, and it will be spilled and the skins will be destroyed. ³⁸But new wine ⌐must be put⌐ into new skins. ³⁹⌐And no one drinking the old wishes for the new; for he says, 'The old is ⌐good⌐.' "⌐

⁶:¹And on a ⌐Sabbath⌐ as he was going through a field of grain, his disciples plucked and ⌐ate some heads of grain, by rubbing them in their hands⌐. ²And some of the Pharisees said, "Why are you doing what is not ⌐allowed⌐ on the Sabbath?" ³And Jesus replied to them, "Surely you have read what David did when he was hungry and those who were with him: ⁴how he went into the house of God and, taking the bread of the presence, ate it and gave it ⌐to those⌐ with him, which was not lawful to eat except for the priests alone?" ⁵And he said to them, "The Son of Man ⌐is Lord of the Sabbath⌐."⌐

[6]On another Sabbath, he entered the synagogue and was teaching. And a man was there also who had a withered hand. [7]And the scribes and the Pharisees were keeping an eye on him to see if he ⌜would heal⌝ on the Sabbath, in order that they might accuse him. [8]But Jesus knew their thoughts and said to the man with the withered hand, "Rise up and stand here." And he rose up and stood there. [9]And Jesus said to them, "I ask you, is it lawful on the Sabbath to do good or to do harm, to save a life or destroy it?" [10]And he looked around on them all, and said to him, "Stretch out your hand." And he did and his hand was restored. [11]But they were filled with mindless rage and discussed with one another what they might do to Jesus.

a. Question about Fasting (5:33–39)
i. Question: Why Do Others Fast and Pray but Not You? (5:33)

5:33   The passage's first issue is its setting in Luke. Reading Luke alone, one could argue that the remarks came at the same time as the meal in the previous unit.[12] But one should probably not read too much into this link. Luke tends to shorten his introductions to these events, as 5:17 and 5:27 show. This "tightening" reflects literary compression and is not an argument for the same setting as 5:27–32.[13] In fact, the verse itself suggests that such compression has taken place, for "they" commented on the practice of the Pharisees' disciples. If no shift had occurred from 5:30–32, then the statement should have used "we" to refer to such practice. Thus, Luke reflects a distinct setting.

This passage presents an encounter between differing religious lifestyles. Luke's reference to "they" is closer to Mark 2:18 here, which notes that "people" come to Jesus, while Matt. 9:14 says it is John's disciples. John's disciples and the Pharisees' followers fast and pray, but Jesus' disciples eat and drink. The remark clearly points out the contrast. What is especially significant is that the Pharisees' practice agrees with the forerunner's followers. The initial impression is that something is haywire with Jesus' disciples.

A few minor differences exist in Luke's presentation. The first difference depends on a textual issue (see additional note). Luke has a statement, rather than a question as in Mark 2:18 = Matt. 9:14. Luke's use of a statement here reflects his summary presentation, a presentation that also allows him at the end of the verse to speak of "eating and drinking," rather than just fasting as in Mark 2:18 =

---

12. Talbert 1982: 65–67 treats 5:30–6:11 as a unit because of the shared theme of controversy and the shared discussion of the new lifestyle of the way with Jesus. Tannehill 1986: 172–76, esp. 173, discusses 5:17–6:11 as a unit of five controversies and notes how Luke tightened the connection in 5:33.

13. This argument applies, no matter what view of Gospel priority one has, since both Matt. 9:14 and Mark 2:18 set out the distinct occasion of the pericope clearly.

Matt. 9:14. The phrase ἐσθίουσιν καὶ πίνουσιν (esthiousin kai pi-nousin) is a stock summary Lucan phrase for charges about Jesus' lifestyle (5:30; 7:34; Schneider 1977a: 139–40; Schürmann 1969: 294). Despite the rewording, the statement functions for Luke exactly as the question does for Mark and Matthew. In fact, Schneider notes that Luke's statement functions like a question in that it is designed to provoke a response from Jesus.

Mark 2:18 is unclear as to who initiated the discussion, while Matt. 9:14 says that John's disciples were involved. The surface impression from Luke, by the placement after Levi's banquet, is that Pharisees were the initiators; but the distinct reference to the Pharisees in the remark makes it likely that Luke has begun a new section. As was noted, if the Pharisees were involved, they would naturally have used "we" to refer to themselves. Luke wishes to portray the remark simply as coming from the crowd and has compressed the setting's discussion. By grouping the Pharisees' disciples and John's disciples, Luke makes clear that an issue of the larger Jewish community is at stake. Luke probably leaves the issue in an indefinite form to portray the community concern (Plummer 1896: 161 [focuses on the concerns of John's disciples]; Marshall 1978: 224; Schweizer 1984: 111).

As noted above, fasting was highly regarded in this period. The OT discusses fasts for specific occasions (Lev. 16:29–34; 23:26–32; Num. 29:7–11; Danker 1988: 127; Behm, TDNT 4:928–29). Individual fasts were taken for differing reasons: some fasted in hope of God's delivery (2 Sam. 12:16–20; 1 Kings 21:27; Ps. 35:13; 69:10 [69:11 MT]), while others hoped to turn aside calamity (Judg. 20:26; 1 Sam. 7:6; 1 Kings 21:9; Jer. 36:6, 9; 2 Chron. 20:3–4).

In combining prayer and fasting, the hope was that God would answer, as often fasting accompanied confession and intercession (Jer. 14:12; Neh. 1:4; Ezra 8:21, 23). The one who fasted reflected a mourner's mood (1 Kings 21:27; Joel 2:12–13; Isa. 58:5; Esth. 4:3; Dan. 9:3). Gesturing was often seen as important (1 Macc. 3:47; Josephus, Antiquities 19.8.2 §349). The usual fast lasted one morning and evening (Judg. 20:26; 1 Sam. 14:24; 2 Sam. 1:12). More severe were the three-day fast (Esth. 4:16) and the weeklong fast (1 Sam. 31:13), where food was forbidden only during the day (2 Sam. 3:35). The three-week fast described in Dan. 10:2–3 was this latter type of severe fast. Needless to say, such fasting would have an influence on the body (Ps. 109:24).

National fasts occurred on the Day of Atonement and the four-day memorial to recall Jerusalem's fall. Thus, fasting held a high place in Judaism's psyche. It occurred frequently and had great significance. In fact, fasting prepared one for all kinds of activity in Judaism. Many apocalyptic materials mention that fasting preceded their visions (2 Esdr. [= 4 Ezra] 5:13, 19–20; 2 Bar. 9.2; 12.5). A vow often was confirmed with a fast (Acts 23:12, 14). Fasting was often regarded as a virtue (T. Jos. 3.4–5; 4.8; 10.1). It even was regarded in some circles as meritorious (1 Enoch 108.7–9; Philo, *Special Laws* 2.32 §197). Only here and there do voices warn that fasting without actual turning from sin is useless (Sir. 34:31 [according to NRSV numbering]). The zealous fasted twice a week, usually on Monday and Thursday. *Didache* 8.1 shows that some in early Christianity took up this practice. Fasting was not permitted on Sabbaths and festival days (Jdt. 8:6; Jub. 50.10, 12). Clearly, this activity had a major role in first-century religious life, so one can see why Jesus' lack of emphasis raised questions.

When Luke focuses on prayer and fasting, the issue is thus not on the periphery of religion. It is a central act of great piety. Luke alone mentions prayer with the fasting, probably because the two activities went together.[14] One fasted in order to spend focused time with God. The remark concerns a serious issue in ancient spiritual life. Still, Jesus defends his disciples' seemingly irreligious practice.

ii. Reply: A Wedding Is Not for Fasting, but . . . (5:34–35)

5:34 Jesus replies with a question that illustrates the disciples' current situation. He uses the picture of a wedding. At this joyous time, he asks, do the attendants of the groom fast? The question is asked with the Greek interrogative particle μή (*mē*, do not) and expects a negative reply: No, the attendants do not fast as long as the groom is present. The picture is clear and the allusions are significant.

The images of the groom and wedding express God's relationship to his people and are often used to allude to messianic times (Isa. 54:5–6; 62:4–5; Jer. 2:2; Ezek. 16; Hos. 2:14–23 [2:16–25 MT]; Marshall 1978: 225). This end-time association existed in Judaism,[15] and the image was also used by John the Baptist (John 3:29). Interest-

---

14. One other Synoptic difference needs notation. Luke uses what some see as the narrower term for petition: δέησις. The distinction that δέησις = petition and προσευχή = prayer is not present in the NT, and the reference in 5:33 appears to be general. For the distinction, see Greeven, *TDNT* 2:807, though he acknowledges that it is harder to argue for the distinction in nouns.

15. SB 1:500–18; Jeremias, *TDNT* 4:1101–3; Bovon 1989: 260. Jeremias notes that nowhere in Judaism is Messiah the bridegroom. Stauffer, *TDNT* 1:654 n. 39, cites 2 Esdr. [4 Ezra] 2:15, 38; Midr. Deut. 3 (200d); *Pirqe de Rabbi Eliezer* 41 (= Friedlander 1916: 322); *Mekilta de Rabbi Ishmael*, tractate *Baḥodesh* 3 on Exod. 19:17 (= Lauterbach 1933–35: 2.219), where God comes forth as a groom to meet Israel his bride. In *Mekilta de Rabbi Ishmael*, tractate *Shirata* 3 on Exod. 15:2 (= Lauterbach 1933–35: 2.26–27), Akiva cites several texts from the Song of Songs as applying to Israel as the bride of God, making it clear that this book was read as a marriage between Israel and God.

ingly enough, Jesus' questioners make reference to John's disciples. Jesus is alluding to the nature of the times and to his own role by this picture. The end has begun to draw near.

Luke uses only the groom image in this verse. The NT also retains the image to refer to features of Jesus' return, another illustration of an image applied to both the "already" and "not yet" time periods (Luke 12:35–36; Matt. 22:2; 25:1; Eph. 5:23–33; Rev. 19:7; 21:2; Rengstorf 1968: 80). When Jesus speaks of the groom's being present, he describes the period of his ministry as characterized by joy. Thus, a fast is not appropriate. In describing the υἱούς (huious, guests; lit., sons) at the wedding, Jesus refers to those who aid the groom at the wedding, an allusion to the intimate relationship his disciples have with him (on νυμφών, nymphōn, see BAGD 545 §2; BAA 1103 §2; for its secular use as "bride chamber," see Tob. 6:14, 17).

At this point, Mark 2:19 makes the explicit statement that when the groom is present those with him do not fast. Luke and Matthew lack this statement and move immediately into when the fast will be appropriate. The quick transition shows that Jesus does not reject fasting. There are a time and place for fasting, but the time of Jesus' ministry is not such a period, because the very event that much fasting commemorates—the deliverance of God's people—is present in him (Schürmann 1969: 295 says, "All fasts are preparation, marriage is fulfillment").

5:35 The double reference to the coming days shows that there is a different kind of period approaching. In that period, the groom is taken from the disciples, and then fasting will be appropriate. Luke alone uses a plural ἡμέραις (hēmerais, days) in the latter part of the verse, but the singular of Mark 2:20b is clearly a collective, referring to a period of time, as the plural in Mark 2:20a shows. Luke's plural matches his earlier use of the plural in the verse. The difference is purely stylistic.

The change in situation produces a change in the nature of the time period and thus in the response. Obviously, the allusion to the groom's being taken away is a reference to Jesus' approaching removal through death. Some see an allusion to Isa. 53:8 here, but only one word is the same, making an allusion uncertain.[16] This reference is one of the first hints of Jesus' approaching death (the initial allusion is in Luke 2:35). The picture is grim: a man is removed from the scene of his wedding (2 Esdr. [4 Ezra] 10:1–4; Danker 1988: 128).

16. For this view are Schürmann 1969: 296; Hendriksen 1978: 309; Wiefel 1988: 121 (perhaps). Against it is Marshall 1978: 226. Bovon 1989: 261 thinks that any specific allusion to the cross or ascension is unlikely and prefers to refer only to the period of the church. The key terms are ἀπαρθῇ in Luke and two forms of αἴρω in Isa. 53.

At the time of Jesus' departure, fasts will again be appropriate. It is debated what Jesus means here. Is this a reference to fasting during the short time between death and the awareness of the resurrection, a period of a few days (John 16:16–22; Hendriksen 1978: 310)? Marshall (1978: 226) argues explicitly for this sense, noting that later church fasts were for guidance, not mourning. The early church, it is argued, did not see the period after the bestowal of the Spirit and the resurrection as a period of mourning. This might well be a correct approach to the passage, though the early church shows evidence of fasting in the period of the Spirit too (Acts 13:2–3; 14:23). Tiede argues that the church did see the need for repentance in the interim, though his formulation has problems.[17] What is clear is that creation is still viewed as unrestored in the early church's view and that one longs for the total restoration that is a part of Jesus' return (Rom. 8:17–30; 1 Cor. 15:20–28; Rev. 19–22). There is a longing for full redemption in the early church. The question is whether this period should be called a period of mourning. It seems slightly better to argue that the groom's physical absence is all that is alluded to here, without trying to limit the time or overpress the figure's significance. With Jesus' departure, the totality of deliverance is still an awaited event for the church (Acts 3:12–26). Jesus' point is that fasting will again become appropriate and an option in this intermediate period, as the church longs for the return and final fulfillment. The tone is important. Jesus allows the return of fasting, but he does not regulate it or make it a test of spirituality (Danker 1988: 128). The church may have variety in practice without requiring conformity. The materials of the early church also reflect this approach to issues of this kind (e.g., freedom over food and days in Rom. 14:5–9 and avoidance of excessive regulation in Col. 2:16–23).

What is key about the change of perspective is that it all turns on Jesus' presence. He is the issue that defines the practice. There is some deep Christology in Jesus' reply, just as there was in the paralytic account. The groom is what really matters, and the audience needs to see that he—Jesus—is the key point.

iii. Jesus' Explanatory Parables (5:36–39)
(1) One Cannot Sew New Cloth on Old (5:36)

5:36 Luke 5:36–39 gives a deeper rationale for the reply. Jesus goes beyond the issue of fasting and prayer, as he explains through three il-

---

17. Tiede 1988: 130 cites Acts 5:31 and 11:18 as evidence of a "new era" of repentance. Acts 1:1–11 discusses Jesus' departure. The problem with this suggestion is that it treats repentance as if it is a fresh theme in Acts, since Tiede speaks of a "new phase" of repentance. But repentance is a constant theme in Luke (5:32; 10:13–15; 15:1–32).

lustrations the religious situation of his ministry. In introducing these pictures, Luke alone notes that Jesus spoke a parable (παραβολή, *parabolē*), a term Luke often uses to refer to a simple metaphor (4:23; 6:39; 12:16, 41; 13:6; 14:7; 18:1, 9; 19:11; 20:9, 19; 21:29).[18] In fact, Jesus gives two extended metaphors and then a proverb to make several related points about the nature of the times. In making these comments, Jesus issues an analysis of his way versus that of tradition found in the Pharisees' and John's disciples (Luce 1933: 135). Here is another text tying John to the old period (7:28–35; 16:16).

Luke's presentation of this first metaphor is slightly different from the picture of Mark 2:21 and Matt. 9:16. Some suggest that he has altered the picture, but this overplays the difference, which is a simple matter of perspective. Mark and Matthew highlight the result of taking unused cloth and sewing it on old cloth. They note that such an action rips the cloth and makes the tear worse. Luke focuses on the picture from the perspective of the new piece of cloth, a difference that heightens the contrast slightly, but still keeps the point made by Mark and Matthew. He notes that the new cloth is torn and that the new cloth does not match the old. All the accounts have the same basic point: the mixture of old and new is destructive and cannot really be done, because the result is damage to both pieces of cloth.[19] Mark and Matthew say in effect that to mix the old and the new makes matters worse for all. Luke says that to mix them is not good, since the new is ripped and the new and old do not fit together. Thus, all accurately summarize the metaphor.

The Lucan picture has a touch of irony in it. It starts off with a piece of old cloth that needs repair. Rather than getting an appropriate piece of old cloth to mend it, a new garment is ruined.[20] The Lucan picture is intended to come across as a little absurd. The results of the effort will even reinforce that mood. This approach to the problem will backfire. One cannot put something new on top of something old (on old-new contrasts, see Seesemann, *TDNT* 5:718).

The phrase εἰ δὲ μή γε (*ei de mē ge*, if he indeed does) is idiomatic, expressing the result of attempting to deal with the damaged old

---

18. Such metaphors are often called "similitudes"; Hauck, *TDNT* 5:753; Marshall 1978: 226.

19. Danker 1988: 128–29 and Luce 1933: 136 overdraw the difference. Marshall 1978: 227 is more balanced.

20. Luke alone refers explicitly to the cloth as καινός, which here means "unused." He uses the term three times in the verse, so it has a touch of emphasis. I translated it "new" to keep the parallelism and linkage clear. It usually refers to a qualitative newness; Bovon 1989: 263. So here it means a new and better teaching. Luke returns to the use of νέος in 5:37–38 in agreement with the Synoptic parallels; Behm, *TDNT* 3:448; Matt. 9:17; Luke 22:20. On this metaphor, see Maurer, *TDNT* 7:961 §4a.

cloth in this manner (the idiom also occurs in 5:37; 10:6; 13:9; 14:32). Two results emerge for Luke: the one taking this approach tears the new cloth, and the old and new cloth do not match. The mix does not work at all.

The points are clear. The ways of Jesus and the traditions of current religion, even though related to the OT, cannot be mixed without significantly damaging the new entity. In addition, the two approaches really do not go together. What Jesus brings is a new approach to God (Nolland 1989: 249 does not see enough distinction here). Jesus will make clear that there is continuity between what he offers and what God promised, but one should have no doubt that what Jesus offers is decidedly new and distinct as well. It is, in every sense of the word, a new approach to viewing how people can come to God, a new period, and a new dispensation. Jesus is the real point of difference, as the previous verses showed. It will take the disciples and the early church a little time to see the implications of what Jesus is saying. The Book of Acts will chronicle the growth of understanding in some detail, especially as it related to circumcision, food laws, and Gentiles. Acts will argue two points at once. A good Jew should become a Christian in continuity with the OT promise (Acts 13:16–41), but what comes is new, too (Acts 10:1–11:18). Jesus brings discontinuity in the midst of continuity.

(2) One Cannot Put New Wine in Old Wineskins (5:37–38)

5:37 Luke uses a threefold οὐδείς (*oudeis*, no one) in 5:36, 37, 39 to mark out the three pictures of the passage. Jesus' second story is about something that no one does: no one places new wine in old wineskins. Wineskins were usually made from sheepskin or goatskin, and the neck area of the animal became the neck of the container. The body portion was skinned, the hair was removed, and the hide was treated to prevent the skin from changing the taste of the contents. Finally, it was sewn together (Josh. 9:4, 13). Over time the skin of such a container would age and become brittle (Gen. 21:14–15, 19; Ps. 119:83; Plummer 1896: 164; Fitzmyer 1981: 601).

Jesus keeps the note of irony in this second picture. He begins by commenting again that no one would do what he is about to describe. The results show why. Someone foolishly might try to put new wine in old skins (note the εἰ δὲ μή γε idiom again). But when the new wine ferments, it expands the container and the skin bursts, being unable to expand because it is brittle. The new wine pours out, and the old skin is destroyed.

The tragic waste is clear. The mood of the metaphor is, "What a loss!" The old and new ways cannot be mixed without harm to both. This illustration is an expansion over the previous metaphor. That illustration dealt with pieces of cloth, but here whole entities are described. Again, the picture is one of lack of continuity between Jesus and what has gone before (Fitzmyer 1981: 601). The point is simply that the gospel cannot be contained within Judaism without destroying both (Marshall 1978: 227). The new ways in which God is dealing with humanity through Jesus cannot be mixed with the old ways. The gospel is a new way. And it is the picture of the gospel as new that is the presupposition for Jesus' being portrayed later in Luke and in Acts as the prophet like Moses (Luke 9:35; Acts 3:12–26). The new prophet will bring a fresh message.

The conclusion of the second picture is stated positively: new wine **5:38** must have new skins; new ways must have new containers. Jesus' teaching will not survive by making it conform to old ways. A new form, a new spirit, and a new approach are required. Old questions are irrelevant. Such a message had relevance beyond the time of Jesus' ministry. In the early church and throughout the new age, to re-Judaize Christianity would have missed the newness of what Jesus brings. The issue raised here is one of the major concerns in the Book of Acts, as the church wrestles with the proper limits of the influence of its Jewish heritage. The focus is not on a return to something old and ancient, but on the presence of something new. This does not mean that some forms of the old worship, like fasting, cannot continue; but it does mean that they are seen differently. The remarks fit the situation in Jesus' ministry, but the significance became timeless for the church's perspective.[21]

(3) Those Attached to Old Wine Do Not Want New (5:39)

The additional note discusses the text-critical problem of whether **5:39** 5:39 is part of Luke's Gospel. This proverb was common in the culture (Sir. 9:10; *m. ʾAbot* 4.20; Marshall 1978: 228).[22] The point is, however, disputed. Some argue that Jesus is saying that the Pharisees will not change, except slowly, while other people may respond quickly (Godet 1875: 1.282). This is thus a call for tolerance: accepting the existence of Judaism, Jesus asks the disciples to recognize that change from the law comes only after reflection. However, in light of Jesus' later rejection of the Pharisees and the mention that

21. Paul raises such issues in 1 Cor. 7:17–24; 8–11; and Rom. 14–15. While not rejecting Jewish worship forms, he did not regard them as required. His approach parallels Jesus'.

22. The Sirach parallel goes the other way by noting that a new friend is like new wine: one does not enjoy it until it has matured. The *ʾAbot* parallel also favors the old over the new. Jesus' reversal of the standard metaphor is one of his typical twists on cultural imagery.

the new wine is not even tried, it is better to see the point as, "You have set your course, you will never change your ways" (Plummer 1896: 164). There is a note of rebuke here in the realization that some people will not alter the way they look at Jesus. They reject the new way he brings. Some people will not taste the new wine of the gospel, since some tastes never change. Rejection of the new message by many in Judaism is very likely. One will not try what one does not sense the need for.

b. Question about Plucking Grain on the Sabbath (6:1–5)
i. Setting: The Disciples Pluck Grain on the Sabbath (6:1)

6:1 There is little introduction to the next event. Luke moves right into the action, which is clearly set on the Sabbath, although the text surrounding the chronological note is one of the most discussed textual problems in the Gospel (see the additional note). Σαββάτῳ (sabbatō, Sabbath) appears to be the most likely text.

The disciples are cutting through a field, probably on its edge. No additional theological significance should be read into the description of the route taken.[23] The account is simply descriptive. As they go, they pick from the stalks, rub them in their hands to break down the grain, and eat. Luke alone adds the detail about rubbing the stalks, while he shares with Matt. 12:1 an explicit mention that they ate. These are merely details, which do not add any significant points to the controversy.[24] The action seems innocent enough, but in the eyes of some, it is not appropriate for the Sabbath, as the disciples are about to discover.

ii. Pharisees' Complaint: This Is Not Lawful (6:2)

6:2 The Pharisees appear and complain. The narrative raises the question how the Pharisees knew that the disciples were plucking the grain or, at least, how they heard about the practice.[25] The impression is given that the Pharisees were keeping a close eye on this group.

The eating of grain from the field in and of itself was not the problem, since Deut. 23:25 [23:26 MT] allowed for such a situation for anyone. The problem was engaging in this activity on the Sabbath (Exod. 20:8–11). The Mishnah dedicates a whole unit to listing what

---

23. So correctly, Carson 1984: 279–80. No path is being made for Jesus as an authority nor is there a reference to excessive travel on the Sabbath to do kingdom preaching.

24. Matthew and Luke use different forms of the verb: Matthew has an infinitive, ἐσθίειν, while Luke has a verbal form, ἤσθιον. Mark 2:23 speaks only of plucking (τίλλοντες) and assumes that eating took place.

25. For a defense of the Pharisees' likely presence in Galilee, see Witherington 1990: 61–66.

is not allowed in terms of Sabbath activity: *m. Šab.* 7.2 (also *m. Pe'a* 8.7). These regulations are "the forty save one," as the Mishnah puts it, and prohibit thirty-nine tasks on the day of rest (Lohse, *TDNT* 7:12–13). According to this detailed and specific list, the disciples were reaping, threshing, winnowing, and preparing food—a quadruple violation! In an interesting twist, later Judaism would not have had a problem with their action as long as a tool was not used to prepare the food (so *b. Šab.* 128a–b; Carson 1984: 280). In fact, in the Mishnah, there seems to be an awareness of how tedious all of this regulation was: "The rules about the Sabbath . . . are as mountains hanging by a hair, for Scripture is scanty and rules many" (*m. Ḥag.* 1.8; Danker 1988: 130; B. Cohen 1930; SB 1:615–18).

The question uses the second-person plural and thus alludes to the disciples' practice. Some argue that Luke directs the question to the disciples here, whereas in Matt. 12:3 and Mark 2:25 Jesus takes the question. But what is happening here is that Jesus and his disciples are being treated as a group. It is a collective comment, so Jesus is ultimately the target. Since they are his disciples, they are seen as following his example (Marshall 1978: 231). The issue simply is Sabbath labor. How is a follower of Jesus to relate to law and the tradition that grew out of it? In Judaism, Sabbath meals were prepared ahead of time to avoid this problem (Jub. 2.19; 50.3, 8–13; SB 2:202–3; Schweizer 1984: 112). The action of Jesus and his disciples is thus a challenge to pharisaic custom. The issue is what is allowed, since ἔξεστιν (*exestin*, permitted) is the key word in the question.[26] The question is actually a warning (Wiefel 1988: 123 and n. 5).

iii. Jesus' Reply: David and the Place of the Son of Man (6:3–5)

(1) Example: The Needs of David and His Men Come above the Law (6:3–4)

Jesus defends the actions of the group against the Pharisees' critique. There is no need to suppose, as Fitzmyer (1981: 608) suggests, that the early Christian community is being defended here. The defense relates to the disciples, though by implication it does allude to the church's practice on the Sabbath. Jesus' teaching about a past issue can be relevant to church issues without requiring a disjunction between the two situations. **6:3**

In appealing to examples from Scripture, Jesus uses one of his common arguments (Mark 12:10, 26; Matt. 12:5 [parallel to this pe-

---

26. Ἔξεστιν will be central in many disputes: Luke 6:2 = Matt. 12:2 = Mark 2:24; note also Matt. 12:12; 14:4; 19:3; 22:17; 27:6; Mark 3:4; 12:14; Luke 14:3; BAGD 275 §1; BAA 556 §1.

ricope]; 19:4; 21:16; Marshall 1978: 231). He words the question in a way to suggest rebuke. The particle οὐδέ (*oude*) expects a positive reply: "Surely you have read, have you not?" The Pharisees are familiar with the biblical account about David. They know the story, but miss a point in it.

The example is from 1 Sam. 21:1–7 [21:2–8 MT] and 22:9–10. Some points that Jesus makes from the OT account are implied from the original. For example, the entry of David into the tabernacle is implied in the remark that Doeg the Edomite, a colleague of Saul, was "detained before the LORD" (1 Sam. 21:7; Plummer 1896: 167). That the bread was intended to feed more than David is suggested by the request for five loaves (1 Sam. 21:3), as well as by the priest's statement that he will give the bread only if the men are ceremonially clean (i.e., if they haven't had sexual intercourse recently; 1 Sam. 21:4). In addition, it is quite possible that the problem that 1 Sam. 21 raised with reference to the law was well known. In order to avoid the problem, some rabbis argued that the bread was not the actual bread of the presence—that is, not the legally restricted, priestly bread— but bread from the previous week.[27] Such an approach, however, cannot explain the priest's question or the language of 1 Sam. 21:6.

6:4   Jesus drives the point home. This incident took place at Nob while Ahimelech was priest.[28] David went to God's house (at this time the tabernacle). At the tabernacle David ate the bread of presence, which was restricted to the priests as part of the twelve loaves set on a table in the Holy Place. It was changed once a week and was prepared by the Levites (Lev. 24:5–9; Exod. 25:30; 39:36; 40:22–23; 1 Sam. 21:6; 1 Chron. 9:32; Hendriksen 1978: 319). In rabbinic tradition, it is suggested that this event occurred on the Sabbath, which is possible since 1 Sam. 21:5–6 suggests that the bread had just been changed (Rengstorf 1968: 81; Lohse, *TDNT* 7:22). If this element is correct, then the illustration is even more appropriate, being a Sabbath violation as well as being an illegal eating of the priestly bread (though the violation is not exact since there was no preparing of the food for David, nor were the disciples eating a forbidden meal). Jesus is working with analogy here. But one cannot be certain that a Sabbath event is in view in 1 Samuel, since no point of it is made

27. Fitzmyer 1981: 609. Josephus, *Antiquities* 6.12.1 §§242–43, does not mention the bread in describing the account. SB 1:618–19 notes the rabbinic accounts; *b. Menaḥ.* 95b cites a remark by Rabbi Shimʾon (ca. A.D. 150).

28. Because of potential misunderstanding, Luke and Matthew omit the reference that Mark 2:26 makes to Abiathar son of Ahimelech, a difficult reference that may be an ambiguous literary reference, rather than a historical one. Most see Mark and Luke removing an error here. So, for example, Fitzmyer 1981: 605 argues for the removal of an error, but it is only an ambiguity, if the reference is literary.

in the OT texts in question (Marshall 1978: 232). Jesus' point is clear: in the OT, there is an apparent violation by David. Even if the details are not the same, the key principle makes Jesus' point.

That Jesus takes the issue beyond tradition with the illustration, however, is clear when the explicit point is made that what David did was not lawful (ἔξεστιν, *exestin*). By law, only the priests had the right to the bread. Jesus is talking about more than pharisaic tradition here. The issue of what is permitted makes this a "legal" dispute. The letter of the law was not followed by David, so does Jesus' remark challenge the scope of the law's application? Is he arguing that the law was never intended to be interpreted so literally that compassion was excluded in a situation of basic need like David's? Jesus knows the law's limits, and his remark shows him to be interpreting the force, intent, and limits of the law. This approach to the law's limitations requires reflection, a point that contemporary theonomists may need to grasp. In effect the argument becomes, "If you condemn my disciples on this one, you also condemn David and his men!" (Danker 1988: 131). Jesus advocates a restricted hierarchical ethic, and David's example is his defense: ceremonial restrictions of law are to give way to human need.[29] The law should not restrict people in their basic tasks, but should encourage them, in the case of the Sabbath, to honor the day. There are situations in which the law can be waived or transcended. David and his men had such a moment. Such a situation faces the disciples. One can overdraw the law's scope. By mentioning the men with David, Jesus establishes the link to the disciples.

Jesus places the officials in a dilemma. If the Pharisees are right, David and his men were guilty. The Pharisees' problem is that the biblical text does not question David's action and neither did the priest at the scene of the "crime." Do the officials want to challenge David and a priest of the OT? While Mark and Matthew both contain additional sayings material at this point, Luke moves right into a summation, since his account is more succinct.[30]

(2) Authority of the Son of Man (6:5)

Jesus' closing remark centers on κύριος (*kyrios*, Lord), which comes at the start of the citation. A literal rendering according to word or-   **6:5**

---

29. Liefeld 1984: 887. Similar examples existed in Judaism, such as the priority of giving birth or burying the dead versus staying ceremonially clean. Witherington 1990: 68 speaks of the Sabbath's being a day of renewal and restoration, so that eating a meal is quite appropriate.

30. Matt. 12:5–7 speaks of another example where the priests work in the temple without profaning themselves; it also mentions the prophetic principle that God desires mercy, not sacrifice. Mark 2:27 refers to the Sabbath's being made for people, not people for the Sabbath.

der is, "Lord is of the Sabbath the Son of Man." The passage has its fullest development in Mark 2:27, which speaks about the Sabbath's being for people and not people for the Sabbath. Many see Mark's point to be humankind's authority over the Sabbath, with the "Son of Man" as a reference to humans in general, since the phrase can have this meaning in Aramaic (Creed 1930: 84–85; see the exegesis of 5:24 and excursus 6). A later rabbinic statement is close to this remark in force; nonetheless, many regard Jesus' remark as a likely reflection of an ancient view: "The Sabbath is given over to you and not you to the Sabbath" (*Mekilta de Rabbi Ishmael*, tractate *Shabbata* 1 on Exod. 31:13 [= Lauterbach 1933–35: 3.198]; Marshall 1978: 232). But Marshall notes that this saying is not a broad reference to all people, but to Israel's special authority. So even here, the application is narrow. The point of Mark's text, which Luke does not have, is that the Sabbath is not to be a master over God's people, but is a service to them (Carson 1982: 62–66). It was created for them and was not created as a burden against them.[31] This approach to Mark 2:27 seems the best way to view its background, which in turn supports its authenticity and its meaning. The Marcan point in the next verse is a form of heightened argument. If the Sabbath is designed for God's people, if the Sabbath is created to serve people, then certainly the representative man, Jesus, has authority over it.

Luke does not have Mark's remark about the Sabbath and God's people. Rather, Luke has a more exclusive christological focus. Mark's intermediate argument is not made, but the deeper issue about Jesus is emphasized. The Son of Man's authority refers to Jesus. Even in Mark, however, this has to be the ultimate point. In chasing the background of the Son of Man, commentators have ignored the contextual clues. In fact, when one detaches this saying from its context because of form-critical or redactional concerns, the logic of the sayings becomes difficult and leads to challenges of the authenticity of Luke 6:5. Lindars (1983: 103–6) seems to argue for the authenticity of Mark 2:27, but cannot accept Mark 2:28 = Luke 6:5 as authentic. He argues that the point about David is not found in David's authority, for if the passage is taken with this christological force, then "Son of Man" must be taken as a messianic title. A messianic force is unlikely at this early point in Jesus' ministry. Thus, Lindars argues that Mark 2:28 is a Marcan saying that is formed in dependence on Mark 2:10.

However, the point becomes clear by keeping a unity in the Marcan remarks, rather than creating a division. The ability of the total

---

31. Hooker 1967: 95–99 is very clear in showing the narrow application of this passage, as well as citing the Jewish background behind it.

context to unify the argument strengthens the argument for authenticity. The key to the argument is the previous Davidic illustration, since the king is a *representative* figure. Jesus' claim to be Son of Man gives the term a representative sense through the contextual linkage. Son of Man need not be explicitly messianic to make the point; it needs only to be representative, which is how the reference to David functions in the analogy. There are, however, implications in the usage that suggest the nature of the authority referred to in this concluding remark. Danker (1988: 131) sees this point clearly: the Son of Man is an authoritative representative on behalf of his people, much as a king would be (Hooker 1967: 100–102; Fitzmyer 1981: 610; Marshall 1978: 232–33). Jesus, as this representative, has authority as Son of Man to evaluate and interpret tradition and law. This is why authority is stressed by the placement of κύριος in the emphatic position. Again, great claims for Jesus are alluded to here. Jesus uses the title *Son of Man* in this context and refers to himself as *this* man for a second time in the Gospel, with David providing the additional backdrop to explain the point (see the exegesis of 5:24 [= Mark 2:10]). Jesus heightens the stakes with the appeal to David, for he suggests by the comparison that the present times are like the times of David. Jesus has such a high stature (Luke 1:32).[32] He is an authoritative representative of the new way. Lindars takes an either/or approach that focuses on a messianic understanding of Son of Man as the only alternative that can really work. In so doing, he misses the unity of the argument that can be found by a more representative emphasis to the title.[33] With the remark, Jesus argues that he is the authoritative representative of the new way (as David was in the old era?) and that he has authority over the understanding and administration of the Sabbath.

c. Question about Healing on the Sabbath (6:6–11)
i. Setting: Officials Waiting to Make a Sabbath Charge (6:6–7)

The next healing occurs on another (ἑτέρῳ, *heterō*) Sabbath, which **6:6** does not necessarily mean the next Sabbath, but simply makes clear that the event would be seen in light of Sabbath traditions. The introduction also temporally separates this event from the previous controversy (6:1) and reveals a topical concern about Sabbath con-

---

32. Danker 1988: 131 alludes to the promises of Ezek. 34:20–24 and 37:24–28 as helpful background. Jesus is more than a prophet or teacher.

33. Borsch 1967: 322–23 also argues for this more representative reading, which is grounded in kingship and not necessarily in explicit messianism. As well, he argues for ties to Adam. The latter connection is less certain here, but Borsch also sees Mark 2:28—and thus Luke 6:5—as authentic.

troversies that links these events. Jesus finds himself teaching in the synagogue again (4:16, 31, 44). In the synagogue is a man whose right hand is withered. His condition probably comes from paralysis, though no details are given.[34] In the Gospel to the Nazareans, the man is a stonemason whose hand has been injured so that his livelihood is destroyed, but there is no way to confirm the origin of this detail (Schneemelcher 1991–92: 1.160; Jerome *Commentary on Matthew* 12:13). What is clear is that the man is not in any mortal danger.

To grasp the tension in this final event of the unit, one needs to appreciate how the Pharisees would have seen the issue of Sabbath healing. In general, healing or medical work was not to be done on the Sabbath, unless a life was in danger, a baby was being born, or a circumcision needed to be performed. Thus, for example, one could do the work of a midwife on the Sabbath (*m. Šab.* 6.3; 12.1; 18.3; 19.2; *m. ʿEd.* 2.5; *m. Yomaʾ* 8.6; *Mekilta de Rabbi Ishmael*, tractate *Shabbata* 1 on Exod. 31:13 [Lauterbach 1933–35: 3.197–99]; Lohse, *TDNT* 7:14–15; SB 1:623–29; 2:533–34; Marshall 1978: 235). The *Mekilta* text argues that since one can kill a burglar on the Sabbath to protect life, so one can save life on the Sabbath. In addition, since one can circumcise and thus sanctify one member of the body on the Sabbath, how much more can one save a life (and the whole body!) on the Sabbath. Someone sick or crippled, without life being threatened, could wait a day for treatment, just as a child born at twilight on Friday could wait to be circumcised until after the Sabbath (*m. Šab.* 19.5). Such waiting would be expected in this situation, as the official's remark in Luke 13:14 makes clear. This situation differs from the events in 4:31–39, where the confrontation with the demon in the synagogue had to be dealt with directly and where the fever in Simon's mother-in-law may have been a case of serious illness. In Luke 6, the event is public and lacks urgency—according to those who hold a traditional approach to the Sabbath.

6:7   The scribes and Pharisees were watching Jesus closely.[35] The graphic term παρετηροῦντο (*paretērounto*) is emotive; it means to spy on or watch out of the corner of one's eye, which adds a sinister note.[36] The Pharisees were watching to see if Jesus would heal on

---

34. BAGD 548 §2; BAA 1112 §2; Van Der Loos 1965: 438–39; Bovon 1989: 274. The term ξηρός means "withered," so that the hand has suffered atrophy. The term also appears in the parallel Matt. 12:10 = Mark 3:3; and Luke 6:8; John 5:3; Matt. 23:15; Heb. 11:29.

35. On the combination scribes and Pharisees, see Luke 5:21; 7:30; 11:53; 15:2; Mark 7:5; H. Weiss, *TDNT* 9:38.

36. Riesenfeld, *TDNT* 8:147; Schürmann 1969: 306 n. 48; Bovon 1989: 274 n. 24; Ps. 37:12 [36:12 LXX]; Dan. 6:12 (with τηρέω); BAGD 622 §1aβ; BAA 1258 §1aβ. Today, παρατηρέω (to watch lurkingly) makes one think of a spy novel.

the Sabbath. A textual issue determines the exact sense: Were they watching for what Jesus did regularly (present tense)? Or were they watching for what his response would be in this one situation (future tense)? In this context, a single action is more likely (see the additional note). Either way, the issue centers clearly on Jesus' healing on the Sabbath.

If Jesus acts, the Pharisees are ready to charge him with working on the Sabbath. The ἵνα (hina) clause gives the purpose of their watching Jesus: they want him to heal on the Sabbath so that they can level a charge against him.[37] Basically, unless a person was near death, the healing could wait (m. Yoma⁾ 8.6).[38]

ii. Jesus' Response: A Question (6:8–9)

Jesus knows what his opponents are thinking, and so he acts. Such references to Jesus' knowledge are common in Luke (5:22; 9:47; 11:17; 24:38; Danker 1988: 132; Schrenk, TDNT 2:97; Friedrich, TDNT 6:844). As elsewhere in Luke (2:35; 5:22; 6:8; 9:47), διαλογισμός (dialogismos, thought) is often negative (Schürmann 1969: 307 n. 51, 128 n. 224; more neutral in force are 9:46 and 24:38). Jesus knows that they want to get him; but he does not back away. The opponents may be secretive; but Jesus is open (Plummer 1896: 169). He turns to the man and tells him to come forward. The man obeys, a point that Luke alone makes. The encounter approaches.

6:8

Jesus takes up the challenge by asking a question. He knows his opponents' thoughts and will characterize their action in contrast to his own. The contrast is expressed in a pair of descriptions, where one element describes what Jesus is attempting to do and the other element is suggestive about how the Pharisees approach the day. Again the issue turns on the term ἔξεστιν (exestin, lawful).

6:9

What Jesus desires to do, and what people should desire to do, is to accomplish good, that is, save a life. Σῴζω (sōzō) here is not a technical term for salvation, but simply refers to deliverance in a general sense—to the restoration and healing that again give the man possession of full physical skills. Using this term in his question shows that Jesus' action is acceptable, since "saving" on the Sabbath was permitted (see n. 38). To do such an act on the Sabbath is morally evaluated as "doing good" (ἀγαθοποιῆσαι, agathopoiēsai).

---

37. The phrase here may reflect an Aramaism; Fitzmyer 1981: 611. On εὑρίσκω, see BAGD 325 §1b; BAA 765 §I.1e.

38. For the background of a possible Sabbath violation, see the discussion above following the discussion of sources and historicity. On Sabbath conflicts related to healing, besides the parallel Matt. 12:10 = Mark 3:2, see Luke 13:14 and 14:3; Beyer, TDNT 3:130.

It is the natural expression of operating on the principle of the law of love.[39]

In contrast stands the Pharisees' condemnatory attitude, not to mention their spying. Because of excessive concern over the Sabbath, they are not willing to let a man be freed from his condition. This attitude and their lying in wait to catch Jesus are described morally in terms of "doing harm" (κακοποιῆσαι, *kakopoiēsai*) or "destroying" (ἀπολέσαι, *apolesai*). It is almost as if the refusal to do good is itself evil (Danker 1988: 133; Marshall 1978: 235; Fitzmyer 1981: 611). The reference to destroying a life may well suggest where their attitude is headed. There is an ironic foreshadowing in this characterization of their position, given what will happen to Jesus. Jesus' reply has an element of precedent in the OT: Isa. 1:11–17; 58:6–14 (Danker 1988: 133; Hendriksen 1978: 322). The intent of the Sabbath was to prevent people from working several consecutive days without rest, to provide time for rejuvenation, and to give time to contemplate God. Certainly it was never intended to prevent one from doing good. The question puts the Pharisees in a dilemma, since the answer is so clear. In effect, Jesus says, "Why delay a healing when good can be done now?" Having laid the groundwork, Jesus turns to demonstrate God's endorsement for doing good on the Sabbath. The endorsement comes with the healing, since God does not respond in such situations to a sinner. If Jesus is right, God will heal the man through him, even though it is the Sabbath. Again, the miracle serves as an audiovisual pointing to truth and its agent.

iii. Act: Jesus Heals (6:10)

6:10 The healing is a success. There is another touch of irony in this verse. Note the amount of labor involved in the healing: Jesus merely speaks a sentence. Such is his authority. Unlike Mark 3:5, Luke does not mention Jesus' anger at the lack of response from the crowd. Luke often lacks such criticism of the disciples and others. Rather, he describes Jesus' gazing at all who are present. The action is for the public, as is the lesson. The right thing is to do good on the Sabbath. He tells the man to stretch his hand out; for the man to obey would mean that healing has occurred. The attempt would show the man's willingness to respond to Jesus. In that request, the "labor" occurs.

The request meets with response, and the stretched-out hand is restored. Danker (1988: 133) notes this is not a reflex response or a

---

39. Luke 6:33 (twice) and 6:35 use the term ἀγαθοποιέω; Ernst 1977: 205; Schürmann 1969: 308; Busse 1979: 140 perceptively notes the conceptual tie to 9:11 and 4:18.

psychosomatic healing, a view he attributes to the excessive rationalism of the nineteenth century. Jesus exercises power on the Sabbath in the synagogue, power that suggests God's endorsement of what he is doing.[40] The account is told from the viewpoint of a spectator, for the man's healing is noted and then he is not mentioned any more. The main characters in this event are Jesus and the opponents. Jesus publicly displays his authority on the Sabbath and leaves it to his opponents to respond. God has shown his power and compassion through Jesus.

iv. Reaction: Decision to Deal with Jesus (6:11)

The officials' response was strong. The graphic term ἀνοίας (*anoias*; lit., mindless) refers to their mindless rage or irrational anger (Schürmann 1969: 309 n. 69; Behm, *TDNT* 4:963, speaks of pathological rage). The reaction was caused by the frustration that God does not hear sinners or Sabbath violators like Jesus, and yet right there in front of them was a Sabbath healing! It also would be difficult to say that Jesus labored on the Sabbath, since he only spoke to the man. They had been confounded by Jesus' action. What could they do?

6:11

In his final comment Luke engages in understatement. He notes that the officials begin to discuss what they might do (ποιήσαιεν, *poiēsaien*) about Jesus.[41] Luke gives no specifics other than to mention that the plotting begins. They are at their wits' end and are not exactly sure what to do, but they have the conviction that something must be done (Marshall 1978: 236). This challenge to their approach to religion and the faith of the fathers is too great to ignore. Mark 3:6 and Matt. 12:14 tell us that they begin to think about how they might destroy him. A turning point has come, since official Judaism registers a negative vote against Jesus.

What do these three pericopes tell about Jesus? Luke 5:33–39 and its dispute over fasting lead to a disclosure about the real distinction between Jesus and what has gone before. Jesus' presence is a time of joy, so that activities like fasting do not fit the occasion. But the real issue is what Jesus brings. What he represents is something new that cannot be mixed with old ways without destroying the new entity. The new way needs new containers. In fact, some people are so wedded to old tastes that they will not be

Summary

---

40. Jesus often heals at synagogues: Mark 1:23–27 = Luke 4:33–36; Mark 1:39 = Matt. 4:23; Mark 3:1–5 = Matt. 12:9–13 = Luke 6:6–10; Matt. 9:35; Luke 13:10–17; Schrage, *TDNT* 7:830 n. 210.

41. Luke uses the optative in indirect questions; BDF §385.1, §386.1; BDR §385.1, §386.1.

interested in the new way. When Jesus is gone, fasting will be appropriate, but optional. In Jesus, something different comes. The reader is asked to pick which wineskin to draw from: the one containing Judaism's old wine or the one containing Jesus' new wine. In addition, one must realize that the two religions cannot be mixed successfully.

In Luke 6:1–5, the first explicit Sabbath controversy in the Gospel has two fundamental points. First, it gives instruction about how Jesus viewed the law and the tradition that grew from it. The law was not to be read with absolute rigidity. There were exceptions to it, when ethical conflicts arose, as the incident with David shows. The Pharisees' question reflects an overapplication of law, even of the Sabbath law, whose roots lay in the Ten Commandments. What is not clear from Jesus' remarks is the more philosophical question: Did Jesus supersede the law here or did he interpret the law in the way it was always intended (and thus did not really violate it at all)? What seems clear from the challenge of the Davidic example is that law is not always to be read in absolute terms. Compassion for life's basic needs is most absolute. David's eating the priests' bread is at most a violation of the letter of the law, as 6:4 makes clear.

Second, Jesus has authority over the Sabbath and also has authority over the law's interpretation. The reason Jesus utters this corollary is that the Pharisees might have been able to object had the argument stopped at 6:4. The objection would then have been, "What gives you the right to make such claims or to compare yourself to David?" By going on to make the christological point, Jesus answers the objection before it can be raised. He claims representative authority. His answer may not be accepted by the leadership, but the choice is clearly placed before them. As with virtually every other pericope in Luke's Galilean section, the point turns on the nature of Jesus' person. As the previous passage showed, Jesus brings something new that those used to old ways will have trouble accepting. The grain issue ultimately turns on something more than the right to eat or Jesus' practice. It turns on who Jesus is. The nature of the times and Jesus' interpretation of them ultimately depend on whether Jesus has authority from God to reveal his ways. If he has such authority, he is to be heeded and new times have come. If he does not, then the objections raised against him expose his ministry as a charade. The basic issue of the passage is not really the disciples' practice, but Jesus' authority. Does Luke's reader believe that Jesus is sent by God? Does the reader see that Jesus is the Son of Man who has authority even over the Sabbath? Does the reader see that Jesus has authority to explain the law?

Luke 6:6–11 continues the emphasis on authority. Jesus teaches about a proper general approach to the law of the Sabbath, while confirming the greatness of his own authority. God's law concerning the Sabbath was never intended to block the doing of good. People are always to be ready to serve others. But more importantly, does Jesus bring something new? The testimony of a restored hand speaks in favor of his claims. However, the testimony hardens the position of some scribes and Pharisees against him. They decide that something needs to be done about Jesus. By choosing rejection, they have missed the point of what has taken place. The opposition's solidification has come, but Jesus' ministry will continue, because the new way he brings does not rest on the authority of religious officials. They may have voted against Jesus, but the restoration of the withered hand reflects a divine vote of confidence for Jesus. The reader is to note the crucial difference.

Additional Notes

5:33. UBS–NA has a declarative statement, with some manuscript support: $\mathfrak{P}^4$, $\aleph^1$, B, L, W. However, manuscript support for a question (with διὰ τί appended to the front of the sentence) is strong: $\aleph^{*,2}$, A, C, Θ, Ψ, Byz, Lect, most Itala. The latter reading is not regarded as original because it looks like a correction made in light of Mark 2:18 or Matt. 9:14, both of which read a question. In any case, the meaning is the same.

5:38. The simple βλητέον (must be put; a verbal adjective from βάλλω) is read in a few manuscripts: $\mathfrak{P}^4$, $\mathfrak{P}^{75}$ (apparently), $\aleph^1$, B, L, family 1, some Syriac. If original, this form is a NT *hapax legomenon* (BAGD 144; BAA 287). Another well-attested reading is βλητέον καὶ ἀμφότεροι συντηροῦνται ([new wine] must be put [in new skins] and both are preserved), read by A, C, Δ, Θ, Ψ, family 13, Byz, and Lect. It may be original, but it looks like assimilation to Matt. 9:17. The presence of additional variants that conform to Matthew increases the suspicion against this reading's being original, for it is difficult to explain the existence of these variants if βλητέον καὶ ἀμφότεροι συντηροῦνται were the original reading. These variants look like attempts to assimilate the Gospel readings. However, the presence of βλητέον in this well-attested longer variant suggests its earlier presence, since other variants lack it. Where would the *hapax legomenon* have come from unless it were original? The text's meaning is not significantly influenced by the decision. If the longer text is chosen, then an additional emphasis on preservation becomes clear. But the longer reading is unlikely to have been original to Luke 5:38.

5:39. Mainly Western manuscripts (D and most Itala) omit the entire verse, making the passage read more like Mark 2:22 and Matt. 9:17. However, widely distributed manuscripts support the inclusion: $\mathfrak{P}^4$, $\mathfrak{P}^{75}$, ℵ, B, C, L, W, Δ, Θ, Ψ, Byz, Lect. The inclusion is also the harder reading, since it lacks Gospel parallels. Thus it should be included.

5:39. Is the wine χρηστός (good) or χρηστότερος (better)? The first reading, printed in UBS–NA, is supported by $\mathfrak{P}^4$, ℵ, B, L, W, one Syriac manuscript; the second by A, C, Δ, Θ, Ψ, Byz, Lect, some Itala, some Syriac. Although difficult to assess because of the omission of Western support for either reading (see the previous additional note), the external evidence slightly favors χρηστότερος. But an argument can be made internally for χρηστός: could the passage be saying that a person is so satisfied with the old wine that the new wine is not even tasted to make a comparison (Plummer 1896: 164; Creed 1930: 84)? Those impressed with this argument will accept the UBS–NA text. The choice is complicated since χρηστός can also be translated "better"; see 9:48 and 10:42, where Luke uses a normal adjective to make comparisons (Fitzmyer 1981: 602). Though the choice of text is not certain, the basic meaning in either case is that the new wine is not accepted. Χρηστός is more likely the original text.

6:1. Many manuscripts (A, C, D, L, Δ, Θ, Ψ, Byz, and many Itala) read a unique term here, δευτεροπρώτῳ, which in context means "second-first" Sabbath (BAGD 177; BAA 354). The attestation is strong enough to suggest that it could be original, but explaining what it means or how it got into the text is difficult.[42] Before deciding the issue, its meaning must be considered.

Four meanings have been suggested for this term (Plummer 1896: 165–66; Fitzmyer 1981: 607–8):

1. It is the first Sabbath in the second year of the seven-year cycle. But if this had been meant, why would Luke introduce it without explanation?
2. It is the first Sabbath of the second month of the year. Again, such a reference is very cryptic.
3. The notation links the Sabbaths in Luke chronologically and is a scribal gloss: 4:31 is the first Sabbath, 6:1 is the second Sabbath, and 6:6 is a third Sabbath (though the term ἑτέρῳ [another] is used in 6:6, not the ordinal "third"; Metzger 1975: 139; Fitzmyer 1981:

---

42. Accepted by Godet 1875: 1.284–85; rejected by Schürmann 1969: 302; Nolland 1989: 255; Ernst 1977: 202 (discussion but no clear choice). Rejecting the reading but attempting to explain its origin are Vogt 1959; Lohse, *TDNT* 7:23 n. 183; Marshall 1978: 230; Wiefel 1988: 122; Bovon 1989: 266–67 (following Metzger 1975: 139). See also Buchanan and Wolfe 1978; Isaac 1981; and Skeat 1988. The reading is noted in the fourth century by Jerome, *Letter* 52.8, who did not know what it meant.

608; Bovon 1989: 266). However, the events that fall between Luke 4 and Luke 6 are problematic to this solution.

4. The phrase alludes to the first Sabbath of Nisan after Passover, which would be the first major Sabbath in the year after Passover and yet would be the second Sabbath of the year. Allusions to this approach are seen in Lev. 23:10–11, 15–16 and at Qumran in 11QTemple^a 18.10–19.9. Also, the time of year—harvest time—would be right for such an event.[43] The question is whether such a technical term existed at this time.

In my view, δευτεροπρώτῳ was probably added to the text and is not original to Luke. The word is rare and possesses an unclear meaning, especially if the existence of such a technical term cannot be firmly established. Manuscripts omitting δευτεροπρώτῳ are $\mathfrak{P}^4$, $\mathfrak{P}^{75}$, ℵ, B, L, W, family 1, many Itala, Syriac. There are two possible explanations for the addition: (1) A scribe, aware of the sacred calendar, may have added the note of the δευτεροπρώτῳ Sabbath (Lohse, *TDNT* 7:23 n. 183) or (2) a scribe may have been counting Sabbaths in this early section of Luke and added the numeral. In fact, in this second view the addition had two stages. First, a scribe, knowing that 6:6 read ἑτέρῳ (another) Sabbath, added πρώτῳ (first) to 6:1. Then a second scribe, knowing about 4:31, added δευτέρῳ (second) to πρώτῳ to yield δευτεροπρώτῳ.

6:1. The text relates that the disciples plucked and ate some heads of grain; only then does it state: "rubbing them in their hands." The original word order and syntactical arrangement of these phrases were evidently somewhat unusual or else four attempts at rearrangement would not exist. The variant readings all attempt to achieve a more logical word order and syntax for the description of handling of the grain. The problem, not discussed in UBS^4, seems to have arisen because the participle ψώχοντες (rubbing) was not appreciated as being syntactically linked to the verb ἤσθιον (ate). The UBS–NA text is correct here.

6:2. A well-attested variant (ℵ, A, C, W, Byz, Lect, Syriac) adds ποιεῖν to the verse, so it translates: "What is not allowed to do." But this is to be rejected because it harmonizes with Matt. 12:2. Also, the infinitive appears slightly redundant. The UBS–NA text is based on $\mathfrak{P}^4$, B, Vulgate. The wording is close to Mark 2:24, but is distinct enough to look like a separate rendering. There is no real difference in the readings (not discussed in UBS^4). Either way, it is a charge against the entire group for violating Sabbath custom.

6:4. The addition of καί (also [to those with him]) is probably correctly re-

---

43. Among those who support this approach are Schürmann 1969: 302; Vogt 1959; Buchanan and Wolfe 1978; and apparently Danker 1988: 130. Marshall 1978: 230 is uncertain of the origin.

garded as a harmonizing variant, since it conforms to Mark 2:26. Regardless of what reading is chosen, the point of the text is the same.

6:5. Manuscript D has an entirely different verse here, which has provoked much discussion (not mentioned in UBS³): D places what is commonly regarded as 6:5 after 6:10 and in its place has an incident about a man working on the Sabbath. Thus, D adds a distinct Sabbath controversy, making a total of three controversies in 6:1–11. Jesus says to the man in this brief incident, "If you know what you are doing, you are blessed; but if not, you are accursed and a transgressor of the law." Plummer (1896: 168) rejects this text, but sees it going back to Jesus (so also Luce 1933: 139–40).[44] The reason it is accepted by some as authentic, though not original in Luke, is that the wording about being a transgressor of the law appears in Rom. 2:25, 27 and James 2:11. The saying is also similar to the Coptic Gospel of Thomas 3, 14. But most reject it (Lohse, *TDNT* 7:23–24). What is clear is that it does not belong here in Luke's Gospel, since it has such little manuscript support. If it was original, how did it so thoroughly disappear from the manuscript tradition?

6:5. An additional καί is present in different locations within the two variations noted by UBS–NA. One well-attested reading (A, D, L, Δ, Θ, Ψ, family 1, family 13, Byz, Lect, most Itala) uses καί to describe the Son of Man's Sabbath authority: ὁ υἱὸς τοῦ ἀνθρώπου καὶ τοῦ σαββάτου (the Son of Man also [is Lord] of the Sabbath). This reading conforms to Mark 2:28, while the UBS–NA text of Luke 6:5 matches Matt. 12:8. The geographical spread of this difficult variant may suggest that it is original, especially given Matthew's popularity in the early church. The other reading (only in UBS³) follows the word order of some Coptic and Ethiopic versions: καὶ τοῦ σαββάτου ὁ υἱὸς τοῦ ἀνθρώπου ([Lord] also of the Sabbath [is] the Son of Man), a translation similar to the above variant but with a distinct word order. This reading, which assumes the Sabbath reference earlier in the verse and attaches καί to σαββάτου is hard to explain if Luke's original order followed Mark and had ὁ υἱὸς τοῦ ἀνθρώπου first. Thus, the second variant indirectly supports the UBS–NA text and tips the scales to that reading. The difference involves only word order and does not change the passage's sense.

6:7. Is the verb for healing a present or future tense? The present tense speaks about what Jesus' habit is, while the future looks only for one event (Luce 1933: 140). The distribution of the manuscripts is fairly even (present: ℵ, A, D, L, W, Ψ; future: 𝔓⁴, B, Θ, family 1, Byz), and either reading is possible. Mark 3:2 reads a future, while Matt. 12:10 expresses the thought as a question using an aorist infinitive. Those who see harmonization as evidence of scribal correction will agree with the present tense in UBS–NA.

44. For more recent discussion, see Kaiser 1968; Schürmann 1969: 304 n. 29; Marshall 1978: 233; Fitzmyer 1981: 610 (who ties it to the apocryphal gospel tradition); Wiefel 1988: 123 (who rejects a connection to Jesus); and Bovon 1989: 267.

5. Choosing of the Twelve (6:12–16)

In the face of rising opposition, the rest of Luke 6 narrates Jesus' organizing of disciples (6:12–16), a summary about his teaching and healing (6:17–19), and an example of his ethical-religious teaching (6:20–49). This teaching will go to all (6:17), but it is intended to set forth the disciples' fundamental love ethic. Despite the opposition mentioned earlier in Luke 6, there are followers. Jesus is training them for the task of following him. From this organizing stage, there will eventually emerge a call to mission in 9:1–6, with a second, larger mission to follow in 10:1–12. The first layer of organization is the call of the Twelve, who will be the first followers sent into mission and from whom almost all the major leaders of the early church are drawn. Thus the text is a major bridge explaining that alongside opposition came Jesus' efforts to tighten his circle of supporters as he prepared them for instruction and mission.

It is debated whether this unit links up with 5:1–6:11 (so Nolland 1989: 264) or 6:17–49 (Fitzmyer 1981: 613). I prefer to call it a bridge, although one should note how easily the selection flows into the next summary passage. Nolland makes too much of the introductory formula in 5:1 and 6:1, since ἐγένετο also appears in 5:12, 17; 6:6; 7:11; 8:1, 22. It is too common an introduction for Luke to have built his literary units around it. Nolland is correct to note that this text is a third call text (5:1–11, 27–32), only here we have a call within the call.

Sources and Historicity

The exact chronological placement of the calling of the Twelve is difficult (Luke 6:12–16 = Mark 3:13–19 = Matt. 10:1–4; Aland 1985: §49). In comparison to Mark, Luke has this event in relatively the same position, though Mark chooses to offer a summary of Jesus' ministry before this account. That Luke saves the summary until after the choosing of the Twelve and uses it to introduce the discourse on the plain (Luke 6:17–19) is simply a difference of arrangement. What is interesting is that Matthew has this event earlier than his parallels of the previous events of Mark and Luke.[1]

---

1. The plucking of grain on the Sabbath (Matt. 12:1–8) and the healing of the man with the withered hand (Matt. 12:9–14) come after the choosing of the Twelve (Matt. 10:1–4).

However, to the calling of the Twelve in Matthew, there is appended in Matt. 10:5–16 an event that appears later in both Luke and Mark—the sending of the Twelve out into mission (Mark 6:7–11 = Luke 9:2–5). Thus, Matthew probably has put together events that were originally somewhat separate in time. Acts 1:21–22 may help, for there the requirements for apostles include having been with Jesus from the early days. If this includes an allusion to Jesus' original selections, then it may suggest that the choosing of the Twelve is early—as reflected in its chronological placement in Mark and Luke. Matthew's placement is a topical one in which he has waited to tell of the calling of the Twelve until he discusses their mission. But to give the event a more precise placement is not possible, given the rearranging that all the Gospels have done in this section.

The Lucan account here is very close to Mark. Luke has only a few additional points. First, he adds that prayer preceded the choice, a point that reflects an emphasis he has throughout his Gospel (3:21 and 5:16 are two earlier examples; note also 9:18, 28–29; 22:40–46; Tannehill 1986: 205–6). Second, Luke notes more specifically than Mark that the choice of the Twelve was out of a larger group of disciples. Mark simply mentions the choice of the Twelve. Luke is also distinct from Matthew at these two points. Finally, with Matt. 10:2 and possibly with Mark 3:14, Luke calls the Twelve "apostles" at this point, though Luke's remark is the most direct.[2] From this group emerges the early church's leadership, and this account makes it clear that they are divinely chosen, the product of an evening of prayer. Luke has used material that parallels Mark, and he may have used some additional source material as well, given the differences in the various lists.[3]

There is little doubt that Jesus had an inner circle, so many do not challenge the account historically. An exception is the study of Guenther, who argues that the notion of the Christian Twelve is an early post-Easter creation.[4] However, the early church would hardly create a list with Judas in it,

2. Matt. 10:2 opens the list of names by noting that "these are the names of the twelve apostles." The phrase οὓς καὶ ἀποστόλους ὠνόμασεν (whom he also named apostles) in Mark 3:14 is bracketed in UBS–NA to express uncertainty concerning its originality.

3. Marshall 1978: 237 notes that Luke may have had an alternate list of the Twelve, but he regards the evidence as weak. Schürmann 1969: 318–19, 323 is confident that Luke had a form of what he calls the "Catalogue of the Apostles" (a name that notes the passage's form), which differed from Mark and derived from Q. Bovon 1989: 278 also sees additional source material here beyond Mark, since the apostolic list had various forms, as Acts 1:13 shows. Nolland 1989: 265 speaks only of the influences of another tradition. Though he is less certain of another full list used by Luke, he thinks one existed because of the inclusion of Judas son of James and the absence of Thaddaeus. The differences in the lists will be noted in the exegesis.

4. Guenther 1985: 31. Nolland 1989: 265–68 has a full discussion, though he sees too much distance between Paul's and Luke's views when he argues that Luke limits the term ἀπόστολος to the Twelve. One of the ways that Luke indicates respect for Paul is by calling him an apostle in Acts 14:4, 14 and by showing that Paul does

yet he is in every list except Acts 1:13, an omission that is a result of his death (Creed 1930: 87). Guenther's study is suspect, because he nowhere explains how a traitor was inserted into a later list of the Twelve. The exegesis of 6:13 discusses the use of ἀπόστολος in this setting. Some suggest allusions to a new exodus motif here, since Jesus goes up to the mountain before acting; but such allusions are too distant to be likely.[5] The account simply narrates the gathering of the Twelve to show the authoritative credibility they have as Jesus' chosen representatives.

The form consists of a summary catalogue, noting Jesus' election of the Twelve (Berger 1984: 224–25).[6]

The outline of Luke 6:12–16 is as follows:

a. Setting: all-night prayer (6:12)
b. Choosing of the Twelve (6:13–16)
  i. Choice of twelve from the disciples (6:13)
  ii. Listing of the Twelve (6:14–16)

A few themes are present here. Relying on God's guidance, Jesus organizes his disciples. The Twelve are chosen in the context of humility, prayer, and guidance. The Twelve, who will become leaders of the church, are consciously chosen and have Jesus' endorsement. Thus, apostolic authority comes early in Jesus' ministry and is grounded in his choice. The church also saw a lesson in the type of prayer that preceded the choice, for the early church repeated the pattern when it made key decisions (Acts 6:6; 13:2–3; 14:23).

Exegesis and Exposition

[12]In these days he went out to the mountain to pray, and through the night he was in prayer with God. [13]And when it was day, he called to his dis-

---

everything that Peter did as an apostle. Nolland decides that the Lucan use reflects a later title. The use of the phrase *the Twelve* as a fixed technical term in the earliest Christian material—even when the Twelve are not present (1 Cor. 15:5)—also speaks for the authenticity of ἀπόστολος here.

5. For this connection are Ellis 1974: 11 and Schürmann 1969: 313 (who mentions Exod. 24:1–2, 9, 12–13, 15–18, with the seventy elders worshiping from a distance as Moses goes up the mountain, as well as 19:3 and 34:2–5); against it are Marshall 1978: 236 and Fitzmyer 1981: 616. Bovon 1989: 279–80 calls it questionable, citing Philo, *Life of Moses* 1.40 §§220–26; 2.14–15 §§70–71; 2.28 §§141–42; 2.30 §153; 2.31 §§159–60; and Pseudo-Philo, *Biblical Antiquities* 11–12, 15, as lacking such a motif. Bovon prefers to see Jesus praying for the preparation and renewal of his people, as Moses had done and as Pseudo-Philo notes.

6. Bovon 1989: 279 see three elements—summary account, short history of an election, and list—that indicate the formation of a community.

ciples and chose from them twelve, whom he also named apostles:
[14] Simon whom he named Peter,
and Andrew his brother,
and James,
and John,
and Philip,
and Bartholomew,
[15] and Matthew,
and Thomas,
and James son of Alphaeus,
and Simon, the one called Zealot,
[16] and Judas son of James,
and Judas ⸀Iscariot⸀, who became a traitor.

a. Setting: All-Night Prayer (6:12)

6:12 Before choosing the Twelve, Jesus withdraws and spends the entire night in prayer. Διανυκτερεύων (*dianyktereuōn*) refers to an all-night prayer vigil and appears only here in the NT (Job 2:9c; Josephus, *Antiquities* 6.13.9 §311; Plummer 1896: 171). The mountain referred to is not specified (Hendriksen 1978: 326 mentions the Horns of Hattin). Many speculate on a motif associated with the mountain: as a symbol for a place of revelation (so Danker 1988: 134–35, citing Exod. 24) or a picture of being close to God (Fitzmyer 1981: 616; Foerster, *TDNT* 5:481). The latter is the more likely, though there is no reason to turn the reference into a mere theological symbol. Jesus' actions follow a long communion with God. This is how Jesus deals with the rise of opposition. Solemnity and a note of guidance open the account. The phrase προσευχῇ τοῦ θεοῦ (*proseuchē tou theou*, prayer to God) is a good example of an objective genitive and makes the point that the prayer is given to God. As noted above, the early church learned to imitate this practice of prayer before decisions (Acts 6:6; 13:2–3; 14:23; 1 Tim. 4:14; 2 Tim. 1:6). Having spent the night in prayer, Jesus is ready to act. He will make a selection from within the circle of disciples and train them for leadership. Perhaps his prayers were for the team he was about to form and the new community that they would build together in the face of opposition.

b. Choosing of the Twelve (6:13–16)
i. Choice of Twelve from the Disciples (6:13)

6:13 The purpose of the prayer becomes evident from Jesus' next action. With the coming of day, Jesus descends and calls his disciples to himself. The number of disciples is not given, but from this group he chooses twelve. Luke alone makes explicit that the Twelve are chosen from a larger pool. The participle ἐκλεξάμενος (*eklexamenos*, electing) functions like a finite verb here ("he elected"). The choice of the Twelve is conscious and calculated. What is amazing about the Twelve is that the inclusion of Judas is part of a divinely guided process (Plummer 1896: 172).

Hendriksen (1978: 327) sees significance in the number twelve: it shows that the church is the new Israel, because Israel had twelve tribes. As a result, the church spans back into the OT (also Tiede 1988: 134, but with less emphasis on the OT connection). Part of assessing this connection turns on what the term *new* means. If it means that the church replaces Israel in God's plan and takes its place permanently, then it is not a correct description.[7] If it means that the church functions in a way parallel to Israel and now is temporary steward of the promise, then the designation is more acceptable. Nothing is made of the number here, though it is clear that in the larger Gospel tradition the Twelve are designed to parallel Israel, for Luke 22:29–30 and Matt. 19:28 show the relationship between the Twelve and Israel in the future. In addition, though there is in Luke an emphasis on continuity with the old period, it is never expressed in terms that say the new Israel is present. Such terminology is only an inference. In fact, the emphasis on newness and the impossibility of mixture in Luke 5:33–39 is against making this alleged Israelite connection too strongly.

The reference to Jesus' calling the Twelve apostles has created much discussion, because in the Gospels the combination ὀνομάζω (*onomazō*, to name) and ἀπόστολος (*apostolos*, apostle) is rare, occurring only here and possibly in Mark 3:14 (see n. 2 above). In the Synoptics, ἀπόστολος is found only at Mark 6:30 and Matt. 10:2 and six times in Luke. The Matthew parallel to Luke 6:13 is an interesting agreement of Matthew and Luke, while Mark 6:30 is a summary remark that may simply be describing the Twelve by their common, current designation, rather than being a suggestion that the title is this old. That Luke uses ἀπόστολος more frequently is not surprising, since he narrates a sequel about the early church and the key role of the apostles (Luke 9:10; 17:5; 22:14; 24:10). In the Synoptic Gospels, the Twelve are more commonly referred to in a nontitular way (Matt. 10:1, 2, 5; 11:1; 20:17; 26:14, 20, 47; Mark 3:16; 4:10; 6:7; 9:35; 10:32; 11:11; 14:10, 17, 20, 43; Luke 8:1; 9:1, 12; 18:31; 22:3, 47). Paul also alludes to the Twelve in a piece of tradition from the early church (1 Cor. 15:5). These data lead some to suggest that ἀπόστολος in the narrow sense of the Twelve or apostle *par excel-*

---

7. Rom. 11 sees a clear future for Israel and a future role in God's plan; Burns 1992. They will be grafted into the vine again one day. For another set of arguments against this Israel-church connection, see Witherington 1990: 128–29, who also notes that the Twelve were called to help gather a community.

lence may be anachronistic in Luke, since its development as a term exclusively referring to the Twelve seems to postdate Jesus' ministry (Plummer 1896: 172; Fitzmyer 1981: 617–18; Bovon 1989: 282 [anachronistic]; Liefeld 1984: 889 [possible]). It is argued that Jesus may have marked out a special group here, but he did not call them apostles in this narrow sense yet. That narrow title came later. Luke telescopes and summarizes the situation here.

Part of what makes a decision difficult are the various ways in which ἀπόστολος is used in the NT (BAGD 99–100; BAA 200). It has a more general meaning of a commissioned messenger and refers to figures outside the Twelve in numerous passages (Acts 14:4; Rom. 16:7; 1 Cor. 9:4–6; 2 Cor. 8:23; Phil. 2:25). Some attempt to show the difference by translating it in these passages as "representative," meaning a commissioned representative. The Jewish concept of sending (שָׁלַח, *šalaḥ*) quite possibly serves as the background for the use of this term. If so, then the representative acts as one with authority equal to the sender (Rengstorf, *TDNT* 1:414–20, 428–29; Fitzmyer 1981: 617; Ernst 1977: 208; Marshall 1978: 238–39; 1 Kings 14:6). The Mishnah phrases the concept this way: "The one sent by the man is as the man himself" (*m. Ber.* 5.5; see also *m. Roʾš. Haš.* 1.3; 4.9; *m. Yomaʾ* 1.5; Witherington 1990: 133–34). This idea of representation also existed in the larger culture (Herodotus 1.21; Josephus, *Antiquities* 17.11.1 §300; MM 70). It is quite possible that Jesus named the Twelve as his commissioned representatives here, as his apostles in the cultural sense, a title of great authority, because of the nature of the one making the commission. In time, that apostleship narrowed into an exclusive office of the select Twelve, a sense different from other apostles mentioned in the NT (e.g., Paul, Barnabas, Epaphroditus, Andronicus, Junia[s], or any other commissioned figure who was not part of the Twelve). Such a description would not be inaccurate nor out of place in light of how their role developed in Jesus' ministry or in light of the broader sense of the term in the culture. It is also possible, though less so in light of its usage, that because the Twelve were always marked out, they were always called apostles and regarded as the greatest of a broader group of apostles from the beginning. This title applied to them so well and uniquely that the title eventually became another way to refer exclusively to them. It seems clear either way that their authority was always regarded as somewhat unique, going back to Jesus' choice of them. Thus, in Luke's usage an apostle needs to be with Jesus from the beginning (Schürmann 1969: 314; Acts 1:21–22). The Twelve chosen by Jesus were called to function as his representatives and mouthpieces for the message of the kingdom (Luke 9:1–6).

ii. Listing of the Twelve (6:14–16)

Luke 6:14–16 is one of four NT lists of the Twelve, the others being **6:14**
Matt. 10:2–4, Mark 3:16–19, and Acts 1:13 (see adjacent table).
These lists have three points of agreement: (1) Peter is always listed
first and Judas is always listed last (except in Acts 1:13 where Judas
is omitted because he is dead). (2) The first four are always Peter,
Andrew, James, and John, though not always in the same order. (3)
There are three groups of four, with the lead position in each group
always occupied by Peter, Philip, and James son of Alphaeus (Plummer 1896: 172; Carson 1984: 237). Luke's list in Acts 1 has the same
names as his list in Luke 6, though in different order. Other differences in the lists will be covered as they arise.

Luke 6:14–16	Matt. 10:2–4	Mark 3:16–19	Acts 1:13
1. Simon Peter	1. Simon Peter	1. Simon Peter	1. Simon Peter
2. Andrew	2. Andrew	3. James son of Zebedee	4. John
3. James	3. James son of Zebedee	4. John	3. James
4. John	4. John	2. Andrew	2. Andrew
5. Philip	5. Philip	5. Philip	5. Philip
6. Bartholomew	6. Bartholomew	6. Bartholomew	8. Thomas
7. Matthew	8. Thomas	7. Matthew	6. Bartholomew
8. Thomas	7. Matthew	8. Thomas	7. Matthew
9. James son of Alphaeus	9. James son of Alphaeus	9. James son of Alphaeus	9. James son of Alphaeus
10. Simon the Zealot	11. Thaddaeus	11. Thaddaeus	10. Simon the Zealot
11. Judas son of James	10. Simon the Zealot	10. Simon the Zealot	11. Judas son of James
12. Judas Iscariot	12. Judas Iscariot	12. Judas Iscariot	—

Σίμωνα (Simon), the first name in the list, is also called Peter
(Πέτρος). Jesus gave him this second name (Matt. 16:18; John 1:42),
but Luke does not make any effort to discuss it. Luke uses the name
Simon for Peter until here, except for Simon Peter in Luke 5:8. For
the rest of his Gospel, Luke will call him Peter (the only exceptions
are 22:31; 24:34). Πέτρος means "rock" and alludes to his leadership
role among the Twelve (Cullmann, *TDNT* 6:100–12; Schürmann
1969: 316 n. 28). Mark 1:29 notes that Peter lived in Capernaum.

Ἀνδρέαν (Andrew), Peter's brother, was also a fisherman. Luke's
only other reference to him is Acts 1:13. John 1:44 notes that Andrew
is from Bethsaida. Otherwise he is mentioned only a few times
(Mark 1:16, 29; 13:3; John 1:40; 6:8; 12:22; Fitzmyer 1981: 618).

Ἰάκωβον (James) and Ἰωάννην (John) are called the sons of Zebedee (Luke 5:10) and the sons of thunder (Mark 3:17). They also are Galilean fishermen and are Jesus' cousins, since their mother, Salome, is Mary's sister (John 19:25 with Matt. 27:56 and Mark 15:40). They worked with Peter and Andrew (Luke 5:10–11). James is one of the early church martyrs (Acts 12:1–2). In one list, John occupies the second place next to Peter (Acts 1:13). He is known in tradition as the "beloved" disciple and is said to have lived a long life (John 13:23; 19:26; 20:2; 21:7, 20).

Φίλιππον (Philip) appears only briefly in the NT (John 1:43–48; 6:5–7; 12:22; 14:8–9). He was from Bethsaida and introduced Nathanael to Jesus. He is portrayed as a rather typical disciple, often struggling to understand what Jesus is doing.

Βαρθολομαῖον (Bartholomew) is a patronym meaning "son of Tolmai." There is speculation that he has another name, with Nathanael of John 1:45 often being put forward as the candidate (Hendriksen 1978: 329 is certain; Plummer 1896: 173 and Marshall 1978: 239 are more cautious). This identification was first made in the ninth century by a Nestorian named Ishodad of Merv, while in the West the suggestion was made by Rupert of Deutz (died 1129; Schürmann 1969: 317 n. 41). Despite the lateness of the suggestion, this identification has several arguments in its favor (Plummer 1896: 173): (1) the patronym probably does not indicate his full name; (2) the Synoptics do not mention Nathanael, while John does not mention Bartholomew; (3) every list except Acts 1:13 places Bartholomew and Philip together; and (4) the other men named in John 21:2 are apostles and Nathanael is among them. Thus, it is quite possible that Bartholomew is Nathanael.

6:15 Μαθθαῖον (Matthew) is the seventh name on the list, which agrees with Mark 3:18 (Matt. 10:3 has Thomas here). Acts 1:13 has Thomas in the sixth position, followed by Bartholomew and then Matthew. As noted in the exegesis of 5:27, Matthew is probably another name for Levi the tax collector (Matt. 9:9–13). After following Jesus, he gave a party for him. When Jesus attended, the Pharisees grumbled about his associating with sinners (5:29–32). Matthew's presence in the group shows the grace and openness of the community.

Θωμᾶν (Thomas) means "twin." He is also known as Δίδυμος (Didymus) (John 11:16; 20:24; 21:2). He is, then, yet another example of a disciple with two names. Thomas's placement in this list parallels Mark 3:18, while Acts 1:13 and Matt. 10:3 have Matthew in this position. John gives the most information about Thomas, including the famous "doubting Thomas" incident (John 11:16; 14:5; 20:24–29). Tradition places his later ministry in either Persia or India (Carson 1984: 238).

Ἰάκωβον Ἀλφαίου (James son of Alphaeus) occupies the same position on all the lists. There is some question as to whether he is mentioned elsewhere. Some suggest that he is James, the Lord's brother (Gal. 1:19). But this is not possible, as John 7:5 makes it clear that Jesus' brother did not believe until later in his ministry (Godet 1875: 1.304–5; Plummer 1896: 173–74). Others suggest that he is James the Lesser (or Younger) of Mark 15:40 (Hendriksen 1978: 330). This identification requires that the names Alphaeus and Clopas (John 19:25) be the same, which is possible but not certain (Plummer 1896: 174). Fitzmyer (1981: 619) rejects the equation, but gives no reason. The exact identification of this James is uncertain. His connection to Alphaeus raises the question of whether Matthew is his brother, a suggestion that requires that Levi son of Alphaeus in Mark 2:14 be Matthew, which is possible (see above on Matthew = Levi). But in addition, the Alphaeus tied to James and to Matthew must be the same man; this is less certain, since the name could be common (Creed 1930: 88; Plummer 1896: 174 is less than certain). Again there is not enough material to decide this question.

Σίμωνα (Simon), in the eleventh position in Matt. 10:3 and Mark 3:18, is called a Zealot (ζηλωτήν, zēlōtēn). This description matches the reference to him in Matt. 10:4 = Mark 3:18: ὁ Καναναῖος (ho Kananaios), from Aramaic קַנְאָן (qanʾān, zealous one) (BAGD 402; BAA 817). The term in Mark was mistranslated as "the Canaanite" in many early English translations, going back to T. Cranmer in 1539 (Plummer 1896: 174). It is clear that Simon the Zealot and Simon ὁ Καναναῖος are the same. The description suggests that he had nationalist political leanings. Josephus describes a fourth party in Judaism, the Zealots, a party to which the reference here might be an allusion (Jewish War 2.8.1 §§117–18; Antiquities 18.1.1 §§1–10; 18.1.6 §§23–25; Stumpff, TDNT 2:882–87; Schürer 1973–87: 2.598–606). Josephus has no sympathy with these political enthusiasts who followed the Pharisees except in their radical political opposition to Rome. In fact, he blamed the Zealots for many of the Jews' political problems with Rome a few decades later. This group was annihilated at Masada in the rebellion against Rome that eventuated in the razing of the temple. Though there is some question whether the party existed this early, Josephus appears to trace their roots to as early as A.D. 6.[8] Those who reject this early reference see

8. Smith 1971 argues for a late origin, but Hengel 1961 argues for ideological unity between the early group and later Zealots, as does Stern 1976: 578–79. Much of Josephus's Jewish War 4 condemns this radical group for their activity in A.D. 66–70; especially descriptive is 4.6.3 §§381–88. Nolland 1989: 271 also prefers a distinction between the Zealot party and Luke's term. Witherington 1990: 81–88, 96–98 supports Hengel. Against this connection is R. Brown 1994: 689–93.

the start of the party in A.D. 66. If this latter view is correct, then Simon was a political zealot without being a member of an identifiable party. It seems likely that Simon was a nationalist Israelite before joining up with Jesus. Thus, among the apostles were a worker for the state (a tax collector) and also one who fiercely opposed the state. Reconciliation was a product of Jesus' work.

6:16 Ἰούδαν Ἰακώβου (Judas son of James) is not the half-brother of the Lord, for when a brother is referred to, ἀδελφός (*adelphos*) is present.[9] In addition, John 7:5 makes it clear that none of Jesus' brothers had responded to him yet. That Thaddaeus occupies the tenth position in Mark 3:18 and Matt. 10:3 leads many to argue that Judas and Thaddaeus are the same person, since so many apostles have two names.[10] Fitzmyer (1981: 619–20) opposes this identification partly because Mark and Matthew have a text variant that gives the name Λεββαῖος (Lebbaios) to Thaddaeus, but a variant is no reason to reject Judas from consideration as a second name. He is often called Jude son of James to distinguish him from the other Judas. Likewise, John 14:22 calls him "Judas, not Iscariot."

Ἰούδαν Ἰσκαριώθ (Judas Iscariot) eventually betrays Jesus, as Luke notes with his remark about Judas's becoming a traitor (22:3, 47–48). He is mentioned often in the Gospels, with John giving the most references (John 6:70–71; 12:4–6; 13:2, 29; 18:2–5; Mark 14:10; Matt. 26:14).

The meaning of the name Iscariot is debated. (1) The reference is to a region in Judea (Josh. 15:25; Jer. 31:24 LXX [48:24 MT]; Luce 1933: 143; Schürmann 1969: 318 n. 51). If so, Judas was likely the only non-Galilean among the Twelve. (2) The name comes from an Aramaic term that means "false one" (Ellis 1974: 110; Torrey 1943; Liefeld 1984: 889 and Marshall 1978: 240 call this view possible).[11] If this is the case, the name is possibly a later description of him. (3) The name is from Latin *sicarius* (dagger man, assassin) (Smith 1971). Again, if this view is correct, the name is probably a late one. (4) The name means Judas the "Dyer" and is a reference to his occupation.[12]

View 1 is most likely and is supported by John 6:71 and 13:26. Most likely Iscariot is a family name, since the genitive is used

---

9. Nor should the name Ἰακώβου ([son] of James) be read as the brother of James; but so T. Beza, an approach rightly rejected by Plummer 1896: 175.

10. Simon-Peter, Thomas-Didymus, Matthew-Levi, Bartholomew-Nathanael (apparently, see the exegesis of 6:14); Plummer 1896: 172, 174; Schürmann 1969: 317–18 n. 49; Jeremias 1971a: 232–33. These variations suggest that the tradition of the list of the Twelve existed in various forms.

11. The view goes back to W. Hengstenberg; Godet 1875: 1.306.

12. Carson 1984: 239 (undecided between this and view 1); A. Ehrman 1978; Arbeitman 1980. Fitzmyer 1981: 620 calls this view highly unlikely but gives no reason.

(Plummer 1896: 175; Godet 1875: 1.306; Fitzmyer 1981: 620). Perhaps the Aramaic allusion (view 2) also existed for the original Semitic audience as a strange irony tied to the family name. But such a Semitic connection would have been lost on Luke's audience. Whatever the meaning of the name, Judas Iscariot, the traitor, completes the list.

Summary

Luke 6:1–16 shows the formation of groups who represent different responses to Jesus. In 6:1–11 the opposition gathers its thoughts and sets its course to oppose Jesus. Meanwhile, in 6:12–16, after a night of prayer, Jesus chooses twelve rather ordinary men to form a commissioned nucleus around him. Jesus brings into this important group a wide variety of men: a fisherman, a tax collector, a political revolutionary, a skeptical man who later wanted clear proof of Jesus' resurrection, and even a future traitor. The choice of Iscariot is not to be seen as an accident, but itself was part of a series of events in which God's hand was at work. With this team assembled, Luke will summarize Jesus' work (6:17–19) and then give a display of what his ethical and eschatological teaching was like (6:20–49). Some have come to him, while others have rejected him. The division shall grow only more intense and eventually more violent. However, some men were to serve him for life and thus received special instruction and authority for that ministry. The leaders of the church did not emerge by accident or vote; they were hand-picked men.

Additional Note

6:16. There is some question as to how to spell Iscariot. The UBS–NA reading, Ἰσκαριώθ, is found in $\mathfrak{P}^4$, ℵ*, B, L, and 33. Other texts (ℵ², A, W, Δ, Θ, Ψ, Byz, Lect) read Ἰσκαριώτην like Matt. 10:4. A few Western texts (D, most Itala) read Σκαριώθ, a variant spelling of the family name. This latter reading lends support to the UBS–NA text since it matches the ending of Ἰσκαριώθ. The weakly attested Western reading might also indicate where the text tradition stood in the West if the initial *iota* dropped out. The meaning of the different spellings, not discussed in UBS⁴, seems to be the same.

III. Galilean Ministry: Revelation of Jesus (4:14–9:50)
   B. Gathering of Disciples (5:1–6:16)
➤ C. Jesus' Teaching (6:17–49)
   D. First Movements to Faith and Christological Questions (7:1–8:3)

C. Jesus' Teaching (6:17–49)

Luke 6:17–49 contains one of the most famous portions of Jesus' teaching. Its influence has spanned generations and cultures. The Sermon on the Plain, to use Luke's description, consists of two subunits: an introductory summary about Jesus' teaching and healing ministry (6:17–19) followed by the sermon proper (6:20–49). The sermon itself has three basic subunits: a prophetic call of blessing and woe (6:20–26), a parenetic section on love and judgment (6:27–38), and a parabolic section that is a call to righteous response (6:39–49). One often thinks of 1 Cor. 13 as the "love chapter" in the Bible, but Jesus' remarks on love in 6:27–36 form the center of his ethic and are even more profound. Such sacrificial love is possible only through faith in God and through a belief that God will balance the scales of justice one day. In short, the sermon is a call to love all humanity in the face of the reality of God's blessing, justice, and character. The experience of God's grace requires that God's children be gracious (Eph. 4:30–5:2). (See pp. 566–67 for an overview of the sermon.)

Sources and Historicity (6:17–19)

Luke 6:17–19 is the fourth summary to appear in the Gospel (4:14–15, 31–32, 40–41). It occupies a position in Luke's sequence very close to that of Mark 3:7–12 in that Gospel. The only difference is that Mark (3:13–19a) relates the choosing of the Twelve after giving his summary, while Luke (6:12–16) has the choosing of the Twelve first. This positioning is simply a matter of each writer's locating a summary in a slightly different position, which is not a problem, since the crowd's general response is described here rather than a portrayal of a single, specific event. Luke chose to let his summary introduce the sermon, while Mark has it in a slightly different position, possibly because he does not mention the sermon (Marshall 1978: 237).

    It should be noted that Mark's omission of the sermon is a problem for those who argue that Mark is both the last Synoptic Gospel and a summary Gospel. Though it is possible that Mark could have omitted any reference to such an occasion, it seems unlikely that he would have done so as a summarizing Gospel, if the other Gospels each had an account of it. This omission is one reason why many writers place Mark first in the historical sequence. An explanation that Mark generally avoids reporting Jesus' teaching does not adequately explain the omission, since Mark does have the Olivet Discourse.

The summaries, though located in similar positions, differ slightly from one another (Fitzmyer 1981: 622; Aland 1985: §48):

1. Luke 6:17 locates his summary on a plain, while Mark 3:7 speaks of the sea, which means teaching by the sea.
2. Mark 3:9 has Jesus teaching in a boat by the sea, while Luke 6:17 has him teaching on land.
3. Luke 6:17–18 alone notes that people came to listen to Jesus, as well as to be healed by him. This difference reflects Luke's emphasis on Jesus as a teacher.
4. Luke has no demonic confession as Mark 3:11 does.
5. Luke 6:19 alone mentions that power went out from Jesus.

These differences represent two ways to summarize this period of Jesus' ministry. In a very real way, the accounts supplement one another and show that Jesus was regarded for both his healing and his teaching ministry. Mark emphasizes the works of healing and the demonic confessions that accompanied them, while Luke concentrates on the variety in Jesus' ministry. Another factor in the difference is that Luke sets the stage for the sermon, so that his account serves as both a summary and an introduction to a specific representative occasion in Jesus' ministry.

Sources and Historicity (6:20–26)

The issue of sources for Luke 6:20–26 is extremely complex and has never been adequately resolved. A century ago, Plummer (1896: 176) suggested that the relationship of Matthew's and Luke's accounts may never be completely resolved because there is so little information to work with. Such caution is admirable in this case and reminds us that conclusions are hardly firm in character.

The discussion centers on at least five differences between Matthew and Luke in this section:[1]

1. Luke has four beatitudes, Matthew eight.[2]
2. The order of the common beatitudes differs, with Luke having Matthew's beatitudes in the following order: 1, 4, 2, and 8 (poor, hungry, grieving, persecuted; Creed 1930: 90; Plummer 1896: 179).
3. The addressees differ: Luke uses the second person while Matthew has the third person (Ernst 1977: 214–15; Marshall 1978: 248;

---

1. Aland 1985: §78. Extrabiblical parallels are the Gospel of Thomas 54, 68–69 and the Acts of Paul 5–6 (Bovon 1989: 295). Thomas's order is poor, persecuted, and hungry.
2. The number of Matthean beatitudes rests on some text-critical issues, but most see eight here.

Guelich 1982: 66). Ernst notes that of forty-five OT beatitudes three are in second-person singular, one is second-person plural, and the rest are third-person plural. Even though third-person beatitudes are thus more common, Manson (1949: 47) still opts for a second-person original. Is it the "harder reading"?

4. The character of those addressed differs slightly. For example, where Luke has "poor," Matthew has "poor in spirit"; where Matthew has "hunger and thirst for righteousness," Luke has "hunger now." This difference causes some to speak of Matthew's wisdom beatitudes in contrast to Luke's beatitudes of eschatological promise.

5. Luke alone has the four woes (Aland 1985: §79).

I will examine these differences in detail in the exegesis, but for now I consider only the source question and related points.

The usual critical approach is to suggest that Q's core sermon contained only four beatitudes (Fitzmyer 1981: 631; Bovon 1989: 295; Bultmann 1963: 109–10; but Ernst 1977: 215 argues that blessing and woes were present in Q). Matthew added a few, while Luke formed the woes to parallel his tradition's four beatitudes.[3] The difference between the second person and third person is seen in various ways and is not tied to the source discussion so tightly. Because the vast majority of OT beatitudes are in the third person, Fitzmyer, Bultmann, and others see Luke changing a third person to a more direct second person. But considering the other differences between Matthew and Luke, this typical appeal to Q may be seen as an oversimplified approach to the sermon tradition.

The issue of the Beatitudes' sequence is further complicated since the beatitude in Luke 6:21b is worded slightly differently from its corresponding beatitude in Matt. 5:4: Luke refers to weepers who laugh, whereas Matthew has mourners who are comforted. This difference indicates the possibility of alternate renderings of the same tradition, and it also raises the possibility that the sermon or some of its sayings existed in various forms in the early church, rather than in one form, a view that seems likely (so also Marshall 1978: 250). What also seems clear is that one of the Gospel authors or the tradition rearranged the order, perhaps for topical reasons. In particular, Luke's order seems to move from a general condition (poor), to a result (hunger), to a response to the result (weeping), to a cause (persecution). Given that Matthew's list is longer and that general characteristics are not in Luke, the arrangement in Luke may well be his doing as a result of shortening the account and making use of the parallel woes, which he found in his version of the sermon.

3. Even Marshall 1978: 247, who is more hesitant than most to recognize additions in the tradition, seems to allow that the woes may be an early church commentary added to the tradition; he calls the arguments for an addition stronger, but without arguing that it is the case.

As for the woes, if the possibility of multiple sources for the sermon is allowed, then we might be dealing simply with an additional feature that Luke found in his sources about Jesus' teaching. A case can be made that they predate Luke (Nolland 1989: 286–87). Note especially the overlap in terminology in Luke 6:24–25 and Matt. 6:2, 5, 16; 5:4 (ἀπέχω, to receive payment, and πενθέω, to mourn). The point is this: putting all the factors together rather than artificially separating them multiplies the possibilities, thus reducing largely to guesswork our ability to determine exactly how the distinctions arose. One should be careful about building historical hypotheses on such multilevel inferences. Plummer's caution about sources and the directions of tradition is appropriate.[4]

For completeness, I note four other approaches to the issue of sources in 6:20–26 before laying out my view (for options, see Marshall 1978: 245).

1. According to Schürmann (1969: 385–86), two originally independent sources were joined together in a pre-Lucan source, with an introduction and conclusion being supplied. The core tradition was what is now Luke 6:27–45. Schürmann believes that Matthew used a very similar source and also made significant additions. Thus, he sees at least three sermon editions in circulation: two independent sources and a conflated source.
2. According to Wrege (1968), only independent oral sources can explain what took place.
3. The differences may be attributed to variation in rendering Jesus' Aramaic into Greek (Manson 1949: 47–48). Manson argues that Luke is closer to the original, while Matthew paraphrases to reveal the force and to give the phrases a more edifying effect.
4. Luke drew his material from Matthew directly (Drury 1976: 131–38). This view defends the two-Gospel hypothesis.
5. Luke made a conscious decision to offer a shortened and mostly law-free version of the sermon for his Gentile audience. He also had access to a distinct source of the sermon that included the woes (Schürmann 1969: 339–41 defends a pre-Lucan source with woes). With four woes in hand, he shortened the Beatitudes to the corresponding four elements—either to place them in rough topical order or to correspond to the order of the woes. In addition, he or his source worded them in the second person to make their application

---

4. It is precisely these kinds of difficulties that cause many in NT studies to move in a more literary direction. Such study concentrates on the "final" text, with the result that many are leaving behind the issues of source, tradition, and historicity. While the focus on the final text that appears in any Gospel is a good and healthy development, the abandonment of historical issues is not so valuable. Still, when one makes a historical judgment on sources, one must recognize that it is simply a judgment.

direct in every case. This direct application was already suggested by the third-person use of beatitudes uttered to an audience of disciples, as well as by the second person in the persecution beatitude of Matt. 5:11–12 = Luke 6:22–23.[5] Again, it must be stressed that such a reconstruction is hypothetical and that, in discussing pre-Gospel sources and the sermon's setting, the tone and remarks in the sermon make sense only if their roots go back ultimately to Jesus himself. Redactional changes reflect more explicitly what was already implied by Jesus and thus would be historically accurate summaries of the Jesus tradition. (For more detail on this position as it relates to the audience of 6:24–25, see the additional note on 6:24–26.)

With regard to the difference in Matthew's "poor in spirit" versus Luke's less explicitly spiritual reference to the poor, one must note that the poor are often described in the OT as pious and persecuted, so that the difference is more superficial than real (see the exegesis of 6:20). The spiritual orientation of the poor is made clear in the comparison of the blessed to the prophets (6:23), while the group that suffers woe is compared to false prophets (6:26). Thus, Luke is referring to spiritual categories, even though the reference looks on the surface to be purely social and economic in character. Such abbreviated references to the blessedness of the poor are common in the NT (1 Cor. 1:26–29; James 2:5). Again, it seems likely that Luke has the original wording or something close to it, while Matthew paraphrases the reference to make explicit the intended spiritual force. The Matthean summary and expansion is appropriate in light of remarks like Luke 6:23, 26. It is not to be forgotten that what we have in the sermon, even in the longer Matthean form, is still a summary, so that the longer version of parallel passages in Matthew may well reflect either additional remarks that Jesus made or clarification of a shorter sermon summary.

On the conjunction of meaning between Matthew and Luke in the Beatitudes, Guelich (1982: 109–11) is helpful, though I am less confident of his ability to determine where Matthew and his sources have worked on the additional beatitudes.[6] It seems that Luke has already shown, by reducing its length, a tendency to edit the sermon. Such reduction also reflects his handling of the beatitudes (e.g., Luke 5:21 = Matt. 5:6). In addition, Jesus uses Isa. 61 in Luke 4:16–19 and the Psalter on many occasions, so Jesus could well be responsible for the longer list of beatitudes.

One other element of Lucan emphasis is to be noted: his use of the term νῦν twice each in Luke 6:21 and 6:25, which is characteristic of Luke and

---

5. It should be noted that others argue for a change to the third person by Matthew, e.g., Manson 1949: 47. Schürmann 1969: 329 argues that Luke's source had a second person, while Jesus used the third person originally.

6. On Guelich's view of Matthew's and the sources' postsermon work to expand the Beatitudes in light of the Psalms and Isa. 61, see pp. 115–18.

is probably Lucan (see the exegesis of 6:21a). Luke brings out explicitly what the original remark said implicitly with its contrast between what is happening in the present (i.e., now, νῦν) and what God will do in the future. The theme of the reversal of circumstances is a key element in the sermon's blessings and sets the theological background for seeing the Beatitudes as an expression of comfort and as a call to enter God's care. The reversal shows that God offers promise of a restored future with him.

That the thrust of these blessings is authentic is not really challenged. Even the often skeptical Jesus Seminar puts 6:20–21 in red type, meaning that it has ties to Jesus; 6:22–23 is in gray type, indicating that the ideas but not the words are Jesus' (Funk and Hoover 1993: 289). They treat the woes as inauthentic, placing them in black type, probably because they are attested at only one level in the tradition (Funk and Hoover 1993: 289–90). But warnings to the rich and others who persecute the disciples are multiply attested themes of Jesus, appearing in L and Q (e.g., Luke 12:13–21; 11:37–54; Matt. 23). This material is also authentic.

Sources and Historicity (6:27–38)

The relationship of Luke 6:27–38 to Matthew's Gospel is also extremely complex and almost impossible to unravel. For someone who sees distinct messages or an anthology here, the issue of relationship hardly needs discussion: it is adequate simply to note how the two authors presented their material and to discuss the origins of the individual pieces. Nevertheless, drawing on my view that Matthew and Luke present two distinct summaries of the same message, I offer some tentative suggestions concerning this relationship.

Matthew's account has six antitheses (starting at 5:21, 5:27, 5:31, 5:33, 5:38, 5:43), while Luke has no such construction. Luke has material that is closely parallel to the fifth and sixth antitheses of Matt. 5:38–48 (Aland 1985: §§58–59, 80). Luke 6:27 may reflect the remnants of an antithetical contrast (Matt. 5:43–44), although it is clearly not in Luke's explicit form.

The issue of how Matthew's antithetical structure emerged is a popular topic in technical discussion. These positions must be examined in order to ask what Luke has done:

1. The antitheses are all Matthean (Suggs 1978; see Strecker 1978: 40 n. 7 for a list of adherents).
2. Some of the antitheses are traditional and some are Matthean, the most popular position being three of each. This position goes back to Bultmann (1963: 134–35), who appeals to parallels, style, and content to argue that antitheses 3, 5, and 6 were redactional and the others traditional. Among those agreeing with this position (for dis-

tinct reasons) are Guelich (1982: 265–68; 1975–76) and Strecker (1978; see p. 39 n. 6 for a list of adherents).

3. All the antitheses are traditional in character so that none of them are the work of Matthew (Jeremias 1971a: 251–53).

While recognizing the complexity of the issue, I agree with Jeremias. One can argue that Luke removed, for whatever reasons, any considerations of the legal discussions that are at the heart of Matthew's treatment. Such omissions may have been the result of working with a distinct source or may have been a conscious choice, since legal concerns would not be an issue for Luke's Gentile audience. In making this choice, Luke removed any need to retain the antitheses, whose function is to express the contrast between Jesus' teaching and contemporary discussion of the law. Luke already lacks material like that in Matt. 6:1–18, so the removal of the antitheses, or perhaps the omission of them in his source, is a possibility, especially if Luke has a distinct summary of the sermon. It seems that the "split character" approach to the antitheses, view 2 above, underplays the summary nature of the materials that recorded the sermon. Such independent summaries, when they circulated, may well have differed as to how they presented the distillation of the sermon's contents. Thus, any differences may reflect not the evangelist's later additions, as much as the perspective of sources or resources available to each writer. Though it is possible that Matthew standardized the antithesis form for all the sayings to make explicit what Jesus' teaching clearly implied in some cases, it seems more likely, given that Luke already has a shortened form of the sermon, that Luke is responsible for omitting the antitheses.

Another major difference between the accounts is the order of the details. What follows is a sequential listing of the Lucan order with the Matthean parallels noted in parentheses (an asterisk indicates material that is out of Matthean order):[7]

* love your enemies (Matt. 5:44)
  turn the cheek (Matt. 5:39)
  give your tunic (Matt. 5:40)
  give to the one who asks (Matt. 5:42)
  ask not from the one who takes (no Matthean parallel)
* Golden Rule (Matt. 7:12)
  if you love only those loving you (Matt. 5:46)
  if you do good only to those who do good to you (Matt. 5:47 [maybe])
  if you lend only to receive (no Matthean parallel)
* love and expect nothing in return (Matt. 5:44)

7. See Bovon 1989: 310 for a slightly different breakdown and with additional comparisons to *Didache* 1.3–5 and Justin Martyr's *Apology* 1.15.9–10; 1.14.3; 1.16.1.

* reward is great in heaven (Matt. 5:45)
   be merciful (Matt. 5:48)

Luke's order differs in the love commands and the promises tied to exhortation. Given the summary form of the materials used, it is impossible to determine the sermon's original order (Schürmann 1969: 345–46 argues for Luke's order as more original). The structure in both Matthew and Luke makes sense, and neither looks more original. It may well be that two distinct summary forms of the sermon existed, with each writer reflecting a distinct summary. However, Luke's choosing to give a shorter account may have caused him to summarize and restructure this material as well. Again, there is no way to be certain of these conclusions, because there is so much diversity in the data.

A couple of smaller items need notation. It seems clear that Luke may well generalize in Luke 6:32, 34 the remarks of Jesus in Matt. 5:46–47. Where Matthew speaks of tax collectors and Gentiles, Luke uses the term ἁμαρτωλοί, which of course is an apt generalization of how Gentiles and tax collectors were seen by Jesus' audience. In fact, Luke does not have any of the disparaging allusions to Gentiles (ἐθνικοί) that Matthew has.[8] The transition at the end of this subunit is also expressed slightly differently: Matt. 5:48 speaks of being perfect as the Father is perfect, while Luke 6:36 speaks of being merciful as he is merciful (see the exegesis for details).

As a briefer treatment of Jesus' teaching, Luke's version is not influenced by Jewish law. It may also reflect the use of different summaries. Luke's handling of the material shows that Jesus' ethics are not related only to a legal or Jewish setting, but are timeless. He reproduces the material for his Gentile audience. Though the original discussion was raised in part out of concerns about following the law, Jesus' ethic transcends that setting. This confirms the view that sees the sermon not as a treatment of law but as a word addressed to disciples of all times. Luke takes the teaching, removes its legal issues, and still presents the ethic that Jesus demands.[9]

Matthew has some parallels to Luke 6:36–38 (Aland 1985: §§59, 68, 80–81): Matt. 5:48 is worded very much like Luke 6:36; Luke 6:37a looks like Matt. 7:1; and Luke 6:38b is worded like Matt. 7:2b. Luke 6:37b–38a has no parallel in Matthew. That an entire chapter of Matthew is skipped in the midst of the Lucan verses looks on the surface like signs of a major rearrangement. But when one notes that none of Matt. 6 parallels Luke's sermon and that Luke does have possible conceptual parallels to Matt. 6 out-

---

8. Three of the four NT uses of this term are in Matthew: 5:47; 6:7; 18:17 (3 John 7 is the other).
9. This point is valid regardless of how one sees the issue of the relationship of the sermons, since the material is still used. If there were two sermons present or if what we have is an anthology, then what is seen in Luke is a sermon less controlled by legal concerns. However, the point is especially true if there was only one sermon.

side the sermon, then perhaps no real skips in sequence have occurred. Instead, Luke has not included, for whatever reasons, the intervening material. Note the Lucan parallels to Matt. 6 outside the sermon:

Matt. 6:7–15 is like Luke 11:1–4 (Aland 1985: §62)
Matt. 6:19–21 is like Luke 12:33–34 (Aland 1985: §64)
Matt. 6:22–23 is like Luke 11:34–36 (Aland 1985: §65)
Matt. 6:24 can be compared to Luke 16:13 (Aland 1985: §66)
Matt. 6:25–34 is similar to Luke 12:22–32 (Aland 1985: §67)

Though such evidence could suggest that Matthew brought Jesus' teaching together into one sermon as a topically arranged summary, I slightly prefer a position that says Jesus taught some of these matters twice and Luke omitted this material in the sermon, because he knew it would appear elsewhere, because his source lacked it, or because it had Jewish legal characteristics that were not of interest to his audience (see excursus 7). The key point of Luke 6:36–38 is that mercy is a basic characteristic of the believer and that mercy means being slow to judge.

The Jesus Seminar rates the material in varying ways: red type for 6:27b, 29–30a; pink type for 6:32, 35a, 37c; gray type for 6:27c–28, 30b–31, 33–34, 35b, 35d, 36, 38d; and black type for 6:27a, 35c, 37a–b, 38a–c (Funk and Hoover 1993: 291–97). Thus, some of the material has contact with Jesus. The Jesus Seminar rejects material in this section usually because it is part of common proverbial stock (e.g., 6:31) or because of differences in Q (e.g., 6:37–38). These judgments ignore the possibility of multiple versions (as noted above) and the likelihood that some of Jesus' teaching did fit the proverbial wisdom of the time. There is no reason to doubt that all of this teaching has roots in Jesus.

Sources and Historicity (6:39–49)

Luke 6:39–42 has parallels in Matt. 10:24–25 and 7:3–5 (Aland 1985: §81). Luke 6:43–45 finds similar sayings in Matt. 7:15–16 and 12:35 (Aland 1985: §82). And Luke 6:46–49 is paralleled in Matt. 7:21, 24–27 (Aland 1985: §83). Thus, each subunit has a parallel within Matthew's sermon, while two of the subunits have additional parallels outside the sermon. Since we are dealing with proverbial statements, the likely reuse of material cannot be ruled out. But, given the complexity of the connections inside and outside the sermon, I wait to examine this relationship until the exegesis of these verses.

The Jesus Seminar also evaluates this material with a high degree of mix: pink type in 6:41–42, 44b; gray type in 6:39, 43–44a, 45a, 46; and black type in 6:40, 45b, 47–49 (Funk and Hoover 1993: 297–99). The major reason for the gray and black classifications is the general use of cultural proverbial imagery (e.g., 6:43–49). These verses were rejected in part because "they do not add materially to the fund of sayings and parables that help us distinguish Jesus from other sages of the period" (pp. 298–99). But this is not a scientific criterion; it is circular reasoning using the criterion of dissimilarity too harshly. The view seems to be, "Someone else said this, so Jesus could not." These examples show just how skeptically the Jesus Seminar applied the criterion. For example, the fruit-tree illustration of 6:43 is not only in two places in Matthew (7:16–20; 12:33–35), but also in James 3:12. Multiply attested, it is still rated gray. One suspects that 6:47–49 is rejected because it elaborates Jesus' teaching slightly. But how else would a divinely directed agent treat his prophetic teaching?

Form critically, Luke 6:17–19 is a summary passage (Fitzmyer 1981: 622; Berger 1984: 333). Jesus' audience comes from ever larger regions. Responses to the reports (4:14) have led to people gathering to hear Jesus; so Luke summarizes. The form of 6:20–26 is a prophetic blessing (Berger 1984: 188–94; Bovon 1989: 296); 6:27–38 is multiple exhortation and encouragement mixed with illustration (Berger 1984: 127, 163–68); and most of 6:39–49 is prophetic admonishment, often using short parables.[10] Jesus presses for a decision and warns that the choice of the teacher one follows is a crucial decision.

The outline of Luke 6:17–49 is as follows:

1. Setting (6:17–19)
   a. Crowds come to hear Jesus and are healed by him (6:17–18)
   b. Why crowds seek healing from Jesus (6:19)
2. Jesus' message: an offer and the call to love (6:20–49)
   a. Prophetic call: blessings and woes (6:20–26)
      i. Four beatitudes (6:20–23)
         (1) To the poor: the kingdom now (6:20)
         (2) To the hungry: satisfaction then (6:21a)
         (3) To the weeping: laughter then (6:21b)
         (4) To the persecuted: heavenly reward (6:22–23)
      ii. Four woes (6:24–26)
         (1) To the rich: consolation now (6:24)
         (2) To the full: hunger then (6:25a)
         (3) To the laughing: weeping then (6:25b)
         (4) To the well-spoken-of who are like the false prophets: woe (6:26)

---

10. Berger 1984: 37, 46–47, 51, 57–58 mentions 6:41–42, 45 as admonishment, while regarding 6:39–40, 43–45, 47–49 as parabolic. Bovon 1989: 330 calls 6:46 a warning.

   b. Parenetic call to love and mercy (6:27–38)
      i. Fourfold call to love your enemies (6:27–28)
         (1) Love your enemies (6:27a)
         (2) Do good to those who hate you (6:27b)
         (3) Bless those who curse you (6:28a)
         (4) Pray for those who abuse you (6:28b)
      ii. Four illustrations of loving (6:29–30)
         (1) Offer the cheek (6:29a)
         (2) Give the shirt with the coat (6:29b)
         (3) Give to the beggar (6:30a)
         (4) Do not demand back what has been taken (6:30b)
      iii. Command to love: the Golden Rule (6:31)
      iv. Three illustrations of radical love (6:32–34)
         (1) If you love only those who love you, what credit is it? (6:32)
         (2) If you do good only to those who do good to you, what credit is it? (6:33)
         (3) If you lend only for return, what credit is it? (6:34)
      v. Summary on love: call to be gracious like God (6:35)
         (1) Love your enemies (6:35a)
         (2) Do good (6:35b)
         (3) Lend and expect nothing (6:35c)
         (4) Reward is great (6:35d)
         (5) Result reflects a relationship with God (6:35e)
         (6) Basis: God's mercy (6:35f)
      vi. Love and the standard of mercy (6:36)
      vii. Four exhortations on judgment (6:37–38a)
         (1) Do not judge and you will not be judged (6:37a)
         (2) Do not condemn and you will not be condemned (6:37b)
         (3) Forgive and you will be forgiven (6:37c)
         (4) Give and you will be given to (6:38a)
      viii. Standard: you will be judged by how you judge (6:38b)
   c. Parabolic call to righteousness, fruit, and wise building (6:39–49)
      i. Call to righteousness: watch whom you follow and where you look (6:39–42)
         (1) Can the blind lead the blind? (6:39)
         (2) The pupil is like the teacher (6:40)
         (3) Remove your own logs before others' specks (6:41–42)
      ii. Call for fruit (6:43–45)
         (1) Good and bad trees (6:43)
         (2) Principle (6:44)
         (3) Good and bad people (6:45)

iii. Call for wise building: put Jesus' word into practice (6:46–49)
   (1) Rebuke: why call me "Lord" and not do what I say? (6:46)
   (2) House on the rock: practicing Jesus' words (6:47–48)
   (3) House on the sand: hearing Jesus' words (6:49)

The introductory subunit 6:17–19 has a few themes. Jesus continues to be popular. His healing continues to draw people to him. The crowd is also interested in his teaching. Luke continues to stress that it is Jesus' power that draws people to him.

The basic theme of the subunit 6:20–26 is God's call and assurance to the needy. There is the promise of grace to those who are like the prophets of old. The reversal of circumstances reflects God's promise when his kingdom and reward come in full. In fact, so certain is this promise that the kingdom can also be promised as already possessed by those aligned with God. Any reward for those who are rich in life now and aligned with the false prophets is limited to this life. Such a limited approach to the current life will have tragic results when God's kingdom comes in full. This ethic is personal in character. One can well wonder, given their OT roots, whether such general social descriptions indicate who often is the most responsive to God's call. Nevertheless, one should be careful not to take these generalized beatitudes and absolutize them, as if one's bank account or social status automatically determines one's spiritual state. The sermon as a whole shows that Jesus is discussing the spiritual condition of one's heart and how the disciple can please God. If the one who comes to God is in dire straits, God promises the hope of reversal. But the promise is not limited to those who suffer lack on earth. All who seek God humbly can find blessing as he seeks to transform them. It just so happens that the audience drawn to Jesus was mostly poor, and so the promise is expressed in terms that relate to them. The Beatitudes declare the hope of God's transformation and blessing to all who will come to receive it.

Themes abound in the heavily ethical subunit 6:27–38. Superior love is the call of the disciple. The disciple's standard of love is to be greater than that of the average person's love. Love involves going the extra step. Love may require enduring injustice. Love means seeing others as we would like them to see us. Love means serving without strings attached or expecting a response.

Full love receives divine reward. Love ultimately expresses itself in graciousness. The believer is called to show compassion, which will help to determine the compassion shown to them. Abundant favor is extended to the one who is giving. The standard of one's evaluation is determined by one's own treatment and evaluation of others. This theme of justice in the eschaton anchors the entire exhortation in a context where disciples are accountable to God for their actions. Love and mercy dominate the subunit, with judgment being tied to mercy. The central exhortations are in 6:27–28, 31, 35–36. This passage is Jesus' equivalent of Paul's chapter on love, 1 Cor. 13.

Many key themes exist in the subunit 6:39–49. Believers need to exercise care about where they go and to examine their source of sight. Believers will be like the teachers they follow. One should deal with one's own major faults and not pick on minor faults of others. The product of one's life is often a reflection of one's spiritual health. It is not hearing Jesus, but doing his teaching that is a reflection of stability and wisdom. Finally, authority is depicted in Jesus' words: his teaching is not something to be merely observed; it calls for response.

Exegesis and Exposition

[17]And coming down with them, he stood on a plateau, along with a great crowd of his disciples and a great crowd of people from all of Judea, Jerusalem, and the district of Tyre and Sidon. The crowd came to hear him and be healed of their diseases, [18]and those who were oppressed with unclean spirits were healed. [19]And all the crowd sought to touch him, because power came forth from him and healed them all.

[20]And lifting his eyes to his disciples he said,

> "Blessed are you poor,
>   for yours is the kingdom of God.
> 21 Blessed are you who hunger now,
>   for you shall be satisfied.
> Blessed are you who weep now,
>   for you shall laugh.
> 22 Blessed are you when men hate you,
>   and when they exclude you and when they revile you
>   and cast out your name as evil
>   on account of the Son of Man.

[23]"Rejoice in that day, and leap for joy, for behold your reward is great in heaven; for so their fathers did to the prophets.

24   "But woe to you who are rich,
      for you have received your consolation.
25   Woe to you who are full now,
      for you shall hunger.
   Woe to you who laugh now,
      for you shall mourn and weep.
26   Woe to you, when all men speak well of you,
      for so their fathers did to the false prophets.

27"But I say to you who are listening: Love your enemies, do good to those who hate you, 28bless those who curse you, pray for those who abuse you. 29To the one who strikes you on the cheek, offer the other also; and from him who takes away your coat, do not withhold even your undershirt. 30Give to all who ask you, and from the one who takes your things, do not demand them back.

31"As you wish that men would do to you, so ⌐do⌐ to them. 32If you love those who love you, what credit is that to you? For even sinners love those who love them. 33⌐And if⌐ you do good to those who do good to you, what credit is that to you? ⌐For⌐ even sinners do the same. 34And if you lend to those from whom you hope to receive, what credit ⌐is⌐ that to you? ⌐Even⌐ sinners lend to sinners to receive the same.

35"But love your enemies, and do good, and lend, expecting ⌐nothing⌐ in return; and your reward will be great and you will be sons of the Most High; for he is kind to the ungrateful and the selfish.

36"Be merciful even as your Father is merciful. 37Judge not and you will not be judged; condemn not and you will not be condemned; forgive and you will be forgiven; 38give and it will be given to you—good measure, pressed down, shaken together, running over, will be put into your lap. For the measure you give will be the measure you get back."

39And he also spoke parables to them: "A blind man is not able to guide a blind man, is he? Will they not both fall into a pit? 40A disciple is not greater than the teacher, but when he is fully equipped, he shall be like his teacher.

41"Why do you see the speck in your brother's eye, but do not notice the plank in your own eye? 42Or how can you say to your brother, 'Brother, let me take out the speck that is in your eye,' when you yourself do not see the plank that is in your own eye? Hypocrite, first take out the plank from your own eye, and then you will see clearly to take the speck out of your brother's eye.

43"For no good tree bears bad fruit, nor again does a bad tree bear good fruit; 44for each tree is known by its own fruit. For figs are not gathered from thorns, nor are grapes picked from brambles. 45The good man from the good treasure of his heart produces good, and the evil man from the evil treasure of his heart produces evil; for out of the abundance of the heart his mouth speaks.

46"Why do you call me 'Lord, Lord,' and not do what I say? 47Everyone who comes to me and hears my words and does them, I will show you what he is like: [48]he is like a man building a house, who dug deep, and laid a foundation upon rock; and when a flood arose, the stream broke against that house, and could not shake it, ʿbecause it had been well builtʾ. [49]But he who hears and does not do them is like a man who built a house on the ground without a foundation, against which the stream broke, and immediately it fell, and the ruin of that house was great."

1. Setting (6:17–19)
a. Crowds Come to Hear Jesus and Are Healed by Him (6:17–18)

6:17 The summary begins by noting that three groups are present: the apostles ("them"), a crowd of disciples, and a crowd of people. The apostles (6:12–16) came down the mountain with Jesus. Many see in this descent an allusion to a "second Moses" motif (Schürmann 1969: 321), while Ellis notes that the apostles may be seen as priests in the Aaronic mold (Exod. 32:1, 7, 15; 34:29). The Aaronic association is clearly not present, since neither Luke nor other NT writers draw such comparisons.[11] The possibility of a new Moses motif does exist in the allusion to Deut. 18:15 in Luke 9:35, in the direct allusion to this OT passage in Acts 3:22, and in an indirect comparison in Acts 7:37. However, Luke does not signal the idea very clearly here, so it is unlikely that it is present.[12]

Jesus is described as standing on a "level place" (τόπου πεδινοῦ, *topou pedinou*). This term is discussed in excursus 7, as is its relationship to Matthew's reference to a mountain. It is perhaps best translated "plateau" to make clear its location in the midst of a mountain setting. Thus, the description is not an obstacle to identifying with the locale of Matthew's sermon. Davies and Allison (1988: 422) disagree, arguing that harmonization is not possible because Luke 6:17 and 6:12 show Jesus coming down the mountain prior to the sermon, while also arguing that a plateau on a mountainside is unlikely to draw a crowd of the sick, being too difficult for them to reach. But neither of these objections is substantive. Luke's language suggests that Jesus descended from the top of a mountain.

11. The closest possibility is the comparison with the priesthood in Hebrews, but here only Jesus is noted. Ellis 1974: 112 accepts the Mosaic imagery but not the Aaronic; Marshall 1978: 241 regards the Mosaic picture as possible; Nolland 1989: 275 argues persuasively against it. Nolland notes that the OT texts are a call to keep people away from the mountain (e.g., Exod. 19:12) and that the OT mountain setting is not related to teaching.

12. Fitzmyer 1981: 623 is skeptical of the new Moses emphasis in Luke, but underplays the Mosaic allusions in Acts. If the motif is present, it is clearer in Matthew than in Luke, though even in Matthew it is not certain. For the motif in Matthew, see Davies and Allison 1988: 423–24; against its presence in Matthew is Carson 1984: 129.

Where the plateau might be with reference to the mountain's height or the surrounding countryside is not clear. So the objection about a mountain climb is also without force. The plateau could be located anywhere on the mountain face, either high up or at the end of a relatively low, reachable incline. Matthew's remark in Matt. 5:1 that Jesus went up the mountain may reflect only a difference in compressing events, since Matthew also has a summary about Jesus' ministry throughout the region before giving the sermon. The language of Luke and Matthew is capable of referring to the same occasion.[13]

Τόπος πεδινός is used of the Shephelah region (Marshall 1978: 242; Geldenhuys 1951: 209 n. 1). Some locate the setting on a plateau west of Tabgha near Capernaum, but there is not enough information to be sure of the locale.[14] In contrast to efforts to locate the exact setting is the approach that regards the plain as purely symbolic of the place where Jesus instructs the people in contrast to instructing the disciples (Mánek 1967; Conzelmann 1960: 44; Ernst 1977: 211; Fitzmyer 1981: 623; Davies and Allison 1988: 422). However, the reference to the plain appears only once in Luke, which hardly establishes a symbolic reference (Marshall 1978: 241). There is no decisive reason to reject the description of the setting. Surely Jesus preached in such locales.

Jesus stood not only with his apostles, but also with a crowd of disciples (ὄχλος πολὺς μαθητῶν αὐτοῦ, ochlos polys mathētōn autou). Luke's reference to Jesus' standing need not conflict with the reference to his being seated in Matt. 5:1, since by the time Jesus completed the healing and turned to teaching, he lifted up his eyes (Luke 6:20) and quite probably, according to the common custom, would have been seated in order to teach (Plummer 1896: 176).[15] Carson (1984: 129) suggests that perhaps the teaching took several days (as in Matt. 15:29–39), but there is no way to confirm this suggestion.[16] This second group of disciples is simply described as great

---

13. Whether in fact the same occasion as Matthew is in view is a separate question that is treated in excursus 7. Of course, those who see different sermons in Matthew and Luke have no problem in dealing with the difference in location. Seeing an anthology is not a problem either, since the setting becomes representative.

14. Hendriksen 1978: 334 argues for this locale; Marshall 1978: 241–42 calls it possible. Davies and Allison 1988: 422 mention Karn Hattin (Horns of Hattin) as another suggestion, but they prefer not to adopt a specific location, since for them the Matthean sermon is a collected representative sermon, as opposed to a sermon in a single place (see excursus 7 for details). Edersheim 1889: 1.524 argues against Karn Hattin.

15. If this approach is taken, then literary compression is probably present.

16. If Carson is right, then the possibility of a sermon compilation is increased, but there is no indicator in Matthew or Luke that a long period is in view. Neither can it be ruled out.

in number. No more details are given. They obviously are more distant from Jesus than are the apostles, but closer than the third group, the people (λαός, *laos*). Only Luke 19:37 mentions a similar gathering. This is a major public event.

Described in some detail, the third group is only tangentially related to Jesus, though they are interested in him.[17] Their presence serves to indicate a deepening popular interest in Jesus. This broad use is one of two Lucan meanings of the term λαός: to refer to God's people (Luke 1:68, 77; 2:32; Acts 15:14; 18:10) and, as here, to refer to those who receive the message with the potential to respond (Luke 7:1, 29; 8:47; 9:13; 18:43; 19:48; 20:1, 9, 19, 26, 45; 21:38; 23:27, 35; Schürmann 1969: 321). The reference to Judea indicates the entire Palestinian region (Luke 4:44; 5:17 [where it is used with Galilee]; Creed 1930: 89; Marshall 1978: 242; Ernst 1977: 212; Fitzmyer 1981: 623; Bovon 1989: 286). The broad scope of the reference parallels the mention of additional regions in the similar summaries of Mark 3:7–8 and Matt. 4:25. The reference to Jerusalem highlights the religious center of the faith where much of the drama surrounding Jesus will be resolved. The reference to Tyre and Sidon may suggest the Gentiles' interest in Jesus (Luke 10:13–14). Such a suggestion is likely but cannot be established, for Luke may be referring here to Jews from these regions.[18] Regardless, Jesus is drawing a wide variety of people, whose level of regard for him differs.

In an effort to see theological significance in this threefold grouping, Ernst (1977: 211) argues for an intentional allusion to the three groups that the church consists of: apostles, disciples, and people (Conzelmann 1960: 44 contrasts people and disciples). True as this point may be, this breakdown does not exist for the church in Acts, so that an intended Lucan parallelism seems unlikely. The third group simply consists of interested people who have yet to make any commitment to Jesus, as their separation from the grouping of disciples makes clear. One is simply to note the variety of people coming to watch and hear Jesus minister.

The people gather for a twofold purpose: to listen to Jesus' teaching and to be healed by him. The reference to healing focuses attention on the people, since there is no indication that the apostles need heal-

17. Strathmann, *TDNT* 4:51. Schürmann 1969: 321 adds to the new Moses motif here by alluding to the people meeting Moses in Exod. 19:12, 14, 17, 21–25; 20:18–21; 24:2; 34:3, 29–30. But how certain is this in light of the various groups noted here? There is no idea of Jesus' receiving new revelation from God in the journey up the mountain, only the picture of communing with him in prayer. As was mentioned above, the OT texts keep people at a distance versus engaging them.

18. Fitzmyer 1981: 624, Schürmann 1969: 322, and Bovon 1989: 286 are certain about the Gentile allusion (Luke 2:31–32; 3:6; 4:25–29). Ernst 1977: 212, Marshall 1978: 242, and Tiede 1988: 136 are more cautious.

ing, and it is those who come to Jesus who are described here.[19] The impression of the passage is that healing is a regular part of Jesus' ministry, which recalls the earlier summary of 4:40–41 (similar summaries occur in 5:15 and 7:21–22). As in 4:40–41, Luke distinguishes between healing of disease and curing of demonic possession. Jesus deals with a variety of evils and has authority over them all.

A key note is struck in the reference to the curing of demon-pos-   **6:18**
sessed people (on possession, see the exegesis of and the second additional note on 4:33). The picture is of a great spiritual battle with spiritual forces. Jesus fights the evil forces that seek to destroy humanity.[20] He overcomes this opposition and releases people from such oppression (in secular usage ἐνοχλέω, enochleō, to trouble, is used for unrest caused by spiritual forces; T. Jos. 7.4; BAGD 267; BAA 540; Heb. 12:15 is the only other NT use). These healings demonstrate his compassion and power and, considered in light of his total ministry, show the breaking in of Jesus' rule and authority (5:19–21, 24; 10:17–20; 11:14–23; Ellis 1974: 112). It is an ability that points to the unique authority of his person as God's chosen agent, though his office is not clearly indicated by this ministry alone, since OT prophets engaged in similar activity. No confession is recorded here by Luke in contrast to Mark 3:11. Luke concentrates simply on the healing, thereby leaving the attention firmly fixed on Jesus.

Jesus compassionately ministers in both word and deed before turning to speak about God's grace and his demands. If the people seek to respond fully to Jesus, then more is required than lining up to be healed (Schürmann 1969: 322; Marshall 1978: 242). In fact, the sermon's placement next to the summary teaches that to follow Jesus is not just to receive, but to give. God's grace is displayed as a gift and then the message is preached. Jesus served and then sermonized about receiving and responding to God's gift. To receive God's grace means being prepared to share it. The eschatology and ethics behind that giving are found in 6:20–49.

b. Why Crowds Seek Healing from Jesus (6:19)

Jesus' ministry was causing quite a crush, since all those seeking   **6:19**
healing wished to avail themselves of the power that they recognized as part of his ministry. The portrait of Jesus as a powerful healer is strong in Luke (5:17; 6:18; 7:7; 8:47; 9:11, 42; 14:4; 17:15; 22:51; Fitzmyer 1981: 624; Schneider 1977a: 149). The power appears to be re-

19. The syntax of 6:17–18 is complex, so my translation paraphrases the passage. Οἵ in 6:18 is resumptive and probably refers back to λαοῦ in 6:17 or to both λαοῦ and ὄχλος, though the latter term resurfaces explicitly in 6:19.
20. Danker 1988: 137 notes that Jesus' ultimate battle is with Satan (Col. 1:12–14).

lated to his special position as the one anointed with the Spirit (Acts 10:38), though in Acts such healings also occur with other figures.[21] The lesson of the Simon Magus episode (Acts 8:9–25) is that such power is not purchasable or requestable, but is sovereignly bestowed. Jesus heals all who come to him, even though their desire to touch him may indicate a perception that Jesus has magical powers that can be released only upon coming into contact with him (Luke 5:17; 8:46; Acts 2:22; contrast the faith expressed in Luke 18:35–43; Grundmann, *TDNT* 2:301; on Jesus' power, see May 1952). Jesus honors a seed of faith that is even slightly misguided.

Thus, as Jesus prepares to address the crowd, three groups are present: apostles, disciples, and the people. They all can hear what he has to say. Jesus does not limit his teaching to insiders only. He will teach all who will hear, so the walk with God is made clear to anyone. The teaching counters the people's focus on healing. God heals and gives graciously, but a walk with God involves serving God, as the sermon will show. One comes to God not just to receive from him, but to respond to him.

With the end of this summary, Luke begins to narrate a sequence of events in 6:20–8:3 that has no explicit parallel in Mark. Most of these events are paralleled in Matt. 7 or Matt. 11. Only Luke 7:11–17 and 8:1–3 have no Matthean parallel, and Luke 7:36–50 is not narrated in the setting where Matthew has it (Matt. 26:6–13) and thus is probably also without a true parallel (see the introduction to 7:36–50). Thus, it is clear that Luke is doing his own arranging in presenting these additional features of Jesus' ministry.

2. Jesus' Message: An Offer and the Call to Love (6:20–49)

Excursus 7 overviews the background of the Sermon on the Plain and considers its relationship to Matthew's Sermon on the Mount. It is important to view the sermon from Luke's frame of reference so that his emphases and themes emerge. With around eighty verses in Matthew's treatment not found in Luke, it is clear that Luke chose to give the sermon in a much briefer form.[22] As these differences and the relationship of Luke to Matthew are dis-

21. Acts 3:1–10 (the lame man healed by Peter); 6:8 (Stephen as a man full of power); 8:6–7 (Philip's healing work in Samaria); 9:34 (Aeneas the paralytic healed by Peter); 9:36–42 (Dorcas raised by Peter); 14:9–10 (the lame man at Lystra healed by Paul [cf. Paul's caveat in 14:15]); 20:9–12 (Eutychus raised by Paul); 28:8–9 (Paul heals many in Malta).

22. This point is valid, no matter how one views the Synoptic problem, because in either view much of the material in Matthew was available to Luke. In fact, for holders of Matthean priority, the remarks that follow are especially valid. It is clear that Luke has made choices in his presentation.

cussed above in the section on sources and historicity, I comment here only on a couple of summary points.

The stress in Luke's version falls on how to treat others. It contains a call to a gracious, loving, and forgiving approach. None of the explicitly Jewish examples of Matthew's sermon appears in Luke's sermon, but the same strong ethical focus is present, as well as a few additions that divide humanity into two groups (esp. prominent here are the woes to the rich in 6:24–26). The accepted or blessed group is compared to the persecuted OT prophets, while the rejected group is compared to false prophets. The spiritual focus in this comparison is sometimes missed in discussions of Luke's sermon. Misguided approaches discuss the poor and meek without any reference to these spiritual concerns and as a result produce a message that does not nuance the sermon properly in a spiritual setting, though it cannot be ignored that these categories do have sociological force.[23]

The call of the sermon is that one should not be preoccupied with the spiritual condition of others, but be diligent about one's own righteousness. In fact, one is to be ready to love, even with what appears to be a self-sacrificing, non-self-protective level of forgiveness. The standard is to do more than the sinner does. The disciple is to be exceptional in love. The disciple should be rich in mercy, just as God is. For Fitzmyer (1981: 630) the sermon's message is that the essence of discipleship is love.[24] He contrasts the gracious attitude of the sermon to the vindictive attitude against enemies at Qumran in 11QTemple[a] 61.12–14. The reason the disciple can love all humanity is that the disciple knows that God will deal justly with all one day. Even the woes of Luke 6:24–26 are grounded in God's final act of justice. It is the sermon's eschatology of hope and justice that lays the groundwork for the disciple's love ethic.

The sermon is a discourse and the outline reflects the formal emphasis of its three main parts: 6:20–26 is prophetic and declarative in force, 6:27–38 is the fundamental exhortation or parenesis, and 6:39–49 contains three parables that teach, warn, and ask for response (see pp. 567–71, 586–87, and 609–10 for overviews of these three parts). Jesus functions as a teacher-prophet in the text.

a. Prophetic Call: Blessings and Woes (6:20–26)

The Beatitudes place the ethical call to disciples in the context of God's blessing. The passage splits nicely into two parts: blessings

---

23. See the discussion of the rich and the poor in the exegesis of 1:51–53 and 4:18 and the introduction to 4:16–30.

24. I agree, only adding the importance of God's promise as the basis for the call.

(6:20–23) and woes (6:24–26). The key to the prophetic declarations is the explanatory remarks that close the two halves of the subunit in 6:23 and 6:26. Identification with the Son of Man is key. Also, the blessed are compared to the prophets of old, while the condemned are compared to the false prophets. Polemic and blessing are side by side. Humankind is divided into two groups: poor and rich, humble and proud, responsive and unresponsive. The rise of division about Jesus in 5:17–6:11 has set the stage for this contrast. Every listener belongs in one of the two camps. The question is, which one?

Virtually every aspect of this subunit and its relationship to Matthew's sermon has generated discussion. Everyone agrees that the blessings (and woes in Luke) form the introduction to both accounts and set their tone, but beyond this, there is great debate. (1) Is it best to describe this section as the qualifications for entry into the kingdom (6:20–23), followed by a description of kingdom adversaries (6:24–26)?[25] (2) Is it best to distinguish Matthew's blessings, grounded in OT and Jewish wisdom background and giving ethical requirements for entrance, from Luke's beatitudes and woes? In this view, Luke's beatitudes derive from eschatological blessings, have an apocalyptic flair, and serve as simple words of promise and comfort.[26] (3) Has Matthew spiritualized a text that Luke addressed to the socially and economically deprived (Plummer 1896: 179 is close to this view)? (4) If this difference does exist, is it a fundamental difference or simply an alternate way to express the same idea with a different nuance (Luce 1933: 144–45; Guelich 1982: 109–11; Ellis 1974: 113; Marshall 1978: 249–50 [apparently]; Hendriksen 1978: 341)? These are some of the issues that must be resolved in the exegesis to understand the passage.

The most basic question is this: does the sermon's introduction operate in the sphere of grace or law? H. Betz and Windisch opt for law, Jeremias for grace.

In H. Betz's view (1985: 19–21), the Matthean blessings are derived from a Jewish Christianity that is concerned about the excessive legalism of the Pharisees and the excessive freedom of Gentile Christianity. Via Matthew's sermon, the early Jewish-Christian church portrayed Jesus as the interpreter of Torah, standing on the side of requirements for righteousness and leaning toward a favorable view of the law, as Matt. 5:17–20 makes clear. This view emphasizes the legal character of the introduction.

---

25. Godet 1875: 1.311. The structure of Matt. 5:3–12 is similar, though it lacks the woes and thus the explicit addressing of adversaries.

26. Koch 1969: 7; Hauck, *TDNT* 4:368 (who suggests this distinction); Fitzmyer 1981: 632–33; Klostermann 1929: 78–79. Guelich 1982: 63–65, 109–11 discusses the options in detail and rejects the absolute distinction.

The view rests on a certain understanding of the early church's history. The picture of Jewish Christianity in conflict with Pauline and Gentile Christianity was an old and favorite characterization for many German scholars of the last two centuries. The view dates back to F. C. Baur in the early nineteenth century and still has many adherents, though the conflict is generally described today with more care than Baur's original description (1831, 1850–51). There is evidence in the NT of some strain between Jewish and Gentile Christians (e.g., the confrontation between Paul and Peter in Gal. 2, the pacifying notes of the Book of Ephesians, and Acts 15). However, the strains never appear to be so severe among the major representatives that a denial of the Gentiles' authentic faith is present.

In addition, that Luke, as a writer to a Gentile audience, uses the sermon seems to preclude its origin as a polemic against Gentile Christianity. Why would a foremost supporter of Gentile Christianity use a piece of polemic from the other side? If, as I hold, the Matthean and Lucan versions do not differ greatly in force, then this view cannot stand. The Jewish flavor of the Matthean version may have causes other than a Jewish-Christian concern for the Gentile church. These causes are rooted in the original setting, where Judaism was subject to the charge of hypocrisy, so that it would be natural for Jesus to call his disciples to be different in their display of righteousness.

Windisch (1951) represents a second option that points to law. He sees the Matthean sermon in the context of OT righteous wisdom, and thus Matthew's emphasis is on questions of law and a proper understanding of it. These commandments set the limits of obedience, which is the basis for salvation. There is no doubt that legal issues are a central part in Matthew's sermon. In fact, such an emphasis is perfectly understandable, given the precross setting of the event, but it is less so if the setting is postcross! Even the suggestion of a Jewish-Christian setting for Matthew or for the sermon does not answer this objection, since Matthew was written in a period when Gentile Christianity was a reality and was already distancing itself from the law. The assumption of sacrifices in Matt. 5:23–24 pictures close, unobstructed contact with the temple. This contact is much more likely in a precross than in a postcross setting. In fact, one senses that the postcross focus in many critical treatments of the sermon hampers the ability of interpreters to come to grips with the message of the sermon. Expecting grace and the cross to be directly manifest in a postcross sermon, but finding them absent, has created all kinds of explanations, none of which are compelling. Perhaps the underlying assumptions about the sermon's origins and shaping by tradition are wrong.

If Jesus is behind the sermon and begins to teach his disciples about righteousness and God's acceptance, how else could he do so before the cross but in terms of law and in contrast to the Pharisees? Stuhlmacher, in discussing Jesus' teaching on righteousness before God, shows that Jesus did treat such a theme and that he was the starting point for the church's reflection on it (Stuhlmacher 1986: 30–49, in an essay entitled "The New Righteousness in the Proclamation of Jesus"). On the other hand, the wisdom emphasis fits a setting that was concerned with evaluating righteousness in relationship to the law, while pointing out that current forms of Judaism majored incorrectly on externals. This setting explains the legal character that dominates much of the Matthean sermon. However, reading a legal emphasis back into the Beatitudes creates the impression of tension, which clouds the issue of how the Beatitudes fit into the sermon.

On the other side of the grace-law controversy stands Jeremias (1963b). He insists that the sermon has to do with God's acceptance and the walk that is to follow such acceptance. The Beatitudes form an invitation or a promise of acceptance, a call of sorts, which holds out the promise of participation in God's blessings. As such, the Beatitudes set the context of the entire sermon. The sermon begins with grace, expressed in Beatitudes. They are followed by a disciple's response, a pattern somewhat parallel to Paul's indicative-imperative, where behavior is a response to God's acceptance. This approach to the sermon is satisfying in that it is able to deal adequately with the present tense in the first beatitude of both Luke and Matthew and the present tense in Matthew's final beatitude (Matt. 5:10). The Matthean present tenses, which begin and end his subunit, serve to emphasize the importance of the currency of the promise and the connection between the present and the future, which the Beatitudes as a whole express.

Thus, God's call in the sermon is to be responsive to him, trust his care, and rest in his promise. One carries out God's desire for righteousness by taking on a certain character and approach to him. In short, the Beatitudes express God's stretching out his hand in promise to those in physical-spiritual distress. He promises to walk with them, if they in turn will give him their hand with trust. He calls the poor, the humble, the meek, the peacemakers, those who desire righteousness, the merciful, the pure in heart, and those who would stand up for God and righteousness. If people seek out God and desire these qualities, they can, God says, come to him and find them. God graciously opens the way for those who seek his face. The audience in both Matthew and Luke consists primarily of disciples, so that the Beatitudes form the preamble to and presuppositions of the rest of the sermon. They declare God's promised acceptance of the disciples for choosing to follow Jesus and enter into this walk (Matt. 5:1; Luke 6:20a). Disciples may be assured that the choice to enter into this walk will meet with blessing. God is committed to them and, in the eschaton, blessing is guaranteed. To one considering becoming a disciple, the Beatitudes say to come into God's promise and seek to be this kind of person. Thus, the Beatitudes express God's grace and set all the following remarks in such a context. At the start of the sermon, disciples can know that they are destined for blessing through the Beatitudes. Precisely how the Beatitudes accomplish this and how Luke presents this emphasis via the contrastive function of the Lucan woes in comparison to Matthew must await the exegesis.

i. Four Beatitudes (6:20–23)

The brief introduction in 6:20a makes it clear that the main audience for Jesus' teaching are those who are following him. That this audience is present, however, does not automatically mean that every point in the sermon relates only to disciples, for it is possible that Jesus could teach them about God's treatment of all or about his judgment upon all. Thus, knowing the audience does not necessarily solve questions raised in the sermon about the scope of the subjects in each remark. For example, the woes of 6:24–26 are clearly intended as a warning to outsiders (Plummer 1896: 182; Marshall 1978: 246). The woes also have relevance to insiders, who can know God will reveal his justice one day.

Each passage within the sermon needs to be evaluated on its own terms to determine its audience. Nevertheless, when a promise of blessing is given and those in the audience are identified by the word *you* and that audience is called disciples, then this part of the promise is made to those who seek a relationship with Jesus. The promise given is not a *carte blanche* promise to all, but is for those who have already shown an interest in Jesus. Thus, the poor inherit the kingdom, while the rich are discussed separately in 6:24 (K. Schmidt, *TDNT* 1:582).

(1) To the Poor: The Kingdom Now (6:20)

The initial beatitude is to the poor. Before discussing the identity of **6:20** the blessed poor, however, the concept of a beatitude needs comment. Declaring someone happy, contented, blessed, or fortunate was common in the ancient world. Dupont (1966a) gives examples from Egyptian culture, and Hauck and Bertram demonstrate its usage in Greek (*TDNT* 4:362–64) and Jewish (*TDNT* 4:364–67) culture. Being blessed refers to a sense of inner happiness at good fortune (Hauck, *TDNT* 4:363, 367). H. Betz (1985: 25) notes four cultural occasions that might produce such a beatitude: religious contexts, secular fortune, exhortations of wisdom, or satire. In OT religious contexts, the idea is joy at experiencing fortune from God's hand, and it is almost always a person who is blessed—not things or states (Fitzmyer 1981: 632–33; Ps. 1:1; 2:12 [2:11 NRSV]; 34:8 [33:9 LXX]; 40:4 [39:5 LXX]). Such OT blessings appear mostly in the Psalter and in Wisdom Literature to exhort one to good behavior, which God honors either now or in the future. Usually, the promise of blessing comes first and then the basis for the blessing or its content is given via a relative clause, a participial phrase, or a ὅτι clause that refers to the blessed in the third person.[27] But second-person beatitudes are also given (Deut. 33:29; Isa. 32:20; Ps. 128:1–2 [127:1–2 LXX]; Marshall 1978: 248). In a few OT texts, blessing is given as a future promise in order to comfort God's people (Isa. 30:18; 32:20; Dan. 12:12; Guelich 1982: 65). In the intertestamental period, the formula has an eschatological usage and stresses the comfort that God gives to his suffering people as he promises to deliver them (1 Enoch 99.10–15; 103.5; 2 Bar. 10.6–7; Guelich 1982: 64–65). The OT-like wisdom beatitude is also common, and it is in the Wisdom Literature that the first known beatitude list appears (Sir. 25:7–10; Bertram, *TDNT* 4:365). In fact, such beatitude lists are rare.

Luke's initial beatitude has three peculiarities: it appears to refer to a state, is given in the less common second person, and is in the present tense. As such the blessing is not future, but already exists. However, this beatitude sets the stage for the ones that follow, which all have a future promise in view. In this way, Jesus' promises, when taken as a whole, wed the present and the future together in a way that is typical of his "already–not yet" eschatological language. What one has now is a token of the full possession later. Jesus' offer is comprehensive in scope, involving both present and future. As such, his promise is an offer of hope extending into the future. This hope enables the disciple to suffer now, because glory awaits later. The promise given here is inaugurated, but it has hardly reached its total fulfillment. The entry point into the promise is the right to belong to the kingdom, which is the honor of those poor who are at Jesus' side and have identified with him. This emphasis is appropriate even if the Aramaic tense originally used here was progressive in force so that the meaning is extended from the present into the future (Marshall 1978: 250). The consistency of the tradition at this point in giving a present tense translation shows that the emphasis is on the currency of the possession of the kingdom.

---

27. "Blessed is/are the one(s) who . . . because (ὅτι). . . ." Guelich 1982: 63 and Fitzmyer 1981: 632–33 discuss the form of beatitudes.

Luke's use of the second person highlights the current, personal possession of the kingdom: *"Yours* is the kingdom of God." As noted in the discussion of sources for 6:20–26, Luke's unique use of the second person brings out the direct application more clearly, while Matthew's third person, being the usual form of such beatitudes, is more likely to be original.[28] Luke is summarizing the real force of Jesus' remarks to his audience, but one could also argue that Matthew generalized an original second-person beatitude, as Marshall (1978: 249) argues by appealing to a prophetic context. If Marshall is correct, then Matthew extended the application beyond Jesus' audience in an analogy: "As with the disciples, so also with Jesus' later followers." This change would show the timeless character of his teaching. Either view is possible; certainty is impossible.

Who are the participants in the promise that are called the poor and are said to have the kingdom? Πτωχός (*ptōchos*, poor) appeared earlier in 4:18 in the citation of Isa. 61:1 and referred to those to whom Jesus proclaimed the good news. In that setting, πτωχός is not merely a socioeconomic term, but also has spiritual content, as its attachment to other ideas in the context makes clear. The interpretive history of Isa. 61 in Judaism also supports this spiritual emphasis (see the exegesis of 4:18).

In addition to its important OT roots, in both Luke 4 and Luke 6 the character of the πτωχός is clearly indicated by the context. Guelich (1982: 67–72) summarizes well the OT background and the NT context of this term:

1. Although in Greek literature the term πτωχός is exclusively socioeconomic in force, its association with the kingdom of God in 6:20 brings in an eschatological flavor that shows it does not merely repeat the pure Greek sense (on Greek usage, see Hauck, *TDNT* 6:886–87).
2. In the LXX, πτωχός translates six Hebrew terms, the most common being עָנִי (ʿānî, poor), which has both socioeconomic and religious connotations that suggest a reference to the pious poor, who look to and depend on God (Ps. 14:6 [13:6 LXX]; 22:24 [21:25 LXX]; 25:16 [24:16 LXX]; 34:6 [33:7 LXX]; 40:17 [39:18 LXX]; 69:29 [68:30 LXX]; Bammel, *TDNT* 6:888).
3. The Torah, Psalms, and Prophets often speak of God's promise in terms of vindication or protection of the pious poor (Exod.

---

28. Bovon 1989: 297 gives three arguments: the form's normal style is in the third person; the remark "blessed are the poor" anticipates a third person; and the fourth beatitude's wording influenced Luke to speak in the second person here. He notes against the third person Jesus' tendency not to use customary style and Matthew's tendency to do so.

22:25–27 [22:24–26 MT]; Deut. 15:7–11; 2 Sam. 22:28; Ps. 72:2, 4, 12; Isa. 3:14–15; 10:2; Jer. 22:16; Ezek. 16:49; 18:12; Amos 8:4; Zech. 7:10), giving the impression that one's compassion and love for a fellow human are measured by one's treatment of the poor.

4. In the LXX (Ps. 24:9 [25:9 Engl.]; 33:2 [34:2 Engl.]) and at Qumran (1QH 1.36; 2.34; 5.13–14), the poor are often associated with the meek or humble, motifs suggested in Luke 1:51–53.

5. Against the suggestion of many, no concrete group in first-century Judaism was called the *Anawim*. The term is best taken as a general description, rather than as a specific sociological reference (Keck 1965).

Guelich's summary definition (1982: 69) is helpful: "*The poor* in Judaism referred to those in desperate need (socioeconomic element) whose helplessness drove them to a dependent relationship with God (religious element) for the supplying of their needs and vindication. Both elements are consistently present, although ʿnwm does place more stress on the latter."

In the context of Luke, the poor often stand in favorable contrast to the rich (1:52–53; 16:19–31), and 6:20 fits that pattern (cf. 6:24). How the two groups as a general rule relate to God is the key to Luke's contrast, which corresponds to the OT usage noted above (1:48–53; 6:20–24; 12:13–21; 14:7–14, 15–24; 16:19–31; 19:1–10). Luke 19:1–10 is an important text, because it is an exception to the pattern and qualifies the negative portrait of the rich (so also 7:1–10). Luke 19 describes a previously immoral rich man who is received by Jesus and pictured as blessed by God because he now has become fair in his tax gathering, has given restitution for his wrong, and has become generous with his wealth. Luke 19 shows that Jesus sees these groups not as absolute, impregnable categories, but as generalized spiritual descriptions, what I call "soteriological generalizations" (see the exegesis of 4:18). The fundamental issue is the condemnation of the rich man's selfish focus on his security versus the poor man's dependence on God (Guelich 1982: 69–70).

More specifically, in 6:20 the near context makes it clear that the religious relationship is not missing, for Jesus addresses the disciples. Also important are the parallel descriptions of the blessed in 6:21–23: the hungry, weeping, and those who occupy positions today like the true prophets of old. They are persecuted because of the Son of Man (6:22). When these descriptions are placed next to Luke's first reference to the poor in 4:18 in terms of Isa. 61:1, then a spiritual dimension for the poor in 6:20 is guaranteed. Thus, Matthew's description of the "poor in spirit" becomes clear. Despite their personal material position, the poor especially picture for Luke both the persecuted remnant mentioned by the OT prophets and the faithfulness of the suffering prophets themselves. Despite the desperation of their external condition, they are blessed because God's kingdom is composed of faithful people who can live above their circumstances and trust God, a theme that appears elsewhere in the NT (1 Cor. 1:26–29; James 2:5).

It is interesting that many of the Lucan beatitudes stress the blessedness of the person who perceives God's plan and so is not offended by Jesus. This blessed disciple understands the promises tied to Jesus (Luke 1:45; 7:23; 10:23–24; 11:28; 12:37–38, 43). That this concern for the poor is to carry over into an expression of the disciples' personal ethics is made clear in the beatitude of 14:14 and the parable that follows it. Luke 14:15–24 shows God's concern to invite even the lowly to the banquet table of God's blessing. It exhorts the disciples to follow him in their concern for the poor, to recognize the poor as candidates for the message. Thus, a paraphrase of this beatitude would read: "Blessed are you materially poor, who nonetheless look to God and his promise, for the kingdom of God is yours." The grace that opens the sermon could not be more manifest in the promise and in the reversal of one's apparent circumstances.

(2) To the Hungry: Satisfaction Then (6:21a)

The second and third beatitudes deal with some of the consequences **6:21a** of being among the poor: hunger and sadness. The pairing of the poor and the hungry is not surprising, since there is ample precedent for it in the OT (Isa. 32:6–7; 58:6–7, 9–10; Ezek. 18:7, 16; Job 22:7; 24:4–11; Ernst 1977: 218). In fact, the hungry, like the poor, are often addressed in comforting terms in the OT (Ps. 37:16–19; 107:9; 132:15; 146:7; Isa. 49:9–10; 55:1–2; Ezek. 34:29; Ernst 1977: 218; Danker 1988: 140; Marshall 1978: 250; Goppelt, *TDNT* 6:18). Another key element in the verse's background is its conceptual tie to Isa. 61:1–3 (Creed 1930: 91). Goppelt describes the hungry:

> The hungry are men who both outwardly and inwardly are painfully deficient in the things essential to life as God meant it to be, and who, since they cannot help themselves, turn to God on the basis of His promise. These men, and these alone, find God's help in Jesus. They are not an existing social or religious group. . . . They are believers who seek help from Jesus because of their own helplessness.

It is important to note that οἱ πεινῶντες (*hoi peinōntes*, the hungry) has both socioeconomic and religious overtones and that errors of interpretation occur when either element is removed. The pairing of οἱ πεινῶντες to eschatological promise in the second part of the verse, the nature of the audience, and the later comparison to the prophets secure a spiritual element in the reference (Ellis 1974: 113; Guelich 1982: 83). Their current condition is highlighted by νῦν (*nyn*, now), which serves to bring out explicitly the greatness of the reversal that God will perform, as the juxtaposition of the condition and the promise suggests. This term is probably Luke's, as he uses νῦν far more frequently (Gospel: fourteen times; Acts: twenty-five times) than does Mark (three times) or Matthew (four times) (Creed 1930: 91). What is "now" will not last forever. In the midst of present poverty and the tension that goes with it, God will give relief (Fitzmyer 1981: 634).

The promise to the hungry, who are also the pious poor, is the promise of satisfaction from God. The reference is not so much to physical filling with food as it is to spiritual satisfaction at being received by God and welcomed as one of his children (Ps. 17:14; 107:9; Luce 1933: 146; Plummer 1896: 180). The imagery is of the satisfaction that comes from being present at God's banquet table (Isa. 25:6; 49:10; Luke 14:15–24; 13:28–29; Schürmann 1969: 331; Fitzmyer 1981: 634; Marshall 1978: 250–51). The parable that pictures this reversal is Lazarus and the rich man in 16:19–31.

The promise is not a political agenda nor a political reversal, but rather the hope of comfort extended to those who elect to participate in God's plan. He leads them into righteousness, while promising to care for them. The point that Jesus is making is that one's fortune is not measured by either current or external criteria (Danker 1988: 140). The key to the present is the security of one's relationship to God as it is brought to fruition in the future. The promise would appeal only to those who have a spiritual perception of reality and the future, to those who have a deep sense of God's being alive and sovereign, and to those who trust that God will act and level out injustice some day. Thus, the promise's spiritual dimension is clear. Matthew's description of this group in spiritually more explicit wording ("hunger and thirst for righteousness") brings out the spiritual quality of those who would be a part of and respond to such a promise (Godet 1875: 1.315; Guelich 1982: 83–84). Again, Luke gives the more original wording, but Matthew accurately brings out its intended force. In effect, the beatitude says: "Blessed are you who sense your lack and depend on God, for God shall accept and reward you in the consummation."

(3) To the Weeping: Laughter Then (6:21b)

6:21b From the condition of the poor, Jesus turns in the third beatitude to the response their position brings now, weeping. Again, as with the previous beatitude, the contrast is between what is lacking now and how that is reversed in the future. The same spiritual perspective of relying on God's work fills this beatitude. The OT background for weeping pictures a person in mourning for a variety of reasons, but primarily for the suffering of painful injustice in a world where God's people are pressured, persecuted, and exiled, just as the prophets were (Ps. 126:5–6; 137:1; Isa. 40:1–2; Luke 6:23; Fitzmyer 1981: 634; Bultmann, *TDNT* 6:43). Those who weep pay a price for depending on God and as a result are scorned (Rengstorf, *TDNT* 1:660 and *TDNT* 3:722–23; Guelich 1982: 80).

Fortunately, that pain is reversed into eschatological joy. Old Testament images for joy are laughter, the removal of grief, and the time of everlasting day (Ps. 126:1–3; Isa. 60:20; 61:3; 65:19; 66:10; Jer. 31:13; Marshall 1978: 251; Ernst 1977: 218). In the Lucan context, the emphasis is on God's total acceptance of the one who currently weeps (Luke 16:19–31; 18:14). The picture is of the removal of woe, like that described in Rev. 21:4; as the future tense in the Lucan passage looks to the consummation, so did the future tense in 6:21a. The laughter here is in stark contrast to the use of γελάω (*gelaō*, to laugh) in 6:25b, where it is a negative term for the rich, who see themselves as independent of God. Beatitudes 2 and 3 recall 1:51–55 and show Jesus' stress on the hope he offers to those who follow him. In effect, this beatitude reads: "Blessed are you who suffer scorn and pain as you identify with God and depend on him, for you shall be fully welcomed by him at his table and shall rejoice."

(4) To the Persecuted: Heavenly Reward (6:22–23)

The fourth beatitude demonstrates that the Beatitudes as a whole **6:22** have a spiritual base and are not just to be taken as socioeconomic in character. Jesus notes the presence of spiritual opposition because of the disciples' commitment to Jesus. Nevertheless, that commitment yields blessing. This recognition of rejection clearly has roots in Jesus' ministry, since already opposition to him exists (6:2, 11). The disciples will also face opposition (Acts 3–4; 7; 21–28). The word is especially comforting to Luke's audience since their choice to follow Jesus had undoubtedly brought them under great pressure (Luke 1:1–4).

There is no reason to regard this teaching as a product of the early church.[29] Many regard this beatitude as added to the original tradi-

---

29. Marshall 1978: 252; Schürmann 1969: 335–36. Jeremias 1971a: 239–40 notes that these warnings of persecution occur in every strand of Gospel tradition, showing their widespread presence and association to Jesus. Schürmann notes conceptual Lucan parallels in 11:49–52 and 12:11–12. They sound like Matt. 5:11. For a pre-Easter setting, he notes Matt. 10:28–31, 34–39; Mark 6:14–29; 11:1–11, 15–18 as giving evidence of pre-Easter tension.

tion, because of the shift to second person in Matthew's version and its added length in comparison to the other beatitudes (Schneider 1977a: 152; Schürmann 1969: 335 #2; Fitzmyer 1981: 634–35). But such a conclusion is hardly required. Daube (1956: 196–201) shows that in Judaism a parallel series often ends with a longer or differently structured line to heighten the conclusion. The length is a way of making the close emphatic. In addition, a change of person often accompanies these kinds of references.[30] In fact, the longer form may reveal a key to the text's meaning in that it is the association to Jesus that unlocks the blessings mentioned in the Beatitudes. The case for the addition of the last beatitude on the basis of line length and person shift is thus to be rejected. As Marshall (1978: 252) notes, the first three beatitudes address the condition of Jesus' disciples, while this final beatitude lists the fate or reaction they face. The teaching has parallels in the epistolary material. Both James 2:7 and 1 Pet. 4:14–16 express similar sentiments about what is occurring to believers. In fact, 1 Peter even shares some of the terms of this passage (Klostermann 1929: 79; J. Schneider, *TDNT* 5:240). Commitment to God's unique representative often produces such reaction, but God promises to respond to those committed to him.

Rejection of the disciples is described by four verbal ideas that depict a gradual heightening of opposition. In a rather paradoxical promise, hostility is said to bring blessing.

The first description of hostility involves hatred (μισέω, *miseō*; Ps. 69:4 [68:5 LXX]; Isa. 66:5; Nolland 1989: 284; Bovon 1989: 303). As the OT texts show, religious opposition to God's people is not unusual. In many Western cultures, religious allegiance is a private affair, and the diversity with which it is held is a given. In ancient culture and in many non-Western cultures today, however, religious convictions are a major element of a person's identity, so that how one views and treats a person is very much related to religious affiliation. For a disciple to align with Jesus was to take a public and potentially offensive stand that would produce reaction, even hatred. A disciple was to realize that God knew of this public reaction.

The second description mentions that disciples will sometimes be excluded (ἀφορίζω, *aphorizō*). But does social separation mean no social contact (Luce 1933: 146)? Is the reference limited to excommunication from the synagogue (John 9:22, 34; 12:42; 16:2; Godet 1875: 1.316)? Or is it both (Plummer 1896: 181)? The term ἀφορίζω is generally broad in scope (BAGD 127 §1; BAA 255 §1; Isa. 56:3).

---

30. Daube notes Isa. 63:7–19; Sir. 47:12–22 (esp. 47:21–22); 48:1–12 (esp. 48:11); and Luke 1:67–79, where shifts of person occur at the end of lists, as well as the structure of 6:37–38, where the last line is longer than the three preceding lines. I already noted Ps. 127:1–2 LXX in the exegesis of 6:20.

When one was banned from the synagogue, sentences ranged from a thirty-day suspension to total expulsion (SB 4:293–333). The terms associated with this ban are *herem* and *nidduy*. The twelfth benediction of the Jewish prayer *Shemoneh Esreh* [Eighteen Benedictions] explicitly curses the Nazarenes and the *minim*, a Jewish reference to Christians (Schürer 1973–87: 2.461). Hare (1967: 48–56) evaluates the view that uses this material to argue for a narrow sense of synagogue ban and shows that many first-century practices of banning, especially the *nidduy*, were not standards directed against the average synagogue attender, but were higher standards directed by the Pharisees against themselves. Thus, Luke is referring to general social ostracism, not a formal synagogue ban, though the ostracism might manifest itself in this way. For example, one might refuse to do business with disciples or fellowship with them over a meal. Hare derives this meaning from some later Jewish and Christian texts displaying this approach to Christians (*t. Ḥul.* 2.20–21 [= Neusner 1977–86: 5.73–75]; Justin Martyr, *Dialogue with Trypho* 138.1; *ʾAbot de Rabbi Nathan* A.2 [= Goldin 1955: 25]). A picture of what this verse is describing is seen in Paul's treatment by some Jews in Acts (14:5–7, 19; 16:19–24).

The third description speaks of being reviled or insulted (ὀνειδίζω, *oneidizō*; BAGD 570; BAA 1155; 1 Pet. 4:14). It refers to the slander and verbal attack that one might suffer for a commitment to Jesus. Schürmann (1969: 333) and Grundmann (1963: 143–44) compare this reference in its original pre-Lucan Palestinian setting to the twelfth benediction of the *Shemoneh Esreh*, which contains a synagogue ban and a curse (Schürer 1973–87: 2.461). Although this text is later than the destruction of the temple in A.D. 70 (Hare 1967: 54), it may reflect elements of earlier practice (SB 4:327–28). As Hare notes, the benediction ostracizes, but it does not excommunicate. Hare, however, may be too skeptical about the texts in John and may be wrong in rejecting such a practice (p. 55).[31]

Ἐκβάλωσιν τὸ ὄνομα ὑμῶν ὡς πονηρόν (*ekbalōsin to onoma hymōn hōs ponēron*, cast out your name as evil) seems to be a summary of the actions taken against disciples (Deut. 22:14, 19; Nolland 1989: 285). The disciple is treated as evil, unclean, and thus as a person with whom one does not associate. To attack a person's name is to strike at the very person. The phrase pictures total rejection.

All of these attacks come on account of the Son of Man, that is, because of the disciple's relationship to Jesus. This phrase has been

---

31. It is unlikely that Christians as a body were banned this early from any synagogue, though individuals might have been. The Book of Acts shows that Christians could still enter the synagogue, until they forced the issue and Jews reacted by turning them out.

used in 5:24 and 6:5 to describe Jesus as the one with authority over sin and over the Sabbath. In the ostracism because of one's tie to Jesus, however, there is blessing from God, despite the rejection of fellow humans.

The parallel in Matt. 5:11 does not mention the Son of Man: the disciple is simply spoken of as being persecuted "on account of me." Whether τοῦ υἱοῦ τοῦ ἀνθρώπου (*tou huiou tou anthrōpou*, the Son of Man) is present in the original tradition is the subject of intense discussion. Marshall (1978: 253) argues that Luke nowhere else inserts a reference to the Son of Man where it is absent in parallel tradition (also Schürmann 1969: 334 n. 62). For Marshall, Matthew does not have the title but a simpler, synonymous reference to Jesus. However, Lindars (1983: 133) cites Luke 22:48 and 24:7 as two examples that refute this view, and Jeremias (1971a: 262–63; 1967) argues that in parallel texts the title *Son of Man* is often clearly the later reading (Colpe, *TDNT* 8:448–49). Counterarguments also exist. Many see Luke using extratraditional materials or sources for his portrayal of the passion and resurrection, so that the passages Lindars mentions may be a reflection of sources, not Luke (Borsch 1967: 337 n. 3). And Guelich (1982: 95) demonstrates Matthew's tendency to refer directly to Jesus in passages where the parallel reference is indirect and in at least one case where the parallel text refers to the Son of Man (Matt. 10:32–33 and Luke 12:8–9; Matt. 16:21 and Mark 8:31; Matt. 23:34 and Luke 11:49). Guelich's references show the Matthean tendency clearly, even if the last set of parallels refers to distinct events. Against Guelich (but without mentioning his evidence), Fitzmyer (1981: 635) argues that since Matthew will add a reference to the Son of Man in texts where parallels do not have it (e.g., Matt. 16:13 = Mark 8:27 = Luke 9:18), he would hardly omit such a reference in Matt. 5:11.

Obviously, there is no way to be certain on this choice, given the mixed evidence of the data. Each reading clearly reflects the sense of the utterance and each version refers to Jesus. It also seems, in light of the Matthean pattern, that he is more likely to have simplified the reference. At any rate, tying oneself to Jesus may yield public rejection, but one can stand reassured that such a relationship yields God's blessing.

6:23   The one command among the Beatitudes now appears. The realization of blessing should yield joy. Matthew 5:12 has a parallel idea, though the wording is slightly different. The basic exhortation is to rejoice in the midst of suffering for Jesus. The command to rejoice contrasts with the references to poverty, hunger, weeping, and violent opposition in the previous verses. The reference to ἐκείνῃ τῇ ἡμέρᾳ (*ekeinē tē hēmera*, that day) is not a day of future judgment or merely of exclusion from the synagogue.[32] Rather, it functions as a parallel to νῦν (*nyn*, now) in Luke 6:21 and alludes to rejoicing at the very moment in which the persecution comes, in whatever form it comes. The term ἐκείνῃ τῇ ἡμέρᾳ is probably a Lucan elaboration on Jesus' meaning (10:12; 17:31; Marshall 1978: 254; Creed 1930: 91). As such, it alludes to all the hostile responses mentioned in 6:22. The aorist imperative in Luke lends a note of urgency to the command ("do this now"), while Matthew's present tense stresses the mere content of the command ("do this").

The attitude of gladness in the midst of persecution and rejection is a key theme in Luke–Acts. Σκιρτάω (*skirtaō*, to leap for joy) was used in Luke 1:41, 44 for John's leaping in Elizabeth's womb on the occasion of Mary's visit. Clearly a positive attitude is described. Willingness to suffer existed in Judaism (2 Macc. 6:30; 4 Macc. 10:20; Jdt. 8:25–27; 2 Bar. 52.5–7; Nolland 1989: 286). Such joy parallels the reactions of various groups to persecution later in Acts (Acts 4:23–31; 5:41; 16:25; 21:13–14; Danker 1988: 141). Such groups counted it an honor to be deemed worthy to suffer for Jesus (Acts 5:41; Carson 1978: 29), a theme that reappears elsewhere in the NT (Rom. 5:2–5; James 1:2; 1 Pet. 1:6; 4:1; Marshall 1978: 254; Klostermann 1929: 79; Nauck 1955).

Two reasons for the exhortation to joy follow, each being introduced by γάρ (*gar*, for). The first is the promise of heavenly reward. Jesus is not holding out a carrot for his disciples to earn, but is reminding them that God is aware of their commitment and will honor it. Thus, the reference is to a promise of present, heavenly vindication. The God who is in heaven knows what they are suffering and honors such faithfulness (Ernst 1977: 221 [of God's great judgment]; Fitzmyer 1981: 635; Liefeld 1984: 891; see esp. Isa. 65:13). The promise calls one to look beyond circumstances, and it encourages one to see God's perspective on suffering endured because of commitment to him (Guelich 1982: 95–96; Preisker, *TDNT* 4:714, 719). Paul holds out the same promise in Rom. 8:18 and 2 Cor. 4:17–18 (Hendriksen 1978: 343). In effect, Jesus says that commitment will be vindicated and rewarded. In other passages where reward is discussed, he makes the point that the disciple is to perform one's duty for God and not focus on earning reward (Luke 17:9; Creed 1930: 92). The concept of rewards is difficult, for they are clearly mentioned as an aspect of motivation. The idea is not to get "brownie points," but to be honored for faithfulness. In other words, the reward deals with the heart behind the service, not the selfish pursuit of the prize (1 Cor. 4:4–5).

---

32. Schürmann 1969: 334 n. 63 shows that the term is not a technical term for the end-time judgment, though he opts too narrowly for a synagogue connection.

The second reason for rejoicing involves an awareness that the disciples' persecution parallels the treatment that God's prophets once received. The pattern of the poor treatment of God's servants and messengers is in view (Godet 1875: 1.316). In previous generations, the ancestors of those mistreating Jesus' disciples mistreated the prophets. So αὐτῶν (autōn, their) here refers to the persecutors of Luke 6:22, who continue the heritage of their ancestors (Plummer 1896: 181). That the nation rejects its messengers is a frequent theme in Luke–Acts (Luke 11:47–51; Acts 7:51–52). The OT also makes this declaration (Jer. 2:29–30; 11:18–21; 20:2; 26:8–11, 20; 37:15–16; 38:4–6; 1 Kings 18:4, 13; 19:10; 22:27; 2 Chron. 16:10; 24:21; Neh. 9:26; Friedrich, *TDNT* 6:834 n. 348). The NT also consistently sounds this note (1 Thess. 2:14–16; Rom. 11:3; Heb. 11:35–38; James 5:10; Guelich 1982: 96; Schürmann 1969: 335 n. 70; Jeremias, *TDNT* 5:714 n. 469). It is part of the history of God's people that they are strongly resisted by those who at first glance should be the most likely to respond. Luke's general reference to all of God's people is paralleled by Matthew, despite the claims of some that Matthew refers to Christian prophets (Marshall 1978: 255 rightly critiques Hare 1967: 116–17). The prophets in view are the ancient parallel group of God's persecuted but faithful servants.

ii. Four Woes (6:24–26)

After the four blessings, Luke relates four woes. The rich, full, laughing, and liked of 6:24–26 contrast with the poor, hungry, weeping, and persecuted of 6:20–23. The parallelism shows that those addressed in these verses are not seen as four separate groups but as one group with four characteristics (Schürmann 1969: 337). The woes serve as a warning and a call of repentance to those who may be tempted to trust too greatly in wealth, comfort, popularity, and possessions.

The audience of this subunit is complex. Luke 6:26 clearly includes a warning to disciples, since the phrase *their fathers* looks to outsiders (as in 6:23). A point of the woes is "do not live as those on the outside live." Your values are not to be their values, which bring woe. But it is an attitude and orientation that is rebuked here, so as the disciples are warned, outsiders are also addressed with the same warning. An attitude of independence from God is the road to destruction. Its reward is fleeting, limited to the present.

The OT provides numerous examples of the woe form: Deut. 27:15–26; Isa. 5:8–23; 30:1–2; 31:1; 33:1; 65:13–16 (which many regard as parallel to this passage, since blessing and judgment are side by side); Amos 5:18; 6:1; Hab. 2:15–20 (Ernst 1977: 220; on the form of OT woe passages, see Gerstenberger 1962). In a few texts of the

OT and Judaism, blessings and woes appear together (Isa. 3:10–11; Eccles. 10:16–17; Tob. 13:12, 14; 1 Enoch 5.7; 99.1–16). Luke is fond of woes, though most of his texts are parallels to similar texts.[33] Woes appear somewhat frequently in the NT as well, especially in Matthew (Mark 13:17; 14:21; Matt. 11:20–24; 23:13, 15, 16, 23, 25, 27, 29; 24:19; 26:24; Jude 11; Rev. 8:13; 12:12; 18:10–12; Schürmann 1969: 337 n. 86 [who argues that Luke does not independently form the sayings]).

(1) To the Rich: Consolation Now (6:24)

Οὐαί (*ouai*, woe or alas) is an exclamation of pain and pity for the misfortune that awaits someone in a certain condition (BAGD 591; BAA 1196). The contrast between woe and blessing is neatly marked out by πλήν (*plēn*, but), a term that Luke uses frequently in his Gospel (fifteen times in Luke, thirty-one times in the NT; BAGD 669; BAA 1345–46; Plummer 1896: 182; Marshall 1978: 255). Both πλήν and οὐαί appear in Matt. 18:7, which shows that the phrase can be of traditional origin (so Marshall). The woe is expressed to warn of danger and the nearness of judgment (Danker 1988: 142).

6:24

The rich are singled out here, a group that Luke often criticizes (1:53; 12:16; 14:12; 16:1, 21–22; 18:23, 25; 19:2; 21:1; Hauck and Kasch, *TDNT* 6:328).[34] But it is important to remember that the parallelism to the poor of 6:20 shows that another generalization is present. Figures like Zacchaeus, Joseph of Arimathea, and Nicodemus show that the rich are not excluded as a class or for merely belonging to a certain socioeconomic group, but for an attitude they often display. The commentary on these remarks is found in parabolic material in Luke's travel section (12:13–21; 16:19–31; note also 1:53; Godet 1875: 1.317; Geldenhuys 1951: 210). James also makes similar comments (2:6–7; 5:1–6). The world's perspective and values are reversed here. What is condemned is a misplaced focus that zeroes in on this life and its possessions without concern for God's desires or fellow humans. The danger of succumbing to things of only temporal value is all too real and deceptive.

The reason for the woe is stated crisply in the ὅτι (*hoti*, for) clause: the rich have already received their consolation. The possessions they garner are all they will have to show for their efforts. Ἀπέχετε (*apechete*, you have received) is a technical commercial term for

---

33. Luke 10:13–15 = Matt. 11:20–24; Luke 11:42–52 is like parts of Matt. 23; Luke 17:1 does not have a parallel woe in the Synoptics; Luke 21:23 = Matt. 24:19 = Mark 13:17; and Luke 22:22 = Matt. 26:24 = Mark 14:21.

34. On this topic in the Synoptics, see T. Schmidt 1987. In arguing against making too much of the criticism, Schmidt is correct, but his book perhaps overreacts in the other direction. More balanced is Pilgrim 1981.

signing or accepting a receipt for payment given (Matt. 6:2, 5, 16; Phil. 4:18; Philem. 15; Luce 1933: 146; BAGD 84–85; BAA 169 §1; Hanse, *TDNT* 2:828). The full payment is their wealth, but nothing will come to them from God in the future. The parables of the rich fool and the rich man who had no compassion for Lazarus both indicate that Jesus views this "riches now" focus as terribly, even destructively, shortsighted (Ernst 1977: 221; Fitzmyer 1981: 636). Again, James has a conceptual parallel (1:9–11). The consolation they have is more like a loser's trophy in the eternal perspective. Where in the future the poor will reap much benefit from their commitment to God and share in an eternal kingdom, spiritually insensitive rich people hold only an empty bag. The term παράκλησιν (*paraklēsin*, consolation) is clearly negative here, although it is often positive in Lucan usage (Luke 2:25; Acts 4:36; 9:31; 13:15; 15:31).

(2) To the Full: Hunger Then (6:25a)

6:25a The second woe gives the condition of the rich. The warning of reversal goes to those who are full. Ἐμπεπλησμένοι (*empeplēsmenoi*, those who are filled) describes the state in which the rich live. They are "sated with the good things of this life" (Plummer 1896: 182; Fitzmyer 1981: 636). Luke 16:19 illustrates the point. They lack for nothing now (as a Lucan qualifier, νῦν twice here parallels its use twice in 6:21). The reason for future woe is that they shall be hungry (note the use of ὅτι again, as in 6:24). In the future, they shall lack for the things they now have in abundance. Conceptual parallels include Luke 1:53 and James 5:1. What they have now, they will utterly lack in the eternal future. The warning reflects OT woes as well (Isa. 5:22; 65:13; Amos 8:11; Plummer 1896: 182; Klostermann 1929: 80). Of course, those who are filled in the future will be the righteous, who may be suffering now (Jer. 31:10–14; Leaney 1958: 136). God will reverse the situation and vindicate the righteous.

(3) To the Laughing: Weeping Then (6:25b)

6:25b The third woe gives the attitude of the rich, derisive laughter now. Again, νῦν shows the contrast—with weeping in 6:21. Γελῶντες (*gelōntes*, those who laugh) is key here. Levity or harmless humor is not in view here. In the LXX, γελάω is often tied to laughter that is boastful, self-satisfied, condescending, or rejoicing in the harm that others experience (Marshall 1978: 256; Rengstorf, *TDNT* 1:659–60; Schürmann 1969: 338 n. 91). For example, Lam. 1:7 uses the term of how the enemies laughed or gloated at Jerusalem's destruction. Jewish Wisdom Literature often uses the term to describe foolish people and their harmful humor (Eccles. 7:6; Sir. 21:20; 27:13). Only in Gen. 21:6 is γελάω used in a positive sense in the LXX. Thus, the picture is of a person of worldly ease who is indifferent because of self-satisfaction (Geldenhuys 1951: 216 n. 10; Godet 1875: 1.317; Grundmann 1963: 145; Fitzmyer 1981: 637). James 5:5 also describes in harsh terms the callous attitude of such a person. But Jesus offers a woe for such people, because (ὅτι, *hoti*) this laughter shall also be reversed. It will become mourning and weeping. The language is reminiscent of Isa. 65:14 and has conceptual parallels in Rev. 18:15, 19. The double description of the reversal in terms of both mourning and weeping intensifies the picture of pain by using two terms to refer to a single idea. The reference to mourning may recall the beatitude of Matt. 5:4 in a reversed direction. The lack of blessing on the callous rich in the eternal future contrasts to what those who weep now will have then (Luke 6:21) and also contrasts to the shallow fullness the rich possess now. The joy of possession now will become the pain of what is lost forever.

(4) To the Well-Spoken-Of Who Are like the False Prophets: Woe (6:26)

The fourth woe contrasts with the fourth beatitude of 6:23. This woe includes a warning to the disciples, as the reference to "their fathers" makes clear. If only the excluded rich were in view, then the verse would read "your fathers." The woe serves as a warning to the disciples, as well as to outsiders, not to fall into the trap of courting acceptance for one's message at the expense of truthfulness, an approach that will make them function more like false prophets. Popularity at the expense of being God's faithful representative is disastrous (Danker 1988: 143). The concept of Jesus' message being unpopular is frequent in the NT (John 15:19; James 4:4; Luke 2:34; 12:51–53; 1 Cor. 1:18–25; 1 Pet. 3:13–17; Ernst 1977: 222).

6:26

The reason (γάρ, *gar*, for) for the woe is that the popularity seeker is in the company of those who set a bad precedent in Israel's history. Israel often courted prophets who gave the message it wanted to hear, rather than giving God's message (Jer. 5:31; 14:13–16; 23:9–15, 27–28; Ezek. 22:23–31; Isa. 30:10; Mic. 2:11; Marshall 1978: 256–57; Leaney 1958: 137; Fitzmyer 1981: 637; Plummer 1896: 183). Seeking such popularity at the expense of God's message is like commending a false prophet. The separation of disciples from their unbelieving ancestry is suggested by the phrase *their fathers*. It shows Jesus' disapproval of those who reject him now, a disapproval that is also highlighted in the emphatic concluding position the phrase has in the verse, just as in 6:23. In fact, 6:23 is the contrastive parallel to this verse. The wording of 6:23b and 6:26b is identical except for προφήταις (*prophētais*, prophets) and ψευδοπροφήταις (*pseudoprophētais*, false prophets).

Although Schürmann (1969: 338–39) relates 6:26 to the current false teachers in the early church, citing 6:39–40, Ernst (1977: 221) prefers a reference to the Pharisees by appealing to Matt. 6:1–5; 23:5. Nevertheless, the warning seems to be broad. Anyone reflecting these values or drawn to them is rebuked. The saying warns of courting the approval of the insensitive yet popular rich (Nolland 1989: 288). Whether Jesus' opponents were guilty of this so that he alludes directly to them is less clear. Courting such popularity was the very problem of messengers of old who departed from God and whom the people wrongly embraced.

The woes show that the world's values and God's values are very different indeed. In addition, whatever treasure one has briefly now may not equate with whatever loss one has forever later. Where is the best place to rest one's well-being: in the short-term present or in the eternal future? That is the issue Jesus raises here. He says that the disciple is to be dependent on God and stand up for him. It may mean poverty, rejection, persecution, and pain now. But one may rest assured that God will bless abundantly. Do not be deceived by the self-sufficient and indifferent way of the rich. They have much now, but they will have nothing later. One can have consolation now and lose it, or one may lack now, only to receive abundant blessing later. Rest assured that God's way is just. Here is the keynote of the Beatitudes and woes: God's blessing is on those who come to him to receive what he generously offers, and that blessing knows no socio-economic limitation. In fact, one's position may be an obstacle to blessing.

b. Parenetic Call to Love and Mercy (6:27–38)

The next subunit contains the main body of the sermon and is full of parenesis (exhortation). The major topic is love. Luke 6:20–26 contained (1) the promise and hope that Jesus offers to those who identify with his message and (2) a warning about those who do not. This passage contains the fundamental exhortation of what a follower is to do. Simply put, the disciple's love for others should be extraordinary in comparison to the way people usually love. The exhortation to love comes in three different forms in 6:27–28, 31, 35. In between the imperatives are two sets of illustrations: four illustrations in 6:29–30 and three illustrations in 6:32–34. With the conclusion of the second set of illustrations, a summary command to love is given in 6:35.

Love is looked at in the subunit from three angles. In 6:27, it is expressed in radical terms as loving those who oppose you. In 6:31, it is expressed in terms of a human perspective: treat others as you wish they would treat you, a classic role reversal. And in 6:35, it is expressed in terms of a divine standard, where love is not the concept expressed, but graciousness is used to define love's generous quality. This ethic clearly made a deep impression on Jesus' followers, as it runs through all characterizations of his teaching (John 13:34–35; 15:12–17; Rom. 12:17–21; 13:10; Gal. 6:2; James 2:8; 1 John 3:11–18).

Luke 6:36–38 turns our attention from how we treat others to how we respond to them. Love includes mercy, following God's own example. This attitude produces a hesitation in judging others, as believers realize that God will treat them in the way they have treated others. The structural pattern in 6:36–38a is a set of four exhortations, two negative and two positive, each of which also has a promise. A note on God's evaluative standard (6:38b) concludes the paragraph.

The placement of 6:36 is disputed, in that it could be viewed as concluding 6:27–35 or as an introduction to the parables of 6:39–49. The syntax of 6:37, which begins with καί (*kai*, and), shows that 6:36 is linked to the following idea of judging in 6:37 (Creed 1930: 95; Klostermann 1929: 82). Yet Nolland (1989: 300) gives compelling reasons for linking 6:36 back to 6:27–35: (1) being like God is the issue in 6:35–36; (2) 6:37–38 is less conceptually compatible with 6:36; (3) the Matthean parallel (5:48) looks backward; and (4) the universal compassion of God (Sir. 18:13; Ps. 145:8–9) models well the compassion that the disciple is called to have. These connections suggest that 6:36 is a hinge verse, but the emphasis goes backward.

The expression of love, the topic of 6:27–35, is still in view in 6:36. Jesus wants disciples to see that mercy (6:36) and generosity (6:35) are related concepts. In the LXX, οἰκτιρμός (*oiktirmos*, mercy) and related terms are tied to the ἔλεος (*eleos*, mercy) word group (Exod. 34:6; Ps. 85:15 LXX [86:15 Engl.]; 102:4 LXX [103:4 Engl.]; Neh. 9:17, 31; 2 Chron. 30:9). Sometimes ἔλεος and χρηστός (*chrēstos*, kind), the term in Luke 6:35, appear together (Ps. 108:21 [109:21 Engl.]). All three terms occur in Ps. 68:17 LXX [69:16 Engl.] and 111:4–5 LXX [112:4–5 Engl.].

But the other point of Luke's connection is the idea of judgment (on Luke 6:36 as a hinge, see Danker 1988: 151 and Fitzmyer 1981: 640–41). Given the shift in the form of the teaching in Luke 6:39 to parabolic description, the subunit 6:36–38 is slightly better seen as a hinge and as concluding the parenetic subunit as one moves from love to judgment. If one is to love, where does that leave pursuit of the truth and judgment? Luke 6:37–49 says not to condemn but forgive, pursue truth by watching whom you follow, deal with your own faults while humbly helping others, and, especially, follow Jesus and his teaching.

i. Fourfold Call to Love Your Enemies (6:27–28)
(1) Love Your Enemies (6:27a)

6:27a The attention now turns to love, but the love exhibited here is not ordinary: it is difficult and superior. It is the love appropriate for a disciple who has experienced God's forgiveness. The verse opens with a contrast and the first of four exhortations. Ἀλλά (*alla*, but) at the beginning of the verse contrasts with the preceding woes. It represents a shift back to the desired activity of disciples.[35] Others speak of a vague recollection of an original antithesis here (Godet 1875: 1.322). Though possible, it is hard to establish, especially since Luke has ἀλλά rather than δέ (*de*, but) like Matt. 5:44. Guelich (1982: 224–25) denies any connection to a possible antithesis, but it is hard to know how one can make such a judgment. There is no doubt, however, that the presentation of the idea in Luke and Matthew comes in distinct forms.[36]

The shift of focus is emphasized by the word order, since ὑμῖν (*hymin*, you) is separated from ἀκούουσιν (*akouousin*, those who listen) (Fitzmyer 1981: 637). In calling the audience listeners, Jesus stresses not just the need to hear the message, but also the importance of responding to it. The force is like his expression, "Let him who has ears, let him hear" (Acts 28:28; Matt. 18:15–16; Luke 9:35; 16:29, 31; Marshall 1978: 258–59; Danker 1988: 143).

The first exhortation is to love one's enemies. Though such a command has similarities with OT sayings, it is unparalleled in its emphatic tone (Exod. 23:4–5; Prov. 17:5; 24:17; 25:21–22; Job 31:29–34; Fitzmyer 1981: 637–38). The law suggested that one should love one's neighbor as oneself (Lev. 19:18). But in Judaism, one's neighbor was someone with similar religious thinking, not one who was opposed and hostile (on enemy, see Foerster, *TDNT* 2:814; Luke 1:71, 74; 6:35; 10:19; 19:27, 43; 20:43). The opposition here is likely tied to the hatred and persecution of Luke 6:22 and thus is largely religious in character (Marshall 1978: 259). In some movements in Judaism, the exact opposite was instructed, as at Qumran, where the right to hate one's religious foes was a given.[37] It is easy to love

---

35. Marshall 1978: 258, however, sees a shift of audience from outsiders to insiders in this verse; so also Ernst 1977: 224. But see T. Schmidt 1987: 141.

36. Such differences lead some to speak of multiple forms of the tradition or of two settings.

37. 1QS 1.10; 2.4–9; 9.21–23; Ellis 1974: 114; Guelich 1982: 226. The leaning of the imprecatory Psalms in this direction is what makes their tone so difficult. Because Jesus' ethic is a heightening of old standards, they appear in antithesis in Matthew. It is right to call for God's justice, but it is also important to seek the best for fellow humans. God's justice is in place and will occur, as the eschatological remarks of the sermon make clear. But the disciple seeks the enemies' transformation and

those favorable to you, but this command to love enemies would be more difficult to carry out. Nonetheless, the early community clearly adopted this approach, as the examples of Jesus (Luke 23:34) and Stephen (Acts 7:58–60) show and as the exhortations of Paul (Rom. 12:16–21; 1 Thess. 5:15) and Peter (1 Pet. 3:9) urge (Plummer 1896: 184).

(2) Do Good to Those Who Hate You (6:27b)

From the general attitude of love, the second exhortation moves to specifics. The disciples are told to do good to those who hate them. Hatred and enemies often appear together to describe those hostile to God's people (Luke 1:71; Ps. 18:17 [18:18 MT]; 106:10). This exhortation and the next have no equivalent in Matthew, leading Fitzmyer (1981: 638) to call the second and third exhortations "Lucan elaborations." But it is quite likely that Luke rendered sources here, for the idea of blessing those who hate you also appears in 1 Pet. 3:9, which may suggest a traditional origin for these exhortations. As Luke 6:33 notes, if we do good only to those who love us, what is unusual about that kind of love (Matt. 5:45–47)? Again, the radical character, as well as the difficulty of what Jesus demands, is clear. In speaking of doing good, Jesus shows that he has in mind more than an intellectual, passive attitude of love toward those who oppose God's people. Rather, active love is in view.

6:27b

(3) Bless Those Who Curse You (6:28a)

The third command moves from actions to words, even words of appeal to God. The idea of blessing is to invoke God's favor on another's behalf or at least appeal to God for that person. As they died, Jesus (Luke 23:34) and Stephen (Acts 7:60) interceded for enemies. In noting their action, of course, one does not exclude the possibility that a harsh warning may need to be sounded, as passages like Luke 6:24–26; Matt. 23; and 1 Cor. 16:22 show. It is important to note what Jesus just said in Luke 6:24–26: people must know that God will be just and that he is displeased with activities that debase others, for they reveal that one is out of touch with God. That Paul can utter a curse like 1 Cor. 16:22 and yet give his life to drawing people to God shows the heart the apostle had for those who would reject him. Cursing reacts to the opponent's religious hostility. It involves an invocation of God or the gods to harm or judge someone (Büchsel, *TDNT* 1:449). The disciples held no right to such invocation, at

6:28a

---

hopes that they may come to know God so that they can enter into God's grace and kindness, while escaping his wrath.

least not at the start of their work (Luke 9:51–56; James 3:9–12). They could acknowledge where people truly stood before God; they could make clear what the justice of God would mean for one who steadfastly refused to listen to God; but they were to seek to benefit their enemies as much as possible (John 20:23; Matt. 16:19; 18:18; Rom. 12:14; 1 Cor. 4:12; Beyer, *TDNT* 2:763).

(4) Pray for Those Who Abuse You (6:28b)

6:28b The extent of such outreach to the opponent is clear from the final exhortation. Jesus commands the disciples to pray for those who abuse or treat them with spite or malice. The reference to harsh treatment is also a reference to persecution (1 Pet. 3:16; Plummer 1896: 185). Intercession to God for the opponent is one of the highest forms of love. Such love is tough love, not because it requires harsh discipline against another as parental love might, but because it requires a sublimation of the self to such a great degree, a sublimation that is not normal for any human. It is a supernatural love, because doing it requires that one reverse all natural instincts. It is a love that can come only in light of a dependence on God.

In fact, not only does Jesus' command stand out against Judaism, though hints of it exist in the OT and elsewhere, it also stands out against some strands of Greek thinking (Lysias, *For the Soldier* 20; Pindar, *Pythian Odes* 2.83–84; Fitzmyer 1981: 637). Lysias said, "I consider it established that one should do harm to one's enemies and be of service to one's friends." Occasionally, however, a different view emerged, so that Jesus' message is not unique (Thucydides 4.19.1–4; Diogenes Laertius 8.23; Seneca, *On Benefits* 4.26.1; Epictetus 3.22.54; Exod. 23:4–5; Prov. 24:17; 25:21; the Babylonian *Counsels of Wisdom* 41–45 [Lambert 1960: 101]; Philo, *On the Virtues* 23 §117; 1QS 10.17–18 [where the call is to punish the enemy with goodness]; T. Ben. 4.3; T. Jos. 18.2; Midr. Exod. 26.2 on 17:8; Fitzmyer 1981: 638; Bovon 1989: 313 n. 19; Nolland 1989: 294).[38] The passages from the Testaments of the Twelve Patriarchs are lessons learned from the example of Joseph in Gen. 39–50. However, Jesus was unique in making such focus a cornerstone of his ethic. He does not follow the other ancients with an appeal to the virtue of such action, nor does he issue a call to maintain solidarity in a com-

---

38. The OT has the call to love the neighbor in Lev. 19:18, but Judaism debated who the neighbor was, as Luke 10:25–37 shows. Bovon 1989: 313 n. 21 cites Seitz 1969–70: 47: "Loving is thus a matter of 'doing mercy,' which is to stop at no frontiers, levelling all barriers erected by national and even religious hostility." The call to love has no racial, national, social, and religious barriers. The disciple is to love all people. The implications of this are far-reaching in any culture in which disciples find themselves.

munity, nor does he appeal to self-interest, but he focuses on the raw power of love as imitation of God (Luke 6:35; Nolland 1989: 296). This is how the disciple is to relate to all humanity.

ii. Four Illustrations of Loving (6:29–30)
(1) Offer the Cheek (6:29a)

Jesus illustrates this love for one's enemies. Saying that 6:29–30 are **6:29a** not precepts but illustrations of principles, Plummer (1896: 185) goes on to say that they cannot be kept as rules but should be read for the spirit they embody: "Resistance of evil and refusal to part with our personal property must never be a *personal* matter: so far as *we* are concerned we must be willing to suffer more and to surrender still more."[39] With regard to our feelings, we ought to be willing to offer the other cheek. But one wonders if Plummer weakens the force of the teaching by softening it to a moral generalization and appealing to the level of feelings.

Schottroff and Stegemann (1986: 112–16) take another approach. They argue that this is a combination of Lucan and traditional material. Luke addressed a concrete situation for the Christian rich. They are to do good to their fellow Christians, even if the latter hate them. They are to exercise charity without expecting return. Schottroff and Stegemann place much weight on 6:35, but their remarks miss the point. First, their interpretation is too focused on a church setting and ignores the sermon's original setting. More importantly, it ignores the context, which is religious persecution for the sake of the Son of Man (6:22). How could this possibly be poor Christians versus rich ones? This suggestion is wide of the mark.

The point is that love involves not defending one's rights and accepting wrongs committed against one by being willing to forgive, with the additional proviso that one is willing to turn around a second time and still offer help—even if that means being abused yet again. Love is available, vulnerable, and subject to repeated abuse. Offering the other cheek is not so much an active pursuit as it is a natural exposure when one reaches out to those who have contempt. Revenge is excluded, while doing good to the hostile is commanded. In the context of persecution, offering the cheek means continuing to minister at the risk of further persecution, as Paul does in Acts 14 and 16.

It should also be made clear that the ethic described is personal and not governmental. John the Baptist allows for the existence of

---

39. This seems similar to a view that Bovon 1989: 318–19 calls the existential view, held by R. Bultmann, P. Ricoeur, and M. Buber. Practically speaking, it leads to a cosmopolitan philanthropy. This kind of activity might be an implication of this passage, but it is hardly the point.

soldiers, which presupposes the right of national self-defense (3:10–14). This fits Paul's comment that governments exist to protect their people (Rom. 13:4; Carson 1978: 51). The personal character of the exhortation is paralleled in Rom. 12:14–21, where love for the persecutor is also commanded.

Still further, it is resources that are especially in view, as the use of money and goods becomes explicit in Luke 6:32–35. Thus, there is application to those who have wealth, but they are but one part of a very broad audience. There are lots of ways to give and be generous in addition to giving money and goods. So Jesus gives four illustrations on loving one's neighbor in 6:29–30.

The first illustration involves turning the other cheek. Some argue that the passage refers to a violent punch to the jaw, because of σιαγόνα (siagona), which often referred to the jaw (Godet 1875: 1.324; Plummer 1896: 185). But by the third century B.C., σιαγών took on the meaning cheek, so that a reference to a punch is not necessary (BAGD 749; BAA 1498; only here and Matt. 5:39 in the NT).

The religious context makes it likely that a slap is intended and that an insult is in view. An ancient slap usually involved the back of the hand and may picture public rejection from the synagogue (1 Esdr. 4:30; *Didache* 1.4; Stählin, *TDNT* 8:263 nn. 23–24; SB 1:342–43; Ellis 1974: 115; Marshall 1978: 260). Τύπτω (typtō, to beat) recurs frequently in Acts in a way that illustrates its use in religious contexts (Acts 18:17; 21:32; 23:2). Such striking is really an abuse of power and a misuse of personal authority (Luke 12:45; 18:13; 23:48). Nevertheless, one is not to fight back in kind, but remain vulnerable to the insult again.

Matthew 5:39 is parallel, but the terminology is distinct. Discussion exists as to which form is original, and most opt for Matthew, especially since Luke elsewhere has details like the right cheek (Luke 6:6; 22:50; Fitzmyer 1981: 638). But the distinct vocabulary may indicate a distinct summary, making the question of the original form a difficult issue to resolve. What is interesting is that both passages use the singular for the illustration, which personalizes the application by making the appeal directly. Nolland (1989: 296) argues that the shift from the plural in the previous Lucan passage argues for Luke's using a combination of sources for the sermon.

(2) Give the Shirt with the Coat (6:29b)

6:29b   The second illustration is similar. If a person takes your outer garment (ἱμάτιον, *himation*), let him also have your undershirt (χιτών, *chitōn*) (on these two types of clothing, see the exegesis of 3:11). The picture is of a robbery and the point is that one should not seek revenge, but again remain potentially vulnerable to a second attack. Missionary travel was potentially dangerous, since robbers lingered on the highways; but one should not cease from missionary work simply because one might get jumped (Ellis 1974: 114–15). Another possibility for the remark's background is that the social ostracism of persecution produced situations where things were taken or damaged. These factors should not stop one from loving and serving one's neighbors.

An apparent parallel exists in Matt. 5:40, but it may not be a genuine parallel. Matthew portrays one who takes the undershirt (χιτών) first and comes back for the coat (ἱμάτιον). Matthew's picture is of an article taken as part of a pledge and then kept after payment with the intent of acquiring the coat also (Exod. 22:25–27 [22:24–26 MT]; Deut. 24:10–11; Amos 2:8).[40] A legal or court setting is likely for Matthew, but the coat could not legally be taken as part of this transaction, since it was protected by the law (Guelich 1982: 222). Luce (1933: 147) holds that Luke is original here. But a case could be made that Luke has taken a legal issue, removed it from the legal context, and made a general application that reflects Jesus' teaching. It is better, however, to recognize distinct summaries that contain distinct illustrations. The Lucan material had been preserved and was in traditional circulation, as allusions in *Didache* 1.4 and Justin Martyr's *Apology* 1.16.1 show (Marshall 1978: 261). Regardless, the point is that although one is exposed to the hostile religious opponent, one should continue to be vulnerable to repeated onslaughts without seeking revenge.

(3) Give to the Beggar (6:30a)

Jesus gives two final illustrations on loving the enemy. The verbs of the illustrations are all present tense, a point that indicates one is always to be prepared to respond in this way. The variety of examples underscores that Jesus is explaining a fundamental principle that reaches into many areas.

6:30a

Giving to the one who asks probably includes a reference to borrowing, as the parallel examples in 6:34–35 show. Danker (1988: 146) stresses that αἰτοῦντι (*aitounti*) should not be translated beg, but refers only to borrowing. Thus, the passage does not deal just with street panhandlers. But a reference just to borrowing is probably too narrow, since the giving of alms is a topic in the message. The giving of alms was considered a reflection of one's piety, and the

---

40. Danker 1988: 145 still sees this background in Luke. Marshall 1978: 261 holds out the possibility of separate sayings.

term for asking (αἰτέω) is general (Matt. 6:1–4; Guelich 1982: 223). In dealing with alms, the focus would be a request by the poor to meet legitimate basic needs. The point is a genuine readiness to meet needs without reference to prejudices. There is a large element of self-denial in aiding anyone who asks in need, a denial that shows a willingness to part with things (Ellis 1974: 115; Plummer 1896: 186). Luke stresses the command's comprehensiveness by alone noting that all (παντί, *panti*) who ask should be treated this way (Luke sometimes uses πᾶς where the Synoptic parallels do not have it: Luke 6:17; 7:35; 9:43; 11:4; Plummer 1896: 185). Jesus' exposition is a reflection of themes already present in the OT (esp. Deut. 15:7–11; Ps. 37:21, 26; Prov. 19:17; 21:26b). Generosity is a fundamental, concrete expression of love.

(4) Do Not Demand Back What Has Been Taken (6:30b)

6:30b The fourth command reflects an absence of retribution for wrong. For even when something is taken, the disciple is not to demand it back. Again, Danker (1988: 146) limits the application to asking for repayment of what is borrowed (ἀπαιτέω, *apaiteō*, to ask for: Sir. 20:15; BAGD 80; BAA 159; Luke 12:20 is the only other NT use). But passages reflecting this principle look broader in scope (1 Cor. 6:7; 1 Pet. 2:21–24; Hendriksen 1978: 350–51). The demand is difficult, but it reflects self-denial that is generous and may win over the hostile one.

Matthew 5:42 refers only to borrowing and has different terminology. While Plummer (1896: 186) speculates about distinct Aramaic renderings here, it is better to see distinct sources and sayings here (with Marshall 1978: 261). Again, the sources are summaries and the differences could represent different portions of the remarks or distinct translations. The 1 Cor. 6 discussion looks as if it applies this exhortation very clearly to a case of legal wrong within the community.

In considering the commands as a group, a question emerges about how literally these commands are to be taken (see Luce 1933: 148 for options). Some totally reject the teaching as unworkable. Others argue that they reflect an apocalyptic worldview that saw the end of the earth as near and so Jesus gave, wrongly, a temporary ethic. Still others speak of the spirit of the commands as the point. Somewhat accurately, the illustrations are described as "hyperbolical command[s]" (Liefeld 1984: 893; Marshall 1978: 261; Hendriksen 1978: 350). They are expressed in absolute terms to shock the listener by giving a vivid contrast to one's own thinking. They also communicate, by their radical character, the importance of the concept. As Marshall notes, to follow 6:29b literally would result in nudism![41] The point is that Jesus' ethical demand is strong, comprehensive, and serious. The world's ethics are to be surpassed, as 6:32–34 will show. But one will accept the demand only if one believes that God will see, that he will reward the faithful, and that he will be just in his final evaluation. Without such a theological view or reality, the ethics of Jesus wilt into futility and foolishness as the follower is exposed with no hope of justice. To commit to a radical love, one must see that God honors such a commitment to reflect his grace (6:35–36).

iii. Command to Love: The Golden Rule (6:31)

Jesus now offers the "Golden Rule," a description of this verse that has been dated back to the eighteenth century (Guelich 1982: 360; Fitzmyer 1981: 639) and to the sixteenth century (Bovon 1989: 321 n. 64). The passage itself is rather straightforward, though the exact wording is a matter of textual dispute (see the additional note). If the reading adopted is correct, then both the wording and placement of the verse differ from Matthew, though the verse's sense is essentially the same. Matthew has the remark later in the sermon (Matt. 7:12) and ties it specifically to the Law and the Prophets. **6:31**

What happened? Some see Luke moving the saying to make a topical subunit on love here (Alford 1874: 499; A. B. Bruce 1897: 506; Fitzmyer 1981: 639). Others argue that Luke's placement is its natural position and that Matthew made the topical move (Godet 1875: 1.325; Schweizer 1984: 123; Marshall 1978: 261; Schürmann 1969: 350). Another possibility exists since the Matthean portion where the statement appears is not paralleled in Luke 6 and since the wording is so different.[42] It is possible that two distinct sayings in the sermon are present, especially since the later Matthean statement relates the rule explicitly to the Law and Prophets, a legal consideration that Luke consistently omits from his version of the sermon.[43] This third possibility strikes me as plausible. If not, a Lucan reorganization is likely, given that he already shortened the sermon to remove legal elements.

---

41. This kind of result is evidence of the remark's rhetorical form. On the variety of applications of this teaching in the NT, see Nolland 1989: 297; Acts 8:2; 9:25; 14:5–6; 22:25; 25:10–12; John 18:22–23. In Acts 22:25 and 25:10–12 Paul seeks legal protection against the unrighteous as he continues to minister. Acts 23:2–3 shows a retaliation for which Paul apologizes (23:5). Acts 4:24–31 shows how the church applied this truth.

42. Luke 11: 9–13 has the material of Matt. 7:7–11; but does not have Matt. 7:12 there.

43. Guelich 1982: 360 notes that the saying fits in both settings, while not explicitly advocating a repetition.

The verse has roots in the OT. In Lev. 19:18, one is commanded to love one's neighbor as oneself. The exhortation in Luke is simple: treat others as you wish they would treat you. That it is stated positively adds to the level of demand. It is not simply a command to avoid unfair treatment that one might not wish for oneself. Rather, it is a command to give the same sensitive consideration to others that one might want others to give. The idea of how we wish (θέλω, *thelō*) to be treated supplies this more demanding standard.

It is sometimes argued that Jesus is unique in this positive emphasis, but an examination of Jewish, Greek, and Roman parallels shows this to be an overstatement (so Ellis 1974: 115; Carson 1978: 112; but see Nolland 1989: 298). The position is right, however, in noting that Jesus is not arguing a utilitarian position that says, "Do this to them so they will do it to you." The love in view here is unconditional. Jesus is not alone in this rule, though the force with which he said it is among the strongest expressions of this idea. There are Jewish (nos. 1–8; SB 1:459–60), classical (nos. 9–11), and Chinese (no. 12) parallels to the Golden Rule:[44]

1. Rabbi Hillel: "What is hateful to you, do not do to your neighbor, that is the whole Torah, while the rest is commentary" (*b. Šab.* 31a).[45] In this form, the wording is very close to Matt. 7:12.
2. Sirach 31:15: "Judge a fellow guest's needs by your own." This statement is given in a positive form, though its scope is limited to hospitality.
3. Tobit 4:15: "What you hate, do to no one." This statement is parallel to Hillel's.
4. Testament of Naphtali (Hebrew version) 1.6: "None should do to his neighbor what he does not like for himself" (Schürmann 1969: 349 n. *d*; Nolland 1989: 298; Charles 1913: 2.361).
5. *Letter to Aristeas* 207: "Just as you do not wish evil to befall you, but to participate in all that is good, so you should deal with those subject to you and with offenders and you should admonish men true and very gently, for God deals with all men with gentleness."[46] This advice is obviously given to someone

44. Homer's *Odyssey* 5.188–89 is sometimes mentioned as a parallel, but it is not nearly as close as the texts cited here.

45. Though the mishnaic text cites Hillel, rabbinic scholars dispute whether such attributions prior to A.D. 70 are trustworthy. At the least, this tradition is old, even if it is not from Hillel; see Neusner 1984: 63–88.

46. The English translations by H. T. Andrews (in Charles 1913: 2.113) and Hadas 1951: 180–81 correctly look like the Golden Rule, while that by R. J. H. Shutt (in J. Charlesworth 1983–85: 2.26) does not.

in power. The relation to the Golden Rule is vague, but interestingly the advice concludes with God's treatment of people, as does Luke 6:36.

6. Philo, *Hypothetica* 7.6: "Whatever things anyone hates to suffer, let him not do." This remark is close to Hillel and Tobit, but there is dispute whether the text is Philo's (see Colson 1941: 407–13).

7. Targum Pseudo-Jonathan on Lev. 19:18: "But you should love your neighbor himself as that though there be (cause for) hatred with you; you may not do (evil) to him: I am the Lord." As one can see, the parallel is distant at best and looks more like Luke 6:27.

8. 2 Enoch 61.2: "That which a person makes request for his soul, in the same manner let him behave toward every living soul." This wording is positive in tone and may come the closest to Jesus' statement in emphasis.

9. Herodotus 3.142: "I will not myself do that which I account blameworthy in my neighbor." This statement is really a personal ethic and is not clearly directed at others. It is the Golden Rule stated in a rather self-focused way. Thus, in tone it is not quite the same.

10. Isocrates, *Nicocles (Cyprians)* 49, 61: "Display no less concern in my interests than in your own. . . . Do not do to others that which angers you when they do it to you." The first quotation is really the Golden Rule in reverse, applying its results to the speaker! It is selfishly or at least inwardly directed. The second quotation is the rule stated negatively and involves only that which invokes irritation.

11. Seneca, *On Benefits* 2.1.1: "Let us give in the manner that would have been acceptable if we had been receiving." This idea is stated positively and is close in tone to Jesus' remarks.

12. Confucius, *Analects* 15.23: "What you do not want done to yourself, do not do to others" (Creed 1930: 94). The parallel is stated negatively, as were those by Hillel and Isocrates.

These parallels show that Jesus called for what many other moralists did: one should treat others with the respect and sensitivity that one would wish from them. Jesus states the rule, however, in the most emphatic and positive form (Nolland 1989: 298). In discussing the rule, Danker (1988: 147) makes a crucial point about its application: Jesus' idea is not, "The way I want things done is the way I should do it to others"—in the sense that if I wish to be left alone, I should be aloof from other people. The rule assumes the note of concern for others expressed in the context by 6:27–30. Thus, it describes a love that is sensitive to others and aware of their preferences. In effect, one may fairly paraphrase the rule this way: "As you wish to be treated with sensitivity to your preferences, so treat others with sensitivity to their preferences."[47]

iv. Three Illustrations of Radical Love (6:32–34)

In the following three illustrations of 6:32–34, Jesus uses negative examples to show that the disciple's love is to be different from the sinner's love. Each illustration takes an example of love and asks what is special about it, given that even sinners love this way. The key phrase is ποία ὑμῖν χάρις ἐστίν (*poia hymin charis estin*, what credit is that to you?) in 6:32, 33, 34. Thus, by raising the matter in this way, the implication is clear that disciples are to exhibit a more demanding love. Each example in this section is paired with the more radically expressed examples of 6:27–30 (Ellis 1974: 115): 6:32 is tied to 6:27a, 6:33 to 6:27b, and 6:34 to 6:30a.

(1) If You Love Only Those Who Love You, What Credit Is It? (6:32)

6:32   The first illustration concerns loving only those who love you. Most of the wording differences in the parallel Matt. 5:46 are stylistic variations. Exceptions include Matthew's use of ἐάν (*ean*, if) instead of Luke's εἰ (*ei*, if) and Matthew's use of μισθόν (*misthon*, reward) instead of Luke's χάρις (*charis*, favor). But since the Lucan term refers to God's favorable response, the meanings of the terms are virtually synonymous, as Luke 6:35 shows (Marshall 1978: 262; Fitzmyer 1981: 640).

There is no hint of a conditional motivation for love in the exhortation. The ancient world often lived on the premise, "Do good to others, so they will do good to you."[48] But Jesus' command is set forth without any such hidden agenda. It is love for love's sake,

---

47. Of course, there are limits to this remark. The preferences one speaks about here are not in moral areas where God's desire is clear, as if people are free to do as they wish without awareness of the moral implications. For how this worked out practically in Jesus' confrontation with the Jewish leadership, see the insightful remarks of Manson 1949: 52–53, who replies to Montefiore's charge (1930: 103–4) that Jesus did not carry out his ethic in practice. Manson emphasizes Jesus' sense of disappointment and sorrow toward his enemies' rejection of him; in addition, Jesus' prophetic challenge shows his regard and concern for his enemies. Manson compares Jesus' relationship with his opponents to that of modern politicians who disagree vigorously in debate but respect one another as people.

48. Marshall 1978: 262; Van Unnik 1966: 289–95; 1 Macc. 11:33; Sir. 12:1–6; *t. Meg.* 3.16 (= Neusner 1977–86: 2.292); Epictetus 2.14.18; Hesiod, *Works and Days* 352; Aristotle, *Rhetoric to Alexander* 1446.

which is why it is so commendable and distinctive. Second Clement 13.4 makes this point explicitly: "For when they hear from us that God says, 'It is no credit to you if you love them that love you, but it is a credit to you if you love your enemies and those who hate you,' when they hear this they wonder at this extraordinary goodness; but when they see that we not only do not love those who hate us, but do not even love those who love us, they laugh us to scorn, and the name is blasphemed." This second-century Christian comment is an excellent commentary on the text and the effects of not following it (also *Didache* 1.3; Ignatius, *Polycarp* 2.1).

The text is clear. If you love those who love you, what is the credit in that? In other words, why should God give a gracious response to such action? Χάρις describes God's favorable response and is equivalent to μισθόν in Matt. 5:46 (Liefeld 1984: 894). Χάρις is probably Lucan in that Luke uses the word eight times, but it does not appear in Matthew or Mark (Schürmann 1969: 353 n. 77; Guelich 1982: 231). For the use of χάρις as the favorable response of God, note the point of Luke 6:35 (Conzelmann, *TDNT* 9:392 n. 152; 1 Cor. 9:16 variant; 1 Pet. 2:19).

Love given only to those who love you is the type of love that sinners have and is nothing special. Luke has ἁμαρτωλοί (*hamartōloi*, sinners) while Matt. 5:46 speaks of τελῶναι (*telōnai*, tax collectors). Schürmann (1969: 353 n. 79) argues that Matthew made the audience more specific, for he alone pairs tax collector and Gentile (Matt. 18:17). But one example hardly establishes a pattern. It is more likely that Luke appropriately generalized the remark in all the examples because a tax collector was viewed in the culture as the exemplary sinner (Fitzmyer 1981: 640; Danker 1988: 148; Rengstorf, *TDNT* 1:328). Matthew's point would be, in effect, that even the most notorious sinner, the tax collector, loves this way, while Luke makes the simple point that sinners love this way. Jesus wishes to highlight the everyday quality of this love, as the introduction to the remark shows. Καὶ γάρ (*kai gar*) is emphatic: "*For even sinners do this!*" The world's standard of love is not enough according to Jesus.

(2) If You Do Good Only to Those Who Do Good to You, What Credit Is It? (6:33)

The second illustration involves doing good and probably parallels 6:32 in structure (depending on a textual issue), while recalling 6:27b. There is no Matthean parallel to this verse, though many see Luke generalizing from Matt. 5:47, where one greets only a relative. It is said that Luke expands the reference to include all doing of good (Marshall 1978: 263; Klostermann 1929: 81). But if a distinct sum-

6:33

mary is present, as I argue, then a distinct saying is possible, as the parallel to 6:27b suggests.

The verse itself is direct. If you do good only for those who do good to you, that love is no different from the love displayed by people in general. There is no favor from God for such limited love. Ἀγαθοποιῆτε (*agathopoiēte*) speaks of concrete acts of good to others. Again, Luke moves from the attitude of love in 6:32 to the visible expression of it in 6:33. Luke loves to record not just the emotion that God desires, but the clear expression of it as well. The term ἀγαθοποιέω is rare in the NT, but is used to describe positive ethical action, usually by God, both in the LXX and NT (Num. 10:32; Judg. 17:13; Zeph. 1:12; 1 Macc. 11:33; 2 Macc. 1:2; Luke 6:9, 33 [twice], 35; 1 Pet. 2:15, 20; 3:6, 17; 3 John 11; Plummer 1896: 187; Grundmann, *TDNT* 1:17). The attitude contrasts with Sir. 12:7: "Help a good person, not a sinner" (Danker 1988: 148).

(3) If You Lend Only for Return, What Credit Is It? (6:34)

6:34   The third illustration involves the lending of money and looks back to 6:30a. There is no parallel to this verse in the corresponding section of Matthew, though Matt. 5:42, which comes earlier in the sermon, has a similar idea. However, Matt. 5:42 already has a parallel in Luke 6:30a. Because Luke 6:34 and Matt. 5:42 use δαν(ε)ίζω (*dan[e]izō*, to lend), some suggest that Luke is aware of Matthew's statement and has framed a third parallel (Klostermann 1929: 81; Bultmann 1963: 96; Fitzmyer 1981: 640). But Matthew uses the middle voice, while Luke has the active. It seems odd that the term appears here in Luke and not in Luke 6:30, if Luke is aware of Matthew's statement, since that is the place to express the agreement. More than likely, Luke has not created the saying (Marshall 1978: 263). In fact, this is another detail that favors an independent source for the sermon.

The verse's structure parallels the two previous examples. If you lend only to those from whom you expect to receive back, what favor does that bring you before God? Δαν(ε)ίζω looks to loaning money, which in a Jewish context would not include interest (Exod. 22:25 [22:24 MT]; Lev. 25:35–37; Deut. 23:19–20 [23:20–21 MT]; Luce 1933: 149; Liefeld 1984: 894). Such no-interest loans protected the poor and were a sign of piety (Ps. 15:5; Prov. 28:8; Danker 1988: 148). Jesus says that to loan only to those who will respond likewise is no different from how sinners loan to sinners. Sinners make safe loans to each other.

The meaning of this safe-loan idea depends on how the end of the verse—"for even sinners lend to sinners in order that they might receive back the same"—is interpreted (Stählin, *TDNT* 3:344–45). Several options are offered for the meaning of the final phrase:

1. It refers to gaining full repayment of principle and interest (Plummer 1896: 187).
2. It refers to repayment of principle only (Bultmann, *TDNT* 2:534, who favors this and the previous view).
3. It refers to a lender who loans so that if a future need arises the lender can get a loan too (Luce 1933: 149; Marshall 1978: 263; Godet 1875: 1.326; Klostermann 1929: 81 [mentions this option]; Liefeld 1984: 894).
4. It refers to both the financial issue (the charging of interest) and the mutuality required before anything is done (Bovon 1989: 317–18 notes five views and prefers this; his fifth view is to lend to non-Christians, but give to Christians).

Marshall (1978: 263) argues against the first two views. Lending with no expectation of repayment makes δαν(ε)ίζω mean "giving a gift," a meaning that the term cannot bear. If view 3 is right, "I loan so that I might get a loan in the future," then the idea is, "I loan so that I can protect my future stability. I loan to protect myself, not to meet a need." The lending becomes motivated by selfish concerns, a perspective that fits Jesus' criticisms. Thus, one should not loan only in hopes of obtaining a future loan (view 3), since there is no credit in making a loan selfishly. The other views force the ἵνα clause in 6:34b to mean, "For even sinners lend to sinners so that they might receive payment back." As Marshall notes, one does not really lend just *for the purpose* of being paid back, which the ἵνα clause must mean in views 1 and 2, but one lends with the hope of being treated similarly in the future, if the need arises.[49] Thus, view 3 is best, though view 4 is possible.

On this understanding, Jesus is saying that the "I'll scratch your back, if you scratch mine" approach to meeting needs is not an example of a disciple's love. One should give without strings attached. Besides, if one meets needs only for people who can meet one's future needs, how do the real needs of the needy, who cannot repay, get met? If the OT law surrounding lending tried to protect the weak of the community, then such conditional lending undercuts that protection (see esp. Deut. 15:7–11).

49. One senses that Bovon's view (#4) is an attempt to avoid this syntactical problem. A purpose clause would mean that the purpose of lending is only to transfer money back and forth.

v. Summary on Love: Call to Be Gracious like God (6:35)
   (1) Love Your Enemies (6:35a)
   (2) Do Good (6:35b)
   (3) Lend and Expect Nothing (6:35c)

6:35a–c Luke summarizes and repeats the three exhortations of 6:32–34: "love your enemies" in 6:35a matches 6:32, "do good" in 6:35b recalls 6:33, and "lend and expect nothing" in 6:35c restates 6:34—illustrations that in turn look back to 6:27, 30. Thus, this verse ties the subunit together, and the exhortations here mean what they did in those verses. But with the exhortations come notes of promise about reward and a relationship with God. The disciple should reflect God's gracious character to the immoral and ungrateful. God does see and honor such righteousness.

The only unusual element is found in the command to lend (μηδὲν ἀπελπίζοντες, *mēden apelpizontes*), a NT *hapax legomenon* that is disputed both textually and lexically (see the additional note). What does ἀπελπίζω mean? Some give it its normal meaning and translate it "despairing nothing" (Plummer 1896: 188; Isa. 29:19; 1 Clem. 59.3; Sir. 22:21; 27:21; 2 Macc. 9:18). The meaning in this case is to lend and not despair or be concerned whether you will see the money paid back. Most, however, see the normal meaning as being foreign to the context and opt for a contextually defined sense, thus making it equivalent to δαν(ε)ίζω in Luke 6:34.[50] The idea is to lend, "hoping for nothing back"; that is, expecting no favor in return. This meaning of the term is better than the first view, because it is less elliptical and matches the idea of 6:34. What that favor would be depends on how 6:34 is taken. If money is seen as the point there, a view I reject, then repayment is not to be expected. If the possibility of borrowing in the future is the point there, then the point of 6:35c is to lend without worrying whether one can receive credit later. The essential idea in either case is to lend without future strings.

(4) Reward Is Great (6:35d)

6:35d God's promise for expressing such love is reward and a relationship with him. Though some equate the reward and the relationship (Godet 1875: 1.326; Guelich 1982: 96), such an interpretation flattens the idea and may even be confusing. The emphasis is not on entry into the relationship with God as reward, since relationship was bound up in the grace-filled invitation of the blessings and woes of

---

50. BAGD 83–84; BAA 167; Godet 1875: 1.326; Creed 1930: 95; Marshall 1978: 264; Fitzmyer 1981: 640; Schürmann 1969: 355 n. 90; Bultmann, *TDNT* 2:533–34.

6:20–26. Rather, the reward is a response to the disciple's demonstration of God's character, which shows one to be a child of the Most High, displaying conduct typical of the Father (Guelich 1982: 230). The reward is God's acknowledgment that he has seen this meritorious love and the faithfulness it reflects. It is the Father's pleasure at evidencing kinship with God. Reward is God's favor/ blessing for doing that which is noteworthy. It is not merit for salvation; but recognition of being a faithful son or daughter (Luke 6:23; Matt. 5:9). The reward reflects χάρις (*charis*, divine favor) in Luke 6:32–34 in response to having done something more. First Corinthians 4:4–5 notes that God's praise comes with the reward. So the reward is not the blessing of life, but the Father's pleasure and affirmation at the disciple's having been a faithful steward by loving in a way that goes beyond the sinner's love.

(5) Result Reflects a Relationship with God (6:35e)

Thus, disciples who love their enemies visibly demonstrate their **6:35e** pedigree to the Father. They have imitated God and shown themselves fully faithful to their Father. In Judaism, a relationship with God was seen as a privilege of members of the divine new era (Sir. 4:10; Ps. Sol. 17.27; 1 Enoch 62.11; T. Moses 10.3; Jub. 1.24–25; Danker 1988: 149; Schürmann 1969: 355 n. 94). For the early church, love is seen as a mark of that relationship (1 John 3:1; 4:7–12; Fitzmyer 1981: 640). Exhortations in the NT Letters to imitate God's character have roots in exhortations like this (Eph. 4:31–5:1).

(6) Basis: God's Mercy (6:35f)

The reason (ὅτι, *hoti*, for) for the exhortation is God's very character. **6:35f** He also is gracious to the immoral and ungrateful, so that anyone who treats people in a similar manner reflects relationship with God. The Father is described as gracious (χρηστός, *chrēstos*, often translated "good" in English versions) frequently in the OT, as well as in the NT (Ps. 25:8 [24:8 LXX]; 34:8 [33:9 LXX]; 69:16 [68:17 LXX]; 86:5 [85:5 LXX]; 100:5 [99:5 LXX]; 106:1 [105:1 LXX]; 109:21 [108:21 LXX]; 119:68 [118:68 LXX]; 136:1 [135:1 LXX]; 145:9 [144:9 LXX]; 1 Pet. 2:3; Rom. 2:4; Matt. 11:30). Psalm 112:4–5 [111:4–5 LXX] places the gracious God and the gracious person side by side, just as this text does.[51] As Plummer (1896: 189) notes, "The moral likeness proves the parentage." Such love reflects God's character to others and shows our identity with God. Jesus' teaching has roots in OT praise of God's character (K. Weiss, *TDNT* 9:487).

51. The term οἰκτίρμων in Ps. 112:4 [111:4 LXX] is the key term in Luke 6:36 as well.

Matthew 5:44–45 has a similar summary, though Matthew includes an additional illustration of God's graciousness about the shining of the sun on the immoral and good, as well as the sending of rain on the righteous and unrighteous. Some argue that Matthew reworked the tradition (Guelich 1982: 229–30), while others suggest that Luke simplified the reference (Plummer 1896: 189; Marshall 1978: 265). Either is possible, but a third possibility also exists. Each writer simply reflected the distinct summaries of his source. The examples already noted in the sermon for such a possibility raise its likelihood here as well. It is hard to know what is the exact relationship between the various wordings, though it is clear that Matthew and Luke make the same point: gracious love is recognized by God and imitates his character.[52] The believer is called to graciously love all, even one's enemies. In fact, such love uniquely marks out God's child.

vi. Love and the Standard of Mercy (6:36)

6:36 The exhortation to love graciously suggests another trait that is reflective of God's character: mercy. This attribute prevents one from being overly harsh in judgment and prevents one from being quick to pounce on the evildoer (Danker 1988: 151). The OT frequently describes God's kind compassion with the term οἰκτίρμων (*oiktirmōn*, merciful): Exod. 34:6; Deut. 4:31; Joel 2:13; Jon. 4:2; 2 Sam. 24:14 [οἰκτιρμός, *oiktirmos*, mercy]; Isa. 63:15; BAGD 561; BAA 1138; Bultmann, *TDNT* 5:159–61, esp. nn. 17, 18, 21, 22). A similar concept is frequent in Judaism: "As our Father is merciful in heaven, so be merciful on earth" (Tg. Ps.-J. on Lev. 22:28; so also *Mekilta de Rabbi Ishmael*, tractate *Shirata* 3 on Exod. 15:2 [= Lauterbach: 1933–35: 2.28] [God has a rule of mercy]; *Sipre* 49 on Deut. 11:22 [= Neusner 1987: 1.164]; SB 2:159; Marshall 1978: 265). The point is the same as in Luke 6:35: the disciples are to imitate their heavenly Father. God's character is the guide for our character.

The relationship to Matthew is much discussed, since Matthew's key term is not οἰκτίρμων but τέλειος (*teleios*, fully mature or perfect). Τέλειος fits Matthew's emphasis, since he presents the sermon in terms of a personal righteousness that exceeds even that of the

---

52. Danker 1988: 150 cites Epictetus 2.14.12–13 to show how the Greeks viewed imitation of the gods: "It is of prime importance for those who would please and obey the deities to be as much like them as lies within their power. If fidelity is a divine characteristic, then they are to be faithful; if generous, they are to be generous; if beneficent, they are to be beneficent; if magnanimous, they are to be magnanimous. In brief, they are to do and say everything in emulation of God." Christianity also has this goal in the context of monotheism, but in addition offers enablement to make it happen (John 14–16).

Pharisees (Matt. 5:20). It also has OT roots (Deut. 18:13; Lev. 19:2 [conceptually]; Schürmann 1969: 360; Creed 1930: 96; Delling, *TDNT* 8:74). The term is unique to Matthew among the evangelists (cf. Matt. 19:21 = Mark 10:21). These features suggest that Matthew chose a synonym for Luke's wording (which reflects the original wording). Nonetheless, opinions remain divided on the relationship (Schürmann 1969: 360 n. 119).

Those who believe that Matthew reflects the original wording allude to an Aramaic wordplay in the Matthean form of the verse and argue that Luke simplified the reference for his audience.[53] Those who favor Luke's wording cite the link to χρηστός in Luke 6:35 and argue for the OT roots of the concept. They also note that Matthew's use of τέλειος uniquely belongs to him (Creed 1930: 96; Marshall 1978: 265; Schürmann 1969: 360; Guelich 1982: 233–34; Matt. 19:21 and nowhere else in the Gospels). Since the saying's placement is so similar, it is likely that the same saying is in view. Matthew has probably chosen τέλειος to express the maturity that is required of one who exercises such mercy (Nolland 1989: 300, citing Dupont 1966b for support).

Luke alone of the evangelists uses οἰκτίρμων, but it appears only here. Interestingly, James 5:11 uses the term, and it is generally recognized that James has many parallels to the sermon material (see excursus 7). Therefore, Luke seems to reflect the original wording, but Matthew gives an accurate rendering of it in terms of the standard of righteousness that Jesus presented in the sermon.

vii. Four Exhortations on Judgment (6:37–38a)
(1) Do Not Judge and You Will Not Be Judged (6:37a)

Mercy expresses itself in terms of a hesitation to hold another down **6:37a** in condemnation. In a real sense the four imperatives of this subunit need to be taken together. In fact, the imperatives come in two pairs followed by a promise. The judgment in view does not refer to a refusal to engage in appropriate ethical evaluation, as numerous NT passages show (in the same sermon: Matt. 7:1–2, with 7:6; also Luke 11:42–44; 20:46–47; John 7:42, 51–53; Rom. 1:32; 1 Cor. 5:5, 11–13; Gal. 1:8–9; Phil. 3:2; Titus 3:2; 1 John 4:1). The idea is rather a judgmental and censorious perspective toward others that holds them down in guilt and never seeks to encourage them toward God. What is commanded is an attitude that is hesitant to condemn and quick to forgive. What is prohibited is an arrogance that reacts with hostility to the worldly and morally lax, viewing such people as be-

53. Black 1967: 181 argues that the play is on the Semitic terms in Matt. 5:47–48: *šĕlam* (peace) and *šĕlim* (whole).

yond God's reach. What is censured by Jesus is an attitude like that of the Pharisee in Luke 18:11–14 (also 5:29–32; Ellis 1974: 116; Marshall 1978: 265–66). Büchsel defines it well (*TDNT* 3:939; see also p. 923):

> What is unconditionally demanded is that such evaluations should be subject to the certainty that God's judgment falls also on those who judge, so that superiority, hardness and blindness to one's own faults are excluded, and a readiness to forgive and to intercede is safeguarded. The emphatic way in which Jesus extended the law of love in this direction has far-reaching consequences. It means that the Church cannot practice discipline with merciless severity (2 C[or]. 11:24). It means that the Church cannot take up a hard, contemptuous and supercilious attitude towards those whom it regards as sinners.

Such an attitude is really self-righteousness and usurps God's role (Rom. 14:10–13; James 2:4; 4:11–12).

Jesus' command has some Jewish parallels, though again Jesus' emphasis is perhaps stronger. In a citation attributed to the late first century B.C. (see n. 45 for a caveat about this date), Rabbi Hillel said: "Judge not your neighbor until you come into his place" (*m. ʾAbot* 2.5). His point is that until one knows the circumstances one should not judge. *M. ʾAbot* 1.6 speaks about regarding someone with mercy: "When you judge any man, incline the balance in his favor." The principle of divine response based on how we treat others surfaces as well in *m. Soṭa* 1.7: "With what measure a man metes, it shall be measured to him again" (Luke 6:38; SB 1:441–42; *b. Šab.* 127b; *b. B. Meṣ.* 59b; Polycarp 2.3; 1 Clem. 13.2).

(2) Do Not Condemn and You Will Not Be Condemned (6:37b)

6:37b   Jesus notes that God promises to treat us as we treat others. God is gracious to those who are gracious. He will not judge those who do not judge. He will not condemn those who do not condemn. He will forgive those who forgive. The demand that the follower be gracious grows out of God's graciousness extended to us. God promises to deal with each person, but the tone of his dealings is influenced by how that person deals with others. The nature of this judgment by God not only involves the ultimate eschatological judgment, but it relates to how he deals with people in life (see 6:38; 11:4; 12:48; esp. 18:30). Jeremias (1963a: 222) shows the association with the thought of rewards (Luke 6:38; 14:14; Matt. 5:12; 6:20; 19:28–29). The righteous and merciful store up heavenly treasure. God is gracious to those who humbly show mercy, but he scorns the proud (James 4:1–10).

(3) Forgive and You Will Be Forgiven (6:37c)

We are to forgive, because God has forgiven us (Eph. 4:32). Schür- **6:37c**
mann (1969: 361 n. 127) makes the point that in living this way one
is not to pretend that another person is innocent when he or she is
guilty; but rather one is not to hold an action permanently against
that other person. It is not acquittal, but amnesty that is in view
(Luke 11:4; Matt. 6:12, 14–15; 18:27–35; 2 Macc. 12:45). It is also
clear that what is in view here is fundamentally an individual ethic
and not a governmental one, since the state is charged with creating
an environment where its citizens are safe. The courts have the right
to sentence the guilty. Jesus did not deny the right of Caesar to exist
nor did he deny the roles of the soldier or tax collector (also John the
Baptist in Luke 3:12–14; 20:20–26 and Paul in Rom. 13:1–4; 1 Tim.
2:1–4). It is also clear that defending moral standards is not prohibited by this teaching. The passage does not deny the right to moral
evaluation. What is warned against is evaluating others with such a
harshness that the result is an unforgiving attitude and an approach
that ceases to hold out hope as if someone is beyond God's reach.
The text's emphasis is on reflecting mercy, being able to forgive, and
refusing to judge harshly.[54]

(4) Give and You Will Be Given To (6:38a)

Jesus also calls for generosity, while giving a promise. The one who **6:38a**
gives will also receive. Jesus notes that generosity will be honored by
God. The reverse of this idea is stated in the NT Letters: those who
treat others harshly can expect their prayers to be hindered (1 Pet.
3:7–12). To the generous, God is generous.

viii. Standard: You Will Be Judged by How You Judge (6:38b)

The promise is graphically illustrated with the image of counting **6:38b**
out grain in abundance. The steps (a good measure, pressed down,
shaken together, and running over) show the overflow of blessing.
Jeremias (1963a: 222 n. 67) describes the process behind the language:

> The measuring of the corn is a process which is carried out according
> to an established pattern. The seller crouches on the ground with the
> measure between his legs. First of all he fills the measure three-quar-
> ters full and gives it a good shake with a rotary motion to make the
> grains settle down. Then he fills the measure to the top and gives it

54. Note how the verse begins with καί, which shows that it elaborates the discussion of mercy in 6:36.

another shake. Next he presses the corn together strongly with both hands. Finally he heaps it into a cone, tapping it carefully to press the grains together; from time to time he bores a hole in the cone and pours a few more grains into it, until there is literally no more room for a single grain. In this way, the purchaser is guaranteed an absolutely full measure; it cannot hold more.

This is the full measure that comes from God into the lap of the one who gives. Κόλπον (*kolpon*, lap) is actually the pocket created by the fold of the robe (Plummer 1896: 189; Nolland 1989: 301; Exod. 4:6; Ps. 74:11 [73:11 LXX]; 79:12 [78:12 LXX]; Isa. 65:6; BAGD 442 §2; BAA 899 §2).

The passive verb ἀντιμετρηθήσεται (*antimetrēthēsetai*, it will be measured back) expresses God's promise to reward the disciple's gracious actions toward others (Fitzmyer 1981: 641; Schneider 1977a: 158). The person's activity sets the standard of God's reaction, which does not so much involve the eschatological judgment of one's salvation before God as it involves God's evaluation of the character of one's life and the pleasure he expresses at the way one has lived. In fact, some of the divine response may spill over into how God treats one in this life (Luke 18:30; Jeremias 1963a: 222; Bertram, *TDNT* 7:69–70; Deissner, *TDNT* 4:634).

Marshall (1978: 267) notes that the imagery is thoroughly Palestinian and that the verse, which has no parallel, could not be from Luke's hand but is from a parallel tradition (also Schürmann 1969: 363). This origin is made even more likely when one notes that Matt. 7:2 uses the phrase at the end of the verse to warn about judgment, while Luke uses it to hold out the promise of blessing. Of course, both applications are legitimate, because a person can measure others either harshly or generously. Luke's positive thrust may relate contextually to the positive call of 6:35. In sum, the standard one uses in relation to others is the standard that God will apply.

Such imagery was common among the ancients (*m. Soṭa* 1.7; CD 2.13; SB 2:221; see Rüger 1969 for the Jewish parallels and Couroyer 1970 for extrabiblical parallels outside of Judaism). The rabbis held that God could measure by one of two balances: justice or mercy (Midr. Lev. 29.3 on Ps. 47:6). Jesus may well be alluding to this option and noting the abundant blessing that comes with generosity, though one should be quick to note that such generosity need not be equated with prosperity, since it is God's forgiveness and absence of condemnation that are in view. In fact, the major blessing is intimate fellowship with God, new relationships with other believers, and the presence of his transforming power in life (Luke 18:29–30). One suspects that effective prayer is the result of such generosity (1 Pet. 3:7–9).

c. Parabolic Call to Righteousness, Fruit, and Wise Building (6:39–49)

The sermon concludes with three parables that warn the disciples to take Jesus' words seriously and use them as a basis of self-examination. The first, 6:39–42, is actually a three-part picture. There is a warning about the ineffectual guidance that a blind person provides for other blind people (6:39). There is a recognition that a pupil becomes like the teacher (6:40). And there is the exhortation to proper self-evaluation before moving to evaluate others (6:41–42). So one should choose one's teachers carefully, make sure one is going in the right direction, and not be too quick to set others straight. This subunit is more proverbial in character than parabolic. Jesus is giving general counsel.

The next subunit makes the point that what one produces reflects what one is spiritually (6:43–45). The exhortation is to examine the quality of one's inner spiritual condition by examining one's product. The product reflects the heart. Again, we are dealing with proverbial truth here, since Jesus will also mention that false teachers are like wolves in sheep's clothing, so that what one sees from them is not necessarily what is inside (Luke 10:3; Matt. 7:15; 10:16). This proverb, however, is not so much concerned with how we are to look at others, but how we are to examine ourselves. Jesus' remarks in this are introspective, and the failure to recognize this emphasis can lead to a false understanding of the text.

The final subunit is a serious call to heed Jesus (6:46–49). The comparison is between two types of people: the person with a house on rock (i.e., the one who practices Jesus' teaching) and the person with a house on sand (i.e., the one who only hears the message but does not practice it). The stress is on introspection and application of what Jesus says. Jesus closes his sermon by saying, in effect, "Will you as a disciple put into practice the love ethic proclaimed here?" His desire is not so much to have his audience examine if people around them love, but to have them look honestly at themselves. Unfortunately, the words often have not been applied in the way they were designed.

The passage is dominated by two rhetorical features: questions and pairs. The questions raise the issue of whom one is following (6:39 [twice], 41, 42, 46). The pairs suggest the issue of following and also divide the imagery of the passage into two parts: good and bad (Bovon 1989: 330). The pairs are two blind people (6:39), the teacher and the pupil (6:40), two brothers (6:41–42), good and bad trees (6:43–44), good and evil people (6:45), and two houses (6:47–49). The pictures move from asking whom one follows to describing two ways of living. The wise way is listening to Jesus, while foolishness fails to heed him.

i. Call to Righteousness: Watch Whom You Follow and Where You Look (6:39–42)
(1) Can the Blind Lead the Blind? (6:39)

6:39 Through various pictures, Jesus pushes the disciples to examine themselves. Luke uses the term παραβολή (*parabolē*, parable) to describe these comparisons (for this term, see the exegesis of 5:36). The first picture contains two rhetorical questions, which are really statements in which the choice of the interrogative particle shows the answer Jesus intends in each case. First is the statement that a blind person is not able to guide another blind person. The particle μήτι (*mēti*, is?) expects a negative answer (Marshall 1978: 268). The blind leading the blind pictures poor spiritual guidance (so ὁδηγεῖν, *hodēgein*, to guide: Acts 8:31; John 16:13; Ps. 25:5 [24:5 LXX]; 86:11 [85:11 LXX]; 119:35 [118:35 LXX]; Michaelis, *TDNT* 5:100). A teacher needs clear vision to avoid leading pupils into a pit, dungeon, or black hole.

There is some debate as to the referent of the blind leader. (1) Does Jesus allude to avoiding false teachers, because to follow them is disaster (Schürmann 1969: 365–79, esp. 365–66; Fitzmyer 1981: 642)? Such a sense would parallel Matt. 15:14 and could fit a context of Jesus' contrasting himself with the Pharisees. However, there is no explicit reference to this group in the passage. (2) Does Jesus call the disciples to examine themselves and realize that only Jesus can lead them (Marshall 1978: 269)? Such an understanding argues against seeing a parallel here to Matt. 15:14, but honors Luke's introspective context, while also alluding to Luke 6:37 and the call not to judge. The point in effect is this: if you try on your own to lead yourself and others spiritually, you are in danger. Jesus is warning against self-righteousness and arrogance. Marshall also argues that the Lucan form of the saying warns disciples, but that the saying's original setting may have been a warning to the Pharisees. This view recognizes both senses in the tradition, but argues that Luke is interested only in the disciples (Rengstorf 1968: 91–92). This approach seems more unifying to the Lucan context of introspection, though the shadow of the false teachers cannot be far off. The setting of Jesus' words in the sermon means that the leaders who lead the wrong way are the Pharisees. What allows a bridge into a church setting is that the Pharisees' error—being arrogant and judgmental—is one that the disciples must watch for and avoid. Jesus says that if you seek to go on your own spiritual intuition or look to other examples you will end up fallen and trapped.

Bovon (1989: 332) brings his own twist to this view. He argues that the audience is believers and the point is this: so long as you are still blind, do not advise. This connects the passage to 6:41–42. Bovon sees tension within the community, where some are seeking to teach and lead in a way that Luke thinks is inappropriate. Bovon compares the situation to that in Corinth, where those gripped by spiritual enthusiasm were trusting their own instincts and going their own way, ignoring those like Paul. The contemporary application may be a point of Luke's concern, but again, this is because Jesus' remark is proverbial and timeless. In fact, the emphasis is following Jesus and watching to whom you entrust yourself.

The argument goes as follows. Luke 6:37–38 leads into the theme with a transition: "Do not judge, forgive"; 6:39 says, "Watch whom you follow"; 6:40 says, "Watch whom you follow, because you will be like your teacher"; 6:41–42 says, "Do not be quick to judge, until you are willing to deal with your own problems"; 6:43–46 says, "Your heart is evident by your fruit, so follow my teaching"; and finally 6:47–49 makes clear that there is one example to follow and that is Jesus' teaching.

The second statement in 6:39 is that, given a blind teacher, both teacher and pupils end up going nowhere, since they fall into the pit. The particle οὐχί (ouchi) expects a "yes" answer. All the blind will fall into the pit. Βόθυνον (bothynon) is a reference to a deep pit, not merely a ditch.[55] As such, the image is strong and describes a dive into a mammoth hole. The blind leading the blind is a walk to disaster. The spiritual process requires care as to where we are going and whom we are following (for Greek and Jewish parallels, see Schrage, *TDNT* 8:275, 285, 292). Simply put, the point is this: since I have warned you about judging (6:37–38)—and the blind person is no guide—there is no authority except Jesus (6:46–49).

As noted, the proverb's usage here is not the same as Matt. 15:14, which addresses the Pharisees directly and has a distinct setting (the parallel in the Gospel of Thomas 34 is like Matthew). Since it is a proverb, there is no need to insist on the same application of it in every use. Jesus could reuse imagery in a variety of ways. Thus, the quest for its original setting is useless, since two distinct uses are present in the NT (contra Michaelis, *TDNT* 5:100 n. 16).

(2) The Pupil Is like the Teacher (6:40)

To solidify the warning, Jesus turns to the importance of choosing an instructor, given that the pupil is like the teacher. In our day, the   **6:40**

---

55. BAGD 144; BAA 288; Matt. 12:11; 15:14; Isa. 24:18; Jer. 48:44 [31:44 LXX]. Its synonym βόθρος is used of a grave or a ritual pit for sacrifices; LSJ 320 notes the βόθυνος = βόθρος equation.

expression "like parent, like child" portrays what one encounters in this passage: "like teacher, like student." In a context where the potential of following a blind teacher is raised (6:39), a point of the passage is to be careful whom you follow.

The picture is laid out in two steps. First, Jesus makes the general point that a pupil is not greater than (ὑπέρ, *hyper*) the teacher.[56] In the ancient world, the teacher-pupil relationship was a personal one, since one learned by oral instruction rather than by books, which were not readily available. One virtually lived alongside the teacher. In addition, these teachers were followed, because they were regarded as authorities (Rengstorf, *TDNT* 4:442; SB 1:577–78; Marshall 1978: 269). One chose not simply to get information or to challenge the teaching, but to follow a teacher by adopting the teaching. Thus, and here is the second step, the disciple becomes like the teacher, because of the nature of the teacher-pupil relationship.

Though the general thrust of the verse is clear, the exact application of Jesus' teaching to his setting is disputed (Marshall 1978: 269–70):

1. Only agreement with the teacher (Jesus) gives the disciples authority to teach (Wellhausen 1904: 25). In this view, the focus of the passage is solely on Jesus' authority. Though this is a point of the passage, the examples from the context (6:43–45) are too negative for the meaning to be this narrow.
2. No pupil will see clearly if following a blind teacher. Thus, the passage is a warning not to follow the Pharisees (Godet 1875: 1.329–30). This view relies on the previous context (6:37–39). Hendriksen (1978: 361 n. 271) objects that, since the verse is stated positively, emphasizing the idea of being fully taught, it is not intended to convey a negative thrust. Hendriksen's criticism, however, fails to deal with the negative imagery that precedes and follows this passage. The problem with the view is the lack of any clear reference in the sermon to the Pharisees.
3. Do not behave differently from Jesus; that is, do not judge. This approach ties the verse into the following verses (Schweizer 1984: 126). One wonders, though, if it deals with the connection to 6:39.
4. Do not go beyond Jesus' teaching, as the false teachers do. This approach has a church setting in view, though one can note

56. On ὑπέρ as a comparative meaning "greater than," see Riesenfeld, *TDNT* 8:515; BAGD 839 §2; BAA 1672 §2.

that such a setting is not required if disciples are the audience (Schürmann 1969: 368–69; Danker 1988: 153; Wiefel 1988: 139 [the Twelve as community, which is too narrow of a setting]).

Which view is most likely to be correct? It would seem that the fourth view has the most going for it. Contextually, 6:40 is a bridge between the danger of following the blind leader and the warning about judging. The connection between those two sections is the danger of attributing too great an authority to oneself. The error of spiritual blindness is often that it thinks it sees. Blind people may think they know where they are going but do not, while those who judge the specks in others are too busy examining others to see their own faults correctly. In both cases the danger is a lack of self-examination and a sense of overconfidence. The solution is to not go beyond the teacher, who will clearly emerge as Jesus in 6:46–49. This sense needs one qualification: even though the Pharisees linger in the background of Jesus' saying, in Luke's day the application would be to anyone who shared their error of arrogance. Luke's point is this: do not err, pick the right teacher (i.e., Jesus or one who truly follows him). The warning is proverbial and fits the setting of Jesus' ministry, though its application is timeless.

This pupil-teacher imagery appears in various passages with various applications, a point that is not surprising for a proverbial saying. Luke 22:27; Matt. 10:24; and John 13:16; 15:20 use this picture or a similar servant-master picture to express the idea that the product is like the producer. Thus, efforts (e.g., Leaney 1958: 138) to decide which saying was given in the original setting and which sayings came later stumble in assuming that Jesus could use this proverb in only one setting and in only one way (so correctly Godet 1875: 1.330; against this is Leaney, who argues that none of the Gospel contexts are original!). Luke 22:27 and John 13:16 argue that one should not set oneself above the teacher, but be a servant. Matthew 10:24 and John 15:20 argue that the servant should not expect to be treated differently than the master. All the examples share an assumption that Jesus' disciples are called to be like him. The history of the relationship of these sayings to one another is simply that they share similar imagery, rather than reflect a development of a single saying.

(3) Remove Your Own Logs before Others' Specks (6:41–42)

Jesus continues to warn about self-righteousness, with an image **6:41** that plays on the picture of sight, as did 6:39. But it is the hyperbolic construction of the rhetorical questions that carries the passage's emotive force. The contrast is a simple one between perceiving a speck and considering a builder's beam.[57] The speck, κάρφος (*karphos*), is a small flake of wood, chaff, or straw (BAGD 405; BAA 823; Plummer 1896: 191). The beam, δοκός (*dokos*), is the main beam of a building (BAGD 203; BAA 408; Hendriksen 1978: 362). Both κάρφος and δοκός are used six times in the NT: three times in Matt. 7:3–5 and three times in Luke 6:41–42. The contrast could hardly be greater. Why is the critic concerned about the dust in someone's eye, when a huge beam protrudes from the critic's own eye? Of course, the speck and beam are figures for personal faults that are worthy of correction. The point is simple: What nerve someone with major problems has to be concerned about minor problems in someone else. The obvious response is that one should not worry about the person with minor problems while one has unresolved major problems to face. One should be self-critical before thinking about being critical of others. Jesus says not to patronize others with your expert advice if you have not dealt with your own problems first (Danker 1988: 153). Rather, consider or take careful notice, κατανοεῖς (*katanoeis*), of your own beam.[58]

6:42 The illustration continues with a second rhetorical question: How is one for whom a major problem still exists able to criticize someone with a small problem? Again, the emotive force of the question gives an answer: What nerve! Ὑποκριτά (*hypokrita*, hypocrite) makes it clear that someone with this attitude stands rebuked. The term ὑποκριτής is descriptive, meaning "play-actor" (Wilckens, *TDNT* 8:567–68; BAGD 845; BAA 1684; Danker 1988: 154; fourteen of its eighteen NT uses are in Matthew; see also Luke 12:56 and 13:15). It suggests an insincerity in someone who fails to deal with self. One pretends that sin offends while ignoring one's own sin (Plummer 1896: 191)! In fact, in Judaism, ὑποκριτής often referred to the godless or deceitful (Fitzmyer 1981: 642; 2 Macc. 6:25; T. Ben. 6.4–5; Ps. Sol. 4.6–7). Foolish arrogance insists on carefully examining others, while not paying any attention to obvious faults in oneself.

The advice that follows is interesting, for it does not tell someone never to deal with other people's problems. Rather, it says to take care of the major problem in your life and then you will be able to help someone else—as if by taking care of your own problem, you can see better to deal sensitively with someone else's problem (Gal.

---

57. The contrast in the verbs at the end of the passage is key. Βλέπω is used figuratively with the meaning "to perceive" in Rom. 7:23; 2 Cor. 7:8; Col. 2:5; Heb. 2:9; 10:25; Michaelis, *TDNT* 5:344.

58. For κατανοέω, see Luke 12:24, 27; 20:23; Acts 11:6; Plummer 1896: 191. Nolland 1989: 307 argues that the force is that one should attend to nonjudgment and love of the enemy, not ethical minutiae. This is correct contextually, but the remark is so proverbial that the application is broader. Sin in general is in view.

6:1). To correct "obscured vision," be self-critical and then take appropriate action. Through those lessons one is better placed to aid others. Thus, after humble self-examining to remove the beam, one can see to help someone else. Διαβλέψεις (*diablepseis*) shows that by working through one's own problems, one can see more clearly.

Jesus' teaching has many cultural parallels (Marshall 1978: 270; Fitzmyer 1981: 642–43; SB 1:446–47). In the fifth century B.C., Democritus said: "Better it is to correct one's own faults than those of others."[59] Jesus' advice goes beyond the Greek philosopher in saying that one should care for other people after dealing with self. About A.D. 100, Rabbi Tarphon is reported to have said: "I should be surprised if there was anyone in this generation who would accept correction. If one says to a man, 'Remove the speck from your eye,' he will reply, 'Remove the beam from yours'" (*b. ʿArak.* 16b; Manson 1949: 58). This is the reversal of the very attitude that Jesus seeks. First, one removes the beam, and then helps the other, who in turn should be ready to be honest in dealing with genuine criticism.

Jeremias (1963a: 167) argues that Jesus really has in mind the Pharisees (as in Luke 13:15), and so the saying is out of place here. But it is more likely that Jesus is warning his disciples not to be like some Pharisees (18:9).[60] The passage has a close parallel in Matt. 7:3–5, where it is part of the warning not to judge. Luke, by interjecting additional material in Luke 6:39–40, has the passage in a similar context, but probably has made an additional point. By removing the plank from one's eye, one is less likely to be a blind leader of the blind (6:39). The eye imagery in these two passages makes this additional point likely. Through his reuse of the image, Luke notes another point of application from the Lord's teaching: those who are ready to aid others are those who have learned to deal with their own faults.

ii. Call for Fruit (6:43–45)
(1) Good and Bad Trees (6:43)

6:43

Jesus now explains why being self-critical and self-correcting is important. The fruit that a teacher produces reflects what is at the core of his or her being, either good (καλόν, *kalon*) or bad (σαπρόν, *sapron*). The fruit a tree produces cannot be different from the char-

---

59. Democritus, *Fragments* 60. Danker 1988: 153–54 also notes Diogenes Laertius 1.36; Menander, *Fragment* 710; Petronius, *Satyricon* 57; and Persius, *Satires* 4.23–24.

60. Hendriksen 1978: 362. Schürmann 1969: 372 notes that the second-person speech is against an original reference to the Pharisees, since they are rebuked in this way only in Luke 14:7–11. In addition, the term ὑποκριτής is not always used of Pharisees, as Matt. 24:51 and Luke 12:56 show. He sees the address as to the disciples, but not limited to them.

acter of the tree itself. Fruit is a picture of the product in one's life (Luke 3:8–9; Hos. 10:13; Isa. 3:10; Jer. 17:10; 21:14; Fitzmyer 1981: 643). Some suggest that fruit is a reference to the type of disciple a teacher produces (Godet 1875: 1.331; Plummer 1896: 191). But this understanding is difficult in light of Luke 6:45, where the person's activity—especially speech—is in view (Marshall 1978: 272; Sir. 27:6). The essential point is this: how can you teach if you have a problem and are self-righteous about it (Hendriksen 1978: 363; Fitzmyer 1981: 643)? The point of connection with the previous verses is marked out by γάρ (*gar*, for), which indicates that this illustration explains the beam-speck image of Luke 6:41–42. Jesus expresses himself in a proverbial form here, so what he says is generally true.

Luke's usage differs slightly from Matt. 7:15–17, where the connection is explicitly to false teachers. It also parallels Matt. 12:33–34. Of course, as Matthew's usage shows, such an image has the potential for multiple application. Luke clearly applies the warning directly to his audience. The application to speech (Luke 6:45) is like that made in both Mark 7:21–22 and James 3:11–12.[61] Thus, Luke's application seems rooted in church tradition that goes back to Jesus. Most agree that the history of this saying's usage is difficult (Creed 1930: 97–98; Marshall 1978: 271–72; Hunzinger, *TDNT* 7:754).[62]

(2) Principle (6:44)

6:44 Jesus gives the explanation, as γάρ (*gar*, for) shows. The nature of the tree is revealed by its fruit. The principle is followed by two more illustrations: figs and grapes do not come from thorn bushes or bramble bushes.[63] The point of the passage agrees with the illustrations of the previous verse: you will produce what you are and not something different. In connecting this text with the previous verses, the idea is to take a careful look at oneself and note the fruit produced. The primary intent is self-examination, not examination of others. Watch what you produce and make sure that the one whom you follow gives good produce. No doubt, such expectations created the basis for selecting church leaders in the Pastoral Letters' list of qualifications (1 Tim. 3:1–13; Titus 1:5–9). The imagery is pastoral and fits a Palestinian setting (Schürmann 1969: 374 n. 194; see Isa. 5:2–4 for the thorns/grapes image). The remark closes with a

61. See also the Gospel of Thomas 45a. On σαπρός as "rotten," "useless," or "of no value," see Bauernfeind, *TDNT* 7:97; Wiefel 1988: 139; Eph. 4:29.

62. The saying's proverbial character makes it difficult to be confident of explanations that argue for development of a single saying.

63. On these plants and the various fruits, see Marshall 1978: 273; Barn. 7.11; Matt. 7:16; Mark 11:13; 12:26; Luke 20:37; Acts 7:30, 35; James 3:12; Rev. 14:18.

technical term for picking grapes, τρυγῶσιν (*trygōsin*, are picked; BAGD 828; BAA 1651; other NT uses: Rev. 14:18–19).

(3) Good and Bad People (6:45)

The previous two verses now find application in two types of people: **6:45** those who produce good because the heart is good and those who produce evil. This generalized twofold division is similar to sections of 1 John. The heart (καρδία, *kardia*) is the key image in the verse and refers to a person as he or she is, especially in the deepest thoughts and being (BAGD 404 §1bε; BAA 820 §1bε; Behm, *TDNT* 3:612 §D2d; Luke 12:34; 24:32). The inner self possesses treasure that is distributed to those around. The image of treasure (θησαυ-ρός, *thēsauros*) here is different from other passages where θησαυ-ρός is used to refer either to externals that one sees as valuable or to storing up God's favor as a reward because he is pleased with what one does (12:33–34; 18:22; Marshall 1978: 273). In 6:45, Jesus says that from the storehouse of one's inner person comes either good or evil. Often, the image of dispensing evil is in view, though some texts refer to a variety of possibilities for fruit (Matt. 15:19; Mark 7:21; Luke 8:5–15; 13:6–9; Tiede 1988: 146). In 6:45, either possibility exists. The images of a clean or a filthy heart also occur later in the book (8:15 [good]; 11:39 [filthy]; Schneider 1977a: 160). A general exhortation sharing a similar theme is Eph. 4:29.

The fundamental principle comes at the end of the verse: what the mouth produces comes from what overflows from the heart. The concern with teaching and speech is evident in the mention of στόμα (*stoma*, mouth). When tied to the heart, the term for abundance (περίσσευμα, *perisseuma*) expresses that what we say is an outgrowth of who we are (Matt. 12:34; Mark 8:8; 2 Cor. 8:14 [twice]; BAGD 650; BAA 1311). The emphasis on speech shows that teaching is still in view, though the principle would be true of all behavior.

The parallel passage to this verse, Matt. 12:34–35, gives the principle first and then describes the two types of people (Klostermann 1929: 84). The wording of these passages is similar: the verbs differ slightly (Luke has προφέρει, *propherei*, produces [its only NT uses are the two in this verse], and Matthew has ἐκβάλλει, *ekballei*, brings forth); the objects in Luke are singular (good, evil), while in Matt. 12:35 they are plural (good things, evil things); and Luke more closely associates the heart and treasure ideas and speaks of "his" mouth. Matthew has the remarks in a clearly distinct setting, while also paralleling some of Luke 6:43–44 in Matt. 7:16–18. Again, it seems more likely that a similar saying appeared in distinct ways in various settings than that one of the writers moved the saying. In addition, James 3:1–10 is similar in conception, and he often alludes to this material (Gospel of Thomas 45b–c is parallel to Luke; cf. Mark 7:14–23).

The subunit shows that one should be able to tell one's spiritual condition by one's own fruit. Luke seeks introspection, not looking at how others live. The context of the entire sermon indicates that another element in the call to love is a process of honest self-evaluation and correction. This is a prerequisite for being in a position to help others.

iii. Call for Wise Building: Put Jesus' Word into Practice (6:46–49)

(1) Rebuke: Why Call Me "Lord" and Not Do What I Say? (6:46)

6:46 As he concludes the sermon, Jesus gives a call to respond in obedience. The rhetorical question and the following parable serve the same purpose: to exhort the disciple to do what Jesus says, and thus be wise (Luke 8:21; James 1:22–25). The mention of speech in Luke 6:45 may have led to the thought of not uttering lightly one's commitment to Jesus (Ernst 1977: 235). Thus, this verse is also a transition. The force is clear. Why give Jesus a title of honor and respect like "Lord" and then ignore what he teaches? In fact, the double invocation of "Lord" is emotive and emphatic, but the life that makes the confession without obedience is without substance, despite the emotion of the appeal. Such an approach is foolish at best and hypocritical at worst.

Some argue that the presence of κύριε (*kyrie*, Lord) reflects the church's highest confession of Jesus' deity and thus reveals that the saying is the church's product rather than from Jesus, since such a high Christology cannot easily be located this early in Jesus' ministry (Fitzmyer 1981: 644). But κύριος need not refer to or be understood simply as a high christological title, since it was a title used for a respected authority, religious or civil (Foerster, *TDNT* 3:1054, 1084–85). In Luke, it probably is perceived as a way to refer to Jesus as a respected teacher, the *mārî* (Aramaic מָרִי) or rabbi-teacher (Foerster, *TDNT* 3:1093; Marshall 1978: 274; Schürmann 1969: 380, esp. n. 4; Creed 1930: 99; Guelich 1982: 398). In this sense there is no difficulty with the saying fitting the setting of Jesus' ministry. It should also be noted that the double address of Jesus as "Lord, Lord" is emphatic and Semitic in character (Foerster, *TDNT* 3:1093; Marshall 1978: 274).[64]

More difficult is the saying's relationship to Matt. 7:21. The Lucan saying occupies the same position in the Lucan sermon as that

---

64. Double vocatives occur in 8:24; 10:41; 13:34; 17:13; 22:31.

saying does in Matthew, but with some notable differences. Matthew has developed the saying on clearly eschatological lines, a usage that suggests that Jesus' authority is greater than that of a teacher, since he exercises eschatological authority as judge. In fact, Matthew has additional verses to draw out this theme. Most explain this additional material as a Matthean development on an original saying like that in Luke (Marshall 1978: 274; Luce 1933: 151; Creed 1930: 98; Schneider 1977a: 161). What can be said with certainty is that Matthew does more with the saying than does Luke.

But Lucan emphases can also explain why Luke may have opted for a shorter version of the saying. The noneschatological character of Luke's saying fits his tendency to play down the end-time judgment. Luke may have used a shorter form to emphasize the present significance of Jesus' teaching and position without desiring to bring out their future significance. Thus, Luke follows his own emphases. In addition, Luke summarizes the sermon throughout in such a way as to emphasize the need for proper introspection by the disciple rather than wariness of false teaching. Accordingly, the eschatological emphasis and the third-person reference to others who may be cast out are omitted to maintain this emphasis. The disciples are challenged directly to make sure that they are not among the group that hypocritically pays respect to Jesus while ignoring his teaching. Thus, it is quite likely that Luke chose to summarize the larger saying to maintain the introspective focus on the present. The abbreviation is consistent with his summarization of the sermon.

This conclusion returns us to the christological question of Matthew's use of κύριος. There is no doubt that Jesus in the Matthean version of the saying portrays himself as an eschatological mediator at the judgment. The issue tied to entry to the kingdom is knowing Jesus, but it also is doing God's will, as a response to him and his teaching. The actions done "in Jesus' name" reflect his position of authority. Though these expressions can be read in terms of full authority—and probably were read that way in the church that emerged after Jesus' resurrection—Jesus' remarks need not have been taken that way originally. They could have simply described his authority as a prophetic or messianic mediator of God's will. For the disciples and crowds who followed Jesus at this early period are portrayed as struggling to understand who he was, and at a minimum they were responding to him as a prophet. In fact, those who failed to appreciate him fully may have responded to him only at this level and thus may have shown that they did not really understand him. If Jesus saw himself as regally messianic in any sense, then the authoritative, mediatorial role he describes here could have been articulated by him, since Messiah was to rule and help administer eschatological righteousness and judgment. The absolute authority Jesus places in his teaching goes in this direction (Marshall 1978: 274). The Christology expressed in Matthew need not be so high as to be impossible for Jesus to declare at this time or to be impossible for this early audience to relate to, even though it is clearly an expression that ultimately possesses high christological overtones and intentions.

Thus, if the Matthean version is original and Luke shortened it, each writer has given emphases from the teaching that are legitimate expressions of Jesus' instruction. Matthew focused on the ultimate implications of the exhortation from an eschatological mediator, while Luke highlighted the present implications of the instruction of this authoritative teacher from God. Their summaries complement one another.

(2) House on the Rock: Practicing Jesus' Words (6:47–48)

6:47   Jesus turns to his concluding parable to illustrate his evaluation of the two types of people. He begins with those who come, hear, and do his teaching. Of course, the teaching in view is especially that of the sermon. In fact, the sermon's unity is shown by the phrase ὁ ἐρ-χόμενος πρός με (*ho erchomenos pros me*, those who come to me), which serves as an *inclusio* for the sermon by answering the phrase οἳ ἦλθον ἀκοῦσαι αὐτοῦ (*hoi ēlthon akousai autou*, they came to hear him) in 6:18, as well as τοῖς ἀκούουσιν (*tois akouousin*, those who hear) in 6:27. The concept of coming to Jesus is frequent in the NT (Matt. 11:28; John 5:40; 6:35, 37; Marshall 1978: 275). Jesus commends those who put into practice his teaching. The idea of hearing and doing the word is common (Luke 8:21; 10:37; 11:28; Mark 4:20; James 1:22–25; Schürmann 1969: 380 n. 7). The structure of the sentence is somewhat broken in that the three nominative participles (ὁ ἐρχόμενος, ἀκούων, and ποιῶν [*ho erchomenos, akouōn,* and *poiōn*], the one who comes, hears, and does) refer logically to the dative τίνι (*tini*, to whom or to what), a construction known as anacoluthon (a broken grammatical construction).[65] Jesus' remark about what this person is like may reflect a direct question in Aramaic.[66]

The passage is paralleled in Matt. 7:24, where it also occupies the same concluding position in that sermon. The wording in the two Gospels is slightly different, but the concept expressed is the same.

---

65. Fitzmyer 1981: 644; BDR §466.3. On this construction, see also Matt. 10:32 and Luke 12:48. In other words, the subject of the start of the sentence (the participles) and that of the subsequent clause ("I [Jesus] will show you") are not the same.

66. Schürmann 1969: 382 n. 19. Luke uses the comparative ὅμοιος in 6:47, 48, 49; 7:31, 32; 12:36.

Luke alone has the image of coming to Jesus, the introduction about showing whom this person is like, and the anacoluthon.[67] Nevertheless, it is clear that Luke and Matthew represent parallel sayings. The point in both Gospels is fundamentally the same: to stress the importance of following Jesus' teaching and to picture the authority of that teaching.

Jesus gives a simple contrastive parable, though Luke gives it in a **6:48** style that has less parallelism than Matthew (Guelich 1982: 403). In fact, each writer has unique details. Luke mentions the foundation that is laid for the secure house in a threefold description that Matthew lacks: the builder digs (ἔσκαψεν, *eskapsen*; BAGD 753; BAA 1505; elsewhere in the NT only at Luke 13:8; 16:3), digs deeper (ἐβάθυνεν, *ebathynen*; BAGD 130; BAA 262; only here in the NT), and lays a foundation on rock (ἔθηκεν, *ethēken*; BAGD 816 §I.1αβ; BAA 1626 §I.1αβ). Matthew 7:24 says only that the builder built (ᾠκοδόμησεν, *ōkodomēsen*) a house. The Lucan picture is more detailed: the builder is digging through topsoil and laying a solid foundation in the rock. Most see Luke's adapting the parable by describing how a house would be built by his Greek audience, rather than how one is built in Palestine (Marshall 1978: 275; Jeremias 1963a: 27 n. 9; Luce 1933: 151). Such a treatment of the parable need not be seen as a problem, since summarizing occurs and the point is not altered by telling the story or using a figure in a way that the audience can appreciate the image. It is a type of contextualizing that does not alter the basic image. The threefold use of καί (*kai*, and) may reflect Semitic style (Klostermann 1929: 85; BDF §471.4) and thus a Semitic source may be present. If so, then one can be less certain of Luke's altering the imagery. Luke may simply have had access to a distinct account as the vocabulary in Luke 6:49 suggests (see the exegesis of 6:49 and n. 72). A certain decision is not possible. Matthew simply summarizes more briefly and speaks of the house on the rock. Nevertheless, for both writers, the house is solidly anchored in the rock and is prepared to face any storm.

Matthew 7:25 describes the bad weather as a typical Palestinian autumn storm in which fierce rains fall on the mountains and the resulting torrents create rivers that crash against the house, along with the winds (Luke has no parallel to Matthew's οἱ ἄνεμοι, *hoi anemoi*, winds).[68] Such a flood is described by Josephus, and Luke

---

67. Bovon 1989: 341 notes correctly that Luke lacks Matthew's apocalyptic thrust, since the First Gospel has the remark in a context about judgment. He argues that Matthew is more original since he is closer to Palestinian weather patterns. But see the discussion (immediately below) on the issue of weather imagery.

68. Guelich 1982: 412, 404; Marshall 1978: 275; Rengstorf, *TDNT* 6:603. For βροχή (only in Matt. 7:25, 27 in the NT), see BAGD 147 and BAA 294.

uses a distinct summarizing term, πλημμύρης (*plēmmyrēs*, high water, flood), to describe it.[69] Luke describes only the overflow water, comparing it to a river that comes against the house. Citing Luke's singular river (ὁ ποταμός, *ho potamos*) as opposed to Matthew's plural rivers (οἱ ποταμοί, *hoi potamoi*), many see in the different descriptions of the water a shift of imagery from a Palestinian mountain flood to a non-Palestinian river flood (Marshall 1978: 275; Fitzmyer 1981: 644). Fitzmyer says that Luke simplifies the image for those who do not know Palestinian weather. Thus, another contextualization is present in this difference. But Klostermann (1929: 85) is less certain of this conclusion. Luke may simply be briefer in describing the flood's origin, so the difference is more a matter of literary compression than a conscious shift of imagery. Luke does not give the source of the river's overflowing; he pictures the flood simply as a single torrent. Again, a certain decision is not possible.

When the waters came they could not shake the house. They were not strong enough to overcome a house with a solid foundation. Again, the wording is common for Luke.[70] The picture of the verse is clear. Anyone who listens to Jesus' words is in a solid position to resist life's trials. Such foundation imagery is common in the NT in a variety of applications (Matt. 16:18; Luke 17:26–31; 1 Cor. 3:10–11; Eph. 2:20; also Isa. 28:16; 1 Tim. 6:19; 2 Tim. 2:19; Heb. 6:1; Rev. 21:14–19; Schürmann 1969: 382 n. 27). Matthew 7:24 says that such a person is wise, a comment that Luke does not have but is clearly implied in his form of the parable.

Schürmann (1969: 381–83) applies the parable's imagery to the final judgment, but there is no decisive eschatological imagery in the passage in Luke.[71] The picture is more proverbial and refers to one's life in general. To listen to Jesus' teaching is to provide a basis to stabilize all of life. Jesus' authority comes through strongly here.

The image of the houses is seen in the rabbis as well, though with slightly distinct details (SB 1:469–70; Creed 1930: 99–100). In *ʾAbot de Rabbi Nathan* A.24 (= Goldin 1955: 103–4), the rabbi tells of two houses, one built with great stones, the other with uncooked bricks. When the storm comes the second house crumbles. In the rabbi's parable, the rock is the law. The difference is instructive of the dif-

---

69. Josephus, *Antiquities* 2.10.2 §250, describes the protection developed to fight swollen rivers in Egypt; also Job 40:23. For πλήμμυρα (only here in the NT), see BAGD 669 and BAA 1345.

70. Ἰσχύω with the infinitive occurs in 8:43; 13:24; 14:6, 29, 30; 16:3; 20:26; and four times in Acts; Plummer 1896: 193; BAGD 383 §2b; BAA 778 §2b.

71. This conclusion fits Matthew more naturally. It might be an implication of Jesus' remarks in Luke, but it is hardly explicit in the context.

fering loci of authority that Christianity and Judaism have. Of course, the image that both Jesus and Judaism use has roots in Ezek. 13:10–16 (Marshall 1978: 276; Nolland 1989: 310).

(3) House on the Sand: Hearing Jesus' Words (6:49)

In contrast to the obedient person stands the person who only hears **6:49** Jesus' teaching. Many such people might have been in Jesus' audience. The verse parallels Luke's account of the obedient person in 6:48, except in contrast. Rather than building a foundation in the rock, this person simply builds on top of the dirt. Rather than standing when the river's flood comes, this house collapses immediately. Luke mentions the instantaneous (εὐθύς, euthys) character of the collapse, and he chooses the heightened prefixed term συνέπεσεν (synepesen, it fell; BAGD 779; BAA 1555; only here in the NT) to emphasize graphically the house's fall. Another NT hapax legomenon for the home's destruction, ῥῆγμα (rhēgma, collapse; BAGD 735; BAA 1471; Amos 6:11; Plummer 1896: 193), adds even more emphasis.[72] Plummer also notes that μέγα (mega, great) trails at the end of the verse and is emphatic. The verse ends with the tragic sound of a huge thud, as the house falls in a great heap.

The picture is of a person with no spiritual roots, because Jesus' teaching is ignored. The parable is primarily a warning, since it ends with the negative example and thus accents it as the climax (Marshall 1978: 275). Luke's readers would see in the parable a warning to not take Jesus' teaching lightly, since the consequences of such a choice are potentially devastating. The passage is proverbial and not exclusively eschatological, so that the nature of the destruction depends on who is applying the passage and the setting in which it is being applied.

The image is closely parallel to Matt. 7:26–27. But there are differences, many of which are parallel to issues discussed in the exegesis of Luke 6:48:

1. Matthew specifically notes that the person does not obey Jesus' words (αὐτούς, autous).
2. Matthew identifies this person as foolish.
3. Matthew speaks of a house built on sand and does not make reference to a foundation.
4. Matthew details the storm as including wind, rain, and torrents.

---

72. The high number of hapax legomena in Luke 6:47–49 suggests the presence of a source. See also Marshall 1978: 274.

5. Matthew picks a synonymous verb for collapse, ἔπεσεν (*epesen*, it fell), though it is a little less emphatic than Luke's συνέπεσεν.
6. Matthew has a synonymous term for fall (πτῶσις, *ptōsis*; BAGD 728; BAA 1457; Luke 2:34 is the only other NT use).
7. Matthew's context is slightly more eschatological than Luke's.

Some of these detailed differences can be explained in terms of the differing images that the authors chose in summarizing the parable, but it seems unlikely that all of them can be explained this way, since the differing terms used are so synonymous. This is especially true of points 5 and 6. Again, evidence suggests that two versions of this parable may have existed and that distinct versions were used by Matthew and Luke. Nonetheless, the parable's point is the same for each: if one only listens to Jesus and does not practice what he teaches, one is spiritually vulnerable and runs the risk of suffering collapse in the midst of trial (Luke) or judgment (Matthew).

Summary   What does this sermon as a whole look like? The Sermon on the Plain has three key parts, beginning with the prophetic declaration of God's promise to those who unite themselves to him. In general, these are the downtrodden of life: the poor, the hungry, the weeping, and the persecuted. For them there is hope: the kingdom is theirs, they will be filled, they shall rejoice, and they shall be rewarded. But for those who ruthlessly oppose God, there is woe. Their riches are their fill, while weeping and suffering are in store for them. The promise acts as a foundation of hope that supports all the succeeding exhortations, because residing in God's blessing and hope enables one both to resist the temptation to fight for one's rights now and to suffer wrong, knowing that one is secure in God's care.

The parenesis calls one to a radical love that subjects itself repeatedly to the abuse that comes from reaching out to one's enemy. The love expressed here constantly seeks to be available, especially to one's adversary. The opposition that Jesus mentions is religious in character. Jesus says to extend continually a hand that offers hope to those who seek to harm one for one's commitment to God and his Chosen One. Love in its essence is the extending of mercy to those around the disciple. This love is to distinguish itself from the world's love. This love does not seek its own welfare nor does it come naturally. It is exceptional. Those who exhibit it show that they are truly children of the Most High, reflecting his merciful character. This means also that one is not to judge, but rather to extend mercy and forgiveness. Mercy and forgiveness have their reward in God's rich blessing of approval.

The parables describe the importance of whom one follows, as well as of how one looks at oneself. Disciples are to look at themselves honestly and introspectively. Since they will be like the teacher they choose to follow and since they will produce disciples after their own kind, they must be sure that they are following the correct teacher. Disciples should be willing and able to take responsibility for their own affairs and faults before seeking to instruct others. The second picture in the sequence says that what disciples produce is a reflection of where their hearts are. Actions picture the kind of character one possesses. Such character is revealed especially in the content of the disciple's teaching. Finally, a contrast warns the disciples to do what Jesus has just taught. The person who does so is like one who builds a solid home that is able to withstand the flood. But the person who only hears is really a tragic figure, since the house built without foundation is lost in the storm. Similarly tragic is the loss one suffers for failing to heed Jesus.

For Luke, the sermon is a call to obey Jesus. It shows Jesus' teaching and authority. The choice is left before the readers: will they follow Jesus and do what he calls them to do? It is clear that Luke believes the choice is not difficult, once one sees what is at stake. A solid, standing home is better than one that will be destroyed. If one thinks through the options, it is obvious that the best choice is to embrace Jesus and his teaching.

It would be well to summarize how my approach fits with the views noted in excursus 7. The sermon gives a believer's ethic at the level of the individual disciple. Luther's concept of the "two realms" has merit, because the state is charged with the responsibility of enabling its citizens to live in peace (Rom. 13:1–5; 1 Tim. 2:1–4). In addition, God uses the state in the OT to operate as a potential source of discipline for other states that are unjust (OT prophets). In contrast, the sermon relates particularly to the area of personal ethics.

The sermon also is set in a gospel-response context, so that to characterize it as law is incorrect. On this point, I agree with Jeremias's description of its function, in that the sermon is a catechism on love grounded in the security of the knowledge of God's blessing. I have tried to explain the force of figures of speech, and I do not see the sermon as engaging in such excessive hyperbole that one should resort to generalizing. When the figures are properly understood, the teaching's force is clear. The absence of personal vengeance is a theme that other NT books pick up on from this sermon (1 Cor. 6:5–8; Rom. 12:17–21). It is possible that such exhortations have their roots in Jesus' teaching. In fact, one can argue that the Lucan form of the sermon is equivalent to the great Pauline chapter on love in 1 Cor. 13. However, it is Jesus' sermon—and not Paul's descriptions—that makes clear the total extent to which the true practice of love should go. For Jesus defines in a most revealing and graphic way what Paul describes. His walk to the cross will picture the commitment of that love, a love that the disciple is to reflect to outsiders.

Additional Notes

6:24–26. Since the people addressed in the woes are not seen as genuine disciples, some speculate on the origin of the woes of 6:24–26. Some regard the tone of the teaching as not fitting an audience of disciples. As a result they see Luke adding the woes to Jesus' teaching at this point (Luce 1933: 146). Other reasons for this position also exist. One of the most important is the lack of any parallel in Matthew. Others mention the second-person form of the woes, while the blessings have mostly a third-person reference (Schweizer 1984: 121). Schweizer also notes that 6:26 is longer than the other woes in 6:24–25. Fitzmyer (1981: 627, 636–37) argues that 6:24–26 is full of Lucan vocabulary.[73] Luke is said to have formed the woes in parallelism to the blessings that he already possessed.

But the situation is not as clear as proponents of Lucan creation suggest. First, given the prophetic form, one need not argue that the remarks are inappropriate to the disciple setting, since OT prophets often called down the nations in condemnation as a note of consolation to the believers they addressed (Isa. 15–23; Amos 1:1–2:3). In addition, many of the curious who came to hear Jesus needed to hear this warning as well, so that an audience exists for these remarks (Marshall 1978: 255–56; the multitude is present, as 6:17, 19, 27 makes clear). The warning also has value to the disciple, whose lifestyle is not to emulate the world's values, which are a snare to be avoided (1 Tim. 6:6–10, 17–19). Thus, the audience does not suggest a Lucan insertion.

Second, Matthew may have omitted the woes because he chose instead to give a full catalogue of virtues and to focus on those that God accepts.

---

73. Bovon 1989: 298 lists other reasons: Luke's knowledge of the woe form (10:13; 11:42–52; 17:1; 21:23; 22:22); Lucan opposition of rich and poor; Lucan opposition of hungry and filled in 1:53; Lucan vocabulary (πλήν, καλῶς εἴπωσιν, and πάντες οἱ ἄνθρωποι); and the second-person address of the woes (which fits Luke's second-person beatitudes). But Schürmann argues that Luke never creates woes and that the verses evidence non-Lucan vocabulary in using πλούσιος and πεινάω; see 1969: 337–38 nn. 86, 88, 96, and 105.

Given Matthew's long list of virtues, a parallel list of woes may have been seen as cumbersome, especially since he will use a long woe list in Matt. 23 (Schürmann 1969: 339). Still another reason for the Matthean omission could be the sermon's early placement in his Gospel, which may have prevented the woes from appearing since no opposition has yet emerged (Plummer 1896: 182).

The issue of the differing length of the woes is like the argument that the fourth beatitude of 6:23 is added because it is longer, an argument refuted in the exegesis. Such variations are not unusual.

More central are the last two factors: the second-person form and Lucan vocabulary. The element of the second person is significant and is probably the strongest argument for Lucan formulation, but it may well reflect only literary balancing by Luke
through a more direct address. If he took the third-person Matthean tradition and paraphrased it into a more direct address in the Beatitudes, why not also here? Another substantial point centers on Lucan vocabulary. Schürmann (1969: 337–39 nn. 86, 88, 96, 103) notes that there are non-Lucan elements in these verses (see n. 73), and he also finds traces of these verses in James 4:9 and 5:1. Thus, it is likely that Luke is following a source here (so Schürmann 1969: 339; Schneider 1977a: 151; Marshall 1978: 247; Grundmann 1963: 144; Wiefel 1988: 132).

6:31. The UBS–NA text has a shorter reading that does not agree with Matt. 7:12. This reading has Alexandrian and some Western support ($\mathfrak{P}^{75}$, B, four Itala manuscripts, Syriac Peshitta). Most manuscripts insert the pronoun ὑμεῖς, which agrees with Matt. 7:12. That the several variants place ὑμεῖς in different positions suggests that it was not original, but was inserted by scribes trying to make the text more like Matthew.

6:33. A parallel structure is obtained by adopting the two variants in the NA apparatus: omitting γάρ from the first line of the verse and including γάρ in the final clause after καί (these variants are not in UBS[4]). Granted, the harder reading would be that in the UBS–NA text, where γάρ is in the first clause but not in the last clause. Nevertheless, internal evidence strongly favors making 6:33 parallel to 6:32 and thus adopting both variants (Marshall 1978: 263).[74]

6:34. Does the question in the verse end with ἐστίν or is the verb omitted and thus implied? The former choice makes the verse parallel to 6:32 and

---

74. Manuscripts reading both variants are A, D, L, Θ, Ξ, Ψ, family 13, Byz, and some Syriac. Manuscript W omits both uses of γάρ, splitting the difference. Omitting the agreement with 6:32 are $\mathfrak{P}^{75}$, ℵ, and B. It is the strength of the strictly Alexandrian witnesses that causes many to go for the omission of agreement, along with the argument of harmonization. Besides fitting the structural harmony of the passage as a whole with its numerous parallelisms (e.g., see the next additional note), the adoption of the variants is supported by wider family distribution.

6:33 and has the support of the widest range of manuscripts: ℵ, A, D, L, W, Θ, Ξ, Ψ, family 1, family 13, Byz.[75] Thus, the verb is original, though there is no difference in meaning between the readings.

6:34. The presence of γάρ as the second word of the final clause where sinners are mentioned would parallel 6:32 and 6:33. The decision of the UBS–NA text to omit γάρ may not be correct. Witnesses attesting to the presence of the term are drawn from a variety of textual families (A, D, Θ, Byz), but the omission is the harder reading and has some manuscript distribution (𝔓[75], ℵ, B, L, W, Ξ). Thus, the choice is difficult, since the variant breakdown is more complex than the other text-critical problems in 6:33–34. The difference in the readings is slight. The presence of γάρ would ensure that καί be read as an emphatic: "For *even* sinners lend to sinners." It may well be that γάρ should be read here, given the breadth of manuscripts with the reading.

6:35. The reading of the UBS–NA text, μηδὲν ἀπελπίζοντες, is clearly the better reading, since it has a variety of manuscript support: A, B, D, L, P, Δ, Θ, Byz, and Itala. Μηδένα ἀπελπίζοντες is read by a less significant group of manuscripts (ℵ, W, Ξ) and probably arose by a double writing of α, an error called dittography (Metzger 1975: 141).

6:48. The UBS–NA reading διὰ τὸ καλῶς οἰκοδομῆσθαι αὐτήν (because it had been built well) is correct, since the image of the Lucan account is of a foundation dug, while the variant τεθεμελίωτο γὰρ ἐπὶ τὴν πέτραν (for he built upon the rock) matches Matt. 7:25 and its more summary description of the house on the rock without mention of the foundation. The variant is read by A, C, D, Θ, Ψ, family 1, family 13, Byz, Lect, some Syriac; while the UBS–NA reading has support in 𝔓[75], ℵ, B, L, W, Ξ, 33, some Syriac. Even Godet (1875: 1.334), who often accepts non-Alexandrian readings, agrees with this judgment, based on internal considerations.

---

75. Omitting the verb are 𝔓[45], 𝔓[75], and B. Note that the switch of one manuscript, ℵ, which here includes the verb (in parallel to 6:32 and 6:33) but does not include the variants that would make 6:33 parallel to 6:32, changes the judgment of text-critics about this variant versus those in 6:33.

III. Galilean Ministry: Revelation of Jesus (4:14–9:50)
    C. Jesus' Teaching (6:17–49)
➤ D. First Movements to Faith and Christological Questions (7:1–8:3)
    E. Call to Faith, Christological Revelation, and Questions (8:4–9:17)

D. First Movements to Faith and Christological Questions (7:1–8:3)

After Jesus' Sermon on the Plain come several pericopes where faith and questions about Jesus' identity are the main issues.[1] There is a pericope about faith (7:1–10), followed by two passages about who Jesus is (7:11–35), followed by two more pictures of faith in action (7:36–8:3). In the last two pericopes, the major subjects are women, showing that Jesus' work has no gender gap. And in the first pericope of the section, a Gentile has faith, showing that there is no racial gap either. Jesus comes for all.

The bracketing of faith around questions about Jesus is effective from a literary perspective. First is an example of faith from a Gentile, then questions about Jesus, and then exemplary responses of faith. The section as a whole presses for the trust that Jesus is worthy to receive. In fact, such worthiness for Jesus is expressed in the centurion's humble remarks about his own unworthiness. The weeping sinful woman responds to God's forgiveness with gratitude for Jesus (7:36–50). Still other women serve Jesus' ministry with their material wealth (8:1–3). Humility, gratitude, and service reflect faith.

In the middle of the unit come John the Baptist's question and Jesus' reply. Is Jesus really God's Promised One to come? Jesus answers by noting that he performs the acts of deliverance and brings the message of God's promise. The OT places his actions in a setting where a positive answer emerges. John was the forerunner; Jesus is the one. He represents the eschatological visitation of God (Nolland 1989: 313). But the response continues to be mixed. As people responded to John, so have they responded to Jesus, despite the differences between the two. For some, regardless of the style of God's messenger, God's way will not do (7:29–35). But for those of faith, there is the commendation of God.

---

1. Tiede 1988: 147–48 sees 7:1–9:50 as a unit (which he calls "Identifying the Messiah of God") in which Luke describes the "christological drama" of demonstrating who Jesus is. Tiede argues that 7:1–50 presents Jesus as the prophet of God. But "the one to come" (7:18–23) is not a prophet, but the promised deliverer. In addition, 8:1–3 deals with response, not proclamation, and therefore belongs with the emphasis of chap. 7. Tiede is right that Christology is a major concern until 9:50, but the chapter divisions, which came centuries after Luke was written, are misleading, and it is therefore better to divide 7:1–9:50 into three units—7:1–8:3; 8:4–9:17; 9:18–50—for reasons that I shall make clear in the exegesis.

1. Faith of a Centurion (7:1–10)

Luke turns to narrate a miracle. His narrative is less concerned with the miracle itself than with the faith of the man who requests Jesus' aid. Thus the story is more a pronouncement on commendable faith than it is concerned with Jesus' power (Fitzmyer 1981: 650). In fact, this focus on characters who respond to Jesus fits well with the chapter's movement as a whole. In Luke 7, Jesus ministers to a centurion, a widow with one child, and a sinful woman. Jesus cares for outsiders.

The account's fundamental structure includes an introduction (7:1–2), the sending of the first emissaries (7:3–5), Jesus' coming (7:6a), the sending of the second emissaries (7:6b–8), Jesus' response at the centurion's faith (7:9), and a note on the healing (7:10). Its connection to 6:47–49 is clear. A man who is building his house on the rock responds to Jesus with concrete faith (Hendriksen 1978: 374). Faith is defined in the passage as a plea to Jesus to offer his aid in the form of his power, even though one is unworthy to receive it (Theissen 1983: 138). Jesus is a picture of power, a man in authority—authority that the centurion understands and describes. This is the third example of faith noted in the book (Mary in 1:45; the four men with the paralytic in 5:20). This first encounter with Gentiles in Luke shows their sensitivity and willingness to respond to Jesus. Faith combined with humility is a commendable, even exemplary characteristic in the centurion. The humility here recalls that of Peter in 5:8, as does the trust of Jesus' authority (Talbert 1982: 83). Jesus willingly responds to such faith.

Sources and Historicity

The account has a parallel in Matt. 8:5–13 (Aland 1985: §85).[1] In fact, Luke 7:6b–9 is very similar in wording to Matt. 8:8–10. Matthew interjects one event between the Sermon on the Mount and this event: the healing of the leper, which Luke had in Luke 5:12–16 before his Sermon on the Plain. As noted earlier, Matthew is somewhat topical in chapters 8–9; thus the leper account probably preceded the sermon, a reflection of Luke's placement (see the introduction to Luke 5:12–16). Mark does not note this event, an

---

1. Since the passage is unique to Matthew and Luke, most speak of Q as the source or at least as one of the sources; Bovon 1989: 346–47; Wiefel 1988: 141–42.

omission that is hard to accept on the premise that Mark was the last Gospel written, especially given Mark's attention to Jesus' miracles (Godet 1875: 1.336).

More controversial is the relation of this account to John 4:46–54 (Van Der Loos 1965: 530–32; Siegman: 1968; Wegner 1985: 34–57). Most see the same event in view because of the parallel wording.[2] Barrett (1978: 244–49) cites John 4:47, 50, 53 as having clear parallels in the Synoptics, especially Matthew. Van Der Loos accepts that they are the same event, while noting eight differences in the accounts. Siegman, who finds it difficult to see only one event, notes nine areas of difference. The major differences are as follows:

1. John 4:46 mentions both Cana and Capernaum, while Luke 7:1 and Matt. 8:5 mention only Capernaum.
2. While Matt. 8:5 and John 4:47 mention the approach of a centurion, Luke 7:3, 6 mentions emissaries. John's term for this person, βα-σιλικός (John 4:46, 49), differs from ἑκατοντάρχης in Matt. 8:5, 8 and Luke 7:2, though the terms can be synonymous (Wegner 1985: 57–72).
3. Matthew 8:6, 8, 13 says that a παῖς (child or servant) is ill (on παῖς meaning "servant," see Matt. 12:18; 14:2). Luke has παῖς in Luke 7:7 and δοῦλος (slave) in Luke 7:2, 3, 10. Besides this potential Synoptic diversity stands John's account, which clearly speaks of a son: υἱός (John 4:46, 47, 50, 53) and παιδίον (John 4:49) (but cf. παῖς in John 4:51).
4. The key difference is that in Matt. 8:7 and Luke 7:6a, Jesus comes in response to an initial request; but in John 4:48, he issues a rebuke. It is possible that Jesus issues a rebuke initially and then the centurion's faith reverses his tone into praise, but this conclusion seems less than likely.
5. Another key difference is Jesus' later reaction. In Matt. 8:10 and Luke 7:9, he marvels at the centurion's faith, a note that John lacks, since the fourth evangelist chooses to note only the healing.
6. The notation of the healing differs in all accounts. Matthew 8:13 notes that the healing came the same hour that Jesus spoke (Matthew also contains an additional saying about the Gentiles at this point, similar to what Luke has at 13:28–29; see the exegesis of 7:9). Luke 7:10 merely mentions the healing. On the other hand, John 4:51–53 notes that the servants report the hour of the healing, so that the royal soldier realizes the healing occurred at the hour that Jesus spoke.

2. Bovon 1989: 346 n. 5 notes that among many Protestant scholars this has been the major position for some time and that only recently have Catholic commentaries like those of Schürmann, Schneider, and Fitzmyer come to accept this approach.

7. Only John mentions that the whole household believed because of the healing.

Of all the differences, the most problematic is the differing tone of John's account and that of the Synoptics. Though a case can be made that the same event is in view, given that Cana and Capernaum are close to one another and that some distance between Jesus and the centurion is assumed in the account, it seems more likely that John is referring to a distinct situation, especially given differences 1, 4, and 5.

Another key difference within the Synoptics is Luke's inclusion of two sets of emissaries, which Matthew lacks. Many regard Luke to have added this detail,[3] while others see a traditional source (Schramm 1971: 40–41, who sees Q and a special Lucan source; so also Wegner 1985: 249–50). Still others argue that Luke had a distinct Q source (Grundmann 1963: 155), while some see Matthew's abbreviating his account.[4] Marshall (1978: 278) makes several points worthy of attention:

1. Matthew does abbreviate accounts (Matt. 9:2, 18–19; 11:2–3; see also Matt. 8:28–34 and 9:18–26 versus their parallels).
2. Messengers sent to represent a figure can be said to speak as the figure (2 Kings 19:20–34). A modern analogy is a press secretary who is perceived as speaking for the president.
3. Appeals to the parallel use of messengers to report Jairus's daughter's death in Luke 8:49 fail because their function is not the same.
4. The possibility of a traditional source concerned with good Jewish-Gentile relations cannot be ruled out.
5. It is debatable if one can argue for a Lucan insertion because of Lucan vocabulary, since there also is non-Lucan vocabulary, as examination of the verses will show.

In sum, one can adequately explain the reference to the messengers without insisting that Luke is responsible for a creative addition. Either Luke had access to additional material or Matthew abbreviated his account (or both).

As with the earlier material involving dialogue related to miracles, the Jesus Seminar puts the words of Jesus in black type, arguing that, although

---

3. Schulz 1972: 237–38 and nn. 410–11, on the basis of Lucan vocabulary in 7:3–6. Most of the cases of Lucan vocabulary depend on Acts, which must also be reckoned to have traditional material, so that some of Schulz's evidence is not as strong as it at first appears. Here also belongs Fitzmyer 1981: 649, who sees as Lucan vv. 1a, 3b–6d, 7a, part of 9, 10a.

4. Schürmann 1969: 395–96; Carson 1984: 200; Liefeld 1984: 897–98. Also noting four options is Busse 1979: 142 n. 3: (1) Luke added the detail, (2) Luke is truer to Q than is Matthew, (3) Luke had another source, and (4) Luke received a pre-Lucan expansion of Q. Busse cannot decide between views 1 and 4. Wiefel 1988: 142 opts for view 4.

the wording of 7:9 is also attested in Matt. 8:10 and so is tied to Q, it does not go back to Jesus (Funk and Hoover 1993: 300). Crossan (1991: 326–28) agrees, by similarly stressing the differences between the Synoptics and John 4. The words were, in the seminar's view, "created by storytellers." But the concept of surprise at Gentile sensitivity to Jesus also appears in Mark 7:24–30 = Matt. 15:21–28. Thus, this concept is multiply attested, even if the wording is not. I agree with Nolland (1989: 315) that "the report has a strong claim to being part of the oldest tradition of the ministry of Jesus." Jesus' remark expresses some surprise at Gentile response, but accepts it. If a Gentile-sensitive Luke had created this saying, such a Gentile response would not have been surprising, so the perspective must be an early one.

The form of the account is variously understood. Bultmann (1963: 38–39) argues that it was an apophthegm or pronouncement story that was clearly a church creation because of the "telepathic healing." He also sees the account as a variation of Mark 7:24–31, written to defend Gentile mission. V. Taylor (1935: 75–76) argues for a "story about Jesus." Fitzmyer (1981: 649) agrees with Bultmann that a pronouncement story is present, though he demurs on Bultmann's comments on historicity, simply saying that such modern questions about the account cannot be answered. He also doubts the connection to Mark. Theissen (1983: 321) calls the account a healing, since it is a miracle (Berger 1984: 309, 314 has this unit in his discussion of miracles, though he dislikes the category "miracle stories"). The issue is whether the miracle or the saying on faith is key. Most acknowledge that the stress is on the exchange between Jesus and the messengers, so the emphasis on pronouncement is appropriate. The evaluation of historicity depends on one's worldview. Why is a "telepathic healing" more difficult than any other healing? Either Jesus healed or he did not. Such power, if it existed, would not be limited by distance.

Tannehill (1986: 111–16) mentions a literary category that has great merit, the "quest story," an account in which someone approaches Jesus in quest of something important for human well-being.[5] The quest itself is the story's dominant concern, and the account ends by noting whether the quest is successful. A quest account focuses on the person who comes to Jesus, unlike other

---

5. This type of pronouncement account is common in Luke: 5:17–26; here; 7:36–50; 17:12–19; 18:18–23 (the only one with a negative outcome); 19:1–10; 23:39–43. Four of these seven accounts (7:36–50; 17:12–19; 19:1–10; 23:39–43) are unique to Luke. (For the view that 7:36–50 is uniquely Lucan, contra Aland 1985: §114, see the discussion of sources for that unit.)

pronouncement accounts, where the saying is the point. Jesus is the authority in such accounts and responds to the one on the quest. Usually there is a difficulty in the request or objectors are present so that the obstacle heightens the drama. In Luke 7, the quest is indirect since messengers for another are involved. The only difficulty present is the potential racial obstacle, which ends up being a nonissue for Jesus.

The outline of Luke 7:1–10 is as follows:

a. Setting: after the sermon, in Capernaum, a sick slave (7:1–2)
b. Jewish elders as emissaries invite Jesus (7:3–5)
   i. Emissaries sent (7:3)
   ii. The centurion is worthy (7:4–5)
c. Jesus goes (7:6a)
d. Other emissaries ask Jesus simply to speak and heal (7:6b–8)
   i. "I am not worthy" (7:6b–7a)
   ii. Authority: "just say the word" (7:7b)
   iii. Authority illustrated (7:8)
e. Jesus praises a Gentile's faith (7:9)
f. The healing is noted (7:10)

The themes are simple. Commendable faith reaches out in trust to Jesus. The passage pictures Gentile faith, Jews who respect a Gentile, the exemplary humility of the centurion, and Jesus' authority. Needless to say, it also illustrates Gentile involvement in Jesus' ministry, as well as Gentile responsiveness. It also shows that racial differences should not be an obstacle, since Jews intercede for a Gentile here and Jesus responds to the quest.

Exegesis and Exposition

[1]After all his words filled the ears of the people, he came to Capernaum. [2]Now a certain slave of a centurion, who was dear to him, was ill and close to death. [3]And having heard about Jesus, he sent to him civil elders of the Jews, asking him to come and cure his slave. [4]And those coming to Jesus were exhorting earnestly, saying, "He is worthy, so that this should be granted him, [5]for he loves our nation and built the synagogue for us."

[6]And Jesus was going with them. And when he was already not far from the house, the centurion sent friends to him, saying, "Lord, do not trouble yourself, for I am not worthy that you should come under my roof. [7]Now neither do I count myself worthy to come to you; but speak the word and my servant ⌜shall be healed⌝. [8]For I am also a man set under authority, having under myself soldiers, and I say to this one, 'Go,' and he goes, and to another, 'Come,' and he comes, and to my slave, 'Do this,' and he does."

⁹And when he heard this, Jesus marveled at him and, turning, he said to the crowd following him, "I say to you, not even in Israel have I found such faith." ¹⁰And when those who were sent returned home, they found the slave in sound health.

a. Setting: After the Sermon, in Capernaum, a Sick Slave (7:1–2)

Luke supplies a transition into the account of the centurion: from the plain located near Capernaum, Jesus journeys into the town. Such transition verses are common in Luke (4:30, 37, 44; 5:11, 16, 26; 6:11, 17; Plummer 1896: 194). This account is clearly set after the sermon, as ἐπειδή (epeidē) shows. The term occurs only here in the NT with a temporal sense and is best translated "after" (Plummer 1896: 194; Klostermann 1929: 85). The picture of Jesus' teaching filling his listeners' ears portrays its importance (19:48) and perhaps alludes to the teaching's authority and penetrating character. At the least, the picture suggests that Jesus' teaching caused reflection and recalls Jesus' closing call to hear in 6:47–49. The term ἀκοάς (akoas) means "ear" here (as in Acts 17:20; 2 Tim. 4:3; Heb. 5:11; BAGD 31 §1c; BAA 59 §1c), but the term has gospel overtones in the early church, where it also means "report" and refers to the content of what went into the ear (see Rom. 10:16; Gal. 3:2; 1 Thess. 2:13; BAGD 31 §2b; BAA 59 §2b). Λαοῦ (laou, people) refers to the entire crowd (cf. ὄχλῳ, ochlō, crowd, in 7:9; Strathmann, TDNT 4:51).

7:1

The account's central figure is the centurion. Yet he never explicitly appears in the Lucan version. Ranked between a decurion who commanded ten soldiers and a chiliarch who had authority over one thousand soldiers, a centurion (ἑκατοντάρχης, hekatontarchēs) under Herod Antipas was in charge of one hundred men (BAGD 237; BAA 477; Van Der Loos 1965: 533 n. 1; ἑκατοντάρχης appears twenty-three times in the NT, nineteen of which are in Luke–Acts: Luke 7:2 [twice], 6; 23:47; Acts 10:1, 22; 21:32; 22:25, 26; 23:17 [twice], 23 [twice]; 24:23; 27:1, 6, 11, 31, 43; Wegner 1985: 60–72). Either mercenary soldiers, tax soldiers, or policemen (Fitzmyer 1981: 651), centurions could be of a variety of nationalities (Josephus, Antiquities 17.8.3 §§198–99; Windisch, TDNT 2:509; Nolland 1989: 316). Sherwin-White (1963: 123–24) notes that Romans did not serve in this capacity in Galilee until A.D. 44. Centurions earned significant amounts of money: in a period where the lowest-paid soldier earned 75 denarii, a centurion earned between 3,750 denarii and 7,500 denarii (Wegner 1985: 63). The soldier's nationality is unclear, though Luke 7:9 makes clear that he is not Jewish (Schürmann 1969: 391 suggests that he might be Syrian). Though it cannot

7:2

be said for certain that he is a proselyte, it is possible that his support of the synagogue (7:5) makes this conclusion tenable. Centurions were not always highly regarded. Danker (1988: 158) notes the remarks of Persius to the effect that centurions were uneducated and uncultured (*Satires* 3.77–85; 5.189–91). This centurion was of a different character and clearly had garnered a high reputation. (Cornelius in Acts 10 is another respected centurion.)

The problem is that the centurion has a slave near death. Matthew 8:6 tells us that the slave is paralyzed, but Luke lacks such detail. Rather, Luke stresses that his life is hanging by a thread. The slave is respected or highly regarded by the centurion, but it is hard to be sure of the exact force of ἔντιμος (*entimos*) (BAGD 269 §2; BAA 543 §2; Plummer 1896: 194; Marshall 1978: 279). If the centurion regarded the servant as an asset or possession, "valuable" is the better translation (1 Pet. 2:4, 6); but if the centurion was the moral, sensitive man that the account suggests, "dear" or "esteemed" may be better (Luke 14:8; Phil. 2:29). The centurion's hesitation in approaching Jesus may have been because of his concern for his slave, as well as his being a Gentile (Plummer 1896: 194; Ellis 1974: 117).

b. Jewish Elders as Emissaries Invite Jesus (7:3–5)
i. Emissaries Sent (7:3)

7:3   The situation is serious, and so the centurion decides to take action. He has heard about Jesus' ministry, including, given the nature of the request, miraculous works like those in 4:31–44 and 5:12–26 (A. B. Bruce 1897: 510; Fitzmyer 1981: 651). But as a Gentile, the centurion may have been hesitant about asking a Jewish teacher for aid, so he sent (ἀπέστειλεν, *apesteilen*) emissaries to make the request for him.[6]

These emissaries are described as "elders of the Jews." Πρεσβυτέρους (*presbyterous*) may refer to synagogue leaders (Godet 1875: 1.337), but it more likely refers to Jewish civil leaders (Plummer 1896: 195; Schürmann 1969: 391 n. 16; Marshall 1978: 280). Alford (1874: 503) mentions that Luke uses a different term for synagogue leaders in Acts 13:15: ἀρχισυνάγωγοι (*archisynagōgoi*). The πρεσβύτεροι are often distinguished from the priests and scribes by Luke (Luke 9:22; 20:1; 22:52; Acts 4:5, 8, 23). Equivalent to γερουσία (*gerousia*, elders) in the LXX, the normal meaning of the term is "prominent social leaders" (Deut. 19:1–13; 21:1–9, 19; Ezra 10:14; Van Der Loos 1965: 534 n. 4; Bornkamm, *TDNT* 6:660–61).

---

6. On the idea of ἀποστέλλω not referring to a special commission, see Rengstorf, *TDNT* 1:403–4. The main reason for rejecting a commission is that the simpler synonym πέμπω is used in 7:10.

Luke indicates three things in referring to the Jewish emissaries. First, he shows how Jews and Gentiles can get along and have respect for one another, a point of great importance for his Gospel. That this detail is his alone fits this concern. Second, by using Ἰου-δαίων (*Ioudaiōn*, Jews), Luke also indicates his audience and perhaps his own ethnic origin, since this term is commonly used only by Gentiles to refer to Jews (Gutbrod, *TDNT* 3:376–77; Marshall 1978: 280; Leaney 1958: 141). Third, the nonappearance of this Gentile figure may well indicate the example of a man who exercises faith without actually having seen Jesus (Talbert 1982: 79).

The emissaries make a simple request. They wish Jesus to come and cure the slave. Διασώζω (*diasōzō*) refers to bringing someone safely through an ordeal or to rescuing someone.[7] This Gentile soldier believes that Jesus has the power to restore his slave, and so he appeals for the teacher's aid.

ii. The Centurion Is Worthy (7:4–5)

The emissaries do not just bring the centurion's request, but they also lobby on his behalf. They attempt to persuade Jesus to come and aid this soldier (of thirty-seven NT uses of παραγίνομαι, *paraginomai*, twenty are in Acts and eight in Luke; Plummer 1896: 195). The text indicates emphatically the length to which these Jews labored on behalf of this Gentile. The adverb σπουδαίως (*spoudaiōs*, earnestly) indicates a seriousness in their efforts (BAGD 763; BAA 1525; 2 Tim. 1:17; Titus 3:13; and Phil. 2:28 are the other NT uses).

7:4

The emissaries implore Jesus by offering a commendation. They describe the centurion as worthy (ἄξιος, *axios*) of benefiting from Jesus' power (BAGD 78 §2a; BAA 155 §2a; Foerster, *TDNT* 1:379–80; Marshall 1978: 280). In fact, this is the only time that the NT uses this term positively to describe a specific person, as opposed to a general group or class of people. The point is made through an unusual qualitative-consecutive relative clause (BDF §5.3b, §379; BDR §379.1.1). The clause that ends the verse is a relative clause describing his worthiness: "This man is worthy so that this request should be granted him." The elders' confidence contrasts with the centurion's own evaluation of himself sent through the friends who come later. They will note that he himself does not feel worthy of a visit to his house (7:6). Such humility Jesus commends later (14:7–11).

The elders' favorable treatment of the man raises the question whether he was a Jewish proselyte. Most regard it as unlikely, since

---

7. BAGD 189; BAA 379–80; Foerster, *TDNT* 7:990 §D.II.1a. Of eight NT uses of διασώζω, six are in Luke–Acts: Matt. 14:36; 1 Pet. 3:20; Luke 7:3; Acts 23:24; 27:43, 44; 28:1, 4; Plummer 1896: 195.

the appeal could have made this status clear to justify the request (so Van Der Loos 1965: 535 n. 3). But it is possible that he was a candidate to be a proselyte, since his sympathy extended to building the synagogue. That he already was a proselyte is less likely, since in 7:5 there is no mention of his loving God. However, there is no way to be certain. At the least he was sympathetic and sensitive to the Jews, as other Gentiles had been. Josephus describes Alexander the Great in similar terms, showing that one need not be a proselyte to receive such respect from Jews (*Against Apion* 2.4 §43; Klostermann 1929: 86; Bovon 1989: 348 n. 20).

7:5   The explanation why (γάρ, *gar*) the elders think this man is worthy of the Jewish teacher's attention follows: he loves the nation. If a proselyte were in view the comment probably would have been that "he loves our God" (Plummer 1896: 195). Here is a Gentile who respects Jewish worship and has affection for the people. A contemporary illustration might be of an anthropologist, ambassador, or soldier sent to a foreign land who grows to respect and love that nation's culture and people. This man may be a God-fearer, but even this is not clear from the remarks, which focus only on Israel's customs (Bovon 1989: 348 places the centurion in this category; note also Finn 1985). If a God-fearer can be defined as a moral, monotheistic Gentile, then perhaps the centurion is a convert in this broad sense.

His affection is evident in the elders' second point; namely, that he built their synagogue. The centurion clearly is a man of means and generosity. This synagogue may have been mentioned already in 4:33 (Fitzmyer 1981: 652). A synagogue has been excavated at Tell Ḥum (Capernaum), but it is dated in the third century A.D., too late to be the synagogue of Luke 7 (Van Der Loos 1965: 536 n. 1; Ellis 1974: 117; Schrage, *TDNT* 7:816 n. 111). Why would a foreign soldier do this? Augustus saw synagogues as valuable, because they maintained order and morality (Josephus, *Antiquities* 16.6.2 §§162–65; 19.6.3 §§300–311). Examples of such Gentile generosity are noted in other Jewish sources (*t. Meg.* 3.5 [= Neusner 1977–86: 2.287 (2.16 in Liebermann's enumeration)]; SB 4:142–43; Creed 1930: 101; Marshall 1978: 280).[8] One inscription of note speaks of a Gentile who built a Jewish house of prayer (Dittenberger 1903–5: #96; Fitzmyer 1981: 652). The type of Jewish and Gentile cooperation that Luke will call for in Acts is previewed here. As well, the favorable portrait of a centurion is frequent in Luke (Luke 23:47; Acts 10).

---

8. Schrage, *TDNT* 7:813–14, 818 n. 123, remarks that such an attitude usually produced a gift to a synagogue. Luke 7 is unique in speaking of the synagogue itself as the gift. Schrage thinks it is a small synagogue.

It is also significant that word about Jesus was reaching socially significant people of all races and was not just limited to the poor.

c. Jesus Goes (7:6a)

A brief comment notes that Jesus accepted the elders' invitation. His **7:6a**
compassion has no racial limits.

d. Other Emissaries Ask Jesus Simply to Speak and Heal (7:6b–8)
i. "I Am Not Worthy" (7:6b–7a)

As word reached the centurion that Jesus was coming, he sent a sec- **7:6b**
ond delegation to meet Jesus. Some argue that this second delegation is simply a literary detail added to the account to make clear the
centurion's humility (Schürmann 1969: 393 n. 23; Fitzmyer 1981:
652). But the point of the second delegation is not that Jesus should
help a worthy, humble man, but that he need not come to the house
to do so. Also, why is a second delegation required to make a statement of humility? Could not the first delegation have made this
point? And if so, why did the centurion not give Jesus this word originally? Such skepticism about the tradition is not necessary. The
narrative is not interested in answering such questions, and any answers are speculative. Perhaps the centurion perceived that starting
off by telling Jesus not to come might suggest that he was embarrassed to have Jesus come to his home. Having made the initial request, he could then tell Jesus that the effort to heal need not be
bothersome. Nonetheless, by telling Jesus not to bother with a journey, the centurion's faith stands out, as well as his humility.

The delegation meets Jesus when he is not far from the house.
The construction οὐ (*ou*, not) with an adjective or adverb is common
in Luke–Acts (Plummer 1896: 195 notes fifteen examples). Luke depicts the friends' message as giving the centurion's exact words. The
term for friends, φίλους (*philous*), is frequent in Luke (12:4; 15:6;
21:16) where parallels lack it (Stählin, *TDNT* 9:159). Their message
is cast in the first-person singular, "I am not worthy." Thus, the verbal agreement with Matthew's report that the centurion said this to
Jesus is not surprising (Matt. 8:8–9).[9] Jesus should not trouble himself to enter the house, because (γάρ, *gar*) the centurion recognizes
that he is not worthy of such a personal visit. Jesus is addressed with
the respectful κύριε (*kyrie*, Lord), a term of courtesy for any significant figure, which here would be equal in force to saying "Rabbi,"

---

9. In Luke, the friends speak for the centurion, and the centurion "speaks with"
Jesus through them. Luke is more detailed here than Matthew, who has probably
telescoped events and thus spoken of the centurion directly.

since a Gentile is speaking, not a Jew (Fitzmyer 1981: 652; Marshall 1978: 281). Schürmann (1969: 393 n. 28) probably correctly notes that Luke's readers would see a little more significance in the term (Luke 5:8; 6:46).

Jesus is not to trouble himself. Σκύλλω (*skyllō*, to trouble) also appears in Mark 5:35 = Luke 8:49 in the account of Jairus's daughter, an agreement that leads some to suggest that Luke added this unit under the influence of that account. But the term's function in the two accounts differs: in Jairus's story Jesus is told not to bother with the daughter, since she has already died. In Luke 8 it means to not come at all for it is too late; in Luke 7 it means that Jesus can heal from where he is.

The key to the verse is the centurion's declaration that he is not worthy to have Jesus step into his house. His sense of unworthiness recalls Peter in 5:8 (Rengstorf, *TDNT* 1:330 n. 96). Two reasons are posited for his hesitancy (Ellis 1974: 117). Some see the soldier as sensitive to a Jew's becoming unclean when entering a Gentile house (Acts 10:28; 11:12; *m. ʾOhol.* 18.7; Danker 1988: 159; Plummer 1896: 196). If this is the concern, then the soldier is not a proselyte, since a proselyte would be like a Jew. In fact, Luke 7:7 is against this view, since the centurion will not come to Jesus either. Others argue that the text shows no concern for ritual purity (which Jesus on occasion ignored; see 5:13), so that the issue is clearly Jesus' person. The centurion simply had a high view of Jesus (so Van Der Loos 1965: 537; Marshall 1978: 281; Derrett 1973: 176). Rengstorf (*TDNT* 3:294–95) goes so far as to see a confession of Jesus' messiahship here. The second view is explicit in the account, since the issue is the man's faith and he testifies to his respect for Jesus in 7:7. However, given that he is not a proselyte, it is unlikely that he sees Jesus as Messiah. Rather, the praise for his faith is a commendation of his recognition that Jesus works through God's power, either as a prophet or as a unique man of God. In this sense his faith is parallel to another centurion's recognition at the cross that Jesus was righteous (23:47). This may not be a full confession, but it is a man opening up to what God is doing in Jesus. The centurion's humility recalls John the Baptist's attitude before Jesus (3:16). Before Jesus, great people—whether Jew or Gentile—pale into insignificance.

7:7a The messengers' report of the centurion's humility continues. He is not worthy to have Jesus come into his home, but neither is he worthy to go to Jesus, a point that shows that defilement by entering a home is not the centurion's main concern. This comment is not in Matthew, because in his telescoping of the account the friends who bring the centurion's message are not mentioned at all (Creed 1930:

102). The wording of this verse is Lucan.[10] But this detail may well reflect sources to which Luke gained access and summarized in his own words. What is clear is that the centurion did not feel worthy of direct contact with Jesus.

ii. Authority: "Just Say the Word" (7:7b)

However, the centurion has not given up asking for Jesus' help. He **7:7b** trusts in Jesus' authority. He recognizes that Jesus has access to God and that all this powerful figure need do is to speak and healing will occur.[11] He has faith that Jesus' command is all that is needed. Παῖς (*pais*) clearly means "servant" in the context (Luke 7:2, 3, 10; 12:45; 15:26; Matt. 8:6, 8, 13; Plummer 1896: 196). The word of Jesus, given unseen and from a distance, can deliver the precious servant from his illness. It is a profound insight that the centurion possesses and expresses: even though physically absent, Jesus can show his presence effectively. The lesson is a key one for Luke's readers, who no longer have Jesus' physical, visible presence.

iii. Authority Illustrated (7:8)

The centurion now explains through his messengers why (γάρ, *gar*) **7:8** he knows that the servant will be healed by the power and authority of Jesus' word. The centurion knows that Jesus' word will be obeyed, even from a distance, and the centurion graphically portrays his understanding with a three-part illustration, which is almost verbally identical with Matt. 8:9 (Luke has the additional word τασσόμενος, *tassomenos*, being set under, subjected to; Delling, *TDNT* 8:28). The issue of authority has been raised already in Luke (4:6, 32, 36; 5:24; Marshall 1978: 282). The centurion's illustration reveals his understanding of Jesus.

The centurion makes a minor-to-major comparison (Fitzmyer 1981: 652–53). Surely if he, as a member of the government's army, is obeyed, so also the spiritual forces that are subject to Jesus will obey his word. The centurion is under another's authority, but nonetheless is in charge of his own forces. The picture parallels Jesus, who ministers for God, serving him with a clear sphere of authority. Just as the soldiers and servant obey the centurion, so will those forces afflicting the centurion's slave obey Jesus. Jesus' work of heal-

---

10. Marshall 1978: 281 notes four expressions that are frequent in Luke: διό, ἐμαυτοῦ, ἀξιόω, and ἔρχομαι πρός.

11. On the authority of Jesus' word, see Matt. 7:29; 8:8; Luke 5:5; Mark 1:25–26; 4:39; Kittel, *TDNT* 4:107. On cures from afar, see the texts frequently discussed with this one: Matt. 8:8, 13; John 4:50–52; Lohse, *TDNT* 9:432. Ps. 107:20 stresses healing by a word; Nolland 1989: 317.

ing has been reported to the centurion, and he accepts the testimony as true. Thus, a soldier of the world's most significant army compliments Jesus' authority and equates it to authority within a military unit (Danker 1988: 159; 1 Esdr. 4:1–12).

e. Jesus Praises a Gentile's Faith (7:9)

7:9 Jesus' response to the request is one of surprise and commendation, especially for the centurion's confident declaration of Jesus' authority. Jesus' reaction is emotional: he is amazed at the soldier. Jesus, portrayed in very human terms, wonders at the quality of a Gentile's response to him (Plummer 1896: 197; Van Der Loos 1965: 539). He is a spectator, commenting to other spectators (Bovon 1989: 351). This is one of only two texts where Jesus is said to be amazed (Mark 6:6; Matt. 8:10 = Luke 7:9; Bertram, *TDNT* 3:40). The centurion's faith leads Jesus to address the crowd (for the syntax of the clause that describes Jesus as turning before speaking, see Fitzmyer 1981: 653).

The reference to turning adds a vivid detail that Matt. 8:10 lacks. Στραφείς (*strapheis*) is common in non-Marcan sections of Luke and as such leads Fitzmyer (1981: 653) to regard it as a Lucan term (7:9; 9:55; 10:23; 14:25; 23:28; in addition 7:44 and 22:61, which have Marcan parallels, use στραφείς, but Mark lacks it). But Marshall (1978: 282) notes that στραφείς is entirely absent from Acts, raising the possibility that the term was in Luke's source. The detail adds color to the account, as Jesus specifically addresses the multitudes who follow him. Jesus' action and remarks say, "Learn from this."

In the paragraph's key saying, Jesus commends the Gentile's faith as something not found in Israel. The faith pictures what will often be the case in Acts: Gentiles respond to Jesus while many Jews reject him. More than this, Luke shows that pious pagans can understand Jesus, who is the completion of the path to God (Talbert 1982: 82–83, though Luke is less optimistic about pagans outside of Christ; see Bock 1991a).

What is it that Jesus commends as unique? It cannot be the centurion's recognition of miraculous power, for that had drawn wide response (4:40–41). This unique faith recognizes Jesus' authority and the power of his word, not only over illness but also in the face of his physical absence and distance. Magical presence or touch is not required for healing, only the power of Jesus' command and will. The centurion recognizes that God's power works through Jesus without spatial limitations. Jesus is entrusted with great authority. It is clear that entrusted power is in view, because of the illustration of 7:8, where Jesus, like the centurion, is a man under authority. In addition, there is the resultant recognition of personal unworthiness. Humility mixed with deep faith describes what Jesus praises. The soldier approaches the man of God on the proper terms. In the commendation, Jesus makes an indirect call to trust him in a similar way. The question in effect is, "Will you trust as the centurion has?" (Schweizer 1984: 131). Such faith brings Jesus' approval.

Several Synoptic issues need to be addressed. (1) The passage is similar in wording to Matt. 8:10 and, depending on how a text-critical problem in Matt. 8:10 is solved, may be exact (see the additional note). (2) Matthew 8:11–13 contains an additional saying that Luke has in 13:28–29. But this saying is of a type that could well have been repeated. The difference in wording between these two accounts and the differences in the sayings adjoining this remark in each Gospel suggest that distinct sayings are likely (Plummer 1896: 197). (3) Matthew also has an additional word of comfort that the centurion can go, because it will be done as he has believed. The omission of this saying in Luke has two apparent causes. First, most obviously, since the centurion does not appear in Luke's account, he cannot be dismissed. Second, Luke's additional knowledge of the sequence of events seems to have caused him to focus on the centurion's confession of Jesus' authority and Jesus' praise of that confession.

f. The Healing Is Noted (7:10)

The slave's healing is reported without any indication of Jesus' command to be healed (Danker 1988: 160; Grundmann 1963: 158). The focus is the centurion's faith, not the healing. Of course, the healing demonstrates Jesus' authority, since the event reflects the authority that the centurion described in 7:8.   **7:10**

The report simply notes that when the messengers returned, the slave was healthy. The subject of the sentence, οἱ πεμφθέντες (hoi pemphthentes, those who were sent), looks back to the second set of envoys in 7:6 (which uses ἔπεμψεν, epempsen; see Schürmann 1969: 394 n. 39). Of course, Luke's account differs from Matt. 8:13, which simply notes that the slave was healed at the moment that Jesus replied. Each author is working with unique materials alongside the sources they share. They each end the account in their own way.

The description of the slave's condition is significant. Ὑγιαίνοντα (hygiainonta) looks to the slave's new-found health, rather than looking back at his being healed (BAGD 832; BAA 1660; Luck, TDNT 8:312; 3 John 2; in the Pastoral Letters, this verb is used eight times of healthy teaching). The emphasis is on what the healing produced. The term is unique to Luke (5:31; 7:10; 15:27) in the Synoptics, leading some to see Luke closing in his own terms (Marshall 1978: 282). This is quite possible, though that Luke does not use the verb in Acts, only the noun (4:10), raises questions as to how Lucan this term is.

Luce (1933: 153) argues that the miracle reflects a later stage of miracle story, since it is done at a distance and thus is an escalated picture of Jesus' power (this view is similar to Bultmann's "telepathic healing" category mentioned in the discussion of sources above). But Marshall (1978: 283) rightly notes that the account is just as miraculous in character as any of the miracle stories. Such miracle stories must be taken together, rather than separated into distinct classes. The element of distance is not an additional difficulty when we assess the historicity of miracles! Clearly the account sets forth the event as part of Jesus' ministry. It is interesting to note that the other Synoptic account where Jesus does not have contact with the healed is Mark 7:24–30, which also involves a Gentile (Marshall 1978: 282).

Summary

The healing of the centurion's slave in Luke 7:1–10 foreshadows the expansion of Jesus' ministry to the nations. The non-Jewish centurion has encountered the ministry of this Jewish teacher and has sought his aid. He has heard of Jesus' work and understands the power and authority that the teacher possesses from God. He senses that he is unworthy of receiving Jesus' help. Jesus commends his insight as unique and offers the faith of this foreign soldier as an example to all. His combination of humility, dependent request, and trusting awareness of God's power is the essence of faith.

The respect that this man received from Jews is a submotif in the account. Surely Jews and Gentiles can get along and share involvement with Jesus. Race makes no difference to God. This theme will receive more comprehensive treatment in Acts, but here the groundwork is laid to show that racial-religious distinctions are not part of the gospel when one responds to Jesus (Eph. 2:11–22; Gal. 3:28–29; Col. 3:10–11).

Above all, what is clear from this account is that Jesus has authority from God that extends over space, distance, and disease. He is gifted by God to a high degree. The healing he gives reveals the authority that he has to reverse the condition of those in need. He need not be physically present to respond. And anyone can share in the benefits that Jesus offers, if faith is exercised. The centurion's faith is an example that should not stand alone. Luke asks his reader to have the faith of the centurion.

Additional Notes

7:7. The harder reading ἰαθήτω (aorist imperative: let him be healed) is supported by $\mathfrak{P}^{75}$, B, and L. Widely distributed manuscripts (ℵ, A, C, D, W, Byz, Itala) read ἰαθήσεται (future indicative: he will be healed), which looks like Matt. 8:8. This impressive variety may indicate the more likely reading, despite the parallel wording in Matthew. Regardless, the meaning of the verse is essentially the same, since Jesus' capability is asserted either way (Fitzmyer 1981: 652).

7:9. If the UBS–NA text of Matt. 8:10 is original (supported by B, W, some Itala, and Syriac), then Matthew speaks of "no one in Israel having such faith," a slightly more personalized, direct, and accusatory summary of what Jesus said when compared to Luke's "not even in Israel have I seen such faith." The essential point is the same: the Gentile's faith is unique. The reading of the UBS–NA text seems to be based on the premise that a scribe is more likely to make the Gospels agree than to make them disagree in wording. However, on the basis of external evidence (ℵ, C, L, Δ, Θ, family 13, 33, Byz, Lect, many Itala, and Vulgate), the more likely Matthean text is the one that agrees with Luke. Nevertheless, if a difference is present, it is not significant, being only a slight difference in emphasis.

2. Resuscitation of a Widow's Son and Questions about Jesus (7:11–17)

Luke turns from faith as the ground for healing to an examination of healing as the basis for popular confession of Jesus. A miracle account unique to Luke (Aland 1985: §86), the raising of the widow of Nain's son illustrates public reaction to Jesus' healing ministry and describes its perception of him as a great prophet (7:16; Fitzmyer 1981: 658; Creed 1930: 102 ["the new prophet"]). Since resuscitation from the dead is involved, the account expands the scope of Jesus' power and authority. This is one of four such accounts in Luke–Acts. Later examples show that apostolic authority is parallel to Jesus' power because it is grounded in him (Luke 8:40–42, 49–56 [Jesus]; Acts 9:36–43 [Peter]; 20:7–12 [Paul]). The point of Luke 7:11–17 is not only that Jesus can overcome disease (as the healing of the centurion's slave showed), but he also has the authority to override death. The miracle is unusual for other reasons: Jesus takes the initiative (so the healing comes at the front of the account), and the public response to this power includes declaration of Jesus' prophetic office and praise to God for visiting his people. When the people conclude that Jesus is a great prophet, they are undoubtedly comparing him to figures such as Elijah and Elisha, who also possessed such miraculous power (1 Kings 17:17–24; 2 Kings 4:8–37).[1] Performing resuscitation evidences the presence of God's power. The action itself need not carry with it ontological implications, as the apostles' and prophets' ability to perform resuscitation shows. Resuscitation from the dead attests the miracle-worker's access to God's power. Confessions commonly follow miracles in the NT (Luke 5:8; Matt. 12:23; 14:33; John 1:49; 6:14; Acts 8:10; 14:11–12; 16:30; 28:6; Theissen 1983: 161). As Acts 14:11–12 shows, such confessions need not be accurate nor exhaustive in their scope.

Another function of this account is to set up the discussion with the envoys from John the Baptist. When Jesus alludes in Luke 7:22 to the dead being raised, he is referring back to this

---

1. Bovon 1989: 357–58 notes the OT similarities (returning the son to the parent, the widow, and recognition that God's messenger is present) and differences (Jesus' taking the initiative, instantaneous resuscitation, and the crowd's response). Bovon references the key study of this passage by Harbarth 1978. For the connections to 1 Kings, see Brodie 1986, though he overdraws the case for framing around this OT book. The differences between the OT and the event reveal that the event controls the details (see C. A. Evans 1990: 115 and Evans in Evans and Sanders 1993: 223–24).

event. Thus, Luke is preparing to declare that a major time of eschatological fulfillment has come.

Sources and Historicity

The issue of resuscitation from the dead is much discussed (SB 1:523, 560; Fitzmyer 1981: 656–57; Creed 1930: 103; Van Der Loos 1965: 559–66; Bovon 1989: 358–60). Several ancient extrabiblical accounts report resuscitation with a note of skepticism: Pliny, *Natural History* 7.37 §124; Philostratus, *Life of Apollonius* 4.45 (third century A.D.); Apuleius, *Florida* 19 (Klostermann 1929: 87; Van Der Loos 1965: 560–61). Jewish parallels (all late) are particularly interesting for their variety in noting who can raise the dead: God (*b. Taʿan.* 2a), righteous people (*b. Pesaḥ.* 68a, citing Isa. 5:17; Mic. 7:14; Zech. 8:4), Messiah (*Pirqe de Rabbi Eliezer* 32 [= Friedlander 1916: 233], citing Ps. 72:17), or the rabbis (Midr. Lev. 10.4 [111d] on Lev. 8:2). Such accounts were also popular in NT apocryphal literature: Acts of Paul 2 [son of Anchares], 3 [Dion], 7 [Artemilla] and Acts of Thomas 30–33, 51–54 (Schneemelcher 1991–92: 2.238, 247, 252, 351–53, 360–62).

These parallels lead some to explain Jesus' actions on naturalistic terms (Luce 1933: 153–54) by appealing to literary explanations or myth or the more naturalistic explanation that Jesus "raised" those who were simply comatose (Van Der Loos 1965: 564–66 notes the options). Marshall (1978: 283), Nolland (1989: 321), and Van Der Loos argue that the ancient parallels prove nothing about the historicity of the Lucan account. Such questions will be answered more by one's preconceptions about the possibility of these kinds of works than they will by the presence of such parallels.

The Jesus Seminar (Funk and Hoover 1993: 300) places the wording of the miracle in 7:13–14 in black type, thus tracing none of it to Jesus. They attribute it to "the invention of the storyteller under the storyteller's license. There is no word or phrase that is likely to have been remembered as coming from Jesus." This is mere assertion that reveals the seminar's preconceptions. Nolland's judgment (1989: 321) that "there seems no good reason for stumbling over the resuscitation of the dead" is sound. The presence of multiple attestation for resuscitation in the Jesus tradition makes it likely that a summary of what he said during such events would also be recalled (see 8:40–56).

Since the unit is unique to Luke, it is part of Luke's special material (Wiefel 1988: 144; two earlier units unique to Luke are 4:14–30 and 5:1–11).[2] Two other uniquely Lucan pericopes related to women follow shortly (7:36–50; 8:1–3).

---

2. Though some see parallels to 4:14–30 and 5:1–11 in the other Gospels, I argue that both of these texts are largely uniquely Lucan, though 4:14–30 is a relocated pericope reflecting both Mark 6:1–6 and special Lucan material (see the discussion of sources for both texts).

The account is a miracle story that can be classified more precisely as a resuscitation (Bultmann 1963: 215, 233–34; Theissen 1983: 321).[3]

The outline of Luke 7:11–17 is as follows:

a. Setting: a funeral procession in Nain (7:11–12)
b. Jesus' healing with compassion (7:13–15)
c. Public confession of a great prophet (7:16)
d. Report in Judea and the region (7:17)

The account is focused on Jesus' care for the needy and his power over death. Jesus takes the initiative and acts compassionately, choosing healing over defilement. The event results in awe for God's work and a public perception of Jesus as a prophet. As a result, news about Jesus spreads.

Exegesis and Exposition

[11]And it happened ⌜thereafter⌝ that he was going into a city called Nain, and his ⌜disciples⌝ and a great crowd were going with him. [12]As he drew near the city gate, behold, a man who had died, an only begotten son to his mother, was being carried out to burial, and she was a widow; and some crowd from the city was together with her.

[13]And when he saw her, the Lord had compassion on her and said to her, "Do not cry." [14]And when he approached, he touched the bier and those removing the corpse stood still, and he said, "Young man, I say to you, arise." [15]And the dead man sat up and began to talk, and he gave him to his mother. [16]And fear seized all, and they glorified God, saying, "A great prophet is raised up among us" and "God has visited his people." [17]And this report concerning him went out into the whole of Judea and into all the region.

a. Setting: A Funeral Procession in Nain (7:11–12)

7:11 Luke connects this event to the previous one only in very general terms. Ἑξῆς (hexēs, thereafter) is a general time reference when it appears without ἡμέρα (hēmera, day).[4] Jesus comes into Nain with his disciples and other observers.

Nain (Vulgate: Naim) is not the Judean city that Josephus refers to in *Jewish War* 4.9.4–5 §§509–20. Neither does it reflect an imprecise understanding of Palestinian geography, as Fitzmyer (1981:

---

3. Fitzmyer 1981: 656 notes that Luke 8:40–42, 49–56; Acts 9:36–43; and perhaps Acts 20:7–12 also are in this form. That it ends with a confession causes Berger 1984: 312 to classify it as epideixis, so the text's goal is the admiration of Jesus.

4. In this context, ἑξῆς refers to an elided χρόνῳ (time); Bovon 1989: 360 n. 28; BAGD 276 §2; BAA 558 §2.

658) rightly notes against Conzelmann (1960: 46). Mentioned only here in the Bible, Nain was a little town and appears to be located at the site of the modern town of Nein, which now has about two hundred residents.[5] Located in Galilee three miles west of Endor, twenty miles southwest of Capernaum, and six miles southeast of Nazareth (Creed 1930: 103; Godet 1875: 1.340; Fitzmyer 1981: 658 [who wrongly locates it southwest of Nazareth]; Marshall 1978: 284), Nein sits at the foot of so-called Little Hermon over the Valley of Jezreel. Bovon (1989: 360 n. 30) notes that the name *Little Hermon* is probably an erroneous Middle Age equation of this site with Mount Hermon. He thinks that Nain might be located at the foot of Mount Moreh (Judg. 7:1), height 1,700 feet. Others refer to Nebi Dahi or Dešebel Dahī (Midr. Gen. 98.12 [62a]; SB 2:161).

Jesus approached the city and drew near the city gate (πύλη, *pylē*), **7:12** which normally served as a defensive fortification, though this town was so small that the entrance was probably decorative.[6] As Jesus entered, he observed a funeral procession. The Way of Life meets the way of death (Grundmann 1963: 159). The verb ἐκκομίζω (*ekkomizō*, to carry out) is used only here in the NT (BAGD 241; BAA 486; Josephus, *Jewish War* 5.13.7 §567; Fitzmyer 1981: 658; Plummer 1896: 198; on the syntax, see BDF §190.4). Such funerals would proceed out of the city gate or boundary to bury the person outside the city walls, where family cemeteries were located.[7] Funerals usually occurred at the end of the day and often on the day of the death (SB 4:578–92; Marshall 1978: 284; Schürmann 1969: 400; see the exegesis of 7:13). This death involved an only begotten son (μονογενής, *monogenēs*), a detail that Luke frequently notes (8:42; 9:38; Büchsel, *TDNT* 4:739; Marshall 1978: 284–85). The mother was also a widow, something that may have been indicated by her clothing or the absence of a husband in the procession (Stählin, *TDNT* 9:449 n. 81; on p. 450 he notes other texts that show widows crying over the loss of loved ones and the loss of protection).

The description of the woman as widowed and childless is important. She has no family now and in effect is an "orphaned parent."

5. Πόλις is used in its broadest sense of inhabited area here and refers to a village; BAGD 685; BAA 1375 §1; Bovon 1989: 360–61 notes the present size of Nein, as does Schürmann 1969: 399.

6. Jeremias, *TDNT* 6:921. No archeological remains of a gate or of the city wall have yet been found; Nolland 1989: 322.

7. Ṣemaḥot 8–11 (= Zlotnick 1966: 57–80; see Lerner 1987: 389–91), an extratalmudic tractate, deals with the deceased. *M. Ber.* 3.1–2 and *b. Ketub.* 17a say that if a procession is small, one is to interrupt the study of Torah to participate, but if the group is large enough, one should continue studying; SB 1:1047–48. Though the *Ketubot* tractate is late, it reveals the importance to Jews of community involvement in mourning.

The emotion in the verse carries deep pathos. The town shares in the grief as they gather with her. Such mourning was seen as an act of love by one's neighbors and was especially significant where a widow was involved (Jer. 6:26; Amos 8:10; Zech. 12:10; SB 4:578). A sad setting greets Jesus in Nain.

b. Jesus' Healing with Compassion (7:13–15)

7:13   Jesus takes the initiative and addresses the woman as he prepares to deal with her tragic situation. He extends to her a word of comfort and asks her to stop crying. Such weeping for the dead is common in the Bible (Gen. 50:1; Deut. 21:13; 2 Sam. 3:32; Mark 5:38–39; Luke 7:32; John 11:31, 33; 20:11, 13, 15; Acts 9:39; Rengstorf, *TDNT* 3:722). The present imperative μὴ κλαῖε (*mē klaie*) asks her to cease weeping (Fitzmyer 1981: 659). Jesus' comfort will include more than others can give to her, and he will offer more than words (Stählin, *TDNT* 5:822). Luke describes Jesus' reaction as the expression of his compassion (ἐσπλαγχνίσθη, *esplanchnisthē*). Several acts of Jesus are attributed to this motive in the other Gospels.[8] Other Synoptic parallels use σπλαγχνίζομαι where Luke does not (Matt. 14:14 = Mark 6:34 = Luke 9:11; Matt. 15:32 = Mark 8:2 [not in Luke]; not used in Acts). Thus, it is likely that this description came to Luke in his source. Jesus' comforting call to cease crying also has a parallel elsewhere in the tradition (John 11:33).

The description of Jesus as Lord is the first use of κύριος (*kyrios*) in Luke's narrative comments with regard to Jesus (Creed 1930: 103–4). The description presents Jesus with the title that will depict his exalted and authoritative position after his resurrection (Acts 2:33–36). Luke is the only Synoptic writer to use κύριος before the resurrection in narrative editorial notes, and he does it often (Luke 7:19; 10:1, 39, 41; 11:39; 12:42a; 13:15; 17:5, 6; 18:6; 19:8a; 22:61 [twice]; Marshall 1978: 285; Klostermann 1929: 88–89; Foerster, *TDNT* 3:1092–93; Schürmann 1969: 401 n. 99; see the exegesis of 5:8). Κύριος indicates the authority that Jesus had during his earthly ministry (Moule 1966; Franklin 1975: 49–55). Nonetheless, it is a reflective use of the term, since the title does not occur for Jesus within the events of his ministry, though the more ambiguous vocative use does appear (see 5:8; 6:46). Luke looks back and characterizes Jesus' acts in terms of the authority that the disciples later came to understand as a reflection of his earthly ministry.

It is debated whether Luke's use of κύριος is his own or reflects

---

8. Matt. 9:36; 14:14; 15:32; 18:27; 20:34; Mark 1:41; 6:34; 8:2; Plummer 1896: 199; Bovon 1989: 362 nn. 43–44. The other Lucan uses of σπλαγχνίζομαι, Luke 10:33 and 15:20, are both in parables.

his sources. Those who argue that Luke supplied the title observe that he alone uses it this way and that this title is found only in Luke in Matthean-Lucan parallel passages (Luke 7:19; 10:1; 11:39; 12:42; 17:5–6; Vielhauer 1965: 34–36 [repr. pp. 154–56]). Those who argue that the title came to Luke from sources argue that he never has the term in Marcan-Lucan parallels.[9] The answer to this question still seems open (La Potterie 1970). In any case, the title reveals Jesus' authority in this event.

To set the scene, it is important to appreciate the nature of burial customs in Judaism (Safrai 1976a: 773–87). First, a person was not prepared for burial until death was certain (Ṣemaḥot 1 [= Zlotnick 1966: 31–33]). Second, a family tore their garments as a sign of mourning and closed the eyes of the corpse to show that death had come (Ṣemaḥot 1.4 [= Zlotnick 1966: 31]). Third, to prevent deterioration the body was anointed and buried quickly (cf. Acts 5:1–11). Generally not kept overnight in the house (m. Šab. 23.4–5; m. Sanh. 6.5; ʾAbot de Rabbi Nathan A.35 [= Goldin 1955: 143], B.39 [= Saldarini 1975: 236]; t. Neg. 6.2 [= Neusner 1977–86: 6.156]; b. B. Qam. 82b), the corpse was wrapped in cloth on a burial plank, not in a coffin, for all to see (m. Moʿed Qaṭ. 1.6; m. Šab. 23.5; Godet 1875: 1.341). Thus, as Jesus approached the woman, the funeral procession was moving out of town, with the mourners present to bury the visible but covered body.[10] In a normal funeral, the service would end with the Shemaʿ and the family would mourn for thirty days (m. Ber. 3.1; on how feasts affected the mourning period, see m. Moʿed Qaṭ. 3.5, 7–9). The funeral procession was emotional, and the widow's tears in such a setting are quite understandable. But Jesus' action will reverse the mood.

Jesus moves to justify his words of comfort. He moves away from **7:14** the widow and approaches the open plank. Interestingly, whenever the term προσέρχομαι (proserchomai, to approach) is used of Jesus' coming to someone, it precedes his acting with authority (Mark 1:31; Luke 7:14; 9:42; Matt. 28:18; J. Schneider, TDNT 2:684; Marshall 1978: 286). As he arrives, Jesus touches the bier, an act that would bring defilement according to the law (Num. 19:11, 16; Sir. 34:30 [according to NRSV numbering]; Marshall 1978: 286; Danker

9. Marshall 1978: 285 notes that Luke 19:34; 22:61; and 24:3 are not exceptions to this observation, though he also notes that the final decision is still open; Creed 1930: 104. Hahn 1969: 81–82 argues that Luke, though introducing the title himself, reflects traditional usage.

10. On mourners, see m. Meg. 4.3; Danby 1933: 206 nn. 9–10. M. Ketub. 4.4 argues that a minimum of two flutes and one wailing woman should be present; also Ṣemaḥot 12.5 (= Zlotnick 1966: 81). T. Judah 26.3 protests against too much extravagance in the funeral procession for Judah.

1988: 161). Cleanliness is next to godliness except where compassion is required. The term for bier, σορός (*soros*), is used only here in the NT and refers to an open coffin, a plank, where the shrouded and anointed corpse lay.[11] Upon Jesus' touching the plank, the pallbearers stopped. In fact, Jesus may have touched the plank to get them to stop (Plummer 1896: 199).

Jesus addresses the dead young man directly, an act that would be humorous or tragic if we were not dealing with a uniquely empowered man of God. Jesus calls to the dead man with personal authority when he says, Σοὶ λέγω (*soi legō*, I say to you). He calls on the corpse to get up (as he will do also to Jairus's daughter and Lazarus: Mark 5:41 = Luke 8:54; John 11:43). Jesus confronts death and illustrates the extent of his authority (John 5:25; 11:25–27, 42).

7:15 Three simple statements mark the healing. First, the dead man sat up. Two terms are key. Referring to the man as ὁ νεκρός (*ho nekros*, the dead man) adds a note of contrast to stress the healing, since dead people do not usually move! And the reference to ἀνεκάθισεν (*anekathisen*, sat up) makes use of a term that appears elsewhere in the NT only at Acts 9:40, where it refers to Tabitha's resuscitation by Peter (Creed 1930: 104). In fact, this medical term is often used extrabiblically to describe the sitting up of someone who was formerly incapacitated by illness (Klostermann 1929: 89; BAGD 55; BAA 108; LSJ 107; MM 34).

Jesus' effortless call to rise up contrasts with OT examples of resuscitation. Elijah stretched himself three times over the boy he revived (1 Kings 17:21), and Elisha touched his child with his staff and then later lay over him (2 Kings 4:31, 34–35). Resuscitation comes easy to this agent of God.

Second, when the man sat up, he began to talk, a point that indicates a return to life. Again, the response is somewhat different from the OT parallels, where in Elijah's case no response is discussed (1 Kings 17:22) and in Elisha's case where the boy sneezed seven times (2 Kings 4:35). A similar detail about speaking is present in Philostratus, *Life of Apollonius* 4.45 (Marshall 1978: 286; Danker 1988: 162).

Finally, Jesus gave the boy back to his mother. The Greek wording agrees verbatim with 1 Kings 17:23—indicating that Jesus' act parallels the great prophet Elijah. Luke's description of the event notes the OT basis for the popular assessment about Jesus as a great prophet (Luke 7:16).

The relationship between mother and son—broken by death—is

---

11. BAGD 759; BAA 1516; Creed 1930: 104; Gen. 50:26; T. Reub. 7.2; MM 581. A plank is in view because the man arises directly upon Jesus' call.

restored by Jesus (Danker 1988: 162). Plummer (1896: 200) and Van Der Loos (1965: 574–75) refer with appropriate skepticism to attempts to explain the account on a naturalistic basis. This is a healing that reveals God's working. Given the character of the healing, what would the popular response be?

c. Public Confession of a Great Prophet (7:16)

The reaction to the display of God's power yields the normal response of fear, φόβος (phobos). Luke often expresses the emotional reaction to God's work in terms of awe and respect (Luke 1:65; 5:26; 8:25, 37; Acts 2:43; 5:5, 11; 19:17; Klostermann 1929: 89; Fitzmyer 1981: 659; Balz, TDNT 9:209). Such respect for God's work reflects an awareness of the event's uniqueness and honors the majesty of the one who has worked. **7:16**

Though fear was present, one could not look upon such an event without comment. The crowd responded first to acknowledge the healer and then to acknowledge the God who sent him. In recognizing such events, they glorified God, another common Lucan description of a response to God's activity (Luke 5:9, 26; 9:43; 13:13; 17:18; 18:43; 23:47; Ernst 1977: 243–44).

In calling Jesus a great prophet (προφήτης μέγας, prophētēs megas), the crowd recognizes the parallel between Jesus' work and that of Elijah and Elisha. At the least, Jesus is among the upper echelon of prophets. But does this confession describe the great eschatological prophet to come, as Bovon (1989: 364–65) argues, distinguishing Luke's meaning (Elijah revived) from the crowd's (a great prophet)? Cullmann (1963: 30) rightly notes that the absence of the definite article makes unlikely an exclusive reference to this great prophet. In fact, 9:19 makes clear that the crowd's understanding bordered on speculation as to where exactly Jesus fit. Thus, an exclusive reference to the great coming prophet is not the point of 7:16. Neither is there anything messianic in this confession (Fitzmyer 1981: 660; but incorrectly Friedrich, TDNT 6:846). Of course, many of Luke's readers believe that Jesus is a prophet and more, but that is not the point here. The picture of Jesus as a prophet is a fundamental one for Luke, but in the Gospel it is almost always on the lips of others who are trying to grapple with who Jesus is (7:39; 9:8, 19; 24:19; Friedrich, TDNT 6:841; Luke 4:24 is the only exception). Luke is careful here as he indicates how the populace assessed Jesus. According to the witnessing crowd, God has raised up a great prophet. The passive verb ἠγέρθη (ēgerthē, is raised up) looks to God's bringing Jesus onto the historical scene (Acts 13:22; John 7:52; Dan. 8:18; Judg. 2:16, 18; 3:9; Marshall 1978: 286; Fitzmyer 1981: 660). The crowd has responded to the event they have seen, which recalls the great prophets of old and points to the renewal of God's miraculous activity for his people. They are no more specific than that.

In speaking of God's activity, the crowd speaks of God's visitation (ἐπεσκέψατο, *epeskepsato*), a term that Luke has used already to express the visit of the Messiah (Luke 1:68, 78; also Acts 15:14). Later, Luke will note that Israel has missed the visitation (Luke 19:44; Schürmann 1969: 403). Ἐπισκέπτομαι refers to God's gracious activity for his people as he utilizes his power on their behalf (Ruth 1:6; Exod. 4:31; Gen. 21:1; Creed 1930: 104; Beyer, *TDNT* 2:605). Such activity would be an encouragement to people who perceived themselves to be largely absent from God's miraculous activity in recent times (1 Macc. 4:46; 9:27; 14:41; Schürmann 1969: 402 n. 103; Plummer 1896: 200). The expression betrays the people's excitement as they reflect on what is happening. Clearly, Jesus is sent from God for them.

The Elijah motif makes one other key point when it is seen as a Lucan theme: through Jesus, God is coming to the aid of the defenseless (Evans in Evans and Sanders 1993: 70–83). Other Elijah texts in Luke allude to a similar concern (Luke 4:25–27; 7:1–10; 9:52–55, 61–62 [negatively]). Those who feel that they are on the outside or who feel abandoned can sense in Jesus the invitation to experience God's renewed presence and blessing. God is visiting his people again, and those who realize his presence and their need can sense that God has chosen to engage them by his grace through Jesus.

d. Report in Judea and the Region (7:17)

7:17 As is his style, Luke closes with a note about how the news spread widely concerning Jesus (Luke 4:14, 37; Matt. 9:26; Mark 1:28; J. Schneider, *TDNT* 2:679). Here, the news went out into Judea (on the use of ἐν, *en*, with the sense "into," see BDF §218; BDR §218.1.3). As in other passages (Luke 1:65; 4:44; 6:17; 23:5; Acts 2:9; 9:31; 10:37), Ἰουδαία refers to the entire region of Judea and Galilee (Ernst 1977: 244). The term is not specific, but probably includes a reference to the region of Perea and specifically the city of Machaerus, where John the Baptist was imprisoned (Josephus, *Antiquities* 18.5.2 §119; Luke 9:7–9). Machaerus is well to the south of Galilee on the other side of the Jordan River, midway down the east side of the Dead Sea. Perhaps the report of Jesus as a prophet stirred John to send the delegation of 7:18–23. Regardless, news about Jesus was sweeping the region, since it had reached areas far south of Galilee (Fitzmyer 1981: 660; Schweizer 1984: 133).

Summary Jesus' raising the widow of Nain's son in Luke 7:11–17 demonstrates two essential qualities. First, Jesus demonstrates his compassion and willingness to reach out and meet the needs of those in distress. He takes the initiative in this account; he comforts the widow; he restores the boy to health. Second, great power is displayed with great ease. The comfort that he offers the widow is real, because he can overpower death's nullifying effects. The extent of his authority reaches to the limits of personal existence. This account, then, represents Jesus' most powerful display of his connection with God.

The crowd concludes on the basis of OT parallels that Jesus is a great prophet, a confession that raises christological questions about who Jesus is. Luke will take advantage of this confession in the next pericope to pursue the issue of Jesus' identity as reflected in his ministry. It is clear that he has prophetic gift, but is he *the* one to come, the one that John prophesied in 3:15–18? Does Jesus offer more to humanity than merely signaling God's visitation? These are the questions that Luke now plants in the narrative. The resurrection of this young man offers answers in terms of power and praise.

Additional Notes

7:11. Elsewhere Luke does not use ἑξῆς with the preposition ἐν and the feminine (Luke 9:37; Acts 21:1; 25:17; 27:18; Luce 1933: 154; Marshall 1978: 284). Thus, on the basis of Lucan style, the variant ἐν τῇ ἑξῆς is unlikely. If the variant is read, then the event is said to occur "the day after" the encounter with the centurion.

7:11. A variant reading speaks of many (ἱκανοί) disciples present (A, C, Δ, Θ, Ψ, family 13, Byz, Lect, some Itala, some Syriac), but this may be influenced by the use of ἱκανός in 7:12. The UBS–NA text, without ἱκανοί, has Alexandrian, Western, and versional support: $\mathfrak{P}^{75}$, ℵ, B, D, L, W, many Itala, some Syriac, Vulgate, and Coptic.

3. Questions about Jesus and John the Baptist (7:18–35)

Luke 7:18–35 comprises three subunits that deal with John the Baptist. Luke 7:18–23 deals with John's question to Jesus. Jesus' reply defines the nature of the times and appeals to his acts and the OT for proof. Luke 7:24–30 gives Jesus' view of John and explains the greatness of the new kingdom in comparison to John. Luke 7:31–35 is a parable of rebuke against Israel for not responding to John or Jesus, despite their difference in style. Nothing will satisfy some.

For Luke's view of Jesus' relationship to John the Baptist, this unit (along with 3:15–22; 16:16; and 1:1–80) is a key text. John is a bridge figure. He is the last of the great prophets of the old period of promise (7:28). Yet he is also inseparably linked to the new period of Jesus (1:14–17, 76–79). Luke 7 gives the first indication of what Jesus thinks of John. In addition, the passage shows that those observing Jesus are struggling to understand the nature of his ministry.

The major issues of 7:18–35 center on the relationship of John and Jesus (Creed 1930: 104–5):[1] (1) What does Jesus think of himself? (2) What does John think of Jesus? (3) What does Jesus think of John? Jesus' works clearly show that he is involved in bringing in the eschaton, since his actions parallel promises made by Isaiah about that period (Isa. 29:18; 35:5; 42:6; 61:1). In fact, the description recalls the Servant of the Lord figure of Luke 4:18–19, who Jesus said was fulfilled in him. Danker (1988: 163) argues that in Luke's Gospel Jesus—not John the Baptist—is Elijah, but the use of Mal. 3:1 in Luke 7:27 to describe John makes this view difficult. It is true that Jesus is the end-time reformer, but Luke clearly compares John to Elijah (Luke 1:17; Webb 1991: 65–66). In Jesus' view, John is the greatest prophet of the old period, but he also is the one who prepares the way for Jesus (7:26–28). Nevertheless, all who follow Jesus will be greater than this forerunner.

The relationship of John and Jesus is later clarified by Luke in Acts 19:1–7, with its mention of disciples who knew only of John's

---

1. Putting Luke 7 in the larger context of 6:20–8:18, Bovon 1989: 369 notes the mix of speaking (6:20–49; 7:18–35; 8:4–18) and action (7:1–17, 36–50), with a summary in 8:1–3. Word and deed are side by side as Jesus moves through Galilee. The arrangement is Luke's, since there is a mix of material from Mark and Matthew, as well as unique Lucan material.

baptism. Luke uses this text to explain how John fit into God's plan as unfolded in Jesus and to deal with any disciples who still found the focus on Jesus hard to accept. It is important, however, to note that these disciples did not struggle with full transition to Jesus once they had heard the whole gospel.[2]

The key question is this: "Is Jesus the Coming One?" This messianic question looks back to Luke 3:15–18. All efforts to limit Jesus' role in 7:18–35 to the eschatological prophet fail. In fact, one could argue that the same messianic emphasis is found in Matthew, though not as explicitly, for if John is greater than a prophet (Matt. 11:9) and Jesus is greater than John, what category is left for Jesus but Messiah?

Another major interpretive question in Luke 7 is the reason that John asks his question (Arndt 1956: 209). Fitzmyer (1981: 664–65) discusses five views in detail, but there are two basic positions:[3] (1) John is trying to engender faith in his disciples (Chrysostom, *Homilies on Matthew* 36 [on Matt. 11:2] [*PG* 57:413–15]; Augustine, *Sermones ad Populum* 66.3–4 [*PG*, 1st series, 38:432–33]); or (2) John is asking for confirmation of Jesus' mission, because he doubts that Jesus is the "one to come"; the doubt is mainly due to the lack of any political or judgment activity in Jesus' ministry (Tertullian, *Against Marcion* 4.18.4–6; Godet 1875: 1.345; Marshall 1978: 289). In favor of the second approach are the allusion to offense in 7:23 and John the Baptist's earlier reference in 3:7–18 to the power and authority of the "one who follows him."

A misdirected description of this passage is to call it John's first step of faith in the Lucan portrayal (Creed 1930: 105; see the exegesis of 7:19 and view 1 there). Luke 1:40–45 speaks against this description, as does, more importantly, the thrust of 3:15–22.[4]

---

2. Why these disciples were in the dark about the Spirit's coming is not made clear in Acts 19. The point seems to be that they did not know about Pentecost. Though many say that these are disciples of John the Baptist, that point is not clear from Acts 19. They may be disciples of Jesus who did not yet know about the Spirit.

3. Fitzmyer's other three options are (1) the question is positive and is John's first hint that he knows who Jesus is (on this, see below); (2) the passage is a reproach by the early church to John's disciples for not responding to Jesus; and (3) the question is a real query, but is not messianic, a view just discussed above and rejected. The passage cannot be a reproach from the early church to John's disciples since the disciples who know only John are not pictured as rejecting Jesus in Luke–Acts, but as responding to him upon hearing about him and without knowing about the Spirit (Acts 19:1–7). If there is such a conflict in the background, Luke has kept it totally hidden.

4. It must be noted, however, that Luke is less explicit about John's awareness of the voice at the baptism than is Matt. 3:17. Luke is not clear about who heard the heavenly endorsement.

John's question is not positive for Luke, but is a query raised out of uncertainty, as 7:23 suggests. Once John had the feeling that Jesus was God's agent, the issue became for him the character of Jesus' ministry. Was Jesus really bringing God's promise with his style of ministry? This style was not what John expected, and this question was asked by others as well. Thus, the second view—that John was seeking confirmation of Jesus' ministry—is best. Jesus' messianic style has raised questions about him. John is not asked to take a first step of faith, but is to be reassured about Jesus. In that sense, he is representative of a reader like Theophilus, who also needs reassurance (1:1–4).

Beyond the nature of Jesus' ministry, Luke makes a final point in 7:31–35. The variety of styles of ministry by God's envoys is not the real cause for some rejecting God's way. John and Jesus had different styles: one ministered in the desert as an ascetic, while the other roamed freely among the people and approached the rejected and sinful of society. Yet both were still rejected by many. Indeed, the response to John was a test of one's response to Jesus. To reject one was to reject the other. In addition, John's rejection was not because of his style, but because of his message. When the style changed, the message was still rejected. The passage argues that one should take note because after Jesus there is no other.

Sources and Historicity (7:18–23)

Luke 7:18–35 has a parallel in Matt. 11:2–19 (Aland 1985: §§106–7). The placement in Matthew is slightly later in terms of the movement of Jesus' ministry, since in Matthew this discussion about John follows sayings that Luke has later.[5] On other occasions, Luke places in a later position remarks that Matthew has earlier (Matt. 10:37–38 = Luke 14:25–27; Matt. 10:34–36 = Luke 12:51–53; Matt. 10:26–33 = Luke 12:2–9; Matt. 10:1–16 = Luke 9:2–5). Carson (1984: 260) suggests that Matthew's arrangement in Matt. 11–13 may be thematic, as in other portions of his work. On the other hand, the sayings in Luke's "journey" section also may have a thematic structure at times. It is difficult to determine the account's exact placement in Jesus' ministry, but it clearly predates Peter's great confession and falls in the latter period of Jesus' early ministry in Galilee, when questions existed about the character of his ministry.

The source of the tradition is usually attributed to Q, since the account is

5. For example, Luke 8:1 and 10:16, whose Matthean parallels come before Matt. 11:2–19 in Matt. 9:35 and 10:40. These accounts are a summary and a proverbial saying, so placement is hard to determine.

shared with Matthew and is very close to Matthew in wording.[6] At the least, the tradition that both writers used has similar origins. Creed (1930: 104) believes that Q is the source and that the origin of that tradition is Palestine. The reason for attributing the tradition to Palestine is that concern for John as a major figure would have been focused there. Marshall (1978: 288), Nolland (1989: 326–27), Witherington (1990: 42–43, 165), and Kümmel (1957: 109–11) argue for the account's authenticity. There is no reason to attribute its origin to the early church, especially since the respected John the Baptist is pictured as wrestling with the character of Jesus' ministry, even though he is God's prophet.

The Jesus Seminar (Funk and Hoover 1993: 301–2) also recognizes the tradition's contact and close agreement with Q. However, they argue that the christological claim defended from Scripture reflects an early church concern, so they reject the authenticity of 7:22–23, printing it in black type. Apparently the assumption is that questions about Jesus' person arose only after he had passed away, an unlikely scenario in light of Jesus' activity during his life. Surely Jesus would have reflected upon and appealed to Scripture to explain who he was. The indirect style of Jesus' reply also fits his style in dealing with the messianic questions in his ministry (e.g., 9:18–21). The remarks reflect the kind of reply that Jesus would make to such a query.

Sources and Historicity (7:24–30)

Luke 7:24–27 contains wording almost parallel to Matt. 11:7b–10, while Matt. 11:7a and 11:11 are parallel to Luke's account in sense but with slightly distinct vocabulary (Aland 1985: §107; Bovon 1989: 370 n. 11 notes the parallel to Gospel of Thomas 78). As noted above, most see Luke and Matthew sharing a similar source (Q) at this point.

Luke 7:29–30 has no Synoptic parallel, but is Luke responsible for this summary or has he received it through the tradition? Marshall (1978: 297) seems to favor its presence in Q, but also notes that Luke's hand has been at work in the text. Fitzmyer (1981: 670–71) argues that these verses can hardly have come from Q and are either from a special Lucan source or from Luke's hand. It is hard to establish the precise literary source of this summary, given how little evidence is available. The remarks in these parenthetical verses could well be Lucan.

Though there are challenges to some elements of the historical portrayal of this account, almost all hold to its general historical value. Even a more skeptical work like Crossan's (1991: 236–37) accepts the authenticity of this material. Fitzmyer (1981: 671) seems to question the historicity of

---

6. For Q as the basic source, see Schürmann 1969: 413, 418; Marshall 1978: 287; Fitzmyer 1981: 662–63; Tiede 1988: 153; Wiefel 1988: 148; Bovon 1989: 369. Those who prefer Matthean priority argue that Luke used Matthew. Luke 7:20–21, 29–30 does not have a parallel in Matthew.

7:28b with its assertion about the "least in the kingdom," because of the way it qualifies 7:28a (so also Bultmann 1963: 164–66). Marshall (1978: 293) notes that John is not denigrated by the statement, but rather the importance of Jesus and the times are elevated by it. In fact, the statement reflects an antithetical parallelism, a balance that is lacking if the statement is removed as inauthentic. Questions are also raised about whether Jesus would use the OT so directly (Mal. 3:1 in Luke 7:27; so Bultmann 1963: 165 calls the parallel Matt. 11:10 "intrusive"). But such objections prejudge too greatly what Jesus did and did not do. Numerous pericopes show Jesus making these kinds of associations and using the OT this way. Only *a priori* judgments deny that Jesus could say this (13:35; 19:46; 20:17). Suggesting that the pericope's messianic flavor is a reflection of the early church, Fitzmyer (1981: 672) argues that Judaism had no hope of Elijah as the precursor of Messiah (he cites *m. ʿEd.* 8.7; *m. B. Meṣ.* 1.8; *m. Šeqal.* 2.5). But is this decisive? If Elijah is related to the eschaton as restorer and peacemaker through Malachi, then can a messianic figure be far away? If Jesus saw himself as greater than Elijah, who else can he be than the greater eschatological restorer? If in any sense Jesus saw John in terms of Elijah or Mal. 3, then this dilemma remains for the nonmessianic position. Thus, as in other texts, Fitzmyer downplays the messianic element too greatly. Finally, the strength of the remarks about John speak for authenticity. Would the church invent such unqualified praise like that in 7:28a?

The Jesus Seminar (Funk and Hoover 1993: 301–2) varies in its assessment of these sayings. Luke 7:24–25 (pink type) is tied to Jesus because in the seminar's view it fits Jesus' social critique of the leadership. Luke 7:26–27 (black type) is rejected because it has no parallel in the Gospel of Thomas and its "forerunner to Messiah" Christology is deemed to be too explicit (for the same reasons given above by others who question its historicity; see my answer to this objection above). Luke 7:28 is presented in gray type, reflecting uncertainty about its authenticity. The seminar admits that the exaltation of John as "the greatest born of women" is not likely to have been a creation of the early church, but it regards 7:28b as problematic and so doubts the whole verse. The handling of this verse illustrates how the Jesus Seminar does not give the Gospel tradition any benefit of the doubt. If Jesus believed his coming brought the eschaton and that John was a bridge to the great new era, nothing in this verse is problematic. The Gospel tradition surrounding the Baptist makes this assumption likely and questions any approach that rejects the credibility of this verse.

Sources and Historicity (7:31–35)

Luke 7:31–35 is present in Matt. 11:16–19 (Aland 1985: §107). The two accounts have similar wording, though there are enough differences, especially in Luke 7:31, 35, to suggest the presence of distinct, but related traditions (for details, see the exegesis). These are two summaries of the same discourse.

In assessing this material, the origin of 7:31–32 in Jesus' ministry has never been seriously challenged (Marshall 1978: 297). However, that the parable's setting applied originally to John and Jesus has been rejected (Bultmann 1963: 172, 199; Fitzmyer 1981: 678; Suggs 1970: 34). It is argued that parables do not normally come with an interpretation and that titles such as Son of Man and wisdom reflect early church theology (e.g., the Jesus Seminar in discussing the son of Adam [= Son of Man] prints the parable in gray type; Funk and Hoover 1993: 302). Others, however, see the material as authentic, with no need to argue that the early church had a creative role in its origination (Jeremias 1963a: 160–62; Marshall 1978: 298; Witherington 1990: 49). Neither the association of the Son of Man nor the connection to wisdom in the passage is a problem (on the Son of Man, see the exegesis of 5:24 and excursus 6; on Jesus as wisdom, see the exegesis of 11:49). The association of Jesus as a glutton and wine drinker is unlikely to have been created by the early church, so that the material's setting does fit Jesus' ministry (Perrin 1967: 120).

The account is a pronouncement story, for Jesus' teaching is the key to the unit (Fitzmyer 1981: 663). The unit actually mixes pronouncement (7:18–23), discourse (7:24–30), and parable (7:31–35) (Berger 1984: 49–50, 81–82 views the account as apophthegm and parable). The remarks are triggered by a question, so the initiative for Jesus' teaching comes from outside. Luke 7:18–23 shows that the crowd's judgment of Jesus as "a great prophet" falls short (Klostermann 1929: 89). As the performer of works of the eschaton, he is more than a prophet.

In 7:24–30, Luke turns from the nature of Jesus' ministry to Jesus' view of John: 7:24–28 shows Jesus calling on his audience to reflect on John the Baptist's role in God's plan, and 7:29–30 is a parenthetical transition into Jesus' comparison of John and himself in the following parable of 7:31–35. It notes the differing reactions to the Baptist's ministry. The passage's major burden is to connect John to the eschatological forerunner of Mal. 3:1, who possesses an Elijah-like ministry. Yet, John's roots in the old era or, better, his role as a transition figure makes him of less significance than anyone who participates in the new era that Jesus brings. The unit, then, stresses the greatness of the fulfillment period. John is a prophet, indeed more than a prophet, a precursor, but he is less than anyone who currently shares in the kingdom of God.

In 7:31–35 Jesus uses a parable to evaluate the generation to which John ministered. The tone is harsh and represents a rebuke of those who chose not to follow John's call. One could call this "the parable of the brats," to show the remark's tone. The generation is compared to children who are unhappy about how things are being done and so refuse to go along. The number of those not responding is large enough that Jesus can characterize them as an entire generation. Only the note (7:35) that wisdom has children adds a positive element. Here is a reminder that some do respond to God's wise counsel and share as family in the benefits of his path.

The outline of Luke 7:18–35 is as follows:

  a. John's question to Jesus about his ministry (7:18–23)
    i. Setting of John's question (7:18–19)
    ii. John's question asked by the envoys (7:20)
    iii. Setting of Jesus' reply (7:21)
    iv. Jesus' reply: call to trust and Old Testament pictures (7:22–23)
  b. Jesus' view of John (7:24–30)
    i. What the crowds did not journey to see (7:24–25)
    ii. John described (7:26–28)
      (1) What John is (7:26–27)
      (2) His greatness and lowliness (7:28)
    iii. Contrasting reactions to John (7:29–30)
      (1) Reception by tax collectors (7:29)
      (2) Rejection by Pharisees (7:30)
  c. Jesus' view of this generation (7:31–35)
    i. Parable of complaining children (7:31–32)
    ii. Application: current rejection of John and Jesus (7:33–34)
    iii. Appeal to wisdom's children (7:35)

Themes abound in this section. Jesus' work testifies to his position as Servant of the Lord, the one to come. The time of eschaton is evidenced by Jesus' works. But even the Baptist struggles to come to grips with the nature of Jesus' ministry. Jesus' work—as much as his words—speaks to the time. This latter theme is like that in John's Gospel. A look at John the Baptist shows that he is a prophet and more than a prophet. He is the Elijah-like forerunner. Yet everyone in the kingdom is greater than this greatest among the prophets. Such is the greatness of the time of fulfillment.

In addition, a contrast reappears between the religious leaders' rejection and the despised tax collectors' reception of John. To reject John is to reject God's plan. The form of John's and Jesus' ministries is not the reason for rejection. Nonetheless, some do respond and show the rightness of God's way in their choice. Jesus' choice to minister to sinners who are sensitive to their sin is a part of God's wisdom, as 7:36–50 also illustrates.

Exegesis and Exposition

[18]And John's disciples proclaimed to him concerning all of these things. And calling two of his disciples, John [19]sent them to ⌜Jesus⌝, saying, "Are you the one who comes or are we to look for ⌜another⌝?" [20]And when the men came to Jesus they said, "John the Baptist sent us to you, saying, 'Are you the one who comes or are we to look for another?' " [21]In that hour he healed many from disease and plagues and evil spirits, and he bestowed sight on many that were blind. [22]And he replied to them, "Go tell John what things you have seen and heard: the blind see, the lame walk, lepers are cleansed, and the deaf hear, the dead are raised, and the poor are hearing the good news, [23]and blessed is the one who is not offended in me."

[24]After the messengers of John departed, he began to speak to the crowd concerning John, "What ⌜did you go out⌝ into the desert to see? A reed blown by the wind? [25]But what ⌜did you go out⌝ to see? A man wearing soft clothing? Behold, those who are beautifully clothed and live in luxury are in the king's courts. [26]But what ⌜did you go out⌝ to see? A prophet? Yes, I say to you, more than a prophet. [27]This is the one concerning whom it is written, 'Behold I am sending my messenger before you, who shall prepare your way before you.' [28]I say to you, ⌜no one⌝ born of women is greater than John, but the least in the kingdom of God is greater than he is." ([29]And when all the people and tax collectors heard, they justified God, by being baptized with the baptism of John. [30]But the Pharisees and lawyers rejected for themselves the counsel of God, by not being baptized by him.)

[31]"To what shall I compare the men of this generation, and what are they like? [32]They are like children who are sitting in the market and who call out to one another, 'We played the flute for you, and you did not dance; we wailed, and you did not weep.' [33]For John the Baptist is come not eating bread or drinking wine, and you say, 'He has a demon.' [34]The Son of Man is come eating and drinking, and you say, 'Behold, a glutton and drunkard, a lover of tax collectors and sinners.' [35]And wisdom is justified by its children."

a. John's Question to Jesus about His Ministry (7:18–23)
i. Setting of John's Question (7:18–19)

Luke's introduction to this section, unlike its Matthean parallel, does not mention John's presence in prison. However, the difference is merely stylistic recasting by Luke in light of his earlier note (3:19–20) that John is in prison (Marshall 1978: 289; Klostermann 1929: 89). Restating John's location now is unnecessary. John's disciples reported to him about Jesus' healings, preaching, and teaching. The extent of the report is indicated by the phrase περὶ πάντων τούτων (*peri pantōn toutōn*, concerning all of these things). The activity of

7:18

texts like 7:1–17 is in view. Josephus notes that Herod the Great imprisoned John at Machaerus, a restored fortress east of the Dead Sea (*Antiquities* 18.5.2 §119; Fitzmyer 1981: 478).

Luke supplies another detail that Matthew does not have: John sends two witnesses to Jesus, which may reflect Deut. 19:15 (Fitzmyer 1981: 665; Danker 1988: 163). If so, then the truthfulness of the witnesses' report given back to John after their visit with Jesus will be guaranteed.[7]

7:19   Upon accepting the text as defended in the additional notes, our key issue centers on why John questioned Jesus. Various views exist on the rationale behind the question:

1. Luce (1933: 155) and Creed (1930: 105) argue that John is hopeful here rather than doubting. John is just now beginning to understand who Jesus is, so he is checking to see if his inference is correct. But to come to this view Luce challenges the historicity of Matt. 3:14–15, as well as of John 1:29. If either of these passages is historical, then seeing John's first flicker of faith here cannot be correct.

2. Liefeld (1984: 900–901) argues that John's doubt is fueled not only by the reports of Jesus' ministry lacking political organization, but also by John's presence in prison, a situation that seems the reverse of "freeing captives from prison," as Jesus' ministry is described in 4:18–19. This difference raises questions for John (Godet 1875: 1.345; Hendriksen 1978: 392–93; Fitzmyer 1981: 664).

3. Plummer (1896: 202), arguing against a view that sees pure doubt as the issue, prefers to argue that John is impatient with Jesus' progress (also Geldenhuys 1951: 226). The problem with this explanation is that impatience is not the issue; Jesus is. Again, it is more natural to see doubt produced by pressure as the background to the question.

4. Arndt (1956: 209) argues that it is John's disciples whose faith needs strengthening. He suggests that 7:22–23 provides no reason to attribute doubt to John. But if a reference to offense is included in what Jesus says to John, then it seems forced not to include John among those who struggle. Even disciples like Peter did not comprehend the full character of Jesus' ministry early on (Matt. 16:22–23).

---

7. The phrase καὶ προσκαλεσάμενος δύο τινὰς τῶν μαθητῶν αὐτοῦ ὁ Ἰωάννης (and calling two of his disciples, John . . .) is in 7:18 in the UBS–NA text and in 7:19 in the Majority Text. English translations also reflect this dual placement: in 7:18: NRSV, GNB, JB/NJB, NIV, NAB; in 7:19: RSV, NEB/REB, ASV, KJV, NASB, Moffatt, Goodspeed.

5. A more skeptical view argues that this account shows that John did not baptize Jesus in order to point to his messianic office since, if he had, the question would not have been raised (Plummer 1896: 202 and Nolland 1989: 326 note this view and tie it to Strauss 1972: 219–34 [originally 1835], who sees Jesus simply baptized as a disciple of John). But such skepticism is not supportable when many accounts indicate that various figures wrestled with the nature of Jesus' ministry even after long exposure to him and confession of him. The account's embarrassing honesty makes its historicity likely. Would the church create such an embarrassing question?

Given that the question's cause is doubt, who then is the Coming One (ὁ ἐρχόμενος, *ho erchomenos*)? For some, the reference to the Coming One, though looking back to 3:15–16, is vague (Luce 1933: 155). There are many figures in Judaism who were seen as coming (Fitzmyer 1981: 666). In this context the possibilities are (1) a great prophet (Luke 7:16; 1QS 9.11; 4QPBless 3), (2) the great prophet of Mal. 3:1 and 4:5 [3:1, 23 MT] (Fitzmyer 1981: 666; Stuhlmacher 1968: 218–25), or (3) the Messiah (Liefeld 1984: 902 [cites John 6:14; 11:27]; Tiede 1988: 153; Marshall 1978: 290 [calls the term vaguely messianic]; J. Schneider, *TDNT* 2:670; Maurer, *TDNT* 6:726).

Luke's answer is clear in light of Luke 3:15–16. John refers to the Coming One because of a question about Messiah. Fitzmyer (1981: 666) argues that this view of Luke 3 does not reflect the original historical context. But it is hard to recast these materials as referring simply to an eschatological figure without reshaping several different traditions, some of which relate to John. Also, 19:38 and 13:35 use the title to refer to a messianic figure (Bock 1987: 112–13, 118, 125). Messianic hope—or, minimally, eschatological hope—is the issue. The question seems to be, "What kind of Messiah would Jesus be, if he is Messiah?" The style of Jesus' messianic mission did not match most forms of Jewish eschatological expectation, producing confusion and doubt. The messianic explanation is natural enough and avoids recasting much traditional material. Old Testament images behind the title include Isa. 40:10; Dan. 7:13 [Theodotion]; Hab. 2:3; and Mal. 3:1; but no explicit quotation is present (Ernst 1977: 246).[8] Ellis

---

8. Schürmann 1969: 408 n. 8, 409 argues that John's question speaks of kingdom hope in general. John's question was, "Do you bring the kingdom and the promise of God?" This may be a correct way to view the question's force, but behind it must lie a messianic implication, when the other options are rejected. This may be why Marshall 1978: 290 speaks of a vague messianic expectation. Wiefel 1988: 149 notes two options for "Coming One": an allusion to Dan. 7:13 [Theodotion] with its apocalyptic judge or to Hab. 2:3, which at Qumran was used with apocalyptic, eschatological force. On Hab. 2:3, see Strobel 1961: 265–77.

(1974: 120) notes that the Coming One was a messianic title in later Judaism (SB 4:858, 860). The question raised here is repeated often in this portion of Luke (7:49; 9:9, 18; Schweizer 1984: 135), and it shows Luke's desire to keep the question of who Jesus is at the forefront. John simply wants to know if Jesus is the expected end-time Messiah. Is he more than the populace thinks (7:16)?

ii. John's Question Asked by the Envoys (7:20)

7:20 Luke 7:20–21 is unique to Luke and shows the question repeated exactly in the form of 7:19—repetition that demonstrates the fundamental nature of this question. Marshall (1978: 290) and Schürmann (1969: 410) argue that Matthew abbreviated his account as was his custom, while others see Luke's expansive hand here.[9] Again it is hard to be sure where the differences lie, but the case for Lucan expansion, outside a term or two of description, is not that strong. Matthean reduction is a better possibility. Regardless, the emphasis intended by the repetition cannot be missed.

John is described as ὁ βαπτιστής (*ho baptistēs*, the baptizer), which summarizes how he was seen (Matt. 3:1; 11:11; 14:2; 17:13; Mark 1:4; 6:14; Luke 7:33; 9:19; Oepke, *TDNT* 1:545). The envoys are portrayed as faithful, for upon their arrival they ask the very question that John gave to them. Παραγίνομαι (*paraginomai*, to arrive, come to) is common in Luke (BAGD 613; BAA 1240–41; twenty-eight of thirty-seven NT uses are in Luke–Acts). It may evidence Luke's hand in the dramatic description of these events, a description that seems natural enough. John was interested in who Jesus was. What would Jesus say?

iii. Setting of Jesus' Reply (7:21)

7:21 In a parenthetical comment, Luke gives the historical setting of Jesus' reply to John. The reference is unique to Luke, though Matthew implies something similar when he speaks of what John's disciples saw (Matt. 11:4; Alford 1874: 506–7). Thus, Luke does not make John's disciples eyewitnesses (but so implies Creed 1930: 106). Luke just makes the point more explicit. The question's setting mentions a variety of healings and exorcisms that show Jesus' authority. The remark also serves to explain why Luke has concentrated on these types of works (Danker 1988: 164). However, the review's lack of attachment to the resurrection of 7:11–17 and the absence of a previous healing of a blind person are against Luke's

---

9. Schürmann 1969: 410 n. 18, 396 n. 49 cites Matthean contraction in 12:2–6, 46–50; 8:14–15, 28–34; 9:18–26; 14:2; 18:1. On arguments for Lucan expansion, see the additional note on 7:20–21.

being responsible for the verse, since that tie would be an obvious one to make.

The list is selective, but representative. It shows the types of things that John was hearing (7:18; Fitzmyer 1981: 667). Ὥρᾳ (*hōra*; lit., hour) refers to a specific recent period of Jesus' ministry during which these events occurred (seventeen times in Luke [e.g., 2:38; 10:21; 12:12]; twenty-one times in Matthew; twelve times in Mark). The envoys saw and heard these activities according to Luke 7:22 (Creed 1930: 106), and they would be eyewitnesses to the answer that Jesus sent to John (Schürmann 1969: 410).

The two terms for illness seem to depict a slight escalation: νόσος (*nosos*) is a general term for illness (BAGD 543; BAA 1100; eleven times in the NT), while μάστιξ (*mastix*) refers to particularly painful afflictions (BAGD 495; BAA 1003; Mark 3:10; 5:29, 34), although it can also refer to torture (Acts 22:24; Heb. 11:36). These illnesses are distinguished from demon possession, as noted in the exegesis of 4:33–34 (see also 8:2 and 11:26; for other healing summaries see 4:40–41 and 6:18; Schürmann 1969: 410 n. 22; Marshall 1978: 290; against Fitzmyer 1981: 667, who argues for no distinction).

The verb ἐχαρίσατο (*echarisato*, to give freely), related to χάρις (*charis*, grace), places the emphasis on the free or gracious exercise of Jesus' power that enables the blind to see: "He graced many with sight" (Plummer 1896: 203). Among the Synoptics, only Luke uses the verb (three times in Luke [7:21, 42, 43] and four times in Acts [3:14; 25:11, 16; 27:24]; Fitzmyer 1981: 668); otherwise only Paul uses it in the NT (sixteen times). This verb shows Jesus' carrying out the ministry described in Luke 4:18–19. It thus links Jesus' activity to that of the Servant figure of Isa. 61, a passage to which further allusion will be made in Luke 7:22. It is another way to refer to the merciful character of God's visit through the horn of David's house (1:68–69), since grace and mercy are both key concepts of the Messiah's activities.

iv. Jesus' Reply: Call to Trust and Old Testament Pictures (7:22–23)

7:22 The envoys are simply to report what they have seen and heard (ἀπαγγέλλω, *apangellō*, to report, occurs twenty-six times in Luke–Acts, eleven of them in Luke; Schniewind, *TDNT* 1:66). The wording in Luke is almost exactly that of Matt. 11:4–5 (Marshall 1978: 291). Matthew has more vivid present tenses ("are hearing and seeing"), repeats the name Jesus, and uses καί (*kai*, and) between each member of the list, but the essential sense is the same. The list's significance is that every activity is a healing of some kind, except the last item about preaching good news to the poor. The phrase πτωχοὶ εὐαγγελίζονται (*ptōchoi euangelizontai*) stands out, not only because it comes last and so functions climactically, but also because of its distinct character (Danker 1988: 164). It alludes to Isa. 61:1 in Luke 4:18 and also looks to Luke 6:20, which gives a beatitude to the poor. Jesus tells John the same thing that he has proclaimed publicly. The miracles depict the arrival of a special time. Blessing is not only individual; it points to a special time period.

The OT background to the list of miracles is found in various Isaianic passages: 35:5–6; 26:19; 29:18–19; and 61:1 (Jeremias 1971a: 103–5; Bock 1987: 112–13, 321; Schürmann 1969: 410 speaks of a "cry of Jubilee" or a "song of salvation" here).[10] In addition, resurrection has just occurred with the widow of Nain's son. The remarks in this summary verse are intended to refer to literal acts of healing and restoration (e.g., healing the blind: Matt. 9:30; 12:22; 15:31; 20:33; Mark 8:25; John 9:10, 25; Schrage, *TDNT* 8:287 §E.II.1). These events show the presence of the eschaton (Isa. 35:5–6 is a picture of paradise, when God's rule is fully manifested; Jeremias, *TDNT* 5:772), for that is the period to which all these Isaianic passages allude. These OT texts look for God's deliverance and the events described in them point to such a decisive time. But does the focus on a specific time and on miraculous events answer John's question about Jesus? There are three ways to construe the reply:

1. Jesus' reply is nonmessianic (Fitzmyer 1981: 667). Jesus is seen as neither affirming nor denying that he is the prophet of the eschaton, *Elias redivivus*. This approach ties into the interpretation of the Coming One and argues that Jesus gives an implied yes to a nonmessianic question (for a rejection of this view, see the exegesis of 7:19). The sense is, "I have come, but not as the fiery reformer you expected." Jesus' answer is not as evasive as this approach suggests.

2. Judaism did expect Messiah to do miraculous works in the eschaton and, thus, Jesus' reply is explicitly messianic. Berger (1973–74) and Duling (1975) trace a Son of David expectation developed on a Solomon typology (see 18:38–39). If such tradition existed (and it seems possible), then Jesus' reply is explicit.

3. Jesus implicitly alludes to a messianic function (Leaney 1958: 145; Godet 1875: 1.347; Arndt 1956: 210; Schürmann 1969: 412, 409 n. 15; Marshall 1978: 292 [who is less explicit, noting that Jesus does not just declare good news, he brings it]). The

10. Only the reference to lepers is not found in these OT texts; Schürmann 1969: 412.

healing points to the messianic age, the great figure of which is Messiah.[11] If the age is present, so is its main figure. The events testify to the presence of a messianic figure like that described in Luke 4:18–19. In fact, Plummer (1896: 203) suggests that the allusion to Isa. 61:1 and preaching clearly indicates that Messiah is in view, not just a prophet.

Either of the last two explanations could be correct. Each answers the question, "Yes, Jesus is the Coming One, the Messiah," though view 2 is more explicit.

Jesus offers a general beatitude that includes John, but goes beyond **7:23** him. Jesus makes a call to faith that is focused only on himself. Anyone (ὃς ἐάν, *hos ean*) not offended by Jesus is blessed. Μακάριος (*makarios*, blessed) is singular, which individualizes the application and focuses on John contextually (Plummer 1896: 203). However, the combination μακάριος and ὃς ἐάν opens Jesus' remark to anyone who responds. It functions as a call, not only to John, but to all who encounter Jesus' remark, including Luke's readers.

Σκανδαλίζω (*skandalizō*) literally means to trip up or be entrapped, but here it is used figuratively of someone who refuses to accept Jesus' claims or to draw near to him. This person is entrapped in sin or tripped up by it (Plummer 1896: 203; BAGD 752–53; BAA 1504–5; Stählin, *TDNT* 7:344, 349–50, 352–55; in Luke only here and 17:2; in the NT twenty-nine times). The terms σκανδαλίζω and σκάνδαλον (*skandalon*) are frequently used in this sense and are often connected with the key OT text Isa. 8:14 (Rom. 9:33; 1 Cor. 1:23; 1 Pet. 2:8). Mark 14:29 illustrates this usage graphically and ironically in describing the fall of Peter, though he later was restored by Jesus.

The key to this beatitude is its personal focus on Jesus. He is the issue, and those who will deal with what God is doing must deal with him. Those who doubt are called to trust in him. It may well be that the absence of a direct word of judgment in Jesus' teaching is part of what threw John off the track (Schürmann 1969: 412). For John, the ax lay at the foot of the tree (Luke 3:9). Such judgment is implied in Jesus' teaching, but it is not the focus of his early public message. John's question is, "Where is the great apocalyptic judge and deliverer?" Jesus' reply shows that his current focus is more a "missionary" concern, since he stresses reaching out to people with good news (9:51–56). This does not mean that judgment is absent;

11. Later Jewish tradition shows a connection between the eschaton and healing: *Pesikta Rabbati* 15.22 (= Braude 1968: 336–37), where Isa. 35:5–6 is used; *Aggadat Bereshit* 69.1 [47b] (see Strack and Stemberger 1991: 339); possibly 1QH 18.14–15.

judgment for those who reject will emerge later, especially in Luke 11–13. In fact, judgment is present all the time, since for some to be blessed means that others are not blessed. When Jesus faces the Jewish leadership's rejection of him, the consequences of that rejection and how Jesus will deal with it will be clear.

b. Jesus' View of John (7:24–30)
i. What the Crowds Did Not Journey to See (7:24–25)

7:24 John's disciples depart and Jesus turns to the crowd to ask some revealing questions about the Baptist. Some suggest that Jesus makes the comments publicly because of the implied rebuke of John in 7:23 (Hendriksen 1978: 395). But it is not entirely clear that 7:22–23 involves a public reply. Jesus may have spoken privately to the messengers. What may have spurred the public response in 7:24–25 is simply the visit of the envoys, since word of their presence may have spread to the crowd.

The questions in 7:24–25 characterize the public reaction to John, whom they associated with the desert (1:80; 3:2, 7; Fitzmyer 1981: 673). Are the remarks figurative pictures of John or are they literal references to the desert and clothes?

The rhetorical questions, if ultimately figurative in force, raise the issue of who John is. First, he is not like a reed (κάλαμος, *kalamos*; BAGD 398; BAA 808–9) that is easily blown about.[12] The figure says that John is neither ordinary nor spineless nor uncertain. That characteristic is not what drove people to go miles to see and hear him. Rather, he was a man of conviction. His arrest by Herod for condemning the ruler's marriage showed his resolve. Taken figuratively, the question stresses John's character and prepares for Jesus' confession of who John is (7:26–27). Marshall (1978: 294) notes that the reed was seen as tender in proverbial contexts.[13]

If the question is literal, then the reference simply notes that people did not journey out to the wilderness merely to see the Jordan River's vegetation (Danker 1988: 166; Godet 1875: 1.348–49; Luce 1933: 157). Taken literally, the question is ironic and notes that more than the scenery drew them to the wilderness. It is hard to know which sense is intended, though a literal reference in 7:25 suggests a literal one here in the parallel. Either view makes contextual

---

12. For a figurative force are Fitzmyer 1981: 671, 673–74; Hendriksen 1978: 395–96; Arndt 1956: 212; Marshall 1978: 294; Ernst 1977: 250; Schürmann 1969: 416 n. 53 (who mentions that such a reed, *Phragmites communis*, could grow to a height of sixteen feet).

13. See 1 Kings 14:15. *B. Ta'an.* 20a stresses tenderness, not resoluteness: "Man should strive to be tender like a reed, not hard like the cedar," a text that commends a characteristic the exact opposite of John's; Manson 1949: 68.

sense. However, there seems to be no need to import the figurative sense, since the text makes good rhetorical sense as a literal reference. What drew you to the desert? It was not the reeds, nor men in soft clothes, for such clothing is found at the palace. Rather, it was a prophet who drew your attention.

Another interpretive issue in these verses is whether τί (*ti*) asks "what?" or "why?" (Marshall 1978: 293–94 has details on Matt. 11:9). If it means "why?" the question mark could be placed after the reference to ἔρημον (*erēmon*, desert) (Luce 1933: 157): "Why did you go out into the desert?" The answer would be, "Not to see a reed." The two questions in 7:24–25 imply a negative response. It is probable that an Aramaic idiom was rendered slightly differently by Matthew and Luke (Schürmann 1969: 416 n. 51). Since it is unusual for an infinitive to serve as the main verb, a "what?" question is more likely for Luke. If so, the ironic answer to the first question ("What did you go out to see?") is a reed; and the ironic answer to the next "what" question, also introduced by τί, is a man in soft clothes (the structure of 7:26 is also parallel to these verses). Jesus' questions gradually reveal John as the reason for the journey.

The questions continue about the issue of why people journeyed out **7:25** to see John. Most of the decisions made about the previous verse apply to this one as well, since they are structurally parallel. Jesus asks the somewhat ludicrous question, "Did you journey out to the desert to see a man from the wealthy class who dressed well?" Of course, the answer is no. John's apparel is not what they went to see. The combination ἱματισμός (*himatismos*) and ἔνδοξος (*endoxos*) refers to expensive clothing, probably of wool or soft linen.[14] Jesus continues: if you want to see expensive clothes, then go to the palace and the king's court. The neuter βασιλείοις (*basileiois*) refers to the palace (Herodotus 1.30; Fitzmyer 1981: 674; Marshall 1978: 294). Plummer (1896: 204) notes that the perspective in this verse is literal, suggesting correctly that the previous verse, which is parallel, should be seen the same way (against this are Hendriksen 1978: 396 and Arndt 1956: 212, who take it as reflecting people without backbone). There is perhaps a distant allusion to John's asceticism not only in the locale of ministry but also in clothes. But Luke does not mention John's clothes, even in Luke 3, in contrast to Mark 1:6, so that it is hard to see an allusion present. Jesus is saying that what drew people to the wilderness was neither the locale nor John's clothes, but his message.

14. On ἱματισμός, see BAGD 376; BAA 764; Exod. 3:22; 12:35; other NT uses are Luke 9:29; John 19:24; Acts 20:33; 1 Tim. 2:9. On ἔνδοξος, see BAGD 263 §2; BAA 530–31; other NT uses are Luke 13:17; 1 Cor. 4:10; Eph. 5:27.

ii. John Described (7:26–28)
(1) What John Is (7:26–27)

7:26   What caused people to go into the wilderness was the presence of a
prophet (Matt. 14:5; Luke 20:6). Jesus gives the first positive reply in
the sequence of three questions starting in 7:24. Indeed no prophet
was like John. He is more than a prophet. The comparative περισ-
σότερον (*perissoteron*, more than) is neuter here and qualifies the
reference to the prophet by elevating John (BAGD 651 §2; BAA 1313
§2; Luke 12:4; 12:48). The greatness of his position is a direct result
of the time in which he served. As a preparer for the Lord, he assumed a position in God's plan as prominent among the prophets
(1:15–17; 3:4–6). He is the greatest yet born (7:28). His greatness is
also demonstrated by Scripture's prediction of his role (Mal. 3:1 in
Luke 7:27; Godet 1875: 1.349; Schürmann 1969: 416). The unfolding
events are controlled by a sovereign God.

   Jesus elsewhere notes that John is Elijah (Matt. 11:14; 17:10–13).
There is a question about the nature of John's office, since the Baptist himself denied that he was Elijah, though he did identify himself
with the prophet who cries out in Isa. 40 (John 1:21–23; Marshall
1978: 295). But it may well be that John did not entirely understand
all that he was bringing to his call, since he clearly did not understand other things about Jesus' ministry (Luke 7:18–20). Or perhaps,
realizing that his ministry was like Elijah's but did not exhaust the
Elijah hope, John replied negatively (Marshall 1978: 295). Luke 1:17
seems to reflect this last attitude and may well suggest that Jesus' remark was part of an "already–not yet" tension. John is the "already
Elijah," while the "not yet Elijah" is still to come (Matt. 17:11).

   This passage sees John as part of Israel's time period. The distinction made in 7:28 between him and those of the kingdom period suggests such a classification of John. However, as Fitzmyer (1981: 674)
notes, John's elevation above the prophets shows that he belonged
to a special time, so that he should be regarded more as a transition
figure than as tied to only one period, especially given the way that
Luke links John and Jesus in Luke 1–2. There are only two periods
for Luke: promise and fulfillment. John simply serves as the bridge
from one era to another. Thus, Jesus describes John as great.

7:27   John's greatness is indicated by the promise of Scripture in Mal.
3:1,[15] a text that appears also in Mark 1:2 and Matt. 11:10. The Malachi passage looks at a commissioned prophet who will prepare the
way for the Lord God. But Luke refers either to the people as a collective group or to Jesus, depending on the antecedent of the pro-

---

15. The perfect tense γέγραπται emphasizes the current validity of the passage.

noun σου (*sou*). The citation in the NT introduces a question with the repeated use of the second-person pronoun, while the LXX and MT use the first person, which makes the prophet go before God, preparing the way by telling the people of God's arrival. The Lucan reference exhibits several differences from Malachi:

1. Malachi's ἐγώ (*egō*, I) is not in Luke.
2. Luke uses the synonymous verb ἀποστέλλω (*apostellō*, I send) instead of Malachi's ἐξαποστέλλω (*exapostellō*, I send).
3. Luke adds πρὸ προσώπου σου (*pro prosōpou sou*, before you) at the end of the first line.
4. Malachi begins the second line with καί (*kai*, and), Luke with the relative ὅς (*hos*, who).
5. Luke uses κατασκευάσει (*kataskeuasei*, will prepare) for Malachi's ἐπιβλέψεται (*epiblepsetai*, he will look upon).
6. Luke has the article τήν (*tēn*, the) before ὁδόν (*hodon*, way) and adds σου after it, yielding "your way."
7. The phrase πρὸ προσώπου μου (*pro prosōpou mou*, before me) is replaced by Luke's ἔμπροσθέν σου (*emprosthen sou*, before you).

These differences show that the LXX is not the source of Luke's citation. Rather, he makes a general reference to Malachi, with the key change being the shift in pronoun. It is clear that the text circulated in this form through the church, since the peculiarities of the text are shared in all the NT citations.[16] But what caused the pronoun change? Who is addressed in 7:27 by Luke's different pronoun? Another OT allusion provides help.

A second OT allusion is made to Exod. 23:20: καὶ ἰδοὺ ἐγὼ ἀποστέλλω τὸν ἄγγελόν μου πρὸ προσώπου σου (*kai idou egō apostellō ton angelon mou pro prosōpou sou*, and, behold, I send my messenger before your face). Using both σου and ἀποστέλλω, this passage speaks of the angel of the Lord going before the people. Following the cloud meant embracing God's protection, while failure to follow resulted in judgment (Exod. 14:19; 32:34; 33:2; Marshall 1978: 296). Exodus 23:20 is generally regarded as background for the second-person pronoun in the NT citations of Mal. 3:1 (Schürmann 1969: 417; but Fitzmyer 1981: 674 expresses doubt about the Exodus connection).

With the allusion to both Malachi and Exodus, the second-person pronoun in the NT may be interpreted in two ways. Godet (1875:

---

16. Matt. 11:10 agrees exactly with Luke except that ἐγώ precedes the initial verb in the verse; Mark 1:2 agrees exactly with Luke except that the final phrase (ἔμπροσθέν σου) is missing. Marshall 1978: 295 suggests that Mal. 3:1 was linked early on in Judaism (via *gezerah shewah*) to Isa. 40:3 by their common use of פָּנָה (*pānâ*, to prepare).

1.350) argues that the antecedent is Jesus, so that God sends the prophet before Jesus-Messiah (also Arndt 1956: 212–13; Stauffer, *TDNT* 3:103; Schürmann 1969: 417; Fitzmyer 1981: 674; Wiefel 1988: 150; Hendriksen 1978: 396). Others argue that the pronoun is a reference to the nation as a collective singular (so σου in Exod. 23:20), and thus the prophet prepares the nation for God's coming in Messiah (Bock 1987: 113–14, 322–23; Danker 1988: 166). By explaining how God comes, either sense is an appropriate expansion of what Malachi describes.

Two points favor a reference to the people. First, the context of Luke 7 indicates that the issue is the nation's response (7:29–35). Second, κατασκευάσει is used also in 1:17, where John is said to prepare a people (κατεσκευασμένον, *kateskeuasmenon*). This parallel guarantees that the reference is to the people. Although John works for God and goes before the Messiah, he also prepares the people for Messiah's coming. The image, influenced as it is by Exod. 23:20, looks at a pattern that pictures the new exodus. The prophet of Mal. 3 is compared to the protection that God gave his people by leading them through the wilderness. To respond to John is to be prepared for God's coming in Messiah and to be protected; failure to respond results in judgment.

The allusion to Mal. 3:1 has good background in the OT and Judaism. The Malachi text alludes to a prophetic figure who will precede God's coming to deliver his people. There is no direct reference to Messiah in the Book of Malachi, but the prophet alluded to by Malachi is part of God's eschatological work. This connection with the eschaton is sufficient to make correct the later Jewish association of this prophet as a predecessor of Messiah. It seems likely that only two figures are in view in Malachi: the prophet-messenger of the covenant and Yahweh, since an explicit reference to Messiah or to the angel of the Lord is missing elsewhere in the book. Thus, in considering Malachi alone, the reader is not prepared for either an angelic or a messianic reference.[17] In addition, Mal. 3:3–5 has a two-event sequence where the messenger ("he") comes first, followed by the Lord's coming ("I"). The eschatological association with Elijah existed also in Judaism.[18] Elijah is not resurrected Elijah, but represents an "Elijah-like" prophet who warns the nation and prepares it

17. For discussion of options, but with a different solution, see France 1971: 91 n. 31, who sees all the allusions in Malachi referring to God. Mal. 4:3 [3:21 MT] may point to Messiah, but a clear reference does not exist; Bock 1987: 322 n. 87.

18. 2 Esdr. [= 4 Ezra] 6:25–28 (where Enoch and Elijah [referred to as "men who were taken up"] are tied to the eschaton); Sir. 48:10 (where it is said that Elijah's return is predicted in the "prophecies of doom"); Midr. Exod. 32.9 (where Exod. 23:20 and Mal. 3:1 appear in the same discussion).

for God's coming by calling out a faithful, ready remnant. Clearly the Jews would understand the allusion and not object to the use of Mal. 3:1 with such a figure. The only question would be whether John was that figure. The differing responses to John show that the Jews answered this question in distinct ways.

(2) His Greatness and Lowliness (7:28)

Jesus praises John as the greatest man ever born.[19] John's position is the result of his mission in announcing the new era. He is, then, viewed as a member of the old order. But this reference does not exclude John from the kingdom. Luke 13:28 looks to the future and makes clear that all the prophets will be in the future kingdom. Luke 7:28 makes reference in its perspective to the present and thus discusses participation in the era of arriving fulfillment, not consummation. John is among those who anticipate the eschaton's arrival with its fulfillment in Jesus. That fulfillment comes in Jesus and is tied to the bestowal of various covenant benefits, like the permanently indwelling Spirit, something that does not occur until Acts 2 (Geldenhuys 1951: 227–28; Danker 1988: 167 [who refers to the benefits of the poor who share fellowship with Jesus]). In fact, all the prophets are said to have longed for such a day (1 Pet. 1:10–12; Matt. 13:17). Failure to note this distinct, rhetorical perspective leads some to argue erroneously that Jesus could not have uttered this verse about John, since it places him outside the sphere of blessing (Creed 1930: 107). But, as Arndt (1956: 213) notes, John is simply viewed as belonging to another dispensation. John is seen only as a prophet who is a forerunner here. He will be in the kingdom, but he does not yet have the benefit of what Jesus offers.

7:28

Though no one of the old era is as great as John, everyone in the new era will be greater than he. Among the fathers, at least as far back as Tertullian (*Against Marcion* 4.18.8), it was popular to take the second half of the verse to refer just to Christ. However, this meaning destroys the parallelism with μείζων (*meizōn*, greater): if John is the greatest person in a group (i.e., those born of women), then ὁ . . . μικρότερος (*ho . . . mikroteros*, the least) also refers to a group.[20] In addition, Jesus would never be the least in the kingdom.

---

19. On γεννητοῖς γυναικῶν, see Job 11:2c [not in MT]; 11:12 [≠ MT's sense]; 14:1; 15:14; 25:4; Büchsel, *TDNT* 1:672. Fitzmyer 1981: 675 gives Qumran parallels from 1QS 11.21; 1QH 13.14; 18.12–13, 16, 23–24. He also notes Gospel of Thomas 46.1. The parallel in Matt. 11:11 is the only other NT use of the phrase.

20. It is likely that μικρότερος is to be taken as a superlative. BDF (§60, §244) discusses the construction, but does not mention this verse. Fitzmyer 1981: 675 erroneously attributes this form of the remark to the early church; see the introduction to 7:18–35. The blessedness of the μικρότερος is frequent in the NT: Matt. 10:42; 18:10, 14; Mark 9:42; Luke 9:48; Nolland 1989: 337.

Reference to a group gives the passage its essential assertion: presence in the kingdom changes and elevates everyone who shares in it (Plummer 1896: 205; Grundmann, *TDNT* 4:535). The point of the remark is not only to explain John's greatness, but above all to show the greatness of the coming era of fulfillment, when all relative scales of evaluation will be completely rewritten. Those reborn in the kingdom are greater than the greatest person born by human generation. It is more significant to be the least member in the era of fulfillment than to have been the greatest prophet (i.e., the "bottom ten" of the new era are greater than "number one" from the old)! Jesus obviously regards these remarks as significant, since he introduces them with the solemn λέγω ὑμῖν (*legō hymin*, I say to you).

The wording of this saying differs slightly from its parallel in Matt. 11:11, though the idea expressed is virtually identical. Matthew has the verb ἐγήγερται (*egēgertai*, has risen), a different word order, ἀμήν (*amēn*, truly), and refers to the kingdom of heaven—all of which reflects his style. A parallel is also found in the Gospel of Thomas 46.1.

iii. Contrasting Reactions to John (7:29–30)
(1) Reception by Tax Collectors (7:29)

7:29 In an aside, Luke summarizes the Jewish response to John: all the people and tax collectors heard. However, the object of ἀκούσας (*akousas*) is missing: what or whom did the people hear? By mentioning that the people responded by being baptized by John the Baptist, the context indicates that they heard John. These comments are probably a Lucan parenthesis, because the remarks are awkwardly placed. Matthew lacks this comment in a section that otherwise parallels Luke fairly consistently. In addition, a reference to responding to John's baptism after hearing this remark by Jesus (assuming no parenthesis) does not fit: John is in jail![21] Though some see in these comments the current crowd's response to Jesus' point about John, such a sense is unlikely, since Jesus would then have to be seen as administering John's baptism (Alford 1874: 508 speaks against this view). Others see the remarks as a continuation of what Jesus said as a historical reflection on John's ministry (Danker 1988: 167; Arndt 1956: 214; Geldenhuys 1951: 228). This is possible, but the problem is that the third-person references in 7:29–30 to the people, tax collectors, and Pharisees seem unnatural for Jesus' address to the crowd. Second-person references to the crowd

---

21. Matt. 21:31–32 shows that such comments were in the tradition. Schürmann 1969: 422–23 argues that the comment may have been in Luke's source.

would be more natural if Jesus was speaking (so Jesus addresses the crowd as "you" in Matt. 21:31–32).

Hendriksen (1978: 399) has the most detailed defense of the view that Jesus is the speaker in 7:29–30: (1) Luke never has a parenthesis within a set of remarks by Jesus, (2) Luke 7:31 follows awkwardly from 7:28, and (3) Matt. 21:31–32 has Jesus speaking. But none of these points is compelling. Against the first point, Luke could express himself this way if he was linking together in a summary fashion remarks made by Jesus. Against the second point, the shift in Luke 7:31 is not awkward. It is a transition into a new image using a parable. Against the third point, Jesus' saying something similar elsewhere need not guarantee that he said it here. In fact, the absence of second-person pronouns in these remarks, unlike Matt. 21:31–32, makes it more likely that Luke 7:29–30 is a narrator's summary. Luke may have been aware of remarks like Matt. 21, so he inserted the historical comment. Although it is possible that Jesus is speaking here, it is more likely that Luke is noting the people's response to John. Luke contrasts the people and tax collectors with the Pharisees in anticipation of Luke 7:31–35.[22] Thus, the parenthesis is a bridge between Jesus' remarks about John (7:24–28) and Jesus' evaluation of the current generation based on their response to the Baptist (7:31–35).

Ἐδικαίωσαν (edikaiōsan, they justified) speaks of people responding favorably to God's overture of forgiveness, because they recognized that God's call for repentance was correct. John baptized those who acknowledged God's justice and vindicated his way (δικαιόω, dikaioō; BAGD 197 §2; BAA 397 §2; Schrenk, TDNT 2:214–15 §C2; Ps. Sol. 8.26–27; 9.2–3; Sir. 18:2). This justification of God contrasts directly with the lack of response by the Pharisees in Luke 7:30, where the contrastive term ἠθέτησαν (ēthetēsan) indicates a rejection of God's ways. Thus, the people and the tax collectors responded to "the counsel of God" (τὴν βουλὴν τοῦ θεοῦ, tēn boulēn tou theou), while the religious authorities did not (Liefeld 1984: 901). The populace becomes a significant part of the many turning to God, as promised in 1:16. The remarks recall passages like 3:1–14, 21 (Ernst 1977: 251).

(2) Rejection by Pharisees (7:30)

The people's response contrasts with that of the Pharisees and scribes, who are portrayed as rejecting τὴν βουλὴν τοῦ θεοῦ. A pop-   **7:30**

---

22. Creed 1930: 108 adds that, if the remarks are Jesus', then the reference to hearing should contextually refer to Jesus' comment about John and not to the response to John's ministry, a connection that is very unlikely, given the reference to John's baptism in 7:29.

ular concept for Luke, the will of God refers here to John's call to repentance, which is marked by one's accepting baptism.[23] The leadership's refusal to accept John's baptism proves their rejection (ἀθετέω, atheteō; Luke 10:16 [four times]; John 12:48; BAGD 21; BAA 39) of God's way of salvation and John's ministry. The phrase εἰς ἑαυτούς (eis heautous) goes with ἠθέτησαν: "rejected for themselves."[24] By rejecting the baptism, they chose not to accept their need for repentance and forgiveness. Whether their refusal was because the source of the message had such a common background or was for another reason, they still missed God's will.

The lawyer-scribes (οἱ νομικοί, hoi nomikoi) were a specialized group of upper-class Jews who gave themselves to the interpretation of the law (see the exegesis of 5:17; Jeremias 1969: 233–45; Luke 10:25; 11:45, 46, 52; 14:3; BAGD 541; BAA 1095; Wiefel 1988: 151). Luke's use of νομικός (as compared to Matthew's common γραμματεύς, grammateus, scribe) would be more intelligible for his Gentile audience, since they knew what a legal expert was (though Luke does use γραμματεύς fourteen times in his Gospel; Plummer 1896: 206). Sirach 38:34b–39:11 (according to NRSV numbering) describes the scribes' task (Stern 1976: 619–21). They were usually Pharisees; though some had priestly background or served at the temple, most came from outside the official priesthood, from occupations such as merchant and artisan. The key to their authority was their knowledge of the law. To be a scribe one had to become ordained after years of study at the feet of a rabbi. For example, Josephus had already engaged in much serious study by age fourteen (Life 2 §9). Three stages were a part of a scribe's schooling. At the beginning, he was simply a pupil who would watch even the gestures of his teacher (m. Suk. 3.9), but later he took on the position of an "unordained scholar," which meant that he had mastered the traditional material and the halakic methods and could make personal decisions on given questions. Upon reaching the age of ordination, he became a full scholar. In this position, he could be called rabbi, make religious decisions, act as judge in civil matters and criminal proceedings, and become a recognized teacher of Torah (1 Macc. 7:12). Thus, in religion, government, justice, and education, these men had a key role. In their hands was the right to interpret and control the reli-

---

23. Of twelve NT uses of βουλή, nine are in Luke–Acts: Luke 7:30; 23:51; Acts 2:23; 4:28; 5:38; 13:36; 20:27; 27:12, 42; elsewhere at 1 Cor. 4:5; Eph. 1:11; and Heb. 6:17. In Luke's use, the phrase centers on what God has done in Jesus; Bovon 1989: 379.

24. Creed 1930: 108. Against this idea is Schrenk, TDNT 1:635, who ties the phrase to God's will, so that the idea is that "they rejected God's will for themselves." Word order favors Creed, though there is not much difference in the options.

gious tradition. Their teaching spread across the land, as is seen in a rabbi's discussion of remarriage (*m. Yeb.* 16.7). It is ironic that those most concerned with the interpretation of the law still missed God's will (Gutbrod, *TDNT* 4:1088). Luke's view of this group can be seen in 3:7–9 and 20:1–8 (Danker 1988: 167).

c. Jesus' View of This Generation (7:31–35)
i. Parable of Complaining Children (7:31–32)

Jesus now turns from evaluating John to describing the current gen- **7:31**
eration. He simply introduces his parable by raising a comparative note (using ὁμοιώσω, *homoiōsō*, and ὅμοιοι, *homoioi*; BAGD 566 §1, 567 §2; BAA 1149 §1, 1150 §2). It is interesting that comparison tends to appear when the kingdom of God or the plan of God is described (Matt. 13:24; 18:23; 22:2; 25:1; Luke 13:18, 20; J. Schneider, *TDNT* 5:189). In fact, the introductory comparison has OT precedent (Lam. 2:13; Isa. 40:18, 25; 46:5; Ezek. 31:2; Fitzmyer 1981: 679).

The reference to "this generation" (τῆς γενεᾶς ταύτης, *tēs geneas tautēs*) is significant in that it generalizes the current response to John and Jesus. Though a distinction will be made among people in Luke 7:35, it seems clear that Jesus is describing the majority response in his rebuke. He is especially critical of the Pharisees and scribes, as the remarks in 7:29–30 indicate (Arndt 1956: 215). The reference is clearly broad, for Luke alone speaks of ἀνθρώπους (*anthrōpous*, men).[25] Danker (1988: 167) points out that in the OT γενεά can indicate a general time period, with either a neutral (Ps. 24:6 [23:6 LXX]; Isa. 61:3 [≠ MT's sense]; also Luke 1:48, 50; 21:32) or negative reference (Gen. 7:1; Ps. 78:8 [77:8 LXX]; 95:10 [94:10 LXX]; also Luke 9:41; 11:29–32, 50–51; 17:25; Büchsel, *TDNT* 1:662–63). Luke intends the negative sense here, as Jesus' rebuke in 7:34–35 makes clear. Danker notes that the remarks are not anti-Semitic, since Jesus is a Jew. Rather, Jesus' rebuke recalls the OT prophets and their message. John and Jesus offered correction so as to improve the nation's walk with their God (Deut. 32:5; Jer. 2:31; 7:29; Ernst 1977: 252; Fitzmyer 1981: 679).

The verse builds around two questions, the first simply raising the comparative issue and the second asking specifically what this generation of people is like. Such double introductions occur on occasion (Luke 13:18 = Mark 4:30; Marshall 1978: 299). Matthew lacks the second question, but then he never has a double introduction, so he may have shortened his version (Schürmann 1969: 423 n. 110).

25. Matt. 11:16 has τὴν γενεὰν ταύτην only. Luke's expanded form is slightly more intense and individualizing; Schürmann 1969: 423 n. 112.

Jesus picks a simple everyday illustration of children at play, thus rebuking the people for being no better than children in their response to God's work (Marshall 1978: 300). This generation is immature and childish. Though saying the same thing, Luke's wording differs slightly from Matthew's:

1. Matthew 11:16 has the feminine singular ὁμοία (*homoia*, like), while Luke has the masculine plural ὅμοιοι (*homoioi*, like).
2. Luke speaks of the marketplace (ἀγορᾷ, *agora*), while Matthew speaks of the marketplaces (ἀγοραῖς, *agorais*).
3. Luke 7:32 has ἀλλήλων (*allēlōn*, one another) (cf. ἄλλος, *allos*, other, in 7:19–20), while Matt. 11:3, 16 has ἕτερος (*heteros*, other).
4. The citation is introduced in Luke with ἃ λέγει (*ha legei*, who say) and προσφωνοῦσιν (*prosphōnousin*, those who call out) is an independent participle, while Matt. 11:16 writes ἃ προσφωνοῦντα (*ha prosphōnounta*, who call out) and the citation is preceded by λέγουσιν (*legousin*, they say).
5. Finally, in Luke the final verb is ἐκλαύσατε (*eklausate*, you wept), while in Matt. 11:17 it is ἐκόψασθε (*ekopsasthe*, you mourned). Schürmann (1969: 424 n. 115) argues that the Matthean term is too Palestinian for Luke's readers, and Schulz (1972: 379 n. 8) agrees.

The last difference is the most striking, but these changes are slight and do not alter the meaning, so it is hard to attribute them simply to one writer's editorial preferences (most of these changes occur because of Luke's reference to ἀνθρώπους). Why, for example, would Luke make such changes in his source if it had agreed with Matthew? An origin in related traditions seems to be the best solution.[26] Of course, as interesting as the source question is, more significant is the text's meaning.

7:32 The imagery—laughing, mourning,[27] playing, dancing—in the "parable of the brats" is clear, though the exact referents are disputed. The dispute centers on two questions (see Luce 1933: 159–60 and Jeremias 1963a: 161–62 for options): (1) Are there two complaining groups or one? (2) Who is complaining, God's messengers or the Jewish rejecters? There are three views:

26. Whatever the character of the tradition called Q, it seems that, if it existed, it had slightly different forms.

27. In the NT, θρηνέω (to mourn) occurs elsewhere at Matt. 11:17; Luke 23:27; John 16:20; Stählin, *TDNT* 3:152–54; αὐλέω (to play an instrument) at Matt. 11:17; 1 Cor. 14:7; ὀρχέομαι (to dance) at Matt. 11:17; 14:6; Mark 6:22; and κλαίω (to cry), among others, at Mark 5:38–39; Luke 7:13; 8:52.

1. If there are two groups, the dance represents Jesus' lifestyle and Jesus is the piper, while the dirge pictures John the Baptist's ascetic ministry (7:33–34). The first group of children (those who have responded to Jesus and John) are complaining to a second group of children who will not play the game no matter what tune the first group uses. In this view, the current generation is compared to the second group of children who do not respond.[28]

2. If only one group is present, then the emphasis is that, no matter what tune is played, some in the group will not play the game (Hendriksen 1978: 400; Danker 1988: 168). In this case, 7:33–34 is an application growing out of the simple picture of uncooperativeness, rather than being an extension of the parable. In this view, the parable has one point of comparison: the leaders are being childish for refusing to join what God is doing (many points of contact exist if two groups are present).

3. A variation on view 2 is to see the leaders as the speakers, the seated children, who are complaining about Jesus and John not playing "by the rules." The point is that the leaders taunt and complain about Jesus and John, because they do not do what the leaders want when they want.[29]

Which view is correct? The solution is complicated by 7:33–34 appearing to describe the messages of John and Jesus as coming in two different tunes (i.e., view 1). But this approach has a major problem as well: the comparison in 7:32 between the rebuked generation and the seated children who utter the complaint. Jesus presents one group and compares the current generation with the seated children—not with any who may have heard them. Thus, the speakers in 7:32 cannot be Jesus with his supporters and John with his supporters.[30] Rather, the Jewish leadership is complaining that John and Jesus do not follow their desires. From the leaders' perspective, God's messengers are at fault for not listening to them. The leaders do not wish to enter the game unless it is played according to their

---

28. Leaney 1958: 145; Godet 1875: 1.354–55; Creed 1930: 108; Schürmann 1969: 423–24; Fitzmyer 1981: 680. Geldenhuys 1951: 231 n. 15 notes that the couplet has rhyme in Aramaic.

29. So Stählin, *TDNT* 3:154; Wilckens, *TDNT* 7:516; Liefeld 1984: 901–2; Plummer 1896: 207; Jeremias 1963a: 162; Marshall 1978: 301; Ernst 1977: 353; Tiede 1988: 158; Bovon 1989: 180; Wiefel 1988: 151; and Linton 1975–76. Nolland 1989: 344 also notes the possibility of an allusion to a real game here, regardless of which view is taken, citing work by Légrasse 1969: 299–301.

30. The order of the images does not fit John and Jesus either, since dancing comes before mourning.

rules. This generation is like children who will play only if they can make the rules. Thus, the third view is preferred to the second, because the complainers picture rejection (7:30), not just lack of cooperation. The irony is strong in the parable. It is the desire of the leaders to dictate and not listen to God's messengers.

ii. Application: Current Rejection of John and Jesus (7:33–34)

7:33   The parable's application is described in terms of John's and Jesus' ministries. The reaction to John was not acceptance, but negative evaluation. Luke highlights John's significance, using the perfect tense ἐλήλυθεν (elēlythen, has come) (Matt. 11:18 the aorist ἦλθεν, ēlthen, came). John's ministry was rooted in God's plan, even though he had an ascetic lifestyle, living in the wilderness and eating only certain foods (Luke 1:15; Mark 1:6). Luke notes that John did not eat bread or drink wine, while Matt. 11:18 speaks of John's refusal to eat and drink, a shorthand way to speak of John's lifestyle.[31] That Matthew also lacks the description of John as ὁ βαπτιστής (ho baptistēs, the baptizer) is interesting given his preference for the term.[32] John's lifestyle was too radical for those uncomfortable with his message (locusts and wild honey were not exactly the average person's diet), and it became a way for them to rationalize their rejection of him by claiming that he was unbalanced and possessed (Hanse, *TDNT* 2:821–22 §C3; Fitzmyer 1981: 681). Jesus will be subject in other settings to similar charges—not accusations centering in lifestyle, but charges that his actions are grounded in the demonic (John 7:20; 8:48; 10:20; Luke 11:19 = Matt. 12:27; Mark 3:22; Plummer 1896: 207).

The use of the second-person λέγετε (legete, you say) shows that some rejecters are in the crowd. Third-person λέγουσιν (legousin, they say) in Matt. 11:18 is a general reference to all rejecters.[33]

The reference to bread and wine has an interesting OT parallel in Deut. 29:6 [29:5 MT/LXX] (Marshall 1978: 301). If this allusion is present, John the Baptist's diet is compared with the diet of the nation in their wilderness wanderings, a time when God was blessing

---

31. Fitzmyer 1981: 680 raises the possibility that ἄρτον (bread) is a generic reference to food, as in 2 Thess. 3:8, 12; Behm, *TDNT* 1:477 §2.

32. Ὁ βαπτιστής occurs twelve times in the NT, seven of them in Matthew: Matt. 3:1; 11:11, 12; 14:2, 8; 16:14; 17:13; Mark 6:25; 8:28; Luke 7:20, 33; 9:19; BAGD 132; BAA 266. Matthew is consistently the shorter edition in this pericope.

33. Luce 1933: 160 and Schulz 1972: 380, with most, argue that Luke made the shift to the second person, but it is hard to know which direction the difference went. If the account has polemical roots, a second-person reference may have been the starting point. Schürmann 1969: 426 calls the remark an indictment of the audience.

the nation with provision of food, so bread and wine were not necessary. But the verb in the LXX is ἐφάγετε (*ephagete*, you ate), not ἐσθίων (*esthiōn*, eating), which complicates making a definite statement about an allusion.

A key note about this rejection is that "many were falling" in Israel by failing to see what God was doing and saying through his messengers (Luke 2:34; Schürmann 1969: 426). There may be an implied rebuke, in that the rejecters were majoring on the minor issues of lifestyle rather than wrestling with the deeper issues of the message. By focusing on the wrong issue they did not get the major concern right. They missed any opportunity to look at themselves and see where they stood before God.

Jesus is contrasted to John. Jesus came in a different style. The Lucan wording is like Matthew with only the two verbs differing: Matt. 11:19 has ἦλθεν (*ēlthen*, he came) and λέγουσιν (*legousin*, they said). Each writer keeps the parallelism with John and uses his own terms from Luke 7:33 and Matt. 11:18. Jesus lived without restrictions on his lifestyle. He ate, drank, and associated with sinners (Luke 7:36–50; 11:37; 14:1; Matt. 11:19; John 2:1–11), as did the disciples (Matt. 9:14 = Mark 2:18 = Luke 5:33; Goppelt, *TDNT* 6:140; Ernst 1977: 253). What the leadership wanted John to do in terms of not living a "separated" lifestyle, Jesus did, but those who rejected him still complained that he lived too loosely and associated with the wrong people, a common complaint in Luke (5:30; 15:2; 19:7). The reference to sinners (ἁμαρτωλῶν, *hamartōlōn*) excludes not only the Pharisees, but also those people who are morally respectable. The charge is that Jesus associates with reprobates.[34] In fact, the charge is serious, for similar behavior can result in stoning according to Deut. 21:20–21.[35] But Jesus in offering God's forgiveness must relate to sinners, a point that Jesus will address directly in Luke 15, repeating a point made in 5:31–32. This characteristic of Jesus' ministry was not appreciated by those who rejected him.

7:34

In referring to the Son of Man (ὁ υἱὸς τοῦ ἀνθρώπου, *ho huios tou anthrōpou*), Jesus points to himself and adds a note of authority to his action (see the exegesis of 5:24; Marshall 1978: 302). That a title is in view here is seen in the parallel reference to John the Baptist as Ἰωάννης ὁ βαπτιστής (*Iōannēs ho baptistēs*) in 7:33. Both John and Jesus are described in terms of the function they perform. The statement's authenticity need not be denied (Marshall 1978: 302).

---

34. Rengstorf, *TDNT* 1:327; Michel, *TDNT* 8:104. On Jesus and table fellowship, see Stählin, *TDNT* 9:161.

35. Fitzmyer 1981: 681 notes that the wording does not equal the LXX, so it is unlikely that Luke has such an allusion in mind.

Whether God's messengers came in asceticism or associating openly with people, they were rejected. The form of ministry did not make any difference in the perception of some. They sang whichever tune they could to defend their rejection. They would always say that John and Jesus did not play by the rules.

iii. Appeal to Wisdom's Children (7:35)

7:35 Those who responded—wisdom's children—are contrasted to those who objected to John and Jesus. Καί (*kai*, but) is contrastive here (Marshall 1978: 303). This characterization looks back to 7:29 and describes wisdom's children as those who justified God by accepting his message. They are the product of divine wisdom and activity. They stand in a different camp than do the Pharisees and lawyers of 7:30–34 who rejected God's counsel. Another way to speak of God's counsel is to call it wisdom, in that the teaching from God's mind is personified as wisdom (Wilckens, *TDNT* 7:516).[36]

One view about the nature of the figure is that the passage reflects the objectors' complaint against Jesus, who is said to lead the way of the foolish.[37] But the connections to 7:29 suggest that Jesus is looking favorably to those who respond to God's messenger (Ernst 1977: 253; Schürmann 1969: 427; Fitzmyer 1981: 681). The wording of Matt. 11:19 differs from Luke's in speaking of wisdom's works (τῶν ἔργων, *tōn ergōn*) instead of children (τῶν τέκνων, *tōn teknōn*). It is hard to explain this difference, other than to suggest that wisdom's works in Matthew's Gospel are referred to in Luke's Gospel in terms of the product—the responding people. In other words, Luke's version lacks the figure. Some suggest that the difference is an alternate translation of the Aramaic (Manson 1949: 71; Schulz 1972: 380 argues that Matthew has made this change). The meaning is not greatly influenced by this difference.

The difference may suggest something else—that Luke and Matthew have distinct versions of the same event. It is hard to explain how this difference would exist if Luke had Matthew's version in front of him. Most regard Luke's version as the original wording, which Matthew has placed in a form that looks back to Matt. 11:2 (Fitzmyer 1981: 681).[38] The difference is sufficiently complex for Creed (1930: 109) to suggest that the Lucan reading is an early tex-

---

36. On "wisdom's children," see Sir. 4:11; Prov. 8:32–33. On wisdom personified, see Prov. 1:20–33; 8:1–9:6; 1 Enoch 42; 2 Esdr. [= 4 Ezra] 5:10; Wis. 7:22–11:1; Schürmann 1969: 427; Nolland 1989: 346.

37. Danker gives this view as an option in 1988: 169, unlike the more definitive statement in the first edition of his commentary (1972: 98–99).

38. If one source is present, this is the likely cause of the difference. For a view that places redaction with Luke, see Witherington 1990: 49.

tual corruption. But it is easier to posit distinct accounts than to posit a corruption for which there is no textual evidence. Both passages say the same thing in different terms. The complainers about John and Jesus do not stand in God's wisdom, but others share in God's knowledge.

Summary

Luke 7:18–23 anticipates Jesus' discussion of John the Baptist by showing that even the Baptist is trying to come to terms with who Jesus is. John asks the christological question in terms of the Coming One, a title that for Luke is understood in his fundamental christological category of Messiah. The answer is indirect but clear: Jesus does the work of the eschaton. Those things that Isaiah associated with God's deliverance are the very things that Jesus does. If Jesus does the work of the eschaton, then his ministry must be what he claims it is. What was predicted in Isa. 61 and alluded to already in Luke 4 is coming to pass. Jesus then is not just a prophetic figure, but also a messianic figure. One is blessed if one is not offended by Jesus' ministry. The envoys, having seen and heard of the activities that the OT described, can testify to that ministry. In many ways, answering this question about Jesus is the most fundamental issue of the early portion of Luke's Gospel.

Beyond this fundamental christological point, this subunit also has a more personal focus. It offers an invitation to the reader through the portrayal of John's struggle. John pictures a man who is sensitive to God and yet struggles to understand who Jesus is. John's question pictures one who is encountering Jesus and reflecting on his ministry. There is no rejection of Jesus here, no unbelief, only an effort to discover who he really is. On that basis, Jesus responds by appealing not to his own words but to the actions of his ministry. Anyone who would come to him can see what he does. To this person, Jesus' reply is found largely in 7:22–23: consider the nature of Jesus' ministry and work; do not be ashamed of him. In drawing near to Jesus and identifying with his ministry, there is the promise of blessing. John's ministry was also an opportunity to respond to God, but where John's was preparatory, Jesus' ministry is crucial. As 7:23 makes clear, the issue is simply how one views Jesus. Luke's reader has only two options: blessing or offense. Put another way, the alternatives are faith or judgment.

The outstanding theme of 7:24–28 is that times are changing. John is the one who prepares the people for God's way in the midst of that change. John is a prophet. In fact, he is at the culmination of the prophets, for Scripture shows him to be the prophet who prepares the people for God's deliverance. However, his greatness is nothing compared to the greatness of those who share in the start of the new era. So great is the shift that the least among the members of the kingdom is greater than the greatest of the old era!

In John's and Jesus' messages is an opportunity to be elevated by God to great blessing. Some take advantage of the opportunity, others do not. The religious elite reject the counsel of God from John, while the people and tax collectors respond to it. With the opportunity to respond comes the responsibility to make a choice of some consequence. John the Baptist is a litmus test of where one stands before God. People who have encountered John are prepared for what God will offer through Jesus. To turn their backs on John is to have turned their backs on the door that God opened. The way of escape into God's gracious arms comes in John's call to recognize one's need for God's forgiveness (pictured in John's baptism). In the admission of what is real or ugly about one's life comes the opportunity for reversal. One can become beautiful before God through the forgiveness he offers. The offered choice also gives an occasion for division among people. Some draw closer to God by recognizing honestly who they are without him, while others turn their backs on him. That sense of division about Jesus, like that in any generation, will become a major concern in the rest of Luke. The reader is to answer the question, "Which side of the partition am I on?"

Finally, 7:31–35 serves to rebuke those who reject John and Jesus. These rejecters are compared to spoiled children, "brats," who sit down and refuse to play any games. They whine that the other children will not play according to their rules and they change their tune constantly as they complain. In contrast to these brats stand wisdom's children who accept God's counsel as represented in John and Jesus. The account asks its readers some basic questions: Where do you stand? What do you think of John and Jesus? Are these messengers of God to be heeded? Will you side with wisdom? Will you be like the complaining children, wanting God to play by your rules? The mood of the passage calls for a choice and a response. In addition, the account sets up the following passage where a "sinner" comes to minister to Jesus, while the complainers continue to grumble about those with whom Jesus associates (7:35–50). Luke continually puts this question before his readers: Do you understand that Jesus is sent from God and that he is called to minister to sinners? Disciples should note the example.

Additional Notes

7:19. Were the envoys sent to Ἰησοῦν (Jesus), supported by ℵ, A, W, Δ, Θ, Ψ, family 1, Byz, Lect, most Itala, most Syriac, and some Coptic, or to τὸν κύριον (the Lord), found in only B, L, C, family 13, some Itala, Vulgate, and some Coptic? Those who retain τὸν κύριον argue that it is more likely to be original because, if Ἰησοῦν were original, it is hard to explain its removal, while the term τὸν κύριον is a reflection of Lucan style (Schürmann 1969: 408 n. 6; Metzger 1975: 143; Marshall 1978: 289; Luke 7:13; 10:41; 11:39; 12:42; 13:15; 16:8). The difference is not of great significance, but manuscript evidence favors Ἰησοῦν. It is possible that a scribe sensitive to the note of John's doubt inserted τὸν κύριον for Ἰησοῦν to keep Jesus' position clear. Though the decision is close, I opt with the textual evidence for Ἰησοῦν.

7:19. Two adjectives meaning "another" are attested in variant readings: ἕτερον (ℵ, B, L, W, Ξ, Ψ) and ἄλλον (A, D, Θ, family 1, family 13, Byz, Lect). Most see ἄλλον as original, because ἕτερον is used in Matt. 11:3. Luke uses both terms frequently: ἄλλος appears eleven times in Luke and eight times in Acts, while ἕτερος appears thirty-three times in Luke and seventeen times in Acts. Some argue that there is a slight difference in meaning for the two terms: ἕτερος means "another of a different kind" and ἄλλος means "another of the same kind." But this distinction is tough to maintain in this context and in Lucan usage in general.[39] The comparison is to the Coming One and not directly to Jesus, so the other one would not be of a different kind but would simply be another person in a different office.

7:20–21. Schulz (1972: 191–92, esp. nn. 127, 129) argues for Lucan expansion, mainly on the basis of vocabulary. The terms in 7:20 suggesting expansion are παραγίνομαι (eight times in Luke, twenty times in Acts, three times in Matthew, once in Mark), ἀνήρ (twenty-seven times in Luke, one hundred times in Acts, eight times in Matthew, four times in Mark), and ἀποστέλλω (twenty-six times in Luke, twenty-four times in Acts, twenty-two times in Matthew, twenty times in Mark). However, ἀποστέλλω is too frequent in all sources to be significant. The redactional terms in 7:21 are θεραπεύω ἀπό (three times in Luke), νόσος (four times in Luke, once in Acts, five times in Matthew, once in Mark), and πνεῦμα πονηρόν (twice in Luke, four times in Acts). However, the Lucan examples of πνεῦμα πονηρόν are clustered in special material in Luke 7–8 (7:21; 8:2), while the Acts examples are in a single pericope (19:12, 13, 15, 16), which could be evidence of tradition. Νόσος is too frequent in Matthew to be called Lucan. The evidence for expansion is not compelling.

---

39. Luke 3:18 and 6:6 seem to ignore any clean distinction. In favor of the distinction are Godet 1875: 1.345 and Plummer 1896: 202; against it are Elliott 1969 and BDF §306.

7:24, 25, 26. The same text-critical problem occurs three times in this sub-unit. External evidence supports the aorist ἐξήλθατε ($\mathfrak{P}^{75}$, ℵ, A [7:24, 25 only], B, D, L, W [7:24, 25 only], Ξ, and family 13) over the perfect ἐξεληλύθατε (A [7:26 only], W [7:26 only], Θ, Ψ, Byz, Lect). The perfect tense is not in Matt. 11:7–9, which makes it the harder reading (A. B. Bruce 1897: 513). The difference in meaning is slight: What *did you go out* to see? vs. What *have you gone out* to see? The choice is difficult, but external evidence slightly favors the aorist.

7:28. Many manuscripts (A, D, Δ, Θ, Ψ, and Byz) read that "no greater prophet (προφήτης) was born of women," which restricts the greatness of John somewhat more than if προφήτης is absent. But other manuscripts ($\mathfrak{P}^{75}$, ℵ, B, L, and W) omit the reference, thus making John "the greatest born of women." The UBS–NA text has this shorter reading. The inclusion of προφήτης fails to recognize that Jesus' point focuses on John's mission, not his person. It seems likely that a scribe added προφήτης to prevent someone from thinking that John is greater than Jesus (Metzger 1975: 143–44).

4. Picture of Faith:
A Sinful Woman Forgiven (7:36–50)

Luke's attention now turns away from John the Baptist, Jesus, and this generation to a fresh dispute: how Jesus and the Pharisees relate to sinners. In a complex, yet vivid account, Luke narrates the anointing of Jesus' feet by a notorious, sinful woman. It is the first of two accounts where women exercise faith in a significant way (8:1–3). In the face of differing reactions, Jesus offers comfort to the woman and also manages to rebuke the Pharisees who complain of his openness to her. The passage illustrates the comment in 7:34 about Jesus' openly associating with sinners. Jesus' parable in 7:41–43 clearly explains why he does so. In addition, Jesus declares the woman's sin forgiven. Thus, the passage has two points of confrontation: association with sinners and the right to forgive sin. Luke 7:36–50 is a picture of forgiveness and faith, but it also adds fuel to the christological debate over Jesus. While many are asking questions about him, he has again claimed to forgive sin (5:24; 7:18–35, 49).

The account contrasts the views of Jesus and the Pharisees on receiving sinners. However, another major theme is the value of God's forgiveness, which in turn produces love and devotion to him. The woman's concrete expression of love is also a major point. Her actions show her faith and bring Jesus' declaration of forgiveness. Her works do not save her, but they give evidence of the presence of faith, which brought about her forgiveness. Authority over forgiveness belongs to Jesus. Finally, the account records the growing division within Israel (2:34; Schürmann 1969: 430).

Sources and Historicity

The relationship of Luke 7:36–50 to other anointing accounts is much discussed. Aland (1985: §114) places Luke 7:36–50 alongside Matt. 26:6–13 = Mark 14:3–9 = John 12:1–8, and many regard the Lucan account as a variant of the event described in those passages. This conclusion needs examination in light of the differences in the accounts:

1. The events have different settings in terms of chronology and locale. The other event occurs in the final week of Jesus' life and takes place in the house of a leper named Simon (Matt. 26:6 = Mark 14:3),

where Pharisees would never dine (in fact, the audience in this later meal is disciples). Luke's version occurs in the earlier Galilean portion of Jesus' ministry and takes place in a Pharisee's house, who also happens to be named Simon (Luke 7:39–40). As Plummer (1896: 209) notes, Simon is one of the most common names of this period (nine NT figures and twenty-nine in Josephus; Schalit 1968: 113). In fact, Simon the Pharisee could not be the same as Simon the leper, since a leper could not be a Pharisee.

2. In Matthew and Mark the woman anoints Jesus' head, not his feet as in Luke. However, John 12:3 does speak of anointing his feet.

3. The identity of the women differs. In John 12:1–3, it is clear that the anointing is by the righteous Mary of Bethany, since she is placed alongside Martha and Lazarus. In Luke, the anointing is by a sinner.

4. The reaction to the event differs: in Matthew and Mark, the complaint is of the waste of the perfume; in Luke the concern is over association with a sinner, which leads to doubt about Jesus' position as a prophet.

5. The unique Lucan parable illustrates the significance of forgiving a sinner and so gives the Lucan account a different perspective.

6. The Lucan account stresses the woman's courtesy to Jesus in contrast to the Pharisee's lack of courtesy. Her act also gives Jesus an opportunity to declare that forgiveness is present. In contrast, the woman's act in Matthew, Mark, and John is seen as a preparation for Jesus' burial and thus as a cause for his commendation.

7. The conclusions differ: an act that Jesus says in Matthew and Mark will be memorialized stands in contrast to the controversy that Jesus' forgiveness in Luke causes among the Pharisees.

This comparison seems to make clear that Matthew, Mark, and John describe the same event, while Luke records a distinct event (Plummer 1896: 209; Ellis 1974: 121; Schneider 1977a: 176 [who calls it special Lucan material]; Schürmann 1969: 441 #2).

Nevertheless, the view that these passages all refer to the same event is old, since Origen refutes it (Plummer 1896: 209 cites Origen on Matt. 26:6). Luce (1933: 161) argues that Luke rewrote the later account to provide an illustration of the pharisaic attitude and placed it in this earlier position. But such an approach is hardly convincing. There seem to be numerous NT examples of Jesus' challenging the Pharisees without having to create an event to make the point. Talbert (1982: 84) implies a similar approach, speaking of a distinctive Lucan form of this tradition, though he rightly notes that within Luke this account illustrates a sinner's proper response to Jesus and thus alludes to 7:29. Alluding only to parallel tradition, this form of the one-incident argument is more sophisticated; it argues that there was one incident, which in the oral tradition was told in various forms (Fitzmyer 1981:

686).[1] Again, how does one demonstrate such a claim? How can one explain the vast differences in the tradition?

Fitzmyer (1981: 684) notes seven and Bovon (1989: 387–88) an additional two points (nos. 8–9) of contact between the two accounts:

1. absence of an expected parallel in Luke 22
2. unnamed anointing woman from the outside
3. Jesus' reclining at the table
4. alabaster perfume (all but John)
5. host with the name Simon (all but John)
6. negative reaction of onlookers
7. Jesus' favorable response to the woman
8. anointing of feet with the use of hair (Luke and John)
9. issue of money (all but Luke)

These points are not compelling, and they ignore important distinctions. The character of the woman, at least in John, differs. The presence of reclining dinner guests is normal for a meal. It is common for expensive perfume to be kept in a special container. The hosts are very different: a leper versus a Pharisee. The reactions differ, as does the nature of Jesus' commendation. Therefore, the accounts are distinct. Marshall (1978: 306) argues that the incidents are distinct and that the two traditions have crossed at points; but his explanation also seems unsatisfactory. The ties with the name Simon, the alabaster jar, and the anointing of the feet are not sufficient to suggest a mixing of details.

The report of the Jesus Seminar places all of the wording of this passage in black type (Funk and Hoover 1993: 303–4), thus rejecting any connection to Jesus. They see the account as parallel to Mark 14:3–9, though they acknowledge that possibly two incidents are fused together in the oral tradition. Luke is said to have composed 7:41–42 and 7:48–50. The seminar's summation is, "All the words put into Jesus' mouth are the fabrication of the storyteller." However, the defense of Jesus' approach to sinners is a multiply attested concept of his ministry (Mark 10:45; Matt. 9:10–13; and Luke 15 are but three examples). That Jesus should tell a parable about the rationale for his associations is not at all improbable. In fact, the contrast to the Jewish leadership's approach speaks to the parable's authenticity. The distinctive nature of this probably unique account of a "sinner story" fits credibly into the teaching and ministry of Jesus.[2]

---

1. Thus, Luke does not use Matthew or Mark, but special material that is a variant of this tradition. Holders of this approach stretch back to Tatian and Chrysostom.

2. For a good summary of the critical discussion, see Nolland 1989: 351–53, who relies on the approaches of Legault 1954, Löning 1971, and Dupont 1980. Nolland also rightly rejects Brodie's midrashic reading (1983) of this text as an internalization of 2 Kings 4:1–37. The points of connection between 2 Kings 4 and Luke 7 are too

The unity of this account is debated. The details will be evaluated as the verses at issue arise. That discussion centers on the mixture of parable and saying in the account, which also touches on the issue of form. The form of the account is complex, because it mixes pronouncement with parable.[3] It contains a controversy account that is illustrated with a parable. Tannehill (1986: 116–18) regards the account as a quest story, though that the woman seeks something from Jesus is not as clear as that she expresses appreciation to him. It might be better to call the account a "gift" story, since Jesus gifts the sinner with a confirmation of her earlier-obtained forgiveness.

The outline of Luke 7:36–50 is as follows:

a. Anointing and reaction (7:36–39)
   i. Setting (7:36)
   ii. Anointing of Jesus' feet by the sinful woman (7:37–38)
   iii. Reaction to the anointing: doubt about Jesus (7:39)
b. Jesus on forgiveness and his defense of the sinner's love (7:40–50)
   i. Jesus' reply: a parable on forgiveness and love (7:40–43)
   ii. Jesus' application to the woman and the Pharisees (7:44–47)
     (1) The woman's acts of love defended (7:44–46)
     (2) Much forgiveness in contrast to little (7:47)
   iii. Jesus' response: forgiveness extended to the woman (7:48)
   iv. The Pharisees' reaction: who is this? (7:49)
   v. Jesus' confirmation: the woman's faith has saved her (7:50)

The text presents numerous themes: Jesus the prophet facing

---

general to be compelling. In addition, the function of oil in the two accounts is too different (2 Kings 4:3–7 versus Luke 7:37–38), and the bowing of the Shunammite in 2 Kings 4:37 is a natural expression of respect, not unlike Luke 5:8. Luke 7:37–38 is filled with emotion, a background that 2 Kings 4 lacks.

3. Bultmann 1963: 20–21 places the discussion in the section on apophthegms and controversy dialogues. He sees 7:48–50 as added later, so that the original key to the passage was 7:47. He also sees the account as a doublet for Mark 14:3–9. Fitzmyer 1981: 686–87 sees the parable inserted into the pronouncement story. The dubious assumption here is that an account cannot mix forms. The argument fails, since without the parable the Pharisee's concerns in 7:39 remain unanswered; Nolland 1989: 351–52. Nolland prefers to call the passage "legend" since it is an example account, but he notes that doing so does not prejudice the account's historicity. Berger 1984: 51–56, 256, 361 speaks of parable and dialogue side by side, and calls the account an apologetic defense of Jesus' attitude toward sinners.

pharisaic skepticism; a follower's faith and love expressed in gratitude and devotion; pictures of the nerve, humility, and sacrifice of faith. The opportunity for forgiveness prevents Jesus' separation from sinners. In turn, sinners know that Jesus can be approached. Great forgiveness leads to great love, while love covers a multitude of sins. Faith is ground for forgiveness and salvation as well as opportunity for peace with God. Much about discipleship is pictured in the silent devotion of this woman.

Exegesis and Exposition

³⁶One of the Pharisees asked him to eat with him, and when he came into the house of the Pharisee, he reclined. ³⁷And behold, a woman in the city, who was a sinner, when she heard that he reclined in the Pharisee's house, brought an alabaster flask of perfume. ³⁸And standing behind him at his feet, weeping, she began to wet his feet with her tears, and she wiped them with the hair from her head, and kissed his feet, and anointed them with perfume.

³⁹And when the Pharisee who invited him saw this, he said to himself, "If this man were ⌜a⌝ prophet, he would know what sort of woman is touching him, for she is a sinner."

⁴⁰And Jesus replied to him, "Simon, I have something to say to you." And he said, "Teacher, speak." ⁴¹"A certain moneylender had two debtors; one owed five hundred denarii, and the other fifty. ⁴²When they did not have anything with which to repay, he freely forgave the debt to both. Now which of them shall love him more?" ⁴³And Simon replied, "I would suppose the one to whom he forgave more." And he said to him, "You have judged correctly."

⁴⁴And turning to the woman he said to Simon, "Do you see this woman? I entered your house, you gave me no water for my feet, but she has wet my feet with her tears and wiped them with her hair. ⁴⁵You did not give me a kiss, but from the time ⌜I⌝ came in she did not cease kissing my feet. ⁴⁶You did not anoint my head with oil, but she anointed ⌜my feet⌝ with perfume. ⁴⁷For which reason I say to you, her sins, which are many, are forgiven, because she loved much; but to whom little is forgiven, he loves little."

⁴⁸And he said to her, "Your sins are forgiven."

⁴⁹And those who were eating with him began to say among themselves, "Who is this, who even forgives sins?"

⁵⁰And he said to the woman, "Your faith has saved you. Go in peace."

a. Anointing and Reaction (7:36–39)
i. Setting (7:36)

7:36 Jesus is still being studied by the Pharisees. So one of their number invites Jesus home for a meal. His name is given in 7:40, when Jesus addresses the host as Simon. By 7:40 it is clear that Jesus' behavior—especially his open acceptance of the sinful woman's actions—is a cause of some concern for the Pharisee. Nevertheless, when the meal invitation comes, Jesus accepts it. He is making himself available to all types of people from all types of backgrounds. Luke alone notes other occasions when the Pharisees invited Jesus for a meal (11:37; 14:1; Luce 1933: 161; Schürmann 1969: 431 n. 4; H. Weiss, *TDNT* 9:36; other meals are in 5:29; 10:38; 19:5). On each occasion with the Pharisees, the mealtime raises an issue that leads Jesus to rebuke his hosts. Though some are certain that the invitation is for a malicious or a less than accepting motive (Morgan 1931: 101–2 calls the invitation uncouth), this point is less than obvious from the text. Later, it becomes clear that certain courtesies were not extended to Jesus upon his arrival (7:44–46), but the tone of Jesus' discussion with Simon is cordial (Godet 1875: 1.357). It is not filled with the hostility that occurs later in his ministry (i.e., 11:37–54). In 7:40, Simon addresses him with the respectful title διδάσκαλε (*didaskale*, teacher). The impression of the text is that this Pharisee is curious, though perhaps skeptical, about Jesus. That Jesus is probably a guest of honor at a banquet suggests an absence of hostility. The city in which the event occurs is not given.

Reclining (κατακλίνω, *kataklinō*) was the normal position for eating a special meal in the ancient Near East (9:14–15; 14:8; 24:30; Marshall 1978: 308). Each person would lie on his side, facing the table, and with body and feet angling away from the table. Such reclining was common at a festive banquet, while family meals involved sitting.[4] Jeremias argues that the occasion suggests a banquet, perhaps a Sabbath meal, in honor of the teacher Jesus, who may also have been viewed as a prophet. Another point that suggests this possibility is the ease with which the woman entered the meal. At special meals the door was left open, so uninvited guests could enter, sit by the walls, and hear the conversation (Talbert 1982: 82; Ellis 1974: 122; SB 4:611–39, esp. 615; 1:726; *b. Ber.* 31b).[5] Ellis also notes that they could beg and snatch leftovers. That the

---

4. Jeremias 1963a: 126; Jeremias 1966: 48–49, esp. 48 n. 4; Sir. 31:12, 18 (speaks of sitting); *m. Ber.* 6.6 (notes two types of sitting). While most of the other texts cited by Jeremias are talmudic, he does note OT texts such as Gen. 27:19; Exod. 32:6; Judg. 19:6; 1 Sam. 20:5, 24–25; 1 Kings 13:20; and Prov. 23:1.

5. The talmudic text is late, but that the woman in Luke is allowed in makes it likely that this was the custom. *B. Ber.* 31b relates a parable of a poor man who requests food from a king, suggesting a form of limited access, since he was able to force his way in to see the king (SB 4:615; Jülicher 1899: 2.291). However, it must be admitted that the parallel is distant. *B. Ber.* 41b relates an exchange between rabbis during a meal, but it is not clear that anyone else is there to hear it. Also relevant is *b. B. Bat.* 8a, where during a famine a rabbi opens his home to students, but not to the unlearned. When chastised by another rabbi for this, the rabbi relents and allows all to enter. The dilemma of the rabbinic passage is whether one should be generous. Thus, the extrabiblical evidence for an open meal is not great. Still, within the text the evidence suggests such an occasion.

woman's action is rebuked and her presence is not suggests a special, public meal.

ii. Anointing of Jesus' Feet by the Sinful Woman (7:37–38)

Luke now introduces the main figure, who causes the discussion. Interestingly, in the entire pericope, this woman says nothing. Her actions speak a thousand words. Luke notes the unusual character of the woman by ἰδού (*idou*, behold). The troublesome thing about the woman is her background: she is a sinner (ἁμαρτωλός, *hamartōlos*). **7:37**

The exact nature of her sin is not spelled out, and she is not further identified. Some associate her with Mary Magdalene and call her a prostitute, but neither point is certain.[6] It is unlikely that this woman is Mary Magdalene, for Mary is introduced fully in the next passage (8:2) without any hint that she is the woman in this account. The exact basis for the woman's description as a sinner is unknown, though she might have gained this reputation because of immorality. If the later Jewish texts recorded in SB 2:162 reflect first-century attitudes, it is possible, though not certain, that she is a prostitute.[7] The other possibilities are that she is the wife of someone with a dishonorable occupation (Schlatter 1960: 259), a woman in debt, or an adulteress.[8]

Sinners figure prominently in Luke (ἁμαρτωλός is found in Luke 5:8, 30, 32; 6:32–34; 7:34, 37, 39; 13:2; 15:1–2, 7, 10; 18:13; 19:7; 24:7—but only eleven times in Matthew and Mark together). This account, the controversy of 5:30–32, and the parables of chapter 15 show why Jesus and Luke are concerned for sinners and are gentle toward them.

The woman's reputation causes the Pharisee to be nervous, but for Jesus her condition simply speaks of her need to be rightly related to God. Black (1967: 181–83) argues that much of the wording in the Lucan account, especially in the parable, can be traced back to Aramaic, where it has numerous wordplays (and, accordingly, the tradition is old). The parable shows the probability that the woman had responded before coming to the meal.

6. Plummer 1896: 210 suggests that she is a prostitute, citing Matt. 21:32 as support. Rengstorf, *TDNT* 1:327, says that this interpretation of the terminology fits rabbinic expression, but gives no specifics at this point; Rengstorf's article shows ἁμαρτωλός to refer to a wide variety of the ungodly, including the Sadducees (*m. Ketub.* 7.6).

7. Ellis 1974: 122. Derrett 1970: 267–68, 275–78 is confident that she is a prostitute (many of the points he makes depend on this view).

8. Jeremias 1963a: 126, 132 opts for either a prostitute or a woman in a dishonorable vocation, by which he means either an immoral or a dishonest vocation; Jeremias 1969: 303–12; Fitzmyer 1981: 689; Black 1967: 181–83. Marshall 1978: 308 notes correctly that the sins seem to be hers, so that her reputation is not because of association with someone else; so also Wiefel 1988: 154, who thinks she is a prostitute, as does Schürmann 1969: 431 n. 8.

The sinful woman is obviously drawn to Jesus and has heard about his ministry, for when she knows that he is eating at the Pharisee's home, she goes to see him firsthand. She brings an alabaster flask filled with perfume (μύρον, *myron*).[9] Aromatic and expensive, such perfume was not the less expensive olive oil (ἔλαιον, *elaion*) normally used for anointing (Schlier, *TDNT* 2:472; Fitzmyer 1981: 689; Esth. 2:12). Of shaped stone or glass (Ben-Dor 1945), the flask preserved the perfume's quality (Pliny, *Natural History* 13.3 §19; BAGD 34; BAA 66; the other NT use of ἀλάβαστρος, *alabastros*, is Matt. 26:7 = Mark 14:3). The woman's coming required great courage. We are not told if she had changed her life before coming to the dinner as some speculate (Hendriksen 1978: 405), but such a conclusion is possible given the devotion that her act implies. What is certain is that Jesus' teaching caused her to think about spiritual matters as her tears in the next verse suggest (Godet 1875: 1.358). If she was not decisively affected before she came, certainly his words to her on this occasion confirmed that God would be gracious to her.

7:38 Luke describes the woman's action in great detail. In fact, virtually every move she makes is presented. She obviously is very meticulous in what she does. But alongside the care that she puts into anointing Jesus is the note of emotion that accompanies her actions. Both humility and devotion are found in her service.

When Jesus sat down to eat, his sandals would have been removed from his dusty feet. As he reclined on his side with his feet away from the table, the woman approached to anoint Jesus' feet, but was so overcome by the opportunity that she had to take care of the tears she shed. The tears are an expression either of her joy at the chance to honor Jesus or of her realization of forgiveness (Schürmann 1969: 432 n. 11 speaks of her thankfulness and love). The weeping is obviously significant, because the term used to describe it, βρέχω (*brechō*, to wet), is also used to describe rain showers (BAGD 147; BAA 294; Matt. 5:45; James 5:17 [twice]; Rev. 11:6; cf. Luke 17:29). This is more than light whimpering. She undoes her hair and wipes the tears away, an action that some might think immodest.[10] Only

9. Luke 7:37, 38, 46; 23:56; BAGD 529–30; BAA 1072; Michaelis, *TDNT* 4:800–801; Schürmann 1969: 432 n. 10. The importance of μύρον is shown by its use as perfume and its presence in the cult to purify priests, in the tabernacle for festal occasions, and by its use in burial to prevent stench and decay; Exod. 30:25–30; Josephus, *Antiquities* 3.8.6 §205; 19.9.1 §358; Luke 23:56. If this perfume were nard (Mark 14:3 = John 12:3), it would have cost about 300 denarii a pound, or the annual wage of a day laborer; BAGD 534; BAA 1080.

10. 1 Cor. 11:5–6; Godet 1875: 1.358. Jeremias 1963a: 126 n. 57 notes that such action in later times could bring grounds for divorce; see *t. Soṭa* 5.9 (= Neusner 1977–86: 3.168) and *y. Giṭ.* 50d (= Neusner et al. 1982–93: 25.254).

then does she kiss his feet and anoint him. Καταφιλέω (*kataphileō*) is the more intense form of the verb used to describe the kiss of the father at the return of the prodigal son (Luke 15:20) and the kiss of the elders upon Paul's farewell in Ephesus (Acts 20:37) (Plummer 1896: 211). The act of kissing and anointing the feet expresses deep reverence (*Joseph and Asenath* 15.11; Nolland 1989: 354).

The woman's mood reveals emotional devotion. Later the action will be described as being motivated by love, a love no doubt fueled by the gracious message that Jesus gave to sinners. These sinners had responded in humility and repentance to God (Luke 7:47; Schürmann 1969: 432 n. 11). Needless to say, the action received much attention. This was no longer an average meal with a teacher. Luke's depiction of the wiping, kissing, and anointing with imperfect tenses, which he often uses, allows the narrative to run in a progression from one act to the next: "She was wiping, was kissing, and was anointing." The impression is that each step took some time. One can imagine the impression it made at the meal.

iii. Reaction to the Anointing: Doubt about Jesus (7:39)

The host is disturbed by the proceedings and begins to doubt Jesus' **7:39** credentials. He reasons that a prophet would be able to discern the type of woman anointing him.[11] In fact, the doubt is expressed rather strongly in a contrary-to-fact condition: εἰ (*ei*, if) and past tenses in both the apodosis and protasis (Talbert 1982: 86; Marshall 1978: 309). In the host's judgment, Jesus is not a prophet, for he let the sinner get too close—or at least closer than he, a Pharisee, would allow. The present tense ἅπτεται (*haptetai*, she is touching) pictures her ongoing contact with Jesus (Plummer 1896: 211), and such continuous contact offends the Pharisee. It may be that the issue was her being unclean as a sinner and thus defiling Jesus by her touch (Marshall 1978: 309; Luce 1933: 161). Jesus' acceptance of her action is what bothers the Pharisee, who exemplifies the doubter and skeptic. It is clear from the host's reaction that the woman had a well-known reputation, though no effort should be made to suggest that Simon had illicit contact with her. He responds as a true Pharisee, not a hypocritical one. What Jesus will receive from sinners, the Pharisee rejects. Luke often uses soliloquy to heighten the drama (15:17–19; 16:3–4; 18:4–5, 11–12; C. F. Evans 1990: 362).

11. Friedrich, *TDNT* 6:844 n. 400, lists a few late Jewish and Christian texts that indicate a prophet's discernment: Pseudo-Clement, *Homilies* 2.6.1; 3.11.2; 3.13.1–2 (where a true prophet is said to be the "one who knows all things"); Midr. Lev. 21.8 (120c) (where Rabbi Akiva "sees . . . in the Holy Spirit" that one of his pupils has received a message from home telling him to marry).

b. Jesus on Forgiveness and His Defense of the Sinner's Love (7:40–50)
i. Jesus' Reply: A Parable on Forgiveness and Love (7:40–43)

7:40 In contrast to the doubt comes the revelation of Jesus' knowledge. Jesus' comment to Simon in the following parable shows quite ironically that Jesus does know what kind of woman is anointing his feet. And he also knows who is questioning his stature. Jesus cordially addresses the host by his first name, Simon, while the host replies respectfully, calling Jesus διδάσκαλε (*didaskale*, teacher). The very prophetic discernment that Simon thought was lacking is doubly manifest, since Jesus knows the woman's identity and the Pharisee's thoughts (Friedrich, *TDNT* 6:844; on Jesus' discernment, see 5:20, 22; 6:8; 9:47; 11:17; 20:23). When Jesus reads minds, a rebuke often follows.

A term of great respect used of the Jewish teachers in 2:46 and of John the Baptist in 3:12, διδάσκαλος now becomes the title used for Jesus by the crowd (8:49; 9:38; 12:13; 21:7), the religious or social authorities (10:25; 11:45; 18:18; 19:39; 20:21, 28, 39), and by Jesus himself (22:11). While the term is generally not used in a hostile sense, often in such addresses the questioner probes in an indirect way that suggests discomfort with Jesus (cf. Nathan's rebuke of David in 2 Sam. 12). It is like calling Jesus rabbi (ῥαββί) (Rengstorf, *TDNT* 2:148–57; Fitzmyer 1981: 690; Bovon 1989: 392 [who mentions a reference to the teacher's authority]). Thus, the tone is cordial, but some tension is present.[12]

The name Simon (Σίμων) is common in the NT, so to argue for confusion between Simon the Pharisee and Simon the leper is not convincing (see the introduction to this unit; Marshall 1978: 310; BAGD 751; BAA 1501–2). As was noted, efforts to see the anointing of Matt. 26:6–13 = Mark 14:3–9 = John 12:1–8 as equal to Luke 7 are unfounded.

7:41 Jesus illustrates his response of forgiveness and explains why he reaches out to sinners (SB 2:163; Wiefel 1988: 155; the rabbis also used monetary comparisons). The parable is introduced simply; two debtors are present, one with ten times the debt of the other (500 denarii versus 50). A denarius (δηνάριον, *dēnarion*) was a soldier's or laborer's daily wage (Matt. 20:2; Tacitus, *Annals* 1.17; Plummer 1896: 212; Heutger 1983: 98). To put these numbers in perspective,

---

12. This is a better way to look at the account than to argue that Simon is rude, insensitive, or uninterested (e.g., Morgan 1931: 103 calls Simon supercilious; Alford 1874: 510 speaks of Simon's disgust).

note that Cicero made 150,000 denarii per year; officeholders under Augustus, 2,500–10,000 denarii per year; and procurators like Pilate, 15,000–75,000 denarii per year (Nolland 1989: 355). So the wages in Luke are middle-class at best. Given the fluctuating values of money across time, it is better to figure the debt in relative terms of basic wages than to figure its current monetary equivalent: about two months' wages versus one-and-three-quarter years' wages (assuming a six-day workweek). The graphic picture will show how great God's forgiveness is. The parable is basic to the story and is not a later addition; it is fundamental to the issue raised in 7:39 (Nolland 1989: 356; Wilckens 1973: 400–404).

Now comes the twist to the story. It is often a characteristic of Jesus' **7:42** parables that they have some striking feature. In this account, the twist supplies the element that Jesus uses to make his point. The moneylender, rather than forcing the debtors to pay, freely forgives the debt.[13] A modern analogy might be the cancellation of a house mortgage or a debt on a car. The verb used for forgiving the debt, χαρίζομαι (charizomai), was a common business term for remitting debt (Fitzmyer 1981: 690; BAGD 876 §1; BAA 1749 §1) and is the very verb that will picture later in Scripture the free offer of God's grace (cf. Josephus, Antiquities 6.7.4 §144).[14] The verse describes the act of a moneylender that is totally out of character for the average debt collector. The forgiving of the debt is unexpected, but would be welcome news to someone with no money to pay it off. The remitting of debt should be seen as extraordinary, despite efforts to appeal to OT precedent (Deut. 15; Lev. 25:8–17) for forgiving such debts (against Nolland 1989: 356). It is the unmerited character of the act that is the basis for the gratitude.

Jesus makes this point by raising a question: Which of the two debtors will respond with greater love?[15] Simon will answer the question correctly in the next verse by noting that, the larger the debt that is forgiven, the larger the gratitude and love that emerge in the response. The joining of love and gratitude in this way through the term ἀγαπάω (agapaō, to love) is indicated in the rest of the parable (7:44–46).[16]

---

13. The phrase μὴ ἐχόντων αὐτῶν introduces a genitive absolute construction: "when they had nothing with which to pay back."

14. Arndt 1956: 219; Luke 7:21 (of a blind person graced with sight); Rom. 8:32; 1 Cor. 2:12; Phil. 1:29; Eph. 4:32 (twice). The verb used in this soteriological sense is largely a Pauline term, while the noun χάρις is more widespread; Acts 15:11; Heb. 4:16 (twice); 1 Pet. 1:10; 2 Pet. 3:18.

15. Parables in Luke 10:36 and Matt. 21:31 also end with questions; Hauck, TDNT 5:754.

16. Fitzmyer 1981: 690 and Marshall 1978: 311 mention that no specific verb for "to thank" exists in Aramaic or Hebrew. Thus, the sense of ἀγαπάω is something like

It is clear from Jesus' following explanation that each part of the parable has a parallel: the moneylender depicts God; the debt is sin; the two debtors depict different levels of sinner: the one who owes less pictures the Pharisee, while the one who owes more represents the woman. The dominant feature in the account is the forgiving of the debt that generates the responses. As Schweizer (1984: 139–40) says, "God, who comes to life in the parable, bursts the bounds of human probability." God is ready and willing to forgive the debts of people and to act graciously beyond expectation. This picture of God's grace motivates Jesus' acceptance of those in dire need and his openness toward sinners. It is this very point that Simon needs to see, as the following verses make clear. The sinner who realizes the nature of the forgiveness received freely will be in a position to love God greatly. It is not what the sinner is that Jesus sees, but what the sinner could be through God's love. It is Jesus' awareness of how God can transform people that makes him, rather than dwell on their past, look forward to what God can make of them. This picture is depicted in a slightly different way in 15:11–32, while rejection of an overly judgmental attitude is depicted in the parable of Matt. 18:23–35 (Schürmann 1969: 434).

7:43 Simon gives an astute response: the one with the larger debt will love more. Jesus endorses the response with the comment that Simon "discerned correctly" (ὀρθῶς ἔκρινας, orthōs ekrinas). Some characterize Simon's reply as less than direct, because of his use of ὑπολαμβάνω (hypolambanō, I suppose). Plummer (1896: 212) speaks of Simon's "air of supercilious indifference," but more aptly Danker (1988: 170) calls it a "grudging admission" (also Delling, *TDNT* 4:15). Maybe Simon knows that Jesus can give surprising responses, and so he is simply being careful (Arndt 1956: 219). Marshall (1978: 311) adds that Simon's caution may have been a result of his training since rabbinic questions like this often contain surprises. In addition, Marshall suggests that Simon may be aware that he has been caught in a trap. Whether the Pharisee sees where Jesus is going, he responds properly, unlike later situations where there will be silence or evasion of an answer (Luke 20:7, 40). Thus, that Simon replies is to his credit. In fact, it is one of the ironies of the account that the answer seems fairly obvious, but Simon is careful in how he states his reply (Ernst 1977: 257). Plummer al-

---

that in Ps. 116:1 [114:1 LXX] or Josephus, *Jewish War* 1.10.2 §198. See Wood 1954–55 and Jeremias 1963a: 126–27. Fitzmyer adds that in 1QH the Hebrew verb for praise (הוֹדָה, *hôdâ*) is constantly used to express thanks. What is present is gratitude that also expresses appreciation and love.

leges that Jesus' reply is close to terminology that Socrates used to finish a line of questioning and betray a blind spot in the opponent's position.[17]

ii. Jesus' Application to the Woman and the Pharisees (7:44–47)
(1) The Woman's Acts of Love Defended (7:44–46)

Jesus addresses the Pharisee and applies the parable to the current **7:44** situation by contrasting Simon's lack of courtesy to the woman's devotion and courtesy. In doing so, the woman's action as described in 7:38 is retold (the same verbs are used in both texts: weep, wipe, kiss, and anoint). In speaking to the Pharisee while turning to the woman, Jesus has the religious leader learn a lesson from the sinner as he draws attention to her.[18] Again, irony is present.

The washing of the feet is the first of three acts that the woman performs but the Pharisee does not.[19] It is debated whether the washing of a guest's feet was required for the host. If it was required (Bailey 1980: 5; Geldenhuys 1951: 234), then the Pharisee was clearly discourteous, but if not, then the woman's actions were extraordinary and more commendable. Marshall (1978: 311–12) suggests that it was not required and when done became an expression of exceptional consideration (Gen. 18:4; Judg. 19:21; 1 Sam. 25:41; John 13:5; 1 Tim. 5:10; Schürmann 1969: 435–36; Alford 1874: 512). Schürmann (1969: 435 n. 31) notes that the citations in SB show that these practices were not required at such meals, so it would be an overstatement to call the Pharisee rude (SB 2:163; 1:427; 4:615; Goppelt, *TDNT* 8:323–24 [esp. n. 63], 328 nn. 93–95). If Simon had performed these acts, a slave would have been likely to do them. At the minimum, it is clear that the woman showed more courtesy and interest in Jesus than Simon did. Simon had done less than he could have done.

---

17. Plummer cites Socrates' phrase as πάνυ ὀρθῶς; so also Godet 1875: 1.359 and Bovon 1989: 393 n. 53. However, no reference is given in any of these sources. A check of Thesaurus Linguae Graecae, an electronic database containing most of the extant ancient Greek literature, did not surface the phrase in Socrates. This classical comparison should not be made until the texts are revealed. However, the general rhetorical pattern does fit a type of Socratic interrogation; see Daube 1956: 152; Aristotle, *Rhetoric* 3.18.2.

18. Plummer 1896: 212 notes that the question whether he sees her (βλέπεις) is also a call to consider her actions.

19. Luke 7:45–46 gives the other actions: kissing the feet and anointing the head with oil. The total lack of response by the Pharisee means that Jesus may be suggesting that the Pharisee has no love, rather than just a little. If so, he is in worse shape than either of the examples in the parable. But I reject this approach for rhetorical reasons (see the exegesis of 7:46).

7:45   Jesus notes a second contrast: a kiss of greeting on the face versus a kiss of respect on the feet. An expression of respect and friendship (Gen. 33:4; Exod. 18:7; 2 Sam. 15:5; 19:39 [19:40 MT]; 20:9), the kiss of greeting was customary, as the NT exhortations about the holy kiss show (SB 1:995–96; Stählin, *TDNT* 9:138; the practice still exists today in parts of Europe, Latin America, and the Middle East). Simon gave no such greeting, but the woman gave it in abundance, kissing Jesus' feet from the point of his arrival. For the woman this was not a sign of friendship, but of humility, appreciation, awareness of Jesus' approachableness, and maybe his forgiveness (Stählin, *TDNT* 9:139). The description looks back to 7:38 by using the same intensive form of the verb καταφιλέω (*kataphileō*).[20] Another sinner will later greet Jesus with such a kiss on the cheek, but his motive will be quite different (22:47–48; Fitzmyer 1981: 691). Jesus' description of the woman kissing his feet from the time of his entry is hyperbole in light of the description of 7:38, but it stresses the constancy of her action.[21] This woman has shown Jesus nothing but respect.

7:46   Jesus makes a third contrast between the Pharisee and the woman: the Pharisee did not anoint Jesus' head with ἔλαιον, *elaion* (BAGD 247; Josephus, *Jewish War* 5.13.6 §565), in all probability inexpensive olive oil that was produced in abundance in the region (Geldenhuys 1951: 236 n. 10; Plummer 1896: 213; SB 1:426–27, 986). Such an act was not required of a host, but would be seen as a special courtesy (Schürmann 1969: 435 nn. 31, 34). Biblical examples of anointing guests include Ps. 23:5; 141:5; Amos 6:6; Matt. 6:17; and Luke 10:34. The woman, however, used the most expensive perfume, μύρον (*myron*), and anointed Jesus' feet (see the exegesis of 7:37–38).

Fitzmyer (1981: 691) notes correctly that one cannot infer from the OT examples that the reference to the anointing of feet is a creative detail, since in the OT feet were washed with water (Gen. 18:4; 19:2; 24:32; 43:24). Schürmann (1969: 436) suggests that Luke 7:44–46, with its pairing of sinner and Pharisee, may have been added to the original account, so that the Pharisee becomes the "little sinner." The major reason for this view is that nowhere else are Pharisees called "little sinners" as 7:47 suggests. But such reasoning is hardly compelling. Jesus tells numerous parables where the religious leadership is taken to task, where they are viewed ironically in a positive sense. The outstanding example is 5:31–32, while

20. Luke 15:20; Acts 20:37. Paul calls it the "holy kiss": Rom. 16:16; 1 Cor. 16:20; Danker 1988: 171.
21. Fitzmyer 1981: 691 rejects a suggestion of a mistranslation of Aramaic here, as argued by Jeremias 1960.

18:9–14 is more direct in its criticism. Luke 5:31–32 has parallels in Matt. 9:13 and Mark 2:17, so an appeal to special Lucan material cannot work. The Pharisees are rhetorically and ironically addressed from their own perspective in a contrast of lack of attention versus devotion. The rhetorical form is why the Pharisee should be identified with the one who has the smaller debt. Just because the Pharisee has "less sin" does not mean that he is excused from seeking forgiveness.

(2) Much Forgiveness in Contrast to Little (7:47)

Jesus contrasts the result of the woman's expression of love with the Pharisee's. The woman's actions cause Jesus to respond and make a point from his parable.[22] The conjunctive phrase οὗ χάριν (hou charin, for which reason) looks back at 7:40–46 and links Jesus' remarks to both the parable and her actions (BAGD 877; BAA 1750; this is the only example in Luke–Acts; other NT uses of χάριν include 1 John 3:12; Eph. 3:1, 14). The parable explains why the woman acted, and her actions testify to the presence of forgiveness, which produced love. Because the woman was forgiven much, she loves much; her love is demonstrated by her actions, so that her great love reflects the presence of great forgiveness. The forgiveness is not a result of the acts; rather, the acts testify to love's presence in gratitude for the previous granting of forgiveness.[23] In fact, the reference to forgiveness in the perfect tense (ἀφέωνται, apheōntai) stresses that she is in a state of forgiveness. A similar saying is found in 1 Pet. 4:8: "Love covers a multitude of sins." Love emerging from forgiveness changes the direction of one's life.

7:47

In addition, Jesus' remarks make clear that he knows who the woman is. Simon had doubted that Jesus was a prophet because he had not discerned this about the woman (7:39). The reference to her many sins shows that Jesus knew all along. Simon should by now recognize that at least a prophet is present. Of course, Simon himself stands in contrast to the woman. For he pictures the one who loves little and thus is forgiven little. This remark is rhetorical: Simon thinks he needs little help and has little need for forgiveness. Jesus' point is that the woman is much closer to God's grace than Simon is. (On the multiple options suggested for the precise sense of the point to Simon, see Nolland 1989: 358–59, who lists six possibilities. Nolland sees Simon unaddressed; I prefer to see a mere com-

---

22. Liefeld 1984: 904 ties οὗ χάριν to λέγω (I say) so that the conjunctive phrase syntactically explains the reason of Jesus' reply, not the reason for forgiveness; Moule 1959: 147.

23. The causal ὅτι clause relates love and forgiveness and makes love the evidence of forgiveness.

parative critique expressed generally.) It takes humility to see one's need for forgiveness, and God honors the humble.

The passage ties together one's spiritual condition and actions, in that actions reflect a previous response to God. The presence of that earlier response allows one to have God's approval. The contrastive remark of Jesus that the one to whom little is forgiven loves little assumes the presence of three elements of forgiveness: God's offer of it, reception of it, and God's confirmation that it was received. The first and third elements, representing the start and finish of the process, are clearly present. The parable illustrates the offer of forgiveness and its receptive response, while 7:48–49 shows the confirmation. But the middle element, which manifests itself as love, is brought out most starkly by Jesus' remark of the contrast between the Pharisee and the woman. God's kindness has produced a response of humble, loving gratitude from the woman, rather than self-exaltation like the Pharisee. An illustration might suffice: the statement "it is raining because the windows are wet" does not mean that the water on the windows is the cause of the rain. Rather, the water on the windows evidences the presence of rain (Marshall 1978: 313; Wiefel 1988: 156; Arndt 1956: 220).[24] That is the sense of the sequence of actions in this verse. Love evidences an awareness of, a reception of, and a response to previous forgiveness. Efforts to argue that the parable and story do not match, so that either the parable or the story is a later addition in the tradition, miss the crucial point made when the two elements are kept together (Geldenhuys 1951: 234; Godet 1875: 1.360–61; Talbert 1982: 87).[25]

Also inadequate are efforts to argue that only two elements, acts of love and forgiveness, are present in the context (Ernst 1977: 258–59; Schürmann 1969: 436–37). Against this approach stand the parable, the second half of 7:47, and 7:50. It is God's initiatory act on behalf of the woman that leads to her transformation in character. It is this previous stage of offer and response that is pictured in the parable, while the woman's actions of love are seen to grow out of that response. It is that very potential for change, initiated by God's offer, that leads Jesus to be open toward sinners and to speak to them about forgiveness. Thus, in 7:50, Jesus refers to the woman's

24. Arndt discusses this sense for ὅτι, which is also found in Luke 1:22; 6:21; 13:2; Gal. 4:6; John 9:16; and 1 John 3:14. This might be called an "evidentiary" use of ὅτι; what is seen is evidence of another spiritual reality, not the cause of it. Love is the product (result) rather than the cause (basis). The rain results in the windows' being wet, so forgiveness results in love.

25. Among those who argue for breaking up the account are Creed 1930: 111–12; Luce 1933: 162–63 (who argues that Luke confused two points here); and Ernst 1977: 258–59.

faith and says that that is what saved her. Only by retaining all of the elements can the entire account hold together. The point is clear: God offers great forgiveness to all to deal with their sin, and those who grasp and receive it realize how much God has done and respond in acts of love. The Pharisee, who is "forgiven little," needs to see God's work as more significant and then his response will be appropriate. Thus, in this final remark to Simon, Jesus expresses the contrast somewhat rhetorically, not to say that the Pharisee was saved, but to show that he had not yet responded sufficiently to God. His "little sin" still needed treatment (5:31–32).

This passage is also the reason that Tannehill's classification (1986: 116–18) of the account as a quest story is not technically correct (see the introduction to this unit). Tannehill views the point of 7:47 as I do, but he argues that 7:48 complicates the picture and reveals what the woman sought: confidence of forgiveness. However, she came and served out of love and gratitude, not with a plea. Jesus gave her what she did not seek. He gifted her with the assurance that God knew why she had acted, despite the Pharisee's protests at the dinner. This is precisely the beauty of God's forgiveness. Given to the humble, it exalts them in assurance—not assurance grounded in self-confidence and pride—but assurance that they can rely on God and respond to him, knowing that he is aware of their heart and that he responds to the humble.

iii. Jesus' Response: Forgiveness Extended to the Woman (7:48)

Jesus reinforces the woman's forgiveness and also encourages her **7:48** by announcing that her sins are forgiven. The perfect tense, ἀφέων-ται (apheōntai, are forgiven), repeats the key verb of 7:47 and denotes that she is in a state of forgiveness. It suggests that the forgiveness began somewhere in the past (Godet 1875: 1.362). The word is designed to reassure the woman and provide confirmation for her in the face of the Pharisees' general rejection (A. B. Bruce 1897: 518; Grundmann 1963: 173; Plummer 1896: 214; against this is Nolland 1989: 359, who sees 7:48–49 as a secondary expansion of this account). These verses are a part of the integral unity of the account, assuring the woman in the face of the dispute now raised publicly by Jesus' remarks. Without Jesus' comment, her action may be viewed as offensive or honorable. Jesus' lending his authority and approval shows it to be an honorable expression of love. Jesus' remark will cause reaction, since the right to forgive sins rests with God. The stakes have risen. Either Jesus is a significant figure commissioned by God for his task or else he is extremely deluded, presumptuous, even blasphemous. There is no middle ground. This is not the first time in Luke that Jesus has forgiven sins, and each time it brought a reaction (5:20–21, 23). Jesus' actions fulfill his commission revealed in 4:18. The woman is reassured before the crowd, just as Theophilus might need to be (1:4).

iv. The Pharisees' Reaction: Who Is This? (7:49)

7:49 Jesus' confirmation of the woman's forgiveness brings a reaction from the theologically sensitive Pharisees. Their response introduces another element into the account: Jesus' identity. This incident now raises questions about Jesus. Who Jesus is has been a major concern of Luke 7 (cf. the remarks of the crowd in 7:16 and the question of John the Baptist in 7:18–20). It will be a major concern in Luke 8–9 and will surface again at Jesus' trial (22:66–71).

The phrase ἐν ἑαυτοῖς (*en heautois*) may mean "among themselves," so that they respond verbally to one another, or "within themselves," so that private thoughts are in view. Many suggest that because Simon's thoughts in 7:39 were private so are these (Plummer 1896: 214; Klostermann 1929: 95). However, it is hard to be certain because of the plural reference here. Probably in view are internal perceptions, indicated not only by the tone of this account but by the parallel 5:22. If the Pharisees expressed themselves verbally, it is unlikely that they did so very loudly, since in many accounts they keep their negative reactions to Jesus largely to themselves. What the plural also shows is that Simon's reaction was not unique. What he thought and reacted to, others in his party had felt as well.

Talbert (1982: 88) argues that by his statement Jesus reveals only that he is acting like a prophet: he knows God's mind and, as a prophet, pronounces that sins are forgiven.[26] In the OT texts (2 Sam. 12:13; Isa. 40:2), however, it is clear that the prophet is speaking for God. Jesus' remarks seem more direct, in that 7:47 begins with "I say to you," as opposed to "the Lord says" or "the Lord will forgive." Josephus (*Antiquities* 6.5.6 §92) sees Nathan functioning as God's mouthpiece in God's action against David. God is the forgiver of sin for a Jew (Bultmann, *TDNT* 1:511, esp. n. 12), and Jesus' direct expression of authority to forgive sins brings the reaction. If Jesus were just claiming prophetic authority, he could have clarified matters easily enough. The reply raises the issue of Jesus' authority in a way that points beyond a prophet. It pushes beyond the account's

---

26. In 4QPrNab, a Jewish exorcist remits sins of the Babylonian King Nabonidus; Dupont-Sommer 1961: 322, esp. n. 3. The problem with this fragmentary Qumran parallel is that the method of expressing forgiveness to the king is not described in the text, but only summarized. Consequently, it can hardly carry the weight of the case for a prophetic understanding in Luke. See the exegesis of 5:24 and Bock 1991c: 117 and n. 26.

picture of Jesus in Luke 7:39, where the Pharisee initially considered the possibility of Jesus' prophetic claims. In fact, the question in 7:49 expresses Jesus' action of forgiveness in a present tense, ἀφίησιν (*aphiēsin*, is forgiving), to show that Jesus is actively declaring such forgiveness.

The Pharisees' attitude is probably like that expressed in 5:21: "Who can forgive sins but God?" In Luke–Acts, the right of Jesus to judge and thus forgive sins is one of Luke's major claims, which shows one must deal with Jesus in order to be accepted by God (Luke 24:47; Acts 10:42; 17:31; on the Son of Man's authority, see Luke 22:69; Acts 7:55–56). Here is raw eschatological authority, and the Pharisees know it. It is not the claim of a mere prophet.

It is hard to know if the question is asked sincerely or as a complaint about Jesus' presumption. The doubts surrounding him, the past hostility toward him, and the lack of response to him favor the likelihood that the question is really a complaint, not a query (Plummer 1896: 214). What is clear is that the question is a fundamental one with which Luke's reader is to grapple (Schürmann 1969: 440). For Luke, it is impossible to be neutral about Jesus. One is either a Pharisee and questions Jesus' authority, or one approaches Jesus humbly as did the sinful woman, seeking with gratitude what he offers.

v. Jesus' Confirmation: The Woman's Faith Has Saved Her (7:50)

Jesus confirms the woman's response one final time, by noting that her faith has saved her. In doing so, he chooses to ignore the Pharisees' questions and yet his response is a challenge to them. Again, the woman is to realize that she stands accepted before God, as this is the point of the perfect tense σέσωκεν (*sesōken*, has saved). The mention of faith also confirms that the starting point of God's forgiving response to her was not her actions but the faith that motivated them (also Luke 8:48 = Matt. 9:22 = Mark 5:34; Luke 18:42 = Mark 10:52; Luke 17:19; Hendriksen 1978: 410; Oepke, *TDNT* 3:211). Faith is key in many Lucan texts (Luke 5:20; 7:9; 8:25; 12:28; 17:6; 18:8; 22:32). Salvation also is a key Lucan theme and is tied to forgiveness of sins (Acts 3:19, 26; 5:31; 10:43; 13:38; 22:16; 26:18; Foerster, *TDNT* 7:990, 997).

The woman is to depart with a sense of God's blessing, as Jesus tells her to go in peace (Mark 5:34 = Luke 8:48). She is to be secure in the knowledge that God has seen her faith (Marshall 1978: 314; Foerster, *TDNT* 2:413). The wording has a parallel in 1 Sam. 1:17 (Schürmann 1969: 439 n. 59; Leaney 1958: 147; Judg. 18:6; 2 Sam. 15:9). God has seen her faith and has reconciled her to himself (Luke

7:50

2:14; Danker 1988: 172). She can be sure that her relationship to God has changed.

Summary In Luke 7:36–50 the actions of a silent, sinful woman speak a thousand words. Why does Jesus associate with sinners? Because in forgiving sinners for a large debt of sin, God is able to transform them into people who display great love. Jesus understands this transformation, and it is at the heart of his mission. When this sinful woman displays an affection fueled by faith and gratitude, Jesus, unlike the Pharisee, is not offended. The woman can know that God has seen her faith and forgiven her sin. In her response, the woman pictures and exemplifies the honorable actions of a forgiven sinner. Faith expresses itself in love, gratitude, and devotion. Faith yields the fruit of forgiveness, which leads to the fruit of action.

The Pharisees' response also comes into view, for their response is not commendable. Their distance from and hostility to those who sin prevent the sinner from ever becoming aware that God can be gracious, that God can transform the sinner. As will often be the case, the Pharisees are negative examples. If one wants to see how not to respond, look to them. Such hostility toward sinners is to be avoided. Honesty about sin is important, but so is a clear message that God has graciously provided a solution to sin for the one who humbly approaches him. The disciple is not special and is not to be proud like the Pharisee. Rather, the disciple is to reflect the trust, which is so commendable in this woman and which represents the starting point of her walk with God.

Finally, there is the question of Jesus. His discernment of the woman's condition and the Pharisee's thoughts indicates that he is clearly a prophet. But he also takes upon himself the right to declare directly that a person's sins are forgiven. This is the authority of God exercised in divine judgment. The fundamental theological and christological question of the passage is asked by the Pharisees: "Who is this who even forgives sins?" Of course, the reader is aware that as far as Luke is concerned Jesus possesses such absolute authority. If the resolution of one's sin lies in Jesus' hands, then one should be responsive to him. It is a wise thing to be responsive to the one who wields the gavel.

Additional Notes

7:39. A few manuscripts (B, Ξ, 205) add a definite article and read ὁ προφήτης, which makes the issue whether Jesus is *the* (end-time) prophet, rather than *a* prophet. The external attestation for this alternative is not strong (Grundmann 1963: 171; Schürmann 1969: 433 n. 17).

7:45. The reference to the woman's kissing Jesus' feet from the moment of his arrival produced a textual variant (not discussed in UBS³) in some manuscripts (L, family 13, some Syriac), εἰσῆλθεν (she came) instead of εἰσῆλθον (I came). By referring to the woman's arrival, not Jesus', a potential conflict with 7:38 was removed. Hyperbole is sufficient explanation of εἰσῆλθον.

7:46. A few manuscripts (D, W, 079, Itala) omit τοὺς πόδας μου (my feet), suggesting perhaps an anointing of the head, but this omission is too poorly attested to be original (Marshall 1978: 312).

5. Picture of Faith:
The Ministering Women (8:1–3)

This brief summary is unique to Luke (Aland 1985: §155), although Luke 8:1 is similar in style to Matt. 9:35 (Mark 6:6b is less parallel). Jesus ministered in a large area, and a variety of women responded to him by providing material support for his ministry. Just as the sinful woman of Luke 7 acted out of love, so other women gave of their resources to Jesus' ministry. The emphasis falls once again on faith's vitality and concrete response.

Women play a major role in Luke's narrative. Talbert (1982: 90) compiled an impressive list of references to women in Luke's Gospel (an asterisk indicates an account unique to Luke):[1]

* Elizabeth (1:5–7, 13, 24–25, 36, 40–45, 56–61)
* Mary (1:26–56)
* Anna (2:36–38)
  Peter's mother-in-law (4:38–39)
* widow of Nain (7:11–17)
* sinful woman (7:36–50)
* women who minister (8:1–3)
  hemorrhaging woman (8:43–48)
* Martha and Mary (10:38–42)
* crippled woman (13:10–17)
* parable of the woman with lost coin (15:8–10)
* parable of widow and judge (18:1–8)
  widow's mite (21:1–4)
  women at the crucifixion (23:49, 55–56)
  women at the tomb (24:10–11)
* report of women at the tomb (24:22–24)

Women were at the center of many of Jesus' illustrations, and, as we see in the list above, Luke has many unique details on this theme. Women played a significant role in responding to and contributing to Jesus' ministry. Material support from women, at least from the wealthy, is not uncharacteristic of religious leaders of the first century (Plummer 1896: 215; Josephus, *Antiquities* 17.2.4 §§41–44; Arndt 1956: 222). The Pharisees also gained sup-

---

1. An additional thirteen women or groups of women are featured in Acts; see Talbert 1982: 91.

port from women, but the way in which they secured help from widows was subject to criticism (Luke 20:47 = Mark 12:40). Apparently it often was used as leverage for power.[2] The common ancient view of women as seen but not heard is reflected more in John 4:27; *Pirqe ʾAbot* 1.5 (= Hertz 1945: 17); *m. ʾAbot* 1.5; *m. Soṭa* 3.4; and *t. Ber.* 6.18 (= Neusner 1977–86: 1.40–41).[3]

Sources and Historicity

This small, uniquely Lucan unit introduces a period of Jesus' ministry where he is constantly on the move (8:1–9:50). After this passage much of the material from here to the end of the Galilean ministry section has parallels in Mark (Bovon 1989: 397). Since Luke 6:20, no Marcan parallels have been present. More importantly, the passage serves as a hinge, since the emphasis on concrete faith finds its final expression here before Luke turns back in 8:4–15 to the issue of responding to the word.

The summary in 8:1–3 shows Jesus carrying out his mission to take the gospel to all (4:43; Marshall 1978: 315). Known as the "tour" section of Luke, 8:1–9:50 precedes the journey to Jerusalem, which starts in 9:51.[4] Teaching and miracles alternate throughout Luke 8–9, with the high point being Peter's confession of Jesus as the Christ (9:20). The unit's burden is to give additional consideration to the question of who Jesus is, and Peter's messianic confession supplies the initial answer that Jesus will use to explain his mission to his disciples. This large unit provides a representation of Jesus' traveling ministry and how people respond to him as he overcomes nature, demons, and death (8:24, 32, 44, 54; Ellis 1974: 123). Jesus ultimately offers deliverance from such opposition for those who have faith (8:25, 48, 50). Meanwhile, lack of such faith is also present (8:12, 25, 37, 45, 53). The contrast between faith and unbelief continues to grow. Luke 8:1–3 introduces the reader to some who are responsive and exemplary, as they contribute their resources to the cause.

2. In the Josephean text just cited, a powerful woman, the wife of Pheroras, paid a fine for some Pharisees, who bargained for her favor by prophesying that God would take Herod's throne from him and give it to them and her! (These Pharisees were slain when the king found out about their view.)

3. Fitzmyer 1981: 696; SB 2:164; Wiefel 1988: 157–58. Grundmann 1963: 174 notes that women could not go into the synagogue or say the *Shemaʿ*. The late Tosepta text just cited gives the remark of a Jewish leader who rejoices that he is not a pagan, a woman, or unlearned. See also Leipoldt 1955: 69–114 and Witherington 1979.

4. There is disagreement about where the journey ends in Luke 19. I prefer 19:44. See the introduction to §IV (9:51–19:44).

The forms of this account are a summary and a catalogue of disciples (Bovon 1989: 397).[5] The outline of Luke 8:1–3 is as follows:

a. Jesus touring the region with the kingdom message (8:1a)
b. The Twelve and the women who support Jesus (8:1b–3)

Luke 8:1–3 shows that Jesus' mission of kingdom preaching continues and reaches both men and women. In fact, women who have responded play a vital role in his material support. Jesus' message reaches up into society as it penetrates Herod's palace.

Exegesis and Exposition

[1]Afterward he went through cities and villages, preaching and proclaiming the good news of the kingdom of God, and the Twelve were with him, [2]and also some women who had been healed from evil spirits and diseases: Mary called Magdalene, from whom seven demons were expelled, [3]and Joanna, the wife of Chuza, Herod's steward, and Susanna, and many others, who ministered to ⌜them⌝ out of their resources.

a. Jesus Touring the Region with the Kingdom Message (8:1a)

8:1a In a Lucan summary statement much like 4:14–15 and 4:43–44, Luke alludes to Jesus' touring ministry.[6] Both large and small settlements received his attention as he moved to cities and villages.[7] The message continued to be the kingdom of God (4:43; 9:2; 16:16). If Luke is to be our guide, then Jesus emphasized that the fulfillment of God's promise was at hand and that God's agent, through whom blessing could be realized, was present (4:16–30; 11:20; 17:21; on preaching and teaching the kingdom, see Friedrich, *TDNT* 2:718).

b. The Twelve and the Women Who Support Jesus (8:1b–3)

8:1b Two sets of travelers accompanied Jesus. The first group was the Twelve, whom Luke introduced in 6:12–16. Jesus did not minister in isolation. Rather, he took with him those who would eventually

---

5. Other Lucan catalogues may be found in Luke 6:12–16 and Acts 1:13; Berger 1984: 224.

6. Καθεξῆς is clearly temporal, denoting events that follow those of Luke 7; BAGD 388; BAA 788. It means afterward, but not necessarily soon afterward, as A. B. Bruce 1897: 518 correctly notes. It appears only in Luke–Acts (Luke 1:3; here; Acts 3:24; 11:4; 18:23). Acts 3:24 speaks of the sequence of prophets following Samuel—which spanned centuries.

7. The phrase κατὰ πόλιν καὶ κώμην (from city to village) has a distributive force and is grammatically linked to the reference to traveling; Fitzmyer 1981: 697; Arndt 1956: 223; Schürmann 1969: 445 n. 5.

share in preaching the message (9:1–6). Much of the wording of the verse is in Lucan style, suggesting that he has framed the summary.[8]

In addition to the Twelve, a group of women traveled with Jesus and **8:2** supported his ministry. Many of these women had benefited from his ministry either through exorcism or healing,[9] three of whom Luke singles out for specific mention. An itinerant ministry like Jesus' was common, and support from women was common; but it was unusual for women to travel with a rabbi.[10] The first woman, Mary Magdalene, was freed from the presence of seven demons.[11] This healing is not presented in detail anywhere in the NT, but Mark 16:9 has a similar summary. After Jesus' act of compassion, Mary decided to serve the agent of God who had healed her. The name Μαγδαληνή (Magdalene) suggests that she was from the region of Magdala, a town on the Sea of Galilee's western shore about three miles north of Tiberias (Godet 1875: 1.365; Arndt 1956: 222; Μαγδαλά is a variant reading in Matt. 15:39). As was argued in the exegesis of 7:37, she was not the sinful woman who anointed Jesus. Nor is it clear that she was immoral, for demon possession was not a sinful condition.[12] Mary stayed faithful to Jesus, for it is recorded that she watched the crucifixion (Matt. 27:55–56 = Mark 15:40 = John 19:25), saw where Jesus was laid (Matt. 27:61 = Mark 15:47 = Luke 23:55), and participated in the anointing of his body (Matt. 28:1 = Mark 16:1; Luke 24:10; Danker 1988: 173).

The mention of Joanna (Ἰωάννα), who also is present with Mary **8:3** Magdalene in 24:10, indicates the scope of Jesus' ministry. Jesus' message had reached into the world of the powerful, for Joanna was the wife of Chuza, who served as ἐπίτροπος (epitropos), an administrative official, in Herod's court.[13] Fitzmyer (1981: 698) suggests that he was manager of Herod's estate. The name Χουζᾶς (Chuza)

---

8. Creed 1930: 112–13 cites καὶ ἐγένετο (it came to pass), καθεξῆς (afterward), διοδεύω (to travel through), εὐαγγελίζω (to preach the good news), and ἀσθένεια (weakness) as Lucan vocabulary.

9. Luke again distinguishes these categories; see the exegesis of 4:33.

10. Talbert 1982: 92–93; Witherington 1979. On the escalated role of women in the later Jewish synagogue, see Brooten 1982.

11. On seven as denoting severe possession, see Marshall 1978: 316; Rengstorf, *TDNT* 2:630–31; cf. Mark 5:9.

12. Tertullian, *On Modesty* 11, identifies the woman in Luke 7:36–50 with the one in Matt. 26:6–13. Gregory the Great identifies the sinful woman with Mary Magdalene (Zahn 1920: 330–32 n. 33 lists the ancient texts). Ephraem the Syrian (*On the Sinful Woman; On Our Lord* 47) equates Magdalene, Mary of Bethany, and the woman of Luke 7—taking the error one step further.

13. BAGD 303; BAA 615; LSJ 669; Josephus, *Jewish War* 1.24.6 §487; *Antiquities* 18.6.6 §194; SB 2:164; Marshall 1978: 317; Fitzmyer 1981: 698; Hoehner 1972: 120, 303–5, 317 n. 4.

has Syrian and Nabatean roots (BAGD 884; BAA 1763). Some suggest that he might be the nobleman of John 4:46–53, but to establish this connection is difficult (Arndt 1956: 223; Geldenhuys 1951: 239–40 n. 5). Herod's foster brother Manaen was another figure in the royal entourage who had contact with Christians (Acts 13:1; Leaney 1958: 150).

The third woman, Susanna (Σουσάννα), is mentioned only here in the NT. Nothing else is known about her. Luke leaves unnamed the other women who minister to Jesus and his disciples through their material resources. The verb διακονέω (*diakoneō*) can mean "to wait tables" (Luke 10:40; 12:37; 17:8; 22:26–27 [three times]; John 12:2; Acts 6:2; BAGD 184 §1, §3; BAA 368 §1, §3; Beyer, *TDNT* 2:85) or "to serve" (Luke 4:39; Mark 1:13, 31; Rom. 15:25; BAGD 184 §2, §4; BAA 368 §2, §4). The more general meaning is supported by the reference to resources in this passage.[14] The women supported the entire group as a reflection of their faith and thereby picture an exemplary response to Jesus.[15] The early church will also be generous in providing for members' needs (Acts 4:32).

Summary Luke 8:1–3 shows the far-reaching impact of Jesus' ministry, stretching even into Herod's house. More significant is that those touched by Jesus' work minister to him and the Twelve through their possessions. Women are prominent in this regard. Whether recipients of exorcism or of his teaching, they contribute to the advance of God's kingdom through their resources. Such assistance was a practical means of helping the mission, thus enabling Jesus' entourage to tour the region.

Additional Note

8:3. What is the scope of the provision? Some manuscripts (א, A, L, Ψ, family 1, 33, some Byz, some Itala, some Syriac, Vulgate) read the singular αὐτῷ (to him) and limit the support to Jesus. Other manuscripts (B, D, W, Γ, Δ, Θ, family 13, some Byz, some Itala, some Syriac) read the plural αὐτοῖς (to them) and thus extend the support to the entire group. The external evidence is divided, but the harder reading is the plural. A singular is found in the distant parallel Matt. 27:55 = Mark 15:41, so that a scribe might make this text similar to those texts (Plummer 1896: 216; Klostermann 1929: 97).

14. So Schürmann 1969: 447 n. 29. Hengel 1963 argues that these women became important witnesses in the church, as their involvement in the resurrection accounts makes clear.
15. The feminine relative αἵτινες makes clear that the ministry of only the women is in view here.

III. Galilean Ministry: Revelation of Jesus (4:14–9:50)
   D. First Movements to Faith and Christological Questions (7:1–8:3)
➤ E. Call to Faith, Christological Revelation, and Questions (8:4–9:17)
   F. Christological Confession and Instruction about Discipleship (9:18–50)

E. Call to Faith, Christological Revelation, and Questions (8:4–9:17)

The fifth section of the Galilean ministry contains two subunits. Mixing teaching and miracle, the section's major topic is Jesus' authority.

The first subunit, 8:4–21, is made up of three pericopes that deal with the call to faith: 8:4–15, the seed parable, raises the issue of response to the word; 8:16–18 uses light imagery to picture the importance of responding to revelation; and 8:19–21 notes that Jesus' true family is made up of those who obey. The word as light calls for faith. The word is responded to in many different ways and faces many obstacles in its reception.

The second subunit of the fifth section, 8:22–9:17, shows Jesus' power and authority in ever-increasing spheres. Jesus can overcome the obstacles that destroy people, for he has power over nature (8:22–25), demons (8:26–39), and disease and death (8:40–56). To further illustrate his authority, Jesus commissions a group to share his message (9:1–6), enabling them to share in his authority and to give miraculous attestation to his message. In response to the spreading reports about Jesus, Herod wonders about Jesus' identity (9:7–9). As this issue is raised, the scene shifts to Jesus' ability to provide for the multitude (9:10–17). Throughout this subunit, Jesus shows the range of his authority. Luke keeps the question of Jesus' identity center stage.

The sixth and final section of the Galilean ministry, 9:18–50, will answer through Peter's confession the question of who Jesus is, and it will define Jesus' ministry through the picture of the suffering Son of Man.

1. Call to Faith (8:4–21)

Coming after the emphasis on faith in 7:36–8:3, this unit is a call to respond. The christological ground for that response was laid in the answer to the question of Jesus' identity in 7:18–35. Luke wishes to reassure his readers that Jesus can and should be trusted.

The three pericopes of this unit all relate to the theme of revelation and response. The seed parable explains various reactions to Jesus' message (8:4–15). Jesus then compares his message to light (8:16–18). Since light is meant to be seen, all should watch how they respond to Jesus' message, for through the word comes the opportunity to receive from God or to lose what one has. Finally, commendation is given to those who respond (8:19–21). Jesus' family consists of those who obey God.

a. Issue of Response: Seed Parable (8:4–15)

The parable of the seed—or, better, the parable of the seed among the soils—is one of Jesus' most well known parables. Regarding an emphasis on the seed's reception in different types of soil as unlikely in the original parable, Jeremias argues that the original parable was about the eschatological harvest and the point was that, despite many obstacles, the kingdom would yield fruit triumphantly.[1] Such fruit would amaze observers, since the growth process was subject to so many frustrations. Thus, sowing describes preaching the kingdom, and the harvest its result. The parable gives confidence that, despite appearances, all will turn out well. The problem with this view is that it reads the imagery too much in light of the kingdom parables of Mark 4 and makes it say much the same thing they do. But the parables in Mark 4 make distinct points: Jesus explains reactions to the kingdom message and then details how the kingdom emerges, despite those reactions. Luke agrees with this sense of the parables (Marshall 1978: 318), but Luke differs from Mark 4 = Matt. 13 by isolating and focusing on a single parable, rather than narrating all the kingdom parables. In this way, Luke can develop a theology of the word of God (Luke 8:4–21) and call people to respond. This focus is unique to him, but it is an appropriate topical use of Jesus' teaching.

Parables or comparisons are not new to Jesus' teaching in Luke's Gospel (5:36–39; 6:39, 41–44, 47–49; 7:41–42; Plummer 1896: 217). However, they are more elaborate and frequent from this point on. This parable is given in three stages. First, the parable is told (8:4–8). Then the reason for Jesus' teaching in parables is revealed (8:9–10). Finally, the interpretation of the parable is given (8:11–15). The entire unit stresses the variety of responses to the word of God, which is present in Jesus' teaching (this is why the title "parable of the soils" is a better name for the passage). Of course, the commendable thing is to respond obediently to the word, to receive it and bear fruit in response to it. But many ob-

---

1. Jeremias 1963a: 150 n. 81 protests against a name like "parable of the seed among the soils," when he complains about the title "fourfold field." On Jeremias's view, see the exegesis of and the additional note on 8:11. The title "parable of the sower" comes from Matt. 13:18.

stacles prevent such a fruitful result, as the variety of soil shows. In fact, the parable is a type of judgment against those who refuse to respond (8:8, 10). The stakes are rising, for rejection leads to a hardening of hearts and judgment from God. A person should not delay responding to the word, for as time passes it may become harder to respond. If one waits, it may eventually become too late.

Sources and Historicity

The parable of the seed among the soils has a parallel in Mark 4:1–20 = Matt. 13:1–23 (Aland 1985: §§122–24). That it is one in a cluster of parables in Matthew and Mark, unlike the Lucan account, may suggest a topical grouping in these books.[2] Regardless, this represents a return to Luke-Mark parallels (the last parallels were Mark 3:13–19a = Luke 6:12–16 and Mark 3:7–10 = Luke 6:17–19). This parable has a grammatical parallel in the Gospel of Thomas 9 and a conceptual parallel in the late-first-century or early-second-century A.D. 2 Esdr. [= 4 Ezra] 8:41–44. In the latter passage, it is said that not all seed sown in the ground takes root and so not all seed sown in the world will be saved.

The relative position of the parable in each Gospel makes difficult the chronological placement of this account, especially if anthologies are present in Matthew and Mark. Even without this possibility, placement is still difficult to determine. Of course, if this is common teaching in Jesus' ministry, its placement could vary. Three later miracles in Luke 8:22–56 appear before the seed parable in Matt. 13 (Matt. 8:23–34; 9:18–26).[3] In addition, Matt. 8–9 has a topical flavor, so that chronological placement becomes difficult to fix from Matthew. On the other hand, Mark and Luke agree in placing these miracles after the seed parable (Luke 8:22–56 = Mark 4:35–5:43). The parables of Matt. 13 = Mark 4 = Luke 8 seem to belong to the "Galilean tour," after Jesus had been engaged in ministry for a while; to specify their locale more than this seems to be unadvised (see the introductions to 8:19–21 and 8:22–25). However, the tighter Matthean connection to the context may well suggest a setting later in the tour (Matt. 13:1). This is one of three detailed parables found in all the Synoptics (the other two are the mustard seed in Mark 4:30–32 = Matt. 13:31–32 = Luke 13:18–

2. Cranfield 1959: 146. The distinct placement of these discourses in Matthew and Mark—i.e., gathered versus being scattered throughout Luke—shows that either multiple traditions about Jesus' kingdom teaching or an anthology of his teaching on the kingdom was available in the church. Matthew and Mark represent a summary of this teaching.

3. Luke's departure from Matthew here poses a challenging problem for those who hold to the two-Gospel hypothesis. The rationale is not clear if Luke has access only to Matthew. The Lucan arrangement seems to suggest additional input from elsewhere.

19 and the wicked farmers in Mark 12:1–12 = Matt. 21:33–46 = Luke 20:9–19).

The question of sources is complex. Most see Luke abbreviating Mark 4 at this point (Marshall 1978: 317–18; Fitzmyer 1981: 700). There are four views on the reason for this abbreviation:

1. Luke made alterations solely on the basis of his theological emphases (Fitzmyer 1981: 700, 706, 710; Carlston 1975: 70–76, esp. 70 n. 1).
2. Luke made alterations for theological reasons, but also used oral tradition for at least 8:9–10 (Schürmann 1969: 457, 461, 465; Ernst 1977: 264, 266–67).[4]
3. Luke used a special source (Schramm 1971: 114–23).
4. Luke knew Mark, but also had access to oral tradition (D. Wenham 1973–74).

As the exegesis will show, the verbal peculiarities of Luke's version are striking in that he often follows neither Matthew nor Mark, while choosing synonymous terminology that need not have a theological motive. In addition, Klostermann (1929: 97) notes other divergences from Mark, the most striking being the absence of a setting in 8:4, the absence of levels of harvest in 8:8, the absence of multiple parables in the unit, and the later use in 8:19–21 of material similar to Mark 3:31–35. While the absence of a setting may be due to the presence of a similar setting in Luke 5:1–3, in many cases it is very hard to explain the nature of Luke's verbal changes, given that they do not differ significantly from the Marcan and Matthean versions.[5] This raises the question of whether Luke used only a tradition like Mark. Marshall (1978: 318) suggests that oral tradition may play a key role here.[6]

Many regard the section on the parable's interpretation as secondary, claiming support from 8:9–10 and the unique Lucan detail and vocabulary in the interpretation.[7] Fitzmyer (1981: 711) notes three vocabulary ele-

---

4. Bovon 1989: 405 is close to this view, though he thinks that Luke had a written source for the interpretation of the parable, while other alterations reflect either oral tradition or Luke's theological emphases.

5. These verbal differences will be detailed in the exegesis. Fitzmyer 1981: 700 notes four striking cases where Luke and Matthew agree against Mark in Luke 8:4–8 (he also notes numerous changes that do not make much difference in meaning). The four Luke-Matthew agreements are an extra τοῦ in Luke 8:5a = Matt. 13:3, an extra αὐτόν in Luke 8:5b = Matt. 13:4, the omission of καὶ καρπὸν οὐκ ἔδωκεν in Luke 8:7 = Matt. 13:7, and ὁ ἔχων in Luke 8:8 = Matt. 13:9. See the exegesis for details and evaluation.

6. D. Wenham 1972. Schürmann 1969: 461 agrees only for 8:9–10. Fitzmyer 1981: 700–701 apparently rejects this suggestion but without clear support.

7. Fitzmyer 1981: 699–702, 706–7, 710–13 represents this approach; so also Bultmann 1963: 199–200 (on the Mark 4 parallel). Fitzmyer argues that the Lucan interpretation focuses more on the soils than on the fate of the seed. The point about vocabulary also applies to the Marcan interpretation, which is also seen as secondary.

ments in support of the secondary nature of the interpretation: (1) ὁ λόγος is uniquely used by Jesus for the Christian message, (2) σπείρω is used for preaching only here, and (3) certain compound adjectives lack Semitic equivalents: πρόσκαιροι (Mark 4:17) and ἄκαρπος (Mark 4:19).

None of these reasons is compelling. (1) The harvest as imagery for kingdom growth is common, as Mark 4 shows. The picture of seed for the kingdom message is a part of that larger metaphor. In fact, it is simply a metonymy of container for contents (message/availability of kingdom). (2) The reference to λόγος, which is a Lucan emphasis, is an appropriate summary description of what the kingdom message is. (3) The lack of Semitic equivalents does not mean these concepts are impossible to express in Semitic, even if single terms do not exist. The communication of such concepts would be simplified in oral tradition for reasons of brevity.

Jesus' teaching in Luke 8:9–10 is also appropriate to the ministry setting (against Schürmann 1969: 461, who sees the parable cheering up the disciples in the early church over rejection of the gospel). Jesus had already met intense rejection in his ministry, and he now needed to explain this to his disciples, who thought he was bringing God's promise. Surely the nation would welcome God's message and messenger. So what was happening? Jesus was almost compelled by circumstances to explain this seeming failure. The mystery character of parables as judgment on the hardening of hearts was relevant not only after the cross. It was a reality in Jesus' ministry as well. It fit the OT emphasis that God's word is a two-edged sword. God's message holds the opportunity for blessing or cursing, depending upon one's response.[8]

The Jesus Seminar takes a mixed approach to this unit (Funk and Hoover 1993: 305–6). They see the base parable in 8:5–8a (in pink type) as probably originating with Jesus. In favor of this link are its wide attestation and certain elements in Jesus' style (nature metaphors, groupings of three, mnemonic devices). They reject a tie to Jesus for the call to hear in 8:8b (in gray type) and the interpretation in 8:9–15 (in black type). The seminar holds that, unlike this text, Jesus taught that the kingdom was not a secret available to insiders only and that he lacked an "us" versus "them" attitude. However, this misrepresents what is taught here, for the issue of mystery is not about the kingdom, but about understanding how it works—a big difference. Jesus' handling of opponents like the Jewish leadership also reflects the reality that opposition ("them") is to be faced. These parables are introduced as an indication of emerging judgment for rejection, a warning that Jesus made earlier (4:25–28). Nothing said here is conceptually impossible for Jesus. The roots of this teaching reach to him and serve to ex-

---

8. In Deut. 28–32 and throughout the prophets, failure to obey brought judgment and exile, and repentance brought deliverance.

plain the varied reactions and extensive rejection that kingdom preaching yields.

In short, the church can translate and explain the parable's force without destroying its connection to Jesus or altering the saying's conceptual authenticity. This is certainly what Luke has done, and Mark and Matthew are no different in their presentations.[9]

This passage is clearly parabolic in form (Berger 1984: 46, 48, 60). It could be called a parable of growth or nature since it compares the word to the growth of seed. The Lucan form is a parable about Jesus' message. Matthew and Mark clearly compare the seed to the kingdom, but Luke doesn't ignore this connection (8:10). See excursus 8 on the issue of parables in Jesus' teaching and in Luke, in particular their definition and classification.

Luke 8:4–15 is structured in three parts: the first gives instruction to the masses, while the last two are given to the disciples. The outline of 8:4–15 is as follows:

   i. Parable of the seed told to all (8:4–8)
     (1) Setting (8:4)
     (2) Seed by the road (8:5)
     (3) Seed on the rock (8:6)
     (4) Seed among thorns (8:7)
     (5) Seed on good soil (8:8a)
     (6) Call to hear (8:8b)
  ii. Function of parables explained to the disciples (8:9–10)
     (1) Question by the disciples (8:9)
     (2) Contrast between the disciples and the rest (8:10)
 iii. Parable of the seed interpreted for the disciples (8:11–15)
     (1) Seed is the word of God (8:11)
     (2) Seed stolen by the devil (8:12)
     (3) Seed without root, fruitless in trial (8:13)
     (4) Seed choked by worry, riches, and pleasures (8:14)
     (5) Fruitful seed growing in the good heart (8:15)

The major theme of the passage is the variety of responses to the word of God caused by a variety of obstacles to the word: spiritual forces, trials, worry, riches, pleasures. Many who hear the word are overcome by these. But there is a decision to be faced when the word is preached. One can also grasp how the word is

9. On the relationship of Luke to Mark, see Marshall 1978: 318. The differences in wording show interpretive paraphrasing by the evangelists in this material, but it is in line with Jesus' original teaching and authentically reflects his teaching. For major arguments defending the authenticity, see P. Payne 1980.

variously received. Jesus gives a call to hear (i.e., obey) the message, which is called the "word" and is associated with the kingdom. The parables represent a warning, since they are present, in part, because of hardness of heart. On the positive side is fruit-bearing at a variety of levels. Fruit is the product of one's patience and holding fast to the word in obedience.

Exegesis and Exposition

[4]When a great crowd was coming together and people from town after town were coming to him, he said in a parable, [5]"A sower went out to sow his seed. And as he sowed, some fell by the road and was trampled on and the birds of the heaven ate it. [6]And some fell on the rock, and as it grew, it withered because it had no moisture. [7]And some fell among the thorns, and the thorns grew with it and choked it. [8]And some fell on the good soil and grew and produced fruit a hundredfold." And saying these things, he cried out, "The one who has ears, let him hear."

[9]And his disciples were asking him, "What might this parable be?" [10]And he said, "To you it has been given to know the mysteries of the kingdom of God, but to the rest, in parables, that seeing they may not see and hearing they may not understand.

[11]"Now the parable means this: The seed is the word of God. [12]The ones along the path are those who have heard; then the devil comes and takes the word from their heart, in order that they might not believe and be saved. [13]Those on the rock are those who, when they hear, receive the word with joy, but they do not have root; they believe for a time and after a while in trial they fall away. [14]And for those falling among the thorns, these are those who hear, but as they go, they are choked by life's worries, riches, and pleasures, and they do not produce fruit to maturity. [15]And as for that in the good soil, they are those with an honest and good heart, who, when they hear the word, hold fast and bear fruit with patience."

i. Parable of the Seed Told to All (8:4–8)
(1) Setting (8:4)

8:4 Jesus is still drawing a great deal of attention as crowds from many towns journey out to hear him. Συνιόντος . . . καὶ . . . ἐπιπορευομένων πρὸς αὐτόν (*syniontos . . . kai . . . epiporeuomenōn pros auton*, gathering together . . . and . . . coming to him) is a double genitive absolute: Jesus taught *as* the crowd gathered and *as* people came.[10] The present tenses in the participles suggest a growth in the crowd's development, since they picture the progress of the crowd's

---

10. Schürmann 1969: 452 n. 57 notes that the construction is Lucan, since only a few of the fifty-six Lucan examples are paralleled in Matthew or Mark. The introduction is Lucan.

coming and the people's gathering. Luke alone notes the varied roots of those in the crowd. Mark 4:1 = Matt. 13:1 mentions that Jesus' teaching occurred by the sea, a detail that Luke lacks (most suggest that Luke does not repeat the scene of Luke 5:1–3; Bovon 1989: 404). In fact, Mark and Matthew note that this teaching was given from a boat. No specific site is given, but it is probably the Sea of Galilee. The wording in each Gospel is somewhat distinct. While five terms are shared in exactly the same form between Mark and Matthew, Luke has no verbal overlap.

In Luke, crowds are often drawn to Jesus. They seem to grow as the account progresses, but this passage begins to suggest that many are interested in him only at a superficial level. The crowd's opposition will surface in Luke 9–13, while the crowd will continue to surround him in Luke 19 (on this theme, see Tannehill 1986: 143–66, esp. pp. 146–47 for Luke 8). The popular masses are shown as uncertain about what they think about Jesus. Ὄχλος (*ochlos*, crowd) occurs forty-one times in Luke, though not every mention is of the crowd tied to Jesus (e.g., in 3:10 the crowd is associated with John the Baptist). The bulk of these uses come before Luke 15, with only seven uses after that chapter and only five of them in 14:25–22:6— this shows how disciple-oriented the Jerusalem journey section of Luke becomes. Luke focuses on the popular ministry here, but later, Jesus' teaching will turn more inward. Disciples must be prepared for what they face on account of their committing to Jesus. The crowds are interested but fickle.

(2) Seed by the Road (8:5)

The parable begins in a field, with a Palestinian farmer sowing **8:5** seed.[11] Through the field runs a well-beaten path over which travelers pass. Sowing took place in the late fall or early winter (October to December), during the rainy season, and the crop sprouted in spring (around April or May) and was harvested around June. This type of labor was forbidden on the Sabbath (*m. Šab.* 7.2; Nolland 1989: 371–72 has a detailed discussion of the process). The imagery of sowing as a figure for God's giving or renewing life is common in Judaism (1 Enoch 62.8; 2 Esdr. [= 4 Ezra] 8:41; 9:31; Hos. 2:23 [2:25 MT]; Jer. 31:27; Ezek. 36:9; esp. Isa. 55:10–11; Nolland 1989: 375–76).

11. Seed as a metaphor for the word is common in the ancient world; Bovon 1989: 407 n. 25; Pseudo-Plutarch, *Liberal Education* 4 (2B); Plato, *Phaedrus* 276B–77A; Klauck 1978: 192–96. Ὁ σπείρων is generic in force and should be translated "a sower"; Arndt 1956: 229. Σπεῖραι is an infinitive of purpose: he went out "to sow his seed." On the generic article, see BDF §252 and BDR §252b.

Between one year's harvest and the next year's sowing, the field was left idle. The order of sowing and plowing is debated: in Palestine, often a field was plowed only after it was sown.[12] This sequence of sowing then plowing has been challenged, but the evidence brought forward is Greco-Roman, not Palestinian (so correctly Fitzmyer 1981: 703, against White 1964). Determining the order is not essential to the parable, since it refers merely to exposed seed on the path.

The sower carried a bag of grain over his shoulder, with the bag in the front. From this bag, he would toss the seed in rows. Of course, not all the seed reached the field. Some (ὃ μέν, *ho men*) would fall on the edge of the road, where it would be walked on by people and devoured by birds looking for food. It is this seasonal practice that Jesus narrates to open his parable. The practice in an agrarian culture is so common that his listeners would immediately picture the story. Of course, the sower in the initial version of the parable pictured Jesus (Marshall 1978: 319).

The verse shares details with the other Synoptics (e.g., seed falling by the path, birds devouring the seed), but Luke alone notes that the seed was walked on. The beginning of the verse is verbally paralleled by Matt. 13:3b–4a. The reference to trampled seed suggests that some of it fell on the edge of the road, but this detail is ignored by Luke when Jesus interprets the parable (Schürmann 1969: 453 n. 63). However, by intensifying the emotive picture, the image may add to the picture of abuse that the seed (i.e., the word) takes (Marshall 1978: 319). Outsiders (birds and travelers) destroy the seed (Wiefel 1988: 160).

(3) Seed on the Rock (8:6)

8:6 A second portion of the seed falls on rock, a thin layer of ground with limestone right under the topsoil, a condition common in the Palestinian hill country. Luke uses the term πέτραν (*petran*) for the rocky ground, while Matt. 13:5 has πετρώδη (*petrōdē*) and Mark 4:5 πετρῶδες (*petrōdes*). This is not a field with many rocks, but a base of rock under the soil. In an unplowed field, such land is not easily spotted (Linnemann 1966: 115–16). At first, all looks fine as the plant sprouts up and grows. But eventually the plant withers. Luke alone attributes the loss to lack of moisture. The root cannot receive water because the ground cannot hold moisture.

---

12. Jub. 11.11, 24; *m. Šab.* 7.2; Linnemann 1966: 115–16; Kistemaker 1980: 17; Jeremias 1966–67; and Jeremias 1963a: 11–12. P. Payne 1978–79 discusses the debate about the Palestinian order of sowing and plowing.

Matthew and Mark speak only of the plant's lacking root, by which they mean the lack of a developed root system (Marshall 1978: 320). In fact, Matthew and Mark are close in wording, with Luke's wording being distinct, though painting the same picture. Luke is aware of the problem being a lack of root, but he holds until the interpretation Mark's description of the seed's lack of root. Interestingly, Luke and Matthew reverse their choice of adjective for "another" from that of Matt. 11:3 = Luke 7:19, where Matthew had ἕτερον (*heteron*) and Luke had ἄλλον (*allon*). Luke does not mention details that Matthew and Mark do: the quick initial growth and the scorching of the plant by the sun (Creed 1930: 114). The point is that ultimately this seed is unproductive.

(4) Seed among Thorns (8:7)

8:7

The third group of seed falls in good ground, but shares that ground with greedy neighbors: thorns. These Palestinian weeds can grow up to six feet tall and often bud with flowers of various colors: red, blue, or yellow (Linnemann 1966: 116). They also take so much nourishment from the ground that nothing else can grow around them. Despite the plowing that would have accompanied the growing season, such thistles inevitably remain. The seed is not purposely mixed with thorns, but when the seed sprouted, thorns are also present (Plummer 1896: 218). Once again, an outside factor has intervened to prevent the seed from producing fruit. A similar warning is found in Jer. 4:3.

Luke's wording is again abbreviated. Mark 4:7 specifies that this seed yielded no grain, a point that Luke saves for the interpretation (Marshall 1978: 320). Matthew 13:7 parallels Luke in lacking this note about yield. In general, however, Matthew's and Mark's wordings are parallel, although interestingly each writer uses a different form of the verb to describe the choking of the seed.[13] Such insignificant differences raise the question whether the source for this material was only written. It is hard to justify such incidental differences.[14] Although most commentators argue that Luke is using Mark's version, it seems likely that this parable had broad circulation with variety of wording.

13. Matt. 13:7 has ἔπνιξαν; Mark 4:7, a compound form, συνέπνιξαν; Luke, yet another compound form, ἀπέπνιξαν. For Luke's term (only here and in Luke 8:33 in the NT), see BAGD 97 and BAA 195.

14. Note also the distinct pronouns for the subject: Matt. 13:7 has ἄλλα, Mark 4:7 ἄλλο, and Luke ἕτερον. Matthew is consciously alluding to the plural, while Mark and Luke have the singular.

(5) Seed on Good Soil (8:8a)

8:8a The fourth group of seed lands on good soil and, overcoming the obstacles present, grows to bear more seed. The yield is a hundredfold.[15] Linnemann (1966: 117) notes that the fruit of a single grain is in view. On average such a seed would bear thirty-five progeny, with some occasionally producing sixty or a hundred pieces of grain.[16] It is interesting that Luke uses four prepositions to describe the different seed: παρά (*para*, by the road), ἐπί (*epi*, upon the rock), ἐν μέσῳ (*en mesō*, in the midst of the thorns), and εἰς (*eis*, into good soil) (Godet 1875: 1.369; Bovon 1989: 412).[17] In contrast to the failure of the other seed, only the last seed penetrates the soil and achieves its goal of becoming fruitful. It depicts God's word bearing fruit and growing (Isa. 55:11; Acts 6:7; Col. 1:6; Schürmann 1969: 454–55). The kingdom message will spread despite obstacles in its way.

Matthew 13:8 = Mark 4:8 has καλήν (*kalēn*, good), while Luke has the synonym ἀγαθήν (*agathēn*).[18] Luke's wording is more abbreviated than the other Synoptics (e.g., he does not mention the thirtyfold and sixtyfold yields) and somewhat distinct from them, though making the same point.[19] The lack of levels of fruitfulness in Luke is explained in various ways (Marshall 1978: 320). Leaney (1958: 151) argues that gnostic levels of spiritual advance are avoided by Luke's approach. However, each seed in Matthew and Mark has a different yield, which is not a picture of the growth of an individual seed, but of many different seeds. Thus, the word yields a variety of responses from a variety of people. Schürmann (1969: 465) suggests that Luke is avoiding the appearance that there are levels of Christians (also Schweizer 1984: 144). This may be correct, but since Luke's account is shorter it is possible to view this just as a stylistic abbreviation with no conscious theological motive.

---

15. Gen. 26:12 speaks of Isaac's hundredfold yield, but that text has no clear connection to Luke. It is debated whether this is a normal or exaggerated yield; Nolland 1989: 371–72 opts for a high yield. On the ancient custom of measuring a yield twice, see Midr. Song 7.3.3. Normal yields ranged from sevenfold to tenfold (Schürmann 1969: 454 n. 78), so that a hundredfold return is exceptional.

16. Plummer 1896: 219 notes that figures as large as three-hundredfold are given for grain in Babylon; Herodotus 1.193.

17. Only Luke has this variation. Matthew uses ἐπί for the last three soils, while Mark has εἰς for the last two. Creed 1930: 114–15 notes a possible Semitism in ἐποίησεν καρπόν (yielded fruit) (see Luke 3:8).

18. Since Luke uses καλός ten times in Luke–Acts, including twice in Luke 8:15, the change is hard to explain. Bovon 1989: 412 n. 54 attempts to explain this variation as emphasizing the ground's quality.

19. It is interesting that in Matt. 13:8 = Mark 4:8, these distinctions are noted in the reverse order: Mark ascends to hundredfold, while Matthew descends to thirtyfold.

(6) Call to Hear (8:8b)

At the end of the parable, Jesus calls "the one with ears to hear" (ὁ   **8:8b**
ἔχων ὦτα ἀκούειν, *ho echōn ōta akouein*) to heed (ἀκουέτω, *akouetō*)
the teaching. Jesus often uses this call to stress the importance of reflecting on his teaching (Matt. 11:15; 13:9, 43; Mark 4:9, 23; 7:16;
8:18 [stated negatively]; Luke 8:8; 9:44; 14:35; Horst, *TDNT* 5:552;
ὦτα [ears] is from οὖς; BAGD 595; BAA 1204–5). The audience is
challenged to respond to the message. Leaney (1958: 151) notes that
the wording reflects a Semitism, but this is disputed, probably correctly, by Fitzmyer (1981: 704). Marshall (1978: 320) notes a conceptual parallel to Ezek. 3:27, and Schürmann (1969: 454) notes a parallel to Isa. 55:10–11, to which should be added Isa. 55:3.

ii. Function of Parables Explained to the Disciples (8:9–10)
(1) Question by the Disciples (8:9)

The disciples are curious as to the parable's meaning and so ask   **8:9**
Jesus to explain it to them. Matthew 13:10 also says that the disciples asked the question, while Mark 4:10 attributes it to "those with
the Twelve." The optative εἴη (*eiē*, might be), introducing an indirect
question, expresses the request to know the parable's sense.[20] The
singular ἡ παραβολή (*hē parabolē*, the parable) shows that the explanation of only the last parable is requested. This singular emphasis
contrasts with the general question about parables found in Matt.
13:10 = Mark 4:10.[21] Here is another instance where Luke's version
has its own focus, yet Jesus' answer using the plural in Luke 8:10
shows that the question as raised in the other Gospels is not ignored. The disciples know Jesus well enough to know that he was
not giving them a lesson in agriculture, but was illustrating something about God. Luke's reply is softer in depicting the response. He
shortens the quotation from Isaiah and lacks any question to the
disciples about their understanding the parable (Fitzmyer 1981:
706).

(2) Contrast between the Disciples and the Rest (8:10)

Jesus explains that the word divides people into two groups and that   **8:10**
parables in particular function this way. The parables reveal to disciples the mysteries of God's kingdom. By committing themselves to

---

20. BAGD 223–24 §II.3; BAA 451 §II.3. This optative is a Lucan expression, since
he uses it so frequently in contrast to the other Synoptics.

21. Matthew stresses why Jesus taught the crowd with parables, while Mark just
notes that the question was about parables and adds specifically that the conversation was given in private. The difference with Luke is easy to explain, since Matt. 13
= Mark 4 has multiple parables; Marshall 1978: 321.

Jesus and his teaching, disciples have access to understanding these parables and can see the parables' connection to each other and to life (Luke 6:20–23; 10:23–24; 1 Cor. 2:12–15). But "the rest" (τοῖς . . . λοιποῖς, tois . . . loipois) do not have access to the symbolism that the parables depict. Thus the parables function as a form of judgment where the story is perceived but not comprehended. Jesus answers by describing the parables' effect, using the plural, rather than the disciples' singular. This shift broadens the question's scope, which had asked only about the seed parable.

The verse contains a key contrastive parallelism and a significant ellipsis. Parables are not just for unbelievers, or else their being recorded in the Gospels for the church does not make sense. The mysteries of the kingdom "are given" (= δέδοται, dedotai, which is elided in the next clause) to the disciples by means of parabolic instruction.[22] Since the parables contain mysteries, they have a positive function for those who embrace Jesus. To those who do not embrace Jesus, the parables are not interpreted and thus remain enigmatic. Thus, it is wrong to see the parables functioning only in a concealing role. Only when a parable is unexplained in terms of how it relates to the kingdom does it have this function. That the disciples have access to the mysteries of God's kingdom in contrast to the crowd shows the twofold function of parables. That the disciples are particularly blessed is seen in the emphatic position of ὑμῖν (hymin, to you) and the perfect tense δέδοται (it stands given).[23] The passive δέδοται makes clear that God has given this gift to the disciples (Fitzmyer 1981: 707).

The judgment on the rest is indicated by their "seeing but not seeing, hearing but not understanding" (βλέποντες μὴ βλέπωσιν καὶ ἀκούοντες μὴ συνιῶσιν, blepontes mē blepōsin kai akouontes mē syniōsin)—a phrase in Isa. 6:9 that alludes to judgment.[24] The concept of judgment because of hardness of heart is found often in the NT (John 3:17–19; 9:39–41; Rom. 1:18–32; 9:17–18; Acts 28:26–27). The parables' purpose for the rest of humanity is to prevent their comprehension of God's plan. Ἵνα (hina, in order that) indicates pur-

---

22. Matt. 13:11 and Luke have a plural reference to mysteries, while Mark 4:11 has the singular. Bovon 1989: 413 sees the influence of oral tradition here.

23. Arndt 1956: 230 notes that no decretal theology is explicit in the reference to one's being given the mysteries, since that would require an aorist tense. But despite Arndt's note, the implication of God's sovereign direction, though not a formal decree, is present. A grammatical parallel to this use of ὑμῖν is found in 1 Cor. 1:18, where ἡμῖν is thrown forward in its clause.

24. Luke does not cite the text explicitly, but summarizes. This is not a softening of the reference, but his typical effort to shorten and summarize. For studies on the use and interpretation of Isa. 6:9–10 in Judaism and the early church, see Hesse 1955; Gnilka 1961; C. A. Evans 1989c.

pose: God in judgment removes the benefit of revelation (Fitzmyer 1981: 708; Stauffer, *TDNT* 3:327; BDF §369.2).[25]

In saying that the parables' purpose is to conceal, there is an assumption, suggested by the allusion to Isaiah, that the concealing takes place for those who are resistant to hearing. Isaiah takes his message to an obstinate nation that is facing judgment and exile for refusing to respond properly to God. Isaiah is told that the people will not respond. In fact, in Isa. 6:9–10 MT God will bring hardness of heart on the people (note the hiphil imperatives in Isa. 6:10), so that response is not possible. However, in the larger context of Isaiah, opportunity for repentance is still offered and the promise of a remnant is made (Isa. 1:21–26; 9:1–7 [8:23–9:6 MT]; 11:1–9; 14:24–26; 17:14; 28:16–17, 29), so the judgment is not comprehensive. Thus, a hardening of the nation in Isaiah does not preclude fulfilling the promise to it.

Codex א of Isa. 6:9–10 LXX, which Matthew cites (as does Acts 28:26–27), speaks only of judgment coming to the nation whose heart is hard. The linkage of God's judgment and human hardness of heart is also evidenced in Isaiah. The ambiguity in how the Isaiah passage was read is reflected in the NT. The rejection comes out more clearly in Matthew's full citation of Isaiah, for Matthew lacks the purpose nuance of Luke, a nuance that Mark 4:10–12 also has. Matthew has a ὅτι (*hoti*, because) clause instead of a ἵνα, which shows that the background of this remark is not the parables considered in abstract from the rest of Jesus' ministry. Rather, the parables are introduced because of the previous lack of response to Jesus' teaching, as the movement in Luke already shows.[26] Matthew and Luke, though nuanced differently, are in essential agreement. Thus, this concealing function of the parables is a response to previous rejection of Jesus, a rejection that has consequences. In short, what the disciples get in parables is insight into the kingdom, but what is given to those who reject God's offer of revelation is a story that prevents them from understanding what God is doing.[27]

---

25. Others suggest that ἵνα indicates result. So Danker 1988: 177 argues that ἵνα expresses not purpose, but tragic realization; but see 9:45 and 11:50. Jeremias 1963a: 17 suggests that the parables' purpose is to fulfill the scriptural promise and thus he sees an ellipse. However, the Isaiah passage is key and is negative. Judgment is expressed here because of hardness of heart.

26. Matthew's difference with Luke and Mark may serve only to relate parabolic teaching to a context larger than the parables themselves. Earlier failure to respond leads to judgment. Isaiah's text points to the analogy between the current rejection and the generations of old, a common theme in Luke (Luke 11:37–54; 13:31–35; Acts 7:51–53) and the NT (Matt. 23).

27. For δέδοται as the elided verbal idea in the clause starting with τοῖς δὲ λοιποῖς, see Fitzmyer 1981: 708.

The exact nature of the mysteries (μυστήρια, *mystēria*) being revealed is determined by the nature and interpretation of each parable. Thus, in the following verses Jesus will explain this parable and give a clue as to the mystery it describes. In this way the disciples will receive divine insight into God's plan (Godet 1875: 1.371; Liefeld 1984: 906; Nolland 1989: 379).[28] Just as mystery in the Book of Daniel was revealed through divine insight into רָז (*rāz*), the Aramaic term for "mystery," so also with the parabolic mysteries in the Gospels. For Daniel, mystery is revelation that is present but not understood.[29] Luke's and Matthew's plural μυστήρια refers to the parts of the plan, while Mark's singular μυστήριον refers to the whole plan as a unit. This is the only use of μυστήριον in the Synoptics (Ellis 1974: 125).

Luke's wording in this verse is close to Matthew, especially in describing the benefits to the disciples. In describing the judgment on the rest, Luke cites a shorter, more paraphrastic form of Isa. 6:9 than do Mark and Matthew, which fits Luke's abbreviated presentation of the whole account. Matthew 13:14–15 has the fullest Isaiah citation. In Mark 4:11, the Isaiah quotation is applied to "those outside," while in Matt. 13:11 it is applied simply to "them."[30] In addition, Matt. 13:12 has a saying that Luke 8:18b = Mark 4:25 saves for a slightly later position. The variety in the tradition's wording of this verse is interesting, especially when placed alongside the several points of difference already noted. D. Wenham (1972: 24–31) argues that Luke and Matthew share a similar, earlier form of the tradition. This is possible, but hard to establish clearly. What is clear is that the amount of Synoptic variation shows the tradition's complexity and the difficulty of tracing its development.

Doubting whether Jesus could say something as exclusive as Isa. 6:9, many attribute the remark to the early church (Luce 1933: 166). This view argues that Jesus could not be the source because parables were present in Jesus' ministry before his rejection by the people. Also, the rejection suggested in the Isaiah quotation is out of character with Jesus' attempt to draw people into the kingdom. But these objections are not telling. It is clear that, as the rejection heightens, Jesus will rebuke those who resist. The Isaiah remark is, thus, both

28. On μυστήριον as revealing God's plan, see Dan. 2:17–23, 27–30; cf. also Ps. 25:14; Prov. 3:32; Amos 3:7; Bornkamm, *TDNT* 4:814–15, 817–18.

29. The Qumran scrolls also refer to the "secrets of God" (רזי אל, *rzy ʾl*): 1QpHab 7.8; 1QS 3.23; 1QM 3.9; 16.9, 14; 17.9, 17 (Fitzmyer 1981: 708). On μυστήριον in the NT, sometimes referring to "new" revelation and other times to "clarifying" revelation, see Bock 1994a: 80–85. In these parables, μυστήριον refers to "clarifying" revelation, which means that additional truth is connected to old promises, since Matt. 13:51–52 compares the mystery kingdom parables to old and new things.

30. On "those outside" as traditional terminology, see Schürmann 1969: 460 n. 110; 1 Cor. 5:12–13; Col. 4:5; 1 Thess. 4:12; 1 Tim. 3:7.

a statement of purpose and a warning that hardness has its cost. Jesus' direct challenges to the Pharisees in Luke 5–6 show this ability to rebuke early on, as do his stronger responses in 11:29–54. (Jesus also has an implied warning to the crowds in 4:25–28.) The question of how long the parables were present in Jesus' ministry is irrelevant to their two-sided function. They may have taken on a greater role as the ministry moved on, and their twofold function may have emerged more clearly as time passed.[31]

iii. Parable of the Seed Interpreted for the Disciples (8:11–15)
(1) Seed Is the Word of God (8:11)

Jesus now turns back to the seed parable. The parable's interpretation is fairly clear in its Synoptic form. But the origin of that understanding is debated. The main issue is whether the original parable had many points (the responses to the kingdom message) or a single point (the kingdom's eventual emergence despite various obstacles). Jeremias (1963a: 77–79, 149–51) argues for a single point (often called the eschatological view); I prefer multiple points (see the additional note). **8:11**

That various factors prevent response to the word is clear in much of Jesus' teaching. Jesus expresses concern about things such as wealth and trials getting in the way. In fact, these concerns sometimes are a dominant theme.[32] Thus, this parable with its multiple points could fit Jesus' teaching. But did the original parable have just one point? The view that argues that parables must have only one point has come under increasing attack (R. Brown 1962; Dahl 1951: 136–37; Black 1959–60). This is not to say every detail needs to be allegorized, but that certain parables have multiple elements of relevance. Such questions no longer can be answered simply by appeal to some global principle. Many of the parables reveal an ability to reflect multiple points, usually one point per main character or object (Blomberg 1990).

A major argument against the eschatological view is that, if the only point is the great harvest of the fourth group of seed, then three-quarters of the parable adds little or nothing to the story.[33]

---

31. Also for authenticity is Marshall 1978: 321. Fitzmyer 1981: 706–7 accepts the assertion as coming from Jesus but not its placement in this setting. For more on the relationship between the Isaiah Targum and the NT, especially Mark, see the additional note. For more on authenticity, see the discussion of sources and historicity in this unit.

32. Luke 12:1–12; 16:1–13, 19–31 are good examples. Parallels exist for most of this material, so this is not a uniquely Lucan theme.

33. It is important to note that Jeremias's complaint is only about the later origin of the parable's interpretation. Jesus does make these interpretive remarks privately

Nor is it necessary to insist that all of Jesus' parables address the same topic; that is, Mark 4:3–20 need not deal exactly with the same theme as do the other kingdom parables. Rather, the kingdom parables complement—but do not repeat—one another. In short, the parable's various themes found in other Gospel passages show the strength of the imagery and the impression that it left on the church. Gerhardsson (1967–68: 166, 186–88), who accepts the interpretation as going back to Jesus, notes that the parable and its interpretation fit "hand in glove" (also Ellis 1974: 126). It seems clear that the basic interpretation belongs to Jesus.[34] Nonetheless, it is likely, given the verbal differences within the tradition, that Luke and the other Synoptic writers paraphrased the teaching in spots to make explicit certain points that were part of Jesus' intention (e.g., 8:12, though such alterations are in all strands of the tradition). Given the interpretation's authenticity, we now turn to the explanation that Jesus gives to the parable.[35]

The seed is the word of God, an association that was also made in Judaism.[36] In the Lucan context (8:10), it is the word from God about the kingdom (K. Schmidt, *TDNT* 1:583). Matthew and Luke have a more condensed introduction to the interpretation than does Mark, who gives an initial rebuke of the disciples before Jesus' reply. Matthew 13:18–19 is explicit in mentioning the word of the kingdom and gives the parable the title "parable of the sower."

(2) Seed Stolen by the Devil (8:12)

8:12   The first group of seed represents the response that never has a chance to germinate. Satan comes and prevents the message from taking root in the heart (i.e., in the person). Luke says that Satan takes the message from (ἀπό, *apo*) their hearts, while Mark 4:15 says

---

to the disciples at a different time from the giving of the parable, but the elements of obstacle are in the original imagery and so demand interpretation as well. This distinction, however, does not entirely resolve the debate, since other points are also raised to argue for the eschatological view.

34. Marshall 1969 notes that the many Lucan touches in the parable do not alter its basic meaning. See the additional note for more defense of the parable's authenticity and a critique of Jeremias's position.

35. Marshall 1978: 324 and Fitzmyer 1981: 713 take the pronoun in the phrase ἔστιν . . . αὕτη as a predicate, yielding, "The parable means this. . . ." Bovon 1989: 407 n. 21 prefers a reference back to 8:9 and translates, "This parable is. . . ." There is little difference in the options. Bovon also notes that this use of the verb recalls Jewish usage, where apocalyptic visions are interpreted. He cites Klauck 1978: 88 n. 273 for details.

36. 2 Esdr. [= 4 Ezra] 9:29–33; Plummer 1896: 220. The imagery of 2 Esdr. [= 4 Ezra] 8:41–44 is close to this parable; Fitzmyer 1981: 712; Schürmann 1969: 463 n. 131. 1 Enoch 62.8 speaks of sowing saints.

that he takes the message that is in (εἰς, *eis*) them. In the battle for hearts between God and Satan, Luke says that some of the failure to respond to the word is the devil's work. As a result, any opportunity for faith and salvation is lost. For such people, hearing is the most that happens. There is no attraction to the message or reflection on it. Birds are often a figure for evil in Judaism (Jub. 11.11–13; Apocalypse of Abraham 13.3–7; 1 Enoch 90.8–13; Nolland 1989: 384).

Luke's wording is close to Mark 4:14–15 in describing the seed as "by the way" (παρὰ τὴν ὁδόν, *para tēn hodon*) and in speaking of the devil's "taking the word" (αἴρει τὸν λόγον, *airei ton logon*). In addition, Luke and Matt. 13:19 refer to the heart. The tradition's complexity is shown by each writer's use of a different term for Satan: ὁ πονηρός (*ho ponēros*) in Matt. 13:19, ὁ σατανᾶς (*ho satanas*) in Mark 4:15, and ὁ διάβολος (*ho diabolos*) in Luke 8:12.[37] Describing the first group with a more vivid present participle, Matt. 13:19 alone notes that lack of understanding precedes the evil one's act.[38] Luke alone mentions faith and salvation, though this may function as a brief explanatory equivalent of Matt. 13:14–15, which cites Isa. 6:9–10.[39]

The Lucan peculiarity of mentioning faith and salvation is often overinterpreted to say that Luke intends all the responses to be seen as "saved." It seems better, however, to say that the spiritual condition of this first seed is clearly a picture of the unsaved; so also the saved condition of the last seed is clear. On the other hand, the spiritual position of the two middle groups of seed is less than clear, possibly on purpose. To discuss the spiritual condition of these groups of seed may, however, take the edge and ambiguity out of the text, an ambiguity that should remain since these two groups of seed are not spoken of with approval by Jesus. In fact, to ask this question of each soil is to misdirect the parable's emphasis. Jesus is not communicating the minimum response required to receive blessing. Rather, he is instructing the disciples on fruitfulness by pointing out

37. Creed 1930: 116 notes that Luke uses both σατανᾶς and διάβολος. In fact, Luke uses each term seven times in Luke–Acts; Bovon 1989: 408 n. 32. It is hard to explain this difference as a conscious change because of stylistic preference; so correctly Marshall 1978: 325.

38. "When anyone hears the word and does not understand"; Kistemaker 1980: 26. This Matthean touch pictures Satan as capitalizing on an initial lack of response. The blame is not only the devil's and may be a point parallel to Luke's mention of the word's being trod under foot in 8:5. The detail is important, because it suggests the danger of taking the word lightly and indicates the exposed position that rejection of God's word produces.

39. So Ernst 1977: 269. Some see a Paulinist touch here. Plummer 1896: 220 suggests that the Lucan conclusion in 8:12 may go back to Paul; Arndt 1956: 230. Others suggest that Luke is using church terminology to make clear what Jesus means, a point that seems likely; Marshall 1978: 325; Fitzmyer 1981: 713.

obstacles that prevent such a response. The fourth seed is the only one that is portrayed favorably. The second and third groups are viewed tragically since opportunity for fruitfulness was present but lost, while the first group is portrayed as never having a good chance. Jesus' point is that only the fourth seed really achieves the goal that the word is intended to produce. Thus, asking the soteriological question of soils two and three results in short-circuiting the parable's force and taking the edge out of its teaching, by forcing it to say too much.

Scripture deals with two concerns on an alternating basis, sometimes side by side and sometimes mixed together: "How does one get in?" and "How is one fully effective?" The emphasis on fruitfulness indicates that the second concern is dominant in this parable. This parable seeks to encourage ethical righteousness, while noting which factors prevent its presence. The issue of "getting in" is largely unaddressed, though it is clear that the first group never gets in the door, while the fourth group clearly does. The position of the two middle groups is less clear, though the context gives some hints about their condition, as the exegesis will show. What is clear is that soils one through three do not have a successful experience with the seed, for they bear no fruit. There is little comfort for them.

The first group of seed also shows that a spiritual battle ensues when the kingdom is preached. As Liefeld (1984: 907) notes, God's and Satan's desires are very different (2 Pet. 3:9). Satan's goal is to prevent belief, as the ἵνα (hina) clause of Luke 8:12b makes clear (Foerster, *TDNT* 7:160): Satan takes the word, *"in order that* they may not believe and be saved."* The obstacles thrown in the way of the other groups of seed show this same battle waged in a more subtle manner.

Another point is important here. This text is not an existential moment-by-moment picture of how one receives the word at various times, but pictures what the word does throughout the totality of one's life. One is not pictured as moving from soil to soil or of being in different soils at different times. Such an implication might be drawn from this imagery, but it is not the point of the parable. The soil represents the different kinds of individuals viewed in terms of their whole life, not the different responses of an individual. Taking one's life as a whole, the parable is designed to produce reflection on the question, "What *single* type of response to the word have I given?" Or, "What various responses to the word exist among people as one looks at the whole pattern of their response?" Jesus is explaining why the word is received in a variety of ways. He notes that many obstacles prevent fruit-bearing, while faithful, patient reception produces fruit.

(3) Seed without Root, Fruitless in Trial (8:13)

The second group of seed faces the first obstacle to fruitfulness: a **8:13** shallow faith that cannot survive the pressure of persecution. The verb εἰσίν (*eisin*, are) is elided and should be supplied (Luke 8:12, 14, 15; Mark 4:16 = Matt. 13:20; Plummer 1896: 221). In these people there is an initial joyous reception of the message, but the reception is superficial, without root, and when persecution comes, they fall away. This verse is clear in what it describes, but its implications are less clear.

The problem is the juxtaposition of two key terms, belief and falling away. Reception of the word and faith for a short time are followed by a falling away. In Luke–Acts, δέχομαι (*dechomai*) frequently indicates a response in faith to the message or a reception of God's messengers (Luke 9:48 [four times], 53; 10:8, 10; 18:17; Acts 8:14; 11:1; 17:11; Schürmann 1969: 464 nn. 140, 145; 237 n. 117; this meaning elsewhere in the NT at 1 Thess. 1:6; 2:13; James 1:21; Bultmann, *TDNT* 6:214 n. 291). The term is limited to describing an initial reception of the word, since it is often associated with the response to a missionary endeavor. In many cases, it is clear that the response is a genuine one. However, the case of Simon Magus in Acts 8 raises the question whether this is always the case and introduces ambiguity into the force of the image.

Ambiguity also comes in the term for falling away, ἀφίστημι (*aphistēmi*), which has no technical function in Luke–Acts in that it normally describes physical departure (Luke 2:37; 4:13; Acts 12:10). However, it does have a clearer force in NT usage. The idea of falling away from faith is found in the NT (1 Tim. 4:1; Heb. 3:12) and LXX (Jer. 3:14; Dan. 9:9) with an extremely negative force.[40] The meaning of the Hebrews text is debated, though it is clear that the failure involves not entering into faith rest, with the potential of abandoning Christ for a return to Judaism (Heb. 3:12–4:9). Luke leaves ambiguous the spiritual condition of the fallen person, since an initial response contrasts with an absence of faith at the end of life.[41] But the situation does not meet with Jesus' approval: it is seen somewhat

40. 1 Macc. 11:43; 1 Enoch 5.4; BAGD 126–27; BAA 254; Schlier, *TDNT* 1:513. Braun, *TDNT* 6:252, says that ἀφίστημι means apostasy.

41. See the note on the soteriology of the parable in the exegesis of 8:12. The question theologically can be put this way: Faith saves, but is temporary faith saving faith? Can one leave Christ and still have the faith that saves? Or to ask it yet another way: Can one be saved without faith, since to fall away from faith is to no longer have it? That is the question this soil raises. It is clear that Jesus is not viewing this soil positively. Another way to say it is, If God "gifts" salvation in Christ, would he give it only to have the person throw it away? This seems unlikely. Regeneration changes the heart with regard to how God and Christ are seen (2 Cor. 6:17; Rom. 8:14–16).

tragically; all the indications are negative. The major point is that this belief is short-lived and unproductive because trial dissolves faith (on this theme in Luke–Acts, see S. Brown 1969: 12–16, 30–31).

The Lucan wording has its peculiarities. It shares with the other Synoptics verbal references to joy and the seeds' lacking root. Mark 4:16 = Matt. 13:20 speaks of an immediate (εὐθύς, *euthys*) response, a note that Luke lacks. Luke alone describes the reception of the word with δέχομαι, though this term is synonymous to λαμβάνω (*lambanō*, to receive), which appears in different forms in Matt. 13:20 (participle) = Mark 4:16 (verb). Luke alone calls the short-term response faith, while Mark and Matthew speak of enduring trial for a while, which of course would be the product of shallow faith. In particular, religious trial against one's faith is meant, such as persecution or teaching that draws one away from trust (Seesemann, *TDNT* 6:31). Only Luke uses πειρασμοῦ (*peirasmou*) for trial. Mark 4:17 = Matt. 13:21 uses both θλίψεως (*thlipseōs*) and διωγμοῦ (*diōgmou*), terms often used in eschatological settings for trial. For the lack of faith, Luke has ἀφίστανται (*aphistantai*), while Matt. 13:21 = Mark 4:17 has forms of σκανδαλίζω (*skandalizō*, to fall away, stumble), though Matthew has the singular and Mark the plural.[42] One could argue that Luke is clarifying the other Gospels at this point to note an unfruitful defection that is an indication of ultimate unbelief, not just a lapse.[43] Confirming this force is the warning of Luke 8:18b, where those who think they have something will find it taken from them. In other words, they end up with nothing. Again, these variations are not significant for the sense, in that all the Gospels are saying the same thing; but the differences do show the difficulty in positing direct literary sources for this account.

(4) Seed Choked by Worry, Riches, and Pleasures (8:14)

8:14 The third group of seed also fails to bear mature fruit. The wording's implication is that a response to the message occurs, but nothing comes to complete fruition because other matters crowd out the word's ability to do its cultivating work. None of the terms used to describe what chokes the plant are frequent in Luke. The term for worry, μέριμνα (*merimna*), appears in Luke only here and in 21:34.[44]

---

42. On σκανδαλίζω as a term of gospel rejection, see Matt. 11:6 = Luke 7:23; Matt. 13:57; 24:10; as a term for a "believer" stumbling into apostasy, see Matt. 18:6 = Mark 9:42 = Luke 17:1–2 (which see for details).

43. Liefeld 1984: 907 cites John 8:31, 44 as examples. If S. Brown 1969: 12–16, 30–31 is correct, then Luke changed the terminology to clarify the text's meaning by leaving out terms capable of being misunderstood.

44. The verbal form is found in 10:41; 12:11, 22, 25, 26. Μέριμνα is excessive self-concern over one's welfare; Bovon 1989: 410 speaks of "egocentric worry."

The Synoptic parallel to Luke 8:14 is Matt. 13:22 (which uses the singular) = Mark 4:19 (plural).[45] Matthew 6:25–34 gives the other side of this dilemma, as it discusses how one can rest in God (Phil. 4:6–7).

The term for riches, πλοῦτος (ploutos), occurs in the Synoptics only in this parable (Hauck and Kasch, TDNT 6:328). However, the related terms πλούσιος (plousios, rich; Luke 6:24; 12:16; 14:12; 16:1, 19, 21, 22; 18:23, 25; 19:2; 21:1) and πλουτέω (plouteō, to be rich; 1:53; 12:21) are more frequent in Luke. Excessive concern for earthly affairs and pleasures is something that Luke frequently notes as a topic of Jesus' teaching (the Pastorals tackle this theme as well: 1 Tim. 6:6–10, 17–19). The term ἡδονή (hēdonē, pleasure) is unique to Luke in the Synoptics.[46] The types of pleasures that Luke has in mind may well be those listed in Luke 7:25; 12:19; 16:19 (Nolland 1989: 386).

Fruitfulness is thus prevented by excessive concern about one's welfare, possessions, and comfort. Godet (1875: 1.373) interprets the three categories in the following manner: μέριμνα is the concern of the poor, πλοῦτος the focus of those who wish to be wealthy, and ἡδονή the pursuit of those already rich. But this interprets the phrases, especially the first one, too narrowly. Jesus says the danger of such distraction is that the word is crowded out and choked off by the energy and priority given to these other concerns.

Fitzmyer (1981: 714) notes a parallel expression in Jewish thought. CD 4.15–5.10 speaks of a threefold obstacle (called "the net of Belial") in which Israel was ensnared: defiling the sanctuary, excessive wealth, and taking two women in one's lifetime—a list distinct from Jesus in particulars but parallel in tone (Kosmala 1965).

Jesus is saying that the seed is choked off and cannot bear mature fruit because of these misplaced priorities of life. Τοῦ βίου (tou biou, of life) may well go with all three distractions (Luke 16:8; 20:34; Marshall 1978: 326).[47] The issue is not that such things are insignificant, but that they are not to have first place and thus destroy one's personal spiritual reception of the word. Plummer (1896: 221) makes the point that the choking of plants is not a sudden, but a gradual process, an observation that makes the image appropriate (Hendriksen 1978: 428 uses the picture of a spreading cancer). Mat-

---

45. Matthew and Mark differ in viewing the worry as a collective unit versus particular cares. The other NT examples are 2 Cor. 11:28 and 1 Pet. 5:7.

46. Other NT uses are Titus 3:3; James 4:1, 3; 2 Pet. 2:13. Mark has the synonymous ἐπιθυμία; Stählin, TDNT 2:924–25; Büchsel, TDNT 3:171 n. 36. Bovon 1989: 410–11 suggests that Luke made the change, because Mark's term can be read positively by a Greek.

47. For βίος as manner of life, see Bultmann, TDNT 2:863 n. 262. For συμπνίγω, see BAGD 779; BAA 1556; Mark 4:7; Matt. 13:22 = Mark 4:19; Luke 8:42. For τελεσφορέω, a NT hapax legomenon, see BAGD 810; BAA 1616; 4 Macc. 13:20.

thew 13:22 = Mark 4:19 mentions the choking, but also refers to the plant's being unfruitful (ἄκαρπος, *akarpos*), rather than speaking of a lack of mature fruit. The point in both cases is simply that the seed does not come to fruition.

Luke's wording is unique, though the thrust of his remarks makes it clear that he gives the same sense as the other Synoptics. Matthew and Mark focus on the fate of the word, while Luke expresses the outcome more directly in terms of the hearers.[48] This tradition shows some fluidity in its wording, but not in its fundamental sense. Such a plant is useless.

(5) Fruitful Seed Growing in the Good Heart (8:15)

8:15 The fourth group of seed has the response that yields fruit. Luke does not mention levels of fruitfulness. He speaks simply of success. There are three keys to that response. The first is the right kind of heart: an honest and good heart (καρδίᾳ καλῇ καὶ ἀγαθῇ, *kardia kalē kai agathē*).[49] The idea is of a moral quality and integrity that makes righteous responses (Grundmann, *TDNT* 1:13–14; Grundmann, *TDNT* 3:544–45; Behm, *TDNT* 3:612 §D2d; Marshall 1978: 327; Fitzmyer 1981: 714; Tob. 7:6; 9:6 [both recension S = Codex Sinaiticus; see NEB for translation]; 2 Macc. 15:12; 4 Macc. 4:1; BAGD 400; BAA 813 §2b). The association of καλός (nine times in Luke) and ἀγαθός (sixteen times in Luke) is not common in the NT (elsewhere only Matt. 7:17). The reference to the heart is not found in Matthew and Mark; Luke elaborated on the sense of the interpretation.

The second key response is holding fast (κατέχουσιν, *katechousin*) to the word, which is another way to speak of faith, since the verb portrays clinging to the word.[50] One does not let go of commitment to God's promise; one perseveres in faith; one is unfailingly wedded to God's promise (Marshall 1978: 327). Perseverance shows up elsewhere in Luke's writings (Luke 18:1, 8; 21:9; Acts 11:23; 13:43; 14:22; Nolland 1989: 387). This is the only theological usage of κατέχω in Luke (the other uses are literal: Luke 4:42; 14:9; Acts 27:40). This term is parallel to παραδέχονται (*paradechontai*, accepts) in Mark 4:20 (which appears in Luke–Acts only at Acts 15:4; 16:21; 22:18) and to συνιείς (*synieis*, understands) in Matt. 13:23 (which Luke uses eight times, mostly negatively, when one does not

---

48. In Luke the hearers are choked, while in Matthew and Mark the word is choked; Luce 1933: 168. The image is similar, for death of the person (the hearer) results in the death of what is in the person (the word).

49. This combination is particularly appropriate for a Greek audience; Bovon 1989: 412 n. 53. It has an ethical thrust here; this is an ethically good person.

50. BAGD 422 §1bβ; BAA 860 §1bβ. Key theological parallels are 1 Cor. 11:2; 15:2; 1 Thess. 5:21; Heb. 3:6, 14; 10:23; Hanse, *TDNT* 2:829.

understand something: Luke 2:50; 8:10; 18:34; 24:45; Acts 7:25 [twice]; 28:26, 27). It is likely that Luke is using terminology that came to him through his sources.

The third response also involves a term unique to Luke, ὑπομονῇ (*hypomonē*, patience), a quality needed to bear up under the pressure of living faithfully. It is the opposite of falling away (ἀφίστημι) in 8:13 (Plummer 1896: 222). In fact, it is the opposite of the responses in the other soils (Hanse, *TDNT* 4:586). Interestingly, ὑπομονή is more of a Pauline than a Lucan term: Luke uses it only twice (here and 21:19), while Paul has half of its NT uses (e.g., Rom. 5:3, 4; 8:25; 15:4; 2 Cor. 1:6; 1 Thess. 1:3; Heb. 10:36; James 1:3, 4; 5:11; Leaney 1958: 153). It is a corollary of hope, or the OT concept of waiting confidently on God (Ps. 33:18; 42:5, 11 [42:6, 12 MT]; 43:5; Isa. 40:30–31). It often refers to patience with regard to God's hope and promise, a sense that it probably has here as well. When one rests in God's promise and hope, one can overcome the obstacles that prevent fruitfulness: trials, worries about wealth, and pursuit of pleasures (James 1:2–4). Conzelmann (1960: 104) argues that the reference to patience is a sign of the delay of the eschaton, but this sees too much in a term that simply refers to clinging to God's hope in the midst of religious pressure and worldly distraction. In this seed, the sowing process has reaped fruit. This is the soil that disciples are to be like.

Summary

The "parable of the sower" is really the "parable of the seed among the soils" or "the responses to the word." Some never even consider the message of the kingdom that God brings through Jesus. The spiritual forces of evil take the message away and the heart is not ready to respond. Others respond initially, but pressure crushes their response. Still others expose themselves to the message but earthly cares, wealth, and pleasure prevent them from following the word in a way that yields fruit. But there are those who have a good heart, persistent faith, and patient response to God's promise. These bring forth fruit and overcome the obstacles that prevent response. The parable is designed to confront the reader and force analysis of how one responds to God's message. Does pressure make one timid or cause abandonment of faith? Does indulging in the pursuit of wealth or undisciplined pleasure come before God? Is faith solid and fruit-bearing?

The parable addresses the broad character of one's response throughout one's life. The subject is one's response to God's promise in a general way and does not directly address particular moments of response. However, it carries with it implications that reflect individual choices, because the little choices may well be evidence of the real nature of one's total faith. Nonetheless, the exhortation to the reader is to be the receptive, faithful, persistent, and patient soil. As a matter of one's life perspective, let the word of God take root and bear the fruit that comes from nurturing that word with undying faith. Be the fourth soil. However, also realize that there are many kinds of ground in the world, that there are many types of responses to the message that Jesus brings. Some people will never be interested in Jesus' teaching. Others will draw close, but will lack constancy or stability in their response. Some may walk away, but others will bear fruit. In fruit-bearers, the word of God expresses itself triumphantly.

Additional Notes

8:10. Jeremias (1963a: 15–18) argues that Mark's form of the Isaiah citation is close to the targumic version, suggesting a Palestinian setting. This point is correct even if the Targum is a later text as Fitzmyer (1981: 709) argues (Horst, *TDNT*, 5:554–55, esp. n. 116, discusses potential parallels to Jewish exegesis). Noting the parallel between the Targum and Mark's form of the text, however, does not establish that Mark's form is the parable's original form (so correctly argues D. Wenham 1972: 25 n. 59, who is against making too much of the targumic connection). However, what cannot be established with certainty may still be possible. In fact, the Targum connection is interesting, for Mark has a causative idea like that of the Targum (and the MT). Though Mark lacks the Targum's relative pronoun for Isa. 6:9, which limits those who are judged to those with hardness of heart, the application of the remark about parables only to "those outside" has a similar effect. Mark also refers to "being forgiven" as does the Targum, while the MT speaks of "being healed," a similar idea in a different image (for details, see C. A. Evans 1989c: 69–71).

8:11. As noted in the introduction to this pericope, some suggest that this text was originally a kingdom parable whose point was simply to focus on the kingdom's triumphant growth, despite the fact that much of the seed never bears fruit (Jeremias 1963a: 77–79, 149–51; Fitzmyer 1981: 711).

Jeremias gives five reasons for attributing the section on the parable's interpretation to the early church. He regards the linguistic arguments as the most telling:

1. The use of ὁ λόγος (the word) reflects a technical term of the church (Mark 1:45; 2:2; 4:33; possibly 8:32; Luke 1:2; Acts 4:4; 6:4; 8:4; 10:36, 44; 11:19; 14:25; 16:6; 17:11; 18:5; Gal. 6:6; Col. 4:3; 1 Thess. 1:6; 2 Tim. 4:2; James 1:21; 1 Pet. 2:8; 3:1a; 1 John 2:7). The use of λόγος by Jesus in this sense occurs only in the passage

on the interpretation of the parable (eight times in Mark, six times in Matthew, and four times in Luke).

2. Jeremias (1963a: 78) mentions nine terms in the Marcan version that do not occur elsewhere in the Synoptics, but occur elsewhere in the NT, especially Paul: σπείρω (to sow) with the meaning "to preach," ῥίζα (root) with the meaning "inward stability," πρόσκαιρος (for a little time), ἀπάτη (deceit), πλοῦτος (riches), ἄκαρπος (without fruit), παραδέχομαι (to accept), καρποφορέω (to bear fruit) in a metaphorical sense, and ἐπιθυμία (desire).

3. The association of sowing with preaching is not typical of Jesus, who usually illustrates preaching with the metaphor of gathering harvest.

4. The parable does not have the eschatological flavor of Jesus' parables, but is more psychological in tone.

5. That the version of the parable in the Gospel of Thomas 9 lacks an interpretation suggests that one was not present originally. Jeremias also notes that the interpretation has allegorical features, which is not like true parables.

Are these objections decisive? The arguments from vocabulary are not compelling. The question remains where the church received such an array of imagery that penetrated so many different writers (e.g., the Synoptics and Paul). This is church imagery simply because it has an early origin in Jesus. Four of the terms that Jeremias mentions are agricultural in flavor and so relate to the basic picture of harvest and planting. Such agricultural imagery tied to a message is common enough, so that there is no reason to refuse the usage to Jesus (see Luke 8:11). If Jesus can speak of the harvest in relation to preaching, then it is natural that the word is the seed. One metaphor implies the other. The other elements of vocabulary do deal with the application of the imagery, but since Jesus rarely interprets a parable, the absence of such terminology elsewhere is not a surprise. One could argue that the very exception proves the point. If Jesus did not interpret this parable, the question remains, why would the church construct an explanation here and not for other parables? The very absence of such examples makes it likely the church rendered a tradition originating with Jesus here, especially since its themes fit Jesus' teaching. As for parables treating only eschatological topics, such a focus is unlikely given the variety of parabolic topics in the various strands of the tradition. Some parables are not eschatological, but describe the spiritual life (7:41–44; 10:25–37; 12:13–21; 14:7–14, 28–33; 15:1–32). Appealing to the Gospel of Thomas is not compelling, given how freely it handles sayings material. In sum, the interpretation of this parable has its roots in Jesus' teaching.

b. Call to Respond to Light (8:16–18)

Challenging his audience to respond to the word, Jesus uses the picture of a lamp to show that all things will be exposed. Some have called this a parable (Geldenhuys 1951: 247), but the saying is more proverbial than parabolic in character. Light comes into the world to reveal. Jesus' teaching is light (Arndt 1956: 231). All will be manifest, so take heed how you hear. Hearing aright will lead to receiving more from God, but failure to hear will mean losing what one already has.

The imagery shows that response to Jesus' teaching is absolutely crucial. He functions as the revealer of truth, and the response to him exposes where the heart is and where one's future with God resides. Some see a missionary thrust here, but this reads the imagery too much in line with the nonparallel Matthean texts (esp. Matt. 5:15).[1] It may be implied that light is revealed through the proclamation of those who share Jesus' teaching, but that is not the thrust of the Lucan passage. Rather, it focuses on Jesus' message.

Sources and Historicity

Mark 4:21–25 also has these sayings in one locale (Aland 1985: §125). In fact, Luke's placement agrees generally with Mark's in coming near the parable of the seed.[2] Luke has similar sayings in 11:33–36, 12:2, and 19:26; but it is probably a misnomer to call these sayings doublets, since Jesus could use similar imagery and sayings in distinct ways (against Fitzmyer 1981: 717; with Liefeld 1984: 909). Thus, to compare the sayings here to their cousins in Matthew or to the later Lucan sayings that share this imagery is not helpful. Many, however, suggest that the three Lucan sayings in 8:16–18 were originally distinct, which would make interpretation of each original saying difficult due to the absence of context (Schürmann 1969: 469 [who also notes the evidence of Palestinian roots in 8:18]; Marshall 1978: 327). Also, Mark 4 is seen as a collection of distinct sayings, since that grouping is also anthological. But it need not be assumed that, because an anthology of parables is present in Mark 4 (a point that is likely), every parable or saying in it was originally uttered in a distinct setting. Taken as a

---

1. So Plummer 1896: 222 sees Luke gathering in one place Matthew's distinct texts.

2. Matthew has similar, distinct sayings in other contexts; but these are not to be seen as parallel to the Marcan sayings: Matt. 5:15; 10:26; 13:12.

unit, these verses can be related to the message and setting they are placed in and can be tied to the parable of the seed, despite the sayings' absence in Matt. 13. In fact, one of the sayings occurs in Matt. 13:12, imbedded in the parable of the seed. This suggests that some of the remarks are tied to this setting and may be a clue that Matthew has done some rearranging. The parables of Matt. 13 show enough peculiarity that Matthew may have omitted some materials while also using distinct material. In addition, that Luke has this passage from Mark 4 but not the other Marcan parables may reflect the influence of his additional source. The passage is well attested in its various forms, suggesting its authenticity.

Even the Jesus Seminar, which is normally skeptical, rates this passage as likely to go back to Jesus, printing most of it in pink type (Funk and Hoover 1993: 306–7). They argue that the sayings are graphic and multiply attested (Mark, Q, Thomas). The one portion that they reject is the exhortation to hear, which they see as an additional insertion different from Mark 4:24. Luke 8:18a is but one example of this multiply attested exhortation (Matt. 11:15; 13:9, 43; Mark 4:9; Luke 8:8a; 14:35). It, too, is conceptually rooted in Jesus.

The form of the remarks is a series of sayings containing a warning.[3] The outline of Luke 8:16–18 is as follows:

   i. The lampstand as a picture of Jesus' public teaching (8:16)
   ii. Secrets to be manifest eventually (8:17)
   iii. A call to hear and a warning (8:18)

Luke focuses on the word, picturing Jesus' message as light openly available to all. Light will eventually reveal all secrets, giving the word a character of judgment as well as light. The need exists to respond with care to Jesus' teaching, which comes with a promise: response brings more spiritual blessing. But a threat also is made: lack of response means losing spiritual insight. Neutrality is not possible.

Exegesis and Exposition

[16]No one after lighting a lamp covers it with a vessel or puts it under a bed, but sets it on a lampstand that those who come in may see the light. [17]For nothing is hid that shall not be manifest, nor is anything secret that

---

3. Bovon 1989: 415 speaks of an antithetical word of wisdom. Bultmann 1963: 81–82, 98 calls the sayings "double-stranded" *mĕšāllîm*, like secular proverbs; also Fitzmyer 1981: 716. Berger 1984: 118 speaks of a warning word for 8:18. Wiefel 1988: 161 also speaks of a *māšāl* (parable), as does Jeremias 1963a: 41, but this is unlikely. Luke seems aware of the proverbial character by his reuse of the material.

shall not be known and come to light. [18]Take heed then how you listen, for whoever has, more will be given to him; and from him who has not, even what he thinks he has shall be taken.

i. The Lampstand as a Picture of Jesus' Public Teaching (8:16)

8:16 The first saying is a proverb or similitude. It is repeated in almost exact verbal form in 11:33 (similar forms are in Mark 4:21; Matt. 5:15; Gospel of Thomas 33). The Lucan uses of λύχνος (*lychnos*, lamp) occur here and in 11:33, 34, 36; 12:25; and 15:8. Given that the saying is a proverb, it can be applied to a variety of situations. Its repetition in the tradition indicates that it should be interpreted contextually in each case.

The image is clear. The purpose of lighting a lamp is not to conceal the light, but to illumine a room so that those who enter can see. Putting the lamp under a cover or bed is foolish and contradictory to the function of light (Marshall 1978: 329). The ancient reference would be to either an open lamp with a candlestick or an oil-burning lamp (BAGD 483; BAA 980; Michaelis, *TDNT* 4:324). An oil-burning lamp is most likely meant here, since it is set on a stand (Fitzmyer 1981: 719; Michaelis, *TDNT* 4:324). The description is too general to assume that Luke describes a Roman-style house with a vestibule (wrongly Talbert 1982: 94 and Fitzmyer 1981: 719; correctly Schürmann 1969: 467 n. 166).[4]

The image is variously interpreted. Many see the saying as an exhortation to the disciples to function as light, to go openly into the world and proclaim the message. This is clearly the force of the remark in Matt. 5:15, where the following verse exhorts them to let their light shine before people. If one sees this saying as a strict parallel to Matthew, then this interpretation is natural (Hendriksen 1978: 430; Plummer 1896: 222).

Others hold to the same thrust and appeal to the previous context, where the parable concerns the fruitfulness of the preached word. Since the section is about the preaching of the word, such an emphasis is only natural (Geldenhuys 1951: 247; Marshall 1978: 328; Schürmann 1969: 467; Fitzmyer 1981: 718; W. Robinson 1966: 132–33).

Another way to view the reference is as a characterization of Jesus' teaching. Jesus' teaching is light; it is given in public and illumines the way to God (Danker 1988: 178; Wis. 6:22; Sir. 39:1–3). Such a reference would concentrate on the manifest revelation of God's will and thus the necessity to respond to it. Disciples in partic-

---

4. Schürmann adds the point that Jesus is saying that these events do not occur in a corner (Acts 26:26).

ular should be responsive. This idea fits nicely with the idea of exposure in Luke 8:17 and the warning to hear and respond in 8:18 (Godet 1875: 1.375; Arndt 1956: 231). Of course, in the context of later ministry, contact with this teaching would come through the missionary enterprise and would suggest its need; but in this early setting the emphasis is on the character, availability, and aid of such light as found in Jesus. Such an emphasis does fit Lucan imagery as well, for 1:78–79 speaks of Messiah as the Rising Sun who illumines the path out of darkness into God's way of peace and 2:32 refers to Jesus as light (φῶς, phōs), as do John 8:12 and 9:5. This interpretation seems the most contextually unifying. Jesus makes the way of God available, and each person is to choose how to respond to it. Seeing the light means being open and responsive to God's Word. If the light is hidden, it is because of the soil on which it falls, not because revelation is unavailable.

ii. Secrets to Be Manifest Eventually (8:17)

Light not only illumines, it exposes. The standards in Jesus' proclamation also examine how people are responding to God. Indeed, Jesus' teaching reveals hidden things and exposes secrets. The second saying focuses on the evaluative and authoritative function of Jesus' teaching, which brings to light people's thoughts. It is a promise that one day all will be exposed and made manifest by God. Truth and light will manifest themselves, and what is hidden will become known.

8:17

What is revealed eventually? Is God's truth to be made obvious to all through the disciples' teaching, so that God's teaching is publicly vindicated (Liefeld 1984: 909; Ernst 1977: 271; Godet 1875: 1.375; Marshall 1978: 330 [citing Matt. 10:26–27]; Fitzmyer 1981: 720; Schürmann 1969: 467)? Or are evil thoughts brought to public attention before God (Schweizer 1984: 146; Arndt 1956: 231; cf. Luke 12:2)? The warning to hear carefully in the next verse fits the latter sense more readily. The only problem with taking light as the exposure of evil thoughts is γάρ (gar, for) at the beginning of the verse: how does 8:17 explain the previous verse? The connection seems to be that God's truth is preached publicly, and it is the function of truth to illumine, to expose reality (8:16). One day the nature of the light as light will become obvious, for it will expose what has previously been hidden. The warning is clear: God's standard will be maintained, revealed, and one day executed—so beware how you respond to the message. In fact, the point of the saying in Matt. 10:26, which Marshall cites as supportive of his view, is against it. In that passage, enemies of God's children are not to be feared, since nothing will happen that will not be revealed and exposed to God for his response. Vindication of the message is not so much the point here, but the threats of judgment and exposure are. The image in Matthew is consistent with this interpretation, as is the image in Luke 12:2, but the saying here must be read in context. The thought is not unlike 2:35 or, in a less eschatological way, Eph. 5:12–14.[5]

Those who argue for a missionary sense say that the disciples are exhorted in Luke 8:18 to take the message to people. Since this is the message's design and their mission, they should take heed how they respond to the call. But the idea of taking everything away from the disciples seems difficult for such an understanding. It seems better to relate the message to the various responses that the soils give and to make clear to the disciples that God will evaluate how each person responds to the word.

The wording of the passage is close to Mark 4:22, except that Luke has relative clauses where Mark has ἵνα (hina, in order that) clauses. The sense in both texts is the same.

iii. A Call to Hear and a Warning (8:18)

8:18 Finally, Jesus gives the warning to hear carefully. Βλέπω (blepō, to see) here means "to take heed" (Michaelis, *TDNT* 5:344 n. 153). Such a proverbial saying recalls 8:8, where the one who has ears is told to hear. Of course, it refers to anyone who hears what Jesus says. The idea is that one should respond to the word's teaching. For those who see a missionary thrust, it is a warning that failure to pursue sharing the message shows they only think they possess faith (Schweizer 1984: 146; Hanse, *TDNT* 2:827). The idea, however, seems to be that those who respond spiritually to the word and receive it continue to get more spiritual blessing, while those who do not receive the word, and thus do not have it, eventually lose whatever they possess (Arndt 1956: 232). They will experience spiritual destitution. Even some who take the previous verses in a missionary light still see the verse as a warning to hearers and would read it as Arndt does (Plummer 1896: 223; Marshall 1978: 330). The idea that someone who receives insight will get more insight parallels OT teaching (Prov. 1:2–6; 9:9; Danker 1988: 178).

The wording is slightly different from Mark 4:25, which exhorts one to take heed of what one hears, that is, to watch the content of the teaching. In Luke, the stress is on how one hears it; but the two ideas are not that distant, since how one regards the content will affect how one responds and what one decides to hear. This final saying occurs again in a similar form in Luke 19:26 in the parable of the

5. A parallel in the Gospel of Thomas 5–6 has Jesus speak of all becoming manifest.

pounds (Matt. 25:29 is conceptually parallel). It emphasizes that to ignore God's teaching is to lose whatever spiritual insight one had or, in Luke's terms, "thinks" (δοκεῖ, *dokei*) one had. Luke's unique use of δοκεῖ heightens the condemnation. The person who is judged is also self-deceived. Mark 4:24 contains the saying of the measure in the middle of this warning, a saying that Luke had in Luke 6:38.

In Luke 8:16–18, Jesus stresses the importance of his teaching **Summary** and its authority. His teaching is public. It is light that can guide. It was not given to be hidden. Neither will this message be lost, for one day it will bring all secrets to light and manifest the thoughts of each one's heart. Therefore, care should be given to respond to it, for spiritual gain or loss is at stake. Jesus is the source of God's way and is the revealer of God's truth, which one day will be the standard that will judge people. The reader is to see that a choice must be made. Either one receives the light, by continually responding to it, so as to open the way for more spiritual blessing—or one faces the exposure of the light later and loses all that one thought he or she had. The choice is left for self-reflection. As Jesus says, "Be careful how you hear."

c. True Family of Jesus (8:19–21)

A short pericope serves to stress the importance of response, just as the previous unit does. Jesus declares his familial allegiance to—and approval of—those who hear and put into practice the word of God. Such emphasis on hearing and doing is common in Luke (6:47, 49; 11:28). It also recalls the command to hold fast to the word and bear fruit in 8:8, 15 (Schürmann 1969: 470). The end of the unit is worded in summary form, as a comparison with the parallels shows. Luke has an abbreviated form of the event as he did with the parable of the seed (Hendriksen 1978: 435). Mark 3:31–35 = Matt. 12:46–50 speaks of those doing God's will as part of Jesus' family. In those Gospels, the remark comes in response to a question. Luke lacks the question and simply has a statement. Luke equates God's will with God's message to focus on the written or oral expression of God's desire. So for Luke, Jesus' family are those who hear and do the word. Luke has also softened any criticism of Jesus' family since his account lacks Mark's mention of the family's doubts (Mark 3:21, 30–31 is tied to the Beelzebub controversy). At the minimum, the action in Mark is an attempt by the family to protect Jesus.

Leaney (1958: 153) attributes the omission of these negative elements to Luke's use of infancy accounts, where family members are told about Jesus so that a negative reaction to Jesus like that in Mark is not possible. This view leaves the impression that either the infancy accounts or Mark's portrayal is wrong. But the Marcan account may express nothing other than frustration with the manner in which Jesus conducts himself. He is not what they are expecting. He lacks the regal look, and his style seemingly will not deliver the people.

Fitzmyer (1981: 722–23) argues that Luke radically changed Mark's meaning by shifting the position of the pericope and eliminating the negative elements, so that Jesus' real family are referred to and are seen as model disciples. But the family is not clearly included in Jesus' remarks (Luke 8:21). Luke does portray the family favorably in his Gospel, but this is a matter of editorial choice, not an alteration of the text's meaning. The essential point of 8:19–21 matches Mark. Luke is generally less harsh in his criticism of Jesus' followers.

Sources and Historicity

The event probably took place toward the end of the Galilean ministry. Luke, unlike Mark 4 = Matt. 13, does not include at this point any more parables after the parable of the seed, but goes on to narrate this account. The Synoptic parallels (Mark 3:31–35 = Matt. 12:46–50) place this event before the parable of the seed in Mark 4:1–20 = Matt. 13:1–23 (Aland 1985: §135; the Gospel of Thomas 99 also has a short version of this saying). With his use of ἔτι in Matt. 12:46, Matthew has a clearer chronological tie to the previous events than does either Mark or Luke.[1] Some translations make it look as if Luke has a fixed setting as well. However, the RSV, which opens with "then" in Luke 8:19, does not reflect the Lucan δέ. Luke appears to have developed a topical arrangement at this point around the theme of hearing the word of God, using this unit to conclude the emphasis (8:4–21). On the other hand, Mark may be using this unit to introduce the same parable section as part of a similar, though distinctly developed, theme on the word of the kingdom. Also, Mark associates the account with the Beelzebub charge, a charge that according to Mark alarmed the family (Godet 1875: 1.377 takes the Marcan link as giving the correct placement). It seems likely that Matthew's placement is the correct chronological one, since the event is not likely to have occurred twice and the key Beelzebub controversy precedes the parables in Matthew as well.[2]

In sum, Luke and Mark have a topical grouping, while Matthew possesses the relative placement in Jesus' ministry (A. B. Bruce 1897: 521; Geldenhuys 1951: 249; Arndt 1956: 232; Plummer 1896: 223 [who says that none of the Gospels specifies the setting]). This is another example of a passage where each Gospel writer arranged the material in such a way that fixing its specific placement in Jesus' ministry is difficult. Luke's arrangement highlights the importance of obeying the word. Mark, who is relatively chronological in sequence, moved the Beelzebub and family remarks forward in Mark 2–4 to juxtapose the themes of rejection and response (Mark 2:1–3:29) with the kingdom parables (Mark 4). This is the most likely scenario, though one can hardly be certain of the conclusion, given the variety of possibilities.

The Jesus Seminar rates this saying as possibly rooted in Jesus, though in Luke's terms (in gray type; Funk and Hoover 1993: 307–8). They note the differences from Mark, Luke's abbreviating of the account, and the "insider" versus "outsider" quality of the saying (this last point was noted in

1. In Matthew, it is clear that Jesus is teaching about the source of his healing power, when this event occurs. The adverb is part of a phrase that reads, "while he was still teaching."

2. Luke has the Beelzebub account later (11:14–23), in a series of accounts where the Pharisees come in for criticism since they do not respond properly to Jesus. If 8:19–21 is really linked to that event, then Luke 11 also confirms my judgment about the Lucan topical placement of 8:19–21.

8:4–15; see the discussion of sources and historicity there). However, Jesus' teaching about hearing and doing the word is well attested (Luke 6:47, 49; James 1:22–25), as is the issue of word over family (Luke 9:59–62; 12:51–53; 14:25–26). There is no reason to question the saying's authenticity (Nolland 1989: 393).

The form of the account is a pronouncement story or apophthegm (Bultmann 1963: 29–30; V. Taylor 1935: 71–72; Fitzmyer 1981: 723; Bovon 1989: 418; Berger 1984: 81, 187 [also speaks of an exhortation and warning]). The outline of Luke 8:19–21 is as follows:

  i. Inability of the family to reach Jesus (8:19)
  ii. Report that the family wishes to see Jesus (8:20)
  iii. Jesus' family: those who hear and do God's word (8:21)

The unit's themes are simple: crowds continue to gather around Jesus; his real family consists of those who respond to him by doing God's word. The saying leaves the listener confronted with a choice. Will he or she be a member of the family? The passage is a call to obey.

Exegesis and Exposition

[19]And his mother and brothers came to him, but they were not able to reach him because of the crowd. [20]And he was told, "Your mother and brothers are standing outside, wishing to see you." [21]And he said to them, "My mother and brothers—these are those who hear and do the word of God."

i. Inability of the Family to Reach Jesus (8:19)

8:19 Luke 8:19 sets the stage for Jesus' key remark in 8:21. No mention is made of the family's motive for coming. As was noted in the introduction, the family's concern in Mark 3:31–35 comes from reaction to Jesus and the direction of his ministry (Geldenhuys 1951: 249).[3] But Luke, with his abbreviated style, simply notes that the crowd prevented Mary and the brothers from getting to Jesus. That we have a new event and setting is clear from the previous remarks to the disciples in private. However, no indication exists about whether the crowd is mixed or favorable. The goal is simply to set the context for Jesus' comment.

---

3. Παραγίνομαι is probably Lucan: twenty-eight times in Luke–Acts, nine times in rest of NT, with three of these being in Matthew and one in Mark. The singular form of the verb reflects occasional Greek style in agreeing with the first subject; BDF §135.1a; BDR §135.1a; Marshall 1978: 331; Luke 8:22; Acts 11:14.

ii. Report That the Family Wishes to See Jesus (8:20)

The family was unable to reach Jesus, so a message was sent to him. **8:20**
Luke's account is abbreviated. In Mark, it seems clear that Jesus was
inside a house during this incident, which in Mark is tied to the Beelzebub dispute (Mark 3:20, 32, 34; Godet 1875: 1.377–78). The Lucan
use of ἔξω (*exō*, outside) might suggest this conclusion as well, but
Luke is not as clear as Mark concerning Jesus' location.

Conzelmann (1960: 48, citing Luke 9:9 and 23:8) and others take
this remark to refer to a request to do signs, which Jesus will reject,
but such a meaning in this context is unlikely.[4] Neither does it depict
symbolically the family's distance from Jesus spiritually (against
Schürmann 1969: 470–71; with Ernst 1977: 272 ["questionable"];
Marshall 1978: 332). There is no concrete indication of such symbolic meanings. The request in Luke is simply to see Jesus, who is
physically separated from his family by the crowd.

iii. Jesus' Family: Those Who Hear and Do God's Word (8:21)

Jesus does not go to the family, but uses the opportunity to teach **8:21**
about his mission. Who is special to Jesus? Those who do God's
word. The remark is not a repudiation of family, as much as it is an
endorsement and exhortation to disciples to be receptive to the
word. The remark makes a rhetorical contrast. Jesus' family are
those who receive God's word, that is, Jesus' message. The combination of hearing and doing has appeared before in Luke (6:47, 49) and
also reflects NT usage, James 1:22–25 being the classic passage on
the theme. Jesus' family is responsive to God's message through
Jesus. Luke is very concrete. Reception of the word is not limited to
intellectual recognition and agreement. It expresses itself in action.
Jesus does not want scribes, but servants.

Luke ties the response to God's word, while Matt. 12:50 = Mark
3:35 speaks of God's will. This is merely a difference of what (God's
will) and where (God's word). The word contains God's will, so that
the expression is Luke's way of rendering the force of Jesus' remarks. Expressing the account this way establishes a link with the
parable of the seed in Luke 8:9, 11, 15 (Klostermann 1929: 99). Luke
also moves directly into the reply since he lacks the rhetorical question, "Who are my mother and brothers?" The point in each Gospel
is clear: those with whom Jesus identifies the most are those who respond to the word. In 11:28, Jesus will utter a beatitude that paral-

---

4. So also Danker 1988: 179 (with a little hesitancy); Ellis 1974: 127. Fitzmyer
1981: 725 rightly rejects this view, as do Schürmann 1969: 470 n. 197; Marshall 1978:
332; and Wiefel 1988: 162.

lels this (Kittel, *TDNT* 4:121). While Luke has not treated the family as negatively as Mark does, both Gospels make essentially the same point. The word is to have first priority, and so one's allegiance is to its message, even over family (9:59–62; 12:51–53; 14:25–26; Danker 1988: 179).[5] At Qumran, the family of God replaces one's human family (1QH 9.34–36). Jesus' remarks are not that strong; but in terms of priority, his remarks reflect the importance that God's message has for him.

Summary   Luke 8:19–21 concludes the focus on the need to respond to Jesus' kingdom word, a unit that started in 8:4. Those with whom Jesus identifies are those who respond to and practice the word. That is where the disciples' commendation resides. The point for the reader is simple: How does one respond to the message Jesus brings? Is the response intellectual comprehension or action? The disciple should see God's call and do God's word. Such a response is commendable before him.

Additional Notes

8:19. Luke seems to indicate that Jesus had siblings, that is, that Mary and Joseph had other children (Tertullian, *Against Marcion* 4.19; Eusebius, *Ecclesiastical History* 2.23; 3.19, 32; 4.22). The question whether Jesus had siblings has a long history of discussion (Arndt 1956: 233–35; Plummer 1896: 224; Danker 1988: 179). One view argues that Mary had no children after Jesus. Epiphanius, the fourth-century defender of Mary's perpetual virginity, holds that Joseph had children by a previous wife (*Haereses* 78 [*PG* 42:699–740]). Jerome argues that these "brothers" are cousins (*Adversus Helvidium* [*PL* 23:193–216]). Fitzmyer (1981: 723–24) notes the ambiguity in Greek and Semitic of the term ἀδελφοί, usually translated "brothers."[6] In the early church, the idea of Joseph's having children by a previous wife was the more popular of the two views that denied younger siblings to Jesus (McHugh 1975). Lightfoot (1896) defends Jerome's view, while Blinzler (1967) has a detailed study of the issue.

Mark 6:3 says that Mary was the mother of James, Joses, Judas, and Simon. But later, Mark uses an unusual grammatical construction (a feminine definite article followed by the names; 15:40, 47; 16:1) to describe a Mary as the mother of Joses, James, and Salome (15:40 finishes with a reference to μήτηρ [mother]). Since the names Joses and James overlap with Mark 6, those who deny that Jesus had siblings argue that Mark 15 is an

---

5. Luke often speaks of the "word of God": Luke 5:1; 8:11; and twelve times in Acts; Schürmann 1969: 267 n. 29.
6. For passages where the term does not denote a nuclear family member, see Matt. 5:22–24 (neighbor) and Gen. 13:8; 14:14; 24:27; 29:12 (kin). The major study of the options is Blinzler 1967.

odd way to identify someone, unless an identification with the figures of Mark 6 is intended. Thus, if Mark 15 and Mark 6 belong together, then the woman in question is not Jesus' mother, since that could have been said in a simpler way. This connection supposedly shows that those mentioned in Mark 6 are Jesus' relatives, a view that takes ἀδελφός there to mean "cousin" or "relative." Of course, the simple solution is to see a distinct Mary in Mark 15 and to take the children's names as common ones that have reference to some well-known church figures who are not the same figures as Mark 6. Fitzmyer (1981: 724) rejects Jerome's solution that ἀδελφός means cousin, because a Greek term for that relation exists (ἀνεψιός; Col. 4:10). He prefers the less specific "relative." But the more likely sense is "brother" or "sibling." The NT never indicates that Joseph was previously married or that he was a widower. Thus, to see a reference to younger siblings is the most natural way to take this reference and the language of Mark 6. Mark 15 refers to a distinct group of people.

8:21. There are two views about the passage's complex grammar: (1) Plummer (1896: 224) argues that οὗτοι (these) is the subject in the sentence, since Luke chooses the anarthrous form of μήτηρ (mother) and ἀδελφοί (brothers). This construction shows that μήτηρ and ἀδελφοί are the predicate. He would translate, "These are my mother and brothers, those who. . . ." (2) Fitzmyer (1981: 725) replies that the reference to μήτηρ and ἀδελφοί is a nominative absolute with οὗτοι simply resuming the reference. He translates, "So [as for] my mother and brothers, they are those who. . . ." Word order seems to be in favor of Fitzmyer's syntactic explanation, but not necessarily his understanding of its force. For his view to work, Fitzmyer must add the phrase *as for*. In addition, Tannehill (1986: 212) argues that the construction parallels the reference to various groups in the interpretation of the parable of the seed, where the phrase *those who* marks out the distinct groupings. This parallelism in the unit is against Fitzmyer's view, since it suggests a distinct group. Thus, Jesus refers to a group other than his real family here.

2. Christological Authority over All (8:22–9:17)

The second unit of the section that runs from Luke 8:4 to 9:17 begins at 8:22. The emphasis now returns to events, not sayings, in contrast to the first unit (8:4–21). Where the earlier unit was a call to faith, here Luke presents a series of revelatory events that show Jesus' power. One should respond to him in faith, because of his power and authority over all areas: he stills a storm (8:22–25), exorcises demons (8:26–39), heals a woman with a flow of blood (8:42b–48), resurrects a dead child (8:40–42a, 49–56), and provides food for the multitude (9:10–17). In between, he commissions the Twelve, thus extending his authority (9:1–6). In addition, his ministry still raises questions about his identity (9:7–9).

Stilling the storm is one in a series of miracles in Luke 8—all centered around the Sea of Galilee (Bornkamm 1963: 53)—that come before the mission of the Twelve in 9:1–6. The deliverance of a demoniac, the healing of a hemorrhaging woman, and the raising of Jairus's daughter follow this miracle, and together they show Jesus' comprehensive power and authority: over nature (8:22–25), over demonic spirits (8:26–39), over disease (8:42b–48), and even over death itself (8:40–42a, 49–56).[1] They review the character of Jesus' ministry that leads to Peter's great confession (Marshall 1978: 332). Only one more miracle, the feeding of the five thousand (9:10–17), intervenes between the sequence of miracles in Luke 8 and Peter's confession. The miracles of Luke 8 also reflect an escalation, since they progress from external threats to more internalized threats, culminating in the direct threat of death itself. Jesus can deal with all these attempts to overwhelm humankind. Schürmann (1969: 472–73) describes these miracles as functioning in much the same manner as the "signs" in John: they show who Jesus is, and they reassure the reader because of the power they reveal.

---

1. This miracle cluster is paralleled in Mark 4:35–5:43; Marshall 1978: 332–33; Fitzmyer 1981: 726–27; Tiede 1988: 170; Wiefel 1988: 163 n. 1.

a. Authority over Nature: Stilling of the Storm (8:22–25)

The stilling of the storm is the second nature miracle in Luke. The previous nature miracle (5:1–11) was a miracle of provision, where the catch of fish pictured the people to be caught by disciples, while this miracle depicts Jesus' protection of the disciples and portrays his authority over creation. The stress comes in the final verse where the christological question is raised: "Who then is this?" The activities of Jesus' life are causing the disciples to reflect on who is in their midst. This miracle gives them reason to raise the question again. In addition, Jesus' power shows that he can be trusted. Even during times when he is seemingly not consciously with them, he is capable of meeting their needs.

Sources and Historicity

The stilling of the storm is part of the triple tradition (Aland 1985: §136; Matt. 8:23–27 = Mark 4:35–41). Mark gives it a definite setting by speaking about its occurring on a day when parables were narrated. This connects it with the teaching of at least some of Mark 4, which comes early in that Gospel.[1]

What is interesting is that Matthew has the miracle account in his topical section (Matt. 8–9), before his parabolic section (Matt. 13). But even more interesting is that Matthew associates the parables of Matt. 13 with the concern of Jesus' family about his teaching (Matt. 12:46–50), which unit precedes this miracle account in Luke and Mark but follows the parabolic teaching of both those Gospels (Matt. 12:46–50 = Luke 8:19–21 = Mark 3:31–35). Thus, Luke and Mark have following the parable of the seed what Matthew places before it.[2] This means that this miracle and the visit by Jesus'

---

1. Those who see an anthology in Mark 4 will see less value in such a chronological note as this; so, e.g., Creed 1930: 119. At the least Mark indicates that the event took place in a setting that followed some type of parabolic kingdom teaching, a setting not unlikely, given that Jesus taught throughout the region.

2. For those who hold to the two-Gospel hypothesis, Luke's placement is a problem. Why would he move the account if Matthew is the only source he had? Also, why does Mark follow Luke and not Matthew? The only possible explanations in this view are that Luke decided on this rearrangement (for reasons that are not clear) or that he had an extra source, the introduction of which cripples one of the cornerstones of the two-Gospel approach: the avoidance of such extra sources.

family were originally chronologically proximate to the parable cluster, but that topical work in all three Gospels makes nailing down the event's exact location difficult.[3] Mark and Luke both agree in placing this miracle after the parable of the seed. Luke and Mark have given the relevant setting for the account as somewhere in the midst of the Galilean period, a placement that also fits Matthew. One cannot be more specific than this about its placement in Jesus' ministry.[4]

Is Matthew's account of this miracle unique, as some argue? Bornkamm (1963: 53) speaks of Matthew's arrangement reflecting an emphasis on the "Messiah of deed" after the "Messiah of the word" is displayed in the Sermon on the Mount. This summary description works for Luke's and Mark's arrangements, though the discourse to which the material is related is parabolic teaching, not Matthew's sermon. Bornkamm argues that for Matthew the placement of the cluster of miracles between sayings on discipleship, as well as certain alterations in the accounts, make this miracle a picture of the dangers and glory of discipleship. Although this emphasis may be more explicit in Matthew than in Mark or Luke, the miracle's function in this Lucan miracle cluster also suggests a discipleship concern, for two reasons. First, the rebuke about little faith in the midst of Jesus' demonstration of authority is a call to believe. Second, the account follows a call to hold fast to the word in Luke 8:15–21, thus showing a concern for discipleship.[5] Matthew's emphasis is not so unique after all.

The Jesus Seminar rates all of the dialogue in this miracle as not tied to Jesus (in black type; Funk and Hoover 1993: 308). This continues their almost automatic tendency to reject teaching tied to miracles (see the discussion of sources and historicity for 4:31–44). But the rebuke for little faith is well attested (Matt. 6:30; 8:26; 14:31; 16:8; 17:20; Luke 12:28), and there is no reason to reject the sayings in this text. The seminar says (p. 310) that the dialogue is "the invention of the storyteller." One suspects that a worldview that excludes the miraculous has spilled over into their assessment of these sayings.

When looking at the event itself, one is struck by the general agreement of the event's portrayal in all three Gospels, although the wording of each

3. See the introduction to 8:4–15, which tentatively argues that the parables were later than their topical placement in Mark 4 suggests. Note also the introduction to 8:19–21.

4. Passages like this one are what makes doing a chronologically sequential life of Jesus so difficult, if not impossible. One can speak of what Jesus did in the various periods of his ministry, but there is too little chronological information to be certain of the order of all of these events.

5. Carson 1984: 214 suggests that the discipleship emphasis is overdrawn, especially when it is treated as Matthew's sole concern. Van Der Loos 1965: 649 argues that calling the boat the "ship of the church" originates in the "ship-yard of the imagination." The miracle pictures spiritual truth, but it is not allegory, nor does it focus only on discipleship.

Gospel has its peculiarities (see the exegesis for details). Nonetheless, Mark and Luke seem to be working with similar versions, and some suggest that the grouping of miracles in Mark 4:35–5:43 predates his Gospel (Fitzmyer 1981: 727; Bultmann 1963: 210; V. Taylor 1935: 39).

Fitzmyer (1981: 728), while noting this text's uniqueness, lists parallels that have been compared to this account (Van Der Loos 1965: 641–44 gives ancient parallels from Greece and Rome as well; also Schenke 1974: 59–69):

1. Antiochus IV Epiphanes, who claimed that the sea would obey him (2 Macc. 9:8)
2. Jonah in the OT (Jon. 1:1–17)
3. a Jewish boy on a boat who invoked God's help during a storm (*y. Ber.* 9.1 [= Neusner et al. 1982–93: 1.316]; SB 1:452)
4. Rabbi Gamaliel, who prayed to calm a storm after confession for making a wrong judgment (*b. B. Meṣ.* 59b)[6]
5. Paul (Acts 27:8–44)

Of course, the Pauline comparison is instructive in showing the uniqueness of this account: Paul did not quell the storm; he only predicted that no life would be lost. In Greco-Roman accounts, power over sea and storm is tied to various figures: Caesar, Caligula, Xerxes, Apollonius of Tyana, Empedocles (Nolland 1989: 398; Porphyry, *Life of Pythagoras* 29). But none of these individuals uses only human power to still a storm. Jesus calms the storm without prayer (Bovon 1989: 423–24).

The power that Jesus displays here is unique for a mortal. Bovon (1989: 423) notes T. Naph. 6 as parallel, but Jacob did not calm the storm there; he simply reappeared at its end. Neither did Jonah calm the storm. Rather, his departure into the sea and eventually into the whale only spared the boat from the sign of God's anger (Van Der Loos 1965: 646 shows that Jonah does not parallel this miracle). The figures in the Jewish examples do quell storms, but it is God who does so—because of the young boy's prayer or as a means of showing divine justification of the righteous, confessing rabbi.

Jesus is unique. The disciples learn to heed Jesus in a moment of severe trial (cf. Luke 8:13) and are forced to consider who it is they trust (Danker 1988: 180). For the one with control over the seas is Yahweh himself (Ps. 29:3; 65:7 [65:8 MT]; 89:9–11 [89:8–10 MT]; 93:3–4; 106:8–9; 107:23–30; Schürmann 1969: 474 and n. 4; Van Der Loos 1965: 644–46). These implications about Jesus are what the disciples struggle to comprehend.

---

6. Theissen 1983: 100 notes Greek parallels in ancient novels. In Greek circles, the rescue involves the appearing of a god; Homer, *Hymns* 33.12; Aristides, *Hymn to Serapis* 33. Such rescues are the affairs of divinity. Marshall 1978: 333 notes a parallel to Virgil, *Aeneid* 4.554–60.

Van Der Loos (1965: 648) argues that the issue is the saving power of Jesus' love. It is this and more. The disciples' question is about the nature of the deliverer, who possesses power like God. Jesus is Savior in all circumstances, but then beyond this understanding of how he functions lies the question of who he is (for more comments on historicity, see below on form).

The account is obviously a miracle story. Bultmann calls it a nature miracle, while others speak more precisely of a rescue miracle.[7] Berger speaks of a text designed to lead to admiration and a demonstration of power.[8] The account has all the basic features of a miracle account: setting, danger, wonder, and reaction (in terms of fear and reflection). In his discussion of the story's authenticity, Fitzmyer (1981: 728–29) raises the question as to what extent the story is mythological. He says it tries to express in human words the impact that Jesus made on his contemporaries: "The symbolism of the story comes through, no matter what one says about its historicity." He concludes: "From the historian's point of view, one can only say that there is no way to prove or disprove it." In one sense, Fitzmyer is right, since one cannot re-create the event or measure what caused the forces of nature to abate. On the other hand, here is a case where the text makes a clear claim of Jesus' authority. The historian's limitations are a result of human inability to analyze the divine by human rules. The text presents a revelation.[9] Nolland (1989: 399) rightly notes that "such events are not the stuff of normal history" but "they may, nevertheless, happen." The passage and the event leave the reader to face the question, "Has God acted through Jesus?" Luke's answer to that question is clear.

7. Bultmann 1963: 215–16; so also Fitzmyer 1981: 727. Bovon 1989: 422 speaks of a "victory of the hero (German *Helden*) over the elements," a rescue miracle, as does Theissen 1983: 321. Bovon says it is like an exorcism, but is distinct.

8. Berger 1984: 312 places the passage in his "epideixis/demonstratio" category. It is a revelatory account designed to create admiration.

9. I question Fitzmyer's view (1981: 543) of the role of miracles. He argues that miracles are not "apologetic proofs of Jesus' mission . . . or of his divinity"; rather they are "powerful manifestations and means whereby the dominion of God is established over human beings in place of the 'dominion of Belial,' freeing them from the evil to which they have been subjected." Miracles show a new phase of salvation history at work. This summary is correct in what it affirms, but needs qualification in what it denies. It is true that miracles are not explicit proofs of deity. Messengers of God did what Jesus did: Moses parted the sea, and Elijah and Elisha performed wonders, including raising the dead. But the bulk of Jesus' miracles and their variety imply his authority. The miracles do not explicitly make Jesus divine, but they do raise the question of his person, as Luke 8 shows. In addition, they defend his mission as grounded in God's power, as 11:14–25 argues. This is not an either/or issue; it is both/and.

The outline of Luke 8:22–25 is as follows:

i. Miracle (8:22–24)
  (1) Setting (8:22)
  (2) Danger (8:23)
  (3) Cry for help (8:24a)
  (4) Rebuke of the wind and coming of the calm (8:24b)
ii. Reaction (8:25)
  (1) Rebuke for lack of faith (8:25a)
  (2) Fear and a question: "who is this man?" (8:25b)

Numerous themes are found in this pericope: the importance of having faith in the midst of trial (which looks back on the earlier teaching of 8:11–15); Jesus' exceptional control over nature and the seas in parallel to Yahweh's acts (which probably generated the disciples' question); Jesus' delivering; awe over the exercise of miraculous power; and the question raised for the reflection of all: "Who is this one who can. . . ?"

Exegesis and Exposition

[22]And on one of these days, he and his disciples got into a boat, and he said to them, "Let us go to the other side of the lake."
So they set out. [23]And as they sailed, he fell asleep. And there descended on the lake a whirlwind, and they were being overcome with water and were in danger. [24]And they went to him and woke him, saying, "Master, Master, we are perishing!" And he awoke and rebuked the wind and the waves of water, and they ceased, and there was calm. [25]But he said to them, "Where is your faith?" And they were afraid and marveled, saying to one another, "Who then is this, that he commands even the winds and water, and they obey him?"

i. Miracle (8:22–24)
(1) Setting (8:22)

The miracle's setting is simple enough. A general temporal note in- **8:22** dicates that on one day during this period, Jesus and his disciples launched out to cross the Sea of Galilee, also known as the Lake of Gennesaret (Luke 5:1; Matt. 14:34; Mark 6:53). Only Luke (8:22, 23) refers to the body of water here as a λίμνη (limnē, lake), while Mark (4:39, 41) and Matthew (8:24, 26, 27) refer to the θάλασσα (thalassa, sea). Luke uses the same term to describe the boat (πλοῖον, ploion) as he did in Luke 5:2, 3, 7, 11. A fishing boat that could hold many disciples would be a substantial vessel. Likely passengers included the Twelve and perhaps the women of 8:1–3 (Fitzmyer 1981: 729).

Geldenhuys (1951: 251) argues that Jesus was tired from the day and sought to withdraw.[10] His resting during the crossing supports this observation. It was not unusual for a boat to have a pillow where those who were not working or fishing could rest (Van Der Loos 1965: 638). Mark 4:38 confirms this picture of the custom.

Giving detail that Luke lacks, Mark 4:35 notes that it is evening and that it is the same day on which Jesus taught in parables. Many argue that Luke recast the setting from Mark. Jesus is already in the boat in Mark 4:1, and so Mark does not mention entering the boat in 4:35. It is suggested that Luke, because he has put a little distance and time between the parables and this incident, mentions embarking on the boat. In fact, some see Mark's setting as artificial, and Luke's as showing a more natural movement (Creed 1930: 119). But such a judgment is not warranted. Mark's "on that day" (ἐν ἐκείνῃ τῇ ἡμέρᾳ, *en ekeinē tē hēmera*) need not assume that Jesus stayed in the boat the entire time or that nothing happened between the parabolic teaching and the departure. In fact, one could argue that the Marcan reference to the evening (ὀψίας, *opsias*) suggests a time lapse and a new setting, as does Mark 4:36, where it says that Jesus left the crowd and went with the disciples in the boat. Thus, the change of setting between Mark and Luke should not be overplayed. It is curious, however, why Luke should be so general about the timing, when Mark is specific.[11] Each has supplied his own distinct introduction and summary of the setting (Matt. 8:23 is even more general in tone).[12] Interestingly, Mark has Jesus suggest going to the other side and then mentions his getting into the boat. Luke has the opposite order. But sequence is not the point here; summary is. Mark also notes that other vessels crossed with the disciples. Ἀνάγω (*anagō*) is the common verb for going out to sea (Arndt 1956: 237; Luce 1933: 170; Schürmann 1969: 475 n. 11; Acts 13:13; 16:11; 18:21; 27:21; BAGD 53 §3; BAA 104 §3).

(2) Danger (8:23)

8:23 The disciples are seemingly on their own. As they sail across, Jesus falls asleep (ἀφυπνόω, *aphypnoō*; a NT *hapax legomenon*; BAGD 127–28; BAA 256–57). His calm mood stands in contrast to the approach-

---

10. Geldenhuys's remark assumes Mark's setting, since Luke does not note that this happened on the day of the parable discourse. His timing is more general. See the next paragraph.

11. All we may have here is a Lucan stylistic introduction. In 5:12, Luke uses an equally ambiguous phrase: "one of the cities." Schramm 1971: 125 raises the possibility of another version of the tradition. It is possible, but not necessary.

12. Fitzmyer 1981: 729 discusses points of Lucan style in the verse: ἐν μιᾷ τῶν ἡμερῶν (on one of those days), ἐγένετο δέ (and it came to pass), and καὶ αὐτός (and he himself).

ing chaos. Πλέω (*pleō*) means "to sail" and may suggest a sailing vessel as opposed to one that is rowed (ἐλαύνω, *elaunō*; Arndt 1956: 237; Plummer 1896: 225; on ἐλαύνω see also Mark 6:48; John 6:19; πλέω occurs elsewhere only at Acts 21:3; 27:2, 6, 24; Rev. 18:17). The storm's arrival is described with a suddenness that fits its character: it is a whirlwind (λαῖλαψ, *lailaps*).[13] The picture is of a storm, bearing severe winds, that produces choppy seas and large waves. Matthew's description of an "earthquake" may be a way to convey the instability produced by the storm, a "quake" on water!

Given the Sea of Galilee's topography, such a storm could descend onto the sea quickly without notice and, at night, could hardly be anticipated. The sea is some seven hundred feet below sea level and is depressed with hills surrounding it. The hills on the east side are particularly steep (Hendriksen 1978: 439–40). Cool air rushing down the ravines and hills around the lake can collide with warm air above the lake and create an instant storm in the confined quarters (Fitzmyer 1981: 729).

The verbs describe the water coming into the vessel as a dangerous situation: "were being overcome" (συνεπληροῦντο, *syneplērounto*) by water and "were being placed in real danger" (ἐκινδύνευον, *ekindyneuon*; Acts 19:27, 40; 1 Cor. 15:30; BAGD 432). The language is personalized when it says "they" were overcome. It is the boat that is filling up with water, but the passengers stand at risk. In fact, it is professional fishermen who are worried. Mark 8:38 adds detail to Jesus' rest in the midst of the storm: he is in the stern, asleep on a cushion. The contrast is striking. The disciples are powerless, while Jesus rests and the storm rages (Bovon 1989: 424–25). Seeing only the circumstances, the disciples doubt and panic, while Jesus rests in the midst of it all (cf. Ps. 121:4). A situation that is fraught with danger in the disciples' view is no cause for worry with Jesus.

(3) Cry for Help (8:24a)

The threat becomes so great that the disciples decide to awaken **8:24a** Jesus. The urgent mood is indicated by the double vocative ἐπιστάτα ἐπιστάτα (*epistata epistata*, Master, Master), a term that Luke always uses in the vocative: 5:5; 8:45; 9:33, 49; 17:13. Such a repeated expression is emphatic and indicates the high emotion running through the cry (like 13:34). The cry for help is simple enough. In the disciples' view, they are on the edge of death.

---

13. λαῖλαψ may be onomatopoetic; so Arndt 1956: 327; Job 21:18; 38:1. The other NT uses are Mark 4:37 and 2 Pet. 2:17; BAGD 462–63; BAA 940. Matt. 8:24 uses σεισμός (earthquake or storm), a term that may make apocalyptic associations with the event; BAGD 746; BAA 1493.

The Gospels differ slightly in their wording of the disciples' request to be saved. Matthew 8:25 calls on the Lord specifically to save them. Mark 4:38 has the disciples complaining to Jesus that perhaps he does not care that they are perishing. Luke's account is the most abbreviated. Interestingly, in Matthew, Jesus is addressed as κύριε (*kyrie*, Lord), in Mark as διδάσκαλε (*didaskale*, Teacher), and in Luke as ἐπιστάτα (*epistata*, Master). Matthew and Luke are similar in force. Of course, given the chaos, the text has many disciples rousing Jesus. Surely several were calling for help.

(4) Rebuke of the Wind and Coming of the Calm (8:24b)

8:24b Jesus acts by rebuking the wind and the waves. Ἐπετίμησεν (*epetimēsen*, he rebuked) is the same verb used to rebuke the unclean spirit in 4:35 and the fever in 4:39. The danger is pictured as a confrontation since the concept of rebuke is present. Nonetheless, one should not see a demonic encounter here, since there is no such note raised (Van Der Loos 1965: 648). The term was used earlier of disease, which Luke distinguished from exorcism. Indeed, such a demonic note here would destroy the progression that runs through the Luke 8 miracles (against Fitzmyer 1981: 730; with Schürmann 1969: 476 and Stauffer, *TDNT* 2:624, 626). Any force hostile to humans can be rebuked by Jesus, whether spirit, disease, or natural forces.

The storm ceases immediately, and there is calm. Creation's testimony to Jesus is a theme in Luke (19:40). Such control over nature is tied in the OT to Yahweh (see the introduction to this unit). God's control of the wind (ἄνεμος, *anemos*) is noted in Ps. 104:3 [103:3 LXX]; 135:7 [134:7 LXX] (cf. Nah. 1:4). Flat seas now emerge from dangerous waves (κλύδων, *klydōn*; Plummer 1896: 226; BAGD 436; BAA 888; James 1:6). The mention of the large waves expresses the nearness of calamity (Wis. 14:3–5), calamity that is overcome by divine protection and power (Ps. 18:16 [17:17 LXX]; Wis. 14:5). The association of waves is also present in Jon. 1, where it also describes the threat to life. These were natural forces that could threaten human life, but Jesus tamed them. Plummer (1896: 226) notes that the seas do not take their time in settling down; they are calmed immediately (ἐπαύσαντο καὶ ἐγένετο γαλήνη, *epausanto kai egeneto galēnē*, they ceased and there was a calm). The OT passage that this event is most like is Ps. 107:23–30. Only a few of the psalm's terms are found in the Synoptic accounts: θάλασσα (*thalassa*, sea) and πλοῖον (*ploion*, boat). But the conceptual parallel is clear (Goppelt, *TDNT* 8:323). God is the one who delivers from peril in the sea.

There are differences of nuance in the taming of the seas. Mark 4:39 includes Jesus' call to the sea to be still, a detail that Matthew and Luke do not have. All mention the calm that results, with Matthew and Mark calling it a "great" calm. Luke and Mark note the silencing in two steps: the activity ceased and there was calm, though Mark's first verbal term ἐκόπασεν (ekopasen, ceased) differs from Luke's synonymous ἐπαύσαντο. Again, the variations are minor differences that do not influence meaning, and yet they paint a complex picture of the source relationship. Was oral tradition available to Luke?

Jesus thus delivers the disciples, who are at risk of perishing. The physical rescue pictures spiritual truth, as the exhortation to faith in the next verse makes clear. The disciples may have felt they were alone, but Jesus was watching over them.

ii. Reaction (8:25)
(1) Rebuke for Lack of Faith (8:25a)

All three Gospels have Jesus turn and rebuke the disciples at this **8:25a** point for their lack of faith.[14] Both Matt. 8:26 and Mark 4:40 note the rebuke in two phases: mention of the disciples' fear and then a rebuke for little faith.[15] Luke simply has an abbreviated report about faith and has slightly lessened the criticism of the disciples, as he often does (Fitzmyer 1981: 730). The point here is clear: the disciples should be able to rest in God's care and to trust Jesus' ability to care for them. The rhetorical form of the question ("Where is your faith?") really makes it a statement: "You should be more trusting." To overcome trial, one must have faith in God's goodness. The faith in view here is not initial faith, but an applied faith that functions in the midst of pressure. It is a faith that has depth of understanding and can be drawn upon in tough times. It is faith that "kicks in" and recognizes that God is in control, even in the face of disaster. It holds fast patiently (Luke 8:15).

(2) Fear and a Question: "Who Is This Man?" (8:25b)

Fear and wonder are a normal response when one becomes aware **8:25b** that God is at work, even when it is through an agent. The ideas of fear and wonder have appeared numerous times already in Luke, and here they are a response to Jesus' mighty work (fear in 1:12, 65; 2:9; 5:26; 7:16; marvel in 1:21, 63; 2:18, 33; Balz, *TDNT* 9:209; Schürmann 1969: 476 n. 27). However, only here are the two placed side by side (Fitzmyer 1981: 730). This action raises not only emotions of

---

14. Matthew has the rebuke of the disciples before the stilling of the storm, a point that suggests that Luke had access to a Mark-like version of this account.

15. But each has distinct wording. For example, only Matthew calls the disciples "little faiths" (ὀλιγόπιστοι). Mark simply asks if they have no faith.

wonder, but also a question. Luke and Mark ask it as, "Who is this then?"[16] Who is this that can command the forces of nature, so that (ὅτι indicates result, not cause) winds and water obey him? This is the climactic question of the account. Matthew and Mark speak of sea and wind, with Matthew using the plural "winds" and Mark the singular; Luke has winds and water. The sense of the question is the same for all three Gospels, but once again source complexity is introduced by the shifts of wording.

Luke leaves the query unanswered. It is a question to be pondered. This certainly is not a normal man. This is at least a prophet, as the parallel with Elijah's handling of weather shows (1 Kings 17:1). But is Jesus merely a prophet? Though on occasion a prophet could perform such wonders, what does it mean that Jesus performs such works so regularly and in so many differing spheres? Who but divinity can handle nature like this? Barriers are being breached here, as with Jesus' other actions. Those who are theologically sensitive know that nature is not in the hands of mere mortals. The Psalms note who controls creation. Regardless of whether one is Jewish or Greek, one knows this to be true. Such common understanding serves as background to answer the question raised by the calmness that Jesus generated. The calmed waves testify to Jesus' identity.

Summary In Luke 8:22–25 Jesus begins a series of miracles that appear to have a threefold function. First, they are to drive home who Jesus really is for the disciples. What God used to do, or what was attributed to him, Jesus now does also (Marshall 1978: 333). More than a teacher or prophet is present. The disciples will continue to struggle with this question, but this account begins to prepare us for the confession of 9:20. Second, the unit continues to demonstrate the authority that Jesus possesses. He will give similar authority to his disciples shortly (9:1–6; Talbert 1982: 95–96). This account shows them how great is the authority that they will receive. Jesus exercises control over forces that otherwise can overcome them. The point is not to promise deliverance from these forces anytime they arise, but to show that when one is allied to Jesus, such forces can ultimately be overcome. There is no enemy too great for Jesus. Finally, the account is designed to call disciples to realize that, however great the peril, Jesus is aware and is able to deliver. It may be deliverance *through* trial, rather than *from* it, but one is to apply faith in such situations. Thus, the position of Jesus allows one to place trust in him. This is the les-

---

16. Matt. 8:27 has a synonymous question: "What sort of man is this?" Luke and Mark have τίς (who?), while Matthew has ποταπός (what sort of?).

son of discipleship that the stilling of the storm teaches. Without a Christology that recognizes Jesus' authority, there can be no real hope in him, for otherwise the hostile waves in life will pull us down, and there is nowhere to turn. The calming of the waves can come only from the one who has the power to restore order.

b. Authority over Demons: Gerasene Demoniac (8:26–39)

The healing of the Gerasene demoniac represents a different kind of miracle. Jesus has exorcised demons previously (Luke 4:31–37, 41; 6:18). But this account is an intensification of this ability—the exorcism of multiple demons from one man.[1] The task is more difficult, as Jesus is outnumbered. Luke tells the story in great detail. Jesus' power here overcomes one of a variety of forces illustrated in the four miracles of 8:22–56. In fact, this series of miracles shows God's reclamation of people through the demonstration of Jesus' unique authority. All forces—nature, demons, disease, and death—that could be regarded as stronger than humanity and that stand opposed to God as rivals to his power are rendered impotent in this section. Relationship to Jesus brings security.

Liefeld (1984: 913) notes seven characteristics of demon possession: (1) disregard for personal dignity in nakedness, (2) social isolation, (3) retreat to basic shelter, (4) demonic recognition of Jesus' deity, (5) demonic control of speech, (6) shouting, and (7) extraordinary strength. The point is not that any one of these is a sign of demon possession, but that the combination portrays it. The list in later rabbinic Judaism was simpler: walking about at night, spending the night on a grave, tearing one's clothes, and destroying what one is given (Van Der Loos 1965: 385; SB 1:491; *y. Ter.* 40b [= Neusner 1982–93: 6.55], as noted by Rabbi Huna, who died in A.D. 297).

One other key element of this passage is that it takes place in Gentile territory. Evidence for this includes the demon's name, the demoniac's unclean lifestyle of living among the dead, the presence of pigs, and the name of God as "Most High" (Bovon 1989: 429). With such a setting, the account previews how all humanity benefits from God's message (Talbert 1982: 97; cf. Luke 2:32; 3:6; 4:25–27). Jesus' ministry goes beyond Israel. Thus, we have a miracle of multiple exorcism and a missionary text. Schürmann (1969: 480) suggests an allusion to Isa. 65:1–5 for aspects of the description of the possessed man (also Pesch 1971: 361).

---

1. Overcoming such forces is important to Luke: Acts 13:6–11; 16:16–18; 19:13–17; Schürmann 1969: 480 n. 54.

Sources and Historicity

The history of this tradition is complex and disputed. The parallel Mark 5:1–20 gives even more detail, while Matt. 8:28–34 is an abbreviated version (Aland 1985: §137). The unique character of the event has generated discussion at various levels.

First, some regard the event as mythical not only because of the demonic subject matter but also because of the incident involving the swine.[2] Marshall (1978: 335–36) is undecided about the nature of the swine account. Does it represent "legendary features" that the early church used to express Jesus' supreme power or Jesus' conscious choice to use the swine to demonstrate graphically that the man had been healed? The latter option is better. It is not the account's burden to answer questions like why Jesus would do such a thing or whether demons have to have such a place to reside (Luce 1933: 170 mentions four such issues and regards the story as a tale). It merely describes what occurred and why. Questioning whether Jesus caused the pigs to stampede, Fitzmyer (1981: 734–35) argues that what is present is the beginning of accretions into the tradition (like that seen in apocryphal material), but he allows with some hesitancy what he calls an "optical demonstration" of the man's liberation. Obviously, how one approaches the entire area of the demonic, in terms of worldview, will determine how one judges the account (Pesch 1971: 349–50 nicely outlines the options).[3] If the demonic is explained naturally in terms of some type of psychological imbalance, then much of the story will be explained on natural terms, though it is difficult to do this with the detail about swine (for which one must then appeal to either legendary accretion or an act of Jesus). Those who accept the realm of the supernatural and the existence of spirits will have fewer problems with the account and will not try to reformulate its rationale. The account's perspective is clear enough: Jesus exercises authority over the destructive forces of evil, and he does so visibly by using the swine, so that the expulsion is clear to all.

The Jesus Seminar views the dialogue in the miracle account as they did the exchanges in 8:22–25: it is the evangelist's invention and, hence, is printed in black type (Funk and Hoover 1993: 308–10). My response to this approach is the same as in the earlier miracle accounts (see the discussion of sources and historicity for 8:22–25). In their discussion, the seminar cites an exorcism by Eleazar reported in Josephus, *Antiquities* 8.2.5 §§46–49. Eleazar used incantations and a ring associated with Solomon (who taught how to perform exorcisms; §§42–45) to effect an exorcism by pulling out the demon through the nostrils of the possessed man. Even a superficial

---

2. Creed 1930: 120 and Luce 1933: 170–71 both call it a "strange story" and a "popular tale"; see also Bultmann 1963: 210–11. Plummer 1896: 228 lists nine explanations offered for the material.

3. For a discussion of the linguistic force of ἔχων δαιμόνια (having demons), see Hanse, *TDNT* 2:821–22.

reading of this account, however, reveals how different its portrayal of exorcism is, with differences of approach being more outstanding than the similarities. Pesch (1971: 363–64) notes that the Bentresh Stele contains a Persian account of an Egyptian exorcism in which the demon requested a banquet feast with the god before agreeing to depart. The theme of asking for a concession before departing looks similar to Luke 8:31, but the calm tone in the Persian account differs greatly from the mood of conflict and threat in Luke.

A second discussion about the tradition concerns the number of demoniacs: two (Matt. 8:28, 33) or one (Mark 5:2 = Luke 5:27)? While many argue for expansion of the tradition (Bultmann 1963: 316), others argue that Matthew has independent material that recalls a second figure (Carson 1984: 217).[4] Mark and Luke simply focus on one of the characters, since that is all that is needed to make the essential point (Godet 1875: 1.381).

The third issue is the locale, which will receive detailed treatment in the additional note on 8:26. This issue is tied to a key textual problem found in all the Gospels. Nonetheless, it should be noted that Matt. 8:28 probably describes the locale as Gadara, while Mark 5:1 = Luke 8:26 has Gerasa. As the dispute also involves what region these names describe, the problem is not only a text-critical issue, but one of ancient geography as well. The geographical reference, on either view, is a general one, since a region (χώραν) is referred to. Thus, speaking of an error in either reference is inappropriate (see Plummer 1896: 227). It should be remembered that the region, whatever the reading, is largely Gentile. This is the key point of the geography.

A fourth issue concerns the event's placement in each Gospel. The placement of this event parallels that of the stilling of the storm (see the discussion of sources for 8:22–25). Luke 8:26–39 = Mark 5:1–20 comes after the parable sequence in Luke 8:4–15 = Mark 4:1–34, while Matt. 8:28–34 comes before the parables of Matt. 13. This event probably came after the parable sequence and seems to follow the stilling of the storm very closely, since Mark 5:2 speaks of Jesus' emerging from the boat and Luke 8:27 speaks of his coming unto land.[5]

The Marcan and Lucan versions stand close to one another, while Matthew appears to have abbreviated the story and used other sources, perhaps even his own recollections.[6] Nolland (1989: 403–5) argues that Mark is Luke's source and that much of Mark's version came to him through the

---

4. This added detail runs against Matthew's tendency to constrict details, and thus suggests a source. Otherwise Matthew's account here is briefer.

5. Arndt 1956: 238 puts all of these events on the same day, while Marshall 1978: 335 suggests an allusion to Ps. 65:7 [65:8 MT] and the "tumult of the people," though the verbal connection is vague. C. F. Evans 1990: 383 notes Ps. 65:5–8 [65:6–9 MT]; 46:2–6; Isa. 17:12–13, which are less than evident. Matt. 8–9 is topically arranged.

6. That Matthew may have accompanied Jesus lends credence to the added detail of the second demoniac. The extent of the agreement between Mark and Luke leads most to see Mark as the source for Luke; so Schürmann 1969: 487; Schramm 1971:

tradition. He sees only Mark 5:3–5, 8, 16 as possible Marcan expansions. The points of scholarly tension in Mark are (1) the location of Gerasa; (2) the tension between 5:2 (meeting Jesus) and 5:6 (still approaching Jesus); (3) whether 5:3–5 is an expansion; (4) the tension between demonic submission in 5:6 and demonic defense in 5:7; (5) the position of 5:8; (6) the shift from singular to plural in 5:9; (7) the use of the swine; and (8) the separate, more missionary theme of 5:18–20. Nolland argues that all of the story's major features in Luke are rooted in Mark's version, since Luke's abbreviated version lacks some of these internal tensions and smooths out the account. (See also Annen 1976: 22–29 and Kertelge 1970: 101.) Thus, each writer tells the story with his own emphases.

The form of the account is a miracle story, more specifically, an exorcism.[7] Bultmann (1963: 210) notes that it has all the characteristics of such an account: (1) meeting with the demon, (2) description of the condition, (3) demon recognition of the exorcist, (4) exorcism, (5) description of the demon's departure, and (6) impression on observers. Fitzmyer (1981: 734) argues that it is more than a simple miracle story because of the "fantastic and grotesque" details that accompany it—remarks that show how uncomfortable moderns can be with parts of this account. Pesch (1971: 349) calls it "not only the most 'stupendous' but also the most scandalous" of Jesus' miracles. Fitzmyer also correctly notes that, because of the ending, the account is really a missionary story and a miracle.[8]

90; Marshall 1978: 335; Fitzmyer 1981: 733; Wiefel 1988: 165–66. Bovon 1989: 432 is so impressed with these agreements that he argues that this account stands against the two-Gospel (or Griesbach) hypothesis. What could have caused Luke to go his own way against Matthew?

7. Bultmann 1963: 210 classifies it as a miracle of healing. Bovon 1989: 432 and Theissen 1983: 321 call it an exorcism. Theissen also speaks of the liberation of an enslaved personality (pp. 89–90). Berger 1984: 311 puts it in his "epideixis/demonstratio" category (where he puts many miracles). He also speaks of the account as a "mandatio" that highlights Jesus' authority and power. Pesch 1971: 354 notes the form elements in Mark: encounter (5:1–2), demon's defensive reaction (5:6–7), exorcist's command (5:8), exit of demon (5:13), crowd amazement and spread of exorcist's fame (5:14a, 18–20).

8. The addition of the missionary emphasis at the end is called secondary on the assumption that multiple forms are not in the original tradition. But most now see that the tradition did reach Mark already in this form. This is an example against the supposed rule, which raises questions about the rule! But for development, see Kertelge 1970: 107. Another key study of this event also seeing stages in the development of the account is Pesch 1972; an earlier English version is Pesch 1971. However, Nolland 1989: 404 rightly sees the double purpose tied to the influence of eyewitness memory, an observation that applies to many fixed-form accounts. The appeal to major stages of development is not necessary.

The outline of Luke 8:26–39 is as follows:

i. Miracle (8:26–33)
   (1) Setting: demoniac introduced (8:26–29)
   (2) Plea of the legion (8:30–31)
   (3) Demons into the swine (8:32–33)
ii. Reaction (8:34–39)
   (1) Reaction of the herders and townspeople (8:34–37a)
   (2) Jesus' departure and instruction to the healed one
       (8:37b–39a)
   (3) Testimony of the healed one about Jesus (8:39b)

The account opens with the destructiveness of evil spiritual forces and shows the tragic picture of the demoniac's isolation. Once again, a demoniac recognizes Jesus' authority. The swine dramatically depict the exorcism's success. The crowd pictures fear that recognizes—but cannot accept—God's presence. The demoniac's remaining at home shows that some are called to go with Jesus; others are called to stay home to testify to him. The account illustrates the importance of personal testimony. Finally, God is active in Jesus for both Gentiles and Jews.

Exegesis and Exposition

[26]And they arrived in the region of the ⌐Gerasenes⌐, which is opposite Galilee. [27]And when he came into the land, a certain man from the city, who had demons, met him; ⌐for a long time⌐ he had worn no clothes and he did not stay in a house but among the tombs. [28]And when he saw Jesus, he cried out, fell before him, and said in a loud voice, "What have I to do with you, Jesus, Son of the Most High God? I beg you, do not torment me." [29]But he ⌐commanded⌐ the unclean spirit to come out of the man. For many times it had seized him, and he was kept under guard, bound with chains and fetters, and yet breaking the bonds, he was driven out into the desert by the demon. [30]Jesus asked him, "What is your name?" And he said, "Legion," for there were many demons in him. [31]And they begged him not to command them to go into the abyss. [32]And a large herd of swine was feeding there on the hillside; and they begged him to let them enter into these. And he gave them permission. [33]And the demons came out of the man into the swine, and the herd rushed down the steep bank into the lake and was drowned.

[34]And when the herdsmen saw what had occurred, they fled and told it in the city and in the country. [35]They went out to see what had occurred, and they came to Jesus and found the man from whom the demons had gone out, sitting, clothed, and of sound mind, at the feet of Jesus; and they were afraid. [36]And those who had seen it told them how the demon-possessed man was delivered. [37]Then all the many people of the region of the ⌐Gera-

senes⌐ asked him to leave them, for they were seized with great fear; so he got into the boat and returned. ³⁸And the man from whom the demons had gone out was begging that he might be with him; but he sent him away, saying, ³⁹"Return to your home and tell how much God did for you." And he went into the entire city, proclaiming how much Jesus had done for him.

i. Miracle (8:26–33)
(1) Setting: Demoniac Introduced (8:26–29)

The geographic setting of the exorcism involves a major textual problem, and the location depends on how it is solved (see the additional note). The reading Γερασηνῶν (Gerasenes) is preferred for Luke. This location is in Gentile territory opposite Galilee. **8:26**

Luke describes the isolation and the possessed man's unusual behavior before he met (ὑπαντάω, hypantaō) Jesus.[9] Three simple items are related about the man from the city. First, he was possessed by multiple demons (δαιμόνια, daimonia, is an accusative plural). Mark 5:2 speaks of an unclean spirit (singular), but the name of the spirit in Mark 5:9 is given as Legion, which leads to the explanation that "many" (πολλοί, polloi) possess him. Luke uses the singular in 8:29. One can speak of the possession as a unity or refer to the individual spirits. **8:27**

Second, the man did not clothe himself, but had roamed around naked for a long time (cf. Acts 19:16). Luke alone mentions this detail, and in 8:35 he will mention the man's being clothed as a sign of the restoration (Schweizer 1984: 150; Arndt 1956: 240). Mark 5:15 notes only that the man is clothed after the exorcism.

Third, the man did not live in the city, but had isolated himself among the tombs, a particularly graphic and somber image. Geldenhuys (1951: 258 n. 4) quotes A. Schlatter that "only deranged people . . . have [a] desire for death and decay." Tombs were often built into hillsides, usually outside the city (Plummer 1896: 229; on demons and graves in Judaism, see SB 1:491–92; 4:516; y. Ter. 40b [= Neusner 1982–93: 6.55]). If the man is Jewish, then uncleanness would result from his presence there (Num. 19:11, 14, 16; Fitzmyer 1981: 737). It would also be ironic that swine, unclean animals, become the haven for the expelled demons, though the irony is less surprising in a Gentile region. Mark 5:2, 5 repeats the mention of the tombs, while Matt. 8:28 briefly notes them. The actions of this man show his desperate condition; but this is only the start of his problems.

---

9. All the parallels (Matt. 8:28 = Mark 5:2 = Luke 8:27) use this term; elsewhere at Matt. 28:9; Luke 14:31; Acts 16:16; and four times in John; Michel, *TDNT* 3:625–26.

8:28   The possessed man cries out to Jesus and falls before him in recognition of his authority (cf. Luke 4:34, 41). Of course, it is not the man who speaks, but the force that possesses him. The question could be paraphrased in one of two ways: "What is there between us?" or "Could you leave me alone?"[10] The confession and prostration, as well as the plea not to torment, give testimony to how transcendent forces, even those opposed to Jesus, see him. Though the falling at his feet would not be worship, since this would be impossible for a demon, these forces show respect to Jesus, because he has a filial relationship to and authority from the Most High God.[11] They know that he has authority over them or can do battle with them. Schürmann (1969: 483) remarks that the demons know about Jesus' sonship, just as Satan did (4:3, 9). Thus, they request Jesus to leave them alone and not torture them (βασανίζω, basanizō; BAGD 134 §2; BAA 269 §2; J. Schneider, *TDNT* 1:563).[12]

The wording matches Mark 5:7 almost exactly, while Matt. 8:29 asks a shortened form of the question and lacks the request. Actually, Matthew asks a second question expressing concern that Jesus may deal with them before "the day," that is, the demon fears judgment before the expected time.[13] The only difference between Mark and Luke is that Mark has already described the man's self-destructive behavior, while Luke withholds these details until after this exchange.

Ellis (1974: 128) notes that at times the ancient world distinguished illness from mental disorder or psychological disease (Herodotus 2.173; 6.84). Hippocrates, however, explained all disease as the result of natural causes (*On the Sacred Disease*; cf. Cicero, *On Divination* 2.28; Van Der Loos 1965: 7 n. 2). Luke's position is clearly different, for he recognizes an additional category. This man is a pawn in a cosmic spiritual battle that pictures spiritual authority. Of course, many ancients of various racial and religious origins viewed the activity of the gods similarly, so all would understand the thrust of Luke's presentation.

---

10. Arndt 1956: 240 suggests something like the latter question; also 1 Kings 17:18.

11. On this title, see Luke 1:32, 35, 76. According to Josephus, *Antiquities* 16.6.2 §163, this was the Gentile way to refer to the God of the Jews; Luce 1933: 172. So also Plummer 1896: 229–30, citing Dan. 3:26; 4:24 [4:21 MT]; 5:18; 7:18; Bovon 1989: 429 n. 4.

12. On demons crying out to resist exorcism, see Grundmann, *TDNT* 3:900; O. Betz, *TDNT* 9:294.

13. This may also be the significance of the request in Luke 8:31 not to be sent into the abyss; Van Der Loos 1965: 387 n. 4. 1 Enoch 56.3; T. Moses 10.11–12; and T. Levi 18 reflect such an eschatological judgment (the T. Moses reference is disputed; see J. Charlesworth 1983–85: 1.932, 933 n. g).

Jesus commands the unclean spirit to depart.[14] This seems to be a **8:29** summary description, since the details follow in 8:30–33 (see the additional note).

By way of background, Luke notes the man's unusual strength. The possession seems to have come and gone in cycles, since there is reference to his being seized (συνηρπάκει, *synērpakei*) many times (πολλοῖς ... χρόνοις, *pollois ... chronois*).[15] Efforts to restrain him had failed, since he broke his bonds and fled to the desert, having been driven there by the demon. Πέδη (*pedē*) is a foot bond (BAGD 638; BAA 1287; elsewhere only twice in Mark 5:4), while δεσμός (*desmos*) refers to a restraint in general (BAGD 176; BAA 352; Bovon 1989: 435 n. 49). We are not told if the bonds were made of hair, cloth, rope, or chains, though Mark 5:4 seems to suggest chains, since it is by shattering (συντρίβω, *syntribō*) that they are removed (BAGD 793; BAA 1582). It was common to bind the hands with chains and the feet with ropes. The possibility of this mixture is indicated by the shift in terminology used to describe the binding (Plummer 1896: 230). The portrayal shows the spirit's strength. The foe is a powerful one that people and chains cannot control.

The Lucan description of the binding comes earlier in the Marcan version. Marshall (1978: 338) notes that Luke's order often differs from Mark's in various pericopes (e.g., Luke 8:42a, 46b, 51b, 55c; 9:14a, 34b, 48c). In Mark 5:4, the description of the man's condition precedes the demon's question to Jesus, a difference that probably reflects the writers' choices. In addition, Mark has details about the destructiveness of the demon that Luke lacks (the man's crying out at night and his bruising himself against the stones). Luke's account stresses the foe's strength, while Mark adds the evil force's destructiveness. The man's presence in the desert shows the tragic isolation that the demon produced.

(2) Plea of the Legion (8:30–31)

The exorcism proper comes after a brief exchange between Jesus **8:30** and the possessed man. The demonic influence speaks through the man in straightforward dialogue. Jesus asks for his name. Plummer (1896: 230) suggests that the request is designed to awaken the man's personality or to show the disciples the extent of the problem (also Godet 1875: 1.335). The reply explains the situation through the name *Legion*, which refers to a large group. The term brings a

---

14. On unclean spirits in the NT, see Hauck, *TDNT* 3:428 n. 12; in Judaism, see Zech. 13:2; T. Ben. 5.2; Jub. 10.1; 11.4; 12.20; T. Sim. 4.9; 6.6.

15. On συναρπάζω, see BAGD 785; BAA 1566; elsewhere only at Acts 6:12; 19:29; 27:15 (of a ship caught in a storm).

military air to the account and thus adds to the note of battle (Bovon 1989: 436 refers to the Qumran War Scroll, which describes legions of troops). The man's plight is the result of multiple possession. It is one against many. The war is on.

In fact, it is one against thousands, if the name Legion is to be taken literally. Λεγιών (*legiōn*) comes from the Latin word for a unit made up of thousands of soldiers (Mark 5:9; Matt. 26:53; Preisker, *TDNT* 4:68).[16] Since the size of a legion varied, the name probably indicates not the exact number of demons; it explains that Jesus faced multiple demons, a point that the swine incident will also demonstrate in Luke 8:32. Bovon (1989: 436) posits that when one thinks in narrative terminology the number indicates "a maximum of demonic concentrations." Mark 5:13 indicates that around two thousand pigs were in the destroyed herd. In fact, the reply may be a diversion, since a number, not a name is given. The demon may be evasive here in hopes of escaping Jesus' reaction. Luke explains the name on the basis of multiple possession, while in Mark 5:9 the demon gives the explanation. The wording in Mark and Luke is very close, but the verbal forms differ slightly.[17] Asking the name is not an effort to gain control of the situation, since many healings have already occurred where no naming was necessary (Luke 4:31–37, 38–41; with Marshall 1978: 338; against Creed 1930: 121; Fitzmyer 1981: 738; and Luce 1933: 172).

8:31 The demons know they are in a bad situation. Despite their numbers and power, they know who has authority. As in 8:28, the demons beg Jesus not to exercise his authority over them and relegate them to the abyss (Schmitz, *TDNT* 5:794 n. 163). Luke alone mentions the abyss, as Mark 5:10 speaks only of their asking not to be cast out of the country and Matt. 8:29 refers to their not being tormented before the time.[18] Mark's less apocalyptic request is not necessarily in conflict with Matthew or Luke here, since Mark is stating positively where the demons would prefer to stay, while Matthew and Luke recount what they wish to avoid.[19]

16. In Augustus's time a legion was about six thousand troops, with an equal number of auxiliary troops; BAGD 467–68 and BAA 950.

17. Mark has ἐπηρώτα (asked) and λέγει (says [historical present]); Luke, ἐπηρώτησεν (asked) and εἶπεν (said). Matthew's shorter account lacks this exchange.

18. Fitzmyer 1981: 739 argues that Mark is more original, but this is difficult to establish, given both Matthew's and Luke's independent indications of distinct apocalyptic imagery ("abyss" and "tormented before the time").

19. Against Van Der Loos 1965: 389, who argues that the request in Mark not to be sent to a "distant country" means a faraway land, not Hades. He does cite a parallel in Tob. 8:3, where the odor of a burning fish so repelled a demon that he fled to the "faraway land" of Egypt (and thus could not seize Tobias). But one cannot be certain of this parallel's influence on Mark.

The abyss (ἄβυσσος, *abyssos*) refers to the abode of the dead in the OT (Ps. 107:26 [106:26 LXX]; also Rom. 10:7). In Luke it is seen as a place where demons or disobedient spirits are kept, and it may well be associated with their being cast into the depths of the sea.[20] This is its only use in the Gospels and could be rendered "Underworld" ("abyss" is a transliteration of the Greek term). Other terms such as Hades (ᾅδης; Luke 10:15; 16:23), Gehenna (γέεννα; Luke 12:5), and Tartarus (ταρταρόω; only 2 Pet. 2:4) may represent parallel concepts (Arndt 1956: 241). In the OT, the abyss originally referred to the depths (חִהוֹם, *těhôm*) of the earth and could be associated with the sea (Gen. 1:2; 7:11; Job 41:32 [41:24 MT]; Ps. 71:20). This association with the sea may suggest why ἄβυσσος is used here, since the demons are destined for the Sea of Galilee (Ellis 1974: 128; Bovon 1989: 437 n. 59). Judaism also saw the deep as a repository for hostile spirits (Jub. 5.6–7; 1 Enoch 10.4–6; 18.11–16). The spirits fear confinement, as illustrated in the restlessness of such beings in Luke 11:24–26 (Fitzmyer 1981: 739). Of course, the point is the extent of Jesus' authority and sovereignty. Ultimately, messianic power is eschatological power over evil, some of which is still to be manifested according to the NT (Luke 7:22–23; Rom. 8:18–25; 1 Pet. 1:3–6; 2 Pet. 2:9–10; Rev. 20:1–14). A cosmic sneak preview takes place in this event.

(3) Demons into the Swine (8:32–33)

The demons make a request. Sure that anything would be better **8:32** than the abyss, they ask to go into a large herd of swine on the hills. Luke only generally describes the number of swine, while Mark 5:13 says there were around two thousand pigs (if Luke has Mark before him, this is another detail that he edits). Although much of the verse's wording is close to Mark, it is given in a slightly different word order. For most, such differences are too small to posit a distinct source.[21]

The demons ask to go into the pigs because they know Jesus' authority. It is interesting that pigs are chosen, since they are unclean animals (Lev. 11:7; Deut. 14:8; Luke 15:15: the "unclean" spirit seeks an "unclean" animal; Danker 1988: 183). But this may be a less important concern, since Jesus is in a Gentile region. The presence of the pigs suggests that either Gentiles or nonpracticing Jews own the pigs (Arndt 1956: 242). Nonetheless, Jesus gives permission. The

---

20. On ἄβυσσος, see BAGD 2 §2; BAA 3; Jeremias, *TDNT* 1:9–10. Perhaps the abyss is equivalent to Tartarus; see Rev. 9:1, 2, 11; 11:7; 17:18; 20:1, 3; cf. Jude 6; 2 Pet. 2:4.

21. Even Schramm 1971: 126 does not posit a distinct source here, though often he does. Some of these differences make one wonder if an oral source is not also behind Luke.

"day" has not yet come when Jesus will deal with such forces decisively, but he will relieve the man of his burden (Ellis 1974: 129).

The motive for the request is not clear. It seems likely that the spirits hoped by their request to avoid confinement. If Jesus would not permit them to indwell a man, an animal would do. Anything was better than the abyss. It was too foreboding a place.

Of course, the transfer of the demons raises questions that the text does not attempt to answer: "How can animals be possessed?" "Why would Jesus allow such a use of animals?" "What happened to the demons?" "Why did the spirits feel compelled to dwell somewhere rather than roaming the earth?" None of these issues are answered here. The text does suggest that demons can possess animals. The pigs serve as a visual demonstration of the man's healing (along with the later evidence of his changed demeanor). In addition, it seems that the man's welfare is more important than that of the beasts. The swine will also bring into play the region's response, but none of these observations answers the questions raised. One must be content to treat the account at the level it is offered and not try to answer questions it does not address (Hendriksen 1978: 447–48; Arndt 1956: 242; Plummer 1896: 232).[22]

8:33 The effect of the exorcism is immediate and visible (Schürmann 1969: 484). The demons depart from the man and enter into the swine. For whatever reason—Luke does not tell us—they rush down to the edge of the bank and fall into the water, where they drown.[23] The exorcism occurs but the destructive consequences are also clear. In addition, it appears the demonic request to go into the swine seems to have done them little good, though the fate of the spirits is not explicitly told (Liefeld 1984: 914). Marshall (1978: 340) suggests that the sea is a "demon-destroying force" and therefore the demons are seen as perishing, a view that is possible (T. Sol. 5.11; 11.6; Hull 1974: 100). At the least, Jesus exercised his control over evil forces yet again, even a force of superior numbers.

The wording is very close to Mark, less so to Matthew. Mark 5:13 speaks of an unclean spirit, while Luke has the plural reference to demons. Mark numbers the swine at about two thousand, while Luke has already spoken of a large herd. Mark speaks of drowning in the sea, using a synonymous verb (πνίγω, pnigō; BAGD 679 §1d;

22. Godet 1875: 1.386 implausibly suggests that Jesus was offended by the swine. For someone who declared all foods clean, this was hardly an issue.

23. Ὥρμησεν in Matt. 8:32 = Mark 5:13 = Luke 8:33 means to rush irrationally or with some emotion; Fitzmyer 1981: 739; Bertram, *TDNT* 5:470; BAGD 581; BAA 1178; elsewhere only at Acts 7:57; 19:29. On ἀποπνίγω (to drown), see BAGD 97; BAA 195; elsewhere only Luke 8:7 (of thorns and thistles that choke); a related verb, συμπνίγω, occurs in 8:14, 42.

BAA 1363 §1d; Bietenhard, *TDNT* 6:456). Matthew 8:32 uses the same verb as Luke to express the demons going out of the man; and he simply notes that "all" the herd died (ἀπέθανον, *apethanon*) in the water. The difference in details simply represents various ways to render the same event.

In dealing with the question of how Jesus could do this, a few points need to be made. Jesus is not responsible for the action of the swine (Danker 1988: 183). It is their demonic possession that brings the destruction. Godet (1875: 1.386–87) argues against demonic possession of an animal by reasoning that animals are not moral agents and therefore cannot be possessed, but the language of the passage clearly refers to the spirits entering into the swine and, at the least, influencing their reaction. Jesus does not command the animals' reaction. It is also clear that the animals were sacrificed for the sake of the man, something that is not out of touch with the OT and its numerous sacrifices. Jesus will later say that people are more important than sparrows (Luke 12:6–7). In addition, it is clear that the removal of evil is always costly. The loss of the swine graphically pictures the cost of purging evil—as will another death on the cross.

ii. Reaction (8:34–39)
(1) Reaction of the Herders and Townspeople (8:34–37a)

The incident caused quite a stir among those caring for the swine. **8:34** This was something that did not happen to your average pig herder! They decide to depart, and in fleeing, they tell what happened. Ἀπαγγέλλω (*apangellō*, to announce) is used three times in the rest of the chapter (8:34, 36, 37), showing that Jesus' ministry produced much talk. Needless to say, they would need to explain the absence of the herd, but the explanation would probably need corroboration. That corroboration comes when those in the city and country go to see what happened.

Mark gives the incident in closely parallel wording. Luke alone speaks of the herders fleeing "when they saw what happened," while Mark 5:14 says that the people who visited following the report "came to see what happened." Matthew 8:33 gives a different form of the same summary, noting that the herders reported on what had happened to the demoniacs.

The trip confirms the herders' report. In a complete reversal of the **8:35** previously possessed man's demeanor, he is now clothed, whereas before he had been naked; he is now seated, whereas before he had been roaming; he is now associating with others as he sits at Jesus' feet, whereas before he sought solitude; he is now of sound mind, whereas before he had been crying out in a loud voice; he is now comfortable in the presence of Jesus, whereas before he wanted nothing to do with him (Geldenhuys 1951: 259 n. 10). The man is seeking instruction from Jesus (Schweizer 1984: 150; Schneider 1977a: 195; Luke 10:39; Acts 22:3) or, at least, is grateful (seen in the reference to sitting at Jesus' feet; Plummer 1896: 232). Instruction is more likely to be correct, given that he wishes to go with Jesus (8:38; Fitzmyer 1981: 739). The emphasis on the man's rationality suggests this conclusion as well.[24] The changed man and the reality that his new condition represents bring fear to those who see it. They know the history of this man and know that something unusual has happened. Healings such as this made a great impression on the apostles (Acts 10:38; Schürmann 1969: 486 n. 98).

Luke's description is more complete than the other Gospels. Matthew 8:34 speaks only of the desire to have Jesus depart and has no mention of the other details of this visit. Mark 5:15 mentions with Luke that the man is clothed and in his right mind, as well as the crowd's fear. Mark also notes that the man had been possessed, a point that Luke makes only by saying that the demons had gone from him. Luke alone mentions that the man is sitting at Jesus' feet, which fits his attention on Jesus the teacher. Again, the differences are not significant in altering the account.

8:36   Those who had seen what had occurred narrate (ἀπήγγειλαν, *apēngeilan* [as in v. 34]) once again how the demon-possessed man was delivered. Ἐσώθη (*esōthē*, he was saved) refers not primarily to salvation in a technical sense, but to physical deliverance as the result of the exorcism (his desire to follow Jesus shows that salvation resulted from the event; Marshall 1978: 340). He is now clearly allied to Jesus. As the observers retell the story, they probably point around to describe what took place (Arndt 1956: 243). The man's presence adds vividness to the recounting. The account, though unusual, is related by eyewitnesses (οἱ ἰδόντες, *hoi idontes*).

Luke agrees with Mark 5:16 in mentioning the event's retelling. Mark uses a related verb to describe the retelling (διηγήσαντο, *diēgēsanto*) and notes that the subject was not only the man but also the swine. The same difference in verbs, but in the opposite direction, occurs in Luke 8:39 = Mark 5:19, an odd variation to say the least. Mark is slightly more detailed in his account than Luke. However, the accounts are again virtually parallel.

8:37a   The final element in the response appears: the people of the region are seized with great fear and so they ask Jesus to leave.[25] This fear

---

24. On σωφρονοῦντα (of sound mind), see Luck, *TDNT* 7:1102, who speaks of the man's being liberated from mania; cf. Acts 26:25.

25. For fear after miracles, see 5:8, 26; 8:25, 47; at the transfiguration, 9:34.

is negative, for it does not lead to faith (Bovon 1989: 440). Luke is not entirely clear why the request is made. Most surmise that the loss of property scared these people into asking Jesus to depart in order to spare the further loss of possessions (Plummer 1896: 232; Geldenhuys 1951: 256).[26] This concern with possessions is clearer in Mark 5:16, where the swine are specifically mentioned in the discussion of the report. Others suggest that the crowd is simply overcome by the supernatural and wants nothing to do with it (Schürmann 1969: 486 speaks of a fear of the numinous). Fitzmyer (1981: 740) argues for both reasons. Luke simply mentions that their fear is so great that they ask him to leave (recorded with alliteration: ἀπελθεῖν ἀπ' αὐτῶν, *apelthein ap' autōn*, to go out from them).[27] Whatever the cause, the region wants nothing to do with Jesus and his power. Luke makes the extent of the fear and rejection very clear when he speaks of the whole region.[28] Jesus does not stay where he is not wanted, and so he departs.

The request to depart is mentioned in all three Gospels. Interestingly, Mark 5:17 = Matt. 8:34 speaks of a request to leave their neighborhood (ἀπὸ τῶν ὁρίων αὐτῶν, *apo tōn horiōn autōn*), while Luke speaks of departing from them (ἀπ' αὐτῶν, *ap' autōn*). Luke also alludes back to all those from the region (περιχώρου, *perichōrou*) who made the request. The term for neighborhood that appears in Matthew and Mark (ὅριον) is used but once by Luke (Acts 13:50), while Matthew and Mark use Luke's term (περίχωρος) elsewhere (Matt. 3:5; 14:35; Mark 1:28; Luke 3:3; 4:14, 37; 7:17; 8:37; Acts 14:6). In addition, Luke alone mentions great fear (φόβῳ μεγάλῳ, *phobō megalō*) as the reason for the request (also in Luke 2:9; Acts 5:5, 11; cf. Mark 4:41; Matt. 28:8). In general, the Gospels agree but have distinct details.

(2) Jesus' Departure and Instruction to the Healed One (8:37b–39a)

The man who had received Jesus' ministry longed to go with him. In **8:37b–38** fact, he was begging (ἐδεῖτο, *edeito*) to go with him. Opinion is divided whether the man wanted to be protected by Jesus (Plummer 1896: 233) or whether he wished to learn from him. Luke does not

26. Arndt 1956: 243 argues that their consciences feared more distress from God's presence. Hendriksen 1978: 449 calls such fear sinful, because they showed no interest in the exorcised man. Danker 1988: 183 notes that a reference to possessions is unstated in Luke.

27. Ὅτι is causal. Fear caused them not to draw near to God and to avoid having anything to do with his messenger. The contrast to the rescued man is instructive.

28. Ἅπαν τὸ πλῆθος is a Lucan expression; see Schürmann 1969: 486 n. 100; Luke 19:37; 23:1; Acts 25:24.

tell us explicitly, though the man's response to Jesus' instruction in
8:39 and his sitting at Jesus' feet in 8:35 suggest that he was ready to
respond to Jesus. This favors the second option (Fitzmyer 1981:
740). Once the healing occurs, this man is not portrayed negatively.

The man's positive response stands in contrast to the people's
negative response, thus ending the account on a positive note (Marshall 1978: 341). Jesus had his own desires for the man, and so
turned down his request. Sometimes when the answer to a request
is no, God has other things in mind (Hendriksen 1978: 449). Jesus'
reply reveals something about the mission of believers: some are to
travel with Jesus away from their home, while others are to remain
where they are and testify to him there. This man is one of the latter.
Not all believers are to serve Jesus in the same way. In fact, although Jesus was departing the region, he was leaving a presence
there.

Mark 5:18 also reports this exchange, though his wording is completely distinct from Luke's. Mark notes that the exchange between
Jesus and the man occurred as Jesus was getting into the boat to depart, while Luke first notes Jesus' departure and then comes back to
conclude the conversation. This difference is not one of substance
but merely reflects editorial selection concerning sequence. One can
hardly imagine that the man departed with Jesus and was then sent
back immediately. Matthew lacks this exchange entirely; but his account is abbreviated anyway, so not much should be made of the
omission.

8:39a Jesus has a task for the man. Rather than traveling with Jesus as a
disciple, the man is asked to witness to his community about what
God did for him. He follows through on Jesus' request and proclaims to the entire city what Jesus did. Mark says that Jesus told the
man to tell about what the Lord (κύριος) did, whereas in Luke, Jesus
tells him to speak of what God (θεός) did—possibly to avoid confusion about whether Jesus or God was meant.

(3) Testimony of the Healed One about Jesus (8:39b)

8:39b Two details about the man's report are significant. First, he
"preached" (κηρύσσων, *kēryssōn*) to the city. The choice of this theologically significant term, κηρύσσω, shows that the man fervently
went about the task: he did not just narrate, he proclaimed the story.
The idea of preaching is a major one for Luke (as it is for all the Synoptics).[29] The man did his job in sharing with those of the village.

29. Luke 3:3; 4:18, 19, 44; 8:1, 39; 9:2; 12:3; 24:47. Of the Lucan examples only
12:3 is not a technical use of the term; also nine times in Matthew and twelve times
in Mark (fourteen times if Mark's longer ending is included).

Second, the man told what *Jesus* did. Though Jesus told him to speak about God (8:39a), he spoke instead about Jesus. He could not help but note the agent whom God used to bring these things to pass. The man pictures the response of one who has been touched by Jesus' ministry and shares that transformation with those who live near him. Preachers of the gospel are not limited to the traveling disciples (Danker 1988: 184). All are called to evangelize (Marshall 1978: 341). The terms ὁ θεός (*ho theos*, God) and ὁ Ἰησοῦς (*ho Iēsous*, Jesus) trail in each clause of the sentence and thus are emphatic (Plummer 1896: 233).

Geldenhuys (1951: 257) reads the last line as showing that the man knew Jesus to be the divine Lord.[30] But such a conclusion is unlikely. Even the disciples, who had been around Jesus for a long time, had not yet reached this insight in Luke's account. It would be unlikely that this man on the basis of a single meeting would understand this point. Rather, what he grasped was that God was working through Jesus in a significant way and that God's power was being demonstrated through him. Even a Gentile can have this perception (Ernst 1977: 278).

One other key point exists. In Gentile territory Jesus permits more open discussion about his ministry, in contrast to his efforts to silence some in Jewish territory from speaking about him. The reason seems to be that there would not be as many Jewish religious representatives present, and so the danger of misunderstanding Jesus' ministry as political would not be as great (Plummer 1896: 233).

Mark identifies the region as the Decapolis, while Luke leaves the city unnamed. As already noted, Matthew lacks the man's subsequent response, so he has no parallel at this point.

Summary

In Luke 8:26–39 Jesus graphically exercises power over the legion of demons. But the account does not stop with the narration of his authority over the spirit world. Some see the execution of his power, are afraid, and want nothing to do with him. This reaction comes despite the thorough transformation of the demon-possessed man by Jesus, which was witnessed by all. Unbelief can be hard to understand sometimes. Those who reject Jesus should contemplate why they are refusing to respond. Nonetheless, unbelief often flees from an encounter with God. The opportunity to draw near to God produces distance instead.

The man stands in contrast: he is ready to follow Jesus; he is at Jesus' feet and wishes to travel with him. However, Jesus has another role in mind. The man is to testify at home to God's good-

30. Hendriksen 1978: 450 speaks more carefully of the man's awareness of the "close relation" between Jesus and God.

ness, which he does enthusiastically. The news about Jesus is spreading into Gentile regions. Some are called to travel with Jesus. Others are called to declare him in their homeland. Those who have responded to Jesus are to identify with this man.

A note of assurance also exists in that Jesus controls vast numbers of spiritual forces allied against him. The man is transformed, despite the efforts of evil to overwhelm him. Jesus' authority comes through clearly. God is working through Jesus and is allied with him. Luke again shows that Jesus can be trusted. Such is his power. Confronted with Jesus, some draw near and others want distance. For Luke, the preference is not found in the opinion of the multitudes, but in one radically transformed man.

Additional Notes

8:26. Before looking at the evidence surrounding a major textual problem about the name of the locality, it might be well to sort out the three locales mentioned in the readings (see the map at §III). (1) The UBS–NA reading in 8:26 is Γερασηνῶν (Gerasa; modern Jerash), a city in the Decapolis region located over twenty miles southeast of the Sea of Galilee. It is generally regarded that this is too distant to be the locale from which the swine go into the sea. Nonetheless, in Mark 5:1 = Luke 8:26, this locale seems to have the best support as the original reading (see below). It is possible that this well-known locale is not the Gerasa referred to by the reading, or that a larger regional reference is intended by this name. (2) Γαδαρηνῶν (Gadara; modern Umm Qeis), the preferred reading in Matt. 8:28, is another city of the Decapolis located about five miles southeast of the Sea of Galilee.[31] (3) Another key variant, Γεργεσηνῶν (Gergesa), may have been generated by a suggestion by Origen (*Commentary on John* 6:24), since only manuscripts later than Origen have this reading (so Metzger 1975: 24 n. 1, but challenged by Fitzmyer 1981: 736–37). Appealing to local tradition and etymology for support, Bovon (1989: 434) opts for this reading. It is generally identified as Kersa (Kursi), which is located on the lake near the cliffs (Marshall 1978: 337). This is possible, though it is poorly attested.

The textual evidence presented in the adjacent table is adapted from Metzger's presentation (1975: 23–24, 84, 145).

In Matt. 8:28, ℵ has a *zeta* (Z) where *delta* (Δ) is expected, thus reading Gazara. Only clearly inferior versional evidence supports the reading Gerasa. Thus, on the basis of external evidence, Gadara is original in Matt. 8:28. In Mark 5:1, one could make a case for Gadara in agreement with Matthew,

---

31. Josephus, *Life* 9 §42, describes Gadara as located "on the frontiers of Tiberias." Some of its coins include a ship; Marshall 1978: 337.

	Γαδαρηνῶν	Γερασηνῶν	Γεργεσηνῶν
Matt. 8:28	(א*), B, C, (Δ), Θ, some Syriac	Itala, Vulgate, some Coptic, some Syriac	א², L, W, family 1, family 13, some Coptic, Byz
Mark 5:1	A, C, family 13, some Lect, some Syriac	א*, B, D, most Itala, Vulgate, some Coptic	א², L, Δ, Θ, family 1, most Lect, some Syriac, some Coptic
Luke 8:26	A, W, Δ, Ψ, family 13, Byz, Lect, some Syriac	𝔓⁷⁵, B, D, Itala, Vulgate, some Syriac, some Coptic	א, L, Θ, Ξ, family 1, some Syriac, some Coptic

but the best Alexandrian and Western witnesses support Gerasa in Mark. In Luke 8:26, the Western and Alexandrian support is aligned toward Gerasa.

Thus, in referring to the locale, Mark and Luke name the region in a different way than does Matthew. Sherwin-White (1963: 128 n. 3) offers the suggestion that Matthew may have given the locale in terms of the region's major administrative center, while the others gave the specific locale of the event. Although this may help advance the discussion, it does not completely resolve the problem, since it is Mark's and Luke's choice—Gerasa—that is disputed as a distant locale. If it is the specific locale, it seems too far away to host the event described.

Other possibilities exist. One could argue for an early corruption that is now lost to us, though this seems unlikely, since three letters in Greek would have to be misread (E ~ A, P ~ Δ, and Σ ~ P; thus, ΓΕΡΑΣΗΝΩΝ ~ ΓΑΔΑΡΗΝΩΝ). It may be that local customs in referring to regions are not well enough understood by us, so that the scene could be referred to in a regional sense by a distant locale like Gerasa. Perhaps those who reacted to the event were spread far and wide in the area. Or perhaps there was another Gerasa in the region that we no longer know about.[32] It could be that the man was from one locale but the event took place in another, given that he had abandoned his home (8:27; there is no way to prove such a possibility). In fact, we do not know for sure why the difference emerged, but the difference between Matthew and Mark = Luke is like that in various writers' references to an event that happened in Denton, Texas, a small city an hour's drive north of Dallas–Fort Worth. One writer might describe it as happening at Denton (the specific location), while another may say it took place at Dallas–Fort Worth (the more well known region). The region of one author may merely be more comprehensive than that of another. Being certain of

32. So Cranfield 1959: 176. Plummer 1896: 227 speaks of Kersa, a locale near the lake, but he rejects Origen's association of it with Gergesa. Arndt 1956: 239–40 and Bovon 1989: 434 accept Gergesa as original in Luke. Liefeld 1984: 914–15 is rightly cautious about a solution, as is Nolland 1989: 407. No clearly superior option exists between reading a regional reference or concluding that Gergesa is intended.

any particular solution is difficult. What is clear is that the event took place in Gentile territory opposite Galilee. It also seems likely that Luke is reading Gerasa.

8:27. A minor text-critical problem, not discussed in UBS[4], concerns χρόνῳ ἱκανῷ (for a long time): Does this temporal indicator refer to how long the man went unclothed or to the duration of his demon possession? The first option, adopted by UBS–NA ($\mathfrak{P}^{75}$, א*,2, B, L, Ξ, (family 1), some Syriac), places καί (and) in front of χρόνῳ ἱκανῷ, yielding "and for a long time he had worn no clothes." The second option places καί after ἐκ χρόνων ἱκαν-ῶν (א1, A, W, Θ, Ψ, family 13, Byz, Itala, and some Syriac) and yields "a man having demons for a long time and had worn no clothes." The decision on external evidence is difficult, but the UBS–NA text seems slightly more likely (Metzger 1975: 145; Fitzmyer 1981: 737).

8:29. The tense of the verb *command* is disputed (Liefeld 1984: 915). The UBS–NA text has the simpler reading, an aorist, παρήγγειλεν (he commanded), following many manuscripts ($\mathfrak{P}^{75}$, B, Θ, Ξ, Ψ, family 13). Some manuscripts (א, A, C, L, W, Γ, Δ) have a harder reading, the imperfect παρ-ήγγελλεν (he was commanding), which may describe the process of the command for exorcism.[33] This latter reading seems more likely, though the sense is little altered by the choice.

8:37. The textual problem as to what region is named almost exactly parallels the manuscript evidence for 8:26. Whatever one decides about the problem in that verse will determine the reading of this verse. It seems likely that Gerasa is in view here in Luke.

---

33. Arndt 1956: 240–41 speaks of many commands; Danker 1988: 182 of an in-gressive imperfect ("he began to command" or "was about to command"), which is probably better; so also Fitzmyer 1981: 738; BDF §328, §329, §331. Bovon 1989: 435 n. 44 calls the choice very difficult, a judgment with which I concur.

c. Authority over Disease and Death: Flow of Blood and Jairus's Daughter (8:40–56)

The final event in the sequence of miracles in Luke 8 is in fact a double miracle, the only such intertwined miracle in the Gospels. The events that lead to the raising of Jairus's daughter are interrupted by the healing of a woman with a flow of blood. This juxtaposition slows the narrative down and introduces tension, as well as adding sympathy to Jairus's plight (Tannehill 1986: 91–92). In a single story, Jesus deals with both disease and death. Such a focus completes an escalating review of his comprehensive authority. Not only can he control nature and demons (8:22–39), but he also can control disease and death. These miracles are part of the revelation of Jesus to his disciples that he can be trusted and that he is the Christ of God (Busse 1979: 230). This passage also combines christological revelation with a call to faith.

Besides Christology, the other key element in the account is faith (which is the key Lucan feature for Theissen 1983: 135). Luke 8:48, 50 emphasizes the importance of believing that Jesus is capable of doing such great acts. When he acts, he shows his gracious compassion (Marshall 1978: 342). Jesus' acts are not demanded; they are requested. Essentially, faith is relying on Jesus to care for his disciples. Jesus can exercise his sovereignty and power for them, a power that Luke will mention again in 9:1 (Busse 1979: 220). Talbert (1982: 96–97) notes that this is the second time such an emphasis on faith and commission is found in Luke: the four miracles of 4:31–5:11 were followed by a call and commission; so also the four miracles in this chapter end with a note on faith and then a commission. Miracles like those in Luke 8 will be repeated in Acts (boat rescue in chap. 27; exorcism in 16:16–18; resurrection in 9:36–43; and healings in 5:15; 19:12).

One other note is important. The sociology of this healing is broad: it includes a synagogue leader, a child, and a woman suffering from a disease that renders her unclean. Whether one is male or female, adult or child, clean or unclean makes no difference to Jesus (Tannehill 1986: 135).

An unusual element is the call for the witnesses to the resurrection to be silent. The silence contrasts with the public nature of

7:11–17, where the crowd concluded that Jesus was a prophet. Jesus does not want to focus his ministry on the miraculous healing he can bring. There are indications in the Gospel tradition at various levels that such concerns distracted the crowd from understanding him (John 6:26; Luke 11:27–29 = Matt. 12:38–39 = Mark 8:11–13). So here he calls for silence. Open declaration of his miracles places the emphasis in the wrong area and yields a less than adequate view of Jesus.[1]

Luke is using the account to communicate a variety of things about Jesus. The account made a deep impression on the later church, for as the story was repeated down the centuries, the woman was given the name Bernice.[2]

Sources and Historicity

The discussion of sources for this account is complex, especially since two events are brought together in one pericope. The Synoptic parallel is Matt. 9:18–26 = Mark 5:21–43 (Aland 1985: §138). Most regard Mark as the source for Luke's account (Schramm 1971: 126–27; Schürmann 1969: 497; Marshall 1978: 341; Fitzmyer 1981: 742). It is clear that Luke's account is much closer to Mark's than to Matthew's more abbreviated version.

Luke has his own peculiarities in this account. Fitzmyer (1981: 743–44) notes eight points where Luke goes his own way:

1. Luke links this event more tightly to the preceding event (8:40).
2. Luke mentions the girl's age early on (8:42).
3. Luke mentions that the girl was an only child, a detail that parallels the account of the son of the widow of Nain (8:42; Tannehill 1986: 92, 94; cf. 7:12; 9:38).
4. Luke describes more gently the doctors who treated the hemorrhaging woman (8:43; cf. Mark 5:26).[3]

---

1. Berger 1984: 117 thinks that the reason for the silence is that Jesus wants this resurrection to be legitimized only as God's act and not through human witness. However, this is hard to see in light of Acts. Perhaps the point here is that this limitation applies to the preresurrection setting, but 7:11–17 is a problem for this perspective. It is simpler to see the silence as protection against a potential misemphasis about Jesus and his ministry.

2. Plummer 1896: 233 cites the Acts of Pilate (= Gospel of Nicodemus) 1.7 as the first text to name her Bernice (= Latin Veronica); Schneemelcher 1991–92: 1.511. This apocryphal work is available in a fifth-century edition, though its roots may reach back to the second century.

3. The extent to which this point is true depends on a textual issue in 8:43 (see the additional note): if the longer text is present, then there is direct criticism of doctors; if the shorter text, then the critique is indirect.

5. Peter speaks for the disciples, whose criticism of Jesus' question is omitted (8:45; cf. Mark 5:31).

6. In Luke 8:46, Jesus notes the power going out from him, while this is Mark's narrative comment in Mark 5:30.

7. Luke 8:53 explains why the crowd laughs, a detail that Mark 5:40 leaves to be inferred.

8. Luke notes the return of the girl's spirit, so that it is clear the girl returns to normal (8:55).

These differences may suggest that Luke either worked over the material,[4] had access to additional material, or had access to other oral descriptions of the event beyond the tradition reflected in Mark.[5]

Whether these two events were originally tied together is a matter of debate. Bultmann (1963: 214–15) argues that two original events were brought together before Mark (Schneider 1977a: 196; see also Fitzmyer 1981: 743, who alludes to the different styles, but takes no clear position). Others regard Mark as the one who put them together (Schürmann 1969: 492 cites Mark 3:20–35; 6:7–30; 11:12–21; 14:1–11, 53–72 as other Marcan examples of combining). A third view regards the account as essentially historical and as originally intertwined (Creed 1930: 122; V. Taylor 1966: 289 [apparently]). Taylor argues that Mark 3:22–26 and 14:3–9 are not the same as this example and that the connective links in Mark 5:35 are not Marcan style, so Mark could not have combined the accounts. Cranfield (1959: 182) calls the accounts historical and Petrine, arguing that the intercalation is not artificial, but due to historical recollection, which means the accounts may have been originally separated, but their union was motivated by genuine reminiscence. The unprecedented character of the mixture of two miracles speaks against an artificial linkage. These events were intertwined. The tradition was probably in this form, and they came to be intertwined through reminiscence.

The Jesus Seminar (Funk and Hoover 1993: 310) treats the dialogue of this unit as it does the dialogues in all the miracles of Luke 8—as "the invention of the storyteller." According to the seminar, the dialogues are not memorable, would not have circulated orally, and so cannot be traced back to Jesus (p. 62). But such an argument assumes that what was said during the miracle was not included when these stories circulated orally. This premise about the general historicity of the miracle accounts should be questioned. Jesus' healing power brought a great amount of attention to his ministry, as the various summaries show (Luke 4:40–41; 6:17–18). Nolland

---

4. Fitzmyer 1981: 743 says that this work has to come from Luke's hand. This is not clear for every detail, though some expressions do reflect Lucan style; see ##3–5.

5. Bovon 1989: 443 and n. 4 acknowledges the possibility of oral sources, especially for 8:44. Schramm 1971: 127 notes that 8:42 with its use of ὑπάγειν (to go) and the direct speech of 8:46 are not Lucan and could be from an oral source.

(1989: 417) notes that the miracles reflect well the popular piety of the period, expressed here in the woman's desire to touch Jesus' garment. In addition, Nolland notes that the resuscitation miracle is not like or built upon OT accounts like 1 Kings 17:17–24 or 2 Kings 4:18–37. This account reflects events that Jesus performed.

The event's placement is also complex. Mark and Luke have it after their parabolic discourses in Mark 4:1–34 = Luke 8:4–15, while Matthew has it before the parables in Matt. 13.[6] Matthew has a second deviation: he has not placed the event right after his description of the Gadarene demoniac (Matt. 8:28–34). Rather, he has linked it tightly to the fasting discussion that appeared much earlier in Luke 5:33–39 (= Matt. 9:14–17 = Mark 2:18–22). Luke and Mark probably moved up this discussion for topical reasons: so they could present in one place Jewish official reaction to Jesus' "unorthodox" associations and practices (see the introduction to Luke 5:33–39). Thus, Matthew's association of these twin healings with this fasting debate is precise, although the fasting debate may have come nearer the parabolic discourse, since Matt. 8–9 has a more topical structure. Complicating matters even more is that Matt. 13:1 links the incident about Jesus' mother and brothers (Matt. 12:46–50 = Luke 8:19–21 = Mark 3:31–35) to the parabolic discourse, saying that they occurred on the same day. In fact, the family's approach to Jesus precedes the Matthean and Marcan parable discourse, while in Luke the meeting follows the discourse.

How can all this be put together? It seems likely that Matthew held off narrating the parabolic discourse until he fully discussed the Jewish rejection of Jesus and John the Baptist, a topical move that also caused him to consider the fasting issue earlier than it actually took place, since it reflects official questioning of Jesus. If so, then Luke and Mark thematically associate these miracles and the family's approach to Jesus with the parables. They are also precise in linking the miracles chronologically, and, in fact, such care may even extend to the association of all these miracles after the parabolic discourse.[7] Matthew also appropriately associates the event topically with the fasting debate, which he has moved up to cover the issue of

---

6. The next event in Mark is the synagogue rejection (Mark 6:1–6a = Luke 4:14–30), while Luke has the mission of the Twelve (Mark 6:6b–13 = Luke 9:1–6). As was noted in the introduction to 4:14–30, Luke probably moved this synagogue account forward in his Gospel to give a representative pericope of what Jesus' ministry was like.

7. In the four-miracle sequence, Mark seems to suggest a tight chronological linkage: "on that day" (Mark 4:35), "they came to the other side" (5:1), and "and when Jesus had crossed again to the other side" (5:21). Only the last link might suggest a break in time, though Jesus' departure at the request of the Gentiles (Mark 5:17) may suggest a quick return. Luke's links between the events are similar, though his initial link is looser: "one day he got into a boat" (Luke 8:22), "then they arrived" (8:26), and "now when Jesus returned" (8:40). Luke's last link may suppose a break, but what was said of Mark also applies to Luke 8:37.

rejection in his topical section of Matt. 8–9, where only some notes of chronology exist (the other pericopes have loose temporal introductions).[8] Beyond these connections, one cannot specify more precisely where things fit, except to suggest that the later portion of the Galilean tour is present (see similar cautions in the introductions to 8:4–15 and 8:19–21). What is important is that the miracles display Jesus' ability to overcome all that can erase human existence: disease and death.

The form consists of a pair of intertwined miracle stories.[9] The outline of Luke 8:40–56 is as follows:

i. Initial request by Jairus (8:40–42a)
   (1) Setting (8:40)
   (2) Request to heal a dying daughter (8:41–42a)
ii. Healing of the woman with a hemorrhage (8:42b–48)
   (1) Setting (8:42b)
   (2) Woman's condition (8:43)
   (3) Woman's action and consequent healing (8:44)
   (4) Jesus' question (8:45a)
   (5) Peter's reply (8:45b)
   (6) Jesus' explanation of the question (8:46)
   (7) Woman's confession and testimony (8:47)
   (8) Jesus' commendation of the woman's faith (8:48)
iii. Raising Jairus's daughter (8:49–56)
   (1) Report of the daughter's death (8:49)
   (2) Jesus' call to believe (8:50)
   (3) Those allowed to go in (8:51)
   (4) Jesus' declaration that she sleeps; call to faith (8:52)
   (5) Crowd's laughter (8:53)
   (6) Call to rise (8:54)
   (7) Raising of the girl (8:55)
   (8) Parents' amazement (8:56a)
   (9) Jesus' call to be silent (8:56b)

The complicated structure yields many themes, key elements being Jesus' power over disease and death and the importance of faith. Faith is seen as a recognition of Jesus' power and good-

---

8. Matthew's arrangement shows that rejection comes despite confirming signs, since after this double miracle are two uniquely Matthean miracles: the healings of the two blind men and of the mute.

9. Bultmann 1963: 214–15 (who argues that they were originally separate); Bovon 1989: 444–45 (who speaks of a "crescendo" in this pairing, especially since it includes two women); Fitzmyer 1981: 743; Theissen 1983: 321. Berger 1984: 314, 317 speaks of a "supplication account" by putting it in his "deesis/petitio" category. It also teaches Jesus' authority, as Berger's placement in the "mandatio" form shows.

ness. There is value in being patient for God's timing. Timid faith is commended in the woman who testifies to Jesus' act, and so a timid faith is deepened. The hesitancy to believe in what Jesus can do is challenged in the Jairus account, where the apparent unbelievability of what Jesus claims is overturned. Rather, one is to see what Jesus can do. Finally, there is the theme of silence, which appears to be limited to the time of Jesus' ministry.

Exegesis and Exposition

[40]When Jesus returned, the crowd welcomed him, for they all were waiting for him. [41]And behold a man whose name was ⌜Jairus⌝ came, and this one was a ruler of the synagogue. And falling before Jesus' feet, he was asking him to come to his house, [42]because he had an only daughter about twelve years old, and she was beginning to die.

As he was going, the crowd pressed him. [43]And a woman who had a flow of blood for twelve years, who ⌜having spent all her living on physicians⌝ was not able to be healed by anyone, [44]coming up ⌜from behind⌝, touched the fringe⌝ of his garment, and immediately her flow of blood stopped. [45]And Jesus said, "Who touched me?" When all denied it, ⌜Peter⌝ said, ⌜"Master, the multitude surrounds you and presses upon you!"⌝ [46]But Jesus said, "Someone touched me, for I know that power has gone out from me." [47]And when the woman saw that she was not yet hidden, she came trembling; and falling down before him, she gave cause why she had touched him; she announced before all the people how she was healed immediately. [48]And he said to her, "Daughter, your faith has saved you; go in peace."

[49]While he was speaking, a man came from the home of the synagogue ruler and said, "Your daughter has died; ⌜no longer⌝ trouble the teacher." [50]When Jesus heard, he said to him, "Do not fear, only believe, and she shall be saved." [51]And when he went into the house he let no one come in with him except Peter, John, James, the father of the child, and the mother. [52]And everyone was weeping and mourning for her. But he said, "Do not cry, for she is not dead, but she sleeps." [53]And they were laughing at him, because they knew she was dead. [54]Having grasped her hand, he called out, "Child, arise." [55]And her spirit returned, and she sat up immediately, and he commanded that something should be given her to eat. [56]And her parents were amazed; but he commanded them to tell no one what had happened.

i. Initial Request by Jairus (8:40–42a)
(1) Setting (8:40)

8:40   Jesus is still causing a stir among those on the western shore of the Sea of Galilee (Creed 1930: 122). Mark 5:21 specifically notes that Jesus and the disciples have crossed the sea and are still located by the sea (Hendriksen 1978: 454). Luke is generally seen to have stylistically simplified Mark's introduction (for Mark's genitive absolute, Luke has a simpler infinitival phrase). On Jesus' return the crowd is receptive to him, since they have been waiting for him (ἀπεδέξατο, *apedexato*, is a positive term; see Luke 9:11; Acts 2:41; 18:27; 21:17; 24:3; 28:30; Plummer 1896: 234; Grundmann, *TDNT* 2:55). The picture is of a populace that desires more exposure to Jesus, both to his healings and to his teaching, as the following events suggest (Mark 6:53–56; Marshall 1978: 343; Schürmann 1969: 489). Crowds are often associated with Jesus' ministry, since Jesus always drew attention,[10] although references to the crowd are rather thin in Luke's discipleship section (9:51–19:44), especially after 13:35. Crowds are present again as Jesus draws near and enters Jerusalem, and they reappear at the crucifixion. In Luke, the crowd observes Jesus' ministry like curious spectators. When Jesus gets serious about teaching his disciples how to live after his departure, references to the crowd are lacking.

(2) Request to Heal a Dying Daughter (8:41–42a)

Not every religious leader rejected Jesus (Danker 1988: 185). Jairus **8:41** was a synagogue leader who sensed that Jesus was being used of God. In fact, ἄρχων (*archōn*, ruler) suggests that he was the main elder in the local synagogue (Schürmann 1969: 489 n. 127; Luke 14:1; 18:18; 23:13, 35; 24:20; eight times in Acts with reference to a synagogue or civic leader [Acts 3:17; 4:5, 8, 26; 13:27; 14:5; 16:19; 23:5]). Mark's related term, ἀρχισυναγώγων (*archisynagōgōn*, synagogue rulers) suggests that Jairus was in charge of arranging the services (Marshall 1978: 343). In fact, Mark 5:22 speaks of "one of" these leaders, which may indicate that Mark has in view the geographical region of the crowd (since only one man headed up each synagogue) or that he is referring to the major figure on the committee of three to seven who ran the synagogue (Arndt 1956: 246; SB 4:145; Luke 8:49 uses Mark's term). Jairus was responsible for the progress of worship (Schrage, *TDNT* 7:847; Wiefel 1988: 168). In this capacity he was neither a civil leader nor a member of the Sanhedrin (Ellis 1974: 130; see the distinctions in 20:1). Jairus was a man of social standing, a leader of the city.

10. For ὄχλος in Luke, see 4:42; 5:1, 3, 15, 19, 29; 6:17, 19; 7:9, 11, 12, 24; 8:4, 19, 40, 42, 45; 9:11, 12, 16, 18, 37, 38; 11:14, 27, 29; 12:1, 13, 54; 14:25; 18:36; 19:3, 39; 22:6, 47; 23:4, 48. In 8:40–56, ὄχλος is synonymous to λαός (people), as 8:47 shows. Ὄχλος recalls the interested group of 8:4, 19. Pointing to 8:47, Bovon 1989: 446 sees a more expectant crowd and speaks of their eschatological hope as they await Jesus, but the term is more neutral here. Schürmann 1969: 489 rightly speaks of their expectation of miracles, as Mark 6:53–56 indicates. See the exegesis of Luke 8:4.

The name *Jairus* means "he will give light" or "may he enlighten," but Luke makes nothing of the meaning.[11] There is no reason to question the presence of the name in the original tradition (Marshall 1978: 343).

When Jairus's daughter fell grievously ill, he sought out the one who had healed so many. Jairus showed his respect by falling to his knees before Jesus as he made the request, an act of significance for one with such a high position (Schürmann 1969: 490). Jairus asked that Jesus make a visit to heal her.[12]

Mark 5:22–23 speaks of Jairus's falling at Jesus' feet and asking him to lay hands on his daughter so that she might be delivered. Matthew 9:18 is close to Mark in the wording of the request, but speaks of Jairus's kneeling before Jesus. Luke summarizes the request in terms of Jesus' coming to the house.

8:42a A transition follows. First, the reason (ὅτι, *hoti*) for Jairus's entreaty to Jesus is given: his only daughter is dying. Luke is fond of noting such details, for he alone describes the dead son of the widow of Nain (7:12) and a possessed boy (9:38) as only sons (Plummer 1896: 234). These details add to the emotion. Luke also has a sense of balance: the widow of Nain account involved an only son and a mother; here we have a father and an only daughter. Also, the daughter is about twelve years old, while the woman who will be healed has suffered from her condition for twelve years (8:43; Rengstorf, *TDNT* 2:322, who regards this note and the accounts as historical). In the first century, a twelve-year-old girl would be approaching marriageable age and entering the prime of life (Plummer 1896: 234; Schweizer 1984: 150; SB 3:374).[13]

But the precious only daughter is not well. In fact, she is beginning to die: ἀπέθνῃσκεν (*apethnēsken*) must be taken as an ingressive imperfect, because in 8:49 the envoy announces that the daughter has in fact died. Some argue that Matt. 9:18 disagrees with Mark 5:23, which speaks of the daughter being "at the end," and also disagrees with Luke in that Matthew has Jairus announce the daughter's death at the beginning of the account, a death that has just (ἄρτι, *arti*) occurred (Schürmann 1969: 490 says that Matthew's rendering is different from Luke's). But this is more of a literary issue

---

11. Num. 32:41; Judg. 10:3; Arndt 1956: 246. Fitzmyer 1981: 745 notes other uses of the name in the first century. Nolland 1989: 419 notes that if the name has Aramaic roots (יָעִיר, Jair), then it means "he [God] will awaken" (1 Chron. 20:5).

12. As usual for Luke's Gospel (four of seven occurrences), παρεκάλει is imperfect: "he was beseeching [him]." On such requests, see Matt. 8:5; 14:36 = Mark 6:56; Matt. 26:53; Mark 1:40; 5:18; 7:32; 8:22; Luke 7:4; Schmitz, *TDNT* 5:794 §F1.

13. Mark notes her age—precisely as twelve, not approximately as in Luke—later in his account (5:42).

than a real problem (Plummer 1896: 234; Arndt 1956: 246). Matthew, as he has before, telescopes the account and does not narrate any report by envoys. Because he lacks this detail, he does not report the death in two stages. Such telescoping occurs often in Matthew throughout this section (e.g., Matt. 8:5–13, 28–34). Mark 5:23 agrees with Luke in rendering the sequence of events, though Mark uses a slang expression to point out that she is near death.[14] The difference between Matthew and the other accounts is a matter of literary choice, since most recognize either that Matthew knew a version like Mark's or that Mark would have known Matthew.

ii. Healing of the Woman with a Hemorrhage (8:42b–48)
(1) Setting (8:42b)

Jesus decides to go. But, as he heads for Jairus's home, he has an encounter that delays his progress and adds to the drama. In describing the interruption, Luke simply notes that the crowd is pressing against Jesus, συνέπνιγον (*synepnigon*) being the same verb used to describe how the thorns choked the word in the parable of the seed (8:14). The crowd is "crushing" Jesus. Mark 5:24 also notes the great crowd's thronging about Jesus, while Matt. 9:19 has an abbreviated version that mentions only that the disciples go with him and ignores the crowd's size. Obviously many are trying to get near Jesus.

8:42b

(2) Woman's Condition (8:43)

Luke describes the woman's condition: she has a flow of blood, a condition she has endured for twelve years. The reference is probably to a uterine hemorrhage, a condition that would make her continuously unclean and that would be the source of continual embarrassment, affecting her ability to live normally with others, since to touch her would make one unclean (Lev. 15:25–31, esp. v. 31; Ezek. 36:17; *m. Zab.* 2.4; 4.1; 5.7; Wiefel 1988: 168 n. 2; Nolland 1989: 419; Marshall 1978: 344). She is shut out from fellowship and religious life. Van Der Loos (1965: 511) mentions some of the remedies applied to this condition: a glass of wine mixed with rubber, alum, and garden crocuses, or a glass of wine mixed with onions. Her sensitive condition also might explain her hesitancy to ask Jesus publicly for help. It is also noted that though efforts had been made to treat the problem, no one had been able to do anything for her.

8:43

---

14. His phrase ἐσχάτως ἔχει equals our slang term "has reached the end." Schürmann 1969: 490 n. 133 notes the idiom in Phrynichus, *Eclogues* 389 (which should be corrected to §368). Mark also notes that Jairus asked Jesus to lay hands on the girl, a point also found in Matt. 9:18. Mark and Matthew cite the request, while Luke only summarizes it.

Mark 5:26 notes these efforts with more detail, since he mentions that she had suffered at the hands of physicians and had spent all her money. As a result, she was worse, not better. Matthew 9:20 merely notes the length and nature of her condition in terms similar to the other accounts.

The verse's point, with or without the textually disputed phrase in Luke about doctors (see the additional note), is that she had suffered in this condition for a long time and could not get help. If the phrase is included, then the tragic situation is painted more graphically. The woman's action will introduce a major interruption for Jesus and really becomes more worrisome when it is announced that Jairus's daughter has died in the meantime.

(3) Woman's Action and Consequent Healing (8:44)

8:44 The woman approaches Jesus from behind. She is trying to avoid any public action and to be as inconspicuous as possible. Perhaps she fears that Jesus will refuse to touch an unclean woman and thus will not heal her (Luce 1933: 174; Danker 1988: 186). However, there is no real condemnation of her action in the text. Some have called her belief superstition in that she thinks she must touch Jesus.[15] Others see the action as a point of faith in that she realizes he holds the key to her cure (Hendriksen 1978: 457). Luke reads her action positively, since the healing comes immediately with her action. Liefeld (1984: 916) suggests that the "smoldering wick" of her faith is fanned into a flame by Jesus' action (other examples of less than ideal but honored faith are Acts 5:15–16; 19:11–12). She touches the edge of his garment (κρασπέδου, *kraspedou*; BAGD 448; BAA 910; Matt. 9:20; 14:36 = Mark 6:56; Matt. 23:5). This may refer to the four tassels that hung from the edge of the garment, two in front and two behind, as a reminder of God's commands (Num. 15:37–40; Deut. 22:12; J. Schneider, *TDNT* 3:904; SB 4:277–92; Bovon 1989: 449 and n. 44). Or it may simply refer to the edge of the garment (Nolland 1989: 419). Nevertheless, the woman is immediately healed. The term ἵστημι (*histēmi*) here refers to the stoppage of blood and has medical overtones (Marshall 1978: 345; P. Oxy. vol. 8 #1088 line 21;

---

15. Luce 1933: 174 is close to this and in addition regards such details as "legendary." He suggests a cure by "auto-suggestion," a rationalistic description that rejects the account's portrait. On the Jewish tradition of healings by touch, see SB 1:520; Schürmann 1969: 491 n. 139. On such an attitude reflecting popular belief, see Nolland 1989: 417. Nolland 1986 shows that the idea of "grace" as reflecting divine power is not a late Hellenistic concept; he cites Homer, *Odyssey* 6.235–36; Martyrdom of Polycarp 12.1; Protevangelium of James 7.3, as well as the OT: Gen. 39:21; Exod. 3:21; 11:3; 12:30; and Ps. 84:11 [84:12 MT]. He notes with particular care Ps. 45:2 [45:3 MT]; Sir. 12:16; Bar. 2.14; and T. Judah 2.1.

Cyranides; BAGD 382 §II.1; BAA 774 §II.1). Years of agony and embarrassment are reversed in one brief touch.

Luke's wording to describe the woman's approach from behind matches the participle προσελθοῦσα (*proselthousa*, coming) in Matt. 9:20 and the adverb ὄπισθεν (*opisthen*, behind) in Mark 5:27 = Matt. 9:20. The description of the touch on the hem of the garment also matches Matt. 9:20. Luke is briefer than Mark, while Matt. 9:21–22 further telescopes the account by having Jesus turn and declare the woman well, after which Matthew notes that she was healed. In other words, Matthew omits Jesus' search to see who touched him.

(4) Jesus' Question (8:45a)

Jesus attempts to expose who it was that touched him, but no one **8:45a** comes forward. The denial by all is a detail found only in Luke (Creed 1930: 123). That Jesus asked this question has prompted speculation whether he knew who touched him. The account is laid out in a matter-of-fact style that gives the impression that he is aware of what is happening around him, and yet he still asks this question. Given the general prophetic portrait of him, it seems unwise to hold that he did not know. If he did know, then the point was to bring the woman to confess. Her realization in 8:47 that she was not hidden suggests that she knew he knew (Liefeld 1984: 916; Plummer 1896: 236; Marshall 1978: 345).[16] Luke 8:47 speaks of her literal "trembling" (τρέμουσα, *tremousa*), indicating her reaction to Jesus' knowledge. Her worst nightmare had come true. Jesus knew what had happened and she would have to speak.

(5) Peter's Reply (8:45b)

Peter stands amazed, given the size and press of the crowd, that **8:45b** Jesus seeks such information, and he reminds him that many are present. The verbs used for the crowd's pressure are descriptive: συνέχω (*synechō*) is also used of holding prisoners in jail or of being locked in a siege (BAGD 789; BAA 1573–74; Luke 22:63; 2 Macc. 9:2) and ἀποθλίβω (*apothlibō*; BAGD 91; BAA 182; a NT *hapax legomenon*; A. B. Bruce 1897: 525) can refer to pressing grapes (Josephus, *Antiquities* 2.5.2 §64). But as 8:46 makes clear, this woman's touch felt different from the crowd's.

Luke narrates elements that Matthew lacks, while Mark 5:30–31 has parallel elements, although each relates the details in a slightly

---

16. Against Van Der Loos 1965: 514, who argues that Jesus did not know. Fitzmyer 1981: 746 argues that the question sounds "stupid," and it does at first glance, as Peter's reaction shows. But, given the emphasis in these accounts on Jesus' control over events, the question calls for reflection about why Jesus would ask it.

distinct order (on the text here, see the additional notes). Mark mentions Jesus' perception of a loss of power first, then follows with Jesus' question. The disciples, not just Peter, then respond with incredulity that Jesus asked the question. Also, Luke's version is less confrontational in tone than Mark's. Last, Jesus peers into the crowd to see who did it. Thus, Mark is more detailed than Luke.

(6) Jesus' Explanation of the Question (8:46)

8:46 Jesus continues to press the issue. Peter's question does make sense: in the midst of a large pressing crowd, how can Jesus complain about being touched? But Jesus persists and explains why: this was not a normal touch, since power had left him (ἐξεληλυθυῖαν, *exelēlythuian*, has gone forth, is a consummative perfect). The type of contact was so unusual that Jesus noticed it. Some have accused the Gospels of having a "magical" flavor. Van Der Loos (1965: 512) speaks of Jesus as a kind of "charged battery" according to this passage (citing Strauss 1972: 459 [originally 1835], who in turn credits H. E. G. Paulus and H. Olshausen for the "magic" description). But this is not the image. Power for Luke is at the heart of what Jesus possesses in his relationship to the Father (Matt. 28:18; Luke 1:35; 4:14, 36; 5:17; 6:19; Van Der Loos 1965: 513). Jesus is the bearer and bestower of God's power (9:1).

In fact, one could argue that Jesus' empowered and empowering function is one of the dominant concepts of Lucan Christology. Jesus is more than a vessel through whom God works. He is the possessor of power and has unique authority (Grundmann, *TDNT* 2:301). This is why Jesus can oppose forces that stand in opposition to humans. The description simply and graphically portrays this function.

But is the woman's view one of magical quality?[17] Throughout Jesus' ministry, the desire to touch Jesus and be healed was common (Matt. 14:36 = Mark 6:56; Mark 3:10 = Luke 6:19). To touch his clothes was to have access to his power, but this is not magical. The point was that contact with this special person healed. If he had power, he could use it and distribute it as he wished (Arndt 1956: 245).[18] There were no incantations, nor was there any intention of drawing attention to the healer. As Van Der Loos (1965: 517 n. 3) asks, "Why should she not do in the press of the multitude what so many had done before her?" The action's success is a reflection of

17. Van Der Loos 1965: 512–15 is right to separate the question of the Gospels' view from that of the woman. See his questions (a) and (d).

18. If this were magical power, why would touch be required? Not everyone who touched Jesus was healed, and he, conversely, healed without being touched.

Jesus' compassion and willingness to heal, as well as a reflection of the crowd's awareness that Jesus bore great power. What is present in her act is the hope of popular piety toward a person who is seen to bear God's power.

Luke gives these details in a slightly different order from Mark 5:30–31 and thus in slightly different wording. But the picture is the same. One difference is that Mark describes the point at which power went out from Jesus (Mark 5:30), while in Luke, Jesus himself makes the remark. Interestingly, the relationship between who summarizes and who cites is exactly the opposite of the situation in Luke 8:42 = Mark 5:23, where Mark cites and Luke summarizes. These merely represent stylistic differences in recounting the story. Matthew makes no mention of these specifics. Mark 5:32 notes that Jesus looked to see who had touched him, a comment that Luke makes implicit when he says in Luke 8:47 that the woman realized she was not hidden.[19] The note of the woman's faith is perhaps a little stronger in Luke, but the point is the same.

(7) Woman's Confession and Testimony (8:47)

Jesus' persistence causes the woman to realize that her actions were **8:47** not hidden (λανθάνω, *lanthanō*; BAGD 466; BAA 947; elsewhere only at Mark 7:24; Acts 26:26; Heb. 13:2; 2 Pet. 3:5, 8). She had not escaped notice, and fear comes over her. Why was she trembling (τρέμουσα, *tremousa*; BAGD 825; BAA 1645; elsewhere only at Mark 5:33; 2 Pet. 2:10)? Τρέμω can refer to trembling or the emotion that accompanies it, fear.[20] Various reasons for her fear are given (Van Der Loos 1965: 517): (1) What would Jesus do? (2) Was he angry that he had been made unclean? (3) Would she have to tell all in front of this crowd? The text does not specify the reason, but it seems that the prospect of Jesus' acting would be the chief cause of concern, for surely she had heard of other cases where unclean people had been healed. In addition, she seems quite ready, once it is clear that Jesus knows, to tell her story. So, trembling, she falls before him and explains why she had touched him, along with the marvelous instant results that followed.[21] The bowing is not a sign of worship, but simply an act of respect and of begging for his mercy. In addition, the testimony to Jesus' work comes freely. She

---

19. Schweizer 1984: 150 sees too much difference here when he argues that Luke leaves it up to the woman to come forward, while Mark has Jesus search for the woman.

20. A variant reading in Acts 9:6 uses τρέμω to describe Saul's reaction to the appearance of the Lord. For the sense of fear, see 2 Pet. 2:10.

21. Note the continued use of ἀπαγγέλλω (to report; 8:34, 36, 47); Schniewind, *TDNT* 1:66 §B. Only in Luke does the woman mention that she touched him.

tells all and notes that she was healed "immediately" (παραχρῆμα, *parchrēma*; 1:64; 4:39; 5:25; 13:13; 18:43; and three times in this pericope: 8:44, 47, 55). Faith has broken through timidity and has openly declared Jesus' act. Jesus initiates, and the woman responds publicly in testimony. Such public declaration by a woman, though not unprecedented in its time, was unusual.[22] Nolland (1989: 420) calls it a "religious testimony."

Mark 5:33 narrates the same details, but in a slightly different form. Mark has the woman fearing, trembling, falling before Jesus, and "telling the whole truth." Luke emphasizes the audience and highlights the confession's content with more detail.[23] Matthew lacks these elements. What is declared openly here contrasts with the request for silence in the next account, possibly due to the nature and situation of this miracle.[24]

(8) Jesus' Commendation of the Woman's Faith (8:48)

8:48 Jesus affirms and encourages the fearful woman in terms that recall his encouragement to the woman who anointed him (7:50). He addresses her as daughter (θυγάτηρ, *thygatēr*) to emphasize his familial relationship to her, a choice of term that is unusual, since Jesus is probably younger than this woman.[25] Then he declares that her faith has brought her into salvation (note the perfect tense σέσωκεν, has saved). The true people of God are being drawn to Jesus. Faith believes God's capability to deliver through Jesus. The healing occurs because she has faith, not because she has enough faith (cf. 17:5–6). In addition, if she thinks that her attitude was unrelated to what had occurred, Jesus reminds her that her faith was important to what had taken place. There is no magic here, only belief in the spiritual action and power of the Almighty God.

She is to depart knowing that her relationship to God is restored. The idea of peace (εἰρήνη, *eirēnē*) associated with Jesus' ministry is

---

22. Hendriksen 1978: 459 says that it was improper for a woman to speak publicly like this, but this is probably too strong. However, such speaking was rare (cf. 2:38). Jesus' question all but required that she speak.

23. Marshall 1978: 346 notes the Lucan terminology in 8:47: the use of the preposition διά with αἰτία (as in Acts 10:21; 22:24; 28:18, 20) and the use of ἐνώπιον with πᾶς (as in Luke 14:10; Acts 6:5; 19:19; 27:35).

24. Marshall 1978: 342 suggests that the scornful Jews of 8:54–56 were not worthy recipients of the report on the resuscitation.

25. According to Arndt 1956: 247, this is the only place where Jesus makes such an address. However, he has missed 13:16, where a woman is addressed as a daughter of Abraham (noted by Tiede 1988: 176). Cf. the description of Zacchaeus as "son of Abraham" in 19:9. Bovon 1989: 450 and n. 50 notes that the term suggests Jesus' authority. See also Ps. 45:10 [44:11 LXX]; Zeph. 3:14; and Lam. 4:21–22. The length of the woman's problem suggests that she is older than Jesus.

key to Luke.[26] The extension of the kingdom message into the Gentile world is also described in terms of peace (Eph. 2:17). Peace here is not an internal, subjective feeling; it is a state that exists between the woman and God because of her faith. Such assurance for a woman who had been ceremonially unclean for twelve years would bring great comfort and encouragement.

Mark 5:34 repeats the reply and adds the point that the woman is healed as well as saved. This Marcan wording clearly distinguishes between Jesus' remarks about her healing and her restored position before God (Foerster, *TDNT* 7:990). Matthew 9:22 mentions Jesus' declaration that her faith has saved her and then mentions the instant healing. This order is a reflection of his telescoping the account. As noted by Arndt (1956: 247), Eusebius (*Ecclesiastical History* 7.18) mentions a commemorative statue at Paneas (Caesarea Philippi) said to stand at the home of this woman, who is associated with this town in church tradition.

iii. Raising Jairus's Daughter (8:49–56)
(1) Report of the Daughter's Death (8:49)

The delay caused by healing the woman's hemorrhage appears to have been costly. As Jesus finishes addressing the woman, a man appears from the synagogue leader's home with bad news: the daughter has died. In stopping to heal a lesser medical condition and forcing a discussion about it, Jesus had allowed a life to be lost. Where are God's justice and Jesus' judgment in this turn of events?

8:49

The envoy suggests that the death means there is no longer need to trouble the teacher (τὸν διδάσκαλον, *ton didaskalon*). This title is a typical description of Jesus in Luke (see 7:40). The envoys from the centurion had a similar desire not to trouble Jesus, but for different reasons (7:6). The envoy from Jairus's house notes that with the death all hope had passed (for the textual issue here, see the additional note).

Though Mark 5:35 is verbally distinct from Luke, the point in the two passages is the same. For example, Mark uses a synonymous prefixed verb for the girl's death, aorist ἀπέθανεν (*apethanen*), in contrast to Luke's perfect τέθνηκεν (*tethnēken*, has died; BAGD 362; BAA 736), thus stressing death's finality more than does Mark's aorist (Marshall 1978: 346). In Mark many come to announce the

---

26. Luke 1:79; 2:14, 29; 7:50; 10:5–6 (those who respond to the kingdom message are called "children of peace"); 11:21 (a nontheological usage); 12:51 (a confrontation text that asserts what Jesus does not bring, because of the division he causes among people); 14:32 (a nontheological usage); 19:38, 42; 24:36; Acts 10:36.

death, while Luke speaks of only one messenger.[27] In addition, the command in Luke is formulated as a question in Mark, "Why trouble the teacher any longer?" These differences are stylistic and present essentially the same picture. Mark's account is generally more complete throughout the pericope, so he mentions many people as present. As was noted in the discussion on 8:42, Matthew differs from Mark and Luke in that he lacks a two-step approach to the account; he does not mention envoys. The difference is simply one of literary choice.

(2) Jesus' Call to Believe (8:50)

8:50   Jesus prepares Jairus for the great work that God will do. He tells Jairus not to fear, not to be anxious that his daughter has died (similar commands not to fear occur in 1:13, 30). Rather, he is to believe, and then salvation—that is, physical deliverance—will follow. The faith called for here is confidence about God's power, compassion, and capability to deliver the child out of death. It is such reliance that is commendable before God. Letting Jesus proceed will show that such faith is present.

Mark 5:36 is parallel, except that it lacks the Lucan promise that "she shall be saved." The introduction to the verse is worded slightly differently, but the idea is the same. Luke's version is stylistically simpler. Also, Mark uses a present imperative for the call to believe, while Luke has an aorist imperative. Luke's tense is slightly more urgent in force and emphasizes the need for faith: "Do not fear, believe" (Marshall 1978: 347; N. Turner 1963: 75). Mark's choice focuses on the duration of the faith asked for: "Only be believing"—but there is no essential difference in what is requested (Fitzmyer 1981: 748). Nolland (1989: 421) suggests that the aorist is used because the faith Jesus calls for here is of a new order. Faith is to prevail over whatever else Jairus faces and feels (Plummer 1896: 236–37). Hendriksen (1978: 460) notes how common it is in Scripture to call people to trust in God's power and character when things seem to be going wrong (Ps. 22:4 [22:5 MT]; Isa. 26:3–4; 43:2; Gen. 22:2 [Abraham]; Exod. 14:10–11 and 32:10 [Moses]; 1 Sam. 17:44–47 [David]; Ps. 27 and numerous lament psalms).

(3) Those Allowed to Go In (8:51)

8:51   Jesus moves to raise the child, but only some of the inner circle of disciples are allowed to come into the house—the first time that Jesus makes such a distinction. The three who come, Peter, John, and

---

27. Mark has ἔρχονται (they came), Luke ἔρχεται (he came). Creed 1930: 123 notes that this is the only historic present in Luke, a common construction in Mark.

James, are the same three who will experience the transfiguration after Peter's confession (9:28). They will also be singled out by Jesus at Gethsemane, though Luke himself lacks this detail at that point (Matt. 26:37 = Mark 14:33). Sometimes Jesus instructs all, sometimes the Twelve, and sometimes some within the Twelve. The reasons why he did this or why he singled out these three are not given (Hendriksen 1978: 461 correctly refuses to speculate on an answer).

The parents also enter with Jesus and the three disciples. The restricted audience fits well with Jesus' later instructions not to tell anyone what occurred. Mark 5:37 says the same thing in slightly different words. Mark lacks mention of the parents entering with Jesus and his disciples, because Mark 5:38 speaks of those who followed Jesus coming into the house, a verbal choice that assumes the family is already present inside (Schweizer 1984: 151). Creed (1930: 124) complains that Luke's inclusion of the parents' entrance into the house makes the story less coherent since the mother has not yet been mentioned and they are entering a house where she already would be. This criticism presses the language too greatly.[28] Luke's point is simply to mention the witnesses who were present during the raising from death. In addition, Mark 5:37 speaks only of the three following Jesus. This has led some to suggest that in Mark only three disciples came to the house, since later (Mark 5:40) the prohibition appears to involve only the crowd at the house (Marshall 1978: 347). Thus, only three disciples came into the house; those excluded in Mark 5:40 and Luke 8:51 are the mourners.[29] Marshall (1978: 347) also notes that Luke has his typical order of Peter, John, and James, while Mark 5:37 has Peter, James, and John (Luke 9:28; Acts 1:13; 3:1, 11; 4:13; Fitzmyer 1981: 749; Schürmann 1969: 494 n. 166). There is no ranking here, just a list of witnesses.

(4) Jesus' Declaration That She Sleeps; Call to Faith (8:52)

Jesus addresses the mourners engaged in the ancient customary ex- **8:52** pressions of grief that accompanied a death (Plummer 1896: 237).[30] One of the terms for mourning, κόπτομαι (koptomai), graphically pictures the beating of one's breast in mourning (Gen. 23:2; 1 Sam. 25:1; Fitzmyer 1981: 749). One did not call for mourners until death took place (Stählin, *TDNT* 3:841–45, esp. pp. 844–45; Rengstorf, *TDNT* 3:724–25). Thus, the presence of the mourners testified to the

---

28. The impression of Mark 5:40 is that the parents were with Jesus as he arrived. Luke's language is compressed.

29. This is certainly the impression of Matt. 9:24, though Matthew lacks a discussion of which disciples attended. Matthew last mentioned the disciples in 9:19.

30. For details on the mourners' customs, see the exegesis of 7:13; also 2 Chron. 35:25; Jer. 9:17–18 [9:16–17 MT].

tragic situation and drew the attention of neighbors to the death that had occurred. It is incorrect to suggest that a coma might explain the mourners' presence, for this is counter to the practice of not having mourners there until death had been established (i.e., one still has a heartbeat while in a coma). Jesus' remarks in Luke 8:52, 55 stand against this view of the text (correctly Liefeld 1984: 917 against Plummer's uncertainty [1896: 237]).[31]

In the midst of these mourners, Jesus remarks that the daughter is not dead but sleeps. This figurative use of καθεύδω (katheudō) appears elsewhere in 1 Thess. 5:10, and another term for sleep, κοιμάω (koimaō), is also used in this sense (John 11:11; 1 Thess. 4:14–15; Bultmann, TDNT 3:14 n. 60; Oepke, TDNT 3:436–37). The difference between these uses is that here the girl is being brought back from death to earthly life, while 1 Thessalonians discusses the bodily transformation out of death that will take place at Jesus' return (Schürmann 1969: 494–95 and n. 170). In Luke, the girl is not beyond Jesus' power to overcome death. Where God is active, death need not be the end of existence nor need it nullify the reality of a future before him. The raising is a sign of God's power to resurrect and makes the point that death is not the end of existence for humans (Schürmann 1969: 495). Jesus' remarks are rhetorical. The "sleep" of the child is not a permanent death, but rather a temporary rest that allows Jesus through resurrection to show his power. The idiom is also used of Lazarus in John 11:11 and of Jacob in Midr. Gen. 96.2 (60e) on Gen. 47:30 (Schürmann 1969: 495 n. 172). The text is clear that a miracle is present.

Both Matthew and Mark paint this scene in their own words. Mark 5:38–39 speaks of the crowd's tumult and loud wailing. Jesus in turn asks the crowd why they are wailing so loudly when the girl only sleeps. Thus, Mark is more critical of the crowd, as is his style. Luke just gives the summary command and lacks the direct criticism. Matthew's account also notes the criticism of the crowd: Matt. 9:23–24 mentions the crowd and the flute-playing that accompanied the mourning (cf. Luke 7:32), and Jesus dismisses the crowd and explains that the daughter sleeps. Of course, this note heightens the drama, for what the mourners were doing was natural following a death. There is some discussion of the locale of this group (Marshall 1978: 347): were they expelled from the house, as Mark 5:40 makes clear, or were they outside? It seems that Luke has summarized Mark's greater detail.

---

31. Van Der Loos 1965: 569 takes Jesus' remark about sleep to indicate a coma, ignoring the use of sleep as a common figure for death (see the next paragraph). There is no indication that the crowd has misread the situation. In fact, this view destroys the parallelism with 7:11–17.

(5) Crowd's Laughter (8:53)

The crowd reacts with derisive laughter (as in Acts 17:32 at Paul's **8:53** teaching on resurrection; Bovon 1989: 452). The reaction is not surprising, given the normally definitive nature of death! Mark 5:39 = Matt. 9:24 mentions the response with the exact same wording. Luke alone adds the explanation that they laughed (κατεγέλων, *kategelōn*, is imperfect: "they were laughing") because (ὅτι, *hoti*, is causal) they knew she was dead. Jesus had turned grief to amusement. Laughter at surprise announcements by God is not unusual in the Scripture (e.g., Sarah's response in Gen. 18:12). But God's power is capable of surprises. Nervousness and the absence of faith at such moments can bring laughter, but amusement is not the end of this story.

(6) Call to Rise (8:54)

Jesus takes very little time to restore the child: he reaches out and **8:54** takes her hand as he addresses her. Such a move would render Jesus unclean by OT standards, but to restore the girl is more important than ritual cleanliness (Num. 19:11). Of course, Jesus does not have to touch the girl (Luke 7:7–8), but does so (cf. 7:14), perhaps to communicate compassion (Isa. 41:13; 42:6; Danker 1988: 188; Fitzmyer 1981: 749). His touch certainly includes the offer of a helpful hand, so that when she revives she can sit up (cf. Acts 9:41). Jesus loudly calls out for the girl to arise, almost as if calling her out of a nap— since he had just called her death sleep. As Luke 8:55 makes clear, Jesus is summoning back her spirit (Acts 7:59 [of one dying]; 9:41; Schürmann 1969: 495; Marshall 1978: 348; also 1 Kings 17:21). The call is similar to the one to the son of the widow of Nain in Luke 7:14, except that there the passive ἐγέρθητι (*egerthēti*, be raised) was used instead of the active ἔγειρε (*egeire*, arise).

Mark 5:41 supplies more detail by giving the Aramaic form of the address to the girl, as well as the Greek translation. The omission of Aramaic is not surprising given Luke's Greek audience (Arndt 1956: 248). Also, Mark 5:41–42 uses κοράσιον (*korasion*, young girl; BAGD 444; BAA 902; Matt. 9:24, 25; 14:11; Mark 6:22, 28 [twice]; never in Luke) to address the girl, whereas Luke has παῖς (*pais*, child). Matthew 9:25 lacks any address by Jesus, but simply speaks of his grasping the girl's (κοράσιον) hand and her being raised.

(7) Raising of the Girl (8:55)

The girl's life is immediately restored. Luke gives three distinct indi- **8:55** cators of this. First, her spirit (πνεῦμα, *pneuma*) returned to her body (Sjöberg, *TDNT* 6:379; Schweizer, *TDNT* 6:415). In ancient expression, the πνεῦμα is the part of a person that survives death and the part of one's being that God works with in resurrection, a work that will also transform a person's body (1 Cor. 15:50–58; Phil. 3:20–21). The Lucan description shows that with death a separation of body and spirit had occurred. Van Der Loos (1965: 571) argues that the return of the spirit indicates only that the vital forces returned to the girl, but this ignores how Luke uses the imagery of the spirit to describe death (Luke 23:46; Acts 7:59).[32] Acts 20:10 uses another expression to refer to the immaterial person: Paul says that Eutychus's "soul (ψυχή, psychē) is still in him" (on the figure involving ψυχή, see Schweizer, TDNT 9:637, 644, 646–47).

Second, with the return of her spirit, life was restored and she rose up in response to Jesus' command. Luke also notes that this took place immediately. Finally, Jesus asks that she be given something to eat. Such a detail makes it clear that there is no hallucination or vision here (Danker 1988: 188; Luke 24:37–43). The girl has been fully and physically restored. Death has been overcome. The request for food reflects Jesus' concern that life return to normal (Plummer 1896: 238). Godet (1875: 1.395) expresses this idea with a literary flair: "He acts like a physician who has just felt the pulse of his patient, and gives instructions respecting [her] diet for the day."

Mark 5:42 relates the immediate recovery and speaks of the girl's walking, an act that amazed those present. Matthew 9:25 lacks any mention of the response and simply notes that the girl arose.

(8) Parents' Amazement (8:56a)

8:56a The healing brought a response of amazement from the very grateful parents. Ἐξίστημι (existēmi, to be amazed) is more common in Acts than Luke (BAGD 276; BAA 559; Luke 2:47; 8:56; 24:22; Acts 2:7, 12; 8:9, 11, 13; 9:21; 10:45; 12:16). The parallel in Mark 5:42 also uses the term, but in Mark the amazement is related first, then the command for silence, and then the command to give the girl food. Matthew 9:26 simply notes that the report of the event went into all the region. Of course, the amazement is not surprising. Resurrections from the dead are not daily happenings, and the possibility had been greeted with doubting laughter. One can imagine the emotional reversal that such an event would bring.

(9) Jesus' Call to Be Silent (8:56b)

8:56b The command for silence seems a little odd. An observer could easily infer what had happened: mourners were present because some-

---

32. Van Der Loos 1965: 572 cites OT precedent (Judg. 15:19; 1 Sam. 30:12); more correct is Schneider 1977a: 199. In Judaism, see 1 Enoch 22.1–14; 39.4–8. Nolland 1989: 422 notes a possible contact with 1 Kings 17:21–22.

one had died, but now that dead person was walking around. What else to conclude but that the dead had been raised? Nonetheless, Jesus tells the parents to say nothing. This contrasts with the instruction to the Gerasene demoniac in Luke 8:39 and the efforts Jesus went to in having the woman with the hemorrhage relate her healing (8:45–47), not to mention an earlier public resurrection in 7:11–17 (Danker 1988: 188). It seems clear that Jesus is concerned about what aspects of his ministry receive attention (4:41; 5:14). Even a normally skeptical commentator like Luce (1933: 175) recognizes the incongruity of the request. Its presence in a variety of sources speaks for its historicity.

But why the request? Jesus knows that he is headed for a different kind of ministry than people will want from him. Excessive focus on his works of power will undermine the type of commitment he will ask from people. He does not need to be raising people on a daily basis. The type of commitment that will be required of them, should they follow him, is one of suffering, not comfort (9:22, 36, 57–62; 10:17–20). People will talk about his works, but they should not be encouraged to focus on elements that only point to deeper issues. There will come a time when the miracles will go public, but their publicity need not be encouraged since they are not at the heart of what Jesus is doing. Rather they point to more significant spiritual realities (11:14–23). Other reasons have been posited for the command to conceal the resurrection: (1) a desire to save the parents from excessive focus on God's act (Plummer 1896: 238), (2) an act of judgment against those who had laughed in 8:53 (Marshall 1978: 342), or (3) an effort to conceal revelation from those who do not believe (Tiede 1988: 177, citing 10:21). But such explanations do not seem to deal adequately with the Lucan portrait of miracles in Jesus' ministry, though reasons 2 and 3 may be partial explanations. In Luke, miracles are a testimony to the nature of the times; they are not intended to be the focus of Jesus' work (7:22). Rather, they picture deeper realities that Jesus offered, as Acts 2:22–36 suggests. It is possible that the hiddenness is a result of judgment, but that is not the major reason. The call to silence makes clear that Jesus does not regard such acts as the center of his ministry, but as only the evidentiary periphery.

Summary

The combined miracles of Luke 8:22–56 attest to Jesus' power over a variety of forces, whether they be forces from without (nature or demons) or within (disease or death). Here, Jesus is able to heal disease. But when one considers the woman's action, an additional note is made: faith, even timid faith, has importance and can mobilize God. This woman was careful not to draw attention to herself, but she also knew that Jesus could heal her. Her faith was more important than her timidity. She eventually relied on him. When confronted and exposed, she openly spoke of what Jesus had done for her.

More interesting is Jairus's perspective. Imagine the faith that he was called on to have. He hoped that Jesus could do something. However, the interruption and delay had seemingly caused all to be lost. Yet, Jesus still called on Jairus to trust. The timing may not have been what Jairus desired, but events were still in God's control through his agent. Others may have thought all was lost—and by all appearances they were. Nevertheless, Jesus had—and has—the authority to reverse appearances and to render the delay meaningless. Several issues stand out in the Jairus account: Jesus' power, faith's importance, and the patience of the one who is called to trust in God. God will do his work in his time. One can be amazed at how God works and the timing that he uses. Jesus' power eventually honors Jairus's patient faith.

In fact, when one considers the four miracles of 8:22–56, it is Jesus' comprehensive power that stands out. This power provides the opportunity for people to see God. Such power exposes the impotency of the forces that oppose God and humanity. The forces may be natural, demonic, disease, or death; yet Jesus is able to reverse them all. The last miracle of resurrection properly comes at the end, for if Jesus has power over death, then one eventually must deal with him and with God. The call in three of these miracles relates to faith (8:25, 48, 50). Jesus is worthy of one's trust. Be assured that what he promises, he eventually will do (1:1–4). Know that God's power is absolute. Death is not the chief end of humans. Facing and knowing God is.

Additional Notes

8:41. The name Ἰάϊρος (Jairus) is lacking in a variant reading in Mark 5:22, but the omission is not well attested (only Codex D and Itala). Nonetheless, some still try to suggest that Luke added the name, an approach decisively refuted by Pesch (1970a). The name does not appear in Matthew.

8:43. The RSV, NIV, and NASB do not translate the phrase ἰατροῖς προσαναλώσασα ὅλον τὸν βίον (having spent all her living on physicians). The UBS–NA text includes it in brackets, which suggests extreme doubt about the originality of the phrase. If it is original, then Luke has summarized some of the detail found in Mark 5:26 and has softened the remarks about physicians. Manuscripts including the phrase are ℵ², A, L, P, W, Δ, Θ, Ξ, family 1, family 13, Byz, and Lect. Other manuscripts read a variation of the phrase by referring to "her own" (ἑαυτῆς) livelihood (ℵ*) or "her" (αὐτῆς) livelihood (C, Ψ). What makes the choice difficult are the texts that omit the phrase entirely: 𝔓⁷⁵, B, D, one Itala manuscript, some Syriac, and a Coptic text—an early Alexandrian and Western agreement that brings together some of the best NT witnesses. It is uncertain whether the phrase was originally in Luke, although the probability is that it was, which is why I have included it.[33]

8:44. Almost all external evidence reads "from behind she touched the hem of his garment" in agreement with Matt. 9:20. This reading has strong Alexandrian, as well as versional and Byzantine support: 𝔓⁷⁵, ℵ, A, B, C, L, P, W, Δ, Θ, Ξ, Byz, Lect, most Syriac, many Itala, Vulgate, and Coptic. The other variants either alter the word order, add a word, omit a word, or omit everything but the reference to her touching. No variant has sufficient external support to warrant acceptance.

8:45. Do all the disciples or does only Peter respond to Jesus' question? If the former, then Luke and Mark are parallel. The evidence for reading Peter only is thin but significant: 𝔓⁷⁵, B, some Syriac, one Coptic manuscript. That the variants that include the disciples are variously worded may suggest that they were added later in a variety of forms to conform to Mark 5:31. In addition, the verb εἶπεν (said), which is not disputed, is singular, which would lead us to expect a singular subject. The variants use either σύν or μετ' to indicate that the disciples "with" Peter also spoke. The shorter reading is slightly more likely to be original, given the likelihood of harmonization, though one must concede that the longer reading is possible. If only Peter speaks, he is portrayed as representing the disciples.

8:45. In mentioning the crowd, did Peter go on to repeat Jesus' question— "and you say, 'Who touched me?'" Such a longer reading brings Luke into conformity with Mark 5:31. The variants render the additional line with distinct wording, giving the impression of various efforts to harmonize Luke and Mark. Paralleling the previous problem, the shorter reading has good support: 𝔓⁷⁵, ℵ, B, L, family 1, one Syriac manuscript, some Coptic. If this reading is not original, then the reading καὶ λέγεις, Τίς ὁ ἁψάμενός μου (and you say, "Who touched me?") is the next best option (A, C [τί], P, W, Δ, Θ, family 13, Byz, Lect, some Syriac, one Coptic manuscript). The point is clear: Peter is astonished that Jesus would seek to ask who touched him in the midst of the crushing crowd.

8:49. Is the Greek negative particle μηκέτι or μή, the second of which would translate "do not trouble"? The choice really makes no difference to the

---

33. Plummer 1896: 235; Marshall 1978: 344; Fitzmyer 1981: 746; Bovon 1989: 445–46 (who argues that Luke may be responsible for it); Creed 1930: 123; and Hendriksen 1978: 466 appear undecided. Arndt 1956: 246 and A. B. Bruce 1897: 525 are for inclusion. Schürmann 1969: 490 n. 137; Ellis 1974: 130; and Luce 1933: 173 omit it.

sense, and to choose between them is difficult. Most regard the agreement between $\mathfrak{P}^{75}$, ℵ, B, and D as decisive for μηκέτι. In addition, that Luke's Gospel uses μηκέτι nowhere else makes it the harder reading (Metzger 1975: 146). What is clear is that all had lost hope with the girl's death. One can imagine how a desperate, yet hopeful Jairus became disappointed and grief-stricken. Frustration mixed with anger may have resulted at this seemingly lost opportunity.

d. Commissioned Authority Revealed (9:1–6)

After his description of Jesus' comprehensive power, Luke describes the commission of the Twelve. They become bearers of the kingdom-gospel message (9:2, 6). This is especially true since they are witnesses to God's power as revealed through Jesus (8:22–56; Tannehill 1986: 210; Talbert 1982: 100). This is the beginning of active ministry for those who have followed Jesus, an initial fulfillment of 5:10 and 6:12–16 (Tannehill 1986: 215–16; Schürmann 1969: 499). Their authority is like Jesus', but it is clearly derived from him. In this brief account, the disciples are told to travel light, stay where they are received, and depart from where they are rejected—bringing either God's blessing or judgment with them. Their message forces a decision; neutrality is the same as rejection. Thus, the account depicts the expansion of ministry to those who will be Jesus' witnesses in the Book of Acts (Luke 24:46–47; Fitzmyer 1981: 752). The disciples are sent out immediately after seeing an impressive series of miracles from Jesus' hand. Yet they are called to a simple life of trusting God as they minister. Marshall (1978: 350–51) notes that such a lifestyle (9:3) contrasted with other missionaries of the Hellenistic world.

This passage is sometimes seen as the start of a new unit running from 9:1 to 9:50.[1] Moessner sees a recapitulation of Moses' career in Jesus, with two dominant themes: rejection by a "stiff-necked" generation and Moses' suffering and death. Moessner argues that the first half of the chapter is positive, while it becomes negative after the transfiguration (9:36). This is correct, though the lack of understanding reaches back into Peter's confession, since Jesus follows the confession immediately with a note that he will suffer. Many of Moessner's points are valid for the latter half of the chapter. O'Toole notes three christological and three ecclesiological themes: (1) Jesus as prophet like Moses and as the Son; (2) an emphasis on the Passion; (3) Jesus' prayer and associ-

---

1. The best cases for this structure are made by Moessner 1983 and O'Toole 1987b. Moessner notes four basic approaches to the unit before making a case that much of the passage previews a "prophet like Moses" motif in the journey section of Luke. O'Toole correctly critiques Moessner as emphasizing the prophet too much at the expense of messianic categories, though for Luke the two concepts are very close, as Acts 3:13–26 shows.

ation with glory; (4) listening to Jesus; (5) the ignorance and weakness of the disciples; and (6) Luke's moderation of the harsh descriptions of disciples. These themes are key to Luke 9. This last point works against Moessner's view slightly. Others also share this division of themes.[2]

However, despite these links, I see the chapter's turning point as the confession, not the transfiguration. So pivotal is this unit that I have made a section break at 9:17, since negative understanding (or lack of understanding) emerged after the confession. This transition shows that Peter's confession, though basic and correct, needs filling out. The disciples still have much to learn. Thus, while many of the thematic points of Moessner and O'Toole have merit, I reject the view that the transfiguration is the turning point of Luke 9. The christological development takes on a new dimension after Peter's confession. Thus, Luke is like Mark.

Nolland (1989: 425) is so impressed with the shift at 9:20 that he breaks the entire section (8:1–9:20) there, treating 9:21–50 as a transitional unit. I agree in seeing 9:21–50 as transitional, but the catalyst to the transition is the confession in 9:18–20, so it must be included with the later unit as well. I prefer to see 9:18–50 as the capstone of this Galilean ministry, with the christological confession and call to discipleship in place before the major shift to Jerusalem in 9:51. As such, 9:1–50 is the culmination of Luke's third section, Jesus' Galilean tour (see the exegesis of these units).

Sources and Historicity

A parallel to this account is found in Mark 6:6b–13 = Matt. 10:1–14, which is part of a much larger commission unit in Matt. 10:1–42 (Aland 1985: §142). Most see Luke following Mark (Schürmann 1969: 504; Marshall 1978: 349; Fitzmyer 1981: 751; Bovon 1989: 454). They argue that Matthew combined some elements that seem to belong to separate events. For example, he has saved the listing of the Twelve until this point (see the introduction to Luke 6:12–16). Elements in the Lucan commission to the larger group of disciples (10:1–16) appear at this point in Matthew (Aland 1985: §99). But this is a minor problem, since the form of the two ministries in Luke is parallel and only Luke details the larger mission. One can assume that the smaller mission operated on a similar basis. However, the Matthean unit is not as composite as many suggest and can be regarded as

2. Wiefel 1988: 170 speaks of Jesus' person and his mysterious suffering as the key to the unit. Schürmann 1969: 498 speaks of the mystery of God's reign becoming evident to the disciples. Bovon 1989: 455 notes points of contact shared with Acts: (1) reception of power from the Lord (Acts 26:15–18), (2) the juxtaposition of preaching and healing (3:1–26), and (3) mission that finds acceptance and rejection (13:51; 18:6).

one commission (Carson 1984: 240–43; Liefeld 1984: 917–18; against Marshall 1978: 349, who speaks of a conflation of two accounts in Matthew, as do most).

Mark 6:1–6a has narrated the Nazareth visit at this point, a position that seems to be more chronologically motivated than the "paradigm" placement of the synagogue account in Luke 4 (see the introduction to 4:16–30). It seems clear that, before Jesus obtained the famous confession of Peter at Caesarea Philippi, he had already sent the disciples out on missions declaring the kingdom of God.[3] The commission's historicity should not be challenged.[4] Luke follows Mark in recounting the commission briefly, but all the Gospels use largely their own wording. Fitzmyer (1981: 751–52) notes seven differences between Mark and Luke, which I shall discuss as they arise.[5] That the account is paradigmatic is indicated by later use of these themes in the NT (1 Cor. 9:14; 1 Tim. 5:18; 3 John 5–7; and in the church fathers: *Didache* 13.1–2; Liefeld 1984: 918). Some of the passage's elements were repeated in the early church's teaching.

The Jesus Seminar (Funk and Hoover 1993: 310–11) treats Luke 9:3–4 as doubtfully linked to Jesus (it's printed in gray type) and 9:5 as not tied to Jesus at all (in black type). Citing the lack of commission in John's Gospel, the seminar rejects the concepts of Jesus' commission and his recruitment of disciples. The seminar does think it possible that these statements reflect Jesus' lifestyle. The rejection of 9:5 is rather amazing, since all the parallels have it; but the seminar regards it as too vindictive for Jesus. In reply, there is no reason to doubt that Jesus involved his disciples in mission work or to question that his instructions to them would mirror his own ministry (Nolland 1993a: 548).[6] The woes of Luke 10:13–15 indicate that Jesus could announce judgment. In fact, that would be part of the reason that the Jewish leadership would want to deal with him: he was perceived as a prophet who threatened their role by warning about God's judgment on those who rejected him. Nolland defends well the historicity of Jesus' warning in Luke 10, and it is only a natural extension from those remarks to 9:5. Acts 13:51 testifies to the precedent that Jesus' remarks created. That

3. On the placement of the account, see Godet 1875: 1.396–97. This explains how the disciples knew how people saw Jesus.

4. Fitzmyer 1981: 753 is too cautious here. Marshall 1978: 350 is correct in calling it "one of the best-attested facts in the life of Jesus," following Manson 1949: 73; also V. Taylor 1966: 302. This tradition contains one of the few sayings of Jesus alluded to by Paul (1 Cor. 9:14).

5. (1) Luke lacks an introduction like Mark 6:6b; (2) Luke speaks of authority over demons and diseases, not just unclean spirits; (3) the Twelve are specifically kingdom preachers; (4) Luke allows no staff and lacks mention of sandals; (5) Luke lacks the introduction in Mark 6:10; (6) Luke has additional instruction about lodging; and (7) Luke lacks mention of preaching and anointing at the end of the account.

6. Interestingly, parts of 10:8–9, which is like 9:3–5 conceptually, show up in the Gospel of Thomas 14.4—but even this is not enough to raise the sayings' credibility in the seminar's eyes.

Jesus' instructions in Luke 9:3–4 contrast with religious practice in Hellenistic culture adds to the case for their authenticity. Thus, these remarks have a strong claim of genuineness.

> Form critics call the account a story about Jesus, because it is mainly narrative.[7] Fitzmyer (1981: 752) notes that the structure has five parts: a conferral of power, commission, rules of journey, rules of lodging, and rules of nonreception. The outline of Luke 9:1–6 is as follows:
>
> > i. Authority and commission given (9:1–2)
> > ii. Instructions about provision and lodging (9:3–5)
> > iii. The mission summarized (9:6)
>
> The major theme is Jesus' sharing of mission with the Twelve. This means bestowing on the Twelve authority over demons and disease, as well as the call to preaching. Their message is the kingdom of God. They engage in the ministry with minimal provision, committing to reside in the place that God provides. God's rejection will come to those who do not respond. The message forces a choice.

Exegesis and Exposition

[1]And when he called ⌜the Twelve⌝ together, he gave them power and authority over all demons and to cure diseases. [2]And he sent them to preach the kingdom of God and to heal ⌜the sick⌝. [3]And he said to them, "Take nothing for your journey, neither staff nor bag, neither bread nor money, neither have two tunics. [4]And whatever house you enter, stay there, and from there go out. [5]And wherever they do not receive you, go out from that city, shaking the dust from your feet as a testimony against them." [6]And going out, they passed through the villages, preaching good news and healing in every place.

i. Authority and Commission Given (9:1–2)

9:1   Jesus now ministers with his inner circle, the Twelve. First he commissions them with authority.[8] The importance of this bestowed authority is something that Jesus develops during his ministry (Luke

---

7. Doubting the account's historicity, Bultmann 1963: 145, 331–32 sees the sayings of Mark 6:8–11 (= Luke 9:3–5) as a church product. He seems to assume incorrectly that a passage cannot have a mixture of narrative and saying material. Berger 1984: 333, 68 speaks of a commission speech and a summary account.

8. Συγκαλέω (to call together) occurs elsewhere in Mark 15:16; Luke 15:6, 9; Acts 5:21; elsewhere in the middle voice at Luke 23:13; Acts 10:24; 28:17; K. Schmidt, *TDNT* 3:496.

10:16, 19–20, 22; 11:19; Grundmann, *TDNT* 2:310 §D3). The power extends into two areas: the disciples can overcome demonic forces, as evidence of the kingdom's nearness (11:18–21), and they will be able to reverse disease, again as evidence of the nature of the times (4:18–19; 7:22). Luke uniquely expresses this authority by combining two terms: δύναμιν καὶ ἐξουσίαν (*dynamin kai exousian*, power and authority). Δύναμις is one focus of Luke's description of Jesus and continues to interest him.[9] In Acts 1:8, Jesus promises the disciples enabling, directing power. Acts 2:22 and 10:38 also look back at Jesus' ministry with this term. Luke is unique among the Gospels in using δύναμις here. Arndt (1956: 250) suggests that authority (ἐξουσία) is the right to do something, while power (δύναμις) is the ability to do it. Such a distinction is technically correct for Luke, but that is not to suggest that the other Gospels, which mention only ἐξουσία, picture commissioned but powerless disciples. Luke uses a more comprehensive hendiadys. What Jesus had done, the disciples will do. The commission here is limited to the Twelve (on the disputed significance of this number, see the exegesis of 6:13 and Ellis 1974: 132–35).

Mark 6:6b–7 = Matt. 10:1 expresses the same provision in different terms. Mark mentions unclean spirits only, while Matthew speaks of casting out unclean spirits and healing all diseases and maladies. Matthew is closer to Luke, but with his own terms, since he (with Mark) speaks of unclean spirits and he alone speaks of maladies here (only Matthew uses the term μαλακία, *malakia*, in the NT: Matt. 4:23; 9:35; 10:1). Mark mentions the commissioning of authority after mentioning the sending out two by two, but this is merely a stylistic variation about events that occurred together.

The commission's nature is indicated by the use of the verb **9:2** ἀπέστειλεν (*apesteilen*, he sent). Ἀποστέλλω is key in Luke–Acts to describe the task to which one is called (Luke 1:19; 4:18 [twice], 43; 7:27; 9:2, 48; 10:1, 16; 11:49; 13:34; 24:49; Acts 3:20, 26; 7:35; 9:17; 10:36; 26:17; 28:28). The task is twofold: the disciples are to preach the kingdom and heal the sick. The details of the kingdom preaching are not given.[10] Luke saves mention of such details until the later mission in Luke 10, but one can suspect that the message here was

---

9. Luke 4:14 (of guidance); 4:36 (over spirits); 5:17, 6:19, and 8:46 (for healing); 9:1 and 10:13 (over demons and miracles); 19:37 (praise for the miracles done by God through Jesus); Ernst 1977: 285; BAGD 207–8; BAA 417–19. Achtemeier 1978 has a good discussion of miracles as a major Lucan theme; he also shows that these miracles are not tied to ancient views of magic nor based on the OT.

10. On the various ways to express the idea of preaching the kingdom, see K. Schmidt, *TDNT* 1:583 §3b, who notes that these expressions are most plentiful in Luke–Acts.

similar, since they are parallel in many other details (10:9–11). If so, the disciples spoke about the nearness of God's kingdom; they challenged people to see the evidence of its power and nearness; they noted that this was a special time; they called on all to repent and enter in. People who refused were to know that God's judgment was drawing near. This message fits not only the later mission, but also Jesus' preaching (like that in 4:16–21). The healings serve only to display the power of God and thus evidence the nearness of the kingdom, as 11:18–21 makes clear. This power will be retained by the Twelve in Acts and extended to others (Schürmann 1969: 501; Acts 3–4; 6:8; 8:5–11; 13:9–12; 14:8–15; 15:12; 19:11–16). Their message in Acts will be similar, except that one new element will be added: the proclamation of Jesus as the exalted mediator of the blessings of promise.

Luke alone summarizes the commission in this manner. Matthew 10:7 relates the commission by citing Jesus directly. He is more detailed than Luke, since he mentions a variety of acts that the disciples are to perform: heal the sick, raise the dead, cleanse lepers, and cast out demons. Mark 6:12–13 gives the mission's twofold task in a concluding summary at the end of his unit and notes that the message was one of repentance (cf. Luke 24:47). Both Matthew and Mark use a synonymous verb for healing, θεραπεύω (therapeuō), while Luke uses ἰάομαι (iaomai), a verb that he often uses along with θεραπεύω.[11] The commission of 5:10 is beginning to be fulfilled: the disciples are "catching people."

ii. Instructions about Provision and Lodging (9:3–5)

9:3 The instructions for the journey are simple: travel light. Jesus gives a general instruction ("take nothing for your journey") followed by four specific prohibitions: no staff, bag, bread, or money. The Twelve are allowed one basic item of clothing: a tunic. They are not to burden themselves with excessive provisions, for their needs will be met by the generosity of people who receive their message. As the note about bread shows, they are to depend upon God for even their most basic needs. The bag, πήραν (pēran), probably refers to the purse that traveling philosophers and religious figures carried to keep the money that they received or for which they had begged (Michaelis, *TDNT* 6:119–21).

The verse's difficulty comes in comparing it to Matt. 10:9–10 = Mark 6:8–9. Matthew prohibits taking gold, silver, copper, bag, san-

---

11. Luke prefers ἰάομαι over the other Gospel writers, using it eleven times, compared to Mark's once and Matthew's four times. Θεραπεύω is used by Matthew sixteen times, by Mark five times, and by Luke fourteen times.

dals, staff, or two tunics—thus agreeing with Luke but with more detail. Mark says to take nothing except a staff: no bread, bag, or money. The disciples can wear sandals, but not two tunics. Thus, Mark allows sandals, while Matthew prohibits them (Luke does not discuss them, although, interestingly, he does mention their absence in 22:35). Mark allows one staff, where the other Gospels exclude it. Various approaches exist to the problem (Liefeld 1984: 919–20; Ahern 1943):

1. The difference comes from Luke's accepting the wording of his source, which most see as Q (Marshall 1978: 352). This approach explains why there is the difference, but leaves the basic problem unaddressed.

2. The Gospel writers have two types of staffs in view: one a walking stick, the other a club to ward off robbers (E. Power 1923). Although this solution is possible, since ῥάβδος (rhabdos) can have various meanings (Fitzmyer 1981: 754), the use of the same term in all three Gospels speaks against it (C. Schneider, TDNT 6:966–70; 1 Cor. 4:21; Heb. 11:21).

3. Mark adapts his wording so that the instructions fit the exodus imagery of Exod. 12:11 or make a connection with 2 Kings 4:29 (Marshall 1978: 352). This is a neat literary solution, but as with view 1, it leaves unaddressed the basic problem.

4. The problem is seen as confusion in the tradition's transmission, since the Aramaic words for "except" (אֶלָּא, ʾillāʾ) and "and not" (וְ]לָא], [wĕ]lāʾ) are close.[12] This is an attempt to get behind the text to the problem's origin, but it too fails by merely blaming the tradition for the problem.

5. Jesus taught that the disciples were not to procure a staff if they lacked one, a solution suggested by κτάομαι (ktaomai, to acquire) in Matt. 10:9 (BAGD 455; BAA 923–24). However, Luke's verb, αἴρω (airō, to take up), is the same as Mark's. It is possible but unlikely that both writers use the verb in distinct senses. This solution would have stronger support if Mark had used κτάομαι.

6. Though the wording is different, the basic meaning is the same, so that there is agreement in sense, but not detail (Plummer 1896: 239). Perhaps an allusion to the linguistic solution in view 5, this approach also leaves the discrepancy (Ellis 1974: 137 simply says that the differences are irrelevant).

12. Black 1967: 216–17. This view goes back to J. Wellhausen's 1903 commentary on Mark. Oepke, TDNT 5:311 n. 6, mentions this view but prefers to see a contradiction here. Oepke notes that Wellhausen rejected this solution in the 1911 edition of his Mark commentary.

7. Jesus said not to take an *extra* staff (Arndt 1956: 250; Hendriksen 1978: 472–73; Godet 1875: 1.399 [who suggests the appropriate Aramaic]). The only problem here is why one would travel with two staffs. Perhaps Jesus used a hyperbolic picture to make the point about traveling light. This may be the answer to the problem, given the picture of the sandals in the account. Though Matthew says that no sandals are to be carried, it is clear that the disciples are to wear sandals, so that the idea of an extra pair is the point.[13] It is unlikely that the disciples would travel barefooted, given the nature of travel in this culture and the reference to their being guests in the homes of other people (Matt. 10:14 = Mark 6:11 = Luke 9:5). Luke 3:16 and 15:22 suggest that wearing sandals was normal. If the staff instruction operates on analogy with the one about sandals, then Jesus prohibited an extra staff and thus made the point both graphically and hyperbolically that no extra provisions were to be taken.

Liefeld makes no clear choice, but this last suggestion seems best. The point of the verse, regardless of the solution adopted, is that the Twelve are to travel light and depend on God. This instruction is reviewed in 22:35–38, where, with the approach of his death, Jesus alters it.

It is interesting that the Jews had similar customs: the Essenes had similar instructions for travel, as did the Jews for temple visitors.[14]

9:4 The instructions on lodging are as simple as those on provisions: the disciples are to go to one place in the village and stay there the whole time. Though it is disputed whether the reference to departure (ἐξέρχεσθε, *exerchesthe*) means a departure from the village, this is more likely than a reference to going out from a house or going out to preach.[15] The disciples' practice of staying in one place contrasts with that of philosophers who went from house to house begging for support (Danker 1988: 190; Luke 10:7; Acts 9:43; 16:15; 18:3, 20).

---

13. Even Oepke, *TDNT* 5:312, esp. n. 7, who sees a problem in the verses, notes that long journeys in Palestine without footwear would be impossible.

14. Fitzmyer 1981: 753–54; Ellis 1974: 137; *m. Ber.* 9.5 (a command with roots in Exod. 3:5); Schürmann 1969: 501 n. 20; Josephus, *Jewish War* 2.8.4 §§124–27 (about the Essenes). On the contrast with the practice of Greek cynics and philosophers, see Schürmann 1969: 502 n. 24 and Bovon 1989: 458 n. 20, who compares the disciples' absence of possessions with the Levites and their being provided for through the tithe (Num. 18:21).

15. For the latter, see Klostermann 1929: 103 (who rejects it) and Luce 1933: 176 (who opts for a reference in Luke to switching homes). Such a remark in either of the alternative senses adds nothing to the instruction but the obvious. The idea of not switching homes is already implied in the command to stay in the house one enters.

Because of abuse in the early church, *Didache* 11–12 gave detailed instructions about how a missionary should be received (Liefeld 1984: 918; Bovon 1989: 458 n. 24).

Matthew 10:11 and Mark 6:10 say virtually the same thing, but each in its own way. Mark separates the instruction on lodging and that on provisions by introducing the lodging remarks with καὶ ἔλεγεν αὐτοῖς (*kai elegen autois*, and he said to them). However, the actual instruction is the same as in Luke, though worded distinctly. Matthew supplies a little more detail by noting that the disciples are to find someone worthy in the village and stay there the whole time. In Matthew, the idea of being worthy (ἄξιος, *axios*) describes someone who receives the message, as Matt. 10:13–14 makes clear. In Luke 10:6, the one who receives a disciple is called a "child [lit., son] of peace" (υἱὸς εἰρήνης, *huios eirēnēs*).

Jesus tackles the question of what the Twelve should do if they get **9:5** no response or no positive reception to their message: they are to depart the city and shake the dust from their feet as a testimony against the people for their rejection (Cadbury 1933). Such an act is a repudiation of their decision and was done by Jews upon leaving pagan territory to shake off "uncleanness" from their feet.[16] Uncleanness is not so much the point here as saying "good riddance." The act warns rejecters of impending judgment if their decision does not change. It expresses their separation from God (Luce 1933: 176–77 [who compares it to the imagery of Jews washing themselves upon return to Israel from an unclean land]; Liefeld 1984: 919; SB 1:571; cf. 10:13–15 and 19:41). To reject the kingdom message was— and is—serious business (10:16).

Except for some verbal differences, the same idea is expressed in Matt. 10:14 = Mark 6:11. Matthew lacks the explanation that the action is done as a testimony against the people.[17]

iii. The Mission Summarized (9:6)

By way of conclusion, Luke summarizes the mission briefly by re- **9:6** ferring to two primary tasks of the Twelve: preaching the good news and healing (so also Acts 13:3 with 14:1–18). These are the same two categories with which Luke introduced the passage (Luke 9:1–2), ex-

---

16. On κονιορτός (dust), see BAGD 443; BAA 900; Luke 10:11; Acts 13:51; 18:6. On ἐκτινάσσω (to shake off), the verb used in the parallel Mark 6:11 = Matt. 10:14, see BAGD 246; BAA 496; Strathmann, *TDNT* 4:503. Even though the tense of the Marcan verb is aorist and the Lucan verb is present (Marshall 1978: 354), there is no difference in sense.

17. The opposite of a testimony against someone is found in 5:14, where the leper is to testify to God's work; Danker 1988: 190.

cept that he now gives them in reverse order (9:2 also spoke about the kingdom). The summary thus forms an *inclusio* with the introduction (Bovon 1989: 460). The equation of kingdom and gospel is important, since one points to the other. The mission presupposes the passing of some time, since the disciples passed through a variety of villages, a point that shows that even small settlements were included (Arndt 1956: 251; Schweizer 1984: 152). Κώμας (*kōmas*, villages) stands in contrast to Jesus' instructions in 9:5 about what to do in the πόλις (*polis*, city). The change may well indicate that the campaign was widespread, hitting cities and villages (8:1; Schürmann 1969: 504).[18] Comprehensiveness is also suggested by the reference to "everyplace" (πανταχοῦ, *pantachou*), which grammatically describes where both the preaching and healing occurred (Plummer 1896: 240). Everywhere the Twelve went, such work resulted. As Schürmann notes, the description depicts the intensity of the ministry in each locale, as opposed to being an indication of the extent of ministry in terms of every possible locale.

Mark 6:12–13 is a similar summary, but with more detail. Mark notes that the disciples' message was one of calling people to repent. They also cast out demons and anointed people with oil as they healed them. Omitting the repentance theme seems odd for Luke, since he uses it elsewhere. Matthew lacks any such summary since he has chosen instead to present Jesus' command directly.

Summary In Luke 9:1–6, Jesus extends his ministry by sharing his authority. With the Twelve, he takes the message to the entire region. Their subject is the kingdom of God, and their confirmation comes in healing and exorcism. By empowering them with his authority, Jesus testifies to their authority as God's representatives. The word goes out to ever larger circles. Rather than many coming to Jesus to hear the message, now Jesus takes the gospel to them.

The disciples are to learn to depend on God as they journey. They are to travel with no extra provisions. They are to live differently from others who travel with a religious message. They are to rely on those who respond to supply their fundamental needs. Their authority is not for personal gain. As they travel, they are to stay in one place, once they enter a city. If there is no response, they are to leave and symbolically say "good riddance" to those

18. Relying on Mark 6:6 and suggesting that Luke 9:5 is influenced by 10:8–11, Bovon 1989: 459 and Schürmann 1969: 504 say that Jesus worked the cities and left the Twelve to train in the towns. But this argument is circular (what is 10:8–11 influenced by?), for the Matthean parallel mentions cities as well (10:5, 11 [probably], 14). It is better to regard the switch as intentional to show ministry in towns and cities. Jesus' woes in Luke 10:13–15 suggest that cities were involved in the mission.

they leave behind. The Twelve thus depart and minister as Jesus' ministry expands in new directions. The reader is to recognize that seeing and hearing the Twelve is seeing and hearing Jesus. The reader also sees that ministry involves a simple lifestyle committed to dependence on God. The disciples' form of ministry stands in contrast to other peddlers of religion and philosophy. Modesty is the rule, ministry is the focus.

Additional Notes

9:1. Many key manuscripts ($\mathfrak{P}^{75}$, A, B, D, W, Δ, family 1, one Itala manuscript, Byz) read δώδεκα (the Twelve). Other variants speak of "his Twelve" (some Syriac and one Coptic manuscript), "his disciples" (a few Lect), "his Twelve disciples" (C^3, Lect, many Itala, Diatessaron), or "the Twelve apostles" (א, C*, L, Θ, Ξ, Ψ, family 13, many Itala, Vulgate, some Syriac). The reading δώδεκα clearly has better manuscript support and is the shorter reading (Marshall 1978: 351; Fitzmyer 1981: 753).

9:2. Two variants describe the sick: ἀσθενεῖς (א, A, D, L, Ξ, Ψ, family 1, Itala, Vulgate, some Syriac) or ἀσθενοῦντας (C, W, Δ, Θ, family 13, Byz, Lect). Matthew 10:8 has the latter form, a participle. A third, shorter reading lacks the object entirely (B, some Syriac). The presence of ἀσθενεῖς in a variety of manuscripts and versions speaks for its inclusion (Arndt 1956: 250; UBS–NA).[19]

---

19. The shorter reading (i.e., ἰᾶσθαι without any object) has been found in critical texts since Westcott-Hort. Recent texts bracket the object, expressing uncertainty about its presence, even though they retain it.

e. Herod's Questions about Jesus (9:7–9)

Luke places Herod's reaction to Jesus after the mission of the Twelve (so also Mark 6:14–16). The impression is that Jesus' regional activity gets Herod's attention. Both Jesus' message and miracles raise the question of who he is. The popular musings that followed the raising of the widow of Nain's son reach Herod (Luke 7:16).[1] He hears and reflects upon the speculations about Jesus as a prophetic figure. The very curiosity and interest that Herod has is the type of reflection that Luke wishes his reader to have. Other "who is this?" questions appear in 7:19–20, 49; 8:25, while Jesus' identity is considered or confessed in 4:34, 41; 7:16; 8:28; 9:7–9, 18–20 (Schürmann 1969: 505).[2] Herod will meet Jesus in 23:6–12. His curiosity here literarily sets up that later meeting (Tannehill 1986: 196–97).

Sources and Historicity

Not only does Mark 6:14–16 supply a parallel, but so does Matt. 14:1–2 (Aland 1985: §143). Matthew's treatment, which is the shortest, follows the discourse on kingdom parables and the crowd's offense at Jesus' teaching. Mark and Luke relate the timing to the mission of the Twelve (Plummer 1896: 240). Matthew simply recounts Herod's opinion that Jesus is a resurrected John the Baptist, something that Mark notes but Luke lacks. Mark describes the public speculation about Jesus: he is either a resurrected John the Baptist, Elijah, or one of the prophets. Mark then notes that Herod agrees with the Baptist option. Luke is close to Mark in giving the popular speculation and Herod's reaction. But only Luke notes Herod's indecision about who Jesus is and his desire to see Jesus. In the present passage Luke only alludes to Herod's slaying of John, whose death Luke has already noted (3:19–20).[3]

1. Talbert 1986: 102 may overplay the differences between Luke and the other Gospels. Matthew and Mark clearly have Herod express the view that Jesus is John the Baptist raised from the dead. Luke has Herod ask only who Jesus is. But this is not really a significant difference; see the exegesis of 9:9. Talbert also notes that this is one of two passages where the question of Jesus' identity is raised directly (9:18 is the other).

2. In recalling the questions of 8:25, 28, this unit looks back to the miracles in Luke 8, which justifies seeing a unit running from 8:22 to 9:17. "Who Jesus is" dominates this section.

3. Fitzmyer 1981: 757 notes six Lucan modifications of Mark: (1) the Lucan use of the title τετραάρχης (tetrarch) (as in 3:1) versus the title βασιλεύς (king); (2) a ref-

As Luke concludes his Galilean section, he will not parallel the material in Mark 6:45–8:26 (Fitzmyer 1981: 756). The next passage, the feeding of the five thousand, is the last event of the Galilean ministry related to Mark. This is known in NT studies as the "great omission," because it is peculiar that so much material would be omitted if Luke used Mark. Solutions include positing that Luke had access to a version of Mark that lacked this material (an "*Ur*-Markus") or that Luke consciously chose to omit this material, mainly because many of the events in it were similar to events already treated. Neither of these explanations is totally compelling. Thus, the presence of the omission is a major problem for those who hold that Mark's is the first Gospel and that Luke used it.[4] Any credible support for Marcan priority must at least attempt to explain this anomaly. The effect of the omission has an impact on Luke 9:7–9, for the differing arrangement moves us quickly from Herod's speculation into the contrastive apostolic confession of Jesus in 9:19–27 (Marshall 1978: 355). In this arrangement, the christological question of 9:7–9 receives a quick answer.

Form critically, the passage is a story about Jesus, since it contains so much narrative and focuses on his person.[5] The outline of Luke 9:7–9 is as follows:

   i. Popular reports about Jesus reach Herod (9:7–8)
  ii. Herod's desire to see Jesus (9:9)

The passage reveals the widening effect of Jesus' ministry. News about Jesus reaches into the palace (cf. 8:3). Popular speculation about Jesus' identity leads to uncertainty at the top of society, as Herod's perplexity about Jesus' identity shows. Herod's

---

erence to τὰ γινόμενα πάντα (all that has happened) instead of just to miracles; (3) a unique reference to Herod's perplexity; (4) the use of threefold ὅτι for the reports of popular speculation about Jesus; (5) the "who is this?" question; and (6) the note about a desire to see Jesus. Most see no sources here outside of Mark; Schürmann 1969: 508; Bovon 1989: 461–62; Schramm 1971: 128.

4. The "*Ur*-Markus" hypothesis attempts to explain the omission, but there is no clear evidence of such a source. One might as well posit oral or other sources. The "doublet" explanation works only for some passages, and thus is not a comprehensive answer. Luke has no real equivalents to Mark 7:24–30; 8:14–21; and possibly 6:45–52. Other passages can be put in the "doublet" category: nature miracles (Mark 6:45–52), healing summaries (6:53–56), legal issues (7:1–23), healings (7:31–37; 8:22–26), miraculous provision of food (8:1–10), and the demand for signs (8:11–13). But Luke can have doublets, as his multiple Sabbath healings show (Luke 4:31–44; 6:6–11; 13:10–17; 14:1–6). See excursus 9.

5. V. Taylor 1935: 147; Fitzmyer 1981: 757. Bultmann 1963: 301–2 does not discuss Luke 9, but the longer parallel of Mark 6:14–29. Berger 1984: 233 speaks of an "uncertain acclamation" present within the account.

curiosity about Jesus leads to a desire to see Jesus. And, as often occurs in this section, there is a reflective "who is this?" question.

Exegesis and Exposition

[7]Now Herod the tetrarch heard all about what was done, and he was perplexed, because it was said by some that John had been raised from the dead, [8]by some that Elijah had appeared, and by others that one of the old prophets had risen. [9]Herod said, "John I beheaded; but who is this about whom I hear such things?" And he was seeking to see him.

i. Popular Reports about Jesus Reach Herod (9:7–8)

9:7   A report comes to Herod about the progress and development of the Jesus movement. Herod Antipas was the political ruler of Galilee and Perea from 4 B.C. to A.D. 39 (Luke 3:1). Matthew 14:1 and Luke use the technical title, τετραάρχης (tetraarchēs, tetrarch), while Mark 6:14 chooses the more descriptive, functional characterization of βασιλεύς (basileus, king) (Marshall 1978: 355; Matt. 14:9 also uses the title βασιλεύς; Schramm 1971: 128). The choice of τετραάρχης might avoid offense to Gentiles since βασιλεύς could be politically volatile. The report reaches Herod in the form of popular attempts to describe who Jesus is. Herod is perplexed by the variety of opinions. The imperfect tense διηπόρει (diēporei, was perplexed or, better, was remaining perplexed) contrasts with the aorist of the report: ἤκουσεν (ēkousen, he heard).[6] Herod was trying to sort out who Jesus was, given the many options raised.

One suggestion is that Jesus is a resurrected John the Baptist. This opinion is Herod's in Mark 6:16 = Matt. 14:2, but Luke lacks such a comment. It appears from the other Gospels this is the suggestion that Herod decided was most likely. Matthew and Mark both mention that Herod was responding to the reports about what Jesus had done, specifically his miraculous works, while Luke's language is sufficiently broad to suggest that the report of the mission reached Herod's ears. Ellis (1974: 137) suggests that the similarity between Jesus' message and John's call to repent is what produced the association with a resurrected John. Herod may have meant "John is Jesus" in a loose sense of "this is like John all over again" (Creed 1930: 127) or "Jesus has the spirit of John" (Schweizer 1984: 153). The only other possibility is a type of reincarnation of John, a belief that has no real parallel and thus is unlikely (Schürmann 1969: 506–7). The remark makes clear that John the Baptist was dead by this point (Fitzmyer 1981: 759).

---

6. Διαπορέω (to be perplexed) is used only in Luke–Acts in the NT: here; Acts 2:12; 5:24; 10:17; BAGD 187; BAA 376.

Two other popular suggestions added to Herod's perplexity. Some **9:8** suggested that Elijah had appeared. It is difficult to know whether this identifies Jesus specifically with Malachi's promised prophet (Mal. 3:1; 4:5 [3:1, 24 MT]) or whether it is an indirect way of saying that Jesus is a prophet of the eschaton.[7] The specific reference to Elijah is more likely, since the third suggestion, that Jesus is one of the old prophets raised, is also general. The Elijah description clearly recognizes that Jesus is from God and probably suggests an awareness that he calls the nation to repent.

The last idea, of a returning prophet of old, was common in Judaism. Prophets who were suggested to be returning include Moses, Jeremiah, and Isaiah (2 Macc. 2:4–7; 15:13–14; 2 Esdr. [= 4 Ezra] 2:18; Matt. 16:14; Fitzmyer 1981: 759). The description reflects popular respect for Jesus (Josephus, *Antiquities* 12.10.6 §413; Delling, *TDNT* 1:487; Friedrich, *TDNT* 6:842 §D.V.3). Jesus as prophet recalls the view of the crowd in Luke 7:11–17.

Mark 6:15 is parallel to Luke here, except in describing Jesus' relation to the prophets of old. Mark says he is like (ὡς, *hōs*) them, not that he is one of them raised. Of course, popular characterizations existed in a variety of forms and therefore could be summarized in various ways. This is, then, simply two ways of saying the same thing, since the idea of a raised prophet may describe only the coming of a figure who mirrors an earlier figure. It could well be that Luke is explaining Mark's remark, since the idea of raising up someone may simply refer to someone coming on the scene (Plummer 1896: 241; Fitzmyer 1981: 759; CD 6.10–11 shows this sense). Since Matthew relates only Herod's opinion, these other popular identifications are not raised by him (if one posits Matthean priority, then Luke has additional source material here).

ii. Herod's Desire to See Jesus (9:9)

Herod's deliberation about the opinions leaves the issue of Jesus' **9:9** identity unresolved. The reply seems to be, "John is no longer with us, I slew him, so who could this be?" The implication is that Jesus is some unidentified agent of God, but Herod cannot be more specific until he sees Jesus. Thus, he has a strong desire to see Jesus and determine who he is (the imperfect ἐζήτει, *ezētei*, expresses this desire with durative force: "He was seeking to see him").

The Lucan passage differs from Matt. 14:2 = Mark 6:16, where Herod suggests that he sees Jesus as John the Baptist raised from the dead. These writers appear to give Herod's resolution of the is-

---

7. On the Elijah hope in Judaism, see Luke 1:17; 7:26–27; Bock 1987: 59–60, 295; Jeremias, *TDNT* 2:936.

sue, not the deliberation that Luke supplies (see Luce 1933: 177–78). Later, Herod has alleged malice and curiosity toward Jesus (Luke 13:31; 23:8–15; Ellis 1974: 137). Luke pursues Jesus' identity against the backdrop of popular uncertainty about who Jesus is. In fact, the disciples wrestled in a similar way with Jesus' identity (8:25; cf. 5:21; 7:20, 49; Fitzmyer 1981: 759). Thus, when Peter gives his confession, it stands out, not only because Luke recounts the confession in closer proximity to Herod's opinion, but also because Luke portrays more consistently the uncertainty over Jesus' identity.

Summary   Luke 9:7–9 shows that the word about Jesus is not only spreading to the palace, it is getting attention there. As is the case with any major popular figure, assessments about him abound. Is he John the Baptist reappeared? Is he the eschatological prophet Elijah? Or is he one of the other prophets? Herod is initially uncertain about which of the options is true and thus wants to see Jesus. Such uncertainty about Jesus is only natural when one views him at a distance through the reports of others. Almost all regard Jesus as sent from God, but who exactly is he? The testimony that counts is from those who encountered him directly, testimony like that the disciples are about to give (9:20). But the issue of Jesus' identity needs to be considered by all. Even those in the highest places have to consider who he is. All must decide where they think Jesus fits.

f. Authority to Provide Revealed (9:10–17)

After the commission of the Twelve and Herod's fundamental question, Luke has the feeding of the five thousand, a miracle that appears in all four Gospels (Matt. 14:13–21 = Mark 6:32–44 = John 6:1–15; Aland 1985: §146). This miracle portrays Jesus' capacity to meet needs and shows that he can provide for life (Ellis 1974: 138). An additional theme is Jesus' ability to provide what the disciples cannot provide for themselves (Marshall 1978: 357). In fact, Jesus is instructing his disciples about trust and his work through them. They are stewards who are to depend upon him (Tannehill 1986: 216). There are OT parallels for what Jesus does here. Both Moses with the manna and quail (Exod. 16; Num. 11) and Elisha with barley bread (2 Kings 4:42–44) were intermediaries for such material provision to the people, though of course the real source was God (Marshall 1978: 357; Ernst 1977: 289; Tannehill 1986: 217). Despite these conceptual allusions, there is no direct verbal relationship between Luke and the OT (Wiefel 1988: 174); rather Luke has strictly a conceptual association with prophetic activity. In addition, some of the event's wording parallels the Last Supper, where bread pictures the teaching about the presence of God's blessing, a theme that indicates the feeding's spiritual point (Creed 1930: 127–28; Luke 9:16–17 with 22:19; possibly 24:30). Luke's version of the account is more succinct than Matthew's or Mark's.

In Luke this miracle precedes Peter's crucial confession that Jesus is the Christ. The general location of the event in all four Gospels is the same, though Luke has no intervening events between the feeding and the confession (see the introduction to 9:18–20 and excursus 9). That confession serves to climax the Galilean ministry. The events after the confession that bring the Galilean section to an end focus on the disciples only, not the public (9:22–50; Plummer 1896: 242; Arndt 1956: 254; Ellis 1974: 138).[1]

---

1. After this passage, only 9:37–43 is a public event, but even there the point is the disciples' failure. Luke 9:10–17 and 9:37–43 are the last two public moments in the Galilean section.

Sources and Historicity

Mark 8:1–10 = Matt. 15:32–39 (Aland 1985: §153) has a second feeding account located closer to Peter's confession. In this second miracle, Jesus feeds four thousand. The two feedings should be kept separate, since the feeding of the five thousand is given in such verbally exact form between the three Synoptics.[2] Luke alludes only to the first of these two feedings, since his narrative verbally ties into the first account only. Still, most argue that the two accounts reflect a single tradition (Fitzmyer 1981: 762; Van Der Loos 1965: 619–20). The basic arguments for one tradition are that the first event, if it really were distinct, would not have been so quickly forgotten, as Mark 8:4 suggests, when the disciples on this supposed second occasion ask from where the food will come. In other words, if Jesus had done this before, surely they would not ask. In addition, for many, the crowd is too great for such an event. However, this approach underestimates the unusual character of Jesus' work, which would take awhile for the disciples to accept as everyday business. So, the disciples' uncertainty on this second occasion is understandable. What Luke's shorter presentation stresses is that Jesus is now turning his attention to the disciples, as he teaches them about following him and ministering through him. The Jesus Seminar (Funk and Hoover 1993: 311–12) treats the dialogue in this unit with the same skepticism with which they evaluated all the miracles, printing, as they do, Jesus' words in black type. But such a facile objection based solely on form should be rejected (see the discussion of sources and historicity for 8:40–56).

This account is considered a miracle story. Some call it a nature miracle (Fitzmyer 1981: 763; Bultmann 1963: 217). However, Bovon (1989: 469) criticizes this classification as too vague, since Jesus does not really act on nature, but rather provides food.[3] He prefers to call it a gift miracle, which is a more precise description (so also Theissen 1983: 321, 103–6). Berger (1984: 255, 317) speaks of a "mandatio," which means Jesus is teaching his disciples to obey him. The outline of Luke 9:10–17 is as follows:

   i. Apostles' report (9:10a)
  ii. Feeding of the five thousand (9:10b–17)
     (1) Setting (9:10b–11)

---

2. Compare Matt. 14:19–20 = Mark 6:39–42 = Luke 9:14–17 in the first feeding account (the Johannine parallel is John 6:1–15). Bovon 1989: 467 notes that the second Marcan feeding and John's single feeding miracle show little influence on Luke 9:10–17. He does note two points of agreement between John's miracle and Luke: (1) the reference to the crowds following Jesus in Luke 9:11 = John 6:2 and (2) the number of the crowd given as five thousand in Luke 6:14 = John 6:10.

3. Schürmann 1969: 524 notes that the account is not a typical miracle account. There is no crowd reaction and no call for help.

(2) Problem (9:12)
(3) Disciples' inability (9:13)
(4) Jesus' provision (9:14–16)
(5) Extent of provision (9:17)

The account notes the success of the apostolic mission, which is short-lived in light of events that follow this account. Jesus continues to draw large followings, and he continues to teach the kingdom and to heal. The disciples are instructed about Jesus and provision. They minister through his provision. Jesus is seen as the provider of life who fully satisfies others with more than what they need.

Exegesis and Exposition

[10]And when the apostles returned, they told him all that they had done. And he took them and withdrew privately to a city called Bethsaida. [11]When the crowds learned about it, they followed him. And welcoming them, he was speaking about the kingdom of God and cured those who had need of healing.

[12]Now the day began to wear away; and the Twelve came and said to him, "Send the crowd away so they may go into the surrounding villages and towns to lodge and get provisions, for we are in a deserted locale." [13]But he said to them, "You give them something to eat." But they said, "We have no more than five loaves and two fish—unless we go and buy food for all these people." [14]And there were about five thousand men. And he said to the disciples, "Make them sit down in groups of about fifty each." [15]And they did so and made them all sit down. [16]Taking the five loaves of bread and the two fish and looking into heaven, he blessed them and broke and gave them to the disciples to set before the crowd. [17]And all ate and were filled, and the leftovers were taken up by them, twelve large baskets of broken pieces.

i. Apostles' Report (9:10a)

Luke accomplishes two things at once. First, he wraps up the mission report on the Twelve, whom he here calls ἀπόστολοι (*apostoloi*, apostles). The return to the issue of 9:1–6 begins a series of quick transitions in this chapter. In a brief space, one sees the mission, the view from the palace, the result of the mission, and the popular response. Upon the disciples' return, they report to Jesus all that had happened. Διηγήσαντο (*diēgēsanto*, they recounted) is a significant term, since it is the verbal form of the noun that appeared in Luke's preface to describe the reports about Jesus' ministry (Fitzmyer 1981: 764–65), although here the report is oral, not written. Thus, the disciples narrate the events of mission. Luke mentions no details other than to speak of what they had done (ὅσα ἐποίησαν, *hosa epoiēsan*), but it seems clear that the mission was a busy one.

9:10a

ii. Feeding of the Five Thousand (9:10b–17)
(1) Setting (9:10b–11)

9:10b Second, Luke sets up the circumstances of the miracle. After such an intense experience, it is natural to seek some rest. So Jesus takes the Twelve and withdraws privately to Bethsaida.[4] They apparently plan to get some solitude and rest, but the desired seclusion does not develop, due to continued interest in Jesus.

Bethsaida was a city in the tetrarchy of Philip, located on the northeast corner of the Sea of Galilee.[5] Mark 6:45 says that immediately after the feeding the disciples were told by Jesus to embark and engage in a journey to the opposite side of the sea to Bethsaida, a district clearly on the lake's west coast. Did the feeding occur in Bethsaida or did the disciples go to Bethsaida after the feeding? Some argue for two Bethsaidas because of this passage. The discussion is complicated by the popular description of this northeastern Bethsaida as part of Galilee, though technically it was in Gaulanitis.[6] This city, then, was outside Herod's jurisdiction (Ellis 1974: 138). The locale's name means "place of hunting," not "place of satisfaction" (so Danker 1972: 112, a view not mentioned in the second edition of his commentary); but Luke makes nothing of the name (Fitzmyer 1981: 765).

The picture of withdrawal for solitude is also noted in Matt. 14:13 = Mark 6:32, where reference is made to withdrawing specifically by boat to a lonely place. What appears to be in view is a withdrawal to the region of Bethsaida as opposed to a stop in the northeastern city per se.[7] Or, perhaps, Jesus and the disciples started in the city and ended up outside of it by the time the crowds arrived (Marshall 1978: 359). By the time of the feeding, a large crowd had come outside the city. The reference in Matt. 14:13 = Mark 6:32 to ἔρημον

4. The idiom κατ' ἰδίαν means "privately, apart, alone" or "lonely" (when referring to an isolated place); BAGD 370 §4; BAA 752–53; Luke 10:23; Acts 23:19, and fourteen times elsewhere in the NT.

5. On the discussion of the exact locale of the city, whether it is on or just north of the sea, see Arndt 1956: 253–54. John 6:1 calls this sea the "Sea of Tiberias."

6. So Arndt 1956: 254 argues for two Bethsaidas; otherwise Fitzmyer 1981: 765–66; Godet 1875: 1.404–5 (who sees many places with this name along the lake, since the name is a generic description); Ptolemy, *Geography* 5.16.4. Cf. Josephus's use of "Gaulanite" in *Antiquities* 18.1.1 §4 and "Galilean" in 18.1.6 §23. A region is addressed, not just a populated locale, as the dilemma about food makes clear. Bethsaida may be nothing more than temporary "headquarters" for mission in the region. Arndt and Godet may be right about the Marcan reference being a distinct locale using a generic name. John 12:21 may confirm the distinction.

7. Arndt 1956: 255 notes that εἰς can mean "toward" as well as "into," though whether Luke is being this precise is uncertain. He may simply be noting the center of activity.

τόπον (erēmon topon) is not a reference to a desert but to a lonely place; thus, the later references to grass are not a problem either (Van Der Loos 1965: 621; Kittel, *TDNT* 2:657–58). Arndt (1956: 253) suggests various reasons for the withdrawal, besides the obvious need for rest after the mission: Herod's attention, the fanaticism of the Galilean followers (John 6:15), and the rising hostility of Jewish opposition, which would create a need to begin preparing the disciples, most especially the Twelve. Luke, however, does not indicate that the disciples knew of Herod's concerns yet. So, for Luke the withdrawal seems to be for privacy and instruction.

The attempt to withdraw was not successful. Crowds still longed to gather around Jesus. When they learned where he was, they went out to him. In Luke's language, they followed him (ἠκολούθησαν, *ēkolouthēsan*). When the crowds came, they were not turned away but "welcomed" (ἀποδεξάμενος, *apodexamenos*) (Plummer 1896: 243; this term also occurs in Luke 8:40 and Acts 28:30). Jesus treated the crowd in his typical manner. He was speaking continually about the kingdom and healing those who needed healing, two key characteristics of his ministry in Luke (4:38–44; 6:17–19; 7:22).[8] Of course, the disciples had just done the same things on their mission (9:6).

9:11

Luke is more detailed in his comments than Mark 6:34 = Matt. 14:14. In distinct wording, Matthew mentions that Jesus had compassion on the crowd and healed the sick. These remarks do not come from the same source as Luke's; or, if they do, each writer has gone his own way in wording the point (Creed 1930: 129; Fitzmyer 1981: 766). Mark also mentions Jesus' compassion, but in addition explains that Jesus had compassion because the people were like sheep without a shepherd, an allusion to Num. 27:17 and 1 Kings 22:17. Mark also mentions that Jesus taught the crowd many things. Schürmann (1969: 513) notes that the Marcan text is influenced by the wording of Ps. 23. Only Luke associates both healing and teaching here and gives the subject of the teaching as the kingdom (Creed 1930: 128). In addition, Jesus is about to provide for the crowd.

(2) Problem (9:12)

As the day winds down, probably nearing sunset, the Twelve perceive the approach of a significant problem.[9] Jesus' teaching continues to hold the crowd, the crowd is large (five thousand men; 9:14),

9:12

---

8. Ἐλάλει could be translated "was continually speaking." On λαλέω (to speak) in Luke, see Jaschke 1971.

9. On ἡμέρα (day) with κλίνω (to decline), see BAGD 436 §2; BAA 887–88. Luke 24:29 speaks of the day "wearing down"; Plummer 1896: 243; cf. Jer. 6:4; Judg. 19:11.

and there is no food or lodging for such a great throng. The NT *hapax legomenon* ἐπισιτισμόν (*episitismon*) refers to basic daily needs (BAGD 298; BAA 604; LSJ 656). The disciples suggest that it is time to wrap up so that all these people can journey into the villages of the surrounding area to find food and shelter. The request seems reasonable enough and reflects the Twelve's sensitivity. However, Jesus sees the problem as an opportunity to teach the disciples something important.

The parallels in Mark 6:35 = Matt. 14:15 are close to one another. Luke's wording is slightly distinct, but says virtually the same thing. Luke is the only writer to suggest the need for lodging as well as for food. This detail is unaddressed in the rest of the account, but the suggestion may be that if food is taken care of, then other types of provision need not be a major concern. In addition, the note about lodging may suggest that the crowd is not made up of just local people. Some have traveled some distance to listen to Jesus (Marshall 1978: 360). Fitzmyer (1981: 766) argues that the note is literary, for where would five thousand people find lodging in this area (also Schürmann 1969: 515, who speaks of haggadic techniques)? This argument overreads the passage to insist that few local people were present. Yet surely many, but not all, who were present would be local. John 6:5 has Jesus initiate the discussion with an awareness of what he would do. Of course, the Synoptics and John have summarized in distinct ways what was a much longer discussion. John has more detail of how Jesus handled the issue as a lesson for the disciples, so John picks up the discussion at a later point.

(3) Disciples' Inability (9:13)

9:13 Next comes Jesus' surprising response. Since the Twelve are sensitive to the issue, Jesus suggests that they solve the problem and provide food for the crowd. This limits the options, as far as the Twelve are concerned: either they share what they have (which is not enough) or they journey into town and pick up enough food for all (which would be quite a task).[10] The one option they do not consider is to ask Jesus to provide the food. The discussion has an OT parallel in 2 Kings 4:42–44.[11] A prophetic picture exists here, though John alone of all the accounts will present the miracle in terms of provision of manna (Exod. 16). Each writer is focusing in on the event with his own emphases.

10. The latter option is expressed as the protasis of a conditional sentence, as is seen by the use of the subjunctive ἀγοράσωμεν with εἰ μήτι: "unless we should go buy"; Marshall 1978: 360; BDF §376.

11. For other OT and rabbinic parallels, see Van Der Loos 1965: 624–27, but these parallels deal more with the constant availability of food.

It is at this point that John 6:5–7 picks up the account. John shares with Mark 6:37 the remark that around two hundred denarii would be needed to buy enough food. This is more than seven months' basic wage, since a denarius was a day's basic wage. Mark gives the mentioned figure, and John notes that it would not be enough to do the job. Luke has no reference to the cost of buying the food and thus makes no point that such a purchase would be expensive. John specifies Philip as the source of the remark. John also notes that the currently available food consists of five loaves and two fish, a remark he notes came from Andrew (Bovon 1989: 471 rightly rejects any symbolic force to the numbers). A limited menu of fish and barley bread was available, but not for five thousand![12] Mark 6:38 = Matt. 14:17 notes the amount of food, as does Luke, though the discussion in Mark and Matthew proceeds in the reverse order of "should we go?" and then the mention of the amount of food currently available. Through literary compression, Mark mentions that the crowd possessed the food, while Luke speaks of the disciples ("we") possessing the food. The disciples have little food available to them. The Gospels communicate the disciples' perception that Jesus' request to provide food is a difficult one. Fitzmyer (1981: 766) notes that on the surface Jesus' request is more unsuitable than the disciples' approach to sending the crowd away. However, OT precedent and recent precedent (i.e., Jesus' bestowing power for mission; Luke 9:1–6) show that the request is not so unusual. By the time of the Book of Acts, the disciples will know from where such authority and provision come (Acts 3:6, 13, 16; 4:10–12).

(4) Jesus' Provision (9:14–16)

Jesus deals with the problem by asking the disciples to have the five thousand men (ἄνδρες, *andres*) sit in groups of fifty, which would result in about one hundred such groups. Why this was done is not clear, though perhaps it would make distribution of the food easier. Some note a parallel to Moses in Exod. 18:21 and Deut. 1:15 (Ellis 1974: 138; Danker 1988: 192; 1QS 2.21–22; 1Q28a [= 1QSa = Rule Annex] 1.14–15; 2.1). However, as Fitzmyer (1981: 767) notes, the parallel is distant, since the groupings in those passages range from one thousand down to ten. Thus, Hendriksen's attempt (1978: 480) to associate the church with the New Israel on this basis misses the mark. Regardless, by separating the crowd in this manner, a good size estimate was possible.

9:14

---

12. John 6:9 mentions barley loaves. On this kind of food, see Van Der Loos 1965: 622 n. 3. SB 1:683–84 notes that barley bread was not well liked.

Matthew lacks any mention of the crowd's preparation. John 6:10 simply mentions they were made to sit and that about five thousand were there. Mark 6:44 notes at a later point that five thousand were present, while 6:39–40 mentions that Jesus commanded them to sit, which they did in groups of fifties and hundreds. Mark also notes that they sat on grass (also Matt. 14:19). This detail, along with John 6:4 (which notes that the Passover was near), places the event in the spring. With regard to the numbers, either Luke's account is briefer (while Mark has more specifics) or Mark notes the result that emerged. The term used of the groupings, κλισία (*klisia*), a NT *hapax legomenon*, simply refers to a reclining group, though it often refers to a group present for a meal (BAGD 436; BAA 888; LSJ 961).

9:15 The disciples follow through on Jesus' instruction. With the crowd clustered in groups, Jesus turns to meet the crowd's need. Some suggest that this is a symbolic picture of the Eucharist (Ernst 1977: 291). In fact, some who hold this liturgical position suggest that this—rather than historical concerns—motivates the account. This approach appears to read meaning into the event, at least in the Lucan version. John 6:14 does describe the event as a sign, and later (John 6:22–59) Jesus calls himself the "bread of life." However, Luke makes nothing of this point, so nothing specifically sacramental exists in his description. Jesus—not a sacrament—is revealed here (Van Der Loos 1965: 634–35).

9:16 Jesus feeds the crowd, and the disciples learn about provision. Jesus breaks the food in front of them and then allows them to distribute it to the people in a picture of mediated provision given by Jesus through the disciples. Thus, while Jesus performs the miracle, the disciples in fact provide food for the crowd, just as Jesus asked them to do in 9:13. They minister through his power and provision, a lesson that will become a focus of Jesus' teaching in Luke 9–19. The events of Acts 2–5 will help them understand what it means. Just as the disciples are "fishers of people" (Luke 5:10), they are also "providers of the basic food of life." Some speak of Jesus' miracles as "acted out parables," an apt description here.

The term λαβών (*labōn*, taking) recalls two other meals that Jesus will have with his disciples, for taking and breaking bread appear in 22:19 and 24:30. The latter passage is only conceptually parallel, since it has no other verbal contact. The basic picture is of Jesus as provider. The thanksgiving that he offers shows his dependence on and gratitude to God. There is a little debate whether Jesus blesses the food or gives thanks "with respect to" the food because God has provided it (Marshall 1978: 362). A metonymy may be present, where food is mentioned for what it reflects: God's blessing and resultant joy. A decision is difficult, though Luce's idea (1933: 180) that blessing food is a magical concept is surely wrong. A standard Jewish blessing, *m. Ber.* 6.1, suggests that Marshall may be correct that thanksgiving to God is offered. Objects are blessed in other NT texts, so that a clear decision is not possible (Mark 8:7; 1 Cor. 10:16; Schürmann 1969: 517 n. 143).

How was food made available? This issue has been greatly debated ever since miracles were first questioned. Various interpretations of the account are set forth (Van Der Loos 1965: 627–31; Arndt 1956: 256; Luce 1933: 181):

1. The absence of any reference to "wonder" by the crowd shows that Jesus' example of sharing led others to share their food (H. E. G. Paulus as cited by Van Der Loos 1965: 627 n. 3). However, according to John 6:14, the crowd does indeed react by describing the event as prophetic. The note about Jesus' person is the functional equivalent to a note about wonder. Its absence in the Synoptics reflects their focus on the disciples as the main figures in the narrative. In addition, not every miracle has a note of wonder (Matt. 9:18–26; Luke 14:1–6; Mark 10:46–52).
2. The supply came from wealthy ladies in the group (P. Nahor as cited by Van Der Loos 1965: 628 n. 3). But no mention of ladies exists in any of these accounts.
3. The stories are simple imitation of OT accounts about Moses (Strauss 1972: 516–17 [originally 1835]; cited by Van Der Loos 1965: 628 n. 4).[13] The account does have OT connections, but they hardly are sufficient to produce it.
4. Jesus broke the food into little bits for everyone and, as a result, all were not really filled (A. Schweitzer as cited by Van Der Loos 1965: 628 nn. 5–6). This was a messianic feast that was transformed into a miracle in its telling.
5. The account is allegorical and symbolic (Van Der Loos 1965: 629).
6. Jesus hypnotized the crowd into believing that they were filled (H. Schäfer and R. Otto as cited by Van Der Loos 1965: 629 n. 2).
7. Jesus is trying to organize another group to forsake all and follow him into the wilderness (R. Eisler as cited by Van Der Loos 1965: 629–30).

Van Der Loos's conclusion (1965: 630) is worth quoting: "It is without doubt a fascinating business to investigate how human ingenuity reaches new heights in its efforts to eliminate the supernatural

---

13. Arndt 1956: 256 mentions 1 Kings 17:15 and 2 Kings 4:5–6, though he rejects the view that this account was created to parallel the OT.

from the story of the feeding." B. Weiss remarks that the text clearly intends the event to be seen as a miracle (as cited by Plummer 1896: 245). The story may reveal more about the interpreter's view of how God works than the interpreter reveals about what really happened.

We are not told exactly how the food grew to feed so many, but it is clear that Jesus was miraculously responsible for it. Most older expositors posit that the food multiplied in Jesus' hands (Augustine) or that it grew in the disciples' hands (Calvin). The imperfect ἐδίδου (*edidou*, he continued to give) suggests that the former is the narrative's perspective (Arndt 1956: 256). Jesus' creative capacity is addressed in the account in much the same way as in the Cana miracle (John 2:1–11). The meeting of needs and the filling of God's people through amazing provision recall OT promises (Ps. 37:19; 81:16 [81:17 MT]; 132:15; 145:15–16; Van Der Loos 1965: 634 n. 4; Fitzmyer 1981: 764). Hauck notes that the food in Exod. 16:18 was just enough for each person, while Jesus' provision had leftovers (*TDNT* 6:59). An event greater than the exodus provision occurs. The people feast at the feet of one who is about to be confessed as Messiah, as he trains his disciples to depend on his ability to meet needs.

The verse's wording is almost verbally exact with Mark 6:41 = Matt. 14:19b. The reference to blessing "them" (αὐτούς, *autous*) is not present in either Matthew or Mark. All five verbal actions are part of all the Synoptics: took (the bread), looked up, gave thanks, broke, and distributed. Noting that all but the second action (looking up) reoccur in the Last Supper accounts, Fitzmyer (1981: 767–68) sees the terms as eucharistic language. However, these actions might be common at any distribution of food and need not have explicitly eucharistic roots. Marshall (1978: 361) notes the differences from the Last Supper: the meal is not a Passover meal; more than the disciples are present; fish as the second element is present, not wine; and no interpretation of the food's significance is given. John 6:11 says that Jesus distributes the food, but that means only that he is the source of the distribution.

(5) Extent of Provision (9:17)

9:17   The account's conclusion reveals the extent of the provision: all present ate and had their fill. The reference to πάντες (*pantes*, all) trailing at the end of the clause is slightly emphatic: "They ate and were filled all." Using large carrying baskets (κόφινος, *kophinos*; BAGD 447; BAA 909), the disciples took up a collection of the leftovers.[14] Baskets like these varied in size, but one account speaks of

---

14. Outside of the four uses in these parallels, κόφινος occurs only in Matt. 16:9 = Mark 8:19.

a basket holding twenty rocks (they were used by the army to collect rocks). In Jewish circles, the firstfruits of harvest were carried in such baskets (MM 357; Hort 1908–9). Josephus humorously describes the Roman soldier's equipment, among which was a basket. So loaded down with equipment was this soldier that Josephus said he was "almost as heavily laden as a pack mule" (*Jewish War* 3.5.5 §95). Another possible meaning of κόφινος is a large sack, but the reference to a basket is customary (Fitzmyer 1981: 769). The clear impression is that the needs of all were thoroughly met.

Ellis (1974: 139) suggests that the number twelve represents one basket for each apostle (Marshall 1978: 363 probably correctly calls this connection incidental). Old Testament connections to the idea of God's provision are plentiful (Danker 1988: 192; Schürmann 1969: 520; Ps. 23; 78:18–29; 105:40; 107:9). In a reversal of the doubt of Ps. 78:19–20, God through Jesus does spread a table of provision in an isolated locale. However, the number twelve is not exploited, as much as it is a striking sum of the excess.[15] Stewardship is also pictured in the feeding (Tannehill 1986: 217–18; Luke 6:21; and the meals of 12:37; 13:28–29; 14:15–24; 22:16, 30). Jesus offers messianic provision through the disciples, something that the allusions to the Last Supper suggest, since there he "passes the torch" (22:19).[16]

Though distinct in wording, Matt. 14:20 = Mark 6:43 also mentions that twelve baskets of leftovers were collected after all were filled. Mark specifies that both bread and fish were picked up. Both Mark and Matthew mention the number of people at this point, rather than earlier, as Luke 9:14 had done. John 6:14 alone mentions the crowd's reaction: they believed this to be a prophet's work and they wished to make him king, an interesting mix of offices.

Summary

Luke 9:10–17 is a major lesson for the disciples. Jesus is the one who can meet needs, and the disciples are called to serve as his ministers in meeting those needs. How will they do it? What the disciples do not do in this account is ask Jesus to provide. They need to realize that for them to minister they need to rely on Jesus. This is the first of many accounts where the disciples' instinctive reactions are wrong. Jesus needs to instruct them so that their instincts do not mislead them. In the transfiguration, some disciples will hear the call to listen to Jesus. The instruction of the next several chapters is designed to prepare them to minister in Jesus' absence. Acts 3–4 shows clearly that they got the lesson.

15. That the other numbers of the account are insignificant makes it likely for this number as well.

16. The image is messianic because of the banquet association. Note especially the explicit connection between teaching and food in Mark 8:14–21. John 6 with its discourse on the Bread of Life is conceptually similar.

Of course, the picture of Jesus creatively supplying these needs has christological overtones as well, especially given the question that Herod raised just prior to this account. In the OT, God was the focus of provision and was the one who filled (Exod. 16; Num. 11; Ps. 78). Jesus now bears this function as he looks to the Father to work through him. Whether this is a prophetic role or a messianic function is not entirely clear from the event itself, but the following messianic confession suggests how the disciples saw it. John 6:15 shows this regal expectation in the crowd's reaction, though Jesus rejects it, because their expectation is too political for his current ministry. The reader is to gain a sense of comfort from the power that Jesus has to care for his own. He or she is to realize, with the disciples, that sustenance is provided through Jesus and that ministry occurs while looking to him. It is a dependent spirit that Jesus wishes to foster in his disciples. When asked to provide, they cannot because they do not know where to go to ask. They are to look at what Jesus has done and realize that he is the source of their life and ministry and that he will give in abundance what is needed.

III. Galilean Ministry: Revelation of Jesus (4:14–9:50)
    D. First Movements to Faith and Christological Questions (7:1–8:3)
    E. Call to Faith, Christological Revelation, and Questions (8:4–9:17)
➤ F. Christological Confession and Instruction about Discipleship (9:18–50)

F. Christological Confession and Instruction about Discipleship (9:18–50)

Peter's confession of Jesus as the Christ brings a major shift in Luke's account. Up to this point the focus has been Jesus' ministry and identity. But with the confession, attention turns to Jesus' instructing the disciples directly and preparing them for his departure and suffering. In fact, such instruction really began with the feeding of the five thousand. Yet, with the confession of Luke 9:20, Jesus begins to discuss his suffering directly. Though the apostles know who Jesus is, as their confession of him as Christ shows, they do not yet know the character of his messianic ministry. After the confession, the nature of Jesus' ministry is a major concern, as Jesus' repeated statements of his coming suffering show. There are six such notes in this middle section of Luke: 9:22, 44; 12:50; 13:31–33; 17:25; 18:31–33 (Tiede 1988: 181).[1] In light of Jesus' rejection, the disciples need to be prepared for rejection.

Luke 9:18–50, the last major unit in §III of Luke's book, begins with Peter's confession (9:18–20), followed by a prediction of Jesus' suffering (9:21–22). Jesus then describes (9:23–27) the "new way" of suffering in which the disciple walks, a surprising revelation in the face of preaching about the kingdom of God and the displays of power that Jesus has been making in Luke 8–9. At the transfiguration, confirmation comes that the disciples have much to learn. The heavenly voice gives the instruction to listen to Jesus (9:28–36). The unit closes with failures by the disciples and continued promise of suffering by Jesus (9:37–50). The disciples' instincts were constantly headed in the wrong direction and needed correction. They needed to learn to follow Jesus and to think the way he does. Greatness is not found in power or position, but in childlike faith.

---

1. The Marcan parallels for the first, second, and sixth passages are Mark 8:31–32; 9:30–32; and 10:32–34. Tiede notes the historical plausibility of Jesus' concluding that he would suffer such a fate. Such a deduction is logical in light of Herod's concern (Luke 9:7–9), the execution of John the Baptist, and the threat that a Galilean prophet-king held for the fragile alliance between Pilate and the high priests.

1. Peter's Confession (9:18–20)

Luke 9:18–20 has a clear christological function. Peter's confession is the first of two key answers to the "who is Jesus?" questions of 8:25 and 9:9. The other answer comes from heaven in 9:35.[1] Peter's confession that Jesus is the Christ contrasts with the popular assessment that he is merely a prophet. It reflects a deeper appreciation of Jesus than do the popular confessions of him as prophet. The disciples have learned from the character of Jesus' ministry who he is, and the reader is to identify with their superior confession.

Sources and Historicity

The confession has parallels in Matt. 16:13–20, a very full account of the event, and Mark 8:27–30 (Aland 1985: §158).[2] The Synoptic accounts are parallel, even down to identical wording in places. Each Gospel functions in similar ways, although Luke puts the event in the context of prayer, reflecting his emphasis. Luke alone omits reference to Caesarea Philippi, a town near the foot of Mount Hermon (Arndt 1956: 257). The wording of the confession differs slightly in each Gospel, but the fundamental category of the Christ is the same (see the exegesis of 9:20).

Bultmann's skepticism (1963: 257–59) about the account's historicity is fueled by Wrede's 1901 work on the messianic secret (see Wrede 1971). Bultmann's two reasons are that Jesus takes the initiative and that his question about the crowd's view is artificial, since Jesus knows what they believe. But when Jesus is teaching, why are such questions for reflection inappropriate (so correctly Schürmann 1969: 530, esp. n. 7)? Jesus is seeing if his disciples know him better than the masses know him (Marshall 1978: 363–64).[3] The remarks of Tiede (1988: 183) are apropos:

> Historical scholarship will debate exactly which titles or roles Jesus and his disciples ascribed to him and what they came to mean after the resurrection, but all the tradition remembers him as an active agent, proclaiming God's righteous

---

1. Tannehill 1986: 214–15 notes that the question appears in various forms in 4:22, 36; 5:21; 7:49; 8:25; and 9:9. He suggests that Jesus' ministry in 8:22–9:17 led to Peter's awareness of who Jesus is.

2. In the parallel in the Gospel of Thomas 13, Thomas is a major figure in the discussion and the wording is very different.

3. Dinkler 1971 defends only Peter's confession and the Satan saying (Mark 8:33 = Matt. 16:23) as authentic. Marshall 1978: 365 correctly accepts the whole unit.

dominion and enacting the fulfillment of scriptural agenda. Exact historical data may be elusive, but Jesus' own acts and words were the foundation of the story by which Christians declared the gospel of God's righteous and glorious rule.

The account is authentic, even though one might wish for more detail about this fascinating exchange. Differences of wording within the Synoptics do not alter the fundamental presentation: Jesus is confessed as Messiah. What is elusive is understanding exactly what the disciples originally meant and what they came to appreciate later. That Jesus in both act and word was the catalyst for their understanding is beyond doubt.

The Jesus Seminar (Funk and Hoover 1993: 312) disagrees, taking all the dialogue in this unit as created, since, in their view, Jesus neither elicited "confessions about himself" nor referred "to himself as the Anointed." Rather, these are early church confessions. But this position can be challenged and rejected. How did messianic confession emerge as so central in the NT if it had no basis in Jesus' ministry? Basic principles of historic causality, not to mention the breadth of messianic tradition in the NT writings, demand an early starting point for this concept in the ministry of Jesus (Marshall 1978: 365; Nolland 1989: 449–50, who rightly challenges Pesch's attempt [1973–74] to argue for a prophetic anointing, not a regal one). The prophetic view ignores the fundamental contrast of this passage (Jesus is the Christ, not one of the old prophets) and the regal emphasis spread throughout the NT tradition. In Judaism, the eschatological Christ is either a regal figure (Ps. Sol. 17–18) or a high-priestly Messiah (11QMelch). But the latter concept makes no impact in the NT, except as it is subsumed in the Davidic regal hope and the use of Ps. 110 in the Book of Hebrews. The NT affirms a regal messianic hope under which prophetic characteristics also fit. The NT tradition is too united on this point to question its veracity.

Form critically, the account is a pronouncement story, though it has a twist: normally Jesus makes the key pronouncement, here a disciple does (Fitzmyer 1981: 772).[4] Berger (1984: 233) rightly calls the text an "acclamation." The outline of Luke 9:18–20 is as follows:

a. Prayerful setting (9:18a)
b. Jesus' question of the disciples (9:18b)
c. The disciples' report of the responses of the crowd (9:19)
d. Peter's confession that Jesus is the Christ (9:20)

4. Bultmann 1963: 257 calls the account a "legend," a supernatural account designed to bring honor to Jesus. This classification is not accurate because there is nothing particularly miraculous in the account nor does it have this category's narrative features. Bultmann's skepticism about historicity probably results in this erroneous classification. Since a disciple makes the pronouncement, the form is somewhat unique, but "acclamation" is a good description. What the disciple acclaims here, heaven will confirm with another acclamation at the transfiguration.

The themes can be stated briefly. Another major event occurs in the context of prayer. The popular assessment of Jesus sees him as a prophet, but the disciples see him as the Messiah—a contrast that is important to Luke. One view is correct and the other is inadequate. However, even the correct view needs additional definition.

Exegesis and Exposition

[18]And it happened that, while he was praying by himself, the disciples were together with him, and he asked them, "Who do the crowds say that I am?" [19]And they replied, "John the Baptist; but others say, Elijah; and others say that one of the old prophets has risen." [20]And he said to them, "But who do you say that I am?" And Peter replied, "The Christ of God."

a. Prayerful Setting (9:18a)

9:18a Finally, the disciples and Jesus get the time alone that they were searching for before the feeding of the five thousand. Jesus is praying, as he often is, before a key moment (Luke 3:21; 5:16; 6:12; 9:28–29; 11:1; 22:41; 23:34, 46; with all but 22:41 unique to Luke; Arndt 1956: 258). The introductory style is Lucan (Marshall 1978: 366 notes the use of καὶ ἐγένετο, *kai egeneto*, and it came to pass), as is the focus on prayer. Of course, Jesus is "alone" (κατὰ μόνας, *kata monas*) in the sense that the crowds are no longer with him.

Luke is similar to the parallel accounts, except that he alone mentions the prayerful setting and he alone omits reference to the locale, Caesarea Philippi.

b. Jesus' Question of the Disciples (9:18b)

9:18b Jesus asks the disciples a simple question: Who do the crowds think that he is? The disciples have just been on a long journey across the land, so surely they will have picked up the speculation. In fact, Luke himself suggested the public view (7:16; 9:7–8). The "who is Jesus?" question has been raised frequently recently (7:49; 8:25; 9:9; Schneider 1977a: 208).

Rather than asking, "Who do people (ἄνθρωποι, *anthrōpoi*) say that I am?" (Matt. 16:13 = Mark 8:27), Luke's Jesus asks, "Who do the crowds (ὄχλοι, *ochloi*) say that I am?" In addition, Matthew asks the question in terms of the "Son of Man," rather than in the first person. The question is the same; the accounts simply use different ways to summarize. In a unique christological emphasis, Luke places this event immediately after the feeding of the five thousand to more closely connect the miracle of provision with the key question of Jesus' identity. Luke's placement also puts the confession close to the mission of the Twelve and Herod's speculation about who Jesus is (see excursus 9).

c. The Disciples' Report of the Responses of the Crowd (9:19)

The disciples reply by noting three general responses: Jesus is John **9:19** the Baptist returned, the eschatological prophet Elijah, or one of the other prophets of old. The basis for each possibility is tied to the prophetic character of Jesus' ministry. From Luke's point of view, these responses are not so much wrong as incomplete. In contrast, Peter's reply centers on Jesus' messianic position. The regal, messianic category that dominated the infancy material returns. The three lesser possibilities match those that were mentioned to Herod (see the exegesis of 9:7–8 and Bovon 1989: 478).

The crowd regarded Jesus with respect, but they still lacked insight into who he really was. For Luke, the crowd refers to those who came out to see Jesus, but did not really follow him (8:4). Apparently some in the multitude considered that Jesus might be the Messiah (John 6:15), but Luke concentrates on where most of the crowd was. The crowd sensed that Jesus was a major eschatological figure.

The parallels are similar. Matthew 16:14 mentions Jeremiah by name (see Jeremias, *TDNT* 3:220 §B4), but all the parallels work with the same three prophetic categories. The accounts are verbally exact, except for the use of differing verbs to introduce the reply[5] and the wording of the last category.[6]

d. Peter's Confession That Jesus Is the Christ (9:20)

Jesus now seeks the disciples' opinion.[7] When Peter speaks, he **9:20** speaks for all the disciples. He is prominent, as in 5:1–11. His reply is simple: Jesus is the Christ of God.[8] The meaning of χριστός (*christos*, Christ) can be broad (M. De Jonge 1966; Bock 1987: 80, 305 n. 105), but for Luke it clearly has Davidic and regal overtones (Luke 1:17 [alluding to 2 Sam. 7:24], 27, 32–33, 68–72; 2:4, 11; Ps. 2:2; Dan. 9:26). What was predicted about Jesus in the infancy materials is be-

5. Matthew has εἶπαν (said); Mark εἶπαν . . . λέγοντες (saying); Luke ἀποκριθέντες εἶπαν (replying said).

6. Matt. 16:14 has Ἰερεμίαν ἢ ἕνα τῶν προφητῶν (Jeremiah or one of the prophets); Mark 8:28 has εἷς τῶν προφητῶν (one of the prophets); Luke 9:19 has προφήτης τις τῶν ἀρχαίων ἀνέστη (one of the old prophets has risen).

7. Note αὐτοῖς (them) and the emphatic position of ὑμεῖς (you) in the question.

8. On the term θεοῦ (of God) as tightly binding Jesus and God, see Stauffer, *TDNT* 3:104 n. 261; Mark 1:24; John 1:29; 6:33, 69; Luke 23:35; 2 Cor. 4:4. Grundmann, *TDNT* 9:532, calls it a genitive of authorship: Jesus is the Christ sent from God. The expression τὸν χριστὸν τοῦ θεοῦ is unique to Luke.

coming a part of the disciples' perception. That a regal, political understanding of Jesus as Messiah is part of the disciples' view can be seen in their question to Jesus in Acts 1:6. Their perception now matches in part that of the hostile demonic forces, as well as the confession of the angels (4:41; 2:11; Marshall 1978: 366). Although Jesus replies in terms of the Son of Man (9:22), he is not rejecting the title that Peter uses. Rather, χριστός needs to be defined in terms of the totality of Jesus' mission, something that Jesus begins to do immediately. The title will not come into view again until the critical events of the last week of Jesus' life, a climactic period in which it will again occupy a central place (20:41; 22:67; 23:2, 35, 39; 24:26, 46). Jesus as Christ is the point of scriptural promises, as 24:46 shows. Χριστός is also a central title in Jesus' trial (22:67) and crucifixion (23:35). This christological point is also made in Acts 3:18 and 4:26–27 (Fitzmyer 1981: 774–75; Tiede 1988: 184).

All three Synoptic accounts portray Peter's answer in messianic terms: "You are the Christ" in Mark 8:29 and "You are the Christ, the Son of the living God" in Matt. 16:16.[9] Matthew follows with a long section unique to him, where Jesus accepts Peter's confession and notes that it is the product of divine revelation. All the Gospels agree that Jesus is the promised eschatological leader who will bring deliverance and fulfillment to those who ally themselves to him. For the disciples, this also ultimately possesses political dimensions (Luke 1:51–55, 69–75; Acts 1:6–11; 3:17–21). John 6:69 speaks of "the Holy One of God" in a similar confession. Jesus will begin a long process of explaining that the political implications of the title are not the current burden of his commission. Suffering comes first. It is important to see that no strong ontological declaration of deity exists in the passage (Marshall 1978: 366–67; Ernst 1977: 295). The way the disciples react to Jesus in the rest of his ministry shows that they do not yet see him as God. The disciples' understanding has not yet been stretched to its limit with regard to Jesus. Only his resurrection will bring them decisively across that threshold. Nevertheless, Peter sees that Jesus is the Christ. This represents a fundamental starting point in seeing who Jesus is.

Summary   Luke 9:18–20 is important for it gives the testimony of those who followed Jesus regularly. They see that he is more than a prophet. The views of the populace at large are not sufficient. Jesus is the promised deliverer sent from God. Although the understanding of

9. An argument for a Matthean conflation of preresurrection and postresurrection titles here is unnecessary, since sonship to God is an OT regal image: Ps. 2; against Fitzmyer 1981: 774, who argues that χριστός is preresurrection and ὁ υἱὸς τοῦ θεοῦ τοῦ ζῶντος (Son of the living God) is postresurrection.

the disciples still needs to grow, they clearly perceive Jesus' importance through the title χριστός. The reader is to identify with their confession. Jesus is the Promised One who brings deliverance. He is the figure of the eschaton. He is the one through whom God is working. He is not the messenger; he is the message.

With this fundamental confession in place, Jesus now begins to develop the disciples' understanding about his mission and the responsibility that grows out of allegiance to him. The way of victory for Messiah is not what they expect. He will triumph by suffering first and ruling later. Thus, the way of following him is not what they expect either. Much of Luke's Gospel from this point on teaches the disciples that they will face suffering and rejection because of their allegiance to Jesus. Jesus shares how they can cope with their controversial confession and how God will help them through it. Then he will show the way to glory.

2. Prediction of Jesus' Suffering (9:21–22)

Peter's confession represents a turning point in Luke's Gospel. The fundamental Lucan questions about Christology that were the focus of the Galilean portrayal are less important after the confession, which reveals the basic answer. Luke has established that Jesus is the Messiah, the Promised One, as well as indicated that Jesus is an eschatological prophetic figure. His followers have confessed his messiahship. New themes now arise: the necessity of Jesus' suffering, his vindication, and the resultant discipleship required of those who will follow him. Suffering and vindication are the theme in Luke 9:21–22, while discipleship is the issue in 9:23–27. These concerns become the main topic until Jesus' arrival in Jerusalem. Additional themes are Jewish rejection, Jesus' destiny, the disciples' walk, the Pharisees' unrighteous walk, the total commitment of discipleship, and a proper understanding of God's program so that one can suffer now in anticipation of glory later.

The promise of Jesus' suffering and vindication is predicted for the first time in Luke. Several more times Jesus announces his forthcoming suffering (9:44; 12:50; 13:31–33; 17:25; 18:31–33). The disciples struggle to grasp what Jesus is saying (9:45; 18:34). Jesus gradually reveals the full scope of his work, but even then the disciples have a hard time understanding it. This is sometimes difficult for modern readers of the account to appreciate, since Jesus' suffering is so basic to the church's message. Two thousand years of history make it hard to appreciate how new Jesus' teaching on Messiah sounded.

Sources and Historicity

The parallel to Luke 9:21–22 is Matt. 16:20–23 = Mark 8:30–33 (Aland 1985: §§158–59). The events are given the same relative location: Jesus' teaching about suffering follows immediately after the confession. Only Luke notes that Jesus was praying before the confession, so that a mood of solemnity is added (Luke 9:18). The subsequent call to discipleship, though directed at disciples, is consciously made before all people (Mark 8:34 = Luke 9:23). Jesus makes clear that to follow him is a serious matter.

The historicity of the command for silence involves one of the great debates of twentieth-century NT studies. Arguing that Mark was responsible for the theme of the "messianic secret," Wrede (1971; originally 1901) holds that only this view explains how so many of the original traditions of Jesus' ministry lacked messianic notes: Jesus deemphasized the messianic office, while the early church confessed it openly after Jesus' resurrection. The Jesus Seminar (Funk and Hoover 1993: 312) reflects a position similar to Wrede's and rejects the sayings of 9:22 as being sourced in Mark, not Jesus (9:22 is printed in black type). Numerous essays have interacted with Wrede's study, which in many ways was a precursor to the redaction-critical studies that emerged in the 1950s.[1] After detailed critical analysis of Jesus' predictions of vindication and resurrection, Bayer (1986: 242–43, 254–56) argues that Jesus is the author of such sayings because he knew that God vindicates the just and because he knew that he himself would bear God's judgment as the Son of Man (Howard 1977 and Bayer's critique of him; 1986: 55–66). There are good reasons for regarding the material as historical (Marshall 1978: 367; Fitzmyer 1981: 778–79 [who argues for a historical core with some later reflection]).[2] Details of this debate are given in the exegesis; for a detailed survey of all sides of the debate, see Nolland's excellent overview (1993a: 459–64). In particular, he notes broad evidence of Jesus' expectation of suffering (Mark 2:19–20; 10:38; 14:58; Luke 12:49–50; 13:32; and the Last Supper accounts) and lists two key works that argue for authenticity: Bayer 1986 and Schürmann 1973. Schürmann argues that Jesus' words and work indicate that he surfaced serious opposition and could well have expected his fate (see also excursus 10).

The material's form is mixed: a command of Jesus combined with a saying of a passion prediction. Berger 1984: 226 speaks of a catalogue where danger is described, a category he calls *"peristasenkatalog."* The outline of Luke 9:21–22 is as follows:

a. Call to silence (9:21)
b. Necessity of Jesus' suffering (9:22)

Two themes are present: the call to be silent about messianic confession and the declared necessity of Jesus' suffering, death, and resurrection. The idea of the necessity of suffering is part of the tradition, since Mark 8:31 = Matt. 16:21 uses δεῖ (*dei*, it is necessary).

1. For the major essays on this theme, see Tuckett 1983, especially the critique of Wrede by Dunn (pp. 116–31, originally Dunn 1970b), who also sees the historical roots of the secret residing in Jesus' ministry.
2. Dinkler 1971, published in the Bultmann Festschrift, defends much of the account's historicity; Dinkler's position is interesting in light of Bultmann's rejection of the account. Fitzmyer 1981: 778–79, however, sees a strong Marcan hand and reflection in Mark's presentation, while Dinkler defends only Peter's confession and the Satan saying.

Exegesis and Exposition

²¹But he commanded and charged them to speak to no one about this, ²²saying, "It is necessary for the Son of Man
> to suffer much,
> and be rejected by the elders, chief priests, and scribes,
> and be killed,
> and on the third day be raised."

a. Call to Silence (9:21)

9:21 Jesus urges silence about Peter's christological confession. Though only Peter answers, all the disciples receive the command (αὐτοῖς, *autois*, them). The major question that emerges is why Jesus would want them to be silent about who he is. The context suggests the answer: this Messiah must suffer before his greatness is completely manifest (9:22). The disciples need instruction on the kind of Messiah that Jesus will be and what is in store for those who follow him in his journey of rejection, exaltation, and glory. God's plan for Messiah is contrary to the disciples' expectations about Messiah. God's people will not experience a glorious messianic rescue from physical enemies in the near future. A confession by Jesus' representatives of his messiahship would be seen as containing an expectation of a political Messiah, which is not Jesus' initial goal (Ps. Sol. 17–18; John 6:15; Ellis 1974: 140; Plummer 1896: 247; Luce 1933: 184; Fitzmyer 1981: 775). Longenecker argues that in Jewish tradition one does not claim messiahship for oneself; rather one should do the works of Messiah and let others proclaim the office.³ While this reason may explain Jesus' hesitancy about his using the title, it does not explain his call for silence on the part of the disciples. Rather, while accepting the confession, Jesus hesitates to have it proclaimed widely and explicitly since misunderstanding is so possible.⁴ Rather than making mere verbal claims, Jesus wants his works and the scriptural promises to testify to him (Luke 4:16–30; 6:1–5; 7:22–23; 24:13–49; note that demons are silenced in 4:41 and human witnesses in 8:56). In addition, such verbal claims should not be made publicly until it is clearly understood by those making the declaration what kind of Messiah is present. Once they understand,

---

3. Longenecker 1970: 71–74 cites the example of Simeon ben Kosebah, who, though seen as messianic, had a reticence to claim the title for himself; also Flusser 1959: 107.

4. Bayer 1986: 163–64. Silence does not mean that Jesus rejects a political messiahship. Jesus is a political Messiah in Luke (Acts 3:14–26). He will exercise such authority one day, but the point is that he will not do so at this time. The misunderstanding that is so dangerous is one of timing, not substance.

then they are to proclaim (24:44–47). Thus, the disciples go public in a bold way after the resurrection (Acts 2:36; 3:18; 4:26; 10:39–43; Fitzmyer 1981: 775).

The parallels also make the same point about silence. Mark 8:30 says the silence is "about him" (περὶ αὐτοῦ, *peri autou*), which contextually must relate to the confession. Matthew 16:20 stresses the content of what is prohibited from being proclaimed, that is, the confession "that he is the Christ" (ὅτι αὐτός ἐστιν ὁ χριστός, *hoti autos estin ho christos*). Luke alone emphasizes the prohibition by using both ἐπιτιμήσας (*epitimēsas*, charged) and παρήγγειλεν (*parēngeilen*, commanded). Bayer (1986: 154–66) defends in detail the pre-Marcan character of the tradition in Mark.

b. Necessity of Jesus' Suffering (9:22)

Jesus explains the reason for silence in terms of the Son of Man's suffering, that is, in terms of his own suffering. Creed (1930: 131) suggests that the reason for the silence is that messianic proclamation will be futile in light of the coming rejection. But it seems more likely that Jesus needs to help the disciples understand the nature of his messiahship. Jesus does not fear rejection, nor does he see it as a futile thing to experience. Rejection will not kill the mission. In fact, his crucifixion will be the result of his own remarks to the Sanhedrin (22:66–71). Jesus does not seek to avoid his coming death.

9:22

This is the first suffering-Son-of-Man saying in Luke. A similar note will appear in 17:24–25. After this, and after the nature of Jesus' messiahship is explained, Luke will speak of the Messiah who suffers (Luke 24:26, 46; Acts 3:18; 17:3; 26:23; Tannehill 1986: 220; note the use of δεῖ, *dei*, must, in Luke 24:26 and Acts 17:3). Jesus instructs the disciples about his mission. Suffering was hinted at before (Luke 2:35; 5:35), but now it is explicit (Liefeld 1984: 923). In fact, the presence of δεῖ shows that Jesus is presenting a commission statement.[5] There is an inevitability to these events. Explicit summaries about Jesus' suffering and resurrection are frequent in Luke.[6] God planned to have the Son of Man experience the things described here. God knew what would happen to the suffering Messiah–Son of Man, Jesus. (On the Son of Man, see excursus 6, Bock 1991c, and Nolland 1993a: 468–74; on the suffering-Son-of-Man sayings, see excursus 10).

---

5. Luke 2:49; 4:43; 13:33; 17:25; 19:5; 22:37; 24:7, 26, 44. Grundmann, *TDNT* 2:23–24, notes that the term speaks of eschatological necessity, with roots in Dan. 2:28, 29 LXX; 2:45 Theodotion.

6. Luke 9:44; 17:25; 18:31–33 (where δεῖ is absent, but fulfillment is expressed); 24:7, 46–47. Other allusions to Jesus' death are in 11:29–32; 12:50; 13:31–35; 20:9–18; 22:19–20, 28; Fitzmyer 1981: 778.

Four infinitives in 9:22 summarize Jesus' career. First, he is to suffer (παθεῖν, *pathein*) many things (17:25; 24:26, 46). No details are given, but the picture refers to the entire process of rejection and persecution, since the handing over to the Jewish leaders and the death on the cross follow later (Marshall 1978: 369). Second, the religious leadership of the Jews will reject him (ἀποδοκιμασθῆναι, *apodokimasthēnai*; 17:25; 20:17). The use of Ps. 118 in Luke 20:17 shows this to be a scriptural theme. The elders, chief priests, and scribes were the three groups who made up the Sanhedrin, the ruling body of Judaism (Fitzmyer 1981: 780; Josephus, *Against Apion* 2.21 §§185–87; Schrenk, *TDNT* 3:269–70; see the exegesis of 5:17 and 7:3). Third, Jesus will be killed (ἀποκτανθῆναι, *apoktanthēnai*; 12:4–5; 13:34; 18:33; 20:14–15). Jesus will also illustrate this theme with a parable in 20:13–15, as well as allude to a pattern of rejection in the history of the nation in 11:47–49. Finally, Jesus will rise (ἐγερθῆναι, *egerthēnai*) on the third day. Interestingly, this final verb does not reappear until Luke 24:6, 34 and the sequel discussion in the Book of Acts (4:10; 5:30). Luke also uses another verb for resurrection (ἀνίστημι, *anistēmi*; Luke 16:31; 18:33; 24:7, 46). Note also how the passive mood is present in the final three infinitives: he will be rejected, will be killed, will be raised. The last infinitive is a "theological passive": humanity's destructive action on a passive Jesus will be reversed in this last action by an active God.

The summary is parallel to Mark 8:31 = Matt. 16:21. In Mark the first three verbs are the same, while the synonym ἀναστῆναι (*anastēnai*, to be raised) is the final infinitive. Mark speaks of Jesus' being raised "after" (μετά, *meta*, with the accusative) three days, rather than "on" (the simple dative) the third day as Matthew and Luke do. The Matthean and Lucan language is more precise, though Mark's expression in fact reflects a synonymous idiom in Josephus.[7] Matthew omits mention of the Son of Man and speaks only of "him" (αὐτόν, *auton*). He also omits the verbal idea of rejection, speaking instead of suffering at the hands of the religious leaders. Matthew and Luke use the same two final infinitives and agree verbally from the third infinitive to the end of the summary. The parallels portray the teaching similarly. Luke, however, lacks Matthew's and Mark's response by Peter and Jesus' subsequent rebuke of him. Luke often softens criticism of the disciples.

7. Josephus, *Antiquities* 7.11.6 §280; 8.8.1–2 §§214, 218; Fitzmyer 1981: 781; Delling, *TDNT* 8:220. However, no allusion to Hos. 6:2 is present in the reference to the third day, since this passage is never directly alluded to in the NT. The reference to ἡμέρα (day) is inclusive in each case, so that Friday, Saturday, and Sunday are in view in both "after three days" and "on the third day."

Luke 9:21–22 represents the first indication that Jesus will walk a **Summary** difficult road. This Messiah is not what people expect. The nation he comes to redeem will largely reject him. The glory that awaits him comes only after intense suffering. In fact, he will die. The power of Messiah, so clearly exhibited in Luke 7–9, will be withdrawn as he humbly submits to rejection. The use of power is forsaken for the way of humility. The reader knows the story, but the contrast Luke has formed is striking, reminding one of the picture of Phil. 2:5–11. The road of glory runs through the cross. Jesus tells his disciples that, though he walks this path in a unique way, he will not walk it alone. Others too will have to bear rejection for following this humble, suffering Messiah, who also holds the power of the Son of Man. Jesus is a mix of strength and weakness, divine mission and humanity. His disciples need to see it all and to understand that this must be. In this necessity comes the assurance that God is at work in Jesus, even in the midst of what seems to be failure. Out of our despair, God often reaffirms our dignity. By dying, we meet life.

3. The "New Way" of Suffering (9:23–27)

Luke turns from passion prediction to disciple response. The commands to carry the cross, lose one's life to gain it, and not be ashamed of the Son of Man show that following Jesus will not be easy. Rejection for Messiah means rejection for his followers. The situation requires that one not be attached to the world, its values, and its acceptance. In fact, such a commitment will require daily diligence. But there is hope: the promise that some will see a glimpse of future glory shows the perspective by which one is able to endure discipleship's present trials. Following Messiah is not easy, but there is great hope at the end of the road. With hope in place, there is basis for faith and love (Col. 1:3–5).

Disciples live in a period where three realities operate: they have a share in blessing and Spirit empowerment "now," but some of those benefits are "not yet" present as they wait for Jesus' return (Talbert 1982: 104–5). In this interim period, a third reality—the forces of the world—still have a powerful presence. To survive involves self-denial, since the forces that opposed Jesus remain opposed to his disciples. Those forces see Jesus and his followers in the same light, so disciples must be ready to follow in his steps. Whether the task is defined as "taking up the cross," "losing one's life," or "not being ashamed of the Son of Man," it is clear that disciples must give themselves to God and rest in his care and acceptance. The world does not embrace those who honor God, but salvation comes to the person who places his or her identity in the hands of the Almighty (Luke 9:24).

Sources and Historicity

The parallel to Luke 9:23–27 is Mark 8:34–9:1 = Matt. 16:24–28 (Aland 1985: §160).[1] In all three Synoptics, these words stand after Peter's confession and Jesus' passion prediction. Many see these as originally separate sayings by Jesus.[2] The Jesus Seminar (Funk and Hoover 1993: 313–

---

1. Bovon 1989: 482 n. 4 sees evidence of oral tradition in Luke 9:25–26. The Gospel of Thomas 55 has a saying like Luke 9:23, while Thomas 67 is like Luke 9:25. 2 Tim. 2:12 is like Luke 9:26.

2. So Bultmann 1963: 82–83. As evidence of the individuality of the sayings, Bovon 1989: 481 notes similar sayings about cross-bearing in Matt. 10:38 = Luke 14:27, about losing one's life in 17:33, and about denying Jesus in 12:9. Fitzmyer 1981: 782 is certain that the sayings were separate.

14) treats the sayings separately: 9:23, 26 (printed in black type) is not rooted in Jesus, while 9:24–25, 27 (in gray type), even though written by the evangelists, may have conceptual roots to Jesus. The more received sayings are proverbial in character, so the seminar regards them as possible for Jesus. But language like "for my sake" leads them to see reformulation by Mark. The seminar also views Luke 9:27 as an allusion to Jesus' exorcism through the mention of his power, though the Gospels lack such a connection. The analysis by individual sayings reflects the seminar's tendency to evaluate this material as isolated sayings. The rejected sayings are seen as too greatly influenced by the realities of the cross and Jesus' rejection to be authentic.

Nonetheless, the basic teaching and its proverbial style suggest that this material could well have been repeated in numerous settings (Luke 14:27; 17:33; John 12:24–25). Luke has conceptual parallels in three locales, indicating both that the theme was important and that the tradition recognized that Jesus said such things both as isolated sayings and in teaching units. One need not make either/or choices here for such a central concept of discipleship. The radical call to discipleship explains the disciples' distinct identity during Jesus' ministry. The appeal to a cross metaphor is not surprising in light of John the Baptist's rejection and the stern opposition already arising against Jesus. The connections are historical (Marshall 1978: 372 sees authentic sayings, though it is not as clear whether he sees this setting as original; see also Nolland 1993a: 476–81, who defends core historicity).

Form critically, the text is a collection of sayings from Jesus (Bultmann 1963: 82–83; Bovon 1989: 481; Berger 1984: 173 [who speaks of a "whoever must be, must do" form in 9:23]). The outline of Luke 9:23–27 is as follows:

a. The "new way" of discipleship (9:23–26)
   i. Call to take up the cross (9:23)
   ii. Call to lose one's life for Christ's sake—only to save it (9:24–25)
   iii. Call not to be ashamed of the Son of Man (9:26)
b. The promise that some will see the kingdom before death (9:27)

Discipleship is not easy, but difficult, for it involves suffering. The cost of total discipleship is the giving up of self for God. There is a call not to be ashamed about Jesus. Self-denial and allegiance to Jesus lead to glory. In contrast, at the judgment there will be a cost for being ashamed about Jesus. Some are promised a glimpse of the kingdom. This preview indicates that eschatological hope for the future is certain. In the context of such hope, one can endure suffering in the world now.

Exegesis and Exposition

[23]And he said to all, "If anyone wishes to come after me, let him deny himself, take up his cross daily, and follow me. [24]For whoever wishes to save his life shall lose it; but whoever loses his life for my sake, this one shall save it. [25]For what does it profit a man to gain the whole world only to lose or forfeit himself? [26]For whoever is ashamed of my words, the Son of Man shall be ashamed of this one when he comes in his glory and the glory of the Father and of the holy angels. [27]I say to you truly, there are some standing here who will not taste death until they see the kingdom of God."

a. The "New Way" of Discipleship (9:23–26)
i. Call to Take Up the Cross (9:23)

9:23   The path of following Jesus, in light of where he is going, is hard. Jesus prepares the disciples for the journey, expressing it simply in terms of wishing "to come after him." This remark sets the context for interpreting what follows.

Discipleship is summarized in three commands: ἀρνησάσθω (arnēsasthō, deny oneself), ἀράτω (aratō, take up), and ἀκολουθείτω (akoloutheitō, follow). The tense sequence (two aorist imperatives followed by a present imperative) shows that fundamental decisions made about the self and about day-by-day bearing of the cross emerge in a continual following of Jesus. In other words, the last act emerges from the others. The disciple's life consists of basic self-denial. Luke 9:24 will reinforce the point made here: to gain life one must give it up. The language is eschatological and relates directly to faith. The essence of saving trust in God is self-denial, a recognition that he must save because disciples cannot save themselves, that life must be given over into God's care and protection. Disciples do not respond to their own personal wills, but to God's. There is a fundamental recognition of allegiance that says, "God needs to direct me; I will not and cannot direct myself." Disciples who follow Jesus will follow him in this attitude. For Paul, when a person in faith asks God to save through Jesus, the petitioner recognizes that Jesus must save from sin and that he imparts life, because the petitioner's life needs redeeming on God's terms. Salvation does not come on one's terms or on one's own merits (Rom. 3–5). Jesus calls this self-denial. Paul's words are no different from Jesus', just less pictorial. Salvation is a gift that God bestows to the one who knows the need for it, who knows one cannot provide it for oneself.

The figure of bearing the cross is much discussed (Fletcher 1964; M. Green 1983 lists over a dozen views; J. Schneider, *TDNT* 7:578–

79, notes six views). The background of the image is clearly a Roman picture of a criminal sentenced to die for a heinous crime. The criminal not only was crucified, but carried his own cross, a picture enacted in Jesus' own death (Fitzmyer 1981: 787 lists contemporary passages: Josephus, *Antiquities* 13.14.2 §380; 17.10.10 §295; 11QTemple[a] 64.10–13; Hengel 1977). Cross-bearing publicly displayed a person's submission to the state. The criminal rebelled against the state, and so bore the penalty of punishment from it. Cross-bearing was a visible, public affair that visualized a person's humility before the state. Thus, the fundamental idea is of submitting to the authority of another—in this case God.

When the image is tied to following Jesus, an additional nuance is suggested: disciples are following Jesus, who although innocent will bear the shame of rejection and death (Luke 9:22). Thus, submitting to God and following Jesus means walking the road of rejection. People may reject and react to the disciple's commitment to God. Ellis (1974: 141) relates the image to Paul's filling up Christ's afflictions (Col. 1:24) and his being crucified with Christ (Gal. 2:20). This association suggests another element in the picture: cross-bearing means that one's independent life is at an end, an element that reinforces the picture of self-denial and submission (Marshall 1978: 373).

The final command is the call to follow Jesus continually. One can go the route Jesus goes if one recognizes the need to place oneself in God's care and submit to him. Such submission includes a willingness to enter into the suffering of rejection. Jesus makes it clear that the essence of discipleship is found in this attitude. To follow Jesus is to recognize this commitment to him. It is to obey him and share in the world's rejection of him. There is no need to deny the authenticity of the statement. The imagery is common, even in a Jewish setting, and the realization that disciples share in the fate of their teacher is also common (Marshall 1978: 374; SB 1:587; Midr. Gen. 56.3 [36c]).

These sayings of Jesus are rendered similarly in Mark 8:34 = Matt. 16:24. Matthew and Mark have the more intensive ἀπαρνησάσθω (*aparnēsasthō*, deny oneself), a verb that Luke uses later for Jesus' denial of the one who denies him and for Peter's denial (Luke 12:9; 22:34, 61). Each writer uses a different verb or verb form for the one who wants to come after Jesus: Matthew has ἐλθεῖν (*elthein*, to come), Mark has ἀκολουθεῖν (*akolouthein*, to follow), and Luke has ἔρχεσθαι (*erchesthai*, to come). Luke alone notes the daily (καθ' ἡμέραν, *kath' hēmeran*) need to take up the cross. Matthew notes that Jesus made his remark to disciples, while Mark speaks of the crowd and the disciples as the audience. Luke simply says that Jesus said it to all, so he and Mark stand together here. Since disciples are the subject, the teaching is intended for them; but all should hear and understand what following Jesus means. Jesus was not above making the difficult nature of the walk clear to outsiders. He wanted all to understand what being allied to him means and what the journey with him involves. Luke 14:27 repeats much of what is said here. Acts 14:22 says a similar thing in a different way. To join with Jesus is to face the opposition of others.

ii. Call to Lose One's Life for Christ's Sake—Only to Save It (9:24–25)

9:24 The description of discipleship continues with the "lose life to gain life" saying. In fact, this verse is the explanation of the previous images (note the use of γάρ, *gar*, for). If one wishes to control one's life, it will be lost because of refusal to submit to God's way. If one wishes to save one's life through the world's acceptance, it will be lost because of a refusal to come to a rejected Jesus, who nevertheless does save (John 12:25; Ellis 1974: 141). The context foresees persecution. One might be inclined to court acceptance with the world by distancing oneself from Jesus (see Luke 14:25–33, esp. v. 26), but such distancing is disaster. One might seek to save one's life by surrounding it with the comforts and protections of life, but this too is dangerous (Luke will develop the idea of excessive attachment to wealth in 12:13–21; 16:19–31; 18:18–30; Hendriksen 1978: 499). The point is that life's comforts and the threat of losing them might keep one from coming to Jesus. If one gives up life for the sake of Jesus, if one gives one's spiritual and physical welfare over to him, then that one will receive life. In fact, life will be saved. Orientation to Jesus (i.e., ἕνεκεν ἐμοῦ, *heneken emou*, for my sake) is a prerequisite for saving life. Though some disciples fulfill this passage in martyrdom, the image of the entire section is figurative and so is the remark here.[3]

Luke will later describe this change in attitude with two terms: repentance (μετάνοια, *metanoia*) and faith (πίστις, *pistis*) (Acts 11:17;

---

3. Luce 1933: 186 is wrong to say that the remark is more literal in Mark than in Luke, for the contexts are identical. Fitzmyer 1981: 788 notes the OT parallels to saving one's ψυχή: Gen. 19:17; 1 Sam. 19:11; and Jer. 31:6 LXX [48:6 MT]; Schürmann 1969: 543 n. 111. Jewish parallels are found in *b. Tamid* 32a ("What shall a man do to live? They replied: Let him mortify himself. What should a man do to kill himself? They replied: Let him keep himself alive [i.e., indulge in luxuries]") and *b. Ber.* 63b ("whoever abases himself for the words of the Torah will in the end be exalted"); SB 1:587–88. Bovon 1989: 482 speaks of the OT picture of the two ways (Deut. 30:15–18) and compares Luke's emphasis to the structure of Luke 6:47–49. Note how the Jewish emphasis on the law is replaced with an emphasis on Christ in the NT.

13:38–39; 20:21; 22:16; 26:18). In turning to God for the forgiveness of sins, one recognizes that one is not to live life as in the past and that one cannot approach God on human terms. Rather, one is to live in light of God's offer of forgiveness and life. Thus, one's spiritual welfare is to rest in God's hands. Paul speaks of faith in describing this reorientation of perspective toward the things of God (1 Thess. 1:9–10; Rom. 1:4–5). The issue is fundamentally one of attitude and allegiance, though there may be failure in its execution at individual points. The NT Letters give ample evidence that faith's outworking is a process that takes time to come to full fruition and is not totally realized until the time of glorification (Phil. 3:20–21; 1 Pet. 1:3–9; Acts 14:22).

The parallels in Matthew and Mark almost agree with each other, except that Mark 8:35 speaks of "for my sake and for the sake of the gospel" and Matt. 16:25 speaks of finding life, not saving it. The meaning of Matthew's synonymous phrase is the same, for he speaks of saving one's life earlier in the verse (cf. Matt. 10:39). Luke specifically mentions "this one" (οὗτος, houtos) will be saved, supplying the term as the subject for the final verb. Luke 17:33 repeats the idea expressed here and relates the idea explicitly to martyrdom, but this is a distinct context, where the general remark is reapplied in a more specific way. There is no need to argue that only a single utterance is behind both texts. The saying is proverbial enough to have been reused.

Jesus describes the risk of not responding to his call. The question **9:25** is rhetorical and expects the answer, "It profits nothing to gain the whole world only to have lost one's life before God." The term for forfeit, ζημιόω (zēmioō), refers to suffering loss, whether through paying a fine, losing a game, or failing in a business deal (Arndt 1956: 260; BAGD 338 §1; BAA 685 §1; MM 273, 341; Stumpff, *TDNT* 2:891; Fitzmyer 1981: 788). The risk is greater in holding on to one's life than in giving it over to God for Jesus' sake. The reference to the soul (ψυχή, psychē) in the previous verse here becomes a reference to the self (ἑαυτόν, heauton), which makes it clear that ψυχή refers to the entire person. One might think that it is a disadvantage to give up one's life, but in fact the opposite is true: to gain the world means to lose life. The NT frequently contrasts what the world offers with what benefits a person spiritually (John 3:17, 19; 1 Cor. 1:20–21, 27–28; Gal. 2:20; 2 Pet. 1:4; 1 John 2:15–16; Sasse, *TDNT* 3:888; SB 1:749). This idea is parallel to what Jesus turned down in the second temptation when he rejected "all the kingdoms of the world" from Satan's hand (Luke 4:5–8).

The parallels are each worded in their own way, though again they express the same idea. Matthew 16:26 = Mark 8:37 has an additional comment where Jesus raises the question of what a person can give in return for the soul. Of course, the soul—that is, the life—is the most that one can offer. It is all that one can offer. Jesus clearly sees discipleship in terms of a shift of allegiance. In a wordplay about this teaching of Jesus, Godet (1875: 1.420) says, "What gain! To draw in a lottery a gallery of pictures . . . , and at the same time to become blind!" It is a shame to live life, only to miss knowing the giver of life. What one possesses in the pursuit of things in this life cannot be possessed permanently. Only God can give such benefits.

iii. Call Not to Be Ashamed of the Son of Man (9:26)

9:26 Jesus continues to explain the nature of discipleship and allegiance that he desires. Γάρ (*gar*, for) is explanatory of 9:25. The danger of gaining the whole world but losing one's spiritual life is real. Essentially, the issue is responding to Jesus' teaching and person. To be ashamed of his words (ἐπαισχυνθῇ . . . τοὺς ἐμοὺς λόγους, *epaischynthē . . . tous emous logous*) is another way to express rejection of his teaching and refusal to confess him publicly (Arndt 1956: 260). Cross-bearing involves public confession of Jesus and acceptance of his teaching's authority (Fitzmyer 1981: 788; Marshall 1978: 376; Bultmann, *TDNT* 1:190; Mark 8:38; Rom. 1:16; 2 Tim. 1:8, 12, 16; 2:12; Heb. 11:16). For example, although Peter initially failed at this (Luke 22:56–60), he eventually turned it around and openly acknowledged Jesus in the Book of Acts, showing that his earlier denial was a denial of nerve and not of heart.

The reference to the Son of Man (ὁ υἱὸς τοῦ ἀνθρώπου, *ho huios tou anthrōpou*) is a reference to Jesus. When tied to Jesus' coming in glory, it indicates his judging authority (Dan. 7:13–14). Thus, Jesus shares the heavenly glory (δόξα, *doxa*), the visible majesty, of the Father, as he represents both him and the heavenly hosts. Jesus is to be heeded because he is also the eschatological judge. There will be vindication and exaltation for Jesus, as there will be for those who respond to him. Marshall (1978: 376–77) notes that the positive idea is not stated explicitly as it is in Luke 12:8, but the implication is clear. In 9:23–27, the emphasis is on not rejecting Jesus and not suffering rejection by him. For Jesus to be ashamed of someone is for him to reject that person. Stephen is the positive example of how Jesus responds to one who confesses him (Acts 7:55–59). Fitzmyer (1981: 789) denies the role of Jesus as judge, preferring to call his role here one of advocate for his own. He contrasts the verse to Matt. 16:27, which refers to Jesus' evaluating every deed that a person does. Technically, this distinction is correct, but the picture still would seem to entail judgment, for if Jesus, heaven's representative, fails to plead for someone, then the reality is that the person will be rejected. Luke describes a general judgment, while Matthew speaks of a particularistic judgment down to every action. What one decides now about Jesus and his teaching determines how he will respond to that person when he returns in majesty to judge. This supreme "judging" position shows that a subordinationist Christology (i.e., where Jesus is less than the Father) is unlikely for Luke, for it is God's prerogative to judge (against Schweizer 1984: 157–58). The Book of Acts shows Jesus returning through God's appointment as the absolute judge: Acts 10:42 reveals Jesus' position, while 17:31 speaks from the perspective of the movement of his career from sufferer to judge. Jesus serves God, but Jesus exercises divine authority.

Luke is closer to Mark 8:38 than to Matt. 16:27, since Matthew has a specific remark on the particular judgment that Christ upon his return brings for every deed. Mark shares with Luke a general remark about the Son of Man and judgment, but only he has an additional remark about the evil and adulterous character of this generation. Otherwise Mark and Luke are virtually identical, except for a few small differences. Mark uses αὐτόν (*auton*, him), while Luke uses τοῦτον (*touton*, this one) in an emphatic position; thus, Mark speaks of "his" shame, that is, the denier's shame, while Luke speaks of "this one's" shame. Mark speaks of Jesus' coming in the Father's glory "with (μετά, *meta*) the holy angels"; and Luke speaks of his coming in the glory of the Father "and (καί, *kai*) the holy angels." The Lucan wording unites the heavenly hosts more closely with the heavenly glory than does Mark's, but both express heaven's presence and authority at the judgment.

Mark and Luke agree that being allied to Jesus prevents rejection by him at the judgment. Matthew 10:32–33 has a similar saying, except it uses ὁμολογέω (*homologeō*, to confess). This Matthean saying is repeated in Luke 12:8–9. The authenticity of the saying in 9:26 is usually tied to that of 12:8–9, which is seen to be the key statement of the pair (Marshall 1978: 377). But it is not entirely clear that these sayings are a doublet. It seems better to treat them as distinct. Luke's repetition of this basic theme reveals his intent to show the idea as a key teaching of Jesus about the spiritual life (see also 17:33). This type of encouragement and warning is something that Jesus could have given repeatedly. As a declaration of Jesus' future glory and the importance of being committed to him, it is a key authentic statement of Jesus (see the exegesis of 12:8).

b. The Promise That Some Will See the Kingdom before Death (9:27)

Jesus' teaching on discipleship closes with a difficult saying: some **9:27** will see τὴν βασιλείαν τοῦ θεοῦ (*tēn basileian tou theou*, the kingdom of God) before they die. The wording and promise are clear enough, but the ambiguity of the phrase introduces an interpretative problem (as does the wording of the Synoptic parallels). The basic question is this: does τὴν βασιλείαν τοῦ θεοῦ refer to (1) the full, consummated, glorious eschatological kingdom of the future, (2) a glimpse of that kingdom's glorious Christ, or (3) the kingdom of the resurrected and exalted Christ (i.e., the church)? Four major views vie for acceptance:[4]

1. Jesus declares his expectation that the full, consummated kingdom will come soon despite his suffering (H. A. W. Meyer, J. Weiss, H. J. Holtzmann, and Kümmel 1957: 25–29). This view is popular among those who see Jesus as a figure who emphasized the instant apocalyptic fulfillment of God's promise in parallel with Jewish hope (see Ellis 1974: 141 and Marshall 1978: 379). The view also argues that Jesus was wrong about the nearness of the kingdom's coming. The view has various subforms depending on whether it is regarded as Jesus' saying or a saying created by the church to explain the return's delay (Grässer 1960 and Schürmann 1969: 551–52 [who holds Mark responsible for it]). Ellis correctly objects to this view. Against it stands the contrast between the rejected, since they are ashamed of Jesus, and the few who will see his kingdom. That only some see the kingdom shows that the final return is not in view. If the final return were in view, then all people present at the return share in it. If this is the apocalyptic return of the king and kingdom, where is its accompanying judgment?

2. The kingdom is the "mystery" or "already" form of the kingdom, which was inaugurated by Jesus at his resurrection (Acts 2:32–36). Many of the views that Plummer mentions fit here: Jesus refers to the resurrection-ascension (Calvin, Beza), Pentecost (Godet 1875: 1.421–22; G. L. Hahn), the spread of Christianity (K. F. Nösgen; Arndt 1956: 261), or the internal development of the gospel (i.e., the inauguration of fulfillment) (Erasmus). Of these subviews, the resurrection-ascension (since in Lucan terms this is a key event) or the Pentecost view (since it shows the significance of Jesus' exaltation) is best (Marshall 1978: 378; Hendriksen 1978: 501–2). This kingdom was a kingdom of salvific power, as the apostolic activity in Acts shows. In addition, Jesus' reply at his trial, where he

---

4. Plummer 1896: 249–50 actually lists seven views, but the four below are the most prevalent. In fact, some of his options are variations of the same view (see view 2). Scholars cited without documentation are listed in Plummer.

mentioned to the Jews that "from now on" the Son of Man would be seated at the right hand of the power of God (Luke 22:69), shows that this near form of the kingdom is intended. If this is the correct view, then Jesus is again alluding to his vindication. The disciples share in the glorious period that he will initiate.

3. The parallel Matt. 16:28 ("Son of Man coming in his kingdom") = Mark 9:1 ("seeing the kingdom of God having come with power") shows that the only time that Jesus came this gloriously in the disciples' lifetime was at the transfiguration (many church fathers; Liefeld 1984: 924). If this view is taken, then some disciples see the transfiguration (i.e., a preview of Jesus' later glory). This special event is also the guarantee of a day when Jesus will fully manifest his power on earth.

4. Jerusalem's destruction is a foretaste of judgment and Jesus' glory (J. J. Wettstein, H. Alford).

Which view is it? Contextually, Luke is clear that the "already" form of the inaugurated kingdom is included in Luke 9:27: if Jesus works by God's power, then his miracles show that the kingdom has come upon those present (11:20; 10:9); the kingdom's beginning and arrival follows John the Baptist (16:16); and the kingdom is "in your midst" in the form of Jesus (17:21). Acts 2 does portray Jesus' resurrection and exaltation as the enthronement of Messiah and a demonstration of Jesus' position as Lord, and Acts 8:12 associates Philip's preaching the kingdom with Jesus' name (Bovon 1989: 486 takes this view, arguing that it is different from Matthew and Mark).

However, one should not entirely exclude the function of the transfiguration as a "preview" experience of where the kingdom program is headed, that is, as the picture of a figure who will fully manifest his authority on the earth in the future, as Luke 21:27 suggests (see also Rom. 14:17; 1 Cor. 4:20; Col. 1:12–14). Luke works in patterns and, for him, the transfiguration is a preview of where the kingdom program ultimately leads. When Jesus refers to seeing the kingdom, he is referring to entering the kingdom and emphasizing the front end of the entry point, a package whose character will conclude with the revelation of a fully glorified Jesus like the one seen in the transfiguration. This combination of views 2 and 3 is actually a fifth view and is likely to be correct (so apparently Ellis 1974: 141).

Why exclude the reference to Jerusalem's destruction? Because Luke does not associate the kingdom's power with this event. He does mention it in association with end-time events, but they are not characterized in Luke 17 or 21 as kingdom events. Rather, they show what its final coming is like. Also, Jesus is not associated with Jerusalem's destruction directly, so it is not in view.

Is this Lucan view that of Matthew and Mark? Danker (1988: 196), Luce (1933: 186), and Bovon (1989: 486) see a different sense. No doubt, the language of the Synoptic parallels is more overtly apocalyptic, which Luke may well have simplified for his Gentile audience. Matthew's reference to the Son of Man and Mark's reference to the kingdom's having come (note the perfect tense ἐληλυθυῖαν, *elēlythuian*) in power both emphasize the authority associated with the realm more overtly than does Luke. But the transfiguration is not the only likely reference, since the coming in power is something whose presence remains, rather than being something whose effect is withdrawn, as the transfiguration view by itself requires. Matthew 26:64 agrees with Luke about Jesus' remarks at the trial: "Hereafter you shall see the Son of Man seated at the right hand of power and coming on the clouds of heaven." In fact, the remarks of 2 Pet. 1:16–21 also suggest the fulfillment of this "pattern-package" view, for in 2 Peter the transfiguration pictures what the apostolic preaching of Jesus was all about, looking ultimately to the dawning of the full eschatological morning.[5] Such a view of the kingdom's inauguration prevents the strictly future-kingdom view (#1) from being correct. It also renders erroneous the suggestion that Jesus erred. If this explanation of the verse is correct, then in Luke, Jesus says that some of those present will experience the beginning of the kingdom's presence in their lifetime. The Synoptic parallels note that this beginning comes with power and looks toward an even more glorious resolution. Who was not present at the inauguration? Who is included in the reference to dying? Judas tasted death through his denial and thereby missed the inauguration of glory. He is the unit's negative illustration: he fails to be a disciple and so misses glory. Thus, the transfiguration will preview the ultimate full glory of the exalted Christ. The kingdom program will end with the glorious Christ visible to all (Luke 9:26). The distribution of its benefits begins with the Spirit's being poured out as earnest after Jesus' resurrection and exaltation (Acts 2; Eph. 1:14; 2 Cor. 1:22; 5:5).

Summary   Luke 9:21–27 follows Peter's significant confession. Jesus begins to prepare the disciples for the future of his ministry, noting that the short-term outlook is grim: he will suffer, be handed over, and killed. But he will be raised as well. Jesus goes into the latter part of his earthly ministry well aware of where he is headed. He will-

---

5. 2 Pet. 1:3, 11, 14 speaks of power and Jesus' lordship now, as we await entrance into the "eternal kingdom of our Lord and Savior Jesus Christ."

ingly takes on the cause for which he came. Design and necessity stand behind what he experienced, so the reader realizes that what happened to Jesus was no surprise.

If one is to follow Jesus, then one had better recognize what allying with Jesus means. It means denying oneself and recognizing that God must deal with one's spiritual and physical needs. It means recognizing that suffering will be included in identifying with the one who was rejected. It means following in Jesus' footsteps. To lose one's life is to gain one's spiritual welfare. To seek to keep one's life and spiritual fate in one's own hands is to risk forfeiting all. It is possible to gain the world and have nothing spiritually, but this is a tragic trade-off. To reject Jesus and his teaching is ultimately to face his rejection. The choice is totally and starkly set out for the reader: Jesus is the issue; he is the choice; he is the authority and Judge with whom one must deal. His path is to be taken—or there is no path at all. To come to him is to recognize that until one comes to know God, one is not what God wants one to be. The call to discipleship reveals what Jesus wants from his people. Luke wants the reader to weigh and consider Jesus' call.

Jesus also offers a promise as the start of the kingdom draws near: many of those in his audience will live to see its beginning, and some will see a preview of the total glory. So also for the reader of Luke both then and now: the starting point has come and the finishing point draws nearer. The path of discipleship, though hard, is not carried out in isolation, since it represents the movement of promise from inauguration to consummation. In the long run, allegiance to Jesus is worth the cost, since the story to come lasts forever.

4. Transfiguration: Divine Confirmation and a Call to Hear (9:28–36)

Following Jesus' instruction about the disciple's sacrificial allegiance, Luke relates a second heavenly communication about Jesus. The transfiguration, like the baptism, involves a divine word about Jesus. In addition, it contains a revelation of Jesus' heavenly glory. He speaks with Moses and Elijah, but only he is transformed. Jesus' lordship and majesty become manifest. The revelation previewing his glory is limited to only a few: Peter, John, and James. After the event, they keep silent about it, but it clearly made a deep impression on Christian tradition (2 Pet. 1:16–21; Apocalypse of Peter 15–17; Acts of Peter 20; Acts of John 90–91; Acts of Philip 60; Bovon 1989: 491–92; Schneemelcher 1991–92: 2.633–35, 303, 180–81; James 1953: 444). This revelation about Jesus is significant, especially coming next to his word of suffering. Jesus will suffer and die, but even so, he is the bearer of heavenly glory.

This is an important time for such an endorsement, because Jesus has just announced his approaching death and warned the disciples of the cost of following him. A word of testimony and reassurance from heaven that Jesus is the messianic, eschatological Son would be an encouragement to them. In addition, the call to "hear Jesus" is a reminder that Jesus needs to instruct his disciples about many things before his "exodus." The disciples need to understand these things before they carry out their task in his absence. Thus, Jesus also functions prophetically as the "Prophet like Moses," another key early Christian title applied to Jesus (see Acts 3:14–26, esp. vv. 22–26). Indeed, the glorious transformation of Jesus alone suggests a transcendence that is not discussed here, but is revealed later. Fitzmyer (1981: 793) notes correctly that more than a Messiah is portrayed here.

Sources and Historicity

Luke 9:28–36 is paralleled in Mark 9:2–10 = Matt. 17:1–9 (Aland 1985: §161). The position of the event is the same in the parallels, located within six (Mark 9:2 = Matt. 17:1) or eight (Luke 9:28) days of the confession at Caesarea Philippi. It is difficult to decide where the transfiguration took place, since no specific locale is mentioned (proposed locations include

Mount Hermon, Mount Tabor, and Mount Meron) and since some time has passed since Peter's confession (see the exegesis of 9:28 for details on the locale).

Luke's version of the transfiguration is shorter at many points than that of Matthew or Mark, but it supplies more detail about what took place in the event itself. For example, by his unique mention of the "exodus," Luke emphasizes the suffering that Jesus is headed toward. This great OT event is a pattern for the ultimate event in God's plan. Christ's death and what happened thereafter recall a salvation of the past. Messiah, passion, and ultimate glory are pictured as part of an exodus, a great journey that Jesus is undertaking (Liefeld 1984: 925). In the transfiguration, one can see heaven's answer to Herod's question about who this man is (Fitzmyer 1981: 793). The answer goes well beyond the categories mentioned in 9:9.

In terms of the parallels, Mark and Matthew are largely in verbal agreement with each other, while Luke generally has used his own vocabulary. It may well be that Luke had unique sources, although some suggest that he made inferences from the account, a point that is difficult to support.[1] The problem of sources in this unit is complex, but the presence of additional source material on the whole is more likely than an appeal to Luke's reworking the material.

The account's authenticity is questioned, mainly because of its supernatural features.[2] Fitzmyer (1981: 795–96) notes four views: a historical occurrence, a vision, a resurrection appearance projected back into Jesus' life, and a symbolic portrayal of Jesus' glory. Ellis (1974: 142) notes a fifth view: it is Christian midrash grounded in Exod. 24:15–16 or 34:35 (Schweizer, *TDNT* 8:369 n. 249). Fitzmyer seems to reject the historical approach, but leaves unspecified the option chosen in its place.[3] Creed (1930: 133) min-

---

1. On the options, see Luce 1933: 186 and Schneider 1977a: 215. Fitzmyer 1981: 791–92 sees Luke's rewriting Mark, as do Schürmann 1969: 563–64; Wiefel 1988: 179; and Neirynck 1973. Plummer 1896: 250 notes signs of Lucan expression in the account. Schweizer 1984: 159 seems to suggest the presence of an additional source, noting the different dating, the journey idea, and the reference to "the" mountain. So also Schramm 1971: 136–39 argues for an additional source, as does Bovon 1989: 488–89, especially for 9:31–33. Bovon even mentions the possibility of oral tradition. Marshall 1978: 381 notes the Lucan peculiarities: Jesus at prayer, change in his facial appearance, exodus, sleep of the disciples, and fear at the cloud's coming. Marshall, like Bovon, suggests that Luke reworked Mark in light of oral sources, since some changes are shared with Matthew (i.e., the facial appearance).

2. Creed 1930: 132–33 cites E. Meyer's complaint about the "rationalistic prejudice" of some critics in the 1920s.

3. Fitzmyer is agnostic on historicity because it is "impossible to say exactly what happened." He rejects a pure historical approach as problematic because it cannot explain Moses' and Elijah's presence, nor can it explain the disciples' denials and defection later in Jesus' ministry. These objections are not decisive, since they underestimate how people react when faced with death and the pressures of extreme persecution. Since the presence of Moses and Elijah is tied to eschatological hope, is Fitzmyer's real objection to their "resurrected" presence? No doubt, the scene's

imally opts for a psychological experience of some kind by the disciples, which might mean a vision (also Luce 1933: 187 and Michaelis, *TDNT* 5:354, 372). It seems difficult to accept this explanation as totally satisfying, for what could engender such an impression? The assumptions that led Wellhausen to classify the text as a resurrection event do not work (Schweizer, *TDNT* 8:369 n. 251).[4] All that is suggested about Jesus is a glorious presence, not a resurrected appearance. Seeing the event as historical and supernatural seems the only way to explain it (Marshall 1978: 381).[5] Nolland (1993a: 496) notes that historical inquiry does not have the tools to substantiate the event, but nothing found in the event represents an insuperable barrier to the possible occurrence of such an event in Jesus' ministry. The tradition, as 2 Peter shows, seems deeply impacted by this event, which is a precursor to resurrection. If resurrection is possible, then nothing in this event is unlikely.

The account is called a story about Jesus (Fitzmyer 1981: 795, following V. Taylor 1966: 386–88). Bultmann (1963: 259–61) calls it a legend because of the supernatural elements (he uses "legend" in its form-critical sense to emphasize the account's supernatural character). Efforts to classify it more precisely have led to a variety of possibilities: enthronement, prophetic vision, apocalyptic vision, divine epiphany, midrash, and cult narrative (Bovon 1989: 490–91). According to Bovon, classification is difficult because of the variety of motifs: apocalyptic revelatory images (Jesus' transformation and the voice from heaven), the Exodus background, regal imagery, and epiphany (heavenly glory manifested on earth; Wiefel 1988: 180).

The outline of Luke 9:28–36 is as follows:

a. Setting (9:28)
b. Jesus' transfiguration and its witnesses (9:29–31)
c. Peter's desire to celebrate the Feast of Tabernacles (9:32–33)
d. Heavenly endorsement of the Son-Prophet (9:34–35)
e. The disciples' silence (9:36)

---

supernatural qualities have influenced how it is seen by interpreters. Fitzmyer also rejects a purely symbolic account, so his view is not clear.

4. Fitzmyer gives four reasons why this view cannot work: (1) it cannot explain the presence of Moses and Elijah; (2) the verb ὁράω (to see; passive = to appear) is not limited to postresurrection events; (3) Jesus' glory is never mentioned in a resurrection account; and (4) the form does not match resurrection appearances. See also Bock 1987: 324 n. 98; Müller 1960: 60; Stein 1976.

5. For the history of interpretation of this passage, see Boobyer 1942: 1–47; Liefeld 1974: 162–65; Baltensweiler 1959. Since no sayings of Jesus appear in this passage, the Jesus Seminar does not discuss it.

Bovon (1989: 490) notes the structure's threefold pairing: the setting and conclusion (9:28, 36), the divine sign (9:29–31) with the divine meaning (9:34–35), and a general human reaction (9:32) with a specific human reaction (9:33).

Many themes are part of this key account: prayer, the revelation of Jesus' glory, his divinely ordained journey into suffering, his being greater than Moses or Elijah (seen in his transformation and the refusal to build booths), the testimony of the law (Moses) and the eschatological prophet (Elijah), the divine testimony to Jesus' sonship, the call to hear him as the "Prophet like Moses," instruction of the disciples, and silence (the proper time for a full testimony is later).

Exegesis and Exposition

[28]Now about eight days after these sayings, he took with him Peter, John, and James and went up on the mountain to pray. [29]And as he was praying the appearance of his face changed, and his garment became dazzling white. [30]And behold, there were two men speaking with him, Moses and Elijah, [31]who appeared in glory and spoke of his exodus, which he was about to fulfill in Jerusalem. [32]Now Peter and those with him were weighed down with sleep, and when they wakened they saw his glory and the two men who stood with him. [33]And as the men were departing from him, Peter said to Jesus, "Master, it is good that we are here; let us make three booths, one for you and one for Moses and one for Elijah"—not knowing what he was saying. [34]And as he was saying this a cloud came and overshadowed them; and they were afraid as they entered the cloud. [35]And a voice came from the cloud, saying, "This is my Son, ⌜the Chosen One⌝, listen to him." [36]And when the voice had spoken, Jesus was found alone. And they kept silent and told no one in those days what they had seen.

a. Setting (9:28)

Luke sets the situation briefly with ἐγένετο (*egeneto*, it came to pass), a common transition term in Luke.[6] It is some (ὡσεί, *hōsei*) eight days after Peter's confession at Caesarea Philippi; Matthew and Mark set the time more exactly at the sixth day. Some suggest that Luke means "about a week," with the days being reckoned inclusively (Creed 1930: 134; Marshall 1978: 382; Fitzmyer 1981: 797).[7]

9:28

6. BDR §442.4b n. 11; BDF §442.5. Grammatically, the temporal note is a parenthetical nominative; BDF §144.

7. Bovon 1989: 493–94 discusses symbolic meanings about the new eschaton or the Feast of Tabernacles (he is uncertain which is indicated). However, the vague reference to "about" eight is against any symbolic meaning, especially since the number is not used elsewhere in this way in Luke. If we did not have Mark and Matthew, would one even raise the question of a symbolic sense?

This difference is peculiar if Luke had only Matthew or Mark as a source; it suggests another source. Only Luke specifically mentions that the transfiguration was after the sayings about discipleship, but this is the impression of Matthew and Mark as well. The Matthean and Marcan reference to six days may allude to Exod. 24:15–16 and thus suggest a second-Moses motif (Liefeld 1984: 926). But Marshall's objections (1978: 382) to this are probably correct: the temporal connection "after six days" in Matthew and Mark is not equivalent to "on the seventh day" in Exodus. On the other hand, the cloud is probably an allusion to the Shekinah glory of Exodus (Marshall 1978: 387; Danker 1988: 200; Fitzmyer 1981: 802). If the allusion to the exodus is present in the parallels, Luke makes nothing else of it. Neither is the tabernacles image of Lev. 23:36 in the background, since Luke 9:33 rejects a tabernacles connection.

Peter, John, and James accompanied Jesus up the mountain. Matthew and Mark have Peter, James, and John—another peculiarity of name order if Mark or Matthew was the only source that Luke had. These three are singled out in other events as well.[8]

Proposed locations for the mountain include the following:

Mountain	Location	Adherents
Hermon	near Caesarea Philippi	Arndt 1956: 262
Tabor	in southern Galilee, six miles from Nazareth	Cyril of Jerusalem (the first clear reference) Jerome Origen, *Exegetica in Psalmos* (on Ps. 88:13) (this text is disputed and may be better called Pseudo-Origen; see *PG* 12:1548) Fitzmyer 1981: 798 Bovon 1989: 494 n. 35 (apparently) Baldi 1955
Meron	northwest of the Sea of Galilee	Liefeld 1974: 167 n. 27

It is difficult to decide, since no specific locale is mentioned and since some time has passed since Peter's confession. Tabor has the strongest support in the tradition.

The third element of the setting is unique to Luke: the mention of prayer. The focus on prayer is common in Luke and adds to the event's spiritual mood. In Luke, when prayer is present, something significant usually follows (e.g., 3:21).

8. Luke 8:51 has the same order as here, but in the Lucan apostolic list in Luke 6:14, James precedes John, so Luke has no fixed order.

b. Jesus' Transfiguration and Its Witnesses (9:29–31)

In the midst of prayer, Jesus is transformed before the three disci- **9:29**
ples. Luke's description of the change in Jesus' face is more specific
than the general reference in Mark 9:2 = Matt. 17:2 to his being
transfigured (μετεμορφώθη, *metemorphōthē*). Matthew also mentions that Jesus' face shone as the sun (ἔλαμψεν . . . ὡς ὁ ἥλιος,
elampsen . . . hōs ho hēlios). Luke lacks a verbal description of what
takes place, literally describing it as "the appearance of his face was
other" (τὸ εἶδος τοῦ προσώπου αὐτοῦ ἕτερον, *to eidos tou prosōpou
autou heteron*, usually expressed in English as "Jesus' face
changed"). It is suggested that Luke omitted the verb μεταμορφόω to
prevent confusion with an epiphany, which might have polytheistic
connotations to a Hellenistic audience (Plummer 1896: 251; Creed
1930: 134; Liefeld 1984: 926).

The point of these descriptions is that Jesus was physically
transformed into a radiant figure whose brilliance extended to his
clothes. Each of the Synoptics mentions in its own way the change
in clothes: Matt. 17:2 speaks of clothes "white like light"; Mark 9:3
mentions "clothes glistening, very white as no bleacher on earth
could bleach them"; Luke simply says "dazzling white" (Danker
1988: 198; Fitzmyer 1981: 799; Fitzer, *TDNT* 7:666).[9] Jesus' glory is
similar to the description of Moses' glory in Exod. 34:29–35,
though the terminology is not parallel. Much in the account (Jesus'
glory, Moses' presence, the cloud, the allusion to Deut. 18:15) suggests an allusion to Jesus as a greater, second Moses, but more than
Moses is intended, since explicit comparison to Moses is rejected
later in the account (cf. 2 Cor. 3:7–18).[10] Danker (1988: 198) argues
against a second-Moses motif of Jesus as new lawgiver, arguing instead for Jesus as a replacement of Moses. However, Jesus as a
prophet to be heard (Luke 9:35) looks to a second-Moses figure.
This new Moses establishes a new order, not new law, in relating
to God and reveals the way to him in this new period. Luke definitely sees Jesus in this light and emphasizes him as the bringer of
a new order (Luke 5:33–39; Acts 3:18–22; 7:35–37; 15:1–29). Contra
Danker (1988: 198) and Schweizer (1984: 160), there is no allusion
to the "righteous one" of Dan. 12:3 (cf. Rev. 3:5) who comes
through apocalyptic tribulation, for there is no apocalyptic image
in Luke.

9. Michaelis, *TDNT* 4:247–48, describes the image as one of heavenly glory; so ἐξ-
αστράπτων (gleaming like lightning); Ezek. 1:4, 7. Conceptual parallels occur in
Ezek. 1:27–28; Dan. 10:6; Luke 24:4; Acts 1:10; Rev. 2:17; 6:2; 20:11; 2 Esdr. [= 4 Ezra]
7:97; 1 Enoch 38.4; 104.2; 2 Bar. 51.

10. Bock 1987: 115–16, 323–24 nn. 96–97. On the apocalyptic imagery, see Behm,
TDNT 4:758; on God's glory, see Ps. 104:2; Hab. 3:4.

9:30 With the transformation also comes the appearance of two major OT figures, Moses and Elijah, who are talking with (συνελάλουν, *synelaloun*) Jesus. Their presence has evoked much discussion (Liefeld 1974: 171–74; Jeremias, *TDNT* 2:938–39). What do they represent?

1. Thrall (1969–70) and Schweizer (1984: 160) argue that they represent different endings to life: Moses was buried by God (Deut. 34:1–8), while Elijah was taken up (2 Kings 2:1–12). Thus, here death before God and translation are contrasted to resurrection. The major problem with this understanding is that Moses' death and Elijah's translation are not mentioned in the passage.

2. They are selected because they are conceived as the great wonder workers of the OT or because they were great prophet-statesmen (Arndt 1956: 263). It is hard to explain their connection on this basis, for many others did miracles and played key roles before the nation. The choice of Elijah for this "statesman" role is especially unclear.

3. Moses represents the Law and Elijah the Prophets (Plummer 1896: 251; Schürmann 1969: 557–58; Wiefel 1988: 180; Bovon 1989: 496). The problem here is not the Mosaic connection, but Elijah's tie to the prophets: why is he considered the representative of the prophets (Danker 1988: 199)? Samuel or one of the major prophets is normally seen in this light (Acts 3:24; Matt. 16:14).

4. The best suggestion is that Moses typifies the prophetic office that Jesus will occupy (as the later allusion to Deut. 18:15 suggests), while Elijah pictures the hope of the eschaton. Jesus will function as a Moses-like formative figure for the people he draws round himself, much as Moses drew together the nation of Israel. With Jesus comes a new period, a new configuration of God's people, a fresh way of relating to God. Thus, Elijah is present as the hope of the eschaton (Mal. 4:5–6 [3:23–24 MT]). Luke makes the Mosaic connection explicit in Acts 3:18–22 and 7:35–37. When the NT mentions Elijah with Jesus, it has in view either the coming of the eschaton or the preparing of the way, the latter concept also appearing in the John the Baptist image of Luke 1:16–17 and Mark 9:12. Perhaps part of the background to this image is the idea that Elijah will rescue the righteous sufferer, as the taunting associated with Jesus' death suggests in Mark 15:36, though this connection is less clear (Danker 1988: 199).[11] Thus, Moses looks back to the ex-

11. Two key studies on the Elijah motif in Luke are Brodie 1987 and C. A. Evans 1987b. Evans argues that Elijah reflects the motif of God's election of his true people.

odus and Elijah looks forward to the fulfillment of promise in the eschaton.[12] It is also suggested that these figures function as OT witnesses to Jesus, which is certainly the impression created by their presence (Marshall 1978: 384, though he accepts view 3). Such a witness function for Elijah caused the Jew Trypho to challenge the Christian Justin's claims about Jesus, since for Trypho Elijah had not appeared but was still expected.[13]

Only Luke notes the glorified condition of the OT saints and their **9:31** topic of conversation: Jesus' "exodus" (ἔξοδον, *exodon*), which was about to come to fulfillment in Jerusalem. Fulfillment (πληροῦν, *plēroun*) is the key theme of this verse; the events discussed are part of God's plan, which will come to pass. In addition, Luke will highlight the Jerusalem journey in 9:51–19:44, by making special note of the city at 9:51; 13:22; 17:11; 18:31; and 19:28.

The ἔξοδος itself recalls the great OT event of salvation and suggests that Jesus is doing something not just equivalent, but even greater. Moses' presence and the refusal to equate Jesus and Moses with the Feast of Booths in 9:33 show Jesus' superiority.[14] The ἔξοδος is variously interpreted (Marshall 1978: 384–85):

1. The term refers only to Jesus' death in Jerusalem, thus reinforcing 9:22 (Liefeld 1984: 927; Arndt 1956: 263; Danker 1988: 199; Michaelis, *TDNT* 5:107; Schürmann 1969: 558 [who speaks of a focus on the fate of death]). While ἔξοδος can refer to death (2 Pet. 1:15; Wis. 3:2; 7:6; BAGD 276 §2; BAA 559–60 §2), the imagery of journey looks beyond the death (which is a focal point of Luke 9:31) to a series of events. The emphasis on fulfillment fits well with this view, which does reflect a major element in the concept but does not exhaust the image.

2. The term refers to Jesus' death and ascension (so 9:51; Plummer 1896: 251; Marshall 1978: 384–85; Fitzmyer 1981: 800; Ellis 1974: 143; Schneider 1977a: 216; Wiefel 1988: 181; Bovon 1989: 496–97). This view has much to commend it, though it may not go far enough.

---

12. In late Judaism, Moses and Elijah are linked eschatologically in Midr. Deut. 3.17 (201c); SB 1:756; Schürmann 1969: 557.

13. Justin Martyr, *Dialogue with Trypho* 8 (ca. A.D. 150). The transfiguration is a counterargument to Trypho's objection.

14. Grundmann, *TDNT* 7:650 n. 31, lists the Lucan expressions for the six phases of Jesus' career: ἔξοδος (exodus) in Luke 9:31; δόξα (glory) in Luke 24:26; ἀναλαμβάνω (taken up) in Acts 1:2, 11, 22; καθῆσθαι ἐκ δεξιῶν τοῦ θεοῦ (seated at the right hand of God) in Luke 20:42; 22:69; and Acts 2:34; ἵστημι (standing) in Acts 7:55–56; and ἔρχομαι (coming) in Luke 9:26 and Acts 1:11.

3. The image argues for repetition of the exodus event (Mánek 1957–58b). This element is present, but it does not really explain the point of comparison between Jesus' ministry and the exodus. This view can be combined with other approaches to the passage.

4. The whole life of Jesus is an "exodus," starting with John's coming and extending to Jesus' departure in Jerusalem (Acts 13:24–31). However, the verse's language (the journey is "about to be" [ἤμελλεν, *ēmellen*] fulfilled in Jerusalem) stands against this option (BDR §356.1 n. 2).

5. The best option, not listed by Marshall, is that the image refers to the entire death-parousia career of Jesus. This is suggested in Luke 9:22, 26 (Bock 1987: 116, 324 n. 99), as well as by the journey image of a lord "gone for a while to return" in certain parables (12:35–37; 19:11–13). Jesus' glorious condition at the time of this discussion also suggests this more comprehensive allusion. Moses and Elijah anticipate what Jesus will fulfill, starting in Jerusalem. Clearly the stress is on his death, resurrection, and ascension—all of which happen in Jerusalem. It is these events as inaugurating a larger program that is the point of the journey motif.

c. Peter's Desire to Celebrate the Feast of Tabernacles (9:32–33)

9:32   Luke adds another unique detail: as Jesus prayed, the disciples drifted off to sleep.[15] (They do this again before Jesus' arrest—21:45.) They awaken to the scene—thus apparently missing most of the conversation[16]—to see Jesus glorified and two men standing with him. What is described is clearly distinguished from a vision or dream (the mention of sleep might indicate that the event occurred in the evening, but that is not certain; if the disciples were tired, they could have fallen asleep at any time). An event without the disciples now becomes more public.

---

15. To indicate sleep, Luke uses ὕπνος (BAGD 843; BAA 1679; elsewhere in Luke's writings twice in Acts 20:9) and βαρέω (to be heavy; BAGD 133; BAA 267; elsewhere in Luke's writings only in Luke 21:34). In 22:45–46, Luke uses the synonymous κοιμάω and καθεύδω. It is clear that the disciples are in deep sleep, for the phrase βεβαρημένοι ὕπνῳ translates literally as "weighed down with sleep." Balz, *TDNT* 8:554, speaks of disciples "drunk with sleep." Bovon's term "second consciousness" (1989: 498) is too visionary in force. He cites Gen. 15:12; Dan. 8:18; 10:9.

16. So διαγρηγορήσαντες (a NT *hapax legomenon*) is an ingressive aorist: "began to awaken fully" (Arndt 1956: 263). BAGD 182 and BAA 365 argue for this ingressive sense, rather than suggesting that drowsiness is the point of the description.

One disciple reacts. With the impending departure of the OT saints, **9:33** Peter tries to prolong the moment with a suggestion that they celebrate the Feast of Tabernacles on the mountain. This key festival in Judaism looked back at God's provision in the wilderness and was regarded as anticipating God's ultimate deliverance.[17] Apparently, Peter understood Moses' and Elijah's presence to have eschatological overtones.[18]

The Feast of Tabernacles was a major event in the Jewish calendar. The festival's main activity involved constructing booths to live in for a week. The rules for the size of the booth were very specific (*m. Suk.* 1). Only men and boys old enough not to need a mother were required to live in the booth, which was to be the "main abode" for that week, with one's house being the "chance abode" (*m. Suk.* 2.9). This time of great joy looked back at God's initial faithful provision of food in the wilderness and at his current provision of harvest (the American Thanksgiving holiday and the German *Erntedank* are loose equivalents). As well, the feast looked forward to God's total provision later. It is this mood of expectation that Peter wants to retain. His remark that the experience is a good thing to share shows his positive frame of mind (Marshall 1978: 386).

What is not clear is whether Peter had in mind reproducing the feast or whether he wanted the booths for something else. Though they recall the imagery of the Feast of Tabernacles, the booths (σκηνάς, *skēnas*) were most likely a way for the visitors to prolong their stay (Marshall 1978: 386 cites Luke 16:9 and John 14:2 as conceptual equivalents tied to heaven). Peter probably wanted to continue the mountaintop experience. It is clear that he had some feel for the special nature of the moment, and his desire to celebrate the occasion and extend it is understandable. Only Luke mentions that Peter's remark came as Moses and Elijah were leaving. Luce (1933: 189) argues that a statement by Peter here is out of place and suggests that Peter raised questions instead ("Is it good for us to be here?" "Should we build three booths?"). However, such interjections by Peter are not unusual (Luke 5:8; 22:33).

But why does Luke say that Peter did not know what he was saying? Most see Peter's error as his desire to build three booths, re-

17. Exod. 23:16; 34:22; Lev. 23:34; Deut. 16:13; Zech. 14:16–21; Marshall 1978: 386; Michaelis, *TDNT* 7:370; *m. Sukka* (esp. 3.9 and 4.5, which call the people to pray to God to deliver them, and 4.8, where Hallel Psalms are sung); Josephus, *Antiquities* 8.4.1 §100.

18. Michaelis, *TDNT* 7:379–80, rejects a connection to the Feast of Tabernacles; but see Boobyer 1942: 76–79; Ellis 1974: 143; Daube 1956: 30–32 (though some of his citations involve material that is much later than this period).

flecting a sense of equality between the three figures. One booth for each luminary stands in contrast to the voice from heaven that follows. By alluding to Deut. 18, the voice makes clear that Jesus is special and that he is the superior successor to Moses (Danker 1988: 200). In addition, Peter may have been rebuked for suggesting that now is the time to celebrate the entry of the eschaton. However, Peter's remarks, though missing the mark in terms of Christology and in terms of timing, do not necessarily represent a conscious attempt to avoid suffering (contra Hendriksen 1978: 506). The need to reject this final option is clear, since up to this point the disciples have not comprehended the force of Jesus' remarks about his impending suffering. They cannot consciously reject what they do not as yet understand.

Matthew 17:4 = Mark 9:5 also notes Peter's remarks. Matthew says that Peter left the celebration up to Jesus' discretion by saying, "If you wish," and adds that Peter himself offered to build the booths. Mark and Luke portray Peter as personally making a request. Matthew omits any rebuke of Peter's remark, while Mark 9:6 notes that fear present with all the disciples formed the background for Peter's remark. The Gospels' portraits are complementary.

d. Heavenly Endorsement of the Son-Prophet (9:34–35)

9:34 Heaven reacts: a cloud comes on the scene and overshadows the participants. The point of this cloud imagery is debated (Liefeld 1974: 169–71):

1. The image is associated with God's eschatological coming on the clouds (Luke 21:27; 1 Thess. 4:17; Ps. 97:2; Zeph. 1:15; Ezek. 30:3; Isa. 4:5; Dan. 7:13–14; 2 Macc. 2:8; 2 Bar. 53; 2 Esdr. [= 4 Ezra] 13:3; Boobyer 1942: 83–85; Ellis 1974: 143). The imagery indicates God's presence in the midst of the period of restoration. With a mood that might be parallel to Luke, 2 Macc. 2:8 expresses a hope for the return of God's glory to the people in the eschaton (Danker 1988: 201).
2. The image reflects the exodus and points to a new period around Jesus like the time of Moses (Exod. 13:21–22; 16:10; 19:16; 24:15–18; 40:34–38; Oepke, *TDNT* 4:908–9; Josephus, *Antiquities* 3.12.5 §290; 3.14.4 §310; Fitzmyer 1981: 802). This latter association is the most natural way to read the passage. The Mosaic connections are explicit, although the return of the cloud does have eschatological overtones, since God's visible presence is in view. In fact, Exod. 40:35 uses the same verb as is used here: ἐπισκιάζω (*episkiazō*, to overshadow) (Luce 1933: 189). So the parallels to Sinai are strong.

3. The cloud pictures God's presence (Bovon 1989: 500 and n. 60 notes that Tg. Neof. 1.3 on Lev. 23:43 speaks of Israel's dwelling in the cloud). It overshadows the disciples, leaving them afraid. Some suggest that only Jesus and his guests were overshadowed, since the voice is described as coming out of the cloud and the disciples appear to be outside observers (Godet 1875: 1.429–30; Plummer 1896: 252–53; Creed 1930: 135; Oepke, *TDNT* 4:908; Marshall 1978: 387). There is no need to make this suggestion, for the disciples could have been overshadowed by the cloud and a voice could still have come from it. In fact, this verse clearly refers to the disciples' coming into the cloud, since it mentions that "they were afraid as they entered the cloud."

The cloud's presence seems to be God's answer to Peter's suggestion: no booths are needed since God has wrapped the disciples in his glory and presence. God's very presence is associated with Jesus, through whom they have access to full communion and presence with God. The cloud's presence leaves the disciples fearful, a normal response to God's action (Luke 1:12; Balz, *TDNT* 9:209–10). With the departure of the cloud after the voice, the OT saints are no longer present (9:36). But to argue that the cloud's purpose was to take them into God's presence is unwarranted, since Jesus did not depart with the OT saints. Given the imagery denoting divine presence, the disciples experienced it as well. Thus, there was no need for a "rapture" to heaven during the event (contra Oepke, *TDNT* 4:908). Both view 2 and view 3 have merit.

The parallel in Mark 9:6–7 = Matt. 17:5–6 is similar. Mark describes Peter's and the disciples' fear first and then notes the cloud's coming, while Matthew lacks any mention of fear, describing only the disciples falling to their faces after hearing the voice and their being filled with awe. Matthew also describes the character of the cloud as "bright" (φωτεινή, *phōteinē*), another description of God's glorious presence. Clearly the experience overwhelms them. One is humbled to meet God so directly.

9:35 The testimony of heaven parallels that given at the baptism (3:22). Both sayings have three structural elements: title ("Son" in both accounts), qualifying description ("beloved" in the baptism; "the chosen" in the transfiguration), and concluding remark ("in whom I am well pleased" in the baptism; "listen to him" in the transfiguration).

The reference to sonship is an allusion to Ps. 2:7, just as the title *Son* at the baptism was seen as derived from the psalm (see the exegesis of Luke 3:22). In the earlier text, the remark was seen as messianic, especially as it is linked to two other Lucan texts (4:1–13, 16–

30).[19] The messianic thrust of the remark is confirmed by the second part of the declaration: ὁ ἐκλελεγμένος (*ho eklelegmenos*, the Chosen One). This wording is found only in Luke, probably as an explanatory reference to strengthen the regal character of the remark, coming as it does after Peter's messianic confession of Jesus. It is God's "amen" to that confession. Mark 9:7 = Matt. 17:5 has ὁ ἀγαπητός (*ho agapētos*, the beloved), as do all three Synoptics' report of the utterance given at the baptism. The Lucan change serves to explain Luke's understanding of the wording and seems to derive from Isa. 42:1, where the reference is to the Servant as God's chosen instrument. When one puts the two titles together, Jesus is identified as the Messiah-Servant, the fundamental christological category that Luke has presented up to this point.[20] The use of the perfect participle shows that Jesus has already occupied the position of the "elect one"; enthronement is not the point here.

Another key feature in the heavenly endorsement is the allusion to Deut. 18:15. Unlike the Matthean and Marcan parallels, Luke's word order directly matches the LXX version of Deuteronomy (αὐτοῦ ἀκούετε, *autou akouete*, listen to him), thus emphasizing slightly the focus of listening *to him*. The allusion to Deuteronomy is important, because it marks out Jesus as a "Prophet like Moses" (Acts 3:19–24). It also indicates that the disciples need instruction from the one who leads the way to God. There are things that the disciples do not yet understand about the one they have confessed. Conzelmann (1960: 57–59) is surely correct to say that the call is to hear Jesus' teaching about his passion and to recognize that Jesus will be a Messiah who suffers. Jesus has much more to reveal about himself.

The reference to Deut. 18 is not used in the voice's remark at Jesus' baptism. The new reference not only identifies Jesus, but declares his role as revealer of God's way through a confession from heaven. Much of the rest of Luke involves the Prophet-Messiah's instruction to his disciples. In effect, the voice says to Peter, "Jesus is not equal to Moses or Elijah; he is greater than they" (Fitzmyer 1981: 803). God is saying, "Sit at his feet, so you can learn from him the way to me."

19. Bovon 1989: 501–2, with most, sees prophetic imagery dominating, but he also correctly speaks of Sinai imagery as key. The emphasis is on God's presence, but the confession is regal and messianic. Luke is not referring only to a "chosen one" like Moses. A synthesis of concepts exists here, not just one image. For Luke, even the "Prophet like Moses" is a regal-like figure, leading a nation to deliverance (Acts 3:17–26; 7:20–43).

20. Bock 1987: 115. Ὁ ἐκλεκτός is the normal OT form: Isa. 42:1 LXX uses it as a description of Israel. In Luke 23:35, the people use ὁ ἐκλεκτός to scoff at Jesus' messianic claim; thus, the regal force for Luke is indisputable.

Another key difference has occurred since the baptism. For Luke and Mark, the second-person remarks made at the baptism were directed at Jesus; but here the third person is used, making clear that the disciples are the intended audience (Danker 1988: 201). It is they who need the heavenly testimony; it is they who need "to hear him."

The remark varies slightly in the accounts. For the second title Matt. 17:5 = Mark 9:7 has ἀγαπητός (beloved), not ἐκλελεγμένος (chosen). Also, the allusion to Deut. 18:15 appears as ἀκούετε αὐτοῦ in Matthew and Mark. Luke makes the saying's force clear by his differences. In addition, Matthew has "the one with whom I am well pleased," tying the remark more closely to the baptism.

e. The Disciples' Silence (9:36)

Everything returns to normal and the "sneak preview" ends. With the culmination of the divine endorsement, the OT saints are gone and Jesus is left alone. The details of the saints' departure are not given. The disciples respond with silence for a time, for which Luke gives no reason. The spirit of the remark is unusual, since in many ancient works of this type such an event would have been proclaimed widely (Plummer 1896: 253 argues that the note is so unusual that it speaks to the event's historicity). Their response suggests that the transfiguration is an event to reflect on, not an event to be paraded in public proclamation. No doubt its implications were much clearer to the disciples after Jesus was raised. At that point they may have felt more comfortable about their understanding of it and so could share its significance more readily. Arndt (1956: 264) notes that they were slow to see the suffering-glory process reflected in the idea of exodus and transfiguration. Other reasons for the silence come from the parallels.

9:36

Luke's conclusion to the event is much briefer than Matthew's and Mark's. Mark 9:8–10 = Matt. 17:8–9 mentions that Jesus commanded the disciples' silence until after the resurrection. The nature of his teaching from this point on in his ministry suggests why. The disciples did not entirely understand, until the resurrection, what God's program for Jesus was. There was great risk that the event might be misunderstood if it was discussed publicly. This conclusion seems likely in light of Jesus' spending much time teaching the disciples about the road of suffering on which he would travel. They struggled constantly with trying to understand him (Luke 9:45). Mark 9:10 makes clear that at this point the disciples did not comprehend what the Son of Man's resurrection meant. Luke's shorter version simply indicates the disciples' silence and suggests it was temporary. In Luke, the event ends with a note of silence and awe. The motif of silence in the face of God's revelation reflects the OT

(Dan. 10:15; Danker 1988: 201). A note of reflection is also present in the perfect ἑώρακαν (heōrakan, they had seen), which suggests that these things lingered with them (Marshall 1978: 389).

Summary Luke 9:28–36 presents the transfiguration as a major event of confirmation. After Jesus received the disciples' confession and warned them about his approaching suffering, three disciples hear the heavenly voice testify to Jesus' uniqueness. Such an endorsement is significant—for the disciples and for Luke's readers. But not only is Jesus endorsed, there is instruction about him. Not only is Jesus pictured as the Messiah-Servant, he is portrayed as the "Prophet like Moses." He is to be heeded. The disciples have much to learn from Jesus. Much of what they hear, they do not expect. So they must listen. The one who follows Jesus must be taught by him about suffering, sharing in that suffering, and pleasing God.

What Jesus says about himself and the way to God is true. The disciples' confession about Jesus is true, but needs filling in. The suffering he promises will occur, for God planned it. It is Jesus' "exodus." But in the face of impending suffering, Jesus' glory reveals who he really is and how he will ultimately manifest himself. Moses, the founding figure of the nation, and Elijah, the prophet of the eschaton, testify to him and are subordinate to him. "Be assured" is the note given to the reader (cf. 1:4). Jesus is who he claims to be. Those who follow him are to heed his new teaching and to trust in his person. Just as the disciples were silent and had time to take in the implications of the transfiguration, so the reader should reflect on Jesus' uniqueness, glory, and authority. When one is with Jesus, one is in the cloud of glory.

Additional Note

9:35. The UBS–NA reading, ὁ ἐκλελεγμένος (the Chosen One), is correct (supported by 𝔓⁴⁵, 𝔓⁷⁵, most Alexandrian witnesses, many Itala). The variant ὁ ἀγαπητός (the beloved) is not in the older manuscripts (supported by C*, A, D ["in whom I am pleased"], W, Byz, Lect) and appears to be an assimilation to Matt. 17:5 = Mark 9:7 (Arndt 1956: 264; Creed 1930: 135; Marshall 1978: 388).

5. The Disciples' Failure and Jesus' Instruction (9:37–50)

Luke now completes his major section on Jesus' Galilean ministry (Luke 4:14–9:50) and also concludes the unit on christological confession and instruction about discipleship (9:18–50). This subunit has three parts, each dominated by the failure of the disciples: the disciples fail to perform an exorcism and are rebuked by Jesus (9:37–43a); they fail to understand a passion prediction (9:43b–45); and they are instructed about greatness and cooperation (9:46–50). The disciples have much to learn. They must listen to Jesus (9:35). Otherwise their instincts will take them in the wrong direction.

a. The Disciples' Failure and Jesus' Reversal (9:37–43a)

The final public act in this unit of Luke is a miracle: Jesus heals a boy possessed by a destructive spirit.[1] Jesus' power and authority dominated this unit, but the present account is not merely another exercise of power. It serves as a contrast between Jesus' power and the disciples' impotence (Schürmann 1969: 567–68; Marshall 1978: 389–90). That the rebuked disciples have much to learn reinforces the command to listen to Jesus, which was given at the end of the transfiguration. Every pericope from here until 9:62 involves instruction, thus subjecting the disciples to constant correction. By the Book of Acts, the disciples will have learned these lessons, so that the miracle also contrasts with their actions in Acts.

In addition, demonic power continues to be overcome by God's Chosen One, even though Jesus begins to turn and face rejection, betrayal, and death. Also repeated is the pattern of mountain scene followed by a demonic encounter (as in 6:12–18; Danker 1988: 203). Ministry, not isolation, is what Jesus is all about. He may spend time before God, but he does not withdraw for long. Above all, the miracle expresses God's compassion through Jesus. It is an exorcism of forces that seek to destroy people (Fitzmyer 1981: 807).

Sources and Historicity

Luke 9:37–43a is paralleled in Matt. 17:14–21 = Mark 9:14–29 (Aland 1985: §163). The Marcan version is the most detailed; Luke is the shortest,

---

1. This is the last of thirteen miracles in the Galilean section:
   unclean spirit cast out (4:33–37)
   Simon's mother-in-law healed (4:38–39)
   miraculous catch of fish (5:1–11)
   leper cleansed (5:12–16)
   paralytic healed (5:17–26)
   centurion's slave healed (7:1–10)
   raising of the widow of Nain's son (7:11–17)
   stilling of the storm (8:22–25)
   Gerasene demoniac healed (8:26–39)
   woman with flow of blood healed (8:42b–48)
   raising of Jairus's daughter (8:40–42a, 49–56)
   feeding of the five thousand (9:10–17)
   healing of a possessed boy (9:37–43a)

lacking four key elements (Matthew also lacks the first three points):[2] (1) the dispute between the scribes and the other disciples (Mark 9:14), (2) the discussion with the father about the length of the illness (Mark 9:21–22), (3) the faith of the boy's father (Mark 9:23–24), and (4) the disciples' private questioning about why they could not heal (Mark 9:28–29). Luke's focus is strictly on the disciples (Ellis 1974: 144) and on Jesus' power and God's work through him.

The placement of the event in all three Gospels is the same, although Luke lacks the discussion about Elijah's coming (Mark 9:11–13 = Matt. 17:10–13; Aland 1985: §162). The question is natural, given Elijah's presence on the mountain; but Luke makes nothing of it, possibly because he tends to focus more on the present aspects of God's program and because he has already noted John's connection to Elijah (Luke 1:17; 7:27). Fitzmyer (1981: 806) lists this unique introduction, lacking as it does the Elijah discussion, as a fifth Lucan difference in this account. Bovon (1989: 507–8) may be right to see the influence of oral tradition on Matthew and Luke.[3]

The discussion of the historicity of this event parallels that of earlier miracles. One additional feature adds to the credibility of this event: the harsh criticism of the disciples. The early church would not have created a story like this. The Jesus Seminar (Funk and Hoover 1993: 314) rejects that the dialogue is rooted in Jesus, printing 9:41 in black type and thus treating the verse as it does all dialogue in miracle accounts. But the nature of the rebuke speaks to its genuine character. Judgments about the historicity of the event reflect a worldview about Jesus' ability to perform miracles in general. Luke presents the reality of this event as a given, using a more condensed account than Mark.

In terms of form, the account is a miracle story, specifically an exorcism (Fitzmyer 1981: 807; Bovon 1989: 506; Bultmann 1963: 211; Theissen 1983: 321). Pronouncement is found in 9:41–42.[4] Warning is found in 9:41 (Berger 1984: 195, 322 calls it an "example narrative as disciple story"). The outline of Luke 9:37–43a is as follows:

2. Theissen 1983: 177 speaks of natural compression for Matthew and Luke, which is the view of those who hold Marcan priority. Busse 1979: 254 n. 3 notes that Luke has 44 percent fewer words than Mark.

3. Schramm 1971: 139–40 also sees another source. Matthean prioritists see Luke working with Matthew and must speak of Marcan expansion. Schneider 1977a: 218 is against another source, but Nolland 1993a: 506 regards it as possible. Nolland (pp. 506–8) also details the scholarly treatment of the parallel in Mark.

4. Bultmann believes that this pronouncement is secondary in Mark, a conclusion based on the false assumption that forms cannot be mixed. Wherever miracle and pronouncement occur together, Bultmann concludes that one element is secondary.

    i. Setting (9:37)
    ii. Request to heal in light of the disciples' failure (9:38–40)
    iii. Jesus' response: rebuke and healing (9:41–42)
    iv. Crowd's response (9:43a)

Luke continues the theme that the disciples still have much to learn. God's power through Jesus is again displayed alongside God's mercy. Jesus' power over demonic forces is reasserted, despite his approaching rejection. There is another call to faith. God is again seen as wonderfully present in Jesus.

Exegesis and Exposition

[37]On the next day, when they had come down from the mountain, a great crowd met him. [38]And behold, a man cried out from the crowd, "Teacher, I beg you to look upon my son, for he is my only child. [39]And behold, a spirit seizes him, and suddenly he cries out; and it convulses him so that he foams and it leaves him with difficulty; it bruises him. [40]And I begged your disciples to cast it out, but they could not." [41]Jesus replied, "O faithless and perverse generation, how long am I to be with you and bear with you? Bring your son here." [42]And while he was approaching, the demon threw him to the ground and caused him to go into convulsions. But Jesus rebuked the unclean spirit, and healed the boy, and gave him back to his father. [43a]And they were all amazed at the majesty of God.

i. Setting (9:37)

9:37   The mountaintop experience ends, and on the next day (Luke's unique detail τῇ ἑξῆς ἡμέρᾳ, *tē hexēs hēmera*, probably indicates that the transfiguration took place at night) Jesus descends with his companions to rejoin the others.[5] When they arrive, a big crowd meets him (συναντάω, *synantaō*, is frequent in Luke–Acts [four of six NT uses]: here; Luke 22:10; Acts 10:25; 20:22; Heb. 7:1, 10; Bovon 1989: 509 n. 23). Only Mark 9:14 notes the dispute between Jesus' disciples and the scribes. The subject of the dispute is not given, but one could surmise that it centered on Jesus or, more probably, on the disciples' failure to heal the boy who is about to be introduced (Luke 9:38). Raphael's last painting, *The Transfiguration*, has this earthly scene of ministry placed below the grandeur of the transfiguration (Plummer 1896: 253–54). Jesus came not to glory in the mountaintop experience, but to touch the needs of people and heal their pain. He did so by overcoming those forces that stand opposed

---

5. Ἑξῆς appears five times in the NT, all in Luke–Acts: Luke 7:11; here; Acts 21:1; 25:17; 27:18; Bovon 1989: 508 n. 21.

to humanity. Marshall (1978: 389) says, "He appears like a visitor from another world who has to put up with the unbelief of men." Of course, Jesus does heal the boy and so reverses a tragic situation, while telling his disciples to depend on God.

Luke's introduction differs from that in Matt. 17:9 = Mark 9:9a, since they include an instruction of silence about the transfiguration and remarks about Elijah, which Luke does not have.

ii. Request to Heal in Light of the Disciples' Failure (9:38–40)

As the crowd meets Jesus, a man cries out to him, requesting that   **9:38** Jesus take a look at his son (ἐπιβλέψαι, *epiblepsai*, means "to have regard for"; Luke 1:48; James 2:3; 1 Sam. 1:11; 9:16; Bovon 1989: 509 n. 28; Danker 1988: 203; BAGD 290; BAA 588; BDR §409.5.7). The reason becomes clear in the following verses: the boy is possessed by a spirit. Adding a note of concern, Luke uniquely mentions that the child is an only son (μονογενής, *monogenēs*), a detail that Luke loves to mention (7:12; 8:42).

Mark 9:16–17 has the man's remarks about the condition of his son given in response to Jesus' question about the dispute with the scribes. Perhaps the dispute centered on the disciples' failure to heal the child. Matthew 17:14–15 has the man come, kneel before Jesus, and tell him about his son. All agree that the son is in serious condition and that the disciples could not heal him. Matthew 17:15 says that the boy suffered terribly by falling into fire and water, a condition that Matthew identifies as epilepsy (σεληνιάζεται, *selēniazetai*; lit., moonstruck; BAGD 746; BAA 1493; Matt. 4:24).[6] Later Judaism debated whether the moon directly caused the disease or indirectly caused evil spirits to roam the earth (Tg. Ps. 121:6 suggests that during the day one is safe, but at night the danger comes; Van Der Loos 1965: 403). The Jews and other ancients saw epilepsy as particularly devastating and as very difficult to cure (SB 1:758; magic rings appear in some ancient accounts; Van Der Loos 1965: 404). Given its supernatural association, the disease caused terror, an important note that adds emotion to the account.

Mark and Luke each describe the symptoms in his own way. Mark mentions the boy's being seized and thrown down by the spirit; his foaming mouth, grinding teeth, and rigid body; and his not being able to speak (he had a "mute spirit"). Luke mentions the spirit's seizing the boy; his crying out, convulsions, and foaming

---

6. On the Jewish attitude toward epilepsy, see Van Der Loos 1965: 401–5, who notes that Balaam and Saul were thought by some to have suffered from the disease (Num. 24:4; 1 Sam. 19:24). David feigned epilepsy before Saul (1 Sam. 21:13 [21:14 MT]). The ancient figure probably alludes to a fear of the influence of the moon. Greek culture also tied epilepsy to the moon's activity.

mouth; his being "shattered"; and the spirit's not leaving him alone. Clearly each writer is summarizing with his own choice of details. The father probably cried out to get Jesus' attention in the midst of the dispute and then told him the problem once he had Jesus' attention. The concerned father seeks physical relief for his son. But Luke's concern is for the spiritual condition of the boy, not just his medical state.

9:39   The spirit (called a demon in 9:42) unleashes destructive power against the boy. The convulsions and foaming at the mouth lead most to see epilepsy as present, or at least a type of nervous reaction that looks like epilepsy (ἀφρός, *aphros*, foam, a NT *hapax legomenon*, is used of epileptic seizures; BAGD 127; BAA 256; Josephus, *Antiquities* 6.12.2 §245; Fitzmyer 1981: 808). The spirit is with the boy over long periods and causes him to bruise himself (συντρῖβον, *syntribon*; BAGD 793 §1b; BAA 1582 §1b), apparently when it throws him down (Mark 9:18). The boy also cries out (Mark 5:5; 9:26; Grundmann, *TDNT* 3:900 §B1). Such destruction by a demonic force is commonly noted in the NT, but this is the first detailed mention in Luke (cf. 4:35). Clearly, the boy is in serious shape. The unique Lucan reference to the spirit's not easily (μόγις, *mogis*) leaving him pictures the situation's severity. The spirit is a regular tormentor. (See the exegesis of 9:38 for the comparison with Matt. 17:15 = Mark 9:18.)

9:40   Something else compounded the son's tragic situation: previous efforts to cast out the spirit had failed. The disciples, presumably the nine who did not go up the mountain, had tried to exorcise the spirit, but were unable to rid the boy of it. The reference to "begging" (δέομαι, *deomai*) repeats the verb of 9:38, where the man asked for Jesus' help (5:12; 8:28; Greeven, *TDNT* 2:40). Plummer (1896: 254) excludes the nine from this failure, on the grounds that such a failure here would be exceptional in light of 9:1. But the natural reading of the text is that this was a bothersome and unusual result. Luke implies their failure, especially since several events in this section expose the disciples' shortcomings. Luke does not dwell on the reasons for the failure. He simply mentions it.

Luke's wording about the request to cast out (ἐκβάλωσιν, *ekbalōsin*) the spirit matches that of Mark 9:18, and Luke's wording about "being unable" (οὐκ ἠδυνήθησαν, *ouk ēdynēthēsan*) to cast the spirit out matches Matt. 17:16 (who adds θεραπεῦσαι, *therapeusai*, to heal). The note of emotion is also strong in Luke, for Luke 9:40 alone speaks of the father "begging" the disciples for aid. Mark 9:28–29 = Matt. 17:19–20 ends the account with a brief reply about the disciples' inability to cast out the spirit, with Matthew attributing the failure to their lack of faith and Mark to a need for prayer. One suggests the other. The disciples may have lacked sufficient trust in and dependence on God to deal with this spirit. They failed to ask God for help. The rebuke noted in Luke suggests an absence of faith, but Luke gives no explicit reason (Creed 1930: 136; Schneider 1977a: 219). It is interesting that the blame is not put on those seeking the healing, but on those offering it. The point of the other Synoptics is that difficult spiritual opposition can be overcome only by prayer. Luke, however, makes nothing of this. Nonetheless, Jesus prevails where the disciples are impotent (cf. 2 Kings 4:31; Schürmann 1969: 569 n. 123; Fitzmyer 1981: 809; Marshall 1978: 391).

iii. Jesus' Response: Rebuke and Healing (9:41–42)

Jesus' reply indicates that something is clearly wrong. He rebukes **9:41** the audience by calling them a faithless and perverse generation, a wearisome situation for him. Does Jesus rebuke all (Marshall 1978: 391; Danker 1988: 203; Arndt 1956: 266) or only the disciples (Schürmann 1969: 570; Ellis 1974: 144)? The language is broad, but given the section's focus on the disciples and their failure to heal, a reference to them is also present. The broader reference is clearer in Mark because Jesus answers a question from the crowd. Luke's language is characteristically broad (7:31; 11:30–32, 50–51; 17:25; 21:32), so all are addressed, but especially the disciples (Plummer 1896: 255 is clearly wrong to exclude the disciples from the rebuke).

Given the lack of faith (ἄπιστος, apistos), Jesus must treat the son. The reference to a perverse generation (γενεά . . . διεστραμμένη, genea . . . diestrammenē) has OT roots (Num. 14:27; Deut. 32:5, 20; Prov. 6:14; Isa. 59:8), with the Lucan version having the most verbal contact with Deut. 32:5. Διεστραμμένη literally means "crooked" and refers to a generation (Büchsel, TDNT 1:663) that strays from walking the right path (Phil. 2:15). The concept of God's "bearing with them" recalls Isa. 46:4 (cf. Num. 11:12).

Mark 9:19 = Matt. 17:17 notes the same rebuke. Matthew, with Luke, speaks of the faithless and perverse generation, while Mark speaks only of a faithless one. All have the double question, though with minor verbal differences. All have Jesus commanding that the boy be brought to him, though Luke diverges from Matthew and Mark in wording the request (Matthew and Mark have φέρετε, pherete; Luke has προσάγαγε, prosagage).[7]

Any doubt about the severity of the condition is removed by what **9:42** happens next. The boy approaches Jesus, but the demon takes con-

---

7. Luke has three of the four NT uses of προσάγω: here; Acts 16:20; 27:27; 1 Pet. 3:18. A similar verbal difference (φέρω ~ ἄγω) appears in Mark 11:2, 7 = Luke 19:30, 35.

trol of him (the subject of προσέρχομαι, *proserchomai*, is the boy, not Jesus—contra J. Schneider, *TDNT* 2:684, citing Mark 1:31 and Luke 7:14). The aorist ἔρρηξεν (*errēxen*) is from ῥήσσω (*rhēssō*, to throw down; BAGD 735 §2a; BAA 1473 §2a; LSJ 1565; Mark 9:18) or ῥήγνυμι (*rhēgnymi*, to tear; BAGD 735; BAA 1471; LSJ 1568; Luke 5:37; rsv). The problem arises from the ambiguity of the verb form, since the aorist of both verbs is identical (Fitzmyer 1981: 810). A reference to being thrown on the ground is more natural for the reaction to the presence of a hostile spirit, especially given the earlier description in 9:39 of the spirit causing bruises on the boy during previous attacks. Once on the ground, the boy begins to have seizures (συσπαράσσω, *sysparassō*; BAGD 794; BAA 1584–85; Mark 9:20).

Jesus deals quickly with the problem: he rebukes the unclean spirit, heals the boy, and returns him to his father (Jesus earlier rebuked a spirit in 4:35 and returned a loved one to his mother in 7:15; on unclean spirits, see Hauck, *TDNT* 3:428 n. 12). It is somewhat unusual for Luke to refer to an exorcism with the term ἰάομαι (*iaomai*, to heal), but Acts 10:38 has a similar expression. Luke usually confines ἰάομαι to diseases (Luke 5:17; 6:18, 19; 7:7; 8:47; 9:2, 11; 14:4; 17:15; 22:51; Acts 9:34; 28:8; Fitzmyer 1981: 810). The difference here may indicate an unusual situation where the demon is exploiting a physical ailment and making it worse.

Mark 9:20–27 contains a much more detailed version of this event. The boy goes into a convulsion. Jesus asks how long the boy has had the condition. "Since childhood" comes the reply. There follows a request for Jesus to heal him. Jesus calls on the father to believe. The father says that he believes and asks for help with his unbelief. As a larger crowd begins coming to the scene, Jesus rebukes the deaf and mute spirit (a description unique to Mark), commanding the spirit to come out permanently. The spirit shrieks, causes convulsions, and comes out of the boy, who now looks like a corpse. Jesus takes the boy's hand and helps him to stand. Luke clearly has a telescoped version. Matthew 17:18 is similar to Luke: Jesus rebukes the demon, it departs from the boy, and he is healed from that hour. Mark emphasizes the key role of faith, the importance of prayer, and the severity of the boy's condition, while Matthew and Luke stress Jesus' healing power. Luke's omission of prayer is interesting, for he normally stresses it. This may be yet another indication of a complex situation with regard to sources.

iv. Crowd's Response (9:43a)

9:43a The crowd's reaction is amazement at God's majesty or greatness (μεγαλειότητι, *megaleiotēti*). Jesus reveals the compassionate exercise of God's power (Acts 10:38).[8] Because Matthew and Mark discuss the disciples' failure to heal the boy, they lack any mention of the crowd's reaction. Rather they have the disciples privately ask Jesus about this failure. Luke's difference allows the account to possess a simpler style typical of a miracle account, and he also softens the criticism of the disciples (as is his custom). The Lucan account focuses on Jesus' power in contrast to the disciples' failure. Luke makes the point that God was praised through the work done by Jesus (the public was amazed earlier in 4:32, and they praised God in 5:25 and 7:16; other public reactions are found in 8:25 and 11:14).

Summary

In Luke 9:37–43a, Jesus returns to the real world of spiritual torment. From the heights of God's mountaintop endorsement, Jesus must confront the demonic opposition that possesses an only son. The disciples could not cope with the problem, but the boy's father still hopes in Jesus. A serious epileptic condition manifests itself before God's chosen agent. Jesus rebukes the spirit, the boy is healed, and God is praised. Even as Jesus faces the prospect of death, he still ministers compassionately, thus showing his power. The disciples still have much to learn as they seek to minister to others, but Jesus is in control. He still overcomes hostile forces. Rejection of him does not alter the nature or extent of his power and authority. Jesus may have to bear with unbelief, but that does not change who he is or what he can do. Jesus still ministers with grace.

8. BAGD 496; BAA 1006; Grundmann, *TDNT* 4:541–42. Μεγαλειότης is used in Acts 19:27 of Artemis; in 2 Pet. 1:16 of Christ; in Dan. 7:27 of the nations; and in 1 Esdr. 1:4 [1:5 NRSV] of Solomon. A related term is found in Luke 1:49.

b. Prediction of Betrayal (9:43b–45)

In contrast to Jesus' power and the crowd's amazement stands his second prediction of betrayal. Luke 9:43b–45 shows Jesus also making another prediction of suffering (9:21–22), but this time the emphasis is on the disciples' failure to understand. It is yet another episode in a series of failures in 9:37–62.

Sources and Historicity

The parallel to Luke 9:43b–45 is Matt. 17:22–23 = Mark 9:30–32 (Aland 1985: §164). The episode shares the same relative position in each Gospel. The disciples are hesitant to ask Jesus about his brief prediction of the suffering of the Son of Man. They know God's agent, but they do not yet understand the divine plan. Matthew 17:23 notes that the disciples were distressed: they understood the content of Jesus' prediction, but not how this could happen to the Messiah they confessed. Marshall (1978: 393) speaks correctly of the Lucan motif of the "suffering secret" here.

The authenticity of this saying is tied to the authenticity of the earlier passion predictions (see the introduction to and exegesis of 9:21–22). The Jesus Seminar (Funk and Hoover 1993: 315) handles this text as they do 9:21–22, regarding the prediction as inauthentic and a creation of Mark (it is printed in black type). The points made for authenticity there apply here, including an extra point. The disciples' lack of comprehension speaks for authenticity, since the early church is unlikely to have created sayings that deprecated their leaders. In addition, the idea of being "handed over" has OT roots (see παραδίδωμι in the LXX of Isa. 53:6, 12; Dan. 7:25; Nolland 1993a: 512). The pattern of righteous suffering stands behind the remarks, strengthening the evidence for authenticity. Though many see Luke simply editing Mark (Schürmann 1969: 574; Ernst 1977: 309; Schneider 1977a: 220), Marshall (1978: 393) sees the possibility of oral sources.[1]

Form critically, the account parallels 9:21–22 and is a passion prediction. The outline of Luke 9:43b–45 is as follows:

   i. The crowd's marvel (9:43b)
   ii. Prediction (9:44)
   iii. Lack of understanding (9:45)

---

1. Marshall distinguishes these oral sources from the presence of another written source, which is Schramm's view; 1971: 130–31.

Themes include a prediction of the crowd's shift from amazement to betrayal of Jesus, a note that bewilders the disciples. Their lack of understanding is tied to God's sovereignty. Jesus is aware of his future and faces it directly. The disciples still need to listen and learn about God's plan.

Exegesis and Exposition

[43b]And as all were marveling at all that he was doing, he said to his disciples, [44]"Let these words sink into your ears, namely the Son of Man is about to be delivered into the hands of men." [45]But they did not understand this saying, and it was concealed from them, that they should not perceive it; and they were afraid to ask him about this saying.

i. The Crowd's Marvel (9:43b)

Luke moves into the final teaching section of the Galilean ministry (9:43b–50) with a short summary note about the crowd's response to Jesus' works. This is a broad summary not restricted to the healing of the possessed boy, but related to all of Jesus' ministry (indicated by the use of πᾶσιν [pasin, all] with ἐποίει [epoiei, he was doing]). "All that he was doing" brought their reaction. There is a focus on the miraculous here, given the previous exorcism, but the reference is broader than miracles because of the scope of Jesus' ministry. In the midst of this popular amazement (cf. 1:21; 2:18, 33; 4:22; 5:26; 7:9; 11:14; 24:12, 41) comes a word about his betrayal. The disciples should not be misled by the popular attention. Things will change. The contrast between marveling and the betrayal could not be greater.

9:43b

Luke's introduction is unique, for he omits any geographical note like that found in Matt. 17:22 = Mark 9:30. Luke creates an initial impression that perhaps these remarks were made in front of the crowds (9:43a); but such a conclusion is not necessary, given the break in the unit, the summary note about the crowd, and the specific mention of disciples as the exclusive audience of the remarks (Arndt 1956: 268). Matthew says that the remark took place as the disciples gathered in Galilee, while Mark says that they were passing through Galilee without public knowledge. It is clear in Mark that Jesus is withdrawing with his disciples to prepare them for what is coming. What Luke's lack of geography and setting allows for is the direct contrast between the crowd's wonder and Jesus' remark (Marshall 1978: 393). They are amazed at him now, but will betray him later. How fickle the crowds can be.

ii. Prediction (9:44)

9:44 The introduction Jesus gives to the disciples indicates the remark's solemnity: "Let these words sink into your ears." The language has biblical roots in Exod. 17:14 and is unique to Luke (Creed 1930: 136; Marshall 1978: 393 [who says it is a Hebraism with no precise equivalent in the LXX]; C. F. Evans 1990: 425 ["take completely to heart"]). The call parallels Jesus' more common phrase: "He who has ears, let him hear" (Luke 8:8 = Matt. 13:9 = Mark 4:9; Luke 14:35; Matt. 11:15; 13:43; Mark 4:23; Horst, *TDNT* 5:553–54; BAGD 595 §2; BAA 1205 §2). The statement that follows is quite simple and gives an explanation (γάρ, *gar*) why Jesus gave the solemn warning, making clear what he wants them to hear. Thus, γάρ should be translated "namely" (Schürmann 1969: 573 n. 143; Marshall 1978: 393).[2] The Son of Man is to be given over into the hands of men. But who will give him over and why? Jesus does not say (the earlier prediction of 9:21–22 gave more detail). A rhetorical contrast exists between "Son of Man" (ὁ . . . υἱὸς τοῦ ἀνθρώπου, *ho . . . huios tou anthrōpou*) and "men" (ἀνθρώπων, *anthrōpōn*) (Fitzmyer 1981: 814). "The man" Jesus will be betrayed by men. The current popular adulation of Jesus is not going to last. The representative man will face rejection from those he seeks to serve. Often God's work is not appreciated by those he loves.

In fact, betrayal draws near. Μέλλει (*mellei*) indicates that the betrayal is "about to come." Matthew 17:22 also uses this term, an agreement that suggests that the Lucan and Matthean forms of this passage are related to one another.[3] If one regards Luke 9:22 as possible for Jesus, there is no reason to doubt the authenticity of this remark (see the exegesis of 9:22; Marshall 1978: 394). In spite of current popularity, Jesus knew where things were headed, so he now begins the process of preparing his disciples. The "exodus" at Jerusalem would occur shortly (9:31).

The prediction's wording in each of the parallels is very close. Luce's contention (1933: 192) that the wording varies greatly is overstated. Mark 9:31 = Matt. 17:22–23 speaks of the "approach of the

---

2. The suggestion that λόγους (words, matters) refers to the recent miraculous events (so Rengstorf 1968: 126) is to be rejected, since γάρ looks ahead.

3. Bayer 1986: 193–94. Appealing to possible oral tradition, Marshall 1978: 394 more cautiously notes that μέλλει reflects an Aramaic participle and thus perhaps the saying's ancient form. Colpe, *TDNT* 8:444, speaks of a possible "unabbreviated special tradition," though he also sees the church developing this tradition. Fitzmyer 1981: 812 sees Luke's dependence only on Mark, though he has trouble explaining Luke's abbreviated prediction. Bayer 1986: 197 makes a good case against the Lucan short form as the original form, arguing that Luke has abbreviated the tradition. Against a second source is Nolland 1993a: 512.

handing over of the Son of Man into the hands of men and of their killing him." Matthew says that the Son of Man will be raised *on* (the simple dative) the third day, Mark that he will rise *after* (μετά, *meta*, with the accusative) three days (on this stylistic difference, see the exegesis of 9:22). Besides this difference, Mark and Matthew differ only in the verbal nuance of the picture of "handing over": Matthew speaks of the handing over as "about to come," while Mark says the Son of Man "is being handed over." Of course, Mark is emphasizing the process growing out of the leadership's current rejection, a rejection that produces betrayal. Matthew, and Luke with him, emphasize the event's approach itself. Luke is shorter and mentions only the handing over. This variation is due to Luke's summarizing.

iii. Lack of Understanding (9:45)

The attention shifts to the disciples' lack of understanding about the **9:45** prediction. Jesus' remark needs explanation since its meaning can be so easily misunderstood. The point is not that the saying was utterly incomprehensible to them (but so Arndt 1956: 267). The picture of the Son of Man's betrayal is a perfectly comprehensible idea. Matthew 17:23 says that the disciples were distressed. In other words, they got the message, but they could not comprehend how this could take place in the context of God's plan for his Chosen One (Ellis 1974: 144). In effect, Jesus was challenging their thinking about how God's deliverer would function. How could this great salvation figure be betrayed? What could God be about? They did not grasp this aspect of Jesus' saying nor did they ask about it. Luke 18:34 shows that they are in the dark even further down the road (Bovon 1989: 519 n. 35). How could Jesus be God's agent and be destined for death at the same time? How did a resurrection fit into all of these events?

Luke adds the point that the disciples did not understand (ἀγνοέω, *agnoeō*; BAGD 11 §3; BAA 20 §3); the meaning of the statement was concealed from them. The implication is that God or some other spiritual force was withholding from them a comprehension of what God was doing through Jesus.[4] The result (ἵνα, *hina*; Mar-

---

4. Note the passive progressive construction: ἦν παρακεκαλυμμένον (was being hidden). Marshall 1978: 394 notes that this construction with ἀπό (from) is a Hebraism; Ezek. 22:26; BDF §155.3. Citing Exod. 7:13–14 ("Pharaoh's heart was hardened"), Tiede 1988: 193 argues that the passive is ambiguous about the concealer's identity. Such remarks are usually tied to God's sovereignty (1 Cor. 1:30; 2:6–9). Regardless, the implication is that such concealment can be overturned only by attention to God's message. Nolland 1993a: 514 holds out the possibility of Satanic binding, noting that by 24:25 the disciples are seen as responsible for failing to understand. Nolland may be right.

shall 1978: 394; BDR §173.3.10, §391.5.11) was a lack of perception (αἰσθάνομαι, *aisthanomai*, is a NT *hapax legomenon*; BAGD 24–25; BAA 46–47), an inability to put the pieces of God's plan together.

For reasons that are not clear, the disciples did not pursue the issue. Were they embarrassed that they could not see the point? Did they fear what the answers might be? What is clear is that they still needed instruction about Jesus, and they sensed something startling in Jesus' remarks. Given their difficulty here, one can see why Jesus told them to let these words sink in. They must pay attention to Jesus' words.

Luke is much more detailed here than Matt. 17:23 = Mark 9:32. Matthew simply speaks of the disciples' great distress, which indicates that the saying's content was clear to them. Mark mentions their lack of understanding and their fear of asking questions (he is close to Luke at this point). However, Luke uniquely stresses the divine concealment. The disciples will gradually get the picture (Luke 10:21–24; 18:34; 24:16–32, 44–47; Danker 1988: 205).

Summary   Jesus' miracles and teaching are drawing a great crowd and great reaction, but all that is set to change. Much of Luke 11–14 will explain what happened. Later in Jerusalem, Jesus will be handed over to die. The disciples are told this, but do not understand. They have no clue what God is doing. It is concealed from them. The time is not right for them to know. Sometimes only after the passage of time does one see what God is doing. The disciples need to be patient. They must listen to and trust God. Jesus knows where his God is taking him. God is in control. God can be trusted to guide his plan, even if it goes down roads no one anticipates or understands. As one travels down such an unknown path, it is important to keep one's ears tuned to God's voice.

c. On Greatness and Cooperation (9:46–50)

The Galilean ministry closes with two related pericopes, both dealing with short teachings of Jesus and portraying the disciples' struggle to understand Jesus' mission. In Luke 9:46–48, Jesus corrects the disciples for arguing over who is the greatest among them. Greatness is not found in stature nor does it come through comparison, but it resides in knowing Jesus. Greatness comes from God, and it can even come on one as little as a child. Jesus will teach this lesson to his disciples again on his last night (22:24–27). In 9:49–50, the disciples are corrected for preventing others from ministering in Jesus' name. What the disciples wish to stop, Jesus allows. He tells them that someone ministering for you is not against you. In each case, the disciples learn that the way of following Jesus does not entail the normal exercise of power. They must learn how to regard each other (9:46–48) and outsiders (9:49–50). The disciples must not be characterized by pride in their ministry. Schweizer (1984: 164) notes that greatness means being the least. Unlike the world, status is not a virtue.

Greatness and exclusive power do not coexist in Jesus' ministry, nor should they in the disciples' ministry. Jesus' greatness is found in the midst of betrayal. The disciples' greatness will come through their connection to Jesus, not by comparison to one another. The ministry is not limited to a small circle. These important lessons create a transition from the Galilean ministry to the Jerusalem journey section of Luke (9:51–19:44).

Luke's version lacks introductory geographical references in both of these scenes, a feature that allows him to heighten the contrast of the accounts more than do the other Gospels. Jesus' coming sacrifice (9:43b–45) stands in contrast to the disciples' quest to be seen as the greatest (9:46–48). Given that 9:46–48 follows a passage about the disciples' misunderstanding, the idea may be that rivalry hinders the disciples from understanding God's plan (Fitzmyer 1981: 815; Tannehill 1986: 227, 254–55; cf. 22:24–27). The greatness of anyone welcomed by Jesus (9:48) stands in contrast to the disciples' refusal to let others minister (9:49–50). Reception of the "least," pictured as the child, means reception of others. Reception of the least also means openness to all. Ecclesiastical snobbery is a vice to Jesus. The disciples have much to learn. Jesus' ministry is not what they expect.

Sources and Historicity

Matthew 18:1–5 = Mark 9:33–37 is parallel to Luke 9:46–48 (Aland 1985: §166). The placement of the pericope in the three Gospels is virtually identical, although Matt. 17:24–27 introduces an intervening event with his unique discussion of the temple tax. It is clear that these accounts deal with the same event, though the reply's original unity is questioned by some (e.g., Fitzmyer 1981: 815–16).

Only one parallel exists to the second unit: Luke 9:49–50 = Mark 9:38–40 (Aland 1985: §167). Mark 9:41 has an additional saying (which is also in Matt. 10:42) about reward going to the one who hosts a disciple. Luke's account is simpler (Bovon 1989: 515 n. 5).

The authenticity of Luke 9:49–50 is disputed (Creed 1930: 138–39). Those who reject authenticity assert that exorcism in Jesus' name would not occur in this period. But given the nature of the mission of the Twelve, such an event is not out of the question. The disciples possessed the right to exorcise demons through Jesus, though whether Luke has summarized its description in traditional church language could be debated.[1] Exorcism by other disciples is not to be rejected by the disciples closest to Jesus.

The Jesus Seminar (Funk and Hoover 1993: 315–16) rejects both sets of sayings, printing all in black type except 9:50b. The seminar recognizes that Jesus probably taught on humility, but it regards the community as having too great a hand in 9:48. By appealing to Luke 10:16 = John 13:20, the seminar holds that the early church recast a remark about disciples in terms of children. The assumption is that the tradition can have only one authentic saying on a topic—an unrealistic assumption for a teacher of wisdom, which the seminar argues Jesus to be. Certainly the most likely material to be preserved of such a figure would be his teaching about relationships. Jesus returns to the theme of the child in Luke 18:15–17. Nolland (1993a: 517) notes that the catchword technique in the Marcan parallel speaks to the tradition's age and reaches back into an oral phase. Nolland (p. 518) also sees early church concerns in these sayings, but it is not clear why this is necessary, given the importance that ancient culture put on status.

---

1. So correctly Luce 1933: 193–94, who is not averse to claiming that sayings are nonhistorical, yet defends historicity here. Marshall 1978: 398 notes the OT conceptual parallel in Num. 11:24–30. To be rejected is Goulder's view (1989: 450) that Luke 9:49–50 is really a subtle defense of Paul before the apostles, a view that looks like F. C. Baur reborn. Goulder is right to reject the view that Jesus endorses non-Christian exorcists here. They cannot act in Jesus' name. Luke has in mind those who have responded to Jesus and have sought to minister for him. He encourages such involvement.

The Jesus Seminar regards Jesus' remark about those not against you as loosely linked to Jesus (9:50b is in gray type), but it rejects the exorcist setting as artificial (thus 9:50a is in black type). Nolland (1993a: 523) rightly defends the idea of "in Jesus' name" as historical, given the role of exorcism in his ministry, not to mention the commissioning of disciples as kingdom preachers through his enablement (9:1–6). This background, as well as the rebuke of the disciples, speaks for authenticity. The openness to others that Jesus calls for here fits his earlier call for humility. The sayings reflect Jesus' community values.

Form critically, both accounts are pronouncement stories, since Jesus' sayings are the key (Fitzmyer 1981: 816, 819; Bultmann 1963: 11, 24–25).[2] Berger (1984: 81) calls both accounts apophthegms (i.e., pronouncements). The outline of Luke 9:46–50 is as follows:

i. Dispute about greatness (9:46–48)
   (1) Dispute (9:46)
   (2) Picture of the child: reception of the "lowly" (9:47–48)
ii. Dispute about the outside exorcist (9:49–50)
   (1) Attempt to exclude (9:49)
   (2) Jesus' reaction (9:50)

Numerous themes exist in these verses. Jesus refuses to compare the disciples to each other. On an ethical note, humility is not served by rivalry. In fact, greatness for a disciple does not come through stature, but through knowing Jesus. Jesus excludes pride or anything other than a functional hierarchy, as seen in the combination of the selection of the Twelve and an openness for others to minister. Those who minister for him need not have traveled with him. Ministry's door is open to all who come to him.

Exegesis and Exposition

[46]And an argument arose among them as to which of them might be the greatest. [47]But when Jesus ⌜perceived⌝ the thoughts of their hearts, he took a child and put it by his side, [48]and he said to them, "Whoever receives this

---

2. The first account is not a chiasmus, against Bovon 1989: 521, who suggests this structure (his categories are correct, but there is no balance since a′ and b′ do not match their opposites):
   a   question (9:46)
   b   nonverbal answer (9:47)
   b′   first indirect answer (9:48a)
   a′   second direct answer (9:48b)

child in my name receives me, and whoever receives me receives him who sent me; for he who is least among you all is the one who is great."

⁴⁹John answered, "Master, we saw a man casting out demons in your name and we ⌜forbade⌝ him, because he is not following with us." ⁵⁰But Jesus said to him, "Do not forbid him, for whoever is not against you is for you."

i. Dispute about Greatness (9:46–48)
(1) Dispute (9:46)

9:46   In a touch of irony, while Jesus is telling the disciples of his approaching suffering and death, they are arguing about their relative importance. His service is contrasted to their pride and self-concern. Without giving details, Luke notes the subject of the argument: Which disciple is greatest?[3] Διαλογισμός (*dialogismos*) should be translated "argument," not "thoughts," since it is combined with ἐν αὐτοῖς (*en autois*, among them). The term may be chosen because each disciple thinks that perhaps he is the greatest (Plummer 1896: 257; BAGD 186; BAA 372; BDR §218.3; a "dispute" is clearly meant in Phil. 2:14 and 1 Tim. 2:8). Given their association with God's agent, they begin to wonder what their position will be when the kingdom comes in its full glory (Matt. 18:1; Grundmann, *TDNT* 4:532–33). The disciples still lack perception about God's plan and their walk with him.

Luke launches into the scene, while Mark 9:33 = Matt. 18:1 gives the setting. Mark notes that Jesus raised the issue after the disciples' debate in a Capernaum home. Matthew lacks a geographic setting, but notes that the disciples asked Jesus for his opinion. A probable reason for Matthew's geographic omission is that his previous discussion (Matt. 17:24–27) of the temple tax is noted as taking place in Capernaum, so that a geographic reference here would be redundant. Luke's lack of a setting allows him to contrast directly the foreboding announcement of approaching betrayal with the disciples' self-focus. When disciples finally understand the cross, such discussions should disappear (Ellis 1974: 145).

(2) Picture of the Child: Reception of the "Lowly" (9:47–48)

9:47   Jesus deals with the dispute through an illustration. He brings a child—a person too young to be regarded as great—to his side (παρά, *para*; BDR §239.1.1). In Judaism, children under twelve could not be taught the Torah, and so to spend time with them was

---

3. Μείζων is superlative, not comparative, since there are more than two disciples (cf. the use of μικρότερος, the least, in 9:48; BDF §244). Luke's characteristic optative εἴη (might be) expresses a question whose answer is uncertain; BDR §267.2.3, §385.2.2; Luke 1:62; 3:15; 6:11.

considered a waste (Oepke, *TDNT* 5:646–47). For example, *b.* ʾ*Abot* 3.10 reads: "Morning sleep, midday wine, chattering with children, and tarrying in places where men of the common people assemble, destroy a man." Jesus' action reverses cultural expectations.

Jesus acts because he knows the disciples' thoughts (ἰδὼν τὸν δια-λογισμόν, *idōn ton dialogismon*).[4] Since the term διαλογισμός in this verse is tied to the mind, internal thoughts are in view, not verbal arguments (as in 9:46). When such a reference to Jesus' knowledge appears, correction usually follows (Mark 2:8 = Luke 5:22; 6:8; 7:39–40 [conceptually]). This event is no exception.

Matthew 18:2 = Mark 9:36 also notes Jesus' use of the child. In Matthew, Jesus calls the child into the midst of the group; in Mark, he takes the child, places it in their midst, and finally takes it into his arms. Thus, it seems clear the child is old enough to understand Jesus, yet young enough to be held by him (on Jesus and children, see Luke 10:21; 17:2; Mark 10:13–16 = Luke 18:15–17).[5] Mark precedes this action with Jesus' statement that those wishing to be first must be last and be the servant of all (Mark 9:35). Luke has his own different saying at the end of 9:48. These differences represent summaries of Jesus' teaching, though it seems odd that Luke should do it his way, if he had Mark. Matthew lacks both of these extra sayings, so it is also hard to see him as Luke's source. This difference causes many to suggest that originally distinct traditions were brought together by Mark (J. Wellhausen [as cited in Fitzmyer 1981: 815]; Bultmann 1963: 149–50). But the saying at the end of Luke and the one at the start of Mark are distinct enough to insist that a conflation of sayings has not occurred. Why would Luke alter either Matthew or Mark if he had them in hand, unless he also had access to additional material? Thus, it would seem that each writer has recounted the event using unique details to which each had access.

9:48 Jesus' illustration prohibits all comparison between disciples. Nowhere does he declare that someone is the greatest. Rather, he speaks simply of greatness. Greatness can be possessed and pursued, but not through comparison.

The reply comes in two parts. First, Jesus notes that greatness is not inherent in a person, but is established by one's relationship to

---

4. Danker 1988: 205 cites the following exchange from Diogenes Laertius 1.36: when the philosopher Thales was asked if one could hide an evil deed from God, he answered, "No, not even the thought."

5. The identity of the child is not given or known. Plummer 1896: 258 mentions a tradition that the church father Ignatius was the child, but this tradition dates from the ninth century: Anastasius Bibliothecarius (*PL* 129:42); Nicephorus Callistus (*PL* 143:848); Lightfoot 1889–90: 2.1.27, 2.2.22. Chrysostom and Eusebius lack this tradition.

Jesus. The child does not have greatness, but receiving it in the name of Jesus is the same as receiving Jesus (ἐμέ is emphatic in ἐμὲ δέχε-ται, eme dechetai: "me he receives"; Plummer 1896: 258). To receive Jesus is to receive the God who sent him. A disciple's relationship with God enhances the value of other persons. Jesus is calling on the disciples to change the way they see people: be kind to the "lowly," act in a way that ignores status. To be open to the lowly means, in effect, to be open to all, since the "mighty" are rarely ignored. To receive someone in the name of Jesus means recognizing the value of that person as God's creature, an attitude that serves to honor God's work (1 Cor. 7:14 may be conceptually similar). Beyond that, to receive such a one is to receive Jesus, who in turn represents God. A moral demand is placed on the disciple to care for others as a result of God's kindness and presence.[6] It is not an optional exercise. When one ministers to people, one receives Jesus and in turn his God (Matt. 25:35–45; Marshall 1978: 397).

Jesus also challenges the way people are evaluated. For him, the least among them is great. The point is that *all* in the community are important and that comparison within the community is to be avoided. If greatness is found in the least, greatness is found in all. All relative scales are removed. Creed (1930: 138) misses the point by saying that the verse says the least is the greatest (Plummer 1896: 258). Love is to be extended to all, for even the least are great.[7]

Each of the Synoptics is different at this point. Matthew 18:3–5 begins with a call to childlike faith and humility. Those coming into the kingdom are to humble themselves as children, an action removing the desire for comparison as well, for greatness is found in humility. Luke 18:17 is similar to Matt. 18:3, while Matt. 18:5 looks like the first part of Luke 9:48. Mark 9:37 has the full first portion of the Lucan saying as it relates to the child's reception and to Jesus' reception. Mark states with Matthew the initial comparison in terms of receiving "one such child" in Jesus' name, and in the second comparison he speaks of receiving "not me, but the one who sent me" (otherwise the saying is close to Luke). The differences allow each

---

6. For a similar intimate linkage of Jesus and God, see Luke 10:16; John 17:3, 18. To receive an emissary is to receive the person who sends the emissary; m. Ber. 5.5 ("a man's emissary is like the man himself"); Philem. 15–18; SB 1:590; Fitzmyer 1981: 817.

7. The concept of reception pictures the open welcome to be given to others. On δέξηται (he receives), see Marshall 1978: 396; Grundmann, TDNT 2:51–52. The term refers to friendly reception or hospitality, which was seen as sacred in the ancient world and in Judaism. B. Šab. 127a says, "Hospitality to travelers is greater than the greeting of the Shekinah." Though hyperbolic, the saying shows the importance of hospitality. Josephus, Jewish War 7.4.1 §63, refers to how Vespasian's reception brought joy and satisfaction.

writer to bring out distinct nuances in summarizing the event. Matthew stresses a call for humility that grows out of a simple faith, a point the other parallels lack. All emphasize the need to receive those who seem to be "lowly." Mark's version focuses on the representative nature of Jesus' remarks ("one such child"). He also highlights receiving God when one receives the lowly ("receives not me but the one who sent me"). Mark 9:35 earlier made a call to the disciples that they should seek to be last and be servants. Luke closes the unit by uniquely indicating that even the least is great. There are no neglectable people for Jesus (Liefeld 1984: 931). Such teaching contains a major lesson for Jesus' followers. All people count, while comparison counts for nothing.

ii. Dispute about the Outside Exorcist (9:49–50)
(1) Attempt to Exclude (9:49)

Following immediately after Jesus' teaching about receiving all, the **9:49** disciples relate that they have excluded someone from ministering. The contrast is stark: they had been told to receive all, but now they refuse to allow someone else to minister. Some time has apparently passed since the previous passage, but the disciples are still in need of instruction. One of the disciples, John, tells about a man casting out demons in Jesus' name. The disciples exercised what they thought was appropriate authority and stopped this exorcist because (ὅτι, *hoti*) he did not follow Jesus with the other disciples. John's remark brings Jesus' response.

Many take the reference to exorcism in Jesus' name as a product of the early church, since this is the first time it appears in Luke. It reappears in 10:17, a summary of the disciples' mission and a description of exorcisms (also Luke 21:12, 17; 24:47; Acts 2:38; 3:6, 16; 4:7, 10, 17, 18; 5:28, 40; 10:43; 19:13 [where some who do not believe in Jesus attempt to use the name and fail]). Given the expression's association with exorcisms by disciples in the midst of mission, it is unlikely that the account refers to a later incident of the early church (but so apparently Fitzmyer 1981: 820, who speaks of a problem emerging in the pre-Marcan church). No doubt the disciples regarded whatever authority they had as coming from Jesus, for he had already commissioned them (Luke 9:1–6). In fact, the exclusive nature of that commission may well have been the reason they tried to prevent this man from performing exorcisms. Jesus' personal provision may also explain why they speak of exorcism in his name. Their reaction is natural, but not necessarily correct. The imperfect ἐκωλύομεν (*ekōlyomen*, we forbade) describes the disciples' efforts and may suggest that they repeatedly tried to get this man to stop (Arndt 1956: 270; for the textual problem, see the additional note).

Mark 9:38 is parallel to Luke, though Luke is shorter. Mark also notes that John raised the issue. Much of Mark's wording matches Luke, although Mark uses διδάσκαλε (*didaskale*, Teacher) to address Jesus, while Luke has ἐπιστάτα (*epistata*, Master), a term unique to him (5:5; 8:24 [twice], 45; 9:33, 49; 17:13). Mark uses a past tense (imperfect) to describe why the disciples rebuked the man: "He was not following us" (οὐκ ἠκολούθει ἡμῖν, *ouk ēkolouthei hēmin*). Luke uses the present, as is common in vivid portrayal of discourse: "He is not following with us" (οὐκ ἀκολουθεῖ μεθ᾽ ἡμῶν, *ouk akolouthei meth' hēmōn*). The meaning is the same. The man's lack of association with the disciples caused them to try to stop his ministry of exorcism.

(2) Jesus' Reaction (9:50)

9:50   Jesus' reply is succinct: the disciples should never give such a prohibition. The present imperative μὴ κωλύετε (*mē kōlyete*, do not forbid) speaks of something that is generally the case (as opposed to one instance). Such people are not to be stopped, for (γάρ, *gar*) someone who is not opposed to the disciples and who ministers at their side is for them, not against them. The point is that someone ministering with the disciples is on their side and should be encouraged (Ellis 1974: 145). The disciples' ministry is not an exclusive ministry, but will draw on many collaborators to complete the task (10:2). There should be no rivalry, but appreciation and cooperation (Liefeld 1984: 931). Numbers 11:24–30 is a similar OT account. The proverbial character of this saying in ancient culture is well known (Fitzmyer 1981: 821; Cicero, *On Behalf of Quintus Ligarius* 33; Suetonius, *Julius Caesar* 75; Plutarch, *Solon* 20.1; Nestle 1912: 84–87).

Luke has a similar saying in 11:23, only there it is stated negatively and in terms of Jesus himself ("the one who is not with me is against me"). In Matt. 12:30 (which is parallel to Luke 11:23), the point is that failure to decide for Jesus leaves one in opposition to him. Only commitment to Jesus allies one to him. Some attempt to argue that this Luke 11 saying stands in contradiction with the one here, but that fails to note their distinct contexts. In fact, the variant form in a fresh context shows that Jesus used the concept proverbially and repeatedly. It was a major theme, whether stated positively or negatively.

Mark 9:39 has more detail: it closes with the saying found in Luke and is verbally identical to Luke, except that it uses the first-person plural, rather than a second-person plural (Schürmann 1969: 579). Luke's form is more directly focused on the disciples. Preceding this saying in Mark is another remark in which Jesus says that no one doing a mighty work in his name is able afterward to speak evil of him. Thus, Mark adds the point that such work encourages those outside the inner circle and leads them to speak well of Jesus. Such work reinforces one's allegiance to Jesus. Fitzmyer (1981: 820) notes Paul's similar exhortations (Phil. 1:15; 1 Cor. 3:5–9). Effective ministry draws one closer to Jesus and should be encouraged.

Three teaching sessions in Luke 9:43b–50 close Jesus' Galilean ministry. They show the disciples struggling to comprehend what following Jesus means. First, Jesus shares his approaching betrayal, but the disciples are unable to perceive how this fits into God's plan. However, they are too uncertain to ask about it. The way of Messiah's suffering is a topic of much future instruction. **Summary**

Next, as they argue about who is the greatest among them, Jesus uses a child to show them that such comparisons should not be made. Rather, if they are related to him, true ministry involves receiving such "lowly" types, as well as recognizing that the least among them is great. The usual ways of discussing and handling power do not apply for Jesus' disciples. As the disciples look at themselves they need to realize that all are great.

Finally, there is the issue of what to do about others, specifically those outside their inner circle. Are they to be excluded from ministry? No, they are not to be prevented from ministering in Jesus' name. Those who minister alongside the disciples share in their task. Interpersonal rivalry is not the trait of a disciple; cooperation is.

In this concluding section, Luke shows that the disciples have much to learn as they "listen to him" (9:35). Jesus not only changes the way disciples see themselves, but he changes the way they see others. Rather than seeking to gain or protect turf, they are to invite others onto it. As Jesus turns to go to Jerusalem and his own betrayal (9:51), such lessons are crucial for those who will carry out his commission in the face of much intense rejection and conflict. Disciples need to be united.

This unit ends the Galilean ministry section of 4:14–9:50, where the concern has been mainly christological. The central question is, "Who is Jesus?" Many miracles show that Jesus is sent from God. Though the crowd has wrestled with prophetic categories, the disciples know better: he is the Christ of God with vast authority. But they too lack understanding, so they must listen to Jesus to understand the type of Messiah that Jesus is and the kind of disciples that he desires. All the while, Jesus teaches about dependence on God, love, acceptance of others, associating with sinners, and his new way to God. Such teaching will also come in the Jerusalem journey section of 9:51–19:44, where Jesus will prepare the disciples for his departure. He will be rejected

(Luke 11–14), since he is the Messiah who must suffer and die. In his absence, the disciples must humbly minister to sinners as they expectantly await his glorious return. That ministry will not be easy. The rejection that Jesus faces will also be the disciples' lot. But with Jesus' return, vindication comes. To confess who Jesus is simply begins the disciples' spiritual journey. Jesus prepares them for the long and winding road ahead.

Additional Notes

9:47. Should the text read εἰδώς (knowing), the perfect participle of οἶδα (to know), or ἰδών (perceiving), the aorist participle of ὁράω (to see)? Either reading is possible, and the basic meaning is the same. Εἰδώς is found in the earlier manuscripts (ℵ, B, 700, some Syriac), while ἰδών has wider distribution (A, C, D, L, W, Δ, Ξ, Ψ, Byz, Itala). The nature of the distribution suggests that ἰδών is more likely.[8]

9:49. Did the apostles attempt to stop the exorcist once or repeatedly? The aorist ἐκωλύσαμεν has wide but late support (A, C, D, W, Θ, Ψ, family 1, family 13, Byz) and therefore is probably not original. The imperfect ἐκωλύομεν, which is not necessarily the harder reading (because of Lucan style), is supported by 𝔓[75] (apparently), ℵ, B, L, Ξ (perhaps in agreement with Mark 9:38, where the same textual problem appears). If the aorist is original, then there was a single attempt to stop the man. However, given Luke's preference for imperfect-tense verbs, the imperfect may simply describe a past event with no repetitive force intended. This variant is not discussed in UBS[3].

---

8. For internal arguments favoring this reading in Matt. 9:4, see Metzger 1975: 24. The UBS–NA committee went the other way in the Lucan passage, but the reasons for treating Luke differently from Matt. 9:4 are not clear. See Metzger 1975: 148.

Excursus 1
John the Baptist and Elijah (1:17)

In the Synoptics and John's Gospel the relationship between John as forerunner and Elijah is a complex theme. The witness motif is the emphasis in John's description of John the Baptist. Talbert's distinction (1982: 27–28) between the forerunner motif of the Synoptics and the witness motif of John is overdrawn. The forerunner's primary task is to witness to the one who follows. Talbert is right that in John the preexistence of Jesus as the Word produces a different and stronger christological emphasis, but the Fourth Gospel's portrayal of John the Baptist's ministry is not greatly distinct from the Synoptics.

Others stress the contrast between Luke's view of John's relationship to Elijah and the view of the other Gospel writers about that connection (Danker 1988: 30–31; Talbert 1982: 27–30). This position argues that Mark (9:13) and Matthew (11:14) identify John with Elijah, while in John's Gospel, John the Baptist denies that he is Elijah (1:21). In fact, some argue that the idea of John as forerunner disappears in John's Gospel, and that he is merely a witness. Also, Luke drops the identification with Elijah, since he omits the reference to John's clothing in Mark 1:6 and the use of Mal. 3:1, which are Elijah motifs. However, Luke keeps the forerunner motif.[1]

What is to be made of this position? This approach to the tradition is right in much of what it observes, but assumes too much from the differences. John's association as a forerunner for Jesus is still clearly asserted by Luke: 7:22–35, especially verse 27, alludes to Malachi and so to the Elijah typology. Luke also compares John's and Jesus' baptisms in 3:16, material that Luke has accepted along with his Synoptic partners. If John is a forerunner, he is a witness. The two positions are not mutually exclusive of one another, but are complementary motifs. It may well be that the emphasis in John's Gospel on the preexistent Christ causes John to deemphasize the description of the Baptist as forerunner, since that could suggest the Baptist existed before Jesus. Yet John still portrays John the Baptist

---

1. R. Brown 1977: 276 argues that the Elijah-like connection for John the Baptist is a late development in the tradition. If there existed an early association of Malachi with John as the angelic announcement suggests and as its repetition in the various contexts shows, then this judgment is not likely.

as the one who testifies to and goes before Jesus (John 1:19–34; 3:22–30, esp. v. 28).

As to the dispute over Luke's acceptance of the Elijah title, this issue also is a matter of nuance. The allusions to Mal. 3 in the Lucan infancy narrative reveal that Luke sees a strong association between Elijah and John the Baptist, not to mention the Malachi citation in Luke 7:27. Luke's "like Elijah" position may serve to clarify Matthew and Mark in that there also continued to exist in Christian circles the hope of Elijah's return at the end, when God will do his final eschatological work (Matt. 17:9–13 is aware of this future Elijah alongside Elijah–John the Baptist). Luke may have feared a misunderstanding that an Elijah identification for John the Baptist would represent a denial of this future Elijah, who is associated in Malachi with the decisive day of the Lord. John the Baptist's denial in John's Gospel may be of this ultimate Elijah as well. What Jesus says in Matt. 17 and what Luke says here is that there is a pattern of ministry like that of Elijah into which John the Baptist fits, without denying that in the end Elijah will return. This dual use of the Elijah motif fits the "already–not yet" tension present in so much of NT eschatology. In the first coming of Jesus, OT hopes "already" are realized. However, the rest of the same hope has "not yet" come and still awaits fulfillment. Thus, the Gospels, though having some differences of nuance, are in essential agreement about the role of John the Baptist. The hope of the return of Elijah at the end is a teaching shared with the OT (Mal. 4:5–6 [3:23–24 MT]) and with Judaism (Sir. 48:10; 2 Esdr. [= 4 Ezra] 6:26; Fitzmyer 1981: 326–27).

Excursus 2
The Census of Quirinius (2:1–2)

A major historical issue in Luke 2:1–7 is the association of a census by Quirinius with Jesus' birth. Virtually every commentary discusses the problem in detail, and it could well be regarded as the most significant historical problem in the entire Gospel. For many, it is the clearest example of historical error in Luke's Gospel.[1]

The objections raised against the account have changed little in the century since the first English edition of Schürer's *History of the Jewish People in the Time of Jesus Christ*.[2] Schürer's isolation of five objections is still a representative listing of the issues that need to be discussed:[3]

1. Nothing is known of a general, empire-wide census in the time of Augustus.
2. No Roman census would require Joseph to go to Bethlehem.[4]
3. There would be no census in Palestine in the time of Herod the Great.
4. Josephus knows of no census before the Quirinian census of A.D. 6. In fact, this Quirinian census is described as an innovation that caused a revolt (*Antiquities* 17.13.2 §§342–44; 17.13.5 §355; 18.1.1 §§1–10), meaning that no census could have come before A.D. 6.
5. Quirinius could not have been governor of a census at the time of Jesus' birth, since the governors' records of this period are well known and Quirinius is not mentioned (Tacitus, *Annals* 3.48; Josephus, *Antiquities* 17.13.5 §355).

Some basic, fixed chronological facts exist. Luke's census is not the one in A.D. 6, because it is tied to the period before Herod the Great's

---

1. For a full discussion, see R. Brown 1977: 547–56 (who rejects the historicity of the reference).
2. Schürer 1890: 105–43. The recent revision of Schürer's work (1973–87: 1.399–427) changes little of the original discussion. Schürer summarizes what was already an old debate, going back at least to Strauss 1972: 152–56 (originally 1835), as noted by Nolland 1989: 99.
3. Both Klostermann 1929: 32–33 and Hoehner 1977: 14 use Schürer as a starting point.
4. Some add that Mary's presence on the journey in her delicate condition is also unnecessary, as well as being unlikely. This will be discussed under view 2b below.

death by Matt. 2:1 and Luke 1:5. Luke and Matthew agree in tying the birth to the reign of Herod the Great. Josephus notes an eclipse that occurred before Herod's death, which allows one to set the date of his passing with some specificity (*Antiquities* 17.6.4 §167; Hoehner 1977: 13). The only eclipse mentioned by Josephus in this period was in March 4 B.C. Josephus also notes that Passover followed Herod's death, which puts the latest he could have died at 11 April 4 B.C. (*Antiquities* 17.9.3 §213; *Jewish War* 2.1.3 §10; Hoehner 1977: 13). Thus, the birth of Jesus and the census must be dated before April 4 B.C.[5]

The date of the Quirinian census mentioned in Josephus is also fixed, since it is dated in the thirty-seventh year after the defeat of Antony at Actium in 31 B.C. (Fitzmyer 1981: 399; Josephus, *Antiquities* 17.13.5 §355; 18.1.1 §§1–2). Thirty-seven years after 31 B.C. is A.D. 6.

Given the differences in the two dates, two things must be settled for another census to be in view. First, could such a census have occurred under Augustus in the time of Herod the Great, when Joseph and Mary would have to journey to Bethlehem (Schürer's first four objections)? Second, can such a census be tied to Quirinius (Schürer's fifth objection)?

The possibility of such a census has been variously assessed, but is not generally regarded as difficult for the following reasons (keyed to Schürer's objections above):

1. Augustus is known to have instituted three censuses in this period.[6] In addition, other censuses of a periodic nature also seem to have been in place at this time.[7] Other cycles at or near this period existed in Syria, Gaul, and Spain.[8] It is clear that Rome was active in registering the people of its empire, whether they were Roman citizens or others. It is not unlikely that Augustus could have issued such an edict for Palestine (Schürmann 1969: 100). Luke's description (2:1) that such an edict is empire-wide may simply reflect the ongoing census process of this period (Plummer 1896: 48; Hoehner 1977: 15).

---

5. Hoehner 1977: 14–27 defends December 5 B.C. or January 4 B.C. as the most likely date of Jesus' birth. Another key chronological element is the mention that Jesus was about thirty years old at the start of his ministry (3:23), which is near the fifteenth year of Tiberius's reign (3:1), around A.D. 27 to 29. This last date yields the period from 10 B.C. to 1 B.C. for Jesus' birth, with the thirty-year mark falling around 5–3 B.C. For Tiberius's date and the date of Jesus' ministry, see the exegesis of 3:1.

6. Hayles 1973: 120; Fitzmyer 1981: 400. On Augustan census activity, see Braunert 1957; Corbishley 1936; Tacitus, *Annals* 1.11; Dio Cassius 53.30.2.

7. For example, Egypt was on a fourteen-year cycle, which seems to go back to 10–9 B.C.; Hayles 1973: 127.

8. These censuses include the entire first century after Christ; Hayles 1973: 128–29. Hayles's article gives numerous primary references.

2a. The problem of Joseph returning to Bethlehem may be explainable on the principle that sometimes the Romans allowed a census to be taken on the basis of local customs, which in a Jewish culture would require an ancestral registration.[9]

2b. Many reasons can be posited for Mary's presence. First, her presence might be required by the Roman census as part of the assessment.[10] Or, it may be that her very state made her going along more necessary, since Joseph would not want to miss the birth. It is also possible that Joseph and Mary married after the birth announcement to Mary and after the pregnancy became known (suggested by Matt. 1:19–21). Luke 2:5 with its use of ἐμνηστευμένη may well mean "unconsummated" (see the exegesis). Thus, Mary might be recently married to Joseph at this time and would naturally be traveling with him. In fact, ancients may not have been so sensitive about a pregnant woman's "tender state" as modern Westerners are. The journey itself corroborates that the census came before the splitting of Herod's empire to his three sons, since if the A.D. 6 census were in view, we would have the unlikely scenario of Joseph and Mary traveling from Herod Antipas's territory (Nazareth) to Archelaus's territory (Bethlehem) to register (Hoehner 1977: 16). Such a mixing of jurisdictions is unlikely.[11]

3. Though Herod the Great's authority in Judea during his reign was great and extended to his minting coins bearing his image, such authority would not prevent an imperial representative from registering the emperor's citizens. Such censuses in vassal kingdoms are not unusual in Roman history.[12] For example, in Samaria taxes were reduced by one-quarter at the beginning of Archelaus's rule—a concession that suggests that

9. Schürmann 1969: 100. R. Brown 1977: 549 allows this as a possibility. What he cannot accept is the reference to Quirinius. The Romans allowed the Jews to keep other customs: tax exemption every seventh year (Josephus, *Antiquities* 14.10.6 §§202–10) and Sabbath observance (*Antiquities* 14.10.20 §§241–43).

10. Hoehner 1977: 15. Hoehner also cites (n. 20) a reference from Ulpian, *Iustiniani Digesta* 1.15.4.2, that required property owners to go to the district where they owned land. Issues of ancestry and land may fit here, even though Joseph lived elsewhere.

11. For one who rejects any historicity to this account, this objection is meaningless, since in this view a census is merely a literary device and not a historical reference of any kind. But the point is still valuable, for the one thing that cannot be present is a confusion on Luke's part that Jesus was born during the A.D. 6 census, since this detail does not fit such a census. Luke clearly has Jesus in an earlier period (1:5). Luke is either clearly wrong, has created an accurate setting for Jesus' birth, or is, as I shall argue, clearly right.

12. Hoehner 1977: 16 cites examples in Syria, Cappadocia, and Nabatea. Tacitus, *Annals* 2.42 and 6.41, discusses Cappadocia, where taxes were reduced by about half.

Roman tax rolls existed before Samaria became part of a Roman province in an area that had been under Herod's rule.[13]

4. The problem of innovation in Josephus's description of the A.D. 6 census is significant, if it is true. However, it assumes that the reason for the revolt against that census was simply that Rome was doing something entirely new. It is not clear that this simple explanation is the real one. As Hoehner (1977: 18) suggests, a previous census patterned after Jewish models most likely produced no reaction and may not have been worthy of Josephus's attention. In addition, it seems clear that part of the grounds for the revolt in A.D. 6 was Archelaus himself, who was unpopular in the region. Rome wanted to confirm its presence visibly, and his support of a Roman-like census would anger those who opposed Rome. It was the Roman presence in a Roman-like census accepted by a Jewish figurehead that produced rebellion. Such a negative reaction to the A.D. 6 census should not be surprising if Roman authority was emphasized and the Roman model of census-taking was followed. Thus, the innovation may not have been the census as such, but its offensive form that more strongly reflected Roman sovereignty.[14] In short, a historian's silence need not mean historical absence, especially when one of the other potential historical witnesses raises other possibilities.

Thus, a census in Herod's time requiring a journey by Joseph and Mary is a possibility based upon what we know of Roman practice. That no other source mentions such a census is not a significant problem, since many ancient sources refer to events that are not corroborated elsewhere and since Luke is found to be trustworthy in his handling of facts that one can check. Since the details of this census fit into general Roman tax policy, there is no need to question that it could have occurred in the time of Herod.

However, there remains the more difficult issue of Quirinius (Schürer's fifth objection), to whom we now turn. Solutions for this

13. Hoehner 1977: 16–17 cites Josephus, *Antiquities* 17.11.4 §319 and *Jewish War* 2.6.3 §96. Hayles 1974: 25–26 posits deteriorating relations between Augustus and Herod as an explanation for the census. The statement by Sherwin-White 1963: 163 n. 4 that such a census in this period is impossible is clearly excessive in light of our partial knowledge of this period.

14. Hayles 1974: 27–28 notes that Josephus does not call the census an innovation and that what was new was the administrative set-up introduced in Judea in A.D. 6. He also notes how Josephus omits the mention of other known censuses, even in his discussion of contemporary history in the *Jewish War*. Josephus, *Antiquities* 18.1.1 §§3–4 speaks of taxation as the problem, but only as an indication of Israel's absence of liberty.

problem may be categorized under three types: lexical, historical, and interpretive (categories that are not always mutually exclusive). Lexical solutions discuss meanings of certain words (e.g., πρώτη, ἀπογράφεσθαι, and ἡγεμονεύοντος) and resolve the issue by adopting a less common meaning for these terms. Historical solutions pay careful attention to the situation of Quirinius in 6 B.C., putting forward the argument either that Quirinius was a governor in this early period (and so was governor of this region twice) or that he held a unique type of authority that could be described as "gubernatorial" in character, if not so in office. Interpretive solutions argue that it is wrong to see Luke as associating Quirinius with this initial census at all. Rather than separating my discussion into these categories, I shall discuss attempts at solutions in terms of their results without undertaking a systematic classification of them.

5a. The argument that Quirinius was governor twice is most forcefully made by Ramsay (1898: 174–96; 1920: 275–300). He argues that Quirinius was governor of Syria from 11/10 B.C. to 8/7 B.C., as well as in the later period, and that he initiated the census in Palestine at a later date (6 B.C.). Ramsay argues that an inscription now called the "Lapis Tiburtinus" refers to Quirinius.[15] But there are problems with this approach. The positing of a delay in the Palestinian census is minor, but more problematic is that the inscription, which is key to Ramsay's position, mentions no specific name, since it is a partial inscription. Thus, the construction of a position based on an anonymous reference makes this position difficult to establish. As Sherwin-White (1963: 165) says, "A headless inscription is at best a dangerous ally who may change sides at any moment." In addition, the association of a governorship in Syria with the known work of Quirinius in the Homonadensian Wars at this general time is also a problem, though the specific date of this conflict is not known. Still, Quirinius's locale during the war is normally tied to Galatia, not Syria. As can be seen, the variables of this position make it difficult to hold. It may be right, but its persuasiveness depends on too many pieces falling precisely into place.

5b. Sherwin-White argues that Quirinius was a legate between Varus and Gaius Caesar in 4 B.C.–1 B.C., since this is the only governorship gap present in the historical data.[16] Thus, though

---

15. Dessau 1892–1916: #918; Dessau 1921. Another relevant inscription on Quirinius is Dessau 1892–1916: #2683, which describes his career in Syria; Nolland 1989: 100.

16. Sherwin-White 1963: 162–71. This conclusion emerges from combining various historical sources, among which Josephus is very important.

Sherwin-White denies a census in the period of Herod, he does regard the reference to Quirinius in this time period as possible. The major problem with this view is that this governorship is too late for Luke's census, since it would follow Herod's death (Hoehner 1977: 20). In this form of the view, Luke is in error with regard to a census, though a lesser error than is normally posited, since Quirinius did rule in this period. This approach does not absolve Luke of error, though it does introduce another possibility.

5c. Might view 5b be made more plausible? Given, as was already defended, that a census under Herod is possible, is it possible that Varus began the census? Could the results and the taxation that came from it have emerged later under Quirinius in the period that Sherwin-White suggests, so that historically his name was attached to the census? It is clear that such a census would take time and could well have overlapped administrations. This suggestion is a constructed solution, but it brings the data together.

5d. A variation of view 5c is offered by Hayles (1974: 29), who suggests that Quirinius was not a legate or a governor but simply the chosen administrator of the census, whose term ran from Saturninus to Varus. This census would have been initiated in 6 B.C. Hayles differs from view 5c simply in seeing two governors involved, with Quirinius working as an administrator of the census, whereas view 5c sees Quirinius as a governor in his own right, who became responsible for the census. The possibility of ἡγεμονεύοντος having the loose meaning of "administrator" is defended by Hayles (1974: 28–29). The assumption in views 5c and 5d is that a major census takes some time to accomplish and requires special administrative skills and authority to complete. Either of these suggestions is possible, though it is difficult to choose between them, given the lack of specific additional evidence.

5e. Stauffer (1960: 30–31) attempts to distinguish technical terms in Luke's account by arguing that ἀπογράφω/ἀπογραφή referred to a tax registration, that is, to the preparing of tax records, while ἀποτίμησις referred to the actual taxation that came from the records in A.D. 6. Thus, Stauffer posits a decade-long taxation process, the initial record-taking phase of which is referred to in Luke 2. The major problem with this suggestion is that the lexical argument does not work. In both Josephus and Luke, the lexical distinctions do not hold up. Luke refers in Acts 5:37 to the revolt associated with the A.D. 6 census with the term he uses in Luke 2, while Josephus in *Antiquities* 18.1.1 §§2–4 uses the terms interchangeably. Thus, a lexical solution that posits a census of over a decade in length is not likely.

5f. Another lexical solution separates Quirinius from the census by arguing that 2:2 contains an ellipse and so fails to mention explicitly a census tied to Quirinius. Also, πρώτη should not be translated "first" but "earlier" (a meaning found in John 1:15, 30). In this view, Luke says that the census is *earlier* than the well-known Quirinius census of A.D. 6.[17] The major problem with this view is that the syntax of Luke 2:2 is cumbersome at best. This view is possible, but is not very likely.

5g. Another lexical solution produces a similar result, in that it separates Quirinius from Luke's census. In this view πρώτη is not to be translated as "first" but "before" (a sense found in John 15:18). Thus, Luke simply says that the census took place *before* Quirinius's governorship (Higgins 1969: 200–201; Nolland 1989: 101–2). The question with the view is whether Luke would use πρώτη in this unusual sense, but it is possible.[18]

The solutions to the Quirinius problem are varied. No candidate is so manifestly superior that it can be regarded as the solution. What one faces is a variety of solutions, any of which could be correct. If one is forced to state a preference, it would seem that the current historical uncertainty regarding the succession of the governorship in Syria is the most likely cause for the lack of clarity in making a choice. The most likely possibilities are my variation of Sherwin-White's solution with the allowance of the beginning of a census in the period of Herod (view 5c) or the solution of Hayles with Quirinius as an administrator of the census (view 5d). But the lexical suggestion of Higgins (view 5g) is also possible. One additional detail is little noted. If πρώτη means "first" (as agree most interpreters), then Luke calls this the "first" census while Quirinius was governor—a remark that could imply knowledge of more censuses under Quirinius. So the one thing Luke may not mean is what scholars who deny historicity argue he means: the later census of A.D. 6. In light of this and the various possibilities, it is clear that the relegation of Luke 2:2 to the category of historical error is premature and erroneous.[19]

17. This view dates back to the seventeenth century and is supported by F. F. Bruce 1972: 32 n. 1. Hoehner 1977: 21 discusses it.

18. This is the view that Hoehner 1977: 21–22 adopts, while Godet 1875: 1.124 calls it unlikely for Luke.

19. It is unfortunate that in both his detailed study (1977: 545–56) and his recent revision (1993), R. Brown, while rejecting Luke's approach, fails to refer to Hoehner or Hayles.

Excursus 3
Date of John the Baptist's Ministry
(3:1–2)

The dates for the rulers listed in Luke 3:1–2 are either undisputed or unknown: Pontius Pilate (A.D. 26–36), Herod Antipas (4 B.C.–A.D. 39), Philip (4 B.C.–A.D. 34), Lysanius (unknown), Annas (A.D. 6–15), and Caiaphas (A.D. 18–36). The range of dates is wide and none of these rulers, except for Tiberius, are cited by the year of their reign or priesthood, so that these references do not fix the chronology (Fitzmyer 1981: 455; Marshall 1978: 132; Schürmann 1969: 150–51; and especially Hoehner 1977: 30–31 and nn. 3–8).

The key date is the citation of the fifteenth year of Tiberius, a reference specific enough to narrow the options. Various issues make figuring the date of his accession difficult (Fitzmyer 1981: 455; Hoehner 1977: 29–37). Fitzmyer notes that five separate questions are involved:

1. Did Luke begin his reckoning from the coregency of Tiberius with Augustus? This date of accession is either 11 (according to Velleius Paterculus 2.121) or 12 (according to Suetonius, *Tiberius* 21). This produces a date of 25/26 for John's ministry.
2. Did Luke reckon the accession year from the death of Augustus (19 Aug. 14) or from the vote of the Senate giving Tiberius power (17 Sept. 14)? This represents a minor question, for in either case John's dates become 28/29, unless one brings in other additional considerations (see points 3–5 below).
3. Did Luke distinguish the accession year by not counting it as one of the regnal years? If he did, this increases the final date by as much as a year, depending on the new calendar year chosen. The result could be a date as late as 29.
4. Did Luke count the partial accession year as the first regnal year, with the second regnal year beginning on the next New Year's Day? To do so decreases the final date by as much as a year, depending on which calendar is used. This gives a date as early as 28.
5. In considering issues 3 and 4, another question is crucial: Which calendar did Luke use to reckon the new year? There are four candidates: (a) the Julian or Roman calendar: January 1; (b) the

Jewish calendar: Nisan 1 (March/April); (c) the Syrian calendar: October 1 (or Tishri 1); or (d) the Egyptian calendar: August 29.[1] As one can see, the issues tied to dating here are very complex.

Hoehner summarizes the factors involved and comments on the resulting positions. (In my summary of Hoehner's discussion, I indicate who holds to which chronology, since there is a great deal of variety.)

a. The earliest date figures Tiberius's reign from the decree that made him coregent with Augustus. This date is variously put at 11 or 12, depending upon whether the dating of Velleius Paterculus or Suetonius is accepted (#1 above). This reckoning yields a date of 25/26 for John's ministry. J. Ussher in the mid-seventeenth century took this approach, so this date has been called the traditional one and is popular (Hendriksen 1978: 194–98, esp. n. 166; J. Ussher, as cited by Creed 1930: 48). This approach ultimately produces an early date for the crucifixion as well, 30 (less frequently 29), when one holds that Jesus had a ministry of a little over three years, as John's Gospel suggests with Jesus' numerous trips to Jerusalem for Passover (John 2:13, 23; 6:4; 11:55). The view suffers from a major problem. There is no evidence in contemporary sources or coins that Tiberius's reign was reckoned in such a fashion (Hoehner 1977: 31, esp. n. 11). As Hoehner notes, the reckoning of Josephus and other ancient historians assumes a starting date later than Tiberius's entry into coregency with Augustus.[2] It is interesting that in arguing for this view Hendriksen appeals to support from Tertullian (*Against Marcion* 1.15), who argues that Jesus appeared in Tiberius's twelfth year, a date that is manifestly reckoned from the full reign of Tiberius (A.D. 14–15) and not from his coregency.[3] The claim that Luke is reckoning actual years of reign would have more credibility if there was evidence that anyone else viewed the "actual" years of Tiberius's

1. Why Fitzmyer lists the Egyptian calendar as a candidate is unclear, since no clear ties to Egypt are present.

2. Hoehner 1977: 32 nn. 12–13, who cites Appian, *Civil Wars* 2.149; Plutarch, *Life of Caesar* 62–67; Suetonius, *Caesar* 81.2; and Josephus, *Antiquities* 18.2.2 §32; 18.6.10 §224; *Jewish War* 2.9.1 §168; 2.9.5 §180.

3. Hendriksen 1978: 198 n. 166. In relation to the accuracy of Tertullian, who in *Against Marcion* 1.15 argued that Jesus appeared in the twelfth year of Tiberius (ca. A.D. 26–27), Eusebius in *Chronicon* 2 notes that Jesus suffered in the nineteenth year of Tiberius (A.D. 33), so that the church fathers do not agree on the dates of Jesus' ministry either, since Jesus did not minister for seven years. Jesus' appearing is probably a reference to his baptism by John.

reign in this way. Thus, this view is not likely. The remaining views all assume that the starting point for Luke's calculation is after any period of coregency.

b. Luke might have used Jewish reckoning, which changes regnal years every Nisan 1 (March/April in our calendar). Thus, whether the first year is figured from the death of Augustus or from the vote of the Senate (# 2 above), the first year of Tiberius's reign is in fact a partial year and the date for his fifteenth year is between April 28 and April 29 (Ogg 1962: 729; Ogg 1940: 196–201). Ogg argues that *m. Roš Haš*. 1.1 calculates dates on this basis, but this tractate and the Talmud argue that only the dates of Israelite kings are figured this way, while foreign kings are dated from Tishri 1 (September/October in our calendar; *b. Roš Haš*. 3a–b, 8a). Hoehner also shows (1977: 32–34) from OT and intertestamental sources that no clear Jewish custom exists. Josephus may have used this method at times, but the question is whether a Gentile, which Luke probably was, would write to another Gentile (Theophilus) and reckon this way. This approach seems improbable.

c. Luke is probably from the region of Syria, specifically Antioch, and thus might have used Syrian reckoning. On this scheme, regnal years would have been reckoned from Tishri 1, so that Tiberius's first year ends up being very short, either from August (Augustus's death) to October or from September (the Senate's vote) to October. This system produces a fifteenth year between fall 27 and fall 28 (Schneider 1977a: 83). This approach would also tend to produce a crucifixion date of 30.[4] Such a date is regarded as fitting the other key chronological point in Luke, which mentions that Jesus was about thirty at the start of his ministry (3:23). It also can fit in the three Passovers during Jesus' ministry (John 2:13; 6:4; 11:55). This is a popular option. The major problem with the view is that it limits Jesus' ministry to a little over two years, if one takes the early crucifixion date of 30. Thus, the view is possible and ought to be the one adopted if one holds that Jesus died in 30. However, that date is not the most likely date for the crucifixion.[5]

4. On the possibility that Luke is from Antioch of Syria, a tradition that Jerome mentions in the prologue of his commentary on Matthew, see Hoehner 1972: 231–32 n. 9; Strobel 1958a; and the introduction to the Gospel of Luke abve, under "Origin and Purpose—Authorship—External Evidence." Schneider 1977a: 83 and Hoehner 1977: 34 do not agree on the month in view in 27: Schneider has Oct. 1 and Hoehner has Sept. 21.

5. Reicke 1968: 183–84 lists the key reasons for a 33 date: (1) the year of Herod Antipas's divorce, which John criticizes, is probably 32 and (2) the removal of the anti-Semitic dictator Sejanus by Tiberius in 31 made Pilate treat the Jews with more

d. One of two possible ways that Romans reckoned regnal years was from the Julian or Roman calendar, that is, from January 1. This approach counts the period of August (or October) 14 to 1 January 15 as an accession year but not the first year of Tiberius's reign and results in a date of 29 for Tiberius's fifteenth year.[6] The ancient Roman historians Tacitus and Suetonius reckoned regnal years in this fashion (Finegan 1964: 271–72). Such a reckoning has an official quality to it that makes it an appealing possibility, since it gives Luke's work the air of formality. It is quite possible that this is how Luke calculated this date, since it fits the Roman perspective of the data and the literary character of his work.

e. The other way to reckon from the Roman perspective is to count fifteen years straight from the accession without appeal to any new calendar year. Such an approach would push back the fifteenth year about three months, between August (versus October) 28 and August (versus October) 29 (Creed 1930: 48; one option of Schürmann 1969: 150). This is the normal, nonformal way the Romans counted regnal years.

The discussion of chronology is complicated, but Luke probably used a Roman approach in figuring the fifteenth year of Tiberius's reign (either view 4 or 5). If that is correct, then John the Baptist's ministry came to public view in the period between late summer to fall 28 and late summer to fall 29. Such a date coheres nicely with the general reference in Luke 3:23 that Jesus' ministry started when he was about thirty. It also fits the portrayal of John's Gospel that Jesus' ministry lasted a little over three years. The time between the start of John the Baptist's ministry and the start of Jesus' ministry is unknown, but it would seem that both ministries together spanned about a five-year period.

---

sympathy. See also Hoehner 1977: 95–111 and the sources and historicity section of 23:6–12.

6. Fitzmyer 1981: 455. Ernst 1977: 137, considering the various options, speaks of fall 27 to fall 29. Hoehner allows this as one of the two possible options.

Excursus 4
Sources and Synoptic Relationships

The use of sources in Gospel studies is a complex issue.[1] One of the goals of this commentary is to outline in detail the verbal relationships between the Synoptics. By any reckoning, a discussion of Luke is the logical place to present key elements in such an analysis, since no matter which of the major theories is accepted, Luke is either in the middle or at the end of the sequence. But the whole question of the order and literary relationship of the Synoptic Gospels to one another is a complex question beyond our scope.[2]

The current dominant approach is based on Marcan priority: Mark came first, followed by Matthew and Luke. This view argues that Matthew and Luke share some teaching material in a source (or sources) called Q and that Luke was the last Synoptic Gospel. However, a growing number of advocates today argue that Matthew was first and Mark was last. Known as the two-Gospel or Griesbach hypothesis, this view challenges the existence of Q and argues that Luke knew Matthew.[3] Others argue for the so-called Augustinian order of Matthew, Mark, and Luke—an order reflected in the Bible.[4] Still others argue for independence.[5]

---

1. For solid overviews of this area, see McKnight 1991b and Stein 1987. McKnight is slightly more confident than I am of Marcan priority, though I still regard it likely that Mark was the first Gospel written. Still, his and Stein's overviews show why many think Mark's Gospel is first. For a comparative study of the two major options in the debate, see Bellinzoni, Tyson, and Walker 1985 and Dungan 1990. A study making significant points about Q and the complex interrelationship of the Gospel writers is Reicke 1986. For the case for Matthean priority, see Farmer 1964.

2. Especially beyond our scope is the detailed analysis of Matthew and Mark that must accompany such a study to make it a full examination of the issue.

3. This view is experiencing a resurgence, at least in America, which was fueled by Farmer's 1964 study. Numerous studies defending the view have come out since Farmer. This camp has caused some in Germany to speak of the *Ur-Marcus* hypothesis again; that is, that the other Gospels worked with an early edition of Mark distinct from the version in our canon. It is hard to know where the discussion is headed.

4. On the history of this discussion, including the church fathers and the various views, see Orchard and Riley 1987. Goulder's detailed 1989 work is unique, arguing that the order is Mark–Matthew–Luke, but that Luke used only Mark and Matthew, not Q. One of the goals of his study is to challenge the existence of Q.

5. Rist 1978. J. Wenham 1992a: 223 dates Matthew in 42, Mark in 45, and Luke in 55 at the latest—dates that are much earlier than typically assigned to the Gospels. Most conservatives place the Synoptics in the sixties, while most others have dates ranging from 60 to 90.

In this commentary, I avoid taking a firm position, since the issue is in my judgment still somewhat open. I think it likely that Mark was first, mainly because it is hard to see Mark as a summary Gospel, coming last, and leaving out huge portions of important teaching, especially when he includes a large teaching unit like the Olivet Discourse (Mark 13). If Mark is not last, then the argument from order tends to suggest that Mark is first. This argument also notes that Matthew and Luke generally follow Marcan order, but never diverge together against Mark. The major problems with Marcan priority are the Matthean-Lucan agreements against Mark and the issue of certain Lucan omissions of Mark that, if Luke used Mark, are hard to explain (see the discussions of sources for 6:12–16; 8:4–15; 8:16–18; 8:19–21; for a sociological critique of Marcan priority, see Meijboom 1993).

In spite of my general agreement with the current consensus on the order of the Gospels, I am also convinced that the literary relationship between Matthew, Mark, and Luke is much more complex than Streeter's 1924 standard four-source theory, which limits sources largely to Mark, Q, Matthean special material (M), and Lucan special material (L). I think his general outline explains much, but I am less confident that the material is limited to these four large groups. Part of this commentary is given over to the phrase-by-phrase analysis of the differences in the Gospels that will show how complex these relationships are. It seems certain that whatever the tradition is that Matthew and Luke share, it is not a single document Q, because of the diversity that exists within the passages attributed to Q—diversity that cannot be explained simply by appeal to the preferences of the Gospel writers. Once Q is broken up, then it is difficult to know the exact nature of the sources, other than to say in a general way that Matthew and Luke are sharing the same tradition stream. I use the symbol Q often, and when I mention it in association with other scholarly studies, it refers to a written source or sources shared by Matthew and Luke. Thus, Q is a convenient way to say that Matthew and Luke share a similar tradition at this point, though not necessarily the same document.

We can be certain that Luke used sources, since he tells us as much in 1:1–4, when he refers to other attempts to give an account of Jesus' ministry. The extent of verbal agreement between the Gospels in passages like 3:7–9 leads many to conclude correctly that the other writers also had access to similar sources or traditions as well. In commenting on his sources, Luke notes that the other accounts he is aware of have roots in the testimony of eyewitnesses, a point that is sometimes minimized in some critical treatments of this area, but that should not be underestimated (see the exegesis of 1:2).

The recognition of sources is, thus, something the texts themselves suggest, though their nature is not specified. In addition, none of the Gospel writers actually give the names of their sources or the location of their writings' audience. These factors make it difficult to know exactly what sources they used, where they wrote, or to whom, though textual comparison can make plausible suggestions. The testimony of church tradition has counted for much in the discussion of authorship. Traditionally, the Gospel of Matthew is seen ultimately as the product of a disciple-apostle, though this is now under challenge.[6] Mark is believed to have had access to Peter, roots that seem to fit Luke's description of his own predecessors. Luke, an associate of Paul, is the third Gospel writer, though this too is challenged by some today. Technical NT introductions deal with such issues of authorship in detail and catalogue the history of the debate about such points.[7]

Thus, I examine the details regarding the source of individual pericopes unit by unit, while recognizing that our ability to be certain of source reconstructions is at best limited. Certainty regarding direct literary dependence or order is difficult to obtain. This commentary simply compares the Gospel accounts to one another, notes differences, and remarks on the differences of emphasis without trying to state confidently who changed what, except where issues of theme or style make such matters clear. However, I also will note how others have viewed these changes and their historical order, an approach that often reflects Marcan priority, because that is how most writers approach this material.

When I attribute an expression clearly to a Gospel writer, I do so because his word usage, style, or theology is so distinctive at the point in question that one can conclude with good probability that the writer's expression is present. Otherwise, what is present are differences of expression that could be attributed to the traditions the Gospel writers used or to the writers themselves. In making comments where writers seem to be sharing the same tradition, I speak of one Gospel writer's point of view in comparison to the other, without always trying to posit a definite historical sequence in each case.

In my judgment, what may often have happened is not that the writer knew the other Gospel as such or the exact verbal form of the

6. Many NT introductions now speak of a product of the Matthean school, rather than of Matthew. I still think it is proper to speak of Matthew as the author.

7. Guthrie 1970 deals with these issues from a conservative, evangelical viewpoint, while the introduction of Kümmel 1975 serves as a good survey of common critical approaches to these issues. See the introduction on "Sources" for these issues as they relate to Luke. Orchard and Riley 1987 detail the ancient testimony of the church on this question.

tradition the other Gospel had, but that he knew the same tradition stream (whether oral or written) reflected in that other Gospel. The uncertainty about precise sources is indicated when numerous differences in a pericope have no clear motive or stylistic preference behind them. If one cannot explain why the text is different, maybe those texts were never the same from the start. These are the premises that guide my analysis, and they were derived from the exegesis that follows.

Thus, this commentary will highlight the theological emphases of each Lucan account as compared to the other Gospels, but the development or historical sequence between the different Gospel writers will not be prominent. Those who are more confident of Synoptic relationships can simply plug in the order they prefer to determine what these historical relationships may have been.

What is important, despite my cautious approach, is that the writings themselves can still be compared and the emphases and teachings can still receive examination with profit. Thus, in speaking of how one writer's wording differs from another's, I deal with the text as it is. I note what one writer is focusing on in comparison to another writer. By such comparisons, the complementary position of each Gospel to the other can be made clear, as each writer presents his own portrait of Jesus. Each writer has emphases that he shares with the others, while also having his own unique points to contribute.

Excursus 5
The Genealogies of Matthew and Luke (3:23–38)

Luke's genealogy differs from the one in Matthew at several levels (Fitzmyer 1981: 495–96; Liefeld 1984: 861; Aland 1985: §19; on the role of genealogies in Jewish culture, see Nolland 1989: 168–69):

1. Matthew goes from the oldest to the youngest generation, while Luke reverses this order. Matthew's order is the normal one for a genealogy, though Luke's has parallels with OT lists where ancestry is the issue (1 Chron. 6:33–38 [6:18–23 MT]; Nolland 1989: 168).
2. They have differing endpoints in the genealogy: Abraham in Matthew versus Adam in Luke.
3. Matthew will stop occasionally to explain the significance of an entry (Matt. 1:2, 5), while Luke never does.
4. Matthew's structure involves names given in three groups of fourteen each, a device that may involve an allusion to the numerics of David's name (Carson 1984: 69–70). On the other hand, Luke's structure seems to be eleven groups of seven names each, though the reason for this structure is not clear.[1] Marshall (1978: 160–61) discusses the suggestion that this structure represents the eleven weeks before the messianic twelfth week. However, he also observes that the scheme goes the wrong way for this point to be made, since the messianic week usually ends the sequence (2 Esdr. [= 4 Ezra] 14:11; 2 Bar. 27.1; 53.6; Apocalypse of Abraham 29.2). Also, the addition of the Son of God as a seventy-eighth name may overthrow this approach.[2]
5. Matthew lists some women (e.g., Rahab and Ruth), but Luke never does—an interesting difference given Luke's attention to women.

---

1. On NT structures with the use of "seven," see Rengstorf, *TDNT* 2:632 §B4d. On other points of Lucan structure, see Nolland 1989: 168 and Goulder 1989: 283–90.

2. Because the exact list of names is so uncertain and because Luke says nothing about the structure, one should be cautious about invoking such precise symbolism. Wiefel 1988: 97 seems to regard this twelfth-week view as possible. Schürmann 1969: 203 n. 119 argues that if it is present Luke is not conscious of it. Nolland 1989: 168 suggests that it was the point of Luke's source, whose order he reversed. But how can one know this? Goulder 1989: 284–85 is strongly supportive of this view, citing 1 Enoch 93.3–10 to stress that the form is to some extent artificial.

6. In the stretch of names from Abraham to Jesus (i.e., where Luke and Matthew overlap), Matthew has forty-one names, while Luke has fifty-seven (Marshall 1978: 158). In the period from David to Jesus, there are only two points of overlap: Shealtiel and Zerubbabel.

All these differences have produced a myriad of solutions as to how the two lists relate to one another. In sum there are six basic approaches to this question:

1. Most opt for a literary and theological approach to this material, regarding any attempt at harmonization as impossible.[3] In this view, both writers relate Jesus to Joseph without any recourse to historical material other than existing biblical materials from 1 Chronicles and Genesis. The point of each account is its theological connection. Matthew points to the king through David and Abraham, while Luke associates Jesus with all of humanity through Adam. Thus, this approach rejects the possibility of a solution. But other attempts to address the problem do exist.

2. Another common approach is to argue that Matthew gives the genealogy through Joseph, while Luke gives the genealogy through Mary (Hendriksen 1978: 222–25; Godet 1875: 1.201). Dating back to Annius of Viterbo in 1490, the view argues that Joseph is not really in view in 3:23, where Luke says that Joseph was "supposed to be" (ἐνομίζετο) Jesus' father. In addition, the absence of the article τοῦ before Joseph's name shows that he is not part of the genealogy. It is also argued that seeing Joseph in the genealogy puts Luke in a double contradiction in that he disagrees not only with Matthew, but also with himself, since he has already made clear that Jesus was born of the virgin Mary (1:27). Finally, it is argued that rabbinic tradition knows of the connection between Heli (also spelled Eli) and Mary.[4] There are many problems with this approach. First, it is not at all clear that the rabbinic reference applies to Mary. In fact, most doubt that it does, because the Miriam referred to

---

3. Schürmann 1969: 200; Fitzmyer 1981: 496; Ernst 1977: 155; Lohse, *TDNT* 8:486 n. 49. Bovon 1989: 189 calls attempts at harmonization excessive rationalization like that in current fundamentalism. C. F. Evans 1990: 252 calls the task "impossible," which is excessively skeptical.

4. *Y. Ḥag.* 77d (= Neusner et al. 1982–93: 20.57–58); Geldenhuys 1951: 154; SB 2:155; Godet 1875: 1.202. Another reference is *y. Sanh.* 23c (38) (= Neusner et al. 1982–93: 31.182). If this view were correct, then the Protevangelium of James 1–5 is wrong to name Mary's father as Joachim. But the origin and value of this NT apocryphal tradition are uncertain.

there is not called the mother of Jesus and thus could be any Miriam.[5] Second, the absence of the article τοῦ can be explained simply because Joseph starts the list. Third, the virgin birth does not prevent legal paternity from passing through the father (Gordon 1977). Thus, no contradiction with the virgin birth exists. Fourth, the most natural way to read the Greek is as a genealogy for Joseph (Carson 1984: 64), given that Mary is not named at all here and that the genitive τοῦ at the front of the list is masculine. To clearly bring in Mary, Luke could have named her and/or changed the opening genitive to a feminine, similar to Matt. 1:16 and its use of ἧς, which makes clear that the Matthean connection is only to Mary.

The remaining views all agree that Joseph's line is addressed by both Luke and Matthew. They disagree on how this is done.

3. The oldest known view is that of Julius Africanus (ca. A.D. 225; cited by Eusebius, *Ecclesiastical History* 1.7), who suggests that Matthew provided the natural line, while Luke provided the royal line, and that the difference in the lists was caused by the principle of levirate marriage (Deut. 25:5–10). According to Julius, Matthan (Matt. 1:15) had a son, Jacob, by way of his wife, Estha. Matthan died and Estha married Melchi (Luke 3:24), who had a son, Heli (Luke 3:23). Heli died without children and his half-brother, Jacob, took his wife by levirate marriage, so that Jacob's sons were tied to Heli's line. In this way, Joseph could be lined up to each list: physically to Jacob but legally to Heli. The problem with this approach is that two names intervene in Luke's list between Heli and Melchi: Μαθθάτ (Matthat) and Λευί (Levi). Such a connection is not impossible, given that Matthew's list is shorter than Luke's, but it is less than likely. Levirate marriage, though not common in the first century, was not completely unknown or else the theological inquiry of the Sadducees in Matt. 22:24–28 does not make sense (Carson 1984: 64; Nolland 1989: 169 [who rejects all levirate-marriage solutions]; M. Johnson 1969: 144–45).

4. A modern variation of this ancient view reverses the focus: Luke gives the physical descent and Matthew the royal descent. Tied to the work of A. Hervey in 1853 and modified by Machen, this approach notes that ancient Judaism argued for a multiple line for David (Tg. Zech. 12:12; Marshall 1978: 158; Machen 1930: 207–9; Hill 1972: 75). The simplest form of this

5. SB 2:155 gives it only a "perhaps," while Geldenhuys 1951: 154 rejects it.

approach argues that Jacob of Matt. 1:15 was childless and so Heli, who had Joseph as his physical son, became the heir. For this approach to work there must be another levirate marriage to Jacob's widow, since Matt. 1:16 seemingly has Jacob as Joseph's father, while Luke 3:23 says Joseph is the son of Heli.[6] However, if Matthew's Jacob and Luke's Heli are brothers, then their father, listed as Matthat in Luke 3:24 and as Matthan in Matt. 1:15, must be the same person. But if these two men, Matthat and Matthan, are the same (as Machen reckons), then their fathers also differ, as the two genealogies note: Eleazar in Matt. 1:15 and Levi in Luke 3:24. Another levirate marriage is required or one must assume that the line through Eleazar became extinct.[7] The introduction of an additional levirate marriage (or an extinct line) is too difficult for Carson (1984: 64–65). But he notes that R. Brown's criticism (1977: 503–4) of ways to harmonize the accounts ignores Machen's work. As one can see, this view is possible, but it is very complicated.

5. Carson (1984: 65) suggests that Matthat and Matthan are not the same person. Machen notes that this configuration requires that Jacob and Heli be half-brothers, a view Machen thinks is less likely. Carson thinks the pieces can fit. He says Levi (Luke 3:24) is the closest heir next to Jacob (Matt. 1:15–16).[8] Carson's explanation can work, but only with an important correction: Levi is not the son of Matthat, Heli is (Luke 3:23).[9] So Heli dies childless as the legal royal heir and is Joseph's uncle. Joseph is the physical son of Jacob by a sister of Heli, who now bears the line. This correction reverses the relationship between Matthew's and Luke's genealogies by going the opposite direction from what Carson suggests. If this configuration is correct, then Matthew gives the physical line and Luke gives the legal and "physical" line. Luke's line is "physical" through Heli's sister, who has legal claim to the line as the

6. Unless one approaches the question like Machen 1930: 207–9, who argues that Jacob and Heli were brothers, so Joseph was Jacob's nephew. When Jacob died childless, the nephew became heir.

7. Machen prefers the latter, a choice that Carson fails to mention in critiquing the view. Thus, Machen sees two childless fathers at the end of Matthew's list: Eleazar and Jacob.

8. For Carson, Levi is an only son; but his sister, who bears the line, marries Jacob. So when Levi dies childless, Joseph, the nephew, becomes the heir physically through Jacob and Levi's sister.

9. Carson appears to have read Luke in the wrong generational direction here or else this is a typo reading Levi in place of Heli. Carson (or his editor) is not the first to get tangled in the complex intersection of these genealogies, nor is he likely to be the last!

nearest relative to Heli. The only problem with this approach through the sister is, How can Joseph then be called the "son" of Heli, since he is not the physical father and a levirate marriage is not present? The genealogy must be seen simply as "legal" at this point, but that is also the only way that Jesus enters in when one assumes a virgin birth, which both Matt. 1:16 and Luke 1:27–35 acknowledge. Another option is that the wife of the childless Heli married Jacob, in which case Joseph was physically born through Jacob, but has ties to the throne also by levirate connections to Heli, his "father." This latter configuration seems the best possibility within this approach.

6. Still another option is noted by Nolland (1989: 170, drawing on U. Holzmeister), who argues that Mary is an heiress of Eli, since she had no brothers. Eli adopted Joseph as son upon marriage, as in other cases where a father had no physical son (Ezra 2:61; Neh. 7:63; see also Num. 27:1–11 [which establishes lines of inheritance]; 1 Chron. 2:34–35). Luke's genealogy reflects adoption. On this basis, the line again becomes "legal" versus physical at this endpoint.

Luke's line may also be the legal one because of the curse of Jeconiah (Jer. 22:30), whose name appears in Matthew but not in Luke. What complicates this particular suggestion about Jeconiah is that Zerubbabel receives the signet ring again, according to Hag. 2:23, an act that probably reverses the Jeconiah curse. At the least, Luke's genealogy excludes Jeconiah from any recognition. So, the Lucan omission could be seen as wiping Jeconiah's memory from the official legal list because of the curse. While one's paternity cannot be denied, one can lose legal right to the inherited line.[10] What emerges from both evangelists' genealogies is that Jesus belongs on the throne no matter which route one takes. Both the physical route and the legal route lead to Jesus.

A clear choice is difficult to establish between the various views that see Joseph's line as present in both Gospels. Views 3–6 are all possible, yet each requires a set of conjectures that cannot be proven. What seems most likely, if one is to take the accounts as historical, is that Jacob (Matt. 1:15–16) and Heli (Luke 3:23) had a close

10. The twentieth-century English Duke of Windsor, Edward VIII, is a classic, similar contemporary illustration of this truth, though he had no children. A closer analogy would be William's becoming king in place of his father, if Charles were to become disqualified for the throne. So then, Luke did not need Nathan to make this point (Nolland 1989: 170, 172, who is for the influence of the Jeconian curse on Luke, so that the evangelist sends the genealogy through Nathan rather than through Solomon).

relationship, though whether as brothers, half-brothers, through the marriage of Heli's sister to Jacob, levirate marriage, or adoption is less clear. It is also clear that other breaks in the listing occurred. What the options show is that it is premature to insist on error here, even though a definite solution does not emerge. Nevertheless, the genealogy's point is obvious. Jesus has a claim to the throne through David and is related to all of humanity through Adam.

Excursus 6
The Son of Man in Aramaic and in Luke (5:24)

There are seven points of current consensus about the Son of Man:[1]

1. The phrase in a few Gospel passages (Luke 21:27; 22:69) is related to Dan. 7:13–14 and in Heb. 2:6 is associated with Ps. 8.
2. The term comes from Aramaic and would have been used by Jesus in an Aramaic form (Fitzmyer 1981: 208–9): בַּר־אֱנָשׁ or בַּר־אֱנוֹשׁ.
3. Technically speaking, the usage in Daniel is not a title, but a description of a human figure who approaches God to receive dominion ("one like a son of man"). In other words, it is not a reference to *the* Son of Man; only the imagery is present. It should not be ignored, however, that the presence of a figure with this description makes the passage capable of generating a title, as is indicated by its later history in the NT, 1 Enoch, and 2 Esdras [= 4 Ezra]. Also, the image of this figure coming on the clouds suggests divinity.[2]
4. There is currently no clear evidence that at the time of Christ the term existed as a formal, specific messianic title in Judaism.[3]

---

1. For more detail about the Son of Man debate and an extended version of this excursus, see Bock 1991c. Key recent studies (with full bibliographies) include Colpe, *TDNT* 8:400–77; Casey 1979; Caragounis 1986; S. Kim 1985; Tödt 1979 (whose work Kim in particular critiques).

2. Bock 1987: 133–35. See the exegesis of 21:27 and 22:69 for details. S. Kim 1985: 17–19 seems to overemphasize the divinity of the figure at the expense of the humanity in the picture. The Dan. 7 imagery suggests deity; it does not declare it.

3. 1 Enoch 46–48, 62–71 and 2 Esdr. [= 4 Ezra] 13 are too late to be related to this period. S. Kim 1985: 19 and n. 25 mentions that a "heavenly," redemptive figure identified alternatively with Enoch, Abel, or Melchizedek may have existed in the ancient Jewish tradition. But he notes that these claims are disputable, since the clear examples are late. He also notes (pp. 20–22) that 4Q246, formerly 4Q243 (= 4QpsDan A^a = 4QpsDan ar^a), may prove this limitation incorrect, but it is too early to know what this text means, since all of it has not been published, and it has many gaps. Fitzmyer 1981: 209–10 argues that 1 Enoch may be relevant as a transitional move to an apocalyptic individualized use, but he treats the point as too unclear to base much on it. Kim (p. 19 n. 25) notes that all undisputed examples from 1 Enoch and 2 Esdras are later than the Gospels. The Son of Man references in Judaism are 1 Enoch 46.3–7; 48.4–10; 62.3–9, 14; 63.11; 69.27–29; 2 Esdr. [= 4 Ezra] 13; *b. Sanh.* 96b; 98a; Midr. Num. 13.14; Midr. ha-Gadol on Gen. 49:10; *Aggadat Bereshit* 4.3; 23.1 (see Strack and Stemberger 1991: 339); *y. Ta'an.* 2.1 [= Neusner et al. 1982–93: 18.183]; *b. Ḥag.* 14a; *Tanḥuma Toledot* 20 (70b) (= Townsend 1989: 167; see also Caragounis 1986: 134–36).

5. Thus, the term as a specific messianic title probably emerged either from Jesus or the early church. The presence of the title in the NT is almost always with the definite article, which suggests a definite reference and a titular use.[4]
6. In this tradition, the key point of association, at least in the Synoptics, is Dan. 7:13–14.
7. In the NT tradition, with the exception of Acts 7:56, the term is found exclusively on Jesus' lips (Rev. 1:13 and 14:14 are similar expressions describing Jesus).

Scholars classify sayings about the Son of Man in the NT in various ways:

1. Most classify them according to content: (a) the present ministry of the Son of Man (of which Luke 5:24 is one example), (b) the suffering Son of Man, and (c) the future return of the Son of Man.
2. Others classify them with regard to their degree of connection to Daniel: (a) no reference, (b) indirect reference or allusion to Dan. 7 (i.e., more than the mere title), or (c) direct reference (i.e., citation of Dan. 7).[5]
3. Perhaps even better is a twofold breakdown: (a) sayings about the authority of the Son of Man and (b) sayings about the rejection of the Son of Man (O. Betz 1985: 13).

The benefit of the third classification is that it deals with biblical concepts, not a mixture of time and function. On the other hand, as suggested by the first classification, the Son of Man sayings do relate generally to Jesus' earthly ministry, death, or resurrection/exaltation.

Regardless of the classification scheme chosen, the category by itself is not sufficient to be the basis for judging a text's historical authenticity. For example, Luke 5:24 makes no direct or clear indirect reference to Daniel. It deals with Jesus' present ministry and with the authority of the Son of Man (so equals 2a and 3a).

The debate over the meaning of the phrase *Son of Man* in its first-century Aramaic setting is complex. A key issue in this debate is the question of what the Aramaic phrase meant in the first century, given that it was not yet a formal title. By itself, the phrase simply refers to a human, just as the idiom *son of a carpenter* refers to a carpenter's descendant. The key participants in this aspect of the recent debate are Fitzmyer (1979b: 143–61; 1979a) and Vermes (1967;

4. One exception to this is John 5:27. The title appears about eight-two times in the Gospels; BAGD 835 §2c; BAA 1665 §2c (both lexicons have bibliography).
5. So Vermes 1973: 178, who discusses classifications 1 and 2 and prefers #2.

1973: 188–91). Both agree that the phrase can have one of two basic senses: "someone" or "man." The debate is whether the term is another way to say "I," so that a speaker indirectly refers to just himself, much like the editorial "we" in English.[6] In other words, does the phrase mean "people in general, including me" or "I and nobody else"? Vermes argues that it can refer exclusively to an individual, while Fitzmyer believes this additional meaning is not attested in material early enough to support the presence of this sense in the first century.[7]

The debate, in my view, may be a huge rabbit trail. This is not to demean the value of discussing the phrase's force in the original Aramaic, but the issue is not as central as many make it. The resolution of the Aramaic origin would settle whether Jesus referred to himself by circumlocution (Vermes) or generically (Fitzmyer). But my contention is that NT usage makes it clear that *either* sense of the Aramaic, even the ambiguous sense, in the original setting and tradition would contain a veiled reference to Jesus. Either way, contextually, the force of Jesus' use would point only to him. But to argue this point requires that the saying is authentic, which needs defense.

Some question whether Jesus used the phrase *Son of Man* of himself. By appealing to Mark 2:27–28, some see the original term as a reference to all people; others see a reference to a figure other than Jesus (both positions are argued by Bultmann 1963: 15–16, 84, 151–52). In Luke 5:24, Bultmann appeals to the plural in the parallel Matt. 9:8, which speaks of authority given to *men*. He sees the Matthean form as the earliest form of this tradition, where the church expresses its authority to forgive sin. This ecclesiastical authority was rewritten in Mark 2:10 and Luke 5:24, using the circumlocution to refer to Jesus. The problem with all these approaches has always been that they cannot explain the consistent tie of the term to Jesus in the NT.

A good example of how the term works is Luke 5:24, where the issue is Jesus' authority. Does either sense of the phrase *Son of Man* here rule out an exclusive self-reference to Jesus? In its more ambiguous sense, the phrase would read, "So you might know that *a man* (or *someone*) has authority to forgive sins on earth." In its other sense, the phrase would mean, "So you might know that *this man* has authority to forgive sins." Since (1) it is a given in Judaism that peo-

6. They speak of circumlocution, which means a "roundabout" way to say something.

7. Fitzmyer 1981: 209–10 retreats slightly from his earlier position, which argued that such attestation is entirely missing from the extrabiblical texts. But he argues that the evidence from Tg. Neof. 1 on Gen. 4:14 and Cairo Targum B is too late to be relevant.

ple do not have this authority (only God does: Exod. 34:6; Ps. 103:12; Isa. 1:18; 43:25; Jer. 31:34) and (2) Jesus is the one who performs the healing in question, the saying is to be applied only to him. The Pharisees in the account get that point clearly, even before the use of the phrase *Son of Man*. Jesus' remark underscores the point. The assumption that Jesus' original remark is ambiguous fails to deal with issues raised by the connection to the event.[8] There is no problem or ambiguity in the Son-of-Man reference. One other point should be made. In Aramaic, it is not clear that a messianic title is present. It is only "someone," that is, Jesus, who does something unique.

It is interesting that Matt. 9:8 (= Luke 5:26) places the crowd's response in very general, ambiguous terms: the crowd offers praise because God had given such authority to *men*. Does this not indicate that a wider original reference for the title is appropriate? The answer is both yes and no. Yes, the reply *does* suggest that the audience heard a general reference. But, no, even in this context, it is the uniqueness of Jesus' action that has drawn attention. The crowd is amazed that "people" have such authority, but it is *Jesus* who amazes them. So the attention is really not on people, but on this man.

Equally important is that the full force of the meaning of a term can be gradually unveiled. In other words, there can be a difference between what Jesus understood a term to mean and how he went about revealing that understanding. I believe that this is the case with Jesus' use of "Son of Man," as the evidence of Luke 5:24 and its Matthean parallel suggests. Jesus' action and saying are a conundrum, like those he often offers his audiences (e.g., the use of Ps. 110 in Luke 20:41–44). It is the second such conundrum in the context (the first was the "which is easier to say" remark in 5:23). The Son of Man saying is a second riddle. He says, assuming the ambiguous use, "Know that *someone* has this authority." But the paradox is that humans do *not* have this authority, as the Pharisees had already noted. So, and this is the question for the crowd, how can Jesus have it? The passage, even if the Son of Man reference were originally ambiguous, still raises the question of who this special man is. What Jesus will eventually suggest by his usage of the term later in his ministry is that the indirect reference to himself as "Son of Man," even in a sense as ambiguous as "a man" or "someone," is really an allusion to the figure of Dan. 7 (Luke 21:27; 22:69). In Luke 5:24, all

---

8. Those who argue that the title is inserted later or is a comment from the evangelist will not be addressed so clearly by this argument, but the handling of that additional issue awaits discussion below. Against an addition of the title in the tradition is the presence of the title in all three renderings of this passage: Luke 5:24 = Mark 2:10 = Matt. 9:6.

that Jesus may have done is introduce the phrase and the concept without elaboration and then display his authority to support his point. But to understand the phrase's force all one really needs is the event and the saying, not its specific background.

What does this discussion mean for Luke 5:24? Jesus, in using the term initially, is suggesting that he is a man through whom God is now working. But this is a unique man, who has a certain unique authority. In Judaism, however, rabbis never associated any man with the authority to forgive sins. Only one currently known Jewish text may be an exception here: 4QPrNab 1.4 (for more detail, see Bock 1991c: 117 n. 26). This Qumran text may refer to the power to forgive sins that came through an exorcist, but the text is fragmentary and the translation is disputed. Jesus' word is either a very rare association or is unique. It hardly is a normative remark, as the reaction to the statement makes clear.

The remark's general force in Luke 5:24 is still related to the frequent force of Jesus' use of the title elsewhere later in the Gospel, which often suggests Jesus' authority. Jesus' thoughts on the Son of Man's authority draw on the picture of the Danielic Son of Man receiving dominion from the Ancient of Days. What this conclusion also indicates is that, when the Gospel tradition takes this general Aramaic phrase that refers to "a man" and renders it in Greek as a specific title (*the* Son of Man), it is being faithful to the semantic force of the usage in the context of the portrayed event, because the activity of *this* man shows him to be unique. The Gospels have not imported to the term more ideas than its original usage had, for it always described the unique position Jesus occupies. Its meaning was always suggested not just by the term itself but by the event that expounded its meaning. The failure to see a connection between event and usage has tripped up some into long excursions of background that really are not central to the issue of authenticity.[9] The connection between event and usage of the term also argues against any attempt to separate the miracle and the saying on the basis of form (see next paragraph). The two pieces are inseparably joined in the account. To remove either piece disembodies the logic of the account.

Two other possibilities about the verse's authenticity need attention. Some argue that this verse is a "suture" to bring together two different accounts and traditions (Fitzmyer 1981: 579; Boobyer 1954; Ceroke 1960). However, the idea of a suture verse is to be rejected, because the verse's themes of authority, sin, and forgiveness

9. If, of course, Vermes is right that the term did mean "I and no other," then the claim is more direct and the meaning is transparent. Matt. 9 suggests either that this is not the force or that the crowd misunderstood the claim. Either option is possible in Matt. 9.

are so intertwined that to view them in this manner does not disentangle the account; rather it leaves a gaping hole (Hooker 1967: 86). This appears to make the verse a victim of the insistence that a mixing of forms is not possible in the early tradition. But pronouncement and miracle have to go together for this miracle to be elevated beyond a "silent" act. Jesus' exposition is central and is what made sense of the action. The remark's omission, despite its syntactical awkwardness, leaves the account vague and incomplete. Without such pronouncements, it would not be clear what Jesus intended by his actions.

Others suggest that Mark inserted an editorial remark that Jesus did not utter.[10] This latter view argues that Mark is giving the significance of this event to his readers in an aside and that Luke follows Mark here. On the surface, this approach is quite possible (Fitzmyer 1981: 579; Mark 13:14b is a syntactical parallel). This suggestion is based on the otherwise unprecedented tie between the Son of Man and forgiveness of sins, which is viewed by some as an association so unlikely in this early ministry setting that it must be a later, accurate reflection of Mark on the true significance of the event. The awkward syntax of the verse also gives credence to this suggestion.

But as good as the reasons are, they are not persuasive. If Jesus had a sense of his unique calling and authority, like that expressed through Isa. 61 in Luke 4:18–19, then such an association, though unique, becomes just as possible here for Jesus as anywhere in his ministry. Once Jesus defined his mission in terms of preaching forgiveness by God's call and in terms of Isaiah's hope, such associations became available for him. His miraculous work only confirms the connection, since in Judaism a sinner is not supposed to receive healing from God, and certainly not through one making false claims.[11]

Thus, it seems unnecessary to appeal to a syntactical, editorial approach, which, if present, seems to have been poorly marked out for the reader (Caragounis 1986: 180–86 has a full and effective critique of this approach). It seems unlikely that only the reader's perception is in view and that Mark intended to suggest the original audience of the healing did not receive this expositional remark. Its presence fits the setting of a controversy, which dominates the passage (Marshall 1978: 215–16 defends the authenticity of the saying).

---

10. Cranfield 1959: 100–101; Lane 1974: 96–98. Of course, what is true of Mark is also true of the parallels in Matthew and Luke.

11. *B. Ned.* 41a. The presupposition here is that God shows his healing mercy only to the righteous. A sinner can count on nothing from God. Neither will God work through one who makes false claims. For this talmudic text, see the exegesis of 5:21.

In summary, the Son of Man in Luke 5:24 can refer to Jesus as a representative man called by God to exercise authority over sin. The authority, however, is one unique to Jesus and as such, upon reflection, means that the representative is unique. In fact, if the healing evidences the verbal claim, then the divine prerogative is exercised uniquely by a man. Jesus' innovations with the Son of Man concept as they emerge from Luke 5:24 and its later NT usage would be (1) the claim to be able to identify the authoritative, heavenly-human figure (as himself!) and (2) the association of that figure with the Son of Man's right to forgive sins. This latter claim also gives evidence of being authentic, because the Son of Man's association with the forgiveness of sins is dissimilar to both Judaism's claims and the early church's language. In other words, the reference is one that goes back to Jesus himself, even if the term was used in its most ambiguous sense. So the representative man is a "unique" man or "the" man through whom God works. As a result, the NT is right to see a titular use for a specific figure, for that is the force of the saying in conjunction with the action. As Hooker (1967: 93) points out, in this account the issue is not the title, but the nature of the authority of the title bearer.[12] I would add that Jesus' actions underlined this authority and defined it. They also helped to explain the force of Jesus' remark. Who "the" man is became clearer as Jesus' ministry proceeded and as the OT background of the phrase *Son of Man* emerged. The authoritative Son of Man was merged with the Suffering Servant portrait of Isa. 52:13–53:12, which is yet a third innovation in Jesus' handling of the phrase. What eventually emerged is that heavenly and human authority were wed together in one unique person, who also suffered. Suffering, forgiveness, divinelike authority, and glory are wed together in the human figure who is uniquely the Son of Man.

Luke 5:24 is an initial glimpse of that union and a major clue to the eventual individual force of the title. The issue of uniqueness is effectively raised by the claim of authority to forgive sins. The claim itself receives confirmation by the paralytic's ability to get up in response to Jesus' call. The event says, put together the remark and the event. If one does, one can know that Jesus is a unique figure. In fact, he exercises divine prerogatives. In the view of this pericope, either Jesus blasphemes as the Jewish leadership claims or he is uniquely related to God. Luke's readers are left to ponder the implications of the choice.

---

12. Hooker's position on authenticity is not entirely clear, although that her remarks end with this observation suggests that she leans toward authenticity.

Excursus 7
The Sermon on the Plain in Luke: Its Relationship to Matthew and Its Theological-Ethical Function (6:20–49)

Issues concerning the Sermon on the Plain are numerous and complex, but one question is basic: Does Luke's Sermon on the Plain equal Matthew's Sermon on the Mount? With a few exceptions, until the time of the Reformation most saw two distinct events.[1] The exceptions were Origen (*Commentary on Matthew* 2) and Chrysostom (*Homilies on Matthew* 15), who used the two sermons interchangeably. However, with the Reformation the discussion about their relationship opened up again. Calvin (1972: 1.168), for example, identified the two sermons as one.

The question involves two separate issues: setting and sources. Taking a general approach that is still helpful, Plummer (1896: 176–78) discusses these issues in great detail and regards a decision as nearly impossible to make. The six basic views break down into three categories: two sermons (views 1–2), the same sermon (views 3–4), or a representative anthology, not a specific occasion (views 5–6):[2]

1. Two distinct messages were delivered to two distinct groups (perhaps Plummer 1896: 176–77 [who argues that the possibility of repetition must be taken seriously]; apparently Walvoord 1974: 43).
2. Two messages were delivered to two distinct groups on the same day (Augustine, *Our Lord's Sermon on the Mount*; J. P. Lange cited by Plummer 1896: 176). Augustine was the first to speak about the "Sermon on the Mount," though the description did not catch on until the Reformation.
3. Matthew and Luke edited two distinct sources of the same sermon (F. E. D. Schleiermacher cited in Plummer 1896: 176;

---

1. Carson 1984: 125–26. Augustine's view that two distinct sermons were present was decisive in the early history of interpretation.

2. Views 5–6 treat the sermon as a unit topically arranged either by the tradition or by the Gospel writers. This summary brings together what Jesus taught on various occasions or unifies what Jesus taught with what the evangelists taught. Thus, the issues of when the sermon occurred and Matthew's relationship to Luke are moot questions.

Luce 1933: 144 [apparently]; Marshall 1978: 245 [#3 seems to argue for multiple versions of Q]).

4. Matthew and Luke edited the same source, with Matthew adding material and Luke omitting some (B. Weiss cited in Plummer 1896: 177; A. B. Bruce 1897: 504; Carson 1984: 126 [who sees Q and other sources as present]).

5. Matthew topically arranged a sermon out of sayings spoken by Jesus on various occasions (Creed 1930: 90; Ellis 1974: 111; Alford 1874: 497 [who opts against such an arrangement for Matthew, since he sees Matthew recording the whole discourse; Alford argues for such arrangement by Luke]; Calvin 1972: 1.168; France 1985: 105–6). This view is not as radical as it may sound, in that topical arrangements of events do occur in the Gospels. Could not a writer arrange sayings into an anthology that represents what Jesus often said? The difference between this view and views 3–4 is that here the responsibility for organizing the sermon is entirely Matthew's, while in the previous views Matthew is guided by a source of a specific sermon. For some, the point of Matthew's arrangement is to show what Jesus said on a variety of occasions, so that "creating" a setting is really forming an appropriate or typical forum for such a sermon.

6. The sermon is a conglomeration of detached sayings brought into an anthology with some additions or alterations by the evangelist. Thus, in this view, the material is both Jesus' and that of the tradition and/or the Gospel writer. As a result, some of the sayings may not go back to Jesus. Many NT scholars take this approach, but they differ on the source that brought together the sayings. Most see Q as responsible (Fitzmyer 1981: 627; Wiefel 1988: 128; Bovon 1989: 291–93), while others give the responsibility to Matthew (Guelich 1982: 33–36 sees Matthew drawing on Q and other materials, as well as doing his own shaping), and still others speak of a pre-Matthean source other than Q (H. Betz 1985: 1–2, 89–91) or of two versions of Q (Strecker 1988: 13) or they argue that Luke used Matthew (so holders of the Griesbach or two-Gospel hypothesis, like Farmer 1964: 221–23). Many give Matthew the responsibility while some appeal to his use of Q (Schürmann 1969: 385; Jeremias 1963b: 16–17 [without mentioning Q]; Hunter 1965: 11–12; Windisch 1951: 26 [without mentioning Q]; W. Davies 1964: 3).

In assessing these categories, it is important to realize why so many suggestions have been made about the sermon. The major factors are these (Carson 1984: 125–26; Godet 1875: 1.294–99):

1. Matthew has much more material than Luke, some 107 verses compared to 30 verses.[3]
2. Luke locates the sermon on a plain, while Matthew has it on a mountain.
3. Luke has the sermon after the choosing of the Twelve, while Matthew has the sermon before their selection.
4. Thirteen sayings in Matthew's Sermon on the Mount are similar to sayings elsewhere in Luke (Guelich 1982: 34):

> Matt. 5:13 ~ Luke 14:34–35
> Matt. 5:15 ~ Luke 11:33
> Matt. 5:18 ~ Luke 16:17
> Matt. 5:25–26 ~ Luke 12:57–59
> Matt. 5:31–32 ~ Luke 16:18
> Matt. 6:9–13 ~ Luke 11:2–4
> Matt. 6:19–21 ~ Luke 12:33–34
> Matt. 6:22–23 ~ Luke 11:34–36
> Matt. 6:24 ~ Luke 16:13
> Matt. 6:25–34 ~ Luke 12:22–32
> Matt. 7:7–11 ~ Luke 11:9–13
> Matt. 7:13–14 ~ Luke 13:23–24
> Matt. 7:22–23 ~ Luke 13:25–27

The differences lead some to suggest two sermons, while others use points 2–4 to argue for an anthology. In fact, between Luke 6:20–49 and what Luke has elsewhere, much of Matthew's sermon is present in Luke. Matthean passages lacking parallels anywhere in Luke are the following (46 out of 107 Matthean verses [43 percent] are not in Luke):

5:4–5	5:21–24	6:1–4	6:19
5:7–10	5:27–30	6:5–6	7:6
5:14	5:31	6:7–8	7:15
5:16	5:33–37	6:10b	7:29
5:17	5:38–39a	6:14–15	
5:19–20	5:43	6:16–18	

In making this list, I read Matt. 5:45 and Luke 6:35 as conceptually parallel, so also Matt. 7:17–20 and Luke 6:43–44. But even after adding these five verses to the list of unique Matthean material, thirty-seven Matthean verses have parallels elsewhere in Luke (these verses together are longer than Luke's sermon).

3. The exact number of Matthean verses depends on how one resolves some text-critical problems. A verse count is, of course, only a relative way to indicate length, since verse numbers were supplied much later.

Those seeing one sermon have explanations for these factors. The shorter Lucan form exists because Luke excised the particularly Jewish material from the sermon as irrelevant to his Gentile audience. Thus, one may not be persuaded by point 1 on the differing lengths of the sermon. Matthew placed the choosing of the Twelve right before the mission that sends them out, a topical arrangement that shows that point 3 is not persuasive either (see the introduction to Luke 6:12–16). Luke's locale for choosing the Twelve is probably more chronologically intended, while Matthew's arrangement is topical. With regard to the mountain (ὄρος) versus a plain (πεδινός), the term used for plain can be used of a level place on the side of a mountain or hill.[4] Thus, the locales may not be in conflict at all. As one can see, each side can assemble credible arguments. Deciding which is right is difficult.

Is an anthology possible? It must be noted that a consensus exists at the critical level that the sermon is really a collection of sayings uttered on several occasions. The major reason for this view is that several of the sayings in Matthew's sermon appear elsewhere in Luke in almost the same verbal form (at the least, 37 of Matthew's 107 verses, or ca. 35 percent of his sermon). Thus, it is argued that either a pre-Gospel source or the evangelist Matthew brought the material together into the Sermon on the Mount. But, as Carson argues, the conclusion made from the Lucan distribution of the Matthean sayings is not free from assumptions and problems.[5] (1) The major assumption is that Jesus said things but once, a poor assumption for any traveling speaker, for an itinerant ministry has repetition. (2) To this is appended an assumption that what Jesus taught on a given theme was recorded only one time. But this idea is certainly suspect, if one argues that there are multiple versions of Q in the early church. In addition, the variant forms of some parables suggest the existence of various versions of Jesus' teaching on a similar theme. (3) There also is an assumption that multiple topics mean multiple sermons. Apparently oral tradition is assumed to keep to one topic at a time. But Jewish prayers like the *Shemoneh Esreh* [Eighteen Benedictions] (Schürer 1973–87: 2.456–61) were long and wide-ranging—yet were memorized. Since the sermon is a summary in either Gospel and since Jesus probably covered a variety of topics in any message as he moved from one locale to the next, there

4. Matthew elsewhere (14:23; 15:29) uses ὄρος to refer to hills; Carson 1984: 129. Luke's πεδινός is not a prairie, but can be a plateau in the mountains: Jer. 21:13; Isa. 13:2; Godet 1875: 1.295; BAGD 638; BAA 1287. See the discussion of sources and historicity in Luke 6:17–19.

5. Carson's four objections (1984: 123–24; 1978: 139–49) are really two objections, each stated in two forms.

is no need to insist that multiple settings for multiple topics are necessary.[6] Of course, challenging these assumptions does not establish the case that an anthology is not present, given the acknowledgment that events and sayings can be grouped together for topical reasons. However, the observations do show that to jump to such a conclusion because of the existing textual factors is not required either. In fact, it would seem slightly more natural to take the approach that a sermonic occasion is intended, since the impression of a definite setting is given in both accounts. What is less clear is whether each evangelist had one specific tradition of the sermon in mind or simply organized a passage that says, in effect, "This is what Jesus' preaching was like." Either view is possible, but neither is provable.

But what of the challenge that Luke (plateau) and Matthew (mountain) do not agree on the setting, so that each writer suggested his own setting? If this objection has merit, then the possibility of a collection of sayings typical of what Jesus said on a given occasion or occasions might be enhanced. However, an examination of the terms shows that this challenge is not airtight. It seems that the anthology approach, though possible, is not necessary. If an anthology is present, it seems best to see the sermon as representative of what Jesus said on many occasions.[7]

Are we dealing with one event or two? Despite the three major differences—Matthew's longer length, Matthew's mountain versus Luke's plain, and Luke's placing the sermon after the choosing of the Twelve, not before as in Matthew—that lead many to argue for two sermons here, four good arguments exist for seeing a single sermon, substantially edited by Luke:

1. Both sermons begin (with the Beatitudes) and end similarly (with the parable about building a house).
2. An event that follows soon after the sermon in both Gospels is the same, the healing of the centurion's servant (Matt. 8:5–13; Luke 7:1–10).[8] Thus, the sermon has a similar position in both Gospels. This point is not without problems either. Matthew has the sermon early in his portrayal of Galilean ministry, since it is his third event, while Luke has it as about the

6. An oral presentation of the Matthean text would take around seven minutes, which suggests a summary, unless Jesus gave exceptionally brief sermons!

7. This approach to anthology, which is possible, would mean that the distinct descriptions of occasions in Luke and Matthew are accurate, since they could indicate distinctive locales when such a representative message was presented.

8. The relative chronological placement of Matt. 8:1–4 (the healing of the leper) was discussed in the introduction to Luke 5:12–16 as a representative healing that Matthew used to introduce his summary of the Galilean ministry. Thus, its presence right after the sermon is not a problem, since its placement is topical.

fourteenth event in his sequence, clearly a later placement. Nonetheless, Godet (1875: 1.297–98) argues persuasively that Luke is more likely to have the more precise placement because several issues in the sermon suggest that Jesus has already challenged the Jewish view of certain matters, a setting that fits Luke's placement and not Matthew's. Matthew moved the sermon up to suggest what Jesus' preaching in this period was like, a point that might also allow Matthew to be presenting an anthology. In addition, the interesting agreement of the placement of the servant's healing may be more than coincidence.

3. The subunits of Matthew's sermon that Luke has follow Matthew's order with one minor exception, Luke 6:31 (Ernst 1977: 213, though he fails to note the exception). But this one difference may involve topical rearrangement (Guelich 1982: 33).

4. Virtually all of Luke is in Matthew, only Luke 6:24–26 being without Matthean parallel (or 90 percent of the Lucan whole).

Such points lead several interpreters to conclude that one sermon is given in two slightly different summarized forms (Carson 1984: 125–26; Marshall 1978: 245 [though with room for recasting by the evangelist]; Hendriksen 1978: 340; Godet 1875: 1.294–99; and Edersheim 1889: 1.526–57). Though the case could hardly be called an established one, this approach seems slightly more likely than any other option, though the next best option is an anthology.

Thus, given that it is likely that the same sermon is present or at least that very similar sermons are present, I now turn to discuss the interpretation of the sermon. What is its theological role?[9] The views on this question are numerous and can be variously grouped (Kissinger 1975 lists over thirty approaches). I start with two general groupings and then proceed to a more focused list to establish my approach. It is important to remember that elements of truth may be found in many of these approaches, even if they are rejected as not holding the single key to unlocking the sermon.

Toussaint (1980: 86–94) lists six basic categories of interpreting the sermon:

1. The soteriological approach argues that the sermon gives a formula for personal salvation (Major 1944: 48). Toussaint rejects the view as being out of step with scriptural teaching, since the sermon's standards make it impossible for anyone to be saved.

---

9. See McArthur 1960: 105–27; Carson 1984: 126–27; Jeremias 1963b: 1–12, 19–23; Hunter 1965: 107–11; Toussaint 1980: 86–94; Bauman 1985; and J. Martin 1986.

2. The sociological view argues that the sermon is addressed to society rather than to individuals (Stamm 1943: 68–69; Ragaz 1945 advocates a Christian socialism). But the context gives no indication that society or any other corporate body is in view. The address is to individuals.

3. The penitential view argues that the sermon gives an ideal that makes one aware of personal sinfulness and leads to repentance. Thus, the sermon is preparatory to salvation. With roots reaching back to Luther, this view is also known as the Lutheran view. Adherents of this view include Kittel (1925) and Gore (1910: 4–5); Pentecost (1980) is sympathetic to this view (J. Martin 1986: 43). Although its point may have pastoral validity, this view has problems. For example, the sermon was uttered to disciples (Matt. 5:1–2 = Luke 6:20) and has much to say about discipleship and ethics. It was not directed primarily to general humanity, just to "get them saved," and it is hardly a sermon about preevangelism. In addition, a reference to salvation, as such, is not present. Persecution of the listeners is assumed (6:22, 26). Nonetheless, it is true that the sermon raises the need for seeking God in light of what God desires. This result might emerge from the sermon, though it cannot be its main intent.

4. The ecclesiastical view, which could also be called the believer's-ethic view, argues that Jesus is setting down ethical standards for those who identify with him—ethics that are valid for every age. Many hold to this view, although in a variety of forms (Hunter 1965 is a popular exposition). Toussaint objects to this view on the premise that the kingdom in view here is an earthly, regal kingdom of OT promise; it is too early for church-age teaching. Toussaint argues that the sermon operates in the context of law (this objection is evaluated below). J. Martin, however, notes several points in favor of this view.[10] First, when Jesus says that the disciples are to teach all that he commanded (Matt. 28:20), certainly this sermon is included, since it is one of the major discourses in the book. Second, Matthew was written to a church audience who naturally would have read the sermon as applying to them. Third, the OT setting of some illustrations like Matt. 5:23–24 is natural, given the sermon's original setting. The principles of the passage are still applicable, even given the theological perspective that emerges after the cross. Proving this point are the parallels to

10. J. Martin 1986: 47–48. Martin's list of reasons is longer than mine, but his other reasons are more supportive than decisive. See J. Martin 1992 for an updated defense.

the sermon in 1 Peter and James.[11] Obviously tied up in the evaluation is the issue of how one sees the kingdom in the Gospels. In Luke–Acts, a total disjunction between OT promise and NT/church fulfillment cannot be maintained, since the church, which is born in Acts 2, is proclaimed as fulfillment of OT promise.[12] This view has much merit.

5. The kingdom view, which is better called the tribulation-kingdom view, is associated with many dispensationalists of the early twentieth century.[13] These older dispensationalists held to the indirect applicability of the sermon for today, because it contains truth for the future, earthly kingdom that Christ will bring in with the millennium. Stated in this way, the view has problems, since it foresees situations that do not fit the millennium: persecution of believers, presence of false prophets, and

11. Jacobean and Petrine similarities to the sermon, both grammatical and conceptual, are as follows (for the Jacobean parallels, see Hartin 1991: 140–72):

James 1:2–4 ~ Luke 6:23
James 1:5 ~ Matt. 7:7
James 1:9–11 ~ Luke 6:24
James 1:17 ~ Matt. 7:11
James 2:5 ~ Luke 6:20
James 2:6–7 ~ Luke 6:24
James 2:7 ~ Luke 6:22
James 3:9 ~ Luke 6:28
James 3:11–12 ~ Luke 6:43
James 3:12 ~ Matt. 7:16
James 3:18 ~ Matt. 5:9
James 4:9 ~ Luke 6:25
James 4:11 ~ Matt. 7:1–5
James 5:1 ~ Luke 6:24
James 5:2 ~ Matt. 6:19
James 5:5 ~ Luke 6:25
James 5:11 ~ Luke 6:36 and Matt. 5:12
James 5:12 ~ Matt. 5:34–37
1 Peter 3:9 ~ Matt. 5:44 = Luke 6:28
1 Peter 3:14 ~ Matt. 5:10 = Luke 6:22–23
1 Peter 3:16 ~ Luke 6:28
1 Peter 4:14 ~ Luke 6:22
1 Peter 5:7 ~ Matt. 6:25

12. Note the use in Acts 2 of Joel 2, Ps. 16, and Ps. 110, along with the allusion to 2 Sam. 7, the Davidic covenant, through the appeal to Ps. 132:11 in Acts 2:30–31. There is parallel teaching in Luke 24:44–47 and Acts 13:16–39, as well as in Paul's defense speeches (e.g., Acts 26:16–23). Acts 13 also appeals to realized Davidic promises; see Bock 1992c; Bock 1994a; O'Toole 1987a: 153–58.

13. So Chafer 1951: 410; W. Kelly 1943: 103–6. Popularly known as Scofieldian dispensationalism, this view was made famous in the *Scofield Reference Bible*. I call this the tribulation-kingdom view because some see the sermon as applicable only in a future kingdom period, while others prefer to see its application beginning in and focusing on the tribulation period.

prayer for the approaching kingdom (see the critique by Toussaint 1980: 90–91). These problems led to a change in the view that focused on the tribulation period, so as to remove the objections about pressure against believers (so D. Campbell 1953: 57–66). If one is to insist on the kingdom-millennium identification, this is a better way to hold this view, but it still seems unsatisfactory in dealing with points made by J. Martin's argument for the believer's-ethic view.

6. The interim-ethic view is Toussaint's choice, a term taken from Schweitzer (1910: 352) but with a vastly different meaning. Schweitzer argues that Jesus composed this ethic for the intense and short period between Jesus' coming and the end. As such it was an "in between time" ethic. According to Schweitzer, Jesus was wrong about the short period to the eschaton. Toussaint adopts the terminology but rejects Schweitzer's view that Jesus was wrong about timing. For Toussaint, the sermon's focus is an "in between" ethic until the promised earthly kingdom comes. It is a life lived in light of the coming kingdom. It is hard to see how this view differs from the believer's-ethic view, since one is still in that interim. But Toussaint's view is distinct, because the only kingdom he sees in the NT is the millennial kingdom. This view is otherwise close to view 4. The only difference is that its point of reference is not directly tied to the church, but rather to the absence of the earthly kingdom.

The above list was compiled by Toussaint, an evangelical scholar. How would another list, more concerned with European interpretation, compare to it? Jeremias's listing of four views (1963b: 1–12, 19–23) gives a good indication (I have added one view, #10, to Jeremias's list to complete the representatives views):

7. The sermon is centered on a "perfectionistic conception of the OT and Judaism" (Windisch's influential 1951 work is the key example). Jesus presented ideal wisdom teaching in the prophetic tradition, a presentation of law in its glory. Jeremias recognizes the truth in this approach but says that it underestimates the difference in tone between rabbinic Judaism and the sermon on such points as loving your enemies and the challenge to the law in the six antitheses (Matt. 5:17–48). Jesus' challenge argued against relating the law merely to externals, at least in terms of its contemporary use in traditional Judaism. Jeremias's objections may overstate the case by relating the sermon too much to rabbinic views of Judaism and the law.

Windisch appealed to the OT prophetic tradition, which clearly called for a response from the heart, not just attention to externals. If one separates the OT ethic from some Jewish applications of it, there is some merit in Windisch's approach.

8. The sermon is an impossible ideal that, when related to Paul, leads one to repentance (so Luther and Kittel). Also known as the penitential view, this view was discussed above under #3.

9. The interim-ethic view of Schweitzer was already discussed above under #6.

10. The "principle-not-rule" approach is advocated by Hermann (1904) with his "ethic of disposition" (German *Gesinnungsethik*) (on Hermann's view, see Bauman 1985: 37–51). Jesus was not giving law, but a general approach to life whose sense must be worked out in each age. Again, there is some merit here, because of the OT setting of many of the examples in the sermon, but this view can become an escape hatch from responding to its ethical demands.

11. The sermon as a catechism for believers is Jeremias's view. It is gospel, not law, in that the Beatitudes make a promise of God's offer of grace, while the rest of the sermon is a response to it. Though Jeremias overdraws the connection to baptism, he is correct in seeing the sermon tied to disciples. It is a call to be a child of God and reflect his character (Luke 6:35–36).

In presenting these two lists from diverse backgrounds, I have indicated my preference for the believer's-ethic view, that is, a teaching designed for all disciples of Jesus. But what does "believer's ethic" mean? This category shows great variety:[14]

12. The absolutist approach takes the sermon literally as a comprehensive and unqualified ethic, as did Tolstoy (cited in Bauman 1985: 11–35). Tolstoy summarized the message in five sets of commands: (a) offend no one and by no act excuse evil in others; (b) be in all things chaste; (c) never take an oath; (d) do not resist evil, bear with offenses, do not judge or go to the law; and (e) make no distinction between countrymen and foreigners. To follow all the sermon consistently, however, is difficult since, for example, lust would bring maiming (Matt. 5:27–30). Though this view is laudatory in its desire, it is unrealistic and fails to appreciate the literary, rhetorical character of the sermon.

14. This list modifies the one in McArthur 1960: 105–27 by combining several related views.

13. The general-principles view attempts to qualify the strong assertions of the sermon. Appeal is made either to the analogy of Scripture, to rhetorical hyperbole, to stressing attitudes over the sermon's specific acts, or to divine will expressing "who I am to be, not what I am to do." This view runs the risk of providing a huge escape hatch to avoid honoring the force of the text. Its merit is that it takes seriously the rhetorical character of the sermon's imagery. The views of Hermann (1904) and Calvin belong here.[15] This approach also seems to fit H. Betz's view, who argues (1985: 1–16) for a comparison to the Greek ἐπιτομή (epitomē) genre, that is, an account that gives a summary teaching of a philosopher and whose point is not the details of the teachings but the process of thinking through the ethical principles portrayed. The goal is to provide suggestions for application in new settings through reflection on past rulings. One wonders how appropriate to a Jewish setting such a comparison is, since Jewish models exist for the sermon's background. However, this general approach does seem to parallel the sermon's focus, which calls for reflection about righteousness and love through examples loaded with OT influence.

14. The higher-standard approach of some Roman Catholics says that some of the sermon applies to all, while the more stringent requirements apply to the clergy or subgroups within it.[16] But nowhere in the sermon are these distinctions made. This view involves theological reflection that attempts to wrestle with the sermon's high ethical level and rhetorical character.

15. The two-realms approach also has roots in Luther (Luther 1956; Guelich 1982: 16–18). It is a reaction to the previous view, as well as to the literal approach of the separatist Anabaptists (or "enthusiasts" as they were known). Arguing against any levels of distinction in the applicability of the sermon, Luther held that the sermon's ethics are only personal and sacred, not institutional. Maintaining a difference between personal application and secular application to govern-

15. For a good example, see how Calvin handles oaths in his treatment (1972: 1.190–93) of Matt. 5:33–37. He concludes that all oaths that profane or abuse God's name are unlawful, but that Jesus does not outlaw every oath here. To make this distinction, Calvin appeals to the teaching of the law where people are to swear in God's name. Thus, analogous Scripture helps to reveal the limits of the figure.

16. The distinction is one that goes back to Aquinas (*Summa* part 2.1, question 108, article 4), who argues for a difference between command (*praeceptum*) and counsel (*consilium*). A command is binding, advice is not—except on those who pursue a special kind of holiness like the monastics. The result is a distinction in Catholic ethics between that which is necessary for gaining eternal bliss and that which aids to that end. See the discussions in Guelich 1982: 15 and Strecker 1988: 15–16.

ment or secular institutions, Luther criticized the Anabaptists for withdrawing from society in order to keep the ethics of the sermon. They abandoned the use of oaths, military service, and sometimes the right to personal property as a result of their view of the sermon. Such interpretation had significant implications for a civil state trying to protect itself. These implications led to Luther's distinction, so that the state could continue to offer protection for its citizens. Luther distinguished between one's office and one's person: office applied to God's ordained order for this world, while person concerned one's relationship to God. Responsibilities to the state must be carried out as a part of one's office, even though one personally might grieve over what must be done. On the other hand, one's person was governed by the ethics of the sermon. The variations found in the Anabaptists and in Luther were the seed plots for the doctrine of the separation of church and state, though Luther surely would not have favored the total removal of religious themes from the secular state (which is a modern application of this doctrine). Again, these distinctions are not in the text, though it can be argued that the sermon is clearly a mandate for believers and for the church made up of believers. Also, a theological deduction about the text is made in order to wrestle with the sermon's demands. It should be noted that Luther also held to a penitential view of the sermon and spoke of the sermon as gospel, because of the comfort and invitation contained in the Beatitudes. For Luther, the sermon was a mixture of gift and duty that contained a call to all humanity and an ethic for all Christians.

16. The interim-ethic approach has been discussed above as #6.
17. What many call the dispensational view is really the tribulation-kingdom view mentioned earlier (#5). The first name for this view ignores that dispensationalists have advocated as many as four different approaches. Lumping together all dispensationalists into one category, as Carson (1978: 155–57) does, is unfortunate.[17] This view did characterize older dispen-

---

17. Any charge today that dispensationalism sees two ways of salvation or sees too great a law/grace contrast in the sermon grossly misrepresents where many of its adherents are now. Such a monolithic view of dispensationalism fails to see the variations that have long been a part of this approach. Gerstner 1991 irresponsibly engages in such confusion and minimizes the significance of such differences, which dispensationalists like C. C. Ryrie and J. D. Pentecost have long noted. Gerstner's charge of antinomianism is a distortion that warps his ability to appreciate the distinctions in the movement. The charge also underestimates the significance of the current discussion about the function of the law within covenant theology, as well as its debate with theonomy; see D. Turner 1991; J. Martin 1986; and J. Martin 1992.

sationalism in the early twentieth century, but it is not representative of many dispensationalists today. The older view is sensitive to the OT setting and the legal flavor of the passage, but, as mentioned earlier, bifurcates the kingdom teaching of the NT too greatly.

18. The penitential view of Kittel was discussed and evaluated under #3.

As one can see, the options are manifold. Some views (13–15, 17) create distinctions to soften or deflect the application of the text in certain areas, while one view (13) takes a literary-theological approach to try to "get behind" the text. One view (12) creates what seem to be unrealistic tensions. Finally, most views (13–18) engage in historical-theological deduction to explain how the sermon relates to the rest of Scripture. The sermon is difficult to classify, but all the views attempt to deal with the sermon's ethical thrust and depth. The options correctly seek to move beyond external spirituality to internal response. But no single approach deals with the sermon's variety of presentation.

The depth of the sermon has produced a wide variety of views. Beyond the recognition that it reflects Jesus' ethical standards for disciples, the sermon defies classification. But most of the sermon reflects a proper response to God's invitation to enter humbly into the blessing of kingdom relationship as offered in the Beatitudes. In short, if one is in the Light, then one should be light (Matt. 5:14–16; Col. 1:9–14). The sermon's focus causes disciples to look to God and to look within, so that they live in a way that honors God and loves fellow humans. Only by accepting God's grace and justice can one live in the way that Jesus calls disciples to live. The sermon is an ethic that leaves justice and retribution to God, while one rests in his grace and love.

The secondary application of the sermon to outsiders—to those not currently related to kingdom promise—comes in the invitation of the Beatitudes followed by a warning against a selfish focus in approaching God, life, and ethics. It is a warning against loving with strings attached, loving for self-gain, or ignoring the call to true righteousness. Indeed, the sermon is a call to exhibit the type of forgiving, giving, grateful, and compassionate love that is like God (Luke 6:36 = Matt. 5:48), which the sermon describes as a righteousness that exceeds the Pharisees (Matt. 5:20). The sermon is a call to believers to love thoroughly. Its interpretation is difficult, but at its center is a mandate to be morally righteous and to love in a selfless, giving way, an ideal that is not to be rejected as unrealistic. Rather it is an exhortation to heed and follow as fully as possible the Lord's will. Oaths are not necessary because one speaks the truth. Wrongs against another are admitted and reconciliation results. Praise from people is not what motivates action, but the desire to please God and meet needs. In short, the sermon is a call to truly be a disciple and follow the Lord. The sermon does give the believer's ethic, similar to Mic. 6:8 in the OT. This ethic is very close to what later NT writers called "the law of love," because the commitment to carry it out requires not only that one love people, but that one trust and love God. It is a life of love for God that will yield a life of righteousness like that described in the sermon. It is that kind of life that is the goal and theological function of the Sermon on the Mount and its Lucan equivalent, the Sermon on the Plain.

Excursus 8
The Parables of Jesus

The term *parable* often indicates a comparison and refers theologically to a story that contains an analogy. About 35 percent of Jesus' teaching is in this form. His parables often describe the human relationship to God, the nature of the kingdom, Jesus' return, the spiritual life, or one's relationship to others. They also note how one is responsible to God for one's actions.

It is difficult to find an agreed-upon definition of parable, since technical and popular definitions vary. From a technical viewpoint, Linnemann (1966: 3–8) discusses the character of a parable and distinguishes it from similitude, illustration, and allegory: a parable is a composed story that describes a particular situation analogous to some theological truth (Luke 18:1–8; also Hauck, *TDNT* 5:752);[1] a similitude is a regular or common event where the emphasis is on its recurring character (11:11–13; 17:7–10); an illustration (often indistinguishable from parable) is an example of some truth where the theological connection is made explicit, rather than being suggested through analogy (10:25–37; 12:16–21; 16:19–31; 18:9–14); an allegory is a complex metaphor, working at many levels simultaneously (see below). Thus, a similitude describes an event that happens regularly in life, while a parable is a creative comparison based on something that happens once in the rhetorical world in which it falls. All the units of a parable are designed to fit together to make a fundamental point, though subsidiary points may be present.[2] In an illustration, the referents in the real world are made clear.[3] Some other literary forms—riddles, symbols, and proverbs—also make comparisons, but generally are not called parabolic (Stein 1978: 34–59).

Kistemaker's popular treatment of parables (1980: xiv–xv) makes clear that some parables are rhetorical and fictive in character, even though what they illustrate is true. He distinguishes three categories: true parable, story parable, and illustration (corresponding, re-

---

1. A parable may reflect the reality of everyday practice or put a twist on it to focus attention on the theological point.
2. This is what causes Blomberg 1990: 171–288 to distinguish one-point, two-point, and three-point parables.
3. In all these examples, the people represent types of real people to whom comparison is made.

spectively, to Linnemann's similitude, parable, and illustration). As one can see, in popular usage several subtypes are subsumed under the name *parable*. Although from a literary point of view a technical distinction can be drawn between similitude and parable, 5:36 shows that the biblical text does not make such fine distinctions, nor do I make them in this commentary.

Allegory is at one end of the parabolic continuum. An allegory is a complex metaphor or extended parable in which the analogy is active at many levels simultaneously. In fact, the meaning of an allegory is not found in the story itself, but in what the symbols in the story represent. Unlike illustration but like parable, an allegory refers indirectly to what it represents: it pictures reality, rather than describing it directly. This factor makes interpretation of an allegory difficult, since it may be hard to distinguish the descriptive background (which is simply given to complete the picture) from a detail that corresponds to theological reality. Some parables do have multiple elements of comparison to reality, though most fall short of full allegory. This sometimes makes the line between allegory and parable difficult to define (e.g., the parable of the wicked farmers reflects many connections to reality and could be called allegorical). The frequent use of allegory in the Bible is to be distinguished from allegorical interpretation. The latter is a method of reading a text as containing multiple symbolic import that the author did not intend.

Parables can be variously classified: by subject matter, theme, or imagery. All these classification schemes have value and complement one another.

Subject categorization of the parables includes the following (Dodd 1961: 122–56): kingdom parables (which describe God's kingdom), *Kyrios* parables (which compare God to an owner or someone in authority), growth parables (which focus on nature, food, or fish and make a comparison with the kingdom), and crisis parables (which generally allude to the tension of awaiting Jesus' return or to the need for immediate decision). The seed parable is a parable of growth that compares the handling of God's message to the growth of seed.

Jeremias (1963a: 115–229) classifies the parables according to the following themes (some texts have more than one theme):

1. now is the day of salvation (5:36–38; 8:16; 11:33) (only in similes and similitudes)
2. God's mercy for sinners (7:41–43; 14:16–24; 15:11–32; 18:9–14)
3. the great assurance (11:5–8; 13:18–19, 20–21; 18:1–8)
4. the imminence of catastrophe (11:34–36; 12:16–21, 49–50, 54–56; 13:6–9)

5. it may be too late (13:6–9; 14:15–24)
6. the challenge of the hour (6:47–49; 11:24–26; 12:58–59; 16:1–8, 19–31; 17:7–10)
7. realized discipleship (10:25–37; 12:24–30)
8. the *via dolorosa* and exaltation of the Son of Man (9:58; 17:24)
9. the consummation (6:20–26; 14:11; 17:26–30)
10. parabolic actions (15:1–2; 19:5–6, 45–48)

In the "too late" category can be placed parables that depict how people respond to the word and that warn them to be careful about rejection. The seed parable is such a parable.

Still another kind of classification is based on the imagery's movement (Crossan 1973: 37–120): advent, reversal, and action.[4]

Parables follow laws of structure (Linnemann 1966: 8–30; Bultmann 1963: 170–201 [who discusses parable with similitude]; Kissinger 1979: 108–10). A parable is usually concise and often revolves around two elements: a person (or people) and an object. It is usually told from the perspective of only one figure, with secondary figures not usually present. Feelings of the figures are only rarely mentioned; but when they are, they are important. Motivations for actions are largely absent. Keys to understanding a parable are direct speech, soliloquy, repetition, contrasts, and the account's ending. Sometimes the main figure's moral character is irrelevant to how his or her action is to be viewed. As one can see, there are many literary features to pay attention to in working with parables.

A parable is ultimately a literary, rhetorical form of argument. Its purposes include instructing believers, hiding truth from those who reject the message, and shocking the listener through its imagery into reconsidering how one sees the world and God. Jesus himself used parables for instruction, exhortation, and defense (Jeremias 1963a: 42–48). Jesus' parables are a major area of NT research and can be studied from various angles.[5]

Luke records many parables, most as part of his emphasis on Jesus' teaching in the "journey to Jerusalem" section (9:51–19:44). In fact, of the sixteen parables in Luke that have no parallel in Mat-

---

4. Advent parables are often kingdom parables that start with "the kingdom is like . . ." (e.g., mustard seed, sower). The title *advent* indicates that the parable describes the kingdom that has come. Reversal parables are often moral parables (e.g., rich man and Lazarus, prodigal son, vineyard, good Samaritan). Action parables are often decision parables (e.g., servant parables, lord parables).

5. Kissinger 1979 overviews recent discussion and gives full bibliographies up to 1977. Blomberg 1990 and B. Scott 1989 update the discussion. Scott attempts a more literary reading of the parables and sees them as a development of the OT מָשָׁל (*māšāl*). His analyses of structure are often helpful, his handling of historical matters less so.

thew or Mark, fifteen of them are in this key unit (Kistemaker 1980: viii–ix; Kissinger 1979: xxii–xxiv). The presence of large numbers of parables in Luke reveals Jesus as a teacher and makes Luke's Gospel a key source for gaining insight into that teaching.

The Lucan parables may be topically classified.[6] In the accompanying table, an asterisk marks uniquely Lucan accounts for which there is no comparable parallel. Note, however, that unmarked texts may have a distinct placement in Luke and may represent, in some cases, distinct parables. For details, see the introduction to each unit.

Text	Parable	Topic	Theme
5:33–39	garments and wineskins	kingdom	newness
6:47–49	two houses	spiritual life	decision to obey Jesus is wise
7:31–35	brats	Jewish leadership	Jewish rejection
* 7:41–44	two debtors	spiritual life	forgiveness, love, and faith
8:5–8	seed	kingdom spiritual life	responses to the word
* 10:25–37	good Samaritan	spiritual life	love for neighbor
* 11:5–8	bold neighbor	spiritual life	prayer and boldness
* 12:13–21	rich fool	spiritual life judgment	money and God
12:35–38	watchful servant	future spiritual life	be awake and responsible
12:39–40	burglar	future spiritual life	be awake and responsible
12:41–46	stewards	future spiritual life	be faithful and compassionate
* 13:6–9	fig tree	Jewish leadership judgment	a short time to decide
13:18–19	mustard seed	kingdom	growth
13:20–21	yeast	kingdom	growth
* 14:7–14	seats of honor	spiritual life	humility
* 14:15–24	great supper	kingdom judgment Jewish leadership	do not refuse the invitation, many others will come
* 14:28–33	tower and warring king	spiritual life	commitment

6. Most of the categories are self-explanatory; "spiritual life" refers to how one—whether inside or outside the community of faith—approaches God.

Text	Parable	Topic	Theme
14:34–35	salt	spiritual life	be useful
* 15:4–7	lost sheep	evangelism	seek the sinner, joy at repentance
* 15:8–10	lost coin	evangelism	seek the sinner, joy at repentance
* 15:11–32	prodigal son/ forgiving father	evangelism	seek the sinner, joy at repentance, do not be harsh on the forgiven
* 16:1–9	shrewd manager	spiritual life	be generous with money
* 16:19–31	rich man and Lazarus	judgment spiritual life	values and money
* 17:7–10	faithful servant	spiritual life	serve dutifully
* 18:1–8	nagging widow	future spiritual life	prayer and trust of God's faithfulness
* 18:9–14	Pharisee and tax collector	judgment Jewish leadership spiritual life	pride and humility
* 19:11–27	pounds	spiritual life	stewardship to God
20:9–19	vineyard	Jewish leadership kingdom	promise to another for now
21:29–33	fig tree	future spiritual life	time is near, so watch

The list, especially the uniquely Lucan material, shows Luke's pastoral concern. He cares about seeking the sinner. He worries about the values held by believers, especially their attachment to money. He wants them to continue to look for the Lord's return and be responsible to God in the meantime. Disciples are to be committed, loving, and prayerful. The thrust of the parables is a call to walk with God and trust him, now and in light of the coming judgment. The impression is that Luke writes to a community under pressure for its faith. They are to hang on and trust God.

Excursus 9
Luke's "Great Omission" (9:18) from Mark 6:45–8:26

With the Petrine confession, Luke again shares parallels with Mark after skipping several possible Marcan parallel passages, if, as many argue, Mark has priority. Luke lacks any material from Mark 6:45–8:26, with the jump from Mark 6:44 to 8:27 occurring between Luke 9:17 and 9:18. Three approaches to Marcan priority defend this omission. (1) This section was missing from Luke's copy of Mark (Streeter 1924: 174–76 discusses and rejects this view). (2) Mark existed in two editions of which the edition that Luke used was the earlier and shorter. This view is a variation on the first view, with the difference being an appeal to two forms of Mark (Grundmann 1963: 189). (3) Luke intentionally omitted this Marcan material (so hold most, including Schürmann 1969: 525–27; Marshall 1978: 364–65; Fitzmyer 1981: 770–71; Wiefel 1988: 176; Danker 1988: 192–93; Luce 1933: 182).

Most who hold to Marcan priority argue that theological reasons forced this arrangement, that Luke shortened his use of Mark to include other material, or that, since equivalent passages to most of the omitted material occur elsewhere in Luke, he intentionally omitted the material here. Schürmann (1969: 525–27) argues (1) that Luke did so to save space for special Lucan material; (2) that "doublets" explain some omissions; (3) that the new structure allows a christological focus; and (4) that a geographical focus that mostly ignores Gentile areas is maintained through the omission.[1]

Fitzmyer argues that Luke keeps to his geographical perspective by focusing on Galilee and omitting the journey into Tyre and Sidon. He specifically rejects other explanations. (1) Noting the size of Luke's two volumes, Fitzmyer rejects Schürmann's view that Luke omitted material to save space. (2) He rejects the view that Luke skipped from Bethsaida in Mark 6:45 to Bethsaida in Mark 8:22, a view that would involve the greatest *homoeoteleuton* of all time. It fails because Luke does not mention a locale in Luke 9:18–20. (3) He rejects the view that removed doublets explain the omission, since some "unique" passages are skipped as well.[2] The geographical ex-

---

1. Schürmann 1969: 527 notes that Luke shows evidence of knowing about the material in Mark, so that theories of a shorter or damaged copy of Mark cannot work.
2. Fitzmyer does not mention specific passages. I suggest that Mark 7:24–30; 8:14–21; and perhaps 6:45–52 belong here.

planation is probably the best one for the Marcan prioritists, but would be more convincing if the passage on the Gerasene demoniac had also been absent from Luke, since it takes place outside Galilee.

The reason for rejecting the other views is that appeal to a mutilated manuscript of Mark looks like special pleading and appeal to two versions of Mark has no evidence for it. Such explanations are unconvincing, and Bovon's uncertainty about motive seems wise.[3]

It is to be admitted that such a skip is otherwise unprecedented in Luke, which should perhaps raise some questions about Luke's use of Mark, questions that Marcan prioritists attempt to answer, though the success of the defense in this instance can be challenged. One can rightly regard this omission as the most problematic detail against Marcan priority. However, no view of Synoptic relationships is problem free. Because the explanation of the omission is more complex than the normal four-source hypothesis tied to Marcan priority, each pericope must be examined on its own terms, and one must be hesitant to be too certain of fixed relationships in limited sources. Such caution is especially appropriate where special Lucan material and Q material are concerned. In the analysis of succeeding pericopes, I hope to show that one must deal with the possibility of oral tradition or streams of tradition in places. Perhaps works like Reicke's *Roots of the Synoptic Gospels* (1986) need further serious consideration. He speaks of "alibi parallels" to describe accounts that look parallel but really are not the same. He also appeals to some interaction between the evangelists on different occasions, but never all three together at the same time. Such a view might make credible the explanation that Luke knew Mark in a shortened form, if one is left unpersuaded by other alternatives tied to Matthean priority. The Marcan gap between Luke 9:10–17 and 9:18–20 is a major element in looking at the relationship of Matthew, Mark, and Luke. This is called the "great omission" for good reason, since it represents the absence of a significant piece of Mark and because it is so hard to know why Luke never referred to at least some of this material.

---

3. Bovon 1989: 477 says that the cause is unclear. He challenges the doublet theory by noting that only Mark 8:1–10 qualifies as a doublet. The walk on the sea (Mark 6:45–52), the Syrophoenician woman (7:24–30), and the detailed dispute over the law (7:1–23) are not doublets. I would note that one could argue that the last account is omitted because of Luke's avoiding issues of the law, as he did in the Sermon on the Plain; but the others still need to be explained, especially the Syrophoenician woman, who as a Gentile fits a favorite Lucan theme.

Excursus 10
Authenticity of the
Suffering-Son-of-Man Sayings
and of the Passion Predictions (9:22)

Whether Jesus spoke about the suffering of the Son of Man is hotly debated. This debate is complex and reflects various positions. Colpe (*TDNT* 8:443–47), for example, argues that the suffering sayings are not authentic and are projected back after the resurrection to describe Jesus. In addition, a variety of views exist regarding the Son-of-Man sayings: (a) Jesus uttered no Son-of-Man sayings (N. Perrin, H. Conzelmann, P. Vielhauer); (b) only apocalyptic Son-of-Man sayings go back to Jesus (C. Colpe, R. Bultmann, H. E. Tödt, G. Bornkamm, F. Hahn); (c) only Jesus' earthly Son-of-Man sayings are authentic (E. Schweizer, who argues that some passion sayings might be authentic); and (d) all groups of sayings go back to Jesus and are authentic (I. H. Marshall, M. D. Hooker, Cullmann 1963: 155–64).[1]

No one holds to the authenticity of just the suffering-Son-of-Man sayings. The major reason these sayings are rejected is that Daniel's Son of Man does not suffer. However, many defend the linkage between suffering and the Son of Man in various ways:

1. The portrait of a suffering Son of Man represents a fusion of the Suffering Servant portrait with this title of Jesus (Ellis 1974: 140; F. F. Bruce 1982: 70).[2] Fitzmyer (1981: 780) rejects the connection with the Suffering Servant, arguing that there is no Jewish precedent for it, an argument that suggests all theological synthesis must have precedent. One cannot rule out a fresh synthesis by Jesus. The problem in linking Isaiah's Suffering Servant with the Son of Man is that Daniel is the explicit point of OT contact for the title Son of Man.
2. The image may be tied to Ps. 118:22 [117:22 LXX], thus linking the suffering Son of Man to the suffering king, as suggested by the picture of rejection in Luke 20:17. This suggestion has

1. See S. Kim 1985: 7–14 for bibliographic details on these scholars. See also excursus 5.

2. The association of the Suffering Servant and the Son of Man is perhaps the most common thread suggested for this link.

merit. However, the connection to the Suffering Servant (view 1) is not explicitly ruled out, since the psalm's concept for rejection has variants in Mark 9:12 and Acts 4:11 (ἐξουθενέω, to reject), which suggests the LXX form of a Servant text, Isa. 53:3, or an independent rendering of it (Marshall 1978: 370; Bock 1987: 199–200).

3. The image may link Ps. 118 with the stone image in Dan. 2, which in turn suggests the Son-of-Man figure of Dan. 7 (Snodgrass 1983: 101, 104–10). This Psalter-Daniel link, though possible, is less clear, since this linkage is not explicitly made in the NT.

4. The Son of Man is a figurative reference to Israel, and he does suffer in Dan. 7 (Hooker 1967). Daniel 7, then, is the only background to the saying. But a suffering Son of Man is doubtful for Dan. 7, as is an exclusive reference to Israel (Bock 1987: 132–37, 336 n. 183).

All recognize that a major theological synthesis is present when the Son of Man is associated with suffering, but what are the elements contributing to the association? Do any of these suggestions have merit?

It appears that three possible elements are at the base of the synthesis: the suffering of the regal figure of Ps. 118, the Suffering Servant of Isa. 53, and the general OT-Jewish theme that the suffering righteous will be vindicated. The regal tie is definitely suggested by NT usage; the Suffering Servant connection is probable, though less clearly demonstrable. To these two basic units, Bayer (1986: 229–42, esp. 238–42) adds another possible association that is broader in scope. He notes the Psalter's emphasis on and early Judaism's attention to the exaltation of the righteous, including, in later texts, the hope of resurrection.[3] Thus, the possibility for a suffering Son of Man exists in the context of Jewish thought about the vindication of the righteous, since the Danielic Son of Man brings such vindication. Though the Son of Man does not suffer in Daniel, he does represent and vindicate those who do. Thus, through a variety of motifs whose roots reach back to the OT, Jesus presents the image of the suffering Son of Man. Rejected king, Suffering Servant, and the vindication of the righteous all serve as background to the development of this title. Once Jesus is associated with the Son-of-Man image and with the righteous, the door is opened for this linkage.

---

3. For vindication texts, see Ps. 3, 8, 9, 18, 27, 32, 56, and others where the righteous have hope of vindication. For resurrection texts, see Wis. 2:12–20; 5:1–7; Bayer 1986: 239 and n. 99.

However, some doubt that Jesus spoke of the Son of Man in Luke 9:22 and thus debate the association of the title with suffering; others doubt whether these predictive passion sayings were given by Jesus at all (Luce 1933: 184). They argue that if Jesus wanted his disciples to know that he was going to die soon, he would have prepared them more explicitly. The objection is this: how could the disciples be so disbelieving upon Jesus' death if he had told them of it ahead of time? Some also argue that, for Jesus to really suffer on people's behalf, it was necessary that he face death in his full humanity, not knowing the outcome. But to suffer humiliation without some knowledge or hope of ultimate vindication would seem foolish. It is lame to argue what Jesus had to go through in order to make an appropriate moral sacrifice. Scripture consistently testifies that the righteous can tolerate suffering because they are confident of God's ultimate vindication (so the psalms in n. 3). As for the disciples' reaction, the text says that they did not understand the utterances, probably because their messianic portrait did not have a "dead raised to life" category. Before the resurrection, it would take an exceptional faith to accept this possibility. Only an empty tomb would reverse the hesitation (for more about the disciples' understanding, see the discussion of the "third day" below).

Fitzmyer (1981: 777–78) opts for a mediating position: a post-church reformulation in light of the passion. But why accept this hypothesis? Jesus can utter the prediction that he would meet with death because he realizes that rejection would lead to his death, just as John the Baptist suffered. He can do so because he sees himself as God's righteous authoritative agent whom God would vindicate. These elements are clearly in Jesus' thinking and are sufficient to make his statement possible. A suffering Son of Man is part of his teaching (Marshall 1978: 368–69). Thus, the authenticity of this general statement about death and resurrection can be defended.

The specific mention of "the third day" is, on the surface, problematic. Even if the disciples understood the remark as an idiom for "immediate" vindication, for Jesus the statement is specific. Association of the third day with Jonah shows that Jesus intended a specific reference (Matt. 12:40; 26:64 [immediate vindication] = Luke 22:69). However, it is clear the disciples did not initially understand the three-day remark as an exact chronological reference. In fact, perhaps it is this detail that they failed to grasp at all until the resurrection had occurred.[4] Luke's portrait is credible in that it honestly shows its "heroes" failing to understand Jesus, which hardly does

---

4. Luke 9:45 and 18:34. In addition, it could hardly be said that the disciples waited for a resurrection after Jesus' death! It is this point that the disciples did not understand about Jesus' prediction, not that he would die and eventually be vindi-

them honor if such an account had been created after the fact. The disciples were asked to assimilate much new truth in a short time before Jesus met his end. They struggled to do so and the text is forthright in saying that they stumbled over such truths. This struggle supports the text's authenticity, for why create such mysteries in an era when many had heard Jesus teach? There is no reason to deny that Jesus made this prediction.

---

cated. Another element in their lack of understanding would be why these events were necessary as a part of God's plan. It is hard to believe that they did not understand the content of Jesus' prediction that he would die and be raised at least at some point. But the disciples wanted Jesus to show his rule immediately and they wanted to share in that rule. They thought that his death killed such hopes. The meaning of Jesus' words is not difficult to understand, but their necessity and their timing are things that the disciples clearly did not perceive originally.

Provisional Bibliography

In a few cases, a year may appear with a "b" tag (e.g., Kilpatrick 1965b) but not the same year with an "a" tag. These items are cited in volume two of the commentary and will be included in the comprehensive bibliography to be printed in that volume.

Achtemeier, P. J.
1978   "The Lukan Perspective on the Miracles of Jesus: A Preliminary Sketch." Pp. 153–67 in *Perspectives on Luke–Acts*. Edited by C. H. Talbert. Danville, Va.: Association of Baptist Professors of Religion/Edinburgh: Clark.

Ahern, B.
1943   "Staff or No Staff?" *Catholic Biblical Quarterly* 5:332–37.

Aland, K.
1985   *Synopsis Quattuor Evangelorum*. 13th edition. Stuttgart: Deutsche Bibelstiftung.

Aland, K., and B. Aland
1987   *The Text of the New Testament: An Introduction to the Critical Editions and to the Theory and Practice of Modern Textual Criticism*. Translated by E. F. Rhodes. Grand Rapids: Eerdmans/Leiden: Brill.

Alexander, L.
1986   "Luke's Preface in the Context of Greek Preface-Writing." *Novum Testamentum* 28:48–74.

Alford, H.
1874   *The Greek Testament*, vol. 1: *The Four Gospels*. 7th edition. London: Rivingtons/Cambridge: Deighton, Bell.

Allison, D. C., Jr.
1987   "Jesus and the Covenant: A Response to E. P. Sanders." *Journal for the Study of the New Testament* 29:57–78.
1992   "The Baptism of Jesus and a New Dead Sea Scroll." *Biblical Archaeology Review* 18/2:58–60.

Annen, F.
1976   *Heil für die Heiden: Zur Bedeutung und Geschichte der Tradition vom besessenen Gerasener (Mk 5,1–20 parr.)*. Franfurter theologische Studien 20. Frankfurt am Main: Knecht.

Arbeitman, Y.
1980   "The Suffix of Iscariot." *Journal of Biblical Literature* 99:122–24.

Arndt, W. F.
1956   *The Gospel according to St. Luke*. St. Louis: Concordia.

Audet, J.-P.
1956   "L'Annonce à Marie." *Revue Biblique* 63:346–74.

Aufhauser, J. B.
1926   *Buddha und Jesus in ihren Paralleltexten*. Kleine Texte für Vorlesungen und Übungen 157. Bonn: Marcus & Weber.

BAA   *Griechisch-Deutsches Wörterbuch zu den Schriften des Neuen Testaments und der frühchristlichen Literatur*. 6th edition. By W. Bauer, K. Aland, and B. Aland. Berlin: de Gruyter, 1988.

Badian, E.
1972   *Publicans and Sinners: Private Enterprise in the Service of the Roman Republic*. Oxford: Blackwell/Ithaca, N.Y.: Cornell University Press.

BAGD   *A Greek-English Lexicon of the New Testament and Other Early Christian Literature*. 2d edition. By W. Bauer, W. F. Arndt, F. W. Gingrich, and F. W. Danker. Chicago: University of Chicago Press, 1979.

Bailey, K. E.
1980   *Through Peasant Eyes: More Lucan Parables, Their Culture and Style*. Grand Rapids: Eerdmans.

Baldi, D.
1955   *Enchiridion Locorum Sanctorum*. 2d edition. Jerusalem: Franciscan Printing Press.

Baltensweiler, H.
1959   *Die Verklärung Jesu: Historisches Ereignis und synoptische Berichte*. Abhandlungen zur Theologie des Alten und Neuen Testaments 33. Zurich: Zwingli.

Barrett, C. K.
1947   *The Holy Spirit and the Gospel Tradition*. London: SPCK.
1978   *The Gospel according to St. John: An Introduction with Commentary and Notes on the Greek Text*. 2d edition. Philadelphia: Westminster/London: SPCK.

Bauman, C.
1985   *The Sermon on the Mount: The Modern Quest for Its Meaning*. Macon, Ga.: Mercer University Press/Louvain: Peeters.

Baur, F. C.
1831   "Die Christuspartei in der korinthischen Gemeinde: Der Gegensatz des petrinischen und paulinischen Christenthums in der ältesten Kirche, der Apostel Petrus in Rom." *Tübinger Zeitschrift für Theologie* 4:61–206. Reprinted in Baur's *Ausgewählte Werke in Einzelausgaben*, vol. 1: *Historisch-kritische Untersuchungen zum Neuen Testament*, pp. 1–146. Stuttgart: Frommann, 1963.
1850–51 "Die Einleitung ins NT als theologische Wissenschaft: Ihr Begriff und ihre Aufgabe, ihr Entwicklungsgang und ihr Organismus." *Theologische Jahrbücher* 9:463–566; 10:70–94, 222–53, 329.

Bayer, H. F.
1986   *Jesus' Predictions of Vindication and Resurrection: The Provenance, Meaning and Correlation of the Synoptic Predictions*. Wissenschaftliche Untersuchungen zum Neuen Testament 2/20. Tübingen: Mohr.

BDB   *A Hebrew and English Lexicon of the Old Testament*. By F. Brown, S. R. Driver, and C. A. Briggs. Oxford: Clarendon, 1907.

BDF   *A Greek Grammar of the New Testament and Other Early Christian Literature*. By F. Blass, A. Debrunner, and R. W. Funk. Chicago: University of Chicago Press, 1961.

BDR   *Grammatik des neutestamentlichen Griechisch*. By F. Blass, A. Debrunner, and F. Rehkopf. Göttingen: Vandenhoeck & Ruprecht, 1984.

Bellinzoni, A., Jr., J. B. Tyson, and W. O. Walker Jr. (eds.)
1985   *The Two-Source Hypothesis: A Critical Appraisal*. Macon, Ga.: Mercer University Press.

Bemile, P.
1986   *The Magnificat within the Context and Framework of Lukan Theology: An Exegetical Theological Study of Lk 1:46–55*. Regensburger Studien zur Theologie 34. Frankfurt am Main: Lang.

Ben-Dor, I.
1945   "Palestinian Alabaster Vases." *Quarterly of the Department of Antiquities in Palestine* 11:93–112.

Benoit, P.
1956–57 "L'Enfance de Jean-Baptiste selon Luc 1." *New Testament Studies* 3:169–94.

Berger, K.
1973–74 "Die königlichen Messiastraditionen des Neuen Testaments." *New Testament Studies* 20:1–44.
1984   *Formgeschichte des Neuen Testaments*. Heidelberg: Quelle & Meyer.

Bertrand, D. A.
1973   *Le Baptême de Jésus: Histoire de l'Exégèse aux Deux Premiers Siècles*. Beiträge zur Geschichte der biblischen Exegese 14. Tübingen: Mohr.

Betz, H. D.
1985   *Essays on the Sermon on the Mount*. Translated by L. L. Welborn. Philadelphia: Fortress.

Betz, O.
1985 *Jesus und das Danielbuch*, vol. 2: *Die Menschensohnworte Jesu und die Zukunftser-wartung des Paulus (Daniel 7,13–14)*. Arbeiten zum Neuen Testament und Judentum 2/6.2. Frankfurt am Main: Lang.

Billerbeck, P.
1964 "Ein Synagogengottesdienst in Jesu Tagen." *Zeitschrift für die Neutestamentliche Wissenschaft* 55:143–61.

Bishop, E. F. F.
1949–50 "Three and a Half Years." *Expository Times* 61:126–27.
1951 "Jesus and the Lake." *Catholic Biblical Quarterly* 13:398–414.

Black, M.
1959–60 "The Parables as Allegory." *Bulletin of the John Rylands Library* 42:273–87.
1967 *An Aramaic Approach to the Gospels and Acts*. 3d edition. Oxford: Clarendon.

Blackman, P.
1983 *Mishnayoth*. 7 vols. 2d edition. Gateshead, N.Y.: Judaica.

Blaising, C. A., and D. L. Bock
1993 *Progressive Dispensationalism*. Wheaton, Ill.: Victor.

Blinzler, J.
1967 *Die Brüder und Schwestern Jesu*. Stuttgarter Bibelstudien 21. Stuttgart: Katholisches Bibelwerk.
1970 "The Jewish Punishment of Stoning in the New Testament Period." Pp. 147–61 in *The Trial of Jesus: Cambridge Studies in Honour of C. F. D. Moule*. Edited by E. Bammel. Studies in Biblical Theology 2/13. London: SCM/Naperville, Ill.: Allenson.

Blomberg, C. L.
1984a "The Law in Luke–Acts." *Journal for the Study of the New Testament* 22:53–80.
1984b "New Testament Miracles and Higher Criticism: Climbing up the Slippery Slope." *Journal of the Evangelical Theological Society* 27:425–38.
1990 *Interpreting the Parables*. Downers Grove, Ill.: InterVarsity.

Bock, D. L.
1985 "Evangelicals and the Use of the Old Testament in the New." *Bibliotheca Sacra* 142:209–23, 306–19.
1986 "Jesus as Lord in Acts and in the Gospel Message." *Bibliotheca Sacra* 143:146–54.
1987 *Proclamation from Prophecy and Pattern: Lucan Old Testament Christology*. Journal for the Study of the New Testament Supplement 12. Sheffield: JSOT Press.
1991a "Athenians Who Have Never Heard." Pp. 117–24 in *Through No Fault of Their Own? The Fate of Those Who Have Never Heard*. Edited by W. V. Crockett and J. G. Sigountos. Grand Rapids: Baker.
1991b "Form Criticism." Pp. 175–96 in *New Testament Criticism and Interpretation*. Edited by D. A. Black and D. S. Dockery. Grand Rapids: Zondervan.
1991c "The Son of Man in Luke 5:24." *Bulletin for Biblical Research* 1:109–21.
1992a "Evidence from Acts." Pp. 181–98 in *A Case for Premillennialism: A New Consensus*. Edited by D. K. Campbell and J. L. Townsend. Chicago: Moody.
1992b "Luke, Gospel of." Pp. 495–510 in *Dictionary of Jesus and the Gospels*. Edited by J. B. Green, S. McKnight, and I. H. Marshall. Downers Grove, Ill.: InterVarsity.
1992c "The Reign of the Lord Christ." Pp. 37–67 in *Dispensationalism, Israel and the Church: The Search for Definition*. Edited by C. A. Blaising and D. L. Bock. Grand Rapids: Zondervan.
1993 "The Son of David and the Saints' Task: The Hermeneutics of Initial Fulfillment." *Bibliotheca Sacra* 150:440–57.
1994a "Current Messianic Activity and OT Davidic Promise: Dispensationalism, Hermeneutics, and NT Fulfillment." *Trinity Journal* 15:55–87.
1994b "The Son of Man Seated at God's Right Hand and the Debate over Jesus' 'Blasphemy.' " Pp. 181–91 in *Jesus of Nazareth: Lord and Christ; Essays on the Historical Jesus and New Testament Christology*. Edited by J. B. Green and M. Turner. Grand Rapids: Eerdmans/Carlisle, Cumbria: Paternoster.

1994c   "The Theology of Luke–Acts." Pp. 87–166 in *A Biblical Theology of the New Testament*. Edited by R. B. Zuck and D. L. Bock. Chicago: Moody.

Böckh, A.

1828–77   *Corpus Inscriptionum Graecarum*. Berlin: Reimer.

Boobyer, G. H.

1942   *St. Mark and the Transfiguration Story*. Edinburgh: Clark.

1954   "Mark ii,10a and the Interpretation of the Healing of the Paralytic." *Harvard Theological Review* 47:115–20.

Bornkamm, G.

1963   "The Stilling of the Storm in Matthew." Pp. 52–57 in *Tradition and Interpretation in Matthew*. By G. Bornkamm, G. Barth, and H. J. Held. Translated by P. Scott. New Testament Library. Philadelphia: Westminster/London: SCM.

Borsch, F. H.

1967   *The Son of Man in Myth and History*. New Testament Library. Philadelphia: Westminster/London: SCM.

Bousset, W.

1926   *Die Religion des Judentums im späthellenistischen Zeitalter*. 3d edition. Edited by H. Gressmann. Handbuch zum Neuen Testament 21. Tübingen: Mohr.

Bover, J. M.

1951   "Una Nueva Interpretación de Luc 2,50." *Estudios Bíblicos* 10:205–15.

Bovon, F.

1989   *Das Evangelium nach Lukas*, vol. 1: *Lk 1,1–9,50*. Evangelisch-katholischer Kommentar zum Neuen Testament 3/1. Zurich: Benzinger/Neukirchen-Vluyn: Neukirchener Verlag.

Braude, W. G.

1968   *Pesikta Rabbati: Discourses for Feasts, Fasts, and Special Sabbaths*. 2 vols. Yale Judaica Series 18. New Haven: Yale University Press.

Braunert, H.

1957   "Der römische Provinzialzensus und der Schätzungsbericht des Lukas-Evangeliums." *Historia* 6:192–214.

Brawley, R. L.

1987   *Luke–Acts and the Jews: Conflict, Apology, and Conciliation*. Society of Biblical Literature Monograph Series 33. Atlanta: Scholars Press.

1992   "Canon and Community: Intertextuality, Canon, Interpretation, Christology, Theology, and Persuasive Rhetoric in Luke 4:1–13." Pp. 419–34 in *Society of Biblical Literature 1992 Seminar Papers*. Edited by E. Lovering Jr. Atlanta: Scholars Press.

Bretscher, P. G.

1968   "Exodus 4:22–23 and the Voice From Heaven." *Journal of Biblical Literature* 87:301–11.

Brodie, T. L.

1983   "Luke 7,36–50 as an Internalization of 2 Kings 4,1–37: A Study in Luke's Use of Rhetorical Imitation." *Biblica* 64:457–85.

1986   "Towards Unravelling Luke's Use of the Old Testament: Luke 7.11–17 as an *Imitatio* of 1 Kings 17.24." *New Testament Studies* 32:247–67.

1987   *Luke the Literary Interpreter: Luke–Acts as a Systematic Rewriting and Updating of the Elijah and Elisha Narrative in 1 and 2 Kings*. Ph.D. diss. Rome: Pontifical University of St. Thomas.

Brooke, G. J.

1985   *Exegesis at Qumran: 4QFlorilegium in Its Jewish Context*. Journal for the Study of the Old Testament Supplement 29. Sheffield: JSOT Press.

Brooten, B. J.

1982   *Women Leaders in the Ancient Synagogue: Inscriptional Evidence and Background Issues*. Brown Judaic Studies 36. Chico, Calif.: Scholars Press.

Brown, R. E.

1962   "Parable and Allegory Reconsidered." *Novum Testamentum* 5:36–45.

1970   *The Gospel according to John (xiii–xxi)*. Anchor Bible 29A. Garden City, N.Y.: Doubleday.

1977   *The Birth of the Messiah: A Commentary on the Infancy Narratives in Matthew and Luke*. London: Chapman/Garden City, N.Y.: Doubleday.

1993   *The Birth of the Messiah: A Commentary on the Infancy Narratives in the Gospels of Matthew and Luke*. Revised edition. Anchor Bible Reference Library. New York: Doubleday.

1994   *The Death of the Messiah, from Gethsemane to the Grave: A Commentary on the Passion Narratives in the Four Gospels*. 2 vols. Anchor Bible Reference Library. New York: Doubleday.

Brown, S.

1969   *Apostasy and Perseverance in the Theology of Luke*. Analecta Biblica 36. Rome: Pontifical Biblical Institute Press.

Bruce, A. B.

1897   *The Synoptic Gospels*. Expositor's Greek Testament 1. London: Hodder & Stoughton.

Bruce, F. F.

1972   *New Testament History*. Garden City, N.Y.: Doubleday.

1974   *Jesus and Christian Origins outside the New Testament*. Grand Rapids: Eerdmans.

1975–76   "Is the Paul of Acts the Real Paul?" *Bulletin of the John Rylands University Library of Manchester* 58:282–305.

1982   "The Background to the Son of Man Sayings." Pp. 50–70 in *Christ the Lord: Studies in Christology Presented to Donald Guthrie*. Edited by H. H. Rowdon. Leicester, Inter-Varsity.

1988   *The Book of the Acts*. 2d edition. New International Commentary on the New Testament. Grand Rapids: Eerdmans.

Buchanan, G. W., and C. Wolfe

1978   "The 'Second-First Sabbath' (Luke 6:1)." *Journal of Biblical Literature* 97:259–62.

Büchele, A.

1978   *Der Tod Jesu im Lukasevangelium: Eine redaktionsgeschichtliche Untersuchung zu Lk 23*. Theologische Studien 26. Frankfurt am Main: Knecht.

Bultmann, R.

1963   *The History of the Synoptic Tradition*. Translated by J. Marsh. New York: Harper & Row/Oxford: Blackwell.

Burns, J. L.

1992   "The Future of Ethnic Israel in Romans 11." Pp. 188–229 in *Dispensationalism, Israel and the Church: The Search for Definition*. Edited by C. A. Blaising and D. L. Bock. Grand Rapids: Zondervan.

Burrows, E.

1940   *The Gospel of the Infancy and Other Biblical Essays*. Edited by E. F. Sutcliffe. London: Burns, Oates & Washbourne.

Busse, U.

1978   *Das Nazareth-Manifest Jesu: Eine Einführung in das lukanische Jesusbild nach Lk 4,16–30*. Stuttgarter Bibelstudien 91. Stuttgart: Katholisches Bibelwerk.

1979   *Die Wunder des Propheten Jesus: Die Rezeption, Komposition und Interpretation der Wundertradition im Evangelium des Lukas*. 2d edition. Forschung zur Bibel 24. Stuttgart: Katholisches Bibelwerk.

Buth, R.

1984   "Hebrew Poetic Tenses and the Magnificat." *Journal for the Study of the New Testament* 21:67–83.

Cadbury, H. J.

1922a   "Commentary on the Preface of Luke." Vol. 2 / pp. 489–510 in *The Beginnings of Christianity*, part 1: *The Acts of the Apostles*. Edited by F. J. Foakes Jackson and K. Lake. London: Macmillan. Reprinted Grand Rapids: Baker, 1979.

1922b   "The Knowledge Claimed in Luke's Preface." *Expositor*, 8th series, 24:401–20.

1926   "Lexical Notes on Luke–Acts, II: Recent Arguments for Medical Language." *Journal of Biblical Literature* 45:190–209.

1933   "Dust and Garments." Vol. 5 / pp. 269–77 in *The Beginnings of Christianity*, part 1: *The Acts of the Apostles*. Edited by F. J. Foakes Jackson and K. Lake. London: Macmillan. Reprinted Grand Rapids: Baker, 1979.

1956–57 " 'We' and 'I' Passages in Luke–Acts." *New Testament Studies* 3:128–32.

1958   *The Making of Luke–Acts*. 2d edition. London: SPCK.

Caird, G. B.
1963   *The Gospel of St Luke*. Pelican Gospel Commentaries. Baltimore: Penguin.

Calvin, J.
1972   *A Harmony of the Gospels: Matthew, Mark and Luke*. Translated by A. W. Morrison and T. H. L. Parker. 3 vols. Grand Rapids: Eerdmans/Edinburgh: Saint Andrew.

Campbell, D. K.
1953   *Interpretation and Exposition of the Sermon on the Mount*. Th.D. diss. Dallas Theological Seminary.

Caragounis, C. C.
1974   "Ὀψώνιον: A Reconsideration of Its Meaning." *Novum Testamentum* 16:35–57.

1986   *The Son of Man: Vision and Interpretation*. Wissenschaftliche Untersuchungen zum Neuen Testament 38. Tübingen: Mohr.

Carlston, C. E.
1975   *The Parables of the Triple Tradition*. Philadelphia: Fortress.

Carroll, J. T.
1988   "Luke's Portrayal of the Pharisees." *Catholic Biblical Quarterly* 50:604–21.

Carroll R., M. D.
1992   "La Cita de Isaías 58:6 en Lucas 4:18: Una Neuva Propuesta." *Kairós* 11:61–78.

Carson, D. A.
1978   *The Sermon on the Mount: An Evangelical Exposition of Matthew 5–7*. Grand Rapids: Baker.

1982   "Jesus and the Sabbath in the Four Gospels." Pp. 57–97 in *From Sabbath to Lord's Day: A Biblical, Historical, and Theological Investigation*. Edited by D. A. Carson. Grand Rapids: Zondervan.

1984   "Matthew." Vol. 8 / pp. 1–599 in *The Expositor's Bible Commentary*. Edited by F. E. Gaebelein. Grand Rapids: Zondervan.

Casey, M.
1979   *Son of Man: The Interpretation and Influence of Daniel 7*. London: SPCK.

Cassidy, R. J.
1978   *Jesus, Politics, and Society: A Study of Luke's Gospel*. Maryknoll, N.Y.: Orbis.

Ceroke, C. P.
1960   "Is Mk 2,10 a Saying of Jesus?" *Catholic Biblical Quarterly* 22:369–90.

Chafer, L. S.
1951   "The Teachings of Christ Incarnate." *Bibliotheca Sacra* 108:389–413.

Charles, R. H.
1913   *The Apocrypha and Pseudepigrapha of the Old Testament in English*. 2 vols. Oxford: Clarendon.

Charlesworth, J. H. (ed.)
1983–85 *The Old Testament Pseudepigrapha*. 2 vols. Garden City, N.Y.: Doubleday.

Chilton, B.
1981   "Announcement in Nazara: An Analysis of Luke 4:16–21." Pp. 147–72 in *Gospel Perspectives*, vol. 2: *Studies of History and Tradition in the Four Gospels*. Edited by R. T. France and D. Wenham. Sheffield: JSOT Press.

Cohen, A.
1948   *The Twelve Prophets: Hebrew Text, English Translation and Commentary*. Soncino Books of the Bible. London: Soncino Press.

Cohen, B.
1930   "The Rabbinic Law Presupposed by Matthew xii.1 and Luke vi.1." *Harvard Theological Review* 23:91–92.

Coleridge, M.
1993   *The Birth of the Lukan Narrative: Narrative as Christology in Luke 1–2*. Journal for the Study of the New Testament Supplement 88. Sheffield: JSOT Press.
Collins, J.
1993   "A Pre-Christian 'Son of God' among the Dead Sea Scrolls." *Bible Review* 9/3:34–38, 57.
Colson, F. H.
1941   *Philo, with an English Translation*, vol. 9. Loeb Classical Library 363. Cambridge: Harvard University Press/London: Heinemann.
Combrink, H. J. B.
1973   "The Structure and Significance of Luke 4:16–30." *Neotestamentica* 7:27–47.
Conzelmann, H.
1960   *The Theology of St. Luke*. Translated by G. Buswell. New York: Harper & Row.
Corbishley, T.
1936   "Quirinius and the Census: A Re-study of the Evidence." *Klio* 29:81–93.
Corrington, G. P.
1993   "Redaction Criticism." Pp. 87–99 in *To Each Its Own Meaning: An Introduction to Biblical Criticisms and Their Application*. Edited by S. R. Haynes and S. L. McKenzie. Louisville: Westminster/John Knox.
Cortés, J. B., and F. M. Gatti
1970   "Jesus' First Recorded Words (Lk. 2:49–50)." *Marianum* 32:404–18.
Couroyer, B.
1970   "De la Mesure dont Vous Mesurez il Vous Sera Mesuré." *Revue Biblique* 77:366–70.
Cranfield, C. E. B.
1959   *The Gospel according to Saint Mark: An Introduction and Commentary*. Cambridge Greek Testament Commentary. Cambridge: Cambridge University Press.
Creed, J. M.
1921–22 "Josephus on John the Baptist." *Journal of Theological Studies* o.s. 23:59–60.
1930   *The Gospel according to St. Luke*. London: Macmillan.
Crockett, L.
1966   "Luke iv.16–30 and the Jewish Lectionary Cycle: A Word of Caution." *Journal of Jewish Studies* 17:13–46.
Crossan, J. D.
1973   *In Parables: The Challenge of the Historical Jesus*. New York: Harper & Row.
1991   *The Historical Jesus: The Life of a Mediterranean Jewish Peasant*. San Francisco: Harper.
Cullmann, O.
1963   *The Christology of the New Testament*. Translated by S. C. Gutherie and C. A. M. Hall. 2d edition. New Testament Library. Philadelphia: Westminster.
Cutler, A.
1966   "Does the Simeon of Luke 2 Refer to Simeon the Son of Hillel?" *Journal of Bible and Religion* 34:29–35.
Dahl, N. A.
1951   "The Parables of Growth." *Studia Theologica* 5:132–66.
1955   "The Origin of Baptism." Pp. 36–42 in *Interpretationes ad Vetus Testamentum pertinentes Sigmundo Mowinckel septuagenario missae*. Edited by A. S. Kapelrud. Oslo: Land og Kirge.
1966   "The Story of Abraham in Luke–Acts." Pp. 139–58 in *Studies in Luke–Acts: Essays Presented in Honor of Paul Schubert*. Edited by L. E. Keck and J. L. Martyn. Nashville: Abingdon. Reprinted Philadelphia: Fortress, 1980.
Danby, H.
1933   *The Mishnah: Translated from the Hebrew with Introduction and Brief Explanatory Notes*. Oxford: Oxford University Press.
Danker, F. W.
1972   *Jesus and the New Age according to St. Luke: A Commentary on the Third Gospel*. St. Louis: Clayton.

1983 "Graeco-Roman Cultural Accommodation in the Christology of Luke–Acts." Pp. 391–414 in *Society of Biblical Literature 1983 Seminar Paper*. Edited by K. H. Richards. Chico, Calif.: Scholars Press.

1988 *Jesus and the New Age: A Commentary on St. Luke's Gospel*. Revised edition. Philadelphia: Fortress.

Daube, D.
1956 *The New Testament and Rabbinic Judaism*. Jordan Lectures 1952. London: University of London/Athlone.

1972–73 "Responsibilities of Master and Disciples in the Gospels." *New Testament Studies* 19:1–15.

Davies, W. D.
1964 *The Setting of the Sermon on the Mount*. Cambridge: Cambridge University Press.

Davies, W. D., and D. C. Allison Jr.
1988 *A Critical and Exegetical Commentary on the Gospel according to Saint Matthew*, vol. 1: *Introduction and Commentary on Matthew i–vii*. International Critical Commentary. Edinburgh: Clark.

De Jonge, H. J.
1977–78 "Sonship, Wisdom, Infancy: Luke ii.41–51a." *New Testament Studies* 24:317–54.

De Jonge, M.
1966 "The Use of the Word 'Anointed' in the Time of Jesus." *Novum Testamentum* 8:132–48.

Delobel, J.
1973 "La Rédaction de Lc., iv,14–16a et le 'Bericht vom Anfang.' " Pp. 203–23 in *L'Évangile de Luc: Problèmes Littéraires et Théologiques: Mémorial Lucien Cerfaux*. Edited by F. Neirynck. Bibliotheca Ephemeridum Theologicarum Lovaniensium 32. Gembloux: Duculot.

Derrett, J. D. M.
1970 *Law in the New Testament*. London: Darton, Longman & Todd.

1973 "Law in the New Testament: The Syro-Phoenician Woman and the Centurion of Capernaum." *Novum Testamentum* 15:161–86.

Dessau, H.
1892– *Inscriptiones Latinae Selectae*. 3 vols. in 5. Berlin: Weidmann.
1916

1921 "Zu den neuen Inschriften des Sulpicius Quirinius." *Klio* 17:252–58.

Dibelius, M.
1956 *Studies in the Acts of the Apostles*. Edited by H. Greeven. Translated by M. Ling and P. Schubert. New York: Scribner/London: SCM.

Dietrich, W.
1972 *Das Petrusbild der lukanischen Schriften*. Beiträge zur Wissenschaft vom Alten und Neuen Testament 5/14. Stuttgart: Kohlhammer.

Dillon, R. J.
1978 *From Eye-Witnesses to Ministers of the Word: Tradition and Composition in Luke 24*. Analecta Biblica 82. Rome: Pontifical Biblical Institute Press.

1981 "Previewing Luke's Project from His Prologue (Luke 1:1–4)." *Catholic Biblical Quarterly* 43:205–27.

Dinkler, E.
1971 "Peter's Confession and the Satan Saying: The Problem of Jesus' Messiahship." Pp. 169–202 in *The Future of Our Religious Past: Essays in Honour of Rudolf Bultmann*. Edited by J. M. Robinson. Translated by C. E. Carlston and R. P. Scharlemann. New York: Harper & Row.

Dittenberger, W.
1903–5 *Orientis Graeci Inscriptiones Selectae: Supplementum "Sylloges Inscriptionum Graecarum."* 2 vols. Leipzig: Hirzel.

Dodd, C. H.
1947 "The Fall of Jerusalem and the 'Abomination of Desolation.' " *Journal of Roman Studies* 37:47–54. Reprinted in Dodd's *More New Testament Studies*, pp. 69–83. Grand Rapids: Eerdmans/Manchester: Manchester University Press, 1968.

1961   *The Parables of the Kingdom*. Revised edition. New York: Scribner/London: Nisbet.

Donahue, J. R.

1971   "Tax Collectors and Sinners: An Attempt at Identification." *Catholic Biblical Quarterly* 33:39–61.

Drury, J.

1976   *Tradition and Design in Luke's Gospel: A Study in Early Christian Historiography*. London: Darton, Longman & Todd.

Duling, D. C.

1975   "Solomon, Exorcism, and the Son of David." *Harvard Theological Review* 68:235–52.

Dungan, D. L. (ed.)

1990   *The Interrelations of the Gospels*. Bibliotheca Ephemeridum Theologicarum Lovaniensium 95. Louvain: Leuven University Press/Macon, Ga.: Mercer University Press.

Dunn, J. D. G.

1970a   *Baptism in the Holy Spirit: A Re-examination of the New Testament Teaching on the Gift of the Spirit in Relation to Pentecostalism Today*. Studies in Biblical Theology 2/15. London: SCM/Naperville, Ill.: Allenson.

1970b   "The Messianic Secret in Mark." *Tyndale Bulletin* 21:92–117. Reprinted in *The Messianic Secret*, pp. 116–31. Edited by C. Tuckett. Philadelphia: Fortress/London: SPCK.

1975   *Jesus and the Spirit: A Study of the Religious and Charismatic Experience of Jesus and the First Christians as Reflected in the New Testament*. New Testament Library. Philadelphia: Westminster/London: SCM.

Du Plessis, I. I.

1974   "Once More: The Purpose of Luke's Prologue (Lk i 1–4)." *Novum Testamentum* 16:259–71.

Dupont, J.

1959   " 'Soyez Parfaits' (Mt., v,48)—'Soyez Miséricordieux' (Lc., vi,36)." Vol. 2 / pp. 150–62 in *Sacra Pagina: Miscellanea Biblica Congressus Internationalis Catholici de re Biblica*. Edited by J. Coppens, A. Descamps, and É. Massaux. Bibliotheca Ephemeridum Theologicarum Lovaniensium 13. Paris: Lecoffre/Paris: Gabalda/Gembloux: Duculot.

1966a   " 'Béatitudes' Égyptiennes." *Biblica* 47:185–222.

1966b   "L'Appel à Imiter Dieu en Matthieu 5,48 et Luc 6,36." *Rivista Biblica* 14:137–58.

1968   *Les Tentations de Jésus au Désert*. Studia Neotestamentica 4. Bruges: Desclée de Brouwer.

1980   "Le Pharisien et la Pécheresse (Lc 7,36–50)." *Communautés et Liturgies* 4:260–68.

Dupont-Sommer, A.

1961   *The Essene Writings from Qumran*. Translated by G. Vermes. Oxford: Blackwell. Reprinted Gloucester, Mass.: Peter Smith, 1973.

Edersheim, A.

1889   *The Life and Times of Jesus the Messiah*. New York: Longmans, Green.

Ehrman, A.

1978   "Judas Iscariot and Abba Saqqara." *Journal of Biblical Literature* 97:572–73.

Einheitsübersetzung

     Einheitsübersetzung der Heiligen Schrift. Stuttgart: Katholische Bibelanstalt, 1979.

Eisler, R. I.

1931   *The Messiah Jesus and John the Baptist according to Flavius Josephus' Recently Discovered "Capture of Jerusalem" and the Other Jewish and Christian Sources*. Translated by A. H. Krappe. New York: Dial/London: Methuen.

Elliott, J. K.

1969   "The Use of Ἕτερος in the New Testament." *Zeitschrift für die Neutestamentliche Wissenschaft* 60:140–41.

Ellis, E. E.

1972   *Eschatology in Luke*. Facet Books, Biblical Series 30. Philadelphia: Fortress.

1974 *The Gospel of Luke*. 2d edition. New Century Bible. Grand Rapids: Eerdmans/London: Marshall, Morgan & Scott.

Epp, E. J.
1966 *The Theological Tendency of Codex Bezae Cantabrigiensis in Acts*. Society for New Testament Studies Monograph Series 3. Cambridge: Cambridge University Press.

Ernst, J.
1977 *Das Evangelium nach Lukas*. Regensburger Neues Testament 3. Regensburg: Pustet.

Esler, P. F.
1987 *Community and Gospel in Luke–Acts: The Social and Political Motivations of Lucan Theology*. Society for New Testament Studies Monograph Series 57. Cambridge: Cambridge University Press.

Evans, C. A.
1987b "Luke's Use of the Elijah/Elisha Narrative and the Ethic of Election." *Journal of Biblical Literature* 106:75–83.

1989c *To See and Not Perceive: Isaiah 6.9–10 in Early Jewish and Christian Interpretation*. Journal for the Study of the Old Testament Supplement 64. Sheffield: JSOT Press.

1990 *Luke*. New International Biblical Commentary 3. Peabody, Mass.: Hendrickson.

Evans, C. A., and J. A. Sanders
1993 *Luke and Scripture: The Function of Sacred Tradition in Luke–Acts*. Minneapolis: Fortress.

Evans, C. F.
1990 *Saint Luke*. Trinity Press International New Testament Commentaries. Philadelphia: Trinity/London: SCM.

Farmer, W. R.
1964 *The Synoptic Problem: A Critical Analysis*. New York: Macmillan. Reprinted Dillsboro, N.C.: Western North Carolina Press, 1976.

Farris, S.
1985 *The Hymns of Luke's Infancy Narratives: Their Origin, Meaning and Significance*. Journal for the Study of the New Testament Supplement 9. Sheffield: JSOT Press.

Feinberg, J. S. (ed.)
1988 *Continuity and Discontinuity: Perspectives on the Relationship between the Old and New Testaments: Essays in Honor of S. Lewis Johnson, Jr*. Weschester, Ill.: Crossway.

Finegan, J.
1964 *Handbook of Biblical Chronology: Principles of Time Reckoning in the Ancient World and the Problems of Chronology in the Bible*. Princeton: Princeton University Press.

Finkel, A.
1963 "Jesus' Sermon at Nazareth (Luk. 4,16–30)." Pp. 106–15 in *Abraham unser Vater: Juden und Christen im Gespräch über die Bibel: Festschrift für Otto Michel zum 60. Geburtstag*. Edited by O. Betz, M. Hengel, and P. Schmidt. Arbeiten zur Geschichte des Spätjudentums und Urchristentums 5. Leiden: Brill.

Finn, T. M.
1985 "The God-fearers Reconsidered." *Catholic Biblical Quarterly* 47:75–84.

Fitzgerald, J. T.
1972 "The Temptation of Jesus: The Testing of the Messiah in Matthew." *Restoration Quarterly* 15:152–60.

Fitzmyer, J. A.
1958 " 'Peace upon Earth among Men of His Good Will' (Lk 2:14)." *Theological Studies* 19:225–27. Reprinted in Fitzmyer's *Essays on the Semitic Background of the New Testament*, pp. 101–4. London: Chapman, 1971.

1972 "The Use of *Agein* and *Pherein* in the Synoptic Gospels." Pp. 147–60 in *Festschrift to Honor F. Wilbur Gingrich*. Edited by E. H. Barth and R. E. Cocroft. Leiden: Brill.

1973–74 "The Contribution of Qumran Aramaic to the Study of the New Testament." *New Testament Studies* 20:382–407. Reprinted in Fitzmyer's *Wandering Aramean: Collected Aramaic Essays*, pp. 85–113. Society of Biblical Literature Monograph Series 25. Missoula, Mont.: Scholars Press, 1979.

1979a   "Another View of the 'Son of Man' Debate." *Journal for the Study of the New Testament* 4:58–68.

1979b   *A Wandering Aramean: Collected Aramaic Essays*. Society of Biblical Literature Monograph Series 25. Missoula, Mont.: Scholars Press.

1981   *The Gospel according to Luke (i–ix)*. Anchor Bible 28. Garden City, N.Y.: Doubleday.

1985   *The Gospel according to Luke (x–xxiv)*. Anchor Bible 28a. Garden City, N.Y.: Doubleday.

1989   *Luke the Theologian: Aspects of His Teaching*. Mahwah, N.J.: Paulist Press/London: Chapman.

Flanagan, N. M.

1978   "The Position of Women in the Writings of St. Luke." *Marianum* 40:288–304.

Fletcher, D. R.

1964   "Condemned to Die: The Logion on Cross-Bearing: What Does It Mean?" *Interpretation* 18:156–64.

Flusser, D.

1957   "Healing through the Laying-on of Hands in a Dead Sea Scroll." *Israel Exploration Journal* 7:107–8.

1959   "Two Notes on the Midrash on II Sam. vii." *Israel Exploration Journal* 9:99–109.

Ford, J. M.

1984   *My Enemy Is My Guest: Jesus and Violence in Luke*. Maryknoll, N.Y.: Orbis.

Fornara, C. W.

1983   *The Nature of History in Ancient Greece and Rome*. Berkeley: University of California Press.

Foulkes, F.

1958   *The Acts of God: A Study of the Basis of Typology in the Old Testament*. Tyndale Old Testament Lecture 1955. London: Tyndale.

Fraenkel, E.

1935   "Namenwesen." Vol. 32 [= 16.2] / cols. 1611–70 in *Paulys Realencyclopädie der classischen Altertumswissenschaft*. Stuttgart: Metzler.

France, R. T.

1971   *Jesus and the Old Testament: His Application of Old Testament Passages to Himself and His Mission*. London: Tyndale/Downer Grove, Ill.: InterVarsity.

1985   *The Gospel according to Matthew: An Introduction and Commentary*. Tyndale New Testament Commentaries. Grand Rapids: Eerdmans/Leicester: Inter-Varsity.

Franklin, E.

1975   *Christ the Lord: A Study in the Purpose and Theology of Luke–Acts*. Philadelphia: Westminster/London: SPCK.

Frey, J.-B.

1930   "La Signification du Terme Πρωτότοκος d'après une Inscription Juive." *Biblica* 11:373–90.

Friedlander, G.

1916   *Pirḳê de Rabbi Eliezer (the Chapters of Rabbi Eliezer the Great) according to the Text of the Manuscript Belonging to Abraham Epstein of Vienna*. London: Paul, Trench, Trübner/New York: Bloch. Reprinted New York: Sepher-Hermon, 1981.

Funk, R. W.

1985   *New Gospel Parallels*. 2 vols. Philadelphia: Fortress

Funk, R. W., and R. W. Hoover

1993   *The Five Gospels: The Search for the Authentic Words of Jesus*. New York: Macmillan.

Gaechter, P.

1955   *Maria im Erdenleben: Neutestamentliche Marienstudien*. 3d edition. Innsbruck: Tyrolia.

Garbe, R.

1959   *India and Christendom: The Historical Connections between Their Religions*. Translated by L. G. Robinson. La Salle, Ill.: Open Court.

Garrett, S. R.
1989   *The Demise of the Devil: Magic and the Demonic in Luke's Writings*. Minneapolis: Fortress.

Gärtner, B. E.
1970–71   "The Person of Jesus and the Kingdom of God." *Theology Today* 27:32–43.

Geldenhuys, N.
1951   *Commentary on the Gospel of Luke*. New International Commentary on the New Testament. Grand Rapids: Eerdmans.

Gerhardsson, B.
1966   *The Testing of God's Son (Matt. 4:1–11 and Par): An Analysis of an Early Christian Midrash*. Coniectanea Biblica, New Testament 2/1. Lund: Gleerup.
1967–68   "The Parable of the Sower and Its Interpretation." *New Testament Studies* 14:165–93.

Gerstenberger, E.
1962   "The Woe-Oracles of the Prophets." *Journal of Biblical Literature* 81:249–63.

Gerstner, J. H.
1991   *Wrongly Dividing the Word of God: A Critique of Dispensationalism*. Brentwood, Tenn.: Wolgemuth & Hyatt.

Gewiess, J.
1967   "Die Mariefrage, Lk 1,34." Pp. 184–217 in *Struktur und Theologie der lukanischen Kindheitsgeschichte*, by R. Laurentin. Stuttgart: Katholisches Bibelwerk.

Glickman, S. C.
1983   *The Temptation Account in Matthew and Luke*. Ph.D. diss. University of Basel.

Glöckner, R.
1976   *Die Verkündigung des Heils beim Evangelisten Lukas*. Walberberger Studien 9. Mainz: Matthias-Grünewald.

Glombitza, O.
1958   "Die Titel Διδάσκαλος und Ἐπιστάτης für Jesus bei Lukas." *Zeitschrift für die Neutestamentliche Wissenschaft* 49:275–78.

Gnilka, J.
1961   *Die Verstockung Israels: Isaias 6,9–10 in der Theologie der Synoptiker*. Studien zum Alten und Neuen Testament 3. Munich: Kösel.
1961–62   "Die essenischen Tauchbäder und die Johannestaufe." *Revue de Qumran* 3:185–207.

Godet, F.
1875   *A Commentary on the Gospel of St. Luke*. 2 vols. Translated by E. W. Shalders and M. D. Cusin. Edinburgh: Clark.

Goldin, J.
1955   *The Fathers according to Rabbi Nathan*. Yale Judaica Series 10. New Haven: Yale University Press.

Goppelt, L.
1982   *Typos: The Typological Interpretation of the Old Testament in the New*. Translated by D. H. Madvig. Grand Rapids: Eerdmans.

Gordon, C. H.
1977   "Paternity at Two Levels." *Journal of Biblical Literature* 96:101.

Gore, C.
1910   *The Sermon on the Mount: A Practical Exposition*. 2d edition. London: Murray.

Goulder, M. D.
1989   *Luke: A New Paradigm*. 2 vols. Journal for the Study of the New Testament Supplement 20. Sheffield: JSOT Press.

Gradwohl, R.
1974   "Sünde und Vergebung im Judentum." *Concilium* 10/10:563–67.

Grässer, E.
1960   *Das Problem der Parusieverzögerung in den synoptischen Evangelien und in der Apostelgeschichte*. 2d edition. Beiheft zur Zeitschrift für die Neutestamentliche Wissenschaft 22. Berlin: Töpelmann.

Gray, G. B.
1899– "The Nazirite." *Journal of Theological Studies* o.s. 1:201–11.
1900

Graystone, G.
1968 *Virgin of All Virgins: The Interpretation of Luke 1:34.* Rome: Tipografia S. Pio X.

Green, M. P.
1983 "The Meaning of Cross-Bearing." *Bibliotheca Sacra* 140:117–33.

Gressmann, H.
1914 *Das Weihnachts-evangelium auf Ursprung und Geschichte.* Göttingen: Vandenhoeck & Ruprecht.

Grigsby, B.
1984 "Compositional Hypotheses for the Lucan 'Magnificat'—Tensions for the Evangelical." *Evangelical Quarterly* 56:159–72.

Grundmann, W.
1963 *Das Evangelium nach Lukas.* Theologischer Handkommentar zum Neuen Testament 3. Berlin: Evangelische Verlagsanstalt.

Guelich, R.
1975–76 "The Antitheses of Matthew v.21–48: Traditional and/or Redactional?" *New Testament Studies* 22:444–57.
1982 *The Sermon on the Mount.* Waco: Word.

Guenther, H. O.
1985 *The Footprints of Jesus' Twelve in Early Christian Traditions: A Study in the Meaning of Religious Symbolism.* American University Studies 7/7. New York: Lang.

Gundry, R. H.
1967 *The Use of the Old Testament in St. Matthew's Gospel, with Special Reference to the Messianic Hope.* Novum Testamentum Supplement 18. Leiden: Brill.
1982 *Matthew: A Commentary on His Literary and Theological Art.* Grand Rapids: Eerdmans.

Gunkel, H.
1921 "Die Lieder in der Kindheitsgeschichte Jesu bei Lukas." Pp. 43–60 in *Festgabe von Fachgenossen und Freunden A. von Harnack zum siebzigsten Geburtstag.* Edited by K. Holl. Tübingen: Mohr.

Guthrie, D.
1970 *New Testament Introduction.* 3d edition. Downers Grove, Ill.: InterVarsity.

Hadas, M.
1951 *Aristeas to Philocrates (Letter of Aristeas).* Jewish Apocryphal Literature. New York: Harper for Dropsie College.

Haenchen, E.
1961 "Das 'Wir' in der Apostelgeschichte und das Itinerar." *Zeitschrift für Theologie und Kirche* 58:329–66.
1971 *The Acts of the Apostles: A Commentary.* Translated by B. Noble, G. Shinn, H. Anderson, and R. M. Wilson. Philadelphia: Westminster/Oxford: Blackwell.

Hahn, F.
1969 *The Titles of Jesus in Christology: Their History in Early Christianity.* Translated by H. Knight and G. Ogg. London: Lutterworth.

Harbarth, A.
1978 *"Gott hat sein Volk heimgesucht": Eine form- und redaktionsgeschichtliche Untersuchungen zu Lk 7,11–17: Die Erweckung des Jünglings von Nain.* Ph.D. diss. Freiberg im Breisgau.

Hare, D. R. A.
1967 *The Theme of Jewish Persecution of Christians in the Gospel according to St Matthew.* Society for New Testament Studies Monograph Series 6. Cambridge: Cambridge University Press.

Harnack, A. von
1900 "Das Magnificat der Elisabet (Luc. 1,46–55) nebst einigen Bermerkungen zu Luc. 1 und 2." *Sitzungsberichte der königlichen preussischen Akademie der Wissenschaften*

zu Berlin 27:538–56. Reprinted in Harnack's *Kleine Schriften zur alten Kirche: Berliner Akademieschriften, 1890–1920*, vol. 1, pp. 439–57. Opuscula 9/1. Leipzig: Zentralantiquariat der Deutschen Demokratischen Republik, 1980.

1907   *Luke the Physician: The Author of the Third Gospel and the Acts of the Apostles*. New Testament Studies 1. Translated by J. R. Wilkinson. London: Williams & Norgate/ New York: Putnam.

Hartin, P. J.
1991   *James and the Q Sayings of Jesus*. Journal for the Study of the New Testament Supplement 47. Sheffield: JSOT Press.

Hayles, D. J.
1973   "The Roman Census and Jesus' Birth: Was Luke Correct?, part 1: The Roman Census System." *Buried History* 9:113–32.
1974   "The Roman Census and Jesus' Birth: Was Luke Correct?, part 2: Quirinius' Career and a Census in Herod's Day." *Buried History* 10:16–31.

Heater, H.
1986   "A Textual Note on Luke 3.33." *Journal for the Study of the New Testament* 28:25–29.

Hemer, C. J.
1989   *The Book of Acts in the Setting of Hellenistic History*. Edited by C. H. Gempf. Wissenschaftliche Untersuchungen zum Neuen Testament 49. Tübingen: Mohr.

Hendriksen, W.
1973   *Exposition of the Gospel according to Matthew*. New Testament Commentary. Grand Rapids: Baker.
1978   *Exposition of the Gospel according to Luke*. New Testament Commentary. Grand Rapids: Baker.

Hengel, M.
1961   *Die Zeloten: Untersuchungen zur jüdischen Freiheitsbewegung in der Zeit von Herodes I. bis 70 n. Chr.* Arbeiten zur Geschichte des Spätjudentums und Urchristentums 1. Leiden: Brill.
1963   "Maria Magdalena und die Frauen als Zeugen." Pp. 243–56 *Abraham unser Vater: Juden und Christen im Gespräch über die Bibel: Festschrift für Otto Michel zum 60. Geburtstag*. Edited by O. Betz, M. Hengel, and P. Schmidt. Arbeiten zur Geschichte des Spätjudentums und Urchristentums 5. Leiden: Brill.
1977   *Crucifixion in the Ancient World and the Folly of the Message of the Cross*. Translated by J. Bowden. Philadelphia: Fortress/London: SCM.
1980   *Acts and the History of Earliest Christianity*. Translated by J. S. Bowden. Philadelphia: Fortress/London: SCM.

Hengel, R., and M. Hengel
1959   "Die Heilungen Jesu und medizinisches Denken." Pp. 331–61 in *Medicus Viator: Fragen und Gedanken am Wege Richard Siebecks*. Tübingen: Mohr/Stuttgart: Thieme.

Herrmann, W.
1907   *Die sittlichen Weisungen Jesu: Ihr Mißbrauch und ihr richtiger Gebrauch*. 2d edition. Göttingen: Vandenhoeck & Ruprecht.

Hertz, J. H.
1945   *Sayings of the Fathers; or, Pirke Aboth*. New York: Behrman.

Hesse, F.
1955   *Das Verstockungsproblem im Alten Testament: Eine frömmigkeitsgeschichtliche Untersuchung*. Beiheft zur Zeitschrift für die Alttestamentliche Wissenschaft 74. Berlin: Töpelmann.

Heutger, N.
1983   "Münzen im Lukasevangelium." *Biblische Zeitschrift* 27:97–101.

Higgins, A. J. B.
1969   "Sidelights on Christian Beginnings in the Graeco-Roman World." *Evangelical Quarterly* 41:197–206.

Hill, D.
1971   "The Rejection of Jesus at Nazareth (Luke iv 16–30)." *Novum Testamentum* 13:161–80.

1972   *The Gospel of Matthew*. New Century Bible. Grand Rapids: Eerdmans/London: Marshall, Morgan & Scott.

Hobart, W. K.

1882   *The Medical Language of St. Luke*. Dublin: Hodges, Figgis. Reprinted Grand Rapids: Baker, 1954.

Hoehner, H. W.

1972   *Herod Antipas*. Society for New Testament Studies Monograph Series 17. Cambridge: Cambridge University Press.

1977   *Chronological Aspects of the Life of Christ*. Grand Rapids: Zondervan.

Holmes, M. W.

1983   "The 'Majority Text Debate': New Form of an Old Issue." *Themelios* 8/2:13–19.

1989   "New Testament Textual Criticism." Pp. 53–74 in *Introducing New Testament Interpretation*. Edited by S. McKnight. Guides to New Testament Exegesis 1. Grand Rapids: Baker.

Holtz, T.

1968   *Untersuchungen über die alttestamentlichen Zitate bei Lukas*. Texte und Untersuchungen 104. Berlin: Akademie-Verlag.

Hooker, M. D.

1967   *The Son of Man in Mark: A Study of the Background of the Term "Son of Man" and Its Use in St. Mark's Gospel*. London: SPCK.

Horsley, R. A.

1987   *Jesus and the Spiral of Violence: Popular Jewish Resistance in Roman Palestine*. San Francisco: Harper & Row.

Hort, F. J. A.

1908–9   "A Note . . . on the Words Κόφινος, Σπυρίς, Σαργάνη." *Journal of Theological Studies* o.s. 10:567–71.

Hospodar, B.

1956   "*Meta Spoudes* in Lk 1,39." *Catholic Biblical Quarterly* 18:14–18.

Howard, V.

1977   "Did Jesus Speak about His Own Death?" *Catholic Biblical Quarterly* 39:515–27.

Hubbard, B. J.

1977   "Commissioning Stories in Luke–Acts: A Study of Their Antecedents, Form and Content." *Semeia* 8:103–26.

Hull, J. M.

1974   *Hellenistic Magic and the Synoptic Tradition*. Studies in Biblical Theology 2/28. London: SCM/Naperville, Ill.: Allenson.

Hunter, A. M.

1965   *A Pattern for Life, An Exposition of the Sermon on the Mount: Its Making, Its Exegesis and Its Meaning*. Philadelphia: Westminster.

Hyldahl, N.

1961   "Die Versuchung auf der Zinne des Tempels (Matth 4,5–7 ≠ Luk 4,9–12)." *Studia Theologica* 15:113–27.

Isaac, E.

1981   "Another Note on Luke 6:1." *Journal of Biblical Literature* 100:96–97.

James, M. R.

1953   *The Apocryphal New Testament*. Corrected edition. Oxford: Clarendon.

Jaschke, H.

1971   " 'Λαλεῖν' bei Lukas: Ein Beitrag zur lukanischen Theologie." *Biblische Zeitschrift* 15:109–14.

Jastrow, M.

1903   *A Dictionary of the Targumim, the Talmud Babli and Yerushalmi, and the Midrashic Literature*. London: Trübner/New York: Putnam. Reprinted New York: Judaica, 1950.

Jeremias, J.

1929a   "Ἄνθρωποι Εὐδοκίας (Lc 2:14)." *Zeitschrift für die Neutestamentliche Wissenschaft* 28:13–20.

| 1929b | "Der Ursprung der Johannestaufe." *Zeitschrift für die Neutestamentliche Wissenschaft* 28:312–20. |

1929b   "Der Ursprung der Johannestaufe." *Zeitschrift für die Neutestamentliche Wissenschaft* 28:312–20.

1931   "Zöllner und Sünder." *Zeitschrift für die Neutestamentliche Wissenschaft* 30:293–300.

1936   "Die 'Zinne' des Tempels (Mt. 4,5; Lk. 4,9)." *Zeitschrift des Deutschen Palätina-Vereins* 59:195–208.

1949   "Proselytentaufe und Neues Testament." *Theologische Zeitschrift* 5:418–28.

1958   *Jesus' Promise to the Nations.* Translated by S. H. Hooke. Franz Delitzsch Lectures 1953. Studies in Biblical Theology 24. London: SCM/Naperville, Ill.: Allenson.

1960   "Lukas 7,45: Εἰσῆλθον." *Zeitschrift für die Neutestamentliche Wissenschaft* 51:131.

1963a   *The Parables of Jesus.* Translated by S. H. Hooke. Revised edition. New Testament Library. Philadelphia: Westminster/London: SCM.

1963b   *The Sermon on the Mount.* Translated by N. Perrin. Facet Books, Biblical Series 2. Philadelphia: Fortress. (British edition: London: Athlone, 1961.)

1966   *The Eucharistic Words of Jesus.* 2d edition. Translated by N. Perrin. New Testament Library. London: SCM/New York: Scribner.

1966–67   "Palästinakundliches zum Gleichnis vom Säemann (Mark iv.3–8 par.)." *New Testament Studies* 13:48–53.

1967   "Die älteste Schicht der Menschensohn-Logien." *Zeitschrift für die Neutestamentliche Wissenschaft* 58:159–72.

1969   *Jerusalem in the Time of Jesus: An Investigation into Economic and Social Conditions during the New Testament Period.* Translated by F. H. Cave and C. H. Cave. London: SCM/Philadelphia: Fortress.

1971a   *New Testament Theology: The Proclamation of Jesus.* Translated by J. Bowden. New Testament Library. London: SCM/New York: Scribner.

1980   *Die Sprache des Lukasevangeliums: Redaktion und Tradition im Nicht-Markusstoff des dritten Evangeliums.* Kritisch-exegetischer Kommentar über das Neue Testament, Sonderband. Göttingen: Vandenhoeck & Ruprecht.

Jervell, J.
1972   *Luke and the People of God: A New Look at Luke–Acts.* Minneapolis: Augsburg.

John, M. P.
1975   "Luke 2.36–37: How Old Was Anna?" *Bible Translator* 26:247.

Johnson, L. T.
1991   *The Gospel of Luke.* Sacra Pagina 3. Collegeville, Minn.: Liturgical Press.

Johnson, M. D.
1988   *The Purpose of Biblical Genealogies, with Special Reference to the Setting of the Genealogies of Jesus.* 2d edition. Society for New Testament Studies Monograph Series 8. Cambridge: Cambridge University Press.

Jones, D. R.
1968   "The Background and Character of the Lukan Psalms." *Journal of Theological Studies* n.s. 19:19–50.

Jülicher, A.
1899   *Die Gleichnisreden Jesu.* 2 vols. 2d edition. Freiburg im Breisgau: Mohr. Reprinted 1960.

Käser, W.
1968   "Exegetische Erwägungen zur Seligpreisung des Sabbatarbeiters Lk 6,5 D." *Zeitschrift für Theologie und Kirche* 65:414–30.

Keck, L. E.
1965   "The Poor among the Saints in the New Testament." *Zeitschrift für die Neutestamentliche Wissenschaft* 56:100–29.

1970–71   "The Spirit and the Dove." *New Testament Studies* 17:41–67.

Kee, H. C.
1967–68   "The Terminology of Mark's Exorcism Stories." *New Testament Studies* 14:232–46.

Kelly, H. A.
1964   "The Devil in the Desert." *Catholic Biblical Quarterly* 26:190–220.

Kelly, W.
1943   *Lectures on the Gospel of Matthew.* Revised edition. New York: Loizeaux.

Kelso, J. L.
1962   "House." Pp. 544–46 in *The New Bible Dictionary*. Edited by J. D. Douglas. Grand Rapids: Eerdmans.

Kenyon, F. G., and H. I. Bell
1907   *Greek Papyri in the British Museum*, vol. 3. London: British Museum.

Kertelge, K.
1970   *Die Wunder Jesu im Markusevangelium: Eine redaktionsgeschichtliche Untersuchung*. Studien zum Alten und Neuen Testament 23. Munich: Kösel.

Kilpatrick, G. D.
1965b   "Λαοί at Luke ii.31 and Acts iv.25, 27." *Journal of Theological Studies* n.s. 16:127.

Kim, S.
1985   *"The 'Son of Man' " as Son of God*. Grand Rapids: Eerdmans. (European edition: Tübingen: Mohr, 1983.)

Kirk, J. A.
1972   "The Messianic Role of Jesus and the Temptation Narrative: A Contemporary Perspective (Concluded)." *Evangelical Quarterly* 44:91–102.

Kissinger, W. S.
1975   *The Sermon on the Mount: A History of Interpretation and Bibliography*. American Theological Library Association Bibliography Series 3. Metuchen, N.J.: Scarecrow/ATLA.

1979   *The Parables of Jesus: A History of Interpretation and Bibliography*. American Theological Library Association Bibliography Series 4. Metuchen, N.J.: Scarecrow/ATLA.

Kistemaker, S. J.
1980   *The Parables of Jesus*. Grand Rapids: Baker.

Kittel, G.
1925   "Die Bergpredigt und die Ethik des Judentums." *Zeitschrift für systematische Theologie* 2:555–94.

Klauck, H.-J.
1978   *Allegorie und Allegorese in synoptischen Gleichnistexten*. Neutestamentliche Abhandlungen n.s. 13. Münster: Aschendorff.

1981   "Die Frage der Sündenvergebung in der Perikope von der Heilung des Gelähmten (Mk 2,1–12 parr)." *Biblische Zeitschrift* 25:223–48.

Klein, G.
1974   "Lukas 1,1–4 als theologisches Programm." Pp. 170–203 in *Das Lukas-Evangelium: Die redaktionsgeschichtliche und kompositionsgeschichtliche Forschung*. Edited by G. Braumann. Wege der Forschung 280. Darmstadt: Wissenschaftliche Buchgesellschaft. (Originally published in *Zeit und Geschichte: Dankesgabe an Rudolf Bultmann zum 80. Geburtstag*, pp. 193–216. Edited by E. Dinkler. Tübingen: Mohr, 1964. Reprinted in Klein's *Rekonstruktion und Interpretation: Gesammelte Aufsätze zum Neuen Testament*, pp. 237–61. Beiträge zur evangelischen Theologie 50. Munich: Kaiser, 1969.)

Kloppenberg, J. S.
1987   *The Formation of Q: Trajectories in Ancient Wisdom Collections*. Studies in Antiquity and Christianity. Philadelphia: Fortress.

1988   *Q Parallels: Synopsis, Critical Notes, and Concordance*. Foundations and Facets Reference Series. Sonoma, Calif.: Polebridge.

Klostermann, E.
1929   *Das Lukasevangelium*. Handbuch zum Neuen Testament 5. Tübingen: Mohr. Reprinted 1975.

Knox, J.
1942   *Marcion and the New Testament: An Essay in the Early History of the Canon*. Chicago: University of Chicago Press.

Koch, K.
1969   *The Growth of the Biblical Tradition: The Form-Critical Method*. Translated by S. M. Cupitt. New York: Scribner.

Köppen, K.-P.
1961   *Die Auslegung der Versuchungsgeschichte unter besonderer Berücksichtigung der Alten Kirche: Ein Beitrage zur Geschichte der Scriftauslegung*. Beiträge zur Geschichte der biblischen Exegese 4. Tübingen: Mohr.

Kosmala, H.
1965   "The Three Nets of Belial: A Study in the Terminology of Qumran and the New Testament." *Annual of the Swedish Theological Institute* 4:91–113.

Kuhn, G.
1923   "Die Geschlechtsregister Jesu bei Lukas und Matthäus, nach ihrer Herkunft untersucht." *Zeitschrift für die Neutestamentliche Wissenschaft* 22:206–28.

Kümmel, W. G.
1957   *Promise and Fulfilment: The Eschatological Message of Jesus*. Translated by D. M. Barton. Studies in Biblical Theology 23. London: SCM/Naperville, Ill.: Allenson.
1975   *Introduction to the New Testament*. Revised edition. Translated by H. C. Kee. Nashville: Abingdon.

Kürzinger, J.
1974   "Lk 1,3: . . . Ἀκριβῶς Καθεξῆς Σοι Γράψαι." *Biblische Zeitschrift* 18:249–55.

Lake, K.
1910   "Christmas." Vol. 3 / pp. 601–8 in *Encyclopaedia of Religion and Ethics*. Edited by J. Hastings. Edinburgh: Clark/New York: Scribner.

Lambert, W. G.
1960   *Babylonian Wisdom Literature*. Oxford: Clarendon.

Lane, W. L.
1974   *The Gospel according to Mark*. New International Commentary on the New Testament. Grand Rapids: Eerdmans.

La Potterie, I. de
1970   "Le Titre Κύριος Appliqué à Jésus dans l'Évangile du Luc." Pp. 117–46 in *Mélanges Bibliques en Hommage au R. P. Béda Rigaux*. Edited by A. Descamps and A. de Halleux. Gembloux: Duculot.

LaSor, W. S.
1972   *The Dead Sea Scrolls and the New Testament*. Grand Rapids: Eerdmans.

Laurentin, R.
1957a   *Structure et Théologie de Luc I–II*. Paris: Gabalda.
1957b   "Traces d'Allusions Étymologiques en Luc 1–2, [part] II." *Biblica* 38:1–23.
1967   *Struktur und Theologie der lukanischen Kindheitsgeschichte*. Translated by P. W. Arnold. Stuttgart: Katholisches Bibelwerk.

Lauterbach, J. Z.
1933–35 *Mekilta de-Rabbi Ishmael*. 3 vols. Philadelphia: Jewish Publication Society.

Leaney, A. R. C.
1958   *A Commentary on the Gospel according to St. Luke*. Harper's (Black's) New Testament Commentaries. New York: Harper/London: Black.
1961–62 "The Birth Narratives in St Luke and St Matthew." *New Testament Studies* 8:155–66.

Légasse, S.
1969   *Jésus et l'Enfant: "Enfants," "Petits" et "Simples" dans la Tradition Synoptique*. Études Bibliques. Paris: Gabalda.

Legault, A.
1954   "An Application of the Form-Critique Method to the Anointings in Galilee (Lk. 7,36–50) and Bethany (Mt. 26,6–13; Mk. 14,3–9; Jn. 12,1–8)." *Catholic Biblical Quarterly* 16:131–45.

Leipoldt, J.
1955   *Die Frau in der antiken Welt und im Urchristentum*. 2d edition. Leipzig: Koehler & Amelang.

Leisegang, H.
1922   *Pneuma Hagion: Der Ursprung des Geistbegriffs der synoptischen Evangelien aus der griechischen Mystik*. Veröffentlichungen des Forschungsinstituts für vergleichende Religionsgeschichte an der Universität Leipzig 4. Leipzig: Hinrichs.

Lentzen-Deis, F.

1970   *Die Taufe Jesus nach den Synoptikern: Literarkritische und gattungsgeschichtliche Untersuchungen.* Frankfurter Theologische Studien 4. Frankfurt am Main: Knecht.

Lerner, M. B.

1987   "The External Tractates." Pp. 367–403 in *The Literature of the Sages,* vol. 1: *Oral Tora, Halakha, Mishna, Tosefta, Talmud, External Tractates.* Edited by S. Safrai. Compendia Rerum Iudaicarum ad Novum Testamentum 2/3. Philadelphia: Fortress/Assen: Van Gorcum.

Liefeld, W. L.

1974   "Theological Motifs in the Transfiguration Narrative." Pp. 162–79 in *New Dimensions in New Testament Study.* Edited by R. N. Longenecker and M. C. Tenney. Grand Rapids: Zondervan.

1984   "Luke." Vol. 8 / pp. 797–1059 in *The Expositor's Bible Commentary.* Edited by F. E. Gaebelein. Grand Rapids: Zondervan.

Lightfoot, J. B.

1889–90   *The Apostolic Fathers.* 5 vols. in 2 parts. London: Macmillan. Reprinted Grand Rapids: Baker, 1981.

1890   "The Brethren of the Lord." Pp. 252–91 in *Saint Paul's Epistle to the Galatians.* 10th edition. London: Macmillan.

Lindars, B.

1983   *Jesus Son of Man: A Fresh Examination of the Son of Man Sayings in the Gospels in the Light of Recent Research.* London: SPCK.

Linnemann, E.

1966   *Jesus of the Parables: Introduction and Exposition.* Translated by J. Sturdy. New York: Harper & Row. (British edition: *The Parables of Jesus: Introduction and Exposition.* London: SPCK.)

Linton, O.

1975–76   "The Parable of the Children's Game: Baptist and Son of Man (Matt. xi.16–19 = Luke vii.31–5): A Synoptic Text-Critical, Structural and Exegetical Investigation." *New Testament Studies* 22:159–79.

Lohmeyer, E.

1959   *Das Evangelium des Markus.* Meyers kritisch-exegetischer Kommentar über das Neue Testament 1/2. Göttingen: Vandenhoeck & Ruprecht.

Lohse, E.

1960   "Jesu Worte über den Sabbat." Pp. 79–89 in *Judentum-Urchristentum-Kirche: Festschrift für Joachim Jeremias.* Edited by W. Eltester. Beiheft zur Zeitschrift für die Neutestamentliche Wissenschaft 26. Berlin: Töpelmann.

Longenecker, R. N.

1970   *The Christology of Early Jewish Christianity.* Studies in Biblical Theology 2/17. London: SCM/Naperville, Ill.: Allenson.

Löning, K.

1971   "Ein Platz für die Verlorenen: Zur Formkritik zweier neutestamentlicher Legenden (Lk 7,36–50; 19,1–10)." *Bibel und Leben* 12:198–208.

LSJ   *A Greek-English Lexicon.* 9th edition. By H. G. Liddell, R. Scott, and H. S. Jones. Oxford: Clarendon, 1968.

Luce, H. K.

1933   *The Gospel according to S. Luke.* Cambridge Greek Testament for Schools and Colleges. Cambridge: Cambridge University Press.

Luther, M.

1956   "The Sermon on the Mount." Translated by J. Pelikan. Pp. 1–294 in *Luther's Works,* vol. 21: *The Sermon on the Mount (Sermons) and the Magnificat.* Edited by J. Pelikan. St. Louis: Concordia. (Originally 1530–32. Reprinted as "Wochenpredigten über Matth. 5–7." Vol. 32 / pp. 299–544 in *D. Martin Luthers Werke: Kritische Gesamtausgabe.* Weimer: Böhlaus, 1906.)

McArthur, H. K.

1960   *Understanding the Sermon on the Mount.* New York: Harper.

Machen, J. G.
1930   *The Virgin Birth*. New York: Harper. Reprinted Grand Rapids: Baker, 1965.

McHugh, J.
1975   *The Mother of Jesus in the New Testament*. Garden City: Doubleday/London: Darton, Longman & Todd.

McKnight, S.
1991a   *A Light among the Gentiles: Jewish Missionary Activity in the Second Temple Period*. Minneapolis: Fortress.
1991b   "Source Criticism." Pp. 135–72 in *New Testament Criticism and Interpretation*. Edited by D. A. Black and D. S. Dockery. Grand Rapids: Zondervan.

Maddox, R.
1982   *The Purpose of Luke–Acts*. Forschungen zur Religion und Literatur des Alten und Neuen Testaments 126. Göttingen: Vandenhoeck & Ruprecht. Reprinted Edinburgh: Clark, 1982.

Major, H. D. A.
1944   *Basic Christianity*. Oxford: Blackwell.

Mánek, J.
1957–58a "Fishers of Men." *Novum Testamentum* 2:138–41.
1957–58b "The New Exodus in the Books of Luke." *Novum Testamentum* 2:8–23.
1967   "On the Mount—On the Plain (Mt. v 1—Lk. vi 17)." *Novum Testamentum* 9:124–31.

Mann, J., and I. Sonne
1940   *The Bible as Read and Preached in the Old Synagogue: A Study in the Cycles of the Readings from Torah and Prophets, as well as from Psalms, and in the Structure of the Midrashic Homilies*, vol. 1: *The Palestinian Triennial Cycle: Genesis and Exodus*. Cincinnati: Hebrew Union College, 1940. Reprinted New York: Ktav, 1971.

Manson, T. W.
1949   *The Sayings of Jesus: As Recorded in the Gospels according to St. Matthew and St. Luke*. London: SCM.

Marshall, I. H.
1968–69 "Son of God or Servant of Yahweh?—A Reconsideration of Mark i.11." *New Testament Studies* 15:326–36.
1969   "Tradition and Theology in Luke (Luke 8:5–15)." *Tyndale Bulletin* 20:56–75.
1970   *Luke: Historian and Theologian*. Grand Rapids: Zondervan/Exeter: Paternoster.
1978   *The Gospel of Luke: A Commentary on the Greek Text*. New International Greek Testament Commentary. Grand Rapids: Eerdmans.

Martin, J. A.
1986   "Dispensational Approaches to the Sermon on the Mount." Pp. 35–48 in *Essays in Honor of J. Dwight Pentecost*. Edited by S. D. Toussaint and C. H. Dyer. Chicago: Moody.
1992   "Christ, the Fulfillment of the Law in the Sermon on the Mount." Pp. 248–63 in *Dispensationalism, Israel and the Church: The Search for Definition*. Edited by C. A. Blaising and D. L. Bock. Grand Rapids: Zondervan.

Mattill, A. J., Jr.
1975   "The Jesus-Paul Parallels and the Purpose of Luke–Acts: H. H. Evans Reconsidered." *Novum Testamentum* 17:15–46.

Mauser, U.
1963   *Christ in the Wilderness: The Wilderness Theme in the Second Gospel and Its Basis in the Biblical Tradition*. Studies in Biblical Theology 39. London: SCM/Naperville, Ill.: Allenson.

May, E. E.
1952   " '. . . For Power Went Forth from Him . . .' (Luke 6,19)." *Catholic Biblical Quarterly* 14:93–103.

Meijboom, H. U.
1993   *A History and Critique of the Origin of the Marcan Hypothesis, 1835–1866: A Contemporary Report Rediscovered*. Translated and edited by J. J. Kiwiet. New Gospel Studies 8. Macon, Ga.: Mercer University Press.

Menzies, R. P.
1991   *The Development of Early Christian Pneumatology, with Special Reference to Luke–Acts.* Journal for the Study of the New Testament Supplement 54. Sheffield: JSOT Press.

Metzger, B. M.
1975   *A Textual Commentary on the Greek New Testament.* Corrected edition. London: United Bible Societies.
1992   *The Text of the New Testament.* 3d edition. Oxford: Oxford University Press.

Meyer, B. F.
1964   "But Mary Kept All These Things . . . (Lk 2,19.51)." *Catholic Biblical Quarterly* 26:31–49.

Michel, O., and O. Betz
1960   "Von Gott gezeugt." Pp. 3–23 in *Judentum, Urchristentum, Kirche: Festschrift für Joachim Jeremias.* Edited by W. Eltester. Beiheft zur Zeitschrift für die Neutestamentliche Wissenschaft 26. Berlin: Töpelmann.
1962–63 "Nocheinmal: 'Von Gott gezeugt.' " *New Testament Studies* 9:129–30.

Miller, M. P.
1969   "The Function of Isa 61:1–2 in 11Q Melchizedek." *Journal of Biblical Literature* 88:467–69.

MM   *The Vocabulary of the Greek Testament Illustrated from the Papyri and Other Non-literary Sources.* By J. H. Moulton and G. Milligan. Reprinted Grand Rapids: Eerdmans, 1980.

Moessner, D. P.
1983   "Luke 9:1–50: Luke's Preview of the Journey of the Prophet like Moses of Deuteronomy." *Journal of Biblical Literature* 102:575–605.
1989   *Lord of the Banquet: The Literary and Theological Significance of the Lukan Travel Narrative.* Minneapolis: Fortress.

Montefiore, C. G.
1930   *Rabbinic Literature and Gospel Teachings.* London: Macmillan.

Moore, G. F.
1927–30 *Judaism in the First Centuries of the Christian Era: The Age of the Tannaim.* 3 vols. Cambridge: Harvard University Press.

Morgan, G. C.
1931   *The Gospel according to Luke.* New York: Revell.

Moule, C. F. D.
1959   *An Idiom Book of New Testament Greek.* 2d edition. Cambridge: Cambridge University Press.
1966   "The Christology of Acts." Pp. 159–85 in *Studies in Luke–Acts: Essays Presented in Honor of Paul Schubert.* Edited by L. E. Keck and J. L. Martyn. Nashville: Abingdon. Reprinted Philadelphia: Fortress, 1980.

Müller, H.-P.
1960   "Die Verklärung Jesu: Eine motivgeschichtliche Studie." *Zeitschrift für die Neutestamentliche Wissenschaft* 51:56–64.

Mussner, F.
1975   "Καθεξῆς im Lukasprolog." Pp. 253–55 in *Jesus und Paulus: Festschrift für Werner Georg Kümmel zum 70. Geburtstag.* Edited by E. E. Ellis and E. Grässer. Göttingen: Vandenhoeck & Ruprecht.

NA   *Novum Testamentum Graece.* 26th edition. Edited by [E. Nestle], K. Aland, and B. Aland. Stuttgart: Deutsche Bibelstiftung, 1979.

Nauck, W.
1955   "Freude in Leiden: Zum Problem einer urchristlichen Verfolgungstradition." *Zeitschrift für die Neutestamentliche Wissenschaft* 46:68–80.

Neale, D. A.
1991   *None but the Sinners: Religious Categories in the Gospel of Luke.* Journal for the Study of the New Testament Supplement 58. Sheffield: Sheffield Academic Press.

Neirynck, F.
1973   "Minor Agreements Matthew-Luke in the Transfiguration Story." Pp. 253–66 in *Orientierung an Jesus: Zur Theologie der Synoptiker: Für Josef Schmid*. Edited by P. Hoffmann, N. Brox, and W. Pesch. Freiburg: Herder.

Nestle, E.
1903   "*Sykophantia* im biblischen Griech." *Zeitschrift für die Neutestamentliche Wissenschaft* 4:271–72.

1912   "Wer nicht mit mir ist, der ist wider mich." *Zeitschrift für die Neutestamentliche Wissenschaft* 13:84–87.

Neu Luther
    Die Bibel nach der Übersetzung Martin Luthers. Stuttgart: Deutsche Bibelgesellschaft, 1984.

Neusner, J.
1977–86   *The Tosefta*. 6 vols. New York: Ktav.

1984   *Judaism in the Beginning of Christianity*. Philadelphia: Fortress.

1986   *Sifré to Numbers: An American Translation and Explanation*. 2 vols. (through §115). Brown Judaic Studies 118 and119. Atlanta: Scholars Press. (Vol. 3 forthcoming by W. S. Green.)

1987   *Sifre to Deuteronomy: An Analytical Translation*. 2 vols. Brown Judaic Studies 98, 101. Atlanta: Scholars Press.

1988a   *Mekhilta according to Rabbi Ishmael: An Analytical Translation*. 2 vols. Brown Judaic Studies 148 and 154. Atlanta: Scholars Press.

1988b   *Sifra: An Analytical Translation*. 3 vols. Brown Judaic Studies 138–40. Atlanta: Scholars Press.

Neusner, J., and B. D. Chilton
1991   "Uncleanness: A Moral or an Ontological Category in the Early Centuries A.D.?" *Bulletin for Biblical Research* 1:63–88.

Neusner, J., et al.
1982–93   *The Talmud of the Land of Israel: A Preliminary Translation and Explanation*. 35 vols. Chicago: University of Chicago Press.

NIDNTT   *The New International Dictionary of New Testament Theology*. Edited by L. Coenen, E. Beyreuther, and H. Bietenhard. English translation edited by C. Brown. 4 vols. Grand Rapids: Zondervan, 1975–86.

Nolland, J.
1979   "Classical and Rabbinic Parallels to 'Physician, Heal Yourself' (Lk. iv 2)." *Novum Testamentum* 21:193–209.

1986   "Grace as Power." *Novum Testamentum* 28:26–31.

1989   *Luke 1–9:20*. Word Biblical Commentary 35a. Dallas: Word.

1993a   *Luke 9:21–18:34*. Word Biblical Commentary 35b. Dallas: Word.

1993b   *Luke 18:35–24:53*. Word Biblical Commentary 35c. Dallas: Word.

North, C. R.
1964   *The Second Isaiah: Introduction, Translation, and Commentary to Chapters xl–lv*. Oxford: Clarendon.

Noth, M.
1928   *Die israelitischen Personennamen im Rahmen der gemeinsemitischen Namengebung*. Beiträge zur Wissenschaft vom Alten und Neuen Testament 3/10. Stuttgart: Kohlhammer.

Núñez C., E. A.
1985   *Liberation Theology*. Translated by P. E. Sywulka. Chicago: Moody.

Ogg, G.
1940   *The Chronology of the Public Ministry of Jesus*. Cambridge: Cambridge University Press.

1962   "Chronology of the New Testament." Pp. 728–32 in *Peake's Commentary on the Bible*. Edited by M. Black and H. H. Rowley. London: Nelson.

O'Neill, J. C.
1959   "The Six Amen Sayings in Luke." *Journal of Theological Studies* n.s. 10:1–9.

1970   *The Theology of Acts in Its Historical Setting.* 2d edition. London: SPCK.

Orchard, B., and H. Riley

1987   *The Order of the Synoptics: Why Three Synoptic Gospels?* Macon, Ga.: Mercer University Press.

O'Toole, R. F.

1984   *The Unity of Luke's Theology: An Analysis of Luke–Acts.* Good News Studies 9. Wilmington, Del.: Glazier.

1987a   "The Kingdom of God in Luke–Acts." Pp. 147–62 in *The Kingdom of God in Twentieth-Century Interpretation.* Edited by W. Willis. Peabody, Mass.: Hendrickson.

1987b   "Luke's Message in Luke 9:1–50." *Catholic Biblical Quarterly* 49:74–89.

Payne, D. F.

1962   "Bethlehem." P. 144 in *The New Bible Dictionary.* Edited by J. D. Douglas. Grand Rapids: Eerdmans.

Payne, P. B.

1978–79   "The Order of Sowing and Ploughing in the Parable of the Sower." *New Testament Studies* 25:123–29.

1980   "The Authenticity of the Parable of the Sower and Its Interpretation." Pp. 163–207 in *Gospel Perspectives*, vol. 1: *Studies of History and Tradition in the Four Gospels.* Edited by R. T. France and D. Wenham. Sheffield: JSOT Press.

Pentecost, J. D.

1980   *The Sermon on the Mount: Contemporary Insights for a Christian Lifestyle.* Revised edition. Portland: Multnomah. (Originally *Design for Living: The Sermon on the Mount.* Chicago: Moody, 1975.)

Perrin, N.

1967   *Rediscovering the Teaching of Jesus.* New York: Harper & Row.

Perrot, C.

1973   "Luc 4,16–30 et la Lecture Biblique de l'Ancienne Synagogue." *Revue des Sciences Religieuses* 47:324–40.

Pesch, R.

1968a   "Levi-Matthäus (Mc 2:14 / Mt 9:9, 10:3): Ein Beitrag zur Lösung eines alten Problems." *Zeitschrift für die Neutestamentliche Wissenschaft* 59:40–56.

1970a   "Jaïrus (Mk 5,22/Lk 8,41)." *Biblische Zeitschrift* 14:252–56.

1970b   *Jesu ureigene Taten? Ein Beitrag zur Wunderfrage.* Questiones Disputatae 52. Freiburg: Herder.

1970c   "Das Zöllnergastmahl (Mk 2,15–17)." Pp. 63–87 in *Mélanges Bibliques en Hommage au R. P. Béda Rigaux.* Edited by A. Descamps and A. de Halleux. Gembloux: Duculot.

1971   "The Markan Version of the Healing of the Gerasene Demoniac." *Ecumenical Review* 23:349–76.

1972   *Der Besessene von Gerasa: Einstehung und Überlieferung einer Wundergeschichte.* Stuttgarter Bibelstudien 56. Stuttgart: Katholisches Bibelwerk.

1973–74   "Das Messiasbekenntnis des Petrus (Mk 8,27–30): Neuverhandlung einer alten Frage." *Biblische Zeitschrift* 17:178–95; 18:20–31.

PG   *Patrologiae Cursus Completus, Series Graeca.* Edited by J. P. Migne. 161 vols. Paris, 1857–66.

Pilgrim, W. E.

1971   *The Death of Christ in Lukan Soteriology.* Th.D. diss., Princeton University.

1981   *Good News to the Poor: Wealth and Poverty in Luke–Acts.* Minneapolis: Augsburg.

PL   *Patrologiae Cursus Completus, Series Latina.* Edited by J. P. Migne. 221 vols. Paris, 1844–55.

Plummer, A.

1896   *A Critical and Exegetical Commentary on the Gospel according to St. Luke.* International Critical Commentary. Edinburgh: Clark/New York: Scribner.

Plymale, S. F.

1991   *The Prayer Texts of Luke–Acts.* American University Studies, series 7: Theology and Religion 118. New York: Lang.

Polag, A.
1982   *Fragmenta Q: Textheft zur Logienquelle*. 2d edition. Neukirchen-Vluyn: Neukirchener Verlag.

Pousma, R. H.
1975   "Diseases of the Bible." Vol. 2 / pp. 132–42 in *The Zondervan Pictorial Encyclopedia of the Bible*. Edited by M. C. Tenney. Grand Rapids: Zondervan.

Power, E.
1923   "The Staff of the Apostles: A Problem in Gospel Harmony." *Biblica* 4:241–66.

Power, M. A.
1912   "Who Were They Who 'Understood Not'?" *Irish Theological Quarterly* 7:261–81, 444–59.

Rad, G. von
1962–65 *Old Testament Theology*. 2 vols. Translated by D. M. G. Stalker. New York: Harper & Row/Edinburgh: Oliver & Boyd.

Ragaz, L.
1945   *Der Bergpredigt Jesus*. Bern: H. Lang.

Ramsay, W. M.
1898   *Was Christ Born at Bethlehem? A Study on the Credibility of St. Luke*. London: Hodder & Stoughton/New York: Putnam.

1920   *The Bearing of Recent Discovery on the Trustworthiness of the New Testament*. 4th edition. London: Hodder & Stoughton.

Reicke, B.
1968   *New Testament Era: The World of the Bible from 500 B.C. to A.D. 100*. Translated by D. E. Green. Philadelphia: Fortress.

1973   "Jesus in Nazareth—Lk 4,14–30." Pp. 47–55 in *Das Wort und die Wörter: Festschrift Gerhard Friedrich zum 65. Geburtstag*. Edited by H. Balz and S. Schulz. Stuttgart: Kohlhammer.

1986   *The Roots of the Synoptic Gospels*. Philadelphia: Fortress.

Rengstorf, K. H.
1968   *Das Evangelium nach Lukas*. Das Neue Testament Deutsch 3. Göttingen: Vandenhoeck & Ruprecht.

Rese, M.
1969   *Alttestamentliche Motive in der Christologie des Lukas*. Studien zum Neuen Testament 1. Gütersloh: Mohn.

Ringgren, H.
1963   *The Faith of Qumran: Theology of the Dead Sea Scrolls*. Translated by E. T. Sander. Philadelphia: Fortress.

Rist, J. M.
1978   *On the Independence of Matthew and Mark*. Society for New Testament Studies Monograph Series 32. Cambridge: Cambridge University Press.

Robertson, A. T.
1923   *A Grammar of the Greek New Testament in the Light of Historical Research*. 4th edition. Nashville: Broadman.

1923–24 "The Implications in Luke's Preface." *Expository Times* 35:319–21.

Robinson, J. A. T.
1957   "The Baptism of John and the Qumran Community: Testing a Hypothesis." *Harvard Theological Review* 50 (1957): 175–91. Reprinted in Robinson's *Twelve New Testament Studies*, pp. 11–27. Studies in Biblical Theology 34. London: SCM/Naperville, Ill.: Allenson, 1962.

Robinson, W. C., Jr.
1966   "On Preaching the Word of God (Luke 8:4–21)." Pp. 131–38 in *Studies in Luke–Acts: Essays Presented in Honor of Paul Schubert*. Edited by L. E. Keck and J. L. Martyn. Nashville: Abingdon. Reprinted Philadelphia: Fortress, 1980.

Roloff, J.
1970   *Das Kerygma und der irdische Jesus: Historische Motive in den Jesus-Erzählungen der Evangelien*. Göttingen: Vandenhoeck & Ruprecht.

Ropes, J. H.
1923–24   "St. Luke's Preface: Ἀσφάλεια and Παρακολουθεῖν." *Journal of Theological Studies* o.s. 25:67–71.

Rüger, H. P.
1969   "Mit welchem Maß ihr meßt, wird euch gemessen werden." *Zeitschrift für die Neutestamentliche Wissenschaft* 60:174–82.

Safrai, S.
1974   "Relations between the Diaspora and the Land of Israel." Vol. 1 / pp. 184–215 in *The Jewish People in the First Century.* Edited by S. Safrai and M. Stern. Compendia Rerum Iudaicarum ad Novum Testamentum 1/2. Philadelphia: Fortress/Assen: Van Gorcum.

1976a   "Home and Family." Vol. 2 / pp. 728–92 in *The Jewish People in the First Century.* Edited by S. Safrai and M. Stern. Compendia Rerum Iudaicarum ad Novum Testamentum 1/2. Philadelphia: Fortress/Assen: Van Gorcum.

1976b   "Religion in Everyday Life." Vol. 2 / pp. 793–833 in *The Jewish People in the First Century.* Edited by S. Safrai and M. Stern. Compendia Rerum Iudaicarum ad Novum Testamentum 1/2. Philadelphia: Fortress/Assen: Van Gorcum.

1976c   "The Synagogue." Vol. 2 / pp. 908–44 in *The Jewish People in the First Century.* Edited by S. Safrai and M. Stern. Compendia Rerum Iudaicarum ad Novum Testamentum 1/2. Philadelphia: Fortress/Assen: Van Gorcum.

1976d   "The Temple." Vol. 2 / pp. 865–907 in *The Jewish People in the First Century.* Edited by S. Safrai and M. Stern. Compendia Rerum Iudaicarum ad Novum Testamentum 1/2. Philadelphia: Fortress/Assen: Van Gorcum.

Sahlin, H.
1945   *Der Messias und das Gottesvolk: Studien zur protolukanischen Theologie.* Uppsala: Almqvist & Wiksell.

Salmon, M.
1988   "Insider or Outsider? Luke's Relationship with Judaism." Pp. 76–82 in *Luke–Acts and the Jewish People: Eight Critical Perspectives.* Edited by J. B. Tyson. Minneapolis: Augsburg.

Sanders, E. P.
1985   *Jesus and Judaism.* Philadelphia: Fortress.
1992   *Judaism: Practice and Belief, 63 BCE–66 CE.* London: SCM/Philadelphia: Trinity.

Sanders, J. A.
1975   "From Isaiah 61 to Luke 4." Pp. 75–106 in *Christianity, Judaism, and other Greco-Roman Cults: Studies for Morton Smith at Sixty,* vol. 1: *New Testament.* Edited by J. Neusner. Studies in Judaism in Late Antiquity 12/1. Leiden: Brill. Reprinted and revised in C. A. Evans and J. A. Sanders's *Luke and Scripture: The Function of Sacred Tradition in Luke–Acts,* pp. 46–69. Minneapolis: Fortress, 1993.

1993   "Isaiah in Luke." Pp. 14–25 in *Luke and Scripture: The Function of Sacred Tradition in Luke–Acts.* By C. A. Evans and J. A. Sanders. Minneapolis: Fortress.

Sanders, J. T.
1987   *The Jews in Luke–Acts.* Philadelphia: Fortress.

Saucy, M.
1994   "The Kingdom-of-God Sayings in Matthew." *Bibliotheca Sacra.* 151:175–97.

SB   *Kommentar zum Neuen Testament aus Talmud und Midrasch.* By H. L. Strack and P. Billerbeck. 6 vols. Munich: Beck, 1922–61.

Schalit, A.
1968   *Namenwörterbuch zu Flavius Josephus.* Supplement 1 to *A Complete Concordance to Flavius Josephus,* edited by K. H. Rengstorf. Leiden: Brill.

Schenke, L.
1974   *Die Wundererzählungen des Markusevangeliums.* Stuttgarter biblische Beiträge. Stuttgart: Katholisches Bibelwerk.

Schlatter, A. von
1960   *Das Evangelium des Lukas aus seinen Quellen erklärt.* 2d edition. Stuttgart: Calwer.

Schmahl, G.
1974   "Lk 2,41–52 und die Kindheitserzählung des Thomas 19,1–5: Ein Vergleich." *Bibel und Leben* 15:249–58.

Schmid, J.
1960   *Das Evangelium nach Lukas*. 4th edition. Regensburger Neues Testament 3. Regensburg: Pustet.

Schmidt, T. E.
1987   *Hostility to Wealth in the Synoptic Gospels*. Journal for the Study of the New Testament Supplement 15. Sheffield: JSOT Press.

Schneemelcher, W.
1991–92 *New Testament Apocrypha*. Revised edition. 2 vols. English translation edited by R. M. Wilson. Philadelphia: Westminster/John Knox.

Schneider, G.
1971   "Luke 1,34.35 als redaktionelle Einheit." *Biblische Zeitschrift* 15:255–59.
1977a   *Das Evangelium nach Lukas*. 2 vols. Ökumenischer Taschenbuch-Kommentar 3. Gütersloh: Mohn.
1977b   "Zur Bedeutung von Καθεξῆς im lukanischen Doppelwerk." *Zeitschrift für die Neutestamentliche Wissenschaft* 68:128–31.

Schoonheim, P. L.
1966   "Der alttestamentliche Boden der Vokabel Ὑπερήφανος in Lukas i 51." *Novum Testamentum* 8:235–46.

Schottroff, L., and W. Stegemann
1986   *Jesus and the Hope of the Poor*. Translated by M. J. O'Connell. Maryknoll, N.Y.: Orbis.

Schramm, T.
1971   *Der Markus-Stoff bei Lukas: Eine literarkritische und redaktionsgeschichtliche Untersuchung*. Society for New Testament Studies Monograph Series 14. Cambridge: Cambridge University Press.

Schreck, C. J.
1989   "The Nazareth Pericope: Luke 4,16–30 in Recent Study." Pp. 399–471 in *L'Évangile de Luc—The Gospel of Luke*. Edited by F. Neirynck. 2d edition. Bibliotheca Ephemeridum Theologicarum Lovaniensium 32. Louvain: Leuven University Press/Peeters.

Schulz, S.
1972   *Q: Die Spruchquelle der Evangelisten*. Zurich: Theologischer Verlag.

Schürer, E.
1890   *A History of the Jewish People in the Time of Jesus Christ*, vol. 2. Translated by J. Macpherson. Edinburgh: Clark/New York: Scribner.
1973–87 *The History of the Jewish People in the Age of Jesus Christ (175 B.C.–A.D. 135)*. Revised edition. 3 vols. Edited by G. Vermes, F. Millar, and M. Black. Edinburgh: Clark.

Schürmann, H.
1964   "Der 'Bericht vom Anfang': Ein Rekonstruktionsversuch auf Grund von Lk. 4,14–16." Pp. 242–58 in *Studia Evangelica*, vol. 2: *Papers Presented to the Second International Congress on New Testament Studies Held at Christ Church, Oxford, 1961*, part 1: *The New Testament Scriptures*. Edited by F. L. Cross. Texte und Untersuchungen 87. Berlin: Akademie-Verlag. Reprinted in Schürmann's *Traditionsgeschichtliche Untersuchungen zu den synoptischen Evangelien*, pp. 69–80. Düsseldorf: Patmos, 1968.
1969   *Das Lukasevangelium*, vol. 1. Herders theologischer Kommentar zum Neuen Testament 3. Freiburg: Herder.
1973   "Wie hat Jesus seinen Tod bestanden und verstanden? Eine methodenkritische Besinnung." Pp. 325–63 in *Orientierung an Jesus: Zur Theologie der Synoptiker: Für Josef Schmid*. Edited by P. Hoffmann, N. Brox, and W. Pesch. Freiburg: Herder.

Schweitzer, A.
1910   *The Quest for the Historical Jesus: A Critical Study of Its Progress from Reimarus to Wrede*. Translated by W. Montgomery. London: Macmillan.

Schweizer, E.
1984   *The Good News according to Luke*. Translated by D. E. Green. Atlanta: John Knox.

Scobie, C. H. H.
  1964   *John the Baptist*. Philadelphia: Fortress.
Scott, B. B.
  1989   *Hear Then the Parable: A Commentary on the Parables of Jesus*. Minneapolis: Fortress.
Seecombe, D. P.
  1982   *Possessions and the Poor in Luke–Acts*. Studien zum Neuen Testament und seiner Umwelt B/6. Linz: Plöchl.
Seitz, O. J. F.
  1969–70 "Love Your Enemies: The Historical Setting of Matthew v.43f.; Luke vi.27f." *New Testament Studies* 16:39–54.
Sherwin-White, A. N.
  1963   *Roman Society and Roman Law in the New Testament*. Sarum Lectures 1960–61. Oxford: Clarendon.
Shin Kyo-Seon, G.
  1989   *Die Ausrufung des endgültigen Jubeljahres durch Jesus in Nazaret: Eine historisch-kritische Studie zu Lk 4,16–30*. Europäische Hochschulschriften 23/378. Bern: Lang.
Siegman, E. F.
  1968   "St. John's Use of the Synoptic Material." *Catholic Biblical Quarterly* 30:182–98.
Sjöberg, E. K. T.
  1938   *Gott und die Sünder im palästinischen Judentum nach, dem Zeugnis der Tannaiten und der apokryphisch-pseudepigraphischen Literatur*. Beiträge zur Wissenschaft vom Alten und Neuen Testament 79 (4/27). Stuttgart: Kohlhammer.
Skeat, T. C.
  1988   "The 'Second-First' Sabbath (Luke 6:1): The Final Solution." *Novum Testamentum* 30:103–6.
Sloan, R. B., Jr.
  1977   *The Favorable Year of the Lord: A Study of Jubilary Theology in the Gospel of Luke*. Austin: Schola.
Smith, M.
  1971   "Zealots and Sicarii: Their Origins and Relation." *Harvard Theological Review* 64:1–19.
Snodgrass, K. R.
  1980   "Streams of Tradition Emerging from Isaiah 40:1–5 and Their Adaptation in the New Testament." *Journal for the Study of the New Testament* 8:24–45.
  1983   *The Parable of the Wicked Tenants: An Inquiry into Parable Interpretation*. Wissenschaftliche Untersuchungen zum Neuen Testament 27. Tübingen: Mohr.
Sparks, H. F. D.
  1936   "The Partiality of Luke for 'Three,' and Its Bearing on the Original of Q." *Journal of Theological Studies* o.s. 37:141–45.
Stamm, F. K.
  1943   *Seeing the Multitudes*. New York: Harper.
Stanley, D. M.
  1959–60 "The Mother of My Lord." *Worship* 34:330–32.
Stauffer, E.
  1960   *Jesus and His Story*. Translated by D. M. Barton. New York: Knopf/London: SCM.
Stegner, W. R.
  1989   *Narrative Theology in Early Jewish Christianity*. Louisville: Westminster/John Knox.
Stein, R. H.
  1976   "Is the Transfiguration (Mark 9:2–8) a Misplaced Resurrection-Account?" *Journal of Biblical Literature* 95:79–96.
  1978   *The Method and Message of Jesus' Teachings*. Philadelphia: Westminster.
  1987   *The Synoptic Problem: An Introduction*. Grand Rapids: Baker.
  1992   *Luke*. New American Commentary 24. Nashville: Broadman.

Stendahl, K.
1954   *The School of St. Matthew and Its Use of the Old Testament*. Acta Seminarii Neotestamentici Upsaliensis 20. Lund: Gleerup/Copenhagen: Munksgaard. Reprinted Philadelphia: Fortress, 1968.

Sterling, G. E.
1992   *Historiography and Self-Definition: Josephos* [sic], *Luke–Acts and Apologetic Historiography*. Novum Testamentum Supplement 64. Leiden: Brill.

Stern, M.
1974   "The Province of Judaea." Vol. 1 / pp. 308–76 in *The Jewish People in the First Century*. Edited by S. Safrai and M. Stern. Compendia Rerum Iudaicarum ad Novum Testamentum 1/2. Philadelphia: Fortress/Assen: Van Gorcum.
1976   "Aspects of Jewish Society: The Priesthood and Other Classes." Vol. 2 / pp. 561–630 in *The Jewish People in the First Century*. Edited by S. Safrai and M. Stern. Compendia Rerum Iudaicarum ad Novum Testamentum 1/2. Philadelphia: Fortress/Assen: Van Gorcum.

Strack, H. L., and G. Stemberger
1991   *Introduction to the Talmud and Midrash*. Translated by M. Bockmuehl. Edinburgh: Clark.

Strauss, D. F.
1972   *The Life of Jesus Critically Examined*. Translated by G. Eliot (from the 4th edition, 1840). Edited by P. C. Hodgson. Philadelphia: Fortress/London: SCM.

Strecker, G.
1978   "Die Antithesen der Bergpredigt (Mt 5:21–48 par)." *Zeitschrift für die Neutestamentliche Wissenschaft* 69:36–72.
1988   *The Sermon on the Mount: An Exegetical Commentary*. Translated by O. C. Dean Jr. Nashville: Abingdon.

Streeter, B. H.
1924   *The Four Gospels: A Study of Origins, Treating of the Manuscript Tradition, Sources, Authorship, and Dates*. London: Macmillan.

Strobel, A.
1958a   "Lukas der Antiochener (Bemerkungen zu Act 11,28 D)." *Zeitschrift für die Neutestamentliche Wissenschaft* 49:131–34.
1961   *Untersuchungen zum eschatologischen Verzögerungsproblem: Auf Grund der spätjüdisch-urchristlichen Geschichte von Habakuk 2,2ff*. Novum Testamentum Supplement 2. Leiden: Brill.
1972   "Das Ausrufung des Jobeljahrs in der Nazarethpredigt Jesu: Zur apokalyptischen Tradition Lc 4:16–30." Pp. 38–50 in *Jesus in Nazareth*. By E. Grässer et al. Beiheft zur Zeitschrift für die Neutestamentliche Wissenschaft 40. Berlin: de Gruyter.

Stuhlmacher, P.
1968   *Das paulinische Evangelium*, vol. 1: *Vorgeschichte*. Forschungen zur Religion und Literatur des Alten und Neuen Testamentes 95. Göttingen: Vandenhoeck & Ruprecht.
1986   *Reconciliation, Law, and Righteousness: Essays in Biblical Theology*. Translated by E. Kalin. Philadelphia: Fortress.

Suggs, M. J.
1970   *Wisdom, Christology, and Law in Matthew's Gospel*. Cambridge: Harvard University Press.
1978   "The Antitheses as Redactional Products." Pp. 93–107 in *Essays on the Love Commandment*. By L. Schottroff et al. Philadelphia: Fortress.

Swartley, W. M.
1983   "Politics or Peace (*Eirēnē*) in Luke's Gospel." Pp. 18–37 in *Political Issues in Luke–Acts*. Edited by R. J. Cassidy and P. J. Scharper. Maryknoll, N.Y.: Orbis.

Sylva, D. D.
1990   *Reimaging the Death of the Lukan Jesus*. Bonner biblische Beiträge 73. Frankfurt am Main: Hain.

Talbert, C. H.

1974   *Literary Patterns, Theological Themes, and the Genre of Luke–Acts*. Society of Biblical Literature Monograph Series 20. Missoula, Mont.: Scholars Press.

1978   *Luke and the Gnostics: An Examination of the Lucan Purpose*. Special Studies Series 5. Danville, Va.: Association of Baptist Professors of Religion.

1982   *Reading Luke: A Literary and Theological Commentary on the Third Gospel*. New York: Crossroad.

Tanenbaum, M. H.

1974   "Holy Year 1975 and Its Origins in the Jewish Jubilee Year." *Jubilaeum* 7:63–79.

Tannehill, R. C.

1972   "The Mission of Jesus according to Luke iv 16–30." Pp. 51–75 in *Jesus in Nazareth*. By E. Grässer et al. Beiheft zur Zeitschrift für die Neutestamentliche Wissenschaft 40. Berlin: de Gruyter.

1974   "The Magnificat as Poem." *Journal of Biblical Literature* 93:263–75.

1985   "Israel in Luke–Acts: A Tragic Story." *Journal of Biblical Literature* 104:69–85.

1986   *The Narrative Unity of Luke–Acts: A Literary Interpretation*, vol. 1: *The Gospel according to Luke*. Foundations and Facets. Philadelphia: Fortress.

Taylor, V.

1935   *The Formation of the Gospel Tradition*. 2d edition. London: Macmillan.

1966   *The Gospel according to St. Mark*. 2d edition. London: Macmillan. Reprinted Grand Rapids: Baker, 1981.

TDNT   *Theological Dictionary of the New Testament*. Edited by G. Kittel and G. Friedrich. Translated and edited by G. W. Bromiley. 10 vols. Grand Rapids: Eerdmans, 1964–76.

Theissen, G.

1983   *The Miracle Stories of the Early Christian Tradition*. Translated by F. McDonagh. Edited by J. Riches. Philadelphia: Fortress/Edinburgh: Clark.

Theobald, M.

1984   "Die Anfänge der Kirche: Zur Struktur von Lk. 5.1–6.19." *New Testament Studies* 30:91–108.

Thomas, R. L., and S. N. Gundry

1978   *A Harmony of the Gospels, with Explanations and Essays*. Chicago: Moody.

Thrall, M. E.

1969–70   "Elijah and Moses in Mark's Account of the Transfiguration." *New Testament Studies* 16:305–17.

Thyen, H.

1970   *Studien zur Sündenvergebung im Neuen Testament und seinen alttestamentlichen und jüdischen Voraussetzungen*. Forschungen zur Religion und Literatur des Alten und Neuen Testamentes 96. Göttingen: Vandenhoeck & Ruprecht.

Tiede, D. L.

1980   *Prophecy and History in Luke–Acts*. Philadelphia: Fortress.

1988   *Luke*. Augsburg Commentary on the New Testament. Minneapolis: Augsburg.

Tödt, H. E.

1979   *Der Menschensohn in der synoptischen Überlieferung*. 4th edition. Gütersloh: Mohn. (An English edition of the 2d German edition [1963] is available: *The Son of Man in the Synoptic Tradition*. Translated by D. M. Barton. New Testament Library. Philadelphia: Westminster/London: SCM, 1965.)

Torrey, C. C.

1943   "The Name 'Iscariot.'" *Harvard Theological Review* 36:51–62.

Toussaint, S. D.

1980   *Behold the King: A Study of Matthew*. Portland: Multnomah.

Townsend, J. T.

1984   "The Date of Luke–Acts." Pp. 47–62 in *Luke–Acts: New Perspectives from the Society of Biblical Literature Seminar*. Edited by C. H. Talbert. New York: Crossroad.

1989   *Midrash Tanḥuma (S. Buber Recension)*, vol. 1: *Genesis*. Hoboken, N.J.: Ktav.

Tuckett, C. M.
1983   *The Revival of the Griesbach Hypothesis: An Analysis and Appraisal*. Society for New Testament Studies Monograph 44. Cambridge: Cambridge University Press.

Tuckett, C. M. (ed.)
1983   *The Messianic Secret*. Issues in Religion and Theology 1. Philadelphia: Fortress/London: SPCK.

Turner, C. H.
1925–26   "'Ο Υἱός Μου ὁ Ἀγαπητός." *Journal of Theological Studies* o.s. 27:113–29.

Turner, D. L.
1991   " 'Dubious Evangelicalism?' A Response to John Gerstner's *Critique of Dispensationalism*." *Grace Theological Journal* 12:263–77.

Turner, M. M. B.
1982   "The Sabbath, Sunday, and the Law in Luke/Acts." Pp. 99–157 in *From Sabbath to Lord's Day: A Biblical, Historical, and Theological Investigation*. Edited by D. A. Carson. Grand Rapids: Zondervan.

Turner, N.
1963   *A Grammar of New Testament Greek*, vol. 3: *Syntax*. Edinburgh: Clark.

Tyson, J. B.
1986   *The Death of Jesus in Luke–Acts*. Columbia: University of South Carolina Press.

UBS³   *The Greek New Testament*. 3d corrected edition. Edited by K. Aland, M. Black, C. M. Martini, B. M. Metzger, and A. Wikgren. New York: United Bible Societies, 1983.

UBS⁴   *The Greek New Testament*. 4th edition. Edited by B. Aland, K. Aland, J. Karavidopoulos, C. M. Martini, and B. M. Metzger. New York: United Bible Societies, 1993.

Van Der Loos, H.
1965   *The Miracles of Jesus*. Novum Testament Supplement 9. Leiden: Brill.

Van Iersel, B. M. F.
1960   "The Finding of Jesus in the Temple: Some Observations on the Original Form of Luke ii 41–51a." *Novum Testamentum* 4:161–73.
1967   "La Vocation de Lévi (Mc., ii,13–17; Mt., ix,9–13; Lc., v,27–32): Traditions et Rédactions." Pp. 212–32 in *De Jésus aux Évangiles: Tradition et Rédaction des le Évangiles Synoptiques*, vol. 2. Edited by I. de La Potterie. Bibliotheca Ephemeridum Theologicarum Lovaniensium 25/2. Gembloux: Duculot.

Van Unnik, W. C.
1960   "The 'Book of Acts' the Confirmation of the Gospel." *Novum Testamentum* 4:26–59.
1964   "Die rechte Bedeutung des Wortes treffen, Lukas 2,19." Pp. 129–47 in *Verbum: Essays on Some Aspects of the Religious Function of Words, Dedicated to Dr. H. W. Obbink*. By T. P. Van Baaren et al. Studia Theologica Rheno-Traiectina 6. Utrecht: Kemink. Reprinted in *Sparsa Collecta: The Collected Essays of W. C. Van Unnik*, vol. 1: *Evangelia, Paulina, Acta*, pp. 72–91. Novum Testamentum Supplement 29. Leiden: Brill, 1973.
1966   "Die Motivierung der Feindesliebe in Lukas vi 32–35." *Novum Testamentum* 8:284–300.
1973   "Once More St. Luke's Prologue." *Neotestamentica* 7:7–26.
1979   "Luke's Second Book and the Rules of Hellenistic Historiography." Pp. 37–60 in *Les Actes des Apôtres: Traditions, Rédaction, Théologie*. Edited by J. Kremer. Bibliotheca Ephemeridum Theologicarum Lovaniensium 48. Gembloux: Duculot/Louvain: Leuven University Press.

Vermes, G.
1967   "The Use of בר נשא/בר נש in Jewish Aramaic." Pp. 310–30 in *An Aramaic Approach to the Gospels and Acts*, by M. Black. 3d edition. Oxford: Clarendon.
1973   *Jesus the Jew: A Historian's Reading of the Gospels*. New York: Macmillan/London: Collins. Reprinted Philadelphia: Fortress, 1981.

Vielhauer, P.
1952   "Das Benedictus des Zacharias (Luk. 1,68–79)." *Zeitschrift für Theologie und Kirche* 49:255–72.

1965   "Ein Weg zur neutestamentlichen Christologie? Prüfung der Thesen Ferdinand Hahn." *Evangelische Theologie* 25:24–72. Reprinted in Vielhauer's *Aufsätze zum Neuen Testament*, pp. 141–98. Theologische Bücherei 31. Munich: Kaiser, 1965.

1966   "On the 'Paulinism' of Acts." Translated by W. C. Robinson Jr. and V. P. Furnish. Pp. 33–50 in *Studies in Luke–Acts: Essays Presented in Honor of Paul Schubert*. Edited by L. E. Keck and J. L. Martyn. Nashville: Abingdon/London: SPCK.

Violet, B.

1938   "Zum rechten Verständnis der Nazareth-Perikope Lc 4$^{16-30}$." *Zeitschrift für die Neutestamentliche Wissenschaft* 37:251–71.

Vogt, E.

1959   "Sabbatum 'Deuteróprōton' in Lc 6,1 et Antiquum Kalendarium Sacerdotale." *Biblica* 40:102–5.

Völkel, M.

1973–74   "Exegetische Erwägungen zum Verständnis des Begriffs Καθεξῆς im lukanischen Prolog." *New Testament Studies* 20:289–99.

1978   "Freund der Zöllner und Sünder." *Zeitschrift für die Neutestamentliche Wissenschaft* 69:1–10.

Walker, W. O., Jr.

1978   "Jesus and the Tax Collectors." *Journal of Biblical Literature* 97:221–38.

Walvoord, J. F.

1974   *Matthew: Thy Kingdom Come*. Chicago: Moody.

Webb, R. L.

1991   *John the Baptizer and Prophet: A Socio-Historical Study*. Journal for the Study of the New Testament Supplement 62. Sheffield: Sheffield Academic Press.

Wegner, U.

1985   *Der Hauptmann von Kafarnaum (Mt 7,28a; 8,5–10.13 par Lk 7,1–10): Ein Beitrag zur Q-Forschung*. Wissenschaftliche Untersuchungen zum Neuen Testament 2/14. Tübingen: Mohr.

Wellhausen, J.

1904   *Das Evangelium Lucae*. Berlin: Reimer.

Wenham, D.

1972   "The Synoptic Problem Revisited: Some New Suggestions about the Composition of Mark 4:1–34." *Tyndale Bulletin* 23:3–38.

1973–74   "The Interpretation of the Parable of the Sower." *New Testament Studies* 20:299–319

Wenham, J. W.

1992a   *Redating Matthew, Mark and Luke: A Fresh Assault on the Synoptic Problem*. Downers Grove, Ill.: InterVarsity.

Westermann, C.

1969   *Isaiah 40–66: A Commentary*. Old Testament Library. Translated by D. M. G. Stalker. Philadelphia: Westminster/London: SCM.

White, K. D.

1964   "The Parable of the Sower." *Journal of Theological Studies* n.s. 15:300–307.

Wiefel, W.

1988   *Das Evangelium nach Lukas*. Theologischer Handkommentar zum Neuen Testament 3. Berlin: Evangelische Verlagsanstalt.

Wight, F. H.

1953   *Manners and Customs of Bible Lands*. Chicago: Moody.

Wilckens, U.

1973   "Vergebung für die Sünderin (Lk 7,36–50)." Pp. 394–424 in *Orientierung an Jesus: Zur Theologie der Synoptiker: Für Josef Schmid*. Edited by P. Hoffmann, N. Brox, and W. Pesch. Freiburg: Herder.

Wilcox, M.

1965   *The Semitisms of Acts*. Oxford: Clarendon.

Wilson, S. G.

1973   *The Gentiles and the Gentile Mission in Luke–Acts*. Society for New Testament Studies Monograph Series 23. Cambridge: Cambridge University Press.

1983   *Luke and the Law*. Society for New Testament Studies Monograph 50. Cambridge: Cambridge University Press.

Winandy, J.
1965   "La Prophétie de Syméon (Lc, ii,34–35)." *Revue Biblique* 72:321–51.

Windisch, H.
1951   *The Meaning of the Sermon on the Mount: A Contribution to the Historical Understanding of the Gospels and to the Problem of Their True Exegesis*. Translated by S. M. Gilmour. Philadelphia: Westminster.

Wink, W.
1968   *John the Baptist in the Gospel Tradition*. Society for New Testament Studies Monograph Series 7. Cambridge: Cambridge University Press.

Winter, P.
1954   "Lc 2:49 and Targum Yerushalmi." *Zeitschrift für die Neutestamentliche Wissenschaft* 45:145–79.
1954–55 "Magnificat and Benedictus—Maccabaean Psalms?" *Bulletin of the John Rylands Library* 37:328–47.
1955   "'Ὅτι *Recitativum* in Luke i 25, 61, ii 23." *Harvard Theological Review* 48:213–16.
1956   "On Luke and Lucan Sources: A Reply to the Reverend N. Turner." *Zeitschrift für die Neutestamentliche Wissenschaft* 47:217–42.
1958   "Lukanische Miszellen, III: Lc 2[11]: Χριστὸς Κύριος oder Χριστὸς Κυρίου?" *Zeitschrift für die Neutestamentliche Wissenschaft* 49:67–75.

Witherington, B., III
1979   "On the Road with Mary Magdalene, Joanna, Susanna, and Other Disciples—Luke 8:1–3." *Zeitschrift für die Neutestamentliche Wissenschaft* 70:243–48.
1990   *The Christology of Jesus*. Minneapolis: Fortress.

Wood, H. G.
1954–55 "The Use of Ἀγαπάω in Luke viii.42, 47." *Expository Times* 66:319–20.

Wrede, W.
1971   *The Messianic Secret*. Translated by J. C. G. Greig. Cambridge: Clarke. (Originally *Das Messiasgeheimnis in den Evangelien: Zugleich ein Beitrag zum Verständnis des Markusevangeliums*. Göttingen: Vandenhoeck & Ruprecht, 1901.)

Wrege, H.-T.
1968   *Die Überlieferungsgeschichte der Bergpredigt*. Wissenschaftliche Untersuchungen zum Neuen Testament 9. Tübingen: Mohr.

Wuellner, W. H.
1967   *The Meaning of "Fishers of Men."* New Testament Library. Philadelphia: Westminster.

Zahn, T.
1920   *Das Evangelium des Lucas*. 3d/4th edition. Kommentar zum Neuen Testament 3. Leipzig: Diechert/Erlangen: Scholl. Reprinted Wuppertal: Brockhaus, 1988.

Zenner, J. K.
1894   "Philologisches zum Namen Nazareth." *Zeitschrift für katholische Theologie* 18:744–47.

Zerwick, M.
1963   *Biblical Greek*. Translated by J. Smith. Rome: Pontifical Biblical Institute Press.

Zlotnick, D.
1966   *The Tractate "Mourning" (Śĕmaḥot): Regulations Relating to Death, Burial, and Mourning*. Yale Judaica Series 17. New Haven: Yale University Press.

Zürcher Bibel
    Die Heilige Schrift des Alten und des Neuen Testaments: Zürcher Bibel. 19th edition. Zurich: Verlag der Zürcher Bibel, 1987.

Editor:	David Aiken
Book designer:	Daniel Knight
Proofreaders:	Anne Berens, Marjory Hailstone, Wells Turner, Ray Wiersma
Text negatives:	Trade Typographers Inc. (Grand Rapids)
Book printer:	Cushing-Malloy Inc. (Ann Arbor)
Binder:	Dekker Bookbinding (Grand Rapids)
Jacket designer:	Koechel/Peterson Design (Minneapolis)
Jacket printer:	Etheridge Co. (Grand Rapids)
Primary typefaces:	New Aster and Franklin Gothic
Paper:	Weyerhaeuser 50# Huskey Offset
Jacket stock:	Westvaco 80# Coated
Cover material:	James River Kivar 2, Black Cabrina Bali